CULTURE AND SACRIFICE

Human sacrifice has fascinated Western writers since the beginnings of European literature. It is prominent in Greek epic and tragedy, and returned to haunt the creative imagination after the discovery of the Aztec mass sacrifices. It has been treated by some of the greatest creative geniuses, including Shakespeare and Wagner, and was a major topic in the works of many Modernists, such as D. H. Lawrence and Stravinsky. In literature, human sacrifice is often used to express a writer's reaction to the residue of barbarism in his or her own culture. The meaning attached to the theme therefore changes profoundly from one period to another, yet it remains as timely an image of cultural collapse as it did over 2,000 years ago. Drawing on sources from literature and music, Derek Hughes examines the representation of human sacrifice in Western culture from the *Iliad* to the First Gulf War.

DEREK HUGHES is Professor of English at the University of Aberdeen.

Alfons Mucha, *Salammbô* (1896)

CULTURE AND SACRIFICE

Ritual Death in Literature and Opera

DEREK HUGHES

CAMBRIDGE UNIVERSITY PRESS
Cambridge, New York, Melbourne, Madrid, Cape Town, Singapore São Paulo

Cambridge University Press
The Edinburgh Building, Cambridge CB2 8RU, UK

Published in the United States of America by Cambridge University Press, New York

www.cambridge.org
Information on this title: www.cambridge.org/9780521867337

© Derek Hughes 2007

This publication is in copyright. Subject to statutory exception
and to the provisions of relevant collective licensing agreements,
no reproduction of any part may take place without
the written permission of Cambridge University Press.

First published 2007

Printed in the United Kingdom at the University Press, Cambridge

A catalogue record for this publication is available from the British Library

Library of Congress Cataloguing in Publication data
Hughes, Derek, 1944–
Culture and sacrifice: ritual death in literature and opera / Derek Hughes.
p. cm.
Includes bibliographical references and index.
ISBN 978-0-521-86733-7
1. Human sacrifice in literature. 2. Human sacrifice in art. I. Title.
PN56.H82H84 2007
810.9′353–dc22 2007007745

ISBN 978-0-521-86733-7 hardback

Cambridge University Press has no responsibility for
the persistence or accuracy of URLs for external or
third-party internet websites referred to in this publication,
and does not guarantee that any content on such
websites is, or will remain, accurate or appropriate.

For Jan

Contents

Plates

Acknowledgments

I am grateful to the Leverhulme Foundation for a one-year fellowship which enabled me to lay the groundwork for this project. A grant from the British Academy enabled me to work on the rich opera holdings of the Library of Congress, and the book could not have been completed without the exceptionally generous research leave granted me by the University of Aberdeen. Many people have placed their time and expertise at my disposal. In the final stages of my work, I was greatly helped and stimulated by all the participants in Professor Sabine MacCormack's seminar 'Europe and the Americas' at the Folger Library (April 2006), and in the colloquium 'Blood, Guts and Ink: Live Sacrifice and Literature' at the University of Leeds (May 2006). Over the years, many individuals have given me indispensable help: David Adams, Pascal Bentoiu, Antje Blank, Michael Burden, Doug Canfield, John Dunkley, Mia Fallone, Karen Friedrich, Rob Hume, Mihaela Irimia, Judy Milhous, John Mucci, Don Neville, A. Dean Palmer, Curtis Price, Claude Rawson, John Rignall, David Symons, and Simon Toll. Linda Bree and Maartje Scheltens of Cambridge University Press have responded patiently and wisely to many queries. By far my greatest debt, however, is to Janet Todd, who meticulously read repeated drafts, and has – as always – been a constant source of knowledge and support.

Some material included in this book first appeared in 'Human Sacrifice in Homer and Dryden's *The Indian Emperour*', in *Dryden and the World of Classicism*, ed. Wolfgang Görtschacher and Holger M. Klein (Tübingen, 2001), pp. 89–98; '"Wie die Hans Heilings": Weber, Marschner, and Thomas Mann's *Doktor Faustus*', *Cambridge Opera Journal*, 10 (1998), 179–204; and in 'Aphra Behn's *Oroonoko* and New World Ethnography', in *A Companion to The Literatures of Colonial America*, ed. Susan Castillo and Ivy T. Schweitzer (Oxford: Blackwell, 2005), pp. 259–74. I am grateful to the original publishers for permission to reuse this material. I am also grateful to many institutions for supplying or granting permission to use illustrations: the Bridgeman Art Library for the Pompeii 'Sacrifice of Iphigenia', Caravaggio's *The Sacrifice of Isaac*, and the illustration from Burnouf's *L'Inde française*; the Scala Group for the Tiepolo Iphigenia; the Bildarchiv Preußischer Kulturbesitz for the red-figure vase and Pompeii mural depicting the dismemberment of Pentheus; the British Library for the 1493 illustration of the death of Pentheus; the Biblioteca Nazionale Centrale di Firenze for the illustration from the Codex Magliabechiano; the Syndics of Cambridge University Library for the illustration from de Bry's *America* and for Arthur Rackham's Brünnhilde; the National Gallery of Ireland for David's *The Funeral of Patroclus*; the Staatsgalerie Stuttgart for Anselm Feuerbach's *Iphigenie*; the Arthur Rackham Estate for permission to reproduce Rackham's Brünnhilde and Undine; the Alfons Mucha Foundation for permission to reproduce Mucha's *Salammbô*; Lebrecht Music and Arts for Franz Stassen's Brünnhilde and Lydia Sokolova; Christie's Images Ltd for Draper's *The Water Nixie*; the Archive of the Salzburg festival (Photo Madner) for the scene from Henze's *The Bassarids*; and Photostage Ltd for the scene from John Buller's *BAKXAI*.

A note on the citation of foreign texts

I give titles of foreign works in the form most generally used in the English-speaking world: *Das Rheingold* and *Götterdämmerung*, but *The Magic Mountain* and *Opera and Drama.* Discussions of foreign literary texts are, of course, based on the original works. These are quoted both in English and in the original language, with the translation coming first unless a specific question of vocabulary is being illustrated. Discursive works are normally quoted only in translation, except in the case of works by an author (such as Wagner) whose creative output is also being discussed. In singling out words for discussion, I use quotation marks when the word is cited in the form used in the text, and italics when citing it in its root form. References to classical prose works are to their universally accepted subdivisions (e.g. *Republic* 391b). Particular texts (invariably the Loeb) are therefore cited only for direct quotations.

CHAPTER 1

Human sacrifice, ancient and modern

Nine dogs had their master that fed beneath his table, and of these did Achilles cut the throats of two, and cast them on the pyre. And twelve noble sons of the great-hearted Trojans he slaughtered with the bronze – and grim was the work he devised in his mind – and to it he set the iron might of fire, so that it would spread. Then he uttered a groan, and called on his dear comrade by name: 'Hail, Patroclus, even in the house of Hades, for now I am bringing to fulfillment all that I promised you before. Twelve noble sons of the great-hearted Trojans, all these together with you the flame devours; but Hector, son of Priam, I will not give to the fire to feed on, but to dogs.'

(Homer, *Iliad*)

[E]very day we saw sacrificed before us three, four or five Indians whose hearts were offered to the idols and their blood plastered on the walls, and the feet, arms and legs of the victims were cut off and eaten, just as in our country we eat beef brought from the butchers. I even believe that they sell it by retail in the *tianguez* as they call their markets. Cortés told them that if they gave up these evil deeds and no longer practised them, not only would we be their friends, but we would make them lords over other provinces. All the caciques, priests, and chiefs replied that it did not seem to them good to give up their idols and sacrifices and that these gods of theirs gave them health and good harvests and everything of which they had need.

(Bernal Díaz del Castillo, *The True History of the Conquest of New Spain*)

THE SACRIFICE OF THE PEERAGE

DEATH OF 45 HEIRS IN THE WAR

(*The Times*, 15 February 1916, p. 8)

Therefore it became the practice to cut out the tongues of the girls three months before they were due to be sacrificed. This was not a mutilation, said the priests, but an improvement – what could be more fitting for the servants of the Goddess of Silence?

Thus, tongueless, and swollen with words she could never again pronounce, each girl would be led in procession to the sound of solemn music, wrapped in veils and garlanded with flowers, up the winding steps to the city's ninth door. Nowadays you might say she looked like a pampered society bride.

(Margaret Atwood, *The Blind Assassin*)[1]

Human sacrifice has preoccupied writers since the beginnings of Western literature. It occurs in the *Iliad*, and pervades the work of Euripides and Virgil. It is present in the Renaissance: for example, a human sacrifice initiates the chain of calamities in Shakespeare's *Titus Andronicus*. By contrast, the optimistic rationalism of the Enlightenment expressed itself in numerous plays and libretti in which civilization frees itself from the superstitious barbarism of human sacrifice: Mozart's *Idomeneo* and Gluck's two *Iphigénie* operas are well-known examples, but they are survivors from a very large field of lesser but cognate works. Self-immolation, whether as an instrument of national destiny or erotic consummation, fascinated the nineteenth century, most notably in the works of Wagner. Then there is Modernist human sacrifice. On 29 May 1913, a diverse audience gathered in the Théâtre des Champs-Elysées to hear – or rather drown out – one of the two seminal works of twentieth-century music, Stravinsky's *The Rite of Spring*. It portrays a human sacrifice.

Human sacrifice is everywhere in Modernist texts: in Eliot's *The Waste Land* and *The Cocktail Party*, in Mann's *The Magic Mountain*, in Lawrence's 'The Woman Who Rode Away' and *The Plumed Serpent*, and in Schoenberg's *Moses und Aron*. Many analysts of modern society begin with speculation about its sacrificial origins: Adorno, Baudrillard, and Girard, for example. Only in the late twentieth century does the theme seem slightly in retreat, perhaps because it feels inadequate to the monstrous horrors which the mid-century witnessed.

By human sacrifice I mean, primarily, the literal, ritual, religious sacrifice of a human victim. To concentrate exclusively on the literal event, however, would be too restrictive. When, in the eighteenth century, Voltaire and others write plays about human sacrifice in ancient or exotic places, they are not primarily writing about the laws of ancient Crete but about the intolerance of contemporary France. A writer may approach things the other way round, portraying a contemporary society, but seeing in its advanced and elaborate structures atavistic processes that recapitulate those of human sacrifice. My subject, therefore, is literary works in which ritual human sacrifice is performed, or narrowly averted, or used as a powerful and deliberate symbol. I am often asked questions such as 'Is judicial execution a human sacrifice?' Such enquiries are, I think, mistaken. The point is not the thing itself but its representation. In the modern world, executions rarely approximate to human sacrifices, but it is perfectly possible for a writer to use the idea of human sacrifice powerfully to interpret the social or psychological dynamics of an execution, as Dickens does in *A Tale of Two Cities*. Not every guillotining, however, is a human sacrifice. Do vampires conduct human sacrifices? Not necessarily, but (in literature) sometimes. Is Clarissa Harlowe a human sacrifice? No. Richardson's novel is full of the language of material, sexual, and moral sacrifice. It explores its spectrum of possibilities, from the trivial and cynical to the essential. In examining the cynical and the trivial, it scrutinizes the ethos of the century in which it first became possible to talk of making financial sacrifices, but it also explores the kinds of personal renunciation which are morally imperative. Nowhere, however (even in portraying the death of the heroine), does it evoke ritual human sacrifice, as Voltaire at times does in his analyses of contemporary France.

In this study, I examine transformations in the literary interpretation of human sacrifice, from Homer to the present day. For my purpose, literature includes music theatre: it would be perverse to study transformations of Euripides without considering his impact on opera, from the eighteenth century onwards; it would be equally perverse to ignore Wagner, whose influence on literature (on, for example, Thomas Mann) is almost as great as his influence on music. If literature and music theatre are deeply interdependent, however, painting raises quite different issues and modes of moral interpretation, and participates in quite different traditions. Timanthes' famous lost painting of the sacrifice of Iphigenia captured Calchas, Odysseus, and Menelaus in various expressions of grief, and registered the still greater grief of Agamemnon by covering his face with a robe.[2] One challenge facing the later painter of the scene was whether he could outdo Timanthes by uncovering Agamemnon's face, or whether he should follow his venerable example, as do the anonymous mural at Pompeii and Tiepolo's fresco at the Villa Valmarana, Vicenza (Plates 1 and 2). This is a tradition, and a technical problem, that has no counterpart in literature and music theatre. Moreover, the Timanthes painting freezes in a single, eternal moment of virtuous grief characters who, in the dramatic tradition, are seen dynamically – and, moreover, in a state of dynamic villainy. Whereas the literary and musico-dramatic traditions are inseparable, the visual arts address different issues and questions, which will not be explored here.

This is a wide-ranging work, but it is not an encyclopaedia. Its subject is evolving traditions, and processes of cultural transformation, and it concentrates on major turning points. It deals with minor works when they are culturally revealing, but it avoids the anomalous, concentrating on texts which enter and influence a substantial tradition. Thus, although many of Euripides' plays deal with human sacrifice, I consider those which have exercised the clearest influence on later literature: *The Bacchae*, in which a mother deludedly sacrifices her son, and *Iphigenia among the Taurians* and *Iphigenia in Aulis*, in which human sacrifice is averted. Indeed, one test of the literary status of human sacrifice in a period is whether librettists and dramatists are more interested in adapting the Iphigenia plays, as they were in the eighteenth century, or *The Bacchae*, as they were in the twentieth. In that century, its influence was evident not only in overt adaptations such as those of Wole Soyinka and of Hans Werner Henze, but also in Thomas Mann's three great engagements with the Dionysiac, *Death in Venice*, *The Magic Mountain*, and *Doctor Faustus*.

Plate 1 The sacrifice of Iphigenia, perhaps after the lost painting of Timanthes (House of the Tragic Poet, Pompeii)

As the traditions develop, other streams enter the current. Sometimes these may be narratives which are not sacrificial in themselves, but inspire sacrificial narratives in others. An example is Friedrich de la Motte Fouqué's novella *Undine*, of 1811, about a knight who is torn between a mortal woman and the water sprite who is at once her opposite and her double. On the night of his wedding to the mortal, he accepts a kiss from her rival, even though he knows that the price of the kiss is death. Though the death is not in itself sacrificial, it palpably influences later erotic self-immolations, in Wagner, Mann, and indeed in Margaret Atwood's *The Blind Assassin*.

This is also, of necessity, a book in which subordinate themes, at first seemingly separate from the main one, gradually gain prominence and become integrated with it. Chief among these is the relationship between sacrifice and systems of calculation or measurement. Initially, sacrifice is not a quantified transaction: a surrender of something to the gods in the

Plate 2 Giambattista Tiepolo, *The Sacrifice of Iphigenia* (1757) (Villa Valmarana, Vicenza)

hope of corresponding reward. Once it is so regarded, however, it becomes possible to see profound psychological or symbolic affinities between the quid pro quo of the sacrificial transaction and the equivalences established in systems of measurement, or in mathematical calculation, or in the determination of exchange value in the marketplace. The iniquities of capitalism, for example, may be imagined to be sacrificial in nature.

Counting in Greek tragedy is associated with the quest for ordered culture, often in opposition to the chaos of human sacrifice (as in the *Oresteia*). In Virgil, however, sacrifice has a positive mathematical dynamic and rationale, in that the one must be sacrificed for the many, and from Shakespeare onwards writers start to see an intrinsic sacrificial principle in the systems of exchange that sustain advanced European societies. At the same time, mathematical systems become key markers of cultural difference: when seventeenth-century writers such as Dryden and Aphra Behn describe the ritualized violence of American cultures, they associate its outlandish nature with alien approaches to mathematics; but they also show that the more advanced numerical and economic systems of the European colonists produce their own corresponding rituals of violence. Human sacrifice and counting are, as it were, the first and second subjects of this book. At first, in the tragedies of Aeschylus and Sophocles, they are opposed, in that counting pre-eminently symbolizes the ordering cultural intelligence that is abolished in the act of human sacrifice. This opposition never disappears: it is present, for example, in *Robinson Crusoe*. More often, however, man in later texts is a sacrificer *because* he is a measurer and enumerator; the primitive compulsion to sacrificial violence is simply reformulated by his most advanced systems of numerical abstraction. The use of counting in Greek tragedy is therefore analysed not because it is, in itself, sacrificial, but because it presents a constellation of ideas – the relationship between man's capacity for numerical order and moral chaos – which was later to explain his capacity for human sacrifice.

Literary human sacrifice rarely has much connection with the real thing. The wealth of ethnographic information recorded by early witnesses of Mexico and Peru proved too alien to be assimilated into the literary mainstream. Though Aztec human sacrifice continues to fascinate, it fascinates as the focus of very Western fantasies, such as those of D. H. Lawrence. As Britain and other colonial powers sought to eradicate *sati* and other sacrificial practices, Wagner concluded *The Ring* with a transfiguring widow-burning, though one with very little reference to reality. Only at one point has there been any substantial interaction between literature and anthropology: in the influence of Frazer's *The Golden Bough* (first edition 1890).

Frazer argued that all primitive cultures are shaped by two fundamental but erroneous innate ideas: that one can cause events by imitating them (for example, sticking pins in an image), or that something that has been in contact with a person – a garment, a hair, even a name – gives power over the person himself. From these principles, he explained the sacrifices that mimetically guarantee the rebirth of the year by casting aside exhausted life. The rites of renewal preserved in the flaying rituals of the Aztecs, the Crucifixion, and the dismemberment of Pentheus in *The Bacchae* all originate in the same innate but mistaken theories of causation: theories that are part of us, because they were part of our own childhood view of the world. Not only did Frazer establish an apparent link between the cult of Huitzilopochtli and the Crucifixion: he established a link whose living force could be felt within the mind of each of his readers, so that his excavation of cultural layers was also a journey down through the layers of the mind to earliest childhood. Suddenly, the multiform cultures of the past and present, in all their outlandish violence, were derived from a single root that we can still feel stirring within us. No wonder he was so influential on the arts. But no other anthropologist has been, and his grand synthesis has long since disintegrated.

Thus, with only passing and opportunistic reference to ethnography, human sacrifice has been a major literary theme throughout the classical period, and ever since the Renaissance. The literary version developed an anthropology of its own, expressing the conflicts, conditions, and self-image of the age in which it was produced: it reflects, for example, changing views of the significance of the body, of individual rights and consciousness, and of the systems of exchange which determine the social value of an individual; of the relationship between the home culture and alien times or nations. The literary concept of the sacrificial transaction thus changes and develops under its own dynamics: one does not look to ancient Greece to describe the difference between Racine's *Iphigénie en Aulide* and Goethe's *Iphigenie auf Tauris*. Although theoretical accounts of human sacrifice rarely interact with literature, however, they can possess their own status as culturally revealing fictions. The idea of human sacrifice is a fundamental starting point in Adorno and Horkheimer's still current *Dialectic of Enlightenment*, though its assumptions about the origins of sacrifice are now mere curiosities.

But what of the Crucifixion in literature? Clearly, a single chapter on the role of Christ in Western literature would be an absurdity, but there are other grounds for treating the Crucifixion as a separate case, largely outside this study; for, until the eighteenth century, it is imagined, represented, and classified quite differently from all other kinds of sacrifice. Not until that century, in works such as Volney's *Les Ruines*, do the Aztec and Christian religions start to seem morally equivalent; not until the age of Frazer do Aztec and Christian sacrifice start to seem identical in their cultural and psychological origins. Similar points can be made about the story of Abraham and Isaac. For much of the Christian era, this was safely unproblematic, since its historical function was to foreshadow God's willingness to

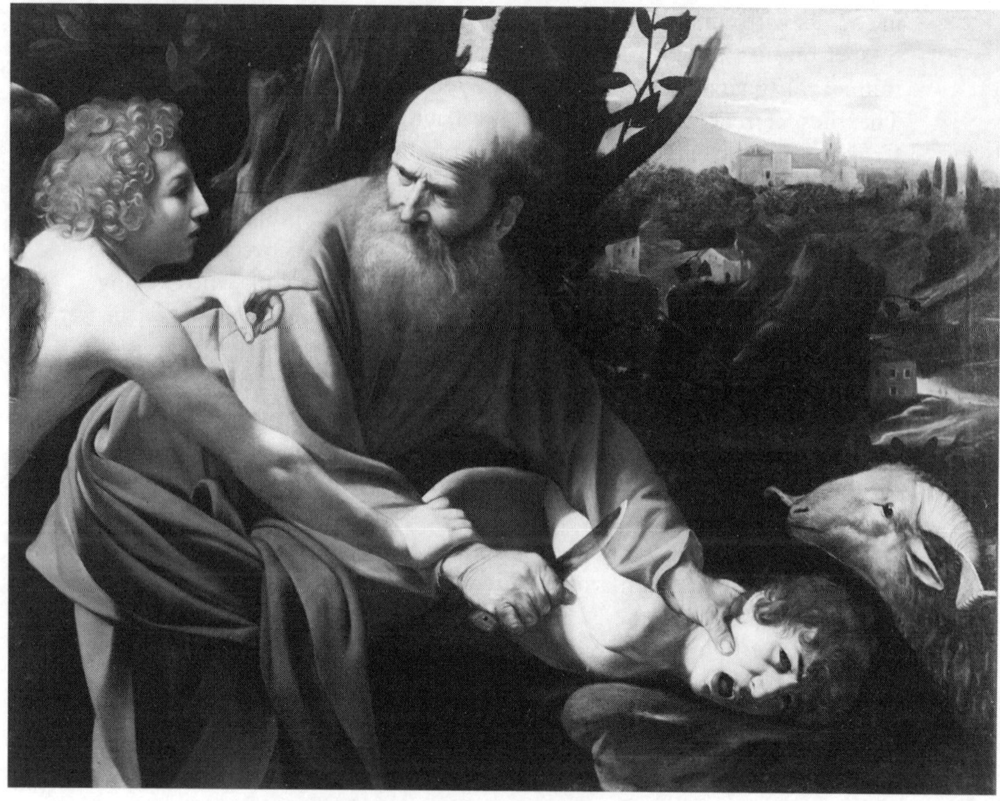

Plate 3 Caravaggio, *The Sacrifice of Isaac* (1603)

sacrifice his son. It becomes problematic when secularized: in, for example, Caravaggio's *The Sacrifice of Isaac* (Plate 3), which emphasizes Isaac's terror and Abraham's reluctance to desist, or in Hobbes's and Spinoza's critiques of the verifiability of divine revelation. Voltaire mocks the absurdity of the Abraham and Isaac story, as does the English deist Thomas Chubb.[3] I shall discuss it here insofar as it is treated as a problematic secular narrative.

THE ORIGINS OF SACRIFICE: THEORIES AND MYTHS

The worshipper experiences the god most powerfully not just in pious conduct or in prayer, song, and dance, but in the deadly blow of the axe, the gush of blood and the burning of thigh-pieces.[4]

In his detailed sociobiological account of the origins of sacrificial practice, *Homo Necans*, Walter Burkert locates the origins of sacrificial ritual in the Palaeolithic rituals of the hunt.[5] Hunting brings the invention of culture, group co-operation, and the division of sexual roles. Man acquires artificially the practices that are instinctive to the great beasts of prey, redirecting intraspecific aggression towards animals of another species (p. 20). The rituals of the hunt involve killing, the expiation of guilt for the death of the animal, and the reassembly of its bones in a kind of resurrection, to ensure the continuity of life. An example of the continuing association of sacrifice and guilt for slaying is provided in the annual Athenian ritual of the Bouphonia (slaying of the ox), after which there was a trial for the murder of the ox. The axe and knife were found guilty and cast into the sea.

In Burkert's account, the development of agriculture perpetuated the ritual need to guarantee the emergence of life out of death. The mentality and symbolism of the hunt shape the rituals sustaining the death and rebirth of the grain, which was guaranteed by blood sacrifice. The hunt became unnecessary, though its primordial importance survives in its persistence as an élite activity. The *Männerbund* of the hunt reconstitutes itself in secret societies, in which the initiand takes the place of the prey and is symbolically killed, through a surrogate animal. Yet, with the decline of the hunt, aggression is no longer safely directed towards another species. If the harvest blood sacrifice in Greece was always (as far as we can see) animal, in other parts of the world it was human. 'Civilized life endures only by giving a ritual form to the brute force that still lurks in men' (p. 45); 'Only *homo necans* can become *homo sapiens*' (p. 212).

Homo Necans is a sweeping and imaginatively compelling account of the origins of sacrifice, detecting survivals of Palaeolithic practice in the narratives of the *Odyssey* and even the rituals of classical Athens. Ever since Frazer and Freud, we have been fascinated with seeing ineradicable survivals of primitive patterns in our own culture, and *Homo Necans* provides a cultural synthesis whose scope and fascination rival that of *The Golden Bough*, while possessing a far sounder basis in scholarship. In the process, Burkert gives new life to a question that is powerfully present from Greek times onwards: that of the relationship between man the sacrificer and man the hunter. Elsewhere, he evokes other instinctual or biological patterns which might be expressed in sacrificial practice: the lizard's 'sacrifice' of its tail when in danger, for example.[6] To some extent, he thus argues, the principle of sacrifice predates the Stone Age, and indeed humanity itself. Yet the expectation of reciprocation implicit in many forms of sacrifice is a distinctively human characteristic, since it involves a sense of time – the ability conceptually to link past and future – that only *Homo sapiens* possesses. Sacrifice thus distinguishes man from the animal, yet expresses itself in that which most closely unites them: the capacity for lethal violence.

Sacrifice is a varied and complex phenomenon, whose nature and origins have been variously explained. Burkert is one interpreter among many, and his work has been challenged on a number of grounds: that, for example, it over-interprets the positioning of animal bones in Palaeolithic sites, or that sacrifice originates in agrarian rather than hunting societies, and is then projected back upon the earlier stages of culture. Greek sacrificial animals were invariably domesticated, and Marcel Detienne has pointed out the degree to which the violence in Greek sacrificial rites is hidden, so as to create an absolute polarity between sacrifice and the hunt.[7] In terms of popular reception, moreover, Burkert's work is outstripped by the far less rigorously argued theories of René Girard, which locate the origins of sacrifice in hypothetical primeval crises, where the community is in danger of collapse as a result of spreading mob violence. The gathering violence is controlled by being focussed on a single individual: a scapegoat in the loose, modern sense of the word; and, in order to break the cycle of reciprocation, it is essential that the victim be not at all connected with any of the foregoing acts of violence. The origins of sacrifice have their own structural logic, but it is the reverse of the logic of justice.[8]

Girard is by no means the only thinker, modern or otherwise, to base a theory of society upon an imaginary account of a primeval state of nature. One feature of his work that has drawn special comment is his use of culturally advanced literary texts such as *King Oedipus* to explicate assumed primitive social and mental states. There are, of course, well-known precedents for this, but Girard does not attempt to show by what chain of cause and effect a text such as *King Oedipus*, most of which is not 'myth' but Sophocles' invention, can express the conditions of man's primal state. His use of classical Athenian texts to illustrate the anthropology of quite other periods is also open to a more elementary challenge: he clearly misreads them.

Sacrifice is often regarded as a transaction with the gods: a gift given in expectation of return. The transaction is, of course, an important feature of sacrifice, though not the only or perhaps the oldest one, and both Girard and Burkert in different ways seek to penetrate to the earliest mental stages of sacrifice. So did Frazer's now discredited key to all mythologies, which derived myth from sacrifices designed to secure the continuity of the vegetative cycle (though some of the cults of dying and risen gods, which he regards as preserving very primitive religious structures, in fact appear to have developed quite late).[9] A more durable theory, also dating from the late nineteenth century, is that of Hubert and Mauss, who argue that 'in every sacrifice an object passes from the common into the religious domain', and that the process of transference involved in sacrifice effects a transformation in the sacrificer.[10] More recently, Miranda Aldhouse Green has pointed out that, originally, to sacrifice (literally make holy) was associated neither semantically nor in practice with giving something up:

> sacrificial activity may originally have been linked with communal feasting, involving both humans and the gods in a sacred partnership, rather than being contingent upon the giving and receiving of gifts. The function of such commensality (collective ritual feasting) was probably associated with the creation of a bond between people and the supernatural world, between the sacrificers and the divine recipient, through the slaughter and consumption of animal victims.[11]

This was the case in ancient Greece. If animal sacrifice in the ancient Middle East was primarily a feeding of the gods, in Greece it was not.[12] The men shared the food, and the gods got the bones, wrapped in fat: an anomaly explained by the myth that Prometheus had cheated Zeus, hiding the flesh of an ox in its stomach, decking out the bones with fat, and tricking him into choosing the latter as his sacrificial portion.[13] When the gods feast with men in Homer, they do so in special or liminal places, such as Ethiopia or Phaeacia,[14] rather than in the known and familiar world. There, sacrifice affirms man's special place, between the animals (who eat flesh raw) and the gods, who do not eat mortal food.

So where do classical myths of *human* sacrifice come from? Myths such as that of Iphigenia do not necessarily preserve memories of actual prehistoric human sacrifice, for which the evidence is debatable. Some scholars now see these myths as explaining rituals of initiation. According to Richard Seaford, for example, myths of violent sacrifice, such as that dramatized in *The Bacchae*, describe the chaos that existed before the establishment of the cult with which the myth is associated, and rituals of initiation can involve an episode of entry into an uncivilized state. In a cult alluded to at the end of *Iphigenia among the Taurians*, 'Athenian girls went out to become "bears" in the uncultivated periphery of Attica, at Brauron, for a ritual in which they were imagined as entering a temporary state of savagery so as to return tamed for the civilized state of marriage'.[15] This play, indeed, portrays the commutation of human sacrifice into a harmless initiation ritual: at the end, the bloody sacrifices practised in the Crimea are transferred to Athens in humanely attenuated form, reduced to a token blood-letting in a rite of passage. Myths such as that of Pentheus in *The Bacchae*, in which a monstrous sacrifice destroys a family or community, place sacrifice at the opposite pole from its constructive function of unifying communities with the divine. Conversely, when, in Book 3 of the *Odyssey*, Telemachus arrives in Pylos to seek advice from Nestor, he arrives in the middle of a sacrifice to Poseidon, in which 500 men consume the flesh of 9 bulls.

The corruption of sacrifice by introducing human victims could be seen as marking a traumatic break with an ideal past, in which men and gods had still feasted together. According to one explanation of the rupture, Tantalus (the great-grandfather of Agamemnon) had the right of feasting with the gods, but in an attempt to prove his intellectual superiority tested them by covertly feeding them the flesh of his own son, Pelops. Only Demeter, preoccupied with the disappearance of Persephone, failed to notice and ate. Pelops was reconstituted, with an ivory shoulder to replace the one eaten by Demeter, and commensality between man and gods was at an end. The story of Tantalus was, indeed, thought to explain the end of the Golden Age. Conversely, when belief in a lost Golden Age started, from the sixth century BC, to yield to a belief in social evolution from a state of brutal savagery,[16] human sacrifice started to typify the primal barbarity which civilization had rejected, but which, perhaps, still threatened to reclaim it. It still, however, marks a dark boundary between two stages of culture.

So why is human sacrifice such a dominant and widespread theme? Until recently, every society has subjected some of its members to public rituals of death, yet none which features in this book has sanctioned human sacrifice. The closest is Rome: this is the last advanced Western civilization to practise human sacrifice, only abolishing it in 97 BC.[17] It is true that human sacrifice figures more prominently and positively in Roman literature and history than elsewhere: for example the father and son Publius Decius Mus were reported to have solemnly devoted themselves to death in battle as sacrifices to ensure victory.[18] In describing the sacrifice by interment of two Gauls and two Greeks, however, Livy describes the rite as un-Roman ('minime Romano sacro'),[19] and Plutarch views it in the same way, stressing that the Romans 'have no barbarous or unnatural practices, but cherish towards their deities those mild and reverent sentiments which especially characterize Greek thought'.[20]

To cultures which practise it, human sacrifice is the highest means of honouring the gods. To those that do not, it is the highest degree of impiety. 'To such a degree of evil could superstition incite men', wrote Lucretius of Iphigenia's sacrifice, only decades after the formal abolition of human sacrifice at Rome: 'tantum religio potuit suadere malorum'.[21] One reason for the abhorrence can be seen in the Greek rituals of sacrifice, which (as explained above) affirm the structure and basis of human life by expressing man's median position between the animals and the gods. The offering of a human victim would pervert and reverse the nature of the sacrifice: Telemachus could not have arrived in Pylos and feasted with Nestor on human flesh. Yet there is more to it than that. All communities need rituals and systems of exchange to make sense of death: it must fit into an intelligible system of circulation, even if it is the end of the road for the dead individual. One of the cultural achievements portrayed in the *Oresteia* is the formulation of a closed and intelligible system of equivalences for managing violent death. If incest in Lévi-Strauss's account is the sexual pairing that blocks and disrupts the cycle of sexual exchange current in a society,[22] enforced human sacrifice is the transaction which deranges the accounting system with which we regularize death. The nature of the monstrous transaction changes with the different configurations of culture, but any system will create the conditions for its own violation, and the process of violation will exercise profound fascination. In literature, such monstrous transactions are often figured as human sacrifice.

CHAPTER 2

Greece

Sacrifice is central to the culture which produced Greek epic and tragedy. Human sacrifice features in many Greek myths, such as those of Iphigenia, Pentheus, or the madness of Heracles. In his commentary on Virgil, Servius preserves a myth about the Homeric hero Idomeneus, king of Crete, that is a variant of the Biblical story of Jephthah and his daughter: that he had vowed to sacrifice the first living thing to meet him on his way home, only to be met by his own son. In Servius' account, Idomeneus was expelled by his indignant people either after performing the sacrifice or after attempting to do so.[1] In most later versions prior to Mozart's opera *Idomeneo*, the sacrifice is accomplished.

Both in Homer and in classical Athens, before and after the development of the *polis*, animal sacrifice is an affirmation of community, as in Nestor's sacrificial feast in the *Odyssey*. Conversely, absence of society is equated with absence of sacrifice: when Odysseus and his companions arrive in the territory of the solitary cave dweller Polyphemus, he eats them raw and without libation to the gods. It was left to later writers, such as Euripides (in his satyr play *Cyclops*), to interpret this episode as one of human sacrifice; Homer does not make the connection. Nevertheless, the absence of sacrifice is itself telling: a sacrificial dedication of a cannibalistic meal to the gods would be even more unthinkable than cannibalism itself.

There are reports of Greek human sacrifice in the classical period. It was believed, for example, that human flesh was mingled with that of animal sacrifices in the worship of Zeus Lycaeus in Arcadia. Archaeology has not provided any confirmation of this belief, though it is significant enough that the Greeks believed that human sacrifice was taking place in their midst. Similarly, Plutarch reported that Themistocles was forced by the mob reluctantly to sacrifice Persian captives before the Battle of Salamis, and that Agesilaus was commanded at Aulis to repeat Agamemnon's sacrifice, but refused and sacrificed a hind instead, thereby angering the locals.[2] Although these stories were also probably false, they again show how close human sacrifice was imaginatively felt to be.[3] There are some signs of prehistoric funerary human sacrifice at Bronze Age graves, but even these are not conclusive. One practice which is certainly attested is the ritual expulsion of the *pharmakos* (human scapegoat): an ugly, criminal, or otherwise dispensable person who was driven out of the city, bearing its pollution, in times of danger. Such figures, clearly, are formational figures in Girard's theory of sacrifice, but according to Dennis Hughes evidence even that *pharmakoi* were ever killed is doubtful (pp. 139–65). It is possible that Pentheus in *The Bacchae* may be treated with some of the ritual formalities appropriate to a *pharmakos*, but that is a symbolic rather than a historic use of the ritual.

Greek and Roman authors do, however, reliably report sacrificial practices abroad. Herodotus records the Taurian custom of sacrificing strangers, claiming that the goddess to whom the sacrifices are made is Agamemnon's daughter, Iphigenia (4.103). Carthaginian child-sacrifice is mentioned in, for example, the pseudo-Platonic *Minos* (fourth century BC), and in Diodorus Siculus. Caesar and Tacitus report the practice of human sacrifice in Gaul and Anglesey.[4] As noted above, moreover, there is clear evidence of human sacrifice at Rome itself until very shortly before its abolition. Human sacrifice was thus not far away, either geographically or chronologically. Even in Greece, as we have seen, there was the suspicion that the Arcadians did it, or that a man as great as Themistocles had done it. It was a potent and menacingly close point of cultural reference.

Myth, ethnography, and history thus meant that human sacrifice was very close to the geographical, legal, and psychological boundaries of civilization. Its abolition was one of the hallmarks of human progress: one of the myths surrounding that great tamer of the wild, Heracles, was that he had ended the Egyptian king Busiris' custom of annual human sacrifice, bursting his bonds while on the altar and killing the king and his son. Human sacrifice is thus associated with the primitive stages of culture. Yet it may also be the price of cultural advance, and it may in some form persist within the most fully advanced culture.

Nevertheless, neither archaeology nor history suggest that Greek myths of human sacrifice preserve any trace of actual sacrificial practices. Myths of sacrificial substitution – such as the miraculous replacement of Iphigenia by a deer at the point of sacrifice – do not represent a historical progression from human to animal sacrifice. It has, indeed, been argued that animal sacrifice preceded human sacrifice, even in cultures which practised the latter. In ritual rather than myth, the animal is not a lesser victim, graciously accepted in place of the human offering. Animal sacrifice affirms humanity's middle position in the triple hierarchy of animals, men, and gods. Human sacrifice negates the structure of the sacrificial ritual and reduces it to chaos. The violence and horror of that negation is glimpsed for a moment in the penultimate book of the *Iliad*. It was to pervade the work of two of the three great Greek tragedians, Aeschylus and Euripides, and leave its mark also on that of Sophocles.

AESCHYLUS AND HOMER

At the beginning of Aeschylus' tragedy *Prometheus Bound*, Power and Force (Kratos and Bia) are overseeing the shackling of Prometheus to the wild rocks of the proverbially waste and uncivilized Caucasus. The work, however, is done not by these embodiments of pure primal violence but by the craftsman god Hephaistos, who regrets the acquired skill that obliges him to torment his kinsman. Only after the artificer has done his work will Prometheus be delivered, first to Tartarus, and then (long after the events of this play) to the predatory eagle who devours his liver.

In the person of the craftsman god, the culture of the gods punishes the inventor of human culture. For Prometheus' crime is to have improved human life by giving men the arts of civilization. He gave them fire (his chief offence), brought them from the caves, and taught them to build houses. He taught letters, numbers, the measurement of time, and the interpretation of omens.[5] For these actions, he is banished to a landscape that negates all culture, and condemned to a continual reliving of that extreme moment of the desert or forest: the moment at which the prey is first conscious of being seized by the predator. Yet this predator embodies the will of the greatest of the gods: the eagle is the 'winged hound' ('ptēnos kuōn') of Zeus.[6] In the bitter concluding dialogue of the play, Prometheus is mocked by Hermes, another contriver god.[7] It is he, the inventor of the lyre and the patron of oratory, who provides the most savagely primitive description of the devouring of Prometheus' flesh, using a verb – *ekthoinasthai* (1025) – whose connotations include public and celebratory human feasting.[8]

In another version of the myth, told in Hesiod's *Theogony*, Prometheus had angered Zeus by tricking the gods into accepting in perpetuity a fraudulent form of sacrificial exchange (sacrifice only being possible after the gift of fire to man). Wrapping the bones of an ox in fat and the flesh in its stomach, he had induced the gods to accept the bones (538–41), turning sacrifice into a sleight of hand in which man, not the gods, ends up as the gainer. For Aeschylus, Prometheus is *philanthrōpos* (11), a benefactor of man. Yet he is paying a just requital (*dikē*) for challenging the monarchy (*turannis*) of Zeus (9–10): a justice which returns the inventor of culture to the landscapes and virtually cannibalistic appetites of the wilderness. When he is delivered to the eagle, he will be flesh in a banquet whose horror approaches that of Thyestes.

During his captivity, Prometheus is visited by the wandering Io. She had been seduced by Zeus, and turned by him into a heifer to keep her from the gaze of Hera. Hera, however, had discovered her, and she is now tormented by a gadfly, which has driven her from the centre of Greece to the wilds of Scythia, and is to take her to the estuary of the Nile. Two victims of Zeus meet, the one immobile, the other incapable of rest, but both forced beneath the limits of the human, both victims of a process whose resolution will take many millennia, yet both foundational figures in the advance of civilization. For Io is the ancestral mother of the Ionians, origin of a lineage that will produce both horror and enlightenment. She is ancestress of Danaus (forefather of the Greeks), who quarrelled with his brother Aegyptus (forefather of the Egyptians) and took a dreadful revenge: pretending a reconciliation, he married his fifty daughters to Aegyptus' fifty sons, commanding each to murder her groom on the wedding night. All but one obeyed. This is a characteristically violent myth of the separation of Greek culture from those of the East; Virgil was to recall it at the end of the *Aeneid*, at another moment of violent cultural formation. A later and contrasting descendant of Io, however, is to be Heracles, the great tamer of the wilderness, who will release Prometheus from his bonds and, in Aeschylus' *Prometheus Unbound*, kill the eagle with the arrow of the huntsman.[9]

In Aeschylus' play, then, the genesis of human culture is threatened from above and from below: from the gods and from the wild, with which the gods seem to be complicit. Culture is itself intrinsically ambiguous, as is shown by the violent myths of the Danaids, and indeed of the profoundly ambiguous figure of Heracles himself. *Prometheus Bound* is not a work about human sacrifice, yet it contained the potential to generate works which were. In his attempt to destroy his creation, Mary Shelley's modern Prometheus, Frankenstein, pursues a quest for child sacrifice across landscapes as desolate as those in which his original is tormented: a pursuit which culminates in the victim's 'sacrifice' of himself. More subtly, Aeschylus' Prometheus, the rebel against god and champion of man, divides in Milton's hands into Satan and the self-sacrificing Son (just as Zeus, tempting Io with seductive dreams, prefigures Satan).

Aeschylus' Prometheus represents both the possibility and the ambiguity of human progress, and his hero became an archetype of both: celebrated by Beethoven, Percy Shelley, and Scriabin; viewed with greater reserve by Mary Shelley and Thomas Mann. Progress does not yet, however, articulate the will of the gods, and it is the conflict between Prometheus' benefactions and their will that make him, potentially, a sacrificial victim. I have started with him because he is both a seminal and transitional figure, the product of a period in which human progress first became formulated as an intellectual possibility, but in which myths preserving an older view were still powerful. The interpretation of human sacrifice was henceforth to remain intimately linked to that of human progress, but the formative sacrificial myths of European literature precede such belief.

The earliest human sacrifice in Western literature is Achilles' slaughter of twelve Trojan captives at the funeral of Patroclus (*Iliad* 23.175–83). Whether it is a reminiscence of actual sacrificial practices, or whether it even is a formal sacrifice, has been debated,[10] yet it certainly passed into later literature as one. Plato's term for the slaughter, 'sphagas', suggests that he saw the killing in this way[11] and, when Virgil imitates it in the *Aeneid*,[12] he is explicitly describing a sacrifice. Later, when Jacques-Louis David painted the funeral (1778), he portrayed a religious ritual of sacrifice with the priest Calchas officiating (Plate 4). Indeed, the snowballing influence of this brief incident ensured that, by the mid seventeenth century, human sacrifice was as stereotypical an epic theme as the quest or the imperialistic war.

Homer's funerary killing is not a regression to the primitive – the idea would have no meaning in the *Iliad* – but it does contribute to a progressive collapse of the systems that order the Homeric world: this is a fragmented milieu of small, unstable social units, in which it is terribly possible to lose one's place and become an exile, a vagabond, or a slave. It is a world where violence is kept in check by honorific systems of exchange: gifts to seal the sacred bond between guest and host, or to put an end to a quarrel; ransoms to redeem captives and place some limit on the potentially infinite violence of war. The collapse started with Paris' abduction of Helen: the wife of his host Menelaus, with whom he should properly have exchanged gifts. It culminates with Achilles' desecration of the corpse of Hector, which he should properly have ransomed. The sacrifice of the prisoners is the penultimate stage in this breakdown of order, for they too ought to have been ransomed. Indeed, immediately before Achilles captures the victims for sacrifice, he defeats, refuses to ransom, and kills an enemy ally whom, on a previous and recent occasion, he had defeated and ransomed. By the juxtaposition of the two episodes, the preparation for sacrifice is clearly linked with the refusal to ransom, marking the breakdown of the system of exchange that in Homer preserves the precarious balance of civilization. Human sacrifice thus first appears in Western literature as the breakdown of an economic system.

The *Iliad*, however, does not mention the most famous sacrifice of the Trojan War: Agamemnon's sacrifice of his daughter Iphigenia at Aulis, in order to appease the goddess Artemis and secure winds that would permit the sailing of the fleet to Troy. Homer may not, indeed, indisputably mention Iphigenia: Iphianassa, one of the daughters Agamemnon offers in marriage to Achilles (9.145, 287), may be Iphigenia, but then again she may not. The first known account of the command to sacrifice Iphigenia was in the lost post-Homeric epic the *Cypria*, which related that Agamemnon had shot a stag and boasted that he surpassed even Artemis. The angry goddess had demanded Iphigenia as a sacrifice, and she had been brought to Aulis on the pretence of marriage to Achilles. But, at the moment of sacrifice, Artemis

> snatched her away and transported her to the Tauri, making her immortal, and putting a stag in place of the girl upon the altar.

> autēn exarpasasa, eis Taurous metakomizei kai athanaton poiei· elaphon de anti tēs korēs paristēsi tōi bōmōi.[13]

Plate 4 Jacques-Louis David, *The Funeral of Patroclus* (1778)

The first surviving reference to a sacrifice of Iphigenia that is consummated is from approximately two centuries later, in Pindar (*Pythian* 11) and Aeschylus' *Agamemnon*. By this time, the representation of human sacrifice had become – and was to remain – inseparably linked to that of human progress. In the *Laws*, Plato postulates social evolution from cannibalism to agriculture, and cites the currency of human sacrifice as an example of man's capacity for such violence (6.781e–782d). The first surviving literary work to link human sacrifice and human progress is the *Oresteia*.

The sacrifice of Iphigenia is described, and deplored, in the first chorus of *Agamemnon* (104–249). It is avenged in the killing of Agamemnon by Clytemnestra, which she explicitly describes as a human sacrifice, answering that of Iphigenia. Agamemnon's concubine, the Trojan princess Cassandra, is also murdered by Clytemnestra, and similarly describes her death as a sacrifice, likening herself to a sacrificial ox. The sequence of deaths proceeding from the sacrifice of Iphigenia has a further and final stage in the killing of Clytemnestra by her son Orestes. Iphigenia's sacrifice is in turn linked to an earlier atrocity: the cannibalistic feast of Thyestes, who had been fed on the flesh of his sons by his brother Atreus, Agamemnon's father. Aegisthus, Clytemnestra's lover and her accomplice in Agamemnon's murder, is a surviving son of Thyestes. Walter Burkert has pointed out that the iconography of the Thyestean banquet as described here imitates that of a sacrificial meal, and indeed that Thyestes literally means *sacrificer*.[14] Moreover, in the (emended) text, the banquet is described as 'androsphageion': a *sphageion* of men (1092). The only surviving use of *sphageion* on its own is as a sacrificial bowl. Coming between the Thyestean feast and the murder of Agamemnon, the sacrifice of Iphigenia is thus the central event of three linked sacrificial acts, which constitute the horrors of the house of Atreus.

Iphigenia is sacrificed to Artemis, the virgin goddess of the hunt. In her primal form, Artemis is the mistress of the beasts, the divinity who provided the kill as a supernatural gift, and 'who of course demanded gifts in return'; if the mistress (or master) of the beasts were annoyed, they 'would deny their gifts, and catastrophe would ensue'.[15] In the *Cypria*, Agamemnon had excited Artemis' wrath by boasting that he was a greater hunter than she. This is the version used by Sophocles (*Electra* 563–76),[16] but here the association between sacrifice and the hunt is stronger and more primitive than in any other ancient version. Even in the *Cypria*'s very early account, the emphasis is on Agamemnon's *hubris* in challenging the divinity, rather than on the sphere of the hunt itself. Here, Artemis so fully belongs to the sphere of the hunt as to recognize the human sphere only in terms of the wild. Two eagles, birds of Zeus, have torn apart a pregnant hare. For the prophet Calchas, this is an omen of the destruction of Troy by Agamemnon and Menelaus: the animal sphere is understood as a symbolic analogy to the human.[17] Not, however, by Artemis, for whom the events of the animal sphere have priority. The eagles were sacrificing ('thuomenoisin') (137) the hare, and she demands Iphigenia as 'another' ('heteran') (151) sacrifice.[18]

This word 'another' is the closest the play comes to suggesting any reciprocity between the death of the hare and that of Iphigenia. Yet the *Oresteia* is a work whose governing problem is reciprocity. The sequence of deaths enforces *poinē* (penalty), *amoibē* (exchange), *tisis* (payment/ vengeance), and *dikē* (apportionment, vengeance, justice). Immediately before her own death, Cassandra poignantly extends the chain of death forwards: 'when for me, a woman, another woman shall be slain, and for an ill-wedded man another man shall fall' ('hotan gunē gunaikos ant' emou thanēi, / anēr te dusdamartos ant' andros pesēi') (1318–19). The pattern of reciprocation is embedded even in the linguistic structure of the play, in its exploitation of the verbal pattern of the *polyptoton*, a doubling pattern in which a word is linked to itself by being immediately repeated in a different form or case – as in the lines just quoted, with their 'woman for woman' and 'man for man' ('gunē gunaikos', 'anēr . . . ant' andros'). Clytemnestra, for example, will pay ('teisai') for Agamemnon's death-blow with another blow: 'tumma tummati' (1430). What emerges here is a concern with the relationship between the structure of the sacrificial exchange and that of language; a concern with a long future, since interpretation of sacrifice necessarily involves attention to the symbolic value given to the victim.

The *Oresteia* manifestly portrays a chain reaction of reciprocated violence. Although the sacrifice of Iphigenia sparks off such reciprocal violence, however, in that it leads to the murder of Agamemnon, it does not itself reciprocate anything. In the human economy, Iphigenia is sacrificed for the worthless Helen, and for the spoils of Troy; in the divine, for a pregnant hare, victim of a demarcation dispute between Zeus and the goddess with the most archaic of spheres. Far from being a reciprocation, the sacrifice confounds one of the most fundamental ordering polarities of our culture, in that it suspends the distinction between the human and the animal.[19] If the blow which fells Clytemnestra is both morally and linguistically paired with the blow with which she felled Agamemnon, the sacrifice of Iphigenia is something which linguistic structure cannot accommodate. Far from using the symmetries of the *polyptoton*, the Chorus keeps employing the negating *a-* prefix, to suggest that it is outside language, outside human structures and systems: it is not to be feasted upon ('adaiton') and without law ('anomon') (151), unholy ('anagnon') and unsanctified ('anieron') (220). The sacrifice itself pushes Iphigenia towards the animal sphere, for her body is raised like that of a she-goat, and a bit is placed in her mouth to deprive her of speech (that is, to prevent the voice previously used at libations from uttering curses); her humanity survives only in her beseeching, unregarded glances. The motive force behind this sacrifice is not reciprocation but desire: the army longs for the sacrifice very eagerly with fierce passion ('orgai periorgōs') (215–16). Both the language and the conduct of the army deny this sacrifice the character of formal ritual. It is the opposite: a triumph of insensate and disordered desire.

Hubert and Mauss write that 'In every sacrifice an object passes from the common into the religious domain' (*Sacrifice*, p. 9). Although the sacrificed Iphigenia passes from one realm to another, the domain to which her body is transferred is the animal as well as the divine. She is caught between two clashing modes of understanding: that of Calchas, for whom animals are symbols of the human, and that of Artemis, for whom the human is a symbol of the animal. Appropriately, therefore, the relationship of priest and victim is patterned upon that of predator and prey: describing her own impending death, Cassandra describes herself almost interchangeably as the victim of sacrifice and of a predatory animal – as a sacrificial ox and the prey of a lioness. Indeed, as Pierre Vidal-Naquet has demonstrated,[20] the events of the play are constantly likened to that antitype of sacrifice, the hunt. In entangling Agamemnon in a cunningly devised shirt, Clytemnestra catches him in a net ('amphiblēstron') (1382), diverting the gifts of culture, the sphere of the goddess Athene, into the service of Artemis. Atreus has fed human flesh to his brother in the guise of animal flesh; Agamemnon has sacrificed his daughter instead of, and in atonement for, an animal. The result of these transgressive substitutions is the cultural collapse depicted in the play.

It is perhaps in keeping with the archaic character of Iphigenia's sacrifice that it is conceptualized not as the giving of a body but as an act of blood-letting. Walter Burkert, indeed, speculates that altars may originally have been accumulations of blood and ashes.[21] Although the play is awash with blood (the Thyestean banquet, for example, produced 'streams of kindred blood' ('homosporois / epirroaisin haimatōn') (1509–10)), there is no awareness of the sacrificed body. In many later treatments of the sacrifice of Iphigenia, the beauty of the victim's body is stressed, as in the reference to the cutting of 'the neck of her lovely body' in Euripides' *Iphigenia in Aulis* ('euphuous te sōmatos deran').[22] But the words *sōma* and *demas* (body) are far more common in *Iphigenia in Aulis* than in *Agamemnon*; when, in the Euripides play, Clytemnestra inconveniently arrives in Aulis with her daughter, the messenger describes her to Agamemnon, in elegant periphrasis, as 'the body of your Clytemnestra' ('sēs Klutaimēstras demas') (417). Aeschylus and Euripides thus show a radical difference in the imagining of what is sacrificed. In Euripides, the body is autonomous, aesthetically independent. In the *Oresteia*, the body is not self-contained, but rather a container: the receptacle of sacred yet terrifying fluids, whose tendency to escape must be fearfully controlled. Blood, naturally, is the chief fluid, though one might add the 'loathly rheum' ('dusphilē liba') (*Eumenides* 54) dripping from the eyes of the Furies. Even the nurse's recollections of tending the infant Orestes are not of a lovable baby but of an insensate, uncontrollably defecating being, like a beast ('boton') (*Libation-Bearers* 753). The body is a thing of fearful power.

Despite the cultural collapse in which cannibalism and human sacrifice erase the distinction between human and animal, the *Oresteia* opens and closes with the gifts of Prometheus: fire and number. At the beginning of *Agamemnon*, the watchman on the roof of the palace observes the signs of the constellations, and of the beacon fires that announce the end of the Trojan War; at the end of *Eumenides*, the equally cast votes of the jurors acquit Orestes. In the palace, the reversion to the sphere of the hunt brings a restricted sense of number, which rarely transcends the twos and the threes that describe patterns of reaction and counter-reaction: Agamemnon's 'I am struck by a second blow' ('deuteran peplēgmenos') (*Agamemnon* 1345) and Aegisthus' boast that he is the 'third' ('triton'), avenging, child of Thyestes (1605); as in *Macbeth*, 'double' (*diplous*) is an important word. Vengeance counts in twos and threes – eagle, hare, Iphigenia – with no structure that transcends the individual reciprocation of death and death. What is distinctive about the higher culture to which the play moves is that it moves beyond the pairing of the eagle and the hare, of the lion and its victim, or the sacrificer and the ox. If the concluding court scene reaches a level of abstraction that goes beyond the sequence of specific predatory or sacrificial acts, however, it does not go beyond the principle of vengeance itself. Athene defends Orestes' killing of his mother:[23] it was Euripides who was to reverse the picture, and (in *Orestes*) portray the matricide as a criminal by-passing of an already established judicial system.

The court of the Areopagus in *Eumenides*, acquitting Orestes with its equally divided votes, moves the community beyond the self-replicating pairing of avenger and victim towards larger, civic patterns that have no precedent in the mountains or forests: patterns which require the abstractions created by Prometheus. Yet the play does not quite portray a movement away from a culture of vengeance to one of law; for the judicial decision, by the narrowest of margins, acquits Orestes of his vengeful killing. What happens is a simplification in the processes of blood retribution: Orestes is right to avenge his father, to whom he is related by blood, as he is not to his mother; for Apollo declares that the child is only a transient guest in the mother's womb, being a creation entirely of the father's seed, and not being (as the Furies claim) of the same blood (*homaimos*) as his mother (*Eumenides* 652–61). The Furies are concerned with punishing not murder – they are unconcerned with Clytemnestra's murder of her husband – but the shedding of kindred blood. Apollo solves the impasse whereby Orestes' vengeance replicates the crime it punishes, but he does not abolish the claims of blood vengeance. Rather, he simplifies their mathematics and ensures that the state is governed by more extensive and widely based categories: distinctions of cultural status, for example (he argues that the crime against Agamemnon was the more serious because he was a great commander) (*Eumenides* 637). In the process, he resolves the endless linguistic symmetries which had mirrored the unstoppable reciprocation of violence. In her death, Clytemnestra had paid for a blow with a blow ('tumma tummati') (*Agamemnon* 1430). In asserting the child's independence of the mother whose womb carries it, Apollo replicates and resolves this verbal pattern, arguing that the mother is a stranger to the child she carried: a stranger to a stranger ('xenōi xenē') (660). The verbal symmetry now separates and distinguishes, breaking the sequence of blows and making possible a directed and contained system of retribution. We then go to the counting of the votes, which spares Orestes from condemnation for murder (literally blood: 'haimatos') (752). In the divided votes, the Promethean gift of number goes beyond the twos and threes of vengeance, replacing the reactive pairing of violated body with violated body with the dialectic of opposing suffrages. In its mathematical balance, the voting of the jurors forms a perfect antithesis to the sacrifice of Iphigenia, with its basis in disordered mob desire.

SOPHOCLES

Of the three great Greek tragedians – Aeschylus, Sophocles, and Euripides – Sophocles has left the fewest surviving plays on the theme of human sacrifice. In in his extant oeuvre it appears only in the surprisingly brief and unproblematic description of the sacrifice of Iphigenia in *Electra*. The titles of his lost works, however, show that he did handle the theme on other occasions: there were two plays on Athamas, for example, and one each on Phrixus and Iphigenia.[24]

Yet, paradoxically, one Sophocles play has in the twentieth century been held to lay bare the most ancient origins of human sacrifice. This is as a result of the work of Freud and, later, René Girard. After using *King Oedipus* to elucidate his theory of the Oedipus complex in *The Interpretation of Dreams*,[25] Freud in *Totem and Taboo* widened Oedipal desire from a critical element in the genesis of neurosis to a foundational force in the genesis of society and its ritual practices. He postulated a primal social state in which the father 'keeps all the females for himself and drives away his sons as they grow up'.[26] Finally, the expelled brothers kill and eat their father, and this primal crime is both expiated and commemorated in the cult and annual eating of the totem animal. This ritual is the origin of animal sacrifice, human sacrifice (a later development) (p. 151), and tragedy.

While rejecting Freud's account of the Oedipus complex, René Girard has also, in *Violence and the Sacred*, seen *King Oedipus* as a key text in disclosing the nature of the sacrificial impulse. According to Girard, sacrifice originates as a means of ending escalating cycles of reciprocal violence in primitive societies. It does so by focussing collective hostility on a single, arbitrarily chosen scapegoat (in the modern, loose sense of the term). In Sophocles' play, Oedipus is the scapegoat who resolves the sacrificial crisis which had been caused by the plague, and whose potential danger is illustrated by the pervasive presence of anger. Anger has dominated Oedipus' life, ever since his quarrel at Corinth with the man who denied he was the son of his apparent parents. The other two male characters, Tiresias and Creon, also grow angry, so that 'The solemnity of the three sages rapidly gives way to fury' (p. 69). Far from presenting individualized tragic character, the play for Girard presents 'The violent elimination of differences between the antagonists, their total identity' (p. 72). It follows that the isolation of Oedipus as the cause of the plague does not proceed from detection of his hidden and unique personal guilt. Rather, it is the arbitrary selection of a sacrificial scapegoat; any of the leading characters would have done just as well. The revelation of parricide and incest is not the emergence of long-buried truth. It is the imposition of 'A particular version of events' (p. 78), 'the camouflaged victory of one version of the story over the other' (p. 73).

Girard's theory of sacrificial origins has not won acceptance among anthropologists, and indeed he offers little empirical evidence in its support.[27] His use of advanced literary texts to explicate primitive social conditions is questionable, the more so because (I believe) he is rather free with the textual evidence. Consider the alleged universality of anger in *King Oedipus*. Three angry men do not make a sacrificial crisis, and in any case only two of them are in fact angry: Creon, far from giving way to 'fury', is a model of patience. One might make the same kind of factual objection to Girard's briefer interpretation of Sophocles' *Ajax* as representing the social dynamics of sacrificial substitution. Resentful at not being awarded the arms of Achilles, the hero has – he thinks – attacked the Greek army at night, and killed the hated Odysseus, among other victims. Athena, however, has visited him with madness, and he has deludedly spent his violence on herds of animals. Observing that Ajax' victims are sheep – 'gentle creatures' and 'traditionally utilized by the Greeks for sacrificial purposes' – Girard argues that 'The institution of sacrifice is based on effects analogous to those produced by Ajax's anger' (p. 9). Yet Ajax' killing spree is not uniquely redirected towards animals, for he kills both herds and herdsman. It is a mere, indiscriminate massacre.

One place where Sophocles does unquestionably deal with ritual human sacrifice, however, is in *Electra*. Here the sacrifice of Iphigenia is largely exculpated, for in this version she is not greedily traded for a bankrupt cause. In contrast to the versions of Aeschylus and Euripides, Agamemnon does not have the option of giving up the war and going home: without the sacrifice, the army is permanently trapped at Aulis, unable to leave in either direction. Sophocles' Agamemnon was not only unwilling to perform the sacrifice but enforced ('biastheis') (575) to do it, so he lacks the guilty compliance that Aeschylus and Euripides attribute to him. Sophocles also weakens Aeschylus' association between the sacrifice and the psychology of the predator, even though he does derive the sacrifice from a hunt, using the version told in the *Cypria*: that Agamemnon had angered Artemis by his boasts after killing a stag. Iphigenia is a compensation ('antistathmon') (571) for the stag, but Agamemnon's crime belongs to the sphere of discourse rather than the hunt, in that he 'chanced to let slip some boastful word or other' ('enkompasas epos ti tunchanei balōn') (569; my translation). The emphasis is on heedlessness rather than culpable hubris: on the ways in which language strays into areas beyond the control of the speaker. Iphigenia dies because of a slip of her father's tongue. In *Agamemnon*, the sacrifice of Iphigenia in recompense for a pregnant hare had shown humanity to be standing on the brink of an incomprehensible wilderness, which had its own laws and could not be translated into human symbols. Here, Iphigenia stands on a different symbolic boundary: between the body and its linguistic representations. Her body must redeem a careless word.

In the *Oresteia*, Orestes had seemingly been trapped by competing obligations of blood, to the father he must avenge and the mother he must kill. The only entrapment in Sophocles' play is in the central one of Agamemnon's helplessness over the sacrifice of Iphigenia. The movements of Iphigenia's sister Electra are restricted, but not supernaturally: she is confined by Aegisthus' political power. Blood is not a common word in Sophocles' play, and it lacks mystery and terror; only in its last occurrence is there any idea of a reciprocal sequence of bloodshed (1419). Clytemnestra's claim on Iphigenia is not the tie of blood but the argument that, in producing her, Agamemnon did not suffer an equality of pain ('ouk ison kamōn emoi'); she has invested more in Iphigenia than he (532–3). Value does not reside in the mysterious absolutes of blood affinity but in the quantifiable demands and – in our looser sense – sacrifices that particular forms of relationship impose. Clytemnestra attempts to assess her stake in Iphigenia by formulating an abstract system of quantification. Agamemnon's stake is lower, and he should not have sacrificed Iphigenia in defiance of her.

Yet abstract quantification tends, in Sophocles, to be treacherous. In addition to Clytemnestra here, the Sophoclean characters who rely on it in other plays are Oedipus in *King Oedipus* and Creon in *Antigone* – all three disastrously. All three apply calculation to major cultural disruptions, and for all three the calculation fails to measure or contain the disruption. Yet, although Sophocles repeatedly portrays the failures of culture, he does not portray culture as intrinsically vitiated by its affinities with the primitive, as Euripides does. Indeed, he could scarcely do more to isolate the sacrifice of Iphigenia from the demands of any human institution, or any human desire, for he portrays none of the passionate bloodlust that Aeschylus so insistently describes. In portraying Iphigenia as sacrificed because of a heedless word, Sophocles suggests that the signs and artefacts of culture are traps of their own nature, not because they preserve some untransformed residue of the wilderness. Oedipus' disaster lies in his greatest triumph, in decoding the Sphinx' riddle of time and number.

In Sophocles' *Electra*, nevertheless, culture triumphs, without the long contest with ancient and irrational divinities portrayed in Aeschylus' *Oresteia*. The consequences of Agamemnon's murder have been structural: Clytemnestra's lover and accomplice, Aegisthus, occupies Agamemnon's throne and hearth, and dissipates his wealth. The deaths of Aegisthus and Clytemnestra purge a corrupt and unjust regime, and there are no avenging Furies. Moreover, although Clytemnestra is described as a sacrifice (*thuēlē*) to Ares (1423), the Chorus explicitly approves the deed, and there is no hint of what Euripides provides when he portrays the killing of Aegisthus in his *Electra*: an animal sacrifice reverting to a human sacrifice; for Euripides' Aegisthus is killed as he officiates at the sacrifice of a bullock. In Euripides and Aeschylus, human sacrifice is the fundamental image of the orgy of slaughter in Argos. In Sophocles it is not: a political crisis finds a political solution; usurpation is punished by tyrannicide.

The other extant Sophocles play to approximate to the theme of human sacrifice is *The Women of Trachis*. Here Heracles, the culture hero who has purged the seas and forests of many evils (1012), has also violated that essential basis of civilization, the sacred bond of hospitality: he has killed the son of his guest–friend Eurytus, sacked his town, and captured his daughter Iole. To the dismay of his wife Deianira, poignantly aware of her own fading beauty, he is in love with Iole. If the gaining of Iole most reveals Heracles' capacity for chaotic violence, that of Deianira had pre-eminently illustrated his ability to master the wild and extend the sphere of culture; for he had overcome his rival, the river-god Achelous, who had opposed him in the forms of a bull, a serpent, and a minotaur. Later, when the centaur Nessus – half-human, half-beast – had attempted to rape Deianira, Heracles had killed the monster with arrows poisoned with the blood of another monster, the Hydra, whom he had killed in one of his labours. Deianira had unwisely believed Nessus' dying advice that his blood would act as a love charm. In an effort to regain Heracles' affections from Iole, she sends him a robe dyed with the blood when he is about to conduct a sacrifice after his expedition: he will appear 'to the gods a new sacrificer wearing a new robe' ('thutēra kainōi kainon en peplōmati') (613). The true effect of the poisoned blood, however, is to dissolve his flesh.

Immediately before the catastrophe, Heracles performs an act of sacred, ritual measurement, marking out altars and the grove in the sacred precinct (a place of transition between the mundane and the divine). Then, in a perverted feast, his flesh starts to be eaten by the poison, at the point when he has sacrificed twelve of the planned one hundred oxen. Heracles' taming of the wild, as exemplified in his defeat of Achelous, is here reversed.

Achelous had appeared as a bull, a serpent, and a minotaur; in the unsacrificed bulls, the Hydra's blood, and the half-beast Nessus these elements recur in different combination, signifying the failure of Heracles' power to impose culture. His death is not sacrifice but anti-sacrifice: a dissolution rather than an offering of the body. Sacred order has been expressed in ritual measurement: the marking out of the holy site, the counting of the sacrificial victims. Many later writers will see in human sacrifice an expression of the human fondness for reductive equations that erase the specificity of the particular individual, but here, number is an expression of the sacred, and the death of Heracles violates the process of sacrificial counting. The ritual turns into completely disordered violence when Heracles, in his agony and rage, dashes out the brains of his companion Lichas, who had brought the robe from Deianira.

Yet the violence of Sophocles' Heracles is not that of Euripides' in *The Madness of Heracles*. In that play, also on the point of conducting a sacrifice, Heracles is seized by a madness which blinds him to the identity of his children, and causes him to slaughter them with the bow with which he had tamed the wilderness. Whereas Euripides emphasizes the fragility of the internal boundary between culture and savagery, however, Sophocles emphasizes that culture cannot impose a permanent identity or significance upon a place or object. The sacrificial space turns into a killing field, and Deianira commits suicide upon what had been her bridal bed. In *Ajax*, similarly, the hero commits suicide with the sword which, in one of the noblest gestures in the *Iliad*, Hector had given him after their duel.

These cultural ambiguities are vested in external, inanimate objects: the sword, the marriage bed, the writing tablet, and the sacrificial space. Sophocles, however, is now regarded as the pioneering explorer of internal space: as the writer who saw into the unconscious, and recorded the primal urges which were to be concentrated in the act of human sacrifice. How far does *King Oedipus* neglect the external and local constructions of culture for the unfathomable universality of the human mind?

As already mentioned, this text – for distinctly dubious reasons – emerged in the twentieth century as a crucial key to the hidden origins of human sacrifice. The 'myth' which it seems to record has also recently acquired other significant resonances: for Jean-Joseph Goux, for example.[28] In his interpretation, Oedipus is the prototype of the autodidact who rejects traditional wisdom, his greatest crime being over-reliance on reason to defeat the irrational, in the person of the Sphinx. It cannot be overemphasized, however, that the plot of *King Oedipus* is not the 'Oedipus myth'; nor can it be overemphasized that there is no such thing as the 'Oedipus myth'. The central element of the play – that Oedipus fulfils an oracle that he will kill his parents and marry his mother, despite his parents' attempt to prevent it – is certainly constant, and indeed the Oedipus story is one variant of a widely diffused folktale (another version of which was used by Thomas Mann in *The Holy Sinner*). This is in turn a subset of a wider group of tales about characters who fulfil an oracle by attempting to avoid it: Apollodorus and Diodorus tell the story of Althaemenes, who attempted to avoid an oracle that he would kill his father, and by doing so fulfilled it.[29] In the analogues to the Oedipus story, however, it is not constant that the hero himself should know of any oracle concerning his future. It is the parents alone who have the oracle: the hero's mind, conscious or unconscious, is not the universal focus of the story. Indeed, the Oedipus story itself has many variants.

For Goux, Oedipus' chief error is to defeat the Sphinx by intellect rather than force; yet, in one version, recorded in the second century AD by the traveller Pausanias, he does just that: 'Oedipus overwhelmed her by the superior numbers of the army he had with him on his arrival from Corinth.'[30] Those for whom Sophocles' play constitutes the 'Oedipus myth' will be surprised to learn that, in some versions, Oedipus remarried after Jocasta's suicide: to Euryganeia (or was it Astymedusa?) (Apollodorus 3.5.8). Euryganeia is mentioned by Pausanias, himself a late authority but quoting a very early source, the lost epic *Oedipodeia* (9.5.11–12). Although plagues are often associated with sexual transgression, the particular association between Oedipus' incest and the plague may well have been an invention of Sophocles, in response to the Athenian plague of 431–427 BC. The final exile of Oedipus, essential to our view of him as a scapegoat, is also optional. So is the unearthing of long-concealed guilt. In the earliest extant version, in the *Odyssey*, the incest is revealed 'at once' ('aphar'),[31] Jocasta commits suicide, but there is no reference to Oedipus' self-blinding, and he continues to rule Thebes, albeit unhappily (11.271–80); his funeral games at Thebes are mentioned in the *Iliad*. In Euripides' *Phoenician Women*, Jocasta and Oedipus are still alive and present in the city during the war of Eteocles and Polyneices, Jocasta killing herself after their death, and the story of Oedipus' continued residence in Thebes persists in Diodorus Siculus (4.65.1).

Sophocles' play is undoubtedly the greatest treatment of the story of Oedipus' parricide and incest. It has been a seminally important document, not only for Freud, Girard, and Goux, but for Hegel and Nietzsche. It is, however, no more an authoritatively typical version of the story than the heavily embroidered versions of Corneille or Voltaire, with their added love interest. If Voltaire added a Philoctetes tormented by unfulfillable love for Jocasta, Sophocles added the Theban plague. One may reasonably say of Sophocles' version, as of Shakespeare's treatment of the Hamlet story, that it is a work in which each age sees a mirror of itself, but the version is unique to Sophocles. It is not collective. It is not myth.

King Oedipus, then, is an extreme example of the capacity of classical texts to acquire deferred sacrificial implications, and in view of the significance given to it by René Girard it can hardly be ignored in a treatment of human sacrifice. Yet it is not about human sacrifice, though it certainly portrays cultural conflicts which in other plays are concentrated in the act of human sacrifice. In view of its equivocal relevance to my theme, I shall briefly indicate what these conflicts are, while enlarging on my dissent from Girard's reading of the play.

King Oedipus, it is agreed, is a tragedy of knowledge.[32] Concern with the intellectual apprehension and control of the universe is manifested in the pervasive vocabulary of knowledge, sight, learning, skill (*technē*), and signifying. Whereas *Oresteia* shows a civilization reduced to the mentality of the hunt, *King Oedipus* at first shows the terminology of the hunt being appropriated for mental enquiry. Hunting is, initially, an intellectual metaphor, distinct from the instincts of the hunting dog to which Aeschylus had allied it. Oedipus complains that the track of the ancient guilt is 'hard to make out by signs' ('ichnos palaias dustekmarton aitias') (109), and that he lacks the token ('sumbolon') to get far on it (221). At this stage, affinity with a hunting animal is not an image of cultural collapse; it is an image of the decoding of signs. A man reading signs is a like dog picking up the scent.

More than any other Greek tragic character, Oedipus is a measurer, priding himself on the skills that (as in the myth of Prometheus) distinguish culture from preculture. Near the beginning, he is anxiously measuring ('xummetroumenon') (73) the time since Creon's departure. Yet the control of the enumerator is slipping, for the city's woes are beyond counting ('anarithma', 'anarithmos') (168, 179). The question of who killed Laius resolves itself into one of number, as Oedipus desperately and vainly tries to establish that his killing of a man at the parting of the three ways differs in decisive details from the killing of Laius: he asks Jocasta how many people there were in the group, and how long a time it is since Laius disappeared. His responsibility for the killing becomes clear when the survivor's original lie, that Laius was killed by many, not one, is retracted. If the survivor had continued giving the same number ('arithmon'), Oedipus would have been exonerated (843–5). When the Theban shepherd meets the Corinthian slave to whom he had given the baby Oedipus, the identification is by counting: he kept him company 'for three whole periods of six months each, from spring to the rising of Arcturus' ('treis holous / ex ēros eis arktouron hekmēnous chronous') (1136–7). Yet, all the attempts to pattern and control through number are shadowed by the repetition of 'nothing' (*ouden*, *mēden*, also meaning 'in no way'), words which (as in *King Lear*) cumulatively suggest the vacancy of existence: 'I *count* you as being *equal* with those who have *nothing* lived' ('hōs humas isa kai to mē- / den zōsas enarithmō') (1187–8; my translation), exclaim the Chorus of humanity in general, with precisely calculating nihilism.

Oedipus' greatest triumph was to solve the riddle of the Sphinx. This is not narrated in Sophocles, but reported by Apollodorus as 'What is that which has one voice and yet becomes four-footed and two-footed and three-footed?' ('ti estin ho mian echon phōnēn tetrapoun kai dipoun and tripoun ginetai?').[33] The riddle is numerical, chronological, and linguistic; its answer is man. Yet, although 'man' is the answer to the Sphinx' riddle, consciousness and knowledge are not part of the definition. They are used to solve the numerical paradox, but the paradox does not imply them. The riddle reduces man to a set of variations upon a moving body. So the play reduces Oedipus.

In seeing the play as a drama of the mind, of atavistic social or sexual impulse, it is easy to underplay its emphasis on the intellectual and physical control of events. Like man in the riddle, Oedipus passes from helplessness – the baby passed from hand to hand on Mount Cithaeron – to power, to physical helplessness again. In the process, he loses control over his name. Perhaps over-ingeniously, Charles Segal argues that Sophocles punningly exploits the similarity between the name *Oidipous* (literally 'swollen-footed') and the Greek word for 'I know', *oida*.[34] It is true, however, that Oedipus' name dwindles in social potency: towards the end of the play, he is named only by the peripheral and the nameless. Yet this is a weakening of the name as an instrument of external power; Oedipus' sense of self disintegrates before outward forces, not before hidden and repressed lusts, and the play explores the command of events, not of desires.

The changes in exterior control are reflected in the uses of an apparently simple and innocuous word: *pempō* (to send). If we are examining the play for repressed incestuous desire, or for the dynamics of a sacrificial crisis, we are unlikely to ask who sends whom; yet the question is of fundamental importance. Oedipus' initial authority as saviour ('sōtēra') (48) of the city is expressed when he states that he *sent* ('epempsa') (71) Creon to Delphi. The polarity of Oedipus and Apollo moves into definition when, as sender ('ho pempsas') of the oracles, Apollo takes over the title of saviour (149–50). Oedipus is commanded by the oracle to send (*ekpempein*) the murderers out of the country (309), and here the word starts to turn against him. It continues to do so, until he asks Creon 'That you shall send me out of the country' ('gēs . . . pempseis apoikon') (1518). As Danielle Allen points out, male offenders in Athens were punished by expulsion (whereas females were punished by immurement, like Sophocles' Antigone).[35] The idea of 'sending' has a ritual and judicial gravity that is hard to preserve in translation. Yet its gravity emphasizes that this is a play about the physical and intellectual control of external events: about the limits of culture rather than the hidden regions of the mind. The relentless isolation of Oedipus as the one who is sent, however, does not identify him as an undifferentiated Girardian scapegoat. The paradoxes of the term are embodied only in him, and the concluding expulsion is enforced by the pressure neither of the community nor of preceding myth. It is uniquely chosen, and uniquely appropriate to this version.

Like Prometheus, the infant Oedipus had been exposed on a mountain, Cithaeron, and at the end of the play he rejects the city for this mountain (1449–54). As the great decoder moves back towards the wilds, hunting ceases to be a metaphor of intellectual activity and reverts to its primitive meaning: eager to identify the murderer of Laius, the Chorus sings of tracking ('ichneuein') the unknown man through the wild woods and caves (475–9). Yet what is it that pushes man from the city to the wilds? Not an interior principle of atavistic savagery. *King Oedipus* does not portray civilization yielding to survivals of ancient instincts. All the cultural flaws are expressed in external ironies: Oedipus is sender and sent, judge and criminal, husband and son, the answerer of the riddle and also its answer. The failures of culture come from gods: from the inexplicable decree of Apollo. The fact that oracles have no cultural or emotional importance for us does not entitle us to airbrush this oracle out of the 'universal' meaning of the text. The oracle suggests that there is a scheme of interpretation that lies beyond human speech and thought; that human beings are peculiarly subject to their representations in language.

The sphere outside culture belongs to the gods, as it belongs also to the animals. The clash between culture and non-culture is expressed in two linked polarities: the city and the mountain, and the sign and the riddle. The riddling Sphinx is normally situated in the mountains,[36] and the Chorus in *Antigone* associates speech with escape from the mountains, claiming that man 'has learned speech and wind-swift thought and the temper that rules cities, and how to escape the exposure of the inhospitable hills':

> Kai phthegma kai anemoen
> phronēma kai astunomous
> orgas edidaxato kai dusaulōn
> pagōn. (354–7)

In solving the riddle, Oedipus has set the city upright: *orthos* (50), a word that recurs throughout the play in its various senses of erect, straight, and linguistically exact. But beyond the clarity of civic speech lie the riddles of the monsters and the gods. When Creon returns from Delphi with the god's commands, they have a stark and simple linguistic symmetry, implying a corresponding simplicity of cause and effect in action: that killing be punished with killing ('phonōi phonon') (100). As in the *Oresteia*, however, such monolithic symmetries are passwords to chaos. Jocasta has borne a husband from her husband and children from her child ('ex andros andra kai tekn' ek teknōn tekoi' (1250); she is 'a wife and not a wife' ('gunaika t' ou gunaika') (1256); Oedipus is both father and brother, child and husband (1406–7); and in the end he wishes to go to a wilderness where none can speak to him (1437).[37] The language of cultural distinction has collapsed into enigma, because of the greater power of the oracle.

Oedipus' tragedy locates him on the boundary between the city and the wilderness; between a state where he controls through linguistic representation and one in which he is controlled by its snares, deceptions, and its subservience to the undecipherable meanings of a higher power. Like Aeschylus' Iphigenia, he stands on the boundary between the restraining systems of culture and an unfathomable violence of which the gods are part, and it is perhaps understandable that the twentieth century should have interpreted him as a sacrificial victim, for we look inward to discover the reasons for cultural failure. So did Aeschylus, deriving the sacrifice of Iphigenia from mob bloodlust (as Euripides was also to do). In *King Oedipus*, and even in *Electra*, Sophocles presents an alternative: to look at the structures and intellectual systems of civilization. It is revealing that, to later readers of Sophocles, these seem powerfully to imply sacrifice.

EURIPIDES

King Oedipus has always been the pre-eminent Greek tragedy, and became so more than ever in the twentieth century, when the authority of Freud superseded that of Aristotle. The other dominant Greek tragedy of the twentieth century was Euripides' *The Bacchae*, which has been the basis for at least six operas and an adaptation by Wole Soyinka. It is also an underlying element in what is perhaps the greatest twentieth-century account of contact between civilization and the mountainous wilds, Thomas Mann's *The Magic Mountain*.

Whereas *King Oedipus* has always been prominent among Greek tragedies, however, and was adapted by writers such as Corneille and Voltaire, *The Bacchae* was resurrected in comparatively recent times. Eighteenth-century dramatists and librettists repeatedly adapted Euripides' two Iphigenia plays, both of which portray averted human sacrifice. They neglected *The Bacchae*, however: there appear to have been no versions of this play between an unpublished opera of 1705[38] and a translation of the opening lines by Hölderlin, dating from 1799. For much of the twentieth century, by contrast, the Iphigenia plays slipped into the background, whereas *The Bacchae* became one of the two Greek tragedies that spoke most to the modern world.

We possess seven plays each by Aeschylus and Sophocles, plus the substantial fragment of Sophocles' *The Searchers*, discovered in 1897. For Euripides, the total is nineteen (including the possibly spurious *Rhesus*). Nine of the surviving plays have titles beginning with the letters epsilon to kappa: they are evidently a segment of an alphabetical collection of the plays, providing a sample whose representativeness is not distorted by aesthetic selection. Of these nine plays, seven portray human sacrifice, or use it as a prominent symbol; an eighth, *Helen*, portrays an Egyptian king who habitually slaughters Greeks. Human sacrifice also features prominently in six of the remaining plays. In addition to the two plays in which she figures as heroine, the sacrifice of Iphigenia is mentioned in four other plays. Clearly, the topic was fundamental to Euripides' thinking about the nature and fragility of civilization.

Detailed discussion of every example is impossible, and I shall concentrate on the three sacrificial plays (the *Iphigenia* plays and *The Bacchae*) which have exerted most influence on the Enlightenment and thereafter, while briefly illustrating the wider concern with human sacrifice in his œuvre.

Euripides repeatedly turns to the idea of voluntary and noble self-sacrifice. That is, the sacrifice has value for reasons that differ from its ritual rationale, and perhaps conflict with it: the demand for sacrifice is cruel and arbitrary, but the individual performs a moral act in giving his or her life for others, so that human nobility asserts itself in the teeth of divine baseness. In *The Suppliant Women*, the widow of a warrior immolates herself on his pyre. In *The Children of Heracles* and *The Phoenician Women*, a young person willingly accepts the role of sacrificial victim in order to save the state (as does Iphigenia in *Iphigenia in Aulis*). Yet the nobility of the victim may contrast not only with the cruelty of the gods but with the tawdriness of the cause. For example, Heracles' daughter is sacrificed to secure victory in *The Children of Heracles*, but the victory is sullied by the dishonourable killing of the captured enemy king. Other sacrifices, in *Hecuba* and *The Trojan Women*, show the ruthlessness of unrestrained power. Euripides is thus exceptional in examining the conflicting social bases of sacrifice: the gap between the generally dark motives of the sacrificers and those of the nobly willing victim, and the victim's delusions about the cause for which he or she is willing to die. On two occasions, in *The Madness of Heracles* and *The Bacchae*, the sacrificial impulse proceeds from a divinely inflicted insanity, which causes parents to slaughter offspring in ignorance of their identity; in the former play, Heracles kills his children in the belief that they are those of his enemy; in the latter, Agave kills her son in the belief that he is a lion. There is a total obliteration of social consciousness; in *The Bacchae*, even the consciousness of belonging to the same species is lost. In *The Madness of Heracles*, Euripides increases the sense of cultural collapse by altering the previously established sequence of events. In earlier versions of the story, Heracles' slaughter of his children had preceded his labours, and been expiated by them, so that savagery was exorcized by the spread of culture. Here, the slaughter follows the clearing of the wilderness and negates its effect: Heracles returns to recreate the wilderness at home, and to find it inside himself. Many Greek tragedies deal with the boundaries between the civilized and untamed landscape; only Euripides presents these as landscapes of the mind.

In contrast to the internalization of the wilderness in *The Madness of Heracles*, *Iphigenia among the Taurians* provides an exceptional dramatization of contact between the Greek culture and a less civilized one. In it, Orestes is still pursued by the Furies for the murder of his mother, despite his acquittal at Athens, and on the advice of Apollo he has come to the Crimea with his friend Pylades, to take a statue of Artemis back to Greece. Only after this will his torments cease. Also in the Crimea is Iphigenia, who has been saved by Artemis from sacrifice at Aulis, but only so that she herself can be a priestess in the goddess's barbarous cult in Taurica, whose inhabitants sacrifice all strangers to the goddess. As Agamemnon nearly sacrificed his daughter at Aulis, so Iphigenia nearly sacrifices her brother here.

The rudimentary civilization of Taurica is an appropriate place for Orestes to confront and overcome the dark history of his own dynasty. One way of interpreting and differentiating the many later rewritings of this influential play is to ask: what does one find in Taurica? What does it mean? For Cavafy, we each have our own private Ithaca.[39] In Dallapiccola's opera *Ulisse*, Circe tells the hero that he would never have encountered the cannibalistic Cyclopes and Laestrygonians 'unless you already had them in your heart' ('se non li avessi avuti già nel cuore').[40] Does one also have Taurica in one's heart? The meaning of this alien space changes with each successive cultural appropriation of it.

The action of *Iphigenia among the Taurians* takes place on the shores of the Black Sea, which the Greeks euphemistically called the Euxine Sea (that is, friendly to strangers). Here, however, euphemism is avoided: the sea is, like the country, consistently *axenos* (hostile to strangers). The play is correspondingly filled with the word *xenos* (foreigner, stranger) – a term that, naturally, is especially applied to Orestes and Pylades. In that Orestes, the displaced foreigner, is nearly sacrificed by his sister, the play gives a literal version of the situation that is explored psychologically in *Heracles* and *The Bacchae*: the transformation of kin into stranger, and consequently into sacrificial victim. Yet *xenos* not only means a foreigner: it also means a suppliant and a guest, both of whom have sacred rights. These sacred rights are, manifestly, violated by the sacrificial custom of Taurica, but they have been just as grossly violated in Greece, in the Thyestean banquet, and the play provides a very bold unsettling of distinction between the Greek and the savage. For there is another word for strangers: *barbaroi* – speakers of incomprehensible tongues. Diminished though it is, the word *xenos* is applied only to Greeks; *barbaros* is applied only to Taurians. But, as Thoas, the Taurian king, exclaims, 'Not even among the barbarians' ('oud' en barbarois') would anyone have dared to murder his mother (1174; my translation). If the language for welcoming the stranger is stripped of its welcome in this *axenos* land and sea, the language for excluding him is unsettled too. The Greek confronts his heritage and identity in an alien land, where the linguistic signposts of strangeness and familiarity have been removed.

Iphigenia among the Taurians is a depiction of exile: not only that of Orestes, Pylades, and Iphigenia, but of the homesick Chorus of Iphigenia's slave women, whose odes without exception deal with Greece and the leaving of Greece. Yet, as they recognize, the ills that the family of Agamemnon are now experiencing derive from a supreme act of inhospitality on Greek soil, the Thyestean banquet. In the wild spaces of the Crimea, Orestes, Pylades, and Iphigenia honour and reconsecrate the primal social impulses of kin and friendship that had been corrupted in Greece itself. They are reconsecrated in a world where primitive violence is seen as a cultural malformation rather than something indelibly atavistic. Iphigenia refuses to believe that the gods demand human sacrifice (*Iphigenia among the Taurians* is one of those self-deconstructing Euripides plays whose characters deny the veracity of the fable in which they figure); instead she believes 'that people here, themselves murderous, ascribe their own fault to the goddess' ('tous d'enthad', autous ontas anthrōpoktonous, / es tēn theon to phaulon anapherein dokō') (389–90). Culture is not menaced by the violence of the gods; on the contrary, such violence is itself a cultural fiction of the Taurians.

One consequence of this change is that blood is once again deprived of the power and terror that it had in Aeschylus. In contrast to the *Oresteia*, with its emphasis on dangerous bodily fluids, *Iphigenia among the Taurians* treats blood as a physical and secular phenomenon. Iphigenia thinks it inconsistent that Artemis should demand blood sacrifice and yet ban those polluted with the blood of childbirth or a corpse from her altars. She does insist on a rite to cure Orestes of pollution, but it is a ruse to delay the sacrifice and enable him to escape.[41] In Aeschylus, the blood-avenging Furies are real presences. In Euripides, their status is unclear, for they are seen only by Orestes in his fits of madness. At its conclusion, however, the play moves towards a new cultural management of blood, for the goddess Artemis is brought from the wild to the civilized spaces of Attica, her rites of sacrifice being commuted into two initiatory rites, one (otherwise unknown) at Halae, involving a token nicking of the neck (1449–67). Sacrificial violence is a product of culture, not the gods, and it can be remedied by culture. It is notable that, in this version, the barbarian king Thoas is himself transformed, heeding the will of Athena and sending the Greeks back to their homeland with his blessing. Here, Euripides achieves a complexity unequalled by any imitator until Goethe, who similarly would treat the sacrificing barbarian with a cosmopolitan humanity.

The date of *Iphigenia among the Taurians* is unknown. One conjecture puts it at round about 412 BC, a time when Athenian hubris had shown itself in the massacre and enslavement of the inhabitants of Melos, who had refused to become subject to Athens, and the disastrous invasion of Sicily. Athens was now fighting desperately for survival against a Sparta which had combined with the old oriental enemy, Persia. If the dating is right, the play is remarkably untouched by contemporary events. Not so *Iphigenia in Aulis*, completed by Euripides' son after his death in 406 BC, two years before Athens's defeat in the Peloponnesian War. This dwells on the irrationality and corruption of war, its greed and mob hysteria. Greed, according to Thucydides, repeatedly induced Athens to reject advantageous peace terms; in the year of the play's first performance, mob hysteria led the Athenians impulsively to execute six of their generals.

This is the version of the Aulis story which is the source, often via Racine's reworking, of most later versions. In the ending, which is certainly not by Euripides, Iphigenia is spared from sacrifice by the substitution of a doe: the resolution in the earliest known version, in the lost post-Homeric epic the *Cypria*. It is probable that Euripides intended this conclusion, but nonetheless the happy ending comes after an unrelenting and unredeemed exposure of the corrupt self-interest of the powerful and of the impersonal frenzy of the mob: of the dynamics that produce sacrifice. Perhaps the most astonishing idea in the play is that the Greek army is so geared up for plunder and slaughter that, if it is not unleashed on Troy, it will rebound and destroy Agamemnon's Argos. Fear that his army will vent its pent-up aggression on his own city is what impels Agamemnon to sacrifice Iphigenia. Fear, including the leaders' fear of their troops, is a fundamental state of mind throughout the play.

Like *Iphigenia among the Taurians*, *Iphigenia in Aulis* denies the veracity of its own myth. In judging the command to sacrifice Iphigenia, the Chorus sees not divine will but unholiness and the rule of might: blasphemy ('asepton') has power, and lawlessness dominates the laws ('Anomia de nomōn kratei') (1092, 1095). Indeed, the commands of the goddess are now unexplained and she is barely imaginatively present in their utterance; for the first time, we do not know *why* she is demanding the sacrifice. The dominant divine force is lust: *Aphroditē*. This features not only in the desire for Helen but also in the appetite for plunder and victory that drives the army to insist on the sacrifice. A terrible passion ('erōs') to make this expedition has seized all Greece (808); the passion which could equally drive the army against Troy or against Argos is an 'Aphroditē' which is driving them mad (1264). The play stresses loss of reason, terror, and disease of the mind, while the dramatic language is consistently rooted in internal processes, expressing a world governed by sensation and desire rather than causes or values.

The great military heroes of Homer are in Euripides powerless before the mob, of whom Odysseus has become the orchestrator. Achilles dare not rescue Iphigenia, for fear of being stoned by his troops; Agamemnon dare not halt the sacrifice lest the Greeks sack his own city. Yet these heroes are also victims of their own baseness and ambition. Agamemnon had schemed and flattered to gain – to buy ('priasthai') – the supreme command (342), and had at first been willing to sacrifice his daughter. The trouble with the desire for gain is that, unlike authority or prowess, it is universal. A world ruled by the desire for gain will always be a world ruled by the mob. (Richard Seaford has argued that the invention of money first made possible an unlimited desire for gain.)[42] More than any previous play, *Iphigenia in Aulis* postulates a relationship between human sacrifice and the marketplace. Agamemnon is prepared to pay ('apoteisai') (1169) the pure Iphigenia in exchange for the worthless Helen and, eventually, the army wishes to exchange Iphigenia for the plunder of Troy.

The portrayal of sacrifice as equivalent to monetary exchange is strengthened by the way in which Euripides imagines the body. This is not the fearful body of the *Oresteia*, leaking dangerous fluids, but the body both as something exchangeable and as something which denotes the unexchangeable individuality of the character. Helen caused wars with her body (1417); Iphigenia gives her body for Greece (1397); when Clytemnestra first arrives in Aulis, she is periphrastically described as 'the body of Clytemnestra' ('Klutaimēstras demas') (417). The body is sharply individualized, but only in order to have its exchange value the more precisely determined.

If the body may be represented by money, it may also be represented by writing. The Chorus mentions the story that Zeus changed his body into that of a swan in order to copulate with Leda and father Helen and Clytemnestra, but adds that the written tablets ('deltois') of the muses may lie (798). At the beginning of the play, Agamemnon has already sent a tablet, commanding Clytemnestra and Iphigenia to come to Aulis on the false pretext that Iphigenia is to marry Achilles. He now sends a tablet countermanding his original summons, but this second message does not get through. Initially, then, Iphigenia's fate rests on two written texts threading competing routes through the roads of Greece; finally, she is exchanged for a deer. The focus is on the victim as someone who can be signified, exchanged, or replaced, and the play is perhaps the first to examine the relationship between sacrifice and the secular sign systems of writing and money. It is curious that, in the eighteenth century, this play should so frequently have been transformed into a text of Enlightenment; that a ruler such as Frederick the Great could use the Iphigenia in Aulis plot to illustrate the cares of the tireless ruler.

In Euripides' play, the illusion of heroic community survives only in the opening chorus of female sightseers from nearby Chalcis, who come to look at and celebrate the heroes. As Helene Foley notes, the chorus presents 'a more glorious world' than that of the strife-ridden army.[43] Yet are there any internal incongruities in this glorious world? In the first antistrophe two Ajaxes are glimpsed – simply sitting together. Protesilaus (the first Greek to die at Troy) is playing with Palamedes at draughts, a game invented by the latter. At the end of the antistrophe Odysseus is glimpsed, doing nothing at all. Odysseus is the villain of this and other plays. At this moment, these heroes are undifferentiated, yet hindsight differentiates many of them. Knowing of a prophecy that the first Greek to step ashore at Troy would be the first to die, Protesilaus had accepted the role; he is the counterpart to Iphigenia, the sacrifice at the other end of the voyage. The greater Ajax had committed suicide after the arms of Achilles were awarded to Odysseus. Palamedes is shortly to die in a judicial murder plotted by Odysseus, whose ruse for avoiding the Trojan expedition he had penetrated and discredited. Palamedes had invented writing, and Odysseus was to turn this invention against him by forging a treasonable letter in his hand, and causing him to be stoned by the army: an actualization of the mob violence that constantly simmers during the play. Palamedes (about whom Euripides and others had written tragedies) is an archetypal example of the dangers of writing: its capacity to produce an infinity of uncontrollable replications of the self; a capacity which leads Iphigenia to the sacrificial altar. The chorus provides a monochrome, untragic version of the heroic world, in which first-raters and second-raters, murderers and victims, occupy an equal role. In the presence of Protesilaus, Odysseus, and above all Palamedes, the impulses that the sacrificial command exposes are seen to be endemic to the larger conduct of the expedition. The chorus looks forward, after all, to a suicide, a judicial murder, and another human sacrifice.

As remarked earlier, *Iphigenia in Aulis* was to be one of the Greek tragedies that most provided a model for Enlightenment tragedy. Euripides' other late tragedy, *The Bacchae*, has little to say to the eighteenth century, but was to be one of the tragedies that spoke most to the twentieth, for it shows a civilization collapsing into a collectivist frenzy. In the play, the young king Pentheus of Thebes tries to suppress the ecstatic worship of Dionysus that is sweeping his city, but he is tricked by the god into spying in female disguise as the Bacchantes (who include his mother) revel in the mountains. He is captured and dismembered, and his mother returns to Thebes bearing her son's head, which she believes to be that of a lion. His killing, by his mother, is described as a sacrifice ('thuma') (1246), and she is the priestess ('hierea') who kills him (1114). All the distinctions of culture are confounded in a perverse sacrificial substitution: not the visible substitution of an animal for a human being, but the unnoticed substitution of a human being for an animal.

In *Agamemnon*, Clytemnestra pays for a blow with a blow: 'tumma tummati'. The structural and emotional symmetry of the isolated verbal pairing masks the chaos which results when the pairings of vengeance are extended in a potentially infinite sequence. Near the beginning of *The Bacchae*, Cadmus, the founding father of Thebes, meets the prophet Teiresias, an old man meeting an old man: 'gerōn geronti' (186). A few lines later, one old man offers to lead the other: 'gerōn geronta' (193). Here, by contrast, the verbal patterns seem reassuring, confirming the shared social and biological roles of the men as elders of the city. Yet they are clad

Plate 5 The death of Pentheus (*c.* 490 BC)

in the fawnskins of Dionysus, trophies of the mountain and the hunt; garments worn equally by men and women, and in the play predominantly by the latter; for another confounded polarity is that of the sexes. The chaos that we see is in radical conflict with the order which we hear. The symmetries of language clash violently with the unmanageable divisions of perception and identity that take over the city.

Figures such as Aeschylus' 'tumma tummati' or Sophocles' 'phonōi phonon' (death with death) express sequential action.[44] Those of Cadmus and Teiresias suggest rather stasis: a reciprocal confirmation of roles, as also happens when Teiresias denounces Pentheus as a fool speaking foolish things ('mōra . . . mōros') (369), or when Dionysus, disguised as his own devotee, claims that he was initiated by the god in person, 'seeing him at the same time as he saw me' ('horōn horōnta') (470). Yet where language offers synonym and tautology, the eye perceives confusion: doubling where there should be unity, and vice versa.

It is hardly necessary to reiterate that the play is full of doublings and splittings of identity.[45] Mesmerized by Dionysus, Pentheus sees two suns. Dionysus appears as his own worshipper, and is also perceived by Pentheus as a bull. Not only do the elders of the city assume alternative identities by dressing like the female bacchanals of the mountain, Pentheus also spies

Plate 6 The death of Pentheus (House of the Vettii, Pompeii)

on the Bacchic orgies dressed as a woman. There are the true maenads whom Dionysus brings with him from Asia, and the false maenads (including Pentheus' mother) whom he intoxicates at Thebes, and finally punishes. The splittings generally affirm a unity of opposites: man and woman, god and animal, Greek and Oriental, nature and culture. They also suggest that the boundaries constructed by *logos* – language, reason, and number – impose forms and divisions that are not sustained outside the mental world, and which can collapse within it. Two old men in the street are a city: but two cities in the same place, or two suns in the sky, are chaos.

The outraged Dionysus seems purely hostile to the culture of the *polis* and of the household: he destroys buildings, and drives women from their homes to the mountains; returning to the city with her son's head in her hand, Agave intensifies the destruction of the civic by wishing to nail the head to the wall of her house. Dionysus is, indeed, regularly dissociated from the city. Though he praises the beauty of the mixed-population

Plate 7 A late medieval version of the death of Pentheus, in Ovid's *Metamorphoses* (Paris: Antoine Vérard, 1493)

cities of Asia, his references to the city (*polis*, *astu*) of Thebes are always hostile and contemptuous, and even the cities of Asia have limited hold on his mind. There is a telling moment when Pentheus asks the stranger what his country is. Dionysus asks if he knows of flowery Mount Tmolus. Yes, replies Pentheus, it encircles the city ('astu') of Sardis (461–3). For Pentheus, the city is an inevitable point of reference; for Dionysus, the mountain is self-sufficient. One might add that, with his image of the encircling mountain, Pentheus here thinks in terms of containment, as he always does: the prison is not only the instrument of his rule but the image of his mind.

Yet what is thc city? In contrast to *King Oedipus*, *The Bacchae* portrays no civic institutions: there is only the civic violence of Pentheus, expressed in the desire to imprison, execute, and hunt. As Helene Foley notes (p. 210), Pentheus ironically suffers the punishments with which he has threatened Dionysus and his followers: beheading (241) and sacrifice (796). The antagonists are thus contrary but complementary exponents of violence: Pentheus imprisons, while Dionysus shatters the prison walls; Pentheus enforces distinctions, while Dionysus dissolves them. Like the *Oresteia*, the play focusses on the idea of *dikē*. In the *Oresteia* this word (initially meaning 'custom') means both vengeance and justice, one of the achievements in the play being to harmonize its meanings. In *The Bacchae*, however, *dikē* is only ever associated with physical punishment. For the first half of the play, up to line 793, it is the exclusive property of Pentheus, and is solely used to suggest containing the threat from women. From Dionysus' pronouncement that Pentheus will render *dikē* in death (847), however, the word is uttered only by him and his acolytes, except when Cadmus recalls that Pentheus visited punishment (*dikē*) on those who tried to wrong (*adikein*) him (1310–26). To which the Chorus replies that Pentheus has received fitting *dikē* (1327). Pentheus uses forcible justice to maintain distinctions of sex and patriarchal authority; Dionysus uses it to confuse them, and finally to return the founder of the city to the condition of a nomad. As Pentheus leaves for his fatal journey to Cithaeron, the Chorus prays for the manifestation of justice. But justice is to come from the 'swift hounds of madness' ('thoai Lussas kunes') on the mountain (977), and the manifestation of justice ('dika phaneros') (992, 1011) is paralleled with the desired manifestation of Dionysus in the form of a bull ('phanēthi tauros') (1017). The revelation of the god's justice is also a revelation of his bestial nature.

Dionysus is not a god of the city, and the words of the city (such as *dikē*) constantly take on a new meaning in the Dionysiac realm. If he introduces two suns and two cities, he also introduces two semantic systems.[46] One of the most contested terms is one of the words that most fundamentally characterizes man as a being capable of culture: *sophia* (wisdom, but also cleverness). Is it wisdom to reject Dionysus, as Pentheus believes, or to accept him? Or is *sophia* to be rejected altogether in favour of pre-rational ecstasy, as the Chorus seem riddlingly to suggest when they assert that that which is *sophos* (wise) is not *sophia* (wisdom) (395). The word first appears amidst the comforting linguistic balance of Cadmus' first greeting to Tiresias. When the old man symmetrically greets the old man, 'gerōn geronti', he hails him as 'sophos' (186); in a slightly earlier verbal doubling, he identifies the approaching Tiresias by recognizing the wise voice of a wise man: 'sophēn sophou' (179) – the first use of the word. The final occurrence of the word *sophos* is, like its first, in a polyptoton, but of a very different effect. Agave exults:

> Dionysus the clever hunter
> cleverly [*sophos sophōs*] urged the maenads on
> against this beast.
>
> Ho Bakchios kunagetas
> sophos sophōs anepēl' epi thēra
> tonde mainadas. (1189–91)

Yet again, sacrifice is here imagined as a reversion from the city to the hunt, the wisdom of the prophet and the lawgiver metamorphosing into the cunning of the huntsman. Not until the twentieth century were later writers able to respond to a vision of culture in which opposites so totally contain each other; to a work which so totally affronts the separations and divisions on which culture depends. What is striking, however, and what no later adaptor matched, is Euripides' exploration of the way in which the vocabulary of the city has a second, shadow self in the wilderness.[47] Language, the gift which is the foundation of culture, automatically reconfigures itself in the image of its opposite.

CHAPTER 3

Virgil to Augustine

In a famous incident at the end of Book 5 of the *Aeneid*, Neptune claims the life of Aeneas' steersman Palinurus as the price for the safe landing in Italy of the rest of the Trojan expedition: one life shall be given for many – 'unum pro multis dabitur caput' (5.815). It is a prime formulation of the modern, secular sense of what sacrifice is.

The death of Palinurus is not a ritual sacrifice: he falls asleep at the helm, and drops into the sea. Yet he is taken by the god, and the sacrifice of one for the sake of many exemplifies the central tenet of Virgil's vision of history: that the imperial mission is greater than any individual. In Euripides, the noble sacrifice of the individual for the state is to be admired even as we view with abhorrence the religious or political system that enforces it. Here the issues seem simpler. Neptune's wishes are inscrutable, but he is elsewhere a benevolent deity, and the payment of one life for many promptly receives its deplorable counterpart in an incident narrated at the beginning of Book 6, as having been engraved by Daedalus on the gates at Cumae: the annual feeding of seven Athenian youths to the Minotaur to avenge the accidental death of Minos' son Androgeos (20–2). In an individualistic tyranny, the many are sacrificed (in a secular sense) for the one without any mathematical ratio or limit. Moreover, they are sacrificed to a semi-human monster whose mingling of human and animal form (like that of the many other monsters in the poem) represents human regress: a confused and primitive state in which reason is lost in instinct. Human progress is here not movement beyond human sacrifice, but towards the right kind of sacrifice: that of the individual for the state. The group of Roman worthies whom Aeneas sees at the end of Book 6 includes several who have killed their children, or sacrificed themselves, for the good of the state, including two (the father and son Publius Decius Mus) who were reported to have ritually undertaken self-immolation in battle, in order to secure victory.

In celebrating the founding and expansion of Rome, the *Aeneid* is, manifestly, a representation of human progress: progress in which the individual plays a decreasingly prominent role. When, in Book 1, Jupiter calms the fears of Aeneas' mother Venus with an exposition of the Roman future (1.254–96), he portrays a transformation of civilization in which the individual is dwarfed by the historical goal: after all his toil and suffering, Aeneas will survive 3 years; his son will reign for 30; Alba Longa, the city he founds, will flourish for 300; and only then will the city of Rome be founded. As the remaining years of Aeneas' lifespan are multiplied tenfold, and then tenfold again, before even the first stone of Rome is laid, the individual dwindles to insignificance in the vast unfolding of imperial destiny. Sacrifice becomes an articulation of the dynamics of history. The subordination of the one to the many is decreed by the structure of time itself.

When Aeneas visits the future site of Rome in Book VIII, its then ruler, the Arcadian King Evander, gives an account of the advance of humanity, though one that is localized to the specific area. First, the inhabitants were hunter–gatherers, scattered throughout the mountains, and ignorant of agriculture and the management of their resources. The exiled Saturn then gathered them together and gave them laws, establishing a Golden Age which has long been lost but whose recovery the poem envisages. Indeed, its establishment has recently been re-enacted, for the Arcadians are commemorating Hercules' killing of Cacus, a half-human monster (like the Minotaur), who breathed fire, stole cattle, and ate human flesh: a foe of culture and of agriculture. Immediately after relating how the priests – the Salii – ritually celebrate his purging of the wilderness, Evander recounts Saturn's earlier civilizing of Latium, so that the two impositions of culture are clearly linked.

Aeneas' visit to the site of Rome counterbalances his visit to the site of its antitype, the matriarchal enemy city of Carthage. This is a land where the fields have not yet been sown, and where hunting still rules: Aeneas' mother Venus appears to her son in the guise of a huntress; Dido at her first appearance is likened to Diana, the goddess of the hunt; and Aeneas himself is reduced to the cultural level of a hunter. At their departure from Troy, the survivors had gathered by the Temple of Ceres, the goddess of corn. During their shipwreck on the African coast, their corn (here metonymically referred to by the name Ceres) (1.177) has become tainted by seawater; it is edible but sterile. At this point, therefore, Aeneas becomes a hunter, slaughtering seven stags (as Odysseus had slaughtered a stag on Circe's island) (*Odyssey* 10.158–84). This pre-agricultural meal is the only one in the poem to follow the ritualized form of a Homeric banquet, and the allusion stresses the primitiveness of Aeneas' cultural condition here. The hunting of the stags is the first act of killing in the poem, and this act of killing forms the basis for the poem's first ritual:

> The others prepare the spoil, the feast that is to be; they flay the hides from the ribs and lay bare the flesh; some cut it into pieces and impale it, still quivering, on spits; others set cauldrons on the shore and feed them with fire. Then with food they revive their strength, and stretched along the grass take their fill of old wine and fat venison.

illi se praedae accingunt dapibusque futuris;
tergora diripiunt costis et viscera nudant;
pars in frusta secant veribusque trementia figunt,
litore aena locant alii flammasque ministrant.
tum victu revocant vires, fusique per herbam
implentur veteris Bacchi pinguisque ferinae. (1.210–15)

Throughout the poem, Saturn's process of civilization is threatened by an atavistic hankering for the hunt, and for the mountains, the caves, or the forest. In Carthage, Aeneas and Dido consummate their love during a hunt, in a mountain cave. After the arrival in Italy, the flashpoint for the war between Latins and Trojans occurs when a tame deer is hunted to death by the Trojans; in the preceding build-up of hysteria, Queen Amata and her fellow women have rushed from the city into the mountains, in feigned Bacchic frenzy. In Book 9, the young male lovers Nisus and Euryalus go on a night mission to take an urgent message to Aeneas, but get diverted into slaughtering and plundering a sleeping group of enemy soldiers. It is a Homeric action, imitating the exploits of Diomedes and Odysseus in Book 10 of the *Iliad*, but on this occasion it is an individualistic glory-trip, deflecting the heroes from their historical vocation. That Nisus is a relic of an obsolescent, individualistic past is indicated by the repeated emphasis on his activities as a hunter.

Euryalus is captured and killed. Nisus gets to the site of Alba Longa – the site of the future – but then realizes that Euryalus is missing, and rushes back into the forest (and the past), pointlessly sacrificing his life in order to kill the killer of his friend. The message they were meant to be taking to Aeneas never gets through.[1] Nisus' death is thus the antitype to that of Palinurus: a sacrifice which impedes the mission instead of enabling it, its tainted sacrificial character prefigured by an incident at the funeral games of Aeneas' father, Anchises, when Nisus, who is in the lead, slips in blood from sacrificed oxen, mixed with dung, but then selfishly trips up the person after him so that Euryalus can win. Proleptically, the polluted sacrificial blood seems to define the later incident as an anti-sacrifice, another elevation of personal passion over public duty. Yet the cause which the two young men neglect did not matter. The undelivered message was unnecessary, for Aeneas was returning anyway. Although their sacrifice impedes rather than enables a cause, the importance of the cause is mistaken.[2] Here, Virgil's ironic view of sacrifice approximates to that of Euripides.

The *Aeneid* is full of deaths which aspire to the condition of formal sacrifice. Indeed, as Philip Hardie notes, 'The narrative begins and ends with a sacrifice';[3] for Aeneas' final, controversial, killing of the enemy commander Turnus is accomplished with the word 'immolat' (12.947).[4] Tempted for a moment to show mercy, Aeneas is plunged into renewed fury when he sees that Turnus is wearing a baldric which he had taken as a trophy after killing Evander's young son Pallas, and sacrifices his enemy to the dead youth. If the first ritual of the poem is the dismemberment of the hunted stag, the last ritual – and indeed the last lines – are devoted to the slicing open of the sacrificed warrior:

'Pallas it is, Pallas who sacrifices you with this stroke, and takes retribution from your guilty blood!' So saying, in burning rage he buries his sword full in Turnus' breast. His limbs grew slack and chill and with a moan his life fled resentfully to the Shades below.

> 'Pallas te hoc vulnere, Pallas
> immolat et poenam scelerato ex sanguine sumit.'
> hoc dicens ferrum adverso sub pectore condit
> fervidus; ast illi solvuntur frigore membra
> vitaque cum gemitu fugit indignata sub umbras. (12.948–52)

In addition to the sacrifices mentioned above, there are also the deaths of Laocöon and Priam, both at altars, and the suicide of Dido, which masquerades as a religious rite. A sacrifice at the beginning of Book 3 is tainted when a branch broken from a tree to adorn a sacrificial altar drips with blood, the blood of Priam's youngest son, who had been sent away from Troy for safety but murdered by his opportunistic host. All these deaths have the character of sacrifice without being fully developed ritual sacrifices. Only once is there a formal human sacrifice: when Aeneas, in imitation of Achilles, captures eight Latin youths for sacrifice at the funeral of his dead protégé, Evander's son Pallas.

Then four youths, sons of Sulmo, and as many reared by Ufens, he takes alive, to offer as victims to the dead and to sprinkle the funeral flame with captive blood.

> Sulmone creatos
> quattuor hic iuvenes, totidem quos educat Ufens,
> viventis rapit, inferias quos immolet umbris
> captivoque rogi perfundat sanguine flammas. (10.517–20)

Turnus is the ninth, deferred, victim in this sacrifice. In the case of the eight youths, the ritual sacrifice is fully accomplished, but is not directly seen; the death of Turnus is seen, but not fully ritualized. Human sacrifice lurks on the margins of the poem, approximated to if seen, not seen if fully accomplished. Yet it is a constant presence, and it is particularly striking that the one incident of formal human sacrifice should take place on the site of Rome, the site that had been purged of its cannibalistic monster by Hercules, and on which Saturn had led men from hunting to agriculture. Human sacrifice is moved to the centre of human progress. By contrast, amidst all the stress on the latent barbarity of Carthage – Dido wishes she had served Aeneas' son to him in a Thyestean banquet (4.602) – Virgil makes no reference to Carthaginian human sacrifice; that practice he associates with Rome.

The *Aeneid* thus traces the traditional sequence of human progress, from the hunt and the cave to the farm and the city, but removes human sacrifice from its traditional place in the cycle. That is a constant: it is not the casualty of progress but its condition. To see the sacrifices of the *Aeneid*, as some critics have done, as a Girardian sacrificial crisis culminating in the death of Turnus does justice to the insensate passion of some of the killings, but oversimplifies the sense that it is an almost objectively inevitable component in progress itself.[5] As is shown by the cycle in which Aeneas' remaining 3 years are dwarfed by the 30 years of his son's reign, and the 300 years' duration of Alba Longa, human sacrifice is a form of mathematical law, determined by the ratio between the individual lifespan and the scale of history.

The question of ritual human sacrifice is most directly confronted in the incident which leads to Troy's downfall. In Book 2, the Greek spy Sinon worms his way into the Trojans' confidence and persuades them to take the wooden horse into their city. He excites their pity by pretending to have escaped a human sacrifice commanded by Apollo's oracle to counterbalance that of Iphigenia, and he does so by invoking the figure of Palamedes: the inventor of writing, unjustly executed after Ulysses had turned his invention against him by forging a treasonable letter in his hand. Sinon represents himself as an associate of Palamedes, persecuted by Ulysses for his dead friend's sake (2.81–194). His tale starts with the death of an agent of human progress, as the cultural advance he introduced became a trap to destroy him. Yet Sinon's narrative is itself, apparently, a narrative of human progress. He has been driven (he claims) from his society to become a refugee skulking in the marshes, but he is then rescued from the wilderness and accepted into a new city. He escapes from a culture of sacrifice, enslaved to the primitive linguistic force of the oath and the oracle, to one of cosmopolitan brotherhood. In short, he largely foreshadows the pattern of later texts such as Mozart's *Idomeneo*, or recapitulates that of earlier ones such as the *Oresteia* or *Iphigenia among the Taurians*.

But not only are the facts of his tale false; its morality is false. Greek literature had portrayed the horror, and often the abolition, of human sacrifice, but Virgil is portraying a civilization founded upon its reinterpretation: a civilization which repudiates Greek individualism. Not only are the Trojans seduced by lies, they are seduced by a false vision of human progress. Sinon portrays Greece as a civilization caught in repetition: the sacrifice of Iphigenia must be counterbalanced by another sacrifice; the theft of the Palladium must be counterbalanced with the offering of the Trojan horse. Body must be counterbalanced with body, sign with sign. Sinon seems to replace repetition with evolution.[6]

Yet what the *Aeneid* offers is both. The speech of Jupiter in Book 1 portrays a thousand-year advance towards global civilization. But the war in Latium, which is necessary to initiate Jupiter's vision, is also characterized by repetition of the past: Aeneas, for example, re-enacts Achilles' funerary sacrifice of captive youths, and the sacrificial killing of Turnus re-enacts Achilles' killing of Hector in the *Iliad*.[7] The factor that induces Aeneas to refuse mercy to Turnus is the sight on him of the belt he had taken from the dead Pallas, the son of Evander, with whom Aeneas felt a special bond, and who had been killed by Turnus on his very first day of warfare. The decorations on the belt depict one of the darkest episodes in Greek mythology. Danaus had quarrelled with his twin brother Aegyptus, and had fled from Africa to the realm of King Pelasgos in Greece. Seemingly, he had agreed to marry his fifty daughters to Aegyptus' fifty sons, but had ordered the brides to murder their grooms on the wedding night. Forty-nine had obeyed. Danaus was the eponymous ancestor of the Danaans (Greeks); Aegyptus, of the Egyptians. The story is an aetiological myth of the separation and polarization of nations and cultures. The representation of this myth is the last object explicitly seen in the poem, so that the union of Trojan and Latin peoples takes place in the shadow of an ancient and terrible myth of origin.[8]

The first event depicted at Carthage is Aeneas' stag-hunt and the carnivorous feast; the last is the self-immolation of Dido. This also concludes the sequence which began with the feast in her palace. Aeneas' arrival in Latium is marked by a vegetarian feast; the last event there is the immolation of Turnus. Aeneas' dealings with Evander's kingdom follow the same sequence: he arrives in the middle of a sacrificial feast; his last contact is to send back the dead Pallas, accompanied by the victims for human sacrifice. The voyage from Sicily to Italy is preceded by nine days of feasting; it concludes with the solitary sacrifice of Palinurus. Or one might extend the pattern beyond the limits of the *Aeneid*: the *Iliad* concludes with a feast; the *Aeneid* with the solitary sacrifice of Turnus. As in Greek culture, human sacrifice is placed in opposition to the community of the feast. The difference is that the feast in Homer is culturally stable: it may be perverted in many ways, but rightly performed only in one. Every feast in the *Aeneid* has a different cultural form, sometimes good, sometimes bad; human sacrifice is constant.

Virgil took a single sacrificial incident in the *Iliad*, and elevated it to a central epic theme, alongside the battle and the quest. As Philip Hardie has shown, his treatment of sacrifice profoundly influenced later Latin poets, and it also proved fascinating for the Renaissance.[9] Writing in the aftermath of the discovery of America, and of the sacrificial cultures of Mexico and Peru, Renaissance epic poets repeatedly dwell on the relationship between Christian civilization and exotic sacrificial cultures, using the Virgilian model, yet reversing (and at times denouncing) the ineradicable presence of human sacrifice in civilization which their model had accepted.

THE EARLY CHURCH

In the immediate aftermath of Virgil, in the earliest period of Christianity, there was no reason to define the Crucifixion in relation to human sacrifice, and indeed the synoptic gospels do not emphasize its sacrificial character. Though Abraham is, naturally, an immensely important figure in the New Testament, his willingness to sacrifice Isaac is only mentioned twice, once as an example of faith (Hebrews 11:17) and once as an example of works (James 2:21). Later, the primary meaning of the sacrifice of Isaac was as a symbol of the Crucifixion, but the connection is only indirectly drawn in the Bible, in that Ishmael (Abraham's son by his concubine Hagar) and Isaac respectively symbolize the Old and the New Testament. The Crucifixion is a ransom or redemption (of man from slavery), with the monetary sense of redemption (*lutrōsis*) far more prominent than it is to our ears. It is a victorious battle. It enables the justification of the sinner: an image of legal penalty which was to be prominent in later accounts (for example, in *The Divine Comedy* and *Paradise Lost*). When it is described as a sacrifice, the point of reference is invariably animal sacrifice, particularly that of the Paschal Lamb. For the Crucifixion shows the insufficiency of the animal sacrifices practised under the Old Law. It is a single sacrifice, after which carnal sacrifice ceases: 'For the law having a shadow of good things to come, and not the very image of the things, can never with those sacrifices which they offered year by year continually make the comers thereunto perfect . . . But this man, after he had offered one sacrifice for sins for ever, sat down on the right hand of God' (Hebrews 10:1, 12).

Primarily, however, the Crucifixion provides atonement or reconciliation achieved with blood, transmuting the rituals of purification with animal blood that are repeatedly ordained in Leviticus. It is a sacrifice, yet its carnal aspect is annulled by the survival of the victim, and it in turn annuls carnal sacrifice altogether. Clearly, however, it is a template against which human sacrifice was to be measured when it was eventually encountered in the sixteenth century, and the rise of free thought in the eighteenth eventually conflated the two forms of sacrifice.

One of the earliest Christian writers to address the question of human sacrifice is Clement of Alexandria (d. *c.* 215). More explicitly than the writers of the New Testament, Clement in his *Paedagogus* sees Isaac as a type of Christ, but the resemblance is in the fact of their survival: that neither was in fact sacrificed (1.5.23). In another work, the *Protrepticus* (*Exhortation to the Greeks*), Clement undertakes an extended comparison of Christianity and Greek and Roman paganism. To some extent, he exploits symmetries between the opposing cults, using the destruction of the mythological serpent at Delphi as a counterpart to Christ's victory over the serpent Satan. In the final chapter, he cites the ending of *The Bacchae* as a summation of that which Christianity is rejecting, using Pentheus' double vision to illustrate the intoxicated ignorance of idolatry. He also (as Milton was to do) compares the sacred mountains of the two religions: 'This is the mountain beloved of God, not a subject for tragedies like Cithaeron, but one devoted to the dramas of the truth, a wineless mountain, shaded by hallowed groves.'[10] Near the beginning, Clement denounces the immorality and cruelty of pagan religion, devoting a chapter to human sacrifice (which for him includes gladiatorial games) (3.36–40). The pagan gods, he argues, are worse than men; the Christian god, far greater. Yet he does not use human sacrifice in the way he uses the Pythian serpent or the sacred mountain: as something which can be translated into a corresponding sacred truth. The sacrifice of Pentheus is not mentioned in Clement's account of *The Bacchae*, and indeed he does not describe the Crucifixion as a sacrifice at all: it is a victory over death and the serpent (11.86–7).

Clement's rebuttal of paganism is an early example of a kind of polemic of which the most substantial and familiar example is St Augustine's *Concerning the City of God, against the Pagans.* This was written in the aftermath of Alaric's sacking of Rome in 410, and confuted those who claimed that Rome had fallen because it had prohibited sacrifice to the old gods. In the process, it provides an extended study of the role of sacrifice in the cities of man and of God. As a meditation on the providential scheme which abandons Rome, *City of God* is, in effect if not intent, a massive answer to the *Aeneid*, and it was so used by Milton in *Paradise Lost.*

Like Clement (though less intensely), Augustine is aware of the former existence of human sacrifice, in Gaul and his own home city of Carthage (7.19, 26), but it is not a primary concern, and it is not a point of reference in considering the Crucifixion. Like Clement, too, he regards Isaac as a type of Christ by virtue of the fact that the sacrifice is averted: 'Abraham, we can be sure,' he writes, 'could never have believed that God delights in human victims'.[11] The essence of the Crucifixion is its total difference from the corporeal, endlessly repeatable sacrifices of the city of man and of the old law. It is different both because of the victim's survival and because of the internalized, non-carnal nature of the sacrifices which it initiates: sacrifices such as the disciplining of the body by temperance.

By stressing the internal and metaphoric character of sacrifice, Augustine redefines the relationship between sacrificial systems and the order of language. Carnal sacrifices are shadows of the true sacrifice, 'just as spoken words are the symbols of things' (10.19; p. 399). The Crucifixion was prefigured by many Old Testament rituals, just as many different words can refer to a single thing (10.20; p. 401). Like language, therefore, carnal sacrifice has what true sacrifice lacks: an infinite capacity for repetitive variation. There is, however, only one true sacrifice.

Like St Paul, Augustine quotes the Psalms ('The sacrifices of God are a broken spirit: a broken and a contrite heart' (Psalm 51:17)) to sum up the paradoxical role of carnal sacrifice in Christianity: 'The offering which . . . God does not want, signifies the offering which . . . God does desire' (10.5; p. 378). The physical sacrifice has two contradictory aspects, as a false sacrifice and a sign of the true sacrifice by which its falsity is measured. Carnal sacrifice thus occupies a different conceptual order from true sacrifice, as a set of infinitely variable false signs by which the true is discovered and understood. It was this distinction that was used when, finally, Europeans once again encountered cultures that practised human sacrifice, and had to interpret that supreme symbol of infinitely repeatable sacrifice: the Aztec skull rack.

CHAPTER 4

The discovery of America

THE CONQUISTADORS AND THE POETS

On their journey to Mexico, Cortés and his companions landed at Cozumel, where they first saw evidence of human sacrifice. They also encountered two Spaniards, shipwrecked some years earlier. One had gone native, but the other, Geronimo de Aguilar, was glad to be ransomed, his knowledge of Mayan proving invaluable in the subsequent conquest. According to the not always reliable López de Gómara, when Aguilar's mother 'hard yt hir son was captiue among people yt used to eate mans flesh, & ever after when she saw any flesh spitted or roasted, she would make an open outcrie, saying, oh I miserable woman, behold this is the flesh of my deare beloued sonne who was all my comfort'.[1] Anthropophagy had re-entered the nightmares of Europe.

It had never entirely gone away. In his account of life among the cannibals of Brazil only a few decades later, the Huguenot Jean de Léry was to narrate the far greater barbarities committed during the French Wars of Religion, when human flesh was consumed, and indeed exposed for sale.[2] And, of course, charges of cannibalism are time-honoured ways of demonizing those we hate: the accusation that Jews drank the blood of ritually slaughtered children resurfaced in Spain in the formative days of the Inquisition.[3] Yet the first explorers did not go primed to project their scapegoating myths onto the heart of darkness. Patterning the New World according to the texts and explanations of the old, Columbus was prepared to expect one-eyed giants in his primitive world,[4] but his acquaintance with classical myth did not drive him to the logical conclusion of associating the primitive with the eating of human flesh, and he was at first unconvinced by reports of anthropophagy.

The experiences of Cortés's followers in Mexico, however, left no room for doubt:

> [A]gain there was sounded the dismal drum of Huichilobos and many other shells and horns and things like trumpets and the sound of them all was terrifying, and we all looked towards the lofty Cue where they were being sounded, and saw that our comrades whom they had captured when they defeated Cortés were being carried by force up the steps, and they were taking them to be sacrificed. When

Plate 8 Aztec human sacrifice in the Codex Magliabechiano, a mid sixteenth-century transcription of an earlier Aztec codex

they got them up to a small square in [front of] the oratory, where their accursed idols are kept, we saw them place plumes on the heads of many of them and with things like fans [in their hands?] they forced them to dance before Huichilobos, and after they had danced they immediately placed them on their backs on some rather narrow stones which had been prepared as [places for] sacrifice, and with stone knives they sawed open their chests and drew out their palpitating hearts and offered them to the idols that were there, and they kicked the bodies down the steps, and Indian butchers who were waiting below cut off the arms and feet and flayed [the skin off] the faces, and prepared it afterwards like glove leather with the beards on, and kept those for the festivals when they celebrated drunken orgies, and the flesh they ate in *chilmole*. In the same way they sacrificed all the others and ate the legs and arms and offered the hearts and blood to their idols, as I have said, and the bodies, that is their entrails and feet, they threw to the tigers and lions which they kept in the house of the carnivores which I have spoken about in an earlier chapter.

When we saw those cruelties all of us in our camp and Pedro de Alvarado and Gonzalo de Sandoval and all the other captains (let the interested readers who peruse this, note what ills we suffered from them [the Mexicans]) said the one to the other 'thank God that they are not carrying me off to day to be sacrificed'.[5]

These are the firsthand memories of Cortés's soldier Bernal Díaz de Castillo. Bernal had twice escaped while being led off to a similar fate, and

Plate 9 A European view of Aztec human sacrifice, in Theodor de Bry, *America*, Part IX (1601)

the spectacle and fear of human sacrifice affected him as no other horror of war did:

> As each day I beheld my companions carried off to be sacrificed, and had seen how they sawed open their chests and tore out their still beating hearts and cut off their feet and arms and ate them, to the number of sixty-two, as I have already said, besides ten of our company whom they had captured before that, I feared that one day or another they would do the same to me, for they had already seized me twice to carry me off to be sacrificed, but it pleased God that I should escape from their power. When I called to mind those hideous deaths, and as the proverb says, 'The little pitcher which goes many times to the fountain, &c.,' for this reason, from that time I always feared death more than ever. I say this because, before going into battle there was a horror and sadness in my heart. (IV, 190)

One recurrent element in Bernal Díaz's horror is his sense that human sacrifice destroys the normal relationship between the body and space. There is a chaotic relationship between the body and the ritual areas in which it was sacrificed: 'the walls were covered with blood' (I, 54); 'the walls and altars stained with blood and the hearts placed as offerings before the Idols . . . he found most of the bodies without arms or legs' (I, 161); 'everything was covered with blood, both walls and altar, and the stench was such that we could hardly wait the moment to get out of it' (II, 77). Bernal was writing sixty years after the event, but the terror of human sacrifice had not left him.

In Bernal Díaz's narrative, abolishing human sacrifice becomes Cortés's mission statement, along with suppressing other moral inversions, such as sodomy: 'desist from your sacrifices, and no longer eat the flesh of your own relations, and cease to commit sodomy' is his advice to one community (I, 221). In literature, too, the abolition of human sacrifice became the mission statement of Christian civilization. The era of exploration inevitably shaped the newly reborn genre of the epic, with Virgil's depiction of Aeneas' imperial destiny forming an irresistible model for celebrating the Christianizing destiny of the crusaders and explorers: figures such as Vasco da Gama, the subject of Camões's *Lusiads*. The year 1492 had witnessed both the defeat of Islam in Granada and the discovery of America by Columbus, who had visited Granada before setting sail. The twin European expansionist drives against the infidel, thus linked by Providence, were repeatedly recombined by poets. The illusions of Islam were stressed in the *Lusiads*. Conversely, in an epic about a crusade, it is normal to have a flash-forward to the voyages of Christian exploration: to prophesy the historical goal to which the events of the poem are moving, as the *Aeneid* moves towards the reign of Augustus.

Frequently, poets at once develop and expurgate the sacrificial theme of the *Aeneid*, giving a sometimes central place to a conflict between Christianity and cultures which are represented as practising cannibalism or human sacrifice (Islam is frequently represented in this way). In the definitive appropriation of Virgil's ideals of empire in the cause of Christian expansionism, Torquato Tasso's epic *Gerusalemme Liberata* (1580), the poet pauses from celebrating the deliverance of Jerusalem to look forward to Columbus's enlightenment of regions blighted by the abominable food ('abominevoli vivande') of cannibalism.[6] His example was widely followed by other epic writers. Pierre Le Moyne's *Saint Louys* (1658), about the Seventh Crusade, portrays Egypt as a land filled with archaeological relics and active survivals of sacrificial cults: Agamemnon-like, the sultan is prepared to sacrifice his daughter, whereas the Christ-like Louis is willing to stand as a sole sacrifice for his people.[7] St Louis's crusading mission is seen as part of a historical process that will result in the conversion of distant regions such as Japan (p. 251).

Like Tasso's epic, Girolamo Graziani's *Il Conquisto di Granata* (1650) portrays the recovery from Islam of a rightfully Christian city, and again associates the contest with Islam with the expansionist mission to the New World. Graziani tampers with chronology to make Columbus return from America to be present when Granada is taken. The experiences he relates include an encounter with a dog-headed, cannibalistic giant (misled by false analogies with Latin, Columbus had thought cannibals possessed the heads of dogs – *canes*).[8] The incident is based on the Polyphemus episode in the *Aeneid*, Columbus picking up a stranded companion, as Aeneas had picked up a stranded Greek. Like his predecessors in Homer and Virgil (but not Euripides), Graziani's giant eats his meals raw ('mense abbominande e crude'),[9] though he is not a solitary. Graziani, however, is not interested in ethnographic contrasts between the raw and the cooked but with providing an allegory of the moral chaos outside Christianity: travellers are lured to the cannibal's den by those commonplace symbols of the illusory beauty of sin, the Sirens. That is, the alien world becomes entirely reconstructed within a Christian schema, doubly filtered: through classical models that have themselves undergone a Christian reinterpretation.

The most explicit challenge to the sacrificial nature of ancient epic was, however, mounted by the Jesuit poet and epic theorist Pierre Mambrun, who between 1652 and 1661 published both a critical work on the epic and a Christian equivalent to the complete Virgilian corpus: a set of Christian Eclogues; a *Georgics* of the soul (the four-book *De Cultura Animi*, describing the four cardinal virtues); and a twelve-book epic, *Idololatria Debellata, sive Constantinus*,[10] which complements the *Aeneid* by portraying the establishment of the Christian Roman empire by Constantine the Great. In the last book of *De Cultura Animi*, 'Fortitudo', Mambrun cites the Trojan War as an example of false fortitude, and selects the human sacrifices of both Achilles and Aeneas as central illustrations of a barbarously vitiated heroic code.[11] In his own epic, moreover, he portrays an evolution beyond sacrificial cultures. Immediately after Constantine's antagonist Licinius has performed a human sacrifice in the last book, for example, God surveys the world from China to Peru, in a vision corresponding to Jupiter's narrative in *Aeneid* 1. The culminating representation of South America is of a land where human blood is – in a corruption of the Eucharist – drunk from golden goblets, and in which water is alien:

> Here mountains swell with gold, and under a rich sky crags raise their head with a yellow summit. Easily moving waters vie with rich sands, and reproach the yellow metal with their angry moisture. A people ignorant of the gods makes war in gloomy gold, and – not rational – drinks human blood in gold.

> Hic montes tumuêre auro, subque aëra diues
> Emisêre caput flauenti vertice rupes.
> Diuitibus faciles lymphæ rixantur arenis,
> Et flauum obiurgant irato rore metallum.
> Nescia gens Superûm tristi bellatur in auro
> Inque auro bibit humanum malè sana cruorem. (p. 310)

The historical mission celebrated in the poem is progress beyond human sacrifice, and the progress is encapsulated in the final lines of the poem, which evoke and reverse Aeneas' sacrifice of Turnus. Defeated by Constantine in single combat, Licinius calls on Christ. The invocation of Christ persuades Constantine to reverse the example of Aeneas and spare his opponent. Instead of the savage immolation of Turnus, there is mercy, authorized by the self-sacrifice of Christ and ending the slaughter of human victims on the altars of false gods (p. 323).

Native American human sacrifice, then, made one great impact on European literature, in that it shaped the prestige literary genre of the Renaissance, the epic. Hence it substantially influenced the nature of *Paradise Lost*, which transmutes the sacrificial aspects of the continental Catholic epic just as much as it transmutes its colonialist and missionary themes. Yet the Renaissance poems have no interest in representing Amerindian cultures, which they simplify into horrific headlines: 'abominevoli vivande'; 'mense abbominande'. Detailed accounts of the cultures remain locked in the works of historians and missionaries, some of which remained unpublished until the nineteenth century (as, for example, did the full version of Bernal Díaz's narrative, and the important accounts of Diego Durán and Bernardino de Sahagún). What remained undiscovered, however, is less interesting than what was published, and yet failed to make any impact on literature.

EARLY ETHNOGRAPHERS

A widely cited authority on the Spanish Americas was the Jesuit José de Acosta, who worked as a missionary in Peru from 1571 to 1587, and who pleaded with Philip II against the oppression of the Native Americans. At one point in his *Natvrall and Morall Historie of the East and West Indies* (1590), he narrates the legends of the successive migrations which had raised Mexico from a region of barbarous, cave-dwelling hunters, without society or agriculture, up to an advanced if cruel culture. On their migration to Mexico (in the thirteenth century), the Aztecs had paused in Culhuacán, whose king had at first tried to destroy them. Realizing the Aztecs' power, however, he had sought alliance, and his new allies had requested his daughter to be their queen, and the mother of their god. The daughter was delivered – and was then sacrificially flayed. To impersonate the goddess, a young man was clad in the girl's skin, and the skin was kept in perpetuity as an idol. To honour the elevation of his daughter, the king of Culhuacán entered the dark chapel with an entourage and rich gifts. By the light of the burning incense, he caught sight of her hair, and rushed out screaming.[12]

What happened next? Not a Renaissance revenge tragedy. The injured king scored a temporary military victory, but Culhuacán was destroyed by the Aztecs. Montezuma's own daughter married the Culhuacán ruler in 1509, and the sacrificed girl did become a goddess, Toci, who was honoured in an annual flaying ritual.[13] If the narrative develops in a distinctly non-Western fashion, however, the tale of the king's visit to the chapel is worthy of Poe, particularly in the sudden visual concentration on the hair illuminated by the flash of incense (compare the 'thirty-two small, white and ivory-looking substances' – the teeth – which conclude *Berenice*).

Like many other details of Mesoamerican sacrifices (such as those collected in the sixteenth century by Cortés's chaplain and apologist, Francisco López de Gómara), the story of the flayed princess was available to writers of Shakespeare's generation; indeed, Acosta was often quoted in the seventeenth century. Despite the literary and judicial fascination with rituals of dismemberment in this period, however, such narratives exercised no hold over the creative imagination, and failed to do so until the impact of Frazer's *The Golden Bough* (first edition 1890). Perhaps one reason for their extremely deferred imaginative appeal is that they did not resonate with any current theories of the body. Frazer provided a synthesis which seemed to link, in a universal set of psychological processes, everything from primitive acts of magic to belief in the Resurrection and communion. We have become fascinated with seeing traces of the primitive, even of the pre-human, in the most complex stages of our social practice. *The Golden Bough* provided this frisson of the *unheimlich*. It is as if we suddenly discovered the face of Huitzilopochtli peering from behind a Bellini Madonna. The alien, however, quite clearly provided different and more limited possibilities in the early modern period.

Seventeenth-century freethinkers or anti-Catholics could certainly draw parallels between the practices of exotic cultures and those of Christianity. To describe the trickery of pagan priests may be a coded way of attacking the Christian clergy; to describe exotic sexual customs may suggest that all forms of sexual morality are local conventions. Yet such analyses of diversity tend to have a homogenizing purpose: 'Priests of all Religions are the same', as Dryden put it.[14] Even the accounts of anti-Christians are not attempts to understand the alien.

How can it be done? The great sixteenth-century ethnographer Bernardino de Sahagún recorded the evidence of his Native American witnesses without intrusive interpretation. In general, however, those who sought to explain could only measure the new ethnological data against familiar but inappropriate templates, seizing fragments that seemed to fit the known structure but dissolving the alien contexture in the process. Like many subsequent writers, some early commentators thought that the Indians were a lost tribe of Israel, and looked for corrupt traces of the Old Testament (as can, for example, plausibly be found in the legend of a tribe seeking its promised land). Diego Durán noted resemblances between the dough images of Huitzilopochtli and the Host (as, from a different point of view, did Frazer (p. 505)), and wondered whether Quetzlcoatl might have been St Thomas. Acosta, by contrast, believed that the Indians had emigrated from Asia and he sought demonic parodies of divine truth, which were equally easily found, but this view similarly denied any intrinsic integrity to the alien culture. There were repeated attempts to rectify and normalize the disturbing symmetries between the religions: Durán notes with approval a plan to convert a sacrificial stone into a baptismal font, 'so that that which was a container for human blood, sacrificed to the devil, may now be the container of the Holy Spirit' (*Aztecs*, p. 119).

Although Acosta does provide a narrative of human progress within Mesoamerica, it is not a seamless one. It is a sequence of invasions, and the consequent movement from the cave to the city does not bring a movement beyond human sacrifice: that only comes with the arrival of the Christians, and the rapid recognition by the conquered that their old religion was absurd, irrational, and demonic. Acosta insists, humanely, on the potential intellectual equality of Africans, Native Americans, and Europeans,[15] but he also (inevitably) insists that the intellects are fulfilled in the same structure of belief. (Early commentators understood the elements of sympathetic magic in some of the Aztec sacrificial rites,[16] but unlike Frazer they regarded them as peripheral and exotic, not corresponding to a fundamental and culturally universal pattern.)

A recurrent theme in Acosta is that of a broken chain of images. Men should not be sacrificed, because men are the images of God. Acosta tells us, as Frazer was to do, of men who impersonate the false gods for a year before being sacrificed: 'they appoynted any slave to be the representation of the idoll, saying that it was his *picture*' (p. 386; italics added). He was reverenced for a whole year as the idol and then sacrificed (p. 387). Man is here divine through arbitrary and casual theatrical casting, rather than through universal carrying of the divine image. Idolatry, which Acosta regularly deplores, is an inflation of the false image: men start by grieving over likenesses of their loved ones, and by a process of cultural distortion the family photograph becomes a divinity. In the tale of the princess of Culhuacán, the process described is the turning of a living being (and image of God) into an 'idol'. If the analogical Christian universe offered a system of correspondences that linked the chain of being from top to toe, Mesoamerican civilization offered a fragmentation of correspondences at every level.[17]

Acosta records that he witnessed the discovery of a giant's skeleton (p. 502). Mexico is rich in fossils: he had perhaps seen the skeleton of a dinosaur.[18] His account of Mexican civilization is like a scattered collection of dinosaur bones; he lacks the pattern according to which he might reconstruct the monster, and show its taxonomic relation to the human. Yet the very misconstruction of the alien religion as a parody of Catholic truth meant that the parody could easily invade the reality. The possibility of cross-contamination was particularly recognized and feared by the Dominican Diego Durán, the most acute recorder of Aztec practices, divided between admiration and fear of the culture he was recording.

Durán pointed out that old practices were surviving within the guise of Christian observances: 'I have heard chants in honor of God and of the saint during the festivities, mixed with ancient metaphors which only the devil, their teacher, understands.'[19] Here, the alien god does peer from behind the image of Christ; but not as a double, as he will later do.

Christians were also capable of contaminating their own rituals. In an anthropologically very interesting work, the Dominican turned Puritan Thomas Gage – a rebel member of a prominent British recusant family – revealed that venal priests in Mexico were making money by degrading Christianity into equality with native religions. The Indians, for example, believed that their souls could be transferred into animals or inanimate objects.[20] Selling a saint's image to an Indian, a priest would tell him that the image was his external soul. Normally, the image remained in the church, but if the owner defaulted on his tithes the 'soul' was banished outside.[21] Gage's book describes a Christian-led synthesis of the two religions, but the synthesis was an inadvertent and corrupt one. Outside the sphere of religion, however, there was an inner compulsion on the part of the invaders to cynical replication of the old customs: a gallows stood on a former sacrificial site; Black African slaves may have been compelled to perform gladiatorial contests on the former Aztec sacrificial stones; and victims were hanged thirteen at a time, in honour of Christ and his disciples.[22] Conversely, crucifixion became an accepted form of human sacrifice among the Native Americans, the last authenticated case dating from 1868.[23]

Human sacrifice in the Americas is conveyed to us through a polyphony of voices. Bernal Díaz provides an intensely subjective engagement with the victims, stirred by the all too credible fear that it might happen to him. Cortés describes the New World in terms of structural relationships, calibrating its degrees of otherness and familiarity with every possible permutation of them: by comparisons with the civilizations of Europe, Asia, and Africa. Bernal Díaz tells us what Montezuma looked like. Cortés, habitually uninterested in personal description, does not: he tells us that, when he was first greeted by Montezuma and his nobles, the party were all dressed alike, except that Montezuma alone wore sandals.[24] Intense subjectivity enters Cortés's narrative only when he describes human sacrifice, though even here he describes not the sight, smell, and terror, as Bernal Díaz was to, but terror distilled into writing. He describes finding an inscription in charcoal at a sacrificial site: '"Here the unhappy Juan Yuste was held prisoner." . . . Surely a sight fit to break the hearts of all who saw it' (p. 184). Similarly, the generally dispassionate accounts recorded by Sahagún at one point acquire a memorable resonance, in imagining the sensations of one who is being sacrificed in ritual combat: 'Then, faltering and fainting, he fell upon the surface, tumbling as if dead. He wished that he might stop breathing, that he might suffer [no longer], that he might perish, that he might cast off his burden of death.'[25]

Human sacrifice was thus a thing of subjective horror. It threatened the Europeans' sense of self, and even (in Bernal Díaz's case) their sense of ordered existence in space. The subjective horror was, in part, due to contact with quite alien views of the body. In Peru, the mummified bodies of sacrificial victims were (like those of the Incas themselves) still regarded as sentient, and were consulted as oracles. The 'idol' in the story of the Princess of Culhuacán is a young man wearing the flayed skin of a woman. The incomprehensible distributions in space of the sacrificed and divided body, narrated by Bernal Díaz and others, reflect cultures which give the body a cosmic and temporal significance that is different from that of Europe. Yet they are both cultures which routinely subject it to extreme violence. How are the forms of violence to be distinguished?

VARIETIES OF VIOLENCE

In Tenochtitlan, Montezuma had a quadruple menagerie consisting of collections of animals, reptiles, fish, and birds, to which were fed parts of sacrificial victims. To us, though not to the original reporters, this is an evocative summation of a culture whose aesthetics are far more closely allied to violence than are ours. Yet the invaders violently destroyed that culture. How does their violence differ from that of their adversaries?

An extreme distinction between the cultures is postulated by Ginés de Sepúlveda, the opponent of Las Casas and defender of Spanish conduct in the New World. His tactic was altogether to deny culture, and indeed humanity, to the Native Americans. In rebuttal of Las Casas's denunciation of Spanish atrocities, Sepúlveda (citing St Augustine) replies that the saving of one soul outweighs millions of deaths. Both religions can provide accounting systems in which mass slaughter is a justifiable debit, but each declares the other to be monstrous and irrational. As always, Cortés formulates the matter with great structural clarity: 'I urged them not to sacrifice living creatures to the idols, as they were accustomed, for, as well as being most abhorrent to God, Your Sacred Majesty's laws forbade it and ordered that he who kills shall be killed' (p. 107). The sacrifice of living beings to lifeless idols is a natural inequality; that killers should be killed is a man-made law, but one of self-evident equity. A greater sympathy with the alien culture is, however, shown by Las Casas, who argued that human sacrifice was an understandable misapplication of an impulse evident in our own heritage, and present in the actions of Jephthah, Abraham, and the Christian martyrs.[26] It is inspired by the impulse to give to the gods that which is most valuable.

The Spanish atrocities reported by Las Casas, however, merited no such defence, for they not only devalued the individual but life itself. 'It happened', he reported, 'that one young man, the son of a chief, was traded for a cheese; on another occasion a hundred natives were exchanged for a single horse.'[27] Native Americans are also hunted with dogs. Although an element of ritualized hunting occasionally enters Mexican sacrifices, and although parts of victims are fed to Montezuma's animals, the Spanish hunts are the opposite of sacrificial ritual: a denial of humanity to human life. The same is true of the parody of the Last Supper, in which thirteen chieftains were hanged in a group, to resemble Christ and the apostles. This degrades in proportion to the magnitude of the original.

Aztec markets were controlled by the gods. As part of the festival of Toci, the god-impersonator would make clothes and go through the ceremonial pretence of selling them in the marketplace. There were specified marketplaces for particular commodities; to sell them elsewhere incurred divine anger.[28] Then this hieratic economy collided with a fully monetized society in which goods and people were universally convertible: convertible into anything. If one of the most haunting images in Bernal Díaz's description of Mexico is of the wild beasts in Montezuma's menagerie, another is of the Spaniards melting down Montezuma's gold and dividing it among themselves with improvised weights and measures. Elaborate systems of measurement were one achievement which distinguished the Europeans from the Native Americans; with their ad hoc weights, however, the Spaniards are blindly aping the systems of their own culture, while converting the forms of another into the universal, impersonal medium of weighed and measured gold.

A hundred natives for a horse. The bodies of the sacrificed were disposed of according to a ritual which makes no sense in any Western system, but which is a system nonetheless:

> they saw open the chest with stone knives and hasten to tear out the palpitating heart and blood, and offer it to their Idols in whose name the sacrifice is made. Then they cut off the thighs, arms and head and eat the former at feasts and banquets, and the head they hang on some beams, and the body of the man sacrificed is not eaten but given to these fierce animals [in Montezuma's menagerie].[29]

What the Spaniards introduce is a general commutability of the body: as food for dogs, as the price of a cheese, or of a hundredth of a horse. In a passage which foreshadows the conclusion of Aphra Behn's *Oroonoko* (1688), Las Casas relates the casual dismemberment of a young Native American prince who refused to enter these processes of exchange:

> When the boy persisted, repeating that he had no wish to leave home, the Spaniard took out his dagger and lopped off first one of his ears and then the other. When the boy again insisted that he did not want to go with him, he hacked off his nose, laughing out loud as he did so as though he were doing no more than pull his hair playfully. (p. 74)

One incident in particular seemed to define the systems of exchange to which the Spaniards subjected the sacrificial culture they were abolishing.

In an unsuccessful attempt to discover more gold, the Spaniards tortured the last emperor, Cuauhtémoc, and one of his noblemen, tormenting the latter to death. This incident is narrated by López de Gómara, though it was omitted from the somewhat expurgated English translation. It was, however, used by Montaigne, and appeared in English in the Florio translation, whence it was borrowed by Dryden for his play about the conquest of Mexico, *The Indian Emperour.* Here the atrocity clearly parallels the sacrificial rites of the Aztecs, showing how radically different cultures have an inbuilt drive to fulfil themselves in human sacrifice. The incident is reused yet again in Marmontel's novel *Les Incas* (1778), an Enlightenment attack upon Christianity and brutal colonialism.[30] Here, the body is precisely what it was not in the Aztec rites: a unit of economic exchange.

There is one area in which Catholicism, and that of Spain in particular, has been felt by non-Catholics to equal the barbarous formality of human sacrifice, and that is in the persecution of heretics. In *The Faerie Queene,* Edmund Spenser writes of the idolatrous 'daily sacrifize' of human beings in the Low Countries and of the sacrificial altar in Orgoglio's castle, 'On which true Christians bloud was often spilt'.[31] The equation of the *auto-da-fe* with ritual sacrifice persists in works such as Charles Maturin's *Melmoth the Wanderer* (1820) and, to some extent, in Schiller's and Verdi's versions of *Don Carlos.*[32]

There is no doubt some similarity between the great public *auto,* held on a feast day, attended by royalty and foreign dignitaries and thousands of sightseers from elsewhere, and the great ceremonies in Tenochtitlan. Yet such events started in 1558, with the appearance of Lutheranism in Spain, and were only common until 1570. The first and bloodiest stage of the Inquisition, caused by reds-under-the-bed fears about Judaizing *conversos,* claimed perhaps 2,000 lives in fifty years,[33] but they were not taken in great public festivities. The aim of the Inquisition was, initially, to reclaim rather than destroy: although acquittal was rare, the percentage of prisoners executed was of the order of 2 per cent. Henry Kamen calculates that, throughout the worldwide Spanish empire in the sixteenth and seventeenth centuries, the average number of executions by the Inquisition was under three persons per annum.[34] One execution, in Peru in 1578, was of Francisco de la Cruz, a friar whose many heresies included the claim that Native Americans could be saved without belief in the Trinity; a leading participant in his examination and condemnation was Acosta.[35] The humane successor of Las Casas, the shuddering narrator of the Princess of Culhuacán's sacrifice, participates in an *auto-da-fe.*

As much as any century, the sixteenth threw into high relief conflicting ideas of what was an acceptable calculus of death. If Sepúlveda considered millions of deaths a fitting price for one saved soul, Acosta destroys one life to suppress a doctrine threatening the salvation of all Native Americans. If we easily equate the mass *autos-da-fe* of the Inquisition's heyday with the mass parade of victims up the sacrificial pyramid, and the thousands of unindividuated skulls on the skull racks, there is no parallel in Aztec culture for the activity which gave the Inquisition its name: the detailed enquiry into faith, with opportunities to recant, which in 98 per cent of cases led elsewhere than to the stake. De la Cruz, for example, was executed after refusing to recant. The Inquisition's terrifying examination of the soul could be seen as diametrically opposed to the fate of the empty skull on the rack, evacuated of inner or outer history. Yet, from another cultural viewpoint, the rival religions can seem remarkably parallel, in that in both cases a tyrannically absolutist creed performs a ritual erasure of individuality. Enforced human sacrifice perverts the accounting systems with which we manage and normalize violent death, just as voluntary and noble self-sacrifice expresses them in their perfection. As these systems change and are reconfigured, so are the forms of death to which we attach the symbol of sacrifice, both monstrous and noble.

'NUMBERLESS WONDERS': MATHEMATICS AND SACRIFICE

If the religious rituals of the Aztecs did not immediately make the leap from the pages of Gómara and Acosta to those of tragedians and poets, there was one aspect of Native American culture that did fascinate early modern Europe. Writing 'The Woman who Rode Away' in the era of Frazer and Freud, D. H. Lawrence appropriated Mesoamerican culture to express his male fantasies about the female death wish: a 'rather dazzling Californian girl from Berkeley'[36] seeks out the role of sacrificial victim in Mexico. The mental structures which preoccupied seventeenth-century intellectuals were, however, rather different. What the New World offered to the age of the Scientific Revolution was an intriguingly alien system of calculation. Here again, however, as with Lawrence, there was selection and distortion: an emphasis on the numerically non-advanced features of 'primitive' cultures. Information about Mayan calendars, time-cycles, and their vigesimal system of counting was available in England in the translations of López de Gómara and Acosta. Acosta notes that the Aztecs had a symbol for zero;[37] the absence of such a symbol from Roman numerals gravely impeded Western mathematics until the introduction of Arabic numerals. In 1643, Roger Williams praised the wonderful mathematical skills of the North American Indians.[38] Yet even the Elizabethan English translator of Gómara downgrades the Indians mathematically. In describing the Indian calendar, for example, he observes: 'yet these simple *Indians* wente neare the marke'. There is no equivalent to 'simple' in the original, which reads: 'yet they too much attained the truth, and agreed with the rest of nations' ('empero demasiado atinaban a lo cierto, y coincidían con las demás naciones').[39]

What increasingly fascinated Europe and Britain were the areas in which the Americans did *not* have their own skills: the Aztecs' inability to measure exact subdivisions of the day, and their lack of measurement of long distances. Their ignorance could, indeed, be magnified. In describing the cultural backwardness of the New World, Montaigne generalized that of the Caribs to that of the entire continent: it 'knew neither letters, nor waight, nor measures, nor apparell, nor corne, nor vines'.[40] While the Aztec possession of a zero excited no interest, writers repeatedly dwelt on the Caribs' inability to count beyond the number of their digits: their inability to ascend from a system based on the body to one of incorporeal abstraction. Carib innumeracy is mentioned time and time again:[41] Behn alludes to it in *Oroonoko*, it is discussed by Locke,[42] and John Ogilby mentions it twice in his monumental compilation *America*.[43] Yet, although Ogilby also describes the calendar of the Mexicans (p. 279), he says nothing about its accuracy, or about their mathematical intelligence. The more the culture of calculation takes hold in the seventeenth century, the more the Other is perceived as unmathematical. When seventeenth-century creative writers did portray in any detail a clash between Native American and European cultures, they did not reproduce exotic details of religious ritual. They portrayed a clash of mathematical systems, leading to a clash of systems of sacrifice.

CHAPTER 5

Shakespeare and the economics of sacrifice

English literature was the first to reflect on the sacrificial implications of a culture increasingly dominated by measurement, statistics, and commercial calculation; a culture that reduced individuals to exchangeable ciphers in a fashion analogous to the transactions of human sacrifice. There are many obvious reasons why the sacrificial power of economic systems should first have been discussed in England, and explored in its literature: the growing commercial prominence of the country in relation to most of its competitors except Holland; the consequent fear that a new moneyed class was threatening the security of the gentry and nobility; the dominant contribution of England to the development of the science of political economy; and the development of a major art form – the theatre – that was not necessarily a channel for aristocratic values and themes.

Protesting in 1615 about the human cost of the East India trade, Robert Kayll complained of the 'labours and liues' that had been 'sacrificed to that implacable East Indian *Neptune*'.[1] Replying in defence of the East India trade, the elder Dudley Digges (a shareholder in the East India Company) sustained the idea of sacrifice to Neptune, but at the same time sanctioned it. In doing so, he put Virgil to a use undreamed of by Tasso and his successors, citing that most memorable statement of the sacrificial principle in the *Aeneid*, when Neptune claims the steersman Palinurus as the price for the safe landing of the remaining fleet:

> (as *Neptune* in the Poet said)
> *Vnus erit amissum tantum quem in gurgite quærent,*
> *Vnum pro multis* [dabitur caput][2]

There shall be one alone whom they seek, lost, in the waters; one life shall be given for many.

In Virgil, however, the lines define the individual's subordinate place in the collective historical cause. Digges writes more like an accountant, entering 'unum caput' in the debit column and 'multis' in the credit. Moreover, whereas Virgil is talking about a single individual, Digges is talking about a ship; about many individuals. Even Kayll talks not about lives but about 'labours and liues': about the sacrifice of productive units. (Though perhaps the first, Digges's was by no means the last use of Virgil to evaluate the human cost of commerce or capitalism. In a passage rich in references to the child mortality caused by industry, Marx parodies Virgil's great line on the struggle required to found Rome: '*Tantae molis erat* [so great was the effort] to unleash the "eternal natural laws" of the capitalist mode of production').[3]

TITUS ANDRONICUS

Number-systems acquire sacrificial potential only in the early modern period; though amply evoked in Greek tragedy, they generally (as in *King Oedipus*) suggest a cultural order that is threatened by the monstrous or the divine. Language, by contrast, has always had fatal power, manifested in the dangers of disclosing one's name, lest it be used in spells and curses. The mere translation of the self into a sign can be dangerous, even when magic has been left behind. Speech and – still more – writing create unmanageably vulnerable replicas of the self that are subject to dangerous, fatal, sometimes sacrificial, forces. The first mention of writing in Western literature was, after all, of a man unwittingly carrying his own death warrant (*Iliad* 6.167–70). In *Iphigenia in Aulis*, the fate of the sacrificial victim is initially dependent on which of two conflicting letters from Agamemnon will reach Clytemnestra. As we have seen, Palamedes, the cultural benefactor who invented writing (or, in some versions, expanded the Greek alphabet), was destroyed by his own contrivance; his death is the starting point of the chain of deaths in the *Aeneid*.

The story of Palamedes also forms an allusive starting point for the first major English work to deal with human sacrifice and its adjunct of cannibalism: *Titus Andronicus*. Like the other early modern English works to be discussed, it portrays human sacrifice as compromising the idea of human progress; like most of the others, it interacts with the *Aeneid*; and, like the ending of the *Aeneid*, it evokes a background of terrible and ancient myth. Recent scholarship has strongly suggested that the first part of the play (the traditional 1.1 and 2.1, combined in Jonathan Bate's Arden edition into 1.1) may be the unaided work of George Peele. Clearly, the whole of the play flows from the human sacrifice which occurs in 1.1, and from the imagery in which it is described. Nevertheless, the symbolic and mythical consequences of that sacrifice are most searchingly portrayed in the later part of the play, more certainly written by Shakespeare.[4]

At the beginning of the play, the Roman hero Titus selects the eldest son of the captive Gothic queen Tamora as a funerary sacrifice for his own dead son. Tamora tries to get him to see the symmetry of the two sons: each has killed enemies in morally and mentally equivalent circumstances. Titus refuses to see the equation; for him, otherness of kind obliterates community of experience. Tamora's son, Alarbus, is 'marked' for sacrifice, and without ever speaking he is led offstage to be dismembered, and to 'feed', and be 'consumed' by, fire.[5] He is, simply, food for flames, the reduction of flesh to the shapeless anonymity of food initiating what is to be recurrent: the dissolution of identity and self-signification. '[M]arked' as a sacrificial victim, he becomes part of an alien system of signs, a letter in a foreign alphabet.

The sacrificial offering of Alarbus generates a number of answering transactions, which similarly deny individuals the power of self-representation, and indeed reveal a society that has lost any symbolic form of currency, and is reduced to trading only in bodily parts. In revenge for Alarbus' death, his brothers Chiron and Demetrius rape Titus' daughter Lavinia, kill her husband Bassianus, and remove her tongue and hands. Two of Titus' sons are framed for Bassianus' murder, and Titus vainly cuts off his hand in the belief that it will buy their lives; later, he dismembers the rapists, feeds them to their unwitting mother, and kills her and Lavinia. In addition to the physical assaults on the organs of signification (the hand and the mouth), there are in the play repeated refusals to listen, and repeated suppressions of speech.

Prior to the murder of Bassianus and rape of Lavinia, the villainous Moor Aaron buries gold and hides a letter with which to incriminate two of Titus' sons. That is, he re-enacts Odysseus' incrimination of Palamedes by forging a treasonable letter in his hand and hiding gold in his tent.[6] In inventing the sign-system with which he was then destroyed, however, Palamedes introduced a decisive cultural advance, and his death illustrates the violent fatality that typically accompanies cultural change in myth. Aaron's ruse represents a point at which culture goes into reverse, and the burying of the gold (although temporary) indicates the regression from a monetary to a bodily economy, in which the only objects of exchange are severed parts of the body, such as the hand with which Titus attempts to buy his sons' lives,[7] and the severed hands with which he is 'repaid' (3.1.235):

> Know that this gold must *coin* a stratagem
> Which, cunningly effected, will beget
> A very excellent piece of villainy. (2.2.5–7; italics added)

Not until late in the eighteenth century would mainland Europe's dramas of human sacrifice measure their crises by the model of a monetary society. Till then, the command to sacrifice challenged a primal economy centred on the body: the proposed victim was typically a blood relative, or the saviour of the sacrificer's life. Starting with Shakespeare, however, English writers began to explore the relationship between monetary and sacrificial exchange. In *The Merchant of Venice*, as in many post-Shakespearean works, the monetary economy itself becomes potentially sacrificial; in *Titus Andronicus*, by contrast, there is a reversion to a pre-civic economy of bodily parts. The only recipient of money in the play is the

Clown whom Titus pays to carry a letter of complaint to the Emperor, Saturninus. 'How much money must I have?', he asks on delivery. '[Y]ou must be hanged', replies Tamora. 'Then I have brought up a neck to a fair end', he laments with odd offhandedness (4.4.45–8). We pass from the deluded expectation of monetary exchange to that visual concentration on an isolated bodily part, the neck. Burying the gold in the earth from which it came, Aaron initiates one of the governing patterns of *Titus Andronicus*: a retrogression of culture. Like a film played backwards, civilization goes into reverse. Children disappear back into their mother's womb. Bodies pop out of graves, and are set 'upright at their dear friends' door' (5.1.136). Mythic horrors burst out of their incarceration in ancient texts, and are re-enacted and intensified. The problem here is not that the body becomes ensnared in symbol, like that of a victim of an incautious sacrificial oath (such as Jephthah's daughter); rather, it reverts to a pre-symbolic, signless state. If Alarbus is, to Titus, simply Other, his brothers lose all separateness and are reabsorbed into their mother's body.

In *Titus Andronicus* the body becomes a passive text. When Aaron sets up corpses before their loved ones' doors, they bear inscriptions carved in 'Roman letters' with his dagger (5.1.139). In part, this reveals what is pervasive: the individual's inability to determine his or her significance. Tamora and her sons try to turn themselves into symbols, posing to Titus as the allegorical personifications of Revenge, Rape, and Murder. They fail to convince, and as a direct consequence the sons lose all form and distinction, dissolved in their mother's stomach. Yet the corpses inscribed with Aaron's dagger illustrate something that is scarcely less pervasive: the withdrawal of the cultural gift of writing, by violence or into violence. Inscribed with Roman letters by a Moor, the corpses are (like Alarbus) mockingly incorporated in an alien sign-system.

Physically, the weapon overwrites the significance of the body; culturally, it replaces the pen. The battleaxes of the Andronici write 'destruction on the enemy's casque' (3.1.170). Horace's famous statement that the man of pure unblemished life ('*Integer vitae, scelerisque purus*') does not need the weapons of the Moor is sent to Chiron and Demetrius wrapped around some weapons (4.2.18–21),[8] and Titus has messages attached to arrows, so that the gods may be bombarded with vain petitions for justice. Writing in the sand with a staff manipulated by her mouth and stumps, Lavinia reinvents the mechanism of writing. Yet she is no Palamedes or Cadmus, devising a sign-system of infinite potential. This is a culture myth in reverse, returning writing to its barest and most stuttering rudiments. The oppressive insertion of the crude, cumbersomely material staff into the wordless mouth emphasizes that writing is not a perpetuation of speech but a pitiful phantom of it; indeed, Lavinia writes in that proverbially transient medium, sand (Titus wishes to use 'a gad of steel' to transfer her ephemeral script to 'a leaf of brass' (4.1.102–6), but never does). No more the custodian of Rome's literary heritage, she is now so fearfully other to the nephew she had taught that he had fled from her and, in a significant moment, thrown his books to the ground. This gesture precedes Lavinia's painful transformation of the earth itself into a rudimentary text.

Many other things return to the earth: Titus' dead sons (1.1.102); Aaron's gold; the sons who fall into the pit in the forest; Aaron himself, who is to be buried from the neck down and die of starvation. Lavinia returns writing to the earth. Titus' message-bearing arrows fall back to earth, and indeed, in his campaign for justice from the gods, he also wishes to delve into the earth and take a petition to Pluto. Return to the earth after death in burial is a necessary ritual of closure, and denial is a severe punishment: for (initially) Titus' rebellious son; for Alarbus; for the bodies that Aaron exhumes; for Aaron, buried before death; and for Tamora, thrown to the beasts and birds of the wilderness. Yet the process of return to the earth wildly escapes the bounds of the ritual that controls and exorcizes it. It mimics (and is in turn mimicked by) the return of sons to their mother's womb. In a chaotic transposition of the processes of life and death, the dead are unburied or exhumed, while the living and the signs that order their lives enter the earth. A key idea in this transposition is the mouth. Mouths as organs of speech are mentioned only in order to be stopped or closed – most poignantly, with Lavinia's writing-staff, where the insertion of the insensately physical supplants the emission of intangible signs.

The first mouth to be mentioned in the play is that of the pit into which the dead Bassianus is thrown, and into which Quintus and Martius (the sons of Titus who are framed for the murder) conveniently fall. It is a critical commonplace to associate this pit with the vagina, and hence with the alleged horror of the maternal as embodied in Tamora.[9] Certainly the blood-stained briars which surround the pit strongly suggest the vagina, but the word 'mouth' even more strongly suggests the mouth. Both are, of course, appropriate: later, Chiron and Demetrius re-enter via the mouth the maternal belly which they had left via the vagina. The violation of Lavinia's vagina is complemented by that of her mouth. This is not symbolism of the vagina via the mouth, but a confusion of functions: the channel that delivers bodies has taken over from the channel that delivers signs, and the latter has become a mere recipient of objects, and indeed bodies. Tamora eats her children, and her unburied body will in turn be eaten by beasts and birds; and Alarbus' sacrificed body 'feed[s]' and is 'consumed' by flames (1.1.147, 132). Non-burial is thus always associated with being eaten: those who do not enter the mouth of the earth enter more devouring mouths. Just as the burial of the gold indicates a transition from a currency of symbols to one of bodily members, just as the descent of books, airborne messages, and the act of writing itself to the ground indicate that the verbal is disappearing into the material, so the fact that the mouth becomes a channel for the body indicates that the body can no longer be translated into signs. Signs degenerate into mere matter. As language dwindles into insignificance, the most notable oral acts are not verbal utterances but the disgorging or reception of bodies. The event which initiates the censoring of the body is the sacrifice of Alarbus.

Either essentially or coincidentally, the unwilling sacrificial victim can become a cipher in another's system of signs. In Acosta's account of the Aztec migrations, the Princess of Culhuacán became an idol. Idomeneus' son and Jephthah's daughter were unwittingly trapped in their fathers' oaths. In *Titus*, victims do not have significance imposed; they have it removed. Their constant re-enactment of myths from Ovid's *Metamorphoses* means that they are always living out deaths that are not their own.

From the time of Aeschylus, human sacrifice has been imaginatively opposed to the idea of human progress. *Titus Andronicus* obviously portrays retrogression, showing a return to the atavistic chaos of myth, and indeed to the Iron Age: '*Terras Astraea reliquit*' ('Astraea deserted the earth') (4.3.4), quoted by Titus before he fires his arrow-borne messages skywards, are the words with which Ovid completes his description of man's descent into the Iron Age (*Metamorphoses* 1.150). If the *Aeneid* counterpoints indubitable progress with relentless repetition of history and myth, *Titus Andronicus* portrays a world caught in regressive cycles of repetition.

The re-enactments of violent, archaic myths – of dismemberment, of return to the wilds, of confrontation with the monstrous, and of transformation into the brute – scarcely need documenting. They reflect the increasing yielding of culture to the primitive, and they occur alike in the part of the play which has been attributed to Peele and in the remainder. Obviously, the action is controlled by the myth of Philomela. In this, the Thracian king Tereus had raped his sister-in-law Philomela and cut out her tongue to prevent her from disclosing the outrage. She, however, had woven the story into a tapestry, and in revenge Tereus' wife Procne had fed their son to him. It is to prevent a repetition of the tapestry ruse that Lavinia's rapists cut off her hands. In addition to this dominant story of rape, mutilation, cannibalism, and loss of humanity, there are (for example) allusions to Hecuba's vengeance upon Polymestor, the murderer of her son Polydorus (by blinding him and killing his sons, whereupon she was turned into a dog) (1.1.139–41); to the incessant rending of Prometheus' liver by a vulture (1.1.516, 5.2.31); and to the transformation of Actaeon into a stag, and his dismemberment by his own hounds (2.2.63–5).

Yet the clash between culture and its collapse seems more subtly explored once the section attributed to Peele has been left behind. In Peele's section, in quick and rather confusing succession, Aaron compares Tamora's lust for him to the bondage of Prometheus in the desolate Caucasus, and describes her both as a Semiramis and as a Siren who will charm Saturninus and shipwreck Rome (1.1.515–23). In each case, the image of an assault on form or culture is clear enough. Yet it is almost distracting to remember that Semiramis, here a potential city-destroyer, features in Ovid (in the Pyramus and Thisbe episode) as the builder of city walls (4.57–8),[10] or that Prometheus is celebrated at the beginning of *Metamorphoses* as the creator of mankind. In each case, a giver of culture undergoes a reversal of role, but the reversal seems unintended and indeed disruptive. Conversely, when Tamora in the role of Revenge promises 'To ease the gnawing vulture' of Titus' mind (5.2.31), the allusion to the Prometheus myth suggests an essential corruption of humanity.

During a hunt in the forest, Tamora and Aaron slip off to be amorously alone, like Dido and Aeneas during their hunt, but are surprised by Bassianus and Lavinia, whereupon there is banter about another hunt: that of the transformed and dismembered Actaeon. While the banter chiefly equates the horns of the stag and of the cuckold, the rending of Actaeon is ominously mentioned. Here every detail fits, and has been prepared for: Demetrius has already said that Lavinia will be hunted as 'a dainty doe' (2.1.26), Aaron that Bassianus' 'Philomel must lose her tongue today' (2.2.43); what the victims take for literary repartee is in fact myth on the point of rebirth. Not only does the myth of Actaeon symbolize the loss of human form in the wilds outside the city; the specific Ovidian context counterbalances and negates the founding of a city. Actaeon was the grandson of Cadmus, the founder of Thebes. Immediately prior to his story, the foundation of the city is described in one-and-a-half throwaway lines: 'Thebes now stood, and you could have seemed, Cadmus, happy in exile' ('Iam stabant Thebae, poteras iam, Cadme, videri / exilio felix') (3.131–2). The establishment of the city is the briefest of preludes to the return to the conflicts of the forest.[11]

Philomela and Procne were princesses of early Athens, sent to the barbarous wilds of Thrace. Pyramus, to whom the dead Bassianus is compared (2.2.231), had left the walled city for the haunts of wild beasts. Repeatedly, the myths suggest the loss of a cultural point of origin. Titus hopes he can move the tribunes and senators as Orpheus had moved the monstrous Cerberus, but he lives up to the example of this archetypal poet only in his dismemberment (narrated in *Metamorphoses* 11.23–84), and thereafter the monsters reign unchecked. Aaron glories in a superhuman strength that could defeat the giants, Hercules (slayer of monsters), or Mars. He here sees himself as the ultimate figure of monstrous force (4.2.95–8). Similarly, when Titus plans the cannibalistic feast, it will be like the battle between the Lapiths and the half-human Centaurs (5.2.203; *Metamorphoses* 12.210–535).

Time and again, then, Shakespeare's mythic examples suggest a reversal of cultural cycle. Yet there is one mythic original who does not conform to this pattern: Lavinia. The original Lavinia, Aeneas' second wife, was the foundational female figure of the Roman race. In the *Aeneid* she is silent. Her Shakespearean namesake has become the guardian and teacher of

Roman literature, instructing her nephew in 'Sweet poetry and Tully's [Cicero's] *Orator*' (4.1.14); but the second Lavinia is violently reduced to the silence of the first. The anomalous myth, of cultural progress, has been constrained to the pattern of its fellows.

The reversal of founding myths and cultural narratives reaches its climax in the last allusion of the play, when a Roman lord asks Lucius to give narrative form to the horrors that have overcome Rome:

> Speak, Rome's dear friend, as erst our ancestor
> When with his solemn tongue he did discourse
> To lovesick Dido's sad-attending ear
> The story of that baleful burning night
> When subtle Greeks surprised King Priam's Troy.
> Tell us what Sinon hath bewitched our ears,
> Or who hath brought the fatal engine in
> That gives our Troy, our Rome, the civil wound. (5.3.79–86)

In its fusion of myths of cultural destruction and rebirth into a single myth of destruction, 'our Troy, our Rome' encapsulates a fundamental pattern of the play. *Titus Andronicus* is a narrative in reverse. It began, as the *Aeneid* ended, with victory and a sacrificial act. It ends where Aeneas' story began.

What, however, of that other foundational figure, Aaron? Why should the villain of this tragedy be named after yet another founding figure?

Aaron first appears in the Biblical narrative as a man gifted in signs, and as the linguistic intermediary between Moses and the people:

> Then the Lorde was very angry with Moyses, and sayde: Doe not I knowe Aaron thy brother the Leuite, that he himselfe shall speake? . . . For loe, he commeth also forth to meete thee: and when he seeth thee, he will be glad in his heart. Therefore thou shalt speake unto him, and put these wordes in his mouth, and I will be with thy mouth, and with his mouth: and will teach you what you ought to doe. And he shall be thy spokesman unto the people, and he shall be, euen he shall be as thy mouth.[12]

Moses may, according to tradition, have '*first the Hebrue letters found*',[13] but it is Aaron who gives voice to the inarticulate writer; who performs a task in the founding of the nation exactly opposite to that which his namesake initiates in the disintegration of Titus' Rome. The eloquent founding figure of the Hebrew nation turns into the eloquent destroyer of 'our Troy, our Rome', Sinon.

THE MERCHANT OF VENICE

Titus Andronicus deals literally with atrocities that persist as powerful symbols in Shakespeare's more mature works. No later work portrays a cannibalistic meal, yet cannibalism is a key metaphor in *Othello* and *King Lear*. No later work portrays a human sacrifice, yet Othello and Brutus (in *Julius Caesar*) attach a sacrificial significance to the murders they commit. The work which most directly transmutes the subject matter of *Titus Andronicus*, however, and which pushes symbolic human sacrifice and cannibalism almost to the verge of the real thing, is *The Merchant of Venice* – a work which, more than any predecessor, explores a homology between monetary transaction and human sacrifice.

In *Titus Andronicus*, the trade in bodily parts appears to be a regression from a more conceptually advanced and symbolic form of currency, not an image of that currency. Yet the commutability of the body and currency was an ancient, and indeed Roman, idea. According to the Twelve Tables, 'The person of a debtor was forfeited to his creditors, who might divide his body among them', though 'No actual occurrence of this . . . was on record in historical times'. There was no penalty for cutting 'more or less than their shares'.[14] Money advanced by a patrician to a plebeian, Marx explains, 'became transformed, through his consumption of the means of subsistence, into his flesh and blood. This "flesh and blood" was therefore "their money".' This law, he adds, is 'worthy of Shylock' (*Capital*, vol. 1, p. 400).

Yet it was not Shylock who made the law. He sees its deadly potentiality, but he does not create it. On the contrary, the Duke of Venice confirms it: as Antonio recognizes, to interfere with the course of the law would destroy the confidence of strangers in Venetian credit and harm 'the trade and profit of the city'.[15]

In *A Theater of Envy* René Girard has extensively postulated a 'symmetry' between Shylock's explicit venality and the covert venality of the Christians, to whom 'Financial considerations have become so natural . . . that they are almost but not quite invisible'.[16] 'Human flesh and money in Venice are constantly exchanged for one another' (p. 245). Shylock is Antonio's 'grotesque double' (p. 246), and the two are caught in the primal cycle of revenge which fulfils itself in the finding of a sacrificial scapegoat: Shylock. Because Antonio and Shylock are doubles, Antonio's 'I am a tainted wether of the flock, / Meetest for death' (4.1.114–15) (which Girard takes as a clear scapegoat image) applies equally to Shylock (p. 252).

It is here necessary to attend to context, however: Bassanio – the friend for whom Antonio contracted his debt with Shylock – has just offered to die in Antonio's place, and Antonio is insisting that he will die in Bassanio's. Antonio's sentiment could only be put in Shylock's mouth by radically altering its application and meaning. This is not evidence that the two men are doubles; quite the reverse. We must also give some weight to the statement with which Antonio follows and parallels it: 'the weakest kind of fruit / Drops earliest to the ground' (4.1.115–16). As it happens, a very similar sentiment occurs in *Titus Andronicus*, when Titus, his brother, and a son debate which of them should volunteer for self-dismemberment, and Titus claims the honour: 'Such withered herbs as these / Are meet for plucking up' (3.1.178–9). The reasons for Titus' self-disparagement are clear: he is past his prime. Antonio's reasons are, by contrast, unspoken, and the unexplained parallel statements create a sense of internal self-disgust and sterility that goes beyond the socially imposed role of scapegoat.

Nevertheless, the context and the image do contain overtones of sacrifice, and they interact with the more explicit sacrificial images associated with Portia, though the primary sense appears to be (appropriately enough) economic dispensability, and possibly guilt at Antonio's love for Bassanio. Although scapegoats and sacrificial lambs were not expected to be 'tainted', the sheep marked out for slaughter, dying in the place of another, inevitably evokes the Crucifixion, even if the constituents of the archetype are startlingly reconstituted and even reversed. Moreover, Antonio's explicit sense of sterile isolation – whatever its cause – obviously aligns him with Shylock, barren breeder of metal out of metal (1.3.129), and perhaps explains his peculiarly intense maltreatment of someone who is, after all, a form of double: a complementary outsider.

Girard's reading of *The Merchant of Venice* is more valuable than his wildly against-the-grain interpretation of *King Oedipus*, with its contention that the final selection of the guilty person is quite arbitrary: that Creon or Teiresias would have fitted the bill just as much as Oedipus. One does not have to accept Girard's relentless denunciation of the Christians as 'even worse than' Shylock, who is at least honest in his vices (p. 248), to find his investigation of parallels between the antagonistic groups useful. Indeed, Shylock's 'Hath not a Jew eyes?' speech is an explicit statement of such doubling, especially in its culminating avowal of the shared passion for revenge: 'The villainy you teach me I will execute, and it shall go hard but I will better the instruction' (3.1.65–6).[17]

Had an Elizabethan gentleman been kicked and spat upon, as Shylock has been by Antonio, his customary (though not legally sanctioned) recourse would have been to seek the death of his opponent in a duel. To an extent, significant but by no means total, Shakespeare defamiliarizes the violence of his own culture by incarnating it in a being of alien origin and beliefs. The fundamental doubling, however, is in the seeming unanimity between the will of Shylock and the decrees of the state. The laws seem to validate interchangeability of monetary and corporeal transactions, and the translation of Antonio's body into the text of the bond. All that Antonio can hope is that Bassanio will provide a contrary text: 'live still and write mine epitaph' (4.1.118).

Whereas the Christians show frequent moral latitude in interpreting oaths, Shylock insists remorselessly on his 'oath in heaven' (4.1.224), a Jephthah both deliberate and exultant in the application of his words. Antonio's body seems to have become one with Shylock's utterances, its integrity or dismemberment dependent upon their interpretation. The unanimity of understanding between the outsider and the system he has infiltrated cannot be broken from within. It is performed by another outsider, and rescue comes less from the resources of the law than from the loopholes that Shylock himself has left; the ancient Roman law of debt left no such loopholes. The only absolute legal prohibition is based on Shylock's status as a stranger in Venice, for it is a capital offence for strangers to compass the death of a citizen. The law both sanctions and prohibits Shylock's 'strange apparent cruelty' (4.1.21): it sanctions it, for fear of offending strangers; it prohibits it, because Shylock is a stranger. The stranger is both needed and exorcized, created and rejected. Shylock cannot be an absolute stranger, like Euripides' King Thoas or the sacrificers of the Princess of Culhuacán; his bargain does partially express the commercial structures and imperatives of Venice.

Girard's forensically severe view of the dominant, racially exclusive, society is more appropriate to a play such as Euripides' *Andromache* than to *The Merchant of Venice*. Yet Shakespeare was the first writer to equal Euripides in showing how controlling groups can create the monstrous strangers who threaten them: a Medea, a Goneril, or an Edmund. The Venetians' insistently punning uses of 'fair' and 'gentle' reveal that their very terminology of value is derived from their sense of non-darkness and non-Jewishness, and that their sense of collective identity needs to be sustained by a process of exclusion (as happens, far more crudely, with all three groups in Marlowe's *The Jew of Malta*). Moreover, Girard is of course right, and scarcely alone, in pointing to the rule of money in Venice. Life and death there are conducted by weight and measurement. When Bassanio and Gratiano wager 1,000 ducats on which of them will father the first child, it is not necessary to follow Girard's darkly accusatory view: that they place one-third of the value on human life that Shylock's bond of 3,000 ducats for Antonio's flesh does.[18] Rather, the extremes of existence are alike governed by numerical and symbolic exchanges where the symbols bear no essential relation to the objects: Shylock demands a pound of flesh for 3,000 ducats; Jessica exchanges for a monkey the ring which her mother gave to her father, and which he would not have exchanged for 'a wilderness of monkeys' (3.1.112–13). Bassanio bought illusory social status by squandering his entire estate, and finances his bid to restore his fortunes, by marriage to the wealthy Portia, with another false display of status, funded by Antonio, who is in turn funded by Shylock. These imaginary circulations have to be grounded somewhere. They are grounded in Antonio's body.

To say that Venice is dominated by such exchanges, however, is not to say that Venetian life is reduced to them; Portia does not marry Bassanio for his seeming wealth but for love. Rather, we see a milieu in which values of faith and love cannot be conceived as absolutes, but (however they are felt) must always be expressed as transactions.

Again, the vocabulary of social value is revealing. *Noble* is a key, if problematic, word in the aristocratic world of the Roman plays; in its various forms, it occurs eighty-seven times in *Coriolanus* and forty-five times in *Antony and Cleopatra*. It occurs seven times in *The Merchant of Venice*, in increasingly inappropriate and economic contexts: the 'noble' Bassanio has impoverished himself by living at a 'noble rate' (1.1.57, 127). When Portia seems likely to enforce the bond, Shylock twice praises her as a 'noble judge' (4.1.242, 249). By contrast, the word *dear* is scrutinized. In *Coriolanus*, there is a marginal distinction between the monetary and emotional uses of the term, the former being associated with the plebeians (though only twice), the latter with the patricians. In *The Merchant of Venice*, however, the economic overtones of the word are always present. Learning of Bassanio's fraudulence and Antonio's plight, and agreeing to help him, Portia says 'Since you are dear bought, I will love you dear' (3.2.312). Claiming his pound of flesh, Shylock says that it 'Is dearly bought, 'tis mine, and I will have it' (4.1.100). They are not, of course, saying the same thing: *have* and *love* are by no means synonyms. But they are saying things that are almost opposite in words that are almost the same (and Portia's choice of words suggests a diminution in her view of Bassanio).

Love and faith are verbally and materially expressed as transactions: the language of value is as conditioned by Venetian economic culture as it is by Venetian pigmentation. This is, of course, revealing. Yet, Girard and many others notwithstanding, the values exceed the terms in which they are expressed. Messy and manipulative as Bassanio's dealings with Antonio and Portia are, the conflict is reductively simplified by the question of whether he should retain the ring which Portia gave him, or bestow it on the lawyer ('Balthazar') who has saved Antonio's life. As Bassanio protests in resisting 'Balthazar's' request for the ring,

> There's more depends on this than on the value, –
> The *dearest* ring in Venice will I give you. (4.1.431–2; italics added)

Unless determined to see the worst in the Venetians at every turn, one must recognize that Bassanio is in an impossible position, for he has been led by his earlier scheming and deceptive monetary treatment of Antonio and Portia into a moral conflict which he now, belatedly, feels with keen agony. The commodity of the ring is a quite inadequate symbol and focus of that conflict. Yet, apparently arbitrarily, the lawyer places a unique and quite meaningless value on the ring. Exchange value is capricious. The fact that the lawyer *is* Portia means, however, that the hidden, human structure of the exchange is contrary to its perceived economic structure. There is, after all, no conflict.

The monetary is in constant conflict with that which it seems to represent: the moral and the symbolic. If 'Balthazar' seems to place an irrational value on the ring which Portia gave to Bassanio, Shylock's daughter Jessica exchanges for a monkey the turquoise ring which her mother gave to her father (effectively exchanging her mother for a monkey). '[A] lady richly left' (1.1.161) is paired with a lead casket, a pound of flesh with 3,000 ducats.

And Bassanio courts Portia with illusory wealth, of which Antonio's body is the surety. Where these exchanges do not explicitly involve the body in a transaction, the involvement is implicit: a mother for a monkey; Portia for Antonio (in the trial scene, Bassanio does indeed express willingness to 'sacrifice' (4.1.282) Portia in order to save Antonio). In view of the constant involvement of the body in such exchanges, we may perhaps look forward to Robert Kayll's attack on the East India trade, for sacrificing 'labours and liues' to Neptune. After all, the argosies which so mysteriously disappear and reappear contained not only merchandise, but 'labors and liues'; and the play does evoke the idea of sacrifice to the sea.

'[C]ontain'd' (2.9.5) in one of the caskets offered in the courtship ritual, Portia is as helplessly translated into an external sign as Antonio. She is a sacrificial victim, whom Bassanio will rescue as Hercules rescued the Trojan princess Hesione from a sea monster:

> Now he goes,
> With no less presence but with much more love
> Than young Alcides when he did redeem
> The virgin tribute paid by howling Troy
> To the sea-monster. I stand for sacrifice. (3.2.53–7)[19]

She is linked to Antonio as a victim of sacrifice, and linked also by the sea, in her case a mythic and ancient source of monsters, in Antonio's a source of commercial danger. Indeed, she is rescued not by a culture hero but by a fortune-hunter who is later willing to 'sacrifice' her life for Antonio's. Yet the original myth is suspect enough. Unlike the parallel myth of Perseus and Andromeda, where the hero rescues the heroine through love and then marries her, that of Hesione is one of multiple fraud. Disguised as mortals, Apollo and Poseidon had built the walls of Troy in return for a promise of gold. King Laomedon refused to honour the debt: the city was flooded, and the king was commanded to offer his daughter to the sea monster. Hercules rescued her, not out of love but because he had been promised divine horses, themselves of rather tainted origin (they had been given to Laomedon by Zeus in compensation for the rape of Laomedon's son, Ganymede). The promise was dishonoured, and Hercules destroyed the city, giving Hesione to Telamon as a reward for helping him: 'Telamon did not depart without honour, for he obtained the gift of Hesione.'[20] The myth links Portia to Antonio, both by emphasizing the fatal, sacrificial power of the sea, and more specifically through the idea of the sacrificial victim atoning for a bad debt. It suggests an ancient and perhaps even an original association between commerce and human sacrifice.

Portia, to repeat, is 'contained' in the leaden casket; yet does the leaden casket stand for her any more significantly than the turquoise ring stands for the monkey? Rejecting gold because of the fraudulence of appearances, Bassanio may (as Girard suggests (p. 245)) be speaking from all too keen personal knowledge. There is possibly a colour- and class-coding in the language of choice, reflecting that in the language of social approval. In its fraudulent glamour, gold is like a 'beauteous scarf / Veiling an Indian beauty' (3.2.98–9); silver is 'pale / and common' (line 103); but lead is moving in its 'paleness' (line 106). However much or little these hints reveal about the motives of the suitor, they scarcely establish a fixed and inevitable symbolic connection between this casket and Portia. The 'meaning' of the caskets is not essential, but determined by the sacrificing father: any of the three could equally have been elected as the right answer.[21] Morocco and Aragon do not reason wrongly; they simply fail to spot the lady. Constantly, the most intimate and complex of human dealings are constrained to fit the binary patterns of the marketplace. Yet life and consciousness cannot be represented in such equations; they can only be sacrificed in them.

CHAPTER 6

Britain and America: Dryden, Behn, and Defoe

The Merchant of Venice is as much a product of the age of exploration as *The Lusiads* or *Gerusalemme Liberata*: notably, one of Antonio's argosies is at Mexico (1.3.18; 3.2.267). Yet Mexico is first mentioned in a speech by the calculating Shylock, when he weighs up Antonio's creditworthiness. Its prime significance is that it represents a high-risk venture; here, as throughout the play, the categories which shape our views of the familiar and alien are monetary. The difference between Bernal Díaz and Montezuma is of Christian and pagan; that between Shylock and Antonio is of usurer and merchant.

Early modern England, however, produced no significant colonial epic, its most lasting representation of the colonial enterprise being Aphra Behn's savagely anti-heroic *Oroonoko*. Naturally, few English writers shared Tasso's and Mambrun's enthusiasm for Catholic expansionism. A century before the appearance of Mambrun's epic celebration of Christian militarism, Bartolomé de las Casas had published his *Short Account of the Destruction of the Indies* (1552), the first and most famous denunciation of atrocities against the Indians, which lamented the rapid loss of Spain's missionary vocation. In 1656, Milton's nephew John Phillips translated this work as *The Tears of the Indians*, in explicit support of Cromwell's campaign in the Caribbean and against Spain, which had started in 1654.[1] Thomas Gage wrote his account of Spanish malpractice in the New World in order to argue that their American subjects would gladly turn to England. He was the motive force behind Cromwell's Caribbean campaign, and he died in Jamaica in 1656.

When a great epic emerged from the ruins of Cromwellian England, however, it rejected imperialistic teleology altogether.[2] Early in Milton's *Paradise Lost* there is an epic catalogue of Satan's disciples, the first named being Moloch, who delights in 'human sacrifice, and parents' tears' (1.393).[3] Obviously, Moloch's pleasure in human sacrifice makes him the exact opposite of the Son, who readily undertakes 'Sacrifice' (3.269) of self. Yet, although Biblical history moves through 'types / And shadows' (12.232–3) to the performance of that sacrifice, it is Moloch who prefigures the dynamics of secular history. Unlike the Catholic epics of crusade and conquest, *Paradise Lost* does not show a world purging itself of human sacrifice: quite the reverse. It does resemble – and perhaps react against – Mambrun's *Idololatria Debellata* in featuring a vision that culminates in the spectacle of the New World: Adam's vision of secular empires, which concludes with the realms of Montezuma, Atabalipa, and the still-unconquered El Dorado (Aphra Behn's Surinam):

> In spirit perhaps he also saw
> Rich Mexico the seat of Motezume,
> And Cusco in Peru, the richer seat
> Of Atabalipa, and yet unspoiled
> Guiana, whose great city Geryon's sons
> Call El Dorado. (11.406–11)

Like Mambrun's New World, this is a realm of gold; but whereas Mambrun uses the gold to illustrate the barbarous idolatry of the natives, here it illustrates the godless greed of the conquerors. These realms will yield not to a missionary zeal for truth but to a lust for riches. Like the vision in *Idololatria Debellata*, Adam's vision is presented not teleologically but spatially: it is a map on which chronological sequence is not recorded. There is, however, an implicit teleology in Mambrun's version, of progression towards the eradication of human sacrifice. The spiritual teleology of *Paradise Lost*, however, is in direct conflict with the unfolding of political and imperial history. The temporal narrative, from the murder of Abel at the sacrificial altar to the triumph of the Son, is one in which the mechanisms of political society inevitably conclude with the exclusion or sacrifice of the scapegoat. The murder of Abel is, indeed, Adam's very next vision after that of El Dorado.

If one has encountered the intensity of the concern with human sacrifice in the French and Italian epics of the mid seventeenth century, its more muted appearance in *Paradise Lost* is likely to come as a surprise, until one realizes that Milton is treating this subject in the way that he treats other conventional epic themes such as the quest and the battle: that is, he completely reverses the approach seemingly demanded by tradition. Far from being triumphantly abolished, human sacrifice remains a steady state in the temporal world. It is overshadowed by the offering of suffering obedience, but this is not primarily represented in sacrificial terms. When he first offers himself as saviour, the Son stands forward 'as a sacrifice / glad to be offered' (3.269–70), counterbalancing Moloch's delight in human sacrifice, but thereafter the idea of sacrifice is absent for eight books, the word occurring only four further times in total: twice to describe Abel's sacrifice (11.437, 450), and twice to describe the inadequacy and purely symbolic nature of the sacrifices prescribed in the Old Testament. One might expect that, when the poem comes to the Crucifixion, the event dimly foreshadowed by the sacrifices of the Old Law, it would be portrayed as the culminating sacrifice, but the contrary is the case. The sacrificial imagery is left behind: the rationale of the Crucifixion is the payment of a legally due penalty.

At the same time as Milton was reinventing, and turning upside down, the Renaissance sacrificial epic, Dryden was reinventing English tragedy, after the lacuna caused by the closure of the theatres from 1642 to 1660. His initial formula was a type of drama derived from epic: the heroic play. His best-known heroic play, *The Conquest of Granada* (1670–1), shares its title and subject with the best mid-century epic of colonialism, Graziani's *Il Conquisto di Granata*, though it is quite different in its emphasis on ruthless power politics. His first heroic play, *The Indian Queen* (1664), was written in collaboration with his brother-in-law, Sir Robert Howard, and is at least nominally set in Aztec America, featuring Montezuma as hero of its totally fictitious plot. Far from being a barbarous and remote alien, however, Montezuma is an obvious image of Charles II, restored to the throne from which he has been villainously deposed. At one point, he is in imminent danger of being ritually sacrificed.

Dryden's first unaided heroic play was a sequel to *The Indian Queen*, *The Indian Emperour* (1665), a portrayal of the conquest of Mexico which (like the later *Conquest of Granada*) provides an Englishman's view of Catholic expansionism. Though little-known today, this is significant as a remarkable attempt to depict the confrontation of two quite conflicting intellectual systems, and to imagine in detail the mental workings of another culture. For Dryden portrays the impact of a (relatively) modern European power on a culture characterized by an absence of all signs except the spoken word. He also contrasts the exchange systems of an advanced economic society with those of pre-commercial man, while showing how they reach the same consummation in human sacrifice. It is an extraordinary exploration of the sacrificial potential in European systems of measurement, enumeration, and economic exchange.

It is well known that an immense change in the technology and cultural dominance of calculation started in the seventeenth century.[4] In a work published in 1686, the founder of political economy, Sir William Petty, reflected on the differing rates of population growth in London and the rest of the country, and predicted a demographic crisis by the year 1842.[5] Individuals become terms in equations whose solution takes centuries. Both Thomas Culpepper the Elder and Sir Josiah Child (governor of the East India Company) argued that the Israelites flourished as God's chosen people because the ban on usury enforced zero interest rates.[6] Historical teleology is equation-driven, as it also is when Petty combats sceptics who complained that the earth did not contain enough matter to resource a general resurrection of the dead: such a resurrection, he calculated, could be completely supplied from two moderately sized Irish mountains.[7]

Culpepper's and Child's explanations of Biblical narrative in terms of economic laws are a long way from the pure providentialism of the Catholic epic poets, even if comparable providentialism remained the dominant doctrine in England. If the calculating mentality could be turned to the interpretation of the Bible, moreover, it could still more be turned to the understanding of New World culture. For, while god-impersonators in human skins did not fire the early modern creative imagination, differences of mathematical mentality did. While Pierre Mambrun and his like locate the alienness of the Aztecs in their parodies of Christian ritual, others were to locate it in an outlandish approach to mathematics and measurement, and to portray Aztec practices as the product of a non-European economic culture. The first to do so was Dryden.

The Aztecs in *The Indian Emperour* are (unhistorically, of course) pre-commercial, without economic infrastructure: they feed themselves by taking fish directly from the lake, and they use gold only for religious purposes, not for currency.[8] More accurately, they have no measures of distance, or of the subdivisions of the day. They count with a mentality that is different from that of the Spaniards. When 500 captives are sacrificed, the significance of the number is in its ritual completeness; it is independent of the particular consignment of captives. By contrast, when the conquistador Cortez boasts the bravery of a nation 'Who with four hundred foot and forty horse, / Dare boldly go a New found World to force',[9] number is abstracted and particularized as a specific measurement of power. Lacking abstract measurements of distance, the Spaniards' Indian guide can only point at the landscape and say that, although the city on the lake is as yet barely visible, they can reach it by noon. The capacities of the body and the cycles of the heavens are the units of measurement: there are no intermediate forms of abstraction separating the individual from his place in the processes of nature. Montezuma believes that the cycle of his life replicates the cycle of the sun, and that he will return to the sun when he dies (5.2.43–8). In a particularly gross cultural misrepresentation, the Indians do not even have metaphor or symbolism, except that which expresses the mimetic oneness of human and natural processes.

First of all, however, we see the New World through the eyes of the recently landed Spaniards, and they can *only* talk in wildly strained metaphor, in order to translate this new and alien place into the likeness of the one they are familiar with. Cortez imagines the genesis of the new continent in terms of the inhibited formalities of a Spanish pregnancy: it is 'As if our old world modestly withdrew, / And here, in private, had brought forth a new' (1.1.3–4). Such strained metaphors used to be considered a general stylistic defect of Dryden's heroic plays, but we might consider that he manages to abstain from them when he portrays the Indians in their uninvaded state. There is a seemingly deliberate distinction: the artificial intermediary of metaphor is presented as the property of economic man.

When we shift to the Indian culture in the following scene, the first thing we witness is the aftermath of a human sacrifice, of 'Five hundred

Captives' (1.2.5), in honour of Montezuma's birthday, followed (in a cyclical movement from death to rebirth) by another ritual of exchange, in which men present garlands to the object of their desire. As the play moves towards its conclusion, we see more religious cruelty, clearly paralleling the opening human sacrifice, but this time inflicted by the Spaniards, under the direction of a Catholic priest. In this final atrocity, Montezuma and his own High Priest are racked in an attempt to get them to reveal the whereabouts of their gold. The presence of the Catholic priest gives the scene a sacrificial character, but the sacrifice is here a commercial transaction: Montezuma's body is to be traded for gold.

When the Spaniards first arrive in the play, the Indian men are presenting garlands to their loved ones in the aftermath of the sacrifice. To some extent this is a symbolic ritual, but one which assumes a mimetic relationship between man, time, and nature:

> Her, who fairest does appear,
> Crown the Queen of all the year,
> Of the year and of the day. (1.2.17–19)

The flowers are natural, analogous signs of the passions they reveal. The ritual, however, quickly goes wrong, and its malfunctioning produces a disruption in the system of natural signs. First, Montezuma offers his garland to an unresponsive object of desire: the villainess Almeria. (In *The Indian Queen*, Almeria's mother had died for unrequited love of Montezuma, and Almeria is eager for vengeance.) In the end, Almeria accepts the garland, but alters its meaning: 'I take this Garland, not as given by you, / But as my merit, and my beauties due' (1.2.85–6). What had seemed a natural sign becomes arbitrary and unfixed, its meaning subject to compact and private perversion, and at this point Montezuma's son Guyomar interrupts the ritual, and introduces the Indians to metaphor in earnest. He has seen the Spanish fleet approaching and, never having seen ships before, and not knowing what they are, he has to translate them into terms derived from his received stock of experience, but strangely and incomprehensibly linked: flying trees, 'floating Palaces' (1.2.111). Then, when the ritual of love resumes and Guyomar makes his contribution, it is significant that he lacks a sign with which to do it: 'I want a Garland, but I'le give a heart' (1.2.134). He gives in metaphor.

Guyomar's explosion of inadvertent metaphor disrupts the appearance of seamless continuity and sympathy between Indian culture and natural process, for he seems to describe inversions of nature – things that, in Montezuma's words, 'float in air and flye upon the Seas!' (1.2.114). The continuity is finally destroyed by the racking of the king, though early in the torture scene Montezuma still believes in the integrity between his life and the processes of nature: he tells the Christian priest that, after his death, the sun his father will let down a beam and draw him back into the endless cycles of day (5.2.43–8).

Here is the essential difference between Indian and Spanish culture: their interpretations of the body, and the economies in which they locate it. In keeping with their commitment to metaphor, the Spaniards have a culture of personation, in which one person artificially substitutes for another, rather as a coin substitutes for a commodity: the Pope 'represents' God (1.2.283); Cortez is an agent of Charles V. Montezuma's culture, by contrast, is one not of representation but of organic and sympathetic mimicry, in which the king participates in the nature of the gods, and the subjects in the nature of the king. As he says to the High Priest when both are being tortured: 'When Monarchs suffer, gods themselves bear part; / Then well may'st thou, who but my Vassal art' (5.2.27–8). On each side, individuals are signs or substitutes, but on the Spanish side the equivalence is artificial, and individuals represent other individuals in a kind of system of currency. On the Indian side, the system is rather of natural transmission and replication (or, equally and interchangeably, reversal). On the Spanish side, bodies are signs; on the Indian, they are clones or duplicates.

This difference between Mexican and European culture governs the difference in sacrificial systems. The Indian victims are unindividuated, with no bodily presence, absorbed in the natural cycle of death and birth that constitutes the birthday rites. The torture of Montezuma and his priest, however, is not a mimicry of any natural cycle: it is a transaction, in which the body is to be traded for gold. It is directed at an individual body, and the pains are particularized in terms of physical law and consequence: 'Pull till my Veins break, and my Sinews crack' (5.2.22); 'My tortur'd Limbs refuse to bear my weight' (5.2.178).

This particularization of the body and its pains makes the king's body an individual atom, with no mimetic relationship to the totality of nature. When, on the rack, Montezuma tells the High Priest that gods and subjects participate in the agonies of kings, the latter reminds him that his kingship was founded on his apparent oneness with the processes of nature, and that he has not been able to sustain this: he swore an oath that the earth would continue to sustain his people, and that oath has been broken (5.2.31–6). When Montezuma dies, moreover, he himself recognizes that his unity with the cyclic movements of nature has gone, and he envisions himself as participating in a quite different set of processes: 'I grow as stiff as cooling Mettals do' (5.2.249). No longer is death a return to the sun. In imagination his body is treated as the plundered gold will be treated: passive, subject to alteration in form and value by other forces. The image confirms that the system of exchange in which the body now figures is one of monetary substitution and equivalence. A world governed by integrated, reciprocally mimetic, and seamlessly linked natural cycles has been replaced by a system of calculation, personation, and commercial exchange. It is an interesting and complex analysis of the impact of

European culture on an exotic and more primitive realm; it is also, perhaps, a meditation on the seventeenth century, and on the death of a divine king in England.

In *Dialectic of Enlightenment*, Adorno and Horkheimer argue that, once the specificity of magic has given way to the generalizing abstraction of myth, there is an alienation from specific natural experience, a translation of the unique into the interchangeable, that is fundamentally the same as the abstracted, general, and mathematical rules of Enlightenment science: 'The world as a gigantic analytic judgment, . . . is of the same mould as the cosmic myth which associated the cycle of spring and autumn with the kidnapping of Persephone' (p. 27).[10] They also argue that the abstractions of logic and science are reflected in an interchangeability of individuals that fosters the oppressiveness of the modern state, and that sacrifice constitutes a very early stage in the process of substitution and abstraction. Writing with an entirely different view of history, Dryden nevertheless saw many of the same organizing elements in it, reflecting on the huge ideological shifts of the seventeenth century and seeing them prefigured in the moment at which primitive man becomes mathematical and economic man.

BEHN

If Dryden imaginatively evoked the systems of a remote culture, he did so without direct experience. The only genuinely alien element in the play was decorative and mute. In *Oroonoko* (1688), her novel set in the English colony of Surinam, Aphra Behn recalls that she had brought feathers back from America, which were used in a performance of *The Indian Queen*; *The Indian Emperour* recycled costumes and scenery from the earlier play. Then, however, over twenty years after the two Dryden plays, the presumed donor of the feathers produced her own reconstruction of non-European cultures, and similarly saw the central distinctions as lying in differing systems of measurement and exchange.

Oroonoko is the story of an African prince. Prior to his enslavement, he has been robbed of his beloved Imoinda by his centenarian grandfather, who marries her. She nevertheless sleeps with Oroonoko, and is sold by her husband into slavery. Oroonoko is also sold into slavery, by an English captain to whom he himself had sold slaves, and is reunited with Imoinda in Surinam. Having led an unsuccessful revolt, Oroonoko beheads the pregnant Imoinda in order to prevent their child from being born into slavery, the killing being repeatedly described as a sacrifice.[11] Afterwards, he is barbarously dismembered by the English, in a death which – in advance – is also termed a sacrifice (p. 111). Unlike Dryden, Behn in *Oroonoko* concentrates on the barbarity of her own countrymen; or, rather, the barbarities released by the relaxation and dissolution of old class distinctions in the new colonial environment. For everything happens in the absence of the proper English governor (though his role and intentions are necessarily unclear).

Apparently, Behn presents us with a narrative of human progress, with the various principal stages juxtaposed in contrasting synchronous cultures: of the Native Americans, the Africans, and the Europeans. Religious consciousness is not part of man's cultural evolution, for pious fraud is fundamental to both the most primitive and advanced societies, the Indian priests performing beneficial tricks of legerdemain in order to cure the sick by force of imagination. Where there has been evolution is in symbolic systems, and one characteristic of the Native Americans is their lack of a numerical culture. Behn, for example, alludes to the Caribs' well-known inability to imagine numbers to which they cannot give physical or bodily expression (by, for example, knotting a cord). On encountering for the first time the elaborately clothed bodies of Europeans, some Indian villagers in *Oroonoko* exclaim: '*Tepeeme*; taking their Hair up in their Hands, and spreading it wide to those they call'd out too, as if they would say (as indeed it signify'd) *Numberless Wonders*, or not to be recounted, no more than to number the Hair of their Heads' (p. 101). This closely recalls the account of the French missionary Antoine Biet, who records that 'When they wish to represent a very big number, to which they cannot count, they say this word *tapoüimé*, and show the hair of their head' ('Quand ils veulent representer vn nombre fort grand, & qu'ils ne peuuent compter, en disant ce mot *tapoüimé*, ils monstrent les cheueux de la teste') (p. 396). Yet there is a difference. Whereas Biet is simply describing an inability to count, Behn is describing an inability to *recount*; she is using a failure of numbering to describe a failure of narrative. She does this because the relationship between numerical and linguistic systems is a fundamental element of the novel, and in its comparison of European and non-European cultures. In a wider sense than that of mere numeracy, Behn portrays Native American culture as one of the body, without the power of symbolic abstraction.

Behn's concern with the relationship between the body and symbolic systems affects her treatment of the topic central to many sacrificial texts: dismemberment. When Carib warriors compete for supreme command of the army, they are asked:

> What they dare do to shew they are worthy to lead an Army? When he, who is first ask'd, making no Reply, Cuts of [*sic*] his Nose, and throws it contemptably on the Ground; and the other does something to himself that he thinks surpasses him, and perhaps deprives himself of Lips and an Eye: so they Slash on till one gives out, and many have dy'd in this Debate. (p. 103)

Behn may or may not have known sacrificial rituals such as that described by Acosta. She would, however, almost certainly have known of the painful initiation rituals (such as flogging) undergone by Native American military commanders (Biet, pp. 376–80), but these bear no resemblance to the ritual she actually describes.

Behn's invented ritual is quite different from these in its significance, and it furthers her interest in the numerical interpretation of the body. The bodies of the competing warriors are economic units: bank accounts consisting of different units – noses, lips, etc. – which can be spent. Like the Indians' uncountable hairs, these severed members bespeak a society whose categories of thought are limited to the concreteness of the body. In the game of bodily strip-poker, a severed nose is a severed nose: it is not a sign; unlike a coin, it cannot represent anything else. Yet again, the body is the only point of reference. And, in order to make it so, Behn replaces known rituals with a fiction of her own.

The practices of Behn's fictitious warriors nevertheless find an all too credible counterpart in the Europeans' punishment of Oroonoko after his rebellion:

> [A]nd the Executioner came, and first cut off his Members, and threw them into the Fire; after that, with an ill-favoured Knife, they cut his Ears, and his Nose, and burn'd them; he still Smoak'd on, as if nothing had touch'd him; then they hacked off one of his Arms, and still he bore up, and held his Pipe; but at the cutting of this other Arm, his Head Sunk, and his Pipe drop'd, and he gave up the Ghost, without a Groan or a Reproach. (p. 118)

The ceremony of the chieftains is not only invented by Behn to express and explore European concerns about the economic management and definition of the body; it is invented as an analogue to European practices. Behn transposes familiar forms of violence into the sphere of the exotic and alien, and thus suspends the distinction between civilization and savagery. Indeed, while the word *barbarous* is used to describe the cultural unfamiliarity of African names and music, it is used in its moral sense only of the Europeans. Banister, the 'wild *Irish* Man' who arranges Oroonoko's execution, is 'a Fellow of absolute Barbarity' (p. 118).

It is noteworthy that, when Behn in *Oroonoko* equates European and exotic violence, she too evokes the idea of human sacrifice. After Oroonoko has led an unsuccessful slave revolt, and been savagely whipped, he kills and mutilates his pregnant wife Imoinda, fearing that she might be raped and their child enslaved: 'the Lovely, Young, and Ador'd Victim lays her self down, before the Sacrificer; while he, with a Hand resolv'd, and a Heart breaking within, gave the Fatal Stroke, first, cutting her Throat, and then severing her, yet Smiling, Face from that Delicate Body' (p. 114).

The killing of Imoinda certainly reveals Behn's frequently dark view of male sexuality, yet it is nevertheless the least appalling of the three human dismemberments in the novel. Whatever its residual horror, moreover, it is something to which Oroonoko has been impelled by the fear of his own Other, the Europeans. The failed sugar planter Richard Ligon reports that black male slaves readily kill wives whom they suspect of infidelity:[12] in his account, sexual violence is nearer to the surface among Black Africans than among whites. Oroonoko's killing of his wife, by contrast, is a reduced and humanized version of the white man's senseless and extreme violence. It is an atrocity imposed by white culture, and an atrocity which Oroonoko and the narrator agree in terming a sacrifice. In addition, Oroonoko applies this same idea of sacrifice to the English treatment of him. After his whipping on the orders of the deputy governor, Byam, he prophetically remarks: '*It had been well for him, if he had Sacrific'd me, instead of giving me the contemptable Whip*' (p. 111). It would be too simple to say that Behn herself is describing the execution of Oroonoko as a human sacrifice. This is a novel of many interwoven voices, and it is significant enough that the term 'sacrifice' should represent the judgment of the Black African on European practices – the African who, in inciting his fellow slaves to rebellion, had described his white masters as '*a degenerate Race*', '*below the Wildest Salvages*' (p. 105).

In his account of his escape from Mexico, Thomas Gage records an encounter with an ingenuously pompous Spanish gentleman:

> *Don Melchor de Velasco*, one day fell into discourse with mee concerning *England*, and our *English* nation, and in the best, most serious and judicious part of his Don-like conference, asked me whether the sun and moone in *England* were of the same colour as in *Chiapa*, and whether *English* men went barefoot like the *Indians*, and sacrificed one another as formerly did the Heathens of that Countrey? ... And whether the women in *England* went as long with child, as did the *Spanish* women? And lastly, whether the *Spanish* nation were not a farre gallanter nation then the *English*? (p. 99)

Do the English perform human sacrifice? *Oroonoko* poses the same question; the answer of the African outsider is 'Yes'.

As noted, the Native Americans' exclamation of '*Numberless Wonders*' expresses a failure to narrate in terms of a failure to count. Like Dryden in *The Indian Emperour*, Behn is portraying a clash between a symbolic and a non-symbolic culture, and two fundamental achievements differentiate the Europeans from the Native Americans. One is abstract number; the other is writing, and a concomitant awareness of language as something independent of reality. Europeans have developed the lie to a degree of sophistication and cultural ingrainedness that is unmatched in the other cultures. They also – uniquely – have history, but this too is deceptive, for the past is treacherous as a guide to the future.

The English attempt to use history to control their powerful and charismatic captive. The narrator (a projection of Behn) tells him the lives[13] of the ancient Romans – presumably from Plutarch – in an attempt to divert his thoughts from his condition. In the event, he concludes from Hannibal's crossing of the Alps that he is capable of leading his fellow-slaves to freedom, and consequently rebels. The narrator had used historical narrative in an attempt to control Oroonoko. She had miscalculated its effects, because she had failed to predict the parallels he would draw from the narrative. In drawing these parallels, Oroonoko also miscalculated. Both are betrayed by Plutarch. Yet, despite the differences in symbolic capacity, the rival cultures have a common bond in the manipulation and violation of the body. If European culture is distinguished by its capacity for written narrative and calculation, these are consummated in a final act of mathematical barbarity: the quartering of Oroonoko's body.

As already noted, when Behn alludes to the rudimentary state of Native American numeracy, she does not discuss it directly, as her predecessors had done; rather, she uses it as a way of disclosing a failure of narrative description. Narrative and number are, of course, often terminologically linked. In English, to *tell* means both to count and to narrate. The Greek word *logos* means *computation*, *word*, *narrative*, and much else. The related verb *legō* means both to *count* and to *recount*, a duality of reference that is exactly reproduced in the English translation, and in *Oroonoko* itself. There is the twice-mentioned 'Account' (balance-sheet) of potential revenge between Oroonoko and his grandfather (p. 79); Behn does not witness the reunion of Oroonoko and Imoinda but receives an 'Account' (narrative) from Trefry (p. 92). And we see both senses of the word when Behn relates both the beauties of Surinam and their economic value: 'it were endless to give an Account of all' (p. 96). When Oroonoko is 'counting up' the sufferings of his fellow-slaves, he is *describing* them in a 'Harangue' rather than literally enumerating them (p. 105). And, when the Native Americans swarm out to see the European visitors, they cry out '*Numberless Wonders*, or not to be re*counted*, no more than to *number* the Hair of their Heads' (p. 101; second and third italics added). In her characters' counting, accounting, and recounting, Behn does seem to be focussing on that very ancient association between numbering and narrative. Number in Oroonoko is the prime point of distinction between the bodily and the abstract. Behn mentally identifies the distinction between physical numeration and symbolic numeration with the difference between experience and history.

Oroonoko is fascinated not only by Plutarch but – earlier – by mathematical abstraction. One pretence used to convince his amorous grandfather that he has resigned Imoinda willingly to him is that he is diverting himself 'with his Mathematicians' (p. 69). He is seduced by counting and recounting: by mathematics and narrative. The first person he meets on arriving in Surinam is the honest but credulous Cornish agent of the governor, Trefry, who was, we are told at once, 'a very good Mathematician' (p. 87). Most significantly, when he first encounters the captain who is to betray him into slavery, the initial attraction is that he is entertained 'every Day with Globes and Maps, and Mathematical Discourses and Instruments' (p. 82): with numbers liberated from the abacus of the body and extended to a global and indeed cosmic scale. Fascinated, Oroonoko does not realize that he is looking at the instruments of abstraction that make possible the transatlantic trade to which he falls victim, a trade which will lead to his being a commodity in the market where slaves are sold at 'twenty Pound a Head' (p. 60). The process then leads to his sacrifice of his wife (p. 115), to prevent the child from entering the cycle of the marketplace, and to the final ritual of dismemberment, in which the body reverts to being an abacus, quartered and distributed through the plantations. The narrative regresses from the generalized to the particular. Whereas most of Behn's contemporaries followed Plutarch in seeing history as a source of generalizing parallel (as Dryden did in *Absalom and Achitophel*), she adopts the opposite approach. Instead of ever-widening circles of generalization, she moves inexorably to the particular: to the fragmented, mutilated body.

If the use of the pen distinguishes European cultures from those of Africa and America, that of the knife unites all three. For the knife is the primary means whereby culture imposes itself on nature. Cutting can be not only destructive, but aesthetic or economically creative. In the first use of the idea in the book, Imoinda's social quality is revealed by her 'delicately *Cut*' body (p. 92; italics added), 'carv'd in fine Flowers and Birds all over', as if 'Japan'd'. Even when Behn directly describes the perpetually blooming trees of Surinam, their flowers appear 'all like Nosegays' (p. 95); the eternal blooms are imagined with reference to *cut* and artificially arranged flowers. Moreover, when Behn goes on to describe the wood of the blossoming trees, the dissecting mind is still more evident: the trees 'have an intrinsick Value above common Timber; for they are, when *cut*, of different Colours, glorious to behold' (p. 95; italics added). Hannibal, whose historical example so fatally bemuses Oroonoko, 'had *Cut* his Way through Mountains of solid Rocks' (p. 106).

The knife, at once creative and destructive, sums up the ambiguities of culture. If cutting can, seemingly, transform Imoinda's body into an inorganic artefact, it also turns her into a decaying corpse, when Oroonoko cuts her throat and then severs her head from her pregnant body. Paradoxically, the newly barren corpse (bearing 'the Fruits of tend'rest Love'), is then covered by the 'Flowers' (p. 114) whose images had adorned it in life; gradually, however, in a peculiarly grim victory of culture over nature, the stench of the cut body overcomes the natural scent of the still growing flowers.

Thus, despite her rejection of genuinely attested Native American rituals of dismemberment, Behn treats the cutting of the body as a fundamental social process. At this basic level, though at none higher, diverse cultures and histories do parallel each other: all violate the integrity of the individual body. The bodies of the Indian commanders and of Oroonoko are alike mutilated; so are the bodies of Oroonoko and the historical figure after whom he is renamed, Julius Caesar. Discovered by the English after his sacrifice of Imoinda, Oroonoko 'cut a piece of Flesh from his own Throat, and threw it at 'em' (p. 116). After the Dutch takeover, the Native Americans will attack, and 'cut in pieces' (p. 100) some of the colonists.

Thus, amidst all the surgery, artistry, and butchery, one thing in particular stands out. Societies, whether in America, Africa, or Europe, have an almost essential tendency to dismember their leaders. The Indian commanders become leaders by self-mutilation. The African slaves who, on Oroonoko's arrival in Surinam, hail him as a king collaborate with the English in torturing his body. Behind Oroonoko's fate lies that of two other leaders: the beheaded Charles I and, as already noted, Caesar. Although Caesar is here evoked as a great conqueror, the text against which we most appropriately set Oroonoko's death is that pious self-deception of Shakespeare's Brutus, full of the imagery of cutting:

> Our course will seem too bloody, Caius Cassius,
> To cut the head off and then hack the limbs, . . .
> Let's be sacrificers, but not butchers, Caius . . .
> Let's carve him as a dish fit for the gods,
> Not hew him as a carcass fit for hounds.[14]

If it is the knife that separates culture from nature, the knife constantly threatens to return it there: to the once exquisitely carved but now rotting corpse among the leaves and flowers. This is why Behn both gives such prominence to the carving of the body and is so creatively free with what she found in the accounts of Native American customs. She is imposing her own unity on the diverse cultures that she inventively records. For Plutarch, a republican and Platonist, the goal is rational balance, both in the individual and in the state. Behn, the pessimistic Tory monarchist, can only contemplate societies with a seemingly inbuilt dynamic towards an opposite goal: 'To cut the head off and then hack the limbs'. In their dependence on the hacking of the body, cultures seem to subsist on the principles of their own destruction, and a sense of foreboding hangs over Behn's narrative. The Surinam she remembers was on the point of falling to the Dutch; it does not feature in the later seventeenth-century surveys of Britain's American 'Isles and Territories' which she may have consulted. The England in which she wrote also seemed likely to fall to the Dutch (and did). And James II seemed likely to join that ominous sequence of earlier destroyed leaders, Julius Caesar, Oroonoko, and his own father, Charles I – the king whose tragedy overshadowed the political world in which Behn wrote, and whom, in dedicating *The Second Part of the Rover* to James, she described as having been '*sacrific'd*' (p. 228).[15] Did the English sacrifice one another, asked Melchor de Velasco. Certainly: in Behn's view, they sacrificed their kings.

DEFOE

[L]et this stand as a Direction from the Experience of the most miserable of all Conditions in this World, that we may always find in it something to comfort our selves from, and to set in the Description of Good and Evil, on the Credit Side of the Accompt.[16]

So wrote Robinson Crusoe after drawing up a balance sheet of the good and evil in his desolate condition. Still more than *Oroonoko*, *Robinson Crusoe* is dominated by the idea of the account, as a numerically, morally, or historically ordered interpretation of experience: '[*P*]*erhaps this is all befallen us on your Account, like* Jonah *in the Ship of Tarshish.* Pray, continues he, *what are you? and on what Account did you go to Sea?* Upon that I told him some of my Story' (p. 15). As Crusoe concludes his narrative, he indicates that it might have a sequel, 'a farther Account' (p. 306), so that *Account* is the last noun in the novel. Other related words repeat the relationship between the numerical, the moral, and the prudential: *measure* and *measures*, *reckon* and *reckoning*. Into this verbally and numerically regimented world come a people who mysteriously leave single footprints (reducing Crusoe to 'un*accountable* Whimsies') (p. 154; italics added), and who hold cannibalistic feasts at which the left-over bones do not add up to a consistent number of bodies. Their visits do not fit the regular calendrical scheme that Crusoe maintains, and Crusoe rescues from them a man who cannot count up to twenty, but whom he promptly assimilates into his symmetrical time scheme by naming him Friday. In *Oroonoko*, European systems of measurement lead to a replication and refinement of the culturally universal impulse to dismember the human body. Defoe's view of things is quite contrary. Dismemberment produces numeric irrationality, violating the order which is archetypally expressed in the double-column account. Yet it is not the cannibalistic savages who are described as conducting human sacrifice. It is the Inquisition in Brazil, where Crusoe achieved his greatest economic success.

If Crusoe tames the wilderness and becomes a paradigm of human progress, he is no innovator; he is not a culture hero. Rather, he applies or recreates the achievements of a co-operative and technologically elaborate culture in conditions of primitive solitude. If he follows the established cultural route from cave-dwelling to building, he is never a dedicated troglodyte, from the outset transforming the cave with artifice. He progresses from hunting to agriculture, but the gun with which he hunts is his prize relic of advanced European culture, and one which makes the most spectacular and definite impact on the desert spaces. 'I believe', Crusoe writes, 'it was the first Gun that had been fir'd there since the Creation of the World' (p. 53). In this sense, Crusoe is the bringer of fire, but he brings it into a world where it already exists, for fire is a distinctive and universal sign of human presence: he is careful lest his fire betray his presence to the cannibals, and the cannibals (and their counterparts, the Inquisition) use fire to cook human flesh. If the knife in *Oroonoko* represents the boundary between culture and nature, in *Robinson Crusoe* the boundary is the gun, which (like Behn's knives) is an instrument of both destruction and signification, serving both to master the island and to signal from a distance. Unlike Behn's knives, however, the gun is never used for evil purposes.

When Crusoe is shipwrecked and initially gunless, he worries that 'I had no Weapon either to hunt and kill any Creature for my Sustenance, or to defend my self against any other Creature that might desire to kill me for theirs: In a Word, I had nothing about me but a Knife, a Tobacco-pipe, and a little Tobacco in a Box, this was all my Provision' (p. 47). His primal needs are to eat, and not to be eaten. Knives are inadequate for either purpose. Although cutting is implicitly important in *Robinson Crusoe*, the knife does not have a consistent and prominent imaginative presence (Crusoe carries a saw and hatchet instead of a sword and dagger (p. 149)). The knife is currency, a trinket to be exchanged with savages, or (like the gun) a maker of signs: Crusoe records the passage of days with notches made with a knife. Man cannot, however, tame the wilderness armed only with a knife, for it lacks the uniqueness and indispensability of the gun: when Crusoe shoots a monstrous beast on the coast of Africa, the inhabitants, 'tho' they had no Knife', skin it with a sharpened piece of wood 'much more readily than we cou'd have done with a Knife' (p. 31). Nevertheless, cutting, like fire, distinguishes man from the animal. After he has salvaged tools, weapons, and powder from the ship, Crusoe reflects that, without them, 'I should have liv'd, if I had not perish'd, like a meer Savage. That if I had kill'd a Goat, or a Fowl, by any Contrivance, I had no way to flea or open them, or part the Flesh from the Skin and the Bowels, or to cut it up; but must gnaw it with my Teeth, and pull it with my Claws, like a Beast' (p. 130).

Cutting divides man from the beast. It is also by definition itself an act of dividing – it will '*part* the Flesh from the Skin and the Bowels' (italics added) – and dividing, separating, and classifying are the essentials of culture. Skinning is perhaps the primary manifestation: it is something that Crusoe does to all animals – even those he cannot classify – except the bear that Friday kills in the Pyrenees, which is left entire only because time is pressing. Skinning turns nature into culture: not only into clothes, but into an item of exchange (Crusoe sells the skins of a lion and a leopard to the Portuguese captain who rescues him). Analogous processes of division and separation characterize all aspects and levels of culture. Crusoe learns 'to part' the grain 'from the Bran, and the Husk' (p. 122). When he discovers how 'to divide' the rainy from the dry seasons (p. 104), he provides a tabulated meteorological account whose design recalls his earlier moral account (p. 106). For separation into opposites is an identical structural presence in all Crusoe's activities, from the skinning of the beast to his double-column spiritual accounting.

His life, both physical and moral, thus either divides naturally into binaries, or else discovers and imposes them: the classifiable and unclassifiable ('many Sorts of Sea Fowls which I did not understand' (p. 72)); 'what was fit for Food, and what not' (p. 53); the eater and the eaten (most important of all); the feast and the fast; his cave and his bower; wet and dry seasons; 'the worst Side of the Island' (p. 110) and 'the other Side of the Island' (p. 86 and throughout); the non-enclosed and the enclosed, one of whose functions is to 'keep the tame from the wild' (p. 146). He distinguishes the operations of tides and currents, and on his return visit 'shar'd the Island into Parts' (p. 305). One of the evils that Crusoe records in his tabulation of good and evil is that he is '*divided from Mankind, a Solitaire*' (p. 66). Yet, in the very act of recording it, he is engaging in a process of intellectual division that sets this isolation in opposition to a greater good.

Mental and moral chaos proceed from failure to differentiate:

> I had, after some Time omitted to *distinguish* the Weeks, by making a longer Notch than ordinary for the Sabbath-Day, and so did not really know what any of the Days were; but now having cast up the Days as above, I found I had been there a Year; so I *divided* it into Weeks, and set *apart* every seventh Day for a Sabbath; though I found at the End of my *Account* I had lost a Day or two in my Reckoning. (p. 104; italics added)

Perhaps the most fundamental distinction of all is that between the different and the same. If Crusoe's knife marks a linear succession of different days, it also marks the recurrent sameness of the Sabbath (Sabbath–weekday being another polarity), and of the first day of the month. The significance of anniversaries in the book is well known. The voyage on which Crusoe is captured by Moors commences on 'same Day eight Year' (p. 40) that he deserted his father (though, later, the actual capture is said to be on 'the same Day'). The escape is on the same day as his first escape from shipwreck, and he survives the second shipwreck on his birthday (p. 133). Indeed, the word most commonly qualified by 'same' is 'day'; the next most common, 'time'. The lost days in Crusoe's account make the repetition, of course, imprecise. What matters is the internalized discovery of providential symmetries in the proliferating differences of experience; symmetries which draw attention to the transformative patterns of cause and effect, sin and punishment. Crusoe keeps his fourth anniversary with the 'same Devotion' as in previous years, but the result of these spiritual exercises is 'a different Knowledge from what I had before' (p. 128).

'[W]e never', writes Crusoe, 'see the true State of our Condition, till it is illustrated to us by its Contraries' (p. 139). When he meditates on the Creation, it is as a series of antitheses:

What is this Earth and Sea . . .?, [A]nd what am I, and all the other Creatures, wild and tame, humane and brutal, whence are we? Sure we are all made by some secret Power, who form'd the Earth and Sea, the Air and Sky. (p. 92)

It is the absence of such division that marks both the cannibals and their counterparts, the sacrificing Inquisition. Possession of the cutting tools gives Crusoe the primary dividing power that puts him above the beast, with its mere teeth and 'Claws'; yet, when he has rescued the Spaniard from the cannibals, he fears that – in a terrible lack of symmetry – his beneficiary might ill reciprocate his kindness by delivering him to New Spain, 'where an *English* Man was certain to be made a Sacrifice, what Necessity, or what Accident soever, brought him thither: And . . . I had rather be deliver'd up to the *Savages*, and be devour'd alive, than fall into the merciless Claws of the Priests, and be carry'd into the *Inquisition*' (p. 244). Englishmen are sacrificed without discrimination, whatever the cause of their arrival. If Crusoe's first importation of the instruments of culture into the island raises him above the clawed beasts, the undifferentiating violence of the priests reverses the process and returns man to their level. In his reflection on the Inquisition, he envisages a succession of imbalance and violated reciprocity, of which the culmination is human sacrifice. More clearly than anywhere else, human sacrifice confounds the accounting systems with which we order death and life.

When Crusoe sees the inexplicable single footprint in the sand, the solitary image offends his sense of differentiation: 'I could see no *other* Impression but that *one*' (p. 154). The footprint is also mathematically absurd. In his panic '*wild* Ideas' (italics added) confuse the distinctions of the landscape, and Crusoe fancies 'every Stump at a Distance to be a Man' (p. 154). Then the processes of differentiation assert themselves. It cannot have been left by the Devil, for the Devil would know that Crusoe lived on 'the *other* Side of the Island' (p. 155; italics added); such a blunder was '*inconsistent* with the Thing it self, and with all the Notions we usually entertain of the Subtilty of the Devil' (p. 155; italics added). He comforts himself with the theory that the footprint may be his own, but measures it against his foot and finds their difference. His first impulse is to destroy all the distinctions he has created: 'to throw down my Enclosures, and turn all my tame Cattle wild into the Woods' (p. 159), but his better thoughts are quite contrary – to improve the separation between the tamed and the untamed with 'a double Wall' (p. 161).

The single, mathematically irrational, footprint is Crusoe's first contact with a human world outside culture, which threatens and dissolves the categories with which he understands and masters nature. In his next stage of contact, when he discovers the relics of the cannibalistic banquet, he thanks God that he was born 'in a *Part* of the World, where I was *distinguish'd* from such dreadful Creatures as these' (p. 165; italics added). When describing this banquet, he lists (but rather uncharacteristically does not enumerate) the 'Skulls, Hands, Feet, and other Bones' (p. 165) that are scattered over the shore. When, on a later occasion, he does count the bodily parts, there is again an anomaly, in that the bones do not add up to bodies: 'I saw three Skulls, five Hands, and the Bones of three or four Legs and Feet, and abundance of other *Parts* of the Bodies' (p. 207; italics added). One may contrast this with the 'Account' which Crusoe gives of the slain mutineers, neatly categorized according to how killed and by whom, and tersely concluding '21 In all' (p. 237). Like Behn in *Oroonoko*, Defoe exploits a conflict between a culture whose fundamental order is numerical and one that is pre-mathematical; Friday cannot count to twenty in English. For Crusoe at first, the cannibals defy any comprehension beyond that of enumeration: at one visitation, he can see that there are nine, and that they are naked; 'but whether they were Men or Women, that I could not *distinguish*' (p. 183; italics added). For Behn and Dryden, the symbolic culture of Europe is driven by its own nature to replicate the annihilating mutilations of the body practised by its most primitive antitypes. Defoe's view is quite contrary. For him, numerical and moral thought are structurally identical. The double-column account is a microcosm and articulation of the morally analysed universe.

What primarily shocks about the cannibals is that they suspend the difference between eater and eaten: they 'would have seiz'd on me with the *same* View, as I did of a Goat, or a Turtle' (p. 197; italics added). Crusoe's long reflections on the morality of killing the cannibals leads him, however, to the conclusion that their sense of sameness and otherness, though mistaken, is homologous with that of Christian Europe, and indeed to some extent replicates cruelties which are culturally sanctioned in his own society:

> They think it no more a Crime to kill a Captive taken in War, than we do to kill an Ox; nor to eat humane Flesh, than we do to eat Mutton . . . these People were not Murtherers in the Sense that I had before condemn'd them, in my Thoughts; any more than those Christians were Murtherers, who often put to Death the Prisoners taken in Battle; or more frequently, upon many Occasions, put whole Troops of Men to the Sword, without giving Quarter, though they threw down their Arms and submitted. (p. 171)

He goes on to reflect that the human sacrifices of the Aztecs – the inequality of offering 'human Bodies' to 'Idols' – did not justify the 'Butchery' of the Spaniards (p. 172). 'Butcher' is a word applied elsewhere only to the cannibals, and clearly suggests nullifying the difference between the human and the animal, as does the reference to the 'Claws' of the Inquisition.

Cannibalism and human sacrifice, then, violate and confound some of the essential distinctions: animate and inanimate (bodies and idols), human and animal. They are also economically misguided. Friday is far more use to Crusoe alive than roasted; cannibalism is the eating of seed-corn. And the oppressions of the Catholic Church restrict trade: Crusoe could only return to his Brazilian estate if he were either prepared to deny his religion or 'be a Sacrifice to my Principles, ... and die in the Inquisition' (p. 303).

Like many works, *Robinson Crusoe* explores the relationship between a sacrificial and a monetary economy. Like earlier British books, though in a new and distinctive way, it portrays a regression to a state prior to money. When Crusoe discovers a hoard of coins on the wrecked ship, he exclaims on their uselessness: 'one of those Knives is worth all this Heap' (p. 57). On discovering another hoard, he 'would have given it all for three or four pair of *English* Shoes and Stockings' (p. 193). To cut rather than tear, to be clothed rather than naked, are far more elemental characteristics of culture than money. In the sphere of transactions, the primary one is not money but the debt created by the sparing or saving of life: the debt that would be dishonoured were the rescued Spaniard to betray his rescuer to the Inquisition. Crusoe repeatedly spares or saves lives (for example, of Friday, Friday's father, the Spaniard, and the English captain), and the ensuing obligations are the essence of his community. In return for his rescue, Friday would (Crusoe believes) 'have sacrific'd his Life for the saving mine' (p. 209). That the primal economy was the giving and receiving of life was to be the fundamental postulate of many Enlightenment treatments of human sacrifice.

The word *inhumane* is throughout the novel exclusively reserved for the cannibals, who do not recognize the sameness of their prey. Conversely, in the passage leading up to that in which he acknowledges Friday's readiness to sacrifice his life, Crusoe observes that peoples outside the geographical limits of Christian revelation nevertheless have 'the same Powers, the same Reason, the same Affections, the same Sentiments of Kindness and Obligation, the same Passions and Resentments of Wrongs, the same Sense of Gratitude, Sincerity, Fidelity, and all the Capacities of doing Good, and receiving Good, that [God] has given to us' (p. 209). The Portuguese captain who rescues Crusoe after his escape from the Moors tells him: '*I have sav'd your Life on no other Terms than I would be glad to be saved my self, and it may one time or other be my Lot to be taken up in the same Condition*' (p. 33). He refuses to take money for his kindness. The word with which Crusoe sums up his behaviour is 'Humanity' (p. 36).

The point about Friday's beguiling and killing of a bear on the journey from Spain to England is that it reasserts the proper relationship between the human and the animal. The bear is described in elaborately mock-human terms: 'a very nice Gentleman, he won't go a Step out of his Way for a Prince' (p. 293). Engaging the animal in mock conversation, Friday entices it along the branch of a tree, on which he then jumps up and down, teaching the bear to '*dance*' (p. 295). The bear will not be dislodged, for it uses its 'Claws' (p. 296), but it is outwitted, and Friday puts a gun to its ears and shoots it dead. The ensuing laughter is the only healthy laughter in the novel (the chief previous instance is the 'Merriment' (p. 183) of the cannibals at their feasts). A perilous battle with ravenous wolves is to follow, but the boundaries of difference have been re-established.

With great justice, Henry Fielding calls the *Odyssey* 'that eating poem';[17] *Robinson Crusoe* is, even more, an 'eating novel'. Eating in the *Odyssey* is always ritual or violated ritual. In *Robinson Crusoe*, it is more a matter of survival. Crusoe's overriding priority is to eat, and to avoid being eaten: by the unclassifiable beasts and (imaginary) cannibals on the coast of Africa, the wolves in the Pyrenees, and the cannibals on the island, where the only beasts of prey are human. Crusoe is closer to the primal and chaotic demands of the wilderness than most Greek heroes. One of the ways in which he orders it is through ritual, and for Defoe ritual is a further expression of man's numerical capacities. The word *first* acquires a new resonance on the island, charting the impact of culture on this undiscovered place: 'I believe it was the first Gun that had been fir'd there since the Creation of the World' (p. 53); 'the first Word I had ever heard spoken in the Island by any Mouth but my own' (p. 119). In his pre-island days, *first* had indicated the undigested changes and inconsistencies of experience ('I could ill reassume the first Penitence, which I had so apparently trampled upon' (p. 11)). Now, in parallel, it charts the introduction of culture into uncultivated external spaces and of religion into Crusoe's mind: he 'Pray'd to GOD, for the first Time since the Storm off of *Hull*' (p. 86); 'This was the first Prayer, if I may call it so, that I had made for many Years' (p. 91); as well as marking the Sabbath with a larger knife mark than usual, Crusoe also marks the first day of the month. As part of this process, he ritualizes eating: 'this was the first Bit of Meat I had ever ask'd God's Blessing to' (p. 91); he fasts on the anniversary of his arrival on the island; and he feeds those he has rescued. Crusoe's mastering of the wilderness includes the sanctification and socialization of instinct by ritual, recognizing the bond between those two semantically distinct but etymologically identical words that pervade the narrative: provisions and Providence, a doublet that links in a single process the divine ordering of the whole and the sustenance of the individual. It would be as impossible to include cannibalism in this verbal spectrum as it would to imagine Telemachus intruding on a cannibalistic feast in Pylos.

Many works have focussed on dismemberment: *The Bacchae*, *Titus Andronicus*, *Oroonoko*, *Robinson Crusoe*. The dismemberment of Pentheus reveals the fragility of the mental categories that sustain civilization; in *Titus Andronicus*, there is a failure of the analogy between body and state; and in *Oroonoko* all forms of social structure seem to require the annihilation of the individual body. In *Robinson Crusoe*, however, the assaults on the physical coherence of the individual are located outside the boundaries of Protestant Europe: in that exotic continent whose lands are divided between the cannibals and the Catholics. The converse is the solitary Crusoe, self-sufficient and whole. Defoe's Protestantism was not to be shared in the Continental Enlightenment, but his confidence in the capacity of civilization to exorcize savagery was.

CHAPTER 7

Lieto Fine: *Baroque and Enlightenment sacrifice*

MONSIEUR AGAMEMNON

Perhaps only a French neo-classicist could have given Agamemnon a *valet de chambre*. Thus did Jean de Rotrou in his *Iphygenie* (1641), which initiated the sequence of Iphigenia plays and operas that appeared regularly on the major European stages until the end of the eighteenth century, most famously in masterpieces by Racine, Goethe, and Gluck. Only a dramatist who had given Agamemnon a *valet de chambre*, moreover, could have had him commence a letter to Clytemnestra with 'Worthy companion of my bed, illustrious blood of so many kings':

> Digne compagne de ma couche,
> Illustre sang de tant de Roys.[1]

The equivalent opening in Euripides is 'O scion of Leda' ('ō Lēdas ernos') (line 116). One notes not only the (to us) inappropriately elaborated expression of social decorum but the detailed network of male identifiers, which turn the mother's daughter of Euripides' version into the guest in a male bed, animated by inherited male blood. Dryden complained of Racine's Hippolyte that the author had 'chosen to give him the turn of Gallantry, sent him to travel from *Athens* to *Paris*, taught him to make love, and transformed the *Hippolitus* of *Euripides* into Monsieur *Hippolite*'.[2] What happens when Thyestes becomes Monsieur Thyeste, and when the Thyestean banquet is served on Sèvres porcelain?

An extreme case of frigidly decorous barbarity is provided in another play about the sacrifice of a daughter, *Jephté, ou La Mort de Seïla* (1676), by M. Venel, Conseiller au parlement d'Aix, which was brought into print by Joseph Leven de Templery. The play is based on the episode in Judges 11, in which Jephthah vows to God that, in return for victory over the Ammonites, he will sacrifice the first living thing that greets him on his return home. He is greeted by his daughter, who is granted two months to lament that she will die a virgin, whereafter Jephthah fulfils his vow – an ending with enough vestigial ambiguity to permit happy-ending versions of the story in the eighteenth century.

In that it was accomplished, Jephthah's sacrifice has always been more problematic than Abraham's. Aquinas, Dante, and others argued that

Jephthah was impious to fulfil his vow, yet the episode was also held to have a blameless symbolic meaning, in that Jephthah represented Christ and his daughter the Church. The story of Jephthah had been influentially dramatized by George Buchanan in *Iephthes* (1542–3), which focusses on the grave problems of religious morality in the sacrifice. It is a chastisement to forestall excessive pride, and the play does not take refuge in typology: the rashness of the father, the anguish of the mother, and the nobility of the daughter are not in any way modified by allegory. This was to remain an influential text, being the basis of Handel's happy-ending version of the story nearly 200 years later. The French play is, however, far simpler.

The Biblical Jephthah was an outsider: 'the son of an harlot', forced by his legitimate brothers into exile, where he consorted with 'vain men' (Judges 11:1–3). His lowly origin is emphasized in Buchanan.[3] In the French play, however, *bienséance* demands that Jephthah be a king, and the play becomes a study of royal responsibilities – perhaps topically, since in the 1670s Louis XIV's lifestyle was still, like that of Charles II, somewhat in conflict with the ideals of the Church. Even so, one is surprised by the extent to which decorum is carried. At the opening, Seïla (the daughter) and her friends are discovered, seated in armchairs ('fauteuils').[4] When Jephté later breaks the dreadful news to her, he gets her to steady her nerves by taking a seat (pp. 44–5). Towards the end, when she goes to request the Biblical two-month stay of sacrifice in order to bewail her virginity, the High Priest's response is the same: 'take a seat, madam' ('Ce fauteuil est pour vous, Madame') (p. 79). The translation of tragic conflict into decorous gesture reappears when Jephté realizes that he is bound by his vow, and dabs his eyes with a handkerchief (p. 56), an action repeated later by Seïla herself (p. 65). Gesture takes the place of thought. As the externalization of emotion shows, this is not a drama of internalized moral experience, and indeed the resolution does not come from within Jephthah at all: a council of priests decides, by a vote of four to three, that the daughter should be sacrificed. At this crucial point, there is no subjective centre in the play. In casting the decisive vote, the High Priest asserts that he ought not to refuse something to God in order to give it to his king (p. 86). For 'God retains his rights over all monarchs, and never defers to human rank':

> Dieu conserve ses droits sur tous les Souverains,
> Et ne se rend jamais à des respects humains. (p. 56)

Seïla dies to prove that the Church is superior to the king.

Jephté is extreme, yet it reveals much about the normal. Jephté's sacrificial vow creates a crisis in a system, and the play works towards rectifying the structure of the system; in the crisis, the conflict is not between the state and the individual chosen for sacrifice, but between monarchic and religious authority. The victim is the medium through which that conflict is explored. To a less preposterous degree, the same is true of Agamemnon's parallel dilemma in Rotrou's *Iphygenie*, where the conflict is schematized into one between his role as father of his daughter and that as father of his people: between nature and *rang* (social rank), and between the two senses of *sang*, as family blood-ties and as the sacrificial blood which he is commanded to shed. The inevitable rhyme of *rang* and *sang* sums up the conflicts of these plays, which represent crises in an aristocratic system. When Rotrou's Agamemnon dithers about the letter he has written, commanding Clytemnestre not to bring Iphygenie to Aulis after all, he shifts between emphasizing his fatherhood – what he owes to his blood ('*deuoir du sang*') (p. 2) – and soldiership, which is also defined in terms of blood: 'only write with a sword, and in letters of blood ('*N'escry que d'une espée, & qu'en lettre de sang*'), he urges himself (p. 2). Rotrou greatly expands the emphasis on Achilles' love for Iphigenia, and entirely removes the irony with which Euripides had treated him. Correspondingly elaborated is Iphigenia's rejection of his love, so that she might embrace the *gloire* of dying for her country. She is, as the formerly unscrupulous and manipulative Ulysses admiringly remarks, the only male in the place (p. 105).

Yet where is the body that is to be sacrificed? Euripides' *Iphigenia in Aulis* emphasizes the bodies of the characters to the point of periphrastically introducing Clytemnestra as 'the body of Clytemnestra' ('Klutaimēstras demas') (line 417). Shakespeare, Behn, and Defoe use dismemberment as a fundamental social and economic metaphor. In the French plays of this period, however, there is plenty of blood, but no bodies; *sang* and its derivatives occur over seventy times in Racine's *Iphigénie*; *corps* occurs twice. In Rotrou, vivid imaginative awareness of the body is confined to the character who remains immovably feminine, despite Agamemnon's attempt to reduce her to a system of male connections: Clytemnestre. As in Euripides (who perhaps invented the story), Clytemnestre denounces Agamemnon for murdering her child by her first marriage, and figuratively ripping out her viscera: '*de ces flancs ouuerts tirastes les entrailles*' (p. 73). Racine's Clytemnestre, similarly, accuses Agamemnon of 'tearing her entrails' ('déchirant [son] flanc') in his plan to sacrifice Iphigenia.[5] In the descriptions of the interrupted sacrifice, however, there is no description of the victim's body; no equivalent to Euripides' concentration on Iphigenia's beautiful throat (line 1516).

Similarly, the French dramatists omit what (independently of each other) Euripides and the English writers make central to their treatment: the sacrificed, dismembered, and circulating body as part of an economic system. The French plays take place in a non-numeric universe: in Racine's play, there is almost no interest in numbers beyond two, the number of rivalry, love, and moral choice. Although the word *prix* (both 'price' and 'prize') and related words run through the versions of Racine and his contemporaries, they never refer to money. In Racine, with only one exception, it refers to the transactions involving the sacrifice or saving of Iphigenia; the exception is the tomb that is the price of Achilles' glory.

Sacrificial drama in this period almost always involves a secret. In Michel Le Clerc's *Iphigénie* (1675), yet another version of the Aulis story, Clytemnestre had silently and secretly vowed Iphigénie to the service of Diane at the moment of her birth, and the goddess is now claiming her promised due.[6] In Simon Joseph Pellegrin's libretto for Montéclair's opera *Jephté* (1732), the daughter is spared from sacrifice, but only when she stops reciprocating 'le feu secret' of the captive enemy commander.[7] Here, the secrets at the heart of the sacrifice are guilty sexual secrets: maiden sacrifice is no longer acceptable, and there has to be some whiff, however faint, of sexual transgression in the prospective victim. These secrets justify the command to sacrifice, and the political order against which the victim offends. By the time that Mozart's Idomeneo laments the 'arcano' that oppresses him,[8] however, the unspeakable secret is the sacrifice itself, which now taints the political order.

One sign of the greater profundity of Racine's *Iphigénie en Aulide* (1674) is the huge increase in the number and kind of secrets that the sacrificial command spawns. To the enigmatic oracle demanding Iphigénie's death, to Agamemnon's deceptions, to the 'secrète horreur' (2.3.580) of Iphigénie's growing suspicions, and to Achille's bewilderment at the 'secret' (2.7.755) which is causing opposition to his love, he adds the mystery of Ériphile, the captive princess from Lesbos, stifling a secret love for her captor, Achille, but driven by 'Une secrète voix' (2.1.516) to follow him to Aulis. She is ignorant of her origins and identity, and may learn these from Calchas, 'who was always privy to the secrets of the gods' ('Qui des secrets des Dieux fut toujours informé') (2.1.456); but she knows from an oracle that disclosure of the secrets will bring death. It does. She is the secret daughter of Helen and Theseus, and she has a secret name: Iphigénie. It is she who is demanded by the oracle, and her passionate, deranged suicide spares Calchas the necessity of sacrificing her.

Whereas the armchairs of the Venel *Jephté* exemplify a world where rank, decorum, and social imperatives have a fixed, palpable force, the proliferating secrets of Racine's *Iphigénie en Aulide* suggest one of insecure surfaces, also exemplified by the situation of its characters on numerous boundaries, particularly that of the formless sea. The demands of *rang* shrink. Although Racine twice uses the *rang-sang* rhyme, he does not use it to represent Agamemnon's dilemma. Instead, he elaborates what had barely been more than a pun in Rotrou, for almost all the conflicts of the play are compressed into the conflicting meanings of *sang* itself: Agamemnon's tie of blood to Iphigénie, and the filial blood that he is obliged to shed. The warring meanings of the word suggest a civilization whose values contain their own opposites. There is something of Virgil's sense of the savagery at the heart of the city, with one telling difference: the death of Dido is one in an unstoppable sequence of sacrifices, whereas the crisis in the Greek camp is resolved by the death of Ériphile, punished for her murderous sexual jealousy of Iphigénie, and her attempt to ensure Iphigénie's sacrifice by betraying her escape plans. She is also, however, doomed by her secret, tainted origin as the illicit 'daughter of Helen's *blood*' ('fille du *sang* d'Hélène') (1.1.59; italics added). The corrupting secrets that legitimate the sacrifice are those of sex and sexual origin: of bad blood.

THE EARLY EIGHTEENTH CENTURY

But what of Iphigenia's afterlife in Taurica? In Euripides' *Iphigenia among the Taurians*, the barbarous heritage of the House of Atreus is finally exorcized in spaces that are on the boundaries of culture. The play provides a vehicle whereby civilization can discover itself in its Other. What did the seventeenth and eighteenth centuries find in Taurica?

What they initially found was a negation of their own ideal systems of power. A fundamental question is the status of Thoas, the Scythian king who enforces the sacrificial customs: whether he is a reassuring antitype of a European *ancien régime* ruler or a dissident's image of just such a ruler. As time goes by, he shifts from one to the other. In 1697, in La Grange-Chancel's *Oreste et Pylade*, he is a barbarous usurper, who uses the sacrificial custom to secure a shaky regime. An oracle given 'En secret'[9] has revealed that he will be deposed when Orestes removes the statue of the goddess; he therefore kills every Greek in case he is Orestes. Secrecy here supports a regime that is insecure because it has subverted legitimate monarchy.[10]

There is no point in detailed description of every largely forgotten play or libretto about Iphigenia. With versions of the Aulis story, the Euripidean happy ending (with or without the substitution of an animal victim) prevails over the Racinian device of a human substitute, though this is used in Apostolo Zeno's popular libretto, first set by Caldara in 1718,[11] and it makes a comeback towards the end of the century: for example, in the *Ifigenia in Aulide* by Ferdinando Moretti, set by (among others) Zingarelli (Milan, 1787) and Cherubini (Turin, 1788). Although each work, however minor, to some extent expands and modifies the overall pattern, it remains true that, in the seventeenth and early eighteenth centuries, the sacrificial custom primarily creates a dislocation in a system of power, either because it expresses the moral disorder of usurpation or because it produces a destructive contradiction between the personal and public roles of the ruler.[12]

At the same time as writers were revisiting the Iphigenia stories in order to explore the tensions within absolute monarchy, they revived a story which had hitherto lain neglected in a footnote, but which was to generate one of the greatest representations of sacrifice of the eighteenth century: the story of Idomeneus, king of Crete, trapped by an incautious vow into the obligation to sacrifice his son, and the subject of one of Mozart's earliest operatic masterpieces.

Idomeneus is an important character in the *Iliad*, but Homer does not mention this story; nor, of course, does he mention that of Iphigenia. Without explanation, Virgil briefly mentions that Idomeneus has been driven out of his home, and had founded a settlement elsewhere; he is one of the many futureless exiles whose destiny contrasts with that of Aeneas (3.121–3). Servius' note elucidating this passage is our earliest source for the story of the imprudent vow, made during a storm at sea. In Servius, Idomeneus is exiled by his subjects after either performing the sacrifice or attempting to do so. This story figures prominently in Fénelon's *Télémaque* (1699), and is the subject of a tragedy by the elder Crébillon (1705) and, prior to Mozart's version, of two operas, by Campra (1712) and Galuppi (1756). These versions are unusual for the eighteenth century in that the sacrifice is accomplished. In Galuppi, the ultimate victim is a villain who happened to meet the returning king a split second before his son, but in the Campra opera Idomenée is (like Euripides' Agave or Heracles) seized by madness, killing his son in the belief that he is sacrificing an animal.[13] Here, incongruously interspersed with pastoral and erotic divertissements, are the horrors that eighteenth-century librettists were increasingly to exorcize from Greek tragedy: the collapse of reason, replacing social consciousness of kin and shared humanity with the total alienness of the wilderness. It was a vision which later librettists were to avoid, until the very end of the century.[14]

The eighteenth-century outlook is more influentially represented by Pietro Metastasio's libretto *Demofoönte* (1733), first performed in Vienna on the nameday of the emperor Charles VI, with music by Antonio Caldara. It was set or adapted over forty times, occasionally in versions which subject the original text to radical political transformation. It portrays the abolition of an annual custom of virgin-sacrifice in Thrace, of which Demofoönte is king, after he has nearly sanctioned the sacrifice of his own long-lost daughter. Characteristically, it shows a ruler triumphing over his baser and more self-serving instincts to become the just and selfless leader of his people; along with the Iphigenia stories, that of Demofoönte becomes one of the major sacrificial narratives of eighteenth-century theatre.

The transformations of this much-set libretto in the eighteenth and early nineteenth centuries are a microcosm of the changing political meanings of human sacrifice throughout the period. First used to glorify an imperial nonentity, it was (for example) appropriated by the more substantial figure of Frederick the Great, who composed three arias for the setting by Graun performed at his opera house in Berlin in 1746. A fiery, radical version, with at times imposing music by Johann Christoph Vogel, was put on in Paris in September 1789, two months after the storming of the Bastille.[15] In 1808, with breathtaking inappropriateness, a revival in Lisbon of a Portuguese setting celebrated Napoleon's birthday, amidst all the horrors and atrocities of the Peninsular War.[16] In Munich in 1811, a setting by Lindpaintner meditated on the threat posed by tyranny to the virtues of the nuclear family. Until the fall of Napoleon, the theme of averted sacrifice could be used to celebrate the enlightenment of absolute monarchs or to deplore their despotism, with even a single libretto mutating to serve contrary political purposes.

LITERARY SACRIFICE AND THE ENLIGHTENMENT

Throughout the eighteenth century, sacrificial plays continued to portray anomalous crises in a potentially just autocracy. By mid-century, however, they were equally likely to portray intrinsic flaws in a corrupt and tottering political system. One of the most successful Iphigenia plays of this time was the *Iphigénie en Tauride* (1757) of Claude Guimond de la Touche (1723–60), which was to influence Gluck's celebrated opera. The author had been a Jesuit novice, and wrote about his experiences in *Les Soupirs du cloître*, posthumously published in 1766. In this work Jesuitism is consistently likened to a cult which conducts human sacrifice.[17] What, I asked earlier, does the writer find in Taurica? Guimond de la Touche found a replica of his own religious life in France.

Earlier French versions of *Iphigenia among the Taurians* had modified Euripides so as to portray Thoas, the sacrificing barbarian king, as a usurper: a violator of a normative system of monarchic power. For Guimond, this was no longer necessary. Thoas is, without contradiction, both a rightful king and a cultural throwback, drawing his inspiration from the example of cannibals. Men, he says, slaughter (*immoler*) each other in wars and eat each other in caves: why should life suddenly become sacred in our relationships with the gods?[18] By contrast with Thoas' vision of a world of violent deeds, Iphigénie and Oreste emphasize the potential of the subjective, and describe the inner sources of a higher morality, pleading the rights of 'nature' (a word which occurs only once in Racine's play) and 'humanité' (e.g., p. 20). The command to sacrifice is thus no longer a structural crisis in a system of power, but a moral crisis whose primary area is internal.

Rang (rank), so important to seventeenth-century French dramatists, consequently loses its importance: it is never a rhyme word, and lacks the social mystique it possesses in seventeenth-century plays. Still more strikingly, blood ceases to have the ambiguity – blood-line, bloodshed – that enabled this single word to encapsulate the conflicting claims of family and the sacrificial duties of the king. Blood in this play is desired, thirsted after, and consumed; it flows in streams, rivers, and floods; people wash in it, or get drunk on it. It is blood in this sense that links Iphigénie with her father. On the way to Aulis for her pretended marriage to Achille, she had had a dream intimating Agamemnon's 'bloody imposture' ('sanglante imposture'); 'I saw him at the altar, violating nature' ('Je le vis à l'autel, outrageant la nature') (p. 5). Now, in Taurica, she has had an ominous dream about the sacrifice of Oreste:

Emerging from the bosom of the dead, my father, murderer of his family, burned again with thirst for his own blood. He seemed to force my trembling hand to pierce his entrails.

> Sorti du sein des morts, mon parricide père
> Sembloit, brûlant encor de la soif de son sang,
> Forcer ma main tremblante à lui percer le flanc. (p. 5)

In the plays of a hundred years before, the piercing of the entrails had represented a distinctively feminine vision of a masculine world ruled by higher abstractions of honour and rank. Now the dismemberment of the body is the primary feature of the world: an archaic world, which Iphigénie's higher feminine morality rejects. The past is a past of blood. At the end of the play, the destruction of Thoas' cult not only destroys a barbarous custom on the fringes of civilization, it liberates Oreste from his own heritage: 'Horror leaves me. All around me seems to be reborn, and I receive a new being in a new world':

> L'horreur me fuit. Tout semble autour de moi renaître:
> Dans un monde nouveau je prend un nouvel être. (p. 44)

The same year of 1757 saw the publication of the unperformed *Iphigenie en Tauride* by the lawyer Jean Baptiste Claude Vaubertrand, which presents an entirely secularized version of the story. Earlier plays take place in a cosmos of cruel gods, relenting gods, or misinterpreted gods. In operas (such as the Campra–Desmarets *Iphigénie en Tauride*) (1704), interludes displaying the gods play an important part in the entertainment. Here there are, simply, no gods. The dynamics of human sacrifice are purely human. Iphigénie escaped from the sacrifice at Aulis with the aid of a slave, not because of the intervention of Diana; she was taken to Taurica not by divine agency but by pirates; Oreste killed his mother not by divine command, but by accident, while killing Aegisthus;[19] and there is no command to recover an image of Diana. Most importantly, Thoas is enforcing the custom of sacrificing strangers in order to keep his subjects from knowledge of the freedoms which exist in other lands. The sacrificial custom is a kind of Berlin Wall. Taurica is the crisis-ridden France of Louis XV, recently embarked on the Seven Years War against that great hero of the Enlightenment, Frederick the Great.[20]

SACRIFICIAL ANXIETIES

But what are these plays about? Did dramatists, for a period of over 150 years, decide that human sacrifice was, in the abstract, a bad thing, and that it improved the mind to see it abolished? As a pressing moral problem, after all, the sacrifice of human victims was not what it had been for the Spanish in the sixteenth century, or was to become again for the British in the nineteenth. In the first period of British rule in India, which commenced in the 1750s, widow-burning was tolerated. The article on 'Anthropophagie' in the *Encyclopédie*, by the abbé Mallet, treated cannibalism not as a monstrous anomaly but as a stage which all cultures pass through. In his discussion of the South Sea islanders, whose closeness to nature he largely idealizes, Diderot briefly discusses cannibalism and human sacrifice as strategies of population control, along with castration and infibulation.[21] He too sees the differences between cannibalistic and non-cannibalistic cultures as essentially chronological. Captain Cook was to investigate human sacrifice with the eye of an anthropological observer, and even perhaps unwittingly to provoke the practices he recorded. He conveys his disapproval, but is aware that he is observing explicable customs. When he met his own *sparagmos*, British indignation at the barbarous fury of his killers could sometimes be tempered with awareness that Cook had rashly offended local decencies: 'For in what country, civilised or savage, would it not be accounted base in a people tamely to suffer their sovereign to be dragged away captive, in order to answer for a crime which he had no share in committing?'[22]

So what is the real focus of horror in these dramas of human sacrifice?

Captain Cook's death, on the far side of the world, was one of the great dismemberments of the eighteenth century. Another took place on the streets of Paris in the very year that Guimond's and Vaubertrand's plays appeared. This was the brutal execution of Robert-François Damiens for a very half-hearted attempt on the life of Louis XV. He was tortured to death over a period of four hours, during which his flesh was torn with pincers, and molten lead and other boiling substances were poured into his wounds. There was an unsuccessful attempt to tear him limb from limb with horses, before the executioner finished the dismemberment with his knife. The punishment had a strong ritual dimension, in that it re-enacted the 1610 execution of François Ravaillac, for the successful murder of Henri IV; indeed, it was so much a re-enactment of the earlier execution that there was irritation at a slight and inadvertent verbal discrepancy between the later and the earlier sentence.

The execution of Damiens has always stood out as one of the worst barbarities of the *ancien régime*. Apparently unaware of the earlier treatment of Ravaillac, William Godwin regarded the tortures as a perverse misapplication of Enlightenment science, writing that 'a council of anatomists was summoned, to deliberate how a human being might be destroyed with the longest protracted and most diversified agony'. He described Damiens as one of the 'Hundreds of victims [who] are annually sacrificed at the shrine of positive law and political institution' (p. 9).[23] The atrocity is again described in *A Tale of Two Cities*[24] and in Peter Weiss's *Marat/Sade*,[25] while an account of it opens Foucault's influential analysis of punishment theory and practice, *Discipline and Punish*. For Foucault, the execution is a defining expression of a system of punishment that was about to pass away. This was a system that assumed a symbolic relationship between the body and the system of authority that had been violated: 'a few decades saw the disappearance of the tortured, dismembered, amputated body, symbolically branded on face or shoulder, exposed alive or dead to public view'.[26] A collection of essays on the Damiens case, *L'Attentat de Damiens*, treats the execution as the sacrificial destruction of a scapegoat. Few people dwell on the execution of Ravaillac, but its re-enactment upon the body of Damiens haunts us, perhaps because this savage *sparagmos* took place in the city of Voltaire, Rameau, and Fragonard. As Henri Duranton writes in *L'Attentat de Damiens*, 'The archetypal situation described by René Girard is recreated in the very midst of the Enlightenment' ('La situation archétypale décrite par R. Girard se réactualise en plein Siècle des Lumières').[27]

The year 1757 thus saw two plays about the abolition of human sacrifice in Taurica, and in both its alien, Asiatic spaces were, in truth, the streets of Paris. In those very same streets was enacted a ritual barbarity which some later interpreters have seen in sacrificial terms. What is the relationship between them?

The answer appears to be that there is none. This profound lack of connection is a lesson against the temptation to assume too tidy a shift of the episteme, or too exact and all-embracing a symmetry between the forms of literature and of history (the kind of relationship that Adorno assumes when he sees in *The Rite of Spring* a foreshadowing of the First World War). If, for us, Damiens is the victim of fanatical violence, many of his contemporaries resolved the pattern differently and saw him as one of its chief embodiments: as representing the very brutal fanaticism that Guimond de la Touche and others were deploring in their sacrificial fictions. Voltaire, for example, wrote of Damiens with consistent contempt, regarding him as having been fanaticized by the Jansenists, and distinguished his treatment from that of unquestionable victims of cruel intolerance such as the Chevalier de La Barre, brutally executed for a minor blasphemy in 1766,[28] or the Huguenot Jean Calas, framed for the murder of his son (who had reconverted to Catholicism) and executed on the wheel in 1762. When imagining sacrifice as something which happens at home, French writers of this period focus particularly on one thing: a reactionary religious cruelty, which operates by exploiting the violence of the mob.

In describing the cases both of Jean Calas and of the Chevalier de La Barre, Voltaire stresses the role of the mob in exacting the sacrifice. Addressing his *Relation de la mort du Chevalier de La Barre* to that great opponent of capital punishment, Cesare Beccaria, he wrote: 'You know, sir, to what extremes the people bring credulity and fanaticism under the too frequent encouragement of the monks' ('Vous connaissez, monsieur, à quel excès la populace porte la crédulité & le fanatisme, trop souvent encouragé par les moines').[29] On 22 April 1773 he wrote to Frederick II, likening the execution of the Chevalier de La Barre to an earlier atrocity, a mass execution of Protestants at Thorn in Poland in 1724. This he describes as a sacrifice to the Virgin Mary: 'I dare to ask you for justice upon the blessed Virgin Mary, to whom were sacrificed so many young scholars in the year 1724' ('j'ose vous demander justice de la sainte Vierge Marie, à laquelle on sacrifia tant de jeunes écoliers en l'année 1724'). Unlike the judges of La Barre, Frederick does not sacrifice anyone to his monks ('n'immole personne à ses capucins').[30]

Voltaire understands the dynamics of what René Girard was to call a sacrificial crisis. He believes that the replications of human sacrifice in modern societies correspond to ancient and exotic rituals because both are dictated by the collective irrationality of the masses. He is also aware of the way in which traces of primitive and violent cultures are preserved and canonized in Holy Writ. In *La Bible enfin expliquée* (1776) he draws attention to many factual absurdities in the story of Abraham and Isaac, and also documents how widespread were the 'horrible sacrifices' of human beings in the time of Abraham. The story loses its protected status as divine narrative, for it is full of nonsense and inconsistencies; it is instead a typical example of a common piece of ancient barbarism, which has managed to lodge itself in the hagiography of the modern world.

Voltaire was already addressing the topic of sacrificial hysteria in his first tragedy, *Oedipe* (1718), and thus to some extent prefigures Girard's reading of Sophocles' play. His most striking innovation, however, was the introduction of Philoctetes as Jocasta's true love, their mutual passion left unfulfilled by her two politic marriages, to Laius and to Oedipus. This modification removes any intrinsically incestuous element in her feelings for Oedipus (which had featured in the version of Dryden and Lee (1678), and was later to dominate Jean Cocteau's *The Infernal Machine*).

In Voltaire's play, Philoctète is the friend and successor of Hercules, slayer of monsters. In Philoctète and Oedipe, the play thus juxtaposes two rival forms of culture hero, one defeating the monsters of the wilderness by force, the other by intellect. They represent the twin ways by which humanity advances culture and civilization: through routes of individual valour and speculation that are more important than the hierarchical systems that sustain the state. Oedipe is (unrightfully, as it turns out) a king, but Philoctète is not. Yet, he claims, his achievements place him above kings: 'A king for his subjects is a god to be revered; for Hercules and me, he is a common man' ('Un roi pour ses sujets est un dieu qu'on révère; / Pour Hercule et pour moi, c'est un homme ordinaire').[31] Nevertheless, both these extraordinary individuals are singled out as sacrificial victims.

On the night of her wedding to Oedipe, Jocaste had a vision of Laïus and the son 'of whom my pious and barbarous injustice had made a secret sacrifice to our gods' ('Ce fils dont ma pieuse et barbare injustice / Avait fait à nos dieux un secret sacrifice') (2.2.113–14). As the panic over the plague increases, so does the clamour for sacrifice: the mob demand the blood of Philoctète on behalf of their gods, while Jocaste and Oedipe are alike willing to sacrifice themselves for Thebes. Sacrifice is thus a social process, driven by the collective superstitions of the rabble, and focussed on the individuals who most stand in opposition to their atavism. The pairing of the two culture heroes emphasizes the struggle of civilization with the primitive, whether located in the wilderness, the mob, or the gods. The final line of the play is Jocaste's: 'I have brought blushes from the gods who forced me to crime' ('J'ai fait rougir les dieux qui m'ont forcée au crime') (5.6.230).

The mob's thirst for human sacrifice is most extensively examined in a later play by Voltaire, *Les Lois de Minos* (1773), which provides his most direct and literal portrayal of ritual human sacrifice. The play is set in Crete, in the aftermath of Idomenée's exile after sacrificing his son. He had believed that his exile would please the mob, but the people are 'inconstant, tempestuous, wild, / exact image of the seas' ('inconstant, orageux, égaré, / Vive image des mers'),[32] and human sacrifice persists: every seven years, a captive must be offered to the shades of Cretan heroes. 'One must grant the people blood' ('Il faut du sang au peuple') (1.3.237), says a nobleman opposed to Idomenée's humane successor, Teucer, who wishes to abolish the custom (and finally does so after discovering, in an echo of *Demofoönte*, that the designated victim is his own daughter). The mob instinct for sacrifice appears in conjunction with another insensate instinct for destruction, with similar claims to be a cultural imperative: the impulse to exterminate primitive peoples; for the sacrificial victim is initially believed to be a member of the primitive, aboriginal Cydonian peoples. Teucer meditates on the combination of advanced culture and barbarism that characterizes the current state of Greek civilization. Advanced Greek culture is an illusion: Greece is still barbarous ('encor barbare') (1.1.44); it has discovered culture ('des arts') and lost nature (1.1.72).

Increasingly, then, human sacrifice indicates the savagery of contemporary systems of government and belief. Culture itself can imply barbarism, in that it conveys the imagined right to dispossess and slaughter less advanced peoples. Yet even so, there is the belief that the savagery can be overcome. How and by whom?

THE PHILOSOPHER KING: FREDERICK II

A particular focus of political hope and idealism in the Enlightenment was Frederick II of Prussia, who had abolished torture and restricted the use of capital punishment. Frederick is praised by Beccaria in his great attack on capital punishment, *Dei Delitti e delle pene*,[33] and by Guimond de la Touche in *Les Soupirs du cloître* (p. 14), and Voltaire spent a tense time at his courts in Potsdam and Berlin from 1750 to 1753. Frederick was a patron of the arts, writer, and composer, whose monumental new opera house in Unter den Linden was the centre of a flourishing operatic culture from 1742 until the start of the Seven Years' War in 1756. Early settings are of Italian librettists, chiefly Metastasio and Zeno, but with the arrival of Leopoldo de Villati in 1747 the emphasis shifted to Italian libretti based on French plays, and sometimes on French drafts supplied by Frederick himself. For Frederick at times worked on libretti or composed arias for works by the chief operatic composer of his court, Carl Heinrich Graun. Given the nature of operatic fashion, it is statistically inevitable that the repertory should have included operas with a sacrificial theme, but it is a theme with which Frederick seems to have had a particular imaginative involvement.

In 1746 Frederick provided three arias for Graun's setting of Metastasio's *Demofòonte*, though here the text is not significantly altered. More interesting is the 1748 *Ifigenia in Aulide*, whose text represents a collaboration between Frederick and his new librettist, Villati. It is avowedly based on Racine, but it dispenses with the troublesome figure of Ériphile, the substitute human victim, in favour of the Euripidean ending, with the substitution of a hind for Iphigenia. What is more striking is that there is no Ulysses or Menelaus in the opera: gone are the self-interested schemers who formulate the corrupt secular rationale for the sacrifice – a rationale which, in Euripides, is its primary feature. Their disappearance means that there are no obstructive or confusing intermediaries between the king and the needs of his people. Like Euripides' Agamemnon, that of Villati and Frederick reflects on the miseries of high office, but the new Agamemnon specifically laments the king's helplessness as servant of his people. Kings must sacrifice everything to the good of their subjects and kingdoms ('al bene / De' lor vassalli e regni').[34] The focus is thus on Agamemnon's inner divisions, and in this conflict the private man wins – he tries to arrange the flight of Ifigenia and Clitennestra – but is thwarted by the vigilant priest, Calcante, and by Ifigenia's own heroic willingness to die for the fatherland. When the goddess Diana descends to stop the sacrifice, she very much emphasizes the private: she is placated 'By the obedience of the father, the courage of the daughter, and the grief of the inconsolable mother':

> Dall' ubbidir del Padre,
> Dal valor della Figlia,
> E dal dolor di sconsolata Madre. (p. 88)

The interests of the state are here absolutely indivisible from those of the private family.

Frederick's most significant operatic venture was *Montezuma* (1755), whose libretto was written in French by Frederick and translated into Italian by Giampietro Tagliazucchi; the music, again, was by Graun. Montezuma, the introductory Argomento proclaims, was 'barbarously sacrificed' ('barbaramente sacrificato') to the cruelty and avarice of the Spanish guests whom he had trusted. Early in the opera, he establishes himself as an enlightened ruler, bound by the laws of his kingdom and solicitous for the welfare of his people. He is then destroyed by an avarice, fanaticism, and duplicity which his own nobler culture has left him unprepared to predict. Inevitably, one of the justifications of Spanish brutality is the allegation that the Mexicans conduct human sacrifice; Montezuma's counter-allegation is that the Christians are fanatically intolerant of those who do not know, or do not share, their own beliefs. Each side accuses the other of religious atrocity, and each hurls at the other the word 'barbaro', yet only the Spaniards visibly merit the accusations, and the opera ends in carnage. In a letter to his friend, the philosopher and art critic Count Algarotti, Frederick remarks that the opera had expressed some mockery of the barbarity of the Christian religion ('quelque lardon contre la barbarie de la R[eligion]. C[h]r[étienne]').[35]

Ifigenia in Aulide and *Montezuma* both portray a solitary, selfless ruler, whose agonies of office are heightened by the destructive imperatives of a bloody religion. It is not the place to analyse the moral complexities and inconsistencies in the career of the enlightened warrior despot, though we might recall that, as an artistic youth, Frederick had remade himself into the warrior desired by his father after the trauma of seeing his best friend beheaded on his father's orders. The sacrificing Agamemnon was, probably, closer to his experience than to that of most Enlightenment librettists; and perhaps not until Wagner is there a more deep-rooted relationship between opera and political ferment.

SENSIBILITY AND SACRIFICE

As noted, one aspect of the Graun–Frederick *Ifigenia in Aulide* is its paring away of external scheming and conflict. A comparable concentration is to be seen in an important setting of *Iphigenia among the Taurians* from the 1760s, Tommaso Traetta's *Ifigenia in Tauride* (Vienna, 1763), to a libretto by Marco Coltellini that was to be much reset by other composers. This is an important opera, influenced by Gluck's *Orfeo ed Euridice*, and in turn clearly influencing Gluck's later *Iphigénie en Tauride*.

In contrast with earlier versions, which show a political system in crisis, the Coltellini–Traetta version uses the subjectivity of the central characters as its organizing principle. For Toante, the sacrificing king of the barbarian land, each victim of the sacrificial custom is simply 'il reo' – 'the guilty one' – and almost all human beings merit the adjective: they are fragments of unexamined otherness, without interiority. Oreste, by contrast, is all interiority, dominated by memory to the extent that it directs the flow of his present experience. He is possessed by the memory of Clytemnestra, feeling that she is killing him and that she is not yet sated with blood. When he first sees Ifigenia, he thinks (in an incident that is copied in the Gluck version) that she is his mother. Ifigenia's sacrificial role means that she must constantly relive the horror of Aulis, and she admits that all the details of the sacrificial ritual are constantly present in her mind.[36]

The Traetta opera provides a new approach to ritual, in that it explores the relationship between ritual and memory. In the drama of Oreste and Ifigenia, the rituals of memory embed the present in the moral traumas of the past. There are no Furies in this opera, only the ever present memory of Clytemnestra, who is a focus of far greater obsession here than in any previous version. There is a conflict between the world as exterior process, as managed by Toante, and the interior life of the Greek characters, where the flow of time and the workings of ritual are shaped by inner factors, which replace the external systems which had been the primary area of conflict in the seventeenth-century plays. In conjunction with the reduced emphasis on systems of authority comes an increased emphasis on the feminine. Ifigenia's friendship with her attendant Dori is given a prominence equivalent to that of Oreste and Pilade, and it is Ifigenia who kills Toante, inducing the Chorus to resolve to follow 'la donna forte' to Argos (Act 3, fo. 83r–v).

Increasingly, then, sacrificial drama explores the consciousness of the unwilling sacrificer and of the victim, at the expense of the system in which they are forced to participate: a system which frequently exploits and is sustained by the collective irrationality of the mob. Rarely is human sacrifice the preserve of barbarous strangers: by mid-century, Taurica bears a striking resemblance to *ancien régime* France, and, in Frederick's and Graun's Mexico, it is Spain that conducts human sacrifice. True, there are libretti which glorify the conquistadors, and even show Montezuma or Atabalipa living happily ever after as the trusted friends and allies of Charles V,[37] but the most popular new inspiration for works about averted sacrifice in the late eighteenth century is an extreme, anti-Spanish idealization of pre-Conquest American civilization: the novel *Les Incas* (1778) by the Encyclopédiste Jean-François Marmontel. This contains an incident of averted sacrifice which inspired many operas and ballets, and also a poem by the Edinburgh poet Elizabeth Scot.[38]

As its title implies, *Les Incas* is about the conquest of Peru. Peru is distinguished from the more brutal civilization of Mexico, but Cortez's devastation of the latter country is nevertheless portrayed with total hostility. Although Pizarro is (surprisingly) given some redeeming qualities, Marmontel portrays the destruction of a rational and exemplary Peruvian culture by ruthless adventurers and hypocritical clerics. The only European embodiments of virtue are Las Casas, transformed into an eighteenth-century man of feeling, and the Spanish soldier Alonzo de Molina, who sides with the Peruvians, and falls in love with the vestal virgin Cora.

Rather like Virgil's Aeneas on the future site of Rome, Alonzo is given an account of social evolution by his host. This is here associated with the culture heroes Manco and his sister Oello, who teach, respectively, agriculture and irrigation, and the domestic arts. Peru is a community of sun-worshippers, and the true form of sacrifice is to imitate the work of the sun by distributing his gifts. The contrary kind of sacrifice is made to beasts of prey, in imitation of their nature. In the pre-agricultural state, some adored the peaceful aspects of nature, but the majority adored its savage elements – the tiger, the lion, the vulture – and the awe of the hunter for the predator survives in the religion of the majority.[39] Like many before him, therefore, Marmontel derives the impulse to human sacrifice from man's history as a hunter.

Aeneas, however, receives his instruction on the future site of Rome: a civilization which will consummate the movement away from the condition of the hunter–gatherer; Alonzo, by contrast, is on a site whose culture is about to be obliterated by the religion of the tiger. For the tiger-god corresponds to the god of the Spanish invaders, who pervert the sacrificial ritual of the Mass to symbolize and ratify the invasion of America: the division of the New World is sealed by a blasphemous communion, in which the Host is divided into three, like the conquered territories.

The most celebrated and imitated incident in *Les Incas* concerns the love of Alonzo and the Peruvian vestal Cora, her violation of her vows, and the abolition of the law that unchaste vestals should be sacrificed by being entombed alive: a law, Alonzo protests, as barbaric as the child sacrifice that the Peruvians have already abolished. In pleading for her, Alonzo tears off her veil, exposes her breasts, and reads the text of her body:

> behold this bosom: it is the sign of the purpose that God has for her. In these twin sources of life, behold her right and sacred duty of being a mother. Thus does the God who made nothing in vain speak and explain himself.

> voyez ce sein: voilà le signe des desseins de son dieu sur elle. A ces deux sources de la vie, reconnoissez le droit, le devoir sacré d'être mere. C'est ainsi que parle et s'explique ce dieu qui n'a rien fait en vain. (vol. II, p. 86)

The sacrificed body is no longer erased. Marmontel is recalling the famous historical incident in which the ancient Athenian orator Hypereides defended the courtesan Phryne by exposing her breasts to the jury,[40] but he turns the defence of extraordinary eroticism into a general defence of the sexual function of the body. The body is a text declaring that humanity fulfils itself in the perpetuation and reproduction of life. 'He is right [has reason]', responds the Inca Ataliba, 'and reason is above the law' ('Il a raison, dit-il, et la raison est au dessus de la loi') (vol. II, p. 86). In the event, the natural law manifested by Cora's body is violated not by the Inca priesthood but by the Spaniards. Alonzo is killed in a Spanish massacre (led by a priest) and Cora dies in childbirth on hearing of his death; the child never opens its eyes to see the sun which has been the object and model of Inca religion.

Without its tragic ending and scene of undressing, this episode gained an independent life not only in Elizabeth Scot's poem but as the subject of operas and ballets, from Italy to Sweden (where Johann Gottlieb Naumann's *Cora och Alonzo* (1782) honoured the wisdom of Gustav III).[41] The main variants in the early versions are the degree of anti-clericalism, and the question of whether the king or the people can take the initiative in ending the sacrifice: is the demand for human sacrifice still driven by the mob, or are the people now the greater source of compassion and wisdom?[42] There is at times a slight reduction in the demonizing of the mob.

Ever since the sixteenth century, it has been commonplace to say that the Christian conquistadors were more barbarous than the heathens they conquered. In his treatment of Catholicism, however, Marmontel is very much of his age, for he provides a secular theory of the evolution of religion, and derives Christianity from a fairly low stage of that evolution. Sacrificial religions originate in the fear and awe that men feel for predatory animals, and Spanish Catholicism is just such a religion. It is no longer, as it was for the historical Las Casas, a perversion of a revealed religion; its alternative is the cult of sensibility embodied in the Las Casas of Marmontel's fiction.

Subversive parallels between Christianity and paganism had, of course, been current since the seventeenth century. For example, the English freethinker Charles Blount repeatedly analysed the absurdities of classical paganism in ways that reflected implicitly upon Christianity.[43] He had, however, no anthropological system, whereas Marmontel sketches an anthropological theory which gives identical psychological and cultural roots to the religions of pre-Conquest America and of Spain. Here, we see the early stages of the kind of thinking that was to lead over a century later to *The Golden Bough*. A far more elaborate and influential example of such an approach was provided by Marmontel's younger contemporary Count Volney, in his *Les Ruines, ou Méditations sur les révolutions des empires* (1791). This attempts to reconstruct the simultaneous development of social and religious codes as humanity emerged from the individualistic condition of the hunter–gatherer, and creates a taxonomy of the various kinds of (deluded) symbolic systems out of which religion is constructed. Volney sees the creation of injustice as almost coeval with the creation of social structures, and examines the close association between social and religious systems. Men sacrifice to gods painted in the image of their despots, and the sacrificial mystery at the heart of Christianity is derived from earlier and more primitive sacrificial customs, such as the sacrifice of a bull to Mithras, itself developed from an astrological sign. Volney's admirer, Percy Bysshe Shelley, was to equate, as mental states, the blind faith of the Christian with the faith that drives the Mexican to sacrifice human victims.[44]

THE PEAKING OF THE TREND

In the years round 1780 the preoccupation with averted sacrifice reached its zenith, and the ballets included in operas meant that audiences sometimes got a double or even treble dose of entertainments on a sacrifice-related subject. Galuppi's *Motezuma* (1772) includes a ballet about Iphigenia. Rispoli's setting of *Idalide* (Turin, 1786), a version of the Alonzo and Cora story, contains *I Barbari Sacrifizj Distrutti*. Paisiello's setting of *Demofoönte* (1775) contains *Iffigenia in Tauride* and *Pizzaro nell'Indie*, and Angelo Tarchi's setting (Crema, 1786) contains *Pizarro Nell'America*.

This is also the period which produced a number of enduring masterworks: Goethe's *Iphigenie auf Tauris* (prose version 1779; verse version 1787), Mozart's *Idomeneo* (1781), and Gluck's *Iphigénie en Aulide* (1774) and *Iphigénie en Tauride* (1779). To these we may add a number of significant minor works: the Piccinni *Iphigénie en Tauride* (1781), and the two versions of *Demofoönte* that were produced in Paris in 1789, with music by Cherubini and by Johann Christoph Vogel, the former with a libretto by Marmontel.

Mozart's *Idomeneo* (1781) has in common with *Les Incas* a deep sympathy with a conquered, non-European civilization: the Asiatic civilization of Troy. The greater barbarism, the custom of human sacrifice, belongs to the conquering Greeks, though this is abrogated when Idomeneo is released by Neptune from the rash vow that obliges him to sacrifice his son. The internal regeneration is complemented by acts of cosmopolitan inclusiveness, in that Idomeneo's son Idamante frees the Trojan prisoners and marries the Trojan princess, Ilia, while the chief representative of the old order, Agamemnon's daughter Electra, ends the opera insane, marginal, and obsolete.

Gluck's libretti, by contrast, locate barbarity in more usual places: the mob, and the oriental savage. His *Iphigénie en Aulide*,[45] like the corresponding opera of Frederick and Graun, dispenses with the scheming Menelaus and Ulysses, concentrating on the conflict between an enamoured Achille and a vacillating Agamemnon. The appetite for sacrifice is voiced only by the Chorus, who represent the sacrificial fanaticism of the crowd. There is similar exploration of mass irrationality in his *Iphigénie en Tauride*. Indeed, the fierce music in the Turkish style that characterizes the barbarous Scythians inspired a reviewer of the first performance to imagine cannibals dancing around their victim.[46] As in Traetta's earlier *Ifigenia in Tauride*, however, the impersonal, violent rituals of the Scythians are interwoven with the subjective ritualizations of the central characters, who progress by re-experiencing the past in the changed context of the present. Like Traetta's hero, Gluck's Oreste superimposes memories of his mother on Iphigénie: indeed, he cries 'ma mère' on first seeing her (p. 152). Unlike the Euripides version, this opera directly portrays the near-sacrifice of Oreste, which becomes another ritual superimposition of the past on the present; for, at the apparent moment of death, Oreste cries, 'In this fashion you died in Aulis, Iphigenia' ('Ainsi tu péris en Aulide, Iphigénie') (p. 266). This fusing of the past with the present provides the moment of recognition that leads to the transcendence of sacrifice. The subjective re-experiencing of the past in the present takes place in an opera much dominated by official ritual, yet the subjective re-enactment frees the characters from the barbarous past that is being relived, while the Scythians are imprisoned in precedent and repetition. This is a work in which we see the individuated consciousness freeing itself from the prison of an impersonal and ritualized culture.[47]

So, pre-eminently, is the greatest version of *Iphigenia among the Taurians*, Goethe's *Iphigenie auf Tauris*, though this culminates in the cosmopolitan inclusion of the alien that the Gluck opera conspicuously denies. It is striking that Goethe, Mozart, and Gluck, three of the greatest creative figures of the period, should almost simultaneously have worked on dramas of averted sacrifice. Beyond its own individual merits as a masterpiece, Goethe's play is important for its idealized representation of Hellenic culture, as a model and symbol for German culture. It has ever since stood as an opposite extreme to the view of Greek culture that came to be represented by *The Bacchae*, and its view is that which Nietzsche was to challenge in *The Birth of Tragedy*, in which he initiated speculation about the dark, pre-Olympian stages of Greek religion: 'The Olympian magic mountain [Zauberberg] now opens up, as it were, and shows us its roots',[48] he wrote; 'Goethe and Schiller were not granted the ability to break open the enchanted gateway leading into the Hellenic magic mountain [Zauberberg]; . . . the furthest reach of their most courageous struggle was that wistful gaze which Goethe's Iphigeneia sends homewards across the sea from the barbaric land of the Taurians' (p. 97). Nietzsche's challenge to the Hellenism represented by Goethe's play is an important strand in Thomas Mann's *The Magic Mountain* (*Der Zauberberg*), which takes its title from Nietzsche's twice-used image of Hellenism. *Iphigenie auf Tauris* thus stands as a definitive literary expression of the Apollonian ideal of Greek culture.

For most of its duration, however, Goethe's play is one of isolation, exile, estrangement, division, and difference; of the quest for self amidst the crumbling of patriarchal and militaristic codes, whose structures at once estrange the woman and replicate themselves in the only roles permitted to her: as sacrificial destroyer, or sacrificial victim. At times, the isolation resolves itself into the image of a desert island, though the significance of this image changes, embracing both the estrangement of the exiled self and its self-sufficiency: Iphigenie initially wants to turn her back on Tauris as on the cliffs of a desert island, though she later begs Thoas to exile her from Tauris to one. Still more, Delos, the 'rocky island inhabited by the God' ('Felseninsel, die der Gott bewohnt'),[49] is the longed-for goal of escape. Yet the idea of the god as inhabitant of a rocky island points to an idea that becomes increasingly prominent: the remoteness of the gods from humanity, their generic alienness to the intimacy of blood sacrifice.

The symbol of the desert island presents an accentuated version of Tauris itself: a remote and uncivilized land, whose unwilling sojourners are persistently drawn to its shore, longing for the unseen lands that lie beyond the horizon. The shore ('Ufer') is as insistent a presence as it was in Racine, but it is no longer the place at which civilization seems to collapse. It is the place where the exiled and isolated individual turns away from the landscape of unfulfilment and gazes towards the imagined home where the isolation ceases, as in Anselm Feuerbach's painting inspired by Goethe's play (Plate 10). *Iphigenie auf Tauris* is a play of boundaries. At the beginning, Iphigenie stands within the dense hedges that mark off the sacred precinct, still a stranger, separated by the sea from her loved ones, remembering the frequency with which she waits on the shore, sighing for Greece: 'During long days I stand on the shore, seeking the land of the Greeks with my soul. In reply to my sighs, the waves bring only dull, roaring noises':

> Und an dem Ufer steh ich lange Tage,
> Das Land der Griechen mit der Seele suchend;
> Und gegen meine Seufzer bringt die Welle
> Nur dumpfe Töne brausend mir herüber. (1.1.11–14)

On the shore of Tauris, the animate consciousness is driven to its last retreat: the sighs for home of the displaced meet the passionless, thoughtless, roar of the waves.

The shore in Racine's *Iphigénie* had represented the boundary between civilization and primitive chaos. Here, it represents the boundary between the self and the other; between the animate and the inanimate. Iphigenie lacks a self-conscious ('selbstbewußtes') life (1.2.110), and has rather fallen into the state of those on the shore ('Ufer') of Lethe: self-forgetting ('selbstvergessend') (1.2.113). One small verbal detail emphasizes the huge transformation in exploring the interiority of sacrificer and victim that had taken place since Racine. *Propre* (one's own) was in Racine a rare word, not used in a positive sense: at the end of the play, Ériphile commits suicide, carried away by 'Her own rage' ('ses propres fureurs') (5.6.1758). In Goethe, the corresponding word *eigen* is a key word of value, as in 'eigen Herz' ('one's own heart') (1.2.211, 4.4.1648). This is a play about the place of subjective consciousness in civilization.

Plate 10 Anselm Feuerbach, *Iphigenie* (1871). This represents Goethe's Iphigenie, longing for Greece

Tauris is a land that sacrifices strangers. It juxtaposes two forms of isolation and estrangement, both associated with boundaries. One is the isolation of the unfulfilled mind on the seashore; the other is that of the victim within the sacrificial precinct. For sacrificer and victim constitute an extreme pairing of self and not-self. If one pole of human existence is as the isolated mind on the seashore, the other is as the alien body on the sacrificial altar. The word *strange* (*fremd*) resonates through the play, as *xenos* does through that of Euripides, going far beyond literal foreignness to embrace the subtler and more various forms of psychological estrangement which the characters experience: Iphigenie's fatherland, for example, has become strange to her. Moreover, the relationship between sacrificer and victim embodies differences that are more profound than those of native and foreigner. Sacrifice is an expression of the sense of difference, and the play portrays a reordering of the perception of difference and community, as part of a quest for individuation and selfhood. The House of Atreus, famously, is a lineage marked by atrocity, starting with the crime of Agamemnon's great-grandfather Tantalus, who had had the privilege of feasting with the gods, and attempted to prove his mental superiority to them by trying to trick them into eating the flesh of his son Pelops. Pelops' milder crimes were to win the hand of Hippodamia in a chariot race by fatally sabotaging the chariot of his opponent, and to murder the charioteer who had assisted the crime. From Pelops sprang Atreus and Thyestes, participants in the family's second cannibalistic banquet; from Thyestes sprang Aegisthus, and, from Agamemnon, Iphigenia, Electra, and Orestes.

Aeschylus pays little attention to Tantalus, but he figures prominently in Goethe. When Iphigenie discloses to Thoas the terrible secret of her ancestry, it is that she is of the race of Tantalus. For Goethe, Tantalus is a Faust figure, frustrated by the boundary that divides men from the gods. The gods cannot mix ('wandeln') with men as with their like ('wie mit ihresgleichen') (1.3.316). Tantalus' attempted sacrifice of his child is an attempt to annul the difference between man and the gods.

A recurrent pattern in *Iphigenie auf Tauris* is the creation of a bond by the destruction of a third party: a process whose dynamics encapsulate the creation of the stranger. In a triangular relationship, two people combine to get rid of the third. It is such a dominant pattern that, when Pylades gives Iphigenie a false account of his and Orest's history, he says that they are a pair of brothers who killed the third brother. This is exactly the story of Atreus and Thyestes, who had combined to murder their half-brother (and blame their stepmother for the crime), had ruled jointly, but had fallen out over desire for a woman. This, in turn, essentially replicates the story of their father, Pelops, who had conspired with his charioteer to murder his rival for the hand of Hippodamia. The charioteer then attempted to rape Hippodamia, and was in turn murdered by Pelops. Agamemnon also died as an unwanted third element in a triangle, but the structure is more interestingly transferred to the next generation, in the sacrifice of Iphigenie. Klytämnestra brings Agamemnon two daughters, and there wants only the blessing of a son. Yet, as soon as the son has arrived 'between the two sisters' ('zwischen beiden Schwestern') (1.3.410), war comes and Iphigenie is sacrificed. Her sacrifice is thus a separation from, even an exchange for, the male child, with whom she is finally united.

This configuration is strikingly repeated throughout *Iphigenie auf Tauris*, taking its simplest and most innocent form in the early youth of Orest and Pylades. This is an idyll of undifferentiated companionship, in which the hostile Other was constituted by the beasts of prey which they pursued, and by the bandits and monsters of which they wished to clear the wilderness. They were nascent culture heroes. Then, however, Orest was specially chosen ('auserkoren') (2.1.707) for a strife that confounded and reversed the simple relationship between the tamer and the wild. For the enemy to be destroyed was not a bandit or monster, but his mother, and in consequence of killing her he himself was to become the prey ('Raube') of the Furies, who follow his tracks like hounds (2.2.855).

In describing his possession by the Furies, Orest is describing a moment of individuation. That is, a moment where the unit is no longer the pair, but the isolated and estranged individual: the solitary consciousness on the seashore. One version of this moment is evocatively described by Iphigenie in her opening reflections: she recalls her earliest youth, when her soul was first forming its bonds with her parents and siblings, until a strange curse ('fremder Fluch') separated ('trennte') her from her loved ones, and rent ('riß') the bond with them in two ('entzwei') (1.2.84–6). The emphasis on the act of separation is considerable, and the idea of splitting into two is to be a fundamental one throughout Goethe's play.

In relationships such as that of Atreus and Thyestes, the pair unites to exclude a third, but then divides itself. The same primitive impulse to individuate the self by destroying its rival impels the house of Thoas to sacrifice strangers, and the house of Atreus to sacrifice its own kin. This three-two-one sequence is a fundamental pattern of the play, though it reconfigures itself throughout the generations. In Pelops and Myrtilus, and Atreus and Thyestes, there is a Girardian mimetic rivalry: initially collaborative pairings are set at odds by rivalry for the same object. Both sides of this pattern – the pairing and the subsequent splitting – are summed up in the ambiguity of the single word *Band* (bond), as something which unites, but also something which imprisons and isolates. Iphigenie's bond with her kin was ruptured; yet in her captivity her soul is welded ('geschmiedet') in her breast as with iron bonds ('Eisenbanden') (1.2.72–3). The kind of individuation experienced by Orest and Iphigenie is more culturally advanced than that of Pelops or Atreus, since it leads to subjective self-realization. In this newer pattern, the woman is no longer a disputed prize, as she was for Pelops and his charioteer, but a being of autonomous consciousness. The three-two-one sequence means that, as in the *Aeneid*, there is a recurrent and embedded mathematical structure in the dynamics of sacrifice, though it here works in the opposite direction: towards the isolation of the individual, rather than towards his dissolution in the mass processes of history.

With the assimilation of woman comes separation from the gods: Orest discovers that he has been sent to Tauris to recover not the image of Apollo's sister but the living body of his own. There is an end to the tormenting illusion of Tantalus, which had produced his violent separation from his own kin: the illusion of similarity with the gods, an illusion which had destroyed Tantalus. The word *göttergleich* (like the gods) runs through the play, but what – in this world of stultifying divisions and dangerous resemblances – is it to be *göttergleich*? In the famous song of the Fates, the gods are blissfully remote from the suffering Titans, feasting on the mountain tops while they languish on the earth, their breath drifting upwards like the smoke of the sacrificed animal ('Opfergerüchen') (4.5.1752). Sacrifice here reaches the gods as a light cloud. Yet sacred violence is the point at which man most interprets the gods in his own image, and is traditionally in most immediate contact with them. The development of a culture more centred on humanity dissolves the religious configurations that make sacrifice seem imperative.

When Orest realizes that his quest is not for a statue but for his own sister, he makes a significant pacificatory remark to Thoas: the image, he says, shall not divide him and the king in twain ('entzweien') (5.6.2107). The movement to oneness takes up an earlier appeal which Iphigenie had made to the king. She had asked him to yield to a universal sense of moral truth, but Thoas at first sarcastically declares himself too uncivilized to hear it: 'do you believe the rude Scythian, the savage, will hear the voice of truth and humanity, which Atreus the Greek did not heed?'

> Du glaubst, es höre
> Der rohe Skythe, der Barbar, die Stimme
> Der Wahrheit und der Menschlichkeit, die Atreus,
> Der Grieche, nicht vernahm? (5.3.1936–9)

Yet he does, and the acknowledgment of a universal, shared morality provides the final resolution to the process of division and individuation that has taken place throughout the play: the discovery of universal moral principles within the individual consciousness. That is the ideal resolution of the three-two-one countdown that has been the fundamental structural pattern of *Iphigenie auf Tauris*.

Myths of sacrifice to Diana generally focus attention on the relationship between the sacrifice and the hunt. Goethe's Diana is remote from the hunt, and is not angry about the death of a deer. Yet the mentality of the hunt is clearly part of the original cultural consciousness of the male characters, explored through the ambiguity of the word *Raub*. It means 'robbery', but also 'rape' (in its sense of abduction): the Greeks besiege Troy to avenge the *Raub* of Helen, but Orest and Pylades initially come to Tauris to steal ('wegzu*rauben*') (5.3.1930; italics added) the statue of Diana. *Raub*, however, also means *prey*: a beast of prey is a *Raubtier*. In their days of unspoilt companionship, Orest and Pylades had tracked predators ('Dem Räuber') (2.1.672). According to Iphigenie, one way in which the culture hero contributes to civilization is to free regions of bandits (*Räuber*) (5.3.1907). Yet, in Orest's madness, the hunter becomes the hunted, his previously free soul becoming the prey ('Raube') of the Furies (2.2.855). Thoas' absolutist tyranny is also founded upon *Raub*, which is again opposed to freedom: he praises the state in which man is completely robbed of freedom ('Der Freiheit ganz beraubt') (5.2.1789).

The untranslatable ambiguities of *rauben* embrace many of the aspects of the world from which civilization is struggling free: a world in which there is a profound psychological and cultural relationship between sacrifice and the hunt. The *Räuber* is both the hostile Other – the enemy, the beast, the bandit – and the insider: the ruler, the hero. *Iphigenie auf Tauris* traces a release from the tangle of competitive instincts that has hitherto shaped every configuration of family or culture; a movement to what is repeatedly identified as the opposite condition to that of the *Raub*: that of the free. The last object of competitive dispute is the image of the god. When that particular and indivisible cult object has been transcended, man is freed into the shared laws of truth and humanity.

CHAPTER 8

The French Revolution to Napoleon

1789

With the masterpieces of Goethe, Gluck, and Mozart, the celebration of averted sacrifice reached its peak. The celebration continued in Paris in 1789, where the storming of the Bastille and start of the French Revolution coincided with two settings of Metastasio's *Demofoonte* that departed radically from the tactful advice to an absolute monarch offered by the original.[1] These were the *Démophon* of Cherubini, with libretto by Marmontel, and that of the talented Johann Christoph Vogel, with libretto by Philippe Desriaux. Cherubini's *Démophon* urges limited reform, whereas the Vogel–Desriaux piece is an impassioned attack on tyranny and fanaticism (exemplified in the grim chanting of the priests of Mars), which asserts the rights of nature and the nuclear family against the arbitrary despotism of the Thracian tyrant. Vogel had died in 1788, but both music and libretto amply capture the mood of revolt, and Desriaux was to throw himself wholeheartedly into the spirit of the time. As 'Citoyen Desriaux', he produced *Alexis et Rosette, ou Les Houlans* [*Ulans*], *Pièce Républicaine*, first performed in August 1793, shortly before the start of the Terror. This idealizes struggle against the Prussian invaders and grimly promises counter-revolutionaries the fate of Lucius Junius Brutus' sons; this was no longer a time to deplore sacrificial deaths.[2] In its transformations from a nameday celebration of a Habsburg emperor, to a manifesto by Frederick the Great, to a firebrand revolutionary text, *Demofoonte* illustrates the infinite adaptability of the sacrificial theme in this period, and the polarized range of historical situations to which it could be applied.

Towards the end of the century, however, the fashion for operatic happy endings started to decline.[3] The drama of averted sacrifice does linger on in the early nineteenth century, and the conservatism of the post-Napoleonic years did bring a resurgence of operas on the Metastasian model: for example, Giovanni Pacini's 1824 setting of Metastasio's by then ninety-year-old libretto *Alessandro nell'Indie*, which concludes with an aborted widow-burning. Nevertheless, interest in the drama of averted sacrifice drops sharply after 1790. For example, Sartori's catalogue of Italian libretti (which includes libretti for revivals) lists twenty-two of *Demofoönte* from the 1770s, seventeen from the 1780s, and nine from the 1790s, all from the first half of the decade. The figures for Iphigenia libretti from the same decades are ten, nineteen, and six.[4] And it is at this point that *The Bacchae* starts to make a return, both in literature and as a key to the understanding of history. Hölderlin, for example, translated part of Dionysus' opening speech in 1799,[5] and in his poem 'Der Einzige' ('The Only One') (1803) described Dionysus as the brother of Christ.[6] At the same time, however, Edmund Burke revived the darker side of Bacchic frenzy as a means of understanding modern history: reflecting on the mob's assault on Versailles, which they 'left swimming in blood, polluted by massacre, and strewed with scattered limbs and mutilated carcases', he deplored the 'Theban and Thracian Orgies' into which a great modern city had descended.[7]

It seemed that the *sparagmos* had returned to the streets of Paris: not ritualized by controlling authority, as in the death of Damiens, but uncontainable, because performed by the mob which was so often the focus of sacrificial fears. It was reported that on 3 September 1792 Marie Antoinette's confidante, the Princesse de Lamballe, had been gang raped, decapitated, and dismembered, her severed breasts and genitalia impaled on a spike and waved before the windows of the Queen's cell. This ranks with the deaths of Damiens and Cook as one of the century's most haunting assaults on the integrity of the body. As a realization of fears about the sacrificial power of the mob within the European city, it was a far more potent object of fear and repulsion. Yet there is one further difference from the dismemberments of Damiens and Cook: this one probably did not happen. Although the Princesse was indubitably murdered, the outrages on her body appear themselves to be sacrificial fictions,[8] but fictions that were appropriate to the time. History was not moving as Voltaire and Guimond de la Touche had wished.

Nevertheless, in Marie Antoinette's native Austria, 1796 saw the première of an opera of aborted sacrifice that was to be one of the most popular German operas between *Die Zauberflöte* (1791) and *Der Freischütz* (1821): Peter von Winter's Singspiel *Das unterbrochene Opferfest* (1796) (*The Averted Sacrifice*).[9] This is somewhat analogous to the Alonzo and Cora plot in Marmontel's *Les Incas*, in that it portrays an English ally of the sun-worshipping Peruvians, who is nearly sacrificed on a trumped-up charge, despite having saved the Inca's life and kingdom from the invading Spaniards. Without much specific political import, the opera thus reflects a period when Austria and England were allied against revolutionary France. Like Goethe's *Iphigenie*, and indeed *Die Zauberflöte*, it is dominated by the idea of saving or rescuing (*Rettung*). The idea had loomed large in the very first Iphigenia opera, Reinhard Keiser's *Die wunderbahr errettete Iphigenia* (1699), and is still dominant in *Fidelio*, whose final chorus insistently celebrates the heroine as *Retterin*, but it was to undergo dark transformations in the Romantic period, where the giving of life can be a gift with a terrible price (as in *Frankenstein*). In Winter's opera, the good characters plan to save from sacrifice the man who has saved Peru. The conflict is not that the father has to sacrifice his child, but that an enlightened and just man has to sacrifice his benefactor. The apparent sacrificial duty thus conflicts with socially constructed bonds (instead of expressing them, as in the early *Iphigenia in Aulis* adaptations). The divine command to sacrifice the hero – still terrifyingly real in Mozart's *Idomeneo* – is here, however, a mere fraud, perpetrated by jealous, vengeful characters. They are defeated by enlightenment and compassion (*Mitleid*), and the opera ends with a confident C-major hymn to the sun.

There was, however, to be one further musical masterpiece about the perfection of civilization, distilling old ideals and transmitting them to a new century: Beethoven's *Eroica* symphony (1803–5). The final movement of the symphony is an immense set of variations on the English dance which concludes Beethoven's earlier ballet, *The Creatures of Prometheus*. Beethoven's Prometheus is not the tortured, sacrificed Prometheus of Aeschylus but the triumphant creator and benefactor of man. The English dance is, conventionally, one in which a nobleman dances with his servants, and its use in the ballet indicates that the creator is at one with his creatures. Earlier, in the second movement, there has been a *marcia funebre*: the funeral march of a hero. There was some agreement in the nineteenth century that the funeral was either from Virgil or from Homer: Berlioz associated the march with the funeral of Pallas, others with that of Patroclus.[10] Both of these funerals include human sacrifices, yet there is no sacrificial episode in the *Eroica* march. This is myth purged of its darker elements and made to express the ideals of an age where dark atavism seemed capable of defeat. As Thomas Mann was later to recognize, it was a brief moment.

SADE

Even as the fashion for fictions of averted sacrifice reached its peak, it is obvious that new literary impulses were formulating more complex and divided views of human nature and its political possibilities. An extreme is, clearly, the Marquis de Sade (1740–1814), who from 1782 onwards published a sequence of works in which virtue is helpless before triumphant vice and in which sexual activity always expresses the natural, and violent, supremacy of the male. At times, the exercise of this violence approximates to sacrifice.

If some of the later Iphigenia works develop a secular, psychological understanding of ritual, Sade provides unprecedented exploration of the ritual element in sexuality, and of the homology between sexual and sacrificial ritual. He scours the customs of ancient and alien lands, in the cultural reports of explorers such as Captain Cook, not to sustain the benignly sceptical moral relativism initiated by Montaigne, but to document the universality of male desire for power and violent sexual gratification, the falsity of the '*systèmes*' of moral society, and the inevitable success of systems built on egocentric strength.

Justine (1791) narrates the extreme suffering and eventual death (by lightning) of the virtuous heroine, and the triumphant prosperity of her immoral sister, Juliette. The primary cause of Justine's sufferings is the unchallengeable prerogative of the male to sexual dominance and violence, a prerogative that includes even the father's right to kill his child. Women are utterly dispensable: 'everywhere I see women humiliated, manhandled, and sacrificed to the superstition of priests, the barbarity of husbands, and the whims of libertines' ('partout je vois les femmes humiliées, molestées, partout sacrifiées à la superstition des prêtres, à la barbarie des époux, ou aux caprices des libertins').[11] The dispensability of the weak is illustrated for Sade by the practice of widow-burning and other forms of human sacrifice, and by more general practices of infanticide, such as the disposal of unwanted infants ('immolés ou abandonnés') in contemporary China (p. 145). This had been noted by Adam Smith, as a horror remote from the economically progressive society he was describing,[12] and was to be cited again by Malthus,[13] as an illustration of something closer to home: the inexorable disparity between the growth of population and the growth of the food supply. For Sade, however, infanticide illustrates a universal principle of power: a child for a parent is of no more consequence than the ejaculation of sperm ('un peu de semence éclose') (p. 145) from which it arose. Such is the justification of the surgeon Rodin as he prepares to anatomize his daughter, claiming that anatomy is best performed on a cadaver of fourteen to fifteen years old, 'expiré d'une mort cruelle' (p. 143).

Nowhere is safe, and Sade systematically erases the old distinctions between wild and civically ordered spaces. Certainly, the forest recurs throughout *Justine* as a space of spontaneous violence: after Justine has rescued a man from bandits, for example, he seems properly and morally grateful – until they enter a forest, whereupon he knocks her out and rapes her. More frequently, however, the spontaneous desires of the forest are systematized in private inner spaces: the domains of the surgeon, the lawyer, the nobleman, the monk. In these spaces, with their associations of scientific or social regulation, the desires acquire a ceremonial and formal character which is not essentially religious, but which is easily assimilated to the rites of the religious life. The ritual character of the orgies comes from the regular, material operations of the body-machine and, consequently, of the processes which are constructed around it: bleeding, dissection, and erotic hanging. In this ritualization of violence and desire, the sacrificial ceremonies of Christianity do become converted into expressions of sexual violence and desire, notably in the monastery of Sainte Marie Des Bois, where (among many other outrages) communion is taken intra-anally, and the image of a crucified and sexually tortured woman is displayed. These are the true rituals of desire, which are disguised and defaced in the pallid rites of Christianity.

In expressing the regularity of the body-machine, the rituals assume a mathematical character, and treat the victims as mathematically interchangeable units. The Comte de Gernande, whose taste is for bleeding his victims, has twelve minions whom he changes every year ('avait douze que l'on lui changeait tous les ans') (p. 269), and his bouts of bleeding assume the character of immutable ceremonies:

All the rituals that I am going to describe to you here, madam, were those required by the Count; they were observed regularly every day, and nothing was changed except the location of the blood-lettings.

> Toutes les cérémonies que je vais vous détailler ici, Madame, étaient celles exigées par le comte: elles s'observaient régulièrement tous les jours, on n'y changeait au plus que le local des saignées. (pp. 269–70)

If, as I have argued in the previous chapter, the operas of Traetta and Gluck treat ritual as a means by which the individual mind organizes experience and copes with the flow of time, Sade uses it to indicate the absence of progression: time, like the body, becomes an endlessly repeated mechanism regulating the movements of the instinct for power. He reduces 'injustice, hatred, and destruction' to the 'regulated, automatic procedures' that Adorno and Horkheimer deemed to be prophetic of Fascism.[14] Sade is a philosopher of (one of his favourite words) *système*. If, in the plays of the mid seventeenth century, sacrifice created a crisis in the public system, in Sade it is the key to the secret system that lurks within the public façades; the secret of the forest that grows inside the monastery or château as well as around its walls.

More immediately influential, however, was another merging of sexuality and sacrificial ritual from an altogether more respectable source: Goethe. In Goethe's ballad 'Die Braut von Korinth' (1797) a youth travels from Athens to Corinth, to enter into a marriage agreed by his and the bride's parents many years ago. He is still a pagan, but Corinth has converted to Christianity. Alone in his bedroom before his wedding day, he is visited by a mysteriously white maiden, who complains that the cult of the Cross has taken over. The old gods have fled, and animal sacrifice has been replaced by the human sacrifice of desire denied: 'victims are sacrificed here: neither lamb nor bullock, but human sacrifice on a huge scale':

> Opfer fallen hier,
> Weder Lamm noch Stier,
> Aber Menschenopfer unerhört.[15]

She complains that, although their fathers' oath promised them to each other, he is now to marry her sister. The spectral maiden and he exchange tokens, she drinks blood-red wine (while refusing bread), and they make love. The woman is the bride to whom he was promised in infancy, but she is dead; he had come to Corinth to marry her surviving sister. But nothing, she declares, can annul the oaths sworn in the temple of Venus. She has claimed her love, and sucked his blood, and he will soon be a corpse. She asks her mother to cremate them, so that they can hurry to the old gods.

The sacrificial mathematics of Goethe's *Iphigenie* had led to a concentration of the individual, the development of culture running variations on the same pattern: a duo emerges from a group of three, only to split in its turn into rival or autonomous individuals. But what happens when there is a further division, within the self? When, with the increasing exploration of subjectivity, the battle between sacrificial and enlightened forces is not on the shores of Taurica, but within the psyche? Or between the self and its double? In 'Die Braut von Korinth', the conflict is not played out on a single, external, and shared landscape. It is now internal: between a daylight, rational world and an alternative, submerged one, where different creatures play in the darker side of the divided consciousness. This was to be the primary model for sacrificial works in the Romantic period.

SCHILLER

There is a particularly complex and influential rethinking of the conflicting impulses within the self in Friedrich Schiller's *Über die ästhetische Erziehung des Menschen* (*On the Aesthetic Education of Man*) (1794). Dismayed by the descent of the French Revolution into barbarity, Schiller contemplates the immense distance that civilization still has to travel, and (like Goethe in *Iphigenie*) uses Hellenic culture as a paradigm of a psychically complete civilization. He attempts to show how man can regain the wholeness of the Greeks; how he can escape from being a specialized component of an impersonal machine, his specialization destroying his totality as an individual. For Schiller, man is impoverished either through overdevelopment of the sensuous drive, which reduces him to 'a unit of quantity, and occupied moment of time',[16] or by the drive for formal analysis, which 'embraces the whole sequence of time . . . annuls time and annuls change'. 'If the first drive only furnishes cases, this second one gives laws' (pp. 80–1). The drives are to be reunified through the instinct for play (*Spieltrieb*), as manifested in artistic creativity.

'Two souls reside in my breast!' ('Zwei Seelen wohnen, ach! in meiner Brust') cried Goethe's Faust,[17] distinguishing the *Trieb* towards sensual pleasure and that towards glory. We no longer look to the Greeks to provide paradigms of the harmoniously unified self, but the model of the two souls or two drives, variously articulated, is to become central to understanding the nature of the sacrificial impulse. In his translation of Euripides' *Iphigenia in Aulis* (1790), Schiller had concluded with the nobility of sacrifice, omitting the happy ending. His mature original dramas, however, tend to show social regeneration as frustrated or complicated by unresolved divisions in the characters and their causes.

In *Don Carlos* (1787–1805), Philip II has married the promised bride of his son, Carlos, and the ensuing personal conflict disastrously impedes the Prince's duty as liberator (*Retter*) of Flanders. Here, in contrast to Verdi's opera, Carlos is killed on his father's orders. The play is dominated by the idea of sacrifice: of crushing personal sacrifice to a system which denies individual emotional and sexual fulfilment; of failed sacrifice to public ideals; of the ritual sacrifice of the *auto-da-fe*; and of the sacrifice of the child by his father. The play traces a long progress from one sacrificial act to another: from an act of childhood friendship in which Carlos had accepted responsibility for a misdeed of his friend, the Marquis of Posa, and undergone a whipping on his behalf, to Posa's repayment of the debt. Pretending that it is he, not Carlos, who is secretly in love with the Queen, he dies in a useless attempt to save Carlos. Nevertheless, Philip II assents to the death of his son after being assured by the Inquisitor that the Crucifixion authorized the sacrifice of sons by fathers: 'to make atonement to eternal justice, the son of God died on the cross' ('Die ewige Gerechtigkeit zu sühnen / Starb an dem Holze Gottes Sohn').[18]

Don Carlos combines the idea of child sacrifice with that of the Oedipus story, most clearly alluded to when Elizabeth – the stepmother to whom Carlos was once betrothed – accuses him of wanting to desecrate his father's corpse and marry his mother. Yet the Oedipus story has been transposed to a culture which so attenuates natural and familial bonds that incest has no horror or forbiddenness. Father and mother are mere names: Carlos' father is a man whom he first saw when he was six, signing death warrants; his 'mother' is his rightful bride. The idea of sacrifice further expresses the disappearance of the personal within an impersonal and hierarchical despotism. A noblewoman is exiled by the King for the indecorum of leaving the Queen alone; the Queen had ordered her absence so that she could see Carlos, but the noblewoman accepts her exile without defending herself, prepared to sacrifice herself ('sich . . . / zu opfern') (3.3.2607–8) in order to protect the Queen. From such casual, cruel individual sacrifices as this to the public orgies of the *auto-da-fe*, the heartless absolutism of Philip creates a system in which the microcosmic bonds of friendship and kin are torn apart, as having no purpose or counterpart in the structures of the state. If God's sacrifice of his son is a supreme sacrifice, Philip's simply abolishes the relationship of father and son.

After its opening scenes in the gardens at Aranjuez, *Don Carlos* moves into a relentlessly built-up culture, whose rooms and secret spaces express and support the restrictive and (in the fullest sense) inquisitive regime of Philip II. With Schiller's *Wilhelm Tell* (1803–4), we move back to the liminal spaces of Greek tragedy: to the boundary between the city and the mountains. The play depicts the revolt which liberates Switzerland from Austrian rule, one expression of the Austrians' arbitrary tyranny being that the governor, Gessler, has placed his hat on a pole, and commanded all the Swiss to bow to it. For neglecting to do so, Tell is made to shoot with his crossbow at an apple placed on his son's head. He hits the apple. In the ensuing rebellion, he kills Gessler with his next shot.

The hat itself is placed in a liminal place: an open space outside Altdorf, where the Austrians are violating the wilderness by building a fortress prison. It is noteworthy that one of the climactic moments in the liberation of the Swiss is the destruction of this prison. The storms and avalanches which are frequently mentioned emphasize the limited degree to which society can control the wilderness, and also call forth the primal qualities of the solitary: Tell ferries away a fugitive from tyranny during a fearful storm that puts off all other rescuers; another storm on the lake liberates him from Gessler, and enables him to kill him. The mountain setting is home to a scattered community whose dispersal gives prominence to that which was erased in *Don Carlos*: the nuclear family. The attempt to destroy it, however, is as strong as in the former play: an Austrian official attempts to rape a married woman; a father is blinded because his son attempted to protect his cattle from theft; and, in the shooting of the apple, a father is forced to gamble with the life of his child. As in *Don Carlos* (and in Schiller's *Kabale und Liebe* and *Die Jungfrau von Orleans*), the conflicts between authority and individuality reach their focus in a point where the father must be ready to destroy the child. The difference is here that the father is unwilling, and that the episode provokes a successful revolt against the oppressive system.

Tell's successful marksmanship in shooting the apple is not an averted human sacrifice, but it stands in significant relationship to the sacrifice of Iphigenia. For, if Tell is not sacrificer, he is that figure who is so often paired with the sacrificer, in both myth and theory: the hunter. In proximity to the rising prison, in a space that is being claimed by the city, he exercises the skills of the hunter in his perfect marksmanship. He is to exercise them again when he shoots Gessler in the mountains, and here the ironic relationship to sacrificial ritual is more fully developed. The death of Gessler is framed by a wedding procession, which (before Gessler enters) Tell is invited to join. Gessler then appears and disrupts the harmonious implications of the ritual, rebuffing a poor woman who begs for mercy for her husband, whereupon Tell shoots the tyrant. After his death, six Brothers of Mercy chant over the corpse, not to sanctify it but merely to reflect on the unpredictability of death and the terrors of judgment. Gessler's death is thus surrounded by ritual, yet the rituals do not touch or transform it. Rather, it is encapsulated in the grim single line of the newly liberated Swiss Stüssi: 'The [sacrificial] victim lies there: the ravens are descending' ('Das Opfer liegt – Die Raben steigen nieder') (4.3.2832). Gessler's corpse has no place in the ceremonies that are enacted in its neighbourhood. It has been returned to the sphere of the hunt, and of the predator.

Eigen in Goethe's *Iphigenie*, it was noted, referred to the inner sphere. Here, often, it refers to the land, or to one's inheritance or hereditary rights (*Erbe*). *Wilhelm Tell* is a play about territory, and this (unlike Greece in *Iphigenie auf Tauris*) is not primarily a territory of the mind. Tell is a solitary and a dreamer; he fails to bow to the hat out of self-absorption, not conscious resistance. He does not take part in the oath at Rütli which is the starting point of the revolt, and is turned into a rebel by the horror of having to shoot the apple from his son's head. The oath which drives him is not the shared one sworn at Rütli but a private one: the oath he swore at the shooting trial, that the next bolt he shot would be aimed at Gessler. His private subjectivity is amply stressed, but it is not the play's centre of gravity. Rather, it makes him at once central and marginal. Partly for this reason, the play leaves us not with a sense of simple social renewal (as Rossini's *Guillaume Tell* (1829) was to do) but with a sense of the troublesome interplay of public and private motives. The shooting trial and the killing of Gessler may have ignited the Swiss revolt, but it would have failed without another, more decisive, event in which the Swiss had no part: the wicked murder of the Emperor by his kinsman. This gives the liberation a moral ambiguity which is excised in Rossini's operatic adaptation of the play, but which dominates Schiller's ending.

In the penultimate scene of the play, Tell's family joyfully await his return. 'Your beloved father returns today' ('heute kommt der liebe Vater wieder!') (5.2.3098), Tell's wife informs her children. No sooner has she spoken than the murderer of the Emperor walks through the door, identified by the coincidence as a potential double of Tell. In a further dislocated use of religious ritual, he is disguised as a monk, but the ritual calm he seems to promise is quickly dispelled by the terror he inspires in the family, and by his evident disorientation: when Tell returns, it becomes clear that the intruder does not know where he is, or where he must go. Tell is then forced to undergo a long and tortured conversation with the man who claims to be his double; a man who also killed in a dispute over inheritance (*Erbe*) (5.2.3165), though an inheritance of a less idealized kind than the homeland. Passionately, and persuasively, Tell distinguishes the actions of ambition from those of the protective father: the former violate nature, the latter fulfil it. Whereas Tell has saved his son, the assassin's name completes the heartless violation of kinship bonds that here, as in *Don Carlos*, is the normal condition of life: Johannes Parricida. The point is not that Tell and Parricida are the same, but that they need to be distinguished. The need to distinguish them is itself troubling; and the fact remains that the assassin's deed is the precondition for the success of the revolt.

Parricida's accomplices have been dispersed, possessed by avenging spirits ('Rachegeister') (5.2.3209), but Tell finally takes pity on the accursed, haunted man and directs him to Rome, where he might find absolution from the Pope. As so often in Schiller, we find a reconstitution of a motif familiar from classical texts (in *Die Jungfrau von Orleans*, for example, he bases the combat between Joan of Arc and the Welshman Montgomery on that of Achilles and Lycaon in the *Iliad*). Here, in Parricida, we see the haunted Orestes of *Iphigenia among the Taurians*, or perhaps the *Oresteia*. Other reconstitutions may be spontaneous and less than allusive: for example, *Wilhelm Tell* and *The Bacchae* that both portray the destruction of a city-based tyranny by forces associated with the mountains and the hunt; both portray the death of the tyrant in the mountains; and both portray the destruction of the prison that supports the tyrant's power. Both, moreover, use the word *city* with careful unusualness. Euripides' Dionysus detests the word. In *Wilhelm Tell*, the word *Stadt* occurs only twice, both being exceptions that prove the rule. The first appearance of the word, in Act 5, is in the description of the Emperor's murder: this took place in a ploughed field, which used to be a city in heathen times.[19] In the final occurrence, Tell directs the assassin to the city of Saint Peter ('Sankt Peters Stadt') (5.2.3233). The City of Man is nowhere present.

These intermittent points of contact with *The Bacchae* (to which one might add Tell's encounter with his mysterious double) are not precise and systematic allusions. Rather, they exemplify the cultural processes which, at this period, were reinstating *The Bacchae* as a culturally living text, for the first time since antiquity, and making sacrifice a felt cultural possibility.

NAPOLEON

Yet the old forms persisted until the end of the Napoleonic period. In 1809, Napoleon was celebrated in Spontini's *Fernand Cortez*, an opera of averted sacrifice (as is Spontini's previous opera, *La Vestale* (1807)). In the previous year, in ravaged Portugal, Napoleon's birthday had been celebrated by a revived setting of that old averted-sacrifice libretto, *Demofôonte* (in which, to recapitulate, an annual custom of maiden sacrifice is abolished after King Demofôonte of Thrace nearly authorizes the sacrifice of his own daughter). Moreover, the four leading German opera composers of the generation before Wagner all set operas on the subject of averted sacrifice or cognate topics: Meyerbeer's first opera was a version of the Jephthah story, *Jephtas Gelübde* (*Jephthah's Vow*) (1812),[20] which (like the earlier settings of Montéclair and Handel) ends the story happily; Peter Joseph von Lindpaintner's first opera, *Demophoon* (1811), was a version of *Demofoonte*, derived from the Desriaux–Vogel version; Louis Spohr's most successful opera, *Jessonda* (1823), has a plot of averted *sati*; and Heinrich Marschner's first opera was a German setting (lost) of *La Clemenza di Tito* (1816). Indeed, Wagner himself revised Gluck's *Iphigénie en Aulide* (1847). In the case of both Wagner and Meyerbeer, these settings contrast with the preoccupation with accomplished sacrifice in their principal works. If most of these operas are minor and obscure, they have a collective interest in documenting the continuing hold of the old subjects shortly before they were to be blown away for ever.

Both the Lindpaintner and the Meyerbeer are firmly focussed on the family rather than the state. In Lindpaintner's *Demophoon*, for example, the impending sacrifice is averted not by a conveniently discovered letter (as in Metastasio) or divine intervention (as in Vogel), but rather by paternal feeling, when Demophoon is overwhelmed by natural love at the sight of his grandson.[21] The nuclear family is also the moral centre of Meyerbeer's *Jephtas Gelübde*. The opera opens with the daughter and her friends celebrating the grape harvest, and one of the strongest moments in the score is a Sarastro-like aria in which Jephtha laments his daughter's seeming fate, and recalls cradling her in his arms. In the Lindpaintner, the threat to the family was from a perhaps formulaic tyranny, but here the threat was far more urgently topical. This is an opera in which refugees are fleeing from an invader; in which the fatherland and homeland are in danger from a nation on the other side of the river. It is an opera in which the central characters face up to the personal cost of national salvation, before finding that – miraculously – there is none; that the God who spared Isaac will not demand the daughter of Jephthah. Nevertheless, it is clearly an opera about Germany and Napoleon.

The librettist of *Jephtas Gelübde* was the aesthetician and folklorist Aloys Schreiber (1761–1841), whose long and varied career included some years as professor of aesthetics at Heidelberg (1805–13). In 1814, after Napoleon's army had been crushed in the Battle of the Nations near Leipzig, Schreiber published a play about Arminius' defeat of the Roman legions, *Marbod und Herrmann; oder, der erste Deutsche Bund* (*Marbod and Hermann; or, the First German Confederation*).[22] This, he admits in his Preface, is a contemporary dramatic parable ('eine zeitgemässe dramatische Parabel'). German culture is under threat from Gallic contamination, and Schreiber looks back to an unspoilt Golden Age: not that of Ovid or Tasso (which had provided Metastasio with his paradigm of ideal justice in *Demofoonte*), but that of the primitive tribesman in the Black Forest, clad in animal skins. This Golden Age is an age of the huntsman.

The world of this triumphalist play is not, then, that of the god who spared Isaac. It is the world of Wotan and the other old gods. 'Only blood can pay atonement to the avenging goddesses,' intones the cast at the end, 'So let German freedom be renewed by blood':

> Und kann nur Blut die Rächerinnen sühnen,
> So laßt aus Blut die Deutsche Freyheit grünen.

The meaning of blood has changed once again. We are far from the frigid ambiguities of *sang* in French neo-classical drama, or its later association with the nobler emotions of the heart. This is blood as a magical fluid, ritually shed. Vengeance and blood sacrifice are embraced as the means to national renewal, and an earlier episode in the play has given us a sample of the kind of vengeance the goddesses require. A prophetess narrates a vision of twelve maidens (the Valkyries), singing as they made a tapestry from human entrails. Their twelve horses scraped the earth with their hooves, each digging a deep grave, whence emerged the bloody, lacerated corpses of Gauls and Romans (p. 24). Twelve eagles fed on the bodies, which had been returned from the sphere of culture to that of the predator. Myth after myth of cultural advance is overturned in this episode.

Yet how different the world had looked to Professor Schreiber at the beginning of his long career. In 1792 he published the closet drama *Szenen aus Fausts Leben* (*Scenes from Faust's Life*), boldly dedicated to Goethe (whose *Faust* fragment had appeared in 1790). Schreiber's play, however, is a *Faust* without Mephistopheles. The sources of Faust's restlessness include horror at the cultural closeness of humanity to the orang-utan,[23] but he is also impatient with the systematizations of the eighteenth century, staring gloomily at the grave of a scholar – evidently a Linnaean classifier – who knew the species of mushrooms and worms (p. 3). Nor can he be enthusiastic about what, in this work, is the highest destiny of the blessed soul: to be the guardian spirit of a benefactor of civilization, such as Joseph Addison (p. 84). Dissatisfied with the European eighteenth century, Faust travels to the East, receives instruction from a Brahmin (who unsuccessfully warns him not to proceed), and undergoes a ritual of initiation rather like that of Tamino in *Die Zauberflöte*. At the end of this he hears of the French Revolution, is told that his joy is premature, but is nevertheless assured that humanity will progress (pp. 95–7). His Faustian bargain, however, has impoverished his own capacity for progress, for it brings a coldness which leaves him incapable of sensibility: incapable, when he returns home, of responding to the love of his mistress and illegitimate son, until he dies and becomes his son's guardian spirit.

The temptation of this Faust is rationalism at the expense of feeling. Rationalism isolates, but sensibility brings experience of a common humanity, and Faust dissents from those who say that there cannot be a copper-coloured Socrates (p. 112). Although he is haunted by the spectre of proximity to the orang-utan, the proximity is cultural, not racial. Whereas in *Jephtas Gelübde* the border is physically protected from foreign invaders, in *Szenen* there is satire of a customs officer who wishes to prevent ideas from crossing the border. In the movement from the cosmopolitanism of this work to the outright German supremacism of *Marbod und Hermann*, this minor writer encapsulates one of the cultural transitions that were radically to reshape the representation and interpretation of human sacrifice.

Meyerbeer's first work was written in Napoleon's menacing but shrinking shadow: it was performed shortly after Napoleon had passed through northern Germany on his way back from the Russian disaster. Works were also, however, produced which celebrated him as the enlightened opponent of human sacrifice. These spectacular divisions in the application of the averted-sacrifice theme prefigure its disappearance as a major cultural phenomenon after 1814.

In 1807 the French army marched into Portugal, seeing itself as the enlightener of a backward country. Yet on 25 July 1808 the soldiers massacred the inhabitants of the town of Evora. The court composer, Marcos Antonio Portugal, was required to supply an opera to commemorate Napoleon's birthday, on 15 August. With remarkably clashing inappropriateness, he revived his 1794 setting of *Demofóonte*, which was produced 'to celebrate the birthday of his majesty the Emperor of France, King of Italy, and Protector of the Confederation of the Rhine' ('per Festeggiare il Giorno Natalizio di sua Maesta L'Imperatore de' Francesi, Re' d'Italia, e Protettore della Confederazione del Rheno'). There are cuts in the libretto, and Demofóonte experiences a greater moral conflict between rigour and tenderness than in Metastasio, but essentially Napoleon, in the midst of his global carnage, was represented with the same text as had instructed Charles VI in clemency in 1733, and Frederick the Great in 1746. This celebration of the abolition of human sacrifice was revived in the year of the events commemorated in the best-known artistic product of the Peninsular War: Goya's painting of the firing squads at work after the Madrid uprising in May 1808.

In Paris at this time, however, there was a more straightforward celebration of Napoleon as the foe of sacrificial superstition. In 1807, Gasparo Spontini had produced his most impressive opera, *La Vestale*, about an unchaste vestal virgin (lover of a military hero) who is spared from sacrificial death by a last-minute sign from the goddess. It is a variation of the Alonzo and Cora story, with the difference that the anticolonialism of the Alonzo and Cora operas has gone: the superstitions of a bigoted priesthood now conflict with the values of secular empire. Spontini was the favourite composer of the Empress Josephine, and his next opera was suggested and to some extent monitored by Napoleon himself. This was *Fernand Cortez ou La Conquête du Méxique* (1809). This stands in striking contrast to the operatic version of the Conquest by Napoleon's military hero, Frederick the Great. Frederick had identified himself with the rationalistic Montezuma, barbarously sacrificed by Spanish greed and superstition. Napoleon, by contrast, is Cortez; in an inelegant role-reversal, the Spaniards become the Mexicans, associated at times with music of a violent barbarism that outdoes Gluck's Turkish music in *Iphigénie en Tauride*.

The threat of human sacrifice permeates the whole opera: of the Spanish prisoners, and then of the Mexican heroine Amazily, who loves Cortez, has accepted Christianity, and who returns to Mexico from the Spanish camp to take the place of Cortez's brother on the sacrificial altar. The sacrifice is averted at the last moment, but not by the intervention of a deity, or the triumph of reason, as (for example) in *Idomeneo*. It is averted by a cannon shot. As in *Robinson Crusoe*, culture emerges from the mouth of a gun. Although *Fernand Cortez* does portray the dissemination of enlightened civilization, it is spread by an individual will to power. When asked by a subordinate what he will oppose to the terrors that surround them, Cortez answers 'The power of my word, and the force of my will' ('La puissance de ma parole[,] la force de ma volonté').[24] Later, when he declares it to be his mission to end the cult of human sacrifice, he concludes 'this land belongs to me, and I shall not leave it any more' ('cette terre est à moi / je ne la quitte plus') (p. 292). Nor does he quit it. For 'who can stop the conqueror in his infinite course, or oppose genius when it is in command of valour' ('dans sa course infinie qui peut arrêter le vainqueur[;] / résister au génie quand il commande à la valeur') (pp. 590–1). Civilization is not spread through the discovery of universally inscribed instincts; it is spread through the power of a single will. In Diderot's *Supplément au Voyage de Bougainville*, the European conquerors were satirically described as coming with '*Ce pays est à nous*' engraved on their swords.[25] The motto that had summed up their infamous acquisitiveness now expresses the Napoleonic thirst for glory.

Fernand Cortez has its English counterpart in a work which uses Aztec human sacrifice to justify the civilizing mission of Britain. This is Robert Southey's long epic poem *Madoc* (1801–5), about the supposed Welsh discoverer of America. Here, the extirpation of human sacrifice among the Native Americans is also a principal theme, and the British win the hearts of the native peoples at the expense of the crueller conquerors, the sacrificing Aztecs, who at the end of the poem are sent on the wanderings that are to take them to Mexico; the advance of civilization permits the uprooting and dislocation of a whole people.

In the same year of 1809, however, an anti-Napoleonic play appeared in Germany, which used the idea of human sacrifice in a completely contrary and far more prophetic way. This is *Die Hermannsschlacht* (*Hermann's Battle*) by Heinrich von Kleist (1777–1811), the most gifted German dramatist of the generation after Goethe and Schiller. Like Schreiber's later *Marbod und Hermann*, this celebrates Arminius' defeat of the Roman legions in the Teutoburg Forest in AD 9.

If sacrificial drama of the eighteenth century had increasingly focussed on the mind of the victim, this play is about the body, sacrificed and otherwise. The Romans plan to plunder the German beauties of their blonde hair and white teeth, to replace the black ones of their own women. The Roman emissary Ventidius tries to start an affair with Hermann's wife Thusnelda (who leads him on at her husband's request), while promising her hair and teeth to the Empress Livia. Finally, thinking that he has an assignation with her, he is locked up with a wild she-bear and torn to pieces. This parallels and to some extent punishes an earlier incident of dismemberment, in which a German girl who had been raped by a Roman soldier is sacrificed by her own father ('Von ihrem eignen Vater hingeopfert'),[26] and then cut into fifteen parts, so that her body might be distributed among the tribal leaders. One element in the cultural clash between German and Rome, therefore, is the question of what to do with the fragmented female body. For the degenerate Romans, it is a source of sex toys, and Ventidius is taught an eternal lesson by being locked up with a real female. For the Germans, the division of the raped girl's body symbolizes the disunity of Germany, and the unnatural horror of its fragmentation stirs the chieftains to recognize that of the land's disunity. If the maiden cannot be made whole, the nation can. The dismemberments planned by the Romans serve the privacy of the bedroom; those of the Germans serve the totality of the state. At the end of the play, in another act of dismemberment, a collaborator prince is summarily beheaded on Hermann's orders. There are thus three divisions or dismemberments of the body, and all three are necessary instruments of national destiny. The *sparagmos* no longer represents civilization dissolving into nightmare. The tearing of the body permits the union of the state.

The beguiling of Ventidius, his seduction into a place where he becomes a victim of the wild, recalls the beguiling of Pentheus, and indeed in his earlier tragedy *Penthesilea* (1808) Kleist had already reintroduced *The Bacchae* into the mainstream of literary influence, for it includes a dismemberment of Achilles by the Amazon queen Penthesilea that is overtly indebted to that of Pentheus by his mother.

Treatments of the Trojan War had increasingly portrayed its savagery as something to be transcended, the great settings of Troy myths from the 1770s and 1780s (such as Goethe's *Iphigenie auf Tauris*) portraying a movement towards civilization and peace; from conflict to simplicity and unity. Kleist's play rather explores the interdependence of conflicting psychosexual forces: the impulses to military and to sexual conquest; to sexual consummation and to *sparagmos*. The opposites modulate into each other, while remaining opposed even in their indissoluble connection. It presents a view of Greek culture that is very different from that of Goethe and Schiller.[27]

According to Greek legend, Achilles killed the beautiful Amazon Penthesilea in battle, but was grief-stricken when he removed the helmet of his victim and saw her beauty. This incident generated a sequence of incidents in Renaissance epic in which a warrior is in love with a warrior heroine on the opposing side, Tasso's story of Tandredi and Clorinda being the most famous of these. Kleist reverts to the original story, yet reverses its outcome, making Penthesilea the killer and Achilles the victim. He has defeated and captured her; they fall in love, but she is rescued by her fellow Amazons. Since Amazons can only have sexual relations with those they conquer in battle, Achilles decides to lose to her, and goes into battle lightly armed. Too late, he realizes that Penthesilea is in earnest. Frenzied, she hunts him with her hounds and, when he is dead, sinks her teeth into his body, as they do. Like Agave in *The Bacchae*, she is gradually brought to consciousness of what she has done.

Many Greek myths besides that of Agave and Pentheus portray an alienating madness in which the killer perceives the victim as something other than human. What is different in Kleist is that the alienating madness represents the gap between man and woman. The sexual isolation of the Amazons had begun when their northern land was conquered by Ethiopians (beings of a different race), who had killed all the men and forcibly possessed the women. On the marriage night of their queen and the Ethiopian king, the Amazons had killed their ravishers, like the Danaïds, whose story is the last narrative glimpsed in the *Aeneid.* If the original myth explains the separation of Greek and North African, and Virgil's appropriation suggests the origins of civilization in barbarous violence, Kleist's suggests rather the atavistic sacrificial forces that are contained in sexuality itself, in both repulsion and attraction. As Sade, and Goethe in 'Die Braut von Korinth', had done in different ways, Kleist extends the idea of sacrificial ritual to encompass the psychology and structure of sexual behaviour.

In *Penthesilea*, the bloody wedding night has its counterpart in the festival of roses at which the Amazons select the temporary partners who will father their children. It commences with the sacrifice of oxen, during which the young captives think that they, too, are to be sacrificed, though the ritual to which they are destined is, rather, sexual. Nevertheless, the Amazon's mind easily turns the red of the roses into that of blood, and indeed one of the remarkable things about the play is its revelation of how one condition may be experienced as its opposite, as when the captive Penthesilea imagines that she is Achilles' captor. In Euripides, the collapse of distinctions indicates the proximity of civilization to the wilderness: of Thebes to Cithaeron. Here, it illustrates the ambiguity of the sex drive, and the way in which that ambiguity controls the rituals and goals of civilization. If Penthesilea violates the protocols of her society in seeking Achilles as a permanent partner, she also perpetuates the terrible origins of these protocols in the fatal wedding night.

The wedding night was now to be, for many decades, the real point of sacrificial danger. Barbarian kings in distant landscapes will, in the nineteenth century, largely be forgotten. The dangers are now fully internalized, lying in desires that the daylight, ordered world normally relegates to nightmares, but which are likeliest to erupt during the rituals that are most designed to contain and sacralize them. 'I shall', the monster in *Frankenstein* says, 'be with you on your wedding-night.'[28]

CHAPTER 9

The secularization of sacrifice

In 1806 the 26-year-old German poetess Karoline von Günderrode committed suicide as a result of unhappy love. Shortly before her death, she had written a sonnet entitled 'The Widows of Malibar' ('Die Malabarischen Witwen'), in an echo of Antoine Le Mierre's once popular play *La Veuve du Malabar* (1771), which portrays the rescue of a young widow from immolation. Le Mierre's opposition to *sati* is, however, replaced by idealization: the immolation consummates love, ends separation ('Trennung'), brings together divided flames of love ('entzweiten Liebesflammen'), and unifies the previously divided elements ('Vereinet die getrennten Elemente').[1]

At this time, the British government in India was discouraging but not outlawing widow-burning. Its officials tried simply to prevent immolation of those who were under age or unwilling, and the first ban, in Bengal, was not imposed until 1829. This initial tolerance was, however, an exception in a struggle against human sacrifice which was conducted throughout the various European empires for the whole of the nineteenth century. In mid-century, the British government official Captain S. Charters MacPherson was reporting on and outlawing human sacrifice among the Khonds in India, the chief form being an annual *sparagmos* to fertilize the fields.[2] Human sacrifice was widespread in Africa.[3]

Despite the toleration granted it until 1829, *sati* as an institution excited abhorrence in the West. Yet the ideal of total erotic surrender and dedication provided by the widow's self-immolation fascinated the nineteenth century. In its desire to escape from 'Trennung', Günderrode's poem anticipates the language of Wagner's *Tristan und Isolde* and of Brünnhilde's immolation in *Götterdämmerung*. The enthusiasm for the fiery *Liebestod* affected even the portrayal of other cultures: Ferdinand Hummel's opera *Assarpaï* (1898), about the conquest of Peru, concludes with a Spanish soldier leaping into the funeral pyre of the Inca Atahualpa's daughter: 'to eternity with you, beloved wife!' ('Zur Ewigkeit mit dir, geliebtes Weib!'), he cries.[4]

Although human sacrifice continued to dominate high art in the nineteenth century, on the whole it has as little to do with the real thing as the ending of Hummel's opera has to do with sixteenth-century Peru. The battle against barbarous sacrifice supposedly occurring in real life appears in second-tier literature (an Indian widow is rescued from burning

Plate 11 Sati, from M. E. Burnouf, *L'Inde française* (1827–35)

in *Around the World in Eighty Days*).[5] As expanding empires tried to wipe the practice off the map, however, human sacrifice gained new, imaginary forms to express the national, racial, and sexual anxieties of Europe itself: *Tristan und Isolde* has permanently conditioned our way of thinking about the erotic. The abolition of *sati* does not do away with a fascination in opera with exotic, self-immolating women, though these are often driven to self-sacrifice by European crassness as well as local superstition: for example, the African queen Selika in Meyerbeer's *L'Africaine* (1865), courted and abandoned by Vasco da Gama; Delibes's Lakmé (1883), courted with too little commitment by an English army officer; and Puccini's Butterfly (1904), courted and abandoned by an American naval lieutenant. In addition, the indignation of oppressed minorities now expresses itself in the portrayal of a quasi-sacrificial intolerance by the dominant culture: in *Les Huguenots* (1836), by the Jewish Meyerbeer, a father unwittingly kills his daughter during the St Bartholomew's massacre; in *La Juive* (1835) by Halévy, another Jew, the heroine's biological father (a cardinal) and her adoptive Jewish father jointly destroy her during a pogrom in fifteenth-century Constance. She is, simultaneously, the daughter of two Jephthahs. In *Les Huguenots*, the blades to be used in the massacre are ritually blessed by monks, the Huguenots are immolated ('on immole nos frères'),[6] and the opera's last words are those of a mob baying the archetypal sacrificial sentiment, 'God wants their blood' ('Dieu veut leur sang') (p. 124). Yet they are a mob far more than they are sacrificers, and the slaughter is carried out not with the consecrated blades but with gunfire: sheer unhallowed violence. Similarly, the mob calling down vengeance on the Jews at the end of *La Juive* is not a religious mob.

In the concluding sacrifice of *L'Africaine*, the abandoned heroine enters the natural 'temple' formed by a manchineel tree and expires from its beautifully scented poison, whose effect is to fill the victim with hallucinations ('Extase mensongère')[7] of entry into heaven. The sacrificial transformation is an intoxicated illusion, and such illusion is characteristic of Selika's realm. One still famous aria from *L'Africaine* is Vasco's 'O Paradis', in which he hails the beauty of the newly discovered land: a 'rediscovered Eden' ('éden retrouvé') (p. 59). He does not know that, immediately before his entrance, his companions have been led to sacrifice, the men on the altar, the women under the manchineel tree beneath which Selika is later to die. For this is a culture which, like Euripides' Taurica, sacrifices all strangers. A flawed Eden, then. The librettist, Scribe, does provide the usual parallel between heathen and Catholic brutality: we have earlier witnessed the cruel narrow-mindedness of the Inquisition in Portugal, which reveals that suspicion of the unfamiliar is universal, and a perhaps deeper-rooted motivation than religion. The final self-immolation of the queen because of sexual rejection, however, takes sacrifice out of the sphere of religion altogether. It is a picture postcard of human sacrifice, and we watch it like jaded but excitable tourists, observing a piece of titillating and faintly sensual exoticism. One of the most striking nineteenth-century developments in the representation of sacrifice is, indeed, to uncouple it from religion.

Until late in the previous century, human sacrifice had principally been associated with religious barbarism, whether of paganism or of Christianity. With the weakening of Christianity, however, there is a sudden explosion and proliferation in the meanings attached to it, the beginnings of which we have already seen in Sade and in Kleist. There was an increasing exploration of the varieties of sexual psychology, and human sacrifice came to be used to represent rituals of erotic submission as well as Sadean domination. In philosophy, too (for example in the work of Hegel and Kierkegaard), the issue is no longer simply explored in the old contexts: Christian versus heathen, Protestant versus Catholic, Deist versus Christian. In addition, the religious fanaticism deplored by eighteenth-century writers broadened out into racial or political fanaticism. This chapter, then, will briefly indicate the vast diversity of new forms into which the sacrificial theme proliferated in the nineteenth century. It thus provides an introduction to the following three chapters, which will trace some major transformations in the nineteenth-century treatment of sacrifice: the changing conceptions brought about by the discovery of the fossil record and of geological time, the innovations of Wagner, and the gradual movement towards the rebirth of Dionysus.

If the subject of *La Juive* was anti-semitism rather than religious fanaticism, Meyerbeer's lifelong distress about the former subject shaped his portrayal of religious intolerance in *Les Huguenots*. In practice, however, few texts can have been more variable in meaning, since its portrayal of Catholicism made it sensitive in some countries, and it was therefore repeatedly rewritten. In Munich it became *Die Anglikaner und Puritaner*, and concludes with the Royalist Duke of Bukingham [*sic*] unknowingly ordering the death of his daughter. In Florence, it became *Gli Anglicani*, and – by contrast – showed Cromwell commanding his child's death. In other versions (*Die Gibellinen in Pisa*, *Die Welfen und Gibellinen*, *I Guelfi ed I Ghibellini*), a Guelf father orders the death of a daughter who loves a Ghibelline.[8] Here, the religious element has been completely jettisoned, and specific religious content is unimportant even in those settings which are transposed to the English Civil War: *Die Anglikaner und Puritaner* and *Gli Anglicani* are reversible Lévi-Straussian structures. *Les Huguenots* is a retraction of the happy-ending version of Jephthah's sacrifice which was the subject of Meyerbeer's first opera. The application of the story, however, is oddly – even absurdly – detachable from any specifically formulated religious context. One cannot imagine Frederick the Great's Montezuma becoming, say, Charles I.

There is another way in which sacrifice may be detached from religion:

> Who now shall content thee as they did,
> Thy lovers, when temples were built
> And the hair of the sacrifice braided
> And the blood of the sacrifice spilt,
> In Lampsacus fervent with faces,
> In Aphaca red from thy reign,
> Who embraced thee with awful embraces,
> Our Lady of Pain?

This is from Swinburne's 'Dolores' (1866).[9] Günderrode had embraced a love-death which transcended physical separation. So does Meyerbeer's Selika, though her ascent towards the beckoning – if ill-assorted – forms of Brahma and Vasco da Gama is a trip fuelled by drugs: a cheap parallel to the death of Wagner's Isolde, which was also first staged in 1865. Especially round this decade of the 1860s, however, the rituals of sacrifice also come to represent the rituals of a sexual submission confined entirely to the present existence of the body. Sacher-Masoch's *Venus in Furs* (1870), for example, uses Apollo's flaying of Marsyas as an archetype of sexual domination. Sade's sexual rituals had been the *ne plus ultra* of the Enlightenment system: impersonal exercises in power on the bodies of sometimes nameless and interchangeable victims. Here, the element of religious ritual suggests personal exaltation and transfiguration: masochism as sacrament. In an admittedly quite different context, Dante had used the flaying of Marsyas to symbolize the transcendence of humanity necessary for him to enter Paradise.[10]

By whatever cultural route, sacrificial scenes later found their way into the sexual fantasies recorded by psychoanalysts. Theodor Reik records that:

> A man of thirty-seven, father of three children, is fully potent sexually only with the aid of varied and different phantasies. I select one at random: To an ancient barbaric idol, somewhat like the Phoenician Moloch, a number of vigorous young men are to be sacrificed at certain not too frequent intervals. They are undressed and laid on the altar one by one. The rumble of drums is joined by the songs of the approaching temple choirs. The high priest followed by his suite approaches the altar and scrutinizes each of the victims with a critical eye. They must satisfy certain requirements as to physical beauty and athletic appearance. The high priest takes the genital of each prospective victim in his hand and carefully tests its weight and form. If he does not approve of the genital, the young man will be rejected as obnoxious to the god and unworthy of being sacrificed. The high priest gives the order for the execution and the ceremony continues. With a sharp cut the young men's genitals and the surrounding parts are cut away.[11]

The association of sexual domination and submission with sacrificial ritual persists in Genet's *The Maids*.

The psychosexual aspects of sacrifice permeated the one major nineteenth-century work to deal in detail with historically attested human sacrifice. This is another product of the 1860s, Flaubert's *Salammbô* (1862). Like Meyerbeer's *L'Africaine* of three years later, it portrays African sacrifice, but it is aimed at stronger tastes than those that Meyerbeer had addressed: at those for whom Selika's soft drugs were insufficiently potent. In a review, Sainte-Beuve noted that it revealed 'Une pointe d'imagination sadique'.[12]

In *La Tentation de Saint Antoine* (final version 1874), Flaubert explores the complex and often sensual roots of the saint's battles with temptation. For example, a penitential self-flagellation quickly becomes ecstatic, and produces a hallucination of oriental voluptuousness: the Queen of Sheba, who has left Solomon to come to him. *Salammbô* also explores a sensual aesthetic of pain. It is set in Carthage, and its scenes of meticulous and extreme violence include one of child sacrifice to Moloch and a prolonged concluding incident of sacrificial dismemberment: here the captured protagonist, the mercenary leader Mathô, is forced to walk through Carthage, with each bystander snatching at him and removing a fragment of his flesh, until he finally meets the sacrificial knife of the priest of Moloch, who offers his heart to the sun. Here, the suffering is particularized with a combination of intellectual detachment and sensory fascination which certainly reveals the heritage of Sade, yet is quite different in its effect. The rituals in Sade express secure, if unacknowledged, principles of power: they are articulations of intelligible and contemporary systems. Here, we glimpse systems – even ones in which violence is elaborately mechanized. We glimpse, but we do not understand, for we are looking at a dead and irrecoverable culture. Sensually detailed as it is in its description of sacrificial and other violence, its subject matter is as alien to contemporary African and Asiatic practices as anything in Wagner or Swinburne.

Flaubert's Carthage is a place outside history, so totally destroyed in 146 BC that it did not participate in the future evolution of the Mediterranean. Nor is the war portrayed one of the famous wars with Rome: the wars that Virgil made central to the teleology of world history. Rather, it was the Mercenary War: a rebellion of mercenaries after the first Punic War as a result of delays in payment, the atrocities of which were outstanding even by the standards of the ancient world. Flaubert portrays a culture of casual, extreme, and predatory cruelty: a history whose only structure appears in a chain of reactive violence, consummated in the dismemberment of the body. This is a civilization which consumes bodies, its architecture and technology devoted to war and the service of cruel gods. Its most elaborate machines are siege engines and the mechanical idol of Moloch, through whose mouth victims are delivered to the fires, in the most literal image of the consumption of the body.

A human sacrifice to Moloch is portrayed at some length. The purpose of the sacrifice is to obtain rain, and it works: the rain comes, and the war is won. Within the narrative structure of the book, the sacrifice is a decisive turning point. Yet it is fraudulent, for one of the victims – ostensibly Hamilcar's son Hannibal – has been replaced by a slave. The Greek historian Diodorus Siculus narrates that the Carthaginians were punished for substituting bought slaves for their firstborn (20.14.4–7). Not so here: though fraudulent, the sacrifice gains the desired result. It presents us with an infinite regression of the incomprehensible: the alien system not only works, but works in violation of its own principles.

Such elusiveness is pervasive, and affects even the portrayal of sexuality. Although *Salammbô* is dominated by the sexual principle, it is expressed in culturally strange forms, such as the stone phalluses and other 'fertility symbols' ('symboles de la fécondation') (p. 81) in the temple of the moon goddess Tanit. The eunuch priest of the sun god, to whom the human sacrifices are made, believes that 'the male exterminating principle' ('le principe mâle exterminateur') (p. 201) is supreme in life. Yet it is when 'the female principle . . . dominated and intermingled everything' ('le principe femelle . . . dominait, confondait tout') (p. 344), during the concluding victory celebrations, that the destructive principle reaches its height. The massive prostitution during the ensuing night is preceded by the day of the most prolonged *sparagmos* in the novel: the death of the central male character, the mercenary leader Mâtho.

On a furtive spying expedition into Carthage, Mâtho had encountered Salammbô, daughter of Hamilcar and priestess of Tanit. He steals the veil of the goddess (a theft which is held to cause Carthage's subsequent misfortunes) but becomes erotically fascinated with her priestess. Salammbô visits him in his camp and recovers the veil, becoming fascinated by him in turn, though her fascination is never simplified as love or sexual desire. With further opacity of historical logic, the single female garment of the veil is invested with almost as much power as all the male violence in the novel.

The day of Mâtho's death coincides with the marriage of Salammbô to the ally of Carthage, Narr'Havas. His journey to sacrificial death is also a journey to her, and her eyes meet those in his terribly unrecognizable face as he dies. Salammbô's marriage is a version of that favourite device of the nineteenth century, the supernaturally interrupted wedding. For not only is it disturbed by the sacrificial victim who represents the alternative object of Salammbô's desires: at the moment at which she raises the goblet to pledge her bridegroom, Salammbô falls dead. 'Thus died the daughter of Hamilcar, for touching the mantle of Tanit' ('Ainsi mourut la fille d'Hamilcar pour avoir touché au manteau de Tanit') (p. 352), the novel concludes. It is a famously enigmatic ending, representing neither our construction of events nor such constructions by characters as we have been able to trace amidst all the incoherent violence of the war. We are left, as it were, with the official explanation of an event for which the novel's customary modes of explanation – the psychological and the physical – do not suffice. The transactions of death are conducted in a foreign currency.

Yet not for long. Alfons Mucha's 1896 lithograph *Salammbô* (frontispiece) treats the sacrificial priestess as an object of voluptuous erotic submission. In 1890, moreover, the French composer Ernest Reyer produced an operatic version of *Salammbô*, with libretto by Camille du Locle, who had already supplied the text for Reyer's earlier opera *Sigurd* (1884). Like Wagner's greater setting of the Nibelung legend, *Sigurd* ends with Brunehild's self-immolation on her husband's funeral pyre. Du Locle then treats *Salammbô* in the same way: commanded to execute Mâtho, the heroine instead turns the knife on herself, and Mâtho then kills himself with the same sword, exclaiming 'je t'adore[,] Et je m'en vais vers toi!' ('I love you, and I am going to meet you!').[13] Just as, in Ferdinand Hummel's opera, the alien world of Atabalipa's Peru adjusts itself to the ethos of Wagnerian *Liebestod*, so Flaubert's narrative here loses its alienness and expresses the romanticization of *sati* that is one of the period's favourite forms of human sacrifice. The opera, like the novel, ends with condemnation of those who touch the goddess's veil, but the words lose their original enigma: they are chanted by a chorus of merciless priests, and overshadowed by the erotic affirmation we have just witnessed. The copy of the vocal score in the Cambridge University Library is dedicated, in the composer's hand, to a celebrated society beauty, Madame Charles Max.

HEGEL AND KIERKEGAARD

Such works perhaps prove what was increasingly to be accepted in the twentieth century: that the impulse to sacrifice is fundamental to the human mind, and provides a means of understanding some of our most advanced institutions. Yet the imagining of sacrifice in literature seems to point more to Dr Reik's consulting room than to Benin or Bengal. Had his patient been reading Flaubert? Reik certainly had, for he wrote his dissertation on him.

With the secularization of sacrifice goes a change in the portrayal of its social functions and operation. Throughout the previous century, sacrifice had been associated with social and religious systems. Sacrificial plays pitted increasingly subjective individuals against increasingly impersonal systems. With the Romantic period all this is blown away. Human sacrifice predominantly becomes a means of exploring and articulating the subjective, though the old oppositions are given new and authoritative form in Hegel. For Hegel, the civilization that is grounded upon human sacrifice is the contrary of that which permits the full evolution of the subjective ethical sense, of which the prime example is Germany. Hegel's view of the evolution of culture is thus essentially compatible with that of Goethe in *Iphigenie*. To say that his view of sacrifice differs from that of Swinburne, Flaubert, or Sacher-Masoch is not to say much. For one thing, he is describing the culmination of civilization of the West, whereas they are losing themselves in dreams of the East. Nor are they analysts of social evolution: for Sacher-Masoch, woman retains her primeval character as savage, despite all advances of civilization ('trotz aller Fortschritte der Zivilisation').[14]

After his famous description of the world-historical heroes – men who embody necessary impulses of historical transformation – Hegel considers the role of individual sacrifice in historical progress. Although we might tolerate the idea that individuals may be sacrificed as means to a great end, he argues, this becomes difficult when we consider the subjective, ethical element of individuals: *means* are things to which we stand in a purely external relation, whereas human beings must share in any ideal aim and cannot be mere means. He analyses various cultures according to the degree to which they accommodate the ethical and subjective, and the degree to which they locate their values in externally and materially expressed systems. The ideal realization of the former is in German culture, which introduces 'an entirely *new Spirit*, through which the World was to be regenerated – the free Spirit, viz. which reposes on itself – the absolutely self determination [Eigensinn] of subjectivity'.[15] The corresponding anti-ideal is in the culture of Black Africans, who according to Hegel lack the category of Universality (p. 93) and have a religion of purely material relations, worshipping 'an animal, a tree, a stone, or a wooden figure'. Unconscious of any universality, they have a 'perfect *contempt* for humanity' (p. 95), which leads them to cannibalism and mass funerary sacrifices. In the more advanced oriental cultures, morality resides in external systems, without being subjectively internalized. An example of such externality of value is the caste system, and the permitted means of ascent within it: the extreme but purely physical ascesis of the yogi. It is this system which permits the self-immolation of widows, and an idea of sacrifice that is supported by a belief in the material interchangeability of individuals: 'An Englishman states that he also saw a woman burn herself because she had lost her child. He did all that he could to divert her away from her purpose; at last he applied to her husband who was standing by, but he showed himself perfectly indifferent, as *he had more wives at home*' (p. 146). 'More wives at home': Siegfried could have said the same; but to what purpose?

Seen in its true nature, the sacrifice of Christ enables man to overcome his attachment to the material and realize his spiritual essence. Yet according to Hegel its meaning has been corrupted by Catholicism, which fetishizes the Host as a thing, and dissipates the sense of the sacred through countless material objects such as saints' relics: 'men looked for a *definite embodiment* of the infinite in a mere isolated object' (p. 393). This deification of the object fuelled the Crusades, which Hegel compares to the Trojan War, and which he regards as barbaric. While the rest of the world was exploring America and India, however, Luther was discovering God: 'Luther's simple doctrine is that the specific embodiment of Deity – infinite subjectivity, that is true spirituality, Christ – is in no way present and actual in outward form, but as essentially spiritual is obtained only in being reconciled to God – *in faith and spiritual enjoyment*' (p. 415). Thus, the evolution of civilization towards one which accommodates the ethical self-realization of the individual is accompanied by a transformation in the idea of sacrifice, from one in which the victim may be treated as a material instrument, with no acknowledgment of a subjective consciousness, to one in which a sacrifice freed from material particularity enables the full realization of an internal moral consciousness. Hegel's account of the changing role of sacrifice in culture, in short, corresponds very closely to its changing role in eighteenth-century tragedy.

In directly considering sacrifice in Greek tragedy, Hegel sees it as part of the general tragic conflict between different ethical imperatives, especially 'between the state, i.e. ethical life in its *spiritual* universality, and the family, i.e. *natural* ethical life':[16] between the public claims that drive Agamemnon to sacrifice Iphigenia and the bond of love that drives Clytemnestra to avenge her (though for Hegel the resolution comes in the avoidance of sacrifice, both in *Iphigenia in Aulis* and *Iphigenia among the Taurians*). The tragedy of Oedipus does not yet reflect permanent and potentially sacrificial impulses of the human mind, as it was to for Freud and René Girard. Rather, for Hegel, it reflects a culture which gives insufficient space to subjective self-consciousness: which 'adheres to the bare fact which an individual has achieved, and refuses to face the division implied by the purely ideal attitude of the soul in the self-conscious life on the one hand and the objective significance of the fact accomplished on the other' (p. 69).

Instrumental sacrifice in Hegel becomes morally outmoded as culture ascends towards an ethical consciousness that is fully individuated but, for that reason, universal, since the value of individual consciousness is universal. The famous opposing view is, of course, that proposed by the Danish philosopher Kierkegaard in *Fear and Trembling*, in his discussion of Abraham's readiness to sacrifice his son. Kierkegaard denies Abraham that which he had always hitherto possessed: the justification of a universal, symbolic status whose imperatives override that of the individual father. In the case of Abraham, 'the single individual as the particular is higher than the universal';[17] it cannot be brought into relationship with the universal.

There is no typology about Kierkegaard's Abraham. He is a purely temporal figure, his experience of sequential time – his seventy years' wait for a son – being an integral part of his significance and suffering. His story does not in any way duplicate the Crucifixion, or any other Biblical event; it is said, for example, to be quite different from that of Jephthah. Kierkegaard's chief points of reference are the stories of Iphigenia, which that of Jephthah's daughter does resemble, and of Lucius Junius Brutus. These, however, are also different, in that the child sacrifice has a clearly formulated external goal: the fathers would not have been understood if they had sacrificed a virtuous child for inner conviction. Nor could the sufferings of Abraham bear the decorum in which tragedians had increasingly wrapped the sufferings of Agamemnon. The sacrifice of Isaac also bears no relationship to monetary sacrifice, for no anguish attaches to money (p. 58), and Kierkegaard destabilizes the story by retelling it in a series of provisional, if unsatisfactory, narratives.

No discussion of human sacrifice in nineteenth-century can omit Kierkegaard's discussion of Abraham, which is after all one of the most famous treatments of the subject in the period. Nevertheless, it bears very little relationship to the way in which sacrifice was being explored in the arts. It goes beyond Hegel in making the individual consciousness not only the site of the moral struggle but the moral criterion by which it is judged. In associating the sacrificial impulse with subjectivity – and in this respect only – Kierkegaard belongs to the era of Wagner and Flaubert (*Fear and Trembling* and *Der Fliegende Holländer* both appeared in 1843). Yet the subjective consciousness is Abraham's. Isaac's consciousness appears most in the provisional and rejected versions of the story, such as the fourth one which culminates in his loss of faith. Moreover, although Abraham's is a consciousness that is divided in its sense of obligation, it is not a consciousness that is divided in its structure. A question one cannot imagine Abraham asking is that of Clara in Hoffmann's 'The Sandman': 'do you not then believe that in cheerful, uninhibited, carefree natures there might also dwell the presentiment of a dark power, that strives like an enemy within our own self to ruin us?' ('glaubst Du denn nicht, daß auch in heitern – unbefangenen – sorglosen Gemütern die Ahnung wohnen könne von einer dunklen Macht, die feindlich uns in unserm eignen Selbst zu verderben strebt?').[18] This presents a self divided between a rational and socially ordered identity and something primitive and formless, barely to be registered in language. Up to this point, the progress of sacrificial drama has been to give priority to the subjective consciousness of the victim, as something which forms the starting point for a new and reconstructed society. From now onwards the subjective consciousness becomes the battlefield. The sacrificial forces are not culturally antiquated ritual practices: they will be permanently recurring features of the dark side of the mind.

CHAPTER 10

Gothic sacrifice

In June 1816, in the Villa Diodati on Lake Geneva, Byron, the Shelleys, and John Polidori amused themselves by the competitive composition of ghost stories; a contest that was ultimately to result in *Frankenstein* (1818) and Polidori's *The Vampyre* (1819). It was a disastrously cold summer, causing global famines, plagues, and unrest, the sense of an apocalypse without divine cause or purpose being vividly caught in Byron's poem 'Darkness', of that year. In view of the preoccupation with geological forces and catastrophe that was to shape much sacrificial literature in the nineteenth century (and to influence the work of Percy and Mary Shelley), it is fitting that the calamities of this year are now known to have been caused by one of the most violent volcanic eruptions of the last 10,000 years: that of Tambora in the East Indies.

The contest in the Villa Diodati was one of two parallel but initially quite separate developments in 1816. The other was the first significant stirring of German Romantic opera. Louis Spohr's *Faust*, completed in 1813, received its first performance under Weber in Prague in 1816, and in the same year E. T. A. Hoffmann's *Undine*, based on La Motte Fouqué's novella of 1811, was first performed in Berlin, with a libretto by Fouqué himself. At first independent, these literary and operatic currents quickly started to intermingle, and there was a latent connection from the start. The inspiration for the ghost story contest was J. B. B. Eyriès's *Fantasmagoriana* (1812), a French translation of some stories from Johann Apel and Friedrich Laun's *Gespensterbuch* (1811–15); one tale in the *Gespensterbuch* which Eyriès did not translate is 'Der Freischütz', the source of Weber's opera. The two currents finally intermingled in 1828, in two sacrificial operas derived from the Polidori tale and heavily influenced by *Der Freischütz*: Heinrich Marschner's *Der Vampyr* (a potent influence on Wagner), and Peter Joseph von Lindpaintner's opera of the same name.

In *Frankenstein*, the monster threatens his creator that he will 'be with [him] on [his] wedding-night',[1] and kills Frankenstein's bride at the promised time. In *The Vampyre*, the heroine marries Lord Ruthven, the vampire of the title, who kills her on their wedding night. In Spohr's *Faust* (which is unrelated to Goethe's), the protagonist attempts to use his demonic powers for good, and rescues a bride from her abductor; he becomes infatuated with her, however, and uses his powers to debauch her on her wedding night. *Undine* also portrays a supernaturally interrupted wedding. Undine is a soulless water sprite, who can only gain a soul by experiencing human love. In infancy, she is substituted for the fisherman's daughter Bertalda, who is in turn adopted by a noble couple. The hero, Huldbrand, arranges to marry Undine, but then rejects her for her human alternative, Bertalda. On the evening of the wedding Undine appears from a fountain and approaches Huldbrand, who insists on kissing her, even though he is warned that the price of the kiss is death. Though the death is not in itself sacrificial, it was to become an influential archetype of the sacrificial love-death: in Hoffmann's opera, though not the novella, the final kiss is indeed termed a 'Liebestod'.[2] The story of Undine is one allusive precedent for the fatal embrace undertaken by Adrian Leverkühn in Thomas Mann's *Doctor Faustus*.

In the Spohr opera, the hero's loyal but constantly betrayed sweetheart finally leaps, despairingly, to a watery death. Unlike the later, very similar, death of Senta in *Der Fliegende Holländer*, however, this sacrifice ('Opfer') cannot save the demonically cursed hero. Faust has been damned by the internal decisions of his own will, and no third-party sacrifice will save him. Like so much opera of this period, this work reads like an advance refutation of Wagner.

The demonically interrupted wedding is commonplace: we have already encountered it in 'Die Braut von Korinth', and the fatal union of Kleist's Achilles with Penthesilea. It recurs in Hoffmann's 'The Mines at Falun' ('Die Bergwerke zu Falun'), Maturin's *Melmoth the Wanderer*, *Der Freischütz*, and the two vampire operas of 1828. A fatally disrupted marriage was to have been the subject of Wagner's first, incomplete (and destroyed) opera *Die Hochzeit* (*The Wedding*), and it recurs in his *Tristan* and *Götterdämmerung*. The motif has classical precedents: notably the bloody wedding night of the Danaïds and the fatal wedding of Jason and Crëusa, who is killed by a poisoned garment given by Jason's rejected first wife, Medea. In these cases, however, the destruction is externally engineered, by a violent and primitive culture. In the present cases, the pattern is different, for the marriage is disrupted by something intrinsic to the desires that are ostensibly being controlled and sanctified: by the bridegroom (*The Vampyre*), the bride's sexual desire (*Faust*), the bride's double (*Undine*), and by the uncontrollable analogue to sexual procreation that Frankenstein had devised. If the interrupted sacrifice is one of the defining themes of Enlightenment opera and theatre, the interrupted marriage replaces it in the Romantic era. I am not, however, making the assumption that it means the same in each of its many occurrences. It is not a spontaneously self-replicating psychological archetype; it is rather a literary convention, recognized and manipulated as such. Yet, inevitably, the convention reflects the larger conditions of the age, where outward landscapes shadow forth inner ones, and where the atavistic impulse comes not from a dark

Plate 12 Arthur Rackham, 'Undine' (1909)

corner of the Black Sea but a dark corner of the mind. Indeed, in Frankenstein's pursuit of the creature, both he and his quarry board the same ship to the Black Sea, but the creature mysteriously disappears: that archetypal site of sacrificial barbarism has for the moment lost its potency (until Dracula's voyage to England commences there). Many sacrificial myths, such as that of Pentheus, are now thought to originate in rites of passage. Marriage is perhaps the rite of passage which has longest retained its aura of mystery and dangerous transition.

There are also other transformations in the imagining of sacrifice at this time. Hitherto, the sacrificial instrument of choice has been the knife: an instrument of culture. Now it is overtaken by more elemental agencies: water, fire, the vampire's tooth. These do more than merely suggest a victory of nature over culture: water, in particular, can represent alternative and suppressed areas of consciousness, as in *Undine*, where the water-world is a mirror (*Spiegel*) of the land.[3] The sea in Racine represents the formlessness outside civilization; in Goethe's *Iphigenie*, the unassimilable alienness outside the consciousness. In both cases, however, it is separate from and opposed to a collective humanity. Now, water denotes boundaries between or even within different psychic states. It is an alternative area for the consciousness to inhabit: an area populated by a doppelgänger figure such as Undine, or by her heirs – Wagner's Rhinemaidens, for instance.

Sacrifice by water can thus suggest entry into a mental state beyond that of one's culture, and the fascination with alternative states is complemented by a tendency to portray otherness – including sexual otherness – as otherness of species. Whereas the Enlightenment increasingly emphasizes the common human character that links Trojan and Greek, European and Native American, characters are now separated by belonging to different orders of being: Frankenstein's creature is a 'new species' (p. 35), pieced together from the charnel house and the slaughter-house; from human and animal. The water sprite Undine is a being of strange nature ('fremdartiges Wesen') (p. 63), who hopes to gain a soul from the love of a mortal. Vampires are non-human. In Wagner's *Die Feen* (*The Fairies*) (1834), about marriage between a fairy and a mortal man, the hero and heroine first encounter each other as hunter and doe; a situation replicated over eighty years later in Richard Strauss's *Die Frau Ohne Schatten*, where the king marries a Peri whom he first encountered as a gazelle while out hunting. In the Wagner work, the hero then enters the heroine's world after losing consciousness in a stream. Eighteenth-century sacrificial literature assumes a cultural or psychological equality between the sacrificer and victim; when men and women seem to belong to different orders of being, the idea of sacrifice is likely to change.

Not only do human bodies belong to different orders of being; they no longer exist in a fixed relation to time and space. The protagonist of Maturin's *Melmoth the Wanderer* (1820) has sold his soul to the devil, and spends his expanded lifespan of 150 years in a vain attempt to find someone who will take the bargain off his hands: he is 'independent of time and place',[4] able to traverse vast distances and pass through impenetrable barriers in an instant. That more famous Satanist, Goethe's Faust, travels in time, whereas Marlowe's Faustus had merely travelled in space. Fouqué's water sprites live a purely material existence, but one which lasts for centuries. Hypnotized at the very point of death, Poe's M. Valdemar remains suspended at that moment for months, until his trance is broken and he dissolves in a putrescent mass.

There were, of course, analogues in the natural world for such frozen perpetuations of the body: fossils. The fossil evidence in the rocks was increasingly seeming to challenge Biblical chronology and narrative, and the stone imprints of ancient life forms could no longer be convincingly interpreted as a record of Noah's flood. To a growing number of interpreters, they showed an earth of great antiquity: life forms that no longer existed, geological periods long past. The mutability and evolution of species were not yet scientifically uncontested facts, but they were powerfully advocated (by, among others, Goethe). In creating a new species, Mary Shelley's Frankenstein was doing something that was not only scientifically but conceptually revolutionary: creating a being who violated the Biblical reading of the geological record. This record also encouraged a sense – which we now know to be true – that life on earth was subject to periodic exterminating catastrophes whose causes were entirely material, and which had nothing to do with the teleology of the Christian Last Judgment. Fears of such extermination haunt the work of Mary Shelley, and, as the century wore on, theories of periodic global catastrophe gave urgency to the need to maintain the human race in the form fittest for survival: to prevent racial degeneration.

So what happens to the imagining of the sacrificial transaction when the destiny of the body is not to ascend in smoke to the nostrils of the gods but to solidify in rocks of unimaginable age? When human destiny is governed not by divine plan but by the lifeless and mindless processes of rock and ice? Or when the lifeless and mindless bodies of executed felons can, seemingly, be re-animated by Galvani's electrical current?

One synthesis of old forms and new fears is provided in the sacrifice by fossilization in E. T. A. Hoffmann's 'The Mines at Falun' – another work from that crucial year of 1816. Here a sailor, Elis Fröbom, is led into becoming a miner by a mysterious old man who is yet another example of unnaturally prolonged life: a miner who disappeared in a mining catastrophe over a century before. The underground, mineral world becomes in his mind a solidified version of the alternative, subaqueous world over which he had floated in his former career as a sailor: an inorganic world that mimics the natural one, stimulating him to hallucinations of beautiful maidens and luxuriant flowers, and its Goddess of the Mines, a replacement for his dead mother. It is also an alternative sphere of consciousness, full of alien and enchanting signs: mysterious writing on the rocks tantalizes the deciphering mind. On his wedding day, Elis Fröbom is irresistibly claimed by the Goddess and her mysterious sign-systems, rushing into the depths of the mine in the belief that he will find a stone engraved with the record of his and his bride's life. He is trapped in a landslide, and on the fiftieth anniversary of his intended wedding his perfectly preserved body is discovered, only to crumble into dust at the touch of his now aged bride.

It is possible to see this story as a flight to the maternal womb from the terrors of sex, but it would be unwise to write off the mineral world as mere disguise for the organic mysteries of the womb. The alien, inanimate solidity of this world is an indispensable part of its nature, and Elis's obsession with it reveals how the human mind can reconstitute not only its shapes but its whole texture of existence in foreign and lifeless media: as though the mind contains its own fossil record. The subterranean world certainly reflects the divided consciousness which Elis (like other Hoffmann heroes) experiences: 'he felt as if he were split into two halves. It was as if his better, actual "I" descended to the midpoint of the globe and rested in the arms of the Queen, while he seeks his gloomy bed in Falun' ('er fühlte sich wie in zwei Hälften geteilt, es war ihm, als stiege sein besseres, sein eigentliches Ich hinab in den Mittelpunkt der Erdkugel und ruhe aus in den Armen der Königin, während er in Falun sein düsteres Lager suche').[5] In part, this division reflects the uncertain boundaries between organic existence and matter: an uncertainty also evident in 'The Sandman', in the hero's love for the mechanical doll, or in 'Mademoiselle de Scudery', where the artist kills in order to reclaim his artefacts. In 'The Mines at Falun', Elis's death has all the overtones of sacrifice. He is claimed by the Mistress of the Mines, as Iphigenia is by the mistress of the animals, and enters her world as a changeless, lapidary object. Here the fossil is imaginatively cognate with the man with the unnaturally prolonged life: Torbern, the miner who had disappeared in the previous collapse of the mines. It is easy to see why Elis's descent into Nibelheim appealed to Wagner, who retained a lifelong fascination with the tale; at the request of the composer Dessauer, he sketched – but did not complete – a libretto based on it. The opera was to conclude with yet another interrupted wedding, as the festivities are halted by the noise from the mine.[6]

FRANKENSTEIN

The creature in *Frankenstein: or, the Modern Prometheus* is another being whose body is released from the normal constraints of time and matter, put together from material that had already gone through the life cycle, mocked by the cycles of fruition around it, and increasingly – in its flight to the Arctic – driven to a barren, mineral, inorganic world of rocks, mountains, and frozen water. The culmination of this separation from the organic is an act of sacrificial self-immolation:

> Do not think that I shall be slow to perform this sacrifice. I shall quit your vessel on the ice-raft which brought me hither, and shall seek the most northern extremity of the globe; I shall collect my funeral pile, and consume to ashes this miserable

> frame, that its remains may afford no light to any curious and unhallowed wretch, who would create such another as I have been ... Light, feeling, and sense, will pass away.[7]

Sacrifice is, again, a return to the world of matter.

Frankenstein reconstitutes and reverses many of the elements of Enlightenment sacrificial narrative. In the latter, characteristically, the seeming obligation to take life in sacrifice conflicts with a contrasting obligation caused by the giving of life: the sacrificer may be the parent of the victim, or may owe his own life to him, and the point of the drama is to evolve a system in which the debt from the giving of life is the primary ordering principle, and the sacrificial taking of life its extreme violation. The owing of life is the fundamental bond from which society is reconstructed in *Robinson Crusoe*, and the primal cultural role of the life-giver is reflected in the preoccupation of German opera and drama with the figure of the rescuer (*Retter*); Leonore's role as *Retterin* of her husband had been jubilantly celebrated in the final chorus of *Fidelio* only four years previously. It is in such a role that Frankenstein first sees himself: 'A new species would bless me as its creator and source; many happy and excellent natures would owe their being to me. No father could claim the gratitude of his child so completely as I should deserve theirs' (p. 35). In *Frankenstein*, however, the giving of life is the fundamental curse. The primal social principle has become something which threatens the very continuance of the human race.

The most critical decision of the book – whether Frankenstein should make the creature a female companion – concerns the giving of life, but its value is entirely undecidable, both for Frankenstein and the reader. The creature might be pacified and restored to the sphere of culture; alternatively, by giving the new species power to reproduce, the creator might ensure the extinction of his own. Yet this moment, where Frankenstein perhaps assures the continuation of the human species, is the most enthusiastically uncontrolled moment of violence in the novel; a wild *sparagmos* in a remote corner of the Orkneys, worthy of far earlier retreats from the city to the wilderness. In the tearing of Pentheus, the difference of species between the slayer and the slain had been a terrible illusion; here, it is fundamental to the act. Yet, if Agave kills her own son, Frankenstein is here killing his friend, and his wife, for it is with this act that he ensures the deaths of Clerval and Elizabeth.

Although the creature is a new and distinct species, he is still Frankenstein's double. Though separate in nature, the two are twinned in their struggle for survival: after the creature has murdered Frankenstein's brother William, the protagonist starts to see him as 'my own vampire, my own spirit let loose from the grave' (p. 57). The obvious and perhaps implicit analogy is with another figure associated with darkness, Caliban, yet it is an analogy which can only work in reverse, for Caliban is impervious to culture. The creature embodies all the ideal social principles of the eighteenth century; he simply violates the aesthetic tastes of the nineteenth.

In Aeschylus, Prometheus was not only the creator of man but the giver of culture: of shelter, language, sign-systems. Here Frankenstein is defective. Like all three of the principal males, the creature is an autodidact. He absorbs culture without a mentor: he lacks cultural as well as biological parentage, though in this respect he is one with his maker. Though he is briefly initiated into civilization, his initiation leads to a rapid reversal of the traditional pattern of social evolution. He starts (and remains) a gatherer, never copying human carnivorousness or fondness for wine, but never cultivating the land either. He cannot form society. When his ugliness causes him to be repelled with horror by a destitute family to whom he has long given unobserved assistance, he restrains his first impulse to act like a predator, by striking his assailant down as a lion destroys an antelope. Inexorably, however, he returns to the most atavistic of social impulses and pursuits, vengeance and the hunt, though in this he again replicates the course followed by his maker. In one of his early letters to his sister, the narrator Walton, a polar explorer, mentions that the master of his ship 'will not hunt (a favourite, and almost the only amusement here)' (p. 8). The mention of this exceptional non-hunting male, however, is quickly followed by the spectacle of the most savage of all forms of hunt, a once-promising scientist hunting his almost-human quarry over the sterile wastes. The old association between the hunt and sacrifice resurfaces: for this hunt culminates in the self-immolation of the prey. Mary Shelley's work appeared in the year of two British expeditions to polar regions, reflecting the confident expansionism of a growing global power. In the novel, however, this is translated into a desperate and solitary regression to human origins.

The quest to the Arctic is one to an area where complex life forms cease, and there is only crystallized water and frigid air. Frankenstein's motive for pursuing the creature is to prevent the extinction of humanity, and the Arctic provides a prophetic confirmation of his fears, for it is an area which prefigures the extinction of life on the entire planet. Recording his own reactions to the visit to Chamounix that inspired the setting for Frankenstein's first colloquy with the creature, Percy Bysshe Shelley had written: 'I will not pursue Buffon's sublime but gloomy theory – that this globe which we inhabit will at some future period be changed into a mass of frost by the encroachments of the polar ice.'[8] This alludes to a theory of inexorable geological catastrophe. By calculations derived from the cooling of two metal spheres, Buffon had calculated that the earth – originally a white-hot fragment of the sun – would take 168,123 years to turn to ice. Life had originated at the poles as they cooled, and the entire earth would eventually be a frigid waste: the time remaining before total glaciation was 93,291 years.[9] In his account of his intellectual growth, Frankenstein records that he read 'Buffon with delight' (p. 24).[10]

It is an apocalypse, but an apocalypse without God. An end of the world that comes about entirely by material process, without divine cause or divine judgment. An end of the world whose processes can be reproduced on a miniature but proportionately accurate scale in the laboratory, and charted with the aid of a clock and a thermometer. Byron portrayed a secular apocalypse in another creation of 1816, the poem 'Darkness', and Mary Shelley herself was to imagine one in *The Last Man* (1826), where dreams of a utopian society following the liberation of Greece give way to the extinction of the human species by plague. Strikingly, the first realization of the scale of the plague is immediately preceded by an inverted version of Buffon's future: the philosopher Merrival predicts that, in 100,000 years, 'The pole of the earth will coincide with the pole of the ecliptic, . . . an universal spring will be produced, and earth become a paradise'.[11] Like that of *The Last Man*, the sacrificial narrative of *Frankenstein* takes place against a larger history made possible by the geological record, in which the death of the individual is overtaken by the death of the species, and that in turn by the ending of all life. Whereas the Christian Judgment transmutes and cancels the death of the individual man, these general and impersonal exterminations no more cancel the death of the individual man than they do that of the individual mammoth. They merely raise it to a higher degree of finality. The plague in *The Last Man* takes away the comfort provided by the imagined continuity of the species: the delusion 'that though the individual is destroyed, man continues for ever. Thus, losing our identity, that of which we are chiefly conscious, we glory in the continuity of our species, and learn to regard death without terror' (p. 230).

The Last Man offers a very precise reversal of the vision of human progress offered by the *Aeneid*. Initially, this vision seems to have been re-enacted, for the West once again conquers the East, Constantinople falls, and Athens is free. Very shortly before Merrival's prediction of a climatic Utopia, 100 millennia hence, there is a utopian statement of a more immediate kind: '[T]he temple of Universal Janus was shut' (p. 219). This refers to the Roman custom of closing the gates of the Temple of Janus when there was peace throughout the borders of the Empire. They were closed three times during the reign of Augustus (and only, according to legend, twice before it), and their closure is the climax of Jupiter's speech in Book 1 of the *Aeneid*, which narrates the progress of civilization to its perfect fulfilment under Augustus. In *The Last Man*, the consummation of civilization leads immediately to extinction, the plague spreading in particular from those ancient and modern archetypes of democratic culture, Athens and America. The penultimate scenes are set in Rome, but a Rome empty of inhabitants. As civilization collapses, there is a reversion to systematic religious killing: a Messianic religious leader promises his followers immunity from the plague, methodically and secretly killing those who display its symptoms.

The old classical accounts of human progress – from hunter–gatherer to citizen – are just as deliberately reversed in *Frankenstein* as in *The Last Man*, for the novel envisages a world in which extinction – of warmth and of life – is not only possible but inevitable. Walton, the Arctic explorer who narrates the novel, is deludedly looking for a temperate, utopian land beyond the polar ice. But dreams of utopian progress and perfection turn, for both Walton and Frankenstein, to ice – or ashes. There is a significant contrast with Percy Bysshe Shelley's contemporary *The Revolt of Islam* (1817–18), despite its anti-utopian concern with the failure of the revolutionary impulse and the repeated return of tyranny after the French Revolution. Towards the end of the poem, its hero and heroine Laon and Cythna (the people, and the seed of the future) are sacrificed by fire, but disintegration into ashes is not (as it is for Frankenstein's creature) the end: after death Laon wakes in an ideal landscape and is taken to the Temple of the Spirit.

Human sacrifice in Percy Shelley is, manifestly, neither a religious nor an exalting experience: it frequently indicates the use of religion to sanctify political oppression, and is consistent with his view that all the manifold gods of the earth are fictions whose purpose is to justify the single human impulse to tyranny.[12] The sacrifice in *The Revolt of Islam* is an exercise of pure power, but it nevertheless prompts a constructive reaction: if not the gateway to a higher state, it is the extreme whose opposite is the higher state. In his early poem *Queen Mab*, Shelley portrays temples whose 'costly altars smoked / With human blood' (7.98–9), and emphasizes the role of Christ's 'sacrifice' in sanctioning massacres (7.142, 176–8). In addition (in the notes) he equates the irrational belief in Christian revelation with the violent and absurd superstitions of exotic religions, including Hindu and Aztec human sacrifice: 'The Mahometan dies fighting for his prophet, the Indian immolates himself at the chariot-wheels of Brahma, the Hottentot worships an insect, the Negro a bunch of feathers, the Mexican sacrifices human victims!' (pp. 824–5). He looks forward, however, to a state of perfect justice: a vegetarian, like Mary Shelley's creature, he foresees a time when man will no longer feed on animal flesh, and in which the 'Happy Earth' will become the 'consummation of all mortal hope!' (9.4). How different from the ending of *Frankenstein*, where the creature's sacrifice will 'consummate the series of my being'; where consummation is merely a return to matter.

While working on the male creature, Frankenstein looks forward to the 'consummation of my toils' (p. 34); during his work on the female, he is in the original version intent on 'the 'sequel' of my labour' (p. 142), sequel becoming 'consummation' in the revision.[13] In both editions, Frankenstein awaits the arrival of the creature on his wedding night, believing that he intended 'On that night . . . to consummate his crimes by my death' (p. 165; p. 158). Obviously, the consummation is the death of the bride, and the occurrence of the word at these three linked violations of normal sexual procreation plays on the sexual sense of the word. Yet, because *consummation* has a primarily sexual meaning today, we must not dull our ears to its earlier, far wider, range of meaning, and not all uses of the word here bear a sexual connotation: 'That is also my victim!' the creature exclaims to Frankenstein, 'In his murder my crimes are consummated' (p. 194); when the creature protests that he suffered more 'in the consummation of the deed' than Frankenstein (p. 194), he is not only describing the death of Elizabeth.

Consummation suggests a teleological view of life. It corresponds to the Aristotelian *telos* (end, goal) or *entelecheia* (full, complete reality). Instructing Milton's Adam in the dynamic actualization of potential which is the purpose of any created being, Raphael describes the growth of the plant from the root to 'the bright consummate flower'.[14] When the creation is complete apart from the making of man, the earth 'Consummate lovely smiled' (7.502). Aquinas uses *consummation* to refer to the end of the world: '*the consummation of the world* will be at the end of the world'; the Day of Judgment is 'the final consummation'.[15] Yet the idea of the *telos* has an ambiguity that is perfectly reproduced in its most common English translation, *end*. An end is a goal, but also an arbitrary termination. The ambiguity of the word runs through the career of that first great exemplar of the Faust figure, Marlowe's Faustus. This is what Mary Shelley offers us. A world without a goal. A world where personal goals turn to ice or ashes: Walton's polar destination simply does not exist. The destination of Walton, Frankenstein, the creature, and the world is – ice.

Mary Shelley's *Frankenstein* is not an exposition of Buffon's work, but it grows out of experiences which called him to Percy Shelley's mind. It charts its own movement between fire and ice, and (like *The Last Man*) is a work about extinction. *Extinguish* and its cognates pervade the work, primarily in opposition to the Promethean fire with which the creature was made: Frankenstein longs to 'extinguish that life which I had so thoughtlessly bestowed' (p. 73). The word has a broader meaning, however, for the novel portrays the creation and sacrificial extinction of a new species: a sacrificial extinction that is necessary to prevent that of the human race. 'I could not sacrifice the whole human race' (p. 163), Frankenstein protests. 'Do not think that I shall be slow to perform this sacrifice', the creature tells Walton, when he meets him on the ice at the end of the novel: 'Light, feeling, and sense, will pass away . . . Soon these burning miseries will be extinct. I shall ascend my funeral pile triumphantly, and exult in the agony of the torturing flames' (pp. 197–8). The sacrifice here methodically undoes the creation of body and the formation of consciousness: it is the reversal of a chemical process, reducing the creature's complex body and infinitely ranging thoughts to the lifeless uniformity of dust.

On first coming to consciousness, the creature had learned, gradually, to distinguish and differentiate. It was some time before he could even 'distinguish between the operations of my various senses' (p. 82). Knowledge becomes a process of distinguishing and associating: realizing that birdsong goes with birds, for example. He learns the difference of the sexes. He learns the use of fire in cooking, and which fruits benefit from cooking and which do not. Yet he also learns from reading Volney the unjust differentiations of power and property that deface human society. And, in culmination, he learns his own utter difference.

Differentiation had, of course, been the foundation of culture in *Robinson Crusoe*: it is there associated with the imposition of cultural order with the knife or the double-column account. Differentiation for Crusoe is always total. Here, the combined process of differentiation and association suggests that both are used in combination to apprehend the world as a set of organic relationships. The principle of pure differentiation is more associated with the kind of science that Frankenstein rejects: 'The professor discoursed with the greatest fluency of potassium and boron, of sulphates and oxyds, terms to which I would affix no idea' (p. 24). The elements of potassium and boron were isolated by Humphrey Davy in 1807–8, the former by means of electrolysis: an, as it were, analytic use of electricity which contrasts with the synthetic use to which Frankenstein puts it. Oxides and sulphates are inorganic compounds first described by Lavoisier in the 1780s, but not until the work of Friedrich Wöhler in 1828 was it realized that organic compounds could also be artificially synthesized; they had previously been thought to have been manufactured by a vital principle. *Frankenstein* emerges in the hiatus between the births of inorganic and organic chemistry. For Frankenstein's is an imagination which delights in the organic; it is a Romantic imagination, thriving on aesthetic interplay and interdependence. And it is in its collision with the intractably alien, extra-mental world of inorganic matter that the tragedy of the novel (and, perhaps, of humanity) resides.

The creature is created with all the benevolent and compassionate impulses that are theoretically necessary for a perfect society. He is a vegetarian, never falling into the carnivorousness that the Pythagoreans associated with human sacrifice, and already in that state that Shelley in *Queen Mab* had associated with the 'consummation of all mortal hope!' Yet he is rejected because he violates the aesthetic canons of beauty; because of an inappropriate interplay of difference and likeness:

> His limbs were in proportion, and I had selected his features as beautiful. Beautiful! – Great God! His yellow skin scarcely covered the work of muscles and arteries beneath; his hair was of a lustrous black, and flowing; his teeth of a pearly whiteness; but these luxuriances only formed a more horrid contrast with his watery eyes, that seemed almost of the same colour as the dun white sockets in which they were set, his shrivelled complexion, and straight black lips. (p. 38)

The creature is the prime example of the clash between the essence of things and the templates of the imagination.

In his flight from society, the creature moves into mountain and Arctic regions whose sublime spaces provided a mirror to Romantic sensibility, as in Percy Shelley's reflections on Mont Blanc, written at the same time as *Frankenstein* was conceived:

> Dizzy Ravine! and when I gaze on thee
> I seem as in a trance sublime and strange
> To muse on my own separate fantasy
> My own, my human mind. (*Mont Blanc*, 34–7)

In the same landscape, Frankenstein experiences a contrary relationship between the self and the landscape. The comfort and exaltation provided by its sublimity is dispelled by a quite different form of encounter with his 'own separate fantasy', in the appearance of the hideous and uncontrollable monster. '[W]hy', Frankenstein asks, 'does man boast of sensibilities superior to those apparent in the brute[?]' (p. 78). Increasingly, however, he loses these sensibilities. In the pursuit of the creature, scenes of aesthetic sublimity degenerate into ones of material terror; for it requires a certain level of culture and economic security to find mountains beautiful. Tracking his quarry, sticking to the courses of streams like a primitive man, Frankenstein experiences the landscape from the standpoint of a rapidly diminishing level of civilization. Writing, one of Prometheus' gifts, the apogee of the creature's cultural education, is used only for the prey to leave derisive messages in a barren landscape.

The novel portrays a conflict between the synthesizing, transforming imagination and the refractory qualities of the material world. In his fascination with Albertus Magnus, Cornelius Agrippa, and Paracelsus, Frankenstein implies that the old synthesis of science and transformative magic is still latent in the age of Sir Humphrey Davy. Magic and alchemy certainly had a profound fascination for the Romantic mind. Goethe had immersed himself in alchemical literature in his youth, and in Part I of *Faust* the protagonist summons up the spirits of the four elements, calling them by the names coined by Paracelsus: Salamander, Undine, Sylph, Gnome. In Part II, in addition, he creates a homunculus of fire. Fouqué's Undine bears the name invented by Paracelsus, and Nathanael's father in 'The Sandman' conducts secret alchemical experiments, which initiate the confused and unstable relationship between Nathanael's consciousness and the world of matter, most extremely expressed in his love for the mechanical doll.

In *Frankenstein*, the power of the magical is seen in the spontaneous reversion to ritual in moments of primitive emotion. When the creature initially gives way to his destructive hatred of humanity, he firstly assaults culture, as manifested in the cultivation of the earth, destroying 'every vestige of cultivation in the garden' (p. 135). He then performs a fire ritual, dancing 'with fury around the devoted cottage' (p. 117) until the precise point at which the moon has set, whereupon he burns the cottage. This ritual is counterbalanced by the final sacrifice, also a ritual of fire. When, after the murder of Elizabeth, Frankenstein dedicates himself to his vengeful hunting of the creature ('as a beast of prey' (p. 176)), he kneels and solemnly invokes another element, the earth: 'I knelt on the grass, and kissed the earth, and with quivering lips exclaimed, "By the sacred earth on which I kneel, . . . I swear to pursue the dæmon . . . [L]et him feel the despair that now torments me"' (p. 178); fellow-feeling can now only be a fellow-feeling of torment. There is thus a sequence of rituals in *Frankenstein*, each marking some relinquishment of culture: the destruction of agriculture, the commitment to vengeance and the hunt, the final sacrifice. In addition, there is one further ritual in the novel. This is the false confession of Justine to the murder of William – forced from her by the threat of 'hell fire' (p. 67).

The rituals centre upon the old elements of earth and fire, and it is difficult to imagine similar rituals with the newly discovered elements: one cannot ritually kiss potassium, or ritually sacrifice oneself with boron. Though central to these rituals of destruction, however, earth and fire are also the elements which predominate in the making of the creature: 'lifeless clay' (p. 36) and Promethean fire. Fire inevitably sums up the ambiguity of culture: in his first encounter with fire, the creature learns about the raw and the cooked, yet the fire destroys culture, and is to destroy him. It is fire that powers the gun. Whereas the gun in *Robinson Crusoe* is the means of imposing culture, it here illustrates the capacity of culture to destroy itself: when the creature rescues a young girl from drowning, a rustic *fires* a gun at him (p. 119). When Frankenstein uselessly 'carried pistols and a dagger constantly about me' (p. 168) after the creature's threat to be with him on his wedding night, the weapons represent his cultural descent into the hunter. It is notable that only at a very late state in his career, when he has become obsessively caught up in the hunt, is Frankenstein identified as a flesh-eater.

It is obvious that fire is both creative and destructive. What is distinctive here is the way in which fire both fascinates the imagination and encapsulates its processes and extremes. Walton 'glow[s]' (p. 4) with enthusiasm for his polar project. Frankenstein is inspired to his dreams of creation by the lightning bolt which reduces an old and beautiful oak to a blasted stump, with which he later comes to identify himself: 'I am a blasted tree; the bolt has entered my soul' (p. 138). At the end, the 'feverish fire' (p. 189) in the eyes of the dying Frankenstein both prefigures the creature's sacrificial pyre and contrasts with 'the warm fire-sides' (p. 190) to which Walton's crew insist on returning. Fire replicates the workings of the Romantic imagination in a way that the science of Lavoisier and Davy does not. It is an imagination that is poetically creative yet materially destructive; the solitary dreamer moves from isolation to desolation, and from desolation to that inevitable fate both of fire and of species, extinction. In the 1831 edition of

Frankenstein, Walton exclaims 'how gladly I would sacrifice my fortune, my existence, my every hope, to the furtherance of my enterprise. One man's life or death were but a small price to pay for the acquirement of the knowledge which I sought; for the dominion I should acquire and transmit over the elemental foes of our race' (p. 35). Though in the first sentence the sacrificial victim is Walton himself, it is no longer exclusively he in the second. No individual must interrupt the visionary scheme. One thinks of the elderly couple of Philemon and Baucis in Part II of *Faust* (1832), who are burned to death because their cottage stands in the way of Faust's scheme to create a 'paradiesisch' realm by ocean reclamation.[16]

Yet, though proposed by Walton, the sacrifice of individuals to an imaginary and utopian goal is more truly the prerogative of Frankenstein. In both characters, we see an imagining of alternative worlds that threatens to obliterate the real one. It is a Romantic impulse, but also a masculine one, worthy of 'the manly and heroical poetry of Greece and Rome' (p. 50). If Frankenstein resembles that earlier visitor to Ingolstadt, the historical Dr Faustus,[17] Walton is transparently based on Dante's Ulysses, who had deserted son, father, and wife for a last voyage into the barren, unpopulated ocean. The visionary solitary is also a sexual solitary, following a drive whose logical goal is the cessation of reproduction and the disappearance of the species. Immediately after the creation of the creature, Frankenstein has a vision of Elizabeth, who turns at his kiss into his mother's worm-eaten corpse: into the decaying matter on which his asexual imagination has forced life.

This incident clearly foreshadows the interrupted wedding night, and also helps to explain it. It may be tempting to see the demonically interrupted consummation as unvaryingly representing the incursion of repressed or unacknowledged desires into officially sanctioned areas of sexuality. That may, frequently, be the function of such episodes, but it is not so here. Rather, Mary Shelley is reworking and giving new meaning to a convention, which she could have found in *Fantasmagoriana*, the book of ghost stories that inspired the contest in the Villa Diodati. In the tale of 'La Morte Fiancée', the hero is fatally seduced on his wedding day by (apparently) the dead sister of his bride; she is really, however, the ghost of a faithless woman who is condemned to tempt men until she finds one who can resist her (an idea to be far more profoundly explored in Wagner's *Parsifal*).[18] The interrupted wedding night in *Frankenstein* is quite different: it represents the extinction of sexuality, as a foretaste of the extinction of the species.

MELMOTH THE WANDERER

An even more complex study of the sacrificial impulse than *Frankenstein* is Charles Maturin's Gothic novel *Melmoth the Wanderer* (1820). Its titular character has, in the mid seventeenth century, made a pact with the devil in exchange for 150 years of life. He is an equivalent to Faust, and another figure whose body is released from its normal relationship to time and space: he is, explicitly, 'independent of time and place'.[19] The novel is an intricate series of multiply embedded narratives which suspends any sense of chronological sequence. These describe Melmoth's consistently unsuccessful attempts to reduce characters to such despairing misery and danger that, in return for immediate rescue, they will release him from his contract and take it upon themselves. The attempt to find a surrogate victim to avert his damnation is, of course, a reversal of Christ's sacrifice, and it is a reversal which finds parallels in many of the cultures portrayed in the novel, particularly that of Catholic Spain: '[B]ut if men were taught to look to the *one great Sacrifice*, would they be so ready to believe that their own, or those of others, could ever be accepted as a commutation for it?' (p. 147). An example of the use of the sacrificial surrogate is the mother who attempts to atone for her youthful sexual transgressions by forcing her sons into a monastic life which they abhor; one of them tells his superior (in vain) that he will not be the sacrificial substitute for the father or brother (p. 96). Sacrifice is seen as being a natural and all but universal consequence of an instrumental view of others: an extreme differentiation of subject and object.

There is a point in the novel at which the skeletons of some of Melmoth's victims appear in a collection along with mammoth bones (and the bones of an alligator); as in *Frankenstein*, sacrifice is once again modified by being seen in the context of geological time and process. The bones are in a collection rather than a layer of rock, but the juxtapositions do suggest a shockingly dislocated context for the sacrificed body, both in the sense that it becomes a curio and in that it ends up in a collection without a system, though one which implies a huge – if imaginatively unpatterned – expanse of time. In a way different from Melmoth's body, these relics are independent of time and place.

What is the relationship of the body to time in the novel? Melmoth's independence of time is, paradoxically, limited by time: it is, in the most etymologically literal and intense sense of the word, temporary. Unlike the Fausts of Spohr and Goethe, he has the old-style contract that is limited by an expiry date. When the deadline is about to run out, he dreams that a mysterious force pushes him over a precipice into the ocean. There is

> a dial-plate fixed on the top of that precipice . . . He saw the mysterious single hand revolve – he saw it reach the appointed period of 150 years – (for in this mystic plate centuries were marked, not hours) . . . His last despairing reverted glance was fixed on the clock of eternity – the upraised black arm seemed to push forward the hand – it arrived at its period – he fell – he sunk – he blazed – he shrieked! The burning waves boomed over his sinking head, and the clock of eternity rung out its awful chime – 'Room for the soul of the Wanderer!' (p. 539)

This is a unique and haunting climax, yet at the same time one which transmutes into infernal nightmare something which had happened in lesser nightmares throughout the novel: constriction of the mind and the body until they become merely part of the mechanisms of time. This phenomenon particularly characterizes the ritualized, repetitive life of the monastery, where monks 'occupied themselves whole hours in taking minutes of their consciences' (pp. 131–2). 'I am a clock that has struck the same minutes and hours for sixty years', confesses one (p. 110). Striking of the clock or tolling of the bell divide and demarcate many episodes of the narrative: when the innocent child of nature, Immalee, falls into the hands of the Inquisition, for example, bells mark the stages of her examination.

In another episode, a young Englishwoman is cheated of the man she loves, and reverts to the soullessly mechanical observances of Puritanism: 'She rose at a fixed hour, – at a fixed hour she prayed, – at a fixed hour received the godly friends who visited her ... Her life was mere mechanism, but the machine was so well wound up, that it appeared to have some quiet consciousness and sullen satisfaction in its movements' (p. 475). For his attempts to be released from the monastery, Monçada (the young monk sacrificed to atone for his mother's sexual transgressions) is imprisoned in the dark without any timepiece. He tries to keep time internally, but fears that he is counting faster than the clock: 'Had I led this life much longer, I might have been converted into the idiot, who, as I have read, from the habit of watching a clock, imitated its mechanism so well, that when it was down, he sounded the hour as faithfully as ear could desire' (p. 147).

In his attempts to become a clock mechanism, Monçada 'oscillated, reckoned, and measured time' (p. 147). A mechanically regular, yet uncontrollable, oscillation between opposite states is another manifestation of the body that has become a timepiece. In a madhouse in Restoration England, for example, there is a lunatic who, for half the day, imagines himself a supralapsarian preacher, secure of salvation, and denounces 'damnation against Papists, Arminians, and even Sublapsarians'; yet 'At night his *creed retaliates on him*; he believes himself one of the reprobates he has been all day denouncing, and curses God for the very decree he has all day been glorifying Him for' (p. 57).

Similar oscillations – between libertinism and austerity, ecstasy and despair – permeate the novel. They suggest the warping of the free flow of life in ways which push it and the body to the condition of the machine, or even of the completely immobile artefact. Characters fall into states of rigour and rigidity, again primarily associated with Catholicism ('rigour' is for Maturin a distinctively Spanish quality), though not exclusively so. Hearing that she is to be forced by her Spanish parents to marry a man she does not love, the erstwhile child of nature, Immalee, freezes into the 'rigidity' of a statue (p. 374). Although the rigidity is in part cultural, it is a cultural custom which accentuates one aspect of the body: its capacity for death. Reproaching a kinsman who is imagined to have dishonoured his family, an Anglican matriarch cries: 'insult not the portraits of your ancestors – insult not their living representative', only to fall at once in the 'rigid constriction' of death (p. 480).

Both these examples of rigidity show the body approximating to the state of an artefact: Immalee becomes like a statue; the matriarch becomes as lifeless as the portraits. Although Maturin shows an immense sensitivity to art, he also equates the abstraction of the body into art with the stilling of the body into death. One of Melmoth's groups of victims is a Protestant family, the Walbergs, lured to Spain on the promise of an inheritance and reduced to desperate indigence. To get food, the son of the family covertly sells his blood to a surgeon, in another version of the sacrificial theme. At one point he is discovered, covered in blood, and with a 'corse-like beauty . . . worthy the pencil of a Murillo, a Rosa'; he is like 'A St Bartholomew flayed, with his skin hanging about him in graceful drapery' (pp. 421–2). The passage crucially depends on the full aesthetic power of the artefacts that are being evoked. Yet there is a terrible gap between the body as representation and the body as experience: this gap is what makes possible instrumental sacrifice. One of the uncanny things about Melmoth is that the gap between him and his representation is suspended, since one feature of his seeming exemption from time is that he continues to remain like his portrait of over a century before. For others, however, the confusion of experience and representation is painful and disorienting. During his imprisonment in the monastery, Monçada is tormented with artificial mimicries of demonic temptations: 'When art assumes the omnipotence of reality,' he says, 'when we feel we suffer as much from an illusion as from truth, our sufferings lose all dignity and all consolation' (p. 157).

'In Catholic countries, . . . religion is the national drama' (p. 165), manoeuvring the body into the condition of the staged image as well as of the painted artefact. In doing so, however, Catholicism distils to extremes the potentialities of other cultures. Yet another of Melmoth's victims is the Englishman Stanton, who is unjustly incarcerated in a madhouse. The fatal encounter with Melmoth occurs in the theatre, at a (historically recorded) performance of Nathaniel Lee's *The Rival Queens* during which the actress Elizabeth Barry had stabbed and wounded her rival and co-star, Elizabeth Bowtell. There is a synthesis between the body as an object of display and as an object of violence whose ultimate expression is the *auto-da-fe*.

Maturin does not present us with an ideal counterpart to these dysfunctional petrifications of the body. He presents us rather with conflicting extremes, a social equivalent to the oscillations he detects in the individual mind. True, the culture of Catholicism pre-eminently nourishes the sacrificial impulse, but there is a primordial and indeed pre-human element that lurks corrosively at the heart of any grouping and, when exposed, leads to human sacrifice: competition for food. One of the most famous episodes in the novel concerns a young man who is forced to become a monk in order to prevent him from making a socially inappropriate marriage.

His beloved joins him in the monastery, disguised as another monk. They are found out, and are locked together in a dark room to die. When the desperation of hunger takes over, the young man sinks his teeth into the flesh of the woman he until recently loved. Hunger can even break up what for Maturin is clearly the ideal social unit: the Protestant nuclear family of the Walbergs. Reduced to the verge of starvation, they start to resent the appetite of their aged father, whose feebleness means that he can only consume and not contribute.

Thus, when the mechanisms of society fail, the relationship between human beings rapidly resolves itself into that of competitors for food, or into eater and eaten. Along with mammoth bones and the skeletons of sacrificial victims, the elderly Jew's collection of curios also contains the skeleton of an alligator. One sacrificial cult mentioned in the book involves the sacrifice of parents to alligators (p. 275), so here the skeleton of a sacrificer lies inertly beside those of the sacrificed. The old Jew's collection of curios holds in a hibernating potential the extremes to which the instrumental use of the body can reduce the human form: a predator; a victim; a lifeless artefact; a fossil.

The closest *Melmoth the Wanderer* comes to an ideal is the initially pure child of nature, Immalee: the daughter of Spanish Catholic parents, shipwrecked in infancy on an Indian island hitherto dedicated to infant sacrifice to the goddess (actually god) Seeva, and growing up in perfect harmony with nature. Her gentle fondness for life makes her the centre of a cult quite different from that of the terrible Seeva, whose idol with twenty serpentine mouths shows the approximation of religious consciousness to that of the reptilian predator.

Immalee lives in a world without difference: 'nothing of that world in which she lived had ever borne a hostile appearance to her'; the flowers, foliage, and birds 'were her friends, and she knew none but these' (p. 280). The 'periodical regularity' (p. 280) of elemental phenomena deprive them of their terrors, so that even the alternation of night and day, 'perhaps the primitive cause of fear in most minds' (p. 280), does not affect her. She lives in an environment whose alternations and cycles create no sense of rupture, no division of the self into separately objectified states, such as are experienced by the lunatic who thinks himself saved by day and damned by night. When Immalee talks about her 'friend', she means her reflection. In Milton's Eden, the reflection is dangerous, drawing its beholder into the deceptive maze of material images and away from God. Although he explicitly patterns Immalee's world upon Milton's Eden, Maturin uses the reflection in a completely contrary way, to suggest a primitivistic harmony between the self and nature. Immalee lives in a prolonged infancy, but her reflection is no more a Lacanian mirror image than a Miltonic one: it suggests that she has not yet experienced difference.

A further aspect of this harmony – and a further departure from Milton – is the absence of language from Immalee's paradise. She remembers language, but has no occasion to use it, and cannot write (p. 318). Language only becomes necessary when the stranger Melmoth enters her world and fascinates her with an unnerving combination of likeness and difference, unusually like her in body, yet utterly different in his outlandish European dress. In order to understand this disruption of her world, she for the first time starts to see it as a set of symbols: 'it was beautiful to see her attempting, from vegetable and animal analogies, to form some image of the incomprehensible destiny of man' (p. 287). She starts to choose desolate, inorganic, volcanic surroundings, surrounding herself with lifeless objects rather than a living landscape that expresses her own identity. Whereas before she loved everything, she now loves only one person. And she experiences a division of the self that recalls the oscillations of the religious madman: 'At night alone she existed' (p. 356).

Language itself becomes an illustration of the sacrificial principle – of the separation of the mind from its organic and immediate relationship with nature, and its acceptance of a system in which one sign can stand for another: the essence of sacrifice. *Melmoth* makes almost comically excessive use of the Gothic convention of the manuscript with gaps, but the device constantly reminds us that to write things is to turn them into unconscious and fragile matter. For language itself constitutes the division of the self from its surroundings, and the division of the self into subject and object. This is a division most spectacularly illustrated in the oscillation of the Puritan madman between hellfire preacher and cursing reprobate: the oscillation is between states of mind, but also states of language, since the lunatic's alternate state is always the prime object of his denunciations. 'To love', Melmoth tells Immalee, '. . . is to live in an existence of perpetual contradictions' (p. 364).

Yet language has another characteristic: repetition. The stranded Immalee grew up 'repeating to herself the few Christian words her nurse had taught her, in answer to the melody of the birds that sung to her' (p. 503), but the capacity of language for repetition becomes ominously intensified when Immalee swears to Melmoth that she will never marry her designated husband: 'I will first be the bride of the grave', she swears, whereupon Melmoth 'required her to repeat the words' (p. 374). (Similarly Elinor, the jilted Englishwoman who loses herself in repetitious Puritan worship, emptily repeats the last words of the lover who left her (p. 477).)

Forced out of her unbroken continuity and interchange with nature, Immalee falls desperately and irreversibly in love with the demonic tempter who has introduced her to difference and to symbolism. Whereas the prelapsarian love of Milton's Adam and Eve is the most perfect fruition in the garden, Immalee's love leads to a complete reversal of her paradise, and of the Miltonic bower: a Satanic wedding in a ruined and isolated chapel, conducted (as it turns out) by a dead priest. The character whose prelinguistic innocence turned a sacrificial site into a recreation of Paradise comes the closest of any character to being Melmoth's sacrificial victim. She always retains her non-predatory nature, and she is not corrupted by suffering in the way that the Walbergs or the young lovers in the monastery are. Once, however, Melmoth ruptures the unity of her world by introducing an opposition of subject and object, of signifier and signified, she embraces the relationship of sacrificed to sacrificer.

Theologically, *Melmoth the Wanderer* opposes the internalized reception of Christ's sacrifice both to the Catholic doctrine of works, which easily leads to the treatment of others as sacrificial instruments, and to the rigours of predestinarianism, which restrict the meaning of the one true sacrifice. Yet what concerns Maturin more than the evils of any creed is the fact of interfaith hostility: the structure of difference. He alludes, for example, to the characters of Testimony and Hothead in John Crowne's Restoration comedy *Sir Courtly Nice* (1685), a Puritan and an Anglican, equally bigoted, who engage in a constant Tweedledum and Tweedledee conflict, the only point of which is the conflict itself (p. 52). No-one, however, actually realizes his apparently simple ideal of internalized sacrifice. The pure Immalee is led by her very purity into marriage to a Satanist, and Maturin seems to suggest that the sacrificial principle is born in the very moment that the consciousness separates itself from the surrounding organism of nature. It is implicit in the genesis of language and, still more, of writing, which creates a division between the self and its representations. It is implicit in the measurement of time, which divides the present self from the past self. To be without time is unendurable, as Monçada discovers during his imprisonment, yet time enslaves man to ritual and repetition, a characteristic it shares with the repetitive nature of language. *Melmoth the Wanderer* appears frustratingly without context, since it is Maturin's only major work. Yet it is fascinating in seeing the sacrificial principle as being dangerously implicit in the acquisition of language and the consciousness of time.

EARLY ROMANTIC OPERA

A year after *Melmoth* there appeared a work which, like *Frankenstein* and Polidori's *The Vampyre*, derives from the book of German ghost stories whose partial translation the Shelley circle had been reading in 1816: Weber's *Der Freischütz*, based on a story in the *Gespensterbuch* of Apel and Laun. The story is well known to opera-lovers. It is set in seventeenth-century Bohemia, in a village and its sinister forest surroundings. The forester Max is in love with Agathe, daughter of the hereditary chief forester, but to gain her hand he must win a shooting contest. Kaspar, a rejected and vengeful suitor of Agathe, has sold his soul to the Black Huntsman Samiel (the Devil), and needs to supply him with another victim (*Opfer*) in order to gain another year on earth. He is trying to entrap Max and has jinxed his marksmanship, so that he now shoots with humiliating ineptitude. Understandably, Max fears that he will perform badly at the shooting trial and consequently lose Agathe. Depressed and impressionable, he is seduced by Kaspar into making a pact with Samiel. This will give him seven magic bullets, to ensure success in the shooting trial. Although six will hit their intended target, however, the seventh will go as the devil chooses.

On the morning of the shooting trial – which is intended to be her wedding morning – Agathe opens the box which should contain her bridal garland, only to find that it contains a funeral wreath. And, when Max aims at a dove in the shooting trial, the dove is a magically transformed Agathe, though the bullet aimed at her – the devil's bullet – claims the life of Kaspar instead. When Max confesses his crime – a crime, he insists, of weakness rather than ingrained evil – the Prince at first banishes him, but is induced by a hermit to show mercy. The custom of the shooting trial is abolished.

It is an opera of averted sacrifice, princely clemency, and the elimination of an archaic and unjust custom: all topics familiar from Metastasio. Yet there are obviously many Romantic features in addition to the famous ghostly effects of the Wolf's Glen scene during which the magic bullets are cast: the demonically interrupted wedding ritual, for example, and the transformation of the bride into a non-human object of the hunt.

Der Freischütz celebrates the triumph of civilization, yet at the same time (not entirely advertently) hints at its fragility. We see the redemption of a village, not a kingdom; a village on the edge of the forest, within which Samiel continues to haunt the Wolf's Glen; a village in a land recently ravaged by the Thirty Years' War. In libretti such as *Demofoönte*, the sacrificial ritual is public, acknowledged, and decisively abolished. The shooting trial, however, is only privately, secretly, and anomalously a ritual of sacrifice, and the sacrificial impulse can no longer be contained by a change in public ritual. Instead of a decisive evolution of civilization, there is here a constant recurring presence of the demonic – or simply the supernaturally alien – within the same physical, mental, and social space that humanity inhabits. The Wolf's Glen remains.

Yet there is one thing that *Der Freischütz* avoids, and that is any sense of doubling between the spirit world and that of human culture, as happens in Fouqué's *Undine*. There is a simple conflict between good and evil. It was not, however, long before the two streams coalesced: before the technique of *Undine* was applied to the subject matter of *Der Freischütz*. Coincidentally, this coalescence also involved a coming together of the two developments of 1816: the ghost-story contest and the emergence of Romantic opera. For, in 1828, there appeared two operas, both called *Der Vampyr*, both ultimately derived from Polidori's *The Vampyre*, both concerned with demonically interrupted weddings, and both influential upon

Wagner, one profoundly and decisively so. Both were by composers who (like Meyerbeer) had begun their careers within the forms and outlook of Enlightenment opera. One was Peter Joseph von Lindpaintner, whose first opera was to a libretto derived from Metastasio's *Demofoönte*; the other, far better known, was Heinrich Marschner, whose first opera had been a setting of Metastasio's *La Clemenza di Tito*.[20] Both composers had by now decisively emerged from the eighteenth century. The Marschner version significantly influenced *Der Fliegende Holländer*, especially in the structure of the overture, the character of its accursed protagonist, and the monologue in which he expounds his fate. It also provided the framework for Wagner's début as an operatic composer. For his first operatic composition to receive a public performance was his rewriting of its tenor aria 'Like a beautiful spring morning' ('Wie ein schöner Frühlingsmorgen')[21] for performance by his brother Albert. Marschner's *Vampyr* is thus a pivotal work in the transmutation of sacrificial themes in nineteenth-century opera.

Polidori's story was based on a fragment of a vampire tale by Byron, and was originally published as Byron's work. Byron repudiated the attribution, and published his own fragment, but the repudiation was not widely known outside Britain, where the tale was still attributed to him; indeed, the title pages of the libretti for both the Marschner and the Lindpaintner operas claim Byron as a source.[22] The heroine of the tale marries a vampire and is killed by him on their wedding night. The death is not here imagined as a sacrifice, but the fatally interrupted wedding night was often portrayed in sacrificial terms, and the transformation into human sacrifice occurs in both the operatic versions.

As well as adapting the Polidori tale, the Lindpaintner opera also seems to draw on that other seminal sacrificial work, Goethe's 'Die Braut von Korinth'. For it portrays the return of a childhood fiancé believed dead (but in fact a vampire). In a hunt to celebrate the forthcoming wedding, the heroine becomes isolated from her companions in a storm, takes refuge in a cave, and is subjected to tempting and disturbing supernatural visions. She is thereby psychologically prepared for the interruption of her wedding by the vampire (given the name of Polidori's hero, Aubri), rejects her destined husband, and spends the rest of the opera in a state of dazed fascination with her tempter, her final descent to Hell only prevented because her father exerts his patriarchal rank and forbids the devil to take her. In the second act, Aubri interrupts another wedding, and entrances the peasant bride, as Don Giovanni had entranced Zerlina. I shall be with you on your wedding-night, indeed. Mesmerically obsessed with a demonic, otherworldly figure, Lindpaintner's heroines foreshadow Wagnerian figures such as Senta and Elsa.

The foreshadowing of Wagner is still more evident in the Marschner *Vampyr* (to which, as noted above, Wagner at the beginning of his career contributed a revised aria). This opera takes over and inflates the sacrificial theme of *Der Freischütz*: in order to gain another year on earth, Lord Ruthven, the vampire, has, within twenty-four hours, to deliver 'Three victims . . . three tender and chaste brides' ('drei Opfer . . . drei Bräute zart und rein') (Act 1, p. 14). Indeed, as he reflects, in extension of the sacrificial language, 'Two victims are already consecrated to me' ('Zwei Opfer sind mir schon geweiht') (Act 1, p. 19). And so they are: only one of the three sacrifices is averted. Prior to that, Ruthven disrupts two weddings and fatally claims the bride. He intends to acquire his third victim (the heroine, Malwina) by marrying her himself, but he misses his deadline and descends to Hell during the preparations for his own wedding.

The chief innovation of this work is in the altered relationship it achieves between the sacrificer and his victims, for he is, potentially, their double as well as their opposite. The D major/minor overture follows the pattern of the *Freischütz* overture (and prefigures that of *Der Fliegende Holländer*) in pitting chromatic, demonic themes against exultantly redemptive music associated with the heroine. Here, the overture plays out the conflict between Ruthven and Malwina, and her eventual triumph. Yet the overture has one very strange feature. As I have argued in detail elsewhere,[23] the heroine's themes are derivatives of the vampire's: she is individuated from within his music. Although the textual relationship between her and Ruthven remains one of uncomplicated antithesis, the initial musical relationship between the damned soul and the pious heart is one of deep and mysterious identity. Here the doubling of *Undine* is applied to the subject matter of *Der Freischütz.*

It is never clear how Ruthven became a vampire. He obviously has a noble past, and the memory of his lost capacity for compassion intrudes even in an aria of bloodlust transparently modelled on Don Pizarro's decidedly uncompassionate vengeance aria in *Fidelio*, 'Ha welch' ein Augenblick'. In an another, anguished, aria, derived from a speech from Byron's *Giaour* that Polidori had quoted in the introduction to *The Vampyre*,[24] Ruthven tells Edgar how his compulsion had driven him to destroy his entire family, including his youngest, favourite daughter (Act 2, pp. 27–33). This is where Ruthven also reveals himself as Edgar's potential double. In the past, he had saved Edgar's life, and at the beginning of the opera a sense of his indebtedness impels Edgar to help Ruthven when he comes upon him after he has been wounded by the father of his first victims. At Ruthven's request, he draws him to where the moonlight can shine on him. He realizes what this request implies, but swears to keep Ruthven's secret, and is bound by the oath even when he realizes that his beloved Malwina is one of Ruthven's designated victims. Ruthven tells his history to impress on Edgar that it might also be his history: it will be if he breaks his oath.

In *Idomeneo*, civilization could evolve beyond the superstitious tyranny of the oath. Not so here. What is yet more striking, however, is the transformation in the figure of the saviour. Mozart's Idamante had earned his release from sacrifice by saving the people from a sea monster. At the end of *Fidelio*, the Chorus insistently hail Leonora as a saviour: 'Retterin'. Here, however, the bestowing of life is as morally complex as it is in *Frankenstein*. The *Retter* of the opera is Ruthven, and the debt he incurs, and claims, is the source of all the danger and horror. Moreover, the word *retten* is repeatedly associated with impotence or irony. The father of Ruthven's first victim begs his servants to save her ('rettet') (Act I, p. 39) even as she is being murdered, and the bridegroom of the second, Emmy, twice begs that she be saved even though he knows that she is really dead. Edgar is despairingly helpless to prevent the death of Emmy, and he is an utterly impotent figure in his protection of Malwina, able only to use delaying tactics and to utter veiled and crazed warnings. Nor is there is a Neptune, Jehovah, or Hermit to release the hero from the consequences of his rash pact; there is simply the primitive, irrational inviolability of the oath. For the sacrificial forces against which the virtuous characters battle are persistent and internal.

Throughout the eighteenth century, attention moved more and more to the subjective consciousness of the sacrificer or victim. Now the subjective consciousness is itself the area of conflict, as characters confront shadowy sacrificers who are in some sense their psychic doubles. Yet the doubled characters tend to be from a radically different sphere of existence – a vampire, water sprite, revenant, or monster – so that the antagonists are now both more alike and more unlike than they had been before. At the same time, there is also frequently a sense of humanity standing precariously on the boundary of a further form of otherness: the inorganic simulacra of life in the fossil record; the mammoth bones that feature in *Melmoth*. All these currents coalesce in the work of the nineteenth century's greatest exponent of sacrifice, Richard Wagner. Indeed, as we shall see, *Parsifal* (his final work) expressed a historical vision that was partly shaped by meditation on the mammoth skeletons in Siberia.

CHAPTER 11

Wagner

WOMANHOOD AND SACRIFICE

The influence of *Der Vampyr* upon Wagner has long been recognized. Ruthven's second victim, Emmy, sings a ballad about a vampire – a pale man ('bleiche Mann') – immediately before the pale man startles her with his entrance (Act 2, pp. 12–13). This device is repeated (down to the phrase 'bleiche Mann') in *Der Fliegende Holländer*. Ruthven's tortured account of the curse under which he labours is the closest parallel in pre-Wagnerian opera to the Dutchman's great monologue, 'Die Frist ist um' ('The term is expired'). And the D minor/major overture is similar both in key structure and in design, pitting the themes of a tortured, cursed male against those of a radiant woman. There are, of course, differences. Unlike Marschner's heroine Malwina, Senta is longingly obsessed with the doomed wanderer, and finally leaps into the sea to redeem him from his curse. In contrast to her predecessors, she willingly submits to sacrifice.

There is a difference that is yet more fundamental. The thematic conflicts of Marschner's overture (like those of its model, Weber's overture to *Der Freischütz*) portray the struggle of opposed moral states, with piety triumphing over the demonic. Wagner's overture imitates this pattern, pitting the themes of the cursed and driven Dutchman against those of the redemptive Senta. Nevertheless, Wagner completely rethinks the patterns he has inherited, for the opposition of damnation and redemption is now identified with one between the male and female, two sexes being imagined as so contrary in their nature as to constitute different psychic conditions and spheres of moral experience. The overture to *Der Fliegende Holländer* is less a conflict between Heaven and Hell than one between the insatiable male drive for conquest and acquisition and the stillness of femininity, more centred on place and person. The restlessly unfulfilled motif of the Dutchman lands on the tonic only to bounce off it, and is subjected to turbulently chromatic modulation; that of Senta tends homeward to the tonic, weaving around it but never escaping its gravitational pull. Weber and Marschner associate their heroines with an exultant piety that is not gender-specific and is eventually shared in the final, mixed chorus. By contrast, not only are the last words of *Der Fliegende Holländer* sung solo by the heroine; no man ever sings the primary form of Senta's motif.

Weber's Wolf's Glen and Marschner's vampire are images of special and extraordinary horror. Roving the seas in his all-male community, in a ship loaded with the gains of global trade, by contrast, the Dutchman embodies something more general: the male expansionist and acquisitive impulse. This is also represented by Senta's father Daland, who within seconds of meeting the Dutchman is so impressed by his wealth that he is prepared to sell him his daughter and accept him as a son-in-law. Securely centred on its point of origin, however, Senta's melody suggests a calm negation of the striving will. This alone can rescue the Dutchman. The different spaces of *Der Freischütz* are the village and the Wolf's Glen; in *Der Fliegende Holländer*, they are the spheres of masculinity and femininity. They are also different stages of culture: in *Opera and Drama*, Wagner was to argue that the period of expansionist exploration of the external world was to be superseded by a more inward exploration of the individual and social life. This process is enacted in *Der Fliegende Holländer*.

The differences between the masculine and feminine spheres are encapsulated in a small musical figure that is associated with both, first introduced in the fourth bar of Senta's motif:[1]

This is the basis both of the all-male seaman's chorus at the end of Act 1 and the all-female Spinning Chorus at the beginning of Act 2 (in the original version of the opera, the one leads directly into the other); here, the girls back home wait for their menfolk to bring back gold from the South Seas. Yet, in the intermezzo between Acts 1 and 2, the melody of the sailors' chorus is set over a rising chromatic scale which persistently changes its harmonic centre of gravity, whereas in the Spinning Chorus it is tonally stable, generating a melody of symmetrically answering phrases. The different harmonic treatments of this tiny three-note phrase encapsulate the differences between male restlessness and unfulfilment and the repose offered by femininity.

'Woman,' Wagner wrote in *Opera and Drama* (1852),

> first gains her full individuality in the moment of surrender. She is the Undine [lit. maiden of the waves] who glides soulless through the waves of her native element, till she receives her soul through love of a man. The look of innocence in a woman's eye is the endlessly pellucid mirror in which the man can only see the general faculty for love, till he is able to see in it the likeness of himself. When he has recognised himself therein, then also is the woman's all-faculty condensed into one strenuous necessity, to love him with the all-dominant fervour of full surrender.

erhält volle Individualität erst im Momente der Hingebung. Es ist das Wellenmädchen, das seelenlos durch die Wogen seines Elementes dahinrauscht, bis es durch die Liebe eines Mannes erst die Seele empfängt. Der Blick der Unschuld im Auge des Weibes ist der endlos klare Spiegel, in welchem der Mann so lange eben nur die allgemeine Fähigkeit zur Liebe erkennt, bis er sein eigenes Bild in ihm zu erblicken vermag: hat er sich darin erkannt, so ist auch die Allfähigkeit des Weibes zu der einen drängenden Nothwendigkeit verdichtet, ihn mit der Allgewalt vollsten Hingebungseifers zu lieben.[2]

Whereas a courtesan ('Buhlerin') cannot 'sacrifice' (*opfern*) herself (*PW*, vol. II, p. 112; *GS*, vol. III, p. 316), the true woman is biologically programmed to sacrifice, because of her child-bearing function:

A woman *who really loves*, who sets her virtue in her *pride*, her pride, however, in her *sacrifice*; that sacrifice whereby she surrenders, not *one portion* of her being, but *her whole being* in the amplest fulness of its faculty – when she *conceives*. (*PW*, vol. II, pp. 114–15)

Ein Weib, das wirklich liebt, seine Tugend in seinen Stolz, seinen Stolz aber in sein Opfer setzt, in das Opfer, mit dem es nicht einen Theil seines Wesens, sondern sein ganzes Wesen in der reichsten Fülle seiner Fähigkeit hingiebt, wenn es empfängt. (*GS*, vol. III, p. 319)

The specific sacrifice of child-bearing (and of death in childbirth) is obviously imaginatively central to Wagner's operas: there is only one mortal mother in the mature operas (Sieglinde in *Die Walküre*), and she dies in childbirth. So did Tristan's mother. Parsifal's mother died through sorrow caused by his male wanderlust, and he cannot remember her until he recovers the memory in the moment of sexual awakening brought about by Kundry. The fathers die also, but in battle. Wagner's self-immolating heroines are doing for their men what they are predetermined to do for their child.

To illustrate the nature of woman, Wagner refers to the character of Undine, in Fouqué's novella. It is a significant imaginative association, for Undine is a being of a different species, striving to be released from her soullessness by the faithful love of a man. Wagner, too, repeatedly explores differences of sex by representing the male and female as beings of different species, and, in doing so, on several occasions reworks the pattern of the Undine story. The structure of her story – a supernatural, watery being, seeking redemption through the love of a mortal of divided affections – is, indeed, that of the Flying Dutchman's, though Wagner reverses the gender roles and grants a happy ending that is denied in the original. (In 1845, however, two years after *Der Fliegende Holländer*, Albert Lortzing's *Undine* supplied the happy ending to Fouqué's story, creating a clemency opera in which the errant hero is finally forgiven and received into the realm of the soulless water nymphs.)

Analogues to the *Undine* story, variously weighted, recur throughout Wagner's work: most obviously, in Brünnhilde's loss of immortality, and her rejection in favour of Gutrune, but also in Tannhäuser's rejection of Venus for her mortal antitype, Elisabeth. In adapting the story of Brünnhilde,

Wagner reshapes it according to the Undine pattern, for Brünnhilde's lost divinity is, essentially, his addition. Although she is described as a Valkyrie in the brief telling of the story in the prose *Edda*, she is a mortal in the *Volsunga Saga* and the *Niebelungenlied* (in the latter, she is a warrior queen who loses her strength along with her virginity). Brünnhilde's original immortality illustrates Wagner's habit of making women radically different in origin and sphere of activity from the men they come to love; Brünnhilde's very identity as a woman is itself a sacrifice. The representation of men and women as beings almost of different species naturally affects the conception of what human sacrifice is. It is not offering an extension of oneself (as Agamemnon must in *Iphigenia in Aulis*) or a fellow being mistakenly stigmatized as Other (as Iphigenia must in *Iphigenia among the Taurians*). Rather, it is entry into a sphere beyond differences of culture and biology.

The strongest analogue to *Undine* is in Wagner's first opera, *Die Feen* (1834), in which the fairy Ada seeks to renounce immortality in order to perpetuate her marriage to her mortal husband Arindal. Like Undine, she is rejected by the mortal she loves, though here the rejection is involuntary, and redeemable: in an anticipation of *Lohengrin*, Arindal is forbidden to ask his mysterious partner's name, and breaks the ban. As a condition of reconciliation, he then has to endure various apparent betrayals by Ada without cursing her, but fails, whereupon she is turned to stone. Eventually, however, he restores her to life with the power of song and finally becomes like her in immortality.

Until their final equalling as immortals, Ada and Arindal have been divided from each other by differences in form, kind, and species. If, towards the end of the opera, Ada is an intelligence trapped in lifeless stone, she had first appeared to Arindal as an animal: while out hunting, he had pursued the most beautiful doe he had ever seen. It had plunged into a river and vanished; he had followed, and awoken in a fairy kingdom. Many symbolic differences – of mortal and immortal, human and animal, animate and inanimate – are piled on to accentuate the literal one of sexual difference; unsurprisingly, separation (*Trennung*) is a key word in emphasizing such differences, as it is in many of the mature operas. The imagining of the woman as a being of alien species (which is hardly peculiar to Wagner) necessitates a profound shift in the understanding of female sacrifice. Equally, it necessitates a shift in imagining the relationship between sacrifice and the hunt; Ada first appeared to Arindal in the guise of an animal whom he was hunting.

SACRIFICE AND THE HUNT

Towards the end of *Die Feen*, insane with guilt at having cursed Ada, Arindal hallucinates that he has run down a doe in the hunt only to recognize the dying animal as his wife: a hallucination within a hallucination that strikingly replicates Agave's more irrevocable hallucination at the end of *The Bacchae*. Despite Wagner's later interest in Greek tragedy, the resemblance is probably accidental, yet it is at the same time revealing. Wagner is returning to a mythic representation of social and indeed human origins that gives the wilderness and the hunt a psychic power that they rarely had in the eighteenth century, and which is equivalent to that in Euripides. In his later prose works, Wagner sees man's transformation into a carnivore and hunter as a calamitous fall, caused by a prehistoric geological catastrophe which drove him from his temperate homeland to sterile, northern territories. In his last opera, *Parsifal*, the hero evolves beyond the role in which he first appears, of hunter, to being custodian of the Grail brotherhood's sacrificial relics. Similarly, his redemption of the seductress Kundry is of a character whose previous incarnations, as Herodias and Gundryggia (a Valkyrie), are figures associated in German legend with the Wild Hunt: he redeems her from her former roles both as temptress and huntress.

The relationship between culture and the activity of the hunt is repeatedly examined in Wagner's operas.[3] When Tannhäuser re-enters male society, he finds himself in the middle of a hunting party; at the end of the following act, he is himself threatened by the weapons of that same group, from which he is rescued by the intercession and the outlook of a woman, the heroine Elisabeth. During his night with Isolde, Tristan is absent from a hunt, whose calls are heard in the distance. Yet the hunt has been planned by Tristan's false friend Melot in order to trap the lovers: they are its true prey, for it is aimed at a nobler quarry ('edlern Wild') than they imagine.[4] As part of Wotan's attempt to reinvent culture from scratch, Siegmund is brought up as a hunter, yet as soon as he meets his feminine double, Sieglinde, his role changes, and he becomes the quarry of Hunding and his dogs. Siegfried also falls victim to Hagen during a hunt – Gunther denounces Hagen as 'the accursed boar / that rent the noble hero's flesh' ('der verfluchte Eber, / der diesen Edlen zerfleischt'),[5] and it is notable that Wagner turns Siegfried into a singularly unsuccessful huntsman; this is in contrast to the *Niebelungenlied*, where Siegfried also dies in a hunt, but one in which he distinguished himself, and of which he is not figured as the victim. Parsifal blunders into Montsalvat as a huntsman who kills a swan; he returns bearing a spear, transmuted from a weapon of blind violence to one of healing.

In the cases of Siegfried and Parsifal, the huntsman is a potentially regenerative reversion to the primitive; *wild*, a largely unfavourable word in Wagner's early operas, is in *The Ring* and *Parsifal* stretched to straddle the ambiguous boundary between savagery and primitive virtue. In other works, such as *Tannhäuser* and *Tristan*, the centrality of the hunt represents the monopolistic elaboration of male instincts in an advanced culture that has atrophied part of its original potential, and the cultural repudiation of the huntsman is at its clearest and starkest in *Der Fliegende Holländer*, where Senta's eventually rejected lover, Erik, is a huntsman. In the Spinning Chorus, the girls mock Senta about him: whereas their lovers bring gold from the South, he only brings game ('Bringt er nicht Gold, bringt er doch Wild') (Act 2.1, p. 103). The hunting is a relic from before a mercantile culture; but Senta goes beyond both. The terms on which she gives herself to the Dutchman are quite different from the commercial deal envisaged by her father.

Yet, in earlier Romantic works, the huntsman normally gets the girl. He does so, for example, in *Der Freischütz* and in *Die Schöne Müllerin*. Marschner's most famous opera, *Hans Heiling* (1833), is a *Fliegende Holländer* in reverse, in which a tormented supernatural figure (a male Undine, like the Dutchman) loses out to the local huntsman, despite the immense wealth he offers in a poor and economically resentful peasant society. Neither the spoils of the hunt, however, nor the goods of its successor, global trade, tempt Senta, and she goes on to an act of self-annihilation which completely reverses the principles on which male societies are built. In *Opera and Drama*, Wagner describes the outward thrust of the age of exploration and intellectual discovery as a necessary stage in the movement beyond the Middle Ages, but argues that it is necessary to go beyond this stage, 'to know the life of Man in the Necessity of its individual and social nature' ('das Leben des Menschen nach der Nothwendigkeit seiner individuellen und sozialen Natur zu erkennen') (*PW*, vol. II, p. 165; *GS*, vol. IV, p. 42). This is what happens in *Der Fliegende Holländer*. Cultural transition beyond the stage of expansionist wandering is the subject of many Wagner operas; the impulse which enables the transition is that to female self-immolation.

PROPERTY AND SACRIFICE

From Euripides onwards, critics of economic man have identified sacrifice with economic exchange: Marx approvingly quotes a reference in the *Daily Telegraph* (17 January 1860) to 'this slow sacrifice of humanity' and compares the all-devouring nature of capitalism to Moloch.[6] Wagner is certainly concerned with the trade in human bodies: indeed, he uses it as a fundamental example of economic transaction (as in the sale of Freia in *Das Rheingold*). He does not, however, use such trade as his model of sacrifice: rather, sacrifice is a self-abnegation that transcends and supersedes the trade in bodies. Daland – like Rocco in *Fidelio* – believes in money as the ruling principle of life, and is willing to sell Senta to the Dutchman. Whereas *Fidelio* moves beyond the cash nexus to a comprehensive political regeneration, however, *Der Fliegende Holländer* moves towards that solitary act beyond society on the boundary of the water: an act of sacrifice.

The opposition between the male property instinct and woman's maternal drive to self-immolation persists throughout Wagner's work, through profound changes of social and philosophic outlook. The conflict is most obvious in *The Ring*. In addition, the self-immolating passions of *Tristan* react against a primitive feudal economy based upon a more active principle of destruction, in which the primal currency is the human head: when Isolde's first lover Morold tries to collect tribute from Cornwall, the tribute ('Zins') that is sent back is his own head (Act 1.2, p. 37); later, accusing Tristan and Isolde of adultery, Tristan's false friend Melot stakes his head on the accusation. Isolde and Brünnhilde, however, do not only bring about a selfless undoing of an egocentric male economy – they also reject the idea of symbolic equivalence on which such economies depend, because they reject the idea of difference which is its precondition. Death brings an absolute identification with the loved one; an identification which is at the opposite pole from the economic convertibility symbolized in *The Ring* by that other product of the Rhinegold: the Tarnhelm, a magic helmet which enables the wearer to shapeshift and become invisible, enjoying a constant transformation of one identity into another. Death transcends that separation of man and woman into different species that had preoccupied Wagner since *Die Feen*. It even transcends language: when unseparated ('ungetrennt') they will also be nameless ('namenlos') (pp. 158–9).

As noted above, the heroine of *Die Feen* first appears to the hero in the guise of an animal: a doe whom he pursues in the hunt. In Act 2 of *Parsifal*, Klingsor's temptresses appear to the hero in the guise of flowers. In each case, the association of the feminine with an alien form is also an association with an alien place: the doe in *Die Feen* leads Arindal into the stream which forms the boundary with the immortal world; the Flower Maidens in *Parsifal* inhabit a magic realm of women ruled by a eunuch. Wagner, indeed, persistently accentuates differences of psychic identity by linking them to conflicting kinds of space or medium: land, subterranean cavities, and most obviously water, from Arindal's immersion in the stream onwards. Even in *Tannhäuser*, the least aquatic of the mature operas, we are introduced to the subterranean world of the Venusberg by a chorus of Sirens, beckoning the seafarer to the shore: 'Naht euch dem Strande'.[7] In Goethe's *Iphigenie* and in *Wilhelm Tell*, water had still represented external spaces beyond the control of the mind. Its transformation to suggest submerged areas of the mind and of sexuality is everywhere evident in Romantic literature and later, and does not need documentation here. What might be observed, however, is that the transformation alters the nature of sacrifice: it is no longer predominantly inflicted by the instruments of culture; its instruments, of fire and water, are themselves images of mental transformation, of evolution beyond the restrictions of current culture.

For, if different natural spaces figure different psychic states, it is because culture has evolved different artificial spaces for the sexes: the Dutchman's ship, the women's quarter in *Lohengrin*, Valhalla, Tristan's castle (inherited from his forefathers, and contrasted with matriarchal Ireland), the

Mastersingers' guild, Klingsor's garden, these are all sexually exclusive spaces. Women retain archaic natural spaces, such as the Venusberg, the depths of the Rhine, or the subterranean domain of Erda. In addition to these archaic realms, they also – for better or for worse – have an unusable cultural past. Isolde deplores her degeneracy of race in losing her mother's power over the sea and storm. Ortrud longs for the old gods; Venus *is* an old god. So is Brünnhilde. If the Dutchman has been frozen in an eternally relived moment, his female counterpart, Kundry, has by contrast a past of varied transformations. Wagner's women carry a burden of psychic history that their culture cannot acknowledge, and it is this suppressed cultural history that intrudes when Wagner uses the motif of the supernaturally interrupted wedding, as he does in *Lohengrin* (in Ortrud's possession of Elsa's mind), in Brünnhilde's disruption of Siegfried's marriage to Gutrune (and to some extent, in Tannhäuser's outburst in praise of Venus at the song contest in praise of chaste love). Whereas a writer such as Polidori uses the device to show the intrusion of private, forbidden desires into the sphere of culture, Wagner shows the marriage ceremony as being invaded by the older, culturally unassimilated, layers of femininity. When Brünnhilde denounces Siegfried at his wedding to Gutrune in *Götterdämmerung*, he reacts to her as though she were a Euripidean Bacchanal, scorning her as a wild woman of the rocks ('wilden Felsen-Frau') (Act 2.4, p. 324).

The primordial manifestations of femininity are ambiguous and at times shrouded in terror, but they also clearly denote a kind of consciousness that precedes the instinct for property: the Rhinemaidens possess the unforged gold, and in *Siegfried* Erda, the eternal woman ('Ewiges Weib') (Act 3.1, p. 254), urges the return of the ring. The feminine is also closer to the origins of language, and more remote from its appropriation to the enforcement and codification of property rights. For Wagner, the more elaborate forms of language were, historically, preceded by an ur-language of sung vocalizations. These are represented in *The Ring* by the chants of the Rhinemaidens and the whoops of the Valkyries, and it is part of Siegfried's primitive virtue that, until the oath of blood-brotherhood, he is not fully separated from the feminine dimensions of language – both in his own vocalizing whoops and in his understanding of the woodbird, the first female voice in the opera; the first, indeed, in Siegfried's life.

In exploring the cultural history of language, Wagner repeatedly reverts to a theme that had been central to eighteenth-century sacrificial opera: the fatal oath. The eighteenth century had treated the oath as something that could be rationally superseded, but Wagner takes a more complex view of its place in culture. Like Jephthah, the Dutchman is the prisoner of a rash oath (as Edgar in *Der Vampyr* also is). Rounding the Cape of Good Hope in a furious storm, the Dutchman had sworn that he would make it even if he had to sail for ever. The Devil heard him, and he is condemned to sail the seas until the Day of Judgment, unless he finds a woman who will be true to him. He is permitted to come ashore once every seven years in order to seek a faithful woman.

Like Idomeneo's oath, and unlike Edgar's, the Dutchman's can be culturally superseded, but in a different way from Idomeneo's: not by moving beyond an order based upon sacrifice, but by moving towards one. Oaths are powerful, but not primitive: rather, they are perversions of the primordial vocalizations that we hear at the beginning of *Das Rheingold*, and to which language periodically reverts. In *The Ring*, these vocalizations are first disturbed by an oath: Alberich's oath renouncing love. Later, in another solemn linguistic act, he places a curse on the ring. These binding linguistic rituals are mirrored in the contractual runes on Wotan's spear and, later, in Siegfried's oath of blood-brotherhood to Gunther. Like Wotan's contract, indeed, Alberich's renunciation is associated with runes: 'Rune magic' ('Runenzauber') (*Rheingold*, sc. 2, p. 82) enables him to make the ring out of the gold, and he uses the 'Ringes Runen' (*Walküre*, Act 2.2., p. 151) to employ it against the gods.

'The soil of history', Wagner had argued in *Opera and Drama*,

> is *man's social nature*: from the individual's need to unite himself with the essence of his species, in order in Society (*Gesellschaft*) to bring his faculties into highest play, arises the whole movement of history. The historic phenomena are the outward manifestments of an inner movement, whose core is the Social Nature of man. But the prime motor of this nature is the *Individual*, who only in the satisfaction of his instinctive longing for Love (*Liebesverlangen*) can appease his bent-to-happiness. (*PW*, vol. II, p. 175)

> Der Boden der Geschichte ist die soziale Natur des Menschen: aus dem Bedürfnisse des Individuums, sich mit den Wesen seiner Gattung zu vereinigen, um in der Gesellschaft seine Fähigkeiten zur höchsten Geltung zu bringen, erwächst die ganze Bewegung der Geschichte. Die geschichtlichen Erscheinungen sind die äußersten Äußerungen der inneren Bewegung, deren Kern die soziale Natur des Menschen ist. Die nährende Kraft dieser Natur ist aber das Individuum, das nur in der Befriedigung seines unwillkürlichen Liebesverlangens seinen Glückseligkeitstrieb stillen kann. (*GS*, vol. IV, p. 50)

Runes represent the social formulations that take man away from the unfettered pursuit of the life-instinct; the runes engraved on Wotan's spear initially commit him to the surrender of Freia, and lead to the ageing of the gods. Siegfried's oath of blood-*brother*hood in *Götterdämmerung* commits him to the loss of Brünnhilde. Brünnhilde has different runes: runes of wisdom, which she teaches to Siegfried. These, however, are defeated by the power of the potion which destroys Siegfried's memory, and separates him from his instinctual past: 'Where are my runes / against this riddle?' ('Wo sind meine Runen / gegen dieß Räthsel?'), she complains (Act 2.5, p. 326). Thus, as part of the separation of social structure from the life-instinct, language, and runes, are torn away from the feminine and become instruments of male power. 'Are they goodly runes?' ('Sind's gute Runen?')

(Act I.2, p. 296), Siegfried punningly asks Gutrune, immediately after drinking the potion. They are not: this is the moment at which the power of society and its linguistic artifices erase Siegfried's primal nature. If the oath in *Idomeneo* represents a primitive and magical conception of language, the contract in *The Ring* represents a cultural cul-de-sac, from which language must be rescued by Brünnhilde's concluding sacrificial act, and the return of the Rhinemaidens.

Throughout the eighteenth century, sacrificial drama had centred more and more upon the self, and its sensations, rights, and possessions; the very individual needs which Wagner associated with the longing for love. A key word in this foregrounding of the self had been *eigen* (one's own): in Goethe's *Iphigenie* its prominence had reflected the growing importance of the personal and the subjective; conjoined with *Erbe* (inheritance), it had in *Wilhelm Tell* represented the national and familial patrimony for which the oppressed Swiss were striving. In *Tristan* and *The Ring*, however, *eigen* and *Erbe* are heavily contested words, representing a network of oppressive property relationships which extend over space and time, but are also capable of transformation to express new – or perhaps older and more natural – ways of forming and representing the self. In his early account of transformations of the Nibelung story, *The Wibelungen. World History as Told in Saga* (*Die Wibelungen. Weltgeschichte aus der Sage*) (1848), Wagner identifies the introduction of hereditary possession as a turning point at which 'the man, his personal excellence, his acts and deeds, lost value, – which passed over to his property' ('verlor der Mensch, seine persönliche Tüchtigkeit, sein Handeln und Thun – an Werth, und dieser ging von ihm auf den Besitz über' (*PW*, vol. VII, p. 296; *GS*, vol. II, p. 154).

The being who forges the ring would win the inheritance of the world as his own ('Der Welt *Erbe* / gewänne zu *eigen*') (*Rheingold* sc. 1, p. 67; italics added). The terms recur in the vocabulary of Alberich, Mime, and Alberich's son Hagen, and the rights of property-ownership also preoccupy Hunding in *Die Walküre*: 'This house and this wife / are Hunding's own', Sieglinde tells Siegmund ('Dieß Haus und dieß Weib sind Hunding's Eigen') (Act I.I, p. 123). The word *eigen* is also used to explore the trap in which Wotan finds himself in *Die Walküre*, of trying in Siegmund to create a free agent who would act 'mit der eig'nen Wehr' ('with his own power') (Act 2.2, p. 152) but would nevertheless execute Wotan's own will. It is a contradiction from which there is no escape: Wotan is caught in his own fetters ('In *eig'ner* Fessel'; italics added) (Act 2.2, p. 148), forced to reject half of himself (his '*eig'ne* Hälfte') (Act 3.3, p. 187) when Brünnhilde executes his desires in defiance of his command.

Eigen, then, does not suggest the subjective self-realization that it does in Goethe. It expresses the systems of division and otherness that are enforced by property. One feature of the potentially regenerative primitivism of Siegmund and Siegfried is that it returns the word to the sphere of the personal, associating it with an exploration of sameness and otherness that is a means of understanding the self rather than distributing property. Like the creature in *Frankenstein* and Maturin's Immalee, both Siegmund and Siegfried take a step towards self-recognition by seeing their own reflection ('eigen Bild').[8] Seeing her image recreated in Siegmund, Sieglinde likens the experience to seeing her own image in the water, and he recognizes her as the hidden image in himself; Siegfried realizes from his reflection in the water that he is not like ('gleich') Mime (*Siegfried* 1.1, p. 202). Brünnhilde is Siegfried's 'heritage and own' ('Erb' und Eigen') (*Siegfried* 3.3, p. 275). When Gunther offers Siegfried joint ownership of his 'Erbe' of lands and vassals, Siegfried dissociates the self from the property nexus, replying that his only *Erbe* is his body (*Götterdämmerung* 1.2, p. 294), and when Brünnhilde finally claims the ring as her inheritance ('Mein Erbe nun / nehm' ich zu eigen') (*Götterdämmerung* 3.3, p. 349), it is to give it to the Rhinemaidens. The language of selfhood and inheritance thus has a fundamental value in *The Ring*, but only when it detaches itself from the system of property and returns to the description of something far more primeval: likeness and love.

As Siegmund and Sieglinde discover these things, the door that separated ('trennte') them from the regenerative power of Spring flies open, love and Spring are united ('vereint'), and the life-instinct is briefly triumphant (*Walküre* 1.3, pp. 134–5). In the event, however, the only escape from the barriers of property rights is that of Tristan and Isolde: sacrificial union in death. At the end of his second visit to Brünnhilde's rock in *Götterdämmerung*, Siegfried asserts Gunther's property rights by placing his sword between him and Brünnhilde: '*separate* me from his bride' ('trenne mich von seiner Braut!') (Act 1.3, p. 308), he commands it. Again, we have a clear opposition between the culture represented by the blade and that necessitated by sacrifice: the sacrificial flame of the funeral pyre undoes the enforcement of property rights by the sword, and permits a final commingling of essence. The fires of love and of the pyre become indistinguishable.

The self-immolation of Brynhild occurs in the *Volsunga Saga*, but it is a straightforward funerary sacrifice which also includes Sigurd's three-year-old son by Gudrun, and reflects a grim and violent level of culture. Gudrun, by no means Wagner's sensitive victim, goes on to marry Atli (Attila), and serve his children to him in a Thyestean banquet. In the *Niebelungenlied*, Siegfried and Brynhild are never lovers, and there is therefore no self-immolation; but Gutrune's equivalent, Kriemhild, does take a terrible vengeance upon Hagen, the fulfilment of which occupies the entire second half of the poem. Wagner abolishes the culturally institutionalized violence which pervades both the *Volsunga Saga* and the high medieval society portrayed in the *Niebelungenlied*, and distils the cultural polarities of the cycle into two contrasting forms of death, which sum up Wagner's imagining of social evolution: Siegfried's death by the spear of

Plate 13 Arthur Rackham, Brünnhilde's Immolation (1910)

Hagen, the hunter, and Brünnhilde's death by the sacrificial flame. The hunt and sacrifice are quite contrary in their nature.

Through works such as Behn's *Oroonoko*, I have argued, we have been accustomed to see the weapon as the emblem and instrument of culture. It

Plate 14 A sterner view of Brünnhilde's immolation, by Franz Stassen (*c.* 1914). Stassen was a friend of Siegfried Wagner, a member of the National Socialist Party, and an artist admired by Hitler

is an illustration of the intrinsic derivation of culture from violence, the reason why it consummates itself in sacrificial acts. In *The Ring*, the weapon is also a symbol of culture, but not of the origins of culture; rather, it symbolizes the point at which culture dissociates itself from the life-instinct. Wotan's spear is engraved with runes; Hagen's spear punishes Siegfried for his perjury (*Meineid*) in sleeping with Brünnhilde and swearing falsely in his oath of brotherhood to Gunther. In order to distract his attention for the spear-thrust, Hagen uses Siegfried's knowledge of bird-speech, which represents his closeness to primal language: he points to some ravens and asks what they are saying, before providing his own interpretation – vengeance. The conjunction of oath and spear wipes out the earlier stage of natural language (restored when Brünnhilde, immediately before her immolation, sends her ravens to announce the end to Wotan). Intervening attempts to make the weapon an instrument of the life-instinct fail. Siegmund pulls the sword Nothung from the trunk of the ash tree in a love scene that is full of affirmative self-naming. It loses its power in the following act, as a result of Fricka's insistence on the sanctity of the marriage oath (*Eid* – a word that is frequently repeated). The shattered sword is reforged in *Siegfried*. It kills the dragon Fafner, potentially ends the reign of private property by liberating the Nibelung hoard, and puts Siegfried in touch with the ur-language; for the taste of the dragon's blood, which it has shed, enables him to understand the speech of the birds. Yet, in *Götterdämmerung*, the sword Nothung engages in an act of blood-letting that counterbalances and eventually annuls the killing of Fafner and its consequences: the oath of blood-brotherhood. The bladeless sacrifice thus transcends both the system of property and the weapons that are its instruments and emblems.

Wagner himself, however, repeatedly changed his mind about the meaning of Brünnhilde's sacrifice. The initial prose sketch (1848) concludes with a decisive transformation of the divine order, showing Brünnhilde as leading Siegfried heavenwards. At the end of *Siegfrieds Tod*, Brünnhilde's monologue describes just such an apotheosis; the gods are to be redeemed – by Siegfried – rather than destroyed. The pyre is, Brünnhilde reiterates, a path to freedom: *frei* is the last word of the text. This ending was quickly revised to promise the gods a peaceful fading away before human deeds: 'a blessed redemption in death!' ('selige Todeserlösung') (p. 362). In the next version, Brünnhilde bequeathed the world to Love; this ending most expresses Wagner's enthusiasm for the philosopher Feuerbach, who treated the divine as a projection of human nature, had praised love as a means of transcending the separateness of individual existence, and denied individual immortality, regarding death as a dissolution of the self. Wagner then underwent a conversion to Schopenhauer's pessimistic view of life as an unfulfilling strife of competing individual wills, from which the only release is through renunciation of desire. In a further version of Brünnhilde's final monologue, she leaves the homes of desire and delusion

('Wunschheim', 'Wahnheim'), having seen the end of all things ('enden sah ich die Welt') (p. 363). Then there is the familiar, final version, in which Brünnhilde is joyfully united with Siegfried in the flames and fulfils her sacrificial destiny as woman (*Weib*) – now the last word of her monologue. Although the *Liebestod* does not redeem the gods, the gold returns to the Rhine, and the divisions enforced by property are at an end.

A useful gloss on Wagner's thinking in *The Ring* is provided by his detailed interpretation of a Greek saga comparable in scale and violence to that of the Nibelungs: that of Thebes. In *Opera and Drama*, he is already discussing ways in which the structure of the state departs from the conditions necessitated by the instincts of the individual, in part because of the internalization of property values. He sees the Theban myth as giving archetypal expression to this internalization, and embarks on a lengthy interpretation of it (*PW*, vol. II, pp. 180–90; *GS*, vol. IV, pp. 55–64). Nature demands that parents should sacrifice themselves for their children; yet custom made it seem natural that Laïus and Jocasta, Oedipus' parents, should sacrifice their child to protect themselves. Although Oedipus' son Eteocles was clearly at fault in breaking his oath to alternate the kingship with Polynices, the burghers saw their own property values more clearly represented by Eteocles, and so the body of the wronged Polynices was outraged, since he was the more appropriate scapegoat (*Sündenbock*) (*PW*, vol. III, p. 187; *GS*, vol. IV, p. 60). Only with the death of Antigone (a paradigm of love), and the self-immolation of Haemon, did the state collapse and Creon revert from tyrant to father.

For Wagner, the tragedy of Oedipus is that of a man who has internalized prohibitions that are purely conventional, and in conflict with the natural life-instinct; the customs of Thebes thus resemble the runes on Wotan's spear in representing the separation of culture from instinct. There is nothing wrong with killing a man in self-defence, or in marrying the queen of a country you have saved; yet the reverence for kin meant that the deeds became execrable once their violation of social prohibition became known, and Oedipus' killing of his father was condemned far above his father's two attempts to kill him. Reverence for kin is, however, an invention of custom, whereas sexual love is not: sexual love is a revolutionary force that breaks down the confinement of the family and drives the individual on a journey towards that which is not formulated by custom. The Greek concept of Fate arose from misunderstanding of the conflict between the necessity of inner nature and the political state.

In Wagner's view, the Oedipus myth encapsulates a false pattern of social evolution from the primitive. The Sphinx had confronted Oedipus with the individual in its subjection to nature; having fathomed the beast-man in the mountains, Oedipus then went – to his own undoing – to confront the social man in the city.

When he stabbed the light from eyes which had flamed wrath upon a taunting despot, had streamed with love towards a noble wife, – without power to see that the one was his father, the other his mother, – then he plunged down to the mangled carcass of the Sphinx, whose riddle he now must know was yet unsolved. – It is *we* who have to solve that riddle, to solve it by vindicating the instinct of the Individual from out Society itself; whose highest, still renewing and re-quickening wealth, that Instinct is. (*PW*, vol. II, p. 183)

Als er sich die leuchtenden Augen ausstach, die einem despotischen Beleidiger Zorn zugeflammt, und einem edlen Weibe Liebe zugestrahlt hatten, ohne zu ersehen, daß jener sein Vater und diese seine Mutter war, da stürzte er sich zu der zerschmetterten Sphinx hinab, deren Räthsel er nun als noch ungelöst erkennen mußte. – Erst wir haben dieses Räthsel zu lösen, und zwar dadurch, daß wir die Unwillkür des Individuums aus der Gesellschaft, deren höchster, immer erneuernder und belebender Reichtum sie ist, selbst rechtfertigen. (GS, vol. IV, p. 57)

I doubt whether any earlier opera composer wrote as extensively as Wagner did about the instinctual and the unconscious, especially in *The Art-Work of the Future* (*Das Kunstwerk der Zukunft*) (1849). If man became human when he 'perceived the difference between himself and Nature, . . . breaking loose from the unconsciousness of natural animal life' ('seinen Unterschied von der Natur empfand, . . . indem er sich von dem Unbewußtsein thierischen Naturlebens losriß') (*PW*, vol. I, p. 70; *GS*, vol. III, p. 43), the life-drive is 'unconscious and instinctive' ('unbewußte, unwillkürliche') by its very nature (*PW*, vol. I, p. 79; *GS*, vol. III, p. 52), and 'The end of Science is the justifying of the Unconscious, the giving of self-consciousness to Life, the re-instatement of the Senses in their perceptive rights' ('Das Ende der Wissenschaft ist das gerechtfertigte Unbewußte, das sich bewußte Leben, die als sinnig erkannte Sinnlichkeit') (*PW*, vol. I, p. 72; *GS*, vol. III, p. 45).

Though doppelgänger figures such as the bride of Corinth, or the two 1828 vampires, represent (or release) concealed and unacknowledged desires, such desires are irremediably alien to rational society, and their sacrificial consequences are an illustration of their deeply non-social character. Despite his unprecedentedly complex representation of the psyche, however, Wagner is concerned with its social expression rather than its concealed private areas; with instinct as the proper basis of society rather than as its perpetual negation. Thus, although he resembles his predecessors in using the figure of the doppelgänger, he uses it in a contrary way. An example is the splitting of Siegfried in *Götterdämmerung*. Having passed through the magic fire and gained Brünnhilde's love, he travels for the first time to society, where he is instantly corrupted. He is given a potion of forgetfulness which wipes out all memory of Brünnhilde, and he falls for Gutrune, the sister of his host Gunther; using the magic of the Tarnhelm, he then assumes Gunther's shape and makes a second journey to the Valkyrie's rock, now winning Brünnhilde for his brother-in-law. Rather than releasing presocial instinct, the splitting shows a rejection of primordial needs for the oppressive artifice of social convention. This is the same process as is followed in Wagner's interpretation of the Oedipus legend, which records another journey from the mountain to society.

The drinking of the potion in *Götterdämmerung* signifies the boundary at which the restrictive artifice of society obliterates primal need; the love potion in *Tristan* works the other way round, releasing primal needs. In both cases, however, the division that is opened up can only be reconciled by the sacrificial unions that conclude these operas. A division that remains unreconciled is illustrated by the doubling at the end of *Lohengrin*, where Elsa dies and her brother immediately steps into her place: the male both doubles and erases the female. The flaw is Elsa's (she will not erase herself in the way that Wagner's other heroines do), but it leads to the confirmation of a male order in which the wandering hero is denied the stasis and fulfilment attained by the Flying Dutchman. The wandering of Wagner's heroes corresponds to a specific stage in the evolution of both civilization and literature, for in *Opera and Drama* Wagner saw the evolution from romance to drama as paralleling the movement from the age of exploration to the investigation of individual and social life: 'the Drama gives us the *man*, the Romance explains to us the *citizen*' ('das Drama giebt uns den Menschen, der Roman erklärt uns den Staatsbürger') (*PW*, vol. II, p. 172; *GS*, vol. IV, p. 48). It is Lohengrin's tragedy that he remains a romance hero.

MYTH, HISTORY, AND GEOLOGY: *PARSIFAL*

Wagner's concern with the loss of cultural and psychic origins gradually led, towards the end of his life, to an at least theoretical espousal of Pythagorean vegetarianism – a desire to return to a point before the emergence of man the hunter:

> Then, falling lower and yet lower, the only worthy food for the world-conqueror appears to be human blood and corpses: the Feast of Thyestes would have been impossible among the Indians; but with such ghastly pictures could the human fancy play, now that the murder of man and beast had nothing strange for it. (*Religion and Art* (1880), *PW*, vol. VI, p. 228)

> Denn immer tiefer verfallend, scheinen Blut und Leichen die einzig würdige Nahrung für den Welteroberer zu werden: das Mahl des Thyestes wäre bei den Indern unmöglich gewesen: mit solchen entsetzlichen Bildern konnte jedoch die menschliche Einbildungskraft spielen, seitdem ihr Thier- und Menschenmord geläufig geworden war. (*Religion und Kunst, GS*, vol. X, p. 227)

Secret communities, such as those of Pythagoras, rediscovered the original nature of man. For Wagner, however, its primary reaffirmation was in the Crucifixion, which redeemed humanity from the degeneration caused by carnivorousness:

his own flesh and blood he gave as last and highest expiation for all the sin of outpoured blood and slaughtered flesh, and offered his disciples wine and bread for each day's meal. (*Religion and Art*, *PW*, vol. VI, p. 231)

sein eigenes Fleisch und Blut gab er, als letztes höchstes Sühnungsopfer für alles sündhaft vergossene Blut und geschlachtete Fleisch dahin, und reichte dafür seinen Jüngern Wein und Brot Zum täglichen Mahl. (*GS*, vol. X, p. 230)

Judaism, by contrast, sanctifies carnivorousness (as well as vegetarianism): humanity fell through eating fruit, and Abel's sacrifice of animal flesh was more acceptable to God than Cain's vegetarian offering (*PW*, vol. VI, p. 241; *GS*, vol. X, p. 241).

The Crucifixion had, for Wagner, always been an archetypal model of sacrificial renunciation. In an early exposition of the Nibelungen legend, *The Wibelungen* (1848), he had espoused Max Müller's interpretation of myth as a representation of the natural cycle, whereby Siegfried's battle with the dragon represents the sun's victory over the forces of winter and darkness (*PW*, vol. VII, p. 263; *GS*, vol. II, p. 119).[9] This victory is temporary, for, as Wagner wrote, the god must fall 'a sacrifice to his deed of blessing us' ('ein Opfer seiner uns beseligenden That') (*PW*, vol. VII, p. 275; *GS*, vol. II, p. 132). Though temporary, the victory is an archetype recreated in many other myths of sacrifice: the 'son of God, called by his nearest kinsmen *Siegfried*', is called

Christ by the remaining nations of the earth; for the welfare of his race, and the peoples of the earth derived therefrom, he wrought a deed most glorious, and for that deed's sake suffered death.

einem Sohne Gottes ..., der seinem nächsten Geschlechte selbst Siegfried, den übrigen Völkern der Erde aber Christus heißt; dieser hat für das Heil und Glück seines Geschlechtes, und der aus ihm entsprossenen Völker der Erde, die herrlichste That vollbracht, und um dieser That willen auch den Tod erlitten. (*PW*, vol. VII, p. 289; *GS*, vol. II, p. 146)

We do not, however, explain a myth simply by reducing it to its original form and ignoring the meanings that gather in the processes of cultural transformation. For early medieval culture, the dragon's hoard became an archetypal image of all 'earthly power' ('aller irdischen Macht') (*PW*, vol. VII, p. 263; *GS*, vol. II, p. 119), before being superseded at the time of the Crusades by the legend of the Grail, which represents a more ideal form of kingship.

If Wagner derives myth from primitive perceptions of the cycles of nature, he also links it to his own, nineteenth-century perceptions of natural process and cycle: to his morbid and baleful sense of racial crisis, and of the geological catastrophes that provoked the crises of civilization. Wagner had enthusiastically devoured Count Gobineau's *Essai sur l'inégalité des races humaines*, which argued that the collapse of civilizations was due to racial interbreeding: only the white race was capable of developing civilization, and one of its virtues was that it had a capacity for renouncing life which exceeded that of other races.[10] In *Hero-Dom and Christendom* Wagner saw the Crucifixion as the supreme expression of this capacity for sacrificial renunciation, and as an evolutionary response to the crisis caused by the racial intermingling in the Roman Middle East. Schopenhauer had suggested that, after major depopulating crises such as famines, more twins were produced than usual, showing the self-regenerative capacity of the species to rebound from crisis. The Crucifixion, similarly, affirms the highest quality of the white races, and the great historical mistake was to link it to the carnivorous religion of the Old Testament. The Catholic Church perpetuates the Judaic takeover of the Crucifixion – for example, in crusading militarism. The Crucifixion is thus completely removed from familiar Christian teleology, and becomes a critical moment in an evolutionary struggle.

The sense of racial crisis is linked to one of geological crisis. Like many of his contemporaries, Wagner saw the history of the earth as being punctuated by periodic catastrophes (Gobineau believed that racial difference was forged in a period of far greater geological activity than that of the present day). There have been previous species, destroyed by geological upheavals, and one reason that racial purification was so imperative was that humanity must be in the best possible shape to meet the next disaster. Although the concluding catastrophe in *Götterdämmerung* is morally rather than geologically caused, it reflects Wagner's sense of a world history punctuated by cataclysm, and of the importance of sacrifice in coping with the upheavals. He was aware that man could contribute to them. Surveying the monstrous growth of arms technology, he speculated that the next great famine might trigger a cycle of destruction that might take us back to 'where world-Historical development began' ('von wo unsere weltgeschichtliche Entwickelung ausging') (*PW*, vol. VI, p. 252; *GS*, vol. X, p. 252).

If culture must ready itself for the next catastrophe, however, it has been shaped by previous ones. In *The Wibelungen*, he postulates a time 'when our earth's Northern hemisphere was about as much covered by water as now is the Southern' ('als die nördliche Halbkügel unsrer Erde ungefähr so mit Wasser bedeckt war, wie es jetzt die südliche ist') (*PW*, vol. VII, p. 259; *GS*, vol. II, p. 116); when the waters retreated to flood the South, there was a northward migration from the Asiatic mountains. Far later, in *Religion and Art*, he writes:

> the human race to which we still belong, has survived, or at least a great portion of it, a violent transformation of the surface of our planet. A careful survey of our earthly ball confirms this: it shews that at some epoch of its last development great stretches of the continent sank down and others rose, while floods immeasurable poured hither from the Southern Pole, only to be arrested by the jutting headlands of the Northern hemisphere, like monstrous ice-guards, after driving before them all the terrified survivors. (*PW*, vol. VI, p. 237)

> das . . . menschliche Geschlecht, welchem wir noch jetzt angehören, wenigstens zu einem großen Theile, eine gewaltsame Umgestaltung der Oberfläche unseres Planeten erlebt hat. Hiervon überzeugend spricht zu uns ein sorgfältiger Überblick der Gestalt unserer Erdkugel: dieser zeigt uns, daß in irgend einer Epoche ihrer letzten Ausbilding große Theile der verbundenen Festländer versanken, andere emporstiegen, während unermeßliche Wasserfluthen vom Südpole her endlich nur an den, gleich Eisbrechern gegen sie sich vorstreckenden, spitzen Ausläufern der sich behauptenden Festländer der nördlichen Halbkugel, sich stauten und verliefen, nachdem sie alles Überlebende in furchtbarer Flucht vor sich hergetrieben hatten. (*GS*, vol. x, pp. 236–7)

Wagner assumes that Siberian mammoth skeletons are the remains of tropical beasts, testifying to a flight from the tropics. The sudden transformation of fertile zones into deserts is the reason that man became carnivorous, for carnivorousness was initially a response to crisis, like cannibalism after shipwrecks (*PW*, vol. vi, pp. 237–8; *GS*, vol. x, p. 237). In *The Wibelungen*, Wagner argued that the migrations from the Asiatic homeland caused by geological upheaval are the reason that so many myths preserve the memory of a walled ur-city, as is contained in Asgard and Montsalvat, the homes of the Norse gods and of the Grail (*PW*, vol. vii, p. 280; *GS*, vol. ii, p. 138).

If Wagner is the first opera composer knowingly to explore the unconscious, he is also the first to confront the idea of long-term geological change, and the extinction of the species; the first for whom the frozen mammoth skeletons in Siberia were an important clue to the meaning of history, and an image of human destiny; for whom the history of the human race is an episode in the sequential flourishing and annihilation of intelligent species. It is telling that the heroine of his first opera, *Die Feen*, should towards the end be turned to stone. She is not fossilized: her petrification represents emotional paralysis rather than mineral inertia. Yet the condition of suspended development is one that would persist in Wagner's work, and be clothed in new meanings as his intellectual and creative personality evolved. Later figures who are frozen in time include the Dutchman, Kundry, and Titurel.

Wagner's musings on the fate of the race and the planet are at their most intense and elaborate at the time he was composing *Parsifal*, and they form the background for his treatment of Christ's sacrifice. *Parsifal* is not normally regarded as a work shaped by a sense of geological fatalism, and the point must not be made too heavily. Yet, like the far earlier *Frankenstein*, it – and its notion of sacrifice – is shaped by the radically different interpretation of time, space, and the destiny of the planet that had been developing since the late eighteenth century. The imagination that formed the lost homeland of Montsalvat had also meditated on that ultimate image of exile from the homeland: the mammoths in the Siberian ice.

For all its seeming representation of timeless and archetypal myth (captured in Wieland Wagner's famous minimalist production at

Bayreuth in 1951), *Parsifal* has a strong sense of the historically specific. Like all Wagner operas, it is a drama of boundaries, with water again being important: the first scene takes place by a lakeside, but not until the baptism of Kundry in Act 3 does water recover its transforming power, as a result of Parsifal's understanding of the meaning of the Cross. *Parsifal* is also, however, on another boundary: the Pyrenees, which separate Europe from Moorish Spain. The palace of the enchanter Klingsor is in an elaborately Moorish architectural style, and Kundry and others wander further East, in their vain search for cures for Amfortas. Situating the opera on the medieval boundary between Europe and the Oriental, Wagner explores what he sees to be the current threat to European racial integrity, and he contrasts the enemy races according to their capacity for sacrifice: Klingsor's castration is a shameful sacrifice (*Opfer*), contrasting with the 'Liebesopfer' that is commemorated on Good Friday.[11]

For the first time, however, sacrifice is not solely associated with women. Parsifal enters the opera as someone to whom the entire world is uncomprehended otherness, and a swan merely something to be shot. His first step forward is through the fellow-feeling with the swan that moves him beyond his role as hunter, and he goes through the process that Wagner outlined in *Opera and Drama*, of understanding himself through fellow-feeling with images of his own condition, leading to an ability to understand his opposites. The critical moment is Wagner's final variant of the interrupted wedding, in Parsifal's thwarted union with Kundry. As a prelude to sexual temptation, she has made him for the first time understand the emotions and priorities of his first opposite, his mother, in the progress through breast-feeding and inevitable separation to her grief and death, caused by his male wanderlust. In this temptation, the comforting image of the mother masks that of the menacing racial alien, and, as it proceeds, Klingsor approaches bearing the spear that had wounded Christ and Amfortas, intending to wound Parsifal with it in turn. Klingsor's version of 'I shall be with you on your wedding-night' is, however, overpowered by a more powerful intrusion: Parsifal's sudden internal understanding of Amfortas's wound; his understanding of the need for sacrifice and renunciation. Klingsor's magic is now powerless, and Parsifal is able to grasp the spear as it hangs motionless in the air. This moment of entry into the sensations of another is the moment at which he starts to understand the world through signs. His first act in the opera had been to destroy a sign: Amfortas had greeted the swan flying over the lake as a good sign ('als gutes Zeichen') (Act 1, p. 54), only for Parsifal promptly to down it. Now, grasping the sacred spear, he makes the sign ('Zeichen') that destroys Klingsor's power (Act 2, p. 243). The Grail brotherhood now controls the meaning of Christ's sacrifice.

CHAPTER 12

The second coming of Dionysus

In his book *Die Wiederkunft des Dionysos*, Joachim Rosteutscher identifies Wagner as one of the prophets of the returning god[1] – inevitably, since in his early period of Wagnerism, Nietzsche sees Wagner as a supreme expression of the Dionysiac. Yet Dionysus figures very little in Wagner's work. There are Bacchantes in the Venusberg, but they are not Maenads. When Wagner discusses Greek tragedy, he associates it with Apollo far more than with Dionysus. The absence of Dionysus from literature before Nietzsche is all the more remarkable given that his return was to be as decisive a feature of twentieth-century literature as collectivist destructive frenzy was to be of twentieth-century politics. This chapter examines the preparations for his return: two novels (*A Tale of Two Cities* and *Dracula*) and three works which reinstate him as a key to representing the irrational, namely Nietzsche's *The Birth of Tragedy*, Frazer's *The Golden Bough*, and Freud's *Totem and Taboo*.

Like *Frankenstein, A Tale of Two Cities* (1859) is in part a response to Arctic exploration. In 1845, Sir John Franklin set out with 128 men in an attempt to discover the Northwest Passage. He was never heard from again, and his ships have not been found to this day. In 1854, however, Dr John Rae interviewed Inuit witnesses, who reported finding bodies in a condition that suggested that the survivors had resorted to cannibalism (accounts which have now been confirmed). The story was widely and indignantly denied, one of the outraged sceptics being Charles Dickens: how can we know, he asked, that the explorers

> were not set upon and slain by the Esquimaux themselves. It is impossible to form an estimate of the character of any race of savages, from the deferential behaviour to the white man when he is strong. The mistake has been made again and again; and the moment the white man has appeared in the new aspect of being weaker than the savage, the savage has changed and sprung upon him. There are pious persons who, in their practice, with strange inconsistency, claim for every child born to civilisation all innate depravity, and for every savage born to the woods and wilds an innate virtue. We believe every savage to be in his heart covetous, treacherous, and cruel; and we have yet to learn what knowledge the white man – lost, houseless, shipless, apparently forgotten by his race, plainly famine-stricken, weak, frozen, helpless, and dying – has of the gentleness of Esquimaux nature.[2]

Dickens collaborated with Wilkie Collins on *The Frozen Deep* (1857), a play about self-sacrifice in an Arctic expedition, in which a rejected lover saves his favoured rival at the expense of his own life. This story forms the germ of *A Tale of Two Cities*, and to this extent it is born in those Arctic wastes that shaped Mary Shelley's imagination, and out of a desire to exorcize that ultimate nightmare of terrifying atavism, cannibalism. The Franklin expedition turned out to be an Arctic *Heart of Darkness*. In Dickens's novel, however, the characteristics of the Arctic are thoroughly assimilated into the cities of temperate Europe: the wilderness (a recurrent image) is economic and mental, and the idea of cannibalism is transferred to the powerful figures who devour the goods of the land.

Like Hegel, though at some distance, Dickens is concerned with societies which do not permit full individuation. For example, the images of petrifaction associated with the *ancien régime* suggest a system which denies all subjective thought or feeling: the palace of the Marquis, whose careless killing of a pauper child sparks off the Revolution, has 'stone balustrades, and stone urns, and stone flowers, and stone faces of men'.[3] The mob has a collectivity which reduces its components to interchangeable ciphers – 'Jacques One and Two', 'Jacques Three', 'Jacques Five-and-Twenty Thousand' (pp. 199, 245) – and a more complex image of interchangeability is the recurrent doubling: the novel hinges on Sydney Carton's remarkable resemblance to the émigré French aristocrat Charles Darnay; the informer Roger Cly, needing a new identity, stages his own funeral and reappears as John Barsad; Doctor Manette oscillates between sanity and the illusion that he is a shoemaker.

The splitting of the self, however, does not (as it often does) produce a doppelgänger who embodies dark and socially unassimilable aspects of the psyche, like Marschner's Ruthven, or Robert Louis Stevenson's Mr Hyde. The doubling of Darnay and Carton is, for example, more allegorical than psychological: if Darnay represents the better self that Carton eventually realizes on the scaffold, Carton is not Darnay's baser self. Rather, that final sacrifice is the point at which Carton breaks loose from his dependent and imitative existence and becomes morally unique.

The dehumanizing interchangeability of persons throughout the novel has, nevertheless, many aspects. One is that people are economically interchangeable: bodies are sold in the 'trade' of the resurrectionists, and, when his carelessly driven coach accidentally kills a poor child, the Marquis believes that he can pay for it. Thus, like much sacrificial literature, this novel considers the kinds of transaction which are appropriate for locating the individual in the community, and it is important that the central, generally benign, mechanism of social interchange is a bank. Yet it is when describing the bank that Dickens describes the economy of death in eighteenth-century London: 'Accordingly, the forger was put to death; the utterer of a bad note was put to Death; the unlawful opener of a letter was put to Death; the purloiner of forty shillings and sixpence was put to Death' (p. 84). Indeed, the bank is situated in close proximity to an expression of atavistic barbarity that, unlike cannibalism, does make it into the novel – a spectacle that was also to form the climax of *Heart of Darkness*: 'the heads [of traitors] exposed on Temple Bar with an insensate brutality and ferocity worthy of Abyssinia or Ashantee' (p. 84).

The juxtaposition of the severed heads with the bank presents an imaginative association of two opposite forms of dehumanization, involving complementary erasures of the person. One is dismemberment: the charges of which Darnay is acquitted in England carry the penalty of hanging, drawing, and quartering; Dickens refers to the punishment of the Chevalier de La Barre for blasphemy (p. 36), which so exercised Voltaire, gives a detailed description of the execution of Damiens (p. 200), and describes the mutilation of the body of the governor of the Bastille (p. 249). The other erasure, counterbalancing the annihilation of the body, is the reduction of individuals to mere categories of general abstraction: after his return to France, Darnay becomes such a category, as emigrant, aristocrat, and prisoner. The two forms of dehumanization are causally linked. For not only is the reduction of the individual to a bodiless category the imaginative precondition of the willingness to tear apart the body: depersonalization and economic interchangeability create the destructive collectivity of the mob which fuels such atrocities.

In a resolutely civic and economically exploited landscape, Dickens contemplates the extremes of horror that Franklin's men had faced in the desolation of King William Island. One already available way to represent the outburst of mass frenzy would be to regard it as Dionysiac. In *Reflections on the Revolution in France* (1790) Edmund Burke had referred to the 'Theban and Thracian Orgies, acted in France',[4] and Carlyle's *The French Revolution* (1837), which was a major source for Dickens, repeatedly recurs to the image of the maenad. Yet Dickens finds classical myth useful only for incidental allusions, as in the title of the chapter which describes the stone life forms that adorn the Marquis's palace: 'The Gorgon's Head'. The idea of Dionysus perhaps influences Dickens in his use of wine as a symbol: for example in Carton's alcoholism, and the centrality of the Defarges' wine shop in the outburst of violence – indeed our first glimpse of France is the breaking of a wine barrel in the street. Yet Dickens edits out all the references to Maenads; Madam Defarge is a monstrous woman, but not a Thracian or a Theban one. The Defarges' wine shop is even explicitly dissociated from Dionysus, who for Dickens is merely the jolly god of the grape: 'No vivacious Bacchanalian flame leaped out of the pressed grape of Monsieur Defarge: but, a smouldering fire that burnt in the dark, lay hidden in the dregs of it' (p. 194).

A Tale of Two Cities has for the English-speaking world become the definitive representation of the French Revolution, and of its sacrificial character. Yet if it confronts the potential for archaic savagery, both in revolutionary France and, by implication, in the dehumanizing industrial society of his own day, it ultimately offers a simple view of human progress; far simpler, for example, than the dialectic interplay of psychological forces that Schiller had proposed in his *Aesthetic Education*. Early in the novel, Dickens reflects on the incommunicable mystery of individual consciousness: 'every human creature is constituted to be that profound secret and mystery to every other' (p. 44). That sense of the secret otherness of consciousness is transformed in the conclusion, where Carton stares ahead into a future landscape which overrides the moral desert around him, and which grows out of the human potential which he is affirming in so pure a form: the mind triumphs over the wilderness. Amidst all the triumphant barbarity, *A Tale of Two Cities* affirms sacrifice as the path to social progress; to definitive rejection of the barbaric city in which severed heads are displayed on its very gateway. Perhaps that is one reason why Dickens, for all his symbolism of wine, has no truck with Dionysus. One recovers from a binge; one is possessed by Dionysus.

DRACULA

In outline, the story of *Dracula* (1897) is old and familiar. A mysterious stranger arrives from the mountains of the East. He is associated with predation, the hunt, and madness (all three are combined in his instrument, the lunatic Renfield, who consumes the blood of trapped animals). He suspends the distinction between man and beast and corrupts the consciousness of kinship (Lucy Westenra is destroyed by her mother, who undoes Van Helsing's protective charms and leaves her daughter unprotected). He is surrounded by a band of possessed women. In short, without any evidence of deliberate textual interplay, the anxieties which shape *Dracula* produce a narrative whose outlines recreate that of *The Bacchae*. Though spontaneous, the parallel does result in one further particular point of reference. Euripides' Dionysus always stands in ironic relationship to the city. When Dracula arranges his arrival in London, he does so under a pseudonym: Count De Ville[5] – Citizen Devil.

Yet there is another familiar narrative pattern too. The questing, Nordic hero battles his way to the mountain lair of an enchanter, sexually sterile but surrounded by tempting women. One of his prime weapons is the communion and its rituals. He removes the threat of pollution to his community and cures the wound that symbolizes that pollution; in this case, the mark burned into Mina Harker's forehead by the communion wafer. Submerged in *Dracula*, also, is the story of *Parsifal*.

The co-existence and merging of these two narratives helps us to see just how intricately and precisely the story of *Parsifal* reverses that of *The Bacchae*: the hero who would purify his society goes into the mountains to confront his mother and the effeminate enchanter who controls the women. *Parsifal* is no more a deliberate variant of *The Bacchae* than is *Dracula*. The structural antitheses between *Parsifal* and *The Bacchae* are of note, not because Wagner intended them, but because they express cultural tensions that were increasingly demanding the return of Euripides' Dionysus. *Dracula* is almost the last study of the Dionysiac to be innocent of the idea of Dionysus.

Dracula is a novel about a vampire. The vampire is not an allegorical representation of something else, such as (as has been suggested) capitalism,[6] but it is widely recognized, and indeed obvious, that the story is infused with contemporary fears of less supernatural (though not less fictitious) threats, of racial degeneration and of the 'New Woman' (pp. 86–7). *Dracula* portrays the sacrificial expiation of pollution – 'There is', Mina says, 'a poison in my blood' (p. 286) – and the novel is permeated by the pseudo-scientific analysis of racial and moral types that was current in the nineteenth century (and which was to feature yet more explicitly in *The Lair of the White Worm* (1911)). Dracula's Transylvania is a 'whirlpool of European races' (p. 33), his agent in Galatz is a Jew (p. 302), and he uses a French pseudonym. By contrast, Quincy Morris's racially suspect name has been thoroughly sanitized by the virile new culture he represents (Quincy is originally a French place name, and Morris means Moorish), and the other vampire hunters have Germanic or Anglo-Saxon names: Van Helsing, Holmwood, Harker, Seward (which was believed to mean Sea-Ward). When Arthur drives the stake into Lucy's heart, he 'looked like a figure of Thor' (p. 192). The vulnerable women, Mina Murray and Lucy Westenra have Celtic names (respectively Scottish and Irish), and Mina's Germanic Wilhelmina is softened into the patronizing diminutive.

In Stoker's last novel, *The Lair of the White Worm*, the racial and sexual threats to civilization are conditioned by a sense of the ancient geological processes to which humanity has been subject. A community is threatened by a vast prehistoric reptile that has evolved the capacity to imitate a beautiful woman, this threat of the primordial being complemented by that of an uncivilized negro servant Oolanga: 'Monsters such as he is belong to an earlier and more rudimentary stage of barbarism.'[7] Dracula to some extent also embodies the geologically primordial, since Transylvania 'is full of strangeness of the geologic and chemical world' (p. 278), and its strange properties may have influenced him. His threat, however, is far more akin to that posed by Oolanga. Despite avoiding direct allegory, the book re-enacts the fear that empire will rebound, and that Britain will be corrupted by the races it conquers. Yet Dracula himself is a testimony to squandered national potential: a soldier and liberator, he has done nothing with his achievements for centuries. His castle contains currency of many nations, all unused and covered in dust, and none less than 300 years old.

The fear that is rendered most explicit, however, is that of matriarchy. Mina refers satirically to the advent of the 'New Woman' in a way that explicitly associates this phenomenon with Lucy's vampirism, and the ship on which Dracula arrives in Whitby is named after the archetypal mother goddess, *Demeter* (p. 79). One positive interpretation of the allusion would be to see the recovery of Mina from Dracula as a version of the Persephone story, though it is hard see why the figure associated with Demeter would be the one who corresponds to Dis in the original narrative, nor why the role that in the myth is performed by the questing mother is in the novel performed by heroic men. Demeter's attribute, corn, is also transferred to the men. When Van Helsing first arrives at Liverpool Street to attend to Lucy, he develops an elaborate simile to the effect that the husbandman does not dig up his corn to see how it is growing (pp. 111–12), and he later describes Dracula as leaving his own barren land to come to one where men teem like 'standing corn' (p. 278) (corn again being associated with the masculine). The gifts of Ceres appear in their highest cultural form in the communion wafer, though Stoker characteristically glances at the capacity of modern technology to redefine ancient symbols: triumphant after tracking down Dracula's London address, Jonathan stops for 'a cup of tea at the Aërated Bread Company' (p. 234).

A more likely significance of Demeter, however, is her association with matriarchy: the cult of Demeter had been interpreted by Johann Jakob Bachofen as evidence of a primeval matriarchal system, which predated the advent of patriarchy, and, although Bachofen had not been translated into English, his ideas were widely disseminated. Confirmation of the concern with matriarchy is supplied by the name of the ship on which Dracula returns to the East, for this is named after a more recent matriarch: *Czarina Catherine* (p. 275).

To what aspects of this formidable and many-faceted figure could Stoker be alluding? The range of possible choices, and his presumed selection within them, are a revealing index of his outlook. It seems hardly to the point that Catherine the Great corresponded with Voltaire and Diderot, or that she invited the composer Giuseppe Sarti to St Petersburg. It seems very much to the point that she (probably) arranged the murder of her husband; that she was a figure of famous sexual excess; that, according to malicious gossip, she had died attempting intercourse with a stallion; and that she ruled an Eastern empire. Thus is one of the great figures of the Enlightenment transformed in Stoker's imagination: into a passage to Castle Dracula and its voluptuous female vampires. The likeness of Dracula and his female band to Dionysus and his Maenads has already been mentioned, and it is perhaps relevant to note that Bachofen saw the Dionysiac cult as a direct successor to Amazonian matriarchy: the weapons of the Amazon cede to the thyrsoi of the Bacchanals, and 'the man-hating virgins become the invincible heroic horde of the phallic lord of Nature'.[8] This seems a fairly good description of Dracula's entourage, though by breastfeeding his charges with blood he shows a corresponding regression to a matriarchal figure.

The racial and sexual fears combine in a single fear: the creation 'of a new order of beings' (p. 263). *Dracula* is yet another work in which women are figured as beings of an alien species, for Lucy is transformed into something terribly inhuman. In both the intersecting pursuits (Dracula's of the Englishwomen, the Anglo-Saxon males' of Dracula and his women), women are the prey of the hunter. In Wagner, such a relationship marks differences of origin and culture beyond which the mind and the community must evolve: the doe which Arindal hunts at the beginning of *Die Feen* turns out to be a superior being who elevates him to her level. In *Dracula*, the association of women with the animal has an opposite character, expressing fear of evolutionary degeneration, a threat that is combated in the three episodes of ritualized death in which the alien species is returned to humanity. In the first two episodes, with Lucy and with Dracula's three followers, the symbols of the Christian sacrifice, the Cross and communion wafer, assist the transformation of flesh, and in beheading Lucy with post-mortem surgical knives (pp. 190–3) Van Helsing again shows how the instruments and symbols of science may acquire the properties of ancient ritual. Van Helsing is also the operator in the killing of the other female vampires. The surgeon doubles as sacrificer. In the improvised and unritualized killing of Dracula, however, we again see a regression from sacrifice to the hunt: after a desperate pursuit, Dracula is dispatched with the Bowie knife of Morris and the kukri of Jonathan; the weapons of the West and the East combine in this final eradication of evil.

These deaths are sacrifices which transfer the victim from one state to another. They also pit culture against the predatory state from which it emerged. Like *Robinson Crusoe*, *Dracula* sets the knife against the tooth: apart from a late incident with knife-wielding gypsies, the knives in *Dracula* are held by the vampire-hunting men, and they are knives with a wide range of cultural properties. Van Helsing, as noted, uses surgeon's knives; the Bowie and kukri knives are not mere weapons, but complex instruments used for skinning, preparing flesh, and shaping wood. On the other side, teeth belong to vampires and their associated animals, the only exception being that moment of desperate cultural deprivation in which the captain of the ship bearing Dracula to England ties knots with his teeth to lash himself to the wheel. Here, however, the tooth is uniquely used to construct rather than divide. In the sacrificial moments of *Dracula*, then, culture triumphs over a recidivist nature, symbolized by the growing teeth of the victims.

But is there in *Dracula* any biological basis for sacrifice, equivalent to child-bearing in Wagner? It appears that there is, and that its basis is breast-feeding. Real female breast-feeding never appears, and indeed Stoker alters vampire legend so that the blood is not taken from the breast, but from the throat: the closest visual approximation to maternal breast-feeding is when the vampire Lucy holds an abducted child to her breast. Yet, as in this incident, we are always implicitly aware of the normative process that never happens.[9]

When, in Castle Dracula, Jonathan seeks somewhere to sleep away from his room, he chooses a room where, he imagines, ladies in former times 'had sat and sung and lived sweet lives whilst their gentle breasts were sad for their menfolk away in the midst of remorseless wars' (p. 41). Immediately, however, he is assailed by the three vampires, trying to fasten on his throat with their animal lips, tongue, and teeth. Shortly afterwards, following a further apparition of the women, he looks out of the window to see a distraught woman tearing her hair, beating her breast, and berating Dracula: 'Monster, give me my child!' (p. 48). She is an impotent Demeter confronting an inflexible Dis. 'I could not pity her', writes Jonathan, 'for I knew now what had become of her child, and she was better dead' (p. 49). Dracula's breast-feeding of his vampire followers seems not so much a compromise of his phallic masculinity as a complete erasure of feminine functions. The novel is essentially a struggle for mastery of the pectoral area, the misuses of the breast being countered with crosses round the neck or stakes through the heart. Again, however, Stoker shows the technological updating of ancient symbols: when the heroes surreptitiously enter Dracula's London residence, the traditional anti-vampire charms are supplemented by electric lamps, fastened to the *breast*.

If Wagner locates the Crucifixion in a scheme of evolutionary racial struggle, Stoker locates it in an economy of fluid exchange: the flowing of Christ's blood against the Antichrist-like Dracula's blood-sucking. Beneficent fluid exchange occurs when Seward has sucked gangrenous poison from a wound in Van Helsing's body (106), and Lucy Westenra receives blood transfusions. The blood transfusions are the most explicitly sacrificial ritual in the book, and again show how old mythic or religious patterns may be preserved in the outlines of modern science (a decorative example is the description of $C_2HCl_3O{\cdot}H_2O$ – chloral hydrate – as 'the modern Morpheus' (p. 97)). 'I would die for her' (p. 114), Arthur says, as he prepares to give blood for Lucy.

Yet the inventions of progress can also be informed by darker presences from the past: witness Dracula's arrival in a railway train, and his use of English legal machinery to establish himself in London. Indeed, Stoker seems to acknowledge that there is a destructively sacrificial potential in scientific research itself: Seward undergoes Frankensteinian temptations as to what means would be justified by the end of understanding the lunatic Renfield (p. 71), and even what discovery might be worth the cost of damnation (p. 61). As Seward's reflections show, this is a culture of calculation. If this is used to positive effect when Mina's knowledge of train timetables proves invaluable in the hunt for Dracula, Dracula too knows his

Bradshaw. In the isolation of his cell, Renfield becomes another Robinson Crusoe, keeping a journal and meticulous totals of his spiders and flies, 'as though he were "focussing" some account' (p. 69). The money that lies unused in Dracula's castle functions equally as a tool of good or evil in England. Similarly, the language and procedures of science and calculation can both reproduce the outlines of old redemptive rituals and lend themselves to infiltration by evil. The rituals of garlic, the wafer, and the crucifix are immutable. Gold is infinitely mutable as coin, but univocal as Cross. The wheat that, when aerated, brings profit to the Aërated Bread Company can when consecrated sear the flesh of vampires. In both cases, their power comes from their translation into another system of exchange: that of blood.

NIETZSCHE AND AFTER

When Stoker wrote *Dracula*, the rebirth of Dionysus was well under way, initiated by Nietzsche's youthful work *The Birth of Tragedy* (1872), which famously sees Greek tragedy as holding in balance the Apolline and the Dionysiac: the former the image-building and individuating faculty and the latter an imageless, collective intoxication, a breakdown of cognitive forms, seen in Bacchic Greek choruses, in the Babylonian Sacaea, and in medieval movements such as the St Vitus's dance. The Dionysiac can manifest itself in the cruel and sensual orgies of Babylon, in which it was believed that a mock king was impaled after a three-day reign, and from which Apollo protected the Greeks, but it also renews the bond between human beings, in the way celebrated in Schiller's 'Ode to Joy'. Dionysiac tragedy dissolves distinctions between individuals and provides 'an overwhelming feeling of unity which leads men back to the heart of nature'.[10] We derive this metaphysical solace from every true tragedy: 'despite all changing appearances, life is indestructibly mighty and pleasurable' (p. 39). For Nietzsche, the Dionysiac entered German culture when Luther introduced the chorale.

Nietzsche replaces Goethe's and Schiller's idea of a calm and harmonious Greek culture with that of a culture in tension, between the violent past, represented in myth by the Titans, and the calm beauty of the Olympians: 'That luminous Olympian company only came to rule so that the sombre sway of *moira*, which determined Achilles' early death and the horrifying marriage of Oedipus, should be hidden by the radiant figures of Zeus, Apollo, Hermes' (p. 125). Tragedy confronted the Apolline Greek with the knowledge that 'his entire existence, with all its beauty and moderation, rested on a hidden ground of suffering and knowledge which was exposed to his gaze once more by the Dionysiac' (p. 27).

This is an early work in a much evolving career, of which it would be inappropriate to attempt any account here. The work introduces Nietzsche's interest in the archaeology of the mind: his interpretation of the psychic life of the individual as recapitulating the earlier stages of culture. '[I]n sleep and dreams we repeat once again the curriculum of earlier mankind', he was to write in *Human, All Too Human* (1878).[11] In the same work, he regards the Crucifixion as one such survival of archaic belief:

> A god who begets children on a mortal woman, a sage who calls upon us no longer to work, no longer to sit in judgement, but to heed the signs of the imminent end of the world; a justice which accepts an innocent man as a substitute sacrifice; someone who bids his disciples drink his blood; prayers for miraculous interventions; sin perpetrated against a god atoned for by a god; fear of a Beyond to which death is the gateway; the figure of the Cross as a symbol in an age which no longer knows the meaning and shame of the Cross – how gruesomely all this is wafted to us, as if out of the grave of a primeval past! Can one believe that things of this sort are still believed in? (p. 66)

In the 'Attempt at Self-Criticism' which in 1886 he added to *The Birth of Tragedy*, Nietzsche identified the Antichrist with the Dionysiac (p. 9).

Though in part associated with the violent stages of Greek culture, Nietzsche's Dionysus is not a deity who exacts sacrifice. When describing the role of Dionysus in *The Bacchae*, Nietzsche confines himself to an enthusiastic account of the Messenger's description of the peaceful Bacchanals, magically drawing milk and wine from the ground. He ignores the later part of the speech, in which the Bacchanals dismember cows and bulls, the blood of the animals dripping from the branches that had previously dripped honey. Yet sacrifice is at least symbolically present in Nietzsche's Dionysiac view of tragedy, for – as Gilbert Murray was to do more literally – he located the origins of tragedy in the myth of the god's dismemberment and resurrection. In part, this is interpreted allegorically, in that Apollo articulates Dionysus into symbols. In equally symbolic senses, the tragic hero re-enacts the sufferings of Dionysus: 'Prometheus, Oedipus etc., are merely masks of that original hero, Dionysos' (p. 51). Prometheus is Dionysiac in his desire to raise all things on his shoulders, and Apollonian in his concern for justice. *King Oedipus* balances the Apollonian and Dionysiac by casting a story of ancient horror in a mystery that is unravelled with serene dialectic; yet Oedipus also breaks through the ordered forms of the Apollonian world, abrogating 'every law, all natural order, indeed the moral world', and founding a new and higher world on its ruins. Referring to the end of *Oedipus at Colonus*, Nietzsche argues that Oedipus here attains a transforming knowledge that 'exerts on the world around him a magical, beneficent force which remains effective even after his death' (p. 47). This interpretation of Oedipus was soon to be overtaken by others, but the fusion of Oedipus and Dionysus is striking testimony to the degree to which Nietzsche turned Dionysus into an archetype of tragic experience, an archetype that was initially regenerative, but gradually became one of terror.

The other prophet of Dionysus, playing a worldly Cadmus to Nietzsche's mantic Tiresias, was Sir James Frazer, whose *Golden Bough* (first edition 1890) proved the key to all mythologies of the early twentieth century. This is one of a number of late nineteenth-century works to move away from the idea of sacrifice as a simple, material transaction with the gods. Edward Burnett Tylor (1832–1917), for example, had argued that sacrifice was originally an ingratiating gift to the gods, but that, as the gods became more remote, it changed into homage without hope of return. William Robertson Smith (1846–94), a major influence on Frazer, suggested that sacrifice originated in a communal meal of animal flesh shared with the god; the idea of sacrifice as tribute or atonement is a later development, arising from the offering of firstfruits after the establishment of agriculture.

At about the same time as *The Golden Bough*, there appeared the far slimmer volume, *Sacrifice: Its Nature and Functions* (1898), by Henri Hubert and Marcel Mauss, which actually endured far longer as an anthropological text. According to Hubert and Mauss, '*Sacrifice is a religious act which, through the consecration of a victim, modifies the condition of the mortal person who accomplishes it or that of certain objects with which he is concerned*' (p. 13). Sacrifice liberates a potentially dangerous spirit in the victim, which is why many sacrificial rituals appease the victim (p. 30). Fertilizing dismemberments, such as those practised by the Khonds in India, fix in the soil a spirit which will make it fertile. Yet, influential as it was within its own sphere, this book made no impact on literature. Its account of the logic of sacrifice was theoretical and psychologically remote, and it categorized by analytic subdivision; Frazer, by contrast, proposed a grand and sweeping synthesis, achieved by deriving all primitive cultures from two false yet universal theories of causation, which everyone could recognize merely by retreating into the outlook of his or her own childhood: the belief in sympathetic and in contagious magic.

As George Eliot recognized when she created Mr Casaubon in *Middlemarch*, the key to all mythologies is a beguiling and age-old obsession. How to explain the tantalizing glimpses of resemblance that link systems of belief that are widely separated in space or in cultural level? Many sixteenth-century observers of Mexico, for example, had noted that the Aztecs had eaten a kind of bread representing the flesh of the god: 'Let the reader note how cleverly this diabolical rite imitates that of our Holy Church', Diego Durán commands.[12] Contemplating the same resemblance, Frazer postulated not satanic parody but essential identity: 'the ancient Mexicans, even before the arrival of Christian missionaries, were fully acquainted with the doctrine of transubstantiation and acted upon it in the solemn rites of their religion' (p. 507).

For Frazer, the reason for such profound and detailed resemblances was that all primitive cultures are shaped by two fundamental but erroneous innate ideas: that one can cause events by imitating them (for example, sticking pins in an image), or that something that has been in contact with a person – a garment, a hair, even a name – gives power over the person himself. A century before, writers and scientists had started to contemplate the ancient figures preserved in the fossil record. Frazer now attempts a geology of the mind: discussing the fundamental and universal beliefs of the ignorant, he writes, 'One of the great achievements of the nineteenth century was to run shafts down into this low mental stratum in many parts of the world, and thus to discover its substantial identity everywhere' (p. 53); 'our resemblances to the savage are still far more numerous than our differences from him; and what we have in common with him, and deliberately retain as true and useful, we owe to our savage forefathers' (p. 218). As humanity moves from primitive to more advanced religions, it simply evolves new reasons for old practices: 'Myth changes while custom remains constant; men continue to do what their fathers did before them, though the reasons on which their fathers acted have been long forgotten. The history of religion is a long attempt to reconcile old custom with new reason, to find a sound theory for an absurd practice' (pp. 493–4).

Frazer does not tell the story of the princess of Culhuacán, the princess whose father arrived at the wedding of his daughter to the god, only to find that the form of the marriage was to flay her and drape her skin over the living body of the god's representative. He does, however, discuss in detail the rituals of which it was the aetiological myth, and he links them to other rituals of dying gods, including those of Dionysus and Christ. There had been previous universal and secular accounts of myth in the nineteenth century: for example Max Müller's interpretation of myth as a representation of the solar cycle. Apart from its comprehensiveness, its amassing and juxtaposition of haunting anecdotes – virgins married to crocodiles, a girl murdered so her fat would furnish candles enabling burglars to operate invisibly – Frazer's has one arresting quality. However artificial and transient the system which he derived from it, belief in sympathetic and contagious magic is part of our childhood view of the world. Not only did Frazer establish an apparent link between the cult of Huitzilopochtli and the Crucifixion: he established a link whose living force could be felt within the mind of each of his readers; the excavation of cultural layers was also a journey down through the layers of the mind to earliest childhood. Suddenly, the multiform cultures of the past and present, in all their outlandish violence, are derived from an innate mental process that we can still feel persisting within us. To know that Wagner accepted Max Müller's solar interpretation of the Siegfried legend does not materially affect our response to *The Ring*. We can hardly read *The Waste Land* without feeling Frazer within it.

Frazer imagines a linear development from magic to religion. At the earliest stages of culture, there was no distinction between the natural and the supernatural. Animals, or kings, were gods: kings were 'expected to give rain and sunshine in due season, to make the crops grow, and so on' (p. 24).

Since their enfeeblement would sympathetically produce the decline of nature, they must be killed before this could happen, and the myth of the dying and risen god originates in these rites of natural renewal: originally kingship was annual, but subsequently kings were killed when their potency declined, or when they could not defeat the challenge of a rival. Later there is a substitute victim: the eldest son, or a mock king, or an animal. (Frazer misinterprets the Babylonian custom of the Sacaea as involving the annual killing of a mock king, rather than a special killing when the king was threatened by ill omens.) The myth of the dismemberment of Pentheus in *The Bacchae* is a distorted recollection of the killing of the king-god himself. Similarly, the sacrificial dismembering of a bull in honour of Dionysus is a survival of the time the bull itself was the god. Frazer links the death and resurrection of Christ to that of Adonis, and even suggests that the Crucifixion may have been the sacrificial killing of a mock king.

The mask of Huitzilopochtli and the face of the Redeemer were now one and the same image, linked in cultural structure through being linked in mental origin. Frazer's successors widened the scope of his synthesis still further. The roots of tragedy, the highest literary form, were traced by Gilbert Murray back to the sacrificial dismemberment of Dionysus. Arguing that 'tragedy originated in a dance, ritual or magical, intended to represent the death of the vegetation this year and its coming return in triumph next year', Murray derived tragic form from a detailed ritual sequence:

> The Dionysiac ritual which lay at the back of tragedy, may be conjectured in its full form to have had six regular stages: (1) an Agon or Contest, in which the Daemon fights against his enemy, who – since it is really this year fighting last year – is apt to be almost identical with himself; (2) a Pathos, or disaster, which very commonly takes the shape of a *Sparagmos*, or Tearing in pieces; the body of the Corn God being scattered in innumerable seeds over the earth; sometimes of some other sacrificial death; (3) a Messenger, who brings the news; (4) a Lamentation, very often mixed with a Song of Rejoicing, since the death of the Old King is also the accession of the new; (5) the Discovery or Recognition of the hidden or dismembered god; and (6) his Epiphany or Resurrection in glory.[13]

In a similar manner, Jessie Weston derived the Grail Legend from ancient fertility ritual, and Jane Harrison in her *Prolegomena to the Study of Greek Religion* attempted to recover the gloomy, pre-Olympian stages of Greek religion. These stages were dominated by fearful expiatory rituals addressed 'not to the Olympians of the upper air, but to snakes and ghosts and underworld beings':[14] beings such as the *Keres* (spirits of evil) (pp. 163–217).

Frazer exposed the savage within, not as a nightmarish literary symbol – a doppelgänger or vampire – nor as a cultural layer broadly outlined with Nietzsche's dithyrambic pen. Rather, in encyclopaedic detail, he showed us the Aztec, or Babylonian, or Troglodyte within, and revealed how close are his ties to the Athenian within us. He also showed how the flaying of the princess of Culhuacán might seminally be present in the fears and superstitions of our childhood; how the most ancient of superstitions still persisted, nearby, in rural Ireland or East Anglia; and how a statue of Demeter in the Fitzwilliam Museum, Cambridge, was still viewed as a potent fertility charm by the inhabitants of Eleusis.

For Frazer, the savage within posed fearful dangers to the permanence of the civilization which the nineteenth century had precariously attained. There was evolution, but there was also the possibility of extinction. His mind again explicitly informed by the categories of geology, he speculated with trepidation about the next catastrophe:

> It is not our business here to consider what bearing the permanent existence of such a solid layer of savagery beneath the surface of society, and unaffected by the superficial changes of religion and culture, has upon the future of humanity. The dispassionate observer, whose studies have led him to plumb its depths, can hardly regard it otherwise than as a standing menace to civilisation. We seem to move on a thin crust which may at any moment be rent by the subterranean forces slumbering below. (p. 54)

Such fears are rational and prophetic. Yet the savage within continues to fascinate us, like a ghost story which we are compelled against our better judgment to read at bedtime. We need an emotional and cultural prehistory to correlate with the impassive record of the rocks and soil. The Bible provided a set of permanent psychological structures with which to refer the whole patterning of history to a primal act of disobedience at the beginning of time. What replaces these when the textual record has yielded to riddles of stone? The identification of imaginary origins creates a sense of homecoming whose satisfaction outweighs the terrors of the home that has been discovered. Discipline after discipline has been devoted to seeing traces of the prehistoric or even prehuman past in our advanced cultures; every railway train now contains a Dracula. The idea that tragedy was the cultural end-product of human sacrifice, or the Grail romance of seasonal fertility rites, proved a stimulus to rethinking and reinventing the forms themselves. Sacrificial ritual was to become not only the subject of literature but even its formal principle.

FREUD: *TOTEM AND TABOO*

Although Frazer created a psychologically unified account of global magic and religion, his eye was on the external practice, and in treating this he established a wide enough channel of influence. A parallel channel, however, was opened by Freud, who relied extensively on Frazer in *Totem and Taboo* (1913) but redirected the focus inward, using Frazer's anthropological data to detect the replication of primitive attitudes in the development and pathology of individual psychological life. For example, taboo is replicated in obsessional neurosis, and the power of totem animals in children's fearful fixation on particular creatures, which Freud interprets as a redirection of fear of the father. He then uses this modern psychoanalytic observation 'as the starting-point of our attempt at explaining totemism'.[15] Totemism is the revering of a particular species of animal, viewed as the ancestor of the clan; eating the totem animal is prohibited except at one annual feast, at which the tribe shares the guilt of devouring it. For Freud, the origin of the practice lay in an Oedipal event among the primal horde, when the sons killed and consumed the hated father who was monopolizing the women of the tribe: a *sparagmos*. The totem is a substitute for the dead father; exogamy is resignation of the men's claim to the women for whom they killed him. Though the protection of the animal expresses remorse for the killing of the father, ambivalence towards him dictated commemoration of the original killing in the communal sacrificial killing of the totem. With the development of the idea of God (also based on the figure of the father), the sacrificial meal becomes reinterpreted as a gift to God. The father is thus doubly present, both as the animal victim and as the God.

Though he does not explain the evolutionary connection, Freud goes on to accept Frazer's account of the regular sacrifice of human gods. Sacrificial ritual, which started in the killing of the father, reverted to human sacrifice: 'The original animal sacrifice was already a substitute for a human sacrifice – for the ceremonial killing of the father; so that, when the father-surrogate once more resumed its human shape, the animal sacrifice too could be changed back into a human sacrifice' (p. 151). The Crucifixion redeems man from the original sin of killing the father, and Freud supports this idea by sidestepping to the *sparagmos* of Dionysus: the idea of original sin is Orphic, and is derived from the myth that the Titans tore the infant Dionysus in pieces, and consumed all but his heart (from which he was reconstituted). Frazer and his followers are thus permitting a very striking interchange of roles. If the tearing apart of Pentheus is, in origin, that of Dionysus, the lacerations of the protagonist's body in *The Bacchae* and the Gospels are alternative versions of the same story. The hero of Greek tragedy is the dismembered father, who takes the primal guilt on himself to relieve the Chorus of theirs.

> In Greek tragedy the special subject-matter of the performance was the sufferings of the divine goat, Dionysus, and the lamentation of the goats who were his followers and who identified themselves with him. That being so, it is easy to understand how drama, which had become extinct, was kindled into fresh life in the Middle Ages around the Passion of Christ. (p. 156)

One consequence of Freud's reworking of Frazer's data is to increase the purchase of the primitive upon the modern mind. Frazer hopes, somewhat gloomily, for an evolution beyond sympathetic and contagious magic. In Freud's account, more elaborate structures of primitive thought are more firmly present in the mechanics of the mind. Obsessional neurosis preserves not only the symptoms but the mental mechanisms of taboo; totemism is a natural feature of childhood; and the Oedipus complex – at least for Freudians – is always with us.

CHAPTER 13

Pentheus 1913

On 29 May 1913, the Ballets Russes gave the first performance of one of the most influential works of early twentieth-century music, Stravinsky's *The Rite of Spring*. This depicts a quasi-Dionysiac human sacrifice to promote the renewal of the earth. Indeed, it has human sacrifice as its formal principle, since the victim – the Chosen One – dances herself to death. The work of art itself becomes the sacrificial instrument. *The Rite of Spring* is the first ballet to be based on anthropological research; to take a scientific sense of the primitive as its starting point. For Adorno, it 'belongs to the years when wild men came to be called primitives, to the sphere of Frazer and Lévy-Bruhl, and further of Freud's *Totem and Taboo*'.[1] Like *Das Rheingold*, it opens by evoking a primordial, prehistoric world, though – unlike Wagner's work – it does not present the primordial world as a recoverable model for the present: rather, its barbarity is presented as an object of detached aesthetic contemplation. Gone is the emphasis on the subjectivity of the sacrificial victim: the Chosen One emerges from the mass, but stands for it and is individuated only by her dance of death. *The Rite* is a portrayal of psychological collectivity, in which ritual itself assumes an identity more powerful than that of its individual participants: there is, writes Adorno, no 'antithesis between the sacrificial victims and the tribe' (p. 158). The photograph of Lydia Sokolova in the 1920 production (Plate 15) freezes her in an impersonally geometric pose.

The Rite of Spring provides an almost perfectly symmetrical contrast with that seminal work of the nineteenth century, Beethoven's *Eroica* symphony, with its celebration of the individual mind, and its elevation of the creative Prometheus, purged of his role as sacrificial victim. By contrast, human sacrifice was to be a major Modernist theme. That other great innovator of early twentieth-century music, Arnold Schoenberg, portrayed it in his opera *Moses und Aron*. A dream of human sacrifice is the psychological centre of Thomas Mann's *The Magic Mountain*, and it also figures powerfully in the Joseph tetralogy. *The Waste Land* portrays a world that has lost the Frazerian rituals of rebirth, and several of Lawrence's works portray human sacrifice as a source of sexual and social renewal. It is everywhere.

For Adorno, *The Rite* speaks to an exhausted bourgeois culture whose 'aesthetic nerves tremble with the desire to regress to the Stone Age' (p. 148).

Plate 15 Lydia Sokolova as the Chosen Virgin in Massine's 1920 production of *The Rite of Spring*

It reflects the depersonalization of the industrial age, and is prescient of the slaughter to come, on the battlefields of the Great War and beyond: 'Human sacrifice, in which the impending domination of the collective is proclaimed, is evoked out of the insufficiency of the individualistic condition in itself . . . It is not only that the work actually resounds with the noise of the impending war, but it further reveals its undisguised joy at the vulgar splendour of it all' (p. 147). Such sinister interpretations mistake distant resonances and analogies, greatly differing in source and intensity, for direct social and psychological links. It is certainly true, however, that an aesthetic of violence and sacrifice survived the First World War (in, for example, the work of the

Futurists, or Georges Bataille's rumoured plan to conduct a human sacrifice)[2] and that its products do at times have an uncomfortably close relationship to the rise of Nazism. Reflecting on the proximity of aestheticism and barbarism in *Doctor Faustus*, Mann wrote (in terms that may embrace *The Rite*) of the dangers in 'The revival of ritual music from a profane epoch' ('Die Erneuerung kultischer Musik aus profaner Zeit').[3]

The First World War is the first war which the British habitually imagined in terms of sacrifice, as can be seen by comparing *The Times*'s reporting of this war with that of the Napoleonic and Crimean wars. Imagery of sacrifice is, it is true, occasionally used of the earlier conflicts, but it is not a dominant mode of thought. In Southey's 'Poet's Pilgrimage To Waterloo', for example, it is specifically evoked only once, and then primarily in connection with the women back home:

> And from the dreadful sacrifice of all,
> Meek woman doth not shrink at Duty's call.[4]

During the period of the Great War, however, *The Times* is full of articles and leaders about sacrifice and self-sacrifice: for example, 'Soldiers' Self-Sacrifice', 'Ties of Heroism and Sacrifice', and 'The Sacrifice of the Peerage'.[5]

'Dulce et decorum est / Pro patria mori' is, as Wilfred Owen wrote, 'The old Lie'.[6] When he wrote 'The Parable of the Old Man and the Young', in which Abraham persists with the sacrifice of Isaac in defiance of the angel, he was addressing an updated version of that lie – that war is noble sacrifice:

> But the old man would not so, but slew his son,
> And half the seed of Europe, one by one.
>
> (*Collected Poems*, p. 42)

In 'one by one' Owen honours what Stravinsky had erased in *The Rite*: the distinct individuality of the victim. The simultaneous stumbling of thousands into the shells and bullets is stretched out into an endless sequence of consecutive, individually experienced moments, dismantling the collectivism of war into its individual tragedies.

Two of the greatest masterpieces of twentieth-century fiction concern the descent into war: Robert Musil's novel *The Man without Qualities*, left incomplete at his death in 1942, and Thomas Mann's *The Magic Mountain* (1924). Both make important use of the image of human sacrifice.

THE MAN WITHOUT QUALITIES

The Man without Qualities is an account of the year 1913. It is a period of glittering decadence, the inhabitants of which cling to the forms of the past and believe in their continued vitality (a failed artist and his sexually neurotic wife are first glimpsed playing Beethoven's 'Ode to Joy' as a piano duet).

Yet it succumbs to enervation, and to the uncertain sense of self induced by the new era of mass-production and unassimilated technological change. It is a time of stagnation after the illusory reinvigoration at the turn of the century: 'As when a magnet releases iron filings and they fall in confusion again' ('Wie Wenn ein Magnet die Eisenspänne losläßt und sie wieder durcheinandergeraten').[7]

The hero of the novel, Ulrich (we never learn his surname), is a *tabula rasa*, without anything to individuate him. He has dabbled in three careers – cavalry officer, engineer, mathematician – all of which have as their essence the furthering of human progress: his motto as an engineer, for example, is 'Mankind walks the earth as a prophecy of the future' (p. 34) ('Die Menschen wandeln auf Erden als Weissagungen der Zukunft' (vol. 1, p. 38)). Yet all hopes of great achievement wither when he reads a report of a sensational racing win, by a 'racehorse of genius' (p. 41) ('geniale Rennpferd' (vol. 1, p. 44)). The cavalryman has been overtaken in the evolutionary race by his mount. There is no point in continuing.

What is at issue is the fate of the extraordinary individual, or any individual, in a culture of mass circulation, where a sense of identity is forged by newspapers, magazine pictures, and street advertisements. What, the novel at one point asks, would happen to Abraham in such a textual culture? What happens to the sacrificer and his victim amidst the endless proliferation of disposable images which decorates the ingenuous march towards the disposable bodies of the Great War? What, indeed, happens to the knife? It too becomes a mass-produced spectator object: Stumm von Bordwehr, a cavalry general too short to sit on a horse and too poor to collect exotic weapons, instead fulfils himself by collecting pocket knives, which he classifies and arranges with a Linnaean precision.

The Man Without Qualities in part traces the activities of the Parallel Campaign: a series of proliferating and increasingly absurd schemes to commemorate the seventieth anniversary of the accession of the Emperor Franz Josef – due in the year 1918. The intention is to overtop celebrations of Kaiser Wilhelm's thirtieth anniversary, also due in that year. Proposals for suitable forms of celebration include one for a Nietzsche Year. The idea of the seventy-year continuum from that year of abortive upheaval, 1848, itself suggests a linear and progressive view of history: the expectation that 1918 will be the fitting consummation of 1848. Progress is a recurrent topic.

Yet the decadent aestheticism and administrative pedantry of Austrian life is overshadowed by universal obsession with the carpenter and sex murderer Moosbrugger. Moosbrugger has used the knife to a more traditional purpose than Stumm von Bordwehr, yet his handiwork is subjected to the same relentless classification: reporters list the slicing of the throat and the breasts, the two stab wounds apiece through the heart and the back, the thirty-five stabs in the belly (p. 67; vol. 1, p. 68). To some extent, Moosbrugger is the savage within: the savage who symbolizes the potential for the barbarism to come. Moosbrugger, Ulrich reflects, is 'a distortion of our own elements of being . . . [I]f mankind could dream as a whole, that dream would be Moosbrugger' ('ein verzerrter Zusammenhang unsrer eignen Elemente des Seins . . . [W]enn die Menschheit als Ganzes träumen könnte, müßte Moosbrugger entstehn') (pp. 76–7; vol. I, p. 76). Bank managers say to their wives at bedtime, 'What would you do now if I were a Moosbrugger?' ('Was würdest du jetzt anfangen, wenn ich ein Moosbrugger wäre') (p. 68; vol. I, p. 69).

Yet Moosbrugger is no more an atavistic figure than the racehorse of genius. As a collective obsession of Vienna, he too is a creation of the press. His case is first introduced as something 'currently much in the news' (literally something which preoccupied the public: 'beschäftigte . . . die Öffentlichkeit') (p. 67; vol. I, p. 67). His near-dismemberment of the prostitute is itself in turn dissected by the cold sensationalism of the press, but then he ceases to be news. When he first sees an aeroplane in the sky, he is astonished; 'But then there was one plane after another, and they all looked alike' ('aber dann kam ein solches Flugzeug nach dem andern, und eines sah wie das andere aus') (p. 579; vol. II, p. 531). Sex murderers have the same mechanical reproducibility: 'Other Moosbruggers were taking their turn; they were not himself, not even the same person every time, but they served the same purpose' ('Andere Moosbruggers kamen an die Reihe; sie waren nicht er, sie waren nicht einmal die gleichen, aber sie leisteten den gleichen Dienst') (p. 580; vol. II, p. 532). There is a man beyond the disposable newsprint: not an archaic and unified drive but a set of confused, disjunct, yet often individually explicable impulses. Yet, for the world, he is what he is on paper.

Moosbrugger had met his victim, a prostitute, at the very boundary of the city and the fields (pp. 72–3; vol. I, p. 3). But he had not then gone on into the wilderness. He had killed her in a sports ground – that modern nursery of genius – on the way back into town: a *sparagmos* in a site of a burgeoning recreational culture, a fitting prelude to the spectator sport he himself becomes. How would he have appeared in earlier ages? '[W]hen he is having one of his seizures,' says the new man, the industrialist Arnheim,

> he is certainly a man possessed by the demonic, which in all virile epochs has been felt to be akin to the divine. In the old days *such a man would have been sent into the wilderness*. Even then he might have committed murder, but perhaps in a visionary state, like Abraham about to slaughter his son Isaac. There it is! We no longer have any idea of how to deal with such things, and there is no sincerity in what we do. (p. 694; italics added)

> Er ist aber in den Zeiten seiner Anfälle ein Sitz des Dämonischen, das in allen starken Jahrhunderten dem Göttlichen verwandt empfunden worden ist. Früher hätte man den Mann, wenn seine Anfälle kamen, in die Wüste geschickt; er würde dann vielleicht auch gemordet haben, aber in einer großen Vision, wie Abraham

den Isaak schlachten wollte! Das ist es! Wir wissen heute nichts mehr damit anzufangen, und wir meinen nichts mehr ehrlich! (vol. II, pp. 636–7)

This is the second time that the sacrificing Abraham has appeared in the novel. Earlier, Ulrich has reflected that:

What we cannot classify as either a fact or a subjective experience we sometimes call an imperative. We have attached such imperatives to the dogmas of religion and the law and thereby give them the status of deduced truth. But the novelists tell us about the exceptions, from Abraham's sacrifice of Isaac to the most recent beauty who shot her lover, and dissolve it again into something subjective. (p. 274)

Man nennt etwas, das weder eine Wahrheit noch eine Subjektivität ist, zuweilen eine Forderung. Man hat diese Forderung an den Dogmen der Religion und an denen des Gesetzes befestigt und ihr dadurch den Charakter einer abgeleiteten Wahrheit gegeben, aber die Romanschriftsteller erzählen uns von den Ausnahmen, angefangen beim Opfer Abrahams bis zur jüngsten schönen Frau, die ihren Geliebten niedergeschossen hat, und lösen es wieder in Subjektivität auf. (vol. I, p. 254)

This is almost Kierkegaard in reverse: Abraham is still a great exception to any universal law, but only like an anomalous pocket knife in the General's collection; a point where the classifying intellect retires in fatigue, and hands over to the subjective and its dissolving vagueness. Thus dissolved, the sacrificing Abraham migrates into an entirely new textual sphere, with its own interchangeability: between the sacrificing patriarch and the jealous mistress.

In Arnheim's formulation, Moosbrugger is not a throwback but a figure who would have a different value in different cultures. There is an inescapable vicious circle: that each culture can be evaluated only by its own standards. 'Human nature', Ulrich reflects,

is as capable of cannibalism as it is of the *Critique of Pure Reason*; the same convictions and qualities will serve to turn out either one, depending on circumstances, and very great external differences in the results correspond to very slight internal ones. (p. 391)

Denn das menschliche Wesen ist ebenso leicht der Menschenfresserei fähig wie der Kritik der reinen Vernunft; es kann mit den gleichen Überzeugungen und Eigenschaften beides schaffen, wenn die Umstände danach sind, und sehr großen äußeren Unterschieden entsprechen dabei sehr kleine innere. (vol. II, p. 361)

The place of human sacrifice in this lottery of cultural evolution is most fully discussed by a group of young Christian-Germanic anti-Semites, who meet at the house of the Jewish doctor Leo Fischel in order to discuss topics such as 'upward humanization' ('Empormenschlichung') (p. 521; vol. II, p. 478), attracting the enthusiasm of his daughter Gerda, who naïvely believes that their aspirations are symbolic rather than racist. In this circle, Ulrich introduces the question of human progress, moral and technological: is the aeroplane an advance on the coach? Morally, the debate focusses on human sacrifice. '[O]nce it has made sense to offer up human sacrifice to the gods, say, or burn witches, or wear powdered wigs,' argues Ulrich, 'then that remains one of life's valid possibilities, even when more hygienic habits and more humane customs represent progress. The trouble is that progress always wants to do away with the old meaning' (p. 528).

Wenn es aber einmal einen Sinn gehabt hat, zum Beispiel den Göttern Menschen zu opfern oder Hexen zu verbrennen oder das Haar zu pudern, dann bleibt das doch ein sinnvolles Lebensgefühl, auch wenn hygienischere Sitten und Humanität Fortschritte sind. Der Fehler ist, daß der Fortschritt immer mit dem alten Sinn aufräumen will. (vol. II, p. 485)

Another participant goes further: 'When you devour an innocent rabbit, that's darkness, but when a cannibal dines reverently and with religious rites on a stranger, we simply cannot know what goes on inside him' ('Wenn Sie einen unschuldigen Hasen verschlingen, ist das finster; wenn aber ein Kannibale unter religiösen Zeremonien ehrfürchtig einen Stammesfremden verspeist, wissen wir einfach nicht, was in ihm vorgeht!') (pp. 528–9; vol. II, p. 485). Elsewhere, Ulrich reflects on the degree to which the language of the primitive hunter survives in the language, alike, of love and of capitalism: to possess (*besitzen*) (p. 610; vol. II, p. 559) is literally to sit upon, the stronger mastering the weaker; to be without an aim or target is, literally, to be without something to kill. Musil seems to be writing like a sociobiologist, tracing the survival of atavistic patterns in modern social behaviour. Yet Ulrich's comment on such traces is almost exactly the opposite of what one would expect: 'a crudely changed meaning has everywhere usurped the function of far subtler messages now quite lost to us, that ever-perceptible but never quite tangible nexus of things' ('sich allerorten der roh veränderte Sinn an die Stelle von bedachtsameren Beziehungen gedrängt hat, die ganz verlorengegangen sind. Es ist das wie ein überall zu fühlender, nirgends zu fassender Zusammenhang') (p. 610; vol. II, p. 559). The subtler meaning is the language of the hunter. We are facing not evolution, not even linear change, but a 'never quite tangible nexus'.

If the Parallel Campaign and the sensationalist fascination with Moosbrugger are conducted on the brink of an abyss that was to open within the year, the anti-Semites gathering in a Jewish household to discuss human sacrifice point to a somewhat more distant abyss, whose full depths Musil (whose wife was Jewish) did not live to see. Yet the debating points remain compelling in the possibilities that they evoke. Moosbrugger is as socially created as he is socially interpreted: the paradox is that the social creation is quite independent of the social interpretation. If Moosbrugger is inseparable – indistinguishable – from the nexus of events that created him, the killer is nevertheless not for an age but for all time. It remains compellingly tempting to transpose him from the deserted Viennese sports ground to the deserted mountain in the land of Moriah, and to see a different culture (and different kind of textual production) as giving him an entirely different form and value, as a heroic sacrificer. There must, Ulrich muses, have been something to be said for powdered wigs and for human sacrifice, 'otherwise so many nice people would never have gone along with them . . . And perhaps we are still sacrificing so many human beings today only because we never clearly faced the problem of the right way to overcome mankind's earlier answers':

> sonst wären doch nicht so viele nette Menschen einst mit ihnen einverstanden gewesen . . . Und vielleicht opfern wir heute gerade deshalb noch viele Menschen, weil wir uns die Frage der richtigen Überwindung früherer Menschheitseinfälle nie deutlich gestellt haben!? (p. 529; vol. II, p. 485)

The man without qualities is the product of a world without archetypes.

THE MAGIC MOUNTAIN

If the sacrificer in the background of *The Man without Qualities* is Abraham, that in *The Magic Mountain* is (not for the first time in Mann) Dionysus. Towards the end of *Death in Venice* (1912), Gustav von Aschenbach had had a nightmare, shortly before (a modern Pentheus) he had assumed the effeminating disguise of dyed hair and cosmetic make-up that prepared him for his last spying mission upon the young god Tadzio. Many details of the dream are taken from *The Bacchae*, and in particular from the first Messenger's speech, describing the Bacchanals' revels on Mount Cithaeron: the Stranger God, the flutes, the torch-light mountain revels, the women in animal skins, the dismemberment of animals. Then, in the following decade, another Mann hero undertook a more literal journey to a mountain: the Hamburg engineer Hans Castorp travels to the sanatorium of Hofrat Behrens in Davos, initially to visit his tubercular cousin Joachim. Quickly, however, he is found to be tubercular himself, and undertakes a seven-year cure on his own account. During this he experiences the perpetual cultural conflict between disciplined, Apollonian order and the formless Dionysiac excess that the Western imagination associates with the East. His own private Orient is the beautiful Russian Claudia Cauchat, with whom he is desperately infatuated, but she reincarnates an earlier and even more illicit passion, for she disturbingly resembles the beautiful Polish boy, Pribislav Hippe, with whom he had fallen in love at school.

The sanatorium in *The Magic Mountain* is an outpost of civilization, staring, at harsh times of the year, into intractable snowy wastes that are beyond the mastery of human technology. In the course of the mountain sojourn, Hans meets an embodiment of Dionysus, Mynheer Pieter Peeperkorn: like Dionysus, a visitor from the East, having returned from a colonial life in Java. Some time before Peeperkorn's arrival, Hans Castorp has made his deepest penetration into the mountains. Lost in the snow he had drifted into a trance, and had a vision of a noble, seemingly utopian society whose secret principle was human sacrifice.

'The Olympian magic mountain now opens up, as it were, and shows us its roots',[8] wrote Nietzsche, discussing what he considered to be the pre-Olympian elements in Greek religion: the stories of Prometheus and Oedipus, for example. Later, writing of German failure to recreate the purity of Greek literature, he claimed that even 'such heroes as Goethe and Schiller were not granted the ability to break open the enchanted gateway leading into the Hellenic magic mountain' (p. 97). The first passage, evoking the dark, pre-Olympian stages of Greek culture, is particularly appropriate, for the Olympian heights of Mann's mountain are strangely subterranean in quality: the Enlightenment rationalist Settembrini keeps referring to its guardian, Behrens, as Rhadamanthus, one of the classical judges of the dead, and Behrens is accompanied by a psychoanalyst, to explore the caverns of the mind. In his dream, Castorp stares into the roots of the mountain.

Many Romantic sacrificers or victims – Melmoth and Elis Fröbom, for example – are in different ways released from participation in time. Some of these, like Fröbom (and Frankenstein's creature), are placed by sacrifice not on the boundary of the human and the divine but of the human and the inorganic, where the eternity the victim faces is geological rather than otherworldly, and where his destiny may be, not translation to Taurica, but fossilization in ancient rock. In his dream in the snow, Hans risks becoming another preserved corpse, like Fröbom. Yet bodies in *The Magic Mountain* are freed from time in a rather different sense, in that time ceases to have any psychological consistency and becomes (as indeed it is) philosophically problematic. Its mental speed expands and contracts capriciously, and its artificial measurements and distinctions are mocked by the natural world, which does not even follow a predictable seasonal cycle. But time belongs far more to the inorganic than to the organic sphere. When Joachim is X-rayed, his flesh fades away before the dissolving beam, yet his ancestral ring, symbol of his place in the span of history, continues to show up, solid and impermeable.

Time is supplanted by another derivative of *tempus*, temperature (*Temperatur*). Temperature regulates the sanatorium, is a universal obsession, and restores what had retreated to the background in Wagner: the numerical classification of the body. Yet number, one of the fundamental constituents of culture, is here a means of imposing intellectual order on bodily dissolution. Released, for a while, from participation in historical time, the body is instead subjected to a numerical scale which gauges its capacity for disease. A cognate system is the Gaffky scale, which measures density of bacilli in the sputum, and even the room numbers become a means of classifying disease and mortality: 'my *moribundus*, number twenty-seven' ('meinem Moribundus . . . auf siebenundzwanzig hier') says Behrens of a dying patient.[9] Temperature is also, however, used to measure the outside, inorganic world, particularly its coldness. The structure of the thermometer scale is thus the common term between the organic and the inorganic worlds, and yet at the same time it establishes their total difference and incommensurability, for the temperature of the outside world seems only relevant insofar as it establishes the degree of its hostility to life. Temperature either denotes the overheated organism or the chill of a world beyond the borders of civilization.

Like *Death in Venice* and *Doctor Faustus*, *The Magic Mountain* is a meditation on the *Liebestod*. In Wagner, it had been a release into pure immateriality from the dividedness of the physical world; in *The Magic Mountain*, it is a byproduct of matter and organic process. Spirit resolves itself into matter, as when Behrens explains physiologically the sensations caused by the experience of holy communion (*MM*, p. 264; *ZB*, p. 243).[10] The spirit world is primarily defended by the violent antagonist of Enlightenment, the Jesuit Leo Naphta, proponent of an autocracy sustained by terror, but it appears only in the vulgar and deranged séances towards the end of the novel, as war looms: the spirit-poet Holger produces descriptive banalities about an uninhabited waterscape (an expanse of pure matter), and the dead Joachim is summoned up, prophetically transformed into a First World War combatant. This is not the immateriality into which Tristan and Isolde escape. Rather, love and death become united by their common origins in the fevered and overheated body, the thermometer becoming an index and symbol of sexual excitement. Immaterial versions of the body become rather X-rays, films, photographs, and gramophone recordings – all, unlike the spirit, concerned with the interpenetration of love and death, all suspensions of the continuity of time. As a memento of his beloved Claudia Cauchat, Hans has an X-ray of her chest.

Towards the end of *The Magic Mountain*, Behrens introduces a gramophone into the sanatorium: another means of playing tricks with the flow of time, which indeed contains its own time-regulating device (*MM*, p. 636; *ZB*, p. 584). The records are the disembodied testaments of a culture obsessed with the relationship between sex and death, and between sex and duty (Dionysus and Apollo). They include, for example, extracts from *Carmen* and *Aida*. As Aida and Radames in the latter opera sing of the opening of the sky and their ascent towards the eternal day, Castorp reflects on the actual biochemical processes – the filling of the lungs with pit gas, for example – that would happen were two people to die in a tomb (*MM*, p. 645; *ZB*, pp. 591–2). One might imagine that Wagner would figure prominently in a work so concerned with the relationship between sex and death in German culture, but his presence is surprisingly subdued. In the record collection, we do not have – as we might at first expect – an extract from *Tristan* (which had given its title to Mann's earlier short story about life in a sanatorium). Wagner is represented by 'Blick' ich umher': the aria from *Tannhäuser* in which Wolfram praises pure and self-sacrificing love, only to provoke Tannhäuser into disturbing the cultured calm of the Wartburg with his praise of Venus (*MM*, p. 641; *ZB*, p. 588). The extract is appropriate to a society in which sex is a disruptive and obsessive force.

The sense of time survives in ritual. This is an ever-present structural feature of life, whether in anniversaries which impose some order on the subjective expansion and contraction of time in the sanatorium or in the almost monastic military rituals to which Hans's soldier cousin Joachim prematurely returns, and which constitute one pole in the conflict between rigorous form and Dionysiac abandon. Yet the rituals assist the development of the disease, and ensure his death; they are themselves the agent of formlessness. Even Settembrini, the Enlightenment devotee of Prometheus and champion of human progress, has his own form of ritualism, being a Freemason, and his opponent Naphta takes pleasure in recalling the more primitive stages and origins of the Masonic cult: their rituals of menacing the breast with swords, in the presence of a deathshead and three tapers, and their debt to the Eleusinian mysteries. Thoth and Hermes Trismegistus, whom Settembrini reveres as the inventors of writing and rhetoric, were, Naphta argues, an ape and moon deity, and a god of death. Mann thus presents a culture devoted to rituals and attenuated images of death, of which human sacrifice is a fitting culmination.

But what, in such a culture, does sacrifice mean? The first important reference to human sacrifice in *The Magic Mountain* applies it to something irrational, inorganic, and geological: the Lisbon earthquake of 1755. Voltaire, Settembrini says, 'protested in the name of reason and the intellect against that scandalous dereliction of nature, to which were sacrificed thousands of human lives' ('protestierte im Namen des Geistes und der Vernunft gegen diesen skandalösen Unfug der Natur, dem . . . Tausende von Menschenleben zum Opfer fielen') (*MM*, p. 250; *ZB*, p. 230). In the multiple hecatombs of the Lisbon disaster, the victims are again swallowed up in geological cycle and time. Voltaire's rage is the rage of the mind before the incomprehensible order of matter, whose forms and processes follow different laws from those of human perception and analysis.

Sacrifice is more usually the intellectual property of Settembrini's opponent Naphta, a Jew turned Jesuit whose father was the ritual slaughterer of the village. This office, originally priestly, implanted in his son an association between religion and cruelty which informs his entire intellectual outlook. In an argument with Settembrini about the ethics of torture and capital punishment, eagerly overheard by the masochist Wehsal, he offers his interpretation of the Crucifixion. Eulogizing spirit, and treating the essential condition of the body as one of disease, he argues that the Crucifixion and atonement signified the embrace of disease, as a route to knowledge and health. Even the sacrifice of Christ becomes an articulation of the diseased state of the body (*MM*, pp. 465–6; *ZB*, p. 425). Nor, Naphta argues, is Settembrini without the sacrificial impulse: despite his opposition to capital punishment and torture, he would be prepared to sacrifice individuals to a higher ideal (*MM*, p. 461; *ZB*, p. 421).

Immediately after this debate, Castorp makes his journey into the snow. Like the discussions with Settembrini and Naphta, it is a journey 'into uncharted and perilous regions' ('ins Weglose und Hochgefährliche') (*MM*, p. 477; *ZB*, p. 436). It also restores the mountain journey to its ancient significance, as a journey beyond the boundaries and possibilities of civilization, into an area which both precludes and predates human culture: in the snow, Hans encounters a 'primeval silence' ('Urschweigen') (*MM*, p. 476; *ZB*, p. 434). Yet the snow is made from water, the fundamental element of life. In contrast to the fevered decay in the sanatorium, it is formally perfect in its icy, crystalline shapes. Again, it shows the unbridgeable difference between the forms of the inorganic world and those grasped at by the animate intellect: in its alien symmetry, the snowflake shows that the structure of the inorganic world cannot be reconciled with that of the conscious mind. Its icy perfection is inimical to life, and reveals that life, and indeed the aesthetic imagination, demand asymmetry and imperfection. Yet in that perfect, lifeless form Hans sees imaged his two greatest encounters with the formless and the Dionysiac: the blue, shining holes in the snow suggest to him the eyes of Hippe, and of Claudia (*MM*, p. 479; *ZB*, p. 437).

Losing consciousness in the snow, he in his trance sees a landscape seemingly quite different from the sterile wastes in which he is lost: a classical, Mediterranean landscape, inhabited by beautiful youths and pursuing every early category of culture except crop-growing and writing. Nevertheless, this formal perfection of culture is as grounded in death as the lifeless symmetry of the snow. There is a temple at whose entrance stand statues of a mother and daughter: they can only be Demeter and Korē, the pre-Olympian, matriarchal goddesses who preside over the Eleusinian mysteries; inside, two old hags are dismembering a child with their bare hands, and talking in an ugly Hamburg dialect. This, then, is the ultimate mystery shown to the initiate: human sacrifice. Here, Hans Castorp gazes into the depths of the Magic Mountain and sees the heart of darkness in Hellenism, and the societies which pattern themselves upon it. As the snow, with its inorganic purity of form, threatens his life, so Hans gives personal imaginative form to the presence of death at the heart of culture, rendered almost inevitable by Mann's analysis of the physiology of culture. Yet the dream is not purely personal. 'Now I know', Hans reflects, 'that it is not out of our single souls we dream. We dream anonymously and communally, if each after his fashion' ('Man träumt nicht nur aus eigener Seele, möchte ich sagen, man träumt anonym und gemeinsam, wenn auch auf eigene Art') (*MM*, p. 495; *ZB*, p. 452). For Musil's Ulrich, the collective dream of humanity was Moosbrugger; for Hans Castorp, it is human sacrifice.

The dream evokes the darker elements in Greek religion, which Nietzsche had influentially described, and rejects the idealistic use of Greece as a symbol of German culture, strongly present in Goethe's *Iphigenie* and Schiller's *Aesthetic Education*. This was a view that was retained (for example) by Nietzsche's opponent, the great Hellenist Ulrich von Wilamowitz-Moellendorff, who in 1877, five years after his demolition of *The Birth of Tragedy*, delivered a lecture 'On the Glory of the Athenian Empire' ('Von des attischen Reiches Herrlichkeit'), to mark the eightieth birthday of Kaiser Wilhelm I. Its celebration of the Athenian empire is explicitly applied to the newly unified Germany, and to the duty of citizens to defend its unity at all costs.[11]

If Hans Castorp's dream alludes to the Eleusinian mysteries, however, why is there no corn in the vision? For the mysteries were sacred to Demeter, the corn goddess. And why would a young engineer from Hamburg dream such a dream? Another work of Wilamowitz perhaps provides the answer. In his essay 'Demeterfest' he contrasts Callimachus' *Hymn to Demeter* with Schiller's poem 'Das Eleusische Fest' (1798), which – he tells us – reluctant schoolboys were required to learn by heart. Callimachus' poem contains the terrible tale of Erysichthon, who for sacrilege against Demeter was afflicted with an insatiable hunger that, finally, reduced him to beggary. As Wilamowitz observes, however, Schiller's poem retains the optimistic faith in brotherly love inspired by the early days of the French Revolution, long after the Revolution had descended into bestiality.[12] In the poem, Ceres roams the earth looking for her lost daughter and arrives in a land without culture, where a tribe of cannibalistic hunters offers her a human sacrifice. She refuses it, and brings culture and humanity to the land, beginning with the growing of corn and concluding with the construction of a temple at whose altar she preaches the values of freedom and humanity. In its celebration of these values it closely resembles the 'Ode to Joy'. As Leverkühn in *Doctor Faustus* was to take back the Ninth Symphony, so *The Magic Mountain* takes back the Enlightenment celebration of averted sacrifice which Hans Castorp learned by rote as a child. This is the point at which the novel most explains and justifies its title: its allusion to Nietzsche's image of 'The Olympian magic mountain' opening up and disclosing its roots. The dream of a reborn Hellenic culture perfecting itself north of the Rhine shrinks to two Hamburg hags dismembering a child.

Hans's vision of sacrifice is followed by the return and death of Joachim, which is in turn followed by the arrival of the novel's equivalent to Dionysus, Pieter Peeperkorn, a charismatic, completely inarticulate Dutchman from Java, who is compared to 'Bacchus himself' ('Bacchus selbst' (*MM*, p. 566; *ZB*, p. 517)). He presides over a heroically drunken festivity, while once again pairing Christ with Dionysus, likening those who will not drink with him to those who abandoned Christ in Gethsemane. Peeperkorn is the lover of Hans's great obsession Claudia, but commits suicide when he realizes that she and Hans had been lovers for a single night: he is like a Frazerian god who must die when his potency wanes. His death is not, however, the end of the Dionysiac, but of the acceptable face of Dionysus. We are moving beyond a culture that can be explained by old mythic symbols, and are left with the frenzy of Dionysus, without its symbolic disguises and attenuations.

The final stages of *The Magic Mountain* show a reversal of old myths of the birth of culture. True to his Enlightenment beliefs, Settembrini has faith in human progress, and a belief in the ancient myths which explain its origins: he repeatedly praises Prometheus, and reveres Thoth and his Greek counterpart Hermes Trismegistus as the givers of writing and rhetoric. Yet the last appearance of the Enlightenment Prometheus is in the vulgar and ignorant Frau Stohr's suggestion that the 'Erotica' symphony be played at Joachim's funeral; and Hermes and Thoth, we have seen, are traced by Naphta back to an ape-headed god and a god of death.

The fate of writing, and of its myths of origin, typifies the fate of culture in *The Magic Mountain*. There is no writing in the classical utopia which Hans sees in his dream, but his chief encounters with the Dionysiac, his infatuations with Hippe and Claudia, both have as their high point the borrowing of a writing implement from the object of desire; and it is when he returns the borrowed pencil that he sleeps with Claudia for the only time, on carnival night. In neither instance, however, is the pencil used for writing. In the earlier one, it is for a drawing lesson; in the later, to participate in a carnival game for drawing a pig blindfold (the Eleusinian mysteries commenced with the sacrifice of a pig). In the cultural collapse at the end of the novel, the gifts of Prometheus and Hermes are taken away. Naphta denies the utility of writing and then of measurement, and the gift of number itself sinks into chaos as the sanatorium is taken over by pointless mathematical fads: squaring the circle, stamp-collecting, the card game of 'elevens'. When told by Settembrini of the approach of war, Hans Castorp is absorbed in his solo card game: 'Seven and four', he replies, 'Eight and three. Knave, queen, king' ('Sieben und vier . . . Acht und drei. Bub, Dame, König') (*MM*, p. 633; *ZB*, p. 581). The world, the narrator says, is in the grip of ape-headed gods. The cultural evolution of Thoth has been reversed.

The final section of the novel shows us Hans Castorp, disappearing for ever from view in the mass slaughter of a First World War battlefield. The descent into war essentially cancels all the dialectic of tradition that has linked European culture to its classical roots. After all the conflicts between Apollonian Europe and the amorphous East, we are left with an illegible signpost on a battlefield, which may be pointing in either direction, east or west (*MM*, p. 713; *ZB*, p. 654). Number, which until the final madness had classified and individuated, even if only with reference to a point on the Fahrenheit scale, is now a means of managing the ratio between human expendability and the physical impetus of the mass attack. This is the final subjection of the body to a system of calculation:

> They are three thousand, that they may be two thousand when the hills, the villages are reached; that: is the meaning of their number. They are a body of troops calculated as sufficient, even after great losses, to attack and carry a position and greet their triumph with a thousand-voiced huzza. (*MM*, p. 714)

> Sie sind dreitausend, damit sie noch ihrer zweitausend sind, wenn sie bei den Hügeln, den Dörfern anlangen; das ist der Sinn ihrer Menge. Sie sind ein Körper, darauf berechnet, nach großen Ausfällen noch handeln und siegen, den Sieg noch immer mit tausend-stimmigem Hurra begrüßen zu können. (*ZB*, p. 655)

Mentally, the narrator transposes the young combatants to the landscape of Hans's dream, imagining 'these youths watering horses on a sunny arm of the sea' ('Rosse regend und schwemmend in einer Meeresbucht') (*MM*, p. 714; *ZB*, p. 656),[13] but what is in fact re-enacted is that other part of the hallucination, the *sparagmos* of the young: two friends are blown up by a shell, and are 'scattered, commingled, and gone' ('vermengt und verschwunden') (*MM*, p. 715; *ZB*, p. 657). This *sparagmos* is, literally, the disappearance of the individual. The Hegelian idealization of German culture as encouraging the supreme realization of the subjective and the ethical has gone. *The Magic Mountain* is the greatest of the twentieth-century responses to *The Bacchae*.

The Magic Mountain has in one of its strands been a dialogue with mythic accounts of cultural formation and human progress. In the epilogue, all relevance of myth ceases: even among ape-headed gods, there are no analogies for what happens. We pass beyond myth into (once more) the sphere of geological catastrophe. The only model for what is happening is that first image of human sacrifice: the blind irrationality of the Lisbon earthquake.

CHAPTER 14

Sparagmos

Especially in the early twentieth century, there was a counter-tendency in the treatment of myth. Instead of allowing it to be obliterated by the massive and impersonal processes of geology, there was a powerful movement to reconstruct science, including geology, according to the evidence of myth – a movement which reached its acme in Germany, under National Socialism. In 1913, for example, the Austrian refrigeration engineer Hanns Hörbiger published the first exposition of his World Ice Theory (*Welteislehre*), which held that many heavenly bodies, including the moon, were made of ice, and that the history of the cosmos was marked by convulsive collisions of fiery and icy bodies; over twenty planets had already disappeared into the sun. The present icy moon had been captured 10,000 years ago, and would in time catastrophically fall to earth, like its predecessors. The last collision and capture was, he argued, amply remembered in myth: in the story of the Flood, the memories of Atlantis, the Apocalypse, and the creation myths of the Icelandic sagas. During the floods, the few hardiest survivors had made it to the mountain tops, and ensured the continuity of the species. The theory was embraced by Hitler and Himmler, for it seemed to provide scientific confirmation of the myth of Atlantis, and validated the idea of a Nordic master race of super-strong survivors, whose character was forged on the icy mountain-tops.[1]

A parallel case is provided by the palaeontologist Edgar Dacqué, who became dissatisfied with the Darwinian idea of the relative recentness of the human species, and attempted instead to trace the human line back to the very beginnings of complex life. His theory was that every geological period has its own dominant animal form: for example, reptilian in the Jurassic and amphibian in the Permian. The ancestry of humanity ascends through these earlier dominant forms, of which we retain traces in both our bodily structure and our mythology. Memories of earlier bodily structures are found throughout the world in the hybrid creatures of ancient legend and art.[2] As in Hörbiger's work, science is shaped by the forms of myth.

In his account of the Kridwiss circle in *Doctor Faustus*, Thomas Mann gives a brilliant characterization of kinds of intellectual abdication that were complicit in the rise of National Socialism: an aesthetic glorification of violence, exemplified in the rantings of the proto-fascist poet Daniel zur

Höhe (Ludwig Derleth), and the enthusiasm for blood sacrifice of the Jewish intellectual Chaim Breisacher. The circle, however, also includes a geologist Dr Egon Unruhe, who uses geological theory to verify the myths of saga. He is based on Edgar Dacqué. He represents a culture which allows objective truth, and individual reason, to be sacrificed to collective myth.

The relationship between geology and eschatology is thus complex. Geology may take over from myth and religion, suggesting that the destiny of the sacrificial is not transference into the sphere of the divine but assimilation into imperceptibly slow inorganic process, with only the dinosaur skeleton providing intimations of immortality. Yet fossilized remains have inspired the formation of myth since ancient times,[3] and the work of Hörbiger, Dacqué, and others shows myth reclaiming the field and seeing itself written in the ancient rocks. Not for nothing is it on the heights of an icy mountain top that Hans Castorp stares into the mythic past.

Nevertheless, a simpler enthusiasm for the Dionysiac and the sacrificial persisted. The earliest of the important overt appropriations of *The Bacchae* is the opera *King Roger* (1926), by the Polish composer Karol Szymanowski, in which a Dionysiac stranger initiates King Roger of Sicily and his wife Roxana into a new and liberating religion. Whereas versions of *The Bacchae* generally show a collapse of the individuating principle, Szymanowski turns inside out the normal Euripidean structure, creating a movement from the opening impersonal ritual chants in a Byzantine church to a process of individuation in a ruined Greek theatre, in which Roxana assumes the guise of a Maenad. There is no delusion or destruction, only liberation. Here, remarkably, the sense of collective violence is entirely on the side of the anti-Dionysiac: it is the church that (unsuccessfully) incites the mob to stone the stranger. In Erich Korngold's *Das Wunder der Heliane* (1927), very similarly, a mysterious stranger offers to restore sexual vitality to a tyrannically repressed kingdom, in which the mob sides with the repressions of its ruler. Instead of a Euripidean *sparagmos*, however, there is a double resurrection, of the executed hero and the tyrant's wife, murdered for loving the stranger.

Another work from the mid-twenties does glorify human sacrifice, in a way that invites comparison with *The Rite of Spring*. This is Egon Wellesz's balletic cantata *Die Opferung des Gefangenen* (*The Sacrifice of the Prisoner*) of 1925, though the musical language is more indebted to early Schoenberg (Wellesz's teacher) than to Stravinsky.[4] Like *The Rite*, it revisits a lost world that has been reconstructed by ethnography, setting an ancient, pre-Columbian folk drama collected in Guatemala by the Abbé Brasseur. The tensions of hostility between the valiant captive and his conquerors are kept in check as he ritually renews himself with food and wine, engages in mock ritual combat, dances with the King's daughter, accepts death as a path to the gods, and is killed by the Eagles and Jaguars (warrior castes). As with *The Rite of Spring*, the ritual predominates, and the piece is explicitly a contemplation of a lost world. It is an exaltation of an individual, but an individual who has no dimensions beyond the ritual which vindicates him. The dance with the Princess is the very reverse of a *Liebestod*: towards the end of the dance, the captive himself voluntarily increases the distance from her, and this farewell to sexuality is followed by a ritual combat and a solo dance. At the moment of death, the victim's face is concealed.

Another sacrificial work from the mid-1920s, though without any tinge of Modernism, is one of the many operas of Richard Wagner's son Siegfried: *Die Heilige Linde* (*The Sacred Lime-tree*) (1924), a post-war meditation on an embattled German culture that has much in common with the Arminius plays of the Napoleonic period. The German chieftain Arbogast has sold out to a Semiticized Rome and consented to the felling of the ancient sacred tree, scornful of the ancient traditions of his race. One tradition that he in particular despises is human sacrifice: the annual sacrifice of the two prisoners-of-war privileged to see the goddess Nerthus in her bath. Far preferable for him is the spectator sport of throwing Christians to the lions in Rome. The aliens in whose power he has placed himself conspire the dismemberment of his kingdom and even his body, demanding the token *sparagmos* of his second toe, and a piece of his nose and ear. Is it significant that the woman who is used to entrap him is called Autonoë, the name of one of the sisters of Agave, who had hunted Pentheus down? Germany is, however, reborn when a new chieftain takes over, and plants another sacred tree, which will last for a thousand years. The opera ends with a chorus in praise of Wotan and Thor. The new leader is clearly Hitler.[5]

Egon Wellesz returned to the subject of violent sacrifice in his own version of *The Bacchae*, *Die Bakchantinnen* (1931), for which he wrote the libretto. The ending is, like that of Euripides, terrifying: the more so because the death of Pentheus is directly represented, instead of being narrated in a messenger's speech. Seizing brands from the sacrificial fire, the torch-bearing Maenads press towards Pentheus in an insensate collective body: they move forward 'like a dark, inescapable mass' ('wie eine dunkle, unentrinnbare Masse').[6] David Symons has suggested that they represent the gathering forces of National Socialism,[7] and torch-bearing crowds had indeed been part of the Nazi ritual from the 1920s. Yet the torch-bearing crowds are the false worshippers of Dionysus, and the opera clearly emphasizes the vivifying aspects of the god. Symons quotes from Wellesz's script for the 1960 BBC broadcast of the opera: 'Here the Greek drama touches the mysterious frontier between true and false belief, between revelation and frenzy. The Maenads, who come with Dionysus are the chosen ones, but the women of Thebes, the Bacchae, who reel in pernicious ecstasy, are the erring ones' (p. 69, n. 35).[8] In the early part of the opera, Dionysus is insistently associated with fire and light, and is far less suspect than Euripides' god. He does not trick Pentheus into going to Cithaeron or into disguising himself, there is no corrupt pragmatism in the worship of Kadmos and Teiresias, the terrifying dismemberment of cattle described by Euripides' messenger is omitted, and the sacrificial fire from which the brands are seized is a fire for vegetable sacrifice. Pentheus embodies an authority based purely on force. Although Dionysos is never morally classified, he is a figure beyond the categories with which Pentheus seeks to regulate his kingdom: a figure, as has been said, of light and fire. Yet soon Wellesz and Korngold would be exiles from Nazism, fleeing from Dionysus and his torch-bearers.

Among major Modernist writers, however, perhaps the most remarkable celebrant of quasi-Dionysiac human sacrifice is D. H. Lawrence. In his late novel *The Plumed Serpent* (1926), the twice-married Kate Leslie visits Mexico and becomes involved with two leaders of a nationalist revolutionary movement, the Spanish American Ramón and the Native American Cipriano, who are reviving the old pre-Christian religion and have taken the names of Quetzlcoatl and Huitzilopochtli. Kate becomes the bride of Huitzilopochtli. We see a Christian church being emptied of its imported, effeminate images, such as that of a passive, victimized Christ, and being rededicated to the old religion: a reversal of the process by which Cortés and later invaders had converted sacrificial sites into Christian chapels. The shock of the desecration causes the death of Ramón's pious wife, Carlota, one of several sacrificial deaths associated with the return to the old ways. Traitors to the movement are, for example, sacrificially killed in the churchyard.

Kate undergoes a different kind of sacrifice. As she approaches the darkened church after its rededication, we finally return to the circumstances of a far earlier narrative: the moment at which Acosta's king of Culhuacán enters the darkened chapel to see (as he thinks) the marriage of his daughter to Huitzilopochtli. Now, a European heroine becomes – like the princess – deified by marriage to the terrible Aztec god. The princess was deified as Toci, Kate as Malintzi – the name of Cortés's Native American mistress and collaborator, who is now reconstituted in reversed form as the European helper of a Native American liberator. Gazing at the darkened and dechristianized church, Kate insistently wonders whether she is 'a sacrifice'.[9] She is: not in the sense that she is flayed but in that she surrenders all individuation, so that 'her own desires were gone in the ocean of the great desire' (p. 115). Wagner had thought that, because of her child-bearing instincts, the woman was hard-wired to self-sacrifice. For Lawrence, female sexual surrender recalls Robertson Smith's interpretation of sacrifice as a collective, regenerative act: 'The blood of the individual', Kate understands, 'is given back to the great blood-being, the god, the nation, the tribe' (p. 375). The individual woman is dispersed in a larger, all-engulfing liquid mass.

Thomas Mann repudiated the alliance of geology and myth, but it is central to Lawrence's creative imagination. Though innocent of Hörbiger's elaborate misconceptions about planetary composition and movement,

Lawrence too believes in the disappearance of vast, Atlantis-like continents in the floods at the end of the Ice Age, which 'drove the peoples to the high places, like the lofty plateaux of Mexico, separated them into cut-off nations' (p. 373).[10] Kate's return to 'the great blood-being' is a process of psychological and cultural restoration, which is identified with a reversal of the geological processes that have obliterated that ancient world before the Flood:

> Sometimes, in America, the shadow of that old pre-Flood world was so strong, that the day of historic humanity would melt out of Kate's consciousness, and she would begin to approximate to the old mode of consciousness, the old, dark will, the unconcern for death, the subtle, dark consciousness, non-cerebral, but vertebrate. When the mind and the power of man was in his blood and his backbone, and there was the strange, dark inter-communication between man and man and man and beast, from the powerful spine. (p. 373)

Here, the records in the rocks are not lifeless impressions of extinct forms: the geological history of the land testifies to the culturally repressed areas of the psyche, and gives promise of their renewal.

A mystic geology also provides the basis for one of the most astonishing celebrations of human sacrifice in the period, Lawrence's short story 'The Woman Who Rode Away' (1924). A 'rather dazzling Californian girl from Berkeley'[11] (she is never named) is married to an older American, who mines silver in Mexico. The mining represents a calculating and mechanical response to the geology of the ancient landscape, and indeed the husband is like a machine whose running is geared to the operations of his mine and to his wife's sexual moods, as though they were entirely equivalent processes: he is a dynamo, 'still full of energy, but dimmed by the lapse of silver from the market, and by some curious inaccessibility on his wife's part' (p. 40). So the woman becomes fascinated by the distant, desert mountains, in their utter alienness of form and origin: 'It looks *so* like nowhere on earth: like being on the moon' (p. 41). She journeys towards the snowy peaks, passing beyond the sterile trumpery of civilization to a world where precarious fertility survives, despite the cold and the altitude.

The Indians have a prophecy that the white men's gods will fall to pieces when a white woman is sacrificed to their own, and that they will then regain control over the sun and the moon: the principles of male and female sexuality. For the moon currently lives in the white woman's cave, and is not happy there. When an Indian tells her that they have lost their power over the sun, she replies that she hopes they get him back. As in an incautious oath story, a verbal inadvertency commits her to sacrifice – though in the role of victim, not priest. This, however, is less an incautious oath than a Freudian slip, indicating her repressed readiness for a sacrifice that is a ritual reaffirmation of male sexuality. The iron-hewn space of the white man's silver mine has thus usurped the psychosexual space of the moon's cave: the more so because, in the old correspondences between the seven metals and the seven planets, silver stood for the moon.

The area outside the vaginal cave in which the woman is sacrificed is dominated by a repeatedly described great shaft of ice. It is a frozen phallus, as though C. S. Lewis's White Witch had abolished not Christmas but the Penis. On the day of the winter solstice, as the sun starts its ascent and shines through the ice into the cave, she is killed by the sacrificial flint knife, which affirms 'The mastery that man must hold, and that passes from race to race' (p. 71). We are accustomed to seeing the knife as the invention that both typifies culture and declares its ineradicable origins in violence; in *The Plumed Serpent,* the domination of the United States is likened to 'the knife of sacrifice' (p. 68). Here, we see a redemption from culture: a geological system which had been an inanimate object of economic exploitation is reordered to recover the archetypal psychic structure of myth, and the woman is killed with stone, on stone, and in stone. To her European, miner's wife's eye, the geological alienness of the landscape had been typified by its likeness to the moon. By the end of the story, she is the moon; like the singer in Schoenberg's second quartet, she breathes the air of other planets: 'Her kind of womanhood, intensely personal and individual, was to be obliterated again . . . [W]omanhood was to be cast once more into the great stream of impersonal sex and impersonal passion' (p. 60).

Like Hans Castorp, Lawrence's woman undertakes a journey to a magic mountain and, amidst the snow, encounters the secret of human sacrifice. Yet the story embodies much of what Mann despised: the rejection of analytic objectivity for a misty surrender to collectivist myth. 'Science strove,' the narrator writes in *Doctor Faustus,* 'on the plane of decent, objective truth, to confute the dynamic lie; but arguments on that plane could only seem irrelevant to the champions of the dynamic' ('man sich mühte, sie auf ganz fremder und für sie irrelevanter Ebene, der wissenschaftlichen nämlich, der Ebene der biederen, objektiven Wahrheit zu widerlegen') (Lowe-Porter, p. 353; *Doktor Faustus,* p. 488). In *Women in Love* (1920), Rupert Birkin (a version of Lawrence himself) champions the opposite cause, defending African art against the resentment and contempt of another mine-owner, Gerald Crich, the lover of Gudrun Brangwen: these expressions of the primitive are to Birkin 'Pure culture in sensation, culture in the physical consciousness, really *ultimate* physical consciousness, mindless, utterly sensual. It is so sensual as to be final, supreme.'[12] Birkin senses that there has been a fatal cultural rupture, a 'death-break' between 'knowledge arrested and ending in the senses' and the equally destructive abstractions of the white races, which are again equated with snow: 'The white races, having the arctic north behind them, the vast abstraction of ice and snow, would fulfil a mystery of ice-destructive knowledge, snow-abstract annihilation' (pp. 253, 254).

Gerald is 'the God of the machine.' (p. 223), reducing human beings to units of productivity: 'He was one of these strange white wonderful demons from the north, fulfilled in the destructive frost mystery' (p. 254). Eventually, Gudrun rejects him for the sculptor Loerke, who is in tune with primitive art, and interprets labour instead of merely managing it: he is working on a great granite frieze for a Cologne factory, representing a carnival-like fair of workers. Again, the issue is of how man responds to the world-order measured by geology: whether he mines coal, or carves granite. For Gudrun, Loerke is a primal geological layer, 'the rock-bottom of all life' (p. 427). And so Gerald becomes the sacrificial victim: 'A strange rent had been torn in him; like a victim that is torn open and given to the heavens, so he had been torn apart and given to Gudrun' (pp. 445–6). It is another victory of the knife: Gudrun chooses the cutter rather than the machiner, with a 'fine, insinuating blade of . . . comprehension' (p. 452), and Gerald stumbles off for a fatal journey into the snow whose deadly abstraction so closely mirrors that of his intellect.

In the act of human sacrifice, man had once been placed on the threshold of the divine. Now, from *Frankenstein* onwards, he is likely to be placed on the threshold of the inorganic. Geology replaces theology as the system within which sacrifice is to be conducted. It is a new and inverted dualism: the crystals of snow mimic the forms of the mind yet represent a pattern of existence which the body cannot enter, save by the kind of frozen immortality that Elis Fröbom gains in Hoffmann's *The Mines at Falun*. Sacrifice for Lawrence is a way of confronting the boundary with the inorganic, of ensuring that the structures of the mind are not fossilized in its forms, and that the circulation of blood can energize the tribe and ensure its arterial connection with the psychic unity of the primitive past.

The past here is indeed another country. In their formalizations and celebrations of violence, works such as 'The Woman who Rode Away' present a world as alien as the Assyrian room of the British Museum; a world which was soon to become real, and at whose callow foreshadowings we may now shudder. It is a relief to turn to a work which sensed more clearly and forebodingly the direction of the future: Schoenberg's *Moses und Aron*, the first two acts of which were composed in 1930–2. The final act, however, remained uncomposed at Schoenberg's death in 1951. The principal character of the work is, of course, the liberator of a Jewish people oppressed in an alien land, but the opera portrays not the liberation of the people but the impasse of the leader: the visionary whose ideas are destroyed by being given sensory form, and for whom there can be no equilibrium between Apollo and Dionysus. He is, perhaps, the leader who composes with twelve notes, related only to each other. Like many operas of the period, such as Pfitzner's *Palestrina* (1917) and Hindemith's *Mathis der Maler* (*Matthias* [Grünewald] *the Painter*) (1938), this is an opera about the role of the artist in a dangerously troubled world.

How does one render in signs a God whose very nature is incompatible not only with signification but also with counting – with numerical extension? In

Plate 16 Schoenberg's *Moses und Aron*, the Dance round the Golden Calf (Berlin, 1959)

his opening address to God, which dwells on his incommunicability, Moses starts by describing him as '*Einziger*' ('unique' – the first word of the opera) and ends with '*unvorstellbarer*' ('inconceivable').[13] The visionary sees God: but how does he translate the truth into the terms of his society, or resolve the impasse that by translating the truth he will falsify it? God gives him the promise that Aron will be his mouthpiece, but the promise that had been so cruelly parodied by Shakespeare's Aaron is here never realized. For this Aron's medium is not the word but the visible and tactile image. Commanded to call forth water from the rock with his word, he instead does so by striking it with his staff. What in the Bible is a simple miracle becomes an act of disobedience. And Aron's greatest sign is the Golden Calf, whose cult becomes one of human sacrifice: a Rite of Spring at the base of Mount Sinai (Plate 16). The gold which is worshipped in the image of the calf derives its mystery not from its particular form, which is transient, but from its combination of permanence and infinite convertibility. It is thus conceptually opposite to the unique, unchanging god of the mountain.

Aron's gift lies in his miraculous ability to transform objects and, consequently, their symbolic meaning: he turns Moses' staff into a serpent, and then interprets the transformation as signifying the distinction between Moses' rigid law and his own cleverness ('*Klugheit*') (p. 140). Down in the world beneath the mountain, Moses' role among his people is itself reversible. He becomes a scapegoat king, quickly changing from the absent leader for whom the crowd longs ('*Wo ist der Führer?*') (p. 154) to the absent leader whom the crowd wishes to tear apart ('*zerreißen*') (p. 160). Whereas the colloquy on the mountain affirms the uniqueness and immutability of God, the dynamic of the Golden Calf episode is of insane proliferation and subdivision: of numerical extension. There is a procession of asses, horses, porters, and wagons, bringing gold, grain, skins, and other things. Then the butchers come with large knives and cut up the animals into pieces, which are distributed for a bout of wild, collective omophagy. Finally, there is an orgy of self-immolation, including that of four naked virgins, the Chorus all the while celebrating the infinite symbolic convertibility of gold:

> Gold is lust!
> Lust is wildness!
> Gold gleams like blood!
> Gold is power.
>
> *Gold gleicht Lust!*
> *Lust ist Wildheit!*
> *Gold glänzt wie Blut!*
> *Gold ist Herrschaft!* (pp. 180–1)

The likeness of gold to blood is the rationale of the sacrificial exchange. The virgins' blood is cold as gold; it must be heated by a kiss from the priests. But then the red blood is shed against the red gold. The endless commutability of gold leads inevitably to the commutation of human sacrifice.

The Golden Calf episode is followed by an unresolved debate between Moses and Aron about the claims of the word and the image. This seems settled – against Moses – when the people are seen following the fiery pillar. This Moses regards as an idolatrous image, and the part of the opera for which Schoenberg composed music ends with Moses' despair at his failure to command the sign: 'O word, thou word, that I lack!' ('*O Wort, du Wort, das mir fehlt!*') (pp. 194–5). In the final act, Moses again confronts Aron, and asserts the primacy of the idea: even the land flowing with milk and honey is a false literalism exploited by the image-maker. Aron falls dead, and the gulf between the idea and its material deformations remains unbridgeable: the pillar of fire and the land flowing with milk and honey are part of the system of sensory symbols which can equally fulfil itself in the human sacrifice to the Golden Calf.

The previous chapter started with *The Rite of Spring*. This one ends with its counterpart, in the work of Stravinsky's greatest rival, repudiating the glorification of sacrifice that had been such a striking, if now irrecoverably alien, feature of musical and literary culture in the previous twenty years. *Moses und Aron* is a work of two periods, composed in 1930–2, first performed (after Schoenberg's death) in 1954. Even the Dance round the Golden Calf was not performed until 1951. By that time, the insouciant glorification of human sacrifice against which it reacted had become impossible.

CHAPTER 15

Hitler and after

In 1933 Dionysus came to power. His greatest atrocity has, in the word Holocaust, become synonymous with sacrifice. The metaphor, however, seems to be derived less from its original, sacrificial sense – the burning of a single lamb in the temple – than from the mass destruction implied in journalistic descriptions of catastrophic tenement fires: descriptions in which 'holocaust' becomes synonymous with 'inferno'. Tzvetan Todorov classified massacre and sacrifice as opposites, since in a massacre the identity of the individual is irrelevant.[1] Apart from Girardian scapegoating, indeed, no model of human sacrifice seems appropriate to the great exterminations of the twentieth century; rather than creating new forms of sacrificial literature, they have superseded human sacrifice as the ultimate touchstones of barbarity. When we require place names to denote the horror where culture collapses, we no longer think of Aulis or Taurica.

Yet speculation about the development of human sacrifice remains a key factor in attempts to understand the evolution of modern society: in, for example, *Dialectic of Enlightenment* (1947), in which Adorno and Horkheimer address the question of how the civilization of Kant could also manifest itself as that of Hitler. Enlightenment, they argue, has through its very methods of abstraction an intrinsic potential to produce its own opposite, for these dissolve the unique and particular and promote the interchangeability, expendability, and alienation of the individual. The hegemony of numbers, starting in Plato's late works, makes interchangeability absolute. Its 'equations dominate bourgeois justice and commodity exchange': 'To the Enlightenment, that which does not reduce to numbers, and ultimately to the one, becomes illusion' (p. 7).

For Adorno and Horkheimer, the first cultural step in this process of alienation from the specific is the movement from animism to myth: to, for example, identifying each year's separate and distinct cycle of spring and autumn with the single event of the kidnapping of Persephone. There is a comparable movement in the substitution of animal for human victims, 'the hind offered up for the daughter' again implying the interchangeability of what was previously unique (p. 10). Human sacrifice is originally of a member of the tribe, so that the blood would flow back to the tribe as energy, and it is associated with a hypothetical stage at which endophagous cannibalism was necessitated by the limited food supply. Once the sacrificial victim is no longer a necessary part of the food chain, however, sacrifice is irrational and in conflict with the principle of self-preservation, needing cunning deception to justify it: 'All demythologization', they write, 'is colored by the inevitable experience of the uselessness and superfluousness of sacrifices' (p. 53). Yet the abstraction of the internally consistent self from its 'dissolution into blind nature' promptly becomes another kind of sacrifice: 'The identically persistent self which arises in the abrogation of sacrifice immediately becomes an unyielding, rigidified sacrificial ritual that man celebrates upon himself by opposing his consciousness to the natural context' (p. 54). The authors go on to examine the consequences of reducing the individual to an interchangeable cipher in, for example, the works of Sade, or in the modern culture industry's lottery of stardom, whose attraction depends upon the potential interchangeability of the star with the similarly interchangeable shopgirls in the audience.

Adorno and Horkheimer's account of the origins of sacrifice, of the substitution of animal for human victims, and of the transition from animism to religion, is now untenably dated. What is interesting is not the specific theory of historical origins, which is unsustainable, but the fact that such a theory is advanced at all: the fact that interpretation of the dialectic tensions of modern society has to start with a vision of prehistoric origins that is as imaginary as Hobbes's state of nature, and that both the original and the modern state are held to be driven by sacrificial processes. In a similar fashion, René Girard's theories – as already noted – are based on an entirely hypothetical account of the prehistoric circumstances in which human sacrifice arose. Georges Bataille adopts a different sequence, seeing all societies as being driven by a need to dispose of their surpluses: the mass sacrifices of the Aztecs are one expression of a universal need that is equally filled in the ritual gift-exchange of the potlatch, or in overinvestment in monasteries, and which underlies the anxieties and divisions of the more complex modern bourgeois culture.[2]

It is curious how many theorists of modern culture seem to need a hypothesis of sacrificial origin. Quasi-sacrificial transactions are also fundamental to Baudrillard's analysis of the capitalist economy, and the place of death in its systems of exchange. Whereas earlier societies had had multiple stakes in their members (in, for example, birth and kinship, or soul and body), in modern political economy the stake is reduced to one: production. Taking the inevitable starting point of a hypothetical prehistoric state of nature, Baudrillard argues that, in earliest times, prisoners of war were originally killed on the spot. Later, they were instead enslaved. Later still, they became paid labour:

> Labour therefore everywhere draws its inspiration from deferred death. It comes from deferred death. Slow or violent, immediate or deferred, the scansion of death is decisive: it is what radically distinguishes two types of organisation, the economic and the sacrificial. We live irreversibly in the first of these, which has inexorably taken root in the *differance* of death.[3]

In the 'evolution from savage societies to our own' (p. 126) the dead are excluded from the symbolic circulation of the group. Savages have no biological concept of death, and incorporate death socially in their rites of passage: for example, a ritual in which young initiands are consumed by their ancestors and then reborn represents death as a cycle of reversible exchange. For us, however, the dead cease to exist: they are fobbed off with immortality. The only death that assumes significance and excites passion is 'violent death which is the sole manifestation of something like the sacrifice, that is to say, like a real transmutation *through the will of the group*' (p. 165). The prime example of this is hostage-taking, which recreates sacrifice 'because we rediscover here a *time* of the sacrifice, of the ritual of execution, in the immanence of the collectively expected death' (p. 165). The rules of symbolic exchange are fulfilled, because the officiating priest – the criminal – is expected to die in return for the hostage.

For Baudrillard, the challenge to the capitalist system is to restore the symbolic circulation of death. In its system of deferred death, capitalism breaks the cycle of gift and counter-gift, which must then be restored by defying '*the system with a gift* [death] *to which it cannot respond save by its own collapse and death*'. An example is the hostage-taker: 'The system must *itself commit suicide in response to the multiplied challenge of death and suicide*' (p. 37). Baudrillard does not explain why the challenge of death obliges the capitalist system to reciprocate in a potlatch of self-destruction. His recent example, of the Twin Towers committing suicide in response to the suicide attack of the terrorists, is a metaphor – and a shocking one – but not an explanation. The pirouettes and elisions of his works (computers as 'transistorised death' (p. 185)?) scarcely show the persuasiveness of human sacrifice as an ur-template of modern social procedures, but they certainly show its seductive power: the recurrent impulse to compel human sacrifice to epitomize the driving forces of modern society. Its potency as an idea extends far beyond its prevalence as a practice, and its formulation as an idea is often tenuously related to its real manifestations. Yet it seems an almost inescapable key to understanding and describing the modern state. It can scarcely be called an archetype, for the configuration varies radically in every detail but one: the question of what transaction merits the taking of life from an unwilling victim. The character of a culture is inseparable from the way in which it answers this question, and an Adorno, a Bataille, and a Baudrillard will always be on hand to report the answer in different ways. Human sacrifice is a specialized and extreme subdivision of the fatal transaction, but it has become a synecdoche for the whole, and this is why it seems unlikely ever entirely to go away.

EURIPIDES UNDER HITLER

By the 1940s, however, the insouciant celebration of human sacrifice was, as I have suggested, over, and two works of the war years show significant changes in adapting the greatest classical tragedies of sacrifice. These are Giorgio Ghedini's opera *Le Baccanti* – composed in 1941–3 and first performed in Milan in 1948, the same year as Ghedini's concerto in memory of the Resistance martyr Duccio Galimberti – and Gerhart Hauptmann's *Atriden-Tetralogie*, which prefaces a reworking of the three *Oresteia* plays with an *Iphigenie in Aulis*.

Whereas Euripides' god appears from his opening speech as a vengeful and punishing god, preoccupied with the past transgressions of Thebes, Ghedini's Diòniso initially appears as a bringer of life in an autumn landscape, briefly mentioning Penteo's hostility, but chiefly seeming to be an energizing deity of vital fluids: lymph will flow through the roots, through the grapes, and through the veins of all creatures. It is in this early part of the text that Ghedini incorporates some details that occur almost halfway through Euripides' play, in the first messenger's speech: the idyllic beauty with which the Bacchanals bring forth wine and milk and honey, and yet tear whole cows apart once they have been attacked by men. The earth will, Diòniso affirms, produce milk – but also blood; flowers – but also serpents.[4] The god explicates his own ambiguity – 'I, Dionysus, blood and wine, laughter and weeping' ('io, Diòniso, sangue e vino, riso e pianto') (p. 10) – and although his ambiguous beauty is certainly powerful and alluring, its manifestation is concentrated in an early part of the play, and is followed by sheer horror.

The transition is the Bacchanals' wild blood sacrifice of a goat in the middle of the city, culminating in the impaling of its head on a thyrsus. Whereas Euripides' Pentheus is a lone voice of disapproval, railing against evils he has not seen, this visible barbarity horrifies the priests and the citizens. When the Bacchanals announce the conventional Dionysiac miracle, that the earth has brought forth milk and wine, the proclaimed miracle is at odds with the violence that we see. It is at this point that Penteo enters, his first words being to protest against the *sparagmos*: 'Victims torn to pieces. Blood and wine throughout the streets of Thebes' ('Vittime dilaniate. Sangue e vino per le strade di Tebe') (p. 62). Although he retains some of the limitations of his Euripidean model, in Ghedini's version the stimulus for his opposition is far stronger and more directly portrayed: in the streets of his capital city, Penteo has seen civilization collapse into bloody collectivist barbarism.

For the first time in an adaptation of *The Bacchae*, we see an explicit conflict between Apollo and Dionysos: the priests of Apollo attempt to purge the horror by purifying the bloodstained steps with water. The opera then follows its Euripidean course, with Penteo in vain trying to prevent an entire civilization from being engulfed by madness. At the end, he takes the place of the goat whose dismemberment had first provoked his resistance: his limbs too are 'dilaniate' (p. 188), and Agave enters with his head on a thyrsus, as she had once carried that of the goat.

Wellesz's Dionysus had been a god of fire and light. Ghedini's is a god of liquid, of formlessness, mingling blood with wine and men with goats; when he urges on the Bacchanals to kill Penteo, he repeatedly calls them 'cagne' ('bitches'). In his primitive communion with vitalizing fluids, he is far more a Lawrentian figure ('In the first time, you can feel the flowers on their stem, the stem very strong and full of sap' (p. 166) says Cipriano/Huitzilopochtli in *The Plumed Serpent*). The final transformation of Cadmo into a serpent confirms Diòniso's hostility to fixity and stability. Although ambiguities remain in both his and Penteo's character, we are for the first time witnessing a Dionysos more terrible than that of Euripides, and more clearly a threat to a civilization based on rational individualism.

At about the same time as Ghedini was composing his opera, the leading German dramatist Gerhart Hauptmann produced his last work, the *Atriden-Tetralogie*. This is a further rejection of the Hellenism of Goethe and Schiller: an exploration of the dark, chthonic aspects of Greek religion that had first been brought into prominence by Nietzsche. For Hauptmann's Greece has been taken over by dark gods, though it emerges into light in the final play, *Iphigenie in Delphi* (1941) (which was in fact written first). In *Iphigenie in Aulis* (1943), however, he portrays a Greece that is entirely in the grip of the chthonic, pre-Olympian divinities: Jane Harrison's beloved Keres ('Keren') are repeatedly invoked,[5] and the fact that the Delphic oracle commands the sacrifice of Iphigenia shows that Apollo himself sides with the darker gods. Hauptmann had compromised with the Nazi regime. As Ritchie Robertson writes, 'This pessimistic rewriting of Goethe's *Iphigenie* can hardly be an anti-Nazi allegory, since it was performed under Nazi rule in 1943, but its relentless power suggests that Greek myth enabled Hauptmann to express symbolically the barbaric realities of the 1940s.'[6]

The action is overshadowed by two events in the immediate past. One is Agamemnon's slaying of the hind sacred to Artemis. Whereas this is ignored in Goethe's *Iphigenie auf Tauris*, the event becomes crucial to defining the irrational bloodlust both of Agamemnon and of the goddess he has offended. Agamemnon is an obsessive hunter, possessed by frenzy of the hunt ('Jagdwut'); Artemis demands human flesh ('Menschenfleisch') in return for the slain doe (p. 10). The other recent event (elsewhere generally ignored, except in Sinon's narrative in the *Aeneid*) is the stoning of Agamemnon's trusted advisor Palamedes (according to some myths, the inventor of the alphabet). At one point, the pile of stones which still covers his body dominates the stage, and he exemplifies the unreasoning, scapegoating fury of the mob: a mob which demands to eat human flesh, and which both clamours for Iphigenia's sacrifice, and indeed for that of all virgins, and yet grievingly crawls and kisses Iphigenia's hand when she has accepted her role as sacrificial victim.

In *Iphigenie*, Hauptmann adopts the usual course of allowing an animal substitution at the last minute, but he could scarcely have done so in a more tragic manner. Throughout the play, it is stressed that Greece – ruled by the blond house of Atreus (*Agamemnons Tod*, p. 132) – has been invaded and taken over by the more primitive and cruel culture of Taurica: a culture of wild cannibals ('wüster Kannibalen') (p. 46). A ship with blood-red sails, used to transport sacrificial victims, lies in the harbour, and in the fourth act its sails loom terrifyingly next to the grave of Palamedes. The priestesses of Hecate emit a smell of decomposition, and it is this ship of the dead that constitutes Iphigenia's escape vehicle, taking her to a half-life, half-death existence as a sacrificial priestess. Yet more horrifying is the actual sacrificial substitution. Although a doe is substituted for Iphigenia, Agamemnon does not realize this, and furiously kills the animal in the belief that it is his daughter. It is thus *The Bacchae* in reverse: there, a mother had killed her son in the belief that he was an animal; here, a father kills an animal in the belief that it is his daughter. If there have been times when the influence of the Iphigenia plays eradicated that of *The Bacchae*, and vice versa, Hauptmann's *Iphigenia in Aulis* is the exception that proves the rule: it is a play shaped by the example of *The Bacchae*.

THOMAS MANN'S *DOCTOR FAUSTUS*

The greatest post-1933 reflection on the workings of Dionysus is, however, Thomas Mann's *Doctor Faustus* (1947). This finally merged two parallel cultural archetypes who had been homologous both in their names (Faustus means 'fortunate' and Pentheus 'woeful') and in their ends, both being victims of a *sparagmos* (described in bloody detail in the *Faustbuch*). Once again, as in *Death in Venice*, surrender to Dionysus becomes for Mann a diseased debasement of that favourite nineteenth-century form of sacrifice, the *Liebestod*.

Mann's Faust is the composer Adrian Leverkühn, whose pact with the demonic consists of a long, voluntarily untreated syphilitic infection, which his brain craves as an exhilarating if destructive liberation from its icy Germanic discipline. The craving is implanted on the very day on which, having renounced his seeming vocation to study theology, he commits his life to music. Arriving in Leipzig late in 1905 to take up his studies, he has a guided tour of the city, among other things visiting Bach's Thomaskirche. But his guide concludes the tour by dumping him in a brothel. Confused, he heads for the piano and tries to work out a harmonic problem: 'Modulation from B major to C major, ... as in the hermit's prayer in the finale of the *Freischütz* ... on the six-four chord on C' ('Modulation von H- nach C-Dur, ... wie im Gebet des Eremiten im Freischütz-Finale, ... auf dem Quartsextakkord von C').[7] Then he rushes out, but not before a prostitute has brushed him on the cheek and indelibly fascinated him.

The main textual irony of the *Freischütz* allusion is obvious: the hero of the opera, Max, has (as explained above) entered a pact with Samiel, the devil, for seven magic bullets in order to win his beloved Agathe at a shooting contest. He has been seduced into the bargain by Kaspar, whose own contract with Samiel is about to expire and who must supply him with another victim to gain a further year of earthly life. It is part of Kaspar's plan that Agathe should be killed with one of the magic bullets, but she is narrowly saved – a late example of the averted sacrifice plot. The Hermit's prayer in the Act 3 finale completes Max's release from his infernal bargain, and from his potential conversion of love into death. The decisive finality of Max's release from the demonic, and from the union of sex and death, contrasts with the transience and delusiveness of Leverkühn's; it is, indeed, while reconstructing the modulation that Leverkühn attracts the attention of the prostitute. Mann's use of *Der Freischütz* here is rather like that of Schiller's 'Eleusische Fest' in *The Magic Mountain*. Both of the earlier works envisage a world purged of sacrificial barbarity, transmitting Enlightenment optimism to the Romantic generation; each is recalled at a later cultural moment which decisively proclaims the vanity of their optimism.

There are more purely musical ironies as well. The keys of B and C between them contain all twelve notes of the chromatic scale, though they are structurally separated and counterbalanced within the framework of tonality. Leverkühn is to devise the procedure of composition with the twelve-note row, in which all twelve notes have equality of status: in Schoenberg's familiar formulation, the '*Method of Composing with Twelve Tones Which are Related Only with One Another*'.[8] Textually and musically, moreover, the Hermit's prayer counterbalances a recent and very different linguistic solemnity: the earlier dying curse of the villain Kaspar. This curse is accompanied by three ascending diminished seventh tremolos, between them including all twelve notes of the chromatic scale, and generating appropriately unstable tonality.[9] In the modulation from B to C (the final modulation in the opera) the twelve notes are rescued from their chromatic amorphousness by an act of Apollonian form-giving, symmetrically segregating the twelve notes into contiguous but opposed keys: the notes that Leverkühn was to equalize in the tone-row.

Der Freischütz is a decisive moment in Mann's account of the development of German culture, as it is in the present book. It represents a point at which Enlightenment still contains and controls the Dionysiac but where the equilibrium is clearly doomed. The tonal structures which are organic in Weber give way to the extreme and (for Mann) artificial rigour of the twelve-note system, whose intense intellectual discipline both opposes and complements the aesthetic and cultural dissolution represented by

Leverkühn's disease. Apollo and Dionysus give way to dodecaphony and syphilis.

In first portraying Leverkühn's contact with Romanticism, long before the Leipzig incident, the narrator, Serenus Zeitblom, provides a significant list of his friend's operatic fare: six operas, representing the transition from the Enlightenment to Romanticism and, in their range, summing up the tension between civilization and the demonic that is central to the book. In the former camp are three operas of rational social rebirth: *Die Zauberflöte*, *Figaro*, and *Fidelio*, praised for its 'lofty humanity and brotherhood' ('erhabene Humanität und Brüderlichkeit'). On the other side, the 'daemony' ('Dämonie') of *Der Freischütz* and 'similar figures of painful and sombre solitude like those of Hans Heiling and The Flying Dutchman' ('verwandte Gestalten schmerzlich düsterer Ausgeschlossenheit wie die Hans Heilings und des Fliegenden Holländers') (LP, pp. 78–9; *DF*, p. 109).[10] Hans Heiling, the principal character of Marschner's 1833 opera of that name, is a male version of Undine and a reverse version of the slightly later figure of the Flying Dutchman: a tormented figure from the spirit world who seeks redemption in the love of a mortal, but is rejected by his bride in favour of the local huntsman. The solitary figures are, of course, proleptic of Leverkühn himself, just as he is portrayed as growing out of the cultural process which they initiate. Looking back in 1918 on his earlier hero, Tonio Kröger (1903), Mann had described him as 'an epigone of romanticism' ('ein Spätling der Romantik'), a true brother of the Undines, the Heilings, the Dutchmen.[11]

The implicit dividing line in the list of six operas is the period between the first performance of *Fidelio* in its final version (1814) and that of *Der Freischütz* (1821). This period has also been a dividing line in the argument of this study. In particular, the year 1816 saw the genesis of *Frankenstein* and *The Vampyre*, the appearance of 'The Mines at Falun', the staging of another version of *Faust*, by Spohr, and of the operatic version of *Undine*, with music by Hoffmann. The common factor of all five is the fatally interrupted wedding, with its unification of death and the sex drive. Of these works, the most obviously important is the one to whose story Mann had alluded in his reflections on *Tonio Kröger*: *Undine*, in which the hero accepts a kiss from his rejected spirit-bride in the knowledge that it will be fatal; that it will be, in the words of the operatic version, a 'Liebestod'.[12] While not itself a story of human sacrifice, *Undine* has provided a template according to which many later sacrificial narratives, including that of Brünnhilde, were to configure themselves. Mann continues this process of configuration – for Leverkühn's fascination with the prostitute is an extended variation on the story of Huldbrand and Undine.

The kiss of the prostitute implants in Leverkühn an irresistible fascination, and a year later he seeks her out, no longer in Leipzig but in Pressburg. Pressburg '(in Hungarian, Pozsony)' ('ungarisch Pozsony genannt') (LP,

p. 150; *DF*, p. 206) was the capital of Hungary when Buda was occupied by the Turks, so it represents another point of tension between Europe and the Dionysiac East. The prostitute warns him that she is infected with syphilis, but he insists on having sex with her and acquires the long, liberating yet destructive, infection that constitutes his pact with the devil. This visit to the prostitute is also associated with an opera, since Leverkühn makes his trip on the pretext of wanting to visit Graz to hear another meeting of West and East, the first Austrian performance (on 16 May 1906) of the recently completed *Salome* (whose première he had heard in Dresden). This is a work which stands on the boundaries of Romanticism and Modernism, as *Der Freischütz* had stood on those of the Enlightenment and Romanticism, and its première is an occasion which brings together the most antagonistic extremes of German culture, attended as it was by (among many others) Gustav Mahler, Arnold Schoenberg, and Adolf Hitler. Indeed, since it is unclear whether Leverkühn actually attends the performance, the infection with syphilis almost *becomes* the experience of *Salome*.

The two brothel incidents are thus associated with two termini in the evolution of Romantic opera, and – obviously – the sex–death linkage that is broken in *Der Freischütz* rages out of control in *Salome*, in which Salome demands John the Baptist's head in order to possess an otherwise unattainable object of sexual desire: the figure of ascetic religious authority no longer exorcizes the fatal potential of sexuality, as Weber's hermit does, but instead becomes its focus. In the beginning is the end, and the beginning and end are both marked by a fatal kiss – for Mann traces a line from the kiss with which Undine had taken away Huldbrand's life to that decadent extreme of the *Liebestod*, Salome kissing the lifeless lips of the Baptist's head. It is noteworthy that it was in exactly this period that Mann's one-time friend, the nationalist composer Hans Pfitzner, was re-editing some of the earliest monuments of German Romantic opera; indeed, in the very year of the Graz performance of *Salome*, Pfitzner published the first ever vocal score of Hoffmann's *Undine*.

The Undine story is most explicitly acknowledged in *Doctor Faustus* through repeated allusions to its sanitized epigone, Hans Christian Andersen's 'The Little Mermaid'. These are principally concerned with the Mermaid's longing for a soul, and obviously reflect the inextinguishable reaching of Leverkühn's soulless art for a condition beyond its own limits. In describing the union of Leverkühn and Esmeralda, for example, Mann's narrator, Zeitblom, detects in Esmeralda's behaviour 'An act of free elevation of soul above her pitiable physical existence' ('einen Akt freier seelischer Erhebung über ihre erbarmungswürdige physische Existenz') (LP, p. 151; *DF*, p. 207), and imagines something like 'a bond of love, which lent to the coming together of the precious youth and that unhappy creature a gleam of soul' ('etwas einer Liebesbindung Ähnliches hier waltete, was der

Vereinigung dieser kostbaren Jugend mit dem unseligen Geschöpf einen Schimmer des Seelenhaften verlieh') (LP p. 150; *DF*, pp. 206–7). But, if this image of the bond which confers soul on the soulless links Esmeralda, and Leverkühn, with the Mermaid, the circumstance which prompts Zeitblom's effusion – the loved one's warning that her embrace brings death – belongs only to the original Undine story, with the closest parallel being provided by the version in Hoffmann's opera, where the fusion of death and love is expressed more compactly than in the novella. 'So I kiss you to death' ('Doch küss' ich dich zum Sterben'), Hoffmann's Undine says (p. 228).

The second brothel incident in *Doktor Faustus* thus progresses both forwards and backwards from *Der Freischütz*. If it duplicates and coincides with one of the latest and most violent fusions of eros and thanatos in Romantic opera, it implicitly traces the fusion back to its prefigurings in the primal and seminal work of the genre, suggesting an inexorable linkage between the beginning and the end: between 'Doch küss' ich dich zum Sterben' and 'I have kissed your mouth, Jochanaan' ('Ich habe deinen Mund geküsst, Jochanaan')[13]

Undine is then a constant shaping presence throughout *Doktor Faustus*. Its underwater mirror-world of soulless creatures is the prime precedent for all the soulless mimetic forms that provide analogues to Leverkühn's compositions, such as the chemicals which Leverkühn's father immerses in diluted water glass, making them sprout like organic forms.[14] (Like Frankenstein's creature and Hans Castorp, Leverkühn stands on the threshold of the inorganic.) The Undine story even furnishes the final event of the novel. At Leverkühn's funeral a mysterious veiled woman arrives, only to disappear as soon as the first earth is cast on the coffin: 'A stranger, a veiled unknown, who disappeared as the first clods fell on the coffin' ('eine unkenntlich verschleierte Fremde, die, während die Erdschollen auf den eingebetteten Sarg fielen, wieder verschwunden war') (LP, p. 489; *DF*, p. 672). Is she Frau von Tolna, the mysterious patroness who would never permit Leverkühn to meet her, or is she Esmeralda herself? The equally possible, and indeed equally necessary, identifications complete the consistent imaginative compulsion to link, or even identify, the two women,[15] who have constantly mirrored each other, like Undine and Bertalda. And the stranger is, subliminally, Undine, who similarly arrives at Huldbrand's funeral as a veiled, initially unrecognized stranger: she is 'deeply veiled' ('tief verschleiert') (p. 93) and 'the veiled woman' ('Die Verschleierte') (p. 94). Then, during a pause for prayer during the construction of the grave, 'the veiled stranger disappeared' ('war die weiße Fremde verschwunden') (p. 94). At Leverkühn's death, as at the fatal embrace years earlier, Esmeralda and Undine coalesce. During the Pressburg visit, Leverkühn is both, ostensibly, watching *Salome* and re-enacting the end of *Undine*, as he again does at his funeral. The beginning contains the end; that is why Esmeralda emerges in association with the modulation to C of the Hermit in *Der Freischütz*.

This is one strand of many in Mann's monumental reflections on the catastrophe which overtook German culture. Yet his purposeful and sustained use of the Undine story in this strand shows how important a point of transition the second decade of the nineteenth century is in his narrative; how important the move from faith in enlightened social rebirth to the cult of the solitary, and to the repudiation of society in the celebration of the *Liebestod*. The love-death here reflects the dissolution of society rather than its transcendence: the actress Clarissa Rodde, an unredeemable Gretchen, commits suicide, driven to it by a Mephistophelean seducer who saw her death as the fitting perfection of his conquest; her sister murders her ex-lover in a tram; Nepomuk Schneidewein, Leverkühn's beloved young nephew, is killed by proximity to his uncle, dying of a meningitis that mirrors Leverkühn's own brain infection. *Schneidewein* means cut-vine. Born in 1923, he dies at harvest-time in 1928, representing a final, mirage-like glimpse of the innocent Dionysian principle.

Leverkühn responds to Nepomuk's death with his last work, and his most explicit repudiation of early nineteenth-century optimism, in that it is a withdrawal of Beethoven's Ninth Symphony (1824). This is the *Lamentation of Dr Faustus*, based on the old *Faustbuch* (which concludes with the *sparagmos* of Faust). In its musical form, it imitates Monteverdi's 'Lamento d'Arianna', the lament of a deserted soul, remote from civilization on the island of Naxos, far from the joyfully united brotherhood of Schiller's ode. Yet it is a fragment of an opera that originally ended with the redemption of Ariadne by Bacchus: that is, Dionysus.

Leverkühn's lamentation is the only fitting testimonial of a Germany that, according to Mann, no longer deserves a *Fidelio* or Ninth Symphony (LP, p. 465; *DF*, p. 640). For a first, private hearing in 1930 Leverkühn gathers together the Kridwiss circle, whose pleasure in the aesthetics of violence is the soil out of which grows the tragedy of Clarissa Rodde and her sister, and the larger tragedy of Germany. Before commencing the play-through, he delivers a long confession of his demonic pact, which is at first taken, and savoured, as part of the performance. Then, as he plays the first chord of the cantata, his mind is erased. It is the final disappearance of the self-conscious moral agent: the twentieth-century equivalent to Faustus's dismemberment.

As in earlier interpretations of the Pentheus legend, the victim becomes interchangeable with the god. The mocking promise of Euripides' Dionysus to Pentheus had been that he would return in his mother's hands ('en chersi mētros') (line 969). Leverkühn enacts both the deceptive and the actual meaning of this promise, returning 'to the maternal, broken' ('gebrochen ins Mütterliche') (*DF*, p. 667).[16] Leverkühn has been gripped by an annihilating madness that obliterates almost all knowledge of kin and culture. Knowledge of kin shrinks to the newborn infant's instinctual clinging to the mother; knowledge of culture to the glimmering instinct for sacrifice. At one point during his madness Leverkühn is prevented from drowning himself: from entering the world of Undine. Zeitblom's interpretation is that this is an attempt to save ('retten') his soul by surrendering his body (LP, p. 488; *DF*, p. 669): a sacrificial exchange. Beethoven's *Fidelio* had been an opera of *Rettung*, and its final chorus had insistently celebrated Leonore as a 'Retterin'. This is all that is left of his great ideals.

Leverkühn's final sacrificial gesture takes us back to the enthusiasms of the Kridwiss circle, whose cult of beautiful violence illustrates how aestheticism can be 'the herald of barbarism' ('Wegbereiter der Barbarei') (LP, p. 359; *DF*, p. 495). Like the comparable circle in *The Man Without Qualities*, this has a Jewish participant, ignorant of the furnace he is helping to stoke. He is Chaim Breisacher, a lover of destructive paradox and a religious reactionary: so reactionary that he deplores the rejection of the carnal worship of a carnal deity, the substitution of symbolic sacrifice for 'the sacrifice of blood and fat, which once, salted and seasoned with savoury smells, fed God, made Him a body' ('das Opfer von Blut und Fett, das einst, gesalzen mit Reizgerüchen gewürzt, den Gott speiste, ihm einen Körper machte' (LP, p. 273; *DF*, p. 377). King Solomon is denounced as 'a progressivist blockhead' ('ein fortschrittlicher Dummkopf') (LP, p. 272; *DF*, p. 376) for countenancing a religion of symbol, and the figure of Christ undergoes profound cultural surgery: another member of the circle, the poet Daniel zur Hohe, adopts the pseudonym of Christus Imperator Maximus in order to extol war and slaughter, and Leverkühn himself increasingly bears a parodic likeness to Christ. All the advanced, symbolic interpretations of sacrifice fall away before the encroachment of barbarism. We are left with empty material gestures that imitate old spiritual forms, like the crystals which Leverkühn's father grows in diluted water glass, which sprout in dead but elaborate mimicry of living growths, even seeking the light. Here, as in the snow scene in *The Magic Mountain*, the crystal represents the realm of inorganic structure on whose threshold life exists; on whose threshold, rather than that of the divine world, the sacrificial victim now stands. This realm is parallel to the world of soulless water sprites portrayed in *Undine*, and to the insentient life forms that swim in the fluid of Leverkühn's brain. And it is these chemical forms to which Leverkühn conforms in his final attempt at sacrifice, in which he becomes a soulless, material being, mechanically seeking the light.

IPHIGENIA IN IRAQ

Man cannot serve both Dionysus and Iphigenia. If the twentieth century has been the century of *The Bacchae*, Iphigenia has largely slipped into the background (*Iphigenia among the Taurians* totally so). There have, to be sure, been adaptations of *Iphigenia in Aulis*: an example is the moving and unjustly neglected opera *Jertfirea Iphigeniei* (*Iphigenia's Sacrifice*) (1968) by the Romanian composer Pascal Bentoiu, which stresses the nobility of the heroine's selflessness. More critical versions have been provided by André Obey and Kenneth Rexroth. Obey's *Une Fille pour du vent* (1953) asserts the unique value of individual life, even in the indiscriminate carnage of a modern territorial war. Although Iphigénie does accept her role as victim, she dies because she can no longer endure Agamemnon's corrupt world. The synchronizing of the sacrifice and the renewed wind is the result merely of intelligent weather forecasting by Calchas; but the wind blows too soon and exposes the trick, even though it does not prevent the sacrifice. In Rexroth's radically reimagined *Iphigenia at Aulis* (1951), Agamemnon and Iphigenia have been lovers, and Iphigenia's proposed marriage with Achilles is initially a façade to conceal the incest of father and daughter. Finally, Iphigenia dies under the knife of her father–lover.[17]

The Iphigenia plays did not, however, impress themselves culturally upon the twentieth century in the way that they did on the eighteenth, and that *The Bacchae* did on the twentieth. As already noted, Hauptmann's version of *Iphigenia in Aulis* – perhaps the most significant twentieth-century adaptation – makes the play closer to *The Bacchae* than any playwright since Euripides himself has done. *Iphigenia in Aulis* has, however, very recently gained new interest as a result of recent Western adventures in the Middle East.

In 1998 the Swiss author Jürg Amann published *Iphigenie, oder Operation Meereswind* (*Iphigenia; or, Operation Sea Wind*), in transparent allusion to the First Gulf War: Operation Desert Storm. This is Euripides' play as filtered through CNN newscasts, and is a study in how the appetite for news creates war. For the first time, the (textually problematic) chorus of sightseers in the original becomes an integral and active part of the reconception. The voice-overs constantly digest and trivialize the action into soundbite headlines, but in doing so they amplify a form of discourse that is present among the characters themselves: it is not Linda Xenakis, the CNN reporter, but Agamemnon himself who comes up with the jingle 'Mein Kind für Wind!' ('My child in exchange for wind').[18] But it is Linda Xenakis who, towards the end of the play, tries out headline after headline before hitting on her decisive masterpiece: 'Iphigenie durch Wunder gerettet' ('Miraculous Rescue of Iphigenia') (p. 73). Although Amann was perhaps unaware of the fact, this nicely echoes the title of the earliest German dramatization of this myth, Reinhard Keiser's *Die wunderbahr errettete Iphigenia* (1699). The title yet again reminds us how important the word *retten* is in eighteenth-century drama, in its typification of the altruistic emotions and actions that bring a new world into being. A rallying cry of the eighteenth century has become the emptiest newspaper-speak of the twentieth.

This adaptation again raises the question of what threshold the sacrificial victim stands on. The divine? An untamed and formless sea, like the Iphigenias of Racine and Goethe? Layers of immemorial rock, like

Hoffmann's Elis Fröbom? In fact, Amann's Iphigenie stands on the threshold of the world of simulations: the hyperreality of disembodied electronic simulacra that led Jean Baudrillard to deny that the Gulf War took place at all. Through the process of sacrifice, Iphigenie is transubstantiated into a headline. Very similar emphasis on the controlling power of media images underlay the English National Theatre's recent production of Euripides' *Iphigenia in Aulis*, in which the Chorus were star-struck camp followers, nervously adjusting their make-up; in which the happy ending made possible a press photo opportunity; and in which the sparing of Iphigenia was in any case overshadowed by the larger horror of the coming war.

The power of images is also a dominant feature of Edna O'Brien's version of the play,[19] though their power is here primarily sexual: hers is a play about males and females, each driven by the sexual dynamics of their group, with individuality taking second place. Women are submissively obsessed with military heroes: the first chorus of Euripides' play, perhaps the earliest portrayal of the cult of celebrity, again comes into its own as a potent shaping influence on the adaptation. Men, by contrast, combine as a mob to possess and master women, whether in their mass courtship of Helen, their clamouring for the sacrifice of Iphigenia, or their stoning of Achilles for attempting to oppose the sacrifice. The sacrifice is accomplished, to exclusively female death shrieks, and the bloodshed spreads to the heavens, falling as rain. In portraying characters who are representatives of sexually typical urges, and readily merge back into an indistinct mob, O'Brien stands at the opposite extreme from the writers of the late eighteenth century, to whom the formation of the individual moral consciousness was paramount.

Taking a lead from Euripides, then, these recent *Iphigenias* portray the overriding of the individual by collective impulses, whether the mass consumption of news or the mob desire for vengeance or profit. Yet are these plays really concerned with *sacrifice*? Hauptmann's play amply shows the psychological power of the pre-Olympian gods. It certainly deals with hysteria and hatred (witness the stoning of Palamedes), but it also shows how these may be experienced as religious emotions. The Enlightenment plays of Voltaire and others are concerned with a process that was driven by religion. The ritual power of sacrifice, however, is of little account in these more recent plays. We rather see what Girard has suggested to be the precursor of sacrificial ritual: the dynamics of the mob. This is the subject of one of the most celebrated sacrificial narratives of the early postwar years, Shirley Jackson's short story 'The Lottery' (1948).

SACRIFICIAL CRISES IN THE MODERN WORLD

Every 27 June, the inhabitants of a small American village gather for a seasonal custom which initially seems to be homely and slightly absurd, like that which was later to be portrayed in the film *Groundhog Day*. It involves the choosing of a member of the village by lot and only at the end do we realize – and witness – the nature of the prize: death by stoning. Because the village is so small, the whole thing can be over between breakfast and lunch. In larger towns, the ritual can take days.

The word 'sacrifice' is never used, and the story depicts not so much ritualized violence as the persistence of violence amidst the decay of ritual. It is a midsummer festival, and the names of its organizers, Mr Summers and Mr Graves, could not be more appropriate to a midsummer sacrifice. Yet the festival misses the solstice by almost a week, and its possible connection with fertility is reduced to an obsolete proverb: 'Used to be a saying about "Lottery in June, corn be heavy soon".'[20] The custom is being abandoned in other towns, but the villagers here cling to the belief that their culture would collapse if the lottery were abandoned: if it speeds the ripening of the corn, without it 'we'd all be eating stewed chickweed and acorns' (p. 230). Without the lottery, man would not even be a hunter–gatherer: he would merely be a gatherer.

The proceedings are over by lunchtime, the convenience of their brevity revealing the decline of their ritual power. Ritual is conservative: Walter Burkert points out that the wooden spear thrown by the Fecialian priests in ancient Rome to mark the beginning of war is a primordial weapon that goes back to Palaeolithic times.[21] Yet here the details of the original ritual – the original box, the use of wooden chips as lots – are dispensable and forgotten. The primordial weapon, however, is remembered: 'Although the villagers had forgotten the ritual and lost the original black box, they still remembered to use stones' (pp. 232–3). This is not a sacrificial ritual: it is a ritual which has lost its sacrificial purpose; the only thing which survives untransmuted from the past is the stone, perhaps the most ancient weapon of all. '[M]en continue', Frazer wrote, 'to do what their fathers did before them, though the reasons on which their fathers acted have been long forgotten' (*Golden Bough*, pp. 493–4). More elaborate forms of culture come and go, but the instincts expressed in the lottery are immutable.

The savagery latent within the commonplace and neighbourly has repeatedly surfaced in the twentieth century, in Germany, the Balkans, and elsewhere. One of the first great British novelists to explore the ineradicable human capacity for evil revealed (for example) by Nazism and Stalinism was William Golding, whose first novel, *Lord of the Flies* (1954), is one of the most celebrated treatments of the subject in modern literature. Here, a group of choirboys marooned on a desert island largely revert to savagery, as Europe is simultaneously doing. The majority quickly return to the mentality of the hunter: his pack instincts, need for a leader, and delight in tracking and the kill. As in 'The Lottery', skill in throwing stones is again a primal and formative capacity, and the categories of the hunter shape the organization of the tribe, unified by fear of a beast in the forest (really the body of a dead parachutist): an object of fear to whom propitiatory sacrifice is offered; an object of hate, who must be hunted and killed. In the rituals which precede the hunt, the actors switch between the roles of prey and hunter. Amidst this reversion to the practices of Stone Age hunters, it is natural to expect a return to human sacrifice, and indeed natural to think that it has happened. Yet it doesn't, quite. What happens rather is that human beings are merged with the prey. The fat, intelligent odd man out and eventual scapegoat, Piggy, is aligned by his name with the principal prey of the hunters, and killed with that primal weapon, a stone. Immediately before the final rescue Ralph, the original and good leader of the group, is also hunted. Simon, another good character, stumbles into the midst of the hunting ritual, sustained by mass chants of '*Kill the beast!*'[22] Simon's message is that the beast does not exist; that it is merely the corpse of a parachutist, but he cannot stop the growing frenzy: 'There was the throb and stamp of a single organism . . . At once the crowd surged after it, poured down the rock, leapt on to the beast, screamed, struck, bit, tore. There were no words, and no movements but the tearing of teeth and claws' (p. 161). It is, yet again, the ending of *The Bacchae*: reason is erased, and the retreat to the 'single organism' of the collective destroys any bond of human identity with the victim. Yet there is a difference. In *The Bacchae* (as in *The Madness of Heracles*) the madness of the hunt invades and degrades a ritual of higher cultural standing. The horror is in the identification of the hunt and sacrifice. Here, the hunt is the thing itself.

One might make a similar point about the scapegoat figure in Golding's later novel *Rites of Passage* (1980), the obsequious, socially insignificant clergyman James Colley, one of the passengers on a voyage from Britain to the Antipodes in the Napoleonic period. Despite his 'sacred office',[23] Colley is the victim of a drunken ritual as the ship crosses the equator. Half-naked, without 'the ornaments of the Spiritual Man' (p. 237), he is forced to kneel before a figure personating Neptune and then immersed in a bag full of bilge. As the ritual proceeds, he hears 'a storm of cheering and that terrible British sound which has ever daunted the foe; and then it came to me, was forced in upon my soul the awful truth – *I was the foe!*' (p. 237).

In *Rites of Passage* the journey to the mountains is replaced by the journey to the upside-down mirror image on the other side of the globe: the Antipodes. The ceremony as the line is crossed is an inverted religious ritual, of Mass and baptism, presented (and partly perceived in the victim's heated mind) as a last judgment. Yet it is ritual only in the sense that destructive parody inevitably retains the structure of what it destroys. The essential feature is the mental and moral isolation of the scapegoat: the terrible moment when he realizes that *he* is the foe; that the whole collective organism of the ship's population is set against him. What destroys him, however, is not this external defilement. He is destroyed by a second incident, only gradually pieced together, in which he gets drunk, appears half naked before his fellow-passengers, urinates in public and, in private, performs an act of fellatio upon his Tadzio, the seaman Billy Rogers, having previously managed to interpret his attraction to the youth as a concern to save his soul. The mechanisms that destroy him are therefore complex. Enlightenment, too, can be a scapegoating process, and the irreligion that in Voltaire protested against human sacrifice here strips the low-born parson of the dignity of office, and exposes him to the combined contempt of the pagan mob and the genteel sceptic. He survives even this until drink makes him see in himself impulses that replicate the pagan ritual which humiliated him. Colley, writes Virginia Tiger, 'is to be likened to Pentheus, who was driven mad and torn to pieces by the Bacchanals when he resisted the introduction of Dionysian worship into his kingdom'.[24]

Golding did actually portray human sacrifice in *The Inheritors* (1955), but he there portrayed it not as a regression to the primitive but as part of the ascent towards symbolic thought. The novel portrays the first encounter between a group of Neanderthals and one of *Homo sapiens*, the former being destroyed by the experience. The Neanderthals do not have the radical separation from the outside, natural world that characterizes human consciousness, their minds forming an unbroken continuum with the natural world, so that they exist in a state of telepathic reciprocity with their environment. *Homo sapiens* has a capacity for symbolic thought and image-making, whereas it is a long time before the Neanderthal protagonist Lok discovers, through human contact, the idea of the 'like'.[25] This idea, however, carries as its inevitable condition that of difference: the humans interpret the Neanderthals as fearful demons, for example. Symbolic thought leads to a more instrumental use of the natural world and, inevitably and immediately, to sacrifice.

A consequence of the Neanderthals' sense of mental reciprocity with nature is that they interpret events according to the model of *giving*. They give the fire wood to eat (p. 39); the fire gives them flame (p. 30). When *Homo sapiens* fires arrows at them, they think the arrows are gifts of twigs. The closest the Neanderthals come to sacrifice is when they make a 'present' of food to 'the ice women' (p. 70), to intercede for a dying companion. The ice women are a large ice formation in a cliff, with some suggestion of human form. Yet again, sacrifice is imaginatively linked to the inanimate realm of geological formations and of ice. In contrast with the snow scene in *The Magic Mountain*, however, the point here is that there is no notion of the inorganic: ice, like fire, needs nutrition, and the chain of sustenance is that which enmeshes the characters in the web of nature.

The sacrifices of *Homo sapiens* are (literally) acts of separation. There is a finger-sacrifice at a hunting ritual which, like the comparable ritual in *Lord of the Flies*, shows human beings alternating between the roles of prey and hunter: a man dances in a stag skin; a stag is slaughtered. Later, a human child is tethered to a human image and left as a sacrifice to the Neanderthals, who do not understand the offering. In both episodes there is a sense of commutability between individual and representation which the Neanderthals do not have. The child is spared, and Golding focusses attention not on this individual transaction but (again) on a collective act of *sparagmos*: the dividing and devouring of the body of a Neanderthal toddler, Liku. '[T]he slaughter of Liku is anything but sacramental', writes Pierre François; 'This "communion" is demonic, because the innocent maternal scapegoat is not killed and eaten for the sake of religious regeneration, but in order to allay hunger in inebriate quarrelsomeness.'[26] Following this rite, 'gifts' – stag's meat and mead (p. 199) – are left by the humans in order to propitiate the Neanderthals, whom they believe to be demons. In drinking the mead, Lok for the first time experiences drunkenness, and its alienating effect produces in him an enhanced sense of understanding the human. The Neanderthals have up to that point experienced the incorporation in natural process that Greek culture associated with the Dionysiac. Here, alcohol dissolves the bond with nature. So does sacrifice. At the end of the novel, when the Neanderthal group have all died and the humans sail off into a mysterious future, it is clear that sacrifice will be an increasing part of the growing culture: 'what sacrifice would they be forced to perform to a world of confusion?' (p. 231). It is, indeed, a consequence of symbolic thought.

Human sacrifice remains popular. In the first half of the twentieth century, the anthropologist Margaret Murray asserted that witchcraft was a channel through which Frazerian Neolithic religions survived into the modern period – an idea explored in the film *The Wicker Man* (1973). The survival of an old, sacrificial religion takes a different form in Peter Ackroyd's novel *Hawksmoor* (1985), in which the rationalism of Wren is mockingly rejected by his successor Nicholas Dyer, who buries a sacrificed child in the foundations of the churches he builds; these events are then transported into the twentieth century, where they are investigated by the detective, Nicholas Hawksmoor. Okonkwo participates in the sacrifice of his surrogate son in Achebe's *Things Fall Apart* (1958).[27] Yet there is a huge retreat from the prominence that the subject had in early Modernism: in Stravinsky, Schoenberg, Mann, Lawrence, and Eliot. We might expect the atrocities of the twentieth century to have generated yet another reformulation of the sacrificial theme, but instead they have supplanted it. There have been many studies of the anthropology and psychology of ritual, whose origins Konrad Lorenz has traced back to animal behaviour.[28] It is a powerful organizing presence in drama (for example, that of Jean Genet) and music theatre (for example, Tippet's *The Midsummer Marriage* (1955)), yet it is now an anthropological or psychosexual phenomenon;

religion has become a minor and archaic subdivision of ritual rather than the thing itself.

The growing difficulties of the sacrificial theme are illustrated by Eliot's postwar experiment with a sacrificial plot in *The Cocktail Party* (1949), in which his lifelong interest in self-discovery through sacrifice leads him, finally, to the portrayal of literal human sacrifice and to a plot oddly parallel to that of 'The Woman Who Rode Away': that is, a young and beautiful Western woman half-deliberately seeks sacrifice by a primitive culture. The play is loosely based on Euripides' play *Alcestis*, in which King Admetus is told that he must die unless another is willing to die in his place; his parents refuse, but his wife Alcestis does give her life for his. She is then brought back from the dead by Heracles. *Alcestis* is thus a variant of the sacrifice-averted plot (death is 'the sacrificer [hierea] of the dead' (line 25)), and was the subject of many later adaptations, including operas by Lully and Gluck. Its concern with wifely self-sacrifice rather than exotic ritual ensured that it was more durable than *Iphigenia among the Taurians*: Egon Wellesz set a version by Hugo von Hoffmanstahl the year before *The Sacrifice of the Prisoner*. Perhaps another reason for its durability is that *Alcestis* seems, pre-eminently, to preserve the supposed origins of drama in sacrificial rituals of rebirth.

In *The Cocktail Party*, the wife returns not from the dead but from a possibly imaginary journey to Dedham. Lavinia Chamberlayne has walked out of a humdrum marriage, discontented with a superficial and humourless husband, Edward. The modern Heracles, the psychiatrist Sir Henry Harcourt Reilly, persuades the couple to remain together, accepting the limits of their existence and themselves. In what at first seems a comic resolution of a sexual quadrangle, Lavinia's lover Peter Quilpe falls in love with Edward's, Celia Coplestone. These two spare lovers, however, go in opposite directions. Peter retreats into the Hollywood world of simulacra, mingles with deracinated Europeans such as the Princess Bologolomsky and the film producer Bela Szogody, and is doing his bit to promote the deracination of his own country – for he is making a film about the most decayed noble house in Britain, 'Boltwell', and is back home to soak up the ambience of decay. The film, however, will not even be made in Boltwell, but in a Hollywood replica of this modern House of Usher.

Celia, however, rejects the possibility of life as a Hollywood actress and joins a strict nursing order on the island of Kinkanja, where she gets caught up in a feud between Christians and pagans arising from a dispute about the sacred status of monkeys. Christians eat monkeys and, as a beneficial by-product, protect their crops from them. They prosper. The pagans regard monkeys as sacred, and their crops are consequently eaten. They do not prosper. Amidst the ensuing insurrection, Celia remains to tend sufferers from plague, is crucified near an anthill, and is largely consumed by the ants. A speech which Eliot soon, but 'not without reluctance', dropped[29] narrated that Celia had then attracted the guilt that the sacrificial victim often attracts. A shrine was erected, at which the inhabitants left offerings of flowers, fruit, and flesh:

> They seemed to think that by propitiating Celia
> They might insure themselves against further misfortune.[30]

Just such ambiguity had characterized the body of another helper against plague, Oedipus: feared for pollution during his life, he was coveted as a protective talisman after his death.

Mark Pizzato is perhaps over-enthusiastic to see Celia's death as a 'Dionysian *sparagmos*', especially as he wrongly reports that she was torn apart and eaten by cannibals.[31] Indeed, perhaps the play's puzzling emphasis on the absence of tigers ('There *were* no tigers', says Alex in the play's second line (p. 7)) points to an absence of the Dionysiac, the tiger (like the panther) being associated with Dionysus.[32] Yet her death *is* a form of sacrificial *omophagia*, and the replacement of the Maenad, or the tiger, by the ant isolates to the exclusion of all else the idea of sacrifice as performed by the brainlessly collective. Like Hauptmann earlier in the decade, Eliot takes a classical model typically associated with the renunciation of sacrifice and reverses it by including a horrifyingly archaic form of the thing the source renounces. If Hauptmann uses the chthonic gods of mythology, Eliot in the anthill creates another form of sacrifice to the earth. Like *The Waste Land*, *The Cocktail Party* evokes a Frazerian pattern of death and regeneration, but the regeneration and the sacrifice are violently unrelated, and its value for the victim is uncertain. As Sir Henry Harcourt Reilly says,

> I'd say that she suffered all that we should suffer
> In fear and pain and loathing – all these together –
> And reluctance of the body to become a *thing*. (p. 163)

The Cocktail Party is, manifestly, a play of ritualized eating and drinking, from the gatherings which give it its title and the inedible 'treat' with eggs which Alex creates for the newly deserted Edward, to the ceremonial glass of wine in Reilly's consulting room, the dispute about the sanctity of monkey flesh, the devouring of Celia, and the edible offerings at her shrine. In the treatment of Celia's crucified body, Eliot obviously plays with the communion, but he also uses the values of hospitality and feasting which are fundamental to Greek culture, and indeed to *Alcestis*: Heracles is an indecorously drunken guest in a grieving household, but he repays his host by rescuing his wife. Heracles' indecorum is replaced, in Eliot's play, by that of guests not knowing, but gradually suspecting, that the host's wife has just walked out on him. But what is the point of ritual? Eliot presents a world in which personality is a series of disjunct moments, memory uncertain, and perception of others a registering of fleeting and deceptive phantasms. The repetitions of ritual mimic continuity and communion instead of confirming it. Robertson Smith's shared sacrificial meal has become the cocktail party, and the participants in the actual sacrificial meal are ants. Even the sacrificed body reverses in significance once it has been sacrificed.

Almost nothing happens in *The Cocktail Party* that is not an attenuation of an originally sacrificial ritual. Like the Princess Bologolomsky, the rituals are now rootless and unfixed. Sacrifice is now a private rather than a social necessity, its impact on the community invisible, its value for the individual inscrutable. Eliot turned a comedy about the reversal of sacrifice into one that is shockingly disrupted by it – disrupted, but not transformed.

If the collective *sparagmos* in *The Cocktail Party* becomes the Lilliputian activity of ants, more direct imitations of Pentheus' fate hold sway elsewhere, as adaptations of *The Bacchae* move increasingly into the mainstream. The play has been adapted by Wole Soyinka (1973), and four postwar operas have been based on it: Harry Partch's *Revelation in the Courthouse Park* (1960); Hans Werner Henze's *The Bassarids*, one of the greatest masterpieces of postwar music theatre; Roy Travis's *Black Bacchantes* (1982); and John Buller's *BAKXAI* (1992) (Plate 17).[33] Buller's powerful piece is a setting of Euripides rather than an adaptation for the modern world, and at times retains the original Greek.

By contrast, *Revelation in the Courthouse Park* is a palimpsest which interweaves with the Euripidean story that of a modern American mother, groupie of the pop star Dion, and her repressed, dominated son, who is turned by her into a gauche misfit: a natural scapegoat, who is murdered by a mob as his mother watches. Dionysus here is a narcissistic 'god of ritualistic and flambuoyant [*sic*] mediocrity'.[34] Pop music is also one point of reference in Wole Soyinka's *The Bacchae of Euripides*. A scene of Dionysiac celebration is described as '*extracting the emotional colour and temperature of a European pop scene without degenerating into that tawdry commercial manipulation of teenage mindlessness*'. The slave leader's '*style is based on the lilt and energy of the black hot gospellers who themselves are often first to become physically possessed.*'[35]

Soyinka is notable for his largely favourable treatment of Dionysos, who empowers a slave revolt in Thebes. The play is nominally set in ancient Greece, with references to the suppression of the Helots in Sparta, and it opens with the spectacle of the skeletal bodies of crucified slaves, the cross being pushed back to the point where it had not yet acquired its symbolism, and where this not-yet symbolic object interacts with the genesis of another religion of rebirth. Nevertheless, there are clear pointers to later tyrannies, both colonial and post-colonial: tyrannies sustained by the idea of a 'master race' (p. 240). They are also based on human sacrifice: there is an annual, and potentially fatal, chasing and flogging of a scapegoat, which

Plate 17 Sarah Walker as Agave in John Buller's *BAKXAI* (1992)

is held to be necessary to the renewal of the year and the prevention of famine. Tragedy in Soyinka's play confronts its own presumed origins in the sacrifice of the Year Spirit, but in this case the ritual is not a direct expression of primal folk psychology, but a means of political and economic oppression: the slave-owners gain the 'profit' (p. 237) of the fertility that is presumed to be consequent, while the slaves are tricked into sacrificing one of their own number. Indignation at the sacrificial custom threatens to produce revolution, and to keep the potential revolution in check Tiresias gambles with his life by assuming the role of scapegoat, wearing a protective Bacchic fawnskin under his sackcloth. The ritual leads directly to the Dionysiac liberation of the slaves and the death of Pentheus, but the chain of cause and effect is political rather than mythic.[36]

Though sacrifice is often in the nineteenth and twentieth centuries associated with assimilation into the inorganic, Soyinka clearly associates it with the organic. Even more than in Euripides, his Dionysos is a god of vital fluids, and of seeds and growth: 'Blessed are they who bathe in the seminal river' intones the Chorus Leader (p. 247). Although Dionysos remains a god of the mountains, he is also a god of rivers. One telling moment of differentiation between Pentheus and Dionysus in Euripides had occurred when Dionysus asked whether Pentheus knew of Mount Tmolus. Yes, replies Pentheus: it encircles the city of Sardis (lines 461–3). Pentheus needs the city as a point of reference, even in locating a mountain, whereas the mountain is self-sufficient for Dionysus. In the corresponding passage in Soyinka, Tmolus has been turned from a mountain into a river: 'have you heard of a river / Called Tmolus', Dionysos asks (p. 267). Pentheus, however, remains (as in Euripides) a guardian of walls and boundaries. Organic life-processes form no part of his thoughts, except when he dismisses them as lechery and drunkenness. Dionysos pinpoints his hostility to the organic when he accuses Pentheus of having 'metallic' thoughts (p. 285), and Pentheus starts thinking in terms of organisms only when he is dressing to spy on the Bacchanals in the mountains.

Soyinka lessens the unscrupulous manipulativeness of Euripides' god in manoeuvring Pentheus into disguising himself as a woman. In Soyinka's version Pentheus calls for his armour, so as to mount an attack on the Bacchanals in the hills. Dionysos masters his mind by divine influence, by giving him alcohol for the first time, and also by showing him two future, complementary expressions of the Dionysiac. One is a loveless wedding ceremony at which the bridegroom is liberated by drink and (like Hippocleides in Herodotus) loses his bride by performing handstands which display his testicles to the onlookers. The other, contrasting, wedding is the one at Canaa, where Christ wears '*an ambiguous thorn-ivy-crown of Dionysos*' (p. 286). The two weddings represent contrasting manifestations of Dionysos, one in a liberation that is accompanied by sensual disorder and one that is a measured affirmation of community. Yet they are troublingly linked. When Dionysos gives Pentheus a cup of wine to commence the process of mastering his mind, the cup is taken from the wedding at Canaa (traditionally the type of communion). Under the influence of its contents Pentheus dons women's clothes, thinking that he is arming himself. This is where he first starts to think in terms of organic process: seeing Dionysos as a bull, he notices 'horns newly / Sprouted from your head' (p. 291). Then he goes off to meet 'sacrifice' at his mother's hands (p. 299).

Soyinka retains Agave's gradual return to sanity and horror, though he reduces Kadmos' criticism of Dionysos to 'Dionysos is just. But he is not fair!' (p. 304), and omits the concluding sentence of exile. Instead, the severed head of Pentheus starts to spout red liquid, which Kadmos thinks to be blood, but which Tiresias finds to be wine. The last spectacle of the play is of Agave drinking the wine which gushes from the head of the son she has sacrificed: a final, troubling absorption of Christ into Dionysos. It is, however, Dionysos who controls the symbols: the cross remains the instrument for punishing and terrifying slaves, and is not historically updated.

Soyinka's play reflects a time when liberators in many parts of Africa were becoming, or giving way to, corrupt dictators. The other outstanding rethinking of the work from the postwar years, Hans Werner Henze's opera *The Bassarids* (1966), is by a creative artist whose work pre-eminently links Modernism to earlier literary and musical traditions: in particular those of the nineteenth century. Henze's early career, for example, shows a remarkable interest in revisiting the formative subjects of early Romanticism: in, for example, works based on La Motte Fouqué's *Undine*, Kleist's *Prinz Friedrich von Homburg* (1809–11), and Hoffmann's 'The Mines at Falun'.[37] The last work inspired *Elegy for Young Lovers*, the libretto of which (like that of *The Bassarids*) was written by W. H. Auden and Chester Kallman. The poet Gregor Mittenhofer draws inspiration from the visions of the deranged Hilda Mack, whose bridegroom disappeared on the Hammerhorn forty years before, the day after their marriage. When the husband's preserved body is recovered from the ice, her visions cease. Mittenhofer instead sends two young lovers up into the mountain to look for edelweiss to inspire him, and conceals information about an impending storm. The 'Elegy for Young Lovers' which their death inspires is read in public at the end of the work, before a statue of Apollo, though we only hear a wordless ensemble of those whose sufferings contributed to the poem. The verbal depiction of the death comes earlier, before it happens, in the last of Hilda's prophetic visions. It is a vision of sacrifice on the gigantic altar of the mountain:

To the Immortal, high
        On their white altar,
        Mortal heat neither
        Simple nor wicked
        Lamb-like is fed.

Paired in the sacrifice,
        Do they die justly
        Though it be fated?
        Never forget the
        Old gods are dead.[38]

Plate 18 The première of Hans Werner Henze's *The Bassarids* (Salzburg, 1966)

Yet again, we have snow and the inorganic, the freezing and preservation of the body here standing for another transformation: translation into the world of simulacra. By contrast, *The Bassarids* ends with an image of Mediterranean lushness: '*Of the palace, only a jagged blackened wall is left. Upon Semele's tomb sit two enormous fertility idols of an African or South Seas type: fetish masks etc. . . . Vines descend and sprout everywhere, wreathing the columns, covering the blackened wall.*'[39] Yes, there is exuberant fertility, but a sense of retrogression is as strong as that of rebirth. Where there was ice in *Elegy for Young Lovers*, here there is fire, reducing a living culture to sterile archaeological remains. There is retrogression, too, at the level of symbolism, the specific intellectual forms of the Olympian divinities yielding to a primitive and impersonal representation of sexual function. This is what the Apollonian Pentheus fears: a world without structure of number or geometrical form, and where even distinction of species is lost. In Dionysus' realm, he had complained, there

> Is no distinction;
> Here is neither
> Square nor circle,
> Even nor odd;
> Men are beasts
> And beasts are men. (p. 23)

This Pentheus is a kind of Akhnaten: a monotheist in a world that is retreating from religion to magic; if Soyinka plays on the homology of Dionysus and Christ, Henze quotes from the *St Matthew Passion* in order to connect Pentheus with Christ.[40] Unlike Wellesz's Dionysus, this one is a god of darkness.

It is well known that the librettists and the composer differed in their view of Dionysus. For Auden, he was a Nazi with nothing to recommend him,[41] yet Henze gave him the most sensuously beautiful melismas uttered by any operatic version of Dionysus since the Stranger in Szymanowski's *King Roger*. Nevertheless, Henze responds fully to the text's realization of crowd dynamics, in all their ambiguity and ugliness. Whereas Euripides opens with the solitary Dionysus, this opera opens with a crowd adulating a leader: the citizens celebrating the accession of Pentheus. After the atrocity, no individual takes responsibility for what collective madness had achieved. We hear the weasel excuses of those who opportunistically got caught up in a wave of national hysteria ('We had no share in his bloody death' (p. 63)), but there is also the implication that in such outbreaks adults revert to the mentality of childhood – a mentality evident in the tone of Autonoe's excuses for her part in Pentheus' death:

> I didn't want to do it.
> Agave made me do it.
> She always was the stronger. (p. 62)

In addition, the librettists accentuate the nostalgia for childhood implicit, but not developed, when Euripides' Pentheus is told that he will be carried home in his mother's hands.

> Oh! How Agave will smile and
> Scold when she bears him
> Home in her arms, her lost babe! (p. 50)

The mentality of childhood is most strikingly present in one of Dionysus' followers: a child carrying an enormous realistic doll which says '*Mamma, mamma*' (p. 24), and whose mechanical cries accompany a hymn in praise of Dionysus' mother Semele. The last event in the opera is the child's smashing of the doll at the foot of Semele's grave.

Any remotely faithful adaptation of *The Bacchae* will portray a mother–son relationship, though it is notable that the freest early adaptations, *King Roger* and *Das Wunder der Heliane*, omit it. As the prop of the doll indicates, however, Auden and Kallman give unprecedented stress to the psychology of the mother–child bond. Dionysus' emotional fixation on Semele is explored in a way that has no precedent in earlier versions; immediately before the child smashes her doll at the foot of Semele's tomb, she is raised from the dead and elevated to divinity by the power of Dionysus. This deification is attested in Greek myth, but not used in any other version of *The Bacchae* that I have seen. In addition, the librettists rival Partch's *Revelation in the Courthouse Park* in stressing the psychologically suffocating nature of Pentheus' involvement with his mother. In particular, Pentheus is tricked into the fatal spying mission because of his fascination with his mother's sexuality, and some unspecified earlier memories associated with it. The fatal journey to Cithaeron becomes a reliving of a primal scene. (Correspondingly, when Cadmus brings Agave out of her Bacchic trance, he acts like a psychoanalyst, recovering repressed memories.)

Another unprecedented feature of this adaptation is the role of Beroe. In myth, she is the old nurse whose form Hera adopted to trick Semele into asking Zeus to appear undisguised. Here, she is the surrogate mother, who loved both Semele and Pentheus, and who pleads in vain for him to Dionysus. She fulfils the cultural role of mother; Zeus and Hera (the enemy of Semele and Dionysus) have the titles of divine father and mother. The opera thus pits cultural and religious symbols which are abstracted from the ideas of fatherhood and motherhood against the literal biological fact of maternity, with all its destructive psychological baggage (fatherhood scarcely figures). Perhaps it is this disappearance of the cultural derivations of motherhood that Beroe laments during her threnody over Pentheus, immediately before Autonoe makes her childish excuses:

> The Mother no longer rules.
> Night and again the night. (p. 62)

In the end, we are left with the '*two enormous fertility idols*', representations of biological procreation and mammary nutrition: even the specificity of the child's doll has gone. These are images, to be sure, but hardly the 'Apolline world of images' (p. 44) of Nietzsche. Here, the birth of tragedy lies in birth itself.

It is now forty years since the première of *The Bassarids*; I remember listening to the first-ever broadcast. Henze quickly struck out in new directions – *The Raft of the Medusa* deals with lives made disposable by class oppression – and in its Freudianism the libretto already seems dated. Yet, if Freud had used one great Greek tragedy to support a view of life as being doomed to tragic conflict by its very origins in the womb, Henze and his librettists sense similar processes of doom in the other of the two Greek tragedies that, more than any others, the twentieth century made its own. In associating collectivist hysteria with a regression to childhood, the librettists have something in common with *Lord of the Flies*, which had appeared in the previous decade. They have one other thing in common: they do not describe the central crime as a sacrifice. In both cases, it is a hunt. Sacrifice requires a level of symbolic thought that is beyond the uterine nostalgia that drives the action, and beyond the state portrayed in the very final words of the opera – retreat into a religious experience that has no need of signs:

> We see not, we hear not:
> We kneel and adore. (p. 66)

In different ways, Soyinka and Auden–Kallman are both rooted in the late nineteenth-century impulses that reinstated *The Bacchae* as a text in which ancient Greek culture pre-eminently spoke to the modern world. *The Birth of Tragedy* is still a useful gloss on *The Bassarids*, as are Frazer and the Cambridge Ritualists – the opera, after all, traces a retreat from myth to fertility ritual, finally confronting us with the origins of tragedy in the process of birth: 'tragedy' in both its literary and its non-literary senses. Soyinka, similarly, uses the idea that tragedy originated in sacrificial ritual, though he employs the idea in an ironic way, to show how the ritual politically triggers the ensuing events. Both write about the violence of the mid twentieth century, in Germany and in Africa, but in part with the interpretative tools of Nietzsche and Freud.

With the recent return to the Iphigenia theme, however, new impulses are coming into play. If the power of mass-produced images has been a concern at least since *The Man Without Qualities*, Amann's emphasis on their sacrificial power, on Iphigenia as a victim offered up to CNN, brings a new element into the reconceiving of Greek tragedy. It is noteworthy that, seemingly independently of each other, recent versions of *Iphigenia in Aulis* give centrality to a feature of the play that had offered little to previous generations: the opening chorus of sightseers, gaping indiscriminately at stars.

The recent Iphigenia plays suggest that we are no longer simply addressing the intrinsic barbarity of our culture but once more contemplating the forces released by conflict with those who are perceived as barbarians from the East. Aspects of that conflict are presenting us with a new version of the offering of human life, in the suicide bomber.

HUMAN SACRIFICE: THE YEAR 2000

The theme remains inexhaustible. The turn of the millennium saw a treatment of human sacrifice by one of the most eminent living writers: *The Blind Assassin* (2000), by Margaret Atwood. I conclude with a quite detailed discussion of this book not only because of the happy convenience of its date, but because it addresses and transforms so many of the cultural and literary traditions discussed in this book: Dionysus, the sacrificial implications of the fossil record, Dido and Aeneas, Tristan and Isolde, and the Great War; it even, surprisingly, contains another version of the Undine story. Atwood's artful interweaving and juxtaposition of the traditions that have figured so largely in this study therefore seems an appropriate point at which to leave the topic of human sacrifice – for the moment.

The Blind Assassin is a multi-generation family novel, in which a paternalistic business (an Ontario button factory) founded in the 1890s falls during the Depression into the hands of the ruthless right-wing industrialist Richard E. Griffen. Iris and Laura Chase, the granddaughters of the founder, also fall into Griffen's clutches, in that he marries the former and sexually abuses the latter. It is his abuse of Laura that constitutes the reworking of the Undine story. Laura and Richard consummate their affair on a boat called the *Water Nixie*, and it is on this boat that he commits suicide when threatened with disgrace. While he lives out a modernized debasement of the story of Huldbrand, his wife similarly recycles another piece of nineteenth-century medievalism: the story of Iseult.

As in the above examples, *The Blind Assassin* tells a story that is filtered through fragments of other stories and iconographies. These are shaped by an overwhelmingly male supremacist past. On her honeymoon, for example, Iris sees the Albert Memorial in London, on which the Prince dominates four women representing four continents. Other filtering narratives include the classical texts, invariably antifeminist, that are taught by the sisters' tutor, the paedophile Mr Erskine; the death of Dido particularly impresses Laura, and becomes a model for her own death. The largely Pre-Raphaelite iconography of the Chase family home, however, is arranged by Iris's grandmother, Adelia, though it stands in an increasingly ironic relationship to the events of which the house is at first the centre, and eventually the margin. The house is named Avilion, from the final resting place of Tennyson's Arthur. (After the collapse of the dynasty, it reverts to a more aggressively male supremacist, though no less ironic, form: an old people's home called Valhalla.) It is Adelia who, in one of 'her wistful Gothicisms', names the family boat the *Water Nixie*.[42] In addition, she installs in the dining room a triptych of stained glass windows representing the story of Tristan and Iseult: a gross beautification of the violent and exploitative sexual triangles that the novel recounts, and an entirely opaque and unreadable sign of the suppressed longings of the grandmother herself. 'I bet you were alleycatting around, . . . I bet you had a secret life', thinks Iris (p. 504). But the secret life remains secret: indeed, considered as an ancient Greek word, *Adelia* means invisibility or unknowability.

At the other end of the narrative scale from these exalted romances are the graffiti which deface the walls of modern Ontario ('*John Loves Mary*') (p. 504), and which are treated as an archetypal expression of the need to memorialize ourselves in narrative ('we carve our names on trees') (p. 95); the news items and society reports in the *Globe and Mail*; and the pulp science fiction novel-within-a-novel, which carries the same name as the novel itself, and concerns rituals of maiden sacrifice on a far distant planet.

At the centre of Atwood's novel are two sexual triangles, in both of which the sisters are rivals. Both the women are involved with the left-wing activist Alex Thomas. In a vain attempt to save the button factory, Iris is sacrificed in marriage to Griffen, and it is he with whom Laura has her under-age affair, consummated in the *Water Nixie*, and leading to his suicide in the same evocatively named boat. When Laura discovers Iris's affair with Alex, however, and hears of his death, she commits a Didoesque suicide by driving her car from a bridge into a ravine, and being burned to death.

The Blind Assassin is published after Laura's death under her name, and becomes a cult classic. We do not see the finished book, but we hear provisional fragments of the narrative told by Alex during assignations with a woman who, we are to assume, is Laura, but who (we are insufficiently surprised to discover) is in fact Iris – the actual author of the fictitious best-seller. An older narrative here intrudes with distracting half-relevance: in the *Aeneid*, we have been reminded, it is Iris who ends Dido's agony on the pyre and enables her to die. Alex's narrative is transparently a commentary on the events of the novel, but is also an escapist trivialization of them by an author who cannot face up to the challenges of socially realistic fiction. The sacrificial narrative does not expose the hidden and essential core of modern society; rather, it caricatures and sensationalizes. The idea of sacrifice, like the carelessly scrawled graffito, is a text overlaid on experience, not a description of the experience itself.

The embedded novel is set in the city of Sakiel-Norn on the planet Zycron, but obviously represents the economic and sexual conflicts of Canada in the Depression: a revolutionary army threatens an oppressive capitalist monarchy; child labourers lose their sight in the effort of making intricate carpets; maiden sacrifice is practised, but merges into prostitution, in that courtiers pay to deflower the victim the night before the sacrifice. The parallels with events in the framing novel are at once obvious and designedly inconsequential: the deflowering of the maiden victims, for example, parallels Iris's marriage to Griffen. Yet the novel distorts as much as it distils, and thus takes its place with the other narratives – Dido and Aeneas, Tristan and Iseult, Mary and John – which influence the events of the story and at the same time intervene between them and us. For there is one narrative that we cannot directly read: the published version of the sci-fi novel, written up by Iris after the deaths of Laura and Alex but published under Laura's name. It becomes a best-seller, and is revealing enough about Richard's affair with Laura to blight his political ambitions and cause his suicide on the *Water Nixie*. As mentioned above, its title is *The Blind Assassin*. The title of the book we are reading is also the title of the book we cannot read.

The indirections of narrative and iconography are well illustrated in a memorial to that other event which attracts repeated imagery of sacrifice: the First World War. The heroines' father Norval, who has lost an eye and a leg in the war, commissions a memorial, but the townsfolk are unimpressed by the unheroic weariness of the statue, and demand that it bear the inscription 'For Those Who Willingly Made the Supreme Sacrifice' (p. 148). The idea of sacrifice has literally become a graffito, laid upon events which it cannot describe. Norval, however, refuses to back down: 'if they didn't watch out he'd go in for bare-naked realism all the way and the statue would be made of rotting body fragments, of which he had stepped on a good many in his day' (p. 148). The artistic alternatives are stone or flesh; statue or *sparagmos*. We return to the question that had overshadowed the end of *The Bacchae*: how to recompose the fragments of the shattered body. Here, however, the question is a metaphor for the nature of narrative itself. It is re-posed throughout the novel, and the image which is here used – of turning life (or death) into stone – constantly recurs. For *The Blind Assassin* is yet another novel which places its characters at the interface with the inorganic and geological.

These alternatives of stone or flesh are incorporated at the cultural heart of Avilion itself, in – appropriately – its library. A mantelpiece had been ordered from France, representing Dionysus and vines, but a Medusa had been delivered by mistake, and was kept because returning it to France would be too much trouble. Those who look on the Medusa, of course, are turned to stone. Once again, the god of spouting blood and torn flesh yields his authority to the impersonal processes of petrifaction. These more truly sum up the final goal of life.

Only the most inattentive reader could miss the book's constant preoccupation with stone, water, and ice. The transformation of mangled flesh into stone in the war memorial is mirrored in the rock garden that is Iris's hobby during her lifeless marriage; the fossils, stuffed animals and the stone monuments (such as the Albert Memorial) that she sees on her honeymoon; and in many other encounters with stone. The town's first industry was limestone; its geological origins in the retreating inland seas are stressed; fossil-hunters scour the area for 'extinct fish, ancient fronds, scrolls of coral'; and Iris often imagines 'the entire town rising out of the shallow prehistoric ocean' (p. 49). Avilion, however, 'is not the standard-issue limestone' (p. 58), but is made of cobblestones rounded by the river; so is the base of the war memorial. The novel thus deals in fragments of stone, fragments of flesh, or fragments of narrative. Water, in rivers and ponds, is also a recurrent image, but not as a source of life. In both the narrative and the quoted poems which intersperse it, it is seen in relation to stone ('Break, break, break, / On thy cold gray stones, O Sea!') (p. 156), or ice ('Kubla Khan') (p. 335), or drowned bodies ('O you who drown in love, remember me') (frontispiece), or sexual unfulfilment ('Mariana') (pp. 155–6). Water belongs far more to the sphere of geology than biology.

Ticonderoga, where the factory stands, is at the confluence of two rivers, the Louveteau ('wolf-cub') and Jogues, the latter named after a *sparagmos*, in that it commemorates a missionary who was tortured, mutilated, and decapitated by the Iroquois, and then thrown into the Mohawk river. In the two names of the mingling rivers, the predator and the dismembered saint coalesce in disorganized meaninglessness. Their combination is recapitulated in the novel's villainess, the chillingly asexual Winifred Griffen Pryor, who affects shoes made from an aquatic predator – the alligator – but is named after another decapitated saint with watery associations: St Winifred was beheaded when she refused the advances of a local chieftain, a spring rising from the place where her head fell, before she was miraculously restored to life. The modern Winifred's own contribution to fountain creation is scarcely less marvellous: at the Xanadu Ball which she supervises in 1936, there is a 'spectacular "Alph, the Sacred River" fountain, dyed a Bacchanalian purple by an overhead spotlight, beneath shimmering crystal festoons in the central "Cave of Ice"' (p. 273). As in the library mantelpiece, the vivifying fluids of Bacchus immediately yield to images of dead petrifaction.

The name Ticonderoga means 'the land between two waters'. Yet not only do two rivers with contradictory names merge: two places do as well. For Ticonderoga is the name of another place in another country: a fort in New York that was the site of several battles in the eighteenth century. Rivers merge, and names migrate. Art, narrative, and naming impose specious unity upon the merging streams, and the scattered fragments of flesh, stone, and paper. Yet, as Ticonderoga is the name of another place, so the narratives are those of other people. This is something that Laura and Iris discover as early as their learning of the alphabet. Iris's letter, 'I', is everyone's. Laura's, 'L', is associated with the following rhyme:

Plate 19 Sir Herbert Draper, *The Water Nixie* (1908) (private collection)

L is for Lily,
So pure and so white;
It opens by day
And it closes at night. (p. 89)

The accompanying picture is of a naked fairy on a water lily. This is the first association between Laura and the water nixie, through a picture which resembles the highly erotic *Water Nixie* by the Pre-Raphaelite artist Herbert Draper (Plate 19), who also painted Tristan and Isolde and Lancelot and Guinevere. Yet Laura is associated with this figure through a name that is not her own: Lily. This dislocation, which occurs in the very process of learning the alphabet, is typical of the novel's displacement of direct naming or narration. The sacrifice, like the lily, is part of this displacement. World War I is not a sacrifice. Nor, any longer, are the ritual killings in Sakiel-Norn. So long the hidden essence of society, sacrifice has here become a trivializing label or scrawl stuck on something that is quite different.

The Blind Assassin is an artfully, ostentatiously allusive work, but it is also – inevitably – one which inherits, absorbs, and reworks without deliberate allusion. Like many earlier works, it places its characters on the boundaries of insensate and inorganic geological processes. It invokes Dionysus. It retells the story of the water sprite and the faithless mortal, though whether the precedent story is that of Undine, or Rusalka, or the Little Mermaid, or none of these, is unclear and ultimately unimportant. It reveals the inexhaustible fascination of the theme of human sacrifice, even as it treats it as no other work discussed in this book does: as an exhausted cliché. This verdict is probably premature.

CONCLUSION

Few questions can be more fundamental than that of what a life is worth. The highest nobility is to lay down one's life for a worthy cause; the greatest tyrannies of the twentieth century are pre-eminently defined by their mass squandering of life in the pursuit of mistaken or evil goals. The modern phenomenon of the suicide bomber presents us with a troubling confusion of the two extremes, and the problem with alien sacrificial cultures is sometimes a sense of the *unheimlich*: of our own values mirrored in vestigial but subliminally familiar form. Thus the early Spanish missionaries laboured to explain and neutralize the parallels between Aztec and Christian practice. Laying down one's life for another is not, literally, sacrifice, though it becomes assimilated to sacrifice as early as Euripides. What is striking is the way in which sacrifice persists as an idea, gathering radically different meanings from generation to generation, acquiring a constantly renewed life of its own as a cultural fiction or ideal in ways that are quite independent of its actual ritual practice. Ritual sacrifice has become a metonym for all transactions in which life is the currency. The equivalences established by the transaction are a mirror both of the values of a culture and of its anxieties.

It is appropriate that sacrifice is often imagined as taking place on or beyond boundaries (the shore at Aulis, the mountain outside Thebes) for it does test the point at which culture most sees itself reflected in barbarism: in which it preserves itself in an act which seems to violate its own premises. New cases test and shift the boundaries: not only the suicide bomber, but – quite different – the uses of embryos in medical research. We continue to be fascinated by the atavistic traces in our minds and cities; by the allegedly sacrificed child's torso in the Thames, for example. Something which can be configured to represent the First World War, the worship of Swinburne's Dolores, and the death of Brünnhilde is likely to be as infinitely durable as it is infinitely variable, for it precedes any specific cultural configuration, arising from conflicts which, if Walter Burkert is right, precede not only society but language and even humanity itself. For any social organization, from the anthill upwards, makes decisions about the value of individual life, whether through evolutionary mechanics or conscious reflection. The ever-changing balance between the two is reflected in the changing representations of human sacrifice.

Notes

1 HUMAN SACRIFICE, ANCIENT AND MODERN

1 Homer, *Iliad*, trans. A. T. Murray, rev. William F. Wyatt, Loeb Classical Library, 2 vols. (Cambridge, Mass., and London: Harvard University Press, 1999), 23.173–83; Bernal Díaz del Castillo, *The True History of the Conquest of New Spain*, trans. Alfred Percival Maudslay, 5 vols. (London: Hakluyt Society, 1908–16), vol. 1, p. 186; *The Blind Assassin* (London: Bloomsbury, 2000), p. 29.

2 Pliny, *Natural History* 35.36.73.

3 Voltaire, *La Bible enfin expliquée par plusieurs aumoniers de S.M.L.R.D.P.* (Geneva, 1776), pp. 53–5. See also Thomas Chubb, 'The Case of Abraham, with Regard to his being commanded by God, to offer his Son *Isaac* in Sacrifice, farther considered', in *Four Tracts* (London, 1734), pp. 84–119.

4 Walter Burkert, *Homo Necans: The Anthropology of Ancient Greek Sacrificial Ritual and Myth*, trans. Peter Bing (Berkeley, Los Angeles, and London: University of California Press, 1983), p. 2.

5 That sacrificial rites were derived from those of Palaeolithic huntsmen was first suggested by Karl Meuli, 'Griechische Opferbräuche', in *Phyllobolia für Peter von der Mühll*, ed. Olof Gigon *et al.* (Basel: Benno Schwabe, 1946), pp. 185–288.

6 Walter Burkert, *Creation of the Sacred: Tracks of Biology in Early Religions* (Cambridge, Mass., and London: Harvard University Press, 1996), p. 41.

7 Marcel Detienne, 'Culinary Practices and the Spirit of Sacrifice', in *The Cuisine of Sacrifice among the Greeks*, trans. Paula Wissing, ed. Marcel Detienne and Jean-Pierre Vernant (Chicago and London: University of Chicago Press, 1989), pp. 1–20.

8 René Girard, *Violence and the Sacred*, trans. Patrick Gregory (Baltimore: Johns Hopkins University Press, 1977).

9 According to Burkert, for example, 'it is in the allegorical writers of late antiquity that Adonis is said to represent "spring" or "crops", and Attis, Osiris, and Persephone are all treated in the same way. Frazer's "god of vegetation" is a post-classic allegory transformed into a genetic theory of religion' (*Structure and History in Greek Mythology and Ritual*, Sather Classical Lectures, 47 (Berkeley, Los Angeles, London: University of California Press, 1979), pp. 99–100).

10 Henri Hubert and Marcel Mauss, *Sacrifice: Its Nature and Functions*, trans. W. D. Halls (London: Cohen and West, 1964), p. 9.

11 Miranda Aldhouse Green, *Dying for the Gods, Human Sacrifice in Iron Age & Roman Europe* (Stroud: Tempus, 2001), p. 19.

12 Richard Seaford, *Money and the Early Greek Mind: Homer, Philosophy, Tragedy* (Cambridge: Cambridge University Press, 2004), pp. 74–7.

13 Hesiod, *Theogony* 538–41, in *Hesiod, Homeric Hymns, Homerica*, trans. Hugh G. Evelyn White, Loeb Classical Library, revised edn (Cambridge, Mass., and London: Harvard University Press, 1936). For an extended analysis of this myth, see Jean-Pierre Vernant, 'At Man's Table: Hesiod's Foundation Myth of Sacrifice', in *The Cuisine of Sacrifice*, ed. Detienne and Vernant, pp. 21–86.
14 G. S. Kirk (gen. ed.), *The Iliad: A Commentary*, 6 vols. (Cambridge: Cambridge University Press, 1985–93), vol. II, pp. 4–13.
15 Richard Seaford, *Reciprocity and Ritual: Homer and Tragedy in the Developing City-State* (Oxford: Clarendon Press, 1991), p. 259. See also Dennis D. Hughes, *Human Sacrifice in Ancient Greece* (London and New York: Routledge, 1991), pp. 79–85, 103.
16 See W. K. C. Guthrie, *The Sophists* (Cambridge: Cambridge University Press, 1971), pp. 55–84.
17 Gladiatorial combats have been thought to originate in funerary sacrifice, but their sacrificial origin is far from certain. See David S. Potter, 'Entertainers in the Roman Empire', in D. S. Potter and J. D. Mattingly (eds.), *Life, Death, and Entertainment in the Roman Empire* (Ann Arbor: University of Michigan Press, 1999), pp. 256–325 (pp. 305–6).
18 Livy 8.6, 9–10; 10.26–30.
19 *Livy*, Loeb Classical Library, 14 vols. (London: Heinemann; Cambridge, Mass.: Harvard University Press, 1919–59), vol. V (1929), ed. and trans. B. O. Foster, 22.57.6.
20 *Marcellus* 3, in *Plutarch's Lives*, trans. Bernadotte Perrin, Loeb Classical Library, 11 vols. (London: Heinemann; New York: Macmillan, 1914–26), vol. V, 3.4. See also *Roman Questions* 283f–284c, where Plutarch claims that the sacrifice was to the spirits, not the gods.
21 Lucretius, *De Rerum Natura* 1.101, trans. W. H. D. Rouse, rev. Martin F. Smith, Loeb Classical Library (Cambridge, Mass., and London: Harvard University Press, 1992). My translation.
22 Claude Lévi-Strauss, *The Elementary Structures of Kinship*, trans. James Harle Bell *et al.* (Boston: Beacon Press, 1969).

2 GREECE

1 *Servianorum in Vergilii Carmina Commentariorum* (Lancaster, Pa: American Philological Society, 1946–), vol. III, p. 61 (only volumes II and III have so far been published).
2 Plutarch, *Themistocles* 13.2–5; *Agesilaus* 6.4–6.
3 The evidence for Greek human sacrifice is surveyed in Dennis D. Hughes, *Human Sacrifice in Ancient Greece.*
4 Diodorus Siculus 20.14.4–6; Caesar, *De Bello Gallico* 6.16; Tacitus, *Annales* 14.30–1.
5 According to G. S. Kirk, Prometheus' role as technological benefactor is probably 'not much older than the sixth century BC, when interest in the evolution of men from a crude and savage state – an idea that directly contradicts the mythical scheme of a decline from the Golden Age – first became prominent' (*The Nature of Greek Myths* (Harmondsworth: Penguin, 1974), p. 140).

6 1022, in *Aeschylus*, trans. Herbert Weir Smyth, Loeb Classical Library, 2 vols. (London and Cambridge, Mass.: Harvard University Press, 1922).

7 Hermes is associated with oratory, the invention of the lyre (the Homeric Hymn *To Hermes*, 24–61), and later with literature in general.

8 *Ekthoinasthai* is derived from the noun *thoinē*, which the Chorus had earlier used to describe pious sacrifice to Zeus (529–30).

9 The centaur Chiron, wounded by a poisoned arrow of Heracles, agreed to take Prometheus' place.

10 Dennis D. Hughes, *Human Sacrifice in Ancient Greece*, pp. 49–56, 65–70.

11 *Republic* 3, 391b, trans. Paul Storry, Loeb Classical Library, 2 vols. (London: Heinemann; Cambridge, Mass.: Harvard University Press, 1930–5).

12 *Aeneid* 10.518–20, in *Virgil*, trans., H. Rushton Fairclough, rev. G. P Goold, Loeb Classical Library, 2 vols. (Cambridge, Mass., and London: Harvard University Press, 1999–2000).

13 *Hesiod, Homeric Hymns, Homerica*, trans. Evelyn-White, p. 495.

14 *Homo Necans*, pp. 104–5.

15 Walter Burkert, *Creation of the Sacred*, p. 142.

16 *Sophocles*, ed. and trans. Hugh Lloyd Jones, corrected edn, Loeb Classical Library, 3 vols. (Cambridge, Mass., and London: Harvard University Press, 1996–8).

17 As it is in *Persians* 205, where the pursuit of an eagle by a falcon prefigures the Greek triumph.

18 Pierre Vidal-Naquet argues that Aeschylus portrays a monstrous confusion of the normally opposed activities of sacrifice and the hunt ('Hunting and Sacrifice in Aeschylus' *Oresteia*', in Jean-Pierre Vernant and Pierre Vidal-Naquet, *Tragedy and Myth in Ancient Greece*, trans. Janet Lloyd (Sussex: Harvester Press; New Jersey: Humanities Press, 1981), pp. 150–74). See also Simon Goldhill, *Reading Greek Tragedy* (Cambridge: Cambridge University Press, 1986), p. 120.

19 Kirk argues that the Greeks, unlike the Egyptians, established very early a hierarchical difference between men and animals: 'the proto-Greeks started on that long process of humanism, of placing man at the centre of the universe, that distinguished them from the Egyptians with their interminable tradition of dreary crocodile-gods and the like' (*The Nature of Greek Myths*, p. 52).

20 'Hunting and Sacrifice in Aeschylus' *Oresteia*'.

21 Walter Burkert, *Greek Religion: Archaic and Classical*, trans. John Raffan (Oxford: Blackwell, 1985), p. 59.

22 1516, in *Euripides*, ed. and trans. David Kovacs, Loeb Classical Library, 6 vols. (Cambridge, Mass., and London: Harvard University Press, 1994–2002). My translation.

23 Danielle S. Allen questions the traditional reading of the *Oresteia* as showing a development towards dispassionate justice (*The World of Prometheus: The Politics of Punishing in Democratic Athens* (Princeton: Princeton University Press, 2000), pp. 18–24).

24 Athamas' second wife, Ino, wished to destroy his children by his first marriage, Phrixus and Helle. She created a famine by roasting the seed-corn, and fabricated an oracle demanding the sacrifice of Phrixus, or Phrixus and Helle. He, or they, were rescued, and carried away on the ram with the golden fleece (which was later sought by the Argonauts). In punishment, Athamas was driven mad and killed his son by Ino. He himself escaped sacrifice.

25 For a trenchant refutation of Freud's reading, see Jean-Pierre Vernant, 'Oedipus without the Complex', in Vernant and Vidal-Naquet, *Tragedy and Myth in Ancient Greece*, pp. 63–86.
26 *Totem and Taboo*, trans. James Strachey (London: Routledge & Kegan Paul, 1950), p. 141.
27 Girard's theories of sacrifice are debated from an anthropological perspective in Robert G. Hamerton-Kelly (ed.), *Violent Origins: Walter Burkert, René Girard, and Jonathan Z. Smith on Ritual Killing and Cultural Formation* (Stanford: Stanford University Press, 1987). Here Girard gives an interesting exposition of his methodology: 'Myths that contain exactly what is needed to reflect a pattern of nonconscious persecution I take at face value and regard as suggestive of the true nature of mythology, and myths that contain something else and therefore do not clearly support my case I regard as having been tampered with' (p. 103).
28 *Oedipus, Philosopher*, trans. Catherine Porter (Stanford: Stanford University Press, 1993).
29 Apollodorus, *The Library* 3.2.1–2; Diodorus Siculus 5.59.1.
30 Pausanias, *Description of Greece*, trans. W. H. S. Jones, Loeb Classical Library, 5 vols. (London: Heinemann; New York: Putnam, 1918–35) 9.26.2.
31 Homer, *Odyssey*, trans. A. T. Murray, rev. George E. Dimock, Loeb Classical Library, 2 vols. (Cambridge, Mass., and London: Harvard University Press, 1995) 11.274.
32 While conceding that Freud's reading is a retrospective reconstitution of the text, Charles Segal has suggested that Freud's investigation of the unconscious and repressed helps to alert us to a concern with hidden or avoided knowledge in the text: why, for instance, does Oedipus make the 'Freudian' slip of referring to one assassin, while the official story is still that he was killed by many (*Sophocles' Tragic World: Divinity, Nature, Society* (Cambridge, Mass., and London: Harvard University Press, 1995), p. 162)?
33 Apollodorus, *The Library*, trans. Sir James George Frazer, Loeb Classical Library, 2 vols. (London: Heinemann; New York: Putnam, 1921) 3.5.7.
34 *Sophocles' Tragic World*, p. 141.
35 Danielle S. Allen, *The World of Prometheus*, pp. 207–9.
36 Euripides, *Phoenician Women* 806; Apollodorus 3.5.8; Pausanias 20.26.2.
37 It was forbidden to speak to one not cleansed of pollution.
38 *Penthée*, with libretto by Charles Auguste La Fare and music by Charles-Hubert Gervais and Philippe d'Orléans.
39 'Ithaca', in *Before Time Could Change Them: The Complete Poems of Constantine P. Cavafy*, trans. Theoharis Constantine Theoharis (New York, San Diego, and London: Harcourt, 2001), pp. 11–12.
40 *Ulisse* (Milan: Suvini Zerboni, [1971]), pp. 165–7.
41 On the low importance of pollution in Athenian homicide law, see Douglas M. MacDowell, *Athenian Homicide Law in the Age of the Orators* (Manchester: Manchester University Press, 1963), pp. 141–50.
42 *Money and the Early Greek Mind*, p. 165.
43 Helene P. Foley, *Ritual Irony: Poetry and Sacrifice in Euripides* (Ithaca and London: Cornell University Press, 1985), p. 79.
44 *Agamemnon* 1430; *King Oedipus* 100.
45 See especially Charles Segal, *Dionysiac Poetics and Euripides' 'Bacchae'*, expanded edn (Princeton: Princeton University Press, 1997), pp. 27–54.

46 Foley, *Ritual Irony*, p. 243.

47 Charles Segal argues that a 'mysterious and perhaps ultimately unformulable coexistence of opposites' is 'the essence of Dionysus' (*Dionysiac Poetics*, p. 20).

3 VIRGIL TO AUGUSTINE

1 For hunting in the *Aeneid*, see J. R. Dunkle, 'The Hunter and Hunting in the *Aeneid*', *Ramus*, 2 (1973), 127–42; E. Vance, 'Sylvia's Pet Stag: Wildness and Domesticity in Virgil's *Aeneid*', *Arethusa*, 14 (1981), 127–38. Vance argues that hunting is a cultural advance, but one with 'potentially regressive' aspects (p. 130); Dunkle, that Virgil contrasts forms of hunting that master nature with those that are merely uncontrolled violence.

2 'If Vergil exposes the deficiencies of his two protagonists, he is also aware of their vitality, their potential as warriors, and their great bond of friendship' (Barbara Pavlock, 'Epic and Tragedy in Vergil's Nisus and Euryalus Episode', *Transactions of the American Philological Association*, 115 (1985), 207–24 (p. 224)).

3 Philip Hardie, *The Epic Successors of Virgil: A Study in the Dynamics of a Tradition* (Cambridge: Cambridge University Press, 1993), p. 20.

4 The killing of Turnus is, for example, defended in Brooks Otis, *Virgil: A Study in Civilized Poetry* (Oxford: Clarendon Press, 1963), pp. 379–82. Nicholas Horsfall denies that a human sacrifice is implied in 'immolat' ('*Aeneid*', in *A Companion to the Study of Virgil*, ed. Nicholas Horsfall, 2nd edn (Leiden: Brill), pp. 214–15). For a more critical view of the killing of Turnus, see, e.g., R. Deryck Williams, 'The *Aeneid*', in *The Cambridge History of Classical Literature*, ed. E. J. Kenney (Cambridge: Cambridge University Press, 1982), pp. 333–69 (pp. 352–3); Hardie, *Epic Successors*, p. 21. S. Farron interprets Aeneas' sacrifice of the prisoners as 'an extremely serious attack on Aeneas and also Octavian' ('Aeneas' Human Sacrifice', *Acta Classica*, 23 (1985), 21–33). The argument is over-simplified, but there is useful documentation of Graeco-Roman attitudes to human sacrifice.

5 Girardian readings are given in Hardie, *Epic Successors*, pp. 19–56; Cesáreo Bandera, 'Sacrificial Levels in Vergil's Aeneid', *Arethusa*, 14 (1981), 217–39.

6 Bandera sees the failure to kill Sinon as the beginning of the sacrificial crisis of the *Aeneid* (p. 235). His argument is rebutted in Rebekah M. Smith, 'Deception and Sacrifice in *Aeneid* 2.1–249', *American Journal of Philology*, 120 (1999), 503–23.

7 In his outstanding *Epic and Empire*, David Quint subtly illustrates the political complexities of the poem's conclusion, but argues that the Trojans progress from repetitious enslavement to their past to re-enactment of the deeds of their conquerors (*Epic and Empire: Politics and Generic Form from Virgil to Milton* (Princeton: Princeton University Press, 1992), pp. 50–96). But should Aeneas increasingly conform to the prime representative of the old Homeric order?

8 As Quint points out (p. 78), the iconography of this baldric was present at the heart of Rome itself: statues of the fifty Danaids adorned the temple of Mars the Avenger, which Augustus built in the new Forum.

9 *Epic Successors*, pp. 49–56.

10 *Protrepticus* 12.92, in *Clement of Alexandria*, trans. G. W. Butterworth, Loeb Classical Library (London: Heinemann; New York, Putnam, 1919), p. 255.

11 St Augustine, *City of God*, trans. Henry Bettenson, ed. David Knowles (Harmondsworth: Penguin, 1972), p. 694 (16.32).

4 THE DISCOVERY OF AMERICA

1 Francisco López de Gómara, *The Conquest of the Weast India (1578)* [trans. Thomas Nicholas], intro. Herbert Ingram Priestley (Scholars' Facsimiles and Reprints: New York, 1940), p. 35. For accounts of the meeting with Aguilar, see also Díaz del Castillo, *True History*, vol. I, pp. 94–103; Hernan Cortes, *Letters from Mexico*, trans. Anthony Pagden, revised edn (New Haven and London: Yale University Press, 1986), p. 17.

2 Jean de Léry, *A History of a Voyage to the Land of Brazil*, trans. Janet Whatley (Berkeley, Los Angeles, and Oxford: University of California Press, 1990), pp. 122–33.

3 Henry Kamen, *The Spanish Inquisition: A Historical Revision* (London: Weidenfeld and Nicolson, 1997), pp. 21–2.

4 Christopher Columbus, *Journal of the First Voyage*, ed. and trans. B. W. Ife (Warminster: Arist and Phillips, 1990), p. 91.

5 Díaz del Castillo, *True History*, vol. IV, pp. 149–50.

6 Torquato Tasso, *Gerusalemme Liberata*, ed. Anna Maria Carini (Milan: Feltrinelli, 1961), Canto 15, stanzas 28–32.

7 Pierre Le Moyne, *Saint Louys, ou la sainte couronne reconquise* (Paris, 1658), pp. 156, 211.

8 *Journal of the First Voyage*, p. 97.

9 Girolamo Graziani, *Il Conquisto di Granata*, Parnasso Italiano, 38–9, 2 vols. (Venice, 1789), Canto 22, p. 237.

10 'The Defeat of Idolatry; or, Constantine'. *Idololatria* is the correct spelling.

11 Pierre Mambrun, *Opera Poetica* (Fixae Andecavorum [Flèche], 1661), pp. 79–82. A separate edition of the epic, *Constantinus, sive Idololatria debellata*, was published in Paris in 1658.

12 Joseph [José de] Acosta, *The Natvrall and Morall Historie of the East and West Indies*, trans. E. G. (London, 1604), pp. 508–11. Acosta's source is Diego Durán: see Durán, *The Aztecs: The History of the Indies of New Spain*, trans. Doris Heyden and Fernando Horcasitas (New York: Orion Press, 1964), pp. 26–7. Durán's work, however, remained unpublished until the nineteenth century. The story is retold, less hauntingly, in John Ogilby, *America* (London, 1671), p. 297.

13 Betty Ann Brown, 'Ochpaniztli in Historical Perspective', in *Ritual Human Sacrifice in MesoAmerica*, ed. Elizabeth H. Boone (Washington, D.C.: Dumbarton Oaks Research Library and Collection, 1984), pp. 195–210.

14 *Absalom and Achitophel*, line 99, in *The Works of John Dryden*, ed. Edward Niles Hooker *et al.*, 20 vols. (Berkeley, Los Angeles, and London: University of California Press, 1956–2002) (hereafter referred to as the 'California Dryden'), vol. II.

15 José de Acosta, *De Natvra Novi Orbis Libri Dvo. Et De Promulgatione Evangelii apvd Barbaros, siue, De Procvranda Indorvm salute, Libri sex* [Cologne, 1596], pp. 151–2.

16 Describing the sacrifice of children to secure rain, Bernardino de Sahagún records that it was a good omen if the child wept on the way to sacrifice

(*General History of the Things of New Spain*, trans. and ed. Arthur J. O. Anderson and Charles E. Dibble, 13 parts (Santa Fe: School of American Research and the University of Utah, 1950–82), Book 2, *The Ceremonies* (1951), Part III, p. 2).

17 For a perceptive discussion of the Aztec view of experienced reality as representation ('a fabrication, and fleeting as a flower'), see Inga Clendinnen, *Aztecs: An Interpretation* (Cambridge: Cambridge University Press, 1991), pp. 214–16 (p. 214).

18 Cf. Durán, *Aztecs*, p. 12.

19 Diego Durán, *Books of the Gods and Rites and The Ancient Calendar*, ed. and trans. Fernando Horcasitas and Doris Heyden (Norman: University of Oklahoma Press, 1971) p. 409. See also pp. 71, 103.

20 For Frazer's discussion of the external soul, see *The Golden Bough . . . A New Abridgement from the Second and Third Editions*, ed. Robert Fraser (Oxford and New York: Oxford University Press, 1994), pp. 750–84. For an example from Central America, see pp. 780–1.

21 Thomas Gage, *The English-American his Travail by Sea and Land: Or, A New Survey of the West-India's* (London, 1648), pp. 148–9.

22 López de Gómara, *Conquest of the Weast India*, p. 350; Durán, *Books of the Gods and Rites*, pp. 11, 180; Bartolomé de Las Casas, *A Short Account of the Destruction of the Indies*, ed. and trans. Nigel Griffin (Harmondsworth: Penguin, 1992), p. 15.

23 Jacques Soustelle, 'Ritual Human Sacrifice in Mesoamerica: An Introduction', in *Ritual Human Sacrifice in MesoAmerica*, ed. Elizabeth H. Boone (Washington, D. C.: Dumbarton Oaks Research Library and Collection, 1984), pp. 1–5 (p. 2).

24 Cortes, *Letters from Mexico*, p. 84.

25 Sahagún, *General History of the Things of New Spain*, Part III, p. 52.

26 See Tzvetan Todorov, *The Conquest of America: The Question of the Other*, trans. Richard Howard (Norman: University of Oklahoma Press, 1999), p. 186.

27 Las Casas, *A Short Account*, p. 72.

28 Durán, *Books of the Gods and Rites*, p. 276.

29 Diáz del Castillo, *True History*, vol. II, pp. 66–7.

30 Jean-François Marmontel, *Les Incas*, 2 vols. (Paris: Bibliothèque Nationale, 1895), vol. I, pp. 75–6.

31 Edmund Spenser, *Faerie Queene* 5.11.19, 1.8.36, in *The Poems of Spenser*, ed. J. C. Smith and E. de Selincourt (London, New York, and Toronto: Oxford University Press, 1912).

32 'I may venture to affirm, that few corruptions of idolatry and polytheism are more pernicious to society than this corruption of theism, when carried to the utmost height. The human sacrifices of the *Carthaginians*, *Mexicans*, and many barbarous nations, scarcely exceed the inquisition and persecutions of *Rome* and *Madrid*. For besides, that the effusion of blood may not be so great in the former case as in the latter; besides this, I say, the human victims, being chosen by lot, or by some exterior signs, affect not, in so considerable a degree, the rest of the society. Whereas virtue, knowledge, love of liberty, are the qualities, which call down the fatal vengeance of inquisitors; and when expelled, leave the society in the most shameful ignorance, corruption, and bondage. The

illegal murder of one man by a tyrant is more pernicious than the death of a thousand by pestilence, famine, or any undistinguishing calamity' (David Hume, *The Natural History of Religion*, ed. John Valdimir Price (Oxford: Clarendon Press, 1976), pp. 61–2).

33 Kamen, *The Spanish Inquisition*, p. 60.

34 Kamen, *The Spanish Inquisition*, p. 203.

35 In *De Promulgatione Evangelii apvd Barbaros*, Acosta argues that all converts should be instructed in the Trinity (5.4).

36 D. H. Lawrence, *'The Woman Who Rode Away' and Other Stories*, ed. Dieter Mehl and Christa Jansohn (Cambridge: Cambridge University Press, 1995), p. 40.

37 *Natvrall and Morall Historie*, p. 435.

38 Roger Williams, *A Key into the Language of America*, edited with a critical introduction, notes, and commentary by John J. Teunissen and Evelyn J. Hinz (Detroit: Wayne State University Press, 1973), pp. 110–13.

39 López de Gómara, *Conquest of the Weast India*, p. 371; and *Historia General de las Indias*, ed. Pilar Guibelalde and Emiliano M. Aguilera, 2 vols. ([Barcelona]: Iberia, 1954), vol. II, p. 368. The English version is a cut and streamlined version of the original, one result being to increase the already considerable hagiography of Cortés.

40 Michel Eyquem de Montaigne, 'Of Coaches', in *Montaigne's Essays*, trans. John Florio, Everyman's Library, 3 vols. (London and New York: Dent and Dutton, 1910), vol. III, p. 141.

41 See, e.g., George Warren, *An Impartial Description of Surinam* (London, 1667), p. 26; Antoine Biet, *Voyage de la France équinoxiale* (Paris, 1664), p. 396; Charles de Rochefort, *The History of the Caribby-Islands*, trans. John Davies of Kidwelly (London, 1666), p. 264; Le Sieur de La Borde, *Relation de l'origine, moeurs, coustumes, religion, guerres et voyages des Caraibes* (n.p., 1684), p. 6.

42 Aphra Behn, *The Works of Aphra Behn*, ed. Janet Todd, 7 vols. (London: Pickering and Chatto, 1992–6), vol. III, p. 101. John Locke, *An Essay Concerning Human Understanding*, ed. Peter H. Nidditch (Oxford: Clarendon Press, 1975), p. 207 (2.xvi.6).

43 Ogilby, *America* (London, 1671), pp. 357, 616.

5 SHAKESPEARE AND THE ECONOMICS OF SACRIFICE

1 Robert Kayll, *The Trades Increase* (London, 1615), pp. 28–9.

2 Dudley Digges, *The Defence of Trade, In a Letter to Sir Thomas Smith Knight, Gouernour of the East-India Companie* (London, 1615), p. 25. This is a slight misquotation of *Aeneid* 5.814–15, which reads 'quem gurgite quaeres' ('whom you seek in the waters').

3 Karl Marx, *Capital*, trans. Ben Fowkes *et al.*, 3 vols. (Harmondsworth: Penguin, 1976–81), vol. I, trans. Ben Fowkes, p. 925. 'Tantae molis erat Romanam condere gentem' ('So great was the effort to found the Roman race' (*Aeneid* 1.33)).

4 MacDonald P. Jackson, 'Stage Directions and Speech Headings in Act I of *Titus Andronicus* Q (1594): Shakespeare or Peele?', *Studies in Bibliography*, 49 (1996), 134–48; 'Indefinite Articles in *Titus Andronicus*, Peele, and Shakespeare', *Notes and Queries*, 45 (243) (1998), 308–10; Brian Boyd, 'Common Words in *Titus*

Andronicus: The Presence of Peele', *Notes and Queries*, 42 (240) (1995), 300–7; Thomas Merriam, 'Influence Alone? More on the Authorship of *Titus Andronicus*', *Notes and Queries*, 45 (243), (1998) 304–8. Boyd argues that Peele wrote 1.1 and 2.1, and that 2.2 and 4.i may be Peele revised by Shakespeare.

5 William Shakespeare, *Titus Andronicus*, ed. Jonathan Bate, The Arden Shakespeare: Third Series (London and New York: Routledge, 1995) 1.1.128, 132, 147.

6 Palamedes was the subject of lost tragedies by Aeschylus and Euripides. His contribution to the alphabet is, for example, mentioned in Pliny, *Natural History*, 7.56.192, and in Barnabe Rich, *The Trauailes and Aduentures of Don Simonides, Tome 2* (London, 1584), sig. Oiii. Ovid merely mentions the burial of the gold (*Metamorphoses* 13.56–60, in *Ovid*, Loeb Classical Library, 6 vols. (Cambridge, Mass., and London: Harvard University Press, 1977–88), vols. III and IV, trans. Frank Justus Miller, rev. G. P. Goold). Arthur Golding's translation, however, adds the forged letter, while merely stating that the gold was 'hidden' (Golding (trans.), *The XV Bookes Entytuled Metamorphosis* (London, 1567; repr. Amsterdam: Theatrum Orbis Terrarum; Norwood, N.J.: Walter J. Johnson, 1977), fo. 158v).

7 Economic language is insistent: 'ransom' (3.1.157, 174), 'redeem' (l. 181), 'purchased at an easy price' (l. 199), 'bought' (l. 200).

8 Horace, *Odes* 1.22.1.

9 E.g. Marion Wynne-Davies, '"The Swallowing Womb": Consumed and Consuming Women in *Titus Andronicus*', in *The Matter of Difference: Materialist Feminist Criticism of Shakespeare*, ed. Valerie Wayne (New York: Harvester Wheatsheaf, 1991), pp. 129–51.

10 For Semiramis as an archetype of murderous and incestuous lust, see Paulus Orosius, *Historiae adversum Paganos* 1.4.

11 Jonathan Bate provides an extensive and useful account of Shakespeare's debts to Ovid, and of their contextual resonance, in *Shakespeare and Ovid* (Oxford: Clarendon Press, 1993).

12 Exodus 4:14–16, in the Bible, ed. J. F. H. (London, 1589) (the Geneva Bible).

13 Rich, *Don Simonides*, sig. Oiii (shortly after the description of Palamedes' contribution to the Greek alphabet).

14 *Harper's Dictionary of Classical Literature and Antiquities*, ed. Harry Thurston Peck (London: Osgood McIlvaine, 1897), p. 1621. The Roman source for this is Aulus Gellius, *Noctes Atticae* 20.1.39–51.

15 *The Merchant of Venice*, ed. John Russell Brown, The Arden Shakespeare: Second Series (London and New York: Methuen, 1955) 3.3.30.

16 René Girard, *A Theater of Envy: William Shakespeare* (Oxford and New York: Oxford University Press, 1991), p. 245. Girard's reading of the play is trenchantly criticized in Richard Levin, 'The New Refutation of Shakespeare', *Modern Philology*, 83 (1985–6), 123–41.

17 'Shylock's bloodthirsty cruelty is presented not simply as produced by the Venetians' treatment of him, but as a precise, deliberate mirror-image of their real concealed nature . . . Shylock shows that his wolvish nature is the foundation of Venetian law' (Kiernan Ryan, '*The Merchant of Venice*: Past Significance and Present Meaning', *Shakespeare Jahrbuch*, 117 (1981), 49–54).

18 See Levin, 'The New Refutation', p. 124.

19 Cf. *Metamorphoses* 11.194–220.

20 '[N]ec . . . Telamon sine honore recessit / Hesioneque data potitur' (lines 216–17).

21 Catherine Belsey argues that 'The answer cannot be deduced from the terms of the puzzle itself' ('Love in Venice', in *The Merchant of Venice*, ed. Martin Coyle, New Casebooks (London and New York: Macmillan and St Martin's Press), pp. 139–60 (p. 149), reprinted from *Shakespeare Survey*, 44 (1991), 41–53).

6 BRITAIN AND AMERICA: DRYDEN, BEHN, AND DEFOE

1 Another translation, *Popery truly display'd*, appeared in 1689, shortly after the deposition of the Catholic James II. Las Casas's book had already appeared as *The Spanish Colonie*, trans. M. S. S. (London, 1583), 'to serue as a President and warning to the xij. Prouinces in the lowe Countries' (sig. ¶2), the Confederacy of Northern Provinces being under Spanish attack. Only Phillips's version has a colonial agenda.

2 For the argument that Milton supported English colonialism, see J. Martin Evans, *Milton's Imperial Epic* (Ithaca and London: Cornell University Press, 1996). For the contrary view, which I favour, see David Quint, *Epic and Empire*, pp. 248–66.

3 John Milton, *Paradise Lost*, ed. Alastair Fowler, corrected edn (London: Longman, 1981).

4 See, e. g., Stuart Sherman, *Telling Time: Clocks, Diaries, and English Diurnal Form, 1660–1785* (Chicago and London: University of Chicago Press, 1996).

5 Sir William Petty, *An Essay Concerning the Multiplication of Mankind: Together with another Essay in Political Arithmetick, Concerning the Growth of the City of London*, 2nd edn (London, 1686).

6 Culpepper, *A Tract Against the high rate of Usury Presented to the High Court of Parliament, Anno Domini 1623*, 4th edn (London, 1668), pp. 20–1; Child, *A Discourse about Trade, Wherein the Reduction of Interest of Money to 4 l. per Centum is Recommended* (London, 1690), p. 28.

7 *An Essay Concerning the Multiplication of Mankind*, p. 26.

8 The Aztecs conducted trade by barter, or with currency such as cacao beans or gold in quills (Richard F. Townsend, *The Aztecs*, revised edn (London: Thames and Hudson, 2000), p. 183).

9 I.I.33–4, in California Dryden, vol. IX.

10 Theodor W. Adorno and Max Horkheimer, *Dialectic of Enlightenment*, trans. John Cumming (London: Verso, 1997), p. 27.

11 Behn, *Works*, ed. Todd, vol. III, pp. 114–15.

12 Richard Ligon, *A True & Exact History of the Island of Barbadoes* (London, 1673), pp. 46–7.

13 The first edition has 'loves'. This is emended in the text printed in Behn's *Three Histories* (London, 1688).

14 William Shakespeare, *Julius Caesar*, ed. T. S. Dorsch, The Arden Shakespeare: Second Series (London: Methuen, 1955) 2.1.162–74.

15 *'[S]acrific'd to the insatiate and cruel Villany of a seeming sanctifi'd Faction'* (Dedication to *The Second Part of the Rover* (*Works*, ed. Todd, vol. VI, p. 229)).

16 Daniel Defoe, *The Life and Strange Surprising Adventures of Robinson Crusoe, of York, Mariner*, ed. J. Donald Crowley (Oxford: Oxford University Press, 1972), p. 67.

17 Henry Fielding, *Tom Jones*, ed. R. P. C. Mutter (Harmondsworth: Penguin, 1966), p. 453 (9.5).

7 *LIETO FINE*: BAROQUE AND ENLIGHTENMENT SACRIFICE

1 Jean de Rotrou, *Iphygenie* (Paris, 1641), p. 15.
2 John Dryden, preface to *All for Love*, in California Dryden, vol. XIII, p. 13.
3 Lines 45–7, in George Buchanan, *Tragedies*, ed. P. Sharratt and P. G. Walsh (Edinburgh: Scottish Academic Press, 1983).
4 Joseph Leven de Templery, *Jephté, ou La Mort de Seïla* (Paris, 1676), p. 12.
5 4.4.1275, in Jean Racine, *Œuvres complètes*, ed. Pierre Clarac (Paris: Éditions du Seuil, 1962).
6 Michel Leclerc, *Iphigénie* (Paris, 1675), p. 64.
7 Michel Pignolet de Montéclair, *Jephté* (Paris, 1732), p. 13.
8 Wolfgang Amadeus Mozart, *Idomeneo*, ed. Heinz Moehn (Kassel, Basel, London, and New York: Bärenreiter, 1973), p. 157.
9 François-Joseph de La Grange-Chancel, *Oreste et Pylade*, p. 96, in *Œuvres de Monsieur de La Grange-Chancel*, 5 vols. (Paris, 1758), vol. I.
10 This play was imitated in *El Sacrificio de Yfigenia. Segunda Parte* (1721) (Barcelona, [1765?]) by the Spanish dramatist Jose de Cañizares (1676–1750), who had written a far more independent version of the Aulis story, *El Sacrificio de Efigenia* (1716) (Madrid, 1758), in which Irifile (Racine's Ériphile) is turned into a spunky feminist who finally marries Ulysses.
11 Apostolo Zeno, *Ifigenia in Aulide* (Venice, 1718), where the death of Elisena (Ériphile) is reported, as it is in the setting by Porta (Monaco, 1738). In the setting by Orlandini (Florence, 1732), Elisena immolates herself onstage.
12 In addition to works mentioned elsewhere, I have read the following plays and libretti based on the Iphigenia plays: Francesco, Count Algarotti, *Iphigenie en Aulide*, in *Discorsi sopra Differenti Soggetti* (Venice, 1755); Anon., *L'Ifigenia* (Venice, 1707); Giuseppe Biamonti, *Ifigenia in Tauri* (Venice, 1804); Giovan Gualberto Bottarelli, *Ifigenia in Aulide* (London, [1770]); Carlo Sigismondo Capeci, *Ifigenia in Aulide* (Rome, 1713); Vittorio Amedeo Cigna-Santi, *Ifigenia in Aulide* (Turin, 1762); John Dennis, *Iphigenia* (London, 1700); Joseph-François Duché de Vancy and Antoine Danchet, *Iphigénie en Tauride* (Paris, 1733) (the libretto of the 1704 opera by André Campra and Henri Desmarets); Benedetto Pasqualigi, *Ifigenia in Tauride* (Venice, 1719); Paolo Rolli, *Ifigenia in Aulide* (London, 1735); Luigi Serio, *L' Ifigenia in Aulide* (Florence, 1784); Mattia Verazi, *Ifigenia in Aulide* (Naples, 1753) and *Ifigenia in Tauride* (Mannheim, 1764). Frequently set libretti often exist in different states.
13 André Campra, *Idomenée* (Paris, 1712); Baldassare Galuppi, *Idomeneo* (Rome, 1756).
14 The opera *Penthée*, with music by Charles-Hubert Gervais and libretto by Charles-Auguste de la Fare, was performed in Paris in 1705. I have not been able to see this opera, whose manuscript is in the Bibliothèque de l'Arsenal de Paris.
15 The opera, however, was completed over a year earlier, since Vogel died in June 1788. The libretto was by Philippe Desriaux.
16 The setting, by the erstwhile court composer Marcos Antonio Portugal, was first performed in 1794.

17 Claude Guimond de la Touche, *Les Soupirs du cloître, ou le Triomphe du fanatisme* (London, 1766), pp. 11–12.
18 [Claude] Guimond de la Touche, *Iphigénie en Tauride* (Paris: Fages, 1805), p. 9.
19 The accidental killing of Clytemnestra had already featured in Pier Jacopo Martello, *L'Ifigenìa in Tauri*, in *Teatro Italiano di Pier Jacopo Martello*, 2 vols. (Rome, 1715), vol. I, pp. 181–2.
20 Frederick is praised by Guimond in *Les Soupirs du cloître* (p. 14).
21 [Denis] Diderot, *Supplément au Voyage de Bougainville*, ed. Michel Delon ([Paris]: Gallimard, 2002), p. 33.
22 John Aikin, *General Biography; or Lives, Critical and Historical, of the Most Eminent Persons of All Ages, Countries, Conditions, and Professions*, 10 vols. (London, 1799–1815), vol. III, p. 133.
23 William Godwin, *An Enquiry concerning Political Justice, and its Influence on Morals and Happiness*, 2nd edn, 2 vols. (London, 1796), vol. I, p. 13. The image of sacrifice occurs in the first edition, but the illustrative example of Damiens is added in the second (*An Enquiry concerning Political Justice*, 2 vols. (Dublin, 1793), vol. I, p. 9).
24 Charles Dickens, *A Tale of Two Cities*, ed. George Woodcock (Harmondsworth: Penguin, 1970), p. 200.
25 Peter Weiss, *Die Verfolgung und Ermordung Jean Paul Marats dargestellt durch die Schauspielgruppe des Hospizes zu Charenton unter Anleitung des Herrn de Sade* (Frankfurt am Main: Suhrkamp, 1981), pp. 36–7.
26 Michel Foucault, *Discipline and Punish: The Birth of the Prison*, trans. Alan Sheridan (Harmondsworth: Penguin, 1991), p. 8.
27 Pierre Rétat (ed.), *L'Attentat de Damiens: discours sur l'événement au XVIIIe siècle* (Paris: CNRS; Lyons: Presses Universitaires de Lyon, 1979), p. 247. Pierre Rétat's chapter 9 (pp. 225–40) and Henri Duranton's chapter 10 (pp. 241–66) deal with the sacrificial aspects of the execution.
28 Voltaire, *Histoire du parlement de Paris*, in Theodore Besterman *et al.* (gen. eds.), *Les Œuvres complètes de Voltaire* (Banbury and subsequently Oxford: Voltaire Foundation, 1968–), vol. LXVIII, pp. 532–44; Voltaire, *Précis du siècle de Louis XV* (Geneva, 1770), pp. 216–27.
29 *Relation de la mort du Chevalier de La Barre* (1766), reprinted (under 'Justice') in V[oltaire], *Questions sur L'Encyclopédie*, 6 vols. (Geneva, 1777), vol. V, pp. 327–40 (p. 330).
30 *Œuvres complètes de Voltaire*, vol. CXXIII, p. 398.
31 2.4.249–50, in *Œuvres complètes de Voltaire*, vol. 1a.
32 1.1.21–2, in *Œuvres complètes de Voltaire*, vol. LXXIII.
33 Cesare Beccaria, *Edizione Nazionale delle Opere di Cesare Beccaria*, gen. ed. Luigi Firpo, 16 vols. (Milan: Mediobanca, 1984–), vol. I, pp. 66–7.
34 Carl Heinrich Graun, *Ifigenia in Aulide* (Berlin, 1768), p. 26.
35 Cited in Carl Heinrich Graun, *Montezuma: Oper in Drei Akten*, ed. Albert Mayer-Reinach, rev. Hans Joachim Moser, Denkmäler Deutscher Tonkunst, 15 vols. (Wiesbaden: Breitkopf & Härtel; Graz: Akademische Druck- u. Verlaganstalt, 1958), p. ix.
36 Tommaso Traetta, *Ifigenia in Tauride*, introduction by Howard Mayer Brown (New York and London: Garland, 1978), Act 1, fo. 61r (acts are paginated separately).

37 The *Montezuma* of Vivaldi (1733) ends happily, for example, as does Galuppi's setting of the popular *Motezuma* libretto by Cigna-Santi (Venice, 1772). There are also settings of the latter libretto by Majo (Turin, 1765), Sacchini (London, 1775), and Insanguine (Turin, 1780), in which Montezuma dies, but without tarnishing Cortez's victory. There are yet more happy endings in Giuseppe Mugnes's *Fernando Cortes, Conquistator del Messico* (Florence, 1789) (librettist unknown) and Giuseppe Giordani's *Pizzaro nell'Indie* (Florence, 1784) (libretto by 'N. N.').

38 Elizabeth Scot, *'Alonzo and Cora' and Other Original Poems* (London: Bunney and Gold, 1801), pp. 64–120.

39 *Les Incas*, vol. I, pp. 184–8. For an account of Manco Capac, the first Inca, and his sister–wife Oello, see Garcilaso de la Vega, *The Royal Commentaries of Peru*, trans. Sir Paul Rycaut (London, 1688), pp. 14–22.

40 Plutarch, *Hypereides* 849e.

41 See Marie-Christine Skuncke, '*Cora och Alonzo*: Upplyst retorik i Peru ['Enlightened Rhetoric in Peru']', in Marie-Christine Skuncke and Anna Ivarsdotter, *Svenska operans födelse: Studier i gustaviansk musikdramatik* (Stockholm, 1998), pp. 89–100 (with English abstract).

42 I have read the following libretti: Giuseppe Foppa's for Francesco Bianchi's *Alonso, e Cora* (Venice, 1786); Ferdinando Moretti's for Salvatore Rispoli's *Idalide* (Turin, 1786) and Giuseppe Sarti's *L'Idalide, o sia Le Vergine del Sole* (Florence, 1788); Carlo Lanfranchi Rossi's for Giacomo Tritto's *La Vergine del Sole* (Naples, 1786); and Giuseppe Bernardoni's for Simone Mayr's *Alonso e Cora* (Vienna, 1804). The 1786 Venice version gives particular prominence to the protests of the people.

43 Charles Blount, *The Two First Books of Philostratus, concerning the life of Apollonius Tyaneus* (London, 1680).

44 Constantin-François de Chasseboeuf, Comte de Volney, *Les Ruines, ou Méditations sur les révolutions des empires* (Paris, 1799), pp. 237–8. Notes on *Queen Mab*, in *The Poems of Shelley*, ed. Thomas Hutchinson (London: Oxford University Press, 1943), pp. 824–5.

45 Julie E. Cumming, 'Gluck's Iphigenia Operas: Sources and Strategies', in *Opera and the Enlightenment*, ed. Thomas Bauman and Marita Petzoldt McClymonds (Cambridge: Cambridge University Press, 1995), pp. 217–42.

46 Quoted in Christoph Willibald Gluck, *Iphigénie en Tauride*, ed. Gerhard Croll (Kassel, Tours, and London: Bährenreiter, 1973), p. viii.

47 The rival Piccinni version is less taut, but similarly contrasts Thoas' coldly objective concern with bloodshed with a social feeling in which the body becomes the vehicle for the discovery of personal emotional bonds in an alien and oppressive place:

> IPHIGÉNIE. il tremble il se trouble . . . il soupire.
> ORESTE. Iphigénie! à peine je respire.
> IPHIGÉNIE. d'où lui vient ce saisissement!
>
> (Niccolò Piccinni, *Iphigénie en Tauride* (Paris [1781]), p. 239).

48 Friedrich Nietzsche, *The Birth of Tragedy and Other Writings*, trans. Ronald Speirs, ed. Raymond Geuss and Ronald Speirs (Cambridge: Cambridge University Press, 1999), p. 23. The debt is noted, for example, in Nietzsche,

The Birth of Tragedy, trans. Douglas Smith (Oxford: Oxford University Press, 2000), p. 140, n. 28.

49 *Iphigenie auf Tauris* (Stuttgart: Reclam, 1970), 4.4.1609.

8 THE FRENCH REVOLUTION TO NAPOLEON

1 See Alison Stonehouse, '*Demofoonte* and Democracy, or the Taming of a French Tyrant', in *Metastasio at Home and Abroad: London (Ontario), 8 January 1996*, ed. Don Neville, *Studies in Music from the University of Western Ontario*, 16 (1997), 135–53.

2 (Paris, [1794]), p. 7.

3 See Thomas Bauman, 'The Eighteenth Century: Serious Opera', in *The Oxford Illustrated History of Opera*, ed. Roger Parker (Oxford: Oxford University Press, 2001), pp. 47–83, 82–3.

4 Claudio Sartori, *I libretti italiani a stampa dalle origini al 1800: catalogo analitico con 16 indici*, 7 vols. (Cuneo: Bertola & Locatelli, 1990–4).

5 Friedrich Hölderlin, *Sämtliche Werke*, ed. Friedrich Beissner, 8 vols. in 14 (Stuttgart: Kohlhammer, 1946–85), vol. V, p. 41.

6 Friedrich Hölderlin, *Poems and Fragments*, trans. Michael Hamburger (London: Routledge and Kegan Paul, 1966), pp. 446–50. See Albert Henrichs, 'Loss of Self, Suffering, Violence: The Modern View of Dionysus from Nietzsche to Girard', *Harvard Studies in Classical Philology*, 88 (1984), 205–40 (pp. 216–18). Giles Fraser, *Redeeming Nietzsche: On the Piety of Unbelief* (London: Routledge, 2002), stresses the importance of Dionysus to the Romantics (p. 57).

7 Edmund Burke, *Reflections on the Revolution in France*, ed. Conor Cruise O'Brien (Harmondsworth: Penguin, 1968), p. 165.

8 See Antoine de Baecque, *Glory and Terror: Seven Deaths Under the French Revolution*, trans. Charlotte Mandell (London: Routledge, 2002), pp. 61–84.

9 Peter von Winter, *Das unterbrochene Opferfest* (Bonn, [1798?]); Winter, *Das unterbrochene Opferfest, . . . Musik . . . von Herrn Peter Winter* (Frankfurt and Munich, 1803) (libretto by Franz Xaver Huber).

10 Thomas Sipe, *Beethoven: Eroica Symphony*, Cambridge Music Handbooks (Cambridge: Cambridge University Press, 1998), pp. 59–60, 100–1.

11 *Justine, ou Les Malheurs de la vertu*, ed. Béatrice Didier (Paris: Livre de Poche, 1973), p. 285.

12 Adam Smith, *An Inquiry into the Nature and Causes of the Wealth of Nations*, ed. R. H. Campbell, A. S. Skinner, and W. B. Todd, 2 vols. (Indianapolis: Liberty Fund, 1981), vol. I, p. 90.

13 T[homas] R[obert] Malthus, *An Essay on the Principle of Population*, ed. Patricia James, 2 vols. (Cambridge: Cambridge University Press, 1989), vol. I, pp. 124–5.

14 Adorno and Horkheimer, *Dialectic of Enlightenment*, p. 104.

15 Johann Wolfgang Goethe, *Sämtliche Werke nach Epochen seines Schaffens*, ed. Karl Richter *et al.*, 21 vols. in 33 (Munich: Hanser, 1985–98), vol. IV.i, p. 867.

16 Friedrich Schiller, *On the Aesthetic Education of Man*, trans. and ed. Elizabeth M. Wilkinson and L. A. Willoughby (Oxford: Clarendon Press, 1967), pp. 78–9.

17 Johann Wolfgang von Goethe, *Faust: erster und zweiter Teil*, ed. Sybille Demmer (Munich: Deutscher Taschenbuch, 1997), Part I, p. 37.
18 5.5267–8, in Schiller, *Sämtliche Werke*, ed. Gerhard Fricke and Herbert G. Göpfert, 5 vols. (Munich: Hanser, 1960–6), vol. II. All citations of Schiller's plays are from this text.
19 'A great, ancient city from heathen times lies underneath' ('eine alte große Stadt / Soll drunter liegen aus der Heiden Zeit') (5.2.2974–5).
20 'Jephtas Gelübde', Add Mss 29, 906, British Library.
21 Peter Joseph von Lindpaintner, *Demophoon* (Munich, 1811), p. 52.
22 In Aloys Schreiber, *Eichenblätter* (Heidelberg: Joseph Engelmann, 1814).
23 [Aloys] Schr[eiber], *Szenen aus Fausts Leben* (Offenbach, 1792), pp. 25, 44.
24 Gasparo Spontini, *Fernand Cortez ou La Conquête du Méxique* (Paris, Imbault [1809?]), p. 97.
25 Diderot, *Supplément*, p. 40.
26 Heinrich von Kleist, *Sämtliche Werke* (Munich: Droemer, 1952), p. 476.
27 The play has even been interpreted as a specific rebuttal of Goethe's *Iphigenie*. Sean Allen, however, argues against the view that 'Kleist deliberately set out to produce a play diametrically opposed in spirit to Goethe's *Iphigenie auf Tauris*' (*The Plays of Heinrich von Kleist: Ideals and Illusions* (Cambridge: Cambridge University Press, 1996), pp. 289–90, n. 27).
28 Mary Shelley, *Frankenstein, or The Modern Prometheus. The 1818 Text*, ed. Marilyn Butler (London: William Pickering, 1993), p. 146.

9 THE SECULARIZATION OF SACRIFICE

1 Karoline von Günderrode, *Der Schatten eines Traumes*, ed. Christa Wolf (Darmstadt and Neuwied: Luchterhand, 1979), p. 88.
2 Samuel Charters MacPherson, *Lieut. MacPherson's Report upon the Khonds of the Districts of Ganjam & Cuttack* (Calcutta: Huttmann, 1842); MacPherson, *An Account of the Religion of the Khonds of Orissa* (London: William Clowes, 1852).
3 Ladislas Segy, *African Sculpture Speaks*, 4th edn (New York: Da Capo, 1975), p. 29; J. D. Page and Roland Oliver (gen. eds.), *The Cambridge History of Africa*, 6 vols. (Cambridge: Cambridge University Press, 1975–85), vol. VI, pp. 234, 236, 271, 290, 345.
4 *Assarpaï* (Berlin, n.d.), p. 32.
5 Jules Verne, *Le Tour du monde en quatre-vingt jours* (Paris: Hetzel, [1884]), pp. 84–98.
6 [Giacomo] Meyerbeer, *Les Huguenots* (Paris: Braun, 1965), p. 100 (libretto, by Eugène Scribe).
7 Giacomo Meyerbeer, *L'Africaine* (Paris: Stock, 1924), p. 79 (libretto, by Eugène Scribe).
8 Charlotte Birch-Pfeiffer, *Die Anglikaner und Puritaner* (Munich, 1838); *Gli Anglicani* (Florence, 1842); *Die Gibellinen in Pisa* (Cassel, 1839); *Die Welfen und Gibellinen* (Vienna, n.d.); *I Guelfi ed I Ghibellini* (Milan, n.d.).
9 Algernon Charles Swinburne, *Swinburne's Collected Poetical Works*, 2 vols. (London: Heinemann, 1924–7), vol. I, p. 167.
10 Dante, *Paradiso* I.19–21.

11 Theodor Reik, *Masochism in Modern Man*, trans. Margaret H. Beigel and Gertrud M. Kurth (New York: Grove Press, n.d.), p. 41.
12 Charles Augustin Sainte-Beuve, '*Salammbô* par Monsieur Gustave Flaubert', *Le Constitutionnel*, 15 decembre 1862.
13 Ernest Reyer, *Salammbô* (Paris: Choudens, [1892]), p. 381.
14 Leopold von Sacher-Masoch, *Venus im Pelz*, ed. Anja and Ralf Bergenson (Flensburg: Stephenson, 2005), p. 69.
15 Georg Wilhelm Friedrich Hegel, *The Philosophy of History*, trans. J. Sibree (New York: Dover, 1956), p. 343.
16 Hegel, *Aesthetics: Lectures on Fine Art*, trans. T. M. Knox, 2 vols. (Oxford: Clarendon Press, 1975), vol. II, p. 1213.
17 Søren Kierkegaard, *Fear and Trembling*, trans. Alastair Hannay (London: Penguin, 1985), p. 84.
18 E. T. A. Hoffmann, *Dichtungen und Schriften*, ed. Walther Harich, 15 vols. (Weimar: Lichtenstein, 1924), vol. VI, p. 64.

10 GOTHIC SACRIFICE

1 Mary Shelley, *Frankenstein . . . The 1818 Text*, p. 146.
2 E. T. A. Hoffmann, *Undine*, vocal score by Hans Pfitzner (Leipzig, [1906]), p. 235.
3 Friedrich de la Motte Fouqué, *Undine* (Stuttgart: Reclam, 1953), pp. 14, 79.
4 Charles Maturin, *Melmoth the Wanderer*, ed. Douglas Grant (Oxford: Oxford University Press, 1968), p. 44.
5 *Dichtungen und Schriften*, vol. IX, pp. 213–14.
6 Marc A. Weiner, 'Richard Wagner's Use of E. T. A. Hoffmann's "The Mines of Falun"', *19th-Century Music*, 5 (1982), 201–14.
7 Mary Shelley, *Frankenstein; . . . The 1818 Text*, p. 197.
8 Mary Shelley and Percy Bysshe Shelley, *History of a Six Weeks' Tour, 1817* (Otley: Woodstock Books, 2002), pp. 161–2.
9 Georges-Louis Leclerc, Comte de Buffon, *Histoire Naturelle, Générale et Particulière*, Supplément, Tome II (Paris, 1775), p. 390.
10 For the Shelleys' interest in Buffon's theories of glaciation, see Kate Flint, *The Victorians and the Visual Imagination* (Cambridge: Cambridge University Press, 2000), pp. 121–3.
11 Mary Shelley, *The Last Man* (Oxford: Oxford University Press, 1994), p. 220.
12 Percy Bysshe Shelley, *The Revolt of Islam* 4063–71, in *The Poems of Shelley*.
13 Mary Shelley, *Frankenstein*, ed. Johanna M. Smith (New York: Bedford Books of St Martin's Press, 1992), p. 139 (the 1831 edition).
14 5.481, in Milton, *Paradise Lost*.
15 Thomas Aquinas, *Summa Theologiae*, gen. ed. Thomas Gilby, 61 vols. (London: Blackfriars, with London: Eyre and Spottiswoode; New York: McGraw-Hill, 1963–76), 1a.73.1, 1a.108.7.1.
16 Goethe, *Faust*, p. 335.
17 '[O]n 15 June 1528, Dr George Faust of Heidelberg was banished as a soothsayer from the town of Ingolstadt' (E. M. Butler, *The Myth of the Magus* (Cambridge: Cambridge University Press, 1993), p. 123).
18 J. B. B. Eyriès (trans.), *Fantasmagoriana, ou Recueil d'histoires d'apparitions de spectres, revenans, fantômes, etc. Traduit de l'allemand, par un amateur*, 2 vols. (Paris, 1812), vol. II, pp. 1–101.

19 Maturin, *Melmoth the Wanderer*, p. 44.
20 Heinrich Marschner, *Der Vampyr ... Klavierauszug* (Leipzig: Hofmeister, [1828?]); Peter Joseph von Lindpaintner, *Der Vampyr ... Vollständiger Klavierauszug* (Leipzig: Peters, [1830?]).
21 Marschner, *Der Vampyr*, Act 1, pp. 34–38 (the acts are paginated separately).
22 Wilhelm August Wohlbrück, *Der Vampyr ... nach Lord Byrons Erzählung frei bearbeitet* (Cologne: Langen, 1840); *Der Vampyr. Nach Lord Byrons Dichtung von C. M. Heigel* (Stuttgart: Hallberger, n.d.).
23 Derek Hughes, '"Wie die Hans Heilings": Weber, Marschner, and Thomas Mann's *Doktor Faustus*,' *Cambridge Opera Journal*, 10 (1998), 179–204.
24 George Gordon, Lord Byron, *The Giaour* 755–86, in *Lord Byron: The Major Works*, ed. Jerome F. McGann (Oxford: Oxford University Press, 1986); [John Polidori], *The Vampyre: A Tale* (London: Sherwood, Neely, and Jones, 1819), pp. xxii–xxiii.

11 WAGNER

1 Richard Wagner, *Der Fliegende Holländer* (Budapest: Könemann, 1993), p. 5.
2 *Richard Wagner's Prose Works*, trans. William Ashton Ellis, 8 vols. (London: Kegan Paul, 1895–9) (hereafter abbreviated as *PW*), vol. II, p. 111; Richard Wagner, *Gesammelte Schriften und Dichtungen*, 2nd edn, 10 vols. in 5 (Leipzig: Fritzsch, 1887) (hereafter abbreviated as *GS*), vol. III, p. 316.
3 Roger Scruton discusses the function of the hunt in Wagner, relating it to the way in which it is used in Greek tragedy (*Death-Devoted Heart: Sex and the Sacred in Wagner's 'Tristan und Isolde'* (Oxford: Oxford University Press, 2004), pp. 171–3).
4 Richard Wagner, *Tristan und Isolde* (Leipzig: Breitkopf and Härtel, n.d.), Act 2.1, p. 146.
5 Richard Wagner, *Götterdämmerung* Act 3.3, p. 346, in *Wagner's Ring of the Nibelung: A Companion*, trans. Stewart Spencer and Barry Millington (New York: Thames & Hudson, 1993). All citations of the libretti of *The Ring* are from this edition.
6 Marx, *Capital*, vol. I, trans. Ben Fowkes, p. 354; vol. III, trans. David Fernbach, p. 521.
7 Richard Wagner, *Tannhäuser und der Sängerkrieg auf Wartburg*, vocal score by Robert Keller (Berlin: Fürstner, n.d.), Act 1.1, p. 29.
8 *Walküre* 1.3, p. 137; *Siegfried* 1.1, p. 202.
9 Max Müller, *Comparative Mythology*, ed. A. Smythe Palmer (London: Routledge; New York: Dutton, 1909), pp. 138–42.
10 [Arthur], Comte de Gobineau, *Essai sur l'inégalité des races humaines*, 2nd edn, 2 vols. (Paris: Firmin-Didot, 1884), vol. I, p. 216.
11 Richard Wagner, *Parsifal*, vocal score by Karl Klindworth (Mainz: Schott, n.d.), Act 1, p. 45; Act 3, p. 288.

12 THE SECOND COMING OF DIONYSUS

1 Joachim Rosteutscher, *Die Wiederkunft des Dionysos: der naturmystische Irrationalismus in Deutschland* (Bern: Franke, 1947).

2 Charles Dickens, 'The Lost Arctic Voyagers' (1854), in *The Works of Charles Dickens: National Edition*, 40 vols. (London: Chapman & Hall, 1906–8), vol. XXXV, p. 428.
3 Dickens, *A Tale of Two Cities*, p. 149.
4 Burke, *Reflections on the Revolution in France*, p. 165.
5 Bram Stoker, *Dracula*, ed. Nina Auerbach and David K. Skal (New York and London: Norton, 1997), p. 239.
6 Franco Moretti, 'A Capital *Dracula*', in Stoker, *Dracula*, pp. 431–44; reprinted from *Signs Taken for Wonders: Essays in the Sociology of Literary Forms*, trans. Susan Fischer and David Forgacs (New York: Verso, 1998), pp. 90–104.
7 Bram Stoker, *The Lair of the White Worm* (Norwood: Deodand, 2002), p. 30. This edition expurgates some of Stoker's racist language.
8 'Die männerfeindliche Mädchen warden des phallischen Herrn der Nature unsiegbare Heldenschar' (Johann Jakob Bachofen, *Gesammelte Werke*, vol. III, *Das Mutterrecht: Zweiter Teil*, ed. Karl Meuli (Basel: Benno Schwabe, 1948), pp. 574–5).
9 For a discussion of breastfeeding in *Dracula*, see Alexandra Warwick, 'Vampires and Empire: Fears and Fictions of the 1890s', in Sally Ledger and Scott McCracken, *Cultural Politics at the Fin De Siècle* (Cambridge: Cambridge University Press, 1995), pp. 202–20 (p. 212).
10 Nietzsche, *The Birth of Tragedy and Other Writings*, p. 39.
11 Friedrich Nietzsche, *Human, All Too Human: A Book for Free Spirits*, trans. R. J. Hollingdale (Cambridge: Cambridge University Press, 1986), p. 17.
12 Durán, *Books of the Gods and Rites*, p. 95.
13 Gilbert Murray, *Euripides and his Age*, with a new introduction by H. D. F. Kitto (London: Oxford University Press, 1965), p. 30.
14 Jane Harrison, *Prolegomena to the Study of Greek Religion* (London: Merlin Press, 1962), p. 28. For an account of Murray, Harrison, and their circle, see Robert Ackerman, *The Myth and Ritual School: J. G. Frazer and the Cambridge Ritualists* (New York and London: Routledge, 2002).
15 Freud, *Totem and Taboo*, p. 131.

13 PENTHEUS 1913

1 Theodor W. Adorno, *Philosophy of Modern Music*, trans. Anne G. Mitchell and Wesley V. Blomster (London: Sheed & Ward, 1973), p. 146.
2 David Johnson, 'Kafka's God of Suffocation: The Futility of "Facing" Death', in Andrew Fagan, *Making Sense of Dying and Death* (Amsterdam and New York: Rodopi, 2004), pp. 89–106 (p. 101).
3 Thomas Mann, *Doktor Faustus. Das Leben des deutschen Tonsetzers Adrian Leverkühn erzählt von einem Freunde* (Frankfurt am Main: Fischer, 1990), p. 495. The translation is taken from Mann, *Doctor Faustus. The Life of the German Composer Adrian Leverkühn as Told by a Friend*, trans. H. T. Lowe-Parker (*sic*, for Lowe-Porter) (Harmondsworth: Penguin, 1968), p. 359.
4 Robert Southey, 'The Poet's Pilgrimage to Waterloo', Part 2.1, stanza 42, in *The Poetical Works of Robert Southey* (London: Longman, 1847), p. 745.
5 30 November 1915, p. 6; 1 January 1916, p. 8; 15 February 1916, p. 8.
6 Wilfred Owen, 'Dulce et Decorum Est', in *The Collected Poems of Wilfred Owen*, ed. C. Day Lewis (London: Chatto and Windus, 1964), p. 55. The quotation is from Horace, *Odes* 3.2.13.

7 Robert Musil, *The Man without Qualities*, trans. Sophie Wilkins (London: Picador, 1995), p. 56; Musil, *Der Mann ohne Eigenschaften*, in *Gesammelte Werke*, 9 vols. (Hamburg: Rowohlt, 1978), vol. 1, p. 57.

8 Nietzsche, *The Birth of Tragedy and Other Writings*, p. 23. The debt is noted, for example, in *The Birth of Tragedy*, trans. Smith, p. 140, n. 28.

9 Thomas Mann, *The Magic Mountain*, trans. H. T. Lowe-Porter (Harmondsworth: Penguin, 1960) (hereafter abbreviated as *MM*), p. 106; Mann, *Der Zauberberg* (Berlin: Fischer, 1964) (hereafter abbreviated as *ZB*), p. 98.

10 Lowe-Porter translates 'Abendmahl' (holy communion) as 'Holy Ghost'.

11 In Ulrich von Wilamowitz-Moellendorff, *Reden und Vorträge*, 3rd edn (Berlin: Weidmann, 1913), pp. 30–66 (see especially pp. 64–6). It was Wilamowitz who, in October 1914, organized the mass declaration by German academics in favour of Germany's entry into the war, which concluded by praising the 'spirit of sacrifice of a harmonious, free German people' ('der Opfermut des einträchtigen freien deutschen Volkes') (*Erklärung der Hochschullehrer des Deutschen Reiches* (Berlin: Dietrich Schäfer, 1914), p. 1).

12 Schiller, *Sämtliche Werke*, vol. 1, pp. 194–200; Wilamowitz, 'Demeterfest', in *Reden und Vorträge*, pp. 271–97 (p. 271).

13 Literally 'in a bay of the sea'.

14 *SPARAGMOS*

1 Hanns Hörbiger, *Wirbelstürme, Wetterstürze, Hagelkatastrophen und Marskanal-Verdoppelungen* (Kaiserslautern: Kayser, 1913); Philip Fauth, *Hörbigers Glacial-Kosmogonie, eine neue Entwickelungsgeschichte des Weltalls* (Kaiserslautern: Kayser, 1913); Brigitte Nagel, *Die Welteislehre: ihre Geschichte und ihre Rolle im 'Dritten Reich'* (Stuttgart: Verlag für Geschichte der Naturwissenschaften und der Technik, 1991).

2 Edgar Dacqué, *Urwelt, Sage und Menschheit: eine naturhistorisch-metaphysische Studie*, 3rd edn (Munich: Oldenbourg, 1925).

3 See Adrienne Mayor, *The First Fossil Hunters: Paleontology in Greek and Roman Times* (Princeton: Princeton University Press, 2000).

4 Egon Wellesz, *Die Opferung des Gefangenen* (Vienna and New York: Universal Edition, 1925).

5 For Siegfried Wagner's early support of Hitler, see Brigitte Hamann, *Winifred Wagner: A Life at the Heart of Hitler's Bayreuth*, trans. Alan Bance (London: Granta, 2005), pp. 51–74. His opera *Der Heidenkönig* (*The Heathen King*) (1913) ends with the averted sacrifice of a king. The opera portrays the conflict between the Poles and the Wends: that is, between a Christian culture and an alien one which has feigned assimilation.

6 Egon Wellesz, *Die Bakchantinnen* (Berlin: Bote & Bock, n.d.), p. 224.

7 David Symons, *Egon Wellesz, Composer* (Wilhelmshaven: Florian Noetzel, 1996), p. 71.

8 I am grateful to David Symons for his helpful correspondence about this opera.

9 D. H. Lawrence, *The Plumed Serpent* (Ware: Wordsworth, 1995), p. 301.

10 See also D. H. Lawrence, 'Fantasia of the Unconscious', in *Psychoanalysis and the Unconscious* (Cambridge: Cambridge University Press, 2004), pp. 63–4.

11 Lawrence, *'The Woman Who Rode Away'*, p. 40.

12 D. H. Lawrence, *Women in Love* (London: Penguin, 1995), p. 79.

13 Karl H. Wörner, *Schoenberg's 'Moses and Aaron'*, trans. Paul Hamburger (London: Faber and Faber, 1959), pp. 112–13.

15 HITLER AND AFTER

1 Todorov, *The Conquest of America*, p. 144.
2 Georges Bataille, *The Accursed Share*, trans. Robert Hurley, 2 vols. (New York: Zone Books, 1988–91).
3 Jean Baudrillard, *Symbolic Exchange and Death*, trans. Iain Hamilton Grant (London, Thousand Oaks, and New Delhi: Sage Publications, 1993), p. 39.
4 Giorgio Ghedini, *Le Baccanti* (Milan and New York: Ricordi, [1948]), pp. 9–10.
5 E.g. pp. 37–8, 63–4, in *Die Atriden-Tetralogie* (Berlin: Suhrkamp, 1949).
6 Ritchie Robertson, 'From Naturalism to National Socialism (1890–1945)', in *The Cambridge History of German Literature*, ed. Helen Watanabe-O'Kelly (Cambridge: Cambridge University Press, 2000), pp. 327–92 (p. 333).
7 Mann, *Doktor Faustus* (hereafter abbreviated as *DF*), p. 191. The translation is taken from Mann, *Doctor Faustus*, trans. H. T. Lowe-Porter (hereafter abbreviated as LP), p. 139.
8 Arnold Schoenberg, 'Composition with Twelve Tones (1)' [1941], in *Style and Idea: Selected Writings of Arnold Schoenberg*, ed. Leonard Stein, trans. Leo Black (London: Faber and Faber, 1984), p. 218.
9 The curse does culminate on a chord of C (to the 'dir' of 'Fluch dir' – 'curse you'). But this chord is eerie and displaced, frustrating an expected modulation to E. The six-four chord reclaims and purifies it. Carl Maria von Weber, *Der Freischütz*, ed. Natalia MacFarren (London: Novello, n.d.), pp. 125–6.
10 Lowe-Porter prints '*Hans Heiling* and *The Flying Dutchman*'.
11 Thomas Mann, *Betrachtungen eines Unpolitischen* (Frankfurt am Main: Fischer, 1956), p. 84.
12 Hoffmann, *Undine*, p. 235.
13 Richard Strauss, *Salome*, vocal score by Otto Singer (London: Hawkes, n.d.), pp. 200–1.
14 The novella *Undine* itself emphasizes a mimetic mirroring between the domains of water and land. The water is 'the liquid mirror' ('den feuchten Spiegel') (p. 14) and 'water-mirror' ('Waßerspiegel') (p. 79), and Huldbrand shoots birds in the 'sea of the air' ('Luftmeer') (p. 28). Undine's menacingly over-protective uncle Kühleborn is 'soulless, a mere elemental mirror of the external world' ('seelenlos, ein bloßer elementarischer Spiegel der Außenwelt') (p. 67).
15 See Victor Oswald, 'Thomas Mann's *Doctor Faustus*: The Enigma of Frau von Tolna', *Germanic Review*, 23 (1948), 249–53; John Francis Fetzer, *Music, Love, Death and Mann's 'Doctor Faustus'* (Columbia, SC: Camden House, 1990), pp. 44, 64–71; Michael Beddow, *Thomas Mann: 'Doctor Faustus'* (Cambridge: Cambridge University Press, 1994), pp. 38–9.
16 Lowe-Porter translates 'Mütterliche' as 'his mother's arms' (p. 486).
17 André Obey, *Une Fille pour du vent* (Paris: Mauclaire, 1953), translated by John Whiting as *Sacrifice to the Wind*, in *Three Dramatic Legends*, ed. Elizabeth Braddon (London: Heinemann, 1964); Kenneth Rexroth, *Iphigenia at Aulis*, in *Beyond the Mountains* (New York: New Directions, 1951).

18 Jürg Amann, *Iphigenie, oder Operation Meereswind* ([Düsseldorf]: Eremiten, [1998]), p. 12.
19 Edna O'Brien, *Iphigenia by Euripides, adapted by Edna O'Brien* (London: Methuen, 2003). It is a new play rather than an adaptation.
20 Shirley Jackson, *Come Along with Me*, ed. Stanley Edgar Hyman (London: Michael Joseph, 1969), p. 230.
21 Burkert, *Structure and History in Greek Mythology*, p. 34.
22 William Golding, *Lord of the Flies* (London: Faber and Faber, 2005), pp. 160–1.
23 William Golding, *Rites of Passage* (London: Faber and Faber, 1980), p. 230.
24 Virginia Tiger, 'William Golding's "Wooden World": Religious Rites in *Rites of Passage*', *Twentieth-Century Literature*, 28 (1982), 216–31 (p. 228).
25 William Golding, *The Inheritors* (London: Faber and Faber, 1961), p. 194.
26 Pierre François, *Inlets of the Soul* (Amsterdam and Atlanta: Rodopi, 1999), p. 106.
27 Chinua Achebe, *Things Fall Apart* (London: Penguin, 2004), pp. 44–5.
28 Konrad Lorenz, *On Aggression*, trans. Marjorie Latzke (London: Methuen, 1966).
29 E. Martin Browne, *The Making of T. S. Eliot's Plays* (Cambridge: Cambridge University Press, 1969), p. 227.
30 T. S. Eliot, *The Cocktail Party* (London: Faber and Faber, 1950), p. 161.
31 Mark Pizzato, *Edges of Loss: From Modern Drama to Postmodern Theory* (Ann Arbor: University of Michigan Press, 1998), p. 52.
32 'In the juvescence of the year / Came Christ the tiger' ('Gerontion', in *The Complete Poems and Plays of T. S. Eliot* (London: Faber and Faber, 1969), p. 37).
33 I have not been able to see *Black Bacchantes*.
34 Harry Partch, *Revelation in the Courthouse Park, After The Bacchae of Euripides*. Facsimile of MS full score, Library of Congress M1500.P292.R5.1960, p. 66.
35 Wole Soyinka, *Collected Plays*, 2 vols. (London, Oxford, and New York: Oxford University Press), vol. 1, p. 248.
36 For a discussion of this play, see K. E. Senanu, 'The Exigencies of Adaptation: The Case of Soyinka's *Bacchae*', in James Gibbs, *Critical Perspectives on Wole Soyinka* (Boulder, Colo.: Lynne Rienner, 1980), pp. 108–12; Patricia Moyer, 'Getting Personal about Euripides', in *Compromising Traditions: Personal Voice in Classical Scholarship*, ed. Judith P. Hallett and Thomas Van Nortwick (London: Routledge, 1996), pp. 102–19 (pp. 113–17). Moyer notes Soyinka's use of 'post-Frazerian' ideas (p. 116).
37 The ballet *Undine* (1957) and the operas *Der Prinz von Homburg* (1960) and *Elegy for Young Lovers* (1961).
38 Hans Werner Henze, *Elegy for Young Lovers . . . Textbook* (Mainz: Schott, 1961), p. 15.
39 Hans Werner Henze, *The Bassarids . . . Text* (Mainz: Schott, 1966), p. 67.
40 Christopher Innes, 'Auden's Plays and Dramatic Writings: Theatre, Film, and Opera', in Stan Smith, *The Cambridge Companion to W. H. Auden* (Cambridge: Cambridge University Press, 2005), pp. 82–95 (pp. 92–3).
41 Peter Burian, 'Tragedy Adapted for Stages and Screens: the Renaissance to the Present', in *The Cambridge Companion to Greek Tragedy*, ed. P. E. Easterling (Cambridge: Cambridge University Press, 1997), pp. 228–83 (p. 269).
42 Atwood, *The Blind Assassin*, p. 63.

Bibliography

Works mentioned in passing are not listed. Opera libretti are listed under the name of the composer, except in the case of those with multiple settings.

PRIMARY WORKS

Acosta, José de, *De Natvra Novi Orbis Libri Duo. Et De Promulgatione Evangelii apvd Barbaros, siue, De Procvranda Indorvm salute, Libri sex*, Cologne, 1596

Acosta, Joseph [José de], *The Natvrall and Morall Historie of the East and West Indies*, trans. E. G., London, 1604

Aeschylus, trans. Herbert Weir Smyth, Loeb Classical Library, 2 vols., London and Cambridge, Mass.: Harvard University Press, 1922

Amann, Jürg, *Iphigenie, oder Operation Meereswind*, [Düsseldorf]: Eremiten, [1998]

Apollodorus, *The Library*, trans. Sir James George Frazer, Loeb Classical Library, 2 vols., London: Heinemann; New York: Putnam, 1921

Atwood, Margaret, *The Blind Assassin*, London: Bloomsbury, 2000

Augustine, St, *City of God*, trans. Henry Bettenson, ed. David Knowles, Harmondsworth: Penguin, 1972

Bachofen, Johann Jakob, *Gesammelte Werke*, vol. III, *Das Mutterrecht: Zweiter Teil*, ed. Karl Meuli, Basel: Benno Schwabe, 1948

Beccaria, Cesare, *Edizione Nazionale delle Opere di Cesare Beccaria*, gen. ed. Luigi Firpo, 16 vols., Milan: Mediobanca, 1984–

Behn, Aphra, *The Works of Aphra Behn*, ed. Janet Todd, 7 vols., London: Pickering and Chatto, 1992–6

Biet, Antoine, *Voyage de la France équinoxiale*, Paris, 1664

Buchanan, George, *Tragedies*, ed. P. Sharratt and P. G. Walsh, Edinburgh: Scottish Academic Press, 1983

Buffon, Georges-Louis Leclerc, Comte de, *Histoire naturelle, générale et particulière*, Supplément, vol. II, Paris, 1775

Burke, Edmund, *Reflections on the Revolution in France*, ed. Conor Cruise O'Brien, Harmondsworth: Penguin, 1968

Campra, André, *Idomenée*, Paris, 1712

Cañizares, José de, *El Sacrificio de Efigenia*, Madrid, 1758

El Sacrificio de Yfigenia. Segunda Parte, Barcelona, [1765?]

Child, Sir Josiah, *A Discourse about Trade, Wherein the Reduction of Interest of Money to 4 l. per Centum is Recommended*, London, 1690

Chubb, Thomas, 'The Case of Abraham, with Regard to his being commanded by God, to offer his Son *Isaac* in Sacrifice, farther considered', in *Four Tracts*, London, 1734, pp. 84–119

Cigna-Santi, Vittorio Amedeo, *Ifigenia in Aulide*, Turin, 1762

Motezuma, Turin, 1765; Venice, 1772; London, 1775; Turin, 1780

Clement of Alexandria, trans. G. W. Butterworth, Loeb Classical Library, London: Heinemann; New York: Putnam, 1919

Columbus, Christopher, *Journal of the First Voyage*, ed. and trans. B. W. Ife, Warminster: Arist and Phillips, 1990

Cortes, Hernan, *Letters from Mexico*, trans. Anthony Pagden, revised edn, New Haven and London: Yale University Press, 1986

Culpepper, Thomas, the Elder, *A Tract Against the high rate of Usury Presented to the High Court of Parliament, Anno Domini 1623*, 4th edn, London, 1668

Dacqué, Edgar, *Urwelt, Sage und Menschheit: eine naturhistorisch-metaphysische Studie*, 3rd edn, Munich: Oldenbourg, 1925

Defoe, Daniel, *The Life and Strange Surprising Adventures of Robinson Crusoe, of York, Mariner*, ed. J. Donald Crowley, Oxford: Oxford University Press, 1972

Desriaux, Philippe, *Alexis et Rosette, ou Les Houlans [Ulans], Pièce Républicaine*, Paris, [1794]

Díaz del Castillo, Bernal, *The True History of the Conquest of New Spain*, trans. Alfred Percival Maudslay, 5 vols., London: Hakluyt Society, 1908–16

Dickens, Charles, 'The Lost Arctic Voyagers', in *The Works of Charles Dickens: National Edition*, 40 vols., London: Chapman & Hall, 1906–8, vol. XXXV

A Tale of Two Cities, ed. George Woodcock, Harmondsworth: Penguin, 1970

Diderot, [Denis], *Supplément au Voyage de Bougainville*, ed. Michel Delon, [Paris]: Gallimard, 2002

Digges, Dudley, *The Defence of Trade, In a Letter to Sir Thomas Smith Knight, Gouernour of the East-India Companie*, London, 1615

Dryden, John, *The Works of John Dryden*, ed. Edward Niles Hooker *et al.*, 20 vols., Berkeley, Los Angeles, and London: University of California Press, 1956–2002

Duché de Vancy, Joseph-François, and Antoine Danchet, *Iphigénie en Tauride*, Paris, 1733

Durán, Diego, *The Aztecs: The History of the Indies of New Spain*, trans. Doris Heyden and Fernando Horcasitas, New York: Orion Press, 1964

Books of the Gods and Rites and The Ancient Calendar, trans. and ed. Fernando Horcasitas and Doris Heyden, Norman: University of Oklahoma Press, 1971

Eliot, T. S., *The Cocktail Party*, London: Faber and Faber, 1950

The Complete Poems and Plays of T. S. Eliot, London: Faber and Faber, 1969

Erklärung der Hochschullehrer des Deutschen Reiches, Berlin: Dietrich Schäfer, 1914

Euripides, trans. and ed. David Kovacs, Loeb Classical Library, 6 vols., Cambridge, Mass., and London: Harvard University Press, 1994–2002

Eyriès, J. B. B. (trans.), *Fantasmagoriana, ou Recueil d'histoires d'apparitions de spectres, revenans, fantômes, etc. Traduit de l'allemand, par un amateur*, 2 vols., Paris, 1812

Fauth, Philip, *Hörbigers Glacial-Kosmogonie, eine neue Entwickelungsgeschichte des Weltalls*, Kaiserslautern: Kayser, 1913

Fouqué, Friedrich de la Motte, *Undine*, Stuttgart: Reclam, 1953

Frazer, Sir James George, *The Golden Bough ... A New Abridgement from the Second and Third Editions*, ed. Robert Fraser, Oxford and New York: Oxford University Press, 1994

Freud, Sigmund, *Totem and Taboo*, trans. James Strachey, London: Routledge & Kegan Paul, 1950

Gage, Thomas, *The English-American his Travail by Sea and Land: Or, A New Survey of the West-India's*, London, 1648

Galuppi, Baldassare, *Idomeneo*, Rome, 1756

Ghedini, Giorgio, *Le Baccanti*, Milan and New York: Ricordi, [1948]

Gluck, Christoph Willibald, *Iphigénie en Tauride*, ed. Gerhard Croll, Kassel, Tours, and London: Bährenreiter, 1973

Gobineau, [Arthur], Comte de, *Essai sur l'inégalité des races humaines*, 2nd edn, 2 vols., Paris: Firmin-Didot, 1884

Goethe, Johann Wolfgang von, *Faust: erster und zweiter Teil*, ed. Sybille Demmer, Munich: Deutscher Taschenbuch, 1997

Iphigenie auf Tauris, Stuttgart: Reclam, 1970

Sämtliche Werke nach Epochen seines Schaffens, ed. Karl Richter *et al.*, 21 vols. in 33, Munich: Hanser, 1985–98

Golding, Arthur (trans.), *The XV Bookes Entytuled Metamorphosis*, London, 1567; repr. Amsterdam: Theatrum Orbis Terrarum; Norwood, N. J.: Walter J. Johnson, 1977

Golding, William, *The Inheritors*, London: Faber and Faber, 1961

Lord of the Flies, London: Faber and Faber, 2005

Rites of Passage, London: Faber and Faber, 1980

Graun, Carl Heinrich, *Ifigenia in Aulide*, Berlin, 1768 (Libretto, by Leopoldo de Villati)

Montezuma: Oper in Drei Akten, ed. Albert Mayer-Reinach, rev. Hans Joachim Moser, Denkmäler Deutscher Tonkunst, 15 vols., Wiesbaden: Breitkopf & Härtel; Graz: Akademische Druck- u. Verlaganstalt, 1958

Graziani, Girolamo, *Il Conquisto di Granata*, Parnasso Italiano, 38–9, 2 vols., Venice, 1789

Guimond de la Touche, [Claude], *Iphigénie en Tauride*, Paris: Fages, 1805

Les Soupirs du cloître, ou le Triomphe du fanatisme, London, 1766

Günderrode, Karoline von, *Der Schatten eines Traumes*, ed. Christa Wolf, Darmstadt and Neuwied: Luchterhand, 1979

Hauptmann, Gerhart, *Die Atriden-Tetralogie*, Berlin: Suhrkamp, 1949

Hegel, Georg Wilhelm Friedrich, *Aesthetics: Lectures on Fine Art*, trans. T. M. Knox, 2 vols., Oxford: Clarendon Press, 1975

The Philosophy of History, trans. J. Sibree, New York: Dover, 1956

Henze, Hans Werner, *The Bassarids . . . Text*, Mainz: Schott, 1966 (Libretto, by W. H. Auden and Chester Kallman)

Elegy for Young Lovers . . . Textbook, Mainz: Schott, 1961 (Libretto, by W. H. Auden and Chester Kallman)

Hesiod, Homeric Hymns, Homerica, trans. Hugh G. Evelyn-White, Loeb Classical Library, revised edn, Cambridge, Mass., and London: Harvard University Press, 1936

Hoffmann, E. T. A., *Dichtungen und Schriften*, ed. Walther Harich, 15 vols., Weimar: Lichtenstein, 1924

Undine, vocal score by Hans Pfitzner, Leipzig, [1906]

Hölderlin, Friedrich, *Poems and Fragments*, trans. Michael Hamburger, London: Routledge and Kegan Paul, 1966

Sämtliche Werke, ed. Friedrich Beissner, 8 vols. in 14, Stuttgart: Kohlhammer, 1946–85

Homer, *Iliad*, trans. A. T. Murray, rev. William F. Wyatt, Loeb Classical Library, 2 vols., Cambridge, Mass., and London: Harvard University Press, 1999

Odyssey, trans. A. T. Murray, rev. George E. Dimock, Loeb Classical Library, 2 vols., Cambridge, Mass., and London: Harvard University Press, 1995

Hörbiger, Hanns, *Wirbelstürme, Wetterstürze, Hagelkatastrophen und Marskanal-Verdoppelungen*, Kaiserslautern: Kayser, 1913

Hume, David, *The Natural History of Religion*, ed. John Valdimir Price, Oxford: Clarendon Press, 1976

Hummel, Ferdinand, *Assarpaï*, Berlin, n.d. (Libretto, by Dora Drucker)

Jackson, Shirley, *Come Along with Me*, ed. Stanley Edgar Hyman, London: Michael Joseph

Kayll, Robert, *The Trades Increase*, London, 1615

Keiser, Reinhard, *Die wunderbahr errettete Iphigenia*, Hamburg, 1699 (Libretto, by Christian Heinrich Postel)

Kierkegaard, Søren, *Fear and Trembling*, trans. Alastair Hannay, London: Penguin, 1985

Kleist, Heinrich von, *Sämtliche Werke*, Munich: Droemer, 1952

La Grange-Chancel, François-Joseph de, *Œuvres de Monsieur de La Grange-Chancel*, 5 vols., Paris, 1758

Las Casas, Bartolomé de, *A Short Account of the Destruction of the Indies*, trans. and ed. Nigel Griffin, Harmondsworth: Penguin, 1992. Translated as *The Spanish Colonie*, by M. S. S., London, 1583; *The Tears of the Indians*, by John Phillips, London, 1656; and *Popery truly display'd*, London, 1689

Lawrence, D. H., *The Plumed Serpent*, Ware: Wordsworth, 1995

Psychoanalysis and the Unconscious, Cambridge: Cambridge University Press, 2004

'*The Woman Who Rode Away' and Other Stories*, ed. Dieter Mehl and Christa Jansohn, Cambridge: Cambridge University Press, 1995

Women in Love, London: Penguin, 1995

Le Moyne, Pierre, *Saint Louys, ou la sainte couronne reconquise*, Paris, 1658

Leclerc, Michel, *Iphigénie*, Paris, 1675

Léry, Jean de, *A History of a Voyage to the Land of Brazil*, trans. Janet Whatley, Berkeley, Los Angeles, and Oxford: University of California Press, 1990

Lindpaintner, Peter Joseph von, *Demophoon*, Munich, 1811 (Libretto, by Ignaz Franz Castelli)

Der Vampyr. Nach Lord Byrons Dichtung von C. M. Heigel, Stuttgart: Hallberger, n.d. (Libretto, by Cäsar Max Heigel)

Der Vampyr . . . Vollständiger Klavierauszug, Leipzig: Peters, [1830?]

Livy, Loeb Classical Library, 14 vols., London: Heinemann; Cambridge, Mass.: Harvard University Press, 1919–59

López de Gómara, Francisco, *The Conquest of the Weast India (1578)* [trans. Thomas Nicholas], intro. Herbert Ingram Priestley, Scholars' Facsimiles and Reprints: New York, 1940

Historia General de las Indias, ed. Pilar Guibelalde and Emiliano M. Aguilera, 2 vols., [Barcelona]: Iberia, 1954

Lucretius, *De Rerum Natura*, trans. W. H. D. Rouse, rev. Martin F. Smith, Loeb Classical Library, Cambridge, Mass., and London: Harvard University Press, 1992

MacPherson, Samuel Charters, *An Account of the Religion of the Khonds of Orissa*, London: William Clowes, 1852

Lieut. MacPherson's Report upon the Khonds of the Districts of Ganjam & Cuttack, Calcutta: Huttmann, 1842

Malthus, T[homas] R[obert], *An Essay on the Principle of Population*, ed. Patricia James, 2 vols., Cambridge: Cambridge University Press, 1989

Mambrun, Pierre [Petrus Mambrunus], *Opera Poetica*, Fixae Andecavorum [Flèche], 1661

Mann, Thomas, *Betrachtungen eines Unpolitischen*, Frankfurt am Main: Fischer, 1956

Doctor Faustus. The Life of the German Composer Adrian Leverkühn as Told by a Friend, trans. H. T. Lowe-Parker (*sic*, for Lowe-Porter), Harmondsworth: Penguin, 1968

Doktor Faustus. Das Leben des deutschen Tonsetzers Adrian Leverkühn erzählt von einem Freunde, Frankfurt am Main: Fischer, 1990

The Magic Mountain, trans. H. T. Lowe-Porter, Harmondsworth: Penguin, 1960

Der Zauberberg, Berlin: Fischer, 1964

Marmontel, Jean-François, *Les Incas*, 2 vols., Paris: Bibliothèque Nationale, 1895

Marschner, Heinrich, *Der Vampyr . . . Klavierauszug*, Leipzig: Hofmeister, [1828?]

Der Vampyr . . . nach Lord Byrons Erzählung frei bearbeitet, Cologne: Langen, 1840. (Libretto, by Wilhelm August Wohlbrück)

Martello, Pier Jacopo, *L'Ifigenìa in Tauri*, in *Teatro Italiano di Pier Jacopo Martello*, 2 vols., Rome, 1715, vol. 1

Marx, Karl, *Capital*, trans. Ben Fowkes *et al.*, 3 vols., Harmondsworth: Penguin, 1976–81

Maturin, Charles, *Melmoth the Wanderer*, ed. Douglas Grant, Oxford: Oxford University Press, 1968

Metastasio, Pietro, *Opere*, ed. Fausto Nicolini, 4 vols., Bari: Laterza, 1912–14

Meyerbeer, Giacomo, *L'Africaine*, Paris: Stock, 1924 (Libretto, by Eugène Scribe)

Les Huguenots, Paris: Braun, 1965 (Libretto, by Eugène Scribe). Adapted as *Die Anglikaner und Puritaner*, Munich, 1838; *Gli Anglicani*, Florence, 1842; *Die Gibellinen in Pisa*, Cassel, 1839; *Die Welfen und Gibellinen*, Vienna, n.d.; *I Guelfi ed I Ghibellini*, Milan, n.d.

'Jephta's Gelübde', Add. Mss. 29, 906, British Library

Milton, John, *Paradise Lost*, ed. Alastair Fowler, corrected edn, London: Longman, 1981

Montaigne, Michel Eyquem de, *Montaigne's Essays*, trans. John Florio, Everyman's Library, 3 vols., London and New York: Dent and Dutton, 1910

Montéclair, Michel Pignolet de, *Jephté*, Paris, 1732 (Libretto, by Simon Joseph Pellegrin)

Müller, Max, *Comparative Mythology*, ed. A. Smythe Palmer, London: Routledge; New York: Dutton, 1909

Musil, Robert, *Gesammelte Werke*, 9 vols., Hamburg: Rowohlt, 1978

The Man without Qualities, trans. Sophie Wilkins, London: Picador, 1995

Nietzsche, Friedrich, *The Birth of Tragedy*, trans. Douglas Smith, Oxford: Oxford University Press, 2000

The Birth of Tragedy and Other Writings, trans. Ronald Speirs, ed. Raymond Geuss and Ronald Speirs, Cambridge: Cambridge University Press, 1999

Human, All Too Human: A Book for Free Spirits, trans. R. J. Hollingdale, Cambridge: Cambridge University Press, 1986

O'Brien, Edna, *Iphigenia by Euripides, adapted by Edna O'Brien*, London: Methuen, 2003

Ovid, *Metamorphoses*, in *Ovid*, Loeb Classical Library, 6 vols., Cambridge, Mass., and London: Harvard University Press, 1977–88, vols. III and IV, trans. Frank Justus Miller, rev. G. P. Goold

Owen, Wilfred, *The Collected Poems of Wilfred Owen*, ed. C. Day Lewis, London: Chatto and Windus, 1964

Partch, Harry, *Revelation in the Courthouse Park, After The Bacchae of Euripides.* Facsimile of MS full score, Library of Congress M1500.P292.R5.1960

Pausanias, *Description of Greece*, trans. W. H. S. Jones, Loeb Classical Library, 5 vols., London: Heinemann; New York: Putnam, 1918–35

Petty, Sir William, *An Essay Concerning the Multiplication of Mankind: Together with another Essay in Political Arithmetick, Concerning the Growth of the City of London*, 2nd edn, London, 1686

Piccinni, Niccolò, *Iphigénie en Tauride*, Paris [1781]

Plato, *Republic*, trans. Paul Storry, Loeb Classical Library, 2 vols., London: Heinemann; Cambridge, Mass.: Harvard University Press, 1930–5

Plutarch's Lives, trans. Bernadotte Perrin, Loeb Classical Library, 11 vols., London: Heinemann; New York: Macmillan, 1914–26

[Polidori, John], *The Vampyre: A Tale*, London: Sherwood, Neely, and Jones, 1819

Portugal, Marcos Antonio, *Il Demofoonte*, Lisbon, 1808

Racine, Jean, *Œuvres complètes*, ed. Pierre Clarac, Paris: Éditions du Seuil, 1962

Rich, Barnabe, *The Trauailes and Adventures of Don Simonides, Tome 2*, London, 1584

Rotrou, Jean de, *Iphygenie*, Paris, 1641

Sacher-Masoch, Leopold von, *Venus im Pelz*, ed. Anja and Ralf Bergenson Flensburg: Stephenson, 2005

Sahagún, Bernardino de, *General History of the Things of New Spain*, trans. and ed. Arthur J. O. Anderson and Charles E. Dibble, 13 parts, Santa Fe: School of American Research, 1950–82

Schiller, Friedrich, *On the Aesthetic Education of Man*, trans. and ed. Elizabeth M. Wilkinson and L. A. Willoughby, Oxford: Clarendon Press, 1967

Sämtliche Werke, ed. Gerhard Fricke and Herbert G. Göpfert, 5 vols., Munich: Hanser, 1960–6

Schoenberg, Arnold, 'Composition with Twelve Tones (1)' [1941], in *Style and Idea: Selected Writings of Arnold Schoenberg*, trans. Leo Black, ed. Leonard Stein, London: Faber and Faber, 1984

Schreiber, Aloys, *Eichenblätter*, Heidelberg: Joseph Engelmann, 1814

Szenen aus Fausts Leben, Offenbach, 1792

Scot, Elizabeth, *'Alonzo and Cora' and Other Original Poems*, London: Bunney and Gold, 1801

Scudéry, George de, *Alaric, ou Rome vaincue*, Paris, 1654

Shakespeare, William, *Julius Caesar*, ed. T. S. Dorsch, The Arden Shakespeare: Second Series, London: Methuen, 1955

The Merchant of Venice, ed. John Russell Brown, The Arden Shakespeare: Second Series, London and New York: Methuen, 1955

Titus Andronicus, ed. Jonathan Bate, The Arden Shakespeare: Third Series, London and New York: Routledge, 1995

Shelley, Mary, *Frankenstein*, ed. Johanna M. Smith, New York: Bedford Books of St Martin's Press, 1992 (The 1831 edition)

Frankenstein, or The Modern Prometheus. The 1818 Text, ed. Marilyn Butler, London: William Pickering, 1993

The Last Man, Oxford: Oxford University Press, 1994

Shelley, Mary, and Percy Bysshe Shelley, *History of a Six Weeks' Tour, 1817*, Otley: Woodstock Books, 2002

Shelley, Percy Bysshe, *The Poems of Shelley*, ed. Thomas Hutchinson, London: Oxford University Press, 1943

Sophocles, trans. and ed. Hugh Lloyd Jones, Loeb Classical Library, corrected edn, 3 vols., Cambridge, Mass., and London: Harvard University Press, 1997

Southey, Robert, *The Poetical Works of Robert Southey*, London: Longman, 1847

Soyinka, Wole, *Collected Plays*, 2 vols., London, Oxford, and New York: Oxford University Press

Spontini, Gasparo, *Fernand Cortez ou La Conquête du Méxique*, Paris: Imbault, [1809?]

Stoker, Bram, *Dracula*, ed. Nina Auerbach and David K. Skal, New York and London: Norton, 1997

The Lair of the White Worm, Norwood: Deodand, 2002

Strauss, Richard, *Salome*, vocal score by Otto Singer, London: Hawkes, n.d.

Swinburne, Algernon Charles, *Swinburne's Collected Poetical Works*, 2 vols., London: Heinemann, 1924–7

Tasso, Torquato, *Gerusalemme Liberata*, ed. Anna Maria Carini, Milan: Feltrinelli, 1961

Templery, Joseph Leven de, *Jephté, ou La Mort de Seïla*, Paris, 1676

Traetta, Tommaso, *Ifigenia in Tauride*, intro. Howard Mayer Brown, New York and London: Garland, 1978

Vaubertrand, Jean Baptiste Claude, *Iphigenie en Tauride*, Paris, 1757

Virgil, trans. H. Rushton Fairclough, rev. G. P. Goold, Loeb Classical Library, 2 vols., Cambridge, Mass., and London: Harvard University Press, 1999–2000

Vogel, Johann Christoph, *Démophon*, Paris, [1790?]

Volney, Constantin-François de Chasseboeuf, Comte de, *Les ruines, ou Méditations sur les révolutions des empires*, Paris, 1799

Voltaire, *La Bible enfin expliquée par plusieurs aumoniers de S.M.L.R.D.P.*, Geneva, 1776

Les Œuvres complètes de Voltaire, gen. eds. Theodore Besterman *et al.*, Banbury and subsequently Oxford: Voltaire Foundation, 1968–

Précis du siècle de Louis XV (Geneva, 1770)

Questions sur L'Encyclopédie, 6 vols., Geneva, 1777

Wagner, Richard, *Der Fliegende Holländer*, Budapest: Könemann, 1993

Gesammelte Schriften und Dichtungen, 2nd edn, 10 vols. in 5, Leipzig: Fritzsch, 1887

Parsifal, vocal score by Karl Klindworth, Mainz: Schott, n.d.

Richard Wagner's Prose Works, trans. William Ashton Ellis, 8 vols., London: Kegan Paul, 1895–9

Tannhäuser und der Sängerkrieg auf Wartburg, vocal score by Robert Keller, Berlin: Fürstner, n.d.

Wagner's Ring of the Nibelung: A Companion, trans. Stewart Spencer and Barry Millington, New York: Thames & Hudson, 1993

Wellesz, Egon, *Die Bakchantinnen*, Berlin: Bote & Bock, n.d.

Die Opferung des Gefangenen, Vienna and New York: Universal Edition, 1925

Winter, Peter von, *Das unterbrochene Opferfest . . . Musik . . . von Hernn Peter Winter*, Bonn, [1798?]

Das unterbrochene Opferfest, Frankfurt and Munich, 1803 (Libretto, by Franz Xaver Huber)

Wörner, Karl H., *Schoenberg's 'Moses and Aaron'*, trans. Paul Hamburger, London: Faber and Faber, 1959

Zeno, Apostolo, *Ifigenia in Aulide*, Venice, 1718; Florence, 1732; Monaco, 1738

SECONDARY WORKS

Ackerman, Robert, *The Myth and Ritual School: J. G. Frazer and the Cambridge Ritualists*, New York and London: Routledge, 2002

Adorno, Theodor W., *Philosophy of Modern Music*, trans. Anne G. Mitchell and Wesley V. Blomster, London: Sheed & Ward, 1973

Adorno, Theodor W., and Max Horkheimer, *Dialectic of Enlightenment*, trans. John Cumming, London: Verso, 1997

Allen, Daniel S., *The World of Prometheus: The Politics of Punishing in Democratic Athens*, Princeton: Princeton University Press, 2000

Allen, Sean, *The Plays of Heinrich von Kleist: Ideals and Illusions*, Cambridge: Cambridge University Press, 1996

Baecque, Antoine de, *Glory and Terror: Seven Deaths Under the French Revolution*, trans. Charlotte Mandell, London: Routledge, 2002

Bandera, Cesáreo, 'Sacrificial Levels in Vergil's Aeneid', *Arethusa*, 14 (1981), 217–39

Bataille, Georges, *The Accursed Share*, trans. Robert Hurley, 2 vols., New York: Zone Books, 1988–91

Bate, Jonathan, *Shakespeare and Ovid*, Oxford: Clarendon Press, 1993

Baudrillard, Jean, *Symbolic Exchange and Death*, trans. Iain Hamilton Grant, London, Thousand Oaks, and New Delhi: Sage Publications, 1993

Bauman, Thomas, 'The Eighteenth Century: Serious Opera', in *The Oxford Illustrated History of Opera*, ed. Roger Parker, Oxford: Oxford University Press, 2001, pp. 47–83

Belsey, Catherine, 'Love in Venice', in *The Merchant of Venice*, ed. Martin Coyle, New Casebooks, London: Macmillan; New York: St Martin's Press, pp. 139–60; reprinted from *Shakespeare Survey*, 44 (1991), 41–53

Boone, Elizabeth H. (ed.), *Ritual Human Sacrifice in MesoAmerica*, Washington, D.C.: Dumbarton Oaks Research Library and Collection, 1984

Brown, Betty Ann, 'Ochpaniztli in Historical Perspective', in *Ritual Human Sacrifice in MesoAmerica*, ed. Elizabeth H. Boone, Washington, D.C.: Dumbarton Oaks Research Library and Collection, 1984, pp. 195–210

Browne, E. Martin, *The Making of T. S. Eliot's Plays*, Cambridge: Cambridge University Press, 1969

Burian, Peter, 'Tragedy Adapted for Stages and Screens: the Renaissance to the Present', in *The Cambridge Companion to Greek Tragedy*, ed. P. E. Easterling, Cambridge: Cambridge University Press, pp. 228–83

Burkert, Walter, *Creation of the Sacred: Tracks of Biology in Early Religions*, Cambridge, Mass., and London: Harvard University Press, 1996

Greek Religion: Archaic and Classical, trans. John Raffan, Oxford: Blackwell, 1985

Homo Necans: The Anthropology of Ancient Greek Sacrificial Ritual and Myth, trans. Peter Bing, Berkeley, Los Angeles, and London: University of California Press, 1983

Structure and History in Greek Mythology and Ritual, Sather Classical Lectures, 47, Berkeley, Los Angeles, and London: University of California Press, 1979

Clendinnen, Inga, *Aztecs: An Interpretation*, Cambridge: Cambridge University Press, 1991

Cumming, Julie E., 'Gluck's Iphigenia Operas: Sources and Strategies', in *Opera and the Enlightenment*, ed. Thomas Bauman and Marita Petzoldt McClymonds, Cambridge: Cambridge University Press, 1995, pp. 217–42

Detienne, Marcel, and Jean-Pierre Vernant (eds.), *The Cuisine of Sacrifice among the Greeks*, trans. Paula Wissing, Chicago and London: University of Chicago Press, 1989

Durand, Jean-Louis, 'Greek Animals: Toward a Topology of Edible Bodies', in *The Cuisine of Sacrifice among the Greeks*, trans. Paula Wissing, ed. Marcel Detienne and Jean-Pierre Vernant, Chicago and London: University of Chicago Press, 1989, pp. 87–118

Easterling, P. E. (ed.), *The Cambridge Companion to Greek Tragedy*, Cambridge: Cambridge University Press, 1997

Evans, J. Martin, *Milton's Imperial Epic*, Ithaca and London: Cornell University Press, 1996

Farron, S., 'Aeneas' Human Sacrifice', *Acta Classica*, 23 (1985), 21–33

Fetzer, John Francis, *Music, Love, Death and Mann's 'Doctor Faustus'*, Columbia, SC: Camden House, 1990

Flint, Kate, *The Victorians and the Visual Imagination*, Cambridge: Cambridge University Press, 2000

Foley, Helene P., *Ritual Irony: Poetry and Sacrifice in Euripides*, Ithaca and London: Cornell University Press, 1985

Foucault, Michel, *Discipline and Punish: The Birth of the Prison*, trans. Alan Sheridan, Harmondsworth: Penguin, 1991

François, Pierre, *Inlets of the Soul*, Amsterdam and Atlanta: Rodopi, 1999

Gibbs, James, *Critical Perspectives on Wole Soyinka*, Boulder, Colo.: Lynne Rienner, 1980

Girard, René, *A Theater of Envy: William Shakespeare*, Oxford and New York: Oxford University Press, 1991

Violence and the Sacred, trans. Patrick Gregory, Baltimore: Johns Hopkins University Press, 1977

Goldhill, Simon, *Reading Greek Tragedy*, Cambridge: Cambridge University Press, 1986

Goux, Jean-Joseph, *Oedipus, Philosopher*, trans. Catherine Porter, Stanford: Stanford University Press, 1993

Green, Miranda Aldhouse, *Dying for the Gods, Human Sacrifice in Iron Age & Roman Europe*, Stroud: Tempus, 2001

Hamann, Brigitte, *Winifred Wagner: A Life at the Heart of Hitler's Bayreuth*, trans. Alan Bance, London: Granta, 2005

Hamerton-Kelly, Robert G. (ed.), *Violent Origins: Walter Burkert, René Girard, and Jonathan Z. Smith on Ritual Killing and Cultural Formation*, Stanford: Stanford University Press, 1987

Hardie, Philip, *The Epic Successors of Virgil: A Study in the Dynamics of a Tradition*, Cambridge: Cambridge University Press, 1993

Harrison, Jane, *Prolegomena to the Study of Greek Religion*, London: Merlin Press, 1962

Henrichs, Albert, 'Loss of Self, Suffering, Violence: The Modern View of Dionysus from Nietzsche to Girard', *Harvard Studies in Classical Philology*, 88 (1984), 205–40

Horsfall, Nicholas, '*Aeneid*', in *A Companion to the Study of Virgil*, ed. Nicholas Horsfall, 2nd edn, Leiden: Brill, 1995, pp. 101–216

Hubert, Henri, and Marcel Mauss, *Sacrifice: Its Nature and Functions*, trans. W. D. Halls, London: Cohen and West, 1964

Hughes, Dennis D., *Human Sacrifice in Ancient Greece*, London and New York: Routledge, 1991

Hughes, Derek, *Dryden's Heroic Plays*, London and Basingstoke: Macmillan, 1981

'"Wie die Hans Heilings": Weber, Marschner, and Thomas Mann's *Doktor Faustus*', *Cambridge Opera Journal*, 10 (1998), 179–204

Innes, Christopher, 'Auden's Plays and Dramatic Writings: Theatre, Film, and Opera', in *The Cambridge Companion to W. H. Auden*, ed. Stan Smith, Cambridge: Cambridge University Press, 2005, pp. 82–95

Johnson, David, 'Kafka's God of Suffocation: The Futility of "Facing" Death', in *Making Sense of Dying and Death*, ed. Andrew Fagan, Amsterdam and New York: Rodopi, 2004, pp. 89–106

Kamen, Henry, *The Spanish Inquisition: A Historical Revision*, London: Weidenfeld and Nicolson, 1997

Kirk, G. S., *The Nature of Greek Myths*, Harmondsworth: Penguin, 1974

(gen. ed.), *The Iliad: A Commentary*, 6 vols., Cambridge: Cambridge University Press, 1985–93

Kirk, G. S., J. E. Raven, and M. Schofield, *The Presocratic Philosophers: A Critical History with a Selection of Texts*, 2nd edn, Cambridge: Cambridge University Press, 1983

Levin, Richard, 'The New Refutation of Shakespeare', *Modern Philology*, 83 (1985–6), 123–41

MacDowell, Douglas M., *Athenian Homicide Law in the Age of the Orators*, Manchester: Manchester University Press, 1963

Mayor, Adrienne, *The First Fossil Hunters: Paleontology in Greek and Roman Times*, Princeton: Princeton University Press, 2000

Meuli, Karl, 'Griechische Opferbräuche', in *Phyllobolia für Peter von der Mühll*, ed. Olof Gigon *et al.*, Basel: Benno Schwake, 1946, pp. 185–288

Moretti, Franco, 'A Capital *Dracula*', in *Dracula*, ed. Nina Auerbach and David K. Skal, New York and London: Norton, 1997, pp. 431–44; reprinted from *Signs Taken for Wonders: Essays in the Sociology of Literary Forms*, trans. Susan Fischer and David Forgacs, New York: Verso, 1988, pp. 90–104

Moyer, Patricia, 'Getting Personal about Euripides', in *Compromising Traditions: Personal Voice in Classical Scholarship*, ed. Judith P. Hallett and Thomas Van Nortwick, London: Routledge, 1996, pp. 102–19

Murray, Gilbert, *Euripides and his Age*, with a new intro. by H. D. F. Kitto, London: Oxford University Press, 1965

Nagel, Brigitte, *Die Welteislehre: ihre Geschichte und ihre Rolle im 'Dritten Reich'*, Stuttgart: Verlag für Geschichte der Naturwissenschaften und der Technik, 1991

Nebeker, Helen E. '"The Lottery": Symbolic Tour de Force', *American Literature*, 46 (1974), 100–8

Oswald, Victor, 'Thomas Mann's *Doctor Faustus*: The Enigma of Frau von Tolna', *Germanic Review*, 23 (1948), 249–53

Otis, Brooks, *Virgil: A Study in Civilized Poetry*, Oxford: Clarendon Press, 1963

Parker, Jan, *Dialogic Education and the Problematics of Translation in Homer and Greek Tragedy*, Studies in Classics, 17, Lewiston, Queenston, and Lampeter: Edwin Mellen, 2001

Pavlock, Barbara, 'Epic and Tragedy in Vergil's Nisus and Euryalus Episode', *Transactions of the American Philological Association*, 115 (1985), 207–24

Pizzato, Mark, *Edges of Loss: From Modern Drama to Postmodern Theory*, Ann Arbor: University of Michigan Press, 1998

Potter, D. S., and J. D. Mattingly (eds.), *Life, Death, and Entertainment in the Roman Empire*, Ann Arbor: University of Michigan Press, 1999

Quint, David, *Epic and Empire: Politics and Generic Form from Virgil to Milton*, Princeton: Princeton University Press, 1992

Reik, Theodor, *Masochism in Modern Man*, trans. Margaret H. Beigel and Gertrud M. Kurth, New York: Grove Press, n.d.

Rétat, Pierre (ed.), *L'Attentat de Damiens: discours sur l'événement au XVIIIe siècle*, Paris: CNRS; Lyons: Presses Universitaires de Lyon, 1979

Robertson, Ritchie, 'From Naturalism to National Socialism (1890–1945)', in *The Cambridge History of German Literature*, ed. Helen Watanabe-O'Kelly, Cambridge: Cambridge University Press, 2000, pp. 327–92

Rosteutscher, Joachim, *Die Wiederkunft des Dionysos: der naturmystische Irrationalismus in Deutschland*, Bern: Franke, 1947

Ryan, Kiernan, '*The Merchant of Venice*: Past Significance and Present Meaning', *Shakespeare Jahrbuch*, 117 (1981), 49–54

Sainte-Beuve, Charles Augustin, '*Salammbô* par Monsieur Gustave Flaubert', *Le Constitutionnel*, 15 décembre 1862

Sartori, Claudio, *I Libretti italiani a stampa dalle origini al 1800: catalogo analitico con 16 indici*, 7 vols., Cuneo: Bertola & Locatelli, 1990–4

Scruton, Roger, *Death-Devoted Heart: Sex and the Sacred in Wagner's 'Tristan und Isolde'*, Oxford: Oxford University Press, 2004

Seaford, Richard, *Money and the Early Greek Mind: Homer, Philosophy, Tragedy*, Cambridge: Cambridge University Press, 2004

Reciprocity and Ritual: Homer and Tragedy in the Developing City-State, Oxford: Clarendon Press, 1991

Segal, Charles, *Dionysiac Poetics and Euripides' 'Bacchae'*, expanded edn, Princeton: Princeton University Press, 1997

Sophocles' Tragic World: Divinity, Nature, Society, Cambridge, Mass., and London: Harvard University Press, 1995

Sherman, Stuart, *Telling Time: Clocks, Diaries, and English Diurnal Form, 1660–1785*, Chicago and London: University of Chicago Press, 1996

Sipe, Thomas, *Beethoven: Eroica Symphony*, Cambridge Music Handbooks, Cambridge: Cambridge University Press, 1998

Soustelle, Jacques, 'Ritual Human Sacrifice in Mesoamerica: An Introduction', in *Ritual Human Sacrifice in MesoAmerica*, ed. Elizabeth H. Boone, Washington, D.C.: Dumbarton Oaks Research Library and Collection, 1984, pp. 1–5

Stonehouse, Alison, '*Demofoonte* and Democracy, or the Taming of a French Tyrant', in *Metastasio at Home and Abroad: London, Ontario, 8 January 1996*, ed. Don Neville, *Studies in Music from the University of Western Ontario*, 16 (1997), 135–53

Symons, David, *Egon Wellesz, Composer*, Wilhelmshaven: Florian Noetzel, 1996

Tiger, Virginia, 'William Golding's "Wooden World": Religious Rites *in Rites of Passage*', *Twentieth-Century Literature*, 28 (1982), 216–31

Todorov, Tzvetan, *The Conquest of America: The Question of the Other*, trans. Richard Howard, Norman: University of Oklahoma Press, 1999

Townsend, Richard F., *The Aztecs*, rev. edn, London: Thames and Hudson, 2000

Vance, Eugene, 'Sylvia's Pet Stag: Wildness and Domesticity in Virgil's *Aeneid*', *Arethusa*, 14 (1981), 127–38

Vernant, Jean-Pierre, 'At Man's Table: Hesiod's Foundation Myth of Sacrifice', in *The Cuisine of Sacrifice among the Greeks*, trans. Paula Wissing, ed. Marcel Detienne and Jean-Pierre Vernant, Chicago and London: University of Chicago Press, 1989, pp. 21–86

'Oedipus without the Complex', in Jean-Pierre Vernant and Pierre Vidal-Naquet, *Tragedy and Myth in Ancient Greece*, trans. Janet Lloyd, Sussex: Harvester Press; New Jersey: Humanities Press, 1981, pp. 63–86

Vidal-Naquet, Pierre, 'Hunting and Sacrifice in Aeschylus' *Oresteia*', in Jean-Pierre Vernant and Pierre Vidal-Naquet, *Tragedy and Myth in Ancient Greece*, trans. Janet Lloyd, Sussex: Harvester Press; New Jersey: Humanities Press, 1981, pp. 150–74

Warwick, Alexandra, 'Vampires and Empire: Fears and Fictions of the 1890s', in *Cultural Politics at the Fin De Siècle*, ed. Sally Ledger and Scott McCracken, Cambridge: Cambridge University Press, 1995, pp. 202–20

Weiner, Marc A., 'Richard Wagner's Use of E. T. A. Hoffmann's "The Mines of Falun"', *19th-Century Music*, 5 (1982), 201–14

Wilamowitz-Moellendorff, Ulrich von, *Reden und Vorträge*, 3rd edn, Berlin: Weidmann, 1913

Williams, R. Deryck, 'The *Aeneid*', in *The Cambridge History of Classical Literature*, ed. E. J. Kenney, Cambridge: Cambridge University Press, 1982, pp. 333–69

Wynne-Davies, Marion, '"The Swallowing Womb": Consumed and Consuming Women in *Titus Andronicus*', in *The Matter of Difference: Materialist Feminist Criticism of Shakespeare*, ed. Valerie Wayne, New York: Harvester Wheatsheaf, 1991, pp. 129–51

Index

The Colour Identification Guide to

Caterpillars of the British Isles

The Colour Identification Guide to

Caterpillars of the British Isles

(Macrolepidoptera)

Jim Porter

VIKING

To my wife,
Karen,
and sons,
David and Philip

VIKING

Published by the Penguin Group
Penguin Books Ltd, 27 Wrights Lane, London W8 5TZ, England
Penguin Books USA Inc., 375 Hudson Street, New York, New York 10014, USA
Penguin Books Australia Ltd, Ringwood, Victoria, Australia
Penguin Books Canada Ltd, 10 Alcorn Avenue, Toronto, Ontario, Canada M4V 3B2
Penguin Books (NZ) Ltd, 182–190 Wairau Road, Auckland 10, New Zealand

Penguin Books Ltd, Registered Offices: Harmondsworth, Middlesex, England

First published 1997
3 5 7 9 10 8 6 4
First edition

Copyright © Jim Porter, 1997

The moral right of the author has been asserted

All rights reserved.
Without limiting the rights under copyright
reserved above, no part of this publication may be
reproduced, stored in or introduced into a retrieval system,
or transmitted, in any form or by any means (electronic, mechanical,
photocopying, recording or otherwise), without the prior
written permission of both the copyright owner and
the above publisher of this book

Filmset in 8½/9pt Monotype Plantin by Cambridge Photosetting Services

Printed in China by South China Printing

A CIP catalogue record for this book is available from the British Library

ISBN 0-670-87509-0

Contents

Preface

Although many works are available describing and identifying the adult insects of the butterflies and larger moths (collectively known as macrolepidoptera) of the British Isles, it is now about one hundred years since a comprehensive guide to their larvae was generally available. This work, which it is hoped will be an on-going project, will not replace Buckler's superb volumes, now very rare and expensive, but will supplement them. Since Bernard Skinner's book, the *Colour Identification Guide to Moths of the British Isles*, is unquestionably the best field guide on moths currently available, it was agreed that a companion volume illustrating the caterpillars would be desirable.

Many books on caterpillars are incomplete, omitting a great many common species, and although the drawn illustrations tend to vary from totally inaccurate to superb, a photograph of the actual live insect is not subject to artistic licence and shows the true structure, colours and markings.

Illustrations of a few resident species have yet to be obtained. Most are internal feeders of the family Noctuidae, which can be notoriously difficult to locate or rear from the egg stage. It is hoped that when these larvae are eventually found and committed to film they may be included in either a separate plate or in later printings, along with any new species that colonize the British Isles in future. Extinct British species are also described and, although photographs may not at present be available, these will also be included when the material is obtained. A few European species, which are unknown to have ever bred in Britain, have been figured because the adults have occurred on occasions and the material was available.

A short description of each larva is included, showing the approximate size when fully developed and indicating any distinguishing characteristics that may support the illustration; although one must remember that many things in nature are not constant and great variation may take place within a species. Unless stated, all of the larvae are figured in the final instar, as many are quite similar when young, although others are totally unidentifiable in the earlier instars and showing tiny green or brown unmarked young caterpillars is impractical in most cases. Some young larvae are distinctly different from the fully developed state and where relevant have been included. Those of the Fox moth are a good example, with the black and yellow-banded young caterpillars being as often observed as the gingery fully grown ones.

The foodplants are mostly listed showing known preferences first, followed by secondary acceptable plants and those with which the larvae may be successfully reared in captivity; always referring to the foliage, unless otherwise stated. For many species unrecorded or unknown pabulums must exist and some, now known, are unexpected and in no way related to the plants on which the larvae usually feed.

The generalization covered by the habits, refers to the time of year in which the larvae usually occur and methods of locating them for first-hand experience. Also in this section are breeding hints and short notes on the habits of the adults, as rearing from captive females often gives one the best chance of seeing some of the more secretive larvae. Knowing an insect's distribution, habitats and present status are all useful hints to recognizing larvae in the field and those with the desire to find certain species may then be guided in the right direction. The final entry on each species describes the method by which the figured larva was obtained and the date of the initial encounter; not necessarily the time when the photograph was taken.

The task of photographing over 850 different macrolepidoptera larvae was immense and could never have been completed without the assistance of many entomologists, both in Britain and on the continent, and the species that were not found or bred by myself have been credited individually to those who have dedicated their efforts to contributing to this work.

Special thanks must go to Steven Church, who from the start of this project assisted me in obtaining many of the illustrated larvae, being single-minded in attempting to supply me with those which I required; and Graham Collins, who not only accompanied me on seemingly impossible ventures to find more species, but also gave me invaluable help and encouragement when writing the text. Also, Bernard Skinner, whose immense knowledge of the British lepidoptera has made the text as accurate as possible and also supplied me with larvae from his many contacts and deliberately searched for a good number himself, before proof-reading what I had written; and Chris Beales for the superb drawing of the 'universal' caterpillar. Finally, I must thank my wife, Karen, and my sons, David and Philip, for tolerating my frequent absences from home while on countless expeditions to try and make this book as complete as possible.

Jim Porter *October 1996*

Acknowledgements

This book could not have been completed without the assistance and co-operation of a great many experienced and dedicated lepidopterists, who gave their own valuable time and effort to obtain a great many different larvae, some of which have never been illustrated before. The least I can do is credit them in the text and thank them all yet again for their invaluable contribution to my work. Their names are listed below:

(SFA) Arnold, S. F.
(BRB) Baker, Brian
(PB) Baker, Peter
(AB) Batten, Alan
(CB) Beales, Chris
(JB) Beeching, Janet
(RAB) Bell, Reg
(EB) Bradford, Eric
(MB) Britton, Mike
(MMB) Brooks, Margaret
(DB) Brown, David
(DJC) Carter, David J.
(MC-H) Chalmers-Hunt, Michael
(RGC) Chatelain, Dick
(SHC) Church, Steven
(SC) Clancy, Sean
(GAC) Collins, Graham A.
(PC) Costen, Peter
(JC) Culpin, John
(AJD) Dewick, A. J.
(BD) Dickerson, Barry
(TJD) Dillon, Terry
(DD) Down, Don
(RD) Dyke, Robert
(BE) Elliott, Brian
(KGWE) Evans, Ken
(MJF) Falconer, Malcolm
(JF) Fenn, John
(AG) Gardner, Andrew
(MG-P) Gascoigne-Pees, Martin
(BG) Goater, Barry
(GdeA) Gomez de Aizpurua, Carlos
(JG) Gregory, John
(MH) Hadley, Mark
(GMH) Haggett, Gerry
(M&JH) Halsey, Mike and James
(AH) Harmer, Alec
(CH) Hart, Colin
(MHy) Harvey, Mike
(GH) Higgs, George
(BH) Holloway, Barry
(AJ) Jenkins, Allan
(WK) Kittle, Bill
(JK) Knight, John
(RL) Largen, Robert
(NL) Lear, Nick
(IL) Lorimer, Ian
(RMcC) McCormick, Roy
(RM) Morris, Roger
(NHM) Natural History Museum, London
(JO) Owen, John
(MP) Parsons, Mark
(AJP) Pickles, Tony
(DWP) Porter, David
(PJP) Porter, Philip
(JMP) Platts, Jim
(CP) Pratt, Colin
(KR) Redshaw, Keith
(JR) Reid, Jim
(IR) Rutherford, Ian
(MRS) Shaw, Mark
(ECLS) Simson, Clive
(BS) Skinner, Bernard
(PS) Smytheman, Peter
(AS) Spalding, Adrian
(BSt) Statham, Brian
(DS) Sterling, Doug
(MJS) Sterling, Mark
(JW) Ward, John
(PW) Waring, Paul
(DJW) Wedd, David
(DEW) Wilson, David
(PQW) Winter, Philip

Introduction

The identity of the caterpillar or larval stage of most British lepidoptera may be confidently determined by its size, colour and markings; and on which plant, when and where it was found.

Larvae may be found by various methods, such as carefully searching leaves, especially on the undersides and on those which show signs of feeding, or by using a torch or powerful lamp after dark, when many species emerge from the daytime retreats to feed with less danger of being destroyed by predators such as mammals, birds, parasitic wasps and other carnivorous insects.

The method known as beating may be very successful for obtaining larvae. Basically it involves placing a large sheet, or even an inverted umbrella, beneath the foliage of trees and shrubs and then rapping the branches suddenly with a strong stick or pole. Continuous thrashing is a pointless act, as most larvae are dislodged on the first contact and those that remain then cling on tightly. Low numbers will be found on windy days, as again the larvae are clasping the leaves more firmly and those that do fall may be blown away, missing the sheet altogether. The contents of the sheet should be carefully watched, as many larvae lie motionless for a short while before moving to betray their presence, and those unwanted should always be carefully shaken back on to the foodplant. Again, beating at night often produces different species that hide by day inside silken spinnings or elsewhere. Specially made folding beating-trays, made of wood braces and a suitably sized black or white cloth sheet, may be purchased from entomological suppliers and are most useful for this method of finding or recording larvae.

To obtain larvae from plants such as heather, grasses or those of a similar height, sweeping can be productive. This involves using a strong framed net with a cloth bag and swiping firmly and steadily about twenty times at the foodplant as low down as is practical, while walking forwards. The contents of the bag may then be examined to find lepidopterous larvae among the debris and myriads of other small creatures knocked from the herbage. When either of the two previous methods is employed during damp conditions, the captive larvae should always be placed on tissue-paper, within the collecting boxes, to absorb all excess moisture.

Most larvae obtained by beating, sweeping or searching will belong to the group known as macrolepidoptera (butterflies and larger moths), to which this book relates. A well-known method of checking if a smaller larva belongs to the microlepidoptera is to gently press the head. If the creature scuttles backwards it is probably a micro; the main exceptions being the *Hepialidae*, *Sesiidae* and *Hypeninae* species. Also larvae of other groups of insects will be found, these usually being distinguished by either the complete absence of abdominal legs (beetles and ladybirds) or an almost complete row of suckers along the underside of the body (sawflies, hoverflies and the like).

When taken in the wild, larvae may be parasitized, by ichneumon wasps and other insects, with some species being more heavily predated than others. The parasite eggs are often injected by means of an ovipositor into the larva, although some lay their eggs externally on the larva's skin to hatch and bore within. Some parasitized larvae look sickly or have dark scars on the body and invariably do not survive. Viruses also attack larvae, especially when kept overcrowded, and any showing signs of unhealthiness or diarrhoea should quickly be separated from the others.

A rewarding and alternative method is to rear the larvae from the egg stage by taking female adult insects into captivity and persuading them to lay. Some species have exacting requirements, such as being supplied with foodplants, rough bark or corrugated cardboard, but many lay freely without any stimulus. Eggs may be laid singly or in batches and many hatch within about a week or so, except those which overwinter. These should be kept either outside in a sheltered spot or placed in the bottom of a refrigerator until the foodplant becomes available in the spring.

Many entomologists prefer to use small clear plastic or card boxes in the field and these are generally ideal for most larvae, except the very large ones. When keeping larvae in captivity, sandwich-boxes or containers of a similar size should be used, with those made from plastic being the best. Jam-jars or metal tobacco-boxes are not suitable as access to the former is difficult for changing food and cleaning, while the latter may begin to rust from moisture within the supplied plants. Captive larvae should never be kept enclosed in direct sunlight as they will be killed by the rise in temperature, although many species can be forced to develop faster by keeping them in a warm environment such as an airing cupboard or a specially made incubator controlled at about 25° centigrade.

Hygiene is a very important factor when rearing larvae, therefore their food should be changed regularly and any frass (droppings) cleaned out daily. If for any reason daily care cannot be given, most larval development can be slowed or stopped by placing them temporarily in the bottom of a refrigerator for a period of up to two weeks.

Successfully hibernating larvae through the winter months is a very hit and miss affair and one's chances are increased by providing them with conditions as natural as possible, such as keeping them outside, protected from excessive damp, frosts and natural enemies, in a prepared pot containing a foodplant and dry withered leaves for shelter; although some species overwinter quite happily on untreated dry wood shavings placed in an outbuilding.

Another method of keeping larvae in confinement is to sleeve them outside on a growing foodplant. In the case of trees or shrubs, a fine netting bag encloses both the larvae and part of the plant, with the frass being cleared out and the larvae transferred to fresh foliage, when necessary. Both sleeves and foodplants grown in prepared pots, which are securely covered with netting, should be regularly checked to eliminate any potential predators and never allowed to become too dry or too damp.

The larvae should not be unnecessarily disturbed while in captivity, especially when about to change skin or pupate; the former condition is often indicated by torpidity and the presence of the new head capsule at the front part of the first segment. When approaching pupation, many larvae tend to lose their markings and begin to shrink and those of many moths should be supplied with sterilized soil in which to change into the dormant phase of their life-cycle. Many entomologists find peat or vermiculite an ideal pupating medium, but I prefer to finely sift earth and then place it in a hot oven for about an hour to kill any bacteria or eggs of earwigs and other predators. During the pupation stage, the insects are best left undisturbed and care must be taken to see that they do not desiccate or become too damp, as both conditions may be fatal.

Prior to the emergence of the adults, many pupae darken and often the wing pattern can be seen through the outer shell of the pupa. The majority of species will then require a good foothold so they can crawl from the pupa and expand their wings without obstructions. Therefore, one or more sides of the pupae container should be covered with netting or scratched corrugated cardboard to allow the emerging insect to develop into a perfect adult. Some butterfly pupae hang from their cremasters (hooks at the tail end, attached to a silken pad) and if these are not hanging freely the resulting adult will often be crippled. Sometimes, fallen pupae or those formed unnaturally at the bottom of the container can be saved by carefully putting a tiny drop of superglue on the cremaster hooks and reattaching them in a hanging position.

All adults that are not required for further breeding or study should be released at the site of capture and not unnecessarily killed or dumped in the garden, as the latter confuses our knowledge of distribution, if they are recaptured or observed by someone else. Some species kept for further breeding will pair without hesitation, while others need exacting requirements such as foodplant, sunshine and a choice of mates. Female adult moths that are attracted to light have usually been fertilized, as many emerge from the pupa and do not fly until they have mated.

Larvae can be preserved by keeping them in glass tubes containing 100 per cent alcohol or by blowing them. The latter method is rather messy and involves killing the larva by freezing or in a killing-jar, and then carefully rolling a cylindrical object, such as a pencil, down the body away from the head until the innards are forced out of the rear orifice. The empty skin is then inflated by blowing air into it and then dried at a warm temperature. This method is not generally recommended as many larval skins lose their shape, colour and markings unless the procedure is expertly carried out. It may, however, be necessary for scientific purposes, such as for specimens to be held in museums or similar establishments.

Nowadays, with relatively cheap but good SLR-type cameras on the market, photographing larvae can be a rewarding and pleasurable method of collecting. Also, the insect will be seen in its natural posture with the colour and markings exactly depicted on film. The majority of photographs included in this work were taken with a Fujica 605 camera, equipped with extension tubes and a standard Photax 131 flashgun, usually mounted on the camera; while the film used was Kodak Ektachrome 100ASA. Most of the larvae were photographed indoors on their respective foodplants under controlled conditions and those that are sensitive to light, crawling about trying to hide themselves, can be made less lively by placing them in the refrigerator for about an hour before filming them.

It is hoped that this work will assist in the recognition and knowledge of the earlier stages of our butterflies and moths and encourage those interested in British natural history to appreciate the crawling feeding-machines that eventually develop into our most popular group of insects.

Larvae Required for Photographs

Although every effort has been made to make this guide as comprehensive as possible, the photographs of the larval stage of just nine resident and about thirty very irregular visitors or extinct species have yet to be obtained. The author and publishers would be most grateful if these could be included in future reprintings of this work to eventually make it complete. The required insects are listed below and I would be most grateful for eggs, larvae or previously taken photographs of any of the following species.

Resident and regular immigrant species

Small Black Arches, *Meganola strigula* D. & S.
Stout Dart, *Spaelotis ravida* D. & S.
The Confused, *Apamea furva* D. & S.
Least Minor, *Photedes captiuncula* Treit.
Crinan Ear, *Amphipoea crinanensis* Burr.
Ear Moth, *Amphipoea oculea* Linn.
Haworth's Minor, *Celaena haworthii* Curt.
Brighton Wainscot, *Oria musculosa* Hb.
Small Marbled, *Eublemma parva* Hb.
Marsh Oblique-barred, *Hypenodes humidalis* Doubl.

Extinct and irregular immigrant species

Dusky Clearwing, *Paranthrene tabaniformis* Rott.
Short-tailed Blue, *Everes argiades* Pall.
American Painted Lady, *Cynthia virginiensis* Drury
Spanish Carpet, *Scotopteryx peribolata* Hb.
Goosefoot Pug, *Eupithecia sinuosaria* Eversm.
Speckled Beauty, *Fagivorina arenaria* Hufn.
Eversmann's Rustic, *Actebia fennica* Tausch.
Radford's Flame Shoulder, *Ochropleura leucogaster* Freyer
The Nonconformist, *Lithophane lamda* Fabr.
Marsh Dagger, *Acronicta strigosa* D. & S.
Scarce Dagger, *Acronicta auricoma* D. & S.
Tree-lichen Beauty, *Cryphia algae* Fabr.
Marbled Grey, *Cryphia raptricula* D. & S.
Scarce Brindle, *Apamea lateritia* Hufn.
Union Rustic, *Apamea pabulatricula* Brahm
Dumeril's Rustic, *Luperina dumerilii* Dup.
Scarce Arches, *Luperina zollikoferi* Freyer
Blair's Wainscot, *Sedina buettneri* Her.
Pease Blossom, *Periphanes delphinii* Linn.
Eastern Bordered Straw, *Heliothis nubigera* H.-S.
Spotted Clover, *Protoschinia scutosa* D. & S.
Pretty Marbled, *Deltote deceptoria* Scop.
Spotted Sulphur, *Emmelia trabealis* Scop.
Spiny Bollworm, *Earias biplaga* Walk.
Tunbridge Wells Gem, *Chrysodeixis acuta* Walk.
Scar Bank Gem, *Ctenoplusia limbirena* Guen.
Purple-shaded Gem, *Euchalcia variabilis* Pill.
Stephen's Gem, *Autographa biloba* Steph.
The Alchymist, *Catephia alchymista* D. & S.
Levant Blackneck, *Tathorhynchus exsiccata* Led.
Lesser Belle, *Colobochyla salicalis* D. & S.
Paignton Snout, *Hypena obesalis* Treit.

Glossary and Abbreviations

aestivation = summer diapause (qv)
anal plate = a chitinous structure located on the rear of the eleventh segment
beating = a method of obtaining larvae by jarring foliage over a sheet
bivoltine = having two generations or broods within a year
claspers = the abdominal and anal segment legs (qv. prolegs)
cocoon = a protective casing around the pupa, constructed with the larva's own silk and sometimes also with the larval hairs
detritus = material, such as soil and plant litter, produced by erosion
diapause = a state of inactivity
dorsal = pertaining to the back
dorsolateral = pertaining to the area above the sides
frass = larval droppings
instar = the stage between larval moults
larva (plural **larvae**) = the second stage in a moth or butterfly's life-cycle, during which all feed and grow, usually changing their skins about four or five times, until fully developed when pupation takes place. Moth and butterfly larvae are commonly known as caterpillars
lateral = pertaining to the side
ovum (plural **ova**) = the egg stage of an insect
pinacula = warts
prolegs = the abdominal legs situated on the sixth to ninth and anal segments
prothoracic plate = a chitinous structure on the top of the first segment
pupa (plural **pupae**) = the third stage in a moth or butterfly's life-cycle, during which no feeding takes place and the bodily liquids break down to reconstruct as the adult insect. Also known as a chrysalis.
pupation = the act of changing from the larval stage into a pupa
rings = body divisions or segments
segment = body divisions, the first three being of the thorax, the others abdominal
seta (plural **setae**) = larval hair or bristle
spinning = leaves or plant matter drawn together with silk to form a larval retreat
spiracles = breathing holes along the sides of larvae, present on the first and fourth to eleventh segments
subdorsal = pertaining to the area between the back and sides
subspiracular = the area immediately below the spiracles
sweeping = a method of obtaining larvae by randomly swiping at chosen herbage with a strong cloth net
thoracic = the first three segments of a larva
true legs = those beneath the first three segments
tubercles = chitinous warts
univoltine = having one generation or brood within a year

MVL = mercury-vapour light (as used for attracting adult moths to a trap)
sp. = species (singular)
spp. = species (plural)
ssp. = subspecies

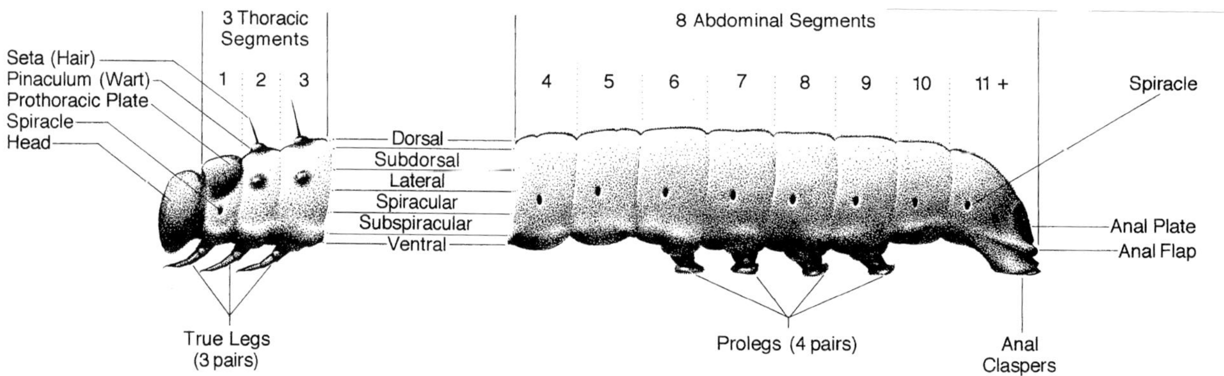

Description of Species

Family: HEPIALIDAE

There are five members of this primitive family, all resident, to be found in the British Isles and all their larvae adopt a subterranean existence, feeding on or inside the roots of their foodplant. Both sexes of adults are freely attracted to light and, although females will lay eggs readily in boxes, it is not normally practical to attempt to rear them through due to the time of development and effort involved. The eggs are scattered at random while the females are flying and are white, changing to black after a short period. Sometimes the larvae will be found by chance and they have been noted on occasions wandering above ground. They all possess the characteristic of microlepidoptera larvae of being able to run backwards when disturbed.

Ghost Moth
Hepialus humuli Linnaeus
Larva. 28–32 mm. Body glossy dirty white, with the head reddish-brown and shining; the prothoracic plate is orange-brown and has raised chitinous plates of the same colour along the body; spiracles very dark brown.
Foodplants. The roots of various grasses and many other plants, including dock, nettle, dandelion and burdock.
Habits. A subterranean species, being in the larval stage from July to May of probably the third year. It is sometimes found by gardeners when turning the soil, and has on occasions been found wandering above ground at night. The pupa is formed underground in the larval burrow and this stage lasts about three to four weeks. The adults fly in June and July, with the females scattering the eggs while flying over herbage. Widespread throughout most of Britain, mainly on open ground and in woodland clearings.
Plate 1: A. Dug from grass roots, fully grown. Late April. (SHC)

Orange Swift
Hepialus sylvina Linnaeus
Larva. 25–30 mm. Body glossy dirty white, head orange-brown with the plates slightly lighter than the head; spiracles dark brown.
Foodplants. The roots of bracken, dock, dandelion and probably other suitable plants.
Habits. A two-year life-cycle spent underground, boring alongside the foodplant roots and feeding slowly, becoming fully grown during May or June and pupating in soil. The adults emerge during July and August and the females distribute their eggs while flying. These drop into the herbage, hatch in about two weeks and the larvae wander to their foodplant and dig into the soil to feed. Widespread over most of the British Isles, being more frequent in the southern counties.
Plate 1: B. Found in soil by dock plants, fully grown. Late May. (SHC)

Gold Swift
Hepialus hecta Linnaeus
Larva. 18–22 mm. Body whitish-grey and wrinkled, with a shining chestnut-coloured head and greyish-brown plates dorsally and laterally on the thoracic segments; the small spiracles are black.
Foodplants. The roots of bracken and possibly grasses.
Habits. This insect has a two-year life-cycle, with the larval stage lasting from July, overwintering twice, until about late May. It is spent entirely underground, feeding on the roots of bracken, and the pupa is also subterranean, being formed close to the ground surface and lasting for about three weeks. The adult insect inhabits open woodland and commons, emerging in June, with the females scattering their eggs over bracken while on the wing. The larvae can be obtained by carefully scraping off the soil around new bracken shoots, often by the side of paths, during April and early May before the vegetation becomes too dense to work. Local, but widely distributed, over much of the British Isles, being most frequent in the south.
Plate 1: C. Found under soil by young bracken, fully grown. Late April.

Common Swift
Hepialus lupulinus Linnaeus
Larva. 20–25 mm. Body greyish-white and glossy, with the head reddish-brown and prothoracic plate orange; each segment has several dark hairs that grow from a very small orange wart; the spiracles are dark brown.
Foodplants. The roots of various wild and cultivated plants, such as grasses, dock, etc.
Habits. One- or two-year cycle, with the larval stage lasting from July to about mid-May, living and feeding mainly underground, but sometimes to be found wandering after dark, probably to find new food when existing supply is exhausted. The pupa is also formed beneath the soil and lasts for about a month, with the adults emerging from late May to July. The dusk-flying females scatter their eggs at random over the herbage. This species can often be a pest of cultivated plants in the garden. Common and widespread throughout most of the British Isles.
Plate 1: D. Dug from grass roots, nearly fully grown. Mid-March.

Map-winged Swift
Hepialus fusconebulosa DeGeer
Larva. 30–35 mm. Body yellowish-white, with the head reddish or purplish-brown, thoracic plates orange and the body warts orange with a short bristle; the large spiracles are black.
Foodplants. The roots and lower stems of bracken, and probably the roots of other plants.
Habits. A subterranean larva, taking two years to develop. The larvae become fully grown in mid-May and pupation takes place just below the surface in a flimsy silken cocoon.

The adults fly in June and July and, as with all members of *Hepialidae*, the females lay their eggs while on the wing, dropping them randomly to the ground among the plants. More frequent in the northern counties of the British Isles, preferring moors, hills and open woodland.
Plate 1: E. Found in soil by young bracken, fully grown. Mid-May. (PQW)

Family: COSSIDAE

The larvae of the three resident members of this family are equipped with powerful jaws and live within the wood or pith of the foodplants. The larval period is at least two years, possibly up to five, although *C. cossus* is regularly forced in captivity by offering softer food alternatives. The males of these species come freely to light, but females of *P. castaneae* and *Z. pyrina* are usually unresponsive.

SUBFAMILY: ZEUZERINAE

Reed Leopard
Phragmataecia castaneae Hübner
(*arundinis* Hübner)
Larva. 40–50 mm. Body dirty whitish, with purplish-brown subdorsal stripes; the head is flat and purplish-brown; prothoracic plate pale brown.
Foodplant. The rootstocks and lower stems of common reed.
Habits. A two-year life-cycle spent inside the roots and lower stems of the foodplant. The larvae become fully grown in May and pupate inside the reed stem, the adults emerging during June. The females lay their eggs in batches on the foodplant and they take about three weeks to hatch, the young larvae boring into the plant. A very local species occurring mainly in the fens of East Anglia.
Plate 1: F. Courtesy of David Wilson.

Leopard Moth
Zeuzera pyrina Linnaeus
Larva. 40–55 mm. Body pale yellow and glossy, with the head dark brown to black and paler in the centre; prothoracic plate and warts very dark brown.
Foodplants. The insides of the stems and branches of sallow, lilac, apple, ash, black currant and cherry. Also recorded from other plants and may cause damage to fruit trees.
Habits. This species spends two or three years as a larva, becoming fully grown about late April. It pupates under the bark during May and this stage lasts for about three to six weeks. The larva can sometimes be found by pulling at dying branches of the foodplant, which may crack to reveal the insect within the wood. It is widely distributed in most of England south of Yorkshire, also occurring in eastern Wales.
Plate 1: G. Found inside split sallow branch, nearly fully grown. Early February.

SUBFAMILY: COSSINAE

Goat Moth
Cossus cossus Linnaeus
Larva. 90–100 mm. Body shining reddish-purple, becoming paler to pink on the sides. The head and prothoracic plate are glossy black and the spiracles are also black.
Foodplants. Insides of the trunks and branches of birch, willow, ash, poplar, oak, apple and many other deciduous trees.
Habits. In the wild the larval stage can take up to five years to be completed. Very young larvae (15–20 mm) can be found just under the bark of suitable trees and then fed up much faster in captivity by using apples or uncooked beetroot and carrot as a softer food substitute. These captive larvae can grow to full size in about six months and then should be kept outside for overwintering and eventual pupation in soil, rotten wood or sawdust placed in their plastic or metal container. In nature the larvae develop slowly, leaving the host tree during the late summer months to wander and find a pupation site, and have frequently been recorded crossing paths during this dispersal period. They spin a strong cocoon under the soil and spend their final winter still as larvae. The pupa is finally formed during May and lasts until the adult emergence period in late June and July. This species is local, but widely distributed, over most of Britain and Ireland.
Plate 1: H. Located under birch bark when very small. Mid-January. Growth completed in captivity by August, using only apples.

Family: ZYGAENIDAE

The British fauna is represented by ten species of moths belonging to this family. The adults are all day-flying and most active in warm sunshine, when they visit flowers to feed. In captivity the females will deposit eggs freely and the slug-shaped larvae of most are not difficult to rear, especially if kept in tubs of growing foodplant. The larvae of the genus *Adscita* graze upon the epidermis of the foodplant leaves, and can be located by the damage caused. Some species of Burnet are capable of overwintering twice. The pupae are usually enclosed in a tough papery cocoon, which in most species is formed low down in plant litter.

SUBFAMILY: PROCRIDINAE

Scarce Forester
Adscita globulariae Hübner
Larva. 12–15 mm. Body pale greyish-brown, with a broad greyish band dorsally, centred by a dark grey incomplete stripe. Head, prothoracic and anal plates all brownish-black; body covered in many white setae.
Foodplants. Common knapweed and greater knapweed.
Habits. Single-brooded, feeding from July to the following May. It has the habit of burrowing between the top and bottom epidermis of the leaves to feed within, causing blotch marks which often give away the location of the insect near to the damage. In June the day-flying adults can be taken and the females induced to lay eggs on potted foodplants. The larvae should then be left outside on potted plants in a sunny place to complete their growth naturally. Distribution of this species seems to be confined to the calcareous areas of Sussex, Gloucestershire, Kent and Wiltshire, where it is very local.
Plate 1: I. Located by close searching, fully grown. Mid-May. (TJD)

Cistus Forester
Adscita geryon Hübner
Larva. 10–13 mm. Body purplish-brown, with a broad pale yellow or cream band dorsally, centred with a bold dark

stripe. Head black and the prothoracic and anal plates very dark blackish-brown; setae dull white.
Foodplant. Common rock-rose.
Habits. A single-brooded species, with the larvae occurring from July to the following May, feeding at first by mining the leaves and later externally, eating the lower surface and leaving the top intact. When fully grown in the spring, the whole of the tiny leaves of their foodplant are consumed. The larvae can be found by close searching or bred from the egg stage by collecting the day-flying females in June and July and introducing them to potted foodplants. This species is locally distributed on calcareous soils from central southern England and northwards as far as Durham.
Plate 1: J. Bred from a netted female adult. Late June. (AJP)

The Forester
Adscita statices Linnaeus
Larva. 12–15 mm. Body variable from pale green to yellowish-green or pinkish-grey to dirty white. Dorsal stripe dull yellowish-green or pinkish-brown; head black and prothoracic plate very dark brown; setae light grey to white.
Foodplant. Common sorrel.
Habits. Single-brooded, being in the larval stage from July to the following May, mining the leaves at first, then grazing the underside and later, before overwintering, feeding on the whole leaf low down on the foodplant. The larvae can be found during May by searching for signs of damage to the larger older leaves. The cocooned pupa is formed low down in the herbage, lasting about three weeks, and the adults can be taken by day for breeding on potted plants. This species is widely distributed, but local, from southern England to Inverness-shire in Scotland, in damp meadows, open woodland and on calcareous hillsides.
Plate 1: K. Bred from a netted female adult. Early July. (JR)

SUBFAMILY: ZYGAENINAE

Scotch Burnet
Zygaena exulans Hohenwarth
Larva. 15–20 mm. Body dark velvety greenish-black, with conspicuous yellow spots subdorsally, two on each abdominal segment. The head is black and the setae almost black.
Foodplants. Crowberry; also recorded on bilberry and cowberry.
Habits. Single-brooded, in the larval stage from August to May, with some individuals taking two years to mature. They mainly feed on the terminal shoots and unripe berries of the foodplant and can readily be found by careful searching. They can be fed up in captivity on bird's-foot trefoil. Care must be taken to separate out larvae that are about to pupate upon supplied heather stems, as they are liable to damage each other when they spin up their cocoons. So far this species has been found only above 700 m on a few mountains in Aberdeenshire.
Plate 1: L. Found by searching, fully grown. Mid-May. (BS)

Slender Scotch Burnet
Zygaena loti Denis & Schiffermüller
Larva. 15–18 mm. Body dull greyish-green, paler on the sides, with four black and two yellow spots on the side of each segment; head black and setae pale grey.
Foodplant. Bird's-foot trefoil.
Habits. A single-brooded species that occurs as a larva from July to the following late May, sometimes overwintering twice. Eggs can be obtained from the day-flying female adults in June and July, and in captivity the larvae are fairly easy to rear on potted foodplant, but should be protected from frost during the winter. The pupa is formed in a cocoon, spun up on the ground. Larvae can also be found by careful searching during May in the known localities. At present this species is only found on grassy slopes by the sea lochs on the islands of Mull and Ulva, where it can be locally common.
Plate 1: M. Bred from a netted female adult. Early July. (AJP)

New Forest Burnet
Zygaena viciae Denis & Schiffermüller
Larva. 14–16 mm. Body bright green, speckled with minute black dots; the dorsal line is whitish and conspicuous, the subdorsal lines are also whitish and there is a conspicuous yellow spot posteriorly on each segment; head black and the setae white.
Foodplants. Bird's-foot trefoil and meadow vetchling.
Habits. Single-brooded, with the larvae feeding from late July to the following early June, and making their cocoons low down among the surrounding herbage, near to the ground. The original British subspecies, which occurred in the New Forest, has been extinct since 1927. The moth has so far been rediscovered in only one small coastal site in Argyllshire, where in some years the population can be extremely small. Quite justifiably, it is protected from collecting by law, but it may possibly remain undetected in other suitable sites elsewhere in Britain.
Plate 1: N. Bred from a female adult found at rest. Early July. (BS)

Six-spot Burnet
Zygaena filipendulae Linnaeus
Larva. 18–22 mm. Body greenish-yellow or yellow, with two large black dorsal spots on either side of each segment, the posterior pair smaller and more elongate. A yellow spot on each segment between the dorsal row and another row of black spots along the side of the larva. Head black and setae short, black or white. Forms heavily marked with larger black blotches are frequent.
Foodplant. Bird's-foot trefoil.
Habits. Single-brooded, occurring as a larva from September to early June, overwintering, sometimes twice, among plant debris. From about mid-May the fully grown larvae that are about to pupate and the cocoons are very noticeable in their exposed positions, such as on grass stems, etc. The adult females taken during July and August readily lay eggs and broods can be successfully reared on potted foodplants. This species is one of the most common of the Burnets and also the most widely distributed, being found throughout England and on the coasts of Scotland and Wales.
Plate 1: O. Found by searching, fully grown. Late May.

Five-spot Burnet
Zygaena trifolii Esper
Larva. 16–20 mm. Body pale whitish-green, often with a yellowish tint; dorsally there are two rows of black spots with a pair on each segment, the anterior of the pair much larger and subquadrate. An inconspicuous pale yellow spot between the dorsal marks and another row of black spots along the sides; head black and setae mainly whitish and short.
Foodplants. Bird's-foot trefoil or greater bird's-foot trefoil.
Habits. Two subspecies of this insect, both single-brooded, occur in Britain, each with a different ecology. Ssp. *palustrella*

inhabits chalk downland and the adults fly from late May to mid-June. The larva feeds low down upon bird's-foot trefoil from late June to early May, and it can be found by careful searching around the lower parts of clumps of the foodplant during the last few days of April to very early May. The tough cocoon is usually well hidden in the herbage close to the ground. Ssp. *decreta* flies between late June and early August and tends to live in marshy areas such as wet meadows, moorland and sometimes coastal cliffs, and is of a mainly western distribution. Its larva is seemingly identical to the downland race, but the development runs about three to four weeks later in all stages. Also it uses the greater bird's-foot trefoil as its foodplant and forms its cocoon high up on the stems of vegetation growing in its habitats.
Plate 1: P. (ssp. *palustrella*) found by close searching underneath the foodplant during the day, fully grown. Early May.

Narrow-bordered Five-spot Burnet

Zygaena lonicerae Scheven
Larva. 17–22 mm. Body pale whitish-green, with two rows of black spots dorsally and other rows of black markings along the sides, between which is a fairly conspicuous yellow spot posteriorly on each segment. The head is black and the setae are very long compared with allied species.
Foodplants. Red clover and meadow vetchling, but also other clovers, vetches and trefoils.
Habits. Single-brooded, occurring as a larva from late July to the following June. The larvae are usually easily found in the spring due to their habit of resting exposed on the foodplant or surrounding vegetation when fully grown. The cocoon is also very obvious, being spun up high on grass stems, etc., with the pupal stage lasting about three to four weeks. The adults fly in sunshine during late June and July, with most females laying readily in captivity. The easiest method to rear them from the egg is on potted foodplant, with dry grass and leaves on the soil for overwintering. This species is widely distributed, and often locally common, over much of England, but apparently absent from the south-western counties and much of Wales.
Plate 1: Q. Swept by day from clover, fully grown. Mid-June. (SHC)

Transparent Burnet

Zygaena purpuralis Brunnich
Larva. 15–18 mm. Body dark olive-green, with a very narrow yellowish dorsal line and two rows of indistinct black spots situated subdorsally at the front of each segment, with a dull yellow spot below. The head is black and the setae mainly pale grey.
Foodplant. Wild thyme.
Habits. A single-brooded insect, being in the larval stage from early July to late May, sometimes overwintering twice. The larvae feed low down on the foodplant and can be located when fully grown by careful searching. Stocks from adult moths can be successfully bred by introducing the newly hatched larvae on to thyme growing on garden rockeries and constructing a netting frame over the brood, then leaving them undisturbed until the following spring. The cocooned pupa is formed during late May near to the ground, and is well hidden, lasting about two to three weeks. This species is locally common on the islands of the Inner Hebrides, a few sites on the western Scottish mainland and in western Ireland.
Plate 1: R. Bred from netted female adult. Mid-June. (CH)

Family: LIMACODIDAE

The woodlouse-like larvae of the two resident species of this family feed on tree leaves and overwinter still as larvae within boat-shaped cocoons spun up on the foodplant. The adults fly at night during the summer months and both sexes are responsive to light. They are restricted in distribution, occurring only in southern England.

The Festoon

Apoda limacodes Hufnagel
(*avellana* Linnaeus)
Larva. 13–16 mm. Body bright bluish-green, covered in minute yellow spots and shaped like a woodlouse. Raised ridges subdorsally, with a complete yellow stripe which is edged with purplish-red spots. The whitish-green head is small and retractile and the prolegs are absent, being replaced by sucker-like structures.
Foodplants. Oak and beech.
Habits. A single-brooded species, the larva of which feeds from July to early October on the upperside of the leaves of its foodplants and can be readily obtained by beating. When fully fed the larva constructs a reddish-brown cocoon attached to the top of a leaf and then overwinters within, not changing into a pupa until the following May. On warm nights during June and July adult females may come to light, and can be induced to lay eggs by using oak leaves as a stimulus. The very small larvae can be difficult to rear, but once they have passed their first instar, seem to settle and thrive. This moth is locally common in mature woodland and on commons in south-eastern England.
Plate 2: A. Bred from female adult to MVL. Early July. (BS)

The Triangle

Heterogenea asella Denis & Schiffermüller
Larva. 10–12 mm. Body pale yellowish-green, with a broad olive-brown diamond-shaped marking dorsally which extends from the head to the anal segment; woodlouse-shaped.
Foodplants. Oak and beech.
Habits. Single-brooded, feeding from about late July to September or even October, usually on the upper surface of the leaf. When fully fed it constructs a hull-shaped cocoon in which to spend the winter, until it is ready to pupate in the following spring. This species seems to be very difficult to breed from the egg, as most of the tiny larvae refuse to feed and quickly die of starvation. They can be obtained by beating, but only infrequently, which probably indicates that they live and feed high in the canopy, well out of reach. The larva moves strangely, gliding over the leaves on the sucker-like prolegs, and the tiny head is retracted into the first segment when resting. Very locally distributed in a few mature woods in Kent, Hampshire, Wiltshire, Buckinghamshire, Oxfordshire, Lincolnshire and Sussex.
Plate 2: B. Beaten from oak, fully grown. Late September. (GAC)

Family: SESIIDAE

This family, commonly known as the clearwings, is represented in the British Isles by thirteen resident species. All the adults fly in sunshine and those of some species are very elusive. The maggot-like larvae live and feed within the wood and pith of their particular foodplants, and obtaining the insect at this stage is often the best way to become familiar with these interesting moths. Locating many of these larvae is not difficult, as most give external signs such as capped emergence holes and larval frass extruding from the plant. Both the larvae and the pupae require fairly damp conditions for successful development, but care should be taken to avoid the growth of moulds, and they must not be disturbed from within the taken piece of foodplant.

SUBFAMILY: SESIINAE

Hornet Moth

Sesia apiformis Clerck

Larva. 28–33 mm. Body yellowish-white, plump and robust, with a faint darker dorsal vessel. The head is shining chestnut-brown and the prothoracic plate yellowish.

Foodplant. The inner wood of poplars, especially black poplar.

Habits. Life-cycle lasts for at least two years, feeding and burrowing between the bark and the wood low down in the trunk or in the roots of the host tree. To search for this species, first detect the old emergence holes (about 8 mm in diameter) from previous years, then carefully remove loose bark near the base of the trunk and sift through the nearby soil to find the fully grown larvae, which sometimes wander a few feet. They spend the last winter and early spring in a cocoon constructed from silk and wood particles and pupate therein during April. Cocooned pupae taken into captivity must be kept moist to avoid desiccation. A local species, being found mainly in south-east England and southern Ireland.

Plate 2: C. Found inside overwintering cocoon from behind the lower bark of black poplar, fully grown. Late January.

Lunar Hornet Moth

Sesia bembeciformis Hübner

Larva. 27–30 mm. Body wrinkled and yellowish-white, with a faint darker dorsal vessel. Head chestnut-brown and prothoracic plate pale yellowish. Seemingly identical to *S. apiformis*.

Foodplants. The inner wood of various species of sallow, occasionally willow and poplar.

Habits. At least a two-year life-cycle, living inside the lower trunk and roots of larger mature sallows. As the larvae become fully grown they bore deeper into the wood and tend to occur about 25–50 cm from the base of the tree. Visible signs of infested sallows are old emergence holes and frass below the bark and on the ground under the tree. During late winter and early spring careful searching should reveal capped tunnels leading to the surface of the bark, behind which the larva will pupate and eventually emerge as an adult moth in July. Widely distributed throughout most of the British Isles.

Plate 2: D. Detected by cutting open infested sallow trunk at ground level, fully grown. Late March. (AJP)

SUBFAMILY: PARANTHRENINAE

Dusky Clearwing

Paranthrene tabaniformis Rottemburg

Larva. 22–25 mm. Body yellowish-white, with a blackish-brown head and prothoracic plate (MBGBI).

Foodplants. The inner stems of poplars, aspen, sallow and sea buckthorn.

Habits. This species, which has not been seen in Britain since 1924, has a life-cycle lasting two years and has never been recorded in this country in the immature stages. It occurred formerly in very small numbers in south-east England; those recorded from Kent were possibly associated with poplar and in Essex it was suspected to be breeding on aspen. Abroad the range covers most of western Europe.

Currant Clearwing

Synanthedon tipuliformis Clerck
(*salmachus* Linnaeus)

Larva. 15–18 mm. Body dull white with a yellowish tinge, dorsal vessel faint and greyish. Head light brown and the prothorax weakly sclerotized and marked with two light brown diagonal streaks.

Foodplants. The insides of the stems of black currant, red currant and sometimes gooseberry.

Habits. Life-cycle probably lasting two years, perhaps taking only one year occasionally. When fully grown the larvae can often be found in the stems of the foodplant feeding on the pith. The external signs of infestation include frass appearing on pruned stem ends and in cracks in the bark, old exit holes from previous seasons and poor leaf growth on stems that may be internally damaged. Widespread over most of England and Wales, but less common than it has been in the past.

Plate 2: E. Found inside 15 mm thick black currant stem, 60 cm from the ground, fully grown. Late April. (MB)

Yellow-legged Clearwing

Synanthedon vespiformis Linnaeus

Larva. 18–21 mm. Body dull brownish-white and with the greyish insides showing through the transparent skin. The head is reddish-brown and the prothoracic segment lightly sclerotized with two faint oblique lines of the same colour as the head.

Foodplants. The inner bark of stumps of newly cut oak; sometimes recorded from birch, beech, elm, cherry and sweet chestnut.

Habits. Probably a one-year life-cycle. The female adults prefer to lay upon freshly cut stumps, but will also continue to use these for one or two more years thereafter. Visible signs of inhabited wood include frass appearing from splits in the bark and between the bark and main wood on the top of the stump. When located the fully grown larvae and cocoons can be extracted by carefully prising off the outer bark in the spring, then keeping the wood and insects in a container with dampish sand in the bottom, to await emergence of the adults from late May onwards. Generally distributed and reasonably common over most of the south of England and in the midland counties as far north as Yorkshire.

Plate 2: F. Found behind bark on an oak stump, about two years after felling, fully grown. Late April. (SHC)

White-barred Clearwing

Synanthedon spheciformis Denis & Schiffermüller

Larva. 25–28 mm. Body dull white with a pinkish tinge, dorsal vessel faint, but visible. The head is dark reddish-brown and shining and the prothoracic segment has two obtuse brown marks.

Foodplants. The inner wood of birch and alder.

Habits. At least a two-year life-cycle, possibly three. Lives inside the lower parts of the foodplant, usually in suckers or young trees, but mature specimens or cut stumps can also be inhabited. The best way to locate this larva is, in April, to find the frass which extrudes from the wood to form small piles at the base of the tree. Then the emergence hole (5 mm diameter) can be found by using a wire brush upon the suspected area of bark to confirm the insect's presence. Local

on heathland and marshy areas in southern England and the West Midlands.
Plate 2: G. Found inside young birch (12 cm thick) close to the ground, fully grown. Late April.

Welsh Clearwing

Synanthedon scoliaeformis Borkhausen
Larva. 27–30 mm. Body dull whitish, with a few tiny brown marks on the sides near to the brown-ringed spiracles. The head is reddish-brown and the prothoracic segment dull orange with two darker marks.
Foodplant. The inner bark of old birch trees.
Habits. Probably a three-year life-cycle, feeding and tunnelling behind the bark of large mature birches, usually at about head height. It can be found by locating the old exit holes which are normally quite obvious, and then using a wire brush to remove the lichens and thin outer bark behind which inhabited mines may be revealed. At present this species seems to occur only in Perthshire, in southern Ireland and in North Wales (where it was first discovered), but possibly exists elsewhere in suitable localities.
Plate 2: H. Obtained from behind bark of a very old tree, nearly fully grown. Early October. (BS)

Sallow Clearwing

Synanthedon flaviventris Staudinger
Larva. 16–20 mm. Body dull yellowish-white. Head yellowish-brown and prothoracic segment yellowish with two diagonal brown streaks.
Foodplants. The insides of the stems and twigs of various sallows.
Habits. A two-year life-cycle, with the fully grown larvae and adult moths only occurring in even-numbered years. They are fairly easy to locate during winter and spring by searching stems between 10 to 15 mm thick, looking for swellings indicating possible damage from larvae feeding within. These stems can then be cut and placed in damp sand to await the emergence of the moths during July or even earlier indoors. Many inhabited galls will turn out to be the longhorn beetle, *Saperda populnea*, which is known to produce very similar swellings in sallow stems. Generally distributed over most of southern England.
Plate 2: I. Found inside stem, fully grown. Mid-February.

Orange-tailed Clearwing

Synanthedon andrenaeformis Laspeyres
(*anthraciniformis* Esper)
Larva. 18–21 mm. Body pale yellowish-white. The head is yellowish-brown and the prothorax lightly sclerotized.
Foodplants. The inner stems of wayfaring-tree and also guelder-rose.
Habits. The life-cycle lasts at least two years, feeding on the central pith of its foodplant when fully grown. During the winter and early spring the larvae can be located by searching for caps constructed over the emergence holes. These are about 5–7 mm in diameter and sunken slightly below the level of the surrounding bark. Sometimes these well-camouflaged caps fall out to reveal the exit hole, which may be plugged with the yellowish frass produced by the larva. If the larva is to be kept, it should be remembered that the stems, normally about 10–40 mm in diameter, must be cut at least 10 cm below the cap as the insect should be in this section. A local species mainly inhabiting downland and wood-edges in southern England.
Plate 2: J. Found inside stem, fully grown. Early March.

Red-belted Clearwing

Synanthedon myopaeformis Borkhausen
Larva. 15–18 mm. Body dirty yellowish-white and tinged brownish. Head shining reddish-brown and prothorax lightly sclerotized with a brownish anterior.
Foodplants. The inner bark of crab apple and cultivated apple; also recorded from pear, cherry, rowan and hawthorn.
Habits. The life-cycle lasts probably only one year and favoured trees may be used for many years. Visible signs of inhabitation are old exit holes, empty pupa cases and small amounts of reddish-brown frass, which collect in bark crevices from the winter to early spring. The adults fly during June and these can be boxed while resting on the host trees during the evening. Widespread and locally common in most of the southern half of England.
Plate 2: K. Located under loose cherry bark on an old roadside tree, nearly fully grown. Early December. (M&JH)

Red-tipped Clearwing

Synanthedon formicaeformis Esper
Larva. 16–20 mm. Body yellowish-white, with the dorsal vessel greyish and more obvious on the middle segments. The head is dark brown and the prothoracic segment lightly sclerotized, with two faint diagonal marks.
Foodplants. The insides of the stems and trunks of osiers, also less often other species of sallow and willow.
Habits. Probably a one-year life-cycle. They can be difficult to locate due to the very little external sign caused by the feeding larvae. Sometimes frass can be found in broken stems or at the edge of a stump and occasionally the foodplant reacts by forming a gall-swelling similar to that made by the larva of *S. flaviventris*. This species occurs in damp areas, most often in southern England and more rarely in the north; also recorded from Wales and the south of Ireland.
Plate 2: L. Found inside osier stem, fully grown. Mid-April. (MP)

Large Red-belted Clearwing

Synanthedon culiciformis Linnaeus
Larva. 17–20 mm. Body dull white and the head reddish-brown and shining. The prothoracic plate is very light yellowish-brown, with two brown diagonal streaks.
Foodplants. The inner bark and wood of birch and occasionally alder.
Habits. Probably a two-year life-cycle. The larvae are fairly easy to locate in birch stumps that have been cut within the previous two to four years, and visible signs include old exit holes and frass extruding from between the inner bark and the main wood of the stump. The cocoons are normally about 3–8 cm down from the exit hole and careful removal of the bark should reveal the larvae or pupae attached to the inside surface. Heathland and open woods are the preferred habitats of this species, which occurs over most of England and Wales, but is more local in Scotland.
Plate 2: M. Located behind bark in a birch stump about 20–25 cm in diameter, fully grown. Early April. (SHC)

Six-belted Clearwing

Bembecia scopigera Scopoli
(*ichneumoniformis* Denis & Schiffermüller)
Larva. 13–16 mm. Body greyish-white and transparent. Head light brown and mottled; dorsal vessel greyish.
Foodplants. The roots of bird's-foot trefoil and kidney vetch; also recorded from horseshoe vetch.
Habits. Feeds from late July to the following early June inside the roots of clumps of the foodplant and is difficult to

locate. Examining isolated plants or those at the edge of more extensive growth is more likely to produce results when searching for larvae. Inhabited roots may be indicated by the presence of frass within or alongside. The adults fly in sunshine during July. Distributed mainly over southern England on chalky soils; colonies also occur in South Wales and in east Yorkshire.
Plate 2: N. Found in the main root of bird's-foot trefoil, fully grown. Late May. (SHC)

Thrift Clearwing

Bembecia muscaeformis Esper
Larva. 11–15 mm. Body yellowish-white with a faintly visible dorsal vessel which appears brownish. The head is reddish-brown and the prothorax pale brown.
Foodplant. The crowns and roots of thrift.
Habits. A one-year life-cycle, normally feeding inside isolated plants growing in rock crevices. Breaking apart sickly looking plants will sometimes reveal the larvae, which sometimes produce small patches of reddish-coloured frass upon the cushions of thrift. During July the adults fly in sunshine and are attracted to the flowers of thrift and thyme. This species is coastal in distribution, occurring only in western England and in Wales, Scotland and Ireland.
Plate 2: O. Found inside crown of foodplant, fully grown. Late May. (SHC)

Fiery Clearwing

Bembecia chrysidiformis Esper
Larva. 18–21 mm. Body dull white and semi-transparent, showing the grey dorsal vessel. The head is chestnut-brown and the prothoracic segment pale yellowish and wider than the head.
Foodplants. The roots of curled dock, water dock and common sorrel.
Habits. The life-cycle lasts two years, with the larvae feeding inside the larger roots of the foodplant. Larvae are often obtained by searching for sickly looking plants during late April and any isolated plants can be more productive. For breeding, these inhabited roots should be replanted in pots to await the emergence of the adults during late June and July. At present this species seems to be found only on the sea-cliffs of Kent, where it is local and uncommon.
Plate 2: P. Found inside the roots of a dock plant, fully grown. Early May. (RD)

Family: HESPERIIDAE

There are eight resident species of Skipper butterflies occurring within the British Isles and the larvae of most of them feed mainly at night on various grasses. These grass feeders possess an anal comb which ejects the frass away from the larval tent. All the species normally have only one generation in a season, but both the Dingy and Grizzled Skipper have been known to produce a second brood under favourable conditions.

SUBFAMILY: HESPERIINAE

Chequered Skipper

Carterocephalus palaemon Pallas
Larva. 22–26 mm. During the early instars the larva is greenish-grey with black marks dorsally. As the larva grows this changes to a whitish-green body and stripes of darker green and white. By the time the larva is fully grown and ready for hibernation it has changed again to straw colour with a darker grey line along the back.
Foodplants. Purple moor-grass, false-brome and tor-grass.
Habits. Single-brooded. The larval stage lasts from about late June to the following April, the insect living at first inside a tube it has constructed by drawing together a grass blade and emerging to feed on the adjacent parts of the same blade. When the food supply is exhausted it moves to another blade and continues the same habits. During October the fully grown larva draws together three or four grass blades and binds them to each other with silk to form the hibernaculum in which it will spend the winter. In early spring it will leave its winter quarters to pupate among loosely spun dry grass, with the adults emerging from the last few days of May to late June. The larva can be found by sweeping at night during August and September or by close searching of the foodplant, looking for signs of feeding and the tube in which it rests. This species used to be found in woods of the midland counties, but died out in the mid-1970s. It still occurs in good numbers in the open birch woodland of western Scotland.
Plate 3: A. Bred from netted female adult and reared on a potted foodplant of purple moor-grass. Early June. (NL)

Small Skipper

Thymelicus sylvestris Poda
Larva. 21–25 mm. Body grass-green, with whitish-green lines along the subdorsal area and the edges of the darker green dorsal line; the posterior parts of the segments are yellowish-green; head yellowish-green, with a faint darker stripe down the centre.
Foodplants. False-brome, Yorkshire-fog, creeping soft-grass and timothy, also probably other grasses.
Habits. Single-brooded, overwintering as a tiny larva within the grass sheath in which the eggs were laid. In the spring feeding commences, with the larva living inside a tube that it has constructed by using silk to draw together the edges of a blade of grass and emerging to feed mainly at night. When larger the larvae can easily be swept during day or night. The pupa lasts about three weeks, with the adults flying from late June to late July. Widely distributed and often common in grassy places over most of Wales, and in England south of Yorkshire.
Plate 3: B. Swept by day from Yorkshire-fog, fully grown. Early June.

Essex Skipper

Thymelicus lineola Ochsenheimer
Larva. 20–24 mm. Body grass-green, with whitish-green lines, being very similar to *T. sylvestris*. Easily separated by the obvious brown and white stripes upon the head.
Foodplants. Cock's-foot, creeping soft-grass and probably other species of grass.
Habits. A single-brooded species that overwinters as a fully formed larva still inside the egg and hatches in the spring. Most of the larval development is similar in habits to *T. sylvestris*, living inside a tube formed of a grass blade. The larva can be located by careful searching and can easily be swept as it becomes fully grown. The pupa is formed among a grass sheath and lasts about three weeks, the adults flying from early July to about mid-August. This grassland species is to be found in most of southern and eastern England; also recorded in Cornwall.
Plate 3: C. Swept by day from cock's-foot, fully grown. Mid-June.

Lulworth Skipper

Thymelicus acteon Rottemburg

Larva. 22–26 mm. Body green, with darker bluish-green lines along the dorsal and subdorsal areas which are edged faintly with whitish-green. The head is also green with two thin yellowish-white streaks.

Foodplants. Tor-grass, and in captivity will accept annual meadow-grass and couch.

Habits. Single-brooded, overwintering as a tiny larva at the place where the egg was laid within a grass sheath. In April it finds a blade of fresh tor-grass and makes a tube by drawing together with silk the edges of that blade. At first it feeds above the tube and then later below, taking out small notches from the margin of the inhabited blade. This habit can be used as a guide when searching for this species. Feeding takes place mainly at night and during this time the larvae can be swept, when larger. The pupae are formed from early June and the adult insect is on the wing from about late June to the middle of August. The distribution is seemingly restricted to the coasts of Dorset, South Devon and Cornwall.

Plate 3: D. Swept at dusk, fully grown. Mid-June.

Silver-spotted Skipper

Hesperia comma Linnaeus

Larva. 23–27 mm. Body dull greyish-olive and grub-like. The head is almost black with two thin orangish lines.

Foodplant. Sheep's-fescue.

Habits. A single-brooded species. After overwintering as an egg, the young larva spins together some fine grass blades of the foodplant and lives within its domicile, very close to the ground. Trying to locate larvae in the wild is very difficult, as the larval tent blends in well with the surrounding grasses. The larvae become fully grown in late June and pupate inside a cocoon spun low down. The adults begin to emerge during late July and linger on, in good seasons, until early September. To breed this species in captivity, a fertile female should be put on to a potted plant, where eggs will normally be laid readily. They must be left outside on the plant in a sunny place through the winter and left to their own devices. Locally distributed, mainly on calcareous soils, in south-eastern England.

Plate 3: E. Bred from a netted female adult. Early August.

Large Skipper

Ochlodes venata Bremer & Grey
(*sylvanus* Esper)

Larva. 26–29 mm. Body dark bluish-green, covered in very short brown bristles. The dorsal line is dark green and the head is large, dull whitish-brown and edged with dark brown.

Foodplants. Cock's-foot, false-brome and probably other wide-bladed grasses.

Habits. Single-brooded, overwintering as a half-grown larva. It feeds slowly from July to about September mainly at night. By day it rests inside a tube made by securing the edges of the grass blade together with silk. When it stops feeding, prior to hibernation, it constructs a more robust tube in which to remain until the following late April. During the spring the larger larvae will utilize several grass blades to form their tubes. At this time of year larvae can sometimes be swept at night when they have left their tubes to feed. The species occurs in the pupal stage from early June, lasting about two to three weeks, with the adult insects flying from about mid-June to late July. This species is generally distributed throughout most of England, Wales and south-west Scotland, inhabiting grassy places.

Plate 3: F. Swept at night, fully grown. Early June. (SHC)

SUBFAMILY: PYRGINAE

Dingy Skipper

Erynnis tages Linnaeus

Larva. 16–20 mm. Body dull yellowish-green, covered with whitish setae, dorsal line slightly darker and spiracles reddish-brown. The large head is brown and purplish.

Foodplants. Bird's-foot trefoil, greater bird's-foot trefoil and horseshoe vetch.

Habits. Single-brooded, with an occasional partial second brood in warmer seasons and in sheltered southern localities. The larvae feed low down on the leaves of the foodplant in a loose spinning and can often be found by careful searching during July and August. When fully grown most larvae construct a hibernaculum in which they remain unchanged until the following April. Pupation then takes place and lasts for about two to three weeks. The main brood of adults flies during late May and June and the females lay eggs readily on potted foodplant. Widely distributed on open ground throughout much of England and Wales; more local in Scotland and Ireland.

Plate 3: G. Bred on potted bird's-foot trefoil, from a netted female adult. Early June. (AH)

Grizzled Skipper

Pyrgus malvae Linnaeus

Larva. 17–19 mm. Body light greenish-yellow and totally covered with short fine whitish bristles, with a thin brownish dorsal stripe and dark olive subdorsal lines; head blackish-brown with obvious setae.

Foodplants. Wild strawberry, silverweed, creeping cinquefoil and tormentil. In captivity it will eat bramble and raspberry.

Habits. Mostly a single-brooded species, with the adults flying in May and June. From about mid-June the newly hatched larva lives and feeds on the upper surface of the foodplant leaf beneath a silken web. As it grows larger the young larva will venture out from its tent to feed nearby and then change its leaf as the food becomes exhausted. By the third instar it is forced because of its size to roll a complete leaf or utilize more than one to stay hidden. Feeding usually takes place during the evenings or early in the morning. During August the fully grown larva makes a loose cocoon low down in the herbage and pupates. Searching for larvae is possible but time consuming, and to breed this species in any quantity a fertile female should be taken for obtaining eggs. Widely distributed on downs, waste land and in woodland rides over central and southern England; more local in the south-western counties, Wales and East Anglia.

Plate 3: H. Bred from netted female adult. Late May. (MG-P)

Family: PAPILIONIDAE

The solitary British resident example of this family is now to be found only locally in the fens and marshes of Norfolk and the larva is unlikely to be mistaken for any other species. It possesses a unique structure, known as the osmeterium, which is eversible and situated upon the top of the first segment. The larva displays this fleshy orange structure when alarmed and it emits a smell that has been described as similar to rotten pineapple.

SUBFAMILY: PAPILIONINAE

The Swallowtail

Papilio machaon Linnaeus

Larva. 40–50 mm. Body whitish-green, with a black band anteriorly on each segment and another, spotted with orange, centrally on each segment. Head yellowish-green marked with black. Young larvae are black with a white marking dorsally and have small warts with setae.

Foodplants. Milk parsley and wild angelica; also other umbellifers, including cultivated carrot leaves in captivity.

Habits. Mainly single-brooded, being found from June to early August, and again in late August and September in good years. In the first three instars the young larva mimics a bird-dropping and rests on the top of the leaves. Later the larvae can readily be found due to their large size on the small leaves of the foodplants. The overwintering pupa is formed upon upright plant stems and can be green or buff with darker markings. The adult females, which mostly fly during late May and June, will readily deposit eggs in spacious breeding cages furnished with foodplant and nectar sources. The British subspecies of this insect can be found, still in good numbers, only in the Norfolk Broads and is at the moment protected by law from being collected.

Plate 3: I. Located by searching on milk parsley, nearly fully grown. Mid-July. (MG-P)

Family: PIERIDAE

This family of butterflies, commonly known as the Whites and Clouded Yellows, is represented in Britain by six residents and four migrants with one species having become extinct. The larvae live conventional life-styles and most of the resident species overwinter as pupae, secured to the chosen site by the cremaster and a silken girdle. Only the Brimstone hibernates as an adult, usually in among ivy or some other evergreen plant. Warmer summers often see an influx of the migrant species, but *C. croceus* is the only one which occurs regularly.

SUBFAMILY: DISMORPHIINAE

Wood White

Leptidea sinapis Linnaeus

Larva. 18–20 mm. Body bright green, with a bright pale yellow stripe along the spiracles and a darker green line along the dorsum. The whole body, including the very slightly darker green head, is covered in tiny pale setae.

Foodplants. Meadow vetchling, bird's-foot trefoil and bitter vetch; may also feed on some other closely related plants.

Habits. Larvae occur in June and July, and again in late August and into September in the south, where the species is double-brooded. Those that occur in the Midlands, Cornwall and Ireland are single-brooded with the larvae to be found in July and August. This species is difficult to find in the wild due to its small size and the habit of resting along the stems of its foodplant, where it is very well camouflaged. Sometimes it may be obtained by carefully putting a net or small sheet under the foodplant and then shaking the plant vigorously. Locally distributed, mainly in open woodland, over much of southern and central England, south-east Wales and most of Ireland.

Plate 3: J. Bred from a netted female adult on potted bird's-foot trefoil. Late May.

SUBFAMILY: COLIADINAE

Pale Clouded Yellow

Colias hyale Linnaeus

Larva. 30–33 mm. Body darkish green and covered in tiny black hairs. The spiracular stripe is whitish, but almost totally obscured by orangish-red markings.

Foodplants. Red clover, lucerne, black medick and also sometimes other species of *Leguminosae.*

Habits. An uncommon migrant species, with the first brood as larvae in June and July, producing a second generation of adults later on in the summer. The larvae from this second brood will normally die out from the cold, but if weather conditions are favourable some will complete their life-cycle to adults or possibly even manage to overwinter successfully in the larval stage. Fertile females lay easily in captivity and then, by keeping the larvae warm, breeding is not difficult.

Plate 3: K. Bred from netted female adult (France). Late July. (MG-P)

Berger's Clouded Yellow

Colias alfacariensis Ribbe

(*australis* Verity)

Larva. 30–33 mm. Body light bluish-green, with pale yellow stripes along the subdorsal area and spiracles; also bold black blotches posteriorly on each of the segments on both sides of the subdorsal stripe.

Foodplants. Horseshoe vetch, and in Europe crown vetch.

Habits. A very rare migrant that bred, probably for the first time, at Portland, Dorset in 1991. Its life-cycle and times of appearance are similar to *C. hyale*, except that it is very unlikely to survive through the British winter in any stage. In captivity eggs should readily be laid by fertile females, and although larval growth is slow to start, in the later instars, given light and warmth, it becomes fairly rapid, often with successful results.

Plate 3: L. Bred from netted female adult (Andorra). Early July. (MG-P)

Clouded Yellow

Colias croceus Geoffroy

(*edusa* Fabricius)

Larva. 32–35 mm. Body green, with a pale yellow spiracular stripe edged with white and orange behind each spiracle. The head is the same colour as the body.

Foodplants. Lucerne, clovers, bird's-foot trefoil and other associated plants.

Habits. A well-known migrant species, occurring in variable numbers depending on the weather conditions. Migration of earlier adults can last from May through to mid-July, so any resulting larvae can be at any time between June and August. Later the second brood or even more migratory individuals could be breeding, making the larval period last from any time between June to late October. Overwintering has never been proven, but it would probably be as a larva if successful. Occasionally, in years when the species becomes abundant, careful searching for eggs and larvae can be very rewarding. Adult females normally lay readily in captivity and as long as the larvae are kept warm and have a fresh food supply, breeding is relatively easy.

Plate 3: M. Bred from netted female adult. Late June. (AH)

The Brimstone

Gonepteryx rhamni Linnaeus

Larva. 32–36 mm. Body dark bluish-green above and yellowish green below, with an obvious whitish spiracular stripe; the whole body is covered in tiny black bristles.

Foodplants. Buckthorn and alder buckthorn.

Habits. A single-brooded species, occurring in the larval stage from early May until about mid-July. In the earlier instars the larva sits upon the upper side of a leaf along the midrib. Later the larva is situated on a larger leaf or a stem and can easily be detected by first locating signs of feeding and then searching carefully. As long as fresh food and space are supplied in captivity, breeding to the adult stage can be successful. Sleeving out on a growing bush is recommended for dealing with larger numbers of larvae. The adults emerge in July and soon go into hibernation in evergreen leaf cover. The distribution of this relatively common species covers most of England as far north as the Lake District, most parts of Wales and many places in Ireland.

Plate 3: N. Found as a fully grown larva. Late May.

SUBFAMILY: PIERINAE

Black-veined White

Aporia crataegi Linnaeus

Larva. 32–36 mm. Body shining grey-black on the sides, dorsally velvet black with orange markings. Whole body is covered in setae and the head is totally black and shining.

Foodplants. Blackthorn, hawthorn, plum and apple.

Habits. Single-brooded. From the eggs laid in batches during July, the tiny larvae live gregariously in silken webs, feeding until the autumn. During October the brood constructs a far stronger hibernaculum in which to spend the winter months, and on resumption of feeding during April, the 5 mm long larvae continue to be gregarious for a while. About the middle of May the larvae tend to become more independent of each other and disperse to complete their growth and pupate. This species became extinct in Britain during the 1920s and although attempts have been made to re-introduce it, none seems to have been successful.

Plate 3: O. Found on blackthorn (S. France), fully grown. May. (MG-P)

Large White

Pieris brassicae Linnaeus

Larva. 40–45 mm. Body greyish, heavily marked and spotted with black, having a conspicuous yellow dorsal stripe and being yellowish laterally.

Foodplants. Cultivated *Brassicas*, wild cabbage, sweet rocket, garden nasturtium and many other associated plants.

Habits. To be found as a larva any time between May and December. This species is at least double-brooded, and the indigenous population is also reinforced by migrants from the continent. The eggs are laid in batches and the larvae are gregarious, feeding on the outer leaves of the foodplant and often becoming a pest to gardeners and farmers. When fully grown they wander off to pupate upon fences, buildings and other sheltered locations. The larvae commonly fall victim to the parasitic wasp, *Apanteles glomeratus*, and will often be found surrounded by the yellow silken cocoons made by the larvae of the parasite after they have finished feeding inside the caterpillar. The distribution of this species covers the whole of the British Isles, and in some years it is much commoner than others.

Plate 3: P. Found on sweet rocket, fully grown. Mid-June. (SHC)

Small White

Pieris rapae Linnaeus

Larva. 25–28 mm. Body bluish-green and finely speckled with small black dots. Dorsal line is pale yellow and thin, the spiracular line is also yellow and incomplete.

Foodplants. Charlock, wild and cultivated cabbage, garlic mustard and other related plants.

Habits. This species is at least double- and often triple-brooded, also migratory, expanding the later populations. The larvae occur from about mid-May until the autumn, and when larger, feeding on the heart of cultivated *Brassicas*, can cause severe damage. They are easy to find and simple to rear in captivity. Pupation takes place in similar sites to *P. brassicae*. Widespread and usually common over most of Britain, but less frequent in Scotland.

Plate 3: Q. Found on cultivated cabbage, half grown. Late July. (SHC)

Green-veined White

Pieris napi Linnaeus

Larva. 24–27 mm. Body bluish-green and covered in tiny black pinacula, each with a seta. The dorsal line is darker and the black spiracles are ringed with bright yellow.

Foodplants. Garlic mustard, lady's smock, hedge mustard, charlock, watercress and other closely related plants.

Habits. Normally a double-brooded species, with larvae from the first generation occurring from mid-May until about late June, and the second from July to August. Northern populations may be single-brooded with larvae from about late June to August. In good years a third generation can be produced in the southern counties. An easy species to breed in captivity, with fertile females laying readily on potted plants. Widely distributed over most of the British Isles and common in many places.

Plate 3: R. Bred from netted female adult on garlic mustard. Mid-May.

Bath White

Pontia daplidice Linnaeus

Larva. 24–27 mm. Body bluish-grey and covered in obvious black pinacula; the subdorsal and spiracular stripes are creamy and marked with orange.

Foodplants. Wild mignonette, hedge mustard and other allied plants.

Habits. A very rare migrant species, with very few recent records. The adults can occur any time from May onwards, so any resulting larvae would be expected from June until the autumn. They are not difficult to rear in captivity, although they should be kept fairly warm. Overwintering takes place as a pupa, usually attached to a plant stem.

Plate 4: A. From commercial stock, taken in Spain. (AJ)

Orange-tip

Anthocharis cardamines Linnaeus

Larva. 29–32 mm. Body bright bluish-green, blending into white on the spiracular area. The pinacula are tiny and mostly black.

Foodplants. The seed pods of garlic mustard, lady's smock, charlock and related *Cruciferae*.

Habits. Single-brooded, occurring as a larva from late May until about early July, spending the winter as a pupa formed among herbage. Probably easiest to find as an egg, as soon after they have been laid they become bright orange and very conspicuous against the green seed pods of the foodplant. Care must be taken when breeding this species as the larvae are cannibalistic, so they must be kept separately. The

adults fly in May and June, and are common and widespread throughout much of the British Isles, preferring the habitats of hedgerows, open woods and lanes.
Plate 4: B. Found in the egg stage on garlic mustard. Mid-May.

Family: LYCAENIDAE

A fairly large family of butterflies, commonly known as the Blues, Coppers and Hairstreaks, with fourteen resident species occurring naturally in Britain. Two species have become extinct, but colonies of introduced foreign stocks are being carefully nurtured by conservation groups; unfortunately neither species is of the original unique British subspecies. The larvae are all woodlouse shaped, and those of many of the Blues have a symbiotic relationship with ants, the larvae supplying the ants with a sweet amino acid solution in return for protection and attention. Many species pupate on the foodplant or close by and the short blunt pupa is secured by the cremaster and a silken girdle.

SUBFAMILY: THECLINAE

Green Hairstreak

Callophrys rubi Linnaeus
Larva. 16–19 mm. Body bright yellowish-green, with oblique yellow stripes and covered in tiny pale setae.
Foodplants. Gorse, broom, bird's-foot trefoil, bilberry, rock-rose and the flower buds of buckthorn and dogwood.
Habits. A single-brooded insect that occurs in the larval stage from May until mid-July, overwintering as a pupa. The larvae can readily be beaten from gorse, broom, etc. and in Scotland are obtainable by sweeping bilberry. These larvae are sometimes cannibalistic, so should not be kept together. The main flight period for the adults is during May and the females will usually lay freely in captivity, if required to do so. Widely distributed over the greater part of Britain and Ireland and usually fairly common.
Plate 4: C. Bred from a netted female adult on bird's-foot trefoil. Late May. (MG-P)

Brown Hairstreak

Thecla betulae Linnaeus
Larva. 16–20 mm. Body pale whitish-green, with thin oblique white stripes along the sides. The whole body has tiny pale setae and the front dorsal area is flattened forming a triangle. The head is tiny and black.
Foodplants. Blackthorn, and in captivity cultivated plum can be used as a successful substitute.
Habits. A single-brooded species that overwinters as an egg. These are laid singly or often in pairs, normally situated on the spine bases or forks between twigs of younger growth. Due to the whitish colour of the eggs they can easily be found during the winter months, with many low down on the foodplant. Collected eggs are best carefully removed with the adjacent bark, and put on to growing foodplant in a sleeve, as the young larvae at first feed inside the developing buds. Later, during May and the first half of June, they can readily be taken by beating. The pupa is formed upon the foodplant and lasts about four to six weeks, with the rarely seen adults flying in late July and August. Local in southern England, south-west Wales and on the Burren in western Ireland.
Plate 4: D. Found in the egg stage. Early March.

Purple Hairstreak

Quercusia quercus Linnaeus
Larva. 15–18 mm. Body warm reddish-brown, with a black dorsal line and oblique black markings on the sides.
Foodplants. Oak, and has been observed ovipositing on holm oak.
Habits. Single-brooded. After overwintering as an egg, the larva hatches in the spring and bores into a developing bud. Later the larva lives inside a loosely spun web and feeds most often at night. During this stage the larvae can easily be beaten until pupation in mid-June. During winter the pale coloured eggs are not difficult to locate, and young larvae can be put on to oak twigs in water until they are large enough to be transferred into boxes to finish their growth. The pupal stage lasts about three to four weeks and the adults fly during July and August. This species is widely distributed over much of southern Britain, but much more local in the north.
Plate 4: E. Beaten from oak by day, nearly fully grown. Mid-May.

White-letter Hairstreak

Satyrium w album Knoch
Larva. 15–17 mm. Body light yellowish-green, with yellow oblique markings along the sides and a twin row of dark grey-green streaks along the dorsal ridge. The whole body is covered in tiny pale setae. A red-marked form also occurs.
Foodplants. Wych elm, common elm and small-leaved elm.
Habits. A single-brooded species that overwinters in the egg stage. The larvae hatch about March and begin to feed upon the developing buds and flowers of elms. When about half-grown the larvae also consume the younger leaves, and rest on the undersides. Around the third week in May most larvae are nearly fully grown and can easily be beaten from their foodplant. When kept in captivity, newly formed pupae should be removed from other still-feeding larvae, as they are likely to be eaten along with the leaves. The pupal stage lasts about three weeks with the adults emerging during late June and July. This insect is widespread, but local, over Britain as far north as Co. Durham, with the preferred habitats being the edges of woods and hedgerows with mature elm growth. It seems to have declined since the advent of Dutch elm disease.
Plate 4: F. Beaten from wych elm, nearly fully grown. Mid-May.

Black Hairstreak

Satyrium pruni Linnaeus
Larva. 15–18 mm. Body bright green, with five twin dorsal ridges which are often tipped with purplish-red. Short white setae cover the body. When smaller the larvae are brown with a paler dorsal area.
Foodplants. Blackthorn, wild plum and in captivity cultivated plums.
Habits. Single-brooded. This species overwinters as an egg and the larvae hatch in early April and begin to feed on the developing flower and leaf buds. By the third instar the larvae are feeding on the leaves and it becomes possible to beat for them. Finding the eggs can be difficult as they match their background very closely in colour and are often laid quite high up. By early June most larvae will have pupated, and in years of good abundance these bird-dropping like pupae may be located on the upperside of the leaves and on the stems. The adults' flight period lasts from the middle of June to mid-July, but many females are reluctant to lay in captivity. The distribution of this species is strange,

considering how widespread its foodplant is. From Oxford in the west and then north-eastwards up to the Peterborough area, in a strip about 25 km wide, are the only localities where it has been found naturally.
Plate 4: G. Beaten from blackthorn, fully grown. Late May.

SUBFAMILY: LYCAENINAE

Small Copper

Lycaena phlaeas Linnaeus
Larva. 15–18 mm. Body dark green, often with a crimson stripe along the dorsal ridge and along the lower edge of the sides. Wholly covered with small white pinacula, each with a short dark seta; head small and brown.
Foodplants. Common sorrel, sheep's sorrel and dock.
Habits. This species has at least two broods and often three or four. It overwinters as a larva and subsequent broods mean the insect can be in this stage at any time during the year. Larvae can be found by careful searching and are normally on the underside of the leaves. Leaves on which the lower epidermis has been eaten and the upper part remains intact, showing as a transparent patch, can be evidence of their presence. It is easy to breed from fertile females on potted foodplant. The adults can fly any time from mid-May to early October, depending on the locality. This species occurs commonly over most of the British Isles, usually on well-drained open ground.
Plate 4: H. Bred from a netted female adult on dock. Late May.

Large Copper

Lycaena dispar Haworth
Larva. 20–22 mm. Body bright green, more yellowish dorsally and having numerous tiny pale tubercles, each with a white seta.
Foodplants. Great water-dock, and will accept broad-leaved dock.
Habits. Single-brooded, overwintering as a half-grown larva among leaf litter close to the ground, during which time it becomes dull in colour with a pinkish tinge. In April, after hibernation, feeding recommences with the larva eating holes in the leaves of its foodplant, until pupation in June. The adults fly during July and early August; formerly occurring in the fens of East Anglia, before it became extinct during about the 1850s. The Dutch subspecies (*batavus*) has been successfully introduced to a fen in Huntingdonshire.
Plate 4: I. From commercial stock.

SUBFAMILY: POLYOMMATINAE

Long-tailed Blue

Lampides boeticus Linnaeus
Larva. 15–16 mm. Body dull greyish, well marked with reddish-brown and the dorsal line also reddish-brown; head and spiracles black.
Foodplants. Everlasting pea, bladder-senna and other plants of the pea family, at first on the flowers and later inside the seed pods.
Habits. A rare migrant to this country, normally not seen until August, when the continental populations have built up. This species has bred several times in Britain, and in good years it might be possible to find larvae by carefully splitting open foodplant seed pods. The larval development is fairly rapid if they are kept warm, and often successful if the food is fresh and clean from a build up of frass. The pupa can last as little as ten days and is formed among the leaves.
Plate 4: J. Found inside bladder-senna seed pod (S. France), nearly fully grown. Early July.

Small Blue

Cupido minimus Fuessly
Larva. 9–12 mm. Body dull greenish-grey, with many obscure pinkish-brown markings and a more obvious brown dorsal line. Wholly covered with setae.
Foodplants. The flowers of kidney vetch and possibly related plants.
Habits. A mainly single-brooded species, the adults of which fly from late May to early July. The eggs hatch in about ten days and the larvae feed up quickly upon the foodplant flowers, becoming fully grown by about mid- to late July. At this time they either leave the foodplant and overwinter in moss or in soil crevices, pupating in the spring, or pupate immediately to form a second generation of adults in August. Flowerheads searched from known colonies in July should produce larvae which then can be left outside in soil, moss and leaf litter-filled pots to overwinter. Most frequently found in southern England, becoming much more local in the north and in Scotland and Ireland.
Plate 4: K. Located in foodplant flowerhead, fully grown. Mid-July.

Short-tailed Blue

Everes argiades Pallas
Larva. 10–11 mm. Body pale green, with a darker dorsal line and vague pale oblique subdorsal marks; head black. They turn dull brown during hibernation (MBGBI).
Foodplants. Gorse, bird's-foot trefoil and other plants of the family *Leguminosae*.
Habits. This very scarce immigrant species has never been proven to breed in the British Isles. It is double-brooded throughout the continent, with the larvae occurring during June and from September to the following April and, like many *Lycaenidae* larvae, they may be cannibalistic during their earlier instars. All records during the present century have been of single specimens, and number fewer than ten, usually occurring during good migratory years and from the southern coastal counties of England.

Silver-studded Blue

Plebejus argus Linnaeus
(*aegon* Schiffermüller)
Larva. 12–14 mm. Body varies from yellowish-green to light brown, always with a broad pale-edged dorsal stripe and often another obvious stripe close to the spiracles. Body totally covered with tiny setae.
Foodplants. Gorse, broom, bird's-foot trefoil, restharrow and probably ling and bell heather.
Habits. A single-brooded insect, the foodplants of which depend on the type of habitat in which it occurs. After overwintering as an egg, often not actually laid on the foodplant but nearby, the young larva feeds at first on the softer parts of the plant such as the flowers, buds and new growth. The larvae have a symbiotic relationship with ants, especially of the genus *Lasius*, but they are not totally necessary for successful development. The pupa is formed on the ground and lasts about a month, with the adults flying mainly in July. Most of the colonies of this species occur on lowland heaths in southern England; in Wales it tends to be more coastal in distribution.

Plate 4: L. Bred from netted female adult on potted bird's-foot trefoil. Early July. (AH)

Brown Argus
Aricia agestis Denis & Schiffermüller
Larva. 10–13 mm. Body light green, with an indistinct purple dorsal line. The subspiracular line is whitish and edged above and below with purple so as to almost obscure the white in many individuals.
Foodplants. Common rock-rose and common stork's-bill.
Habits. A double-brooded species, with larvae occurring during June and July, and again in August and September, overwintering when half grown and completing their growth in the following spring. The best way to obtain larvae is to encourage a fertile female to lay on potted foodplant, but they can be found by careful searching. The pupal stage lasts about three to four weeks, and the adults are on the wing in late May and June, and those of the second generation from late July to late August. This butterfly is widely distributed on open ground over most of southern England, but in Wales it tends to be mainly coastal in occurrence.
Plate 4: M. Bred from netted female adult on rock-rose. Late May. (MG-P)

Northern Brown Argus
Aricia artaxerxes Fabricius
Larva. 10–13 mm. Body light green, with a darker green dorsal line. The subspiracular line is purplish and centred obviously with white.
Foodplants. Common rock-rose and probably other closely related plants.
Habits. This species is single-brooded, with the larvae feeding from July until September, when they hibernate in plant litter, about half grown, until the following April. During the spring completion of the growth is steady and they are ready to pupate by early June. The adults can be found throughout most of July and females lay easily on potted foodplant. This should be left outside and undisturbed until the following spring for the best results. During mid-May larvae can be found by close searching at known localities. A local species occurring mainly on limestone districts on the Pennines, in northern England and in central and eastern Scotland.
Plate 4: N. Located on rock-rose, fully grown. Mid-May. (MRS)

Common Blue
Polyommatus icarus Rottemburg
Larva. 12–15 mm. Body bright green, with a darker green dorsal line and a whitish lateral stripe; spiracles white, setae light brown dorsally and white on the sides.
Foodplants. Bird's-foot trefoil, black medick, restharrow, greater bird's-foot trefoil, red clover and other species of *Leguminosae*.
Habits. A double-brooded species in the southern parts of Britain and univoltine in the north. Larvae hibernate when they are about half grown, low down among plant litter. Feeding recommences during the spring and, in the south, the larvae are fully grown by early May. The next generation of larvae is to be found during late June and July. In the northern populations they may not be ready to pupate until June. Breeding from fertile females is easy and eggs are readily laid on potted plants. Searching or sweeping at dusk for larvae can also produce good results as this species is normally common where it occurs. Widely distributed over nearly all parts of the British Isles.

Plate 4: O. Swept from bird's-foot trefoil, fully grown. July. (GAC)

Chalkhill Blue
Lysandra coridon Poda
Larva. 14–17 mm. Body bright green, with a double row of yellow markings along the dorsal ridge and a yellow marked subspiracular line. Wholly covered with tiny pinacula, each bearing a short seta; spiracles black.
Foodplants. Horseshoe vetch; also may accept bird's-foot trefoil, kidney vetch and clovers.
Habits. Single-brooded, overwintering as an egg. The larvae hatch in April and feed up at night to maturity by June. In the wild they have a relationship with ants, but these are not necessary for breeding this species in captivity. As most colonies are large, the larvae can often be located by searching around the bases of horseshoe vetch plants in the day. The pupa is formed on the ground and lasts about a month, with the adults flying during July and August. Mainly a downland insect, distributed over the chalk and limestone regions of most of the southern counties in England.
Plate 4: P. Found at base of foodplant, fully grown. Mid-June. (SHC)

Adonis Blue
Lysandra bellargus Rottemburg
(*thetis* Rottemburg)
Larva. 13–16 mm. Body dark green, with a double row of bright yellow marks along the dorsal ridge and a bright yellow subspiracular line. Body is wholly covered in dark setae and the spiracles are black.
Foodplant. Horseshoe vetch.
Habits. A double-brooded species that overwinters as a young larva. In late March the larvae begin to feed again by day and night, and are fully grown by around early May. From the second instar they are constantly attended by ants, which are attracted to the sweet secretions emitted from the larvae, although ants are not necessary for successful breeding in captivity. The pupa is formed on the ground, lasting three to four weeks. Larvae from the spring generation occur during late June and July, with the resulting adults being on the wing in August. These larvae can be found by careful searching, but breeding from an adult female should result in a better chance of obtaining stocks. A local species, being found on calcareous soils in southern England.
Plate 4: Q. Bred from netted female adult on potted plant. Late May.

Mazarine Blue
Cyaniris semiargus Rottemburg
(*acis* Schiffermüller)
Larva. 13–15 mm. Body pale green, with a darker dorsal line, other less distinct darker lines in the subdorsal region and on the sides and vague pale subspiracular marks; head black.
Foodplants. Red clover, gorse, kidney vetch and other leguminous plants.
Habits. A single-brooded insect that probably became extinct in the British Isles during the early part of this century. Since then a few individual adults have been observed in southern England and been considered to be immigrants. The larval stage lasts from about August to the following May, with feeding at first on the flowers and seeds of the foodplants and then on the developing shoots during the spring, after hibernation. The species is stated to be quite common in many parts of continental Europe.

Plate 4: R. Bred from netted female adult (Belgium). Late May. (MHy)

Holly Blue

Celastrina argiolus Linnaeus

Larva. 14–17 mm. Body yellowish-green, with variable amounts of reddish markings dorsally and laterally. The form without any red colour is far commoner than the marked individuals. The body is completely covered by short whitish setae.

Foodplants. Holly, ivy buds, dogwood and gorse.

Habits. Usually double-brooded and overwinters as a pupa spun up on the foodplant. The adults emerge in May and from the eggs laid in the spring, mainly on holly, the larvae feed from late May until early July on the young soft leaves and the drupes. The second-brood ova are laid on developing ivy buds and the larvae feed on these and on the flowers during late August and throughout September. The best way to obtain larvae is to beat mature, south-facing ivy bushes in September. They should not be kept overcrowded as they have mild cannibalistic habits. The more northern populations may be univoltine, with the larvae feeding on holly and spending from July until the following spring as chrysalides. Normally common and widespread over southern Britain and Ireland; it does occur in northern England, but is far less frequent.

Plate 5: A. Beaten from mature ivy. Mid-September.

Large Blue

Maculinea arion Linnaeus

Larva. 14–15 mm. Body glossy dirty white with a small black marking dorsally near the head.

Foodplant. Wild thyme (see habits).

Habits. This species has one of the strangest life histories of any of the British lepidoptera. From the eggs laid in July, the larvae hatch and spend their first three instars feeding upon the flowers of the foodplant. At this stage, during August, they are pale pink with thin white lines, well camouflaged among the florets. The larvae then leave the foodplant, go to the ground and wait to be discovered by the ants (*Myrmica* species), which will act as hosts for the rest of the larval development. The tiny larvae are taken into the brood chamber of the ants' nest and spend the next nine months feeding upon the eggs, larvae and prepupae of the ant. The ants usually tolerate the larvae as they supply them with an amino acid solution excreted from a small gland situated upon the seventh abdominal segment. Larvae may die or be killed while inside the ants' nest, but the survivors pupate about late May still underground. About four to six weeks later, when the adult insect emerges, it makes its way to the surface, crawls up a plant and expands its wings. Distribution was mainly centred in south-west England, but the species had become extinct by 1979. Since the mid-1980s attempts have been made to re-establish colonies by using the Swedish subspecies which is similar to the British race. At present this insect is protected from collecting by law.

Plate 5: B. Courtesy of Jeremy Thomas.

Family: NEMEOBIIDAE

The larva of this species resembles those of the *Lycaenidae*, rather than those of the fritillaries, this name coming from the likeness of the adult to the orange and black marked *Nymphalidae*. The pupa is attached to the herbage by the cremaster and a silken girdle and can be recognized by the creamy colour and black dots. Although many recent works classify this species within the *Lycaenidae*, it is treated separately in this book.

SUBFAMILY: RIODININAE

Duke of Burgundy Fritillary

Hamearis lucina Linnaeus

Larva. 16–17 mm. Body light brown, with a dark brown dorsal stripe that has a blackish spot centrally on each segment and more dark brown marks along the sides. The whole body is covered in dark setae.

Foodplants. Cowslip, primrose and in captivity garden *Primulas*.

Habits. A single-brooded species that is in the larval stage from about early June until early August. During late May the eggs can readily be located on the underside edges of the larger leaves growing in the half-shade. The larva feeds at night usually on the upper surface of the leaves and hides at the plant bases during the day. It hibernates as a pupa formed low down among the herbage, and although adults have been known to hatch in captivity during the autumn, they usually emerge the following May. Most females will lay freely in confinement. This species is local in woodland and on downland mainly in southern England; colonies also exist in North Yorkshire and south Cumbria.

Plate 5: C. Found in the egg stage on cowslip. Late May. (MG-P)

Family: NYMPHALIDAE

This family is represented by fourteen resident species, although it seems one, the Large Tortoiseshell, is probably extinct in the British Isles as a resident. Two species, the Red Admiral and the Painted Lady, are probably the most likely migrant species that the layman is familiar with, both occurring in fluctuating numbers every year. The majority of the larvae possess branched spines and many are gregarious in habits. The pupae of all the species hang inverted, attached solely by the cremaster, and those of some are delicately marked with metallic spots.

SUBFAMILY: LIMENITINAE

White Admiral

Ladoga camilla Linnaeus
(*sibylla* Linnaeus)

Larva. 26–28 mm. Body bright green, with pairs of brown branched spines on most segments dorsally; white along the spiracles on the abdominal segments. The brown head and the body are covered with white pinacula.

Foodplant. Honeysuckle.

Habits. Single-brooded, being in the larval stage from August to the following spring. During the early instars, in August and September, the signs of larval feeding are obvious as they eat the leaf edges, leaving the midrib intact. Overwintering takes place inside a hibernaculum formed from a honeysuckle leaf spun with silk to a stem. These can also be located during the winter months by searching. In April feeding recommences and the larvae are fully grown about the end of May or early June. To find them at this stage, locating eaten leaves is often a good indication and then careful searching may be successful. The pupal stage

lasts three to four weeks, with the adults flying from late June to early August. This species is widely distributed in woodland over most of southern England.
Plate 5: D. Found on shaded trailing honeysuckle, fully grown. Late May. (SHC)

SUBFAMILY: APATURINAE

Purple Emperor

Apatura iris Linnaeus
Larva. 35–40 mm. Body bright green, with oblique yellow stripes along the sides. The head is strange in structure, with two forward-facing pink-tipped horns.
Foodplants. Grey sallow, goat willow and crack willow; also recorded from other sallows and aspen.
Habits. A single-brooded insect. In July and August the eggs are laid upon the upper surface of leaves, normally in partial shade, and these can be found by diligent searching or observing females ovipositing. The young larvae feed until about October, always on the top of a leaf, and then they change from green to brownish ready for hibernation. During the winter months they lie fully exposed upon a silken pad located at the fork of a twig or near to a bud. They are about 10–15 mm long and can be found during this period. During April the larvae begin to feed again, on the opening buds and young leaves, and they become fully grown by the middle of June. Beating for the larvae is possible but not very successful, as they have a strong grip and are not easily dislodged from their foodplant. When breeding very young larvae in captivity, it is advisable to keep them in a sleeve on a growing bush and they must be overwintered outside. This species is to be found mainly in central southern England, where it is often not uncommon in the larger deciduous woods.
Plate 5: E. Found in the egg stage on grey sallow. Mid-July. (ECLS)

SUBFAMILY: NYMPHALINAE

Red Admiral

Vanessa atalanta Linnaeus
Larva. 32–36 mm. Body variable from dull olive-green to black, with a row of pale yellow markings on the abdominal segments near to the spiracles. All the segments have branched spines of the body colour.
Foodplants. Common nettle, small nettle and pellitory-of-the-wall.
Habits. A regular migrant species, with the adults normally arriving from mid-May onwards throughout the summer. The earliest larvae occur in June and often build up in numbers until they are killed by frosts in the autumn. Depending on the temperature, the larval stage lasts about twenty-five days and the larvae can easily be found by locating nettle leaves that have been spun up to form a tent. Leaves that have been rolled should be ignored as these are probably inhabited by a larva of one of the Pyralid moths, *Pleuroptya ruralis* or *Eurrhypara hortulata*, which are both common on nettle.
Plate 5: F. Bred from netted female adult. Early June. (MG-P)

Painted Lady

Cynthia cardui Linnaeus
Larva. 28–33 mm. Body velvety black, with yellow crescent-shaped markings on the abdominal segments in the spiracular region and covered in short branched yellow and black spines; head black.
Foodplants. Spear thistle, marsh thistle, common nettle, creeping thistle and viper's bugloss.
Habits. This species is a frequent migrant which starts to appear most years in about May or June. The larvae from these earlier individuals or later adults can be found from June until the autumn, when they die from the cold weather. The larval stage lasts about a month, and until the last instar the larvae can be found in silken webs on the underside of the leaves. Populations are usually much higher during a good summer.
Plate 5: G. Bred from netted female adult on nettle. Early June. (MG-P)

American Painted Lady

Cynthia virginiensis Drury
Larva. 27–32 mm. Body black, with yellowish-green transverse bands, white subdorsal spots on the abdominal rings and dull red pinacula from which the branched black spines emanate; head black (Wright).
Foodplants. Various species of *Compositae*, including thistles and cudweeds.
Habits. A very scarce immigrant species that has occurred as an adult in the British Isles about fifteen times during the present century. It is mainly a North American insect which has migratory habits and is now known to be breeding in the Canary Islands and Portugal, from where some of the British specimens could have originated. In Portugal it is considered to be double-brooded, with the larvae occurring in June and July, and from November to February, living solitarily inside a spinning among the foliage of the foodplant.

Small Tortoiseshell

Aglais urticae Linnaeus
Larva. 27–32 mm. Body yellowish-grey, but often varying darker or lighter, with a blackish dorsal line and markings on the sides. The short spines are mainly yellowish and the head is black with yellow dots.
Foodplants. Common nettle, small nettle and in captivity hop.
Habits. A double-brooded insect. After overwintering as an adult insect, this species lays its eggs in large batches on the undersides of foodplant leaves. The young larvae live gregariously in conspicuous webs and are easy to find during May and June, and those of the second generation in late July and August. During the final instar the larvae disperse and feed exposed on nettles. Large numbers of these larvae can easily be reared in captivity by using plant propagators or even a large cardboard box covered with netting, but hygiene is important. This species is widely distributed and often common over most of Britain.
Plate 5: H. Found as a larva, fully grown. Late May.

Large Tortoiseshell

Nymphalis polychloros Linnaeus
Larva. 35–40 mm. Body greyish-black, with a broad orangish dorsal area that is centred by the black dorsal line. The sharp branched spines are orange and the head is shining black.
Foodplants. Common elm, wych elm, grey sallow, goat willow, poplars, aspen, osier and pear.
Habits. A single-brooded species, overwintering as an adult. During May and June the larvae live gregariously in a conspicuous web, and begin to disperse shortly before they are ready to pupate. When breeding them in captivity they

should be sleeved out on growing foodplant until they are fully grown, then transferred into spacious containers with netting over the top, so they can hang up to form the pupae. This stage lasts about three to four weeks, with the adults emerging in July and early August, and feeding briefly before hibernation. This species is now very rare in Britain and possibly does not breed here at the present time. Many recent records probably relate to migrants or escapes from foreign breeding stocks which are easily obtainable.
Plate 5: I. From commercial stock (S. France).

Camberwell Beauty

Nymphalis antiopa Linnaeus
Larva. 45–50 mm. Body black, with a conspicuous brick-red spot on most of the segments dorsally. The head and spines are black and the body is dusted with tiny whitish dots.
Foodplants. Sallows, willows, poplars, birch and elm.
Habits. This rare migrant species overwinters as an adult and larvae have yet to be found occurring naturally in this country. In Europe the larvae live gregariously in a silken web during May to July, and disperse to pupate when fully grown. Livestock should be put into a sleeve for development and moved into netting-covered containers when ready to pupate.
Plate 5: J. Bred from netted female adult (S. France). Mid-May. (MG-P)

The Peacock

Inachis io Linnaeus
Larva. 38–42 mm. Body totally velvety black, with many tiny white dots. The head and spines are also black.
Foodplants. Common nettle; also recorded from hop.
Habits. Single-brooded, overwintering as an adult. From about late May until July the larvae can be found living gregariously in obvious silken webs and when fully grown they disperse to pupate. Breeding in captivity is easy as long as the larvae have fresh food, space and netting on which to hang up to pupate. After spending about three weeks in this stage, the adults begin to emerge in late July and most hibernate after feeding for a short period. This species is widespread and common throughout most of England, up to the Scottish border. In Scotland it is less frequent and mainly confined to the south-west.
Plate 5: K. Located as a larva, fully grown. Late June.

The Comma

Polygonia c-album Linnaeus
Larva. 30–34 mm. Body greyish, heavily marked with orangish-brown, except on the abdominal segments which are totally white dorsally. The head is black and the branched spines are either orange or white.
Foodplants. Common nettle, sallows, elms and hop.
Habits. A double-brooded species that overwinters as an adult. Larvae from the first generation occur during May and June and are solitary in habits. When small they live on the underside of a leaf, but after they take on the coloration of a bird-dropping they move to the upperside. The second-brood larvae repeat the cycle during late July and August. Due to their solitary habits and wide dispersal, obtaining larvae in any quantity is difficult, unless bred from a fertile female. Occasionally they are beaten from elms and sallows when looking for other species on the same foodplants. This species is distributed over southern England as far north as Yorkshire and Wales.
Plate 5: L. Bred from netted female adult, on nettle. Early May. (MG-P)

SUBFAMILY: ARGYNNINAE

Small Pearl-bordered Fritillary

Boloria selene Denis & Schiffermüller
Larva. 20–23 mm. Body brownish-grey, with small black markings and many ochreous branched spines. The head is black and along the spiracles is an indistinct yellowish wavy stripe.
Foodplants. Dog violet and marsh violet; also in captivity most kinds of violets and pansy.
Habits. Normally a single-brooded species that overwinters as a half-grown larva on the ground sheltered by leaf debris. After hibernation the larvae feed up on the new plant growth, and are fully grown about early May. During the spring they can be found by diligent searching after the location of eaten leaves. They are also easy to breed from adult females, which fly during June and early July, readily depositing eggs on potted foodplant. Kept warm the larvae will not hibernate and continue to feed for about six weeks and then pupate. In warmer years, especially in the south-west, some larvae will complete their growth naturally, and produce a second generation of adults which fly in August. Widespread, but mainly of a western distribution, over most of England, Wales and Scotland.
Plate 5: M. Bred from a netted female adult on dog violet. Early June.

Pearl-bordered Fritillary

Boloria euphrosyne Linnaeus
Larva. 22–25 mm. Body velvety black, with a twin row of contrasting yellow spines along the subdorsal area. The head is black and along the spiracles the body is mottled with grey.
Foodplants. Dog violet, marsh violet, sweet violet and in captivity other species of violets and pansy.
Habits. A single-brooded insect that occurs in the larval stage from June to the following spring, hibernating when half grown among leaf litter. During the first warm days of March the larvae become active and start to bask in sunshine and feed on the fresh growth. Indication of their presence is violet leaves that have been eaten leaving just the stem intact, and close searching should then locate them. Obtaining eggs in confinement is easy, but the larvae should be kept on potted plants as they refuse to feed up during the summer. During the autumn dry leaves should be put in the plant tub for the larvae to overwinter successfully. A woodland species that is generally distributed over most of southern and western England, Wales, Scotland and the Burren in Ireland.
Plate 5: N. Bred from netted female adult on potted violets. Mid-May. (AH)

Queen of Spain Fritillary

Argynnis lathonia Linnaeus
Larva. 28–32 mm. Body black, with many tiny pale dots; the branched spines are ochreous and the head is light brown, mottled darker.
Foodplants. Dog violet, wild pansy and many other related violets and pansies; also recorded on borage and lucerne.
Habits. A very rare migrant species that has probably bred in Britain in the past. The adults could occur during any of the summer months, but most records tend to be in August and September. In the far north of its range, in Sweden, it has been suggested that this species can overwinter as either

a larva, a pupa or an adult. Overwintering has never been proven in the British Isles. Females readily lay eggs in captivity and any resulting larvae should be kept warm and given light as they seem to require this for successful development.
Plate 5: O. From commercial stock (N. Spain).

High Brown Fritillary
Argynnis adippe Denis & Schiffermüller
(*cydippe* Linnaeus)
Larva. 38–42 mm. Body black, with an obvious broken white dorsal line, and branched spines of a light ochreous colour. The head is also ochreous and mottled with black.
Foodplants. Dog violet and sweet violet; in confinement it will also accept other associated *Viola* species.
Habits. Single-brooded, being in the larval stage from April to June. The eggs are laid during July and August on or near the foodplants, and the species overwinters in this stage. During early April the eggs hatch and the larvae feed up to be fully grown in about two months. The larvae can be found in the spring and they are fond of basking in sunshine. Any eggs that are obtained from adult females should not be kept in too damp an environment as this may cause fungal attack. This species seems to be declining rapidly and the only areas where it is likely to be found regularly are on the western side of Britain. It is presently protected by law from being collected.
Plate 5: P. Found as a larva while basking, half-grown. Late May. (MG-P)

Dark Green Fritillary
Argynnis aglaja Linnaeus
Larva. 38–42 mm. Body velvety black, with a distinct row of brick-red spots along the sides. The head and the branched spines are also black.
Foodplants. Hairy violet, dog violet, marsh violet and related species.
Habits. A single-brooded species, being in the larval stage from August to the following May or June. The eggs are laid in July and August, and the larvae hatch after about twenty days, immediately hibernating among plant litter. As soon as the spring warmth starts, the tiny larvae begin to feed upon the fresh growth and reach full size by about late May. They may be located in the wild by searching for partly eaten leaves and bare stems. Also they can be bred from adults, by using plant tubs with established violets and dry dead leaf litter spread over the soil for hibernation. Although this species has been declining in the south for a few years, it is still widely found and fairly common over most of the British Isles.
Plate 5: Q. Bred from netted female adult on dog violet. Late July. (AH)

Silver-washed Fritillary
Argynnis paphia Linnaeus
Larva. 38–44 mm. Body greyish-brown, with a broad pale yellow dorsal line that is centred with a thin brown line. The long branched spines are light brown and the head is dark brown and mottled.
Foodplants. Dog violet, sweet violet and in captivity other species of violet and pansy.
Habits. During July and August the female butterflies lay their eggs upon the north side of tree trunks, among mosses and lichens, about a metre from the ground. After about two weeks the larvae hatch and immediately hibernate in the bark crevices. In the spring they move to the ground and start to feed upon the new foodplant growth and are fully grown by early June. They bask in sunshine on leaf litter and bare ground and where populations are high they can be found by close searching. To obtain eggs from females in captivity, pieces of loose bark and hanging strips of netting inside the plant tub are recommended and they should then be left outside to overwinter naturally. This mainly woodland species is most often found south of a line between London and North Wales; in Ireland it is widespread over the whole country.
Plate 5: R. Bred from netted female adult on dog violet. Late July. (SFA)

SUBFAMILY: MELITAEINAE

Marsh Fritillary
Eurodryas aurinia Rottemburg
Larva. 25–30 mm. Body black, liberally speckled with white dots. The head and short branched spines are also black.
Foodplants. Devil's-bit scabious and rarely honeysuckle; in captivity it will also accept teasel and snowberry.
Habits. Single-brooded, occurring as a larva from late June to the following mid-May. During June the adult females lay eggs in large batches on the underside of the foodplant leaves and during July and August, when the larvae are still tiny, they construct a tent from leaves and silk and live within this structure. They consume only the lower epidermis of the tent leaves, which soon turn brown and are readily located. Hibernation starts early and the half-grown larvae spend the winter together in a silken web that must not be disturbed. After hibernation they are still gregarious and are conspicuous while they bask in sunshine upon plants. They become fully grown in about mid-May and pupate for about three to four weeks. Fertile females will lay eggs in captivity on foodplants grown in plant tubs and they are fairly easy to breed through by leaving them to develop naturally. This species is most often found in the western parts of England, Wales and Scotland and more generally over all parts of Ireland.
Plate 6: A. Found by searching, fully grown. Mid-May.

Glanville Fritillary
Melitaea cinxia Linnaeus
Larva. 24–28 mm. Body black with many white dots. The head is chestnut-brown and the short branched spines are black.
Foodplants. Ribwort plantain, sea plantain and buck's-horn plantain.
Habits. A single-brooded species, being in the larval stage from late June to the following spring. The eggs are laid in batches and the young gregarious larvae live in silken webs on the foodplant. They feed and bask in sunshine up to early September, when they construct a more substantial web among the herbage in which to overwinter. During early April they once again become active, move away from the web and complete their growth by about early May. Feeding takes place mainly in the sunshine and in cold and damp weather they become dormant. Breeding in captivity is usually easy as long as the stock is sheltered from frosts during the winter and is given adequate space and light. At present this species occurs naturally only on the southern coast of the Isle of Wight, but the population seems to be stable.
Plate 6: B. Found by searching, almost fully grown. Late April.

Heath Fritillary

Mellicta athalia Rottemburg

Larva. 23–27 mm. Body blackish and heavily mottled with greyish-white markings. The head is black and along the back are many pale orange tubercles which have numerous black bristles emitting from them.

Foodplants. Cow-wheat, foxglove, ribwort plantain and germander speed-well. Also recorded are yarrow and greater plantain.

Habits. Single-brooded, occurring as a larva from July to the following spring. The eggs are laid in batches during June and July, and the larvae hatch after about twenty days, at first living gregariously in a flimsy web. Soon they disperse to a certain extent and continue to feed until about September. During hibernation they are usually solitary inside a dead rolled leaf on the ground among plant litter. Many may die while overwintering from fungal disease caused by dampness. In the spring they recommence feeding and spend a lot of time basking in sunshine. In dull or cool weather they shelter in leaf litter below their foodplants. They become fully grown between mid-May and mid-June depending on their geographical location, and pupate for about three weeks. This species now occurs in woodland in north Kent and on heaths and grassland in the West Country. It is protected from collection by law as it is a vulnerable insect.

Plate 6: C. Found in leaf litter, nearly fully grown. Mid-May.

Family: SATYRIDAE

Eleven species are to be found in the British Isles, all resident and with no migratory tendencies. The larvae feed mainly at night on various species of grass, are of a conventional shape and can often be distinguished from other groups by the presence of the twin anal points. Overwintering is always completed in the larval stage, except for *P. aegeria* which also has the capability of hibernating as a pupa. The pupae of most species are attached solely by the cremaster to grasses and other plants and are usually green or brown. Although this family is considered by many works to be part of the *Nymphalidae*, it is treated separately here.

Speckled Wood

Pararge aegeria Linnaeus

Larva. 25–30 mm. Body bright green, with a darker green dorsal line that is edged with pale green. The whole body is covered in tiny white setae. The short anal points are pale green.

Foodplants. Grasses, especially cock's-foot, false-brome, Yorkshire-fog, annual meadow-grass and common couch.

Habits. This species is at least double- and often treble-brooded and it may overwinter either in the larval or pupal states. Larvae can occur at any time during the year and during the warmer months they can be swept in shady areas, mainly at night. From early May, in the south, the adults will be on the wing and most females lay very freely in captivity, with the larvae needing no special attention for successful rearing. Mostly a woodland insect, being widespread and often common over most of southern and central England, parts of Wales, Ireland and western Scotland.

Plate 6: D. Bred from netted female adult. Late May.

The Wall

Lasiommata megera Linnaeus

Larva. 23–27 mm. Body bright green, with a distinct thin pale spiracular line. The short anal points are whitish and the dorsal line is darker green.

Foodplants. Couch, cock's-foot, annual meadow-grass and other species of broad-bladed grass.

Habits. This double-brooded species overwinters as half-grown larvae that feed up in the early spring to produce adults around late May. The next generation of larvae occurs from mid-June until late July, and after pupating for about three weeks, the adults emerge in August. Although this species is not uncommon, it is rarely abundant enough to be found in the larval stage, so stocks may best be obtained by getting females to lay in captivity, which they do readily. The species is found over most parts of England, Wales and Ireland on open ground, but seems to have declined over the last decade.

Plate 6: E. Bred from netted female adult. Late July.

Mountain Ringlet

Erebia epiphron Knoch

Larva. 18–20 mm. Body bright bluish-green with a darker green dorsal stripe and whitish stripes along the subdorsal and spiracular regions. The short anal points have a pinkish tinge.

Foodplants. Mat-grass, and in captivity will also accept annual meadow-grass and sheep's-fescue.

Habits. This single-brooded montane species overwinters as a third instar larva, deep in among the grass tussocks. In late March the larvae start to become active again and sometimes bask in sunshine. They feed at night and can be found in the spring, becoming fully grown by about late May. The pupa lasts about three to four weeks, with the adults emerging in late June and July. Captive females often lay eggs and the larvae can be bred through by being left outside on potted plants and protected from severe frosts. This species is restricted in distribution to the mountains of the Lake District and those of central Scotland.

Plate 6: F. Courtesy of Carlos Gomez de Aizpurua.

Scotch Argus

Erebia aethiops Esper

Larva. 24–26 mm. Body pale ochreous, with a darker brownish dorsal line and a broken row of marks of the same colour along the subdorsal area. The head is slightly darker than the body and has a small black spot on the 'cheek'. The anal points are short and ochreous.

Foodplants. Purple moor-grass, blue moor-grass and tufted hair-grass, and in captivity it will feed on annual meadow-grass and other grasses.

Habits. This single-brooded species overwinters as a small larva in among the plant debris in sheltered locations. Activity starts again during March, and by late June most will have pupated. From about mid-May the larvae are large enough to be found or swept from their foodplants after dusk and the adults fly during very late July and throughout August. The females will often lay freely in confinement. This insect is easy enough to breed from the egg and the larvae should be kept outside in grass clumps and dead leaves to hibernate successfully. In England there are only two known localities, both in the north-west, but in Scotland it is widely distributed, especially in the west.

Plate 6: G. Swept at night, nearly fully grown. Early June. (RL)

Marbled White

Melanargia galathea Linnaeus

Larva. 28–30 mm. Body dull yellowish-green or ochreous-brown, with a darker dorsal line. The head is ochreous and the anal points pinkish. The body and head are wholly covered in short pale setae.

Foodplants. Grasses, especially sheep's-fescue, red fescue and also probably tor-grass. Larger larvae will accept many other grasses.

Habits. A single-brooded species that occurs in the larval stage from August to the following spring. The eggs, which are scattered at random while the female is on the wing, are laid in July and early August and the larvae hatch in about three weeks and immediately hibernate upon dry grass stems. In late winter they begin to feed at night and will not be fully developed until around mid-June. Most colonies are large and the larvae can readily be swept from grasses after dark. During the day they hide among grass clumps and may be located by careful searching. This species is widely distributed on open ground over central and southern England and also occurs in Yorkshire and South Wales.

Plate 6: H. Swept at night, fully grown. Early June.

The Grayling

Hipparchia semele Linnaeus

Larva. 26–32 mm. Body light ochreous, with a conspicuous blackish-brown dorsal line and warm-brown stripes in the subdorsal region. The head is light brown and striped darker and the anal points are small and brown.

Foodplants. Grasses, depending on the habitat, including fescue, couch, hair-grass, marram, false-brome and annual meadow-grass.

Habits. Single-brooded, overwintering as a half-grown larva on or in the soil, and if the weather is mild may sporadically feed. In the spring it normally feeds by night and will be fully developed by early June to early July depending on the locality. The larvae can easily be swept or located by torchlight well up on the foodplants, and captive larvae must be given loose soil in which to pupate for successful breeding. The pupa lasts for about four weeks and the adults can be seen during July and August. The distribution of this insect tends to be mainly coastal, but many colonies occur inland on sandy soils and other suitable open habitats throughout the British Isles.

Plate 6: I. Swept at night, fully grown. Early June.

The Gatekeeper

Pyronia tithonus Linnaeus

Larva. 23–26 mm. Body light green or pale pinkish-ochreous, with a darker dorsal line of green or brown depending on the larval colour form. The head is always pinkish-ochreous and the short anal points are pale.

Foodplants. Grasses, especially cock's-foot, couch, fescue, annual meadow-grass and other grasses.

Habits. A single-brooded species that occurs as a larva from August to June. After feeding until October the half-grown larvae hibernate at the bases of their foodplants. During the spring they tend to feed only at night and may easily be swept from grasses growing in among scrub and in woodland rides, until they pupate in mid-June. The adults fly in July and August and most females will lay freely in captivity. The resulting larvae should then be left outside on potted grasses to develop naturally. This species is widespread and often common over most of southern Britain.

Plate 6: J. Swept at night, nearly fully grown. Late May.

Meadow Brown

Maniola jurtina Linnaeus
(*janira* Linnaeus)

Larva. 25–28 mm. Body bright green with a dark green dorsal line. The spiracles are small and pinkish and below them is a thin obscure white line; body is ventrally dark green and the anal points are white.

Foodplants. Annual meadow-grass, couch, sheep's-fescue, and also probably most other species of grasses.

Habits. From the eggs laid between June and September, the larvae of this single-brooded species feed steadily until the first frosts. During the winter months they do not hibernate, but continue in mild weather to be active, feeding on whatever grasses are available. During the spring, feeding mainly at night, the growth becomes more rapid and the pupation period lasts from late May until about early August, when the very last larvae mature. The protracted emergence of the adults lasts from mid-June to early September and the females will usually lay freely in captivity. This species occurs commonly all over Britain and Ireland, except in the highest of upland districts.

Plate 6: K. Swept at night, fully grown. Early June.

Small Heath

Coenonympha pamphilus Linnaeus

Larva. 18–20 mm. Body green, with a darker dorsal stripe and a yellowish spiracular line. The head is green and the long anal points are pinkish.

Foodplants. Grasses, especially annual meadow-grass, sheep's-fescue and mat-grass; also recorded from many other grass species.

Habits. Depending on the season and latitude of the population this species may be single-, double- or even treble-brooded. Overwintering is always in the larval stage but the size can vary greatly. The larvae are most easily obtained by sweeping at night, and in captivity most adult females will lay readily on grasses. The larvae need no special conditions in which to develop. This is probably the most widely distributed of our butterflies, being found in almost all parts of Britain and Ireland, tending to inhabit mainly open ground.

Plate 6: L. Bred from netted female adult. Early July. (SHC)

Large Heath

Coenonympha tullia Müller
(*typhon* Rottemburg)

Larva. 22–26 mm. Body green, with a very dark green dorsal line that is bordered with almost white stripes. In both the subdorsal and spiracular regions are more whitish stripes, the head is dark green and the longish anal points are tipped with pink.

Foodplants. Cotton-grass, white beak-sedge, purple moor-grass, and in captivity will also accept annual meadow-grass and sheep's-fescue.

Habits. A single-brooded species, with the larva feeding from July to late September and then hibernating within the grass clumps when about half grown. In late March it becomes active again and feeds during the day and night until pupation takes place during early June. In the spring the larvae can be obtained by searching or sweeping in peat bogs and on mosses. The adults are on the wing during late June and July and most females will lay freely in confinement if supplied with foodplant. This northern species is widespread in Scotland and Ireland, but much more local in England and Wales where many colonies have been lost by the destruction of its particular habitats.

Plate 6: M. Swept at night, fully grown. Late May.

The Ringlet

Aphantopus hyperantus Linnaeus

Larva. 21–24 mm. Body ochreous, with a brown dorsal line that becomes obscure on the thoracic segments. Below the black spiracles is a light ochreous line and the anal points are of the body colour.

Foodplants. Grasses, especially cock's-foot, tufted hair-grass and wood-sedge. Also accepts many other grass species in captivity.

Habits. A single-brooded species the larva of which overwinters when about half grown and feeds when the conditions are mild enough. It is active mainly at night, and during the spring it can readily be swept or found by torchlight, high up upon grasses. Pupation takes place near ground level during early to mid-June and lasts about a month. The adults fly in July, and from eggs laid in captivity the larvae should be left to develop naturally on potted grasses. Widely distributed in southern and central England, Wales and Ireland; more local in the north and in southern Scotland.

Plate 6: N. Swept at night, fully grown. Late May.

Family: DANAIDAE

The only example of this mainly tropical group occurs in Britain as a vagrant from North America or southern Europe. It is a great wanderer, each season travelling thousands of miles between breeding and hibernation sites, but is unlikely ever to establish itself in Britain due to the foodplants not occurring naturally here. The larvae, pupae and adults carry toxins which are accumulated by the larvae as they feed upon the poisonous foodplants. The bright green pupa is formed hanging inverted by the cremaster.

The Milkweed or Monarch

Danaus plexippus Linnaeus

Larva. 55–60 mm. Body very pale green, heavily banded with black and yellow. A pair of long black filaments are present on the thoracic segments and also a shorter pair near the rear of the body.

Foodplants. Milkweeds, which do not grow naturally in Britain.

Habits. This is a very rare migrant species that has probably never bred in the wild in this country. When it occurs it is usually in late summer and its origin could be from either America, the Canary Islands or even southern Spain, where it has been reported as breeding. It is a popular species in commercial butterfly houses and some records are almost certainly due to escapes from these establishments. In America it overwinters as an adult in the southern states and Mexico, congregating in huge gatherings upon trees.

Plate 6: O. Commercial stock from the United States.

Family: LASIOCAMPIDAE

The British fauna is represented by ten regularly found species of moths in this family, commonly known as the Eggars; one other species may still occur, but the last record was in 1965. All of the larvae are hairy and some species should be carefully handled as the hairs can cause irritation to sensitive skin. All form pupae enclosed in tough cocoons and most of these are located among the herbage or on the foodplants.

December Moth

Poecilocampa populi Linnaeus

Larva. 42–48 mm. Body bluish-grey, lightly tinged with green on the anterior part of each segment. Behind the greyish head is a russet mark and the whole body is covered in greyish setae.

Foodplants. Birch, oak, poplar, elm, hawthorn, blackthorn and various other deciduous trees.

Habits. A single-brooded species that overwinters in the egg stage. The larvae hatch in about mid-April and feed at first upon the buds and young leaves. They develop steadily throughout the spring and are fully grown by about June. Larger larvae can often be found basking on tree trunks or by beating at night, when they are more active. Pupation takes place under loose bark or on the ground in leaf litter and the adults emerge between late October and early December. This species is widely distributed over most of the British Isles, but less frequent in the northern areas.

Plate 7: A. Beaten from oak, nearly fully grown. Mid-May.

Pale Eggar

Trichiura crataegi Linnaeus

Larva. 37–43 mm. Body normally greyish-black, with lighter markings that are variable in colour and intensity. Many larvae have orangish dashes along the sides and near to the spiracles, while others have yellowish bands dorsally and white markings in the subdorsal region. All larvae are covered in long thin brownish or grey hairs.

Foodplants. Hawthorn, blackthorn, sallow, birch, bramble, heather and bilberry. Also recorded from other deciduous trees.

Habits. This single-brooded species overwinters as an egg, laid in large batches in the autumn upon twigs of the foodplant. From these, the varied and colourful larvae feed up between April and June, and pupate among dead leaves on the ground or sometimes in crevices under bark. The easiest way to obtain them is to beat from mid-May onwards. In the north and in Scotland, the life-cycle may take two years to complete, and they spend the second winter as nearly fully grown larvae, finishing the development in the following spring. The adults fly at night during September and both sexes are attracted to light. Widely distributed in the southern parts of Britain, but less frequent and much more local in the Midlands and the north. In Ireland it is very local in occurrence.

Plate 7: B. Beaten from blackthorn, nearly fully grown. Late May.

Small Eggar

Eriogaster lanestris Linnaeus

Larva. 45–50 mm. Body velvety black, with reddish-brown marks dorsally, that are bordered by conspicuous whitish lines. The head and thoracic legs are black, the prolegs are reddish-brown and the body is wholly covered in fine brownish hairs, some of which are quite long.

Foodplants. Hawthorn, blackthorn and dog rose.

Habits. A single-brooded insect that inhabits hedgerows and open woodland. The adults fly very early in the year, during February and March, and from the resulting eggs the gregarious larvae live inside silken webs from early May until July, when they become fully grown and then disperse. These conspicuous grey webs may be found on bushes growing in hedgerows and the larvae pupate in strong ochreous cocoons that are spun up on the foodplant twigs and branches. Most adults emerge in the following year, but some overwinter up to three times before hatching. At present this

once fairly common insect has become local and its range has contracted to occur only as far north as Yorkshire, but in Ireland the population has stayed more stable and it is locally common.
Plate 7: C and R. Found on hawthorn, fully grown. Early July. (AB)

The Lackey

Malacosoma neustria Linnaeus
Larva. 50–55 mm. Body blue, with a conspicuous thin white dorsal line that is bordered with stripes of black and orangish-red. The head is darker blue with two black markings and along the spiracular area are dense gingery hairs.
Foodplants. Hawthorn, sallow, bramble, blackthorn, apple, oak and other trees.
Habits. Single-brooded, overwintering as an egg. These are laid in batches in a ring around the foodplant twigs during July and August and hatch in the following April. The small larvae first construct a silken web, in which they live gregariously. The growth is rapid and by mid-June most larvae are fully grown and then disperse to find sheltered sites in which to pupate. The pupa is formed inside a tough yellow cocoon and lasts about three to four weeks. The larvae of this fairly common species are most often found by beating and when the populations are large they are frequently seen moving rapidly across paths, roads and other open ground as they disperse. Widespread over most of southern England, Ireland and Wales, but much less frequent in the north.
Plate 7: D. Beaten from blackthorn, nearly fully grown. Late May.

Ground Lackey

Malacosoma castrensis Linnaeus
Larva. 46–52 mm. Body brownish-black, and liberally marked with pale blue along the sides; also there are thin wavy orangish lines along the top and sides and many gingery hairs. The head is greyish and without spots.
Foodplants. Sea lavender, sea wormwood, sea plantain and many other saltmarsh plants. In captivity they accept sallow, plum and blackthorn.
Habits. Single-brooded. After overwintering as eggs, the young larvae hatch in April and live gregariously in a silken web. When they are larger they start to disperse and live in loose colonies among the plants growing on the salterns. In the known localities the larvae can easily be found by searching and once the first is located many others can be seen nearby. During fine weather they bask in sunshine and become very conspicuous, and any taken into captivity should be given plenty of light and air; spraying them daily with a lightly salted water solution is said to be beneficial. About early July they pupate inside a tough silken cocoon and this stage lasts about a month, with the light-responsive adults flying in late July and August. This species is very local to the saltmarshes of Kent, Essex and Suffolk. Also recorded in South Devon.
Plate 7: E. Found while basking, fully grown. Late June.

Grass Eggar

Lasiocampa trifolii Denis & Schiffermüller
Larva. 55–65 mm. Body blackish, heavily obscured by dense gingery hairs dorsally and greyish-white hairs along the sides. The head is greyish-white marked with ginger and black.
Foodplants. Sallows, bramble, heather, broom, bird's-foot trefoil, blackthorn, tree lupin, false oat-grass and many other plants.
Habits. A single-brooded species that overwinters as an egg. The larvae hatch in late March and feed up on various plants to become fully grown by about mid- to late June. They are probably easiest to obtain when they are large by beating or searching, and in captivity they prefer light and space for successful development. The cocooned pupae last about four to six weeks and both sexes of the adults respond to light traps, with the females usually laying freely in captivity. Mainly coastal in distribution in the southern counties from Kent to Cornwall and in Lancashire. Also in Glamorgan in South Wales.
Plate 7: F. Found on bramble, fully grown. Early June. (SHC)

Oak Eggar

Lasiocampa quercus Linnaeus
Larva. 65–80 mm. Body blackish-brown, heavily covered with pale greyish-white hairs dorsally and light brownish hairs on the sides. The head is speckled grey and brown and the spiracles are obvious and white. The young larvae are greyish-blue with orange diamond-shaped marks along the back. In some northern populations a melanic form of the larva occurs.
Foodplants. Heather, bramble, sallows, broom, blackthorn, hawthorn, ivy and bilberry are among the many acceptable plants.
Habits. Single-brooded, inhabiting heaths, commons, moors and other open ground. The eggs are laid during July and August and hatch after about two to three weeks. In the south this species hibernates as a half-grown larva and completes its growth in the spring, becoming fully fed and pupating, inside a tough cocoon, about early June. More northerly populations, especially those in Scotland, adopt a two-year life-cycle. The first winter is spent as a small larva and the second as a pupa. The male adults fly in sunshine, while the females often visit light traps at dusk and lay eggs readily in confinement. The offspring can then be bred up quicker by using bramble at first and then ivy, when other foods become unavailable during the winter. This species is widespread and locally common over most of Britain.
Plate 7: G and H. Bred from a female adult to MVL. Late July.

Fox Moth

Macrothylacia rubi Linnaeus
Larva. 60–70 mm. Body densely covered in long dark brown hairs, except along the back where the hairs are shorter and reddish-brown in colour and there are some greyish ones along the sides. The young larvae are quite different, with conspicuous yellow bands and shorter dark brown hairs.
Foodplants. Heather, bramble, bilberry, sallows and many other plants.
Habits. A single-brooded species, of which the larvae occur from about mid-June to the following April. During late May and June the grey egg batches of this species can often be found high up on a grass stalk, but these frequently produce only tiny wasps which have parasitized the brood. The eggs that survive predation hatch in about two to three weeks and the larvae feed steadily throughout the summer and become fully grown by late September, when they hibernate among leaf litter. During late March and April they become active and spend time basking, but do not feed again. Pupation takes place at the base of grass tussocks and other low sheltered spots, lasting about a month. In captivity the larvae can be difficult to overwinter and they should be left outside

as naturally as possible for any hope of success. This species occurs throughout the British Isles, preferring open habitats.
Plate 7: I and J. Found basking on heathland, about half grown. Late August.

The Drinker

Euthrix potatoria Linnaeus
Larva. 60–70 mm. Body greyish-black, with abundant orange speckling in the subdorsal region. Along the dorsal area there are many short tufts of very dark brown hair and near the spiracles tufts of white hairs.
Foodplants. Common reed, cock's-foot, reed canary-grass and other wide-bladed species of grass.
Habits. Single-brooded, being in the larval stage from August to the following June. During August to October the small larvae feed until they are about 25 mm long and then enter hibernation at the bases of the grass tussocks and among leaf and reed litter in their damp habitats. During mid-April feeding recommences and they become fully developed by about June. They feed mainly at night, but can readily be found during the day by close searching of the lower parts of the foodplants. Those taken in the spring are easy to rear in captivity, pupating in a cocoon for about a month, with the adults emerging in July and both sexes being attracted to light. This species is widely distributed over most of Britain and Ireland, but less frequent in the north.
Plate 7: K. Found on reed-stem, almost fully grown. Late May.

Small Lappet

Phyllodesma ilicifolia Linnaeus
Larva. 45–55 mm. Body bluish-grey, often with a broad brown dorsal stripe, edged conspicuously with white and having transverse bands of orangish-red; setae gingery; head grey.
Foodplants. Bilberry; also recorded on birch, sallow and other trees in continental Europe.
Habits. A single-brooded insect that occurs in the larval stage from June to the middle of August and has not been recorded in the British Isles since 1965. In the past the larvae have been found mainly in places where bilberry abounds, such as on moorland and in open woodland. Although speculation exists as to whether this species is now extinct, it has always been uncommon and local, therefore colonies could still survive at low densities in Britain. This species overwinters as a cocooned pupa, with the adults flying during late April and May, and the more recent records come from North Devon and Somerset.
Plate 7: L. Courtesy of Carlos Gomez de Aizpurua.

The Lappet

Gastropacha quercifolia Linnaeus
Larva. 75–90 mm. Body mainly grey, with very dark blue thoracic segmental divisions and an orangish fringe of hair above the legs along the whole body. Dorsally speckled with a few small orange pinacula and sometimes marked with light grey to white along the back.
Foodplants. Blackthorn, hawthorn, buckthorn, sallow, plum and apple.
Habits. A single-brooded species, occurring as a larva from August to the following spring. The young larvae feed at night until they are about 20 mm long in October, and then hibernate low down on the trunk of their foodplant. During the winter they can sometimes be found in such locations and, if kept, they should be sleeved outside. During April they start to feed again at night and become fully grown by late May. During May their size makes them fairly easy to find by torchlight while they feed on the young growth of the outer twigs of the foodplant and during the day they can be located at the trunk bases fairly readily. The cocooned pupa is formed in plant litter, lasting about four to six weeks, with the adults being attracted to light during July. Captive stocks, bred from the eggs, can often be forced to complete their life-cycle in about four months by keeping them warm, but the resulting adults are usually undersized. This species is widespread, but rarely common, in the hedgerows and scrub habitats of southern Britain.
Plate 7: M. Found at base of blackthorn, fully grown. Mid-May. (MB)

Family: SATURNIIDAE

The sole British example of this mainly tropical family is to be found throughout the country and the fully grown larva is unmistakable. It belongs to the same group as the Silkworm, *Bombyx mori*, which is kept in captivity worldwide for commercial purposes.

Emperor Moth

Pavonia pavonia Linnaeus
Larva. 60–65 mm. Body bright green, with a white tuberculated black band around the middle part of each segment. The head is green and black bristles emit from the tubercles. The young larvae are black and marked with orange and light yellowish-green.
Foodplants. Heather, sallow, bramble, hawthorn, meadowsweet, blackthorn and hazel, with many others accepted.
Habits. Single-brooded, with the larvae hatching from the eggs during late May and becoming fully grown by about late August. When they are smaller they can be swept from some of their foodplants, such as heather, but otherwise they must be found by searching. The overwintering pupae are formed in conspicuous tough ginger-coloured cocoons which are frequently located high up in the heather and are often found by chance in moor and heathland localities. During late April and May, the male adults fly in sunshine and occasionally females come to light traps; these will normally lay eggs without any special conditions. This species is widespread in most open ground habitats throughout most of the British Isles.
Plate 7: N and O. Bred from female adult to MVL on sallow and bramble. Early May.

Family: ENDROMIDAE

The larva of the single British example of this family is in some ways similar to those of certain *Sphingidae*, but lacks the horn-like structure on the eleventh segment. The males fly in sunshine and, along with the females, attend light traps soon after dusk.

Kentish Glory

Endromis versicolora Linnaeus
Larva. 50–60 mm. Body yellowish-green, with a conspicuous hump on the last segment and oblique yellow stripes along the whole body.
Foodplants. Birch and alder.
Habits. A single-brooded insect, occurring as a larva from

about June to mid-August. The adults fly in April and May, and the purplish-brown eggs are normally laid in clusters upon the twigs of scrub birch in its moorland habitats where they can be very conspicuous on the budding foodplant. When small, the larvae will congregate together on bare twigs when not feeding, but later, when they are fully grown in late July, they can be located by finding the stripped leaves and large pieces of frass on the ground beneath. The pupa is spun up in a cocoon among leaf litter or just underground and the insect may overwinter up to three times before emergence. At present this species seems to be local on moorland in Inverness-shire, Aberdeenshire, Morayshire and Perthshire, but may still occur in its old haunts in the Wyre Forest of the West Midlands of England.
Plate 7: P and Q. From an egg batch found on birch. Late May. (BH)

Family: DREPANIDAE

Six species of the Hook-tip family are regularly found in Britain and their larvae feed on tree leaves and have the anal claspers modified into a raised point. They usually inhabit woodland and commons, and all overwinter as cocooned pupae formed among leaves.

Scalloped Hook-tip
Falcaria lacertinaria Linnaeus
Larva. 23–26 mm. Body mottled greenish-brown without any anal claspers, instead the last segment becomes a raised point; on the second and third thoracic segments are double tubercular structures.
Foodplant. Birch.
Habits. A double-brooded species, with the larvae occurring from early June to mid-July, and again from mid-August to about late September. They feed on the upperside of the leaves and can easily be beaten from lower branches of the foodplant, often preferring younger trees. They pupate in spun up leaves upon the trees in summer, and the later brood does the same on leaves that will fall to the ground in late autumn. The adults fly during May and late July to August, with both sexes being attracted to light. In Scotland it is single-brooded and its season follows about two weeks behind the spring generation in the south. Widely distributed over most of Britain.
Plate 8: A. Beaten from birch, fully grown. Mid-September. (DWP)

Oak Hook-tip
Drepana binaria Hufnagel
Larva. 22–25 mm. Body ochreous, with a paler diamond-shaped mark dorsally above the prolegs. On the third thoracic segment is a twin-pointed structure and the anal claspers are absent.
Foodplant. Oak.
Habits. The larval periods of this double-brooded species are in June and July, and again in late August and September. They feed and rest on the upperside of leaves and they can readily be beaten from the foodplant. Also, they are easily bred from light-trapped females, which fly in May and August. Pupation takes place in a cocoon spun up in leaves and they overwinter in this stage. To be found in most parts of England and Wales as far north as Westmorland, in woods, heaths and commons.
Plate 8: B. Bred from female adult to MVL. Mid-August. (M&JH)

Barred Hook-tip
Drepana cultraria Fabricius
Larva. 19–22 mm. Body ochreous with a dark-edged diamond-shaped mark of pale ochreous dorsally above the prolegs. The hump on the third segment is smaller than that on *D. binaria* and the larva seems to be of a slimmer build.
Foodplant. Beech.
Habits. A double-brooded species, with the larvae to be found in June and July, and those of the second generation in September. They can be beaten, but populations are rarely large enough to obtain many by this method. During May and August the adult females come readily to light and will often lay eggs if given fresh foodplant leaves. As with all Hook-tips the pupa is formed in a silken cocoon spun in the leaves and overwinters in this stage. It is a locally common species in most of southern England, especially on chalk.
Plate 8: C. Bred from female adult to MVL. Mid-August. (M&JH)

Pebble Hook-tip
Drepana falcataria Linnaeus
Larva. 19–24 mm. Body bluish-green with ochreous and brown markings on most of the back. There are twin humps on the segments from two to five and the head is yellowish and banded with brown; anal claspers are absent.
Foodplants. Birch and alder.
Habits. Usually a double-brooded species, except in Scotland, where its univoltine life-cycle runs about two weeks later than the normal spring populations. Between late June and late July, and during September, the larvae can easily be beaten from birch, especially at night. For most of the day they rest on the underside of a leaf with the edges turned in with silken threads and they can be found by silhouetting the leaves against the sky. Females will lay in captivity and no special conditions are required for successful rearing. This species is widespread over most parts of Britain, but seems to be less frequent in Ireland.
Plate 8: D. Beaten by day, fully grown. Late September. (PJP)

Dusky Hook-tip
Drepana curvatula Borkhausen
Larva. 18–22 mm. Body laterally green, dorsally brown with a purplish bloom, and pairs of small reddish projections along the subdorsal areas, from which short black setae emanate; spiracles white, ringed with black; head whitish, heavily banded with dark brown; anal claspers absent.
Foodplants. Birch, alder and oak.
Habits. A double-brooded suspected immigrant species, of which adults have been recorded in Britain on nine occasions. In Europe the larvae occur during June and July, and again in late August and September, and may produce a third brood when kept warm in captivity. They are very easy to rear, pupating in a silken cocoon among the foodplant leaves, for overwintering when necessary. The adults have occurred in May and in late July and August with both sexes coming to light.
Plate 8: E. Bred from a female adult to MVL (France). Mid-August. (WK)

Scarce Hook-tip
Sabra harpagula Esper
Larva. 22–25 mm. Body brown, with greenish-yellow dorsal saddle markings on the abdominal segments. The head is heavily marked with reddish-brown and the anal claspers are absent, being replaced by a reddish-brown point.

Foodplant. Small-leaved lime.
Habits. A single-brooded species, with the larvae occurring from about mid-July until the last become fully grown during September. They seem to feed on the higher branches of the trees, as trying to obtain them by beating is mostly unsuccessful, even in their best localities. During late June and July the female adults will occasionally come to light, but most seem reluctant to lay in captivity. If eggs are obtained, the best method to rear them is to sleeve out the young larvae on growing food and let them develop naturally. Pupation for overwintering will take place in spun leaves. Very local, in the large mature woods of Monmouthshire and Gloucestershire.
Plate 8: F. Bred from a female adult to MVL. Early July. (RMcC)

Chinese Character
Cilix glaucata Scopoli
Larva. 15–18 mm. Body variegated with reddish-brown and brownish-grey with a raised hump on segment three. The anal claspers are absent and are replaced by a dark brown point.
Foodplants. Hawthorn, blackthorn, bramble, apple and pear.
Habits. Double-brooded, with larvae to be found from mid-June to mid-July, and those of the second generation from late August and throughout September. They can easily be beaten from hawthorns and blackthorns that grow in hedgerows and in scrubby places. Both sexes of the adults come to light during May and late July and August, and eggs are readily laid by captive females. Pupation takes place inside a cocoon spun up in leaves or sometimes under loose bark, the pupae overwintering when necessary. This species is generally distributed in England, Wales, southern Scotland and Ireland.
Plate 8: G. Bred from a female adult to MVL. Early June. (RM)

Family: THYATIRIDAE

This family is represented in Britain by nine species. All overwinter as pupae, except *C. diluta* which does so in the egg stage. The adults of all species respond well to light and many also come to sugar and flowers to feed. Some of the larvae construct domiciles from the foodplant leaves in which to hide during the day, emerging at night to feed.

Peach Blossom
Thyatira batis Linnaeus
Larva. 28–33 mm. Body light reddish-brown marked with darker brown. Upon the third thoracic segment is a double raised structure and several more pyramid-shaped structures on segments five to nine.
Foodplant. Bramble.
Habits. Normally a single-brooded species, with the larvae occurring from early July until about mid-September. Adult females will come to sugar and light, from late May to mid-July, and given fresh foodplant they will often produce eggs. Finding larvae in the wild is difficult as they feed mostly at night and bramble is awkward to beat, but they can sometimes be found by torchlight. A few individuals occasionally produce a small second brood in the autumn. The insect overwinters as a pupa, formed in a cocoon just under the soil, and is generally distributed over much of Britain.
Plate 8: H. Bred from a female adult to MVL. Late May. (RM)

Buff Arches
Habrosyne pyritoides Hufnagel
(*derasa* Linnaeus)
Larva. 32–36 mm. Body of a warm reddish-brown with a conspicuous yellowish spot on the side of segment four and a smaller spot on segment five. The dorsal line is darker brown and the head paler brown.
Foodplant. Bramble.
Habits. The larvae of this single-brooded species can be found from late July until mid-October when the very last are fully grown. They feed mainly at night and can be found by searching brambles with a torch, especially those growing beneath trees. Pupation takes place in the ground inside a loose cocoon, and occasionally they have been known to hatch in the autumn, but most remain in this stage until the following June or July. The adults will come freely to light traps and the females lay eggs in captivity. This insect is widely distributed over most of England as far north as Cumbria, also occurring in Wales and Ireland.
Plate 8: I. Found at night, fully grown. Early September. (SHC)

Figure of Eighty
Tethea ocularis Linnaeus
Larva. 33–37 mm. Body greyish-white, with a yellowish plate behind the orange head.
Foodplants. Poplar and aspen.
Habits. From the eggs laid during June and July, the larvae of this single-brooded species are to be found until late August. The females can be obtained at light traps and by sugaring, especially on poplar trunks, and they will lay in captivity upon fresh leaves. The larvae feed at night and can be beaten, or during the day they can be found between two leaves spun flatly together. The insect overwinters as a pupa in a cocoon, still between leaves that eventually fall to the ground. To be found in England as far north as Cumbria and in eastern Wales.
Plate 8: J. Beaten at night, nearly fully grown. Late July.

Poplar Lutestring
Tethea or Denis & Schiffermüller
Larva. 32–37 mm. Body yellowish-white, with a yellowish-orange plate on the first segment. The head is orange and the greyish dorsal vessel is just visible.
Foodplants. Aspen and occasionally poplar.
Habits. The larva of this single-brooded species can be found between flatly spun leaves between mid-July and September. After dark it leaves its retreat and feeds in the open and then can readily be beaten. During June and early July both sexes of the adult come to sugar and light, and eggs should be laid if fresh foodplant is available to the captive females. Pupation takes place in a cocoon between the leaves and the insects overwinter in this stage. Widely distributed over most of the British Isles, but local in Ireland.
Plate 8: K. Found between spun leaves, fully grown. Mid-August.

Satin Lutestring
Tetheella fluctuosa Hübner
Larva. 26–30 mm. Body blackish-green and lightly dusted with tiny pale marks; below the spiracles is a mottled whitish-green stripe. The head is dull yellow-brown and marked with black.

Foodplant. Birch.
Habits. A single-brooded species, the larvae of which can be located inside spun up leaves on the foodplant from late July until the middle of September. At night the larva leaves its retreat to feed and can then be obtained by beating. During June to early August females that come to light can sometimes be encouraged to lay eggs, but the very young larvae seem reluctant to develop. In September pupation takes place in a cocoon spun between leaves that eventually fall in autumn. This species is local, mainly occurring in the south-east, the Midlands, Cumbria, Wales, central Scotland and western Ireland.
Plate 8: L. Bred from a female adult to MVL. Mid-July. (SHC)

Common Lutestring
Ochropacha duplaris Linnaeus
Larva. 21–24 mm. Body dark green dorsally, with a darker central line and laterally pale whitish-green. The head is dull orange and the obvious thoracic plate is shining black.
Foodplants. Birch, and sometimes alder and oak.
Habits. A single-brooded species, the larvae of which can be found in their spun up leaves between late July and early October. They can be beaten after dark, when they emerge to feed in the open, and are easy to rear in captivity. The female adults come frequently to light in June and July, with most readily laying in confinement. Pupation is inside a silken cocoon among leaves and they spend the winter in this stage. The species is generally distributed throughout the British Isles.
Plate 8: M. Bred from a female adult to MVL. Early July. (SHC)

Oak Lutestring
Cymatophorima diluta Denis & Schiffermüller
Larva. 23–28 mm. Body yellowish-white, with a visible grey dorsal vessel and a shining black head. The thoracic plate is bone coloured.
Foodplant. Oak.
Habits. Single-brooded. After overwintering as eggs, laid upon oak twigs, the larvae hatch during May and become fully grown by about early July. During the day they hide inside a strong spinning of leaves and cannot often be dislodged by beating. These spinnings can be found, but it is better to wait until dusk when the larvae emerge to feed, to obtain them by beating. In late August and September the adults come to sugar and light, but the females are reluctant to lay in captivity and even when eggs are obtained the young larvae do not often survive. This woodland species is locally common over much of England and Wales, but less frequent in the northern counties and in southern Scotland.
Plate 8: N. Beaten at dusk, fully grown. Early July. (MJF)

Yellow Horned
Achlya flavicornis Linnaeus
Larva. 28–33 mm. Body olive-green, liberally spotted with white and with a thin greyish dorsal line. The head is reddish-brown and the plate is grey and black with a white central mark. Pale green underneath the body.
Foodplant. Birch.
Habits. The larvae of this early spring species can easily be found in spun up birch leaves between mid-May and mid-July. Sometimes they can be beaten by day, but this method is more successful after dark when they leave their spinnings to feed. Pupation takes place on the ground in a flimsy cocoon among leaf litter or just in the soil and they overwinter in this stage. The adults emerge in March and April, with both sexes being attracted to light and most females laying freely in confinement. Widespread and generally common over most of the British Isles, especially in woodland and on heaths.
Plate 8: O. Bred from a female adult to MVL. Early April.

Frosted Green
Polyploca ridens Fabricius
Larva. 30–35 mm. Body yellow, mottled with light green and white spots dorsally. The head is orange and has small pale yellow marks.
Foodplant. Oak.
Habits. A single-brooded insect, the larva of which can readily be obtained by beating, especially at night, from late May until about mid-July, from the main boughs of mature oaks. During the day it hides on the underside of a leaf that has been loosely folded with silken threads. In April and early May light-trapped females lay well in confinement and the tiny larvae should be given fresh soft oak leaves to start their growth. No special conditions are necessary for the rest of the development. The cocooned pupa is formed in leaf litter on the ground and it may overwinter more than once in this stage. It is locally common in southern England, but less frequent further north.
Plate 8: P. Beaten at night, fully grown. Late June.

Family: GEOMETRIDAE

A large family consisting of about 300 British species, almost all of the larvae having the characteristic of the absence of the first three pairs of prolegs, moving by a looping process of arching and straightening the body. The majority feed openly upon the foodplant, with a few species boring into the flowers or seed capsules, but the larvae of quite a few common species are unknown in the wild, especially those of the subfamily *Sterrhinae*, being very retiring in their habits. Overwintering most frequently occurs in the pupal stage, although there are many exceptions. The adults are not strong flyers and they are active mainly at night, but a good proportion can be obtained during the day by disturbing them from herbage and branches. Many are attracted to light, a few also to sugar, with most females laying eggs freely in captivity, and generally the larvae are not difficult to rear.

SUBFAMILY: ARCHIEARINAE

Orange Underwing
Archiearis parthenias Linnaeus
Larva. 24–26 mm. Body green, with six thin white stripes along the back and sides and a bold white line beneath the black spiracles; the head is yellowish-green.
Foodplants. Birch and rowan.
Habits. A single-brooded day-flying insect that occurs as a larva from April to June. From the eggs laid in March and April, the larvae hatch after about three weeks and begin to feed at first on the catkins. Later they feed upon the young leaf growth and rest during the day in a loose spinning between the leaves. They can be beaten, especially at night. By early June most will have pupated in a cocoon spun upon the surface of dead or rotten wood and in this stage they overwinter. In captivity the fully fed larvae should be given rough cork or rotten wood for their pupation. Widely

distributed over most of Britain, especially in mature woods and on heathland.
Plate 8: Q. Bred from female adult netted by day. Early April.

Light Orange Underwing
Archiearis notha Hübner
Larva. 22–25 mm. Body green and variably marked with black laterally. There are two pale dorsal lines and another greenish-white line below the spiracles; the head is green and marked with black.
Foodplant. Aspen.
Habits. A single-brooded day-flying species, the larvae of which can be found between spun leaves from early May to mid-June, and at night they may be beaten when they have left their retreats to feed. When fully grown, the larva pupates in a strong cocoon that is spun using rotten or decaying wood particles as well as the larva's own silk. It remains in this stage normally until the following spring, but has been known to overwinter up to three times before emerging. In captivity the day-flying female moths lay readily and the fully grown larvae must be supplied with rough cork or soft bark for successful pupation. A local species found mainly in southern England.
Plate 8: R. Bred from female adult netted by day. Mid-April. (BE)

SUBFAMILY: OENOCHROMINAE

March Moth
Alsophila aescularia Denis & Schiffermüller
Larva. 24–28 mm. Body pale green, with many thin white stripes along the back and a pale yellow subspiracular line. The head is green and on the fifth abdominal segment is a small rudimentary proleg which will distinguish this species from most other *Geometridae* larvae.
Foodplants. Oak, hawthorn, blackthorn, birch and many other deciduous trees and shrubs.
Habits. Single-brooded. During March and early April, at night, the wingless females of this moth can be beaten from foodplant branches and they lay readily in captivity. The larvae hatch about late April and no special conditions are required for their development. During May and June larvae can also be beaten from the many foodplants and pupation takes place in the soil in a slight cocoon. In confinement these should be kept outside in the shade to avoid them drying out. The moth occurs over most of the British Isles.
Plate 9: A. Beaten from oak, nearly fully grown. Late May.

SUBFAMILY: GEOMETRINAE

Rest Harrow
Aplasta ononaria Fuessly
Larva. 14–16 mm. Body bright green, with many short pale bristles, each growing from a tiny yellow tubercle; the head is also green.
Foodplant. Common restharrow.
Habits. A mainly single-brooded species. From the eggs laid in late June and July, the majority of larvae feed from late July until September and then hibernate low down on the foodplant while they are still small. In the spring they become active again and are fully grown by about late May. A few larvae feed up quickly and produce a second brood of adults during late August and September. Pupation takes place in a loose spinning at the base of the foodplant or adjacent herbage. The larvae can sometimes be swept from or found on their foodplant during the late summer or in the spring. A very local species which seems to be confined to the coastal areas of south-east Kent.
Plate 9: B. Swept at night, nearly fully grown. Mid-May.

Grass Emerald
Pseudoterpna pruinata Hufnagel
Larva. 25–28 mm. Body dark green, with a conspicuous white spiracular stripe that often has a pink tinge. The dorsal line is darker than the body and there are pale lines in the subdorsal region. The head is cleft and tipped with pink and the anal point is also tipped pink.
Foodplants. Broom, gorse and petty whin.
Habits. A single-brooded species that hibernates as a small larva, usually among its foodplant. During the spring feeding recommences mainly at night and the larvae become fully grown by around early June. When larger, the larvae are normally easy to obtain by beating or sweeping, and pupation takes place in a cocoon among plant litter. This stage lasts about a month with the adults flying from mid-June to August. Generally distributed throughout the British Isles, except in the north of Scotland.
Plate 9: C. Swept from broom at night, fully grown. Late May.

Large Emerald
Geometra papilionaria Linnaeus
Larva. 28–33 mm. Body yellowish-green, covered in tiny white pinacula and having a green cleft head tipped with reddish-brown. Along the back are four pairs of reddish-brown tipped humps and another shorter structure near the rear of the body. During the winter the whole larva assumes the reddish-brown of birch twigs.
Foodplants. Birch and sometimes alder, beech and hazel.
Habits. A single-brooded species that spends the winter as a small larva, fully exposed upon a silken pad on the twigs of its foodplant. Prior to hibernation the small larvae are green and when the leaves fall in autumn they change to reddish-brown to be camouflaged from predators. They resume feeding in about mid-April and most are fully grown by late May. During this time they can easily be beaten from the branches of the foodplant and in the wild they pupate among leaf litter. The adults fly from late June to early August and both sexes respond well to light. Widely distributed throughout most of the British Isles.
Plate 9: D. Beaten from birch, fully grown. Mid-May. (DD)

Blotched Emerald
Comibaena bajularia Denis & Schiffermüller
(*pustulata* Hufnagel)
Larva. 17–20 mm. Body reddish-brown, liberally marked with darker brown and black, also with three thin dark brown lines dorsally. The body has short bristles to which the larva attaches with silk small pieces of dry leaf and bud scales to hide almost totally from any predators.
Foodplant. Oak.
Habits. Single-brooded. During late July and August the larvae hatch from the eggs and feed slowly until they hibernate in the autumn. Activity starts again in the spring as soon as the oaks begin to bud and by early June most will have pupated in a slight silken cocoon among leaf litter. From mid-May, when the larvae are nearly fully grown, they can readily be beaten from oaks in mature woodland. Their camouflage is excellent and the debris on the beating tray must be watched for movement to detect these larvae. Dur-

ing late June and July the adults are on the wing, but the females are infrequent at light traps. This species is widespread over southern England as far north as Yorkshire; it also occurs in east Wales.
Plate 9: E. Beaten from oak, nearly fully grown. Late May. (M&JH)

Essex Emerald

Thetidia smaragdaria Fabricius
Larva. 27–29 mm. Body light brown, mottled with darker brown and very wrinkled; it has a blackish-brown dorsal line and adorns itself with fragments of the foodplant.
Foodplants. Sea wormwood, and in captivity wormwood and southernwood.
Habits. This single-brooded insect overwinters as a half-grown larva among the dead and curled leaves on the lower part of the foodplant. During September the larvae can be located by careful searching and then transferred to growing plants in tubs to overwinter as naturally as possible. In the spring feeding recommences and they become fully grown by about late May, but they seem to be much more difficult to locate after hibernation. The pupa lasts about three to four weeks, with the adults flying from mid-June to early July. An extremely local species, being found only on the saltmarshes of Essex and Kent, it seems to be on the verge of extinction in this country. Due to its status it is at present protected by law from collecting.
Plate 9: F. Located by searching, half grown. Mid-September. (MH)

Common Emerald

Hemithea aestivaria Hübner
Larva. 26–30 mm. Body variable in colour, one form being green with reddish-brown on the thoracic segments and anal segments, another being ochreous with dark brown chevrons on the back and an incomplete black dorsal line. Often there is an obvious dark marking on segment five; the head is deeply cleft and mostly brown.
Foodplants. Hawthorn, oak, sallow, blackthorn, birch and many other deciduous trees and shrubs.
Habits. A single-brooded species that overwinters as a small larva. During the spring, when they are feeding again, the larvae can easily be beaten from their foodplants and most are fully grown by about late May or early June. Pupation takes place in a spinning among the leaves of the foodplant and lasts for about three weeks. The adults fly during late June and July, being frequent visitors to light traps. Widely distributed and fairly common in England as far north as Cumbria, also in Wales and Ireland.
Plate 9: G. Beaten at dusk from oak, fully grown. Mid-May. (AJP)

Small Grass Emerald

Chlorissa viridata Linnaeus
Larva. 21–24 mm. Body whitish-green, with an incomplete pinkish-brown dorsal line. The head is cleft and the points are marked with brown.
Foodplants. Heather, birch, creeping willow and in captivity it will also accept most species of sallow.
Habits. Single-brooded, occurring as a larva in July and August. From the eggs laid in June and early July the larvae feed up quickly and by late August most will have pupated. The winter is spent in this stage; the pupae are usually spun up in plant debris or on the foodplant. During June and early July the adults can easily be disturbed from heather, with the females laying readily in confinement and no special conditions being required for successful rearing of the larvae. These can also be swept from heather or beaten from their other foodplants quite easily. This very local species frequents damp heathland in southern England and the boggy mosses of Cumbria.
Plate 9: H. Bred from netted female adult. Mid-June. (SHC)

Sussex Emerald

Thalera fimbrialis Scopoli
Larva. 28–30 mm. Body light green, normally with a bright pink dorsal line and a cleft brown head. Behind the head are two brownish points and the anal flap is also brown; low down on the seventh abdominal segment is a maroon mark.
Foodplants. Wild carrot, yarrow, ragworts and probably many other plants.
Habits. Single-brooded, with the larval period lasting from late August until about the following June. During the winter the larvae hibernate low down on the foodplant or nearby among plant litter. Before and after the hibernation these larvae can be swept or found fairly readily. Those found in the autumn should be kept outside on potted plants in a frost-protected environment and the survival rate should be high. During July and August females sometimes come to light and they can also be found after dark resting on tall grasses; they will lay in captivity. The only known colony of this species is on the shingle area of southern Kent and is at present protected by law from being collected.
Plate 9: I. Bred from a female adult to MVL. Late July. (RD)

Small Emerald

Hemistola chrysoprasaria Esper
(*immaculata* Thunberg)
Larva. 27–30 mm. Body yellowish-green, with indistinct white lines and minute white tubercles; sometimes with a reddish dorsal line. The head is brownish and deeply cleft and the first segment has a twin-pointed structure facing forwards.
Foodplants. Traveller's-joy and garden species of *Clematis*.
Habits. After hatching from the egg in August, this single-brooded species overwinters as a small larva upon its foodplant. In April feeding resumes and most larvae will be fully grown by early June. Beating during the spring is the most productive method of obtaining these larvae and sometimes they can be quite common. The pupa is formed inside a loose spinning and lasts about one month before emergence. Locally common in southern and eastern England, especially on chalk.
Plate 9: J. Bred from a female adult to light. Mid-July. (JMP)

Little Emerald

Jodis lactearia Linnaeus
Larva. 18–22 mm. Body darkish green, with small yellow-ringed red blotches along the dorsal line between the segments; the head is brown and deeply cleft.
Foodplants. Birch, hawthorn, oak, bilberry and various other plants.
Habits. From the eggs laid during May and June, the larvae of this single-brooded species feed up steadily between July and September on a great variety of foodplants. They are easy to obtain by sweeping and beating in the wooded habitats that they prefer. Pupation takes place in a loose spinning among the leaves and they spend the winter in this stage. They are widely distributed over England, Wales and Ireland, but more local in western Scotland.
Plate 9: K. Swept from bilberry, fully grown. Early September.

SUBFAMILY: STERRHINAE

Dingy Mocha

Cyclophora pendularia Clerck
(*orbicularia* Hübner)

Larva. 20–24 mm. Body bluish-grey, and heavily marked with olive-green along the back. Laterally there are vague brown markings on the middle segments and the head is mottled with reddish-brown.

Foodplants. Sallows, especially the small-leaved species.

Habits. A double-brooded species that overwinters as a pupa. The larvae occur from mid-June to mid-July and those of the second brood from late August until about the end of September. The larval development is rapid, with the insects feeding by day and night fully exposed upon the leaves. They can be taken by beating and the female moths come to light, during May and late July to late August, readily laying eggs in captivity. This very local species seems to be found only in Dorset, Hampshire, southern Wiltshire and Shropshire, and is declining in numbers.

Plate 9: L. Bred from a female adult to MVL. Late July. (DB)

The Mocha

Cyclophora annulata Schulze

Larva. 20–23 mm. Body green, with yellow between the segments, two thin pale lines along the centre of the back and a pale brownish head. There is also an ochreous form of the larva.

Foodplants. Maple and in captivity sycamore.

Habits. Double-brooded. Throughout July and again in late August and September the larvae of this species can often be obtained by beating maple boughs in calcareous localities. From mid-May to mid-June and in August the female adults will come to light and they will often lay in captivity when given foodplant as a stimulus; the larvae require no special conditions for successful development. Overwintering is in the pupal stage. Locally distributed in most of southern England.

Plate 9: M. Beaten by day from maple, fully grown. Late July.

Birch Mocha

Cyclophora albipunctata Hufnagel
(*pendularia* auctt.)

Larva. 22–26 mm. Body green, with yellow between the segments and a brown head and claspers, or ashy-grey with russet marks dorsally between the segments and a dark brown head. Both colour forms are common.

Foodplant. Birch.

Habits. The larvae from the main brood of this species can easily be beaten from the foodplant during late June and July, and those of the partial second generation, in the south, during September and early October. They overwinter in the pupal stage and the preferred habitats are woods and heathland. The adults fly in May and June, also in August, and are freely attracted to light. Widely distributed and fairly common over most of the British Isles.

Plate 9: N. Beaten by day, fully grown. Late September.

Blair's Mocha

Cyclophora puppillaria Hübner

Larva. 21–24 mm. Body yellowish-green, with yellow between the segments, minute yellow dots all over and a reddish-brown head; or the body is ochreous and paler between the segments with the head brown. The green form is more frequent.

Foodplants. Evergreen oak and common oak on young fresh growth. In captivity it has been known to accept privet, *Myrtus* and *Cistus*.

Habits. A migrant species that most years turns up sparingly at light between August and October. Females are often fertile and will lay eggs readily in captivity, if given leaves as a stimulus. The young larvae prefer to eat the soft fresh growth of the foodplants and during the autumn evergreen oak is probably the best choice. If they are kept warm, they grow rapidly and many successive broods may be obtained. The most likely place to encounter this species is on the south coast.

Plate 9: O. Bred from a female adult on privet. Early October. (DD)

False Mocha

Cyclophora porata Linnaeus

Larva. 20–24 mm. Body various shades of green or ochreous with paler colour between the segments and an indistinct paler line low down along the sides. Some larvae have dark lines along the subdorsal region.

Foodplant. Oak.

Habits. A double-brooded species, with the larvae occurring from mid-June until late July, and those of the partial second generation during September and early October. Females attend light traps during May to mid-June and late August to mid-September, and eggs may be obtained. When trying to obtain stock beating can also be successful. They overwinter in the pupal stage among plant litter. This species is local and usually uncommon in the southern parts of England and in Wales.

Plate 9: P. Bred from a female adult to MVL. Early September. (SHC)

Maiden's Blush

Cyclophora punctaria Linnaeus

Larva. 22–25 mm. Body of a shade of green or grey, with distinct yellow oblique markings along the back. The dorsal line is faint and darker than the main body and the head is heavily mottled with brown.

Foodplants. Oak and possibly birch.

Habits. The larvae of this double-brooded species can readily be beaten from oaks during late June and July and again during September. The adults come to light in May, June and August, and the females will often lay eggs in captivity; the resulting larvae need no special conditions to develop. The winter is spent as a pupa in leaf litter. Widely distributed over much of Britain except the northern parts of Scotland.

Plate 9: Q. Beaten by day, fully grown. Late September.

Clay Triple-lines

Cyclophora linearia Hübner

Larva. 21–23 mm. Body bluish-grey, with russet coloured blotches that are edged with cream along the subdorsal area and a few small russet dots along the back. The dorsal line is thin, pale and edged with brown. A rare colour form is green with a brown head and anal claspers.

Foodplant. Beech.

Habits. Normally a single-brooded species, with the main bulk of the larvae feeding from late June until about late August. A partial second brood sometimes occurs and the larvae from this will be found during September and October. Adult females often come to light in June and early July, and these frequently lay in captivity; the larvae can also be beaten from their foodplant. They pupate in leaf litter and

overwinter in this stage. Locally common in much of southern England as far north as Cheshire; also found in South Wales and parts of Ireland.
Plate 9: R. Bred from a female adult to MVL. Mid-June.

Blood-vein

Timandra griseata Petersen
(*amata* auctt.)
Larva. 18–22 mm. Body greyish-brown, with much darker brown mottling. The dorsal line is obvious and greyish-brown, as are several oblique lines along the back. The body tapers from the fourth segment to the head.
Foodplants. Dock, sorrel, knotgrass and orache.
Habits. Double-brooded, with the larvae occurring in July and then from September through until the following April. The easiest way to obtain stocks of this species is to breed from female moths; these will lay in confinement if supplied with the foodplant, and rearing the larvae is usually successful. Pupation takes place in a cocoon among plant litter. Common and generally distributed over southern England and most of Wales, but local and less frequent in Ireland and the border counties.
Plate 10: A. Bred from a moth netted at dusk on dock. Mid-May. (M&JH)

Lewes Wave

Scopula immorata Linnaeus
Larva. 22–25 mm. Body ochreous dorsally, with a pale line that is edged with brown especially on the last segments. A brown stripe subdorsally and the spiracles are obvious and coloured black.
Foodplants. In captivity knotgrass, plantain, dandelion and dock.
Habits. In Britain the larval stage lasted from August to the following May, and the larvae probably hibernated among plant litter. The species occurred in one heathy wood in East Sussex, until the habitat was greatly changed, and it has not been seen since 1961. In captivity the larvae feed up quickly, pupate in plant debris and produce adults in September.
Plate 10: B. From a female adult netted by day (S. E. France). Early July.

Sub-angled Wave

Scopula nigropunctata Hufnagel
Larva. 26–29 mm. Body ochreous, with a thin brown dorsal line and two thin pale lines along the sides. The underparts are dark brown and the head is round and the same colour as the body.
Foodplants. In captivity traveller's-joy and dandelion.
Habits. A single-brooded species that occurs as a larva from August until the following May. In the wild the foodplants are unknown and overwintering probably takes place among plant debris. In July both sexes sometimes come to light or can be disturbed from foliage during the day, and the females will often lay in captivity. Larvae can be forced to develop faster by keeping them warm and supplied with fresh food and no special conditions are required for breeding them. Pupation takes place between spun leaves. Very local, occurring in southern Kent and south-east Sussex.
Plate 10: C. Bred from female adult to MVL on dandelion. Late July. (BS)

Lace Border

Scopula ornata Scopoli
Larva. 17–20 mm. Body light reddish-brown, heavily marked with black dorsally, except on the last segments. Along the lower side is a whitish line and the brown mottled head is streaked with brownish-white.
Foodplants. Common thyme, marjoram and in confinement garden mint.
Habits. Double-brooded, with the larvae occurring from mid-June until mid-July and again from late August, through the winter, until about late April. Females can be flushed up during sunny days and sometimes they come to light. In captivity they often lay eggs and the larval growth will be rapid as long as they are kept warm. The pupa is spun in a loose cocoon on the foodplant. This local species seems confined mainly to the North Downs of Kent and Surrey, and Norfolk and Gloucestershire.
Plate 10: D. Bred from a female adult netted by day. Early June.

Tawny Wave

Scopula rubiginata Hufnagel
Larva. 19–22 mm. Body light greyish-brown, with an indistinct pale dorsal line that has black and ochreous markings either side of it on the middle segments. On the first three segments there is a blackish stripe subdorsally and there is a pale line below the spiracles.
Foodplants. In captivity knotgrass and dandelion; perhaps trefoils.
Habits. A double-brooded species, being in the larval stage from mid-June to mid-July and those of the second generation from late August until the following early May. In the wild the foodplant is unrecorded, but they thrive on knotgrass in captivity. Pupation takes place in a flimsy spinning on the leaves and lasts about eighteen days. A very local species that is restricted to the Breck and coastal sandhills of Suffolk.
Plate 10: E. Bred from a female adult to MVL. Early June. (BS)

Mullein Wave

Scopula marginepunctata Goeze
(*conjugata* Borkhausen)
Larva. 26–29 mm. Body ochreous; on the back there is a twin brown line along the centre, which is bolder on the last three segments.
Foodplants. Plantains, yarrow, mugwort, knotgrass and probably other low-growing herbaceous plants.
Habits. Double-brooded in the south and univoltine farther north. The larvae, which normally occur from September to May and during July, can occasionally be swept from their foodplants, especially mugwort. The best way to obtain stock is to take females at light; they lay eggs freely in confinement and the larvae need no special conditions for successful development. Mainly distributed along the south and west coasts as far north as Ayrshire, also in the London area and Ireland.
Plate 10: F. Bred from a female adult to MVL. Late June. (JG)

Small Blood-vein

Scopula imitaria Hübner
Larva. 25–28 mm. Body reddish-ochreous or greyish-brown, with a pair of dull brown stripes dorsally on either side of the darkish incomplete central line. It also has obvious black spiracles.
Foodplants. Privet, chickweed, dandelion and knotgrass are all accepted in captivity; probably also other low-growing plants.
Habits. Single-brooded, feeding steadily from late August until early October and then entering hibernation usually on its foodplant until the spring. It then finishes its development

on the fresh growth and pupates by about late May on the ground among moss and plant litter. Eggs are laid readily in confinement and the larval development can be shortened by keeping them warm. Widely distributed in southern areas, Wales and the Midlands, but less common in northern England and Ireland.
Plate 10: G. Bred from a female adult to MVL, on chickweed. Mid-July. (BS)

Rosy Wave
Scopula emutaria Hübner
Larva. 25–28 mm. Pale ochreous, with a distinct brown dorsal line that has darker points anteriorly on each of the middle segments. The spiracles are black and noticeable; and the underparts are dark brown.
Foodplants. Sea beet and in confinement knotgrass and dandelion.
Habits. A univoltine species, with the larval stage lasting from August until the following late May. Although this species sometimes comes to light, it is more readily obtained by finding the insects by torchlight, at rest on plant stems. Females lay freely in captivity and young larvae should be overwintered outside on dry wood shavings in a box. The pupa is formed in plant litter and lasts about three weeks. A local moth that inhabits mainly coastal marshes and bogs as far north as Yorkshire.
Plate 10: H. Bred from a female adult found at night. Early July. (BS)

Lesser Cream Wave
Scopula immutata Linnaeus
Larva. 24–27 mm. Body pale ochreous, with the segments ringed with many tiny ridges that are slightly darker. The dorsal line is greyish-brown and the spiracles are black.
Foodplants. Meadowsweet, common valerian and in captivity knotgrass and groundsel.
Habits. Single-brooded, with larvae feeding at night from late August to October and again in the spring, until fully fed in about late May. They spend the winter and pupate in plant debris. The easiest way to obtain stocks of this species is from adults netted at dusk. The females lay readily and if the larvae are kept warm they complete their growth in about three months. Locally common in marshes and in damp areas over much of England, Wales and Ireland.
Plate 10: I. Bred from female adult netted at night. Late July. (JR)

Cream Wave
Scopula floslactata Haworth
Larva. 26–30 mm. Body pale ochreous on the sides blending to ochreous-brown dorsally. The light brown head is notched and has a black marking.
Foodplants. In captivity docks, dandelion, knotgrass and persicaria.
Habits. A single-brooded species, with the larva overwintering when it is fully grown. Probably easiest to obtain by getting eggs from females that come to light and can also be disturbed from foliage and then netted during the day. The larvae feed steadily throughout the summer and in October they can be put outside in plant tubs with growing dock, leaf litter and light soil and left to hibernate naturally. They are widely distributed and fairly common over much of the British Isles.
Plate 10: J. Bred from a female adult netted by day. Early June.

Smoky Wave
Scopula ternata Schrank
Larva. 24–26 mm. Body light ochreous on the sides blending dorsally to reddish-brown. The underparts are dark brown and the segments are ridged. A greyish form of the larva occurs frequently.
Foodplants. Heather and bilberry.
Habits. From the eggs laid in June and July, the young larvae hatch after about three weeks and grow slowly until they hibernate in early October. Feeding recommences in April and they are fully grown by about late May. During the spring they can easily be obtained by sweeping in their heathland habitats, and pupation takes place among leaf litter or just in the soil. To be found in Scotland, Wales, northern parts of England and on Exmoor, in the south-west.
Plate 10: K. Swept from bilberry by day, fully grown. Late May.

Bright Wave
Idaea ochrata Scopoli
Larva. 14–16 mm. Body ochreous, with two narrow parallel brown lines along the centre of the back, and tapering towards the head.
Foodplants. In captivity knotgrass and dandelion.
Habits. Single-brooded, being in the larval stage from late July until about the following mid-May, overwintering when half grown. The best way to obtain stocks of this species is to breed from an adult female. These can be disturbed from herbage during dry days and they also sometimes come to light, especially on warm still nights. Eggs are readily laid, and by keeping the larvae warm they will develop rapidly, producing a second generation of adults within a few months. A very local species that inhabits the coastal sandhills of Kent, Essex and Suffolk.
Plate 10: L. Bred from a female adult netted at dusk. Early July. (JMP)

Purple-bordered Gold
Idaea muricata Hufnagel
Larva. 16–18 mm. Body greyish-brown, with a variable amount of small black markings dorsally.
Foodplants. Marsh cinquefoil and in captivity it will accept knotgrass and dandelion.
Habits. Single-brooded. From the eggs laid in June and July, the larvae hatch after about three weeks and develop steadily until hibernation in the autumn. Feeding recommences in the spring and most are fully grown by late May. During late June and July females can often be taken by disturbing them from heather during the day and they will lay freely in confinement. By keeping the larvae warm they can be forced to grow faster and pupate in plant litter in about three months. A local species found mainly in wet heathland, bogs and fens as far north as Cumbria and Yorkshire.
Plate 10: M. Bred from a female adult netted by day. Early July. (SHC)

Least Carpet
Idaea vulpinaria Herrich-Schäffer
(*rusticata* auctt.)
Larva. 14–16 mm. Body greyish-brown, with a strange circular ochreous structure formed of tiny pinacula, on the dorsal areas of the fifth to ninth segments. Also there are paler blotches laterally.
Foodplants. Ivy, traveller's-joy, groundsel and garden alyssum; also knotgrass in captivity.
Habits. A single-brooded species that overwinters as a half-

grown larva. The adults come frequently to light and the females lay easily when in confinement. The larvae will feed up quickly if kept warm and produce a second brood in about three months. This species seems to be most frequent in the south London area, also occurring regularly in north Kent, Surrey and south-west Essex.
Plate 10: N. Bred from a female adult to MVL on groundsel. Mid-July.

Dotted Border Wave
Idaea sylvestraria Hübner
Larva. 17–20 mm. Body ashy-grey dorsally, with indistinct darker markings along the back. The underparts are blackish-brown.
Foodplants. In confinement knotgrass, bramble, plantain and dandelion.
Habits. Single-brooded, with the larvae occurring from early August, through the winter, until the following late May. Best obtained from adult females taken at light or flushed by day from foliage or heather. They lay freely in captivity, but rearing the young larvae can be difficult. They seem to do better if kept warm and forced through their larval stage, offered both fresh and withered leaves of plants. A heathland species that is mainly found in southern England, elsewhere it occurs more locally in the West Midlands, Cumbria and Yorkshire.
Plate 10: O. Bred from a female adult to MVL on knotgrass. Early July. (BS)

Small Fan-footed Wave
Idaea biselata Hufnagel
Larva. 16–18 mm. Body variable in colour of some shade of brown or grey, with brownish-black markings dorsally. The body, which tapers towards the head, has a few tubercles, each one with a short seta growing from it.
Foodplants. In captivity dandelion, knotgrass, bramble and plantain.
Habits. A single-brooded species with the larvae occurring in the wild from August until the following late May. The best method to obtain stock is from an adult female. These can be collected at light traps or by disturbing them from foliage during the day. In captivity they lay eggs freely and the larvae can be forced to develop faster by keeping them warm and supplying them with withered leaves, which they prefer. Pupation takes place in leaf litter and lasts about a month. The species is widely distributed and fairly common over most of the British Isles.
Plate 10: P. Bred from a female adult to MVL. Early July. (JMP)

Rusty Wave
Idaea inquinata Scopoli
Larva. 11–13 mm. Body ochreous, with a faint pale dorsal line, darker dorsal blotches on the fourth to eighth segments; pinacula tiny, mostly ochreous on the last three rings and each with a short black seta; head blackish-brown.
Foodplants. Dried herbs and withered plants.
Habits. A single-brooded insect that has probably been imported on occasions with plant matter, such as dried flowers, herbs and packing material, from the continent. The larval stage lasts from August to the following April and neither the adults nor the earlier stages have ever been confidently recorded in the wild in the British Isles.
Plate 10: Q. Located among dried flowers. (JB)

Silky Wave
Idaea dilutaria Hübner
Larva. 13–14 mm. Body dull greyish, with ochreous markings dorsally and along the sides, especially on the last rings. Along the back is a double row of tiny pinacula which are more obvious on the final four segments.
Foodplants. Common rock-rose and in confinement knotgrass, dandelion and persicaria.
Habits. Single-brooded, overwintering as a small larva. This species can be found as adults, in July, by flushing them from plant growth during dry warm days, especially in the evening. The females lay readily in captivity, if supplied with a little knotgrass or rock-rose, and the eggs hatch after about three weeks. Some broods can be forced through to a second generation with heat and they will hatch during the winter months. A very local species that seems to occur only on the coast on the Great Orme in North Wales and in one locality near Bristol.
Plate 10: R. Bred from a female adult netted by day. Early July. (BS)

Dwarf Cream Wave
Idaea fuscovenosa Goeze
(*interjectaria* auctt.)
Larva. 14–16 mm. Body greyish-brown, with paler areas of ochreous. The dorsal line is indistinct except on the last few segments and along the middle part of the back are vague cross-shaped darker markings.
Foodplants. In captivity bramble, knotgrass and dandelion.
Habits. Single-brooded, overwintering as a small larva among leaf and plant debris, probably feeding if the weather is mild. It is easily bred in captivity by obtaining eggs from fertile females. These sometimes come to light but are more readily found by lightly tapping about in the herbage during the day. The larvae can be forced by keeping them warm and a second brood will emerge in the winter. This species is widely distributed over most of England and Wales.
Plate 11: A. Bred from a female adult to MVL. Mid-July.

Isle of Wight Wave
Idaea humiliata Hufnagel
Larva. 15–18 mm. Body light brown with many tiny tubercles especially on the dorsal area. The head is darker brown.
Foodplants. In captivity knotgrass, dandelion and dock.
Habits. Single-brooded and overwintering as a small larva. Adult females can readily be disturbed from herbage during the day and they will lay freely in captivity. If kept warm the larval growth is rapid and they can be forced through to a second generation in about three to four months. This species used to occur on the southern coast of the Isle of Wight, but it seems to have become extinct about 1931. It is possible that it has been overlooked from some other localities since then.
Plate 11: B. Bred from a female adult netted by day (Switzerland). July.

Small Dusty Wave
Idaea seriata Schrank
Larva. 15–18 mm. Body variable shades of brown, with darker markings along the dorsal area and brownish underneath. On the fifth segment is a conspicuous black spot laterally.
Foodplants. Ivy and in captivity dock, dandelion and knotgrass.
Habits. A double-brooded species that overwinters as a small larva. Like most Waves this insect is rarely found in

the larval stage and to obtain stock one must breed from a female adult. They are not often attracted to MV light, but can easily be found on fences and shop windows during the day. Eggs may be laid readily in captivity and by keeping the larvae warm they will become continuously brooded. Widely distributed and often common throughout England, Wales and eastern Scotland.
Plate II: C. Bred from a female adult found by day. Early July.

Single-dotted Wave
Idaea dimidiata Hufnagel
Larva. 16–18 mm. Body light brown, with a dark brown dorsal line that becomes indistinct and white on the thoracic segments. Also vague brown oblique markings on the middle rings.
Foodplants. Burnet-saxifrage, cow parsley and in captivity will accept dock, dandelion and knotgrass.
Habits. Single-brooded, with the larvae occurring in the wild from August, through the winter, until about the following late May. Easily reared in confinement with the larvae preferring withered leaves; they can be forced to develop faster by keeping them warm. Pupation takes place in plant litter surrounded by a loose cocoon. Widely distributed in damp places over most of England, Wales, southern Scotland and Ireland.
Plate II: D. Bred from a female adult to MVL. Mid-July. (SHC)

Satin Wave
Idaea subsericeata Haworth
Larva. 20–23 mm. Body variable shades of brown, with a thin light grey dorsal line that is bordered with dark brown. On the ninth segment is a distinct dark brown blotch in the subdorsal area and the middle rings have clouded brown dorsal blotches.
Foodplants. In captivity plantain, dandelion, dock and knotgrass.
Habits. Usually single-brooded, but also with a partial second generation when conditions are favourable. The majority of the larvae occur in this stage from early August to the following mid-May, probably overwintering among the plant debris. Adults are readily disturbed from foliage by day or can be netted at dusk; the females lay freely in captivity. By keeping the larvae warm they will grow rapidly and pupate among the foodplant in about six weeks. This species is widespread and fairly frequent over much of southern Britain, but more local further north.
Plate II: E. Bred from a female adult to MVL, on plantain. Mid-June.

Weaver's Wave
Idaea contiguaria Hübner
(*eburnata* Wocke)
Larva. 18–21 mm. Body light brown, with a series of dark brown elongated diamond-shaped markings along the back, except on the first three rings. On the thoracic segments is a short blackish line subdorsally and the underparts are dark brown.
Foodplants. Heather and crowberry, and in confinement knotgrass, dandelion and chickweed.
Habits. Single-brooded, with the larvae occurring from August to the following May, overwintering when about half grown. Both sexes of the adults come to light and the females normally lay eggs quite readily. When kept warm in captivity the larvae will feed up rapidly and pupate among loose soil and plant litter to produce another generation in the same year. A very local species only to be found in the upland areas of north-west Wales.
Plate II: F. Bred from a female adult to MVL on knotgrass. July. (ECLS)

Treble Brown Spot
Idaea trigeminata Haworth
Larva. 16–19 mm. Body dull greyish-brown, with a variable amount of lighter ochreous markings and many forward-facing greyish setae.
Foodplants. In captivity knotgrass, ivy, plantains and various other low-growing plants.
Habits. Generally a single-brooded species that has a partial second generation occurring later in the summer. The larvae overwinter when about half grown and are rarely found in the wild. Fertile females will come to light and eggs can often be obtained in confinement. If the larvae are kept warm they will develop rapidly and pupate among loose soil and leaf litter within a couple of months. Widespread over most of southern England and also in south-east Wales.
Plate II: G. Bred from a female adult to MVL on knotgrass. Late June.

Small Scallop
Idaea emarginata Linnaeus
Larva. 18–20 mm. Body various shades of ochreous or brown, with a whitish-grey dorsal line and vague lines of the same colour subdorsally. Along the back are indistinct cross-shaped markings on the middle segments.
Foodplants. Bedstraw and in captivity dandelion, groundsel, dock and knotgrass.
Habits. A single-brooded species that overwinters as a small larva among the plant debris. Like most Waves this species is best reared from the egg and these can be obtained from females taken at light or netted while flying slowly at dusk in their damp habitats. Larval development can be shortened by keeping them warm and supplying them with withering leaves, which they seem to prefer. In the wild the larvae occur from August to May, but in confinement the full life-cycle can take as little as three months. Widespread, but local, over most of central and southern England and in Wales.
Plate II: H. Bred from a female adult netted at dusk. Early July.

Riband Wave
Idaea aversata Linnaeus
Larva. 20–22 mm. Body various shades of brown or grey, with a very faint dorsal line and frequently obvious darker cross-shaped marks along the back.
Foodplants. Knotgrass, chickweed, dandelion, dock and a variety of low-growing herbaceous plants.
Habits. Mainly a univoltine species, with a partial second brood in the southern parts of its range. The larvae occur in the wild from mid-July through to the following May, overwintering when still quite small. In captivity the larval growth is normally rapid and can take less than two months to complete. Pupation usually takes place in a loose cocoon in leaf litter and lasts about three weeks. Widespread and generally common over most parts of the British Isles.
Plate II: I. Bred from a female adult to MVL on dandelion. Late June.

Portland Ribbon Wave
Idaea degeneraria Hübner
Larva. 18–21 mm. Body shades of ochreous, with variable

amounts of brown or russet dorsally. Also along the back are cross-shaped markings on the middle segments and a faint paler dorsal line.
Foodplants. In captivity it will accept knotgrass, dandelion and dock.
Habits. A single-brooded species that is most easily obtained by netting females at dusk during July, and inducing them to lay in captivity. Like most other species of Waves the larvae can often be forced with warmth to produce a second brood during the same year. Sometimes the larvae insist on hibernating, and they should be kept outside on dry leaf litter and wood shavings in a cool place, until they become active again in the spring. A very local moth, occurring regularly only on Portland, in Dorset.
Plate II: J. Bred from a female adult to MVL. Early July. (SHC)

Plain Wave
Idaea straminata Borkhausen
(*inornata* Haworth)
Larva. 19–21 mm. Body variable shades of brown, often with the rear four segments noticeably lighter in colour than the rest. Dorsally there are cross-shaped marks on the middle segments and a darker line centrally on the last three rings.
Foodplants. In captivity dandelion, persicaria and knotgrass; also probably other herbaceous plants.
Habits. Single-brooded, with the larvae occurring from August until the following late May, overwintering when about half grown. The easiest way to obtain stocks is from a fertile female. These will come to light and sometimes lay readily in captivity. The larvae are not difficult to rear and can be forced to develop faster by keeping them in the dark and warm. From these a second generation of adults can be had by late September. Local, but widely distributed, over most of the British Isles.
Plate II: K. Bred from a female adult to MVL on dandelion. Mid-July. (SHC)

The Vestal
Rhodometra sacraria Linnaeus
Larva. 18–22 mm. Body variable shades of green or ochreous dorsally, and often with whitish underparts. The darker markings are usually brown or reddish-brown on the back, obvious centrally on the last few segments and subdorsally on the thoracic rings. The head is ochreous and striped with reddish-brown.
Foodplants. Knotgrass and in captivity dock.
Habits. A southern European species that frequently migrates to this country. The insects are continuously brooded, but die out during the winter. Females come to light freely and can also be flushed out of herbage by day; they lay readily in captivity. The larvae must be kept warm and their growth is rapid, completing the life-cycle in about two months. Pupation takes place among leaf litter and lasts about two weeks.
Plate II: L. Bred from a female adult to MVL on dock. Late August. (KGWE)

SUBFAMILY: LARENTIINAE

Oblique Striped
Phibalapteryx virgata Hufnagel
Larva. 16–19 mm. Body brown, of various shades, dorsally with a thin darker central line, also with an indistinct yellow subdorsal line. Greenish-white to pale yellow below the black spiracles.
Foodplants. Lady's bedstraw and probably other species of bedstraw.
Habits. The larvae of this double-brooded species can easily be swept from the foodplant during late May and June, and again from mid-August until about the end of September. They feed up quite quickly and prefer to pupate in loose soil or plant litter. This is the stage in which they spend the winter months. Locally distributed, mainly on coastal sandhills and chalk downland in central southern England and in the Breckland of East Anglia.
Plate II: M. Swept at night, fully grown. Late June.

Oblique Carpet
Orthonama vittata Borkhausen
(*lignata* Hübner)
Larva. 20–23 mm. Body brownish-grey with a thin dark brown dorsal line and a pale stripe along the spiracular region that is bordered above by a darker line.
Foodplants. Marsh bedstraw, heath bedstraw and other associated species.
Habits. A double-brooded species, except in the far north of its range where it is univoltine. In the larval stage from September until late April, and during July from the first brood. In the north, from August to early June with the development being slower. Females do not often come to light, but can frequently be taken by net, while fluttering about in their marshy habitats. They will lay in captivity and the larvae are not usually difficult to rear in confinement. Widespread, but local, over most parts of the British Isles.
Plate II: N. Bred from a netted female adult. Early June. (JMP)

The Gem
Orthonama obstipata Fabricius
Larva. 17–20 mm. Body extremely variable in colour and markings, basically green or brown with paler underparts. Along the subdorsal area is an incomplete dark line that can be reduced to mere dashes and dorsally there are normally vague chevrons of a paler colour. Also there are small greyish tubercles on the body, mainly at the rear end.
Foodplants. In captivity groundsel, knotgrass, dock and will probably accept many other kinds of herbaceous plants.
Habits. A frequent migrant species that occurs mainly at light at any time during the warmer months of the year. This is one of the easiest species to breed in captivity, and as long as the insects are kept warm, they will produce one generation after another with continuing success. This species is most likely to be found in the southern coastal counties.
Plate II: O. Bred from a female adult to MVL on groundsel. August. (BS)

Balsam Carpet
Xanthorhoe biriviata Borkhausen
Larva. 24–26 mm. Body greyish-green, green or brownish, with a variable amount of black marking along the dorsal area. Many individuals have a short black dash on the anterior part of the middle segments along the faint dorsal line, often followed by another dark marking.
Foodplants. Orange balsam and in captivity touch-me-not and small balsam.
Habits. A double-brooded species, with the rapid growing larvae occurring in June and again in August and September. The adults fly naturally in the afternoons and evenings on fine days and are easily netted. Females will lay in captivity and the larvae are easy to rear, pupating in moss or leaf litter. The one problem with breeding this species is that the

picked foodplant wilts very quickly, so stems should be brought home in water and then the leaves can be put into sealed plastic containers in the refrigerator, until needed. The larvae can also be located by searching for eaten leaves and then finding them nearby on the plant. Very local in damp waterside habitats in Middlesex, Surrey, Buckinghamshire, north Hampshire, Kent, Berkshire, Norfolk and Cambridgeshire.
Plate 11: P. Found on orange balsam, nearly fully grown. Mid-June.

Flame Carpet

Xanthorhoe designata Hufnagel
Larva. 23–25 mm. Body dark blackish-green dorsally except on the last few segments where the colour is brown. Along the middle parts of the back are a few wedge-shaped brownish marks and the underparts are ochreous.
Foodplants. Wallflower, cabbage and other associated species.
Habits. The larvae of this double-brooded species occur from early June to mid-July, and again in late August and September. They can easily be bred from female moths, which come readily to light traps or may be disturbed from foliage during the day. The larvae can sometimes be found by careful searching of the foodplants. The larval stage lasts about a month and they pupate in a silken cocoon for overwintering. A widespread species to be found over most of the British Isles.
Plate 11: Q. Bred from a female adult to MVL. Early June.

Red Carpet

Xanthorhoe munitata Hübner
Larva. 25–28 mm. Body bright green or ochreous, with a variable amount of black markings dorsally, including dashes in the dorsal line on the middle segments. There are other small black markings between the spiracles, below which the body is paler.
Foodplants. Lady's-mantle and in confinement groundsel, chickweed and bedstraw.
Habits. A single-brooded insect that occurs in the larval stage from August, through the winter, until late May. Mainly a moorland species that is best reared from the egg to obtain stocks. The females can readily be disturbed from rocks and stone walls during the day or they can be netted at dusk when they become active. They lay freely in captivity and the larvae can be forced to develop faster by keeping them warm. Pupation takes place in a cocoon among plant litter and lasts for about three weeks. Widely distributed over most northern counties of England, Wales and Ireland; also occurring over most of Scotland.
Plate 11: R. Bred from a female adult netted at dusk. Late July. (IR)

Red Twin-spot Carpet

Xanthorhoe spadicearia Denis & Schiffermüller
Larva. 20–23 mm. Body ochreous, with a variable amount of dark olive-brown markings on the dorsal area. The underparts are frequently plain and paler than the rest of the body.
Foodplants. Lady's bedstraw, goosegrass, knotgrass and various other herbaceous low-growing plants.
Habits. This species overwinters as a pupa, spun up among leaf litter. In southern England it is double-brooded, with the larvae being found during July and September, but mainly it is univoltine with the larvae from late June until late August. They are difficult to find in the wild and the best way to obtain stocks is from an adult female; these come to light and may also be collected by disturbing them from foliage during the day. Generally distributed and normally common throughout most of the British Isles.
Plate 12: A. Bred from a female adult to MVL. Mid-June.

Dark-barred Twin-spot Carpet

Xanthorhoe ferrugata Clerck
Larva. 22–25 mm. Body of various shades of ochreous, with darker blackish-brown markings dorsally, especially upon the middle segments and subdorsally on the thoracic segments.
Foodplants. Dock, dandelion, bedstraw and other low-growing plants.
Habits. A double-brooded species, with the larvae occurring from late June and throughout July, and those from the second brood in September. They are most easily obtained by breeding from an adult female. These can be light-trapped or found during the day by tapping about in the herbage and then netting them. No special requirements are needed for successful breeding and they will pupate among moss or light leaf litter to pass the winter months. Widely distributed over most of Britain.
Plate 12: B. Bred from a female adult to MVL. Early June. (SHC)

Large Twin-spot Carpet

Xanthorhoe quadrifasiata Clerck
Larva. 23–27 mm. Body greyish-brown with obvious darker markings on the middle segments dorsally. The underparts are pale ochreous, mottled lighter and the spiracles are black.
Foodplants. Bedstraw, chickweed, dock and other low-growing plants.
Habits. Single-brooded, with the larvae occurring from about August, then overwintering when still small, until late May. They are difficult to find in the wild, but can sometimes be swept in the spring in places where the moth is common. During late June and July the females will come to light and larvae from these can easily be bred in captivity. If kept warm the larvae can be forced to feed up in about two months. A woodland species that is locally common in many places mainly in the southern half of Britain, especially on chalky soils.
Plate 12: C. Bred from an adult female to MVL. Early July. (JMP)

Silver-ground Carpet

Xanthorhoe montanata Denis & Schiffermüller
Larva. 22–25 mm. Body greyish-brown, with a variable amount of blackish-brown markings along the central dorsal area, especially on the middle segments. There is a pale stripe along the subdorsal region and the underparts are pale brown.
Foodplants. Bedstraw, primrose, chickweed, groundsel and other low-growing herbaceous plants.
Habits. Single-brooded, occurring as a larva from July until the following May. Usually the moths are fairly common and are readily disturbed by day from herbage. They lay freely in captivity and by keeping the larvae warm they will complete their growth within about three months. Occasionally they will be found at random while sweeping or searching for other species. They are easy to breed with no special conditions necessary for their survival. To be found in most parts of Britain and Ireland.
Plate 12: D. Bred from a netted female adult. Early June.

Garden Carpet

Xanthorhoe fluctuata Linnaeus

Larva. 21–24 mm. Body variable from light green to olive and also different shades of brown. The amount of dorsal markings is also extremely variable from almost totally absent to boldly obvious, especially on the middle segments. The spiracles are black and the larva is always paler on the underparts.

Foodplants. Mainly plants of the *Cruciferae*, including cabbage and garlic mustard.

Habits. During the summer months this species is continually brooded, but it always overwinters as a pupa. The total number of broods depends on the climate and latitude of the population, from three in the south to one or two in more northern localities. The larvae are easy to breed from the egg and many generations can be obtained in captivity by keeping the larvae warm. In the wild they pupate in the soil, but also in plant litter and tissue-paper in confinement. To be found throughout most of the British Isles.

Plate 12: E. Bred from a female adult to MVL on cabbage. Mid-May.

Spanish Carpet

Scotopteryx peribolata Hübner

Larva. 20–24 mm. Body yellowish-grey, sometimes green tinged, with an incomplete black dorsal line, black subdorsal lines and a whitish lateral line (Seitz).

Foodplants. Gorse and broom.

Habits. Single-brooded, occurring in the larval stage from September to May. Although usually regarded as a very rare immigrant, it is possible that this species could become established if given the right conditions. It is well established in the Channel Islands and unknown colonies could already exist on the mainland of Britain. The adults occur during late August and September and may be disturbed from the foodplants during the day.

Chalk Carpet

Scotopteryx bipunctaria Denis & Schiffermüller

Larva. 21–24 mm. Body ochreous, with a bluish-grey dorsal line and subdorsal lines, also parallel dark grey markings on the middle segments underneath.

Foodplants. Clovers and various trefoils.

Habits. A single-brooded species, with the larvae occurring from late August until the following early June, overwintering when still quite small, probably low down on the foodplants. Females can be obtained at light or flushed during the day, and these will lay readily on picked plants in captivity. The larvae can be forced by keeping them warm and in the dark, and they complete their development in about three months. Mainly found on limestone and chalk soils over most of southern England and Wales, but more local farther north to the Co. Durham coast.

Plate 12: F. Bred from a netted female adult. Early July. (SHC)

Shaded Broad-bar

Scotopteryx chenopodiata Linnaeus
(*limitata* Scopoli)

Larva. 20–23 mm. Body bluish-grey, with thin whitish stripes on the back and sides. Below the black spiracles is a broader whitish line and there are a few black dots scattered over the upper parts and in the spiracular area.

Foodplants. Clovers, vetches and probably trefoils.

Habits. The larvae of this single-brooded species occur from August through to the following June, overwintering when about half grown. Although the larvae of this fairly common insect are rarely found in the wild, they are easy to obtain from the egg stage, by disturbing fertile females from the herbage during the day. Keeping them warm and in the dark will often result in the larvae feeding up within a few months, to pupate among moss and plant litter. Widely distributed and frequent over most parts of the British Isles.

Plate 12: G. Bred from a netted female adult on clover. Early July. (SHC)

Lead Belle

Scotopteryx mucronata Scopoli

Larva. 20–24 mm. Body generally light grey, with a variable amount of black markings dorsally. These often consist of dashes along the dorsal line, bordered by parallel twin spots. The spiracles are black and the head is square shaped.

Foodplants. Gorse, broom, petty whin and dyer's greenweed.

Habits. A single-brooded species, with the larvae occurring from August to March, feeding throughout the winter whenever the weather is mild enough. They can be bred from the moth, but this is a long and laborious task unless they are sleeved upon growing foodplants. Larvae can be obtained more easily by searching their foodplants from October to mid-March, at night by torchlight. In captivity they pupate readily on the foodplant and this stage lasts about two months. The distribution of this species covers the western and northern parts of the British Isles, mainly heath and moorland localities.

Plate 12: H. Found at night, nearly fully grown. January. (BS)

July Belle

Scotopteryx luridata Hufnagel

Larva. Seemingly identical to the previous species, *S. mucronata*, but with the distribution and season frequently different.

Foodplants. Gorse and petty whin.

Habits. A similar life-cycle to the previous species, but running about six weeks later on average. This species is as likely to be found on downland and commons, as on the heathery localities that seem to be preferred by *S. mucronata*. Widely distributed on open ground over most of the British Isles.

Plate 12: I. Bred from a female adult netted by day. Mid-July. (M&JH)

Ruddy Carpet

Catarhoe rubidata Denis & Schiffermüller

Larva. 24–27 mm. Body light grey or greyish-brown with obscure paler markings along the back and an obvious blackish dorsal line on the last few segments. The small spiracles are black, the underparts paler and there is often a black marking in front of the first back leg.

Foodplants. Lady's bedstraw, hedge bedstraw and probably other associated plants.

Habits. Single-brooded, overwintering as a pupa. The larvae occur during July and August and are best obtained by breeding from a female moth. These occasionally come to light traps, but are obtained more easily by netting at dusk or disturbing them from herbage during the day. They lay freely in captivity and no special conditions are required to rear the brood. To be found mainly in southern England and Wales, preferring bushy downland, sea-cliffs and other open areas.

Plate 12: J. Bred from a female adult netted at dusk. Early June. (BS)

Royal Mantle

Catarhoe cuculata Hufnagel

Larva. 23–26 mm. Body pale yellow or yellowish-green, with two broad purplish or black stripes along the subdorsal regions. The head is light green and speckled with brown.

Foodplants. Hedge bedstraw, lady's bedstraw and probably other associated plants.

Habits. A single-brooded species with the larvae feeding, mainly on the flowers of bedstraw, from late July until about early September. Occasionally they can be swept, especially at night, but are much easier to obtain from adult females that may be light-trapped or taken while flying at dusk. They feed up steadily and pupate among plant litter in about six weeks, overwintering in this stage. Generally a local insect that is mainly found on chalky or limestone soils over most of southern England and East Anglia; also occurring in Perthshire, Fifeshire and on the Burren in Ireland.

Plate 12: K. Bred from a female adult to MVL. Early July. (MP)

Small Argent and Sable

Epirrhoe tristata Linnaeus

Larva. 19–22 mm. Body reddish-brown, with a thin dark brown dorsal line and a broader pale brown stripe along the subdorsal area.

Foodplants. Heath bedstraw and in captivity other species of bedstraw.

Habits. Mostly single-brooded, with a partial second generation in the south-western and Irish populations. Normally occurring as a larva from late June until about mid-August and pupating among plant litter or light soil for the winter. On fine afternoons and at dusk the adults will fly and can be netted to obtain stocks for rearing. The females lay freely in confinement and the larvae need no special conditions for successful development. Mainly of a northern and western distribution and often fairly common where it occurs.

Plate 12: L. Bred from female adult netted by day. Early July.

Common Carpet

Epirrhoe alternata Müller

Larva. 21–24 mm. Body basically brown of various shades, with a distinct dorsal line marking only on the last few segments, lighter coloured chevrons on the middle segments and thin pale stripes subdorsally on the thoracic segments.

Foodplants. Hedge bedstraw, goosegrass, lady's bedstraw and other associated species.

Habits. In the south this species has the main brood of larvae during June and July, and those of the partial second generation during September. Further north, where it is univoltine, the larvae normally occur during July and August. Occasionally they can be found in the wild by searching or sweeping, but they are obtained more easily by breeding from a fertile female. These will lay eggs freely in captivity and the larvae are easy to breed through to the pupal stage. Throughout its range this species overwinters as a pupa, being widely distributed and often common over most of the British Isles.

Plate 12: M. Bred from a female adult to MVL. Late May. (SHC)

Wood Carpet

Epirrhoe rivata Hübner

Larva. 21–25 mm. Body light- or greyish-brown, with paler chevrons along the back, which are most distinct on the middle segments. Paler lines are also visible in the subdorsal region on the thoracic segments and on the last few rings.

Foodplants. Hedge bedstraw and lady's bedstraw.

Habits. A single-brooded species, being in the larval stage from late July to late September, and overwintering as a pupa in a flimsy cocoon spun up in the soil and plant debris. The larvae are obtained most easily by getting eggs from an adult female; these sometimes come to light and can often be disturbed from foliage during the day. Widespread in scrubby places, but rarely common, over much of southern England, but more local and much less frequent in northern England and southern Scotland.

Plate 12: N. Bred from a female adult to MVL. Early July. (AJ)

Galium Carpet

Epirrhoe galiata Denis & Schiffermüller

Larva. 22–26 mm. Body light brown, with a dark brown dorsal line that is most obvious on the thoracic segments and on the last few rings. Often there is a bold paler line along the subdorsal region and another pale area beneath the small brown spiracles.

Foodplants. Lady's bedstraw, hedge bedstraw and other associated plants.

Habits. Double-brooded in the south, with the larvae occurring during late June and July, and again in September. Northern populations are normally univoltine, with the larvae in August. They all overwinter as pupae, and these are formed in light cocoons among soil particles. In some places, especially on the south coast where they are common, the larvae can be found or swept at night. Female adults frequently come to light and can also be tapped out of herbage by day. They will lay freely in captivity and no special conditions are needed for successful development of the larvae. This species is mainly coastal in occurrence, but in southern England it can also be found inland on calcareous soils, and also sometimes on moorland in the north.

Plate 12: O. Located at night, fully grown. Mid-July.

The Many-lined

Costaconvexa polygrammata Borkhausen

Larva. 22–26 mm. Body reddish-brown, with pale dorsal and subdorsal lines and darker coloration to the posterior parts of the abdominal rings; underparts pale brown, irrorate with black.

Foodplants. Bedstraws.

Habits. An extinct resident, not uncommon in some of the Cambridgeshire fens during the middle part of the last century. The reason for its apparent extinction is unclear, as the foodplants still occur in profusion and although many fenland habitats were drained during this period, most bedstraws do not need especially damp conditions to survive. The species was probably double-brooded with the larvae occurring in May and July to August.

Plate 12: P. Bred from a female adult to MVL (France). (WK)

Yellow Shell

Camptogramma bilineata Linnaeus

Larva. 20–23 mm. Body pale bluish-green, with a yellow tint between the segments. The dorsal line is darker green and bordered by paler whitish-green, also a few other thin pale lines along the back and sides. A less frequent ochreous form sometimes occurs.

Foodplants. Chickweed, docks, various grasses and other low-growing plants.

Habits. A single-brooded species, with the larvae feeding slowly from late July until the following late May. Throughout the winter when the weather is mild they continue to

feed at night upon whatever is available, and from about January to May they can be swept fairly readily or be found by torchlight. They pupate in light soil or plant litter and this stage lasts about six weeks. Widely distributed over most of lowland Britain and Ireland.
Plate 12: Q. Swept at night, nearly fully grown. Late February.

Yellow-ringed Carpet
Entephria flavicinctata Hübner
Larva. 20–22 mm. Body green or reddish-brown, with distinct chevron markings that are blackish and centred with pink and yellow along the dorsal surface. The body is rough and wrinkled and has many small tubercles each with a single short bristle.
Foodplants. Stonecrop, saxifrage and roseroot.
Habits. Double-brooded in Ireland, coastal western Scotland and the Hebrides, but univoltine in central and northwest Scotland and in the English localities of the Yorkshire Dales and Herefordshire. In the single-brooded populations the larvae occur from September until the following early June, and those of the bivoltine moths from September to early May and again during June and July. The species inhabits rocky screes, gullies and old quarries where the foodplants grow from cracks in the rocks. The larvae can readily be obtained by shaking the plants over a small tray or a net, especially during the spring, and breeding them through in captivity is not difficult. The pupa is spun up in the foodplant and lasts about three weeks.
Plate 13: A. Tapped from hanging foodplant, fully grown. Late May.

Grey Mountain Carpet
Entephria caesiata Denis & Schiffermüller
Larva. 22–26 mm. Body green or reddish-brown, with dark brown chevrons centred with lilac and yellowish-orange along the greater part of the dorsal area and a pale stripe below the spiracles.
Foodplants. Heather, bilberry and in captivity sallow and knotgrass.
Habits. A single-brooded species that occurs as a larva from August to early June, overwintering when still quite small. During May the larvae can easily be swept from their foodplants and often in large numbers. They will pupate in a loose cocoon that is spun up among the leaves of the plants and this stage lasts about a month. Widespread in moorland and mountain habitats over most of the northern parts of Britain, also occurring locally in Ireland and South Wales.
Plate 13: B. Swept from heather, fully grown. Late May.

The Mallow
Larentia clavaria Haworth
Larva. 27–30 mm. Body light green, with black spiracles and tiny white short bristled tubercles. Thin darker lines along the back of which the central one is occasionally purplish.
Foodplants. Common mallow, marsh-mallow and garden hollyhock.
Habits. A single-brooded species that overwinters as an egg. The larvae feed at night from April until about early June, before pupating in the soil for the next three months. They may be located at night by torchlight or bred from female adults, that come to light and can be netted at dusk during September. Generally distributed over most of England and Wales; also found locally in Ireland and southern Scotland.
Plate 12: R. Bred from a female adult netted at dusk. Mid-September. (RM)

Shoulder Stripe
Anticlea badiata Denis & Schiffermüller
Larva. 24–27 mm. Body green or olive-brown dorsally, with a few tiny white tubercles. The underparts are distinctly paler, the spiracles black and the head is orangish-brown with two dark spots.
Foodplants. Dog rose, sweet briar and probably other related plants.
Habits. The larvae of this single-brooded species can readily be beaten from their foodplant from late April to mid-June. Pupation takes place in a silken cocoon among loose soil and lasts until the following March or April. Due to the risk of the pupae drying out during the summer, they should be left undisturbed outside in a shaded place. Widely distributed over most of the British Isles, but less common and more local in Scotland and Ireland.
Plate 13: C. Beaten from dog rose, fully grown. Late May.

The Streamer
Anticlea derivata Denis & Schiffermüller
Larva. 24–28 mm. Body yellowish-green, with reddish-brown dorsal marks, that vary from bold dashes all along the back to almost absent. The legs are marked with brown and the head is also mainly brown.
Foodplant. Dog rose.
Habits. A single-brooded species, with the larvae occurring from mid-May until mid-July, and being easily obtained by beating. During April and early May adult females often come to light and in captivity they lay eggs freely on wild rose leaves and buds. The larvae will eat the flowers as well as the young leaves and complete their growth in about six weeks. Pupation takes place in a flimsy cocoon spun among loose soil particles and lasts until the following April. To be found throughout most parts of the British Isles.
Plate 13: D. Beaten from the foodplant, fully grown. Mid-June.

Beautiful Carpet
Mesoleuca albicillata Linnaeus
Larva. 26–30 mm. Body dark green with obvious pinkish chevrons, that are bordered with brown, along the dorsal area. The head is green, but heavily marked with brown and the rear extremity of the larva is also brown.
Foodplants. Bramble and raspberry.
Habits. Single-brooded, with the nocturnal feeding larvae from mid-July to about early September. During the day they rest upon the under surface of the foodplant leaves and they are difficult to obtain in the wild as bramble is awkward to beat and uncomfortable to search. Female adults readily come to light traps and they often lay freely in confinement. The larval development takes about five weeks and the overwintering pupa is formed in the soil. Widespread over most of the British Isles.
Plate 13: E. Bred from a female adult to MVL. Early July. (SHC)

Dark Spinach
Pelurga comitata Linnaeus
Larva. 22–24 mm. Body greyish-brown, and heavily marked with blackish mottling above the very wavy pale spiracular line.
Foodplants. Goosefoot and orache.
Habits. A single-brooded species, with larvae occurring from

late August until mid-October. They can be swept from the foodplant, especially at night when they become more active, but are more readily obtained from light-trapped adults. The females lay on picked plant in confinement and no special conditions are required for the larval development. Pupation takes place in a cocoon in the soil and lasts throughout the winter, until the following July or August. Widely distributed over much of England, Wales, Ireland and southern Scotland.
Plate 13: F. Bred from a female adult to MVL. Late July.

Water Carpet
Lampropteryx suffumata Denis & Schiffermüller
Larva. 21–23 mm. Body pale brown to ochreous, variably marked with dark brown chevrons along the dorsal area. The dorsal line is visible on the thoracic segments where it is pale and on the last few rings where it is black. The underparts are paler and the small spiracles black.
Foodplants. Hedge bedstraw, goosegrass, lady's bedstraw, heath bedstraw and other allied plants.
Habits. The larvae of this single-brooded species normally occur from early May in the south, until about late June in Scotland. They can sometimes be found at night by torchlight or by sweeping, but rarely in any quantity. During April and May the adults fly freely at dusk and will often come to light traps. In captivity eggs are often laid and the easily bred larvae take about four weeks to become fully grown. The cocooned pupa is spun up among plant debris and lasts for ten months. Generally distributed in woods and scrubland over most of Britain.
Plate 13: G. Bred from a female adult to light. Late April. (SHC)

Devon Carpet
Lampropteryx otregiata Metcalfe
Larva. 18–20 mm. Body of various shades of brown, with the white dorsal line distinct on the thoracic segments, and appearing as a thin black line upon the last few segments. Also dark brown chevrons dorsally and a ring of small dark tubercles on the centre segments.
Foodplants. Marsh bedstraw, fen bedstraw and possibly other allied species.
Habits. A double-brooded species, with the larvae occurring from late June to the end of July, and again from early September to the middle of October. They are most easily obtained from adult females, which can be disturbed from herbage by day, netted at dusk or sometimes come to light, seeming to prefer actinic traps. They will lay freely in captivity and the larvae grow to full size in about a month. The cocooned pupa is formed in leaf litter and the insect will overwinter in this stage. A local species found mainly in the south-western parts of England and in Wales.
Plate 13: H. Bred from a female adult to MVL. Early August. (RMcC)

Purple Bar
Cosmorhoe ocellata Linnaeus
Larva. 19–22 mm. Body light or pinkish-brown, with a pale spiracular line and paler chevron markings along the dorsal region. The spiracles are small and black, and the head is generally light brown.
Foodplants. Hedge bedstraw, marsh bedstraw and other associated species.
Habits. The larvae of this species can sometimes be obtained by sweeping from late June to late July, and those of the partial second generation, in the south, during September. The adults come readily to light or can be flushed out during the day, and the females lay eggs freely in confinement. The larvae are easy to rear, and after about four weeks of feeding spin up their overwintering cocoons, changing into pupae about April. Widespread and fairly common over most of the British Isles.
Plate 13: I. Bred from a female adult to MVL. Late June. (SHC)

Striped Twin-spot Carpet
Nebula salicata Hübner
Larva. 17–19 mm. Body ochreous with dark brown dorsal and spiracular lines, between which are other indistinct brown lines and a brown raised tubercle subdorsally on each segment. The underparts are pale and the head is mottled with brown.
Foodplants. Heath bedstraw and other related species.
Habits. Mostly a univoltine species, the larvae of which feed at night from July onwards until about six weeks later, when they become fully grown. At this point of their life-cycle they construct a silken cocoon among plant litter and then spend the winter in a dormant state, until finally changing into pupae during April or May. In some populations, especially those on low ground, there is a second generation, from which the larvae will occur from early September. The larvae can be swept, but are obtained most easily by breeding from adult moths which are often disturbed from rocks during the day. Mainly to be found on moorland in the northern and western parts of Britain.
Plate 13: J. Bred from a female adult disturbed by day. Early July.

The Phoenix
Eulithis prunata Linnaeus
Larva. 26–28 mm. Body green or greyish-brown, with reddish-brown chevrons along the dorsal area. There is a distinct swelling of the third thoracic segment which is also ringed with a darker colour.
Foodplants. Black currant, red currant and gooseberry.
Habits. A single-brooded species that overwinters in the egg stage. The larvae hatch during April and feed up steadily at night to become fully grown by around early June. This species is mainly associated with gardens, and although frequent, is rarely common enough to make searching for larvae worth while. Both sexes of adults come readily to light traps and the females lay freely on picked foodplant. No special conditions are required for successful breeding and the larvae normally spin up to pupate among moss or leaf litter, which should be supplied when they are full size. Local, but widespread, over most of Britain.
Plate 13: K. Bred from a female adult to MVL. Late July. (SHC)

The Chevron
Eulithis testata Linnaeus
Larva. 23–25 mm. Body light ochreous, with an almost black dorsal line and indistinct thin whitish lines in the subdorsal and spiracular regions.
Foodplants. Sallows, aspen, birch and creeping willow.
Habits. From mid-May until about late June the larvae of this univoltine species can readily be beaten from its foodplants. They are easy to rear in captivity and will pupate in cocoons spun up on the plant or in leaf litter. They can also be bred from fertile females, which are most easily obtained by searching on plant stems after dark, with a torch. The eggs will be laid upon twigs and they should be kept outside

for overwintering. Widespread and frequent over most of the British Isles.
Plate 13: L. Bred from a female adult, found at night. Early August. (M&JH)

Northern Spinach
Eulithis populata Linnaeus
Larva. 22–25 mm. Body green, with variable amounts of brown markings dorsally, from almost absent to totally obscuring the ground colour. The most noticeable marks are the chevrons along the back and it also has a distinctive swelling and darker ring on the third thoracic segment.
Foodplant. Bilberry.
Habits. A single-brooded species that overwinters as an egg. The larvae occur from mid-April until June, and are easily taken by sweeping the foodplant in moorland habitats. They grow rapidly in confinement and pupate among foodplant leaves or in plant litter. This stage lasts about three to six weeks depending on the temperature. Usually fairly common where it occurs, mostly in western and northern parts of the British Isles.
Plate 13: M. Swept by day, nearly fully grown. Late May. (JMP)

The Spinach
Eulithis mellinata Fabricius
Larva. 22–24 mm. Body pale green, with a yellow tint between the segments. The lines are indistinct, being darker on the dorsal area and paler subdorsally. The spiracles are tiny and white.
Foodplants. Black currant and red currant.
Habits. Single-brooded. After overwintering in the egg stage, the larvae hatch in April and develop quickly, becoming fully grown by late May. They feed mainly at night and can sometimes be found resting under the leaves during the day. From mid-June to early August the adults come to light and most females will lay freely in captivity. The eggs should be kept outside in a dark cool place, until they are ready to hatch in the following spring. Generally distributed over most of England and Wales, very local in Scotland and seemingly only in the Dublin area of Ireland.
Plate 13: N. Bred from a female adult to MVL. Early July. (JMP)

Barred Straw
Eulithis pyraliata Denis & Schiffermüller
Larva. 23–26 mm. Body bluish-green, with a darker green dorsal line and an almost white stripe along the subdorsal area.
Foodplants. Goosegrass and other species of bedstraw.
Habits. A single-brooded species that overwinters as an egg. The larvae occur from mid-April to mid-June and are best obtained by breeding from a fertile female. These will often come to light traps and can sometimes be disturbed from herbage during the day. The eggs should be kept outside and rearing this insect is easy. The pupa is spun up among plant debris and lasts up to two months. Widespread and fairly frequent over most of the British Isles; local in northern Scotland.
Plate 13: O. Bred from a female adult to MVL. Mid-July. (JMP)

Small Phoenix
Ecliptopera silaceata Denis & Schiffermüller
Larva. 23–25 mm. Body green with a darker dorsal line that is reddish-brown and most obvious on the last rings, a dark coloured head, small black spiracles, and a darker last segment that has a few pale tubercles.
Foodplants. Rosebay willowherb, broad-leaved willowherb and other allied species; also recorded from enchanter's nightshade.
Habits. Mainly a single-brooded species, with the larvae occurring from late June until late July, and pupating for the winter among plant litter. A second generation is frequent in southern populations, with the larvae from late August and throughout September. They can be found or swept from the foodplant, but are easier to obtain by collecting eggs from females, which can be light-trapped or flushed from the herbage by day. Fairly common in England and Wales, but to be found in smaller numbers in Scotland and Ireland.
Plate 13: P. Bred from a female adult to MVL. Late May. (SHC)

Red-green Carpet
Chloroclysta siterata Hufnagel
Larva. 23–26 mm. Body yellowish-green, often with a series of pink dashes along the dorsal line and sometimes pinkish below the spiracles; the long twin anal points are also pink.
Foodplants. Oak, birch, rowan and, less often, other deciduous trees.
Habits. A single-brooded species, with the larvae feeding from early June to early August. They can sometimes be beaten from the foodplants, but are more readily obtained by breeding from an adult female. They hibernate in the adult stage, with the males dying off before the winter. So any female moths taken in the spring, most often at light, will normally lay freely in confinement. The larvae need no special conditions and become fully fed after about six weeks. Pupation takes place in plant litter and this stage lasts about a month. Found over most parts of the British Isles, but more frequent in the west and north.
Plate 13: Q. Bred from a female adult to MVL. Mid-May. (SHC)

Autumn Green Carpet
Chloroclysta miata Linnaeus
Larva. 24–27 mm. Body yellowish-green, with an indistinct darker green dorsal line. The anal points are pinkish-brown and on the underparts there are mottlings of the same colour.
Foodplants. Birch, sallow and other deciduous trees.
Habits. Single-brooded, occurring as a larva from June to August, having a very similar life-cycle to the previous species, *C. siterata*, with only the hibernating female adults surviving to the spring. It is probably most frequent on the moors of Scotland, where the moths can often be found by day resting on deer-fence posts. They also come to light, sugar and sallow bloom in reasonable numbers. Confined females lay freely on picked foodplant leaves and breeding the species is easy. Widely distributed over most of Britain, but rare in the south-east.
Plate 13: R. Bred from a female adult to sugar. Late April. (JMP)

Dark Marbled Carpet
Chloroclysta citrata Linnaeus
Larva. 24–26 mm. Body green, with yellow between the segments, a darker green dorsal line that is bordered with pale green and whitish subdorsal lines. The anal points are whitish-green or tipped with pink and have been described as being blunt.
Foodplants. Bilberry, birch, sallow, wild strawberry and probably other plants.

Habits. A single-brooded species, with the larvae occurring from mid-April until about the middle of June. They can be beaten or swept from their foodplants during the day and will then feed up, needing no special conditions in captivity. Pupation takes place in plant litter or among the leaves and this stage lasts about a month. This species can also be obtained from the adult moths which can be disturbed from rocks and tree trunks by day or taken at light traps after dark. To be found in most parts of Britain, preferring moors and woodland habitats, but local in the south.
Plate 14: A. Swept from bilberry, nearly fully grown. Late May. (DB)

Arran Carpet
Chloroclysta concinnata Stephens
Larva. 23–25 mm. Body green, with a dark green dorsal line and a whitish stripe subdorsally. Many individuals have pink to purple markings along the spiracular region and the sharp anal points are also of this colour.
Foodplants. Heather, bilberry and in captivity garden strawberry.
Habits. Speculation exists as to whether this is a true species or a univoltine race of *C. truncata*. It overwinters in the wild as a small larva and feeds up in the spring to become fully grown by around the middle of June. The adults are most often found on high moorland, resting on heather after dark, but can also be located during the day upon rocks. Females lay readily in confinement and the larvae will often feed up to produce a second generation in the same year. Only recorded from the Isle of Arran, Kintyre, Buteshire and South Uist.
Plate 14: B. Bred from a female adult found at night. Late July. (JR)

Common Marbled Carpet
Chloroclysta truncata Hufnagel
Larva. 24–27 mm. Body green, with a dark green dorsal line and a variable amount of pinkish-purple markings along the sides. The subdorsal line is whitish and the sharp anal points are often pink.
Foodplants. Sallow, birch, bilberry, dock, bramble and many other plants.
Habits. Mostly a double-brooded species that occurs as a larva from September to May and again during July and August. Those of the higher-ground populations in Scotland and parts of Ireland are univoltine, being in the larval stage from late August until about June. They can readily be swept or beaten from the foodplants and are easy to breed through in captivity. The adults regularly come to light and the females will lay freely in confinement when given leaves as a stimulus. Widespread and often common over much of the British Isles.
Plate 14: C. Bred from a female adult to MVL. Mid-May. (BS)

Barred Yellow
Cidaria fulvata Forster
Larva. 19–21 mm. Body green, with yellow between the segments and a series of fine white lines along the back. The spiracular line is broader and tends towards yellowish and the first two thoracic segments have a small series of ridges in the subdorsal area.
Foodplants. Dog rose and in captivity garden roses.
Habits. This univoltine species overwinters as an egg, and from early May to the middle of June the larvae can readily be beaten from their foodplant, growing in woods and on scrubland. They feed up steadily in confinement and no special conditions are necessary for their development. Pupation lasts for about three weeks inside a flimsy cocoon. Widespread, but sometimes local, over most of Britain.
Plate 14: D. Bred from a female adult to MVL. Late June. (JMP)

Blue-bordered Carpet
Plemyria rubiginata Denis & Schiffermüller
(*bicolorata* Hufnagel)
Larva. 20–23 mm. Body yellowish-green, with two contrasting broad pale whitish stripes along the back. The head is green and the anal points are widely separated and curve slightly inwards.
Foodplants. Blackthorn, alder, plum, birch, apple and other trees.
Habits. A single-brooded insect, with the larvae occurring from late April until early June. They can easily be beaten from the foodplant by day and are easy to rear in captivity. During the winter months this species can be obtained by searching for the tiny pinkish-white eggs, that are laid singly or in pairs, upon the forks of the twigs on the foodplants. In Scotland, where the moths are darker, the eggs can often be found on riverside alders and this keeps the naturalist busy during the day while on early season collecting trips. Generally distributed over most of the British Isles.
Plate 14: E. Beaten from blackthorn, fully grown. Late May.

Pine Carpet
Thera firmata Hübner
Larva. 22–23 mm. Body darkish green, exactly the same colour as pine needles, with thin white lines subdorsally and below the spiracles. The head is reddish-brown on the sides and a hint of this colour is to be found laterally on the thoracic segments.
Foodplants. Scots pine and possibly other associated species.
Habits. This single-brooded species overwinters either as an egg or as a tiny larva upon the foodplant. When they are larger, from late May to mid-July, the larvae can readily be beaten from the lower boughs of the more mature trees and rearing them in captivity is easy. The females often come to light traps and will lay eggs if given foodplant as a stimulus. Widespread, but sometimes local, over most of Britain.
Plate 14: F. Bred from a female adult to MVL. Mid-August. (SHC)

Grey Pine Carpet
Thera obeliscata Hübner
Larva. 20–22 mm. Body dark green, with whitish lines along the subdorsal area and below the spiracles. The head is green and the thoracic legs are pink.
Foodplants. Scots pine, spruces and firs.
Habits. A double-brooded insect, with the larvae occurring from about late September, through the winter, until about early June, and again in July and August. They can easily be beaten, sometimes in large numbers, from the lower branches of their foodplants and need no special attention for successful development in captivity. The adults are often common at light and females will lay readily upon picked foodplant. Most numerous in conifer plantations throughout much of the British Isles.
Plate 14: G. Beaten from Scots pine, fully grown. Late May.

Spruce Carpet

Thera britannica Turner
(*variata* auctt.)
Larva. 19–22 mm. Body dark green, with a yellow stripe below the spiracles, a green head and mainly green thoracic legs.
Foodplants. Norway spruce, Sitka spruce, Douglas fir and Western hemlock.
Habits. Double-brooded, with the larvae overwintering when small and then feeding up in the spring, to be fully grown by about late May. The second generation is in this stage from late June and throughout July. They can readily be beaten from the foodplant and are easy to rear in captivity. The adults can be obtained at light or flushed from the lower branches of spruce during the day. Generally distributed over England and Wales, but local in Scotland and Ireland.
Plate 14: H. Bred from a female adult to MVL. Early June. (SHC)

Chestnut-coloured Carpet

Thera cognata Thunberg
Larva. 18–20 mm. Body green with a broad bluish-white dorsal line, a pure white subdorsal line and another white line below the spiracles. The head is light brown and the thoracic legs are pinkish.
Foodplant. Juniper.
Habits. A single-brooded species, with the larvae overwintering while still very small. During the spring their development becomes more rapid and most are fully grown by about early June, when they will pupate in a spinning on the foodplant or in the needles below the bushes. They are easiest to obtain by beating during the last week of May, and no special conditions are needed for rearing them to the adult stage. Locally common in central Scotland and western Ireland, also occurring in Cumbria, Co. Durham, Yorkshire and in a few counties of west Wales.
Plate 14: I. Beaten from juniper, fully grown. Late May.

Juniper Carpet

Thera juniperata Linnaeus
Larva. 20–22 mm. Body green with a broad bluish-white dorsal line, a yellowish-white subdorsal line and a white line that is edged with crimson below the spiracles. The head is mainly green and the thoracic legs are pinkish.
Foodplant. Juniper.
Habits. Single-brooded, overwintering in the egg stage. In Scotland and Ireland the larvae hatch about mid-July, and become fully grown in late August and early September. Those of the populations occurring in southern England are in the larval stage from late August to late September, developing slightly faster. The pupa is spun up in a cocoon among the leaves or in the litter beneath the foodplant. The adult moths are best found with a torch, resting on the foodplant after dark, and the females will lay on picked juniper leaves. Also the larvae can be beaten during the late summer and are easy to rear in captivity. Local in Scotland and western Ireland, also still to be found in decreasing numbers on calcareous soils in southern England.
Plate 14: J. Beaten from foodplant, fully grown. Late September. (RL)

Cypress Carpet

Thera cupressata Geyer
Larva. 22–25 mm. Body green, with a yellow tinge between the segments and broad rings of white along the dorsal area.
Foodplants. Monterey cypress and in captivity *Cupressus leylandii.*
Habits. A double-brooded species that has recently colonized some parts of coastal southern England, especially Dorset and the Isle of Wight. It overwinters as a larva, probably feeding whenever the weather is mild, and can be beaten from the foodplant in the spring. By about late May most larvae are fully developed and pupation takes place, lasting for around three to four weeks. The summer generation of larvae occurs from July to September, but the best way to obtain stocks is from light-trapped females. These will lay in captivity and any resulting larvae are best reared on sleeved foodplant if possible.
Plate 14: K. Bred from a female adult to MVL (Guernsey). Late June. (PC)

Netted Carpet

Eustroma reticulatum Denis & Schiffermüller
Larva. 22–24 mm. Body light green, with a faint darker dorsal line that is sometimes reddish; also there are pale opaque subdorsal stripes and a small head. Many individuals are mottled with a pinkish colour along the sides.
Foodplants. Touch-me-not and in captivity orange balsam.
Habits. A single-brooded species that feeds mainly at night during August and September and overwinters as a cocooned pupa in leaf litter. In July the adult moths can be taken at light or netted at dusk when they fly around their foodplants in damp habitats. The larvae can be difficult to breed in captivity, as they seem to insist on having only very fresh foodplant to eat. Picked balsam keeps best if the stems are put in water or in sealed boxes in the refrigerator, but even then they only last for a few days. Very local in distribution, being found only in the Lake District and North Wales.
Plate 14: L. Bred from a female adult netted at dusk. Late July. (DS)

Broken-barred Carpet

Electrophaes corylata Thunberg
Larva. 24–26 mm. Body green, with dorsal markings from purple to black that are most obvious on the thoracic and last few segments. The large cleft head is green.
Foodplants. Birch, hawthorn, oak, blackthorn and other deciduous trees.
Habits. A single-brooded species that overwinters as a pupa in the soil. From the eggs laid in May and June the larvae are slow to develop, sometimes still being found as late as the first week of October. From about mid-August onwards they can easily be beaten from their foodplants and no special conditions are necessary for successful rearing in captivity. Widely distributed in woods and on heaths over most of Britain and Ireland.
Plate 14: M. Beaten from birch, fully grown. Mid-September.

Beech-green Carpet

Colostygia olivata Denis & Schiffermüller
Larva. 16–18 mm. Body pale ochreous, with lines of greyish-brown along the dorsal area. Also there are many brownish tubercles, each with a short bristle, all over the stout wrinkled body.
Foodplants. Hedge bedstraw, heath bedstraw, lady's bedstraw and other related plants.
Habits. Single-brooded, hibernating as a small larva, probably low down on the foodplant or in plant litter nearby. Feeding resumes in the spring and most larvae will be fully developed by late May, when pupation takes place in the soil or detritus. In July and August the adults can be flushed

from rocks or tree trunks during the day and sometimes they come to light traps. The females will lay in captivity and ideally the larvae should be overwintered outside on a potted foodplant. Some individuals can be forced to grow faster by keeping them warm and they should pupate during the winter months. Very local in southern Britain, occurring mainly on calcareous soils, but more widespread in the north on moorland; also present in small numbers in western Ireland.
Plate 14: N. Bred from a female adult to MVL. Early August. (BS)

Mottled Grey
Colostygia multistrigaria Haworth
Larva. 18–20 mm. Body ochreous, with many grey lines on the dorsal area that almost obscure the ground colour. Between the segments it is ringed with orange, the spiracles are black and the underparts plain ochreous.
Foodplants. Lady's bedstraw, heath bedstraw and other bedstraws.
Habits. A single-brooded species that occurs as a larva during May and June. The larvae can often be swept, especially at night, from open habitats. When they pupate in captivity, they should be kept out of doors in a shaded place, to avoid the pupae drying out during the summer months. They overwinter in this stage and the adults hatch in the early spring. In the wild they can be found at night resting upon plants, and the females will lay on picked bedstraw. Widely distributed over most of Britain and Ireland.
Plate 14: O. Bred from an adult female to MVL. Early April. (SHC)

Green Carpet
Colostygia pectinataria Knoch
Larva. 18–20 mm. Body brown or greyish-brown, with dark grey chevron markings on the five middle segments; the dorsal line is grey and indistinct, except on the paler last few rings. Also there are a few bristle-bearing black tubercles along the back.
Foodplants. Hedge bedstraw, lady's bedstraw and other allied species.
Habits. Mainly a single-brooded insect, with a partial second generation in the southern counties. The larvae occur from about late June through to the following early May, overwintering in plant debris when about half grown. The easiest way to obtain stocks is from a fertile female moth; these can easily be flushed by day from foliage and herbage. They will deposit eggs upon picked foodplant and, if kept warm, the larvae will develop rapidly in confinement. No special conditions are necessary for rearing them and they will pupate in moss or between tissue-paper. This species is widely distributed and fairly common over much of Britain.
Plate 14: P. Bred from a female adult to MVL. Early June. (SHC)

July Highflyer
Hydriomena furcata Thunberg
Larva. 19–22 mm. Body dull white, with large square-shaped markings of brown to black along the dorsal area and mottlings and lines of the same colour subdorsally and along the sides. The head is chestnut-brown and on the first segment is an obvious brown chitinous plate.
Foodplants. Sallow, hazel, bilberry and heather and probably other plants.
Habits. A single-brooded species that overwinters in the egg stage. The larvae hatch in the early spring and feed upon the fresh growth, hiding by day spun up among the leaves. During May and early June they can easily be found by searching by day, and at night, when they have left their spinnings to feed, they can often be swept from bilberry and heather in large numbers. Rearing them in confinement is easy and pupation takes place in moss, soil or plant litter and lasts about three weeks. Breeding large stocks can be rewarding as the resulting adults come in many different forms. Widespread and sometimes abundant all over Britain except on very high ground.
Plate 14: Q. Found in spinning by collecting fallen sallow catkins, about one-third grown. Early May.

May Highflyer
Hydriomena impluviata Denis & Schiffermüller
(*coerulata* Fabricius)
Larva. 20–22 mm. Body light brown, with a dark brown dorsal line and square-shaped markings along the middle segments of the back; the sides are mottled with dark brown. The head and prothoracic plate are dark brown and the underparts are pale greyish.
Foodplant. Alder.
Habits. Single-brooded, with the slow-growing larvae feeding from early July to as late as mid-October, but most are fully developed by late September. Except when they are very young, they spend the day hidden between spun leaves, emerging after dark to feed. Beating the alder branches at night can be successful, especially in damp woods where the populations can be high. They can be found by day in their spinnings, but rarely in any numbers. Pupation takes place in a cocoon under the loose bark or in the soil and the insect overwinters in this stage. Widespread, but usually local, over most of the British Isles.
Plate 14: R. Beaten at night, nearly fully grown. Late August.

Ruddy Highflyer
Hydriomena ruberata Freyer
Larva. 20–22 mm. Body light reddish-brown or brownish-grey, with three grey lines on the dorsal area, the middle one being the most obvious. The spiracles are black, the head brown and the prothoracic plate light brown, centred darker.
Foodplant. Sallow.
Habits. A single-brooded species, with the larvae feeding steadily from late June to early September. During the day they hide in a spinning between the leaves, emerging at night to feed. They can be obtained by careful searching; also beating after dark can be successful. In May and June the adults can be flushed from sallow bushes on calm days, and the females will lay readily on foodplant leaves in captivity. Rearing the larvae is easy. Pupation takes place in a cocoon among moss or plant litter and in the wild lasts throughout the winter. To be found locally in most parts of Britain, being more frequent in the north.
Plate 15: A. Bred from a female adult flushed by day. Early June. (SHC)

Slender-striped Rufous
Coenocalpe lapidata Hübner
Larva. 22–24 mm. Body ochreous, with a light grey dorsal line and other, less distinct, grey mottlings and lines along the back and sides. The spiracles are black and there are also a few black dots scattered over the greater part of the insect.
Foodplants. In captivity buttercup, dandelion and traveller's-joy; possibly various grasses or bedstraw in the wild.
Habits. Single-brooded, overwintering in the egg stage. The larvae hatch during April and May, and become fully developed by about early August. They are best obtained by

netting a female at dusk during September and then keeping the eggs outside in natural temperatures for the winter. The larvae are normally not easy to rear but using potted buttercup seems to be a good method. Pupation should take place in light soil or plant litter and lasts about a month. A local species occurring in central and northern Scotland and also in northern parts of Ireland.
Plate 15: B. Bred from a netted female adult. Mid-September. (RAB)

Small Waved Umber
Horisme vitalbata Denis & Schiffermüller
Larva. 24–27 mm. Body greyish-brown, with a dorsal line that is most distinct on the thoracic and last segments, and adapted into blotches on the middle parts of the back. The spiracles are black and the large flat head is darker centrally.
Foodplant. Traveller's-joy.
Habits. A double-brooded species, with the larvae occurring from early June to late July, and again during September to early October. They are easily beaten from the foodplant and grow rapidly in captivity, needing no special conditions to rear them. Pupation takes place in plant litter and those of the later brood overwinter in this stage. Widely distributed in southern England and South Wales.
Plate 15: C. Bred from a female adult to MVL. Mid-June.

The Fern
Horisme tersata Denis & Schiffermüller
Larva. 25–28 mm. Body light brown, with an incomplete dorsal line that is bold on the thoracic and last few segments, and formed into blotches on the middle rings. Subdorsally there is a vague pale line and the largish flat head is darker centrally.
Foodplants. Traveller's-joy, also possibly buttercup.
Habits. Single-brooded, with the larvae feeding from late July to about mid-September and overwintering as pupae in leaf litter or soil. The larvae can readily be beaten from the foodplant and stocks can also be obtained easily from adults, which come to light or can be disturbed from hedgerows during the day. In captivity the eggs are normally laid on foodplant leaves and rearing the larvae through their development to pupation is easy. This species tends to inhabit bushy places and scrub, mainly on calcareous soils in southern England.
Plate 15: D. Bred from a female adult to MVL. Early July. (SHC)

Pretty Chalk Carpet
Melanthia procellata Denis & Schiffermüller
Larva. 24–26 mm. Body light brown, with three darker lines along the dorsal area, the central line being the narrowest. Also various other mottlings of dark brown on the sides, black spiracles and a largish flat head that is striped with reddish-brown.
Foodplant. Traveller's-joy.
Habits. A single-brooded species, with the larvae occurring from late July until about mid-September. They can readily be beaten from the foodplant and require no special breeding conditions. Also the adults come to light and often eggs can be obtained by stimulating the females with picked foodplant. The larval development lasts about six weeks and pupation takes place in plant litter or light soil for overwintering. Widespread over much of southern Britain, as far north as Lincolnshire.
Plate 15: E. Bred from a female adult to MVL. Early July.

Barberry Carpet
Pareulype berberata Denis & Schiffermüller
Larva. 20–22 mm. Body greyish to reddish-brown, with an indistinct dorsal line that is most obvious on the last few segments where it is bordered by a plain pale ground-colour. Around the posterior part of each segment is a row of small tubercles and the head is small and dark brown.
Foodplant. Barberry.
Habits. Double-brooded, with the larvae to be found from mid-June to mid-July, and again in late August and throughout September. They can easily be beaten from the foodplant and seem to prefer fresh or young leaves for their development. Pupation takes place in a loose cocoon among leaves, and the second generation overwinters in this stage. The adults can be flushed from barberry bushes by day and will also come to light. The females lay readily in confinement. At present this extremely local species, which seems to be on the verge of extinction, is protected by law from collecting. It still occurs in Suffolk, Gloucestershire, and probably in Hampshire, and may also exist undiscovered elsewhere in southern England.
Plate 15: F. Beaten at night, fully grown. Mid-September.

White-banded Carpet
Spargania luctuata Denis & Schiffermüller
Larva. 25–28 mm. Body pale green or brown, often with a row of dark cross-shaped markings along the back on the abdominal segments. The dorsal line is darker, but often almost absent.
Foodplant. Rosebay willowherb.
Habits. A double-brooded species that overwinters as a pupa among plant litter. From mid-June to late July and again in September the larvae can be swept carefully from their foodplant, and rearing them in captivity is easy. The adult moths come to light and can also readily be disturbed from herbage during the day. Given a foodplant leaf, the females will often deposit eggs and, if fertile, these may hatch very quickly, especially if kept warm. The pupae from the first brood have been known to remain in this stage until the following spring. Locally distributed in Kent, East Sussex and East Anglia.
Plate 15: G. Swept by day, nearly fully grown. Late June. (GAC)

Argent and Sable
Rheumaptera hastata Linnaeus
Larva. 20–23 mm. Body brown, with a thin darker dorsal line, darker between the segments and a darker line subdorsally. The head is black or very dark brown.
Foodplants. Birch, and larvae of the northern subspecies also bog myrtle.
Habits. Single-brooded, being in the larval stage from late June to mid-August in the south, and from early July to early September in the more northern populations. The larval stage lasts about five weeks and is spent inside a spinning of leaves on the foodplant. In the north, when feeding on bog myrtle, the larvae can be found by careful searching on the terminal leaves, but they often tend to be parasitized. The adults fly naturally in sunshine; the females will readily lay eggs on picked leaves in captivity, and rearing them is not difficult. Pupation takes place in the spinning and lasts throughout the winter months. In the south this species seems to be local and infrequent, but it can be more readily obtained on moorland and hillsides in Scotland.
Plate 15: H. Bred from a netted female adult. Early June.

Scarce Tissue
Rheumaptera cervinalis Scopoli
(*certata* Hübner)
Larva. 26–28 mm. Body grey, with three faint broken white lines along the back. The head is orange and the black spiracles are each surrounded by an orange blotch; the underparts are very pale grey.
Foodplants. Barberry and cultivated *Berberis*.
Habits. A single-brooded species, being in the larval stage from early June until about late July. The easiest method of obtaining the larvae is by beating the foodplant, especially in July when they are larger. In captivity rearing the larvae is easy, and pupation for the winter takes place in a cocoon among leaf litter. The adults fly in May and occasionally they come to light. They are widely distributed, but local, over much of southern England and Wales; most frequent in East Anglia.
Plate 15: I. Beaten by day, nearly fully grown. Early July. (SHC)

Scallop Shell
Rheumaptera undulata Linnaeus
Larva. 20–22 mm. Body various shades of brown or ochreous, with a distinct broad stripe along the subdorsal area and a thin pale edged dorsal line. The spiracles are pale and ringed with brown, the head is also brown.
Foodplants. Sallows, aspen and bilberry.
Habits. Single-brooded, with the larvae feeding at night from late July to early October. During the day they hide in a silken spinning usually on the terminal shoots of their foodplants. These can be found by close searching and the larvae can also be taken by beating and sweeping at night. The adults readily come to light and can be disturbed from foliage on calm days; the females will lay in captivity if supplied with foodplant as a stimulus. Rearing the larvae is easy and they pupate in light soil, moss or plant litter for overwintering. Mainly a woodland species inhabiting most of Britain, except central and northern Scotland.
Plate 15: J. Bred from a female adult to MVL. Early July.

The Tissue
Triphosa dubitata Linnaeus
Larva. 28–30 mm. Body green, with four thin whitish lines along the dorsal area, a broader yellowish line along the spiracles and yellow between the segments.
Foodplants. Buckthorn and alder buckthorn.
Habits. A single-brooded insect that overwinters as an adult moth inside caves, tunnels and undisturbed buildings. From mid-May to early July, the larvae can be found by carefully searching the foodplant for leaves spun together, inside which they hide during the day; also beating at night can sometimes produce larvae in small numbers. Rearing the larvae in captivity is not difficult and when they are fully grown they should be given finely sifted soil in which to pupate. Widespread, but usually infrequent, over most of southern and central Britain.
Plate 15: K. Located by searching, nearly fully grown. Mid-June.

Brown Scallop
Philereme vetulata Denis & Schiffermüller
Larva. 21–23 mm. Body greyish, with a broad black dorsal line in which there are two thin white stripes; vague orange markings laterally and black underparts.
Foodplant. Buckthorn.
Habits. Single-brooded, with the larvae occurring during May and early June after overwintering in the egg stage. Although adult females occasionally visit light traps and will lay in confinement, probably the best way to obtain larvae is by searching for their spinnings or by beating at night. The larvae are easy to rear and pupation takes place in a cocoon in the soil, lasting about a month. Widespread in the south-central and south-east parts of England, but less frequent in the Midlands, northern England and South Wales.
Plate 15: L. Located inside spun leaves, nearly fully grown. Mid-May.

Dark Umber
Philereme transversata Hufnagel
(*rhamnata* Denis & Schiffermüller)
Larva. 25–28 mm. Body green, with a conspicuous white spiracular line and purplish-black anal legs from which the colour often extends below the spiracular line for the last three segments. The dorsal line is darker and the head is dark brown; sometimes the whole body is clouded with purplish-brown. A totally different form occurs with a pale grey body, a broad blackish-brown dorsal stripe and yellow and black mottlings laterally.
Foodplant. Buckthorn.
Habits. A single-brooded species, with the larvae hatching from the overwintering eggs about late April and becoming fully grown by mid-June. They can easily be beaten at night when they have left their spinnings to feed or they may be searched for by day when dormant inside their retreats. The adults come to light and fertile females will readily lay eggs on the foodplant twigs. Widely distributed over much of southern England, also occurring locally in the Midlands, northern England and South Wales.
Plate 15: M. Beaten at night, about half grown. Mid-May.

Cloaked Carpet
Euphyia biangulata Haworth
(*picata* Hübner)
Larva. 26–28 mm. Body ochreous, with many wavy light grey lines, black spiracles and a slightly forked brown marked head.
Foodplants. In captivity chickweed and stitchwort.
Habits. Single-brooded, with the larvae occurring from late July until about mid-September. To collect stocks of this species the best method is to obtain a fertile female. These will come to light and can also be taken by disturbing them from foliage during calm days. In captivity they will deposit eggs upon picked foodplant, and rearing the larvae is easy as long as they are supplied with fresh food. Pupation takes place in leaf litter and the insects spend the winter in this stage. A very local species, being found in southern England, Wales and Ireland.
Plate 15: N. Bred from a female adult to MVL. Mid-July. (SHC)

Sharp-angled Carpet
Euphyia unangulata Haworth
Larva. 26–28 mm. Body ochreous, with broad cross-shaped grey markings on the back, including a darker short mark on the anterior part of the middle segments on the obscured dorsal line. The underparts are pale with a greyish central line and black mottling towards the spiracles.
Foodplants. In confinement chickweed and stitchwort.
Habits. A similar life-cycle to the previous species, *E. biangulata*. The larvae feed from mid-July to September and pupate for the winter in loose soil particles. This species is best obtained by breeding from an adult female trapped at

light or flushed from vegetation; they will lay readily on fresh foodplant in captivity. As long as the larvae are supplied with fresh food, rearing is normally easy. Locally distributed in woodland in southern England, Wales and most of Ireland.
Plate 15: O. Bred from a female adult to MVL. Early July.

November Moth
Epirrita dilutata Denis & Schiffermüller
Larva. 20–22 mm. Body usually bright to dark green, variably marked with bold reddish-brown blotches, also a pale whitish line below the spiracles. Very similar to the next two species, *E. christyi* and *E. autumnata*.
Foodplants. Blackthorn, birch, oak, elm, hawthorn, apple, ash and other deciduous trees.
Habits. A single-brooded species, overwintering in the egg stage. The larvae hatch as soon as the leaves begin to bud in April and most become fully developed by about mid-June. Pupation takes place in a cocoon just under the soil, and the insect remains in this stage until hatching in late autumn. The larvae are easily beaten from the foodplants, and need no special conditions to be reared successfully. In captivity the pupae should be kept outside in a shaded place, so they do not dry out during the summer. Generally distributed and often common over most of the British Isles.
Plate 15: P. Beaten from blackthorn, fully grown. Early June.

Pale November Moth
Epirrita christyi Allen
Larva. 20–22 mm. Body usually bright green inclining to yellowish-green, variably marked with clouded reddish-brown blotches, also with a whitish line below the spiracles. This species can be difficult to distinguish from the previous and next species, *E. dilutata* and *E. autumnata*.
Foodplants. Beech, sallow, hawthorn, oak, hornbeam, maple, blackthorn, hazel and other deciduous trees.
Habits. A similar life-cycle to the previous species, *E. dilutata*, with the methods of obtaining and rearing the insect exactly the same. It tends to be more of a woodland species, being found less often in gardens, hedgerows and on heathland. Widespread over most of England, Wales, southern Scotland and also occurring in Ireland.
Plate 15: Q. Beaten from beech, fully grown. Early June.

Autumnal Moth
Epirrita autumnata Borkhausen
Larva. 20–23 mm. Body usually bright green inclining to bluish-green, sometimes marked with rose-red or russet markings or blotches, also with a pale line below the spiracles. Difficult to separate from the previous two species, *E. dilutata* and *E. christyi*.
Foodplants. Birch and alder, possibly also other deciduous trees.
Habits. A parallel life-cycle to the previous two species, but being the least common of the three, more difficult to obtain. It can be beaten, especially from birches growing in heathland localities. It seems to be widespread over most of Britain, but difficulty in differentiating this species from the others causes much confusion as to the exact status in distribution.
Plate 15: R. Beaten from birch, fully grown. Early June.

Small Autumnal Moth
Epirrita filigrammaria Herrich-Schäffer
Larva. 17–20 mm. Body dark velvety green, with a conspicuous yellow subdorsal line and a light yellow line below the spiracles. The dorsal line and the head are dark green.
Foodplants. Heather and bilberry.
Habits. A single-brooded species that overwinters in the egg stage. The larvae occur from mid-April until late May and are easily swept from their foodplants in moorland and hillside habitats. They are easy to rear in captivity and pupate in the soil, but should be kept in a shaded place outside to avoid desiccation during the summer. Locally distributed in Scotland, North and mid-Wales, Ireland and the northern counties of England.
Plate 16: A. Swept by day, nearly fully grown. Early May.

Winter Moth
Operophtera brumata Linnaeus
Larva. 18–20 mm. Body usually bright green, with a darker dorsal line and yellowish-white lines in the subdorsal and spiracular regions. The head is light green and often devoid of any black markings and the spiracles are reddish-brown.
Foodplants. Oak, apple, blackthorn, birch, sallow, hawthorn, hazel and many other deciduous trees and shrubs.
Habits. Single-brooded, overwintering as an egg. The larvae hatch during April and bore into the developing buds, feeding within until the food supply is exhausted and then moving to another bud or on to the young leaves. Throughout most of this stage they can be searched for in their spinnings between the leaves and they become fully grown by early June. At this time they can easily be beaten, sometimes in large numbers, from the many foodplants. Rearing in captivity is easy, but the subterranean pupae must be kept outside in a shaded place to avoid them drying out in the summer months. Occasionally this species reaches pest proportions in orchards and bands of a sticky compound may be seen on tree trunks to prevent the wingless females from reaching the buds to deposit eggs. Widely distributed and often very common over most of Britain and Ireland.
Plate 16: B. Beaten from oak, fully grown. Late May.

Northern Winter Moth
Operophtera fagata Scharfenberg
(*boreata* Hübner)
Larva. 18–21 mm. Body green, inclining to yellowish-green with an indistinct darker dorsal line and paler lines subdorsally and in the spiracular region. The head is usually wholly brownish-black and the spiracles are black.
Foodplants. Birch, alder, apple and other deciduous trees.
Habits. A single-brooded insect that overwinters in the egg stage. In May the larvae are fairly easy to obtain by searching birch leaves for their spinnings and they can also be beaten, especially at night, when becoming fully developed. Rearing them is easy. Pupation takes place in a silken cocoon in the soil and these should be left outside in the shade for the summer. Widespread over most of Britain, but probably not occurring in Ireland.
Plate 16: C. Beaten from birch, fully grown. Late May.

Barred Carpet
Perizoma taeniata Stephens
Larva. 18–22 mm. Body light reddish-brown, with X-shaped dark markings along the dorsal area and undulating brown lines along the lateral region; pinacula small, black, with short black setae that face forwards on the anterior part of the segment and those at the back facing rearwards; head pale brown, heavily mottled darker.
Foodplants. Unknown in the wild, possibly the flowers and seed pods of various mosses, but may accept garden nasturtium, flowers of herb-robert, knotgrass, ivy-leaved toadflax and chickweed in captivity. Successfully reared on self-heal.

Habits. A single-brooded species, with the larvae occurring from early August until the following late May, overwintering when still quite small, probably in plant litter. During July the adult females may be disturbed by day by tapping moss and lichen covered branches. Eggs are deposited freely in confinement upon almost any vegetation and last about ten days. The larvae are considered difficult to rear in captivity. While most larval fatalities take place before the winter, if hibernation is successful they should feed and grow more rapidly and survive through to pupation. Also it has been suggested that larvae are vulnerable to frost and moulds on the foodplant. A local insect, being found in damp woods mainly in western and northern parts of Britain.
Plate 16: D. Bred from a netted female adult. Mid-July. (GMH)

The Rivulet

Perizoma affinitata Stephens
Larva. 12–15 mm. Body pinkish-white, with a black head, a dark brown prothoracic plate, a pale brown anal plate and light brown spiracles.
Foodplant. The flowers and seed capsules of red campion.
Habits. Single-brooded, with the larvae feeding at first, during July, inside the flowers and later in the seed capsules of the foodplant. They become fully grown by about mid-September and then pupate in the soil for the winter. They can be obtained by picking off the dying flowers and soft seed capsules from the plant during late August and early September and keeping these in a well-ventilated container. White paper should be put under the spread-out plant so the inhabited pieces can be identified from the larvae's frass beneath. They can then be put into boxes that have a layer of sifted soil at the bottom for pupation. This species is generally distributed over most of England, Wales, southern Scotland and much of Ireland, except the south-west.
Plate 16: E. Located in picked foodplant flowers, fully grown. Late August.

Small Rivulet

Perizoma alchemillata Linnaeus
Larva. 10–13 mm. Body purple, with a broad yellowish dorsal stripe that is centred darker and greenish underparts. The head is very dark brown and the prothoracic and anal plates are also brown.
Foodplants. The flowers and seeds of hemp-nettle and probably also woundwort.
Habits. A single-brooded species, being in the larval stage between mid-July and early September. They can easily be reared by introducing fertile female adults on to potted foodplants that are covered by a netting cage. They should deposit eggs freely and all that needs to be done is to make sure that the growing larvae do not run out of food. Pupation takes place in the soil and lasts through the winter until the following June. To be found over most of the British Isles, especially in woods and on commons.
Plate 16: F. Bred from a female adult to MVL. Late June. (SHC)

Barred Rivulet

Perizoma bifaciata Haworth
Larva. 12–15 mm. Body of various shades of brown, with a thin incomplete dark brown dorsal line and a series of dark brown dashes along the subdorsal area. On the back are many tiny blackish dots that are each surrounded by a ring of pale coloration. The head and the underparts are mainly dark brown.
Foodplants. The ripening seeds of red bartsia; also recorded on eyebright.
Habits. Single-brooded, with the larvae occurring from about mid-August until the last become fully grown in late October. The eggs are laid on the old flowers or developing seed capsules and upon hatching the young larvae burrow inside the capsule and feed on the plant matter within. At this point of their development the larvae look like small yellow grubs. After changing into the final instar they are too large to hide totally in a capsule and live on the outside of the plant, burrowing their head and front segments into the capsules to feed on the seeds. While being mainly external on the plant, during October, they can often be obtained readily by sweeping. Pupation takes place in loose soil and the insects normally remain in this stage until thc following July or August, but have been known to overwinter for up to five times. Locally distributed over most of Britain, except northern Scotland, being more frequent in the southern counties.
Plate 16: G. Swept by day, fully grown. Mid-October. (BS)

Heath Rivulet

Perizoma minorata Treitschke
Larva. 10–12 mm. Body yellowish-green to yellowish-brown, with a faint brown dorsal line, a distinct subdorsal line and a broad brown line in the spiracular region, between which are various mottlings and indistinct wavy light brown lines. The head, prothoracic and anal plates are all dark brown. Another form has the sides and underparts bright green.
Foodplant. The seeds of eyebright.
Habits. A single-brooded species, with the larvae living and feeding within the flowers and seed capsules of the foodplant, from about mid-August and throughout September. They can be bred by introducing fertile females to potted foodplant or by collecting the withering flowers and seeds and placing them on white paper on which to observe the frass from larvae inside inhabited capsules. In the final instar the larvae also rest on the outside of the capsule relying on their camouflage to remain undetected by predators. Pupation takes place in a cocoon in light soil and lasts throughout the winter, until the following July or August. Locally common in Scotland, very local in northern England and also occurring on the Burren in western Ireland.
Plate 16: H. Found in picked eyebright, fully grown. Mid-September. (MB)

Pretty Pinion

Perizoma blandiata Denis & Schiffermüller
Larva. 12–14 mm. Body light yellowish-green to yellowish-brown, with a purple or brownish-red stripe along the dorsal area, that varies in width between individuals. The head is dull green and marked with tiny pinkish-brown dots.
Foodplant. The flowers and seeds of eyebright.
Habits. Single-brooded, with the larvae occurring from early August to about mid-September, feeding at first on the flowers and later on the developing seeds of the foodplant. This species can be searched for in the egg stage – these are oblong and flattened in shape and coloured bright yellow. They are deposited on or just by the flowers during July. The larvae can be obtained by picking the eyebright and laying the plants on paper to detect which are inhabited, as the frass accumulates below the seed capsules. In the final instar the larvae are too large to secrete themselves inside the capsules and feed with only their head and front segments bored into the plant. The pupa is formed in a cocoon just under the soil and this stage lasts until the following summer.

Widespread and generally frequent over much of Scotland and also occurring locally in Ireland and the Lake District of England.
Plate 16: I. Located in picked plants, fully grown. Early September. (IL)

Grass Rivulet

Perizoma albulata Denis & Schiffermüller
Larva. 10–13 mm. Body dull yellow, inclining to greenish-yellow, with a faint darker spiracular line, a black head and brownish prothoracic and anal plates.
Foodplant. The ripening seeds of yellow rattle.
Habits. A single-brooded species, with the larvae occurring from mid-June to early August, living and feeding totally inside the seed capsules of the foodplant. They can be obtained by searching for discoloured seed capsules, in which there should be a developing larva, or by picking many plants at random, placing them on paper and waiting for the larva's frass to appear below the separated stems. The larval growth from the egg takes about a month, and pupation takes place in the soil, lasting through the winter, until the following late May or June. Widespread and locally common over most of the British Isles.
Plate 16: J. Found in picked plant, fully grown. Early July.

Sandy Carpet

Perizoma flavofasciata Thunberg
Larva. 15–17 mm. Body bluish-grey, with obvious brownish-purple stripes subdorsally and in the spiracular region. The head is dark brown and the thoracic and anal plates are also brown.
Foodplants. The ripening seeds of red campion, white campion and bladder campion.
Habits. Single-brooded, with the larvae feeding inside the seed capsules of the foodplants from about mid-July to early September, before pupating in the soil to overwinter. Breeding this species from the adult is easy, although the food must be checked regularly for mould or desiccation. The larger larvae can be taken by collecting the seed capsules during the first half of August, spreading them on paper and observing which have frass beneath after about two days. This species is widely distributed and reasonably common throughout most of the British Isles.
Plate 16: K. Bred from a female adult netted at dusk. Late June. (SHC)

Twin-spot Carpet

Perizoma didymata Linnaeus
Larva. 22–24 mm. Body green with a faint narrow darker dorsal line, a whitish spiracular line and yellow between the segments; also there are a few small black tubercles each with a short dark bristle.
Foodplants. Bilberry, sallow, heather, willowherb, docks and many other herbaceous plants.
Habits. A single-brooded species that overwinters in the egg stage. The larvae hatch about early April and most are fully grown by the first week of June, when they pupate in a cocoon among leaf litter. They are probably easiest to obtain by sweeping bilberry in heathy woods in the northern and western counties of Britain and they require no special conditions to be successfully reared in captivity. In the wild the insect spends about a month as a pupa, but it may hatch within about ten days in confinement. The female adults, which will lay eggs freely on plant twigs, can often be found at night resting on plants or be located on rocks and tree trunks by day. Locally common over most of Britain, but less frequent in the south-east.
Plate 16: L. Swept from bilberry, fully grown. Late May.

Marsh Carpet

Perizoma sagittata Fabricius
Larva. 18–20 mm. Body green, with an olive-green ridged structure on the fifth to tenth segments and pinkish subdorsally on the thoracic segments and sometimes on the last few rings.
Foodplant. The ripening seeds of common meadow-rue.
Habits. A single-brooded species, with the larvae occurring from late July until about mid-September, feeding externally on the ripening seeds of the foodplant. The best time to obtain the larvae is in late August and very early September, when they are large enough to be carefully swept or searched for on plants growing in damp ditches. Rearing them in captivity is not difficult, but the subterranean cocooned pupae must not be disturbed or they may dry out before hatching in the following June and July. Very local, being found mainly in East Anglia; also recorded from Nottinghamshire and Yorkshire.
Plate 16: M. Found by close searching, fully grown. Late August. (JR)

Slender Pug

Eupithecia tenuiata Hübner
Larva. 14–16 mm. Body dull greenish-white, with indistinct blackish markings along the dorsal area. The head is almost black and the first segment is marked with brown dorsally.
Foodplant. The catkins of sallow.
Habits. A single-brooded species that overwinters as an egg, and the larva of which feeds inside the catkins of various species of sallow, during March and April. The easiest way to obtain these larvae is to collect fallen catkins, then place them on white paper and in about two days search for the larval frass which will appear beneath those that are inhabited. Pupation takes place in plant litter or soil and lasts about six weeks in the wild. Widespread over most of Britain.
Plate 16: N. Found in fallen catkins, fully grown. Late April. (CH)

Maple Pug

Eupithecia inturbata Hübner
Larva. 15–16 mm. Body light green, with a series of reddish-brown or dark green diamond-shaped markings along the centre of the back, also vague pale green lines in the subdorsal and spiracular regions.
Foodplant. The flowers of field maple.
Habits. Single-brooded, overwintering in the egg stage. The larvae hatch during early May and feed up quickly on the flowers of the foodplant, becoming fully developed by about early June. They can be readily obtained by beating the lower boughs of mature maples, especially those growing in woodland rides and along hedgerows in late May. Rearing the larvae in captivity is easy and they pupate in cocoons among the flowers or in plant litter and spend about four weeks in this stage. Widespread and reasonably frequent over most of England and Wales.
Plate 16: O. Beaten from maple, fully grown. Late May.

Haworth's Pug

Eupithecia haworthiata Doubleday
Larva. 13–15 mm. Body light greyish-green, with a blackish dorsal line, an indistinct dark subdorsal line and a small

brown head; some individuals are suffused with a pinkish tinge.
Foodplants. The flower buds of traveller's-joy, and cultivated *Clematis* in captivity.
Habits. A single-brooded species, with the larvae living and feeding within the foodplant flower buds during July and August. The larvae can be collected by searching for buds that have a small brown hole in the side, where the larva has gained entry into the capsule and is living within, or they can be beaten, especially when they are nearly fully developed. Those inside buds should be left in a ventilated container with fine soil on the bottom for pupation, and supplied with fresh food if necessary. They will overwinter as cocooned pupae and hatch in the following June. Locally common and widespread over most of England, Wales and Ireland.
Plate 16: P. Found in picked buds, fully grown. Early August. (GAC)

Lead-coloured Pug

Eupithecia plumbeolata Haworth
Larva. 16–18 mm. Body greenish-yellow, with an obvious undulating dorsal line and narrower subdorsal lines that are usually dull purple.
Foodplants. The flowers of common cow-wheat, and has been recorded from yellow rattle.
Habits. Single-brooded, occurring as a larva from late June until about mid-August and pupating in leaf litter or soil for overwintering. The larvae are probably easiest to obtain by picking the foodplant flowers in late July and early August from localities where the species is known to occur. The foodplant will last a few days in sealed containers and must be replaced when it seems to be wilting or the larvae may die. Mainly a woodland species, being found over much of England and Wales and locally in Ireland.
Plate 16: Q. Found on picked foodplant, fully grown. Late July.

Cloaked Pug

Eupithecia abietaria Goeze
(*pini* Retzius)
(*togata* Hübner)
Larva. 20–22 mm. Body dull pinkish, with a visible darker dorsal vessel, a brown head and a dark-brown prothoracic plate. On the back and sides are a few small greyish tubercles.
Foodplants. The inner parts of the cones of Norway spruce and allied conifers.
Habits. A single-brooded species, with the larvae living and feeding totally inside the larger cones of mature examples of Norway spruce from late June to about mid-September. Inhabited cones tend to be those which are high up on the trees, and it is possible to use binoculars to ascertain whether they are tenanted by observing the reddish-brown frass emitting from between the cone-scales. The difficulty is getting to the cones, either by using a ladder or by climbing the tree. Occasionally these cones, which may contain more than one larva, are blown to the ground by gales and can be obtained safely. Pupation takes place in a flimsy cocoon in plant litter and lasts throughout the winter. The adult insect flies in June and early July and will come to light traps. Very irregular in its distribution and could turn up in any mature spruce plantation; recently recorded as a resident from Northumberland, Co. Durham, Inverness-shire, Northamptonshire and Warwickshire.
Plate 16: R. Taken from tree-top cones, nearly fully grown. August. (BS)

Toadflax Pug

Eupithecia linariata Denis & Schiffermüller
Larva. 18–20 mm. Body yellow or green, with reddish-brown markings across the segments in the dorsal area, although some individuals have these marks greatly reduced or absent. The body colour seems to be determined by that of the foodplant, as those fed on purple garden *Antirrhinum* soon change to that colour.
Foodplants. The flowers and seed capsules of common toadflax and in captivity those of garden *Antirrhinum*.
Habits. Single-brooded, with the larvae feeding at first inside the flowers and later externally on the seed capsules. They are to be found during August and September, either by collecting the flowering stems and placing them in a well-ventilated container, adding fresh food as necessary, or by careful sweeping when the larvae are larger and feeding externally. Pupation takes place in fine soil and lasts through the winter until the following July. Widespread over most of England and Wales, but local in Scotland.
Plate 17: A. Found in picked plants, about half grown. Late August.

Foxglove Pug

Eupithecia pulchellata Stephens
Larva. 21–22 mm. Body usually green, but sometimes brownish, with a darker dorsal line of variable thickness, thinner dark lines subdorsally and usually a brown head.
Foodplant. The stamens of the flowers of foxglove.
Habits. A single-brooded insect, with the variable larvae living inside the foodplant flower, feeding on the stamens after boring in through the side and securing the open mouth of the flower with silk. They can be located from late June to about mid-August by carefully searching for discoloured flowers, and are normally easy to rear in captivity. Pupation takes place in the soil and lasts through the winter until the following May or June. Widespread and generally common over most of the British Isles.
Plate 17: B. Located by searching, fully grown. Early August. (SHC)

Marbled Pug

Eupithecia irriguata Hübner
Larva. 19–21 mm. Body green, inclining to yellowish-green, with reddish-brown markings that are bordered with dull yellow along the dorsal area.
Foodplant. Oak.
Habits. Single-brooded, with the larvae occurring from about late May to early July, feeding openly on the foliage of the foodplant. They can readily be beaten from mature oaks, and adult females, which can be found on oak trunks by day or light-trapped at night during May, will lay eggs freely in confinement. The larvae need no special conditions for rearing and pupate in the soil to overwinter. A very local species occurring only in southern England and probably being most frequently found in the New Forest.
Plate 17: C. Bred from a female adult to MVL. Early May. (JMP)

Mottled Pug

Eupithecia exiguata Hübner
Larva. 23–25 mm. Body bright green, with a reddish-brown dorsal line that varies in intensity and a reddish-brown spiracular line, below which the underparts are very pale green.
Foodplants. Hawthorn, blackthorn, dogwood, rowan and probably other trees and shrubs.

Habits. A single-brooded species, of which the slow-developing larvae occur from late June to early October before pupating in a cocoon formed just under the soil, to overwinter. They can readily be beaten during August and September and are easy to rear in captivity, needing no special attention. Fairly common and widely distributed over most of Britain.
Plate 17: D. Bred from a female adult to MVL. Early June. (M&JH)

Pinion-spotted Pug

Eupithecia insigniata Hübner
Larva. 24–26 mm. Body bright green, with a reddish-brown dorsal line that is expanded posteriorly on each segment to form an elongated triangle. The largish round head is green and some individuals also have a brownish spiracular line.
Foodplants. Hawthorn and possibly apple.
Habits. Single-brooded, with the larvae occurring from about mid-June until early August. They can be beaten and seem to prefer mature trees on which to feed. Once obtained they are easy to rear and pupate for overwintering among loose soil particles, plant litter or moss. A very local species, being found over most of southern England as far north as Yorkshire; probably most frequent in East Anglia and on the Chilterns.
Plate 17: E. Beaten from hawthorn, fully grown. Late July. (BS)

Valerian Pug

Eupithecia valerianata Hübner
Larva. 20–22 mm. Body dull green, with indistinct thin greyish-green dorsal and subdorsal lines.
Foodplant. The flowers and ripening seeds of common valerian.
Habits. A single-brooded insect, with the larvae feeding fully exposed upon the flowerhead of the foodplant during July and the first half of August. They can readily be obtained by carefully shaking valerian flowerheads over a net and then examining the contents of the bag. They are easy to rear and the foodplant keeps fresh in water or in sealed containers in the refrigerator. Pupation takes place in plant litter and lasts throughout the winter months, with the adults emerging during the following May or June. Locally common in damp woods, fens and wet meadows throughout most of Britain and western Ireland.
Plate 17: F. Shaken from foodplant, fully grown. Late July.

Marsh Pug

Eupithecia pygmaeata Hübner
(*palustraria* Doubleday)
Larva. 16–18 mm. Body green or ochreous, with indistinct darker dorsal and subdorsal lines; the head is usually brown or brownish-green.
Foodplants. The flowers and seed capsules of field mouse-ear and probably also other associated plants.
Habits. Single-brooded, with the larvae occurring from mid-June to late July. This species is best obtained by careful searching of the foodplant in localities which it is known to frequent. The young larvae feed inside the tiny flowers, but when they are larger they live exposed with only their head and front segments inside the seed capsules, on which they partially bore to eat the seeds. They can be swept, but this method tends not to be very successful. Once obtained the larvae feed rapidly and will pupate among plant litter for overwintering and the adults should emerge in the following spring, but have been known to remain in this stage for another year. A very local species that is to be found in East Anglia, the South Midlands and northwards, seemingly being absent from the southern counties; also recorded from parts of Ireland.
Plate 17: G. Found by searching, nearly fully grown. Early July. (MB)

Netted Pug

Eupithecia venosata Fabricius
Larva. 22–24 mm. Body ochreous, with a darker greyish-brown dorsal line and sometimes with a visible brown subdorsal line; the head is dark brown.
Foodplants. The ripening seed capsules of bladder campion and sea campion.
Habits. A single-brooded insect, with the larvae living and feeding mostly inside the flowers and ripening seed capsules of the foodplant from about mid-June to the end of July, or even later in the more northern populations. They can readily be obtained by picking the flowering parts of the plant in early July and placing these in a well-ventilated container, adding fresh stems as necessary. They can also be swept carefully from the plants at night. Pupation takes place in the soil and lasts through the winter until the following May or June, but sometimes they remain in this stage for another year. Widespread and generally common over most of Britain, being more frequent on calcareous soil and on the coast.
Plate 17: H. Found inside picked capsules, fully grown. Mid-July. (IR)

Pauper Pug

Eupithecia egenaria Herrich-Schäffer
Larva. 23–25 mm. Body green, with the dorsal vessel showing through the skin as a darker line; yellowish where the segments join and the head is brownish-green.
Foodplants. The flowers of small-leaved lime and large-leaved lime and in captivity those of the common lime.
Habits. Single-brooded, with the larvae occurring from late June and throughout most of July. They can be beaten from the mature flower-bearing trees and female adults come readily to light traps, laying freely in captivity on fresh lime flowers. The larvae are easy to rear, feeding and growing rapidly and they take to the flowers of common lime, preferring the stamens, in confinement. The cocooned pupa is formed in among plant litter or just under the soil and lasts through the winter until the following late May or June. A very local species, at present recorded only from the Wye Valley area and in south-west Norfolk.
Plate 17: I. Bred from a female adult to MVL. Late June.

Lime-speck Pug

Eupithecia centaureata Denis & Schiffermüller
Larva. 21–23 mm. Body colour extremely variable, being basically green, brown or grey usually with a reddish, brown or grey dorsal line and often with other markings along the back and sides.
Foodplants. The flowers of ragwort, mugwort, goldenrod, burnet-saxifrage, traveller's-joy, scabious, knapweed, yarrow and many other plants.
Habits. This species has two broods that are so protracted that they overlap during the summer months. The larvae can be found at any time from late May until late October and can readily be swept from the flowers of their many accepted foodplants. Rearing them in captivity is very easy; they will pupate in loose soil or plant litter, overwintering when necessary in this stage. Widely distributed and often common over most of the British Isles.

Plate 17: J. Swept from ragwort, fully grown. Early September.

Triple-spotted Pug

Eupithecia trisignaria Herrich-Schäffer

Larva. 17–18 mm. Body dull green, with darker green dorsal and subdorsal lines, a whitish line just below the spiracles and a black head.

Foodplants. The flowers and ripening seeds of wild angelica and occasionally hogweed.

Habits. A single-brooded species, with the larvae occurring from early August until about late September. They can easily be obtained by shaking the flowerheads of the foodplant over a net or beating tray and then examining the contents that have fallen from the plant. They are fairly easy to rear in captivity and they pupate for the winter among loose soil particles or plant litter. A local insect, being found mainly in the southern counties of England, Cambridgeshire, East Anglia and parts of the Midlands.

Plate 17: K. Shaken from angelica flowers, about one-third grown. Late August. (GAC)

Freyer's Pug / Edinburgh Pug / Mere's Pug

Eupithecia intricata Zetterstedt

Larva. 22–24 mm. Body green, with a dark green dorsal line, yellowish subdorsal lines and a broader white line in the spiracular region. The head is green in the southern subspecies, brownish in the others.

Foodplants. Various species of cypress (southern England), and juniper (north-west England, Scotland and western Ireland).

Habits. This species is separated into three distinct races within the British Isles. They are: Freyer's Pug (*E. intricata arceuthata*) found in the southern half of England, Edinburgh Pug (*E. intricata millieraria*) in north-west England and Scotland and Mere's Pug (*E. intricata hibernica*) on the Burren in western Ireland. The larvae of all three subspecies seem to be identical except for the head colour. Those of the southern and Scottish races can readily be beaten from their respective foodplants from early August to about late September. The Irish race feeds up quicker, most larvae being fully grown by mid-September, and these can be taken by shaking over a tray the prostrate junipers on the higher ground of the Burren. They all pupate in cocoons spun up among the foodplant leaves and overwinter in this stage.

Plate 17: L. (ssp. *arceuthata*) Beaten from cypress, fully grown. Late September. (M&JH)

Satyr Pug

Eupithecia satyrata Hübner

Larva. 22–24 mm. Body ground colour variable, being shades of green, yellow, brown or pink, often with bold darker chevrons and dashes over the back and sides.

Foodplants. The flowers of knapweed, thyme, meadowsweet, stork's-bill and other herbaceous plants.

Habits. A single-brooded species, with the variable larvae occurring from late June to early September. They can be swept from flowers or bred from fertile females, which will lay eggs freely on potted foodplants in captivity. The females can be netted after disturbing them from herbage on calm warm days during late May and June. They will also come to light and on moorlands they can be found at rest upon fence posts. Rearing the larvae is fairly easy, with no special methods being required and they will usually pupate in plant litter or sifted soil for overwintering. Widespread, but local, mainly on open ground over most of Britain.

Plate 17: M. Bred from a netted female adult on thyme. Early June. (JR)

Wormwood Pug

Eupithecia absinthiata Clerck

Larva. 18–20 mm. Body ground colour variable, usually of some shade of brown, green or ochreous with a darker dorsal line that is swollen in shape posteriorly on each segment, subdorsally another darker line and often dark dashes along the sides.

Foodplants. The flowers of ragwort, mugwort, yarrow, wormwood, goldenrod, goosefoot and many other herbaceous plants.

Habits. A single-brooded species, being in the larval stage from late July to about mid-October. The larvae can readily be swept from the flowers of many plants, especially those of the family *Compositae*, and are easily reared in captivity. Pupation takes place in a cocoon just under the soil and lasts throughout the winter. Widely distributed and usually common over most of the British Isles.

Plate 17: N. Swept from ragwort, fully grown. Mid-September. (GAC)

Ling Pug

Eupithecia goossensiata Mabille

Larva. 16–19 mm. Body dull purplish-pink with a slightly darker dorsal line and purplish-brown triangular dorsal markings that are most obvious on the middle segments.

Foodplant. The flowers of heather.

Habits. Single-brooded, with the larval period from late July to about the middle of September. The larvae can easily be swept from mature plants of heather, especially when most are nearly fully grown in late August and early September. They are easy to rear in captivity, pupating in a cocoon for the winter in fine sifted soil. Many authors consider this insect to be a form of the previous species (*E. absinthiata*), but the adult is slightly different, and the larvae are smaller, thinner and constant in colour and markings. Also they can occur on the same ground and at the same flight period as *E. absinthiata* without a natural mixed pairing ever being proven. Widespread on heaths and moorland throughout most of Britain and much of Ireland.

Plate 17: O. Swept at night, nearly fully grown. Late August.

Currant Pug

Eupithecia assimilata Doubleday

Larva. 22–24 mm. Body green or greenish-grey, with a darker dorsal line, slightly paler subdorsal lines and yellow where the segments join.

Foodplants. Red currant, black currant and wild hop.

Habits. A double-brooded species, with the larvae occurring from early June to about mid-July, and again from late August and throughout most of September. They can be located by searching the foliage of the foodplants for the many holes that the larvae make while feeding from the underside of the leaves, and may also be taken by beating. They grow quite rapidly, taking about three to four weeks from the egg to becoming fully developed and pupation takes place in a cocoon just under the soil, lasting through the winter months. To be found in gardens and on waste ground over most of the British Isles.

Plate 17: P. Located by searching, fully grown. Early July. (JR)

Bleached Pug

Eupithecia expallidata Doubleday

Larva. 22–24 mm. Body usually of shades between green and yellow, with a darker coloured dorsal line that swells in the middle part of each segment and less distinct subdorsal lines.

Foodplant. The flowers of goldenrod.

Habits. Single-brooded, with the larvae feeding externally on the flowers of the foodplant from late August to about mid-October. They can easily be obtained by sweeping the foodplant and the larvae are not difficult to rear in captivity. The pupa is formed inside a cocoon just under the soil, and the insect spends the winter and through to the following July in this stage. Local, mainly in woodland rides, over much of the British Isles, especially in the south, but probably absent from northern Scotland.

Plate 17: Q. Found on picked flowers, fully grown. Late September.

Common Pug

Eupithecia vulgata Haworth

Larva. 22–23 mm. Body various shades of green or light brown, with a series of elongated diamond or triangular darker markings along the dorsal area.

Foodplants. Sallow, yarrow, bilberry, hawthorn, ragwort and various other plants.

Habits. A double-brooded species, with the larvae occurring during June and July and those of the second generation from late August to early October. They can readily be swept or beaten from their many foodplants and are very easy to rear in confinement. Pupation takes place in plant litter or loose soil, and those of the second brood overwinter in this stage. Widely distributed and fairly common over most of Britain and Ireland.

Plate 17: R. Bred from a female adult to MVL. Late May. (SHC)

White-spotted Pug

Eupithecia tripunctaria Herrich-Schäffer
(*albipunctata* Haworth)

Larva. 22–23 mm. Body usually yellow or yellowish-green, with triangular-shaped dark brown markings along the dorsal area, dark brown triangles along the sides and a thin subdorsal line of the same colour.

Foodplants. The ripening seeds of wild angelica, wild parsnip, goldenrod, cow parsley and the flowers of elder.

Habits. The larvae of this species can easily be swept or beaten from its many foodplants from late June to late September, and are easy to rear in captivity. They will pupate in plant litter or loose soil and they overwinter in this stage until the following May. The adults will come to light, but rarely in any numbers, and females will lay readily in confinement. Widespread over much of the British Isles, being more frequent in the southern counties.

Plate 18: A. Swept from angelica, half grown. Late August. (GAC)

Campanula Pug / Jasione Pug

Eupithecia denotata Hübner

Larva. 20–22 mm. Body light brown, with slightly darker dorsal and subdorsal lines, between which are oblique brown markings along the back; the head is small and mainly dark brown.

Foodplants. The seed-heads of nettle-leaved bellflower, giant bellflower and garden *Campanulae* (ssp. *denotata*), and sheep's-bit (ssp. *jasioneata*).

Habits. This single-brooded insect is represented by two subspecies in the British Isles. The Campanula Pug (*E. denotata denotata*), which is generally distributed over southern and eastern England and parts of South Wales and Ireland, feeds on bellflowers and may be taken by collecting the seed-heads during August and September, and keeping the larvae on fine sifted soil for pupation, in well-ventilated boxes. The Jasione Pug (*E. denotata jasioneata*) is to be found on or near the coast in south-west England, Wales, the Isle of Man and parts of Ireland, and feeds on sheep's-bit. It can be obtained by searching or sweeping and should be reared using the same methods. Both races spend the winter as pupae and the adults emerge during late June and July.

Plate 18: B and C. (ssp. *denotata*) Found on picked bellflower, nearly fully grown. Late August.
(ssp. *jasioneata*) Found inside dry sheep's-bit flowerhead. Late August.

Grey Pug

Eupithecia subfuscata Haworth
(*castigata* Hübner)

Larva. 24–26 mm. Body of shades of brown, with a darker row of diamond-shaped markings along the dorsal area; also covered with exceedingly small greyish-white pinacula. The underparts are dark brown and grey.

Foodplants. The flowers and leaves of various plants, including yarrow, mugwort, sallow, hawthorn, ragwort, goldenrod and knapweed.

Habits. Mainly a single-brooded species, but often having a partial second generation in the late summer. The larvae can be taken by beating, sweeping and searching during any time from late June to October from many different plants and in most places where they are common. Rearing them in captivity is easy and they pupate in soil or plant litter to overwinter. To be found throughout most of the British Isles.

Plate 18: D. Bred from a female adult to MVL on sallow. Late May. (M&JH)

Tawny Speckled Pug

Eupithecia icterata de Villers

Larva. 24–26 mm. Body greyish-brown, with dark brown dorsal blotches and a whitish-grey stripe along the centre of the underparts; also covered in minute pale pinacula.

Foodplants. The flowers and leaves of yarrow and sneezewort; also possibly tansy.

Habits. A single-brooded species, with the larvae occurring from mid-August to about mid-October. They may readily be swept from the foodplant, especially at night. During July and August adult females will often be taken at light and these will lay eggs freely on picked foodplant in captivity. Rearing the larvae is not difficult and they pupate in the soil to overwinter. Widespread and moderately common over most of the British Isles.

Plate 18: E. Bred from a female adult to MVL. Late July.

Bordered Pug

Eupithecia succenturiata Linnaeus

Larva. 24–25 mm. Body greyish-brown or reddish-brown, with a series of darker lozenge-shaped markings along the back and an obvious wavy subdorsal line of the same colour.

Foodplant. Mugwort.

Habits. A single-brooded species, with the larvae occurring from mid-August to about mid-October. When they are small, the larvae feed upon the dark green upper surface of the foodplant leaves with the lower grey surface remaining intact. They are night-feeders, hiding at the base of the plant

during the day, and can sometimes be obtained by sweeping after dark. During July and August both sexes of the adult moths will come to light and the females often lay freely on picked foodplant in captivity. The larvae are easy to rear and pupate in soil for overwintering. Widely distributed over most of the British Isles, being less frequent and local in the north.
Plate 18: F. Bred from a female adult to MVL. Early August.

Shaded Pug
Eupithecia subumbrata Denis & Schiffermüller
Larva. 24–26 mm. Body light brown or green, with a distinct darker dorsal line and faint thin slightly darker subdorsal and lateral lines.
Foodplants. The flowers of hawk's-beard, scabious, ragwort and other herbaceous plants.
Habits. Single-brooded, being in the larval stage from early July to about mid-September. The adults can be obtained during June and July by disturbing them from herbage and later they will come to light. Females will lay eggs in confinement, but breeding from the egg is a long and laborious task, unless potted foodplants are used. Obtaining stocks by sweeping is an easier method and usually the larvae are in good numbers where they occur. Rearing this species is easy and pupation takes place in soil for overwintering. Widely distributed, but local, over most of Britain, preferring open rough flower-covered ground.
Plate 18: G. Swept from hawk's-beard, fully grown. Early September.

Yarrow Pug
Eupithecia millefoliata Rössler
Larva. 16–18 mm. Body pale brown, darker anteriorly and posteriorly with dark brown chevrons on the dorsal area that are most obvious on the middle segments.
Foodplant. The seed-heads of yarrow.
Habits. A single-brooded species that occurs in the larval stage from late August to late October. The best method of obtaining this insect is to sweep vigorously the brown dying foodplant heads, during early to mid-October. Once obtained they will feed up on the dry seed-heads in a well-ventilated container, and pupate in a cocoon among plant litter or fine soil. They remain in this stage throughout the winter until the following June or July. A very local moth, being found mainly in coastal and saltmarsh localities, from Dorset to both sides of the Thames Estuary.
Plate 18: H. Swept from seed-heads, fully grown. Mid-October.

Plain Pug
Eupithecia simpliciata Haworth
(*subnotata* Hübner)
Larva. 19–20 mm. Body usually bright green, but sometimes pale brown, with indistinct darker dorsal markings and wholly covered with tiny greyish-white speckling and lines.
Foodplants. The ripening seed-heads of goosefoot and orache.
Habits. Single-brooded, with the larvae occurring from early August to late September. They can be obtained during September by careful sweeping or by placing a small sheet or tray under the foodplant and then brushing the seed-heads, causing the camouflaged larvae to fall. The female adults will often come to light in about July, and these will readily lay eggs upon the plant heads in confinement. Pupation takes place in loose soil and lasts throughout the winter. Widespread over much of England, being most common in the south; also occurring in Wales and Ireland, where it is very local.
Plate 18: I. Swept at night, nearly fully grown. Early September.

Goosefoot Pug
Eupithecia sinuosaria Eversmann
Larva. 17–20 mm. Body green, wholly covered with white speckling and having a reddish tip to the anal segment (Hoffmeyer).
Foodplant. The flowers and ripening seeds of goosefoot.
Habits. A single-brooded species that has been recently recorded twice as an adult in Britain. The larval stage lasts from about late July to September, before overwintering as a pupa, and careful sweeping of the foodplant on coastal waste ground would probably be the best method of discovering any colonies of this mainly Scandinavian and eastern European insect.

Thyme Pug
Eupithecia distinctaria Herrich-Schäffer
Larva. 24–26 mm. Body green, with a distinct broad reddish-purple dorsal line and a dull green head.
Foodplant. The flowers of thyme.
Habits. A single-brooded insect, with the larvae occurring from late July to about mid-September. They can often be located by carefully searching clumps of the foodplant, watching for movement; another quite productive method is to place a small tray or net carefully under loose hanging thyme and gently shake and brush the plant so the larvae drop off into the trap. Rearing them in captivity is easy, but many may be parasitized. The pupa is formed in a cocoon just under the soil and lasts through the winter until the following June or July. A local species, being found mainly on the south and west rocky coasts from the Isle of Wight to western Scotland, and inland on the Derbyshire Dales, Cumbria and parts of central Scotland; also to be found in western Ireland.
Plate 18: J. Found by searching, about half grown. Mid-August. (BSt)

Ochreous Pug
Eupithecia indigata Hübner
Larva. 22–23 mm. Body glossy light brown, with a slightly darker dorsal line, slightly paler subdorsal lines and a reddish-brown head.
Foodplants. The buds and fresh shoots of Scots pine, and possibly larch, juniper and cypress.
Habits. Single-brooded, with the larvae feeding from about early June to mid-September. During late April and May the adults will readily come to light and the females will usually lay eggs freely in captivity. Rearing from the egg is a long and laborious task, unless they can be sleeved on a growing tree. The larger larvae can be beaten in July and August, especially from the more mature trees, and are easily reared in confinement, preferring to feed on the young male inflorescences. Overwintering takes place in the pupal stage and this species is widely distributed throughout Britain and Ireland, occurring most frequently in central Scotland and East Anglia.
Plate 18: K. Bred from a female adult to MVL. Late May. (M&JH)

Pimpinel Pug

Eupithecia pimpinellata Hübner

Larva. 22–24 mm. Body usually light green, with purplish dorsal and subdorsal lines that are variable in intensity; another common form of the larva is wholly reddish-purple over the dorsal area with a pale whitish-green stripe laterally.

Foodplant. The ripening seed capsules of burnet-saxifrage.

Habits. A single-brooded species, the larvae of which feed steadily from late July to early October. They can readily be obtained by sweeping or shaking the foodplant flowerheads over a net during September, when the larvae are nearly fully grown and easier to see among the debris. Rearing them is not difficult, but often many are parasitized, and pupation for overwintering takes place in a silken cocoon just under loose soil. Mainly to be found on calcareous soils over much of southern England as far north as Yorkshire; also occurring locally in Ireland.

Plate 18: L. Swept from seed-heads, fully grown. Late September. (SHC)

Narrow-winged Pug

Eupithecia nanata Hübner

Larva. 20–22 mm. Body variable in colour, being of shades of white, green and pink with an obvious darker dorsal line and markings of reddish-brown, green and crimson liberally and often boldly over the back, sides and underparts.

Foodplant. The flowers of heather.

Habits. Mainly a single-brooded species, with a partial second generation occurring later in the summer. The larvae can easily be swept, sometimes in large numbers, from heaths and moors at any time from mid-June to late September. They are very easy to rear in captivity and usually pupate in loose soil particles. Many will emerge within three weeks if kept warm, but in the wild the later pupae will overwinter and the adults appear from late April to June. Widespread and usually common in suitable habitats over most of Britain and Ireland.

Plate 18: M. Swept from heather, fully grown. Early July.

Scarce Pug

Eupithecia extensaria Freyer

Larva. 28–30 mm. Body green, with an indistinct darker dorsal line that tends to broaden slightly at the middle part of each segment, a darker green subdorsal line and an obvious white spiracular line that is often marked with reddish-brown; also wholly covered in minute white pinacula.

Foodplant. The leaves and flowers of sea wormwood.

Habits. Single-brooded, with the larvae occurring from early August and throughout much of September. The easiest way to obtain this species is to sweep or shake the foodplant carefully into a net. Once in captivity the larvae are very easy to rear and pupation takes place in a silken cocoon among plant litter for overwintering. Very local, being found on the saltmarsh edges of north Norfolk, Lincolnshire, south-east Yorkshire and north Essex.

Plate 18: N. Swept from foodplant, fully grown. Early September. (SHC)

Ash Pug

Eupithecia fraxinata Crewe

Larva. 25–27 mm. Body dull green or purplish-brown, with a whitish spiracular line that often has dull purple markings slightly above on the middle segments; some individuals have markings along the dorsal area.

Foodplants. Ash and sea buckthorn.

Habits. A double-brooded species, the larvae of which can be taken by beating from mid-June to late July, and again from late August and throughout September. They are to be found in two very different types of habitat: those on the coastal sandhills of east and south-east England, using the spiny shrub sea buckthorn as the foodplant, are the easiest to obtain, being much more localized and often in good numbers. The other race feeds on the leaves of ash and is widely distributed over most of Britain, but usually at a very low density. The larvae are easy to rear in captivity and will pupate for the winter in loose soil. In the wild the pupae of the ash-feeding race have been found under moss and bark at the base of mature ash trees in woods and hedgerows.

Plate 18: O. Beaten from sea buckthorn, fully grown. Mid-September.

Golden-rod Pug

Eupithecia virgaureata Doubleday

Larva. 19–20 mm. Body variable in colour, being shades of yellow, brown or greyish with distinct bold dark brown triangular or horseshoe-shaped markings along the back, also a series of brown triangular marks on the sides that are separated from those on the dorsal area by a dull white.

Foodplants. The flowers of goldenrod and ragwort, and in captivity the larvae of the first brood will accept the leaves of hawthorn.

Habits. A double-brooded insect, the larvae of which have only been found in the wild during September and early October, by sweeping or searching on the flowers of goldenrod and ragwort. The natural foodplant of the first-brood larvae, occurring in June and July, has yet to be proven, but they will readily accept fresh hawthorn leaves for their development. Pupation takes place in a cocoon under the soil and they overwinter in this stage. Widely distributed over much of Britain, but more frequently recorded from the western half of the country.

Plate 18: P. Found on ragwort, fully grown. Late September. (JR)

Brindled Pug

Eupithecia abbreviata Stephens

Larva. 24–26 mm. Body usually of some shade of light brown, with a distinct row of dark brown chevrons or triangular-shaped markings along the middle of the back.

Foodplants. Oak and sometimes hawthorn.

Habits. Single-brooded, with the larvae occurring from mid-May to about early July and being beaten readily from the foliage of larger oaks. During April and early May the adults of this species come to light, sometimes in large numbers, and the females will lay eggs freely upon the buds and young foodplant leaves. The larvae are easy to rear in confinement and pupate in cocoons just under the soil for overwintering. Generally distributed over most of the British Isles, being especially common in oak woods in the southern counties.

Plate 18: Q. Beaten from oak, fully grown. Late June.

Oak-tree Pug

Eupithecia dodoneata Guenée

Larva. 22–24 mm. Body orangish-brown or pale yellowish-green, with a darker dorsal line and often darker triangular-shaped markings along the centre of the back. Usually these marks are less intense than those of the previous species (*E. abbreviata*).

Foodplants. Hawthorn, feeding mainly on the calyx of the hips, oak and possibly evergreen oak.

Habits. A single-brooded species, with the larvae feeding

from mid-June to about early August. They can be obtained by beating the older mature hawthorns in woods and hedgerows during the last half of July, or by netting female adults at dusk during May as they fly about the foodplants. They also come to light in small numbers and most lay eggs freely in confinement. The larvae are fairly easy to rear in captivity and pupate just under the soil for overwintering. Locally distributed over much of the southern half of England and Wales, also most of Ireland.
Plate 18: R. Bred from a female adult to MVL. Late May. (SHC)

Juniper Pug
Eupithecia pusillata Denis & Schiffermüller
(*sobrinata* Hübner)
Larva. 16–18 mm. Body green or brown, with a darker dorsal line and variably marked with blotches, chevrons and lines of dark brown, red and yellow along the back and sides; the spiracular line is usually whitish and obvious.
Foodplants. Junipers, including the cultivated varieties.
Habits. Single-brooded, overwintering in the egg stage, with the colourful and varied larvae occurring from mid-April to about mid-June, feeding on the fresh shoots of the foodplant. They can easily be beaten, often in large numbers, and are very easy to breed in confinement, pupating in a silken cocoon spun up among the juniper needles. The pupal duration is variable, with some individuals emerging after about three weeks and others, that pupated at the same time, remaining in this stage for up to three months. Generally distributed over most of the British Isles wherever its foodplant is well established, but possibly absent from the Burren in western Ireland.
Plate 19: A. Beaten from wild juniper, fully grown. Early June.

Cypress Pug
Eupithecia phoeniceata Rambur
Larva. 20–22 mm. Body bright green or pinkish-brown, with darker dorsal markings and variegated paler markings and blotches; also a reddish-brown dash on the anal flap.
Foodplants. Monterey cypress and in captivity and probably in the wild *Cupressus leylandii*.
Habits. A recent colonist to the British Isles that has established itself all along the south coast on the ornamental Monterey cypresses grown in gardens. It is single-brooded, with the cryptically coloured larvae feeding from October and throughout the winter, until the eventual pupation of the very last by about April or May. They can readily be beaten from the lower boughs of mature trees and in captivity usually feed up faster, especially on the budding shoots, and form their cocoons during the winter. In the wild the adults have been recorded in every month between May and October, with the peak emergence during August and September.
Plate 19: B. Bred from a female adult to MVL. Late August. (SHC)

Channel Islands Pug
Eupithecia ultimaria Boisduval
Larva. 21–25 mm. Body green, with a series of dull yellow lateral markings and small crimson subdorsal spots; anal flap crimson, edged with yellow. A buff form occurs regularly, with pinkish brown markings dorsally and maroon lateral marks; head as body colour in both forms.
Foodplant. The flowers and foliage of tamarisk.
Habits. A single-brooded insect, being in the larval stage during July and August, and possibly again in the autumn from moths of a premature emergence. This species is a recent colonist to the British Isles, the first insect being taken in 1988 in Hertfordshire, and was established in Guernsey, Channel Islands, from 1984. At present the breeding range is wholly coastal, the species being found so far in East and West Sussex and south-east Hampshire. Larvae may be found by beating and overwintering takes place in the pupal stage, with the adults flying from late June to early August.
Plate 19: C. Beaten from tamarisk, fully grown. Early August. (BS)

Larch Pug
Eupithecia lariciata Freyer
Larva. 24–26 mm. Body light brown or green, with a darker dorsal line, a faint subdorsal line and a pale whitish or yellowish line along the spiracles.
Foodplant. Larch.
Habits. A single-brooded insect, with the larvae occurring from about mid-June to early August. They can readily be beaten, especially from mature stands of larch and are easy to rear in confinement. The adults come readily to light and females will often lay eggs freely, if supplied with fresh shoots as a stimulus. Pupation takes place in plant litter or soil and lasts throughout the winter until the following May. Generally distributed and fairly common over most of Britain.
Plate 19: D. Beaten from foodplant, nearly fully grown. Mid-July.

Dwarf Pug
Eupithecia tantillaria Boisduval
(*pusillata* auctt.)
Larva. 20–22 mm. Body reddish-brown, with a darker dorsal line which is most obvious on the thoracic and last few segments, indistinct subdorsal lines and a slightly paler spiracular line.
Foodplants. Norway spruce, Douglas fir and western hemlock.
Habits. Single-brooded, being in the larval stage from late June to the end of August. When they are becoming fully developed, the larvae can readily be beaten from the foodplants and are not difficult to rear in captivity, or eggs can be obtained from adult females which often come to light traps. The cocooned pupa is formed in the soil and lasts until the following May, after overwintering. Widespread, but local, over most of Britain and possibly established in Ireland with an increasing number of recent records.
Plate 19: E. Bred from a female adult to MVL. Early June. (SHC)

The V-Pug
Chloroclystis v-ata Haworth
(*coronata* Hübner)
Larva. 16–18 mm. Body light greenish or light brown, with a series of reddish-brown triangular-shaped marks on the dorsal area, subdorsal lines of the same colour and sometimes reddish-brown marks along the spiracles.
Foodplants. The flowers of dog rose, hemp-agrimony, yarrow, bramble, mugwort, goldenrod and many other plants.
Habits. A mainly double-brooded species, with the larvae occurring from about mid-June to mid-July, and again from late August to early October. The northern populations are univoltine, with the larval period being from late June to about the middle of August. They can easily be swept from their many foodplants and the adults will often come to light, the captive females laying freely on suitable flowers.

It is an easy insect to breed in confinement, so long as the larvae are supplied with fresh food. Pupation usually takes place in a cocoon just under the soil, overwintering when from the autumn larvae. Widespread over most of the southern half of England, to be found locally in northern England, Wales, southern Scotland and Ireland.
Plate 19: F. Bred from a female adult to MVL. Late May. (SHC)

Sloe Pug

Chloroclystis chloerata Mabille
Larva. 10–12 mm. Body dull greenish-white, often with a reddish-purple dorsal line that is most obvious on the thoracic and first abdominal segments.
Foodplant. The flowers of blackthorn.
Habits. Single-brooded, overwintering in the egg stage, with the maggot-like, well-camouflaged larvae feeding on the fresh flowers of the foodplant, sometimes in a loose spinning, from the last week of March and throughout April. They can readily be beaten, especially from the higher branches of mature blackthorn when the flowers are at full bloom, and are very easy to rear. In captivity the larval development is rapid and pupation takes place among plant litter and lasts about a month. To be found locally in southern England and occurring as far north as Yorkshire and Westmorland.
Plate 19: G. Beaten from foodplant, fully grown. Mid-April.

Green Pug

Chloroclystis rectangulata Linnaeus
Larva. 12–13 mm. Body green, usually with a dorsal line that is dark green or dark reddish-purple.
Foodplants. The flowers of apple, blackthorn, pear and cherry.
Habits. A single-brooded species that overwinters as an egg upon the twigs of its foodplants. The larvae occur from April until about late May, sometimes loosely spinning together the flower petals, and can easily be obtained by beating. Rearing them in confinement is not difficult and they pupate for about a month among plant litter or finely sifted soil. Generally distributed over most of the British Isles and sometimes quite common in the southern counties.
Plate 19: H. Beaten from blackthorn, fully grown. Mid-May.

Bilberry Pug

Chloroclystis debiliata Hübner
Larva. 10–12 mm. Body green, with a dark green dorsal line and a dark brown head.
Foodplant. Bilberry.
Habits. A single-brooded species that spends the winter in the egg stage and hatches about mid-April, then develops rapidly, becoming fully grown by about late May. During the day the larvae rest among spun leaves, usually on terminal shoots, and can be located by careful searching. After dark they can often be swept in good numbers when they leave their retreats to feed. They are easy to rear and will pupate in cocoons, spun up just under loose soil or among the foodplant. Locally common in England, Wales and southern Ireland.
Plate 19: I. Swept at night, about half grown. Early May.

Double-striped Pug

Gymnoscelis rufifasciata Haworth
Larva. 14–16 mm. Body very variable in colour, being of whitish, light green or brownish, often with darker diamond or triangular dorsal markings and other darker dashes and marks along the sides; the head is small and usually brownish.
Foodplants. The flowers of many plants, including heather, bramble, rowan, garden buddleia, holly, ragwort, broom and gorse.
Habits. This species is double-brooded, with a partial third brood in the southern counties. The larvae can occur at any time between early May and late October and feed upon a great variety of different flowers. They are easy to obtain by rearing from eggs laid by light-trapped female moths and can also be swept from flowers, especially during June and again in August, when the larval populations are at their peak. Widely distributed and reasonably common over most of the British Isles.
Plate 19: J. Bred from a female adult to MVL. Late July.

Dentated Pug

Anticollix sparsata Treitschke
Larva. 20–22 mm. Body bright green, with a distinct whitish spiracular line and several vague whitish lines along the back and sides. The head is dull green and between the segments it is yellow.
Foodplant. Yellow loosestrife.
Habits. A single-brooded insect, with the larvae occurring from late July to about mid September, feeding mainly on the leaves, but sometimes the flowers of the foodplant, preferring those growing in the shade. In late August or early September the larvae can be located by carefully searching plants that have the small distinctive feeding holes in their leaves, with the larvae resting nearby underneath, or they can be swept vigorously in known localities, sometimes with moderate success. In captivity the larvae are not difficult to rear, but the overwintering pupae seem to require dampish conditions for successful emergence of the adults in the following June and July. Very locally distributed in the southern parts of England, as far north as Yorkshire.
Plate 19: K. Swept from foodplant, nearly fully grown. Late August.

The Streak

Chesias legatella Denis & Schiffermüller
(*spartiata* Herbst)
Larva. 28–30 mm. Body green, with thin darker dorsal line, a broader dark subdorsal line and a whitish spiracular line that inclines to yellowish along the top edge and between the segments.
Foodplant. Broom.
Habits. After overwintering in the egg stage, the larvae of this single-brooded species feed externally on the leaves of broom from late April to about mid-June. They can often readily be obtained by beating and are usually fairly easy to rear in captivity. Pupation takes place in the soil and lasts through the summer, until the adults emerge between mid-September and early November. Widespread and generally common over most of the British Isles.
Plate 19: L. Beaten, almost fully grown. Late May.

Broom-tip

Chesias rufata Fabricius
Larva. 26–28 mm. Body green, with a thin darker dorsal line, a thin whitish subdorsal line and clear white spiracular line.
Foodplant. Broom.
Habits. A single-brooded species, with the larvae occurring from about early July to September. They can easily be beaten, especially at night when they are more active, and although they are easy to rear, they tend to suffer heavily from parasitism. The adults have a protracted emergence

period lasting from mid-April to late July, and they can be obtained by searching mature foodplant bushes after dark or be taken at light traps. Pupation takes place in the soil and lasts throughout the winter months, sometimes lying over for a second year. A local insect, being found on heaths and commons in most of England, Wales and northwards to central Scotland.
Plate 19: M. Beaten at night, fully grown. Early September.

Manchester Treble-bar

Carsia sororiata Hübner
(*paludata* Thunberg)
Larva. 16–18 mm. Body reddish-brown, with a fine darker dorsal line and a broad conspicuous pale yellow spiracular stripe.
Foodplants. The flowers and leaves of bilberry, cranberry and cowberry.
Habits. A single-brooded insect that occurs in the larval stage from late April to about mid-June. The larvae can be obtained by sweeping or carefully searching on the foodplants, especially at night when they become more active, and the cocooned pupa is formed among plant litter and lasts about a month. The adults can be netted on warm calm days and the females will often lay eggs in confinement, these lasting through the winter. This species is to be found on moorland and mosses in northern England and Scotland; also locally in parts of Ireland.
Plate 19: N. Swept at night, nearly fully grown. Late May.

Treble-bar

Aplocera plagiata Linnaeus
Larva. 32–34 mm. Body variable shades of brown or grey, with a darker dorsal line that is most obvious on the thoracic and last abdominal segments and a pale thin line below the spiracles that contrasts with the dark brown underparts. Probably indistinguishable from the following species (*A. efformata*), but it has been suggested that the anal plate is reddish-brown, instead of drab in colour.
Foodplants. Various species of St John's-wort.
Habits. Mainly double-brooded, with the larvae occurring from late June to early August, and again from mid-September, throughout the winter, to early May. Those of the univoltine northern populations are in the larval stage from mid-August until the following early June. They can readily be swept and are also easy to rear from the eggs freely laid on picked foodplant by the females, which can be flushed from herbage during the day. Pupation takes place in loose soil and lasts about three weeks. Widely distributed over most of Britain and Ireland.
Plate 19: O. Bred from a netted female adult. Late May.

Lesser Treble-bar

Aplocera efformata Guenée
Larva. 30–32 mm. Body light brown or greyish, with a darker dorsal line and a whitish subspiracular line. Seemingly identical to the previous species (*A. plagiata*), but possibly distinguishable by the drab-coloured anal flap.
Foodplant. St John's-wort.
Habits. A double-brooded species that has a life-cycle in parallel with the previous species (*A. plagiata*), and the methods of obtaining and rearing the larvae are exactly the same. The distribution is somewhat different, the species occurring commonly in southern England, but in northern England and Wales tending to be local.
Plate 19: P. Bred from a netted female adult. Early June. (RM)

Chimney Sweeper

Odezia atrata Linnaeus
Larva. 22–24 mm. Body bright green, with a thin dark green dorsal line that broadens and becomes purplish in colour on the last segments. Below the thin whitish spiracular line the underparts are dark green, inclining to paler along the middle ventral area.
Foodplant. The flowers and seeds of pignut.
Habits. A single-brooded species, overwintering in the egg stage, and with the larvae occurring from about mid-April to early June, feeding solely on the flowers and seeds of the foodplant. During mid- or late May they can easily be swept from localities this day-flying species is known to inhabit. They are easy to rear and pupation takes place in loose soil, lasting about a month. Widely distributed over most of the British Isles, inhabiting open ground, but very local in southern England and East Anglia.
Plate 19: Q. Swept from foodplant, fully grown. Late May. (BH)

Grey Carpet

Lithostege griseata Denis & Schiffermüller
Larva. 22–24 mm. Body green, with a distinct broad white spiracular line and a brownish anal flap; the mottled head is mainly brownish-green.
Foodplants. The seed pods of flixweed and treacle mustard.
Habits. Single-brooded, with the larvae occurring from late June to about mid-August and being easy to sweep from the foodplant. They are not difficult to rear in captivity, with the cocooned pupae being formed just under the soil for overwintering. The adults are readily disturbed from their foodplants and surrounding herbage by day and the females will often lay eggs when sleeved upon growing flixweed. A very local species inhabiting only the Breckland district of East Anglia.
Plate 19: R. Swept from foodplant, fully grown. Late July. (CH)

Blomer's Rivulet

Discoloxia blomeri Curtis
Larva. 20–22 mm. Body yellowish-green, usually with a conspicuous brown or reddish-brown dorsal blotch on the thoracic segments, another marking of the same colour on the sides of the middle segments and a fainter dorsal mottling on the last two rings on the back.
Foodplant. Wych elm.
Habits. A single-brooded insect, the larvae of which occur from late July to about mid-September. They feed distinctively upon the leaves by making large ragged holes, and may be beaten during the latter part of August. The adults will often come to light in June and July, and fertile females will deposit eggs quite readily on picked leaves. The young larvae are notoriously difficult to rear, refusing to eat and constantly crawling up to the light until they die from starvation. Many beaten larvae tend to be parasitized, but the healthy individuals will pupate in a cocoon just under the soil for overwintering. A local woodland moth, being found mainly in central and western England and in Wales.
Plate 20: A. Beaten, nearly fully grown. Late August. (JK)

Welsh Wave

Venusia cambrica Curtis
Larva. 20–22 mm. Body yellowish-green, with bold brown blotches on the underparts, especially on the thoracic segments and on the middle part of the body, which in the latter often extend on to the sides and dorsal area.

Foodplant. Rowan.
Habits. Single-brooded, with the larvae occurring from late July to late September. They can readily be obtained by beating, especially from isolated trees growing on moorland, and are fairly easy to rear in captivity, usually pupating among plant litter or loose soil for overwintering. The adults can be found from late June to August on rowan trunks during the day and will also come to light. The females will lay in captivity and sleeving the larvae on growing foodplant can be successful in rearing them. Locally distributed over the western and northern parts of the British Isles.
Plate 20: B. Beaten from rowan, about half grown. Late August. (GAC)

Dingy Shell

Euchoeca nebulata Scopoli
Larva. 16–18 mm. Body yellowish-green, often marked with a broad blackish or brown stripe along the dorsal area, but this may be totally absent. The subdorsal line is usually conspicuous and pale yellow.
Foodplant. Alder.
Habits. A single-brooded species, with the larvae occurring from early July to late August. They can easily be beaten from their foodplant and are usually easy to rear. During June the adults can be flushed from alder foliage or light-trapped at night and the females will lay eggs upon picked young leaves in captivity. Pupation for overwintering takes place in moss on the lower trunks and also on the ground nearby. To be found, not uncommonly, in damp woodland and marshy habitats over most of England and Wales.
Plate 20: C. Beaten at night, fully grown. Mid-August.

Small White Wave

Asthena albulata Hufnagel
(*candidata* Denis & Schiffermüller)
Larva. 12–15 mm. Body pale green, usually with reddish-pink blotches and colouring along the sides and underparts, especially on the middle segments and on the legs; also with a few short black bristles on the back.
Foodplants. Hazel, birch and hornbeam.
Habits. Usually a single-brooded insect, but a partial second generation often takes place in southern England. The colourful larvae occur from late June to mid-August and sometimes again in September, and can be taken in small numbers by beating. The adults are not often attracted to light, but can readily be disturbed from foliage during the day or netted at dusk when they begin to fly naturally. The females deposit their tiny eggs along the edges of the foodplant leaves but the young larvae can be difficult to rear. Pupation takes place among plant litter and normally lasts throughout the winter months. Generally distributed in woodland over most of the British Isles, but local and infrequent in Scotland and parts of Ireland.
Plate 20: D. Beaten from hornbeam, fully grown. Early August.

Small Yellow Wave

Hydrelia flammeolaria Hufnagel
Larva. 16–18 mm. Body light green, with an indistinct darker dorsal line and pale yellow between the segments. The head is yellowish and glossy.
Foodplants. Maple and alder.
Habits. Single-brooded, with the larvae occurring from late July to about mid-September, usually feeding at night on the leaves of maple, but those of the northern populations on alder. They can readily be beaten from their foodplants and are not difficult to rear in captivity, eventually pupating in a loose cocoon among leaf litter for overwintering. The adults can easily be disturbed from foliage by day and they are attracted to light, with the females laying freely on picked maple leaves in confinement. A fairly common species in southern England and in Wales, but more local and less frequent in the northern counties to central Scotland.
Plate 20: E. Beaten by day, fully grown. Early September.

Waved Carpet

Hydrelia sylvata Denis & Schiffermüller
(*testaceata* Donovan)
Larva. 18–20 mm. Body yellowish-green, with bold colourful marblings of pink, purple, brown and whitish over most of the dorsal area, extending down the sides and beneath on the middle segments.
Foodplants. Birch, alder, sallow and sweet chestnut.
Habits. A single-brooded species, with the attractive larvae occurring from about late July to mid-September. They can be taken by beating or females can be flushed from foliage by day or light-trapped at night. They will often lay eggs if given fresh leaves as a stimulus, and the larvae are usually easy to rear in confinement. The cocooned pupa is formed among leaf litter on the ground and lasts through the winter until the following June. A local and usually uncommon insect, being found mainly in the southern and western counties of England; also in Wales and parts of southern Ireland.
Plate 20: F. Bred from a female adult to MVL. Late June. (BS)

Drab Looper

Minoa murinata Scopoli
Larva. 15–16 mm. Body usually blackish, and covered with white tubercles which emit a cluster of short spiny yellowish-white bristles; along the sides of the middle segments are some dull orange marks and the head is often dark brown.
Foodplant. Wood spurge.
Habits. Mainly single-brooded, with the distinctive larvae feeding from late June to early September. They can be taken by sweeping and then reared without difficulty on growing plant or stems kept in water. The adults fly in sunshine during May and June, and the females will lay eggs freely upon the flowers and leaves of the foodplant, if sleeved in captivity. A local species occurring in open woodland in southern England, south-east Wales and the south-west Midlands.
Plate 20: G. Bred from a netted female adult. Early June. (BS)

The Seraphim

Lobophora halterata Hufnagel
Larva. 23–25 mm. Body pale green, with an obvious pale whitish or sometimes yellowish subdorsal line, tiny yellow spiracles and long whitish anal points.
Foodplants. Aspen and occasionally other species of poplar.
Habits. A single-brooded species, the larvae of which occur from mid-June and throughout most of July, resting by day on the undersides of the leaves. They can readily be beaten and are very easy to rear in captivity with their development taking about four weeks from the egg. The cocooned pupa is formed just in the soil and lasts throughout the winter months until the following May. Widely distributed over most of the British Isles, being most frequent in southern England and central Scotland.
Plate 20: H. Beaten from aspen, by day, fully grown. Mid-July.

Barred Tooth-striped
Trichopteryx polycommata Denis & Schiffermüller
Larva. 22–23 mm. Body dark green, with a whitish subspiracular line and tiny obvious pale spiracles, also inclining to yellow between the rings.
Foodplants. Wild privet, ash and possibly honeysuckle.
Habits. Single-brooded, with the larvae occurring from mid-April to about early June. The larvae can be beaten, but usually they are in low numbers and difficult to obtain in any quantity. During late March and early April the adults can be found resting on wild privet bushes at night and they are also occasionally attracted to light. The females often lay freely in confinement and the larvae are normally easy to rear on garden privet, although some broods suffer badly from virus infection and all may die. The subterranean cocooned pupae must be kept outside in a shaded place or they are likely to dry out during the summer months. A local species that seems to be decreasing, found in scattered localities from southern England northwards to Staffordshire, also Yorkshire and Cumbria and in western parts of Scotland.
Plate 20: I. Bred from a female adult found at night. Early April.

Early Tooth-striped
Trichopteryx carpinata Borkhausen
Larva. 22–24 mm. Body bright green, with a distinct broad whitish or yellowish spiracular line.
Foodplants. Birch, sallow, alder and honeysuckle.
Habits. A single-brooded species, with the larvae feeding from mid-May to early July. They are usually common throughout their range and can readily be beaten from the foodplants. Rearing the larvae in captivity is not difficult and they will eventually pupate in soil to last through the winter until the following April or May. The adults come frequently to light and the females will lay eggs freely on picked foodplant buds or leaves. Widely distributed over most of the British Isles.
Plate 20: J. Beaten from birch, fully grown. Late June.

Small Seraphim
Pterapherapteryx sexalata Retzius
Larva. 24–26 mm. Body whitish-green, with three dull white dorsal lines, a light green cleft head and long pinkish-white anal points.
Foodplant. Sallow.
Habits. Usually a double-brooded species, with the larvae occurring from mid-June to mid-July, and again from about mid-August to mid-September. North of the Midlands this insect is mainly univoltine and the larvae are to be found from early July to mid-August. They can readily be beaten from the foodplant and are very simple to rear in captivity, growing rapidly and pupating in moss or plant litter for overwintering when necessary. Generally distributed over southern England and East Anglia, but more local and less common in Wales, northern England and parts of Scotland and Ireland.
Plate 20: K. Beaten from sallow, fully grown. Early September.

Yellow-barred Brindle
Acasis viretata Hübner
Larva. 17–18 mm. Body green, often variably marked dorsally with reddish-brown or crimson blotches and some individuals are flushed greatly with this colour.
Foodplants. The flowers, leaves and buds of ivy, holly, wild privet and dogwood.
Habits. Mainly a single-brooded species, with the colourful larvae occurring from mid-June to late July, and in the south, where there is a partial second generation, again in September. They feed on a variety of plants, sometimes in a loose silken web, and can often be obtained by beating. They are normally easy to rear in captivity and pupate in a cocoon for overwintering. The adults are attracted to light and the females will lay freely on fresh buds or flowers. Widely distributed, usually in small numbers, over most of Britain, but very local in the northern parts of its range.
Plate 20: L. Beaten at night from ivy, fully grown. Mid-September.

SUBFAMILY: ENNOMINAE

The Magpie
Abraxas grossulariata Linnaeus
Larva. 28–32 mm. Body white, with rows of large black spots along the dorsal and lateral areas and also a conspicuous orange spiracular stripe. The head and thoracic legs are black. A wholly blackish rare form is known to occur.
Foodplants. Currants, gooseberry, blackthorn, hawthorn, sallow, hazel, *Euonymus* spp. and other trees and shrubs.
Habits. A single-brooded species that overwinters as a small larva upon its foodplant. During the spring larval growth becomes rapid and most larvae are fully grown by about mid-June. They can readily be beaten from their foodplants and rearing them in confinement is usually very easy. The black and orange-ringed pupa is spun up in a cocoon among the foodplant leaves and lasts about a month, with the adults coming freely to light during July and early August. Widely distributed over most of the British Isles and usually fairly common in occurrence.
Plate 20: M. Beaten from blackthorn, fully grown. Early June.

Clouded Magpie
Abraxas sylvata Scopoli
Larva. 28–30 mm. Body white, with patches of pale yellow dorsally and on the lateral area, and seven broad evenly spaced black stripes along the back and sides. The black head is followed by a ring of yellow and the final segment is also black.
Foodplants. Wych elm, English elm and possibly hazel.
Habits. Single-brooded, with the larvae occurring from about mid-July to as late as early October in some seasons. Normally the majority of the larvae are fully grown by early September and they can be beaten from the boughs of the larger mature elms growing in mixed woodland. The adults will come to light traps and fertile females will often deposit their eggs upon a picked foodplant leaf in confinement. Young larvae seem to do best if sleeved upon a growing plant and the eventual pupation takes place in soil or leaf litter, and lasts through the winter months until the following May or June. A widely distributed but quite local species, being recorded throughout most of England, Wales, southern Scotland and parts of Ireland.
Plate 20: N. Bred from a female adult to MVL. Late June. (SHC)

Clouded Border
Lomaspilis marginata Linnaeus
Larva. 18–21 mm. Body green, with indistinct darker dorsal, subdorsal and lateral lines, and pale green underparts; also a few minute black pinacula, an inconspicuous yellow

spiracular stripe and a purplish-brown anal flap; head green, with bold purplish marks.
Foodplants. Sallow, aspen, poplar and hazel.
Habits. A single-brooded species, with the larvae occurring from about mid-July to mid-September. In the southern counties this species can be very common in damp woodland and the larvae can often be beaten in large numbers during late August. They are very easy to rear and the cocooned pupa is formed in the soil for overwintering. The adults fly in June and July, with both sexes coming freely to light traps. Generally distributed over most of Britain and Ireland.
Plate 20: O. Beaten from sallow, fully grown. Early September. (DWP)

Scorched Carpet

Ligdia adustata Denis & Schiffermüller
Larva. 20–22 mm. Body green, with a distinctive brown marking laterally on the fifth and sixth segments, and a buff-coloured head that is mottled with darker brown; usually the first proleg is mainly brown and there are a few brownish blotches along the centre of the back. An ochreous form is known to occur.
Foodplant. Spindle.
Habits. A double-brooded species, with the larvae occurring from mid-June to late July, and again in late August and September, except in the northern univoltine populations which are larvae from early July to mid-August. They can be beaten from their foodplant or bred by taking females, which are attracted to light in small numbers, especially in scrubland habitats. They are usually easy to breed in captivity and pupate in plant litter or loose soil for overwintering when necessary. Widespread over most of England and Wales, but mainly very local in the more northern parts of its range and in Ireland.
Plate 20: P. Bred from a female adult to MVL. Early June. (SHC)

Peacock Moth

Semiothisa notata Linnaeus
Larva. 22–24 mm. Body glossy greenish-brown to olive-brown, with a darker subdorsal line and a brown head.
Foodplants. Birch and sallows.
Habits. A mainly single-brooded species, with the larvae occurring from late June to early August, but also as a partial second brood in September in southern England. They can be beaten with much effort, but are more easily procured by obtaining eggs from a light-trapped fertile female. Rearing the larvae is usually easy and if kept warm they will hatch from the pupae in about three weeks in captivity. In the wild the pupa is formed among plant litter and lasts throughout the winter until the following late May or June. This is a local insect, being found in woodland in the southern half of England, much of Wales and central and western Scotland; also in Co. Cork and Co. Kerry in Ireland.
Plate 20: Q. Bred from a female adult to MVL. Mid-June.

Sharp-angled Peacock

Semiothisa alternaria Hübner
Larva. 22–25 mm. Body variable in colour, usually being shades of green, brown or grey, with a faint paler dorsal line, with indistinct thin wavy lines along the back and sides, and sometimes darker markings laterally.
Foodplants. Sallows, willows, blackthorn, sea buckthorn and alder.
Habits. A double-brooded species, with the second generation being partial but usually in good numbers. The larvae can be obtained by beating during July and again in September, and are not difficult to rear in confinement. The pupa is formed in a cocoon just under the soil and overwinters when necessary. The adults will attend light traps in small numbers, with captive females often depositing eggs quite freely on picked foodplant. A rather local species, being found mainly in woodland and on sandhills in the southern counties of England and south-east Wales.
Plate 20: R. Beaten from sea buckthorn, fully grown. Mid-September. (GAC)

Dusky Peacock

Semiothisa signaria Hübner
Larva. 23–26 mm. Body deep green, with a darker dorsal line and an orange-tinged yellowish lateral line; head green, marked with orange.
Foodplants. Norway spruce, Scots pine and other conifers.
Habits. A single-brooded scarce immigrant species that has been recorded in Britain as an adult on eleven occasions. Abroad the larvae occur in August and September, pupating in a silken cocoon for overwintering, with the adults flying the following late May to mid-July.
Plate 21: A. Bred from a female adult to MVL. (JF)

Tawny-barred Angle

Semiothisa liturata Clerck
Larva. 24–26 mm. Body green, with a darker green dorsal line that is bordered with paler colour, distinct whitish subdorsal and spiracular lines and a pale brown head that is heavily mottled with darker brown.
Foodplants. Scots pine, Norway spruce, Western hemlock and other associated coniferous species.
Habits. Double-brooded, with the larvae occurring from late June to early August, and again in September and early October, except in the univoltine northern populations where they are to be found in July and August. They are usually quite common in pine plantations where they occur, and can be taken by beating, especially from the boughs of the more mature trees. Rearing this species in captivity is usually very easy, the larvae pupating in silken cocoons formed among plant litter or moss for overwintering. Generally distributed over most of the British Isles.
Plate 21: B. Beaten from Western hemlock, fully grown. Late September. (SHC)

Latticed Heath

Semiothisa clathrata Linnaeus
Larva. 22–24 mm. Body bright green, with fine wavy whitish lines along the back and sides and a broad white stripe just below the tiny black spiracles.
Foodplants. Clovers and trefoils.
Habits. Mainly a double-brooded species, being in the larval stage during June and July, and again from mid-August and throughout September. In the more northern parts of its range and in Ireland this insect is usually single-brooded, with the larvae occurring during July and August. They can readily be obtained from eggs laid by females netted as they fly in sunshine over open ground or taken at light in small numbers. No special requirements are necessary for successfully rearing the larvae and pupation takes place in the soil, lasting through the winter. Widely distributed in England, Wales, southern Scotland; also occurring locally in northern and western Ireland.
Plate 21: C. Bred from a female adult to MVL. Late May.

Netted Mountain Moth
Semiothisa carbonaria Clerck
Larva. 20–22 mm. Body bright green, with thin incomplete whitish lines along the back and sides, a greenish-white spiracular stripe, yellowish-green head and a distinct purple-coloured anal flap.
Foodplants. Bearberry; also stated to accept sallow, birch and bilberry in captivity.
Habits. A single-brooded species, being in the larval stage from about late May to early July. In other works this larva is described as being shades of brown with wavy dark lines; this is probably not correct. The specimen illustrated was bred from a female netted in sunshine, and all the resulting larvae (about thirty) were green, with the distinctive purple anal marking. They would not accept any food except the fresh tips of bearberry leaves, although offered all of the stated alternatives, and also heather and knotgrass. About half died during their development, most when young from an unknown cause and a few when larger as the supplies of foodplant became exhausted. Fresh plant of a cultivated variety was obtained and the remaining larvae took to this quite happily and pupated in moss for overwintering. To be found locally on moors and hillsides in the highlands of central Scotland.
Plate 21: D. Bred from a netted female adult. Late May. (SHC & GAC)

Rannoch Looper
Semiothisa brunneata Thunberg
Larva. 18–20 mm. Body reddish to greyish-brown, with a darker dorsal line that is edged paler, also a conspicuous yellowish-white spiracular line and a brown head that is mottled darker.
Foodplant. Bilberry.
Habits. A single-brooded species that overwinters in the egg stage. The larvae occur from late April to late May and can easily be swept from the fresh leaves of the foodplant. They are distinctive, even when very small, by the white spiracular line contrasting against the otherwise very dark body, and they feed up rapidly in confinement, some becoming paler as they reach full development. Pupation takes place in a loose cocoon among leaf litter and lasts about three to four weeks. During July the adult females can be found at night resting on the tips of bilberry and they will often lay eggs upon the stems, just below the buds. Locally distributed in the old pine and birch woods of central Scotland, with occasional migrants being taken elsewhere, especially on the eastern side of Britain.
Plate 21: E. Swept from bilberry, about half grown. Mid-May.

The V-Moth
Semiothisa wauaria Linnaeus
Larva. 24–26 mm. Body brown or green, with a conspicuous yellow stripe along the spiracles, darker lines and paler mottlings along the back and black tubercles that have short black bristles.
Foodplants. Black currant, red currant and gooseberry.
Habits. A single-brooded insect, overwintering as an egg. The larvae hatch from about mid-April and develop steadily, feeding at night, with most becoming fully grown by mid-June, when they pupate in a cocoon spun up among the foodplant leaves. They can sometimes be obtained by careful searching under the leaves during the day and they are easy to rear in confinement. During July the adults will attend light traps in small numbers, but many females seem reluctant to lay eggs in captivity. Widespread over most of Britain, but probably less common than in the past when the foodplants were far more popular in gardens and allotments.
Plate 21: F. Bred from a female adult to MVL. Early July. (GAC)

Frosted Yellow
Isturgia limbaria Fabricius
Larva. 24–26 mm. Body green or brown, with a broad stripe of dull yellow along the spiracles, a darker dorsal line and thin lines of dull yellow along the rest of the dorsal and lateral regions.
Foodplant. Broom.
Habits. This species probably became extinct in Britain about 1914, but could still remain undiscovered in these islands. The adults fly in sunshine around their foodplant and captive females will lay freely on picked leaves. They are mainly double-brooded, with the larvae occurring in June and September, with univoltine races inhabiting more northern and montane regions. The larvae are easy to rear and pupate in a cocoon spun up in the soil, and in this stage they will overwinter when necessary, sometimes for more than one year.
Plate 21: G. Bred from a netted female adult (Central France). Early July.

Little Thorn
Cepphis advenaria Hübner
Larva. 20–22 mm. Body reddish-brown, with a more or less distinct pale wavy line along the spiracular area, often with a pale marking subdorsally at the join of the fourth and fifth segments.
Foodplants. Bilberry, bramble and dog rose.
Habits. A single-brooded species, with the larvae occurring from late June to about early August. In late May and June the adult females, which are easily disturbed from herbage by day and come to light after dark, will freely deposit eggs upon foodplant leaves in captivity and the resulting larvae are usually not difficult to rear, preferring bilberry as their main foodplant. They can also be swept from this plant, especially after dark, from heathy woodland localities which the moth is known to inhabit. The cocooned pupa is formed just under the soil and lasts throughout the winter months. Widespread, but local, over most of southern England and in Wales, as far north as Yorkshire; also recorded from south-west Ireland.
Plate 21: H. Swept at night from bilberry, fully grown. Late July.

Brown Silver-line
Petrophora chlorosata Scopoli
Larva. 28–30 mm. Body light green or pale brown, with numerous darker thin wavy lines along the back and sides. A pale area below the small black spiracles and a head that is usually light brown and mottled darker.
Foodplant. Bracken.
Habits. A single-brooded insect that occurs in the larval stage from about mid-June to early September, although most have finished developing and have pupated in the soil by late July. The adults are usually common wherever they are found in May and June, and are readily flushed by day from the foodplant and surrounding vegetation; later they can become annoyingly abundant at light. The females will deposit eggs quite freely on picked bracken, and rearing the larvae is easy. They can also be swept at night, often in good

numbers, during mid-July. Widespread over most of the British Isles.
Plate 21: I. Bred from a female adult to MVL. Late May. (SHC)

Barred Umber
Plagodis pulveraria Linnaeus
Larva. 32–35 mm. Body light brown, with a pair of parallel projecting structures dorsally on the eighth segment and often a smaller pair on the next ring. The head is cleft and pale brown.
Foodplants. Sallow, birch and hazel.
Habits. Single-brooded, with the larvae feeding from mid-June to about the middle of August. They can be beaten from the foodplants, but rarely in any numbers, as this species seems to occur at a low density in most places and the eggs are not concentrated in large batches. During May and June the adult females can be netted at dusk or light-trapped and these will usually lay eggs quite freely in captivity if given foodplant leaves as a stimulus. Rearing the larvae is fairly easy and pupation will take place just under the soil for over-wintering. Widespread over most parts of Britain and Ireland.
Plate 21: J. Bred from a female adult to MVL. Late May. (KGWE)

Scorched Wing
Plagodis dolabraria Linnaeus
Larva. 36–38 mm. Body shades of grey, with reddish-brown blotches and a single projecting hump dorsally on the eighth segment.
Foodplants. Birch, oak, sallow and beech.
Habits. A single-brooded species, being in the larval stage between late June and about early September. The larvae are sometimes beaten when attempting to obtain other species, but are rarely frequent enough to warrant taking any numbers by this method. The females do not seem to respond greatly to light, but may be collected by sugaring or by disturbing them from foliage by day. They will readily deposit eggs on foodplant leaves in captivity and rearing the larvae is not difficult. Pupation takes place in a cocoon on the ground and lasts throughout the winter until the following May or June. Widely distributed in woodland over most of the British Isles, but local in the north and in Ireland.
Plate 21: K. Bred from a female adult flushed by day. Mid-June. (M&JH)

Horse Chestnut
Pachycnemia hippocastanaria Hübner
Larva. 26–28 mm. Body grey, with reddish-brown diamond-shaped markings along the centre of the dorsal area, that are sometimes extended to almost obscure the ground colour. The underparts are wrinkled and usually ashy-grey in colour. The spiracles are black and the one on the first segment is noticeably larger.
Foodplant. Heather.
Habits. Double-brooded, with the second generation being partial but usually fairly numerous. The larvae occur from late May to early July, and again during September. They are easily swept, especially at night when they are feeding near to the tips of the foodplant. By day they remain motionless on the lower parts of heather, but can sometimes be found by careful searching. They do not seem to do well in captivity, often dying of an unknown cause before reaching the end of their development. In the wild pupation takes place in loose sandy soil and lasts through the winter. The adults frequently come to light traps and sometimes can be flushed on calm warm days in late April, May and August. Locally distributed on the heathlands of southern England.
Plate 21: L. Swept at night, fully grown. Mid-September. (SHC)

Brimstone Moth
Opisthograptis luteolata Linnaeus
Larva. 28–32 mm. Body usually dark reddish-brown or bright green, with two extra rudimentary pairs of prolegs on the seventh and eighth segments. On the back there is a hump on the sixth segment, that tends to be visibly smaller and reddish on individuals of the northern green larva.
Foodplants. Blackthorn, hawthorn, rowan and many other deciduous trees.
Habits. In southern Britain this species seems to adopt a life-cycle that produces three broods every two years, so the larvae can occur at any time and they can overwinter as either pupae or larvae. In the northern parts of its range the adults fly in June and July, producing larvae that feed between July and September, pupating throughout the winter months. These univoltine larvae are often green and the size of the hump on the sixth segment is much reduced in size, compared with those of the southern insects. Also, the green form of the larva is either absent or very scarce in southern Britain. Certainly more research is necessary to determine the factors that cause the larvae of the supposedly same species to be structurally different. It is an easy species to obtain by beating and to rear in captivity, being usually common throughout most of the British Isles.
Plate 21: M and N. Brown form – beaten from blackthorn, nearly fully grown. Early May. (SHC) Green form – beaten from rowan, nearly fully grown. Late August. (GAC)

Bordered Beauty
Epione repandaria Hufnagel
Larva. 26–28 mm. Body reddish or greyish-brown, with the fifth segment swollen and having several small humps across dorsally. The indistinct dorsal line is slightly darker, the subdorsal line paler and most obvious on the third and fourth rings; vaguely marked with a darker colour on the back.
Foodplant. Sallow.
Habits. A single-brooded species, with the larvae occurring between early May and mid-July, after overwintering in the egg stage. They can be beaten, especially in June when they are larger, and are usually easy to rear in confinement, pupating in leaf litter for about three weeks. The moths often inhabit damp places and can be netted at dusk or attracted to light from July to September. The females will deposit eggs on the foodplant twigs and these should be kept outside in the shade to avoid them hatching too early in the spring. Generally distributed throughout the British Isles.
Plate 21: O. Bred from a female adult to MVL. Early August. (SHC)

Dark Bordered Beauty
Epione paralellaria Denis & Schiffermüller
(*vespertaria* Fabricius)
Larva. 26–28 mm. Body greyish-brown, with the fifth segment slightly swollen dorsally; between this and the last segment are pairs of tiny white points along the back and the white subdorsal line is conspicuous on the thoracic and first abdominal segments.
Foodplants. Creeping willow and aspen; will accept most sallows in captivity.
Habits. Single-brooded, overwintering in the egg stage. The

larvae hatch in May and feed steadily until they become fully developed in about late June or early July. They can be taken by careful searching and are not difficult to rear in captivity. Pupation takes place in a cocoon among leaf litter and lasts nearly a month. A very local insect, being found only in a few localities in Yorkshire, Northumberland and eastern Scotland.
Plate 21: P. Found by searching, nearly fully grown. Mid-June. (CH)

Speckled Yellow
Pseudopanthera macularia Linnaeus
Larva. 20–22 mm. Body green, with a darker dorsal line and several fine whitish lines along the back and sides; the broad spiracular line is also white, edged above with a darker green shading.
Foodplants. Wood sage, dead-nettle, woundwort and yellow archangel.
Habits. A single-brooded species, with the larvae occurring from mid-June to about early August. The easiest way of obtaining stocks of this insect is to net a fertile female. From mid-May to late June these fly readily in sunshine and will lay freely on picked or potted foodplant placed in dappled sunlight. The larvae are easy to rear and feed up rapidly in confinement, pupating among leaf litter to overwinter. Generally distributed, mainly in open woodland, over most of the British Isles, being more local and less frequent in the north.
Plate 21: Q. Bred from a netted female adult on red dead-nettle. Early June.

Lilac Beauty
Apeira syringaria Linnaeus
Larva. 28–30 mm. Body coloured various shades of brown, with tiny short greyish bristles, two unusual long curled structures emitting from the seventh segment dorsally and smaller pairs of humps on the fifth and sixth rings.
Foodplants. Honeysuckle, ash and wild privet.
Habits. A single-brooded species that hibernates as a small larva, camouflaged upon its foodplant. During the spring, from mid-April to about late May, the larvae can sometimes be beaten, especially from the large clumps of honeysuckle that grow upon old stumps and against large tree trunks. Another successful method of obtaining them is to shine a torch at them on a still night. Startled, they drop about 3 cm on a thread and sway gently. They are easy to rear when larger, but can be difficult to overwinter unless kept sleeved outside. The pupa is formed in a flimsy cocoon spun up on the twigs of the foodplant. A widely distributed insect found in woodland over most of England, Wales and Ireland.
Plate 21: R. Bred from an adult female. Early July. (KGWE)

Large Thorn
Ennomos autumnaria Werneburg
Larva. 48–52 mm. Body greyish or greenish-brown, with short humps dorsally on the fifth and eighth segments and laterally on the sixth ring. Wholly mottled with darker and lighter brown and the flat squarish head is grey.
Foodplants. Oak, elm, birch, sallow, hawthorn and many other deciduous trees.
Habits. Single-brooded, overwintering in the egg stage. The adults fly during September and early October, and respond well to light traps with a good percentage being females. These will deposit eggs freely in captivity and rearing the larvae, that hatch in late April or early May, is usually very easy. They often take a long time to develop, with some still feeding in early August. They can be beaten from localities where the moth occurs in good numbers. Pupation takes place in a cocoon spun up between the foodplant leaves and lasts about four to six weeks. A local species occurring mainly in woodland of the coastal counties of southern and eastern England and also in Hertfordshire and Cambridgeshire, probably with the native population reinforced by immigration.
Plate 22: A. Bred from a female adult to MVL. Mid-September. (DEW)

August Thorn
Ennomos quercinaria Hufnagel
Larva. 45–48 mm. Body light brown to brownish-green, with humped structures dorsally on the fifth and eighth segments, a slight swelling on the lower side of the sixth ring and small twin points on the top of the eleventh segment.
Foodplants. Beech, blackthorn, oak, birch, hawthorn and other deciduous trees.
Habits. A single-brooded species, occurring as a larva from early May to about mid-July. The larvae feed at night, resting twig-like on the stems by day and are easily beaten from the foodplants. Rearing them in captivity is usually not difficult and they pupate among the leaves for about a month. From mid-August to the middle of September both sexes of the adults will come to light and the females will lay neat rows of square-shaped eggs along the foodplant twigs, the insect remaining in this stage throughout the winter months. Widespread, but local, over most of England, Wales, Ireland and southern Scotland.
Plate 22: B. Bred from a female adult to MVL. Late August. (BS)

Canary-shouldered Thorn
Ennomos alniaria Linnaeus
Larva. 43–47 mm. Body reddish-brown, with a slightly darker back and small hump-like dorsal structures on the fifth and eighth segments.
Foodplants. Birch, alder, sallow and other deciduous trees.
Habits. Single-brooded, overwintering as an egg deposited upon the foodplant twigs. The larvae hatch during early May and feed mainly at night until they are fully grown in about early July. They can readily be taken by beating and are very easy to rear in confinement, pupating among plant litter for between one and three months. The adults will frequently come to light, but the majority are males. To be found fairly commonly throughout most of the British Isles, especially in woodland and gardens.
Plate 22: C. Bred from a female adult to MVL. Late August. (M&JH)

Dusky Thorn
Ennomos fuscantaria Haworth
Larva. 45–48 mm. Body light brown or greenish-brown, with obvious hump-like structures on the fifth and eighth segments that are darker, and often a dark streak on the sub-dorsal area of the second segment.
Foodplants. Ash, and probably privets, which are accepted in captivity.
Habits. A single-brooded species that overwinters in the egg stage. The larvae occur between early May and mid-July and can be obtained by beating. They are usually easy to rear in confinement and pupate among the leaves of the foodplant. During August and September the adults come readily to light and the females will lay eggs freely upon the twigs of ash. This insect is widely distributed throughout

England and Wales, as far north as Lancashire and Co. Durham.
Plate 22: D. Bred from a female adult to MVL. Early September. (M&JH)

September Thorn

Ennomos erosaria Denis & Schiffermüller
Larva. 40–42 mm. Body grey or brownish-grey, with brown swellings of various sizes laterally on the second, fifth and sixth segments and dorsally on the fifth, eighth and eleventh segments.
Foodplants. Oak, birch and lime.
Habits. A univoltine insect that overwinters as an egg, deposited upon the foodplant twigs. Towards the end of April the larvae hatch and feed mainly at night, resting twig-like by day, until they become fully developed by around early July. Pupation takes place in a spinning among the leaves and some adults hatch after about three to four weeks while more emerge later, during September. The earlier adults are paler and smaller than the others, giving rise to speculation about there being two distinct ecological races within the species. The larvae can readily be taken by beating and adult females will often deposit eggs in captivity on supplied twigs or corrugated cardboard. Widely distributed over most of southern Britain, but more local and more uncommon in the north to Inverness-shire; also in southern Ireland.
Plate 22: E. Bred from a female adult to MVL. Early August. (M&JH)

Early Thorn

Selenia dentaria Fabricius
(*bilunaria* Esper)
Larva. 38–40 mm. Body brown or brownish-grey, variably mottled with darker colour and having pairs of conical-shaped structures dorsally on the swollen seventh and eighth segments.
Foodplants. Blackthorn, hawthorn, sallow, birch, alder and various other deciduous trees.
Habits. Mainly a double-brooded species, except in the north where there is only one generation each year. It occurs as a larva from mid-May to late June, again in August and September, and in northern Britain from June to August. The larvae can readily be obtained by beating and are usually very easy to rear in captivity; also keeping the pupae warm will often result in a third brood. The cocooned pupa is normally formed in leaf litter and the insect overwinters in this stage when necessary. Widespread and usually common over much of Britain.
Plate 22: F. Beaten from blackthorn, about half grown. Early June. (SHC)

Lunar Thorn

Selenia lunularia Hübner
(*lunaria* Denis & Schiffermüller)
Larva. 38–40 mm. Body brown or greenish-brown, with a paler dorsal line; the fifth and eighth segments are swollen and have small twin conical-shaped structures dorsally.
Foodplants. Ash, birch, oak and other deciduous trees.
Habits. A single-brooded woodland species that is in the larval stage from about late June to late August, feeding mainly at night and resting, resembling a twig, throughout the day. The larvae can be beaten, but rarely in any numbers, as populations tend to be low where they occur. Larger stocks are more readily obtained by light-trapping a female adult; these will freely deposit eggs in captivity and rearing the larvae is usually not difficult. The overwintering pupa is formed among plant litter or just under the soil in a cocoon and lasts until the following May or June. Local, but widespread, over most of the British Isles.
Plate 22: G. Bred from a female adult to MVL. Early June. (SHC)

Purple Thorn

Selenia tetralunaria Hufnagel
Larva. 39–42 mm. Body of some shade of brown, with the fourth, fifth, seventh and eighth segments swollen and having wart-like structures.
Foodplants. Oak, ash, alder, birch and many other deciduous trees.
Habits. Mainly a double-brooded species, with the nocturnal-feeding larvae occurring from late May to early July, again in August and September, and during June and July in the northern populations where it has only one generation in a year. The best method of obtaining stocks is from a light-trapped female, but the odd larva is often found on the beating tray, while trying to collect other species from the foodplants. The cocooned pupa is formed just under the soil or moss and will last throughout the winter when necessary. This insect is more often found in the southern counties of England and Wales, but is also recorded locally as far north as Ross-shire in Scotland.
Plate 22: H. Bred from a female adult to MVL. Mid-May. (SHC)

Scalloped Hazel

Odontopera bidentata Clerck
Larva. 42–45 mm. Body of various shades of brown or grey, with a darker dorsal line, a slight hump dorsally on the eleventh segment and often a triangular-shaped dark marking on the fourth ring.
Foodplants. Hawthorn, blackthorn, oak, birch, sallow, lime, privet, pine and many other trees.
Habits. Single-brooded, with the larvae occurring from early June to as late as September. They can often be taken by beating, but rarely in any numbers. Larger stocks can readily be obtained by breeding from fertile female adults, which often attend light traps in reasonable numbers. The larvae are very easy to rear in captivity, but can often take a long time to become fully developed. The overwintering cocooned pupa is formed under moss or plant litter and lasts until the following late April or May. Widespread and fairly common over most of the British Isles.
Plate 22: I. Bred from a female adult to MVL. Late May. (M&JH)

Scalloped Oak

Crocallis elinguaria Linnaeus
Larva. 42–45 mm. Body of various shades of brown or grey, with a row of diamond-shaped darker markings along the dorsal area that are usually indistinct and a small prominence on the top of the eleventh segment.
Foodplants. Sallow, hawthorn, blackthorn, bilberry, heather, oak and many other deciduous trees and shrubs.
Habits. A single-brooded species that overwinters in the egg stage. The larvae hatch from late March and feed up steadily, mainly at night, until they are fully developed by about early June, or later in more northern localities. Where they occur they are usually quite common and can readily be obtained by beating the many different foodplants that this species accepts. The cocooned pupa is formed under moss or in loose soil and lasts about three weeks. Both sexes of the adult will respond to light and the females will lay

freely in confinement, upon supplied twigs. Widespread over most of the British Isles, but yet to be recorded from Orkney or the Shetland Islands.
Plate 22: J. Beaten at night, about half grown. Mid-May.

Swallow-tailed Moth

Ourapteryx sambucaria Linnaeus
Larva. 50–54 mm. Body of some shade of brown, with a structural swelling on the sides of the sixth segment and dorsally on the eighth ring.
Foodplants. Hawthorn, blackthorn, ivy, privet and various other trees and shrubs.
Habits. Single-brooded, occurring as a larva from late August to about early June. Throughout the winter the small larvae hibernate among crevices upon the foodplant and feeding resumes when the buds start to open during the early spring. They are night-feeders, remaining motionless upon the twigs by day, and can sometimes be obtained by beating. The pupa is formed in a loose spinning hanging from the twigs of the foodplant and lasts about a month. During late June and July the adults can be attracted to light and the females lay freely in captivity. Keeping the larvae warm and feeding them on ivy or privet will frequently result in them feeding up in about four to five months, ignoring the hibernation period. To be found over most parts of England, Ireland, Wales and southern Scotland.
Plate 22: K. Beaten from hawthorn, nearly fully grown. Late May. (SHC)

Feathered Thorn

Colotois pennaria Linnaeus
Larva. Body usually of some shade of grey, mottled with a darker colour and having small twin parallel conical-shaped structures on the top of the eleventh segment.
Foodplants. Hawthorn, birch, oak, blackthorn, sallow and other deciduous trees and shrubs.
Habits. A single-brooded species that overwinters as an egg, laid in batches upon the twigs of its foodplant. These hatch during early spring and most of the night-feeding larvae are fully developed by about mid-June. They can readily be taken by beating after dark, especially in May when they are larger. Rearing them in confinement is usually very easy and they pupate just under the soil, until the adults emerge in October. These come to light on mild nights, males in good numbers and the females less frequently. Widespread and fairly common over most of the British Isles, but local and less frequent in the north.
Plate 22: L. Beaten at night, nearly fully grown. Late May. (AJP)

Orange Moth

Angerona prunaria Linnaeus
Larva. 48–50 mm. Body light brown and mottled darker, with large pointed conical-shaped projections on the eighth ring and smaller structures on the fourth and eleventh segments.
Foodplants. Hawthorn, blackthorn, honeysuckle, birch and other trees and shrubs; also readily accepting garden privet and lilac in captivity.
Habits. A single-brooded species that hibernates as a one-third grown larva upon its foodplant. Feeding resumes in the spring and the development is rapid, with most larvae becoming fully grown by late May. Sometimes they can be beaten, but rarely in any numbers as the species is usually not frequent enough in its wooded habitats. A better method of obtaining stocks is to take a female adult; these fly during late June and July. They can sometimes be flushed from foliage during the day and occasionally come to light traps on warmer nights. Eggs are usually laid freely and the larvae are fairly easy to rear, as long as they are kept outside for overwintering or fed on privet and kept warm for forcing through. Mainly a southern insect, occurring locally as far north as Lincolnshire; also recorded from southern parts of Ireland.
Plate 22: M. Bred from a female adult to MVL. Early July. (M&JH)

Small Brindled Beauty

Apocheima hispidaria Denis & Schiffermüller
Larva. 37–40 mm. Body various shades of brown or grey, with wart-like structures on the dorsal and subdorsal areas of segments four to eleven, those on the fifth and eleventh being the most prominent.
Foodplants. Oak; also recorded from elm, hazel and sweet chestnut.
Habits. Single-brooded, occurring in the larval stage from late April to about the middle of June, feeding mainly at night and resting on the twigs by day. The larvae can be beaten from the boughs of trees growing in larger mature oak woods and are usually easy to rear in captivity, but the subterranean pupae should be kept outside in a shaded place for the summer and eventual overwintering. During March the adult wingless females may be searched for by day hiding in crevices in oak trunks, and at night they can be found by torchlight, sometimes while pairing with the fully winged males. Locally common and widespread in the southern half of England and Wales, and northwards, but less frequent, to Cumbria and Yorkshire.
Plate 22: N. Beaten from oak, about half grown. Mid-May (BS)

Pale Brindled Beauty

Apocheima pilosaria Denis & Schiffermüller
(*pedaria* Fabricius)
Larva. 38–42 mm. Body various shades of brown or grey, with wart-like structures on the dorsal and subdorsal areas of the fourth to eleventh segments, with those of the fifth and sixth being the largest. Also on these two segments are pale ochreous oblique marks from the subdorsal to dorsal region, in front of the warts.
Foodplants. Oak, hawthorn, blackthorn, birch, lime, sallow, apple and various other deciduous trees.
Habits. A single-brooded insect, with the larval development lasting from mid-April to about mid-June. The larvae are night-feeders, resting camouflaged on the foodplant twigs by day, and can readily be taken by beating. Usually they are very easy to rear in confinement, but the pupae, which are formed in a cocoon under the soil, should not be kept indoors as they are liable to dry out during the summer. The wingless females can be located at night during late January to early March, resting on tree trunks, and they will often lay eggs freely on supplied twigs or netting. Reasonably common over most of England and Wales, also occurring less frequently and locally in Scotland and Ireland.
Plate 22: O. Beaten at night, nearly fully grown. Late May.

Brindled Beauty

Lycia hirtaria Clerck
Larva. 52–56 mm. Body ashy-grey, with many russet streaks and mottlings along the back and sides, a thin yellow collar behind the head and small yellow spots on the middle segments.

Foodplants. Sallow, oak, elm, lime, birch, alder, hawthorn and various other deciduous trees.
Habits. Single-brooded, with the highly parasitized larvae occurring from early May to about mid-June. They are usually easy to obtain by beating from trees and bushes growing in woods, hedgerows and parkland and are not difficult to rear in captivity. The pupae are formed under the soil and should be left outside to avoid desiccation during the summer. After overwintering the adults, which are fully winged in both sexes, hatch in March or April. Although the females rarely come to light, they can be found by searching tree trunks, fences and walls during the day. This species is to be found over most of the British Isles, being less frequent and more local in the north and in Ireland.
Plate 22: P. Beaten from sallow, nearly fully grown. Late May.

Belted Beauty

Lycia zonaria Denis & Schiffermüller
Larva. 38–40 mm. Body light greyish-green, heavily speckled with tiny dark grey to black dots and lines and having a distinct broad pale yellow spiracular stripe.
Foodplants. Plantain, clovers, bird's-foot trefoil, creeping willow, yellow iris, burnet rose; also readily accepting most sallows in captivity.
Habits. A single-brooded species that is in the larval stage from May to mid-July and can readily be obtained by sweeping, especially at dusk or after dark when the larvae begin to become more active. They are usually not difficult to rear in captivity and prefer to pupate in loose soil, but will successfully spin up among the leaves or tissue-paper placed in their breeding cage. Keeping the pupae outside avoids drying out and most adults hatch the following March, with some remaining as pupae for up to four years. In the wild the wingless females can often be located on wooden posts and low vegetation by day or night, and they usually deposit eggs freely in confinement. A very local moth, being recorded at present from coastal localities only in Caernarvonshire, Cheshire, Argyllshire, the Hebrides and western Ireland.
Plate 22: Q. Swept at night, less than half grown. Early June. (SHC)

Rannoch Brindled Beauty

Lycia lapponaria Boisduval
Larva. 40–42 mm. Body light grey, heavily dusted with dark grey dots and having irregular pale yellow lines along the back, in which blotches are formed mainly on the middle rings. The black spiracles are bordered below by more yellow markings that form a broken line.
Foodplants. Bog myrtle, heather, bell heather and cross-leaved heath; also readily accepting hawthorn, sallow and birch in confinement.
Habits. Single-brooded, with the larvae occurring from about mid-May to early August, feeding mainly at night when they are larger. They can readily be swept, especially from bog myrtle, in their moorland habitats at the end of May when they are still tiny, often being taken in good numbers. At this point of their development they are completely black and will move rapidly about in the bottom of the sweep net. In captivity their growth becomes more rapid, feeding up within about a month if kept in the dark and supplied with sallow as an alternative foodplant. They are usually easy to rear but the subterranean pupae must be kept outside to avoid desiccation, remaining in this stage normally until the following April, but sometimes for up to four years. In the wild the wingless females can be located resting by day on fence posts and heather and bog myrtle plants, frequently laying eggs freely on twigs in captivity. Locally common in Perthshire, Inverness-shire and also has been found in Argyllshire.
Plate 22: R. Swept by day, about one-fifth grown. Late May.

Oak Beauty

Biston strataria Hufnagel
Larva. 52–55 mm. Body grey, clouded and marked with brown, with wart-like structures on the eighth segment subdorsally; the cleft head and anal segment are reddish-brown.
Foodplants. Oak, hazel, aspen, elm and other deciduous trees.
Habits. A single-brooded species, with the night-feeding larvae occurring from about mid-May to mid-July. These can often be obtained by beating and are usually easy to rear in captivity. During March and April the female adults will occasionally come to light traps and may deposit eggs around the buds of supplied oak twigs. The pupa is formed in the soil and lasts throughout the winter months. This woodland insect is generally distributed over most of Britain, but less frequent and more local in the north and in Ireland.
Plate 23: A. Bred from a female adult to MVL. Mid-April.

Peppered Moth

Biston betularia Linnaeus
Larva. 55–60 mm. Body brownish-grey, brown or brownish-green to green, with a deeply cleft brown head, a pair of wart-like structures dorsally on the eighth segment and large reddish spiracles.
Foodplants. Lime, birch, sallow, hawthorn, rose, oak and various other plants, mainly trees.
Habits. Single-brooded, with the larvae feeding mainly at night from early July to about mid-September on a wide range of suitable plants. They are often obtained by beating, especially in woodland, parks and gardens. The adults fly throughout June and July and the females will attend light traps, but rarely as often as the males. Eggs are easily obtained in captivity and rearing the larvae is not difficult. The overwintering pupa is formed just under the soil and can sometimes be found by digging. It can be identified by its size, reddish colour and very sharp anal point. A rather common species distributed over most of the British Isles, but more local in Scotland.
Plate 23: B. Bred from a female adult to MVL. Early July. (SHC)

Spring Usher

Agriopis leucophaearia Denis & Schiffermüller
Larva. 24–26 mm. Body greyish-green, pale green or olive, with lighter subdorsal lines and often darker markings on the back and sides; in the more heavily marked darker individuals there are sometimes two conspicuous blackish spots dorsally on the second segment.
Foodplants. Oak and occasionally apple.
Habits. A single-brooded species that is most easily obtained in the larval stage by beating. The eggs begin to hatch during early April and the young larvae start to feed on the developing buds in a spinning and then later on the leaves, becoming fully grown by about early June. They are fairly easy to rear in confinement, and the subterranean pupae, that last until the following February, should be kept outside in a shaded place. The wingless female adults can be located by torchlight resting upon oak trunks after dark and will deposit eggs freely on twigs in captivity. Widely distributed

and often common over most of England and Wales; more local in southern Scotland to Inverness-shire.
Plate 23: C. Beaten from oak at night, fully grown. Late May. (GAC)

Scarce Umber
Agriopis aurantiaria Hübner
Larva. 28–30 mm. Body greyish, with a broad dorsal stripe consisting of dull brownish-orange and fine irregular lines of paler colour, also a variable amount of brownish-black markings on the sides that sometimes extend into the dorsal area; the head and legs are reddish-brown.
Foodplants. Birch, blackthorn, hazel, beech, oak and many other deciduous trees.
Habits. A single-brooded species that overwinters in the egg stage. The larvae occur from about mid-April and most are fully developed by the middle of June, and are readily taken by beating. Rearing them in captivity is not difficult but they should be allowed to pupate under soil in a container that can be left outside throughout the summer months. The adults normally hatch in October or November and the almost wingless females, which can be found at night on trunks of the foodplant, will often lay freely on bark or cardboard. Fairly common and widely distributed, mainly in woodland, over most of England and Wales; also occurring locally in Scotland and Ireland.
Plate 23: D. Beaten from blackthorn, fully grown. Late May.

Dotted Border
Agriopis marginaria Fabricius
Larva. 28–30 mm. Body shades of brown, ochreous or green, often with cross-shaped blackish markings along the back, most obvious on the middle segments. The head is dark or reddish-brown and some individuals have a distinct dark subdorsal line.
Foodplants. Blackthorn, hawthorn, oak, birch, sallow and many other deciduous trees.
Habits. Single-brooded, being in the larval stage from mid-April to about the middle of June. The larvae are easily obtained by beating and present no difficulties when being reared in captivity. The pupa is formed under the soil and overwinters, seeming to be more successful if kept outside and left to the natural weather conditions. The adults hatch in the early spring and the vestigial-winged females are to be found at night upon tree trunks; they usually deposit their eggs quite freely on twigs or bark in confinement. Generally distributed over most of the British Isles.
Plate 23: E. Beaten from blackthorn, fully grown. Early June.

Mottled Umber
Erannis defoliaria Clerck
Larva. 28–32 mm. Body greyish, heavily marked with reddish-brown, with a wavy black subdorsal line that has pale yellow blotches below. The head is reddish-brown and the white spiracles are ringed with black.
Foodplants. Oak, birch, blackthorn, hawthorn, sallow, hazel and various other deciduous trees.
Habits. A single-brooded species that occurs in the larval stage from April to late June. The larvae are usually very easy to beat due to the abundance of this species where it occurs. Rearing in captivity is easy and the pupae do best if kept outside in natural conditions until the adults emerge during the late autumn. The wingless females can readily be located upon tree trunks at night and they will usually lay their eggs freely on twigs or cardboard in captivity. Widely distributed over most of the British Isles, being most common in the southern counties of England and in Wales.
Plate 23: F. Beaten from oak, fully grown. Early June.

Waved Umber
Menophra abruptaria Thunberg
Larva. 36–38 mm. Body of various shades of brown, with darker brown dorsal markings and inconspicuous paler subdorsal lines. Also slight swellings dorsally on the ninth to eleventh segments that are darker.
Foodplants. Privet and lilac; also accepting ash and birch in captivity.
Habits. A single-brooded insect that occurs in the larval stage from early June to about early September, taking a long time to develop even when kept warm in captivity. In the wild the larvae can be taken by beating, but rarely in any numbers, or stocks can be obtained from female adults. These come sparingly to light and are more readily located by searching tree trunks and fences near to privet bushes from late April to early June. Pupation takes place in a tough cocoon spun up on the foodplant twigs and lasts throughout the winter. Widespread in gardens, woods and parkland over much of England and Wales, being less frequent in the northern parts of its range.
Plate 23: G. Bred from a female adult to MVL. Mid-May.

Willow Beauty
Peribatodes rhomboidaria Denis & Schiffermüller
Larva. 38–40 mm. Body ochreous or light reddish to greyish-brown, with an indistinct darker dorsal line and sometimes markings of darker brown on the back. The head is cleft and the blackish-ringed white spiracles are larger on the first and eleventh segments, also having two small structures on the underparts of the fifth segment.
Foodplants. Privet, ivy, yew, hawthorn, birch, gorse and many other trees and shrubs.
Habits. Normally a single-brooded species, with the larvae hatching from the eggs in July and August and usually overwintering when still fairly small. In southern counties some individuals feed up rapidly in about six weeks and pupate in a strong cocoon attached to the twigs, producing a partial second generation. Those that have hibernated recommence activity in the spring and will become fully developed by about early June. From late June to mid-August both sexes of the adult come to light and the females will often lay freely in confinement. The larvae are not difficult to rear and can be forced by keeping them warm and in the dark. Generally distributed over most of the British Isles.
Plate 23: H. Bred from a female adult to MVL. Late July. (SHC)

Feathered Beauty
Peribatodes secundaria Esper
Larva. 38–40 mm. Body light reddish-brown, with an indistinct dorsal line and paler subdorsal lines that often have darker markings below.
Foodplants. Norway spruce and in captivity Scots pine, Western hemlock, Douglas fir and Lawson's cypress.
Habits. This single-brooded insect is a recent colonist that has been found in coniferous woods in south-east England since 1981. The larvae occur in the wild from late August to the following early June, overwintering on the foodplant when about a quarter grown. The larvae can be beaten during the spring and in July and early August the adult females will come to light traps, laying eggs readily in confinement

upon picked foodplant. The larvae are easy to rear and will continue to develop without hibernating, if kept warm and supplied with fresh food. Pupation takes place in a cocoon spun up on the plant and lasts about a month.
Plate 23: I. Bred from a female adult to MVL. Late July. (BS)

Lydd Beauty
Peribatodes manuelaria Herrich-Schäffer
Larva. 32–35 mm. Body grey, brownish-grey or greenish-grey, with a variable amount of markings, pairs of small projections subdorsally on the fourth to eleventh rings and also having a pair of fleshy humps on the underparts of the fifth segment.
Foodplants. Birch, oak, blackthorn, privet and other trees and shrubs.
Habits. A single-brooded rare immigrant species that has been recorded twice in the British Isles as an adult. On the continent the larvae occur from about September to the following early June, overwintering when about one-third grown, probably pupating among leaf litter, with the adults flying in July and August. Occasionally some larvae may be forced in captivity to complete their development by October.
Plate 23: J. Bred from a female adult to MVL. Early August. (KR)

Bordered Grey
Selidosema brunnearia de Villers
(*ericetaria* de Villers)
(*plumaria* auctt.)
Larva. 28–30 mm. Body grey or brownish-grey, with a dark dorsal line and many other fine darker lines along the back and sides, pale whitish areas along the back and square-shaped mottled head.
Foodplants. Heather in heathland localities and bird's-foot trefoil on downland and other habitats; also flowers of sorrel. Recorded on the continent as accepting broom, clover, restharrow and dock.
Habits. Single-brooded, occurring in the larval stage from about early September to the following early June, overwintering when about one-third grown. During May they are to be obtained by sweeping, especially from heather, which is the main foodplant in Britain. The adults fly in July and August and both sexes attend light traps, with the females laying freely on picked plant in captivity. The larvae are easy to rear, being kept outside on potted foodplant during the winter, and the pupa is formed inside a silken cocoon just under loose soil and lasts for about six weeks. Widely, but locally, distributed in suitable localities over much of the British Isles.
Plate 23: K. Swept at night, nearly fully grown. Early May. (SHC)

Ringed Carpet
Cleora cinctaria Denis & Schiffermüller
Larva. 36–38 mm. Body green, with a broadish darker dorsal line and paler subdorsal lines of about the same width, also irregular thin whitish lines along the rest of the back and darker mottlings and lines laterally.
Foodplants. Birch, bilberry, bog myrtle and heather.
Habits. A single-brooded species, with the larval stage lasting from about late May to early August, depending on the latitude of the population. The larvae can be swept or beaten from their foodplants, but are probably easiest to obtain in good numbers from eggs laid by a fertile female. During May these can often be located by day at rest on tree trunks or old wooden posts and at night they come to light traps or even sugar. They usually lay eggs readily in captivity, especially if supplied with picked foodplant as a stimulus. The resulting larvae are very easy to rear, pupating in leaf litter or just under loose soil for overwintering. Mainly inhabiting lightly wooded heathland and moors in central southern England, central Scotland and parts of Wales and Ireland.
Plate 23: L. Bred from a female adult found on birch trunk. Late May. (JMP)

Satin Beauty
Deileptenia ribeata Clerck
Larva. 40–42 mm. Body usually dark brown, sometimes paler, with a variable amount of lighter mottlings and markings on the dorsal area; underparts pale brown.
Foodplants. Yew, Norway spruce, Douglas fir, pines, oak and birch.
Habits. A single-brooded insect that overwinters as a small larva upon its foodplant. During the spring its growth becomes more rapid and most are fully grown by about late May. They are readily taken by beating in late April and May, especially at night when they are more active, from old yew trees growing on the edges of woods. Both sexes of the adult come to light during July but the females can be reluctant to lay eggs in captivity. If these are obtained, the resulting larvae take a long time to mature, usually refusing to feed up faster, even if kept warm and in the dark. Those larvae taken in the spring are easier to rear, pupating just under loose soil for about a month. A woodland species, being widely distributed over much of England, Wales and southern Scotland, but local in the northern parts of its range; also recorded from Cos. Kildare, Wicklow and Leix in Ireland.
Plate 23: M. Beaten from yew, fully grown. Late May.

Mottled Beauty
Alcis repandata Linnaeus
Larva. 36–38 mm. Body of some shade of brown, with variable amounts of darker markings and mottling on the back and sides. The dorsal line is present and fairly indistinct and on the underparts is a dark centred broad pale stripe; the black-ringed pale spiracles are larger on the first and eleventh segments.
Foodplants. Bilberry, heather, birch, blackthorn, bramble, honeysuckle, birch, dock and many other plants.
Habits. Single-brooded, being in the larval stage from about mid-August to late May, overwintering while still quite small. The larvae often come out of hibernation before the leaves have developed and feed upon the soft bark of the foodplant or can be given bramble or heather throughout this period in captivity. During the spring they can readily be swept or beaten from the foodplants at night and often in good numbers. They are not difficult to rear and pupate in a loose cocoon among leaf litter for about four weeks. Both sexes of the adults come to light and females lay eggs freely in confinement. Widely distributed and fairly common over most of the British Isles.
Plate 23: N. Swept at night, fully grown. Late May.

Dotted Carpet
Alcis jubata Thunberg
(*glabraria* Hübner)
Larva. 24–27 mm. Body bright pale green, with rows of black spots along the back and sides and a pale green head marked with black.
Foodplants. Beard lichen and probably other associated species.

Habits. A single-brooded species, being in the larval stage from late August, through the winter, until the following early June, feeding mainly on the newest growth of the lichen. The larvae can be obtained by beating from the thinner boughs or by lightly brushing the lichens with a soft feather-duster over a beating tray. Often they are difficult to rear in captivity, requiring moist food at all times and unless they can be sleeved out, are impractical to rear from the egg stage. They are said to pupate under the moss and lichens on the host trees and this stage lasts about four to six weeks. This insect inhabits the ancient woodlands, mainly on the western side of England, Scotland and most of Wales, where the lichens grow abundantly upon the old mature trees.
Plate 23: O. Beaten from lichen on oak, fully grown. Early June. (BS)

Great Oak Beauty
Hypomecis roboraria Denis & Schiffermüller
Larva. 46–48 mm. Body greyish to reddish-brown, with a large hump-like structure on the fifth segment and a smaller one on the eleventh segment dorsally; also another hump on the sixth segment ventrally. The cleft head is reddish-brown.
Foodplant. Oak.
Habits. A single-brooded insect, occurring as a larva from about early August to the following late May, after hibernating while still quite small (about 18 mm) upon the twigs of the foodplant. During the early spring, in mild weather, the larvae feed upon the softer parts of the bark of the oak twigs, and later become fully active as the buds begin to develop in April. During the spring they can be beaten, especially after dark, when they are feeding. Pupation takes place under the soil in a silken cocoon and lasts about a month. Both sexes come to light and the females will lay in captivity if given space and picked foodplant, but the larvae can be difficult to overwinter unless sleeved on growing foodplant. Locally distributed over most of the southern half of England and in south-east Wales.
Plate 23: P. Bred from a female adult to MVL. Early July. (M&JH)

Pale Oak Beauty
Serraca punctinalis Scopoli
Larva. 42–44 mm. Body of various shades of brown, with lighter and darker mottlings and two prominent wart-like structures on the slightly swollen fifth segment dorsally. The brown head is slightly notched and the small pale spiracles are ringed with black.
Foodplants. Oak, less often birch, and occasionally sallow and sycamore.
Habits. A single-brooded species, with the larvae occurring from about early July and throughout most of August, feeding mainly at night when larger. They can be taken by beating, especially from the lower boughs of mature trees, and larger stocks can be obtained more easily by taking a light-trapped female during June and early July. They will often lay freely in confinement and rearing the resulting larvae is usually very easy. The overwintering pupae are formed under the soil and are best kept outside in natural weather conditions. Widely distributed in deciduous woodland over most of southern England and parts of Wales.
Plate 23: Q. Bred from a female adult to MVL. Late June.

Brussels Lace
Cleorodes lichenaria Hufnagel
Larva. 26–28 mm. Body darkish or greyish-green, liberally mottled with black, grey and brown on the back and sides and small paired structures along the dorsal area, most prominent on segments five, eight and nine.
Foodplants. Various lichens that grow on oaks, hawthorn and blackthorn, and on rocks.
Habits. Single-brooded, being in the larval stage from about late August to the following late May. The larvae are easiest to obtain by beating during the spring, and at this point of their development are easy to breed, pupating in a cocoon for about four to five weeks under moss or lichens. During late June and July eggs can be obtained from light-trapped female adults, but the larvae from these are more difficult to rear due to the requirement of fresh foodplant and their insistence on overwintering. Locally common, mainly in south-west England, Wales and parts of Ireland; rare or very local elsewhere in southern England and Scotland.
Plate 23: R. Beaten from lichen on hawthorn, fully grown. Late May. (SHC)

Speckled Beauty
Fagivorina arenaria Hufnagel
Larva. 26–32 mm. Body reddish- or greyish-brown, marked paler, with slight dorsal and lateral protuberances on the abdominal segments (Hoffmeyer).
Foodplants. Lichens growing on oak, birch and possibly other trees.
Habits. A single-brooded insect that was recorded from Hampshire and Sussex until 1898 and is now probably extinct. The larvae were stated to occur during August and September, before overwintering in the pupal stage. The species is still well established in northern Europe and Scandinavia.

The Engrailed
Ectropis bistortata Goeze
(*biundulata* de Villers)
Larva. 32–34 mm. Body of various shades of brown or grey, with a greater or lesser amount of brown or black markings, also often with mottlings of brownish-orange or dull yellow on the back and sides. The third segment is slightly swollen laterally and the eleventh segment has two small warts dorsally.
Foodplants. Oak, birch, sallow, aspen and various other trees and shrubs.
Habits. Mainly a double-brooded species, except in the northern parts of Britain where it is univoltine. The larvae occur from late April to June and again in the south from late July to early September. They can readily be beaten from their foodplants and are very easy to rear in captivity. Overwintering is spent in the pupal stage under the ground, and the adults emerge in the early spring and come freely to light traps. Female adults deposit eggs freely in captivity and the second generation can be found on the wing during July. Widespread and usually common in woodland and scrubland over the greater part of the British Isles.
Plate 24: A. Beaten from sallow, fully grown. Early September.

Small Engrailed
Ectropis crepuscularia Denis & Schiffermüller
Larva. 32–34 mm. Body of various shades of brown or grey, mottled and speckled with darker brown or black with some individuals having yellow or orangish-brown markings. The third segment laterally swollen and eleventh segment humped dorsally.
Foodplants. Birch, sallow, beech, larch and other trees and shrubs.

Habits. Single-brooded, with the larvae occurring from about mid-June to early August, usually between the broods of the previous similar species, *E. bistortata*. They can be beaten, especially at night when more active, and are not difficult to rear in confinement. The adults, which fly from mid-May to mid-June, come sparingly to light, but can be obtained by searching tree trunks during the day. Stocks can be reared from the females that will lay eggs on picked foodplant placed in spacious containers. The pupa is formed in a silken cocoon just under the soil and the insect overwinters in this stage. Widely distributed, but local, over much of the British Isles, most frequent in the southern counties.
Plate 24: B. Bred from a female adult to MVL. Early June. (SHC)

Square Spot

Paradarisa consonaria Hübner
Larva. 38–42 mm. Body greenish-brown or light brown, often with distinct oblique blackish markings subdorsally mainly on the middle segments; head chestnut-brown with darker mottlings.
Foodplants. Birch, beech, oak, pine, yew and various other trees.
Habits. A single-brooded insect, with the larvae occurring from mid-June to about mid-August. They can often be taken by beating or are obtained by breeding from adult females taken at light or located by day at rest on tree trunks during May and early June. The larvae are easy to rear and pupate for overwintering under the soil in a loose cocoon. A locally common woodland species, being found over much of the southern half of the British Isles as far north as Westmorland.
Plate 24: C. Bred from a female adult found on trunk by day. Mid-May.

Brindled White-spot

Paradarisa extersaria Hübner
(*luridata* Borkhausen)
Larva. 38–40 mm. Body green or brownish-green, with dark-brown dorsal raised structures on the fourth and eighth segments; head large and round.
Foodplants. Oak, birch and occasionally lime.
Habits. Single-brooded, being in the larval stage from late June to about early September. The larvae can be obtained by beating, but larger stocks can be bred by using light traps to attract fertile adult females during June. Most will deposit eggs in captivity, if supplied with fresh foodplant leaves, and rearing the larvae is usually not difficult. When fully grown they will pupate for overwintering in a cocoon formed just under the soil. A woodland species locally common over most of southern England and much of Wales.
Plate 24: D. Bred from a female adult to MVL. Mid-June.

Grey Birch

Aethalura punctulata Denis & Schiffermüller
Larva. 28–30 mm. Body green or brown, with a darker dorsal line and several fine paler lines along the back and sides. The greenish head is mottled darker and some individuals have darker blotches dorsally.
Foodplants. Birch and occasionally alder.
Habits. A single-brooded species that occurs as a larva from about late May to the end of July. The larvae can readily be obtained by breeding from light-trapped female adults, which are also easy to find by day by tapping thin birch trunks in May and early June. They will lay eggs freely in captivity and the larvae are usually very easy to rear. During July the larvae can also be taken by beating, especially from trees growing along the edges of woodland rides. The winter is spent in the pupal stage, in a cocoon just under the soil. Widespread and fairly common over most of England and Wales; less frequent and more local in Ireland and Scotland.
Plate 24: E. Bred from a female adult to MVL. Mid-May. (M&JH)

Common Heath

Ematurga atomaria Linnaeus
Larva. 28–30 mm. Body variable in colour, being of shades of green, brown or grey, some with light and darker mottlings and lines, while others are almost unmarked.
Foodplants. Heather, heath, trefoils, vetches and clovers.
Habits. A single-brooded insect that often has a substantial partial second generation, especially in the more southern parts of its range. The larvae occur from about mid-June and can readily be taken, sometimes in large numbers, by sweeping heather, until the last pupate in about mid-September. They are very easy to rear in confinement and prefer to form their pupae just under fine sandy soil in a loose cocoon for overwintering. From May to July or August both sexes of the adults fly freely in sunshine and netted females will deposit eggs on sprigs of the foodplant placed in cages kept in the light. Widespread and generally common on heaths and downland over most of the British Isles.
Plate 24: F. Swept from heather, fully grown. Early September.

Bordered White

Bupalus piniaria Linnaeus
Larva. 28–32 mm. Body green, with a broad white dorsal line, finer whitish subdorsal lines and a yellowish spiracular line. On the paler green underparts are a further two less distinct yellowish lines; head green and striped with whitish.
Foodplants. Scots pine and other pines.
Habits. Single-brooded, with the larvae occurring from late June to about early September and being very easy to beat, sometimes in large numbers, from the foodplant. They are not difficult to rear in confinement and pupate beneath the soil and plant litter for overwintering. During May and June both sexes of the adults can be obtained by tapping the lower boughs of pines and then using a net to capture them. The darker-coloured females lay freely on picked plant in cages. Widespread and generally common in pine woods over most of the British Isles.
Plate 24: G. Beaten at night, fully grown. Early September.

Common White Wave

Cabera pusaria Linnaeus
Larva. 28–30 mm. Body shades of light green, with a few small pinkish-red markings along the back; the anal legs are often also pinkish. Another form is of shades of brown, with dorsal marks of whitish colour and the central part of the flattened head greenish.
Foodplants. Birch, sallow, oak, alder and various other trees and shrubs.
Habits. A double-brooded species in southern Britain and univoltine in the north. The larvae occur from late June to September and can be taken by beating, and are also easy to obtain by breeding from the adult stage. Both sexes are attracted to light and females lay freely on picked plant in captivity. The larvae are easy to rear and pupate among plant litter for overwintering when necessary. Generally distributed throughout the British Isles.
Plate 24: H. Beaten from birch, fully grown. Mid-September.

Common Wave
Cabera exanthemata Scopoli
Larva. 27–30 mm. Body usually light green, with a darker green dorsal line in which there is often a blackish mark anteriorly on each segment. Subdorsally there is a whitish-green stripe and the first anal leg is sometimes marked with a darker colour. Brown forms with darker dorsal markings do occur, but never in such frequency as the green larvae.
Foodplants. Sallow and aspen.
Habits. A mainly single-brooded species that often has a partial second generation in the more southern parts of its range. The larvae occur from about mid-June to mid-July and in late August and September in the south, with those in the north in July and August. They can easily be beaten from the foodplant and light-trapped females should lay in confinement if supplied with sallow leaves as a stimulus. The larvae are very easy to rear and prefer to pupate in plant litter or fine soil. Overwintering takes place in the pupal stage and lasts until May or June. Widely distributed in damp places over most of the British Isles.
Plate 24: I. Bred from a female adult to MVL. Late May.

White-pinion Spotted
Lomographa bimaculata Fabricius
Larva. 24–27 mm. Body green, with a varying amount of reddish or brown dorsal markings and a green head that is finely speckled with dark reddish-brown.
Foodplants. Hawthorn, blackthorn and probably plum.
Habits. A single-brooded species that occurs in the larval stage from late June to early August and can often be taken by beating. The larvae are usually easy to rear in captivity and willingly pupate among plant litter or fine soil for overwintering. During May and June the adults can be light-trapped or disturbed from foliage by day, but many females seem to be reluctant to deposit eggs in captivity, even when given space and sleeved foodplant. Widely distributed in woodland and scrub over much of southern and eastern England, South Wales, the Lake District and part of southern Ireland.
Plate 24: J. Beaten from hawthorn, fully grown. Late July.

Clouded Silver
Lomographa temerata Denis & Schiffermüller
Larva. 24–26 mm. Body green, with a distinct row of whitish or red-edged pale dashes along the dorsal area. The head is glassy green with a pair of reddish triangular marks on the sides.
Foodplants. Blackthorn, hawthorn, plum, apple and aspen.
Habits. Single-brooded, occurring as a larva from about late June to mid-August. The larvae can be taken by beating, usually in small numbers, and most female adults seem to lay quite freely in captivity. During late May and throughout June the females will come readily to light traps and can also be obtained by disturbing them from foliage during the day. The larvae are easy to rear and the overwintering pupae are formed on the ground among plant debris. Widely distributed and moderately common in England, Wales and Ireland, local in Scotland.
Plate 24: K. Bred from a female adult to MVL. Early June. (M&JH)

Sloe Carpet
Aleucis distinctata Herrich-Schäffer
Larva. 24–27 mm. Body light green or greyish-brown, with pale green or whitish areas on the seventh and eighth segments. In both colour forms there are indistinct V- or X-shaped darker markings dorsally.
Foodplant. Blackthorn.
Habits. A single-brooded species, with the larval stage lasting from about mid-May to early July. In some localities the population can be fairly concentrated and the larvae can be beaten in good numbers. Elsewhere the insect can be widely scattered over a large area and the best way to obtain stocks is from a fertile female. During April both sexes of the adult respond to light traps, but are often much easier to find by searching the outer twigs of larger blackthorn bushes at night. Eggs should be laid on picked foodplant and rearing the larvae in captivity is not difficult. Pupation takes place in a cocoon spun up among plant litter or in loose soil and lasts through the winter. Local, but sometimes common where it occurs, mainly in the south-east of England.
Plate 24: L. Bred from a female adult to MVL. Late April. (SHC)

Early Moth
Theria primaria Haworth
(*rupicapraria* auctt.)
Larva. 23–25 mm. Body whitish-green to darker greyish-green or brown, with distinct white dorsal lines and darker squarish markings along the back.
Foodplants. Blackthorn and hawthorn.
Habits. Single-brooded, occurring in the larval stage from about early April to late May. The larvae are often obtained by beating and are easy to rear in captivity. The pupa is formed just under the soil or in among leaf litter inside a loose cocoon and lasts until the following January or February. The adult females are almost wingless and can be found resting on the bare twigs after dark; they usually lay eggs freely in confinement. Widely distributed throughout England, Wales and the northern parts of Ireland, more local in southern Scotland.
Plate 24: M. Beaten from blackthorn, fully grown. Mid-May.

Light Emerald
Campaea margaritata Linnaeus
Larva. 36–40 mm. Body usually greyish-brown, but sometimes greenish, with a distinguishing fringe of hair-like structures all along the lower parts; the eighth segment has a rudimentary pair of legs.
Foodplants. Birch, beech, oak, elm, hawthorn and other deciduous trees.
Habits. Generally a single-brooded species, with a partial second generation occurring in southern England. The larval stage lasts from late August to the following late May, overwintering exposed on the foodplant. Sometimes the brood from earlier emerging adults feed up quickly during late July and early August to produce more moths in late August and September. They can readily be beaten during the spring and are not difficult to rear. The cocooned pupa is formed in plant litter and lasts about a month. Both sexes of the adult come to light traps and females will often deposit eggs in good numbers on foodplant leaves. Breeding from this method is most successful when the larvae are sleeved outside on growing plant. A usually common woodland species distributed throughout most of the British Isles.
Plate 24: N. Beaten from birch, nearly fully grown. Early May.

Barred Red
Hylaea fasciaria Linnaeus
Larva. 30–34 mm. Body greyish, with brown mottlings and

paler markings dorsally, also pairs of small raised wart-like structures along the back.
Foodplants. Scots pine, Douglas fir, Norway spruce and other conifers.
Habits. Single-brooded, being in the larval stage from about early September until the following late May, overwintering on the foodplant while still quite small. During the spring the larvae can be beaten, especially from the boughs of more mature conifers growing along the edges of woodland rides or on open heathland. At this point of their development they are easy to rear, but are more difficult to breed from the egg as they take a long time to grow and need to be sleeved outside in natural conditions for the winter. Pupation takes place in plant litter and lasts from three to six weeks depending on the temperature, with the light-responsive adults emerging from mid-June to early August. Generally distributed and fairly common throughout much of the British Isles.
Plate 24: O. Beaten from Scots pine, fully grown. Late May.

Irish Annulet
Odontognophos dumetata Treitschke
Larva. 27–30 mm. Body brownish-grey, with an incomplete black dorsal line that is modified into triangular-shaped blotches, edged posteriorly with pale yellow, on the fourth to seventh segments; head greyish, heavily freckled with black.
Foodplant. Buckthorn.
Habits. A recently discovered single-brooded species that occurs in the larval stage from April to mid-June, after overwintering as an egg. The larvae may be obtained by careful searching of the lower parts of the foodplant during the day and are not difficult to rear in captivity, pupating for about four to six weeks in a silken cocoon. The adults fly in August and are attracted to light. The Burren district in western Ireland is the only place from which the species has been recorded.
Plate 24: P. Located on foodplant, almost fully grown. Early June. (BS)

Scotch Annulet
Gnophos obfuscata Denis & Schiffermüller
(*myrtillata* Thunberg)
Larva. 24–26 mm. Body shades of grey, lighter on the underparts, variably marked with darker on the dorsal area. The spiracles are black and there is often a brownish tinge between them, also a pair of small raised structures dorsally on the eleventh segment.
Foodplants. Heather, heath, dyer's greenweed, saxifrage, stonecrop and other herbaceous plants.
Habits. A single-brooded insect, occurring in the larval stage from late August to early June, overwintering when about half grown. The larvae can be taken, usually in small numbers, by sweeping the foodplants at night during the spring. They are also frequently found when shaking and tapping saxifrage and stonecrop over small trays, when attempting to obtain larvae of *E. flavicinctata*, in the rocky gullies and quarries of central Scotland. In July both sexes of the adult come to light, and the females lay readily in confinement on picked foodplant, but rearing from the egg is a long and laborious task unless the larvae can be left upon potted plants to develop naturally. Larvae collected after hibernation seem to thrive well and pupate among plant litter for about a month. Local, but widespread, in central and northern Scotland and parts of western Ireland.
Plate 24: Q. Tapped from hanging saxifrage, fully grown. Late May. (BS)

The Annulet
Gnophos obscurata Denis & Schiffermüller
Larva. 22–25 mm. Body grey or brown, with variable amounts of paler V-shaped markings dorsally, obvious black spiracles and black-marked twin structures on the top of the eleventh segment.
Foodplants. Heather, trefoils, common rock-rose, cinquefoil and other herbaceous plants; also in captivity garden strawberry.
Habits. Single-brooded, being in the larval stage from September to the following late May, overwintering when still small, probably feeding when the weather is mild. The larvae are most successfully obtained by sweeping or finding them during the spring, as the species is usually difficult to bring through the winter in captivity. Pupation takes place in a cocoon formed just under the soil or in plant litter and lasts about six weeks. A mainly coastal insect occurring all round the British Isles and also on downs and heathland in southern parts of England and Wales.
Plate 24: R. Bred from a female adult to MVL. Early August. (JR)

Black Mountain Moth
Psodos coracina Esper
Larva. 15–18 mm. Body grey, with black chevrons dorsally on segments four to seven, a reddish-brown subdorsal line and wavy black marks above the pale lateral line; head reddish-brown.
Foodplants. Crowberry and possibly cowberry, bilberry and heather.
Habits. It is probable that this species has a two-year life-cycle, due to the fact that the adults occur in much greater numbers during odd-numbered years. The first winter is almost certainly spent as a small larva and the second could be either as a nearly fully grown caterpillar or even a pupa; most likely the former, although Seitz states the second winter is passed in the pupal stage. The larvae have been found during May under reindeer moss on the mountain tops in central Scotland. The adults emerge during June and July and on sunny days the males fly and the females can be found crawling over the rocks and lichens. Eggs are laid freely and sometimes larvae can be forced to develop faster by keeping them fairly warm although they rarely survive to pupate.
Plate 25: A. Bred from a netted female adult. Mid-July. (DB)

Black-veined Moth
Siona lineata Scopoli
Larva. 36–40 mm. Body ochreous, with a darker dorsal line and variable amounts of black speckling on the back.
Foodplants. Probably marjoram; will accept knotgrass, dock, bird's-foot trefoil and chickweed in captivity.
Habits. Single-brooded, with the larvae occurring from July to the following May. The adults fly from late May to early July and the day-flying females have been observed laying eggs upon marjoram, bird's-foot trefoil and the blades of tor-grass in the wild. Captured females will readily lay eggs in captivity, with the larvae thriving on knotgrass and developing quickly if kept warm, to pupate in a spindle-shaped cocoon after about three months. If to be reared naturally, introducing the larvae to a mixture of marjoram and tor-grass in a large plant pot can be successful. They become dormant in the autumn, when about half grown, and recommence feeding when the temperature becomes sufficiently warm during the spring. An extremely local species, being

known from only a couple of localities in Kent. It is protected from collecting by law.
Plate 25: B. Bred from a netted female adult (S. E. France). Early July.

Straw Belle
Aspitates gilvaria Denis & Schiffermüller
Larva. 28–30 mm. Body ochreous to greyish-ochreous, with a few tiny black dots, a darker dorsal line and a whitish line along the spiracles; there are two obvious anal points.
Foodplants. Thyme, cinquefoil, wild parsnip and other herbaceous plants, accepting knotgrass readily in captivity.
Habits. A single-brooded species, being in the larval stage from September to the following June, overwintering when still very small. During July and August the adults are readily disturbed from the herbage on warm days, and the females will often lay eggs on foodplant in captivity. If the larvae are kept warm and in the dark they will grow rapidly, pupating in a flimsy spinning after about two months. In the wild the larvae hibernate while small and most of their development does not take place until the spring plant growth has increased and the weather is warmer. A very local insect confined to the downs of Surrey and Kent and also occurring in good numbers in parts of western Ireland.
Plate 25: C. Bred from a netted female adult. Early August. (MC-H)

Yellow Belle
Aspitates ochrearia Rossi
Larva. 28–30 mm. Body ochreous, greyish or pale brown, with a darker dorsal line, and thin paler lines in the subdorsal and spiracular regions; there are a pair of short anal points.
Foodplants. Wild carrot, restharrow, toadflax, plantains and other low-growing plants. In captivity it thrives on knotgrass.
Habits. A double-brooded insect, with the larvae occurring from September to May, and again from late June to early August. They can readily be collected by sweeping and can be distinguished by the way they roll in on themselves when alarmed. Rearing them in captivity is usually very easy and the pupa is formed in a loose cocoon on the foodplant or in plant litter. Eggs can be obtained from adult females, which are not difficult to find resting, wings closed, upon grass stems and herbage after dark. Locally common, mainly on the coast, in southern England and South Wales. There are also inland colonies in the Breckland of Norfolk and Suffolk.
Plate 25: D. Swept at night. Late April. (SHC)

Grey Scalloped Bar
Dyscia fagaria Thunberg
Larva. 30–35 mm. Body greyish-brown, mottled with reddish-brown and whitish, with a distinct dark-brown horn on the eleventh segment and small paired wart-like structures on the seventh to ninth rings dorsally.
Foodplants. Heather and heaths.
Habits. Single-brooded, occurring in the larval stage from about July to the following May, overwintering when small and feeding up rapidly in the spring. The best method to find the larvae is by sweeping during April and early May, especially at night when they are more active and are higher up on the foodplant. The cocooned pupa is formed in plant litter and lasts around three weeks. From late May to July adult females can be found at night at rest on heather, and any stocks obtained from their eggs are best put on to potted plants and left to develop naturally. Widely distributed on heath and moorland over much of Britain and Ireland.
Plate 25: E. Swept at night, fully grown. Late April. (MB)

Grass Wave
Perconia strigillaria Hübner
Larva. 32–36 mm. Body shades of brown or grey, with lighter and darker mottling and distinct twin wart-like structures on the fifth to eighth segments, those on the eighth being the most prominent.
Foodplants. Heather, heath, broom and the flowers of gorse.
Habits. A single-brooded insect, being in the larval stage from August to the following late May, overwintering when still small. Where it occurs in southern England, this will often be the commonest species taken in the sweep net during the spring, and larvae collected at this time of year are easy to rear in confinement, but frequently parasitized. In June and July adults can be disturbed by day or found from dusk onwards, and females lay readily. Breeding from the egg is a long process and best done by leaving the larvae outside on a potted heather plant. The best localities are on heathland in south-east England, but the species also occurs elsewhere in England, Wales, Ireland and southern Scotland.
Plate 25: F. Swept from heather, fully grown. Mid-May.

Family: SPHINGIDAE

Mainly, the larvae of this popular family of moths are to be distinguished by the presence of the horn that is situated dorsally on the eleventh segment. Britain has nine residents, two regular migrants and seven species that occur as rare immigrants or vagrants. The larvae of most species are usually very easy to rear in confinement and most overwinter as pupae on or in the ground. The adults fly at night and are strongly attracted to light, except for the genera *Macroglossum* and *Hemaris* which are active in sunshine, and the eggs are mainly laid singly or in pairs upon the leaves of the foodplant.

SUBFAMILY: SPHINGINAE

Convolvulus Hawk-moth
Agrius convolvuli Linnaeus
Larva. 90–105 mm. Body brown or sometimes green, mottled with black, and having oblique yellowish lateral stripes and a curved black horn on the top of the eleventh segment; spiracles large and black. Bright green in the earlier instars.
Foodplants. Field bindweed and allied plants.
Habits. A regular migrant species, occurring more commonly in the southern coastal counties, with the adults flying from June to November, and frequently being taken by light-trapping. Although many adults will be females, they often have a reluctance to lay in captivity, and the larvae are rarely met with in the wild in Britain. If eggs are obtained, these and the larvae should be kept in a warm environment and rearing them is fairly easy, with the growth being rapid. The pupa has a long curled proboscis sheath and is formed in the soil, lasting about three to six weeks given continued warmth.
Plate 25: G. Bred from a female adult to MVL. Early September. (DB)

Death's-head Hawk-moth
Acherontia atropos Linnaeus
Larva. 100–125 mm. Body yellow, yellowish-green or brown, with purplish-grey oblique lateral stripes and a small yellow or brown granulose horn dorsally on the eleventh segment.
Foodplants. Potato and other species of *Solanaceae*, also accepting privet and ash in captivity.
Habits. A fairly regular, but uncommon, migrant to the British Isles, with the adults occurring from about May to September. The huge larvae are more often found by chance in allotments and potato fields from August to October, and deliberately searching for them is usually unproductive. In captivity they are fairly easy to rear if kept warm, and are a popular species with commercial breeders. Pupation takes place under the soil and lasts about a month to six weeks.
Plate 25: H. Bred from commercial stock.

Privet Hawk-moth
Sphinx ligustri Linnaeus
Larva. 70–85 mm. Body bright green, with purple-edged white oblique stripes laterally and a mainly black curved horn on the eleventh segment.
Foodplants. Privet, ash and lilac.
Habits. A single-brooded resident species that occurs in the larval stage from July to September. The larvae can be obtained by light-trapping female adults in June and July; they lay readily in captivity and the larvae are usually very easy to rear. Larger larvae can also be located in the wild by looking for the insect's droppings beneath privet and lilac bushes on suburban pavements. The shining brown pupa is formed deep in the soil and possesses a short proboscis sheath, and it may overwinter more than once before emergence. Generally distributed, especially on calcareous soils and in towns, over much of southern England and in Wales.
Plate 25: I. Bred from a female adult to MVL. Late June. (SHC)

Pine Hawk-moth
Hyloicus pinastri Linnaeus
Larva. 70–80 mm. Body dorsally and ventrally reddish-brown, heavily marked with white and dark brown on the back and sides and dark green also on the sides. The horn is dark brown to black and the head orange-brown. The earlier instars are green, striped with white.
Foodplant. Scots pine.
Habits. Single-brooded, being in the larval stage from about late June to mid-September. The larvae have been obtained by beating the branches of mature pines. From May to July the adults regularly come to light and the females will freely deposit eggs in confinement. The larvae are usually easy to rear, but some broods do fail due to viruses. The foodplant should not be put in water as this is said to be fatal to the larvae. The pupa is formed below the fallen pine-needles or just under the soil and lasts throughout the winter. This species is mainly to be found in the pine woods of Dorset, Hampshire, Surrey, West Sussex and East Anglia.
Plate 25: J. Bred from a female adult to MVL. Mid-June. (SHC)

Lime Hawk-moth
Mimas tiliae Linnaeus
Larva. 60–65 mm. Body yellowish-green dorsally and bluish-green on the sides, with oblique yellow lateral stripes and a slightly curved blue horn that is coloured pale yellow and red beneath; the green triangular head is marked with white stripes.
Foodplants. Birch, lime, English elm and alder.
Habits. A single-brooded species, being found as a larva from about late June to early September. The adults of this insect can readily be obtained by light-trapping and are often found at rest on trunks and fences by day from May to July. Most females will lay eggs freely and birch or elm are the better plants to rear the larvae on in captivity, as they last longer and the larval frass is less messy. Just prior to pupation, the larva changes to a dull purplish and orange colour and leaves the host tree to burrow into the soil beneath. During the winter months these pupae can be found in good numbers just under the soil. Inhabiting parks, gardens and woodland, this species is widely distributed in southern England.
Plate 25: K. Bred from a female adult to MVL. Early June.

Eyed Hawk-moth
Smerinthus ocellata Linnaeus
Larva. 65–75 mm. Body bluish-green, with whitish oblique stripes laterally, large red spiracles and a blue horn.
Foodplants. Sallow, willow, apple, aspen and rarely poplar.
Habits. Single-brooded, occurring as a larva from about late June to September, feeding mainly at night. The larvae can be found by careful searching, especially when they are larger and are stripping the leaves from branches of the foodplant. They can also be obtained, in larger numbers, by light-trapping female adults which fly from early May to mid-July. Eggs should be laid freely if the moth is kept in a netting cage or even a paper bag. It is an easy species to rear in confinement and the subterranean pupa, that lasts throughout the winter, can sometimes be located at the base of the foodplant. Generally distributed over much of England and Wales; also recorded from Ireland.
Plate 25: L. Bred from a female adult to MVL. Late June. (RM)

Poplar Hawk-moth
Laothoe populi Linnaeus
Larva. 60–70 mm. Body yellowish-green, with yellow oblique lateral stripes, red-brown spiracles and a yellow horn.
Foodplants. Sallow, poplar, aspen and willow.
Habits. Mainly a single-brooded insect, being in the larval stage from June to September. The larvae can be located on the foodplant and are easy to rear in captivity, eventually pupating under the soil for overwintering, although a few may emerge the same year to produce a small second generation. The adults fly from May to July, and later, and respond well to light, with the females laying freely in captivity. The pupae can be obtained, sometimes commonly, from the soil beneath foodplant trunks during the winter months. Widely distributed over most of the British Isles.
Plate 25: M. Found on sallow, about half grown. Late July.

SUBFAMILY: MACROGLOSSINAE

Narrow-bordered Bee Hawk-moth
Hemaris tityus Linnaeus
Larva. 38–45 mm. Body green, with brown lateral blotches, brown dorsal marks and a purplish-brown horn.
Foodplant. Devil's-bit scabious.
Habits. The larvae of this single-brooded, day-flying species may be obtained by close searching of the foodplant from late June to about mid-August. They live on the underside of the leaves and sometimes betray their presence by eating

out small round holes which can be observed from above. Once located they are usually fairly easy to rear, especially if kept on potted foodplant. The pupa is formed in a flimsy cocoon just under the soil and lasts throughout the winter. The adults fly from mid-May to mid-June in sunshine and eggs may be obtained from females by sleeving them over foodplants and supplying nectar-bearing flowers, such as bugle and red valerian. An extremely local species being found in woodland rides, marshes and wet moorland over many parts of the British Isles.
Plate 25: N. Located on foodplant, nearly fully grown. Late July. (RGC)

Broad-bordered Bee Hawk-moth

Hemaris fuciformis Linnaeus
Larva. 45–53 mm. Body green, with tiny yellow warts, brown-ringed orange spiracles and a greyish-brown horn; underparts brown.
Foodplant. Honeysuckle.
Habits. Single-brooded, occurring as a larva from about late June to the middle of August. The larvae can be found by searching the foodplant, looking especially for the tell-tale small round holes which often indicate signs of feeding by this species, when smaller. In captivity the larvae are fairly easy to rear, pupating for the winter just under the soil. In May and June the adults fly in sunshine and captured females may deposit eggs on sleeved foodplant, if supplied with flowers for feeding. A second generation has been known during August in exceptionally hot summers. Widespread, but local, in open woodland over much of southern England; also recorded in South Wales.
Plate 25: O. Found on trailing foodplant, about half grown. Mid-July. (AJ)

Humming-bird Hawk-moth

Macroglossum stellatarum Linnaeus
Larva. 60–65 mm. Body green or brown, with tiny white warts, a whitish subdorsal line, yellow subspiracular stripe and a brown-tipped black horn on the eleventh segment.
Foodplants. Hedge bedstraw, lady's bedstraw, wild madder and probably other related plants.
Habits. A regular migrant species that overwinters as an adult, but probably not in this country. Its arrival usually begins in the spring with the resulting larvae being found from June until the autumn, with the peak often occurring during August. When larger they feed mostly at night and can be found by searching with a torch on the clumps of foodplant, especially on the south coast where the insects occur most frequently. They are easy to rear in captivity and keeping the pupae warm should result in the adults emerging in about four weeks. It is a day-flying species, often seen hovering over red valerian and buddleia on warm sunny days. Captured females will often deposit eggs if given sunshine, space, foodplant and flowers, but the green eggs can be difficult to see among the flowers and buds of the bedstraw.
Plate 25: P. Bred from a netted female adult. Late July. (AH)

Willowherb Hawk-moth

Proserpinus proserpina Pallas
Larva. 50–60 mm. Body pale grey, with heavy brown mottling along the dorsal area and red spiracles enclosed by bold black blotches; caudial horn absent, being replaced by a small yellow ring; head blackish.
Foodplants. Willowherbs, evening primrose and purple loosestrife.
Habits. A single-brooded species that has occurred as an adult in Britain on two occasions, in May 1985 and July 1995. Abroad it inhabits waste ground in central Europe, ranging as far north as the Ardennes, overwintering in the pupal stage.
Plate 49: A. Courtesy of Per Stadel Nielsen.

Oleander Hawk-moth

Daphnis nerii Linnaeus
Larva. 90–110 mm. Body yellowish-green, with a blue-bordered white subdorsal line, a large white blotch on the thoracic segments laterally and a fleshy yellow horn. A brown form also occurs.
Foodplants. Oleander and periwinkle, also accepting privet in captivity.
Habits. A very infrequent migrant species, being absent in most years. The early stages have never been found in the British Isles and most of the adult records have occurred between August and October, at light. This insect is sometimes bred in commercial butterfly-houses, because of its size and bright colours, and livestock sometimes becomes available to enthusiasts. Naturally distributed mainly in North Africa and Asia.
Plate 25: Q. From commercial stock.

Spurge Hawk-moth

Hyles euphorbiae Linnaeus
Larva. 70–85 mm. Body shining black, with a red head and broad dorsal line and pairs of large cream blotches along the sides; the horn is red, tipped with black.
Foodplants. Various species of spurge.
Habits. A very uncommon migrant species, flying mainly in June, that was reported as breeding in the British Isles several times during the last century. It is a common species in central and southern Europe and very occasionally migrates to this country, there being only a few records in the last twenty years. The larval stage lasts about two months, usually from late May to August, and the species overwinters as a pupa in the soil. Most years livestock is freely available from dealers and it is a popular insect with the breeders.
Plate 25: R. Found by day on foodplant (Switzerland). Mid-July. (MG-P)

Bedstraw Hawk-moth

Hyles gallii Rottemburg
Larva. 70–80 mm. Body dark olive-green, with conspicuous cream lateral spots, a red-brown head and dorsal line; the horn is reddish. An almost black form also occurs.
Foodplants. Bedstraw, willowherb and *Godetia*; also stated to accept *Fuchsia*.
Habits. A fairly regular migrant species that occasionally breeds in Britain. Most records tend to come from the eastern counties, and many larvae were found in Norfolk between 1955 and 1958 and in southern England in 1973. The adults usually occur between May and August, most frequently in light traps, and captive females will often lay in confinement. Rearing the larvae is usually easy, and they can be searched for in the wild from July to September, with the best chance being in coastal localities. Overwintering is in the pupal stage just under the soil. This species has become temporarily established in the past and hopefully will do so in the future.
Plate 26: A. Bred from a female adult to MVL. Early July. (SC)

Striped Hawk-moth

Hyles livornica Esper
(*lineata* Fabricius)
Larva. 80–95 mm. Body green to almost black, with yellowish-green dorsal and subdorsal lines, darker banding, a greenish head; the red or orange horn is tipped with black.
Foodplants. Bedstraw, knotgrass, snapdragon, dock, *Fuchsia* and grape-vine.
Habits. A frequent migrant species that sometimes occurs in good numbers, such as in 1943 when over 540 were found all over Britain. Most years the records are only a handful, mainly on the south coast and the larvae seem to be found only in the better years. The adults fly in May and June, coming to light. There is a partial second generation in August. Any larvae should be looked for during June and July and again in the autumn. Rearing them in captivity is not difficult and pupae kept warm will often emerge after about four to five weeks, with those in the wild overwintering.
Plate 26: B. Bred from continental stock (Spain). (AJ)

Elephant Hawk-moth

Deilephila elpenor Linnaeus
Larva. 80–85 mm. Body green or brown, heavily speckled with grey and with distinctive black and pinkish eye-spots on the fourth and fifth segments laterally; the small horn is black with a pale tip.
Foodplants. Willowherb and bedstraw, also *Fuchsia* and other plants.
Habits. Mainly a single-brooded species, sometimes with a small second generation, being found in the larval state from about late June to September. When larger the larvae can readily be found when feeding at night, while during the day they usually hide among the lower herbage. Both sexes come freely to light from May to July, and the females will often lay eggs, if kept in a cage and supplied with foodplant. Rearing this species is considered easy and the pupa is formed beneath the soil for overwintering. Generally distributed over most of England, Wales and Ireland; local in south and west Scotland.
Plate 26: C. Bred from a female adult to MVL. Mid-July. (GAC)

Small Elephant Hawk-moth

Deilephila porcellus Linnaeus
Larva. 50–55 mm. Body greyish-brown, sometimes green, lightly speckled with dark brown or black and having a distinct pink and black eye-spot laterally on the fourth segment and a smaller one on the following ring; the horn is rudimentary, almost absent.
Foodplants. Bedstraw; has been recorded on willowherb and purple loosestrife.
Habits. Single-brooded, occurring as a larva from late June to early September, feeding mainly at night and hiding by day among the lower herbage. The larger larvae can be located by torchlight, especially on downland and golf courses, where the cover is often sparse. From May to July the adults come readily to light and most females willingly lay in captivity. Rearing the larva requires no special conditions and the pupa is formed just under the soil for overwintering. Widespread on open ground over much of the British Isles, being more frequent in the south.
Plate 26: D. Bred from a female adult to MVL. Early June. (RM)

Silver-striped Hawk-moth

Hippotion celerio Linnaeus
Larva. 70–75 mm. Body grey, green or brown, variably speckled with black and having a pale yellow and black eye-spot laterally on the fourth ring and a smaller yellowish spot on the next segment. The thoracic parts have a pale subdorsal line and the horn is dark brown or black.
Foodplants. Bedstraw, willowherb, *Fuchsia*, Virginia creeper and grape-vine.
Habits. An uncommon immigrant species that usually occurs sparingly in most years. The adults can arrive as early as May, but most records are from August onwards. They are attracted to light and flowering plants, and the females can be enticed to lay eggs by giving them space, warmth and foodplants. The larvae can be bred more rapidly if kept warm and they pupate on or under the ground in a slight cocoon. It would not be practical to deliberately search for the larvae of this species in Britain due to their rarity, but those that have been found have mostly occurred in October.
Plate 26: E. Bred from a female adult to MVL. September. (SHC)

Family: NOTODONTIDAE

This family is represented in the British Isles by over twenty regularly found resident species. Most of the larvae are easy to rear in captivity and those of the *Cerura*, *Furcula* and *Stauropus* genera are strange-looking creatures having their anal claspers modified into appendages. The adults are nocturnal, with the males being freely attracted to light traps, although the females of some species can rarely be obtained by this method. The pupae are formed in a cocoon, either under the soil or on the bark of trees.

Buff-tip

Phalera bucephala Linnaeus
Larva. 65–75 mm. Body black and yellow, with a shining yellow-marked black head, grey and yellow stripes and abundant greyish setae.
Foodplants. Oak, sallow, lime, elm and many other deciduous trees.
Habits. A single-brooded species that occurs in the larval stage from about mid-July to early October and later. The eggs are laid in batches under the leaves and the larvae are gregarious until the final instar, sometimes totally stripping the leaves from the branches. They can readily be obtained by beating and are very easy to rear in confinement. From late May to late July, both sexes of the adults come to light, usually after midnight, and the females need no encouragement to deposit their eggs. The pupa is formed under the soil and can be dug from the bases of the foodplant trees during the winter months. This woodland and waste ground species is usually common and generally distributed over most of the British Isles.
Plate 26: F. Beaten from hazel, fully grown. Mid-September. (SHC)

Puss Moth

Cerura vinula Linnaeus
Larva. 60–65 mm. Body bright green, with a purplish-brown saddle-shaped dorsal marking that is clearly edged with white; the anal claspers are modified into a pair of long thin structures from which red whip-like flagellae extrude when alarmed.

Foodplants. Sallow, willow, aspen and poplar.
Habits. Single-brooded, being in the larval state from about early June to September. The early stages of this insect can easily be located by searching the upperside of the leaves for the reddish-brown hemispherical eggs, usually laid in pairs, or the empty shells, in which case the larvae should be nearby. The adults are attracted to light from May to July, and most females deposit eggs readily. Rearing this species is not difficult, but overcrowding should be avoided. When the larvae turn purplish, prior to pupation, they should be supplied with bark, cork or corrugated cardboard so they can form their tough cocoons, constructed by mixing their silk with the chewed wood, for overwintering. Widespread, but less common than in the past, over much of Britain and Ireland.
Plate 26: G. Found in the egg stage. Mid-June.

Alder Kitten

Furcula bicuspis Borkhausen
Larva. 33–37 mm. Body bright green, with a reddish-brown saddle-shaped dorsal marking that is edged with yellowish-white and extends to the spiracle on the seventh segment and half-way on the sixth ring; the anal claspers are modified into long thin structures.
Foodplants. Birch and alder.
Habits. A single-brooded species that occurs in the larval stage from about late June to late August, sometimes later. It can be searched for as an egg, purplish, laid in pairs on the top side of the leaves, or as a larva. The larvae's grip is quite strong and they are difficult to beat. It is not an easy species to rear, many broods failing due to viruses, and the best method seems to be to avoid overcrowding and sleeve them out on birch or keep on stems in water. Although the male adults come readily to light in late May and June, the females are less responsive, but they do lay freely in captivity. Bark or cork should be supplied for pupation, as the larvae use these for constructing the cocoons in which they overwinter. In the wild these can be found on the stems and trunks of the foodplants, but they are difficult to detect. A local woodland insect, being mainly found in south-east and south-west England, the West Midlands, Norfolk and south-east and central Wales.
Plate 26: H. Bred from a female to MVL. Mid-June. (AJ)

Sallow Kitten

Furcula furcula Clerck
Larva. 32–35 mm. Body bright green, with a purplish-brown saddle-shaped dorsal mark that is edged and mottled with yellow; anal claspers modified into long thin appendages.
Foodplants. Sallow, willow and sometimes aspen and poplar.
Habits. Mainly a double-brooded species, being in the larval stage in June and July, and again from late August to late September, except in Scotland and Ireland where it is single-brooded and larvae feed during July and August. This is the commonest of the Kittens and it can be found by locating the dark purple eggs, laid in pairs on the upperside of the leaf, or by searching carefully for the larvae. In May and June, also during August, the adults come freely to light and breeding this insect in captivity is usually easy, as long as the larvae are not too overcrowded. Pupation requirements are identical to others in this genus: supplying bark or a similar wood material for the construction of the tough cocoon. Generally distributed over much of the British Isles.
Plate 26: I. Bred from a female adult to MVL. Late May.

Poplar Kitten

Furcula bifida Brahm
Larva. 34–38 mm. Body bright green, with a brown saddle-shaped dorsal marking that extends to the sides on the sixth and seventh segments and is edged with yellowish-white; the anal claspers are modified into long thin structures.
Foodplants. Aspen and poplar; also recorded on sallow.
Habits. A single-brooded insect that can be found as a larva from about late June to mid-September. Searching for the purplish-black eggs laid upon the upperside of the foodplant leaves can be a successful method of obtaining this species and the empty shells could mean larvae nearby. From late May to July both sexes will come to light, and the females usually lay readily in captivity. The larvae are fairly easy to rear if not overcrowded and should be given bark to make their silk and wood cocoons for overwintering. A declining species, found most often in the south of England, but also distributed throughout most of England and eastern parts of Wales.
Plate 26: J. Bred from a female adult to MVL. Early June. (DB)

Lobster Moth

Stauropus fagi Linnaeus
Larva. 55–65 mm. Body reddish-brown, with a large head, long thoracic legs, raised humps on the fourth to seventh segments and a greatly swollen anal segment that has the claspers modified into long thin structures. The young larvae could be described as ant-like in appearance.
Foodplants. Beech, oak, birch and hazel.
Habits. Single-brooded, occurring as a larva from about late June to September. The larvae can be beaten when small and are not too difficult to rear in captivity. Between May and July the adults come readily to light and the females usually deposit eggs freely. After hatching the young larvae spend several days feeding solely upon their empty eggshells and must not be disturbed during this period; later they are especially vulnerable to interference when changing their skins. Sleeving the larvae upon a growing foodplant is the best method for successful rearing and they pupate for overwintering in a cocoon spun up among the leaves. Widely distributed, in mature woods, over most of southern England and parts of Wales; also recorded from south-west Ireland.
Plate 26: K. Bred from a female adult to MVL. Late June. (SHC)

Iron Prominent

Notodonta dromedarius Linnaeus
Larva. 35–38 mm. Body green, with a brown dorsal stripe on the first to seventh segments and raised humps on the fourth to seventh and eleventh segments; subspiracular line pale yellow and the head speckled with brown.
Foodplants. Birch, alder, oak and hazel.
Habits. Generally a double-brooded species, except for some northern populations which are univoltine. The larvae can readily be beaten from their foodplants from about mid-June to late July and again in September and early October, and mainly in August in the north. The adults come to light in May, June and August, and females usually lay eggs freely in confinement. This insect is easy to rear with no special conditions being necessary and pupation for overwintering takes place under the soil in a slight cocoon. Widely distributed, mainly in woodland and on heaths, over most of the British Isles.
Plate 26: L. Beaten from birch, fully grown. Late September.

Large Dark Prominent
Notodonta torva Hübner
Larva. 38–43 mm. Body grey, brown on the rearmost segments, with the darker dorsal stripe more obvious on the first seven segments and having raised structures dorsally on the fifth, sixth and eleventh rings; head pale grey with dark speckling.
Foodplants. Aspen, poplar and birch.
Habits. This double-brooded species has been recorded twice in the British Isles. The first one, in 1882, was found as an egg or larva in Norfolk and the second was an adult attracted to light in Sussex in 1979. On the continent the larvae occur during July and again in late August and September, before overwintering as pupae. The adults fly mainly in May and August.
Plate 49: B. Courtesy of Per Stadel Nielsen.

Three-humped Prominent
Tritophia tritophus Denis & Schiffermüller
(*phoebe* Siebert)
Larva. 35–40 mm. Body green, brownish-green or grey, with paler dorsal and lateral lines; rearward-facing humps on the sixth to eighth segments and another hump, directed forwards, at the end of the body; head as body colour with darker speckling.
Foodplants. Aspen and poplar.
Habits. A very infrequent immigrant species that is double-brooded on the continent, with the larvae occurring in June and September, overwintering as a cocooned pupa in the soil. Larvae are reported to have been found in the last century and since 1900 there have been seven records of adults, mostly at light, with the most recent being in 1992.
Plate 49: C. Courtesy of Per Stadel Nielsen.

Pebble Prominent
Eligmodonta ziczac Linnaeus
Larva. 35–40 mm. Body grey, with a brown dorsal stripe on the first to seventh segments and raised structures on the sixth, seventh and eleventh rings. There is often an orangish patch laterally on the last few abdominal segments.
Foodplants. Sallow, poplar, aspen and willow.
Habits. Mostly double-brooded, occurring as a larva in June and July, and from late August and throughout September, except in the north where the univoltine population is in this stage during July and August. The larvae can be obtained by beating and are usually very easy to rear in confinement, pupating underground for the winter when necessary. The adults are attracted to light during May and June, also again in August, and the females often lay freely without any persuasion. Widespread and fairly common over most of Britain.
Plate 26: M. Found in the egg stage. Late May.

Tawny Prominent
Harpyia milhauseri Fabricius
Larva. 35–40 mm. Body green, speckled with tiny pale green dots and a yellow dorsal stripe on the thoracic rings, a forked structure on the humped fourth segment and other smaller similar structures on the fifth to eighth and eleventh rings; laterally, a brown marking on the seventh and eighth rings; head pale brown.
Foodplants. Oak, holm oak and sometimes beech.
Habits. A single-brooded immigrant species that has been recorded twice as an adult in southern Britain. On the continent the larvae occur from late June to the middle of August and overwinter as cocooned pupae behind bark or in crevices, with the adults flying in the following May and June.
Plate 26: N. Bred from a female adult to MVL (France). Early June. (PQW)

Great Prominent
Peridea anceps Goeze
(*trepida* Esper)
Larva. 40–45 mm. Body green, with oblique red-edged yellow lateral stripes, thin broken yellow dorsal lines and a glassy green head that has an obvious brown line on the sides.
Foodplant. Oak.
Habits. A single-brooded species that exists in the larval state from about late May to early August. The larvae can sometimes be beaten, but rarely in any numbers, suggesting that they feed in the canopy of the trees. From late April to the middle of June the adult males are strongly attracted to light, the females less so, although most lay freely if required. It is not a difficult species to rear and the insects pupate well into the soil for overwintering. An inhabitant of mature oak woods, widely distributed in southern England and parts of Wales; also found locally in the Lake District and western parts of Scotland.
Plate 26: O. Bred from a female adult to MVL. Mid-May.

Lesser Swallow Prominent
Pheosia gnoma Fabricius
Larva. 34–37 mm. Body glossy purplish-brown, with a bold yellow spiracular stripe and an obvious hump on the eleventh segment.
Foodplants. Birch, and has been known to accept sallow in captivity.
Habits. A double-brooded species that can readily be beaten during June and July, and again from late August and throughout September. The adults respond well to light, with many of them being females, and these should readily lay eggs on the top of supplied birch leaves, if breeding is required. The larvae can be easy to rear, as long as they are not too overcrowded and are given fresh food. Winter is spent as a pupa, spun up in a firm cocoon under the soil. Generally distributed and fairly common over most of the British Isles.
Plate 26: P. Bred from a female adult to MVL. Mid-May. (SHC)

Swallow Prominent
Pheosia tremula Clerck
Larva. 36–40 mm. Body green, with a broad yellow spiracular line or light brownish-green, ringed with reddish-brown; there is a humped structure on the eleventh segment.
Foodplants. Sallow, aspen, poplar and willow.
Habits. Double-brooded in the south, with the larvae occurring from June to mid-July and again in September, and during July and August in the north, where the insect is single-brooded. The larvae can be taken by beating and larger stocks can be obtained by light-trapping the adult females in May and June, and later in August. These often lay freely in captivity and the larvae are usually fairly easy to rear. The cocooned pupae are formed under the soil, for overwintering when necessary. Widespread over most of Britain and Ireland.
Plate 26: Q. Bred from a female adult to MVL. Early August.

Coxcomb Prominent
Ptilodon capucina Linnaeus
Larva. 33–36 mm. Body bright green, with a pair of red

conical structures on the top of the eleventh segment and a yellow spiracular line.
Foodplants. Oak, birch, sallow, hazel and many other deciduous trees.
Habits. A double-brooded insect, being in the larval stage during June and July and again from mid-August to about late September. The larvae can readily be collected by beating and the adults fly from early May to June and also in August, with both sexes being attracted by light. Rearing this species in captivity is very easy, with the subterranean cocooned pupa lasting through the winter. Generally distributed over most parts of the British Isles.
Plate 26: R. Beaten from sallow, about half grown. Early September.

Maple Prominent

Ptilodontella cucullina Denis & Schiffermüller
Larva. 30–34 mm. Body bright green, with a darker dorsal line that is broadest on the thoracic segments and a humped structure on the eleventh segment that is tipped with brown. A brown form of the larva sometimes occurs.
Foodplants. Field maple, and may accept sycamore in captivity.
Habits. Single-brooded, occurring as a larva from about late June to late August, which can readily be taken by beating. The adults fly from mid-May to late July, but the females are usually scarce at light. When taken these often lay eggs in confinement and rearing the larvae is not difficult as long as the food is kept fresh. Pupation for the winter months takes place in leaf litter or just under the soil in a flimsy cocoon. To be found mainly on calcareous soils in the south and south-eastern counties of England and in East Anglia.
Plate 27: A. Beaten from field maple, nearly fully grown. Late July.

Scarce Prominent

Odontosia carmelita Esper
Larva. 35–38 mm. Body bright green and wrinkled, with faint paler lines, a red-marked yellow spiracular line and bluish-green underparts.
Foodplant. Birch.
Habits. A single-brooded species, the larvae of which can be beaten from late May to about mid-July. The adults will come to light during April and May, but the females infrequently. If taken these will often deposit eggs in captivity and rearing the resulting larvae is not difficult as long as they are supplied with fresh foodplant. The pupa is formed in a cocoon under moss or just under the soil, and lasts throughout the winter months. A woodland and heathland insect, occurring mainly in southern England, Nottinghamshire, the Forest of Dean, the Lake District, the Highlands of Scotland and south-west Ireland.
Plate 27: B. Bred from a female adult to MVL. Late April. (GAC)

Pale Prominent

Pterostoma palpina Clerck
Larva. 37–40 mm. Body bright green and wrinkled, with many faint white lines and a yellow spiracular line that is edged above with dark grey.
Foodplants. Sallow, poplar and aspen.
Habits. Double-brooded in southern parts and single-brooded in the north. The larvae occur from late June to late July and again in late August and September, or from late June to early August where univoltine. They can readily be beaten or found by searching and are easy to rear in confinement. In May and June and August the adult males will come freely to light, but the females much less so. The overwintering pupa is formed in a cocoon on or just below the ground. Generally distributed over most of England and much of Wales; local in Scotland and Ireland.
Plate 27: C. Beaten from sallow, nearly fully grown. Mid-September.

White Prominent

Leucodonta bicoloria Denis & Schiffermüller
Larva. 35–38 mm. Body green, whitish dorsally, with yellow subdorsal and spiracular lines; spiracles black and obvious.
Foodplant. Birch.
Habits. This single-brooded species is claimed to have been taken in Staffordshire during the last century, and has been recorded from the mature birch woods of Co. Kerry in Ireland, where it has not been seen since 1938, but may possibly still exist. The larval stage lasts from June to August, and the larvae have been collected by beating the lower birch branches. Not a difficult insect to rear in confinement, with the pupa being formed under the soil for overwintering.
Plate 27: D. Bred from a female adult to MVL (France). Mid-June. (DEW)

Plumed Prominent

Ptilophora plumigera Denis & Schiffermüller
Larva. 33–36 mm. Body pale green, with whitish-green sides and white subdorsal and spiracular lines.
Foodplant. Field maple.
Habits. Single-brooded, being in the larval stage from about late April to early June. The larvae can be beaten, especially from the more mature trees, and are fairly easy to rear in captivity. The cocooned pupae, spun up among leaf litter, should be kept outside in a shaded place to avoid desiccation during the summer months. The adults emerge during November and early December, and although the males come freely to light soon after dusk, the females much less frequently so and normally around midnight. The eggs are laid upon the foodplant twigs and overwinter. A local species, being mainly found in woodland on calcareous soils in south and south-east England.
Plate 27: E. Bred from a female adult to MVL. Mid-November. (RL)

Marbled Brown

Drymonia dodonaea Denis & Schiffermüller
Larva. 35–38 mm. Body light green and glossy, with a pair of thin pale yellow lines along the back and a broader orange-marked pale yellow spiracular line.
Foodplant. Oak.
Habits. A single-brooded species that occurs as a larva from late June to early September. The larvae seem to be difficult to beat, even in woods where the moth is abundant, suggesting that they are probably canopy feeders. In May and June the adult males come readily to light, but the females rarely respond. Occasionally a female can be taken by this method and then it should lay freely on oak leaves, if required to do so. No special conditions are necessary for rearing the larvae and they pupate for overwintering in tough cocoons just under the soil. These can be obtained by digging at the base of the trees in winter. Generally distributed, in mature oak woods, over much of England and Wales; also recorded locally in western Scotland and parts of Ireland.
Plate 27: F. Bred from a female adult to MVL. Early June. (BS)

Lunar Marbled Brown

Drymonia ruficornis Hufnagel

Larva. 36–40 mm. Body green, with yellow subdorsal lines and an obvious bright yellow spiracular line; head darker green. The penultimate instar larva is green, boldly striped with bright yellow.

Foodplant. Oak.

Habits. Single-brooded, being in the larval stage from about late May to late July, and can sometimes be beaten from the branches of mature oaks. In late April and May both sexes of the adult are attracted to light and most females will lay eggs freely in captivity, if supplied with budding oak leaves. Rearing the larvae is usually very easy and the overwintering pupa is formed in a cocoon just under the ground. These cocoons can be obtained by digging at the bases of larger oaks during the winter months. Generally distributed and fairly common in southern England and parts of Wales; less frequent and more local in the north, southern Scotland and in Ireland.

Plate 27: G. Bred from a female adult to MVL. Early May.

Dusky Marbled Brown

Gluphisia crenata Esper

Larva. 24–27 mm. Body green, with a broadly separated pair of yellow dorsal lines between which are a series of crimson spots, mainly on the abdominal rings; head darker green, finely spotted.

Foodplants. Aspen and poplars.

Habits. A single-brooded insect in the northern part of the range that was possibly still resident in the British Isles during the nineteenth century, with three reputedly authentic records between 1839 and 1853. The British records were of two adults in June and a larva in August. It overwinters as a pupa between spun leaves. A further adult was recorded in late July 1995 in the Channel Islands.

Plate 49: D. Courtesy of Per Stadel Nielsen.

Small Chocolate-tip

Clostera pigra Hufnagel

Larva. 24–26 mm. Body bluish-grey subdorsally, marked with orange on the back and sides and having an obvious raised black spot on the top of the fourth and eleventh segments; setae light brown.

Foodplants. Aspen, willows and sallows.

Habits. Double-brooded in the south and in Ireland, single-brooded in the north. The larvae occur mostly during late May and June, and again in late August and September, except those of the northern populations which occur during late July to September. They can readily be found by searching the foodplants for leaves that are spun together forming a retreat in which the larvae spend the day. At night, when they leave these retreats to feed, they can be beaten. During May and August the adult females come to light traps and normally lay freely in captivity, if supplied with foodplant. Rearing this species is not difficult if given fresh food or sleeved on a growing plant, and the pupa is formed in a cocoon between the spun leaves for overwintering when necessary. A local insect, being found in widely scattered localities throughout much of Britain and Ireland.

Plate 27: H. Bred from a female adult to MVL. Mid-May. (DB)

Scarce Chocolate-tip

Clostera anachoreta Denis & Schiffermüller

Larva. 33–37 mm. Body dark grey, with a black dorsal line, orange-brown dorsal patches, and a russet-coloured raised structure on the fourth segment that is flanked by two obvious white raised spots; setae light brown.

Foodplants. Sallow, aspen, poplar and willow.

Habits. A double-brooded insect that occurs as a larva from about late May to mid-July, and again in September. The larvae can be obtained by beating at night or by searching for their retreat of spun leaves during the day. The adults fly in late April and May and those of the second brood in August, with both sexes responding well to light traps. Most females will lay freely and rearing the larvae is very easy, developing rapidly and pupating among the leaves for overwintering. This species became established in south-east Kent between about 1858 and 1912, then seemed to disappear except for odd records between the 1950s and early 1970s. In 1979 it re-established itself at Dungeness and seems to still persist, annually, in small numbers.

Plate 27: I. Found between sallow leaves, fully grown. Mid-July. (MJF)

Chocolate-tip

Clostera curtula Linnaeus

Larva. 30–34 mm. Body dark grey, with orange patches dorsally and raised black humps on the fourth and eleventh segments; setae pale grey.

Foodplants. Poplar, aspen and willow.

Habits. Mainly double-brooded, being in the larval stage during May to about mid-July, and again from late August to early October. Univoltine in Scotland, with the larvae in July and August. They can easily be located by searching aspens and poplars for leaves spun together, in which they hide during the day, and when larger can often be beaten at night, when out of their retreats feeding. During May and August the adult moths come to light and most females will lay freely on foodplant. Rearing this species in captivity is fairly easy and the larvae pupate for overwintering in cocoons spun up between the leaves. Widely distributed in southern and eastern England; also recorded from Aberdeenshire and Inverness-shire in Scotland.

Plate 27: J. Found between spun poplar leaves, fully grown. Late September. (RM)

Figure of Eight

Diloba caeruleocephala Linnaeus

Larva. 38–43 mm. Body bluish-grey, with bright yellow dorsal marks and spiracular line; large black pinacula, each bearing a long black bristle.

Foodplants. Blackthorn, hawthorn, apple and associated trees.

Habits. A single-brooded species, the larvae of which can readily be beaten from about mid-May to mid-July. These are easy to rear in captivity as long as they are given soil and plant litter in which to pupate. The cocooned pupae should be left outside in natural weather conditions and not disturbed. The adults emerge during October and early November, and both sexes will come to light. The eggs are laid upon the bare twigs and last throughout the winter until the following spring. Widely distributed and fairly common, in woods and hedgerows, over most of England and eastern parts of Wales; local in Scotland and scarce in Ireland.

Plate 27: K. Beaten from blackthorn, about half grown. Early June.

Family: THAUMETOPOEIDAE

Oak Processionary

Thaumetopoea processionea Linnaeus

Larva. 20–25 mm. Body grey, with a blackish-grey dorsal stripe and long white irritating setae emanating from reddish-orange pinacula; spiracular line whitish; head brownish-black.

Foodplant. Oak.

Habits. A single-brooded rare immigrant species, of which several male adults have been taken at light in the southern coastal counties during recent years. On the continent the larvae occur during May and June after overwintering as eggs, and live gregariously in spinnings on the foodplant trees, sometimes causing considerable damage to the foliage. The pupae are formed within the spinnings, with the adults flying in July and August.

Plate 27: L. Courtesy of Carlos Gomez de Aizpurua.

Family: LYMANTRIIDAE

Eight species of this family are to be regularly found in the British Isles, with two others occurring as vagrants; one other became extinct during the last century. The larvae are all very hairy, with those of *E. chrysorrhoea* being a notable pest species, the popular press often reporting plagues of dangerous caterpillars affecting the health of people, sometimes justifiably, as the larval hairs can cause a severe case of urticaria in those with a sensitive skin. All species lay their eggs in batches, often covered by scale from the female's abdominal tuft, and those of the wingless females of the genus *Orgyia* are located on the outside of the empty cocoon. Most of the adults fly at night, and although the females are less attracted to light, they often lay eggs freely in captivity.

Reed Tussock

Laelia coenosa Hübner

Larva. 30–35 mm. Body grey, with a black dorsal stripe, dorsal tufts of dull yellow hairs on the fourth to seventh segments, a pair of forward-facing black tufts of hair on the first ring and a rearward-facing tuft at the end of the body; head pale brown.

Foodplants. Branched bur-reed, great fen-sedge and common reed.

Habits. A single-brooded species that became extinct in the British Isles about 1879. It formerly inhabited the fens of Cambridgeshire and Huntingdonshire, with the larvae occurring from August to the following early June, overwintering when about half grown. The pupae were formed in tough brown cocoons upon the foodplants, with adults emerging during July and early August. On the continent it is still found locally in France, Spain, Denmark and northern Germany.

Plate 49: E. Courtesy of Per Stadel Nielsen.

Scarce Vapourer

Orgyia recens Hübner

Larva. 35–38 mm. Body black or dark grey, marked with white, a bold orange-red spiracular line and brown tufts of bristles on the fourth to seventh segments dorsally.

Foodplants. Hawthorn, oak, sallow, bramble and many other deciduous trees and shrubs; also recorded on meadowsweet and water dock.

Habits. Mainly a single-brooded species, being in the larval stage from August to the following late May. The best method of obtaining the larvae is by beating during the spring, although many may be parasitized. The adult males fly in sunshine from about mid-June to mid-July; the females are wingless. Sometimes a difficult species to breed with some stocks being susceptible to viruses, and overwintering is best done by leaving the brood outside in a sleeve. A very local insect that used to be widespread in southern England, now to be found mainly in woods and hedgerows in Yorkshire, Lincolnshire and Norfolk.

Plate 27: M. Beaten from hawthorn. Late May. (RAB)

The Vapourer

Orgyia antiqua Linnaeus

Larva. 36–40 mm. Body dark bluish-grey, marked with red spots and having yellow tufts of bristles on the fourth to seventh segments dorsally; tufts of black bristles also emanate from the first and eleventh rings.

Foodplants. Hawthorn, blackthorn, birch, oak, lime, bilberry, tamarisk and many other deciduous trees and shrubs.

Habits. Mostly single-brooded, but often with a second generation in the south of England. The larvae can readily be beaten from May to August and are very easy to rear in confinement. The males fly in sunshine from July to early October, with the wingless females depositing their large egg batches on the outside of their empty cocoons. These batches can sometimes be found on tree trunks, fences and buildings during the winter months, especially in cities where the larvae occasionally become a pest. Generally distributed over most of Britain and Ireland; less frequent in the north.

Plate 27: N. Beaten from lime, about half grown. Early June.

Dark Tussock

Dicallomera fascelina Linnaeus

Larva. 40–45 mm. Body black, covered with yellowish hairs and having black-tipped white tufts of bristles dorsally on the fourth to seventh segments.

Foodplants. Heather, broom, sallow, bramble and many other plants.

Habits. Single-brooded, being in the larval stage from late August to the following early June, overwintering in a silken tent when still quite small. Possibly with a two-year cycle in Scotland. The larvae can readily be obtained by sweeping and beating, but if taken in the autumn they can be difficult to overwinter, unless kept outside on a potted plant or in a sleeve. Those collected in the spring usually survive to the adult stage, although many will be parasitized. The cocoon is spun up in the herbage and lasts about a month. During July and August both sexes of the adult come to light and the females often lay freely in confinement. To be found on moorland, heaths, shingle beaches and coastal sandhills mainly in southern England, Cheshire and Lancashire and the Scottish Highlands; also rarely recorded in Ireland.

Plate 27: O. Swept from heather and bilberry, nearly fully grown. Late May.

Pale Tussock

Calliteara pudibunda Linnaeus

Larva. 42–46 mm. Body greenish-yellow or even bright yellow, with black hairs and having yellow tufts of bristles dorsally on the fourth to seventh segments, each separated by a black ring, these being more obvious as the larva curls.

Foodplants. Oak, birch, lime, blackthorn and many other deciduous trees.
Habits. A single-brooded insect, with the slow-growing larvae occurring from about late June to early October. They can be taken by beating and are usually easy to rear in captivity, overwintering as a pupa in a silken cocoon spun up among the leaf litter. The adults fly in May and June, the males being especially attracted to light, the females less so, but with most willing to deposit eggs in confinement. Mainly a woodland species, usually common in England and Wales; local in Ireland.
Plate 27: P. Bred from a female adult to MVL. Late May.

Brown-tail

Euproctis chrysorrhoea Linnaeus
Larva. 38–42 mm. Body almost black, with brown hairs, a series of white marks subdorsally and a pair of red spots dorsally on the ninth and tenth segments.
Foodplants. Bramble, sallow, blackthorn, hawthorn and other deciduous trees and shrubs.
Habits. Single-brooded, being in the larval stage from about late August to the following early June, overwintering in a grey tough communal web spun up on the foodplant twigs. These nests are very conspicuous on the bare plants during winter, and in the spring the larvae often swarm over the leaves and are very easy to find. No special conditions are necessary to rear them in captivity, but one should be aware that the larvae and their cocoons are covered in irritating hairs and should not be handled if possible. The adults fly in July and August, with both sexes coming freely to light and the eggs are laid in large batches, covered by the hairs from the female's abdomen. Mainly a coastal species, often locally abundant from Hampshire to Suffolk, with some colonies being found well inland; also occurring as far north as Yorkshire and westwards to the Isles of Scilly.
Plate 27: Q. Found on bramble, about half grown. Early May.

Yellow-tail

Euproctis similis Fuessly
Larva. 40–43 mm. Body black, with black hairs on the back and grey hairs laterally, twin broken red lines dorsally and white markings subdorsally.
Foodplants. Blackthorn, hawthorn, oak, sallow and other deciduous trees.
Habits. A single-brooded species that occurs as a larva from about late August, living gregariously until the larvae form their individual hibernacula to overwinter within. Feeding resumes in April, and by early June most will have pupated inside their cocoons. During the spring they can readily be beaten and are very easy to rear in captivity. Both sexes of the adults come freely to light and the females cover their egg batches with the hairs from the end of their abdomen. A common species throughout most of England and Wales; less frequent in southern Scotland and Ireland.
Plate 27: R. Beaten from oak, fully grown. Late May.

White Satin Moth

Leucoma salicis Linnaeus
Larva. 42–46 mm. Body grey on the sides and black dorsally, with a row of conspicuous creamy-white blotches along the centre of the back and rows of reddish bristle-bearing structures along the subdorsal and spiracular areas.
Foodplants. Sallow, poplar, aspen and willow.
Habits. Single-brooded, in the larval stage from about late August to late June, overwintering when still small, gregariously in a silken web. In the spring feeding recommences, with the larvae venturing from the web to nearby leaves. During May and June they can readily be beaten and are easy to rear in captivity. The pupa is formed in a cocoon that is usually spun up in bark crevices on the foodplant tree. In July and August the adults will come to light traps and in some localities the moths are common enough to be found resting under leaves by day. Generally distributed over much of England and eastern Wales, being most frequent in parts of Essex, Kent and east London.
Plate 28: A. Beaten from sallow, fully grown. Mid-June.

Black V Moth

Arctornis l-nigrum Müller
Larva. 43–46 mm. Body greyish, with tufts of white hairs laterally and dorsally on the fourth, fifth, ninth and tenth segments, those on the sixth to eighth rings coloured orangish-brown; dorsal and subdorsal lines orange.
Foodplants. Sallow, poplar, elm, lime and other trees.
Habits. A single-brooded species that occurs as a larva from August to May, overwintering in the first instar. The larvae can be beaten during the spring and rearing them in captivity is not difficult, pupating in a silken cocoon spun upon tree trunks. The adults fly in late June and July, with the males being more responsive to light. This species temporarily established itself on the Essex coast from 1947 to 1960, and may well do so again.
Plate 28: B. Beaten from lime, fully grown (France). Late May. (DEW)

Black Arches

Lymantria monacha Linnaeus
Larva. 37–40 mm. Body grey, with whitish hairs and a broad mainly black dorsal marking that is grey on the seventh to ninth segments.
Foodplant. Oak.
Habits. A single-brooded species, the larvae of which can readily be beaten from late April to about mid-June. They are not difficult to rear in captivity and the cocooned pupa is spun up, naturally, in bark crevices on oak trees. The adults fly in August, with mainly males coming to light. The females can sometimes be obtained by searching oak trunks by day, and freely lay the overwintering eggs on bark. Mostly inhabiting mature oak woods in the southern half of England.
Plate 28: C. Beaten from oak, nearly fully grown. Early June. (SHC)

Gypsy Moth

Lymantria dispar Linnaeus
Larva. 40–50 mm. Body dark grey with light brown hairs, heavily marked with black dorsally, also having reddish spots on the top of the sixth to eleventh segments centrally and pairs of dark blue pinacula on the first to fifth rings.
Foodplants. Most species of deciduous trees, especially apple, plum and sallow; the extinct British population fed on bog myrtle and creeping willow.
Habits. Single-brooded, occurring as a larva from April to about late June. The original British population, which was found in the fens of Huntingdonshire, Cambridgeshire and Norfolk, became extinct about 1907; and although the larvae can readily be beaten on the continent, it is unlikely that this species will naturally breed again in Britain, due to the large-bodied females being unable to fly. Captive larvae are easy to breed and there have been attempts to re-introduce them, but so far none successful. Perhaps this is fortunate, as they can be a major pest of forests and orchards in Europe and

North America. The cocooned pupa is spun up on the trunks and lasts about four to six weeks, with the adults emerging in August. The females lay the overwintering egg batches on their empty cocoons and nearby bark and the tiny larvae can be dispersed by winds during April. The day-flying males also fly at dusk, and there are sporadic reports of suspected migrants being caught at light traps, especially on the south coast.
Plate 28: D. Found on blackthorn, fully grown (France). (MG-P)

Family: ARCTIIDAE

Over thirty species of this family are found in the British Isles. The larvae of the subfamily *Lithosiinae* are predominantly feeders on algae and lichens and many are not easy to find in the wild. Many of the subfamily *Arctiinae* are very hairy, being commonly known as woolly-bears and these are often observed basking in sunshine or dashing across open ground as they search for a pupation site. Most of the adults fly at night and are attracted to light. Many species lay their eggs, sometimes in batches, quite freely in confinement. The cocooned pupae are formed above ground, usually in plant litter and most hatch after about a month, except the few species that overwinter in this stage.

SUBFAMILY: LITHOSIINAE

Round-winged Muslin

Thumatha senex Hübner
Larva. 15–18 mm. Body black, with dense tufts of light brown hairs that are tipped with black; head shining and black.
Foodplants. Various algae, lichens and mosses, especially dog lichen.
Habits. A single-brooded species that occurs in the larval stage from about late August to the following late May, overwintering when still very small. The larvae are fairly easy to rear in captivity and will develop faster when kept warm and in the dark, becoming fully grown in around four to six months. They must have adequate ventilation or mould will form upon the foodplant, growing on bark or twigs, this eventually killing the larvae. The pupa is formed in a cocoon consisting of silk and the larval hairs, lasting about a month. The dusk-flying and light-responsive adults fly during July and August, and most females will lay freely in confinement. A marsh and fenland species, being found mainly in southern and eastern England; elsewhere local or uncommon.
Plate 28: E. Bred from a female adult to MVL. Late July. (SHC)

Dew Moth

Setina irrorella Linnaeus
Larva. 18–22 mm. Body dark grey, with conspicuous orange diamond-shaped markings along the dorsal area and more pale orange marks on the sides.
Foodplants. Various black and orange lichens that grow on pebbles and rocks.
Habits. Single-brooded, being in the larval state from August to the following early June, overwintering when about quarter grown. The larvae can readily be obtained by close searching in known localities during May, as they feed and bask in sunshine fully exposed. During dull or wet weather they congregate beneath the stones and can often still be located, but in smaller numbers. At this point of their development they are easy to rear to the adult stage, although the larvae have been known to devour the newly formed pupae of their companions if the lichens are in short supply. The adults emerge in late June and July, and the males fly in the afternoon sun and later again at dusk, coming to light in small numbers. A very local species, mainly occurring on the coasts of Kent, Hampshire, the Isle of Wight, the Isle of Man, western Scotland and west Wales; also inland colonies on the North Downs of Surrey and in the Burren region of Ireland.
Plate 28: F. Found on shingle, fully grown. Late May. (RL)

Rosy Footman

Miltochrista miniata Forster
Larva. 14–18 mm. Body dark grey, densely covered with grey hairs on the first to seventh segments and slightly paler hairs on the other rings.
Foodplants. Various algae, lichens and mosses; also accepting withering dandelion and lettuce in captivity.
Habits. A single-brooded insect, the larval stage of which lasts from August to the following late May, continuing to feed during mild weather during the winter months. In the spring the growth becomes more rapid and the larvae can occasionally be found by carefully searching among the leaf litter. The light-responsive adults fly in late June and July, with the females depositing eggs freely in confinement. The resulting larvae can be forced to develop faster by keeping them warm and in the dark, eventually pupating in a cocoon constructed of silk and the larval hairs, for about four weeks. Mainly a woodland species, most often recorded in the southern parts of England and Wales.
Plate 28: G. Bred from a female adult to MVL. Mid-July.

Muslin Footman

Nudaria mundana Linnaeus
Larva. 12–15 mm. Body dark grey, with dull yellow markings along the dorsal area, long grey hairs and a large black spot on the top of the seventh segment.
Foodplants. Various small green and black lichens growing on stones and branches of isolated trees and bushes.
Habits. Single-brooded, occurring as a larva from August to early June, overwintering when still quite small. During the spring the larvae can be found under the top stones of dry-stone walls, especially where there is shelter from nearby trees. At this stage the larvae can easily be reared in captivity, pupating in a flimsy silken cocoon that is often spun up in crevices. The adults fly during July, with the males coming freely to mercury-vapour light and the females seeming to prefer low-power light sources such as torches and Tilley lamps. Local, but widely distributed, throughout most of Britain, but much less frequent in the south-eastern counties.
Plate 28: H. Found under stones on wall, fully grown. Late May.

Red-necked Footman

Atolmis rubricollis Linnaeus
Larva. 25–28 mm. Body greenish-grey, with many small raised dull orange pinacula and sparse long brown hairs.
Foodplants. Algae and lichens, especially those growing on oak, beech, larch and other conifers.
Habits. A single-brooded species, in the larval stage from about early August to the middle of October, which can readily be taken by beating the boughs of the foodplants' host trees. The larvae are usually not difficult to rear in captivity and the cocooned pupa is spun up on twigs, in crevices

or leaf litter for overwintering. The adults emerge during June and early July, with both sexes coming to light in small numbers and sometimes, on calm sunny days, the moths will fly in swarms above the tops of large trees. A local woodland insect found mainly in southern England and Wales.
Plate 28: I. Beaten from *Cupressus*, about half grown. Early September. (SHC)

Four-dotted Footman

Cybosia mesomella Linnaeus
Larva. 22–25 mm. Body black, with dense black or dark-brown hairs; head shining and black.
Foodplants. Various lichens and algae growing on heather, sallow and other plants; also accepting the leaves of sallow, bramble, dandelion and heather after hibernation.
Habits. Single-brooded, occurring as a larva from about mid-August to the following late May, overwintering in plant litter when still quite small. The larvae are easiest to obtain by rearing them from a captured female adult, these being readily flushed from the herbage on warm sunny afternoons during late June and July. Most will lay eggs freely in captivity and the resulting larvae can often be forced to develop faster by keeping them warm and in darkness, becoming fully grown in about four months. The pupa is formed in a loose cocoon among plant litter or in bark crevices and normally lasts about four to six weeks. This species mainly inhabits heaths, mosses and commons over most parts of southern England and Wales; local in the north and parts of Scotland.
Plate 28: J. Bred from a netted female adult. Early July. (SHC)

Dotted Footman

Pelosia muscerda Hufnagel
Larva. 20–23 mm. Body dark greyish-brown, with a black dorsal line, short brown setae and vague reddish marks on the prothorax and eleventh segment dorsally; head black.
Foodplants. Various algae and lichens, probably growing on sallows and plant litter.
Habits. A single-brooded insect, the larva of which occurs from about late August to early June and probably is most readily obtained by rearing from a light-trapped female. These fly in late July and early August, laying freely in captivity if given algae-covered sallow twigs as a stimulus. The larvae are quite easy to rear, becoming fully grown in about four months if kept warm, pupating in a double cocoon for about four to six weeks. A very local species that is only known at present from the sallow carr areas on the Norfolk Broads, with the occasional records from elsewhere in the south-east being attributed to vagrants from the continent.
Plate 28: K. Bred from a female adult to MVL. Late July. (GAC)

Small Dotted Footman

Pelosia obtusa Herrich-Schäffer
Larva. 17–20 mm. Body almost black, with black dorsal and subdorsal lines and a shining dark brown head; setae black.
Foodplants. Probably algae and lichens growing on reeds and plant litter, accepting green algae (*Desmococcus*) on bark in captivity.
Habits. Single-brooded, occurring as a larva from late August to the following late June, hibernating on silken pads on the underside of plant litter, when still quite small (about 7 mm long). Feeding, mostly at night, resumes in late April and is slow at first, with the growth becoming rapid from about early June until pupation. This can be a difficult species to rear in confinement and if overwintering is attempted the larvae may survive if placed outside in a sheltered place with algae-covered bark, in small plastic boxes that are covered with fine netting so that the moisture level and ventilation are as natural as possible. The pupa is formed in a double cocoon, lasting about two to four weeks. The adults fly in late July and early August, inhabiting mature reed-beds, with the males responding to light and females being found at rest on the reeds after dark. Since being discovered in Britain during 1961, this elusive little moth has been found to be established, very locally, only in the Norfolk Broads.
Plate 28: L. Bred from a female adult found at rest. Late July. (CH)

Orange Footman

Eilema sororcula Hufnagel
Larva. 18–22 mm. Body mainly black, marked with red and yellowish-white dorsally and having an obvious white bar across the top of the eleventh segment; head black and setae greyish.
Foodplants. Various algae and lichens growing on the branches and trunks of oak and beech.
Habits. A single-brooded species that is in the larval stage from late June to about the middle of September. This insect can be so exceedingly local that, if known from a particular individual tree, the larvae can readily be found by searching. Often a light trap placed under such a tree in late May or early June can produce a good number of adults and in a trap only yards away this species will be absent. Fertile females usually lay freely in confinement and the larvae are quite easy to rear, pupating in a flimsy cocoon for overwintering. Mainly found in the mature woodlands of southern England and south-east Wales.
Plate 28: M. Bred from a female adult to MVL. Late May. (SHC)

Dingy Footman

Eilema griseola Hübner
Larva. 25–28 mm. Body black, with orange markings subdorsally and more extensive orange patches on the first, second and eleventh segments dorsally; head black and setae brownish.
Foodplants. Various lichens and algae; also accepting withered sallow and dandelion leaves in captivity.
Habits. A single-brooded insect, the larvae of which occur from about August to the following late May, overwintering in plant litter. They are occasionally accidentally taken during the spring when beating sallows for other species, but are most readily obtained by rearing from light-trapped females. These fly over marshy ground and in damp woodland throughout July and the first half of August, and usually deposit eggs freely in confinement. If the resulting larvae are kept in the dark and fairly warm, they may complete their growth within about four to five months, with the cocooned pupa lasting about a month to six weeks. Widespread and locally common over much of southern England and parts of Wales.
Plate 28: N. Bred from a female adult to MVL. Late July. (SHC)

Hoary Footman

Eilema caniola Hübner
Larva. 22–26 mm. Body greyish-brown, with a black dorsal line, a row of bright orange markings subdorsally and short grey setae.

Foodplants. Various lichens and algae growing on rocks; also stated to feed on bird's-foot trefoil and other leguminous plants.
Habits. Single-brooded, being in the larval stage from September to the following late June, probably feeding throughout the winter whenever the weather is mild. The larvae can be found at night during the spring and are not difficult to rear to the adult stage, with the cocooned pupa being formed in crevices. The light-responsive adults fly from late July until early September and most females will lay freely in captivity. Overwintering larvae should be protected from frosts and extreme cold as the south-western coastal distribution could indicate they are not tolerant of prolonged low temperatures. To be regularly found only on the coasts of Devon, Cornwall and western Wales.
Plate 28: O. Found at night on rocks, over half grown. Early June.

Pigmy Footman

Eilema pygmaeola Doubleday
Larva. 15–18 mm. Body dark greyish-brown, with a black dorsal line, dull orange subdorsal marks and short brown setae; head black.
Foodplants. Various lichens and algae growing on pebbles, posts and the ground; also accepting withering young sallow leaves in confinement.
Habits. A single-brooded species that occurs in the larval stage from August to the middle of the following June, overwintering when still very small. During the spring the larvae can be taken in small numbers by sweeping grasses at night, when they wander about in their open ground habitat, and by day they have been located beneath fallen posts and other debris while hiding from the light. The larvae are fairly easy to rear when taken at this point of their development and the loosely cocooned pupa lasts about four to six weeks. Both sexes of the adults come freely to light from mid-July to mid-August, and the females will probably lay freely in captivity if required. A locally common insect that is recorded most often from the coasts of Kent and Norfolk.
Plate 28: P. Swept at night from grasses, fully grown. June. (RM)

Scarce Footman

Eilema complana Linnaeus
Larva. 23–26 mm. Body dark brown, with an indistinct black dorsal line, conspicuous orange marks subdorsally with those on the thoracic segments being faint; brownish-grey setae; head black.
Foodplants. Various lichens and algae; also accepting knotgrass and withered sallow, bramble and dandelion leaves in captivity.
Habits. Single-brooded, occurring as a larva from August to early June, overwintering when still quite small. Feeding recommences in April and during the spring these larvae are often taken accidentally when beating for other species. The adults fly in July and August, with both sexes being strongly attracted to light. Most females lay freely in confinement and the resulting larvae can be forced to develop faster by keeping them warm and in the dark. The cocooned pupa lasts about a month and is usually spun up in a crevice or among plant litter. Generally distributed and often common in woods and on heathland, downs, cliffs and sandhills over much of central and southern England and in Wales; local in Ireland, mainly on the south and west coasts.
Plate 28: Q. Found on lichen-covered rock, fully grown. Early June.

Northern Footman

Eilema sericea Gregson
Larva. 23–26 mm. Seemingly identical to the previous species (*E. complana*).
Foodplants. Various lichens and green algae.
Habits. In keeping with current opinions, this Footman has been illustrated for completeness, but it is almost certainly a northern moss-inhabiting race of the previous species. Its life-cycle and the rearing methods used in captivity are the same as for *E. complana* and although some adults are slightly different in markings, the genitalia cannot be used to distinguish this moth as a separate species. Those individuals credited with being *E. sericea* all come from peat mosses in north-west England, North Wales and the Isle of Man, where *E. complana* seems to be absent.
Plate 28: R. Bred from a female adult to MVL. Mid-July. (GAC)

Buff Footman

Eilema deplana Esper
Larva. 20–24 mm. Body black, with a broad greyish-white dorsal stripe that is interrupted on the third, seventh and eleventh segments by black markings.
Foodplants. Various lichens and green algae growing on branches of oak, yew, hawthorn and other trees.
Habits. A single-brooded species that occurs in the larval state from September to the following late June, overwintering when still very small. During the spring the larvae can be taken in small numbers by beating the thinner branches of woodland trees, especially oaks and yews. They are usually not difficult to rear in captivity when taken at this point of their development, and pupate in a cocoon spun up on the bark or among lichens in a crevice. The adults fly from about mid-July to early September and both sexes come readily to light traps. Locally distributed over many parts of southern England and Wales; also recorded from south-west Ireland.
Plate 29: A. Beaten from oak, nearly fully grown. Early June. (SHC)

Common Footman

Eilema lurideola Zincken
Larva. 23–26 mm. Body black, with a distinct orange spiracular line along the abdominal segments and mainly black setae dorsally and brown setae on the sides.
Foodplants. Lichens and algae growing on trees, bushes, walls, rocks and fences; also accepting withering sallow, bramble and dandelion leaves in captivity.
Habits. Single-brooded, being in the larval stage from August to the following late May, overwintering when still small. Feeding recommences during April and the larvae are often found or taken by beating during the spring. They are fairly easy to rear in captivity, pupating for about four to six weeks in a cocoon usually located in a bark crevice. The light-responsive adults fly in July and August and most females lay eggs freely in confinement if required. Widely distributed and often common over most of England and Wales, also recorded from the eastern parts of Scotland; mainly coastal and on the Burren in Ireland.
Plate 29: B. Found on oak trunk, fully grown. Late May.

Four-spotted Footman

Lithosia quadra Linnaeus
Larva. 32–36 mm. Body black, with a mainly yellowish-white dorsal area that has conspicuous orange pinacula and bold black marks on the third, seventh and eleventh segments; head black and setae mainly greyish.

Foodplants. Various lichens and green algae growing on trees and rocks.
Habits. A single-brooded species that occurs as a larva from September to about the following late June, overwintering when small. These colourful larvae can be beaten, especially from oak boughs, during the spring and larger stocks can also be obtained by breeding from light-trapped female adults that fly during August and most of September. Eggs are usually laid freely in captivity and the larvae may be forced to complete their growth in about four months by keeping them warm and in the dark. The pupa is formed inside a loose silken cocoon, often naturally in a bark crevice, and lasts up to six weeks. The resident populations of this insect are centred on Hampshire, Devon, Cornwall, Pembrokeshire and south-west Ireland, with records of probable migrants occurring elsewhere.
Plate 29: C. Bred from a female adult to MVL. Late August. (SHC)

SUBFAMILY: ARCTIINAE

Feathered Footman

Spiris striata Linnaeus
Larva. 28–30 mm. Body black, with a distinct brick-red dorsal line and mainly black setae; head black.
Foodplants. Many species of low-growing herbaceous plants, including dandelion and knotgrass.
Habits. This species was recorded from Britain on a few occasions during the nineteenth century, but has not been seen here since. It is fairly common on dry heathy soils in southern Europe and the day-flying adults can easily be netted during June and July. Naturally they occur as larvae from August to May, living and hibernating gregariously in a silken web, but in captivity will readily feed up quickly in about three to four months if kept warm. The cocooned pupa lasts about a month.
Plate 29: D. Bred from a netted female adult (S. France). Early July. (MG-P)

Speckled Footman

Coscinia cribraria Linnaeus
Larva. 28–30 mm. Body dark brown, with a greyish-white dorsal line, reddish-brown laterally and longish black and grey setae; head blackish-brown.
Foodplants. Various low-growing herbaceous plants, especially dandelion.
Habits. A single-brooded species that occurs in the larval stage from late August to the following June, overwintering when still quite small. The larvae have been stated to bask while sitting on grass stems during the spring and could probably be taken by sweeping or searching. Most of the adults fly during late July and early August and although the males come freely to light, the females need to be searched for as they rest upon the heather. This species has declined greatly in the last decade, and now seems to inhabit only some of the heaths in east Dorset.
Plate 29: E. Courtesy of Carlos Gomez de Aizpurua.

Crimson Speckled

Utetheisa pulchella Linnaeus
Larva. 26–30 mm. Body black, with a conspicuous yellowish-white dorsal line, small orange-red markings and a mainly brown head; setae long, black dorsally and white on the sides.
Foodplants. Various herbaceous plants, readily accepting forget-me-not and borage in captivity.
Habits. Occasionally specimens of this continuously brooded sub-tropical insect occur as migrants in the British Isles, with most recorded from July to October. These moths can readily be disturbed from the herbage on sunny days and later also come to light traps. Fertile females usually lay eggs freely in captivity and the larvae are fairly easy to rear when given sunshine and warmth. Breeding them on a sleeved potted plant kept in a well-ventilated greenhouse is a good method for success. The cocooned pupa should also be kept warm and lasts for about two to three weeks. In temperate regions the larva overwinters, feeding in mild spells, but probably will not tolerate frosts or prolonged low temperatures.
Plate 29: F. Bred from the adult female moth to light. (GH)

Wood Tiger

Parasemia plantaginis Linnaeus
Larva. 30–35 mm. Body blackish-brown, with mainly long dark brown hairs and those on the fourth to sixth segments being orange or gingery; head black and spiracles small and dark.
Foodplants. Mostly on low-growing herbaceous plants, especially plantains, dandelion, dock and groundsel.
Habits. A single-brooded insect, being in the larval stage from August to the following early May, or late May in the north, hibernating when about half grown. During the spring the larvae can often be found on south-facing slopes, basking on the bare ground or herbage and are very easy to rear in captivity, but many taken at this time may be parasitized. The cocoons have also been found spun up on the heather in moorland localities. During June and July the females can easily be disturbed from the herbage on warm sunny days, and most will deposit large batches of eggs in collecting-boxes. If the resulting larvae are kept warm, they frequently become continuously brooded in captivity, pupating for about three to four weeks. Widespread, but local, on moors, downland and open woods throughout most of Britain, although rarely recorded nowadays from the south-east.
Plate 29: G. Bred from a netted female adult. Late June. (SHC)

Garden Tiger

Arctia caja Linnaeus
Larva. 55–60 mm. Body dark brown and densely covered in long mainly white hairs mixed with shorter black hairs dorsally, and reddish hairs along the sides; a series of distinct white marks in the spiracular region and a black head.
Foodplants. Mostly various herbaceous plants, including plantains, dock and dandelion; often recorded on bramble, and other shrubs and bushes.
Habits. Single-brooded, occurring as a larva from August to the following late June, hibernating when about one-third grown. During the spring the larvae can frequently be found basking or resting exposed upon the herbage and, when fully fed, sometimes rushing across paths and other open ground while dispersing to their pupation sites. They are very easy to rear in confinement with the pupa, enclosed in a cocoon of silk and larval hair, lasting about a month. During July and August both sexes of the adult come freely to light and any resulting stocks reared from eggs can frequently be forced by warmth to produce continual broods. A widely distributed and sometimes common species, being found over most of the British Isles.
Plate 29: H. Found basking on grasses, nearly fully grown. Late May.

Cream-spot Tiger
Arctia villica Linnaeus

Larva. 55–65 mm. Body almost black, with dense long brown hairs and a brownish-red head and prolegs.

Foodplants. Various low-growing herbaceous plants.

Habits. A single-brooded species, being in the larval stage from about late July to the following early May, feeding sporadically throughout the winter whenever the weather is mild enough. Most larvae are fully grown by about mid-April and they then spend a while basking in the sunshine until pupation. Larvae collected at this time are often parasitized and the survivors do best when placed in a netting-covered wooden box filled with soil, leaf litter and foodplant, left in a sheltered sunny location. From late May to late July both sexes come freely to light and the females lay readily in captivity. Some broods can be forced by keeping them warm, but not as often as some of the other members of this family. Generally distributed, mainly on downs, sandhills and sea-cliffs in southern England, occurring more frequently on the coast.

Plate 29: I. Bred from a female adult to MVL. Late June. (SHC)

Clouded Buff
Diacrisia sannio Linnaeus

Larva. 35–38 mm. Body dark brown, with an orange-marked yellowish-white dorsal line and light brown setae; head dark brown.

Foodplants. Heather and various species of herbaceous plants.

Habits. Single-brooded, occurring as a larva from July to the following late April or May, feeding slowly throughout the winter whenever the weather is mild. These larvae can be swept from heather in the spring, and are usually easy to rear, with the cocooned pupa being spun up on the foodplant. The adult males are easily disturbed from herbage on warm sunny days during June and July, and the more sluggish females regularly lay batches of eggs on picked plants in confinement. Kept warm the larvae can be forced to produce a second generation in about four months. Widespread on heaths, moors and downland over much of Britain and Ireland.

Plate 29: J. Swept from heather, nearly fully grown. Late April. (JMP)

White Ermine
Spilosoma lubricipeda Linnaeus
(*menthastri* Denis & Schiffermüller)

Larva. 40–45 mm. Body brownish-black, with an orangish-red dorsal line and long dark brown setae; head and prolegs black.

Foodplants. Various low-growing herbaceous plants.

Habits. Single-brooded, with an occasional small second generation in warmer years. The larvae can be found from late July to September by shaking and then searching at the bases of low-growing plants along walls and fences. They are very easy to rear, pupating in a silken cocoon for overwintering. The adults fly from late May to July, with both sexes being attracted to light and most females depositing batches of eggs freely in captivity. Widespread and often common over most of the British Isles.

Plate 29: K. Bred from a female adult to MVL. Mid-June.

Buff Ermine
Spilosoma luteum Hufnagel

Larva. 40–45 mm. Body dark grey, with pale grey dorsal and subdorsal lines and light brown setae; head light brown.

Foodplants. Various low-growing plants; also accepting sallow, blackthorn and bramble in captivity.

Habits. A single-brooded insect, being in the larval stage from about late July to September, overwintering as a cocooned pupa spun up among plant debris. From late May to July both sexes of the adults come to light and the females are so willing to lay eggs that batches of these are often to be found on the sides of egg-boxes placed inside light traps. The larvae are very easy to rear and this species can be induced to become continuously brooded in captivity, when kept warm. Found commonly throughout most of Britain.

Plate 29: L. Bred from a female adult to MVL. Late June.

Water Ermine
Spilosoma urticae Esper

Larva. 40–45 mm. Body dark brown, with a pinkish-brown dorsal line and deep brown setae; head and prolegs pale brown.

Foodplants. Many different low-growing marsh plants, including water dock, water mint and yellow iris; also readily accepting dandelion and other docks in confinement.

Habits. Single-brooded, being in the larval stage from about mid-July to early September, overwintering as a pupa in a silken cocoon spun up low down among the herbage. The adults emerge during June and July and both sexes are attracted to light, with the females usually laying their large batches of eggs quite freely in captivity. This insect is fairly simple to rear at home and some larvae can be forced to produce another generation by keeping them warm. A local species found mainly in the marshes, fens and salterns of East Anglia, Essex, Kent and Sussex.

Plate 29: M. Bred from a female adult to MVL. Early July. (RM)

Muslin Moth
Diaphora mendica Clerck

Larva. 35–38 mm. Body grey, with pale brown dorsal and subdorsal lines and orangish-brown setae; head dull orange.

Foodplants. Various low-growing herbaceous plants, including dandelion, dock, chickweed and plantain.

Habits. A single-brooded species that occurs as a larva from mid-June to about early September. The larvae may be found by searching at the bases of the foodplants and are easy to rear in captivity. The adults fly in May and early June, and although the dark-coloured males come freely to light, the females seem unresponsive to this kind of lure. Occasionally the females can be seen flying in the sunshine, but are more likely to be observed after being disturbed from the herbage. Batches of eggs are laid readily in captivity and a second generation can be obtained by keeping the stock warm. In the wild overwintering is in the pupal stage, spun up in a cocoon among plant litter. Widespread and fairly common over much of the British Isles; less frequent and more local in Scotland and Ireland.

Plate 29: N. Bred from a female adult netted by day. Late May. (SHC)

Ruby Tiger
Phragmatobia fuliginosa Linnaeus

Larva. 33–36 mm. Body grey, with a pale orange dorsal line and a series of marks of the same colour along the subdorsal region; pinacula black or grey with tufts of mainly light brown setae; head black.

Foodplants. Various herbaceous plants, including plantain, dock, heather, chickweed and dandelion.

Habits. Mainly a single-brooded species, having a partial second generation in the southern parts of its range. The larvae occur from July to the following spring, overwintering when in the final instar and can be found basking on warm sunny days during the autumn and again in April and early May, prior to pupation. Most larvae collected during the autumn will insist on hibernating and this can be done by keeping them in boxes placed outside in a sheltered place. They are not likely to feed again before spinning their cocoons. The adults fly in May and June, and again in August, and both sexes often come to light traps; also they sometimes fly in sunshine on calm days. Generally distributed in all kinds of habitats over much of the British Isles.
Plate 29: O. Bred from a female adult to MVL. Mid-May. (SHC)

Jersey Tiger
Euplagia quadripunctaria Poda
(*hera* Linnaeus)
Larva. 45–55 mm. Body almost black, with a broad orange dorsal stripe, cream subdorsal marks and large conspicuous brownish-orange pinacula from which pale brown setae emanate; head black.
Foodplants. Various low-growing plants, including dandelion, ground ivy, dead nettle, plantain and common nettle.
Habits. A single-brooded insect that occurs in the larval stage from September to the following June, overwintering when still very small. The adults are on the wing from late July to about late August; they fly naturally in sunshine and also can be obtained by finding them at rest on walls and fences or disturbing them from the herbage in dull weather. Later they come to light and most females will lay freely in confinement. Rearing the larvae can be difficult, as most broods insist on hibernating. This should be done by keeping the brood in a netting-covered pot with growing foodplants, located in a frost-free location such as a shaded greenhouse. Occasionally some larvae will continue to feed without hibernating and become fully grown in about four months. Activity recommences about late March and from this point their growth is rapid, until pupating in a silken cocoon for about four to six weeks. This species is found mainly along the coastal regions of South Devon between Seaton and Brixham and is fairly common in most years.
Plate 29: P. Bred from a female adult found by day. Early August.

Scarlet Tiger
Callimorpha dominula Linnaeus
Larva. 42–48 mm. Body black, with a white-marked yellowish-orange dorsal stripe and a less obvious line of the same colours along the sides; head black and setae black and grey.
Foodplants. Comfrey, bramble, meadowsweet and other herbaceous plants; also recorded on sallow and blackthorn.
Habits. Single-brooded, being in the larval stage from about late July to the following May, hibernating when still fairly small. These conspicuous larvae are easy to find in the spring, especially when feeding on comfrey growing along river banks and in water-meadows. At this stage they are simple to rear in captivity and pupate for about a month inside a cocoon spun up on the foodplant or nearby in plant litter. The adults fly in sunshine during June and July, and sometimes come to light traps. In captivity the females usually lay eggs quite freely and the rearing of stocks is most successful when the broods are kept on potted foodplant for a natural development. Locally common in damp places, mainly in central, southern and western parts of England and south and west Wales.
Plate 29: Q. Found on comfrey, nearly fully grown. Early May.

The Cinnabar
Tyria jacobaeae Linnaeus
Larva. 24–28 mm. Body yellow, with a bold black band on each segment; head, prolegs and setae black.
Foodplants. Ragwort; also recorded on groundsel and colt's-foot.
Habits. A single-brooded species, occurring as a larva from July to early September. The larvae can readily be found on ragwort growing upon open ground and are very easy to rear in captivity, as long as they are not kept overcrowded. The pupa is formed in a loose cocoon located just under the soil or moss, lasting throughout the winter months. From May to July the adults can be attracted to light and they may also easily be disturbed from the vegetation by day. Generally distributed over much of England, Wales and Ireland; local and mainly coastal in southern parts of Scotland.
Plate 29: R. Found on ragwort, fully grown. Mid-August.

Family: NOLIDAE

This family of small moths is represented by five species occurring in the British Isles. In all of them the larvae have the first pair of prolegs absent and all pupate in a tough silken cocoon, usually located on the foodplant stems, bark or in plant litter. The adults come in small numbers to light and although the females lay freely in confinement, some species can be difficult to rear from the egg.

Small Black Arches
Meganola strigula Denis & Schiffermüller
Larva. 13–16 mm. Body pale pinkish-brown, with a broad yellowish dorsal line that is edged with dark brown and has a dark blotch on the sixth segment; setae pale brown.
Foodplant. Oak.
Habits. A single-brooded insect, the larvae of which probably hatch from the egg in August and overwinter when still very small in a crevice. In the spring the growth is completed, feeding on the upperside of the leaves, and they become fully grown by about the first week in June. The boat-shaped cocoon is formed upon bark and lasts about a month, with the light-responsive adults flying during July. A very local species inhabiting oak woods in southern England.

Kent Black Arches
Meganola albula Denis & Schiffermüller
Larva. 14–18 mm. Body pale buff, with darker subdorsal lines and pairs of dark-based raised pinacula on the second to sixth segments. Setae long and mostly pale grey in colour.
Foodplants. Dewberry, raspberry, strawberry and bramble.
Habits. Single-brooded, occurring as a larva from August to June, overwintering while still very small. In captivity the larvae are not difficult to rear and can be forced to develop faster by keeping them warm. The adults fly during late June and July and often come to light, with the females laying eggs freely when required to do so. Mainly coastal in distribution, being found in southern and eastern England; also occurring inland in open woodland in Hampshire, Berkshire and Surrey.
Plate 30: A. Bred from a female adult to MVL. Mid-July. (JMP)

Short-cloaked Moth

Nola cucullatella Linnaeus

Larva. 12–15 mm. Body dark grey, with a distinct white dorsal line that is interrupted on the fourth segment; head dark brown, pinacula brown and setae pale grey.

Foodplants. Blackthorn, hawthorn, apple and plum.

Habits. A single-brooded species, being in the larval stage from August to the following late May, overwintering in a crevice when very small. The larvae can readily be taken by beating during the spring and are very easy to rear in captivity, pupating in a tough boat-shaped cocoon for about a month. The adults fly in late June and July and are frequent visitors to light traps. This is the most widespread and common of this group of moths, inhabiting commons, woods and hedgerows throughout most of England and Wales.

Plate 30: B. Beaten from hawthorn, fully grown. Mid-May.

Least Black Arches

Nola confusalis Herrich-Schäffer

Larva. 13–16 mm. Body very pale buff, with blackish triangular markings on the fourth, sixth, tenth and eleventh segments; head and pinacula orange and setae whitish.

Foodplants. Lime, holm oak, oak, and will accept blackthorn leaves in captivity. Not lichens as often stated.

Habits. Single-brooded, occurring as a larva from June to August, overwintering in the pupal stage in a cocoon spun up upon bark. The adults fly during late May and June, coming readily to light, and the females will often lay their tiny eggs on tissue-paper or leaves when required. Rearing the larvae in confinement can be difficult at first due to their size, but once half grown they usually survive to pupate. To be found locally in woods and parks throughout most of the British Isles.

Plate 30: C. Bred from a female adult to MVL. Early June. (SHC)

Scarce Black Arches

Nola aerugula Hübner

(*centonalis* Hübner)

Larva. 13–15 mm. Body grey, with a thin pinkish-orange dorsal line edged by blackish wedge-shaped markings; head dark brown and setae pale grey.

Foodplants. Trefoils, vetches and clovers.

Habits. A single-brooded irregular migrant species that may establish itself temporarily on the south and east coasts. It occurs in the larval stage from August to June, overwintering when small and the boat-shaped cocoon is formed among plant litter and lasts about a month. The adults come freely to light during July and August, and any attempt to rear this species would probably best be done on potted plants that are kept protected from low temperatures and frost. The larvae can be forced in captivity. Almost all of the recent records of this species have been from southern coastal localities.

Plate 30: D. Bred from a female adult (Belgium). Early August. (JW)

Family: NOCTUIDAE

A large and diverse family consisting of about 350 species to be found regularly in the British Isles. The larvae of most species are cylindrical in shape and are active mainly at night, hiding by day among plant litter, under leaves or within spinnings. Many adopt a secretive existence, living and feeding within the foodplant stems or among roots, and are unlikely to be encountered unless deliberately searched for. Some larvae of the subfamilies *Plusiinae*, *Catocalinae* and *Hypeninae* have the anterior pairs of prolegs either absent or rudimentary and these characteristics can often be helpful when trying to determine the species. The adults of almost all species fly at night and are attracted to light, with many also feeding from flowering plants or coming to sugar. Generally the females will deposit eggs in confinement, especially when given foodplant as a stimulus, and most noctuid larvae are not difficult to rear in captivity, although special conditions must be provided for those which feed internally on plants or within roots.

SUBFAMILY: NOCTUINAE

Square-spot Dart

Euxoa obelisca Denis & Schiffermüller

Larva. 35–38 mm. Body greyish-brown, with a pale grey dorsal line and less distinct incomplete subdorsal lines of the same colour; head brown and prothoracic plate darker brown, with a pale central mark.

Foodplants. Various herbaceous plants, accepting plantain, bedstraw and dandelion in captivity.

Habits. A single-brooded species that probably occurs as a larva from about March to July, with the life-cycle in the wild not being fully known so far. In captivity eggs that are obtained in August and September from the female adults often hatch in February or March and the larvae can be difficult to rear. The pupa is most likely formed just under the soil and lasts about a month. Mostly distributed around the cliffs and rocky coasts of the south and west parts of Britain and Ireland.

Plate 30: E. Bred from a female adult to MVL. Late August. (SHC)

White-line Dart

Euxoa tritici Linnaeus

Larva. 35–40 mm. Body dark greyish-brown, with a pale grey dorsal line and very faint greyish subdorsal marks; head dark grey or brown and the prothoracic plate is dark brown marked dorsally and subdorsally with a pale stripe.

Foodplants. Various herbaceous plants, including chickweed, plantains and dandelion.

Habits. Single-brooded, occurring as a larva from March to July, after overwintering in the egg stage. From late May the nocturnal larvae can sometimes be found when feeding, especially on the low-growing plants among sand dunes and on heathland. At this stage they are not difficult to rear and pupate in the soil for three to four weeks. The adults fly from July to late August, and are attracted to light and flowering plants. Some females will lay in captivity, but the young larvae are often unwilling to start feeding and die quickly. Widespread throughout most of Britain, although mainly coastal in its occurrence in Ireland.

Plate 30: F. Found at night, nearly fully grown. Late May.

Garden Dart

Euxoa nigricans Linnaeus

Larva. 38–44 mm. Body ochreous, with a pale grey dorsal line that is bordered with smudges of darker grey and has indistinct grey markings laterally; head light brown marked darker; prothoracic plate mainly pale brown.

Foodplants. Various herbaceous plants, including clovers, dandelion, plantains and docks.

Habits. A single-brooded species that overwinters as an

egg. The larvae can hatch as early as February and they develop slowly, feeding at night until becoming fully grown by about mid-June. They can be found in the wild where the populations are large, such as on agricultural ground and in gardens and allotments; and the adults are attracted to light in July and August. Eggs can be obtained from the females and it is not a difficult species to rear in captivity, with the cocooned pupa being formed in the soil, lasting about three to four weeks. Generally distributed over most of the British Isles, being more frequent on open ground and in the eastern counties.
Plate 30: G. Bred from a female adult to MVL. Late July. (JMP)

Coast Dart
Euxoa cursoria Hufnagel
Larva. 38–42 mm. Body pale greyish-brown, with a dark-edged thin grey dorsal line; head and prothoracic plate orangish-brown, marked with black.
Foodplants. Sea sandwort, sand couch and other herbaceous plants, accepting plantain and dandelion in captivity.
Habits. Single-brooded, probably overwintering as an egg, with the larvae feeding at night throughout the spring and early summer until July. They can readily be located during the day by carefully sifting through the sand around the bases of the foodplants growing among the coastal sand dunes. When reared in captivity from this stage of their development, they will readily accept plantains; sand from their natural habitat should also be supplied for them to burrow into by day and eventually pupate within. The pupa lasts about a month and the adults, which fly between late July and early September, are more often found at flowering marram and other grasses than at light. Locally distributed on the Suffolk coast northwards to Caithness and from Cheshire northwards to Cumberland; widespread on the north and west coasts of Scotland and parts of Ireland.
Plate 30: H. Located in sand beneath foodplant, fully grown. Late June.

Light Feathered Rustic
Agrotis cinerea Denis & Schiffermüller
(*denticulatus* Haworth)
Larva. 35–40 mm. Body greyish-brown, with an indistinct pale dorsal line and large black spiracles; head and prothoracic plate almost black.
Foodplants. Various herbaceous plants, including wild thyme, accepting dandelion and plantain in captivity.
Habits. A single-brooded insect, the larvae of which feed from late June to September, then overwinter fully grown before pupating in the early spring. The adults fly in May and June, with the females more likely to be found at sugar than attracted to light. These will often lay eggs freely in captivity and the larvae are quite easy to rear, although they should be left outside with soil and plant litter in which to overwinter. Locally widespread over the southern parts of England, north to Derbyshire; also occurring in parts of Wales and rarely in Ireland.
Plate 30: I. Bred from a female adult to sugar. Late May. (RM)

Archer's Dart
Agrotis vestigialis Hufnagel
Larva. 38–43 mm. Body light brown, with a distinct grey-edged pale dorsal line and vague pale markings surrounding the spiracles; head orangish-brown with dark streaks and the prothoracic plate is dark brown dorsally with pale orange stripes.
Foodplants. Various grasses and herbaceous plants, readily accepting dandelion and bedstraw in confinement.
Habits. Single-brooded, occurring as a larva from September to the following June, feeding throughout most of the winter except when very cold. The adults fly from about late July to early September and both sexes are attracted to light and sugar. Most females will lay freely in confinement and the larvae can be encouraged to develop faster by keeping them warm and in the dark, becoming fully grown in about three months. The pupa is formed beneath the soil and lasts about four to six weeks. Generally distributed around the coasts of Britain and Ireland; also occurring locally inland, especially on heaths and sandy soils.
Plate 30: J. Bred from a female adult to MVL. Late August.

Turnip Moth
Agrotis segetum Denis & Schiffermüller
Larva. 45–50 mm. Body greyish-brown, with a slightly darker dorsal line and more obvious subdorsal mottling; spiracles and pinacula brownish-black and the head is brown with darker streaks.
Foodplants. The roots and lower stems of various herbaceous and cultivated plants.
Habits. Single- or double-brooded, with the mainly subterranean larvae feeding from July to the following spring, many overwintering when fully grown. The adults mostly fly during May and June, and those of the partial second generation in the autumn; also the resident population is often reinforced by immigrants from the continent. Both sexes are readily attracted to light, sugar and flowering plants and most females will lay freely in confinement. The larvae are usually very easy to rear, accepting all parts of dandelion or plantain, and by keeping them warm and in the dark most will become fully developed in about six to eight weeks. Pupation takes place underground and this stage lasts about three to six weeks. This usually common species, that sometimes becomes a pest of root crops, is widely distributed over most parts of the British Isles.
Plate 30: K. Bred from a female adult to MVL. Mid-June.

Heart and Club
Agrotis clavis Hufnagel
(*corticea* Denis & Schiffermüller)
Larva. 35–38 mm. Body greyish-brown, with a vague dark-edged dorsal line and dark pinacula; head brown with four broad black streaks and the prothoracic plate is slightly paler than the body.
Foodplants. Various herbaceous plants, including dandelion, dock, knotgrass and clover.
Habits. Single-brooded, being in the larval stage from about August to the following spring, feeding at first on the leaves and later the roots of the foodplants, while overwintering fully grown in an earthen cell. The adults fly during late June and July, with both sexes coming freely to light. Most females will lay eggs in captivity if required to do so, and rearing the larvae is usually fairly easy. When fully grown they should be supplied with light soil and then left outside to hibernate and pupate naturally. Locally common in gardens, on sandhills and in other open ground habitats over much of the British Isles, being most frequent in the southern counties.
Plate 30: L. Bred from a female adult to MVL. Early July. (SHC)

Heart and Dart
Agrotis exclamationis Linnaeus

Larva. 37–40 mm. Body reddish-brown, with a fine dark-edged pale dorsal line and darker subdorsal line; head brown with a pair of dark streaks and the black spiracles are large and obvious.

Foodplants. Various herbaceous plants.

Habits. Mostly single-brooded, although sometimes a few larvae feed up and emerge as adults in the autumn. Normally the larval stage lasts from July to the following spring, the insects becoming fully grown by about October and then overwintering in an earthen cell in which they later pupate. The adults mostly fly during June and July and can be abundant at sugar and light, with most females laying freely in captivity. The larvae are easy to rear and, if kept warm, will often pupate immediately and produce moths after about a month. Widely distributed over most parts of the British Isles.

Plate 30: M. Bred from a female adult to MVL. Late June.

Crescent Dart
Agrotis trux Hübner

Larva. 37–40 mm. Body grey, with a faint paler dorsal line and darker laterally. The head is light brown with large black markings and the prothoracic plate is almost black with a paler dorsal stripe.

Foodplants. Various herbaceous plants, accepting dandelion, plantain, dock, knotgrass and sliced carrot in captivity.

Habits. A single-brooded species that occurs in the larval stage from late August to the following spring. Most larvae are fully grown by about November and feed little, if at all, during the winter. They are most readily obtained by rearing from an adult female; these fly during July and August, responding well to light traps or sugar patches. Captive moths should be given corrugated cardboard or crumpled tissue-paper on which to oviposit, and rearing the larvae is usually not too difficult, with many feeding up rapidly to produce more adults in the autumn. Mostly to be found on the coastal cliffs of southern and western England, Wales and Ireland; also occurring in the Isle of Man and in Morayshire, Scotland.

Plate 30: N. Bred from a female adult to MVL. Late July. (SHC)

Dark Sword-grass
Agrotis ipsilon Hufnagel

Larva. 43–47 mm. Body greenish-grey, with an indistinct dorsal line and a vague pale brownish subdorsal line; head almost black, and prothoracic plate and spiracles black; there is a series of four black pinacula on the first two segments and underparts are very pale grey.

Foodplants. Various herbaceous plants, accepting dandelion and plantain in captivity.

Habits. A regular immigrant species that is recorded most frequently during the autumn. The larval stage lasts about a month to six weeks and is most likely to occur during July and August from the earlier arrivals. These adults can readily be taken at light, sugar and flowering plants from about May to November, although the females kept during the autumn are invariably sexually immature and will not deposit eggs in captivity. If eggs are obtained, the resulting larvae are very easy to rear when kept warm, and like most other associated species pupate in an earthen cell for about three to four weeks. This insect is to be found most often in the southern coastal counties, but has been recorded from most parts of the British Isles.

Plate 30: O. Bred from a female adult to light. Early July.

Shuttle-shaped Dart
Agrotis puta Hübner

Larva. 30–33 mm. Body light brown, with a faint grey dorsal line and darker subdorsal lines; head brown, with blackish marks; spiracles small and black.

Foodplants. Various herbaceous plants, including plantains, dandelion, docks and knotgrass.

Habits. At least double-brooded, with the larvae occurring from autumn to the following April and throughout the summer months, feeding at night and hiding on or in the soil during the day. The adults fly from late April to June, again in July and August and once more in smaller numbers during the autumn. They are readily attracted to light, sugar and flowers, and captive females usually lay quite freely. The larvae are very easy to rear and pupate in the soil for about three to four weeks. A common to abundant species inhabiting gardens, waste ground, open woods and marshes, being found over most of southern England and lowland parts of Wales.

Plate 30: P. Bred from a female adult to MVL. Late May.

Sand Dart
Agrotis ripae Hübner

Larva. 35–38 mm. Body pale ochreous, with a dark-edged pale dorsal line, darker subdorsal lines, bold black spiracles and brown pinacula; head light brown.

Foodplants. Sea rocket, prickly saltwort and other foreshore plants, accepting sliced carrots in captivity, when larger.

Habits. A single-brooded species that occurs in the larval stage from August to October, then overwintering in a cocoon beneath the sand, until eventually pupating in the spring. Throughout September and October the night-feeding larvae can be found in good numbers by carefully sifting through the sand beneath the plants that grow on the foreshore. They can then be reared by placing them in a container, such as a large plastic sweet-jar, filled with sand from their habitat with pieces of sliced carrot on the surface, on which they can feed. The sand should be deep and the larvae must not be disturbed during the winter months. During the spring a few sticks can be carefully pushed into the top of the sand for the adults to crawl up when they emerge during June and July. Locally common on coastal sandhills throughout England and Wales; also recorded from Scotland and parts of Ireland.

Plate 30: Q. Located in sand beneath foodplant, nearly fully grown. Mid-September. (SHC)

Great Dart
Agrotis crassa Hübner

Larva. 33–38 mm. Body greyish-brown, with an indistinct grey-edged pale dorsal line, small brown subdorsal pinacula and largish black spiracles; head brownish-orange, with a pair of bold black streaks.

Foodplants. The roots of grasses and low-growing plants, accepting carrot roots in captivity.

Habits. A single-brooded insect that was possibly established during the last century on the once extensive marshland to the east of London. Recently several adults have been light-trapped in Dorset and elsewhere, these probably being immigrants from France where the insect is not uncommon. The larval stage lasts from September to the following spring and although the larvae are not too difficult to keep in captivity, they usually do not survive to pupate. The adults fly in August and both sexes are attracted to light.

Plate 30: R. Bred from a female adult (France). Mid-August. (AJP)

Purple Cloud
Actinotia polyodon Clerck
Larva. 32–36 mm. Body reddish-brown, with an obscure yellowish dorsal line and oblique dark brown subdorsal streaks; spiracular line bold, lemon-yellow; yellow subdorsal dashes on the prothoracic plate and last segment; head pale brown.
Foodplant. The flowers, seeds and leaves of St John's-wort.
Habits. A single-brooded insect in northern Europe, of which fifteen have been recorded in the adult stage in the British Isles. The insects are considered to be immigrants and breeding in the wild has never been proven in Britain. The larval stage lasts from June to August, feeding on the underside of the leaves during the first instar and dropping on silken threads if disturbed. The larvae are considered not to be difficult to rear in captivity and overwintering takes place as a subterranean pupa, with the adults flying during the following May and June.
Plate 31: A. Bred from a female adult to MVL (C. France). Mid-May. (PQW)

The Flame
Axylia putris Linnaeus
Larva. 34–38 mm. Body greenish-grey, with the fourth, fifth and eleventh segments slightly swollen, a series of small brownish dorsal spots and dark subdorsal marks on segments four, five, and nine to eleven; head dark brown.
Foodplants. Various herbaceous plants, including docks, dandelion, bedstraw, common nettle, knotgrass and plantains.
Habits. Mainly a single-brooded species that occurs as a larva from July to September, overwintering as a cocooned pupa just under the soil. The main brood of adults is on the wing during June and July, with both sexes being readily attracted to light and most females laying eggs freely in confinement. The larvae are not difficult to rear and those kept indoors will often pupate for about three weeks, emerging in the autumn, as do a small proportion in the wild. Widespread and moderately common over much of England, Wales and Ireland; local in southern Scotland.
Plate 31: B. Bred from a female adult to MVL. Late June.

Portland Moth
Actebia praecox Linnaeus
Larva. 42–46 mm. Body dark grey, with pale triangular dorsal markings, distinctly orange in the subdorsal region and pale underparts; head light brown with a pair of thin black lines; prothoracic plate pale brown.
Foodplants. Creeping willow, tree lupin, trefoils and other herbaceous sand-dune plants, accepting most species of sallow and willow in captivity.
Habits. A single-brooded species, occurring in the larval stage from September to the following late June. It feeds at night and during the day hides in a burrow under the sand. During the spring these burrows can sometimes be located by the presence of a small mound of sand and the trail leading from the foodplant. The cocooned pupa is formed under the sand and lasts from six to eight weeks, before the adults emerge in late August and September. These may readily be taken at light and flowering plants and although eggs can be obtained, this insect is not easy to rear; although putting the tiny larvae on to suitable potted plants growing in fine sandy soil could be successful. A local species mostly inhabiting coastal sandhills and a few inland sites on sandy soil in Lincolnshire and Nottinghamshire; also recorded from the Spey valley in Scotland and on the coast of Ireland.
Plate 31: C. Found under sand close to plantains, fully grown. Early June. (MH)

Eversmann's Rustic
Actebia fennica Tauscher
Larva. 35–40 mm. Body brown, with a slender pale subdorsal line, blackish laterally and having a pale stripe in the spiracular region; head, prothoracic and anal plates black (Spuler).
Foodplants. Willowherb and other herbaceous plants.
Habits. A single-brooded scarce immigrant species that occurs in the larval stage from September to the following June and has been recorded six times as an adult, most coming from the eastern side of Britain. The adults fly mainly in August and abroad the species occurs in northern Europe, western Siberia and North America.

Flame Shoulder
Ochropleura plecta Linnaeus
Larva. 32–35 mm. Body pale brown or greenish-brown, with a dark-edged thin pale dorsal line and an indistinct darker subdorsal line; head orangish-brown and underparts pale ochreous.
Foodplants. Various herbaceous plants, including groundsel, plantains, docks, dandelion and knotgrass.
Habits. Usually double-brooded, with the larvae occurring in June and July, and again in September and October, then almost certainly overwintering in the pupal stage. These nocturnal larvae are sometimes found by accident when searching for other species, and are very easy to rear in captivity. The adults fly in May and June, and those of the second brood in August and September, both sexes being attracted to light and ragwort flowers, and most females laying freely in confinement. This common species is widely distributed over most of the British Isles.
Plate 31: D. Bred from a female adult to MVL. Early June. (SHC)

Radford's Flame Shoulder
Ochropleura leucogaster Freyer
Larva. 33–37 mm. Body greyish-brown, with fine whitish dorsal and subdorsal lines; lateral line broad and yellowish (Forster and Wohlfahrt).
Foodplants. Various herbaceous plants, including trefoils.
Habits. A very scarce immigrant species that has recently been recorded five times as an adult in the British Isles. On the continent its range covers much of southern Europe, being double-brooded with the larvae occurring from late October to the following March and again in the summer months.

Plain Clay
Eugnorisma depuncta Linnaeus
Larva. 45–48 mm. Body greyish-brown, with a pale thin interrupted dorsal line and a broad very pale yellow line below the spiracles; head brown with a black streak.
Foodplants. Various herbaceous plants, including dock, stitchwort, common nettle and primrose.
Habits. A single-brooded species that occurs in the larval stage from September to about late May, overwintering in grass stems and similar sheltered locations immediately after hatching from the egg. During the spring feeding commences and the larvae can be found at night feeding and resting upon their foodplants. Pupation takes place in a cocoon just beneath the soil and lasts about six to eight weeks, with the adults emerging in July and August. Both sexes are attracted

to light and sugar, but many females are reluctant to lay in captivity, even when fed and supplied with netting and crumpled tissue-paper in which to oviposit. The young larvae should be put into a refrigerator until January, then brought into a warm room and they can then be reared successfully. A local woodland species, being found most frequently in central and eastern Scotland; local and rare in Wales, northern and south-west England.
Plate 31: E. Located at night on common nettle, fully grown. Mid-May. (BS)

Northern Rustic

Standfussiana lucernea Linnaeus
Larva. 45–48 mm. Body brown, heavily irrorate with dark greyish-brown and pairs of pale markings on each of segments four to eleven in the subdorsal region; head dark brown with a pair of black streaks. In the penultimate instar, body pale brown with dark chevrons dorsally.
Foodplants. Various grasses and herbaceous plants, including harebell, stonecrops and saxifrages, accepting dandelion in captivity.
Habits. Single-brooded, occurring as a larva from October to about the following May, overwintering when still quite small. During the spring the larvae have been found at night resting on rocks near to the foodplant. The adults fly from July to September, with the females disappearing, probably to aestivate, during most of August. Both sexes are attracted to light, sugar and flowering plants, especially wood sage, red valerian and ragwort, and some females lay their egg batches quite freely on netting, sponge or crumpled tissue-paper in captivity. The larvae are notoriously difficult to rear and most die of an unknown cause before reaching half grown. Mainly coastal in distribution, being found on rocky cliffs, also in quarries and on mountain scree in northern and western Britain and Ireland; also locally on the south coast at Folkestone Warren, Kent and Eastbourne, Sussex, and from the Isle of Wight to Cornwall.
Plate 31: F. Bred from a female adult to MVL. Mid-September. (SHC)

Dotted Rustic

Rhyacia simulans Hufnagel
Larva. 45–48 mm. Body light brown, with a paler dorsal line and dark brown dashes along the subdorsal region of the abdominal segments; head pale brown.
Foodplants. Unknown in the wild, accepting couch and other grasses, dandelion, dock, knotgrass and bramble in captivity.
Habits. A single-brooded species, being in the larval stage from September to the following spring. The adults fly from late June to late September, aestivating during late July and August in outbuildings, caves, tunnels and other cool locations. Both sexes are attracted to light and flowering plants, and although some females may deposit eggs in captivity, the larvae are usually very difficult to rear. To be found locally throughout most of Britain, but subject to great fluctuations in numbers and distribution.
Plate 31: G. Bred from a female adult to MVL. Mid-September. (PQW)

Large Yellow Underwing

Noctua pronuba Linnaeus
Larva. 46–52 mm. Body greyish-brown or greenish-brown, with an indistinct dorsal line, oblong-shaped blackish markings subdorsally on the abdominal segments above a pale line and a brown head that is marked with black.
Foodplants. Various herbaceous plants and grasses.
Habits. Single-brooded, occurring as a larva from September to the following early May, feeding during the winter whenever the weather is mild enough. During the early spring the larvae are very easy to find or sweep at night when they are active and feeding. Rearing them in captivity is very easy and they prefer to pupate just under the soil in a silken cocoon. This stage usually lasts between one and three months depending on the temperature and local conditions, with the light- and sugar-responsive adults flying from late June to early September or even later. Widely distributed and often common throughout almost all of the British Isles, except on the very highest ground.
Plate 31: H. Found at night, fully grown. Late April.

Lunar Yellow Underwing

Noctua orbona Hufnagel
Larva. 35–40 mm. Body brown, with a conspicuous white dorsal stripe and buff subdorsal lines, above which are black oblong markings, boldest on the abdominal segments; head brown with black marks.
Foodplants. Various herbaceous plants and grasses, accepting cock's-foot and later dandelion in captivity.
Habits. A single-brooded species, being in the larval stage from September to the following April, feeding slowly throughout the winter months in mild weather. These larvae can be found or swept, mainly at night, from February onwards, while resting on short fine-bladed grasses, and once brought into captivity their development becomes more rapid. Usually an easy species to rear, but some individuals die from an unknown cause and they are quite often parasitized. The pupa is formed in a flimsy cocoon beneath loose soil and lasts about a month in captivity and up to three months in the wild. The adults begin to emerge about late June and soon aestivate, reappearing in late August and September. Both sexes are attracted to light and sugar, and most females will lay readily in confinement. A very local and declining species, being found mainly in the Breck district of East Anglia, downland areas of Wiltshire, the border counties of England and Scotland and the Findhorn sandhills of Morayshire.
Plate 31: I. Swept at night, about one-third grown. Early February.

Lesser Yellow Underwing

Noctua comes Hübner
Larva. 38–44 mm. Body greenish-grey or greyish-brown, with a thin pale dorsal line and black triangular marks subdorsally on the tenth and eleventh segments; subspiracular line pale and broad; head brown streaked with black.
Foodplants. Various herbaceous plants and also various deciduous trees, especially in the spring.
Habits. Single-brooded, occurring as a larva from August to the following May, or even early June in the north. During the spring these mainly nocturnal larvae can readily be found, feeding on the foodplant buds, especially birch, hawthorn, blackthorn and bog myrtle, fully exposed in the torchlight. They are usually very easy to rear and should be supplied with fine soil in which to form their cocooned pupae. This stage lasts about a month and the adults emerge from late June to late August, with both sexes being freely attracted to light, sugar and flowering plants. Females lay readily in captivity and the larvae can be forced through by keeping them warm and in the dark. A common and widespread species, being found over most of the British Isles.
Plate 31: J. Found at night on birch, fully grown. Early May.

Broad-bordered Yellow Underwing
Noctua fimbriata Schreber

Larva. 47–53 mm. Body ochreous, with a pale bar across the eleventh segment and conspicuous white spiracles that are surrounded with black spots on the fourth to ninth segments; head brown.

Foodplants. Various herbaceous plants, also the young buds and foliage of various trees during the spring.

Habits. A single-brooded insect, the larva of which occurs from about September to the following spring, overwintering on or near the ground, feeding during mild weather. During April most of these larvae are fully grown and they can readily be found at night, when their plump pale bodies are very conspicuous on the twigs of birch, blackthorn and sallow. In captivity they are fairly easy to rear and pupate in loose soil for about two months. The adults emerge in July, then aestivate for a period before reappearing in August and lingering on until September. They are attracted to light and sugar, with the females laying freely in confinement. Larvae from these can be forced with warmth. Widespread and generally common over much of the British Isles.

Plate 31: K. Found at night on birch, fully grown. Late April.

Lesser Broad-bordered Yellow Underwing
Noctua janthe Borkhausen
(*janthina* Denis & Schiffermüller)

Larva. 37–40 mm. Body brown, with a fine yellowish-white dorsal line and vague darker chevrons along the back, with those on the tenth and eleventh segments being more distinct and a pale thin bar across the hind parts of the latter; head brown.

Foodplants. Various herbaceous plants, also bramble, sallow, birch, blackthorn and other shrubs and bushes.

Habits. Single-brooded, occurring in the larval stage from September to the following April, overwintering when about half grown. Although this species is fairly common, the larva is not found in the spring as often as its close relatives, probably preferring to feed low down among the developing herbaceous plants. Most have pupated underground by May and the light-responsive adults can be found between late July and early September. Most females will readily deposit eggs in confinement and the resulting larvae are easy to force through by keeping them warm and in the dark. Widespread throughout most of the British Isles, and sometimes abundant in the mature woodlands of southern England.

Plate 31: L. Bred from a female adult to MVL. Late August.

Least Yellow Underwing
Noctua interjecta Hübner

Larva. 35–40 mm. Body ochreous, with dark-edged dorsal and subdorsal lines, a brown spiracular line and black-marked brown head.

Foodplants. Various herbaceous plants and grasses, accepting dock, chickweed, dandelion and blackthorn in captivity.

Habits. A single-brooded species, being in the larval stage from about September to the following May, overwintering when about half grown. The larva is not often seen in the wild, but occasionally the odd one can be found at night, when searching for other species. The adults fly during July and August, and come to light in small numbers. Most females are content to lay their egg batches in confinement and the resulting larvae are not difficult to rear, with some individuals accepting being forced to develop faster if kept warm. A local insect that is widely distributed mainly over the southern parts of England, Wales and Ireland.

Plate 31: M. Found at night on blackthorn, fully grown. Early May.

Stout Dart
Spaelotis ravida Denis & Schiffermüller

Larva. 38–42 mm. Body brown or brownish-grey, with a series of yellowish markings along the subdorsal area and a pale spiracular line.

Foodplants. Unknown in the wild, but almost certainly various low-growing plants, including dock, dandelion and sow-thistle, which are accepted in captivity.

Habits. Single-brooded, probably occurring as a larva from about September to the following late May. The larvae, which are exceedingly difficult to rear, could possibly be found during the spring by careful searching of various suitable foodplants at night. The adults emerge during late June and early July, and quickly go into aestivation, reappearing during August and September. Both sexes respond to light and flowering plants, but the females are very reluctant to deposit eggs in captivity. Those eggs that are obtained tend to hatch about December and the young larvae feed slowly for about two weeks before dying from an unknown cause. It has been suggested that they need to be kept outside, on growing foodplants in netting-covered tubs and even then they die just before pupation. This species is cyclic in its abundance and distribution, with East Anglia and the midland counties of England being the strongholds.

Double Dart
Graphiphora augur Fabricius

Larva. 44–48 mm. Body reddish-brown, with a series of small white tubercles along the subdorsal area and a dull yellow band across the rear part of the eleventh segment; head dark brown with black markings.

Foodplants. Various herbaceous plants in the autumn, and the young foliage of hawthorn, blackthorn, birch and sallow in the spring.

Habits. A single-brooded insect that occurs in the larval stage from about August to mid-May, and later in the north. The larva is rarely met with during the autumn, probably due to its size and feeding low down on herbaceous plants. About April the development becomes more rapid and at this time the larvae can readily be found at night up on the bare twigs of bushes, feeding on the new buds and young leaves. At this stage they are very easy to rear in confinement and pupate in the soil for about a month. The adults fly in June and July, with both sexes coming to light, sugar and flowering plants, and most females can be induced to lay eggs by feeding them and supplying netting on which to oviposit. Generally distributed over most parts of the British Isles.

Plate 31: N. Located at night on blackthorn, fully grown. Early May.

Rosy Marsh Moth
Eugraphe subrosea Stephens

Larva. 37–40 mm. Body purplish-brown, with a distinct white dorsal line, a yellow subdorsal line that is bordered with orange below and black above and a broad white subspiracular stripe; head brown marked with black.

Foodplants. Bog myrtle, accepting most species of sallow and willow in captivity.

Habits. Single-brooded, occurring as a larva from September to the following late May, June or even early July, overwintering when still very small. During the late spring the larvae may be found at night, feeding and resting on the

upper parts of the foodplant, with their broad white lateral stripe making them very conspicuous. Taken into captivity at this stage, they are very easy to rear, pupating in loose soil for about a month. The adults fly in late July and August, and respond well to both light and flowering plants. A very local species, at present being found only in the acid boggy areas of west Wales, although it did occur in the fenlands of East Anglia until becoming extinct during the last century.
Plate 31: O. Courtesy of Paul Waring.

Cousin German

Paradiarsia sobrina Duponchel
Larva. 30–34 mm. Body reddish-brown, with a faint dorsal line in which there is a series of yellowish-white spots, most obvious on the fourth to ninth segments; a pale spiracular line and head pale brown marked darker.
Foodplants. Bilberry, heather and in the spring birch.
Habits. A single-brooded species, being in the larval stage from September to the following June, overwintering when still very small. During the spring the development becomes rapid, although these larvae are rarely met with until about the latter part of May. They can then be found at night, usually feeding on the young leaves of birch scrub that grows among bilberry at the edges of woods. Most collected at this time seem to survive and they prefer to pupate in moss or loose soil for about four to six weeks. The adults fly in late July and August, being attracted to light and heather flowers. A very local species restricted in distribution mainly to the highlands of Scotland.
Plate 31: P. Found at night on birch, nearly fully grown. Early June. (BS)

Autumnal Rustic

Paradiarsia glareosa Esper
Larva. 30–35 mm. Body light brown, with a thin pale dorsal line, vague subdorsal lines and a broad straw-coloured subspiracular line; head reddish-brown marked with black.
Foodplants. Various herbaceous plants and grasses, also the young foliage of birch, sallow and other trees in the spring.
Habits. Single-brooded, occurring as a larva from about October to the following May, feeding throughout the winter whenever the weather is mild enough. From January onwards the larvae may be swept at night from short grasses and can readily be distinguished by the yellowish lateral stripe and their posture of curling the front part of the body. Later, as the trees begin to bud, they can be found, again at night, on the bare twigs of scrub birches. At this stage they are usually very easy to rear in confinement and pupate in a loose cocoon just under the soil. The adults fly during August and September, with both sexes coming to light in reasonable numbers and most females will lay freely in confinement. Widespread, but local, mainly on sandy soils and moorland over much of the British Isles.
Plate 31: Q. Found at night on birch, nearly fully grown. Early May. (GAC)

True Lover's Knot

Lycophotia porphyrea Denis & Schiffermüller
(*varia* de Villers)
Larva. 27–30 mm. Body reddish-brown, with a series of bold white marks that are surrounded by dark brown on the abdominal segments along the dorsal area and yellowish-white subdorsal marks; head dark brown.
Foodplants. Heather and bell heather.
Habits. Single-brooded, being in the larval stage from August to the following May, overwintering among plant litter when nearly fully grown. During the late autumn and early spring, the larvae can easily be obtained by sweeping, especially at night, and although they are often difficult to overwinter in captivity, those taken in the spring usually present no problems to rear. The cocooned pupa is formed on or just under the soil and lasts from four to six weeks, with the adults flying from June to August. These come freely to light and heather flowers at night and can often be seen flying in sunshine during the afternoon. Generally distributed and often common on heaths and moorland throughout the British Isles.
Plate 31: R. Swept at night, nearly fully grown. Mid-September.

Pearly Underwing

Peridroma saucia Hübner
Larva. 40–45 mm. Body various shades of brown, with an indistinct dorsal line that may be marked with small yellowish spots and a dark marking on the eleventh segment, followed by a yellowish blotch. Subdorsally thin black marks and grey clouding around the black spiracles; head brown, irrorate with black.
Foodplants. Various herbaceous plants, including dandelion, dock and plantain.
Habits. A regular immigrant species that occurs most frequently as a larva from about July to late October and although rarely met with in the wild, the larvae are very easy to rear from the adult females, which can be taken at light, sugar and flowering plants between June and October. The larvae feed mostly at night, and if kept warm and in the dark, they become fully developed in about four to six weeks and pupate in a cocoon just under the soil for about a month. Recorded throughout the British Isles, being far more frequent in the southern coastal counties of England.
Plate 32: A. Bred from a female adult to sugar. Early September. (M&JH)

Ingrailed Clay

Diarsia mendica Fabricius
(*festiva* Denis & Schiffermüller)
Larva. 30–34 mm. Body reddish-brown, occasionally olive-green, with a vague pale dorsal line and black wedge-shaped markings along the subdorsal area of the abdominal segments; head dark brown and spiracular line broad and pale brown.
Foodplants. Various herbaceous plants, including dock, plantain, heather, bilberry and bramble.
Habits. Single-brooded, occurring as a larva from about August to the following May, overwintering while still quite small and being most frequently found in the spring. At this time the larvae can be found at night, feeding on the developing plants and are very easy to rear in confinement, pupating for about a month just under the soil. The adults fly from June to early August, with the females laying their egg batches quite freely in captivity. Keeping the resulting broods warm will force most to continue feeding and pupate by about November. Widely distributed and often common over most parts of the British Isles.
Plate 32: B. Bred from a female adult to MVL. Early July. (SHC)

Barred Chestnut

Diarsia dahlii Hübner
Larva. 32–35 mm. Body of various shades of brown, with darker diamond-shaped markings along the dorsal area and indistinct thin greyish dorsal and subdorsal lines; head dark brown speckled with black.

Foodplants. Various herbaceous plants, including dock, plantain and dandelion, and in the spring the young shoots of bilberry, birch and sallow.
Habits. A single-brooded insect that occurs in the larval stage from about September to the following early spring. The larvae are rarely met with in the wild, even in places where the species is locally common, but are very easy to obtain by rearing from adult moths. These fly during August and September, and both sexes respond well to light and can also be found feeding on flowering plants, such as heather and wood sage. The females freely lay their egg batches in captivity and the larvae grow quickly if kept warm and supplied with dock or dandelion, to produce more adults by about December. Found mainly in light woodland on acid soils in the Midlands, northern England and Scotland. Local and rare in the south, except in parts of Surrey where it is locally common; also recorded from Ireland.
Plate 32: C. Bred from a female adult to MVL. Early September.

Purple Clay

Diarsia brunnea Denis & Schiffermüller
Larva. 30–34 mm. Body reddish-brown, with a conspicuous yellowish-white bar across the eleventh segment and a series of dark marks along the thin vague dorsal line. The spiracular line is broad and paler than the body and the head is mainly brown.
Foodplants. Various herbaceous plants before hibernation and the young foliage of birch, blackthorn, sallow, bilberry, bramble and other plants in the spring.
Habits. Single-brooded, being in the larval stage from about August to the following early May, overwintering when still quite small and being less often met with before hibernation. During the spring the growth becomes rapid and these larvae can then be located at night when up on the bare twigs of budding bushes and can also readily be swept from bilberry in some localities. At this stage of their development they are easy to rear and pupate just under the soil for about a month to six weeks. The light-responsive adults fly from about late June to early August and most females deposit eggs readily in captivity, with the resulting larvae often being forced through by keeping them warm. Generally distributed and fairly common in woodland throughout Britain and Ireland.
Plate 32: D. Found at night on blackthorn, fully grown. Early May.

Small Square-spot

Diarsia rubi Vieweg
Larva. 28–32 mm. Body various shades of brown, with a thin dark-bordered pale dorsal line, small black spiracles and paler underparts; head pale reddish-brown.
Foodplants. Various herbaceous plants, including dandelion, plantain, dock, chickweed and heather.
Habits. Double-brooded in southern parts of its range, occurring in the larval stage in June and July and from September to late April. Single-brooded in the north, with larvae from August to May. Although not often found in the wild, these larvae can be obtained by rearing from the adults. These come to light and sugar during May and early June, and again in late August and September, except those of the northern populations which fly in late June and July. Most females lay freely in captivity and the larvae are easy to breed, becoming continuously brooded if kept warm. Common and widely distributed in the southern parts of England, Wales and Ireland; more local, and the distribution frequently confused with following species, *D. florida*, in the north of England and Scotland.
Plate 32: E. Bred from a female adult to MVL (Sussex). Late May. (SHC)

Fen Square-spot

Diarsia florida Schmidt
Larva. Seemingly identical to the previous species, *D. rubi*.
Foodplants. Probably various herbaceous plants, accepting dandelion and dock in captivity.
Habits. Much speculation exists as to whether this is a true species or merely a single-brooded race of the previous insect, *D. rubi*. In the southern parts of Britain it inhabits fens and boggy ground, sharing the habitat with *D. rubi* but flying in late June and July, between the two broods of that species, and having the habit of not coming to light traps until after midnight, whereas *D. rubi* attends from dusk onwards. The adults are extremely similar and they cannot be separated by examination of the genitalia, although they are generally larger, have paler hindwings and an orange tint to the forewings. Fertile hybrids have been obtained in captivity and rearing *D. florida* is very easy, although it is reported to manage only two broods each year even when kept warm. In Scotland the situation is even more confusing, as here *D. rubi* is univoltine and very few moths of any species respond to light before midnight in July, due to the very short hours of darkness.
Plate 32: F. Bred from a female adult to MVL (Norfolk). Early July. (JF)

Northern Dart

Xestia alpicola Zetterstedt
Larva. 30–35 mm. Body in penultimate instar purplish-brown, with a thin pale dorsal line and a series of black dashes along the top edge of the paler subdorsal line; head dark brown, irrorate with black. Final instar duller, wrinkled and leathery.
Foodplants. Crowberry and possibly heather.
Habits. Adopting a life-cycle that lasts two years, overwintering twice as a larva. The adults fly from late June to August and the eggs hatch in about two weeks with the larvae feeding slowly, overwintering in their first year when very small and in the second year probably in the penultimate instar. They can be located by careful searching under the lichens and moss that cover their montane habitats, during April and early May of the year in which they are due to emerge. The pupa is formed without any cocoon in the moss during late May or June and lasts from four to eight weeks. It occurs mainly on the mountain tops of the Scottish Highlands in even numbered years and those of the Pennines and Cheviots in odd years.
Plate 32: G. Found under reindeer-moss, nearly fully grown. Early May. (MB)

Setaceous Hebrew Character

Xestia c-nigrum Linnaeus
Larva. 35–40 mm. Body greenish or greyish-brown, with a thin white interrupted dorsal line and a series of wedge-shaped dark markings along the subdorsal area of the abdominal segments; the spiracle on the eleventh ring is larger and obvious; head pale brown with darker streaks.
Foodplants. Various herbaceous plants, including plantain, dandelion, common nettle, dock, groundsel and chickweed.
Habits. Double-brooded, occurring as a larva during the summer, and again from about September to the following early spring, probably feeding during the milder winter

weather. The larvae are not often found in the wild due to their nocturnal habits and to feeding on low-growing plants, but occasionally they are located when searching for other species. The adults mostly fly in May and June, and later in greater numbers, probably being reinforced by immigrants, from late August to October. They come readily to light and sugar, with most females depositing eggs quite freely in captivity. The larvae are very easy to rear and do better if kept warm. Pupation takes place under the soil in a loose cocoon and lasts about a month. Widely distributed throughout most of the British Isles, often common in the southern counties of England.

Plate 32: H. Bred from a female adult to MVL. Early September.

Triple-spotted Clay

Xestia ditrapezium Denis & Schiffermüller

Larva. 37–40 mm. Body various shades of brown, with an indistinct pale dorsal line and wedge-shaped dark markings subdorsally on the last few abdominal rings, behind which on the eleventh segment is a black-edged pale bar across the dorsal area; head light brown.

Foodplants. Various herbaceous plants before hibernation and the buds and young foliage of birch, sallow, blackthorn and bramble in spring.

Habits. A single-brooded species, in the larval stage from August to the following May, overwintering when about one-third grown. The larvae are easiest to find at night during the spring, when feeding higher up on the bushes and brambles, and taken into captivity they are very easy to rear. The pupa is formed in a flimsy cocoon on or just under the ground and lasts about four to six weeks. The adults fly during July, come freely to light, sugar and flowering plants, with most females depositing eggs freely in confinement. The larvae may be forced through by keeping them warm, in the dark, and supplied with plantain and bramble leaves. Widespread, but rather local, over much of the British Isles, mainly inhabiting open woodland and commons.

Plate 32: I. Found at night on birch, fully grown. Early May. (JMP)

Double Square-spot

Xestia triangulum Hufnagel

Larva. 37–40 mm. Body ochreous to reddish-brown, darker anteriorly, with an indistinct dorsal line, a pair of bold black wedge-shaped marks subdorsally on the tenth and eleventh segments and a thin black-edged pale bar across the eleventh ring behind the wedges; head brown, with darker marks.

Foodplants. Various herbaceous plants, including dandelion, dock and plantain, also birch, bramble, sallow, hawthorn and blackthorn during the spring.

Habits. Single-brooded, occurring as a larva from about August to the following early May, overwintering when about half grown. It is easiest to find during the spring by searching at night on the developing foliage of brambles and on the stems of small bushes of birch and blackthorn, although some larvae may be parasitized. The subterranean cocooned pupa lasts for about four to eight weeks, with the light- and sugar-responsive adults flying in June and July. Eggs are usually laid freely in confinement and the larvae can often be forced by keeping them warm. Generally distributed and fairly common over most of Britain and Ireland.

Plate 32: J. Found at night on bramble, fully grown. Late April.

Ashworth's Rustic

Xestia ashworthii Doubleday

Larva. 36–40 mm. Body dark greyish-black, with a series of jet-black rectangular markings along the subdorsal area and white spiracles; head and thoracic legs orangish-brown.

Foodplants. Heather, foxglove, wild thyme and other herbaceous plants, accepting sallow, especially the catkins, in captivity.

Habits. A single-brooded species, being in the larval stage from August to the following early June, overwintering when still small. During the spring the larvae can be located resting fully exposed on their foodplants or on nearby rocks, basking in sunshine, although they feed mostly at night. Brought into captivity they are very easy to rear and willingly accept most sallows as an alternative foodplant. The pupa is formed in a loose cocoon, under moss or soil and lasts about four to six weeks. The adults fly from late June to August, with both sexes being attracted to light and sugar, and the females usually lay their egg batches quite readily in captivity. The resulting larvae can be forced to produce more adults by about December. A locally common species, being found in the mountain regions of North Wales, usually on the lower slopes and scree.

Plate 32: K. Bred from a female adult to MVL. Early August. (SHC)

Dotted Clay

Xestia baja Denis & Schiffermüller

Larva. 37–42 mm. Body light reddish-brown, with a thin pale dorsal line and a series of V-shaped dusky marks along the dorsal area, those on the tenth and eleventh segments being most distinct; head orangish-brown, marked with dark brown.

Foodplants. Various herbaceous plants such as dandelion, primrose and dock in the autumn, the developing foliage of birch, blackthorn, sallow, bog myrtle and bramble during the spring.

Habits. Single-brooded, occurring as a larva from about August to the following late May, overwintering when still quite small. The larvae are most easily found during the spring when feeding at night on the buds and young leaves of birch saplings, blackthorn and bog myrtle, especially in open woodland and on heathland. The pupa is usually formed by late May, just under the soil in a flimsy cocoon, and lasts until the adults emerge in late July and August. These come to light and sugar, with most females laying freely in captivity and the resulting larvae can be forced to develop faster by keeping them warm. Generally distributed and fairly common over most parts of the British Isles.

Plate 32: L. Found on birch at night, nearly fully grown. Late April.

Square-spotted Clay

Xestia rhomboidea Esper

(*stigmatica* Hübner)

Larva. 35–40 mm. Body glossy light brown, with a thin white dorsal line, in which are small dark marks between the abdominal segments and darker wedge-shaped marks subdorsally on the tenth and eleventh rings. The spiracular line is narrow and white; head reddish-brown, marked darker.

Foodplants. Probably herbaceous plants and birch and bramble. Accepting dock, dandelion, plantain and sliced carrot in captivity.

Habits. A single-brooded insect, occurring in the larval stage from September to about the following May, overwintering when still quite small. The larvae are rarely met with

in the wild, but can be obtained by rearing them from the egg. The adults fly in August and are frequently taken while feeding on the flowers of burdock, wood sage and ragwort, although they do come to light in small numbers. The females can be persuaded to lay in captivity by supplying them with dock leaves, crumpled tissue-paper and flowering plants from which to take nectar. The eggs hatch in about two weeks and the larvae are not too difficult to rear, especially if forced by keeping them warm. The larvae form a cocoon under the soil and lie dormant for several weeks before pupating and they must not be disturbed during this period. A very local species inhabiting woodland, especially on calcareous and gravel soils, where the undergrowth is sparse, mostly in the southern half of England; also recorded sparingly from Scotland and Wales.
Plate 32: M. Bred from a female adult on burdock. Early August. (JMP)

Neglected Rustic
Xestia castanea Esper
(*neglecta* Hübner)
Larva. 33–36 mm. Body green, with a fine paler dorsal line and a broad white spiracular stripe, or reddish-brown, with a pale brown spiracular stripe. Both colour forms seem to occur in about even numbers.
Foodplants. Heather, bell heather and cross-leaved heath, accepting sallow, hawthorn and blackthorn in captivity.
Habits. A single-brooded species, being in the larval stage from about September to the following May, overwintering when still very small and sporadically feeding during mild spells. In the spring the larvae can readily be obtained by sweeping and are very easy to rear in captivity. Around mid-May they become fully grown, burrow in loose soil and spend about six weeks lying dormant before changing into pupae and should not be disturbed during this period. The adults emerge in August and September, with both sexes being attracted to light and the flowers of grasses, heather and ragwort. A heath and moorland insect, being found in most suitable places throughout the British Isles.
Plate 32: N. Swept from heather, nearly fully grown. Late April. (GAC)

Six-striped Rustic
Xestia sexstrigata Haworth
Larva. 30–34 mm. Body brown, with a dark-edged pale dorsal line and pale subdorsal lines that are edged above with a series of narrow black marks. Above the spiracles is a dark area and below a pale brown area. No characteristics have yet been found to distinguish this larva from the next species, *X. xanthographa*.
Foodplants. Various herbaceous plants, accepting dandelion, dock, groundsel and plantain in captivity.
Habits. Single-brooded, occurring as a larva from September to the following spring, probably feeding in mild weather throughout the winter. These larvae are rarely recorded in the wild, probably due to the reluctance of entomologists to collect up specimens of what they expect to be the abundant caterpillars of *X. xanthographa*, which so far cannot be distinguished from this less common insect. The adults fly during July and August, coming to light, sugar and flowering plants, with the females laying readily in captivity. The resulting larvae are easy to rear and can be forced through by keeping them indoors, pupating in soil for about six to eight weeks. Widely distributed and fairly common, especially in damp places, throughout most of the British Isles.
Plate 32: O. Bred from a female adult to MVL. Early August. (SHC)

Square-spot Rustic
Xestia xanthographa Denis & Schiffermüller
Larva. 32–36 mm. Body brown, with a dark-edged pale dorsal line and pale subdorsal lines, narrow black marks subdorsally on the abdominal rings and dark above and pale below the spiracles. Indistinguishable from the previous species.
Foodplants. Various herbaceous plants and grasses.
Habits. A single-brooded species, being in the larval stage from about September to the following spring, feeding throughout the winter in mild weather. The abundant larvae are easily found at night by searching or sweeping and are very easy to rear in captivity. They form a cocoon just under the soil or moss, changing into pupae after about six weeks, and the adults emerge between mid-July and September, being very common at light traps, sugar and flowering plants. The females lay eggs freely and the larvae can be forced in confinement. Occurring almost everywhere, especially on open ground, in the British Isles, except upon the tops of northern hills and mountains.
Plate 32: P. Bred from a female adult to MVL. Late July.

Heath Rustic
Xestia agathina Duponchel
Larva. 27–30 mm. Body brown or green, with distinct yellowish-white dorsal and subdorsal lines and a series of bold dark markings along the top edge of the latter; spiracular line broad and yellowish and the head is pale brown.
Foodplants. The young shoots of heather and will accept sallow leaves in captivity.
Habits. Single-brooded, being in the larval stage from late September to the following June, overwintering when still very small. From about May onwards the larvae can readily be swept at night from their foodplant, and although not easy to rear, will accept sallow leaves to supplement their requirement for fresh young heather shoots. Many larvae do not survive being taken into captivity, dying from an unknown cause when just about fully grown, although some may successfully pupate among plant litter on or just under the soil. This stage lasts about three months with the adults flying in late August and September, coming to light and heather bloom in reasonable numbers. A heath and moorland species, occurring in suitable places throughout the British Isles.
Plate 32: Q. Swept at night, nearly fully grown. Early June. (MB)

The Gothic
Naenia typica Linnaeus
Larva. 40–45 mm. Body greyish or reddish-brown, with a vague pale dorsal line, a thin wavy black spiracular line beneath which the underparts are distinctly paler and dark clouding dorsally and laterally on the tenth and eleventh segments; head brown, irrorate with darker brown, and spiracles pale orange.
Foodplants. Various herbaceous plants, including dandelion, plantain, dock and primrose, also accepting blackthorn, sallow and apple.
Habits. A single-brooded insect, occurring as a larva from July to the following early spring, feeding in mild weather throughout the winter months. After hatching from the egg, the larvae are at first gregarious, dispersing as they grow larger. They are not often found in the wild due to their retiring nocturnal habits, but are sometimes recorded when

searching for other species. After pupating in the soil for about two to three months, the adults emerge during June and July, and although they rarely attend light traps, they can readily be taken at sugar and flowering plants, just after dark. Most females will lay eggs freely in captivity and the larvae are easy to rear, accepting being forced by being kept warm. Widespread, inhabiting gardens, waste ground, damp woods and marshes throughout much of Britain and Ireland.
Plate 32: R. Bred from a female adult to sugar. Early July.

Great Brocade
Eurois occulta Linnaeus
Larva. 53–58 mm. Body dark purplish-brown, with a conspicuous undulating white spiracular line in which there are pinkish-orange mottlings and a series of black marks above; head brown, marked with black.
Foodplants. Bog myrtle, birch and sallow; also various herbaceous plants.
Habits. Single-brooded, being in the larval stage from September to the following early June, overwintering when still very small. During April the small larvae can sometimes be found by day at rest upon the bare stems of bog myrtle growing in damp places in their moorland habitat. When larger, in late May and early June, they must be looked for well after dark, when they ascend the foodplants to feed upon the fresh growth. Taken into captivity, they are easy to rear, pupating in a silken cocoon beneath the soil for about four to six weeks. The adults fly during July and early August and both sexes will come to light and sugar. The resident population occurs in the central and western highlands of Scotland, others taken elsewhere are most often immigrants from northern Europe.
Plate 33: A. Found at night, almost fully grown. Late May.

Green Arches
Anaplectoides prasina Denis & Schiffermüller
Larva. 43–47 mm. Body various shades of brown, with a distinct pale yellowish dorsal line and a black-edged bar across the eleventh ring; pale underparts and head orange-brown with darker stripes.
Foodplants. Various herbaceous plants, especially primrose, bramble, honeysuckle, bilberry and dock. Also recorded on birch and sallow.
Habits. A single-brooded species, occurring as a larva from August to the following early May. During the spring the larvae can easily be found at night by torchlight, feeding upon their foodplants. They are not difficult to rear in confinement and pupate in the soil for about six to eight weeks. The adults fly from late June and throughout July, and come readily to light and sugar. Most captive females will freely lay eggs and the resulting larvae can be forced by feeding them on dock and sliced carrots. Widespread, mainly in open deciduous woodland, over most of the British Isles.
Plate 33: B. Bred from an adult female to MVL. Early July. (RM)

Red Chestnut
Cerastis rubricosa Denis & Schiffermüller
Larva. 40–44 mm. Body reddish-brown, with a series of large blackish marks along the back and distinct yellow dashes along the subdorsal area; spiracular stripe yellowish; head brown, marked with dark brown. Young larvae are reddish-brown, with a broad distinct yellowish-white spiracular line.
Foodplants. Various herbaceous plants, including dock, bedstraw, chickweed, groundsel and bilberry; also accepting sallow.
Habits. Single-brooded, being in the larval stage from late April to June, overwintering in a tough silken cocoon under the soil. The larvae are not often found in the wild, but eggs are easily obtained from a fertile female. These fly during March and April, and come readily to light and sugar, with most laying freely in confinement. Widely distributed, mostly in woodland and on moors, over most of the British Isles.
Plate 33: C. Bred from a female adult to MVL. Early April.

White-marked
Cerastis leucographa Denis & Schiffermüller
Larva. 35–40 mm. Body green, irrorate with yellowish-white dots and a series of darker oblique markings along the dorsal area; spiracular line dark and thin, head green, marked darker. A brown form also occurs less frequently.
Foodplants. Sallow, dock and chickweed in captivity.
Habits. A single-brooded species, occurring from late April to June as a larva, pupating in the soil for overwintering. The larvae have possibly never been recorded in the wild, but may be easily bred from eggs laid by female adults by supplying them with a mixed diet. These fly during April in open deciduous woodland, respond well to light and visit sallow blossom in good numbers. A local species, being found mainly in south-east England, on the Chilterns and in the southern half of Wales.
Plate 33: D. Bred from a female adult to MVL. Mid-April. (SHC)

SUBFAMILY: HADENINAE

Beautiful Yellow Underwing
Anarta myrtilli Linnaeus
Larva. 24–28 mm. Body bright green, marked all over with dashes of white, and laterally yellow; greenish-brown head.
Foodplants. Heather and bell heather.
Habits. Mostly double-brooded in the south, with the larvae from April to October, overwintering as either a larva or a pupa, usually the latter; univoltine in the north, with the larvae occurring from July to September. These may readily be swept by day or night from heather and are very easy to rear in captivity, although prone to parasitism. The pupa is formed in a tough cocoon on or just under the soil and usually lasts about a month, unless overwintering. The adults fly from late April to August, and in June and July in the northern populations, by day in bright sunshine. Widely distributed and not uncommon on heaths and moors throughout most of the British Isles.
Plate 33: E. Swept by day, fully grown. Early July.

Small Dark Yellow Underwing
Anarta cordigera Thunberg
Larva. 27–33 mm. Body purplish-grey, with bold yellowish-white dorsal and subspiracular lines and a black-streaked orange-brown head; darker blotches dorsally.
Foodplants. Bearberry, sometimes accepting bilberry in captivity.
Habits. A single-brooded species that occurs as a larva from late May to about mid-July, overwintering in the pupal stage. The nocturnal larvae have possibly never been found in the wild, although they can be reared in captivity. The adults fly from mid-May to early June in sunshine and can also be located on deer-fence and railway posts early in the morning, in the evening and in dull weather. Females will often produce eggs when kept in cages, supplied with foodplant and flowers. The resulting larvae are not difficult to rear to full growth, but most tend to die just before pupa-

tion. Locally distributed in the valleys of the Scottish Highlands and Aberdeenshire.
Plate 33: F. Bred from a female adult found by day. Late May. (GAC)

Broad-bordered White Underwing

Anarta melanopa Thunberg
Larva. 32–35 mm. Body light reddish-brown, with a dark-bordered white dorsal line, distinct white subdorsal and spiracular lines and a series of blackish oblique marks subdorsally on the fourth to eleventh segments; head brown.
Foodplant. Crowberry, cowberry, bearberry and bilberry; also accepting knotgrass and sallow in confinement.
Habits. Single-brooded, occurring in the larval stage from about late June to early August, overwintering as a pupa. The adults fly in sunshine during late May and June, and although most females will deposit eggs freely in captivity when supplied with flowers and foodplant, the larvae can be difficult to rear to maturity. The eggs hatch after about two weeks and the young larvae will thrive at first when using knotgrass as a substitute food. When about half grown many seem to die from an unknown cause, but a few may survive to spin up a cocooned pupa among the plant debris. This species is mostly restricted to the higher slopes and tops of mountains in Argyll, Caithness, Galloway and the Scottish Highlands; also recorded from the Cheviots in England.
Plate 33: G. Bred from a female adult netted by day. Early June. (BS)

The Nutmeg

Discestra trifolii Hufnagel
Larva. 35–40 mm. Body various shades of green or brown, with a broad pale spiracular line that is often tinged with pink. The intensity of the dorsal line is variable and there are often dark marks along the top edge of the pale subdorsal line; head brown.
Foodplants. Goosefoot, orache, dock, dandelion and other herbaceous plants.
Habits. Double-brooded in southern Britain and mainly univoltine in the northern half of the country, with the larvae occurring from about late June and July and again in September and October, pupating under the soil in a fragile cocoon for overwintering. They can sometimes be found at night when active and feeding, but are more easily obtained by rearing from an adult. These fly in May and June, again in August and September in the south, and mostly in July elsewhere, coming freely to light, sugar and flowering plants. The larvae are easy to rear in confinement, readily accepting dock and dandelion rather than their rather messy favourite natural foodplants of the family *Chenopodiaceae*. Frequent and fairly common in south-eastern England, local from the Midlands northwards.
Plate 33: H. Bred from a female adult to MVL. Early June. (RM)

The Shears

Hada plebeja Linnaeus
(*nana* Hufnagel)
Larva. 32–36 mm. Body greyish-brown, with vague pale dorsal and subdorsal lines and a series of dark brown subdorsal markings; head brown. The penultimate instar is dark brown with blackish mottlings.
Foodplants. Various herbaceous plants, including dandelion, chickweed, knotgrass and hawkweed.
Habits. Mainly single-brooded, with a partial second generation in the southern parts of Britain. The larvae occur in July and August, and sometimes again in September, but are rarely found in the wild due to their retiring nocturnal habits. They are much easier to obtain by rearing from the adult. These fly mainly in May and June, coming to light, sugar and flowering plants, with most females readily laying eggs in captivity. The larvae are fairly easy to rear, with no special conditions being necessary, and pupation takes place in a cocoon under moss or among leaf litter for overwintering. Widely distributed, mainly on open ground, over much of the British Isles.
Plate 33: I. Bred from a female adult to MVL. Early June.

Pale Shining Brown

Polia bombycina Hufnagel
(*nitens* Haworth)
Larva. 45–50 mm. Body greyish-brown, with a thin vague pale dorsal line that is edged with grey and indistinct diamond-shaped darker dorsal mottlings; head pale brown, spiracles orange bordered with black.
Foodplants. Various herbaceous plants; accepting dandelion, knotgrass, dock, sow-thistle and sliced carrot in confinement.
Habits. A single-brooded insect, probably occurring as a larva from July to the following spring. The life history in the wild is apparently unknown and unlike the other species in this genus it seems not to have been recorded feeding on budding trees in the spring. The adults fly in June and July, with both sexes coming to light, sugar and flowers, and most females will freely deposit eggs in captivity. These hatch after about two weeks and the resulting larvae are very easy to rear, especially if kept warm and in the dark, producing more adults during the winter. A declining species, mostly inhabiting open ground, especially on calcareous soils, being most frequently recorded from the southern and eastern counties of England.
Plate 33: J. Bred from a female adult to MVL. Late July.

Silvery Arches

Polia trimaculosa Esper
(*hepatica* Clerck)
(*tincta* Brahm)
Larva. 47–52 mm. Body reddish-brown, with a thin pale dorsal line, bordered with darker brown and vague diamond-shaped darker dorsal markings; head brown, prothoracic plate pale reddish-brown.
Foodplants. Various herbaceous plants; also birch, bog myrtle, sallow and hawthorn in the spring.
Habits. Single-brooded, being in the larval stage from about August to the following May, overwintering when about half grown. The larvae may be obtained by searching birch saplings after dark during April and May, and those taken by this method are very easy to rear in captivity. Pupation takes place in a weak cocoon spun up on or just under the soil, and lasts about two to four weeks depending on the temperature. During late June and July the adults will be on the wing and both sexes respond well to light and sugar, with the females depositing their egg batches quite freely in captivity. Some of the resulting larvae can be forced to produce a second generation during the winter months. Locally common in woods and on heaths in parts of southern England and on moors in the highlands of Scotland; local elsewhere and seemingly absent from Ireland.
Plate 33: K. Located at night on birch, nearly fully grown. Late April.

Grey Arches
Polia nebulosa Hufnagel
Larva. 48–54 mm. Body various shades of brown or grey, with an indistinct pale dorsal line within dark diamond-shaped blotches and dark oblique marks laterally; head reddish-brown with dark streaks.
Foodplants. Various herbaceous plants, including dandelion, dock and primrose, and during spring the fresh growth of birch, sallow, blackthorn, honeysuckle, bramble and other plants.
Habits. A single-brooded species, the larva of which occurs from August to the following May, overwintering when less than half grown. The larvae are most readily found during the spring by searching birch saplings, honeysuckle and bramble after dark, and are very easy to rear in captivity. Also larvae obtained from adult moths will accept being forced to develop faster by being kept warm and produce more adults during the winter. The cocooned pupa is formed on or just under soil and lasts about a month, with the adults flying in June and July and coming freely to light and sugar. Widely distributed, mainly in open woodland, over much of the British Isles.
Plate 33: L. Bred from a female adult to MVL. Late June. (BS)

Feathered Ear
Pachetra sagittigera Hufnagel
(*leucophaea* Denis & Schiffermüller)
Larva. 36–42 mm. Body buff-coloured, with a paler dorsal line, a broader pale subdorsal line and variable rows of darker markings along the back and sides; head orangish-brown, speckled darker.
Foodplants. Various grasses, especially those of the genus *Poa*.
Habits. Single-brooded, occurring in the larval stage from July to April, feeding throughout the winter during mild weather. The larvae can be located at night from early February to April, and at this stage are often fairly easy to rear in confinement. The pupa is formed on the soil in a flimsy cocoon and the adults emerge in June, coming to sugar and flowering plants, less often to light. Females are stated to lay freely in boxes, but overwintering the larvae in captivity is usually difficult. This species used to be found on the chalk downland of southern England; it was last recorded in 1963 and despite many attempts to relocate this moth, none has so far been successful.
Plate 33: M. Bred from a female adult (Belgium). Mid-June. (JW)

White Colon
Sideridis albicolon Hübner
Larva. 42–46 mm. Body pale bluish-green, with a paler spiracular line, the darker dorsal vessel showing indistinctly through the skin and paler between the segments; head yellowish-green or yellowish-brown, spiracles white, ringed with black.
Foodplants. Various low-growing plants, including dandelion, dock, goosefoot, sea rocket and chickweed.
Habits. A mostly single-brooded species, the larva of which occurs from late June and throughout July, and those of the partial second generation during September. The larvae can be located by searching in the sand and soft soil beneath their foodplants during the day and by torchlight after dark, but are most easily obtained by rearing from an adult moth. These fly in late May and June, sometimes again in August, and are readily attracted to light, sugar and flowering plants. Most females will deposit eggs freely in captivity and the larvae are generally very easy to rear. The winter is spent as pupae, these being formed deep in the sand inside a flimsy cocoon and this habit should be noted to successfully rear this species to the adult stage. Widely distributed on coastal sandhills throughout most of Britain, with inland colonies occurring on sandy soil in the Breck of East Anglia and in Hampshire and Surrey.
Plate 33: N. Bred from a female adult to sugar. Mid-June.

Bordered Gothic
Heliophobus reticulata Goeze
(*saponariae* Borkhausen)
Larva. 43–48 mm. Body pale brown, with a thin pale dorsal line and darker lines and mottlings on the back and sides; head orange-brown with a pair of black stripes and spiracles small and whitish, ringed with grey.
Foodplants. Unrecorded in the wild, accepting knotgrass and soapwort in captivity.
Habits. Single-brooded, being in the larval stage from about late June to early September, overwintering as a pupa. The larval foodplant in the wild is apparently unrecorded, although the insects will readily accept knotgrass in captivity. The larvae are best obtained by rearing from an adult female, these being attracted to light, sugar and flowers from late May to July. Many females refuse to lay in captivity and even when eggs are obtained the larvae can often be difficult to rear. Widely distributed, but very local, over the southern half of England; also recorded on the coast of south-west Ireland.
Plate 33: O. Bred from a female adult to MVL. Late June. (JMP)

Cabbage Moth
Mamestra brassicae Linnaeus
Larva. 45–50 mm. Body various shades of brown or green, with a dark-edged thin pale dorsal line, a dark dorsal marking on the slightly humped eleventh segment and a broad pale spiracular line; head usually light brown and spiracles white, edged with black.
Foodplants. Various wild and cultivated plants, especially those of the cabbage family.
Habits. Double- or sometimes treble-brooded, with the larvae being recorded during almost every month of the year, but being most frequent in the summer and autumn when numbers have built up from the spring brood. This species usually overwinters as a cocooned pupa in soil, but many insects pass this period in the larval stage. The larvae are well known as a pest of cultivated *Brassicas*, boring deep into the heart of the plants and causing considerable damage and mess from the frass. The adults are on the wing from late May to October in overlapping broods and are strongly attracted to light, sugar and flowering plants. Captive females readily lay large egg batches and the resulting larvae are very easy to rear. Generally distributed over most parts of the British Isles, being most frequent in the south.
Plate 33: P. Bred from a female adult to MVL. Early July.

Dot Moth
Melanchra persicariae Linnaeus
Larva. 42–46 mm. Body various shades of green or brown, with an obvious darker prothoracic plate that is traversed by the pale dorsal line, oblique markings dorsally to just above the white spiracles and reversed oblique lines below; head usually pale brown and also having a distinct hump on the eleventh segment.
Foodplants. Various herbaceous plants, including common

nettle, dock, plantain, dandelion, common toadflax and sow-thistle; also recorded on sallow and larch.
Habits. A single-brooded insect, being found in the larval stage from August to October, overwintering as a pupa in a cocoon beneath the soil. The larvae can readily be found by searching or by shaking clumps of herbaceous plants over bare ground and are very easy to rear in captivity. The adults fly mainly from late June to early August, are freely attracted to light, sugar and flowers and most females will readily deposit eggs in confinement without any encouragement being necessary. Generally distributed in gardens and on waste ground over much of England and Wales; less frequent and local in southern Scotland and Ireland.
Plate 33: Q. Bred from a female adult to MVL. Mid-July.

Beautiful Brocade
Lacanobia contigua Denis & Schiffermüller
Larva. 38–43 mm. Body brown or green, with narrow dark-edged pale dorsal and subdorsal lines and a series of cross-shaped brown markings along the back. The spiracular line is dark brown, edged below with a paler stripe of light brown or even white in some individuals; head green or greenish-brown, spiracles white.
Foodplants. Various trees and low-growing plants, including birch, sallow, heather, bog myrtle and dock.
Habits. Single-brooded, occurring as a larva from about late July to the middle of September. The larvae can readily be obtained by beating small birches and by sweeping heather and bog myrtle during the day. They are usually easy to rear in captivity, pupating in a flimsy cocoon under the soil for overwintering. The adults fly in June and July, coming freely to light and sugar and most females will lay in confinement if required. Widely distributed, inhabiting woods, heaths and moorland over much of the British Isles.
Plate 33: R. Bred from an adult female to MVL. Late June. (RM)

Light Brocade
Lacanobia w-latinum Hufnagel
Larva. 40–45 mm. Body greyish or reddish-brown, irrorate with darker specklings and having paler dorsal and spiracular lines; head reddish-brown, marked with black and the small spiracles are dull brownish-white.
Foodplants. Various plants, including broom, dyer's greenweed, dock, knotgrass and common persicaria.
Habits. A single-brooded species, being in the larval stage from about late June to late August, overwintering as a pupa in the ground. These nocturnal larvae are sometimes found while searching by torchlight, although larger stocks are more easily obtained by rearing them from the adult. These fly from mid-May to early July, responding well to light and sugar, with most females laying freely in confinement. The larvae seem to do well in captivity and they thrive on knotgrass, but overcrowding should be especially avoided. Widely distributed, mainly on open ground, over most of southern England; also recorded from parts of Wales, northern England and Scotland, where it tends to be local and uncommon.
Plate 34: A. Bred from a female adult to MVL. Early June.

Pale-shouldered Brocade
Lacanobia thalassina Hufnagel
Larva. 38–43 mm. Body reddish-brown, with indistinct pale dorsal and subdorsal lines and a series of darker slightly oblique markings along the back. The broad spiracular line is orangish, edged above with white; head pale brown.
Foodplants. Various trees and other plants, including oak, sallow, birch, hawthorn, blackthorn, honeysuckle and broom.
Habits. Single-brooded, occurring as a larva from about late June to early September, although most have pupated for overwintering by the middle of August. The larvae can sometimes be taken by beating at night, but rarely in numbers, and the best way to obtain this larva is by rearing from an adult. These are on the wing from late May to early July and come to light and sugar, especially in woods in the south and on moors in the northern parts of their range. Most females seem to lay freely in captivity and rearing the larvae is usually very easy. Widespread throughout most of the British Isles.
Plate 34: B. Bred from a female adult found on fence post. Early June.

Dog's Tooth
Lacanobia suasa Denis & Schiffermüller
Larva. 40–44 mm. Body olive-green or brown, with a darker dorsal stripe, a series of short dark oblique markings along the back and a thin dark line along the spiracles below which is a broad pale yellowish stripe; head brownish-green or pale brown.
Foodplants. Various low-growing plants, such as dock, dandelion, plantain and knotgrass.
Habits. A single-brooded insect in the north, double-brooded in the south, being in the larval state from about late June and July and again during late August and September, overwintering in the ground as a cocooned pupa. These nocturnal larvae are not often met with in the wild, but are easy to obtain by breeding from an adult moth. These are attracted to light, sugar and flowering plants from late May to July, also again about early August to early September in the south. The females usually lay eggs freely in captivity and the resulting larvae will feed up quite quickly becoming fully grown in less than two months. This species prefers to inhabit damp places, such as coastal estuaries, moorland and waste ground, occurring over much of England and Wales; also recorded locally in southern Scotland and in Ireland.
Plate 34: C. Bred from an adult female to MVL. Late August. (RL)

Bright-line Brown-eye
Lacanobia oleracea Linnaeus
Larva. 40–45 mm. Body green or light brown, with slightly darker dorsal and subdorsal lines and heavily dusted with tiny white dots; also having fewer, but larger, black dots. The spiracular line is distinct, yellowish-white, and the head is usually greenish-brown.
Foodplants. Various herbaceous plants and shrubs, including goosefoot, orache, dock, dandelion, knotgrass and plantain.
Habits. Generally single-brooded, often with a second generation in the more southern parts of its range. The larvae are most frequent during July to early September, when they can often be swept at night from goosefoot and orache which seem to be the favoured foodplants. They are very easy to rear in confinement and pupate for overwintering in a loose cocoon just under the soil. The adults fly mainly during June and July, with both sexes being readily attracted to light and the females usually laying their egg batches freely if required. Occasionally this species can be a pest to the growers of tomatoes, with the larvae boring into the fruit and causing damage. Widespread and often common over most of the British Isles.
Plate 34: D. Bred from a female adult to MVL. Late June.

The Stranger
Lacanobia blenna Hübner

Larva. 35–40 mm. Body dark olive-green or grey, wholly covered with minute black and white dots and with a broad distinct white-edged yellowish-orange subspiracular line.

Foodplants. Sea beet, prickly saltwort and other seashore plants.

Habits. A single-brooded species that has never been recorded in the larval stage in Britain. Three adults were recorded in the Isle of Wight between 1857 and 1876 and another in Sussex during 1868.

Plate 34: E. Courtesy of B. Goater, via D. J. Carter. (NHM)

Glaucous Shears
Papestra biren Goeze
(*glauca* Hübner)
(*bombycina* sensu Hufnagel)

Larva. 42–46 mm. Body brown, with a vague pale dorsal line, darker dorsal V-shaped markings and sometimes small white spots in the subdorsal region of the first few abdominal segments; spiracular line usually paler and head reddish-brown. Earlier instars are green with yellowish dorsal, subdorsal and spiracular stripes.

Foodplants. Bog myrtle, sallow, heather, bilberry and other plants.

Habits. A single-brooded species, with the larvae occurring from about mid-June to late August, overwintering as a cocooned pupa on the ground. The larvae can often be taken by sweeping or beating, especially at night when they are most active, and are then fairly easy to rear in captivity. The cocooned pupae need more attention as they quite often desiccate if kept too dry. Keeping them outside during the winter in sealed boxes containing slightly damp moss often helps them survive. The adults fly from about mid-May to mid-July, depending on the season and locality, are strongly attracted to light and also come to sugar. The females will lay their egg batches freely on corrugated cardboard or tissue-paper. A moorland insect, being widespread in Wales, northern England, Scotland and Ireland; also recorded locally in south-western England.

Plate 34: F. Bred from a female adult to MVL. Late May.

Broom Moth
Ceramica pisi Linnaeus

Larva. 40–45 mm. Body green or brown, with broad white-edged yellow stripes subdorsally and along the spiracles; head brownish-green or pale brown.

Foodplants. Various herbaceous plants and sometimes trees, including broom, dock, plantain, common toadflax, common persicaria, bracken, birch and elm.

Habits. Single-brooded, being in the larval stage from about late June to mid-September, overwintering in the soil as a cocooned pupa. These easily distinguished larvae are readily found by searching or sweeping, especially at night when more active. They are very easy to rear in captivity, but overcrowding should be avoided. The adults fly from mid-May to July, coming freely to light and the females will lay in captivity without any encouragement. Widely distributed and fairly common over most of the British Isles.

Plate 34: G. Found at night on toadflax, fully grown. Early September.

Broad-barred White
Hecatera bicolorata Hufnagel
(*serena* Denis & Schiffermüller)

Larva. 33–36 mm. Body various shades of green or brown, with darker diamond-shaped markings along the dorsal area and a lighter spiracular stripe; head lighter in colour than the body.

Foodplants. The flowers and buds of various plants in the family *Compositae*, especially hawkweed and hawk's-beard; accepting many other herbaceous plants in captivity.

Habits. A single-brooded insect, occurring as a larva from about late July to late September, pupating in the soil for overwintering. These larvae can readily be taken by careful sweeping or found by examining hawkweed and hawk's-beard flowers that grow on open ground such as meadows, downland and wasteland. They are fairly easy to rear in captivity, requiring dryish conditions for pupation. The adults have a protracted emergence period lasting from late May to early August, with the peak being around early July. Although they come to light and females often lay freely on picked flower buds, breeding this species from the egg is often not practical, as the young larvae seem to require growing flowers to survive. Widespread and fairly common in England and much of Wales; local in Scotland and mainly coastal in Ireland.

Plate 34: H. Located by searching, nearly fully grown. Early September.

Small Ranunculus
Hecatera dysodea Denis & Schiffermüller

Larva. 32–35 mm. Body reddish-brown or pale green, with a darker dorsal stripe and each segment having a pair of small dark dots dorsally; head darker than body, spiracles small and black; underparts pale brown or green.

Foodplants. The flowers and seeds of wild and cultivated lettuce.

Habits. Single-brooded, with the larvae occurring during July and August, overwintering as a pupa just under the soil. This species was to be found in Britain until it died out during the first half of this century. Most insects were recorded from East Anglia and the London area, with others being reported from elsewhere in England. The species inhabited waste ground and gardens and the exact reasons for its apparent extinction are obscure. It seems to be declining in northern Europe, so climatic factors or changes in land usage could be the cause.

Plate 34: I. Bred from a female adult to MVL (S. France). Late June.

The Campion
Hadena rivularis Fabricius
(*cucubali* Denis & Schiffermüller)

Larva. 32–36 mm. Body brownish-green, with an indistinct white dorsal line and a series of darker oblique markings along the back. Small white spots subdorsally and the head is small and light brown. Some individuals have the brown coloration absent from the last few segments and the earlier instars are green with yellow between the rings.

Foodplants. The ripening seeds of various campions.

Habits. A mostly single-brooded species, with the larvae occurring in June and July, and again in August and September in southern England, where there is a partial second generation. These larvae can readily be obtained by picking at random the seed capsules of the foodplants during late July and August. These should then be put into a ventilated box and fresh food introduced as necessary. When larger the larvae are too big to live inside the capsules, and hide by day close to the ground. They should be searched for or swept after dark when feeding. The pupa is formed in a slight cocoon just under the soil for overwintering, although may hatch after about three weeks if kept warm. The adults mostly fly during late May and June, coming to light and flowering plants, and the females should be supplied with budding campion flowers if eggs are to be obtained. Generally distributed and fairly common over much of the British Isles.

Plate 34: J. Located in white campion seed capsules, about half grown. Early July. (JR)

Tawny Shears

Hadena perplexa Denis & Schiffermüller
(*lepida* Esper)

Larva. 34–38 mm. Body usually brown or ochreous, with broad distinct paler dorsal, subdorsal and spiracular lines; head light brown and small, spiracles pale brown, ringed darker.

Foodplants. The ripening seeds of bladder campion, sea campion, Nottingham catchfly and sometimes white campion and rock sea-spurrey.

Habits. A mainly single-brooded species, being in the larval stage from about late June to late August, and later in the southern counties of England where there is a partial second brood. These larvae can be taken by picking the foodplant seed capsules during July and by searching and sweeping at night later in August, as most larvae leave the plant during the day to hide on the ground. They are fairly easy to rear in captivity and prefer dryish conditions in which to pupate in a cocoon under moss or soil for the winter. The adults fly mostly from late May to early July and are freely attracted to light and flowers of the larval foodplants. Widely distributed, usually inhabiting open dry ground, over much of England and Wales; mainly coastal in Ireland.

Plate 34: K. Found in picked campion seed capsules, when still small. Late June. (CH)

Viper's Bugloss

Hadena irregularis Hufnagel

Larva. 30–35 mm. Body yellowish-brown, with paler dorsal, subdorsal and spiracular lines and a series of darker chevrons along the back; head light brown, spiracles black.

Foodplants. The ripening seeds of Spanish catchfly, accepting in captivity the flowerheads of garden carnation and sweet william.

Habits. Single-brooded, occurring as a larva during July and August, overwintering in the ground as a cocooned pupa. At first the larvae feed inside the flowers and seed capsules of the foodplant. Later when too large to stay hidden, they leave the plant during the day, ascending again at night to feed; often highly parasitized. The adults come to light and flowering plants, with the protracted flight period being from late May to mid-July. In Britain it has only been recorded from the Breck of East Anglia and at present this species seems to be on the verge of extinction in this country, with its rare and decreasing foodplant also being vulnerable.

Plate 34: L. From Poland, courtesy of Paul Waring.

Barrett's Marbled Coronet

Hadena luteago Denis & Schiffermüller

Larva. 30–35 mm. Body dull white, with an orangish-brown head, pale yellow prothoracic and anal plates and black spiracles; the greyish dorsal vessel shows through the skin.

Foodplants. The lower stems and roots of sea campion and rock sea-spurrey, accepting lettuce roots in captivity.

Habits. A single-brooded species, being in the larval stage from about July to the middle of September, overwintering as a pupa among the foodplant roots. The young larvae hatch from the eggs and bore down into the plant feeding and growing as they descend. By August they are completely underground living in the soil alongside the roots on which they feed. At this time they can be located by finding sickly looking plants, especially those in rock crevices, and many of those tenanted will break off at the crown when gently pulled. The larvae brought into captivity at this stage are usually very easy to rear in sealed containers with roots and soil. The adults emerge during June and July, coming to light and flowering plants. A coastal species found locally on the cliffs of Devon, Cornwall and south-west Wales; also recorded from Co. Waterford and Co. Cork in Ireland.

Plate 34: M. Found in soil under sea campion, almost fully grown. Late August. (SHC)

Varied Coronet

Hadena compta Denis & Schiffermüller

Larva. 30–34 mm. Body greyish-brown, with a darker dorsal stripe and specklings of dark greyish-brown over the back and sides; head reddish-brown, underparts drab, spiracles pale, ringed darker.

Foodplant. The ripening seeds of sweet william.

Habits. Single-brooded, occurring in the larval stage from July to early September, overwintering as a cocooned pupa in the soil. When small these larvae live within the seed capsules and when larger hide beneath the plant by day, feeding at night. They can be obtained by picking these capsules and placing them spread out on paper in ventilated containers (watching for larval frass), or by searching around the bases of plants from late July onwards. They are easy to rear in confinement by providing them regularly with fresh plants. The adults fly in June and early July, coming to light, and the females can be induced to lay on growing plants placed under netting cages. A frequently recorded species in the gardens of south-eastern and eastern England.

Plate 34: N. Located in picked seed capsules, half grown. Late July.

Marbled Coronet

Hadena confusa Hufnagel
(*conspersa* Denis & Schiffermüller)

Larva. 33–37 mm. Body various shades of brown, with a darker dorsal stripe and darker chevrons along the back, these being most distinct on the fourth to sixth segments; head brown with darker stripes, prothoracic plate mainly dark brown.

Foodplants. The ripening seeds of bladder campion and sea campion.

Habits. Mainly single-brooded, being in the larval stage from about early July to the middle of August, overwintering, sometimes twice, in the soil as a cocooned pupa. These larvae can be obtained by carefully sweeping or searching the foodplants after dark during early August; also they can be taken when smaller by picking the seed capsules of campions during July. They are usually easy to rear in confinement when kept in ventilated boxes and supplied with fresh plants periodically. As with all seed capsule feeders, care should be taken to eradicate any earwigs or other predators from the picked plants. Most of the adults fly from late May to early July, slightly later in the north and occasionally a few appear as a probable partial second brood in south-eastern England during late August and early September. Widespread, mainly on calcareous open ground, over much of Britain; coastal in Ireland.

Plate 34: O. Swept at night, fully grown. Early August.

White Spot

Hadena albimacula Borkhausen

Larva. 32–36 mm. Body light brown, with a series of dark brown triangular dorsal markings and numerous dark specklings laterally; head light brown, marked with blackish, spiracles pale brown, ringed with black.

Foodplants. The ripening seeds of Nottingham catchfly, accepting garden carnation and sweet william in confinement.

Habits. A single-brooded species, the larva of which occurs from late June to the end of August, overwintering as a pupa just beneath the soil. The larvae only live within the flowers and seeds when very small, soon becoming nocturnal and hiding by day on the ground. During early August they can be swept carefully or searched for after dark, when they ascend their foodplant to feed. Generally they are fairly easy to rear in captivity, preferring dryish conditions to pupate. Both sexes of the adults come freely to light and flowering plants during June and early July. A local insect, being found mostly on shingle beaches and cliffs along the south coast of England.

Plate 34: P. Swept at night, nearly fully grown. Late July.

The Lychnis

Hadena bicruris Hufnagel

Larva. 35–40 mm. Body of various shades of brown, with a fine pale dorsal line, a series of darker chevrons along the back that can vary greatly in intensity and darker specklings laterally; head pale brown, spiracles pale brown edged with black.

Foodplants. The ripening seeds of campions and associated plants, especially red campion.

Habits. Mostly single-brooded, with the larvae occurring from about late June to early August, and again in September in the south where it has a partial second generation. They can readily be found by close searching of their foodplants during July, and especially more so at night when they are larger as many leave the plant during the day. They are usually very easy to rear in captivity, pupating in a slight cocoon just under the soil for overwintering. The main brood of adults fly from late May to July, with both sexes responding well to light and suitable flowers. Widespread and generally common over much of the British Isles.

Plate 34: Q. Found at night, fully grown. Late July. (SHC)

The Grey

Hadena caesia Denis & Schiffermüller

Larva. 40–44 mm. Body brownish-grey or grey, with vague darker diamond-shaped dorsal markings and darker lateral mottlings; head light brown with dark stripes, spiracles pale brown.

Foodplant. The ripening seeds and leaves of sea campion.

Habits. Probably single-brooded, occurring as a larva from June to September, overwintering in the pupal stage just under the soil in a fragile cocoon. The larva feeds in the seed pods of the plant until about one-third grown, after which it lives under the plant and feeds exclusively on the leaves. Larvae should be searched for on plants growing in rock crevices close to the sea, and are not difficult to rear. The adults have been recorded from late May to August and come freely to light and campion flowers to feed. A local insect, inhabiting the rocky coasts of the Isle of Man, Argyllshire and the Hebridean islands of Scotland, and those of southern and western Ireland.

Plate 34: R. Found in picked foodplant capsules, less than half grown. Early August. (DB)

The Silurian

Eriopygodes imbecilla Fabricius

Larva. 30–35 mm. Body light brown, with a dark-edged pale dorsal line, a thin dark subdorsal line and another thin dark brown line along the spiracles; laterally specked with dark brown and the head is yellowish-brown and streaked darker.

Foodplants. Almost certainly herbaceous plants, accepting dandelion and plantain in captivity.

Habits. Single-brooded, being in the larval stage from August to the following May, probably overwintering when about half grown. The early stages seem to be unrecorded in Britain, although the larvae are very easy to obtain and rear from female moths. These can be found flying rapidly over their hillside habitat on warm afternoons during late June and July and most will deposit eggs freely in captivity. The resulting larvae seem to do well and feed up in about ten weeks if kept warm, to produce more adults during October. At present this species is restricted to north-west Montgomeryshire, where it was discovered in 1972. With more research in similar habitats, this moth could be recorded from elsewhere.

Plate 35: A. Bred from a female adult netted by day. Early July.

Antler Moth

Cerapteryx graminis Linnaeus

Larva. 28–33 mm. Body glossy greyish-brown, with a distinct dark-edged pale dorsal line, a less obvious pale subdorsal stripe and a broad pale spiracular line; head light brown, blotched with black; prothoracic and anal plates black, striped with pale brown.

Foodplants. Various grasses and sedges, including sheep's-fescue, mat-grass, purple moor-grass, preferring hard-bladed varieties.

Habits. A single-brooded species, occurring in the larval stage from about late March to June, after overwintering as an egg. During May and June the larvae can readily be swept, especially at night on upland grassy slopes where the populations can be very large. Taken into captivity, they are not difficult to rear, although some tend to die from an unknown cause just before pupation. The pupa is formed in an earthen chamber just below the ground, lasting about four to six weeks, with the adults flying in July and August. They are active by day, flying in the morning, and later can be found feeding and resting on flowering plants, such as ragwort and thistle. They fly again at night, coming to light in good numbers and also attending sugar patches. The eggs are laid by scattering them at random while on the wing. To be found throughout most of the British Isles, mainly inhabiting open ground such as hills, moors and downland.

Plate 35: B. Swept at night, about half grown. Late May.

Hedge Rustic

Tholera cespitis Denis & Schiffermüller

Larva. 32–36 mm. Body glossy greyish-brown, with distinct paler dorsal, subdorsal and spiracular lines; head pale brown, marked with black. Often being distinguished from the previous and next species by having three (not one) faint pale lines laterally between the subdorsal and spiracular stripes.

Foodplants. Various grasses, including mat-grass and tufted hair-grass, preferring the hard-bladed species.

Habits. Single-brooded, occurring as a larva from about mid-March to mid-July, after overwintering as an egg. During May and the first half of June the younger green and white striped larvae can easily be swept at night, when feed-

ing higher up on the grass blades. Later they are more difficult to obtain by this method as they live and feed closer to the ground. Brought into captivity, they are not difficult to rear as long as soil is provided for pupation. The pupae are formed in an earthen cell, lasting about four to six weeks. The adults fly during late August and early September, and although the males respond to light, females are more readily taken at sugar and flowering plants just after dark. Widely distributed, but local, over most of the British Isles, except northern Scotland.
Plate 35: C. Swept at night, about half grown. Late May.

Feathered Gothic

Tholera decimalis Poda
(*popularis* Fabricius)
Larva. 36–42 mm. Body greyish-brown with distinct black-edged broad pale dorsal, subdorsal and spiracular lines; head brown, mottled with black. Sometimes more rough-textured than the previous two species (*C. graminis* and *T. cespitis*).
Foodplants. Various hard-bladed grasses, including sheep's-fescue, mat-grass and those of the genus *Poa*.
Habits. A single-brooded insect, of which the larva occurs between March and July, after overwintering as an egg, these being scattered by the female moth while flying. The green and white striped larvae of the earlier instars can readily be taken by sweeping at night during May and early June; although later, when they have attained their drab coloration, they can be found at the bases of grass clumps. They are fairly easy to rear in confinement, requiring soil in which to pupate for about a month inside an earthern cell. The adults fly during late August and throughout September, with mainly the males coming to light and both sexes to sugar and flowers. Widely distributed, mainly on open ground, over much of Britain and Ireland; local in Scotland.
Plate 35: D. Found in grass clump, nearly fully grown. Late June. (SHC)

Pine Beauty

Panolis flammea Denis & Schiffermüller
(*piniperda* Panzer)
Larva. 37–42 mm. Body dark green, with obvious white dorsal, subdorsal and spiracular stripes, the latter being edged below with orange; head light brown, mottled darker.
Foodplants. Scots pine and other pines.
Habits. Single-brooded, occurring in the larval stage from May to about mid-July. Can be taken readily from early June onwards by beating. The larvae are easy to rear in confinement, pupating in a fragile cocoon among plant litter or sometimes in a bark crevice, for overwintering. The adults fly from mid-March to early May, both sexes being attracted to light and sallow blossom, with the females depositing their eggs on the twigs and at the bases of pine needles. Widespread and generally common over much of Britain; sometimes a pest species in the conifer plantations of northern Scotland.
Plate 35: E. Beaten from pine, nearly fully grown. Late June.

Silver Cloud

Egira conspicillaris Linnaeus
Larva. 40–45 mm. Body greyish-brown, with many small greyish-white dots, a darker dorsal line and a pale reddish-brown spiracular stripe; head light brown, speckled darker.
Foodplants. Unrecorded in the wild, accepting dock, knotgrass, trefoils, sallow, elm and blackthorn in captivity.
Habits. A single-brooded species, of which the larva occurs from late May to about the middle of July. The larvae have yet to be found in the wild, but can often be obtained by breeding from female moths. The main flight period is between late April and mid-May, with both sexes coming to light and feeding on blackthorn blossom. Many females will lay their egg batches in captivity, although rearing some broods can be difficult, with the larvae becoming soft and squashy before dying when about half grown. Those that survive pupate for overwintering inside a silken cocoon formed in the soil. Local, but not uncommon, mainly inhabiting the open woods and orchards of Gloucestershire, Herefordshire, Somerset and Worcestershire; also recorded from Warwickshire and Monmouth, but seems to have declined in these counties.
Plate 35: F. Bred from a female adult to MVL. Early May. (JMP)

Small Quaker

Orthosia cruda Denis & Schiffermüller
Larva. 28–32 mm. Body various shades of dull green, or rarely brown, with a distinct white dorsal line, a narrower white subdorsal line and a yellowish spiracular line, also each segment darker anteriorly; head pale bluish-green with black speckles and prothoracic plate black with white stripes.
Foodplants. Various trees, including oak, sallow, hazel, blackthorn and hawthorn.
Habits. Single-brooded, being in the larval stage from about mid-April to the middle of June. The larvae can easily be obtained by beating, especially at night when out of their daytime retreat of spun leaves, and are usually very easy to rear in confinement. Overcrowding should be avoided as they have cannibalistic tendencies, and the subterranean pupae are best kept outside in a shaded place to avoid desiccation during the summer. The pupae overwinter, with the bulk of the adults emerging between mid-March and mid-April, and coming freely to light, sugar and sallow blossom. Widely distributed, preferring wooded habitats, over most of the British Isles, although local in Scotland and Ireland.
Plate 35: G. Beaten from oak, nearly fully grown. Late May.

Blossom Underwing

Orthosia miniosa Denis & Schiffermüller
Larva. 34–38 mm. Body bluish-grey, with a broad yellow or brick-red dorsal stripe, a thin subdorsal line of the same colour and a broad spiracular line. Also a series of black spots dorsally; head pale brown, marked darker.
Foodplants. Oak, and when larger various herbaceous plants.
Habits. A single-brooded species, occurring as a larva from about late April to mid-June, most readily obtained by beating. At first the young larvae live gregariously in a silken web, feeding on the soft young oak foliage. Later they disperse and either continue to feed on oak, also consuming the oak-galls, or feed up on low-growing plants. They are not difficult to rear in captivity, although they have been known to cannibalize each other if not supplied with sufficient food. The cocooned pupa is formed in an earthen cell and lasts throughout the winter, until the adults emerge during late March and April. These come freely to light, sallow bloom and sometimes sugar, with most females laying their egg batches readily in captivity. Mainly inhabiting mature oak woods in southern England and in Wales, also recorded locally in the Lake District; scarce in Ireland.
Plate 35: H. Bred from a female adult to MVL. Late April. (GAC)

Northern Drab
Orthosia opima Hübner
(*advena* auctt.)
Larva. 40–45 mm. Body purplish-brown, with an indistinct pale dorsal line, a broad yellowish subdorsal line and an obvious yellow spiracular stripe; head pale brown, spiracles white and underparts pale green.
Foodplants. Various trees, shrubs and herbaceous plants, including sallow, birch, dyer's greenweed, ragwort and mugwort, and sea lavender on salt marshes.
Habits. Single-brooded, being in the larval stage from about early May to late June or July. The larvae can often be obtained by locating the conspicuous untidy grey egg batches that are laid on dry grass stems and other herbage during late April and early May, as the larvae are not as easily found as related species in the wild. They usually do quite well in captivity, although some broods fail to survive, dying when about half grown from an unknown cause. The pupa is formed in a cocoon under the soil and lasts through the winter. During late April and most of May the adults can be light-trapped or be found feeding on blackthorn blossom, with the females laying freely on netting in confinement. Widely distributed, but local, mostly in open ground throughout England, Wales, Ireland and southern Scotland.
Plate 35: I. Bred from ova found on grass stem. Early May. (BS)

Lead-coloured Drab
Orthosia populeti Fabricius
Larva. 37–42 mm. Body glossy bright green, with a distinct white dorsal line and vague white subdorsal and spiracular lines; head brownish-green, marked with black.
Foodplants. Aspen and occasionally other poplars.
Habits. A single-brooded insect, of which the larvae occur from about late April to mid-June, feeding at first within the catkins and later at night on the foliage. During the day they can be located between pairs of spun leaves, usually high up, and can be beaten at night when active. They are reasonably easy to rear in confinement, pupating in a cocoon formed under the moss or soil until the following spring. The adults emerge during late March and April, both sexes coming to light and sallow bloom, with the females laying freely if supplied with budding aspen twigs and netting. A local woodland species mainly found in southern and central England, parts of Wales and central Scotland.
Plate 35: J. Bred from a female adult to MVL. Mid-April. (M&JH)

Powdered Quaker
Orthosia gracilis Denis & Schiffermüller
Larva. 40–44 mm. Body deep green or brownish-green, with thin whitish dorsal and subdorsal lines and a broad yellow spiracular stripe above which is a line of black mottlings; head light brown, spiracles white, ringed with black.
Foodplants. Bog myrtle, sallow, meadowsweet and other plants.
Habits. Single-brooded, occurring in the larval stage from about mid-May to July, living at first in a spinning formed at the terminal leaves of the foodplant. Later, when larger, these nocturnal-feeding larvae can be found or beaten at night, after spending the day hidden on the ground among the plant debris. In captivity they are fairly easy to rear, pupating in a cocoon under the soil for overwintering. The adults fly between mid-April and late May, coming readily to light, blackthorn blossom and sallow catkins, with most females laying their egg batches freely in confinement, if required to do so. Generally distributed, especially in damp places, over much of the British Isles.
Plate 35: K. Bred from a female adult to MVL. Early May. (SHC)

Common Quaker
Orthosia cerasi Fabricius
(*stabilis* Denis & Schiffermüller)
Larva. 35–40 mm. Body bright green, liberally speckled with yellowish-white dots and with a white dorsal line, less obvious white subdorsal and spiracular lines and a distinctive yellow band dorsally across the eleventh segment; head green.
Foodplants. Oak, sallow, hawthorn, birch, blackthorn and other deciduous trees.
Habits. A single-brooded insect, being in the larval stage from about early April to mid-June, feeding at first within the developing buds, then hiding by day inside spun terminal leaves and fully exposed when in the last instar. The larvae are readily taken by beating, especially at night, and are usually very easy to rear in captivity. The cocooned pupa is formed just under the soil and lasts throughout the winter until the following March or April. Both sexes of the adult come commonly to light, sugar and sallow blossom and the females often deposit their egg batches in confinement without any encouragement. A widely distributed and often common species throughout much of the British Isles; more local in Ireland and northern Scotland.
Plate 35: L. Beaten from birch, fully grown. Late May.

Clouded Drab
Orthosia incerta Hufnagel
Larva. 37–42 mm. Body bluish-green, speckled with tiny white dots and with bold white dorsal and spiracular lines, a less distinct white subdorsal line and a green head.
Foodplants. Oak, sallow, blackthorn, hawthorn, elm, birch and other deciduous trees.
Habits. Single-brooded, occurring as a larva from about late April to the middle of June, feeding at first on the developing buds and later on the foliage at night, spending the day hidden in spun terminal leaves. The larvae can be beaten, especially at night when more active, and during the last instar live fully exposed, usually on the underside of the leaves. They do well in confinement, pupating inside a cocoon under the soil for overwintering. The adults fly mainly during March and April, coming readily to light and sallow bloom, occasionally to sugar. Generally distributed and often common in woodland over much of the British Isles.
Plate 35: M. Beaten from birch, fully grown. Early June.

Twin-spotted Quaker
Orthosia munda Denis & Schiffermüller
Larva. 35–40 mm. Body dark greyish-brown, sprinkled with white dots and also with a reddish-brown dorsal area and a broad spiracular stripe of the same colour; head light brown, spiracles light brown, ringed with black.
Foodplants. Oak, elm, sallow, birch, blackthorn, aspen, poplar, honeysuckle and other trees and plants.
Habits. A single-brooded species, being found as a larva from about mid-April to the middle of June. These mainly nocturnal feeders are often encountered when beating for other species and, when larger, can be located in bark crevices during the day. They are easy to rear in captivity, forming the overwintering cocooned pupae just under the soil. The adults fly during March and April, being attracted to light,

sugar and sallow blossom. Mainly to be found in woodland over much of the British Isles.
Plate 35: N. Beaten from oak, fully grown. Late May.

Hebrew Character
Orthosia gothica Linnaeus
Larva. 42–47 mm. Body green, with fine white dorsal and subdorsal lines and a broad white spiracular stripe, edged above with black; head bright green; spiracles white, ringed with black.
Foodplants. Various trees, shrubs and herbaceous plants, including oak, sallow, birch, blackthorn, hawthorn, common nettle, clover, bilberry and meadowsweet.
Habits. Single-brooded, occurring as a larva from about mid-April to the middle of June, and up to a month later in the northern parts of its range. At first the larvae feed on the developing buds and later, mainly nocturnally, on the foliage. They are not beaten as often as would be expected for such a common insect, although those obtained by this method or bred from the egg are very easy to rear in confinement. The pupa is formed in a cocoon just below the ground and lasts throughout the winter, with the bulk of the adults emerging during March and April, although they linger on until late May in Scotland and parts of Ireland. These attend light traps, sugar and sallow blossom soon after dark and the females usually lay egg batches freely in captivity. Widespread, and usually common to abundant, throughout most of the British Isles.
Plate 35: O. Bred from a female adult to MVL. Late March. (GAC)

Double Line
Mythimna turca Linnaeus
Larva. 44–48 mm. Body ochreous, with a dark-edged pale dorsal line and a series of cross-shaped darker markings dorsally on the abdominal segments. Below the spiracles the body is paler than the rest; head pale brown, heavily mottled with darker brown.
Foodplants. Various grasses, including cock's-foot, woodrush and wood meadow-grass.
Habits. A single-brooded species that occurs in the larval stage from August to the following May, overwintering when still quite small. During late April and May the larvae can sometimes be found at night when active and feeding, after spending the day hidden at the bases of grass tussocks. The cocooned pupa is formed in the soil and lasts about four to six weeks, with the adults flying from mid-June to mid-July, coming freely to light and sugar. Females can be induced to lay their egg batches in captivity by supplying them with broad-leaved grass stems and a small piece of pear or apple on which to feed. Rearing the resulting larvae is usually fairly easy and they can be forced to feed up in about two months by keeping them warm and in the dark. This woodland insect is most frequently recorded from the south-western peninsula of England and from west Wales, although it still occurs in declining numbers elsewhere in southern England.
Plate 35: P. Bred from a female adult to MVL. Early July. (BS)

Brown-line Bright-eye
Mythimna conigera Denis & Schiffermüller
Larva. 35–40 mm. Body ochreous, with a dark brown-edged white dorsal line, a brown subdorsal line that is edged below with yellowish-white and a paler spiracular line; head pale brown with two clear dark stripes.
Foodplants. Various grasses, including cock's-foot, common couch and those of the genera *Poa* and *Festuca*.
Habits. Single-brooded, being in the larval stage from August until the following May, overwintering when small and readily found at night during the spring, being easy to rear when taken at this stage of development. The pupa is formed in a cocoon just below the soil and lasts about four to six weeks, with the adults coming to light, sugar and flowering plants during July and August. The females lay freely on suitable grass stems, and it is possible to force some broods through to a second generation by keeping them warm. Widespread and reasonably common throughout much of Britain and Ireland.
Plate 35: Q. Bred from a female adult to MVL. Late July. (SHC)

The Clay
Mythimna ferrago Fabricius
(*lythargyria* Esper)
Larva. 40–45 mm. Body ochreous, with somewhat similar markings to the previous species (*M. conigera*). Although a good deal of individual variation occurs, the larvae can often be distinguished by their larger size and less clear dark markings on the head.
Foodplants. Various grasses, especially cock's-foot, and *Poa* species; also accepting dandelion, plantain and other herbaceous plants.
Habits. A single-brooded species that occurs as a larva from about August to the following mid-May, overwintering when still small. During the spring the growth becomes more rapid and the larvae can often be found or swept at night from grass tussocks growing along the edges of woodland rides. They are not difficult to rear in confinement, pupating for just over a month in a subterranean cocoon. The adults fly from late June to early August, both sexes coming in good numbers to light, sugar and flowers, with most females laying freely in captivity if supplied with suitable grass stems. The resulting larvae can be forced with warmth. Widely distributed and fairly common over much of the British Isles.
Plate 35: R. Bred from a female adult to MVL. Mid-July.

White-point
Mythimna albipuncta Denis & Schiffermüller
Larva. 35–40 mm. Body usually ochreous or putty coloured, with dark-edged pale dorsal and subdorsal lines, the latter with finely marked dark streaks above; head pale brown, mottled with darker brown; spiracles whitish, ringed with black.
Foodplants. Various grasses, preferring cock's-foot and other soft-bladed varieties.
Habits. A migratory species that may temporarily establish itself on the south coast of England during milder winters. Most of the records of adults occur during August to October, coming to light and sugar, and from these larvae are often obtained. The eggs are laid on grass-heads or within the sheaths and hatch quickly if given warmth, with the growth of the larvae being quite rapid if also kept at about 20–25° centigrade. In captivity they are easy to rear and can become continuously brooded. The pupa is formed in a cocoon among moss or loose soil and can last as little as fourteen days in an incubator.
Plate 36: A. Bred from a female adult to MVL. Mid-September. (BS)

The Delicate

Mythimna vitellina Hübner

Larva. 38–42 mm. Body usually ochreous or some similar shade of pale yellowish-brown, with a fine dark-edged pale dorsal line and the subdorsal lines are often white, although in many paler-coloured individuals they are quite obscure; head pale reddish-brown, spiracles black.

Foodplants. Various grasses, especially soft-bladed species such as cock's-foot and those of the genus *Poa*.

Habits. A regular migrant to the British Isles, of which the larvae are most readily obtained by rearing from adult moths. These tend to occur more frequently on the coasts of south-western England, mainly being recorded at light traps between the end of August and the middle of October, although they have been taken in most of the other months. The females often lay freely in supplied grass sheaths, especially if fed with a small piece of pear or apple and kept in a warm environment. Given continuous warmth the eggs hatch in less than two weeks and the easily reared larvae can become continuously brooded in captivity. It is probable that this species breeds naturally on the south coasts of Devon and Cornwall from earlier arrivals.

Plate 36: B. Bred from a female adult to MVL. Late August. (BS)

Striped Wainscot

Mythimna pudorina Denis & Schiffermüller
(*impudens* Hübner)

Larva. 43–48 mm. Body ochreous, with a dark-edged pale dorsal line and often with a distinct series of bold black dashes along the subdorsal region; head very pale brown, marked with darker brown stripes.

Foodplants. Common reed, purple moor-grass, cock's-foot, reed canary-grass and other broad-bladed grasses.

Habits. A single-brooded species, of which the larvae occur from August to the following mid-May, overwintering when still very small. During April and early May they can be located by searching at night and most tend to be found on or close to the ground. Taken at this stage of their development they can be relatively easy to rear in captivity, pupating in a cocoon among plant litter or just under the soil for about four to six weeks. The adults fly from mid-June to mid-July and are frequently taken in light traps situated on damp heathland and in marshy places and can also be found soon after dusk feeding on flowering grasses. Fairly common in southern England, also occurring elsewhere as far north as Yorkshire; local in south-western Ireland.

Plate 36: C. Found at night, fully grown. Early May.

Southern Wainscot

Mythimna straminea Treitschke

Larva. 42–46 mm. Body ochreous, with a greyish-edged pale dorsal line and other indistinct greyish and pale lines along the subdorsal and lateral areas; head straw-coloured; spiracles white, ringed with black.

Foodplants. Common reed and reed canary-grass, sometimes accepting other broad-bladed grasses in confinement.

Habits. Single-brooded, occurring in the larval stage from August until the following late May or early June, overwintering when still very small. The larvae resume feeding in early April and during May can be swept or searched for on reed-blades at night, hiding by day in old hollow stems or among the reed litter. Although difficult to rear from the egg, those taken when nearly full grown often survive in captivity, if given fresh food and litter in which to form their cocooned pupae. The adults, which fly during July and early August, can be taken at light, sugar and flowering grasses. Mainly to be found locally in the southern half of England, with isolated colonies elsewhere in the Midlands, northern England, Wales and Ireland.

Plate 36: D. Found at night, fully grown. Late May.

Smoky Wainscot

Mythimna impura Hübner

Larva. 36–40 mm. Body ochreous, with a grey-edged whitish dorsal line, a fine whitish subdorsal line, edged darker above and below which are a pair of thin orangish-brown lines; subspiracular line grey; dorsally and laterally sprinkled with small black pinacula; head pale brown, marked with blackish-brown and the spiracles are pinkish, ringed with black.

Foodplants. A wide variety of grasses, including cock's-foot, annual meadow-grass, common reed and tufted hair-grass.

Habits. Mainly a single-brooded species, the larvae of which occur from about late July to the following late May, or even mid-June in Scotland. They overwinter when small and can readily be found or swept, sometimes in good numbers, at night during the spring. They are very easy to rear in captivity and those bred from the egg can often be forced by keeping them warm, reflecting their ability in southern England to feed up and produce a small second generation of adults during September. The pupa is formed in a cocoon beneath the soil, with the main emergence of adults taking place between late June and mid-August, these coming freely to light, sugar and flowering plants. A widespread and common insect occurring throughout most of the British Isles.

Plate 36: E. Swept at night, nearly half grown. Late March. (SHC)

Common Wainscot

Mythimna pallens Linnaeus

Larva. 40–44 mm. Body ochreous, with a grey-edged white dorsal line, a pair of white subdorsal lines between which are dull orange lines; head pale brown, marked with darker brown. Similar to the previous species (*M. impura*), but more slender in build.

Foodplants. Various grasses, especially the broad-bladed species.

Habits. Double-brooded in southern parts of its range, with the larvae occurring from September to the following May, and again during the summer. North of the Midlands, this insect is univoltine with the larval period being from August to about mid-June. When small the larvae are semi-gregarious living in spun terminal blades of grasses. Later they disperse, hiding in the bases of grass clumps by day, and may then readily be found or swept at night. Pupation takes place in a slight cocoon just below the soil and lasts about a month. The adults are on the wing from late June to October in two overlapping broods in the south, and from mid-July to late August elsewhere. They come freely to light, sugar and flowering plants, especially grasses. Widely distributed and fairly common over much of the British Isles.

Plate 36: F. Bred from a female adult to MVL. Early July. (SHC)

Mathew's Wainscot

Mythimna favicolor Barrett

Larva. 40–44 mm. Body ochreous or pinkish-brown, with a pale dark-edged dorsal line and a pair of pale subdorsal lines. Similar to the previous species (*M. pallens*), but usually darker and richer in colour.

Foodplants. Common saltmarsh-grass, and accepting a wide variety of broad-bladed grasses in captivity.

Habits. Single-brooded, with the larval stage lasting from about August to the following mid- to late May. The larvae can be located during the first half of May by searching or sweeping at night on the grasses growing on banks immediately above the saltmarsh. The adults fly from mid-June to mid-July and can be taken at light or when feeding at flowering plants. Most females will freely deposit their eggs in captivity and the resulting larvae can be forced with moderate warmth. Much speculation exists as to whether this is a true species or a saltmarsh-inhabiting race of the previous species (*M. pallens*), as cross pairings have been observed in the wild and the genitalia of the adults is similar. To be found on the coastal saltmarshes of south-east England from Hampshire to Suffolk.
Plate 36: G. Found at night, nearly fully grown. Early May.

Shore Wainscot

Mythimna litoralis Curtis
Larva. 42–46 mm. Body pale ochreous, with a fine dark-edged pale dorsal line and usually an obvious brown subdorsal stripe, below which is often a fine pale line; head light brown, almost unmarked.
Foodplants. Marram, and accepting annual meadow-grass and tufted hair-grass when in captivity.
Habits. A single-brooded species, occurring in the larval stage from about August to the following late May, overwintering when still quite small. During the spring the larvae can be obtained by searching at night or by carefully sifting through the sand below marram plants during the day. They are fairly easy to rear in captivity if supplied with about 10–15 cm of sand from their habitat in which to hide by day and eventually pupate. These pupae should not be disturbed and usually last from three to six weeks. The adults fly from late June to about late August and come freely to light, sugar and flowering marram grasses. Locally common in suitable habitats around the coast of England and Wales; also in southern Scotland and Ireland.
Plate 36: H. Found at night, fully grown. Late May.

L-album Wainscot

Mythimna l-album Linnaeus
Larva. 30–35 mm. Body ochreous, with a grey-bordered fine white dorsal line and a broadish brown subdorsal stripe, below which is another white line; head light reddish-brown, finely speckled with darker brown.
Foodplants. Various grasses, especially the soft broad-bladed varieties.
Habits. A double-brooded resident species that is reinforced by migration. The larvae occur from October to the following late May, and again in August, overwintering when still very small and probably feeding during milder nights. They have been found during the spring by careful searching or sweeping after dark on the cliff edges, where the populations are at their greatest, and in captivity they are usually very easy to rear, pupating for about three to six weeks in a subterranean cocoon. The light-responsive adults fly first in July and later from mid-September to late October, when they can also be taken on ivy bloom and over-ripe blackberries. Female adults lay freely in confinement if given space and foodplant as a stimulus and the larvae can easily be forced with moderate warmth. Since establishing itself in south Devon and Cornwall during the 1930s, this once rare migrant species has now spread along the coast to Hampshire and the Isle of Wight, although it is not often seen more than a mile from the sea.
Plate 36: I. Bred from a female adult to MVL. Late September. (SHC)

White-speck

Mythimna unipuncta Haworth
Larva. 38–43 mm. Body variable in colour, being of some shade of ochreous or brown. The dorsal and pair of subdorsal lines are thin and whitish, the latter being separated by a pinkish-orange stripe and bordered above with darker mottlings; a thin dark line along the spiracles and the head is light brown, marked darker.
Foodplants. Various grasses, preferring couch and cock's-foot in captivity.
Habits. An immigrant species that temporarily establishes itself on the south coasts of Devon and Cornwall and in the Isles of Scilly during milder winters. The adults have been recorded during most months of the year, although the majority of those observed are from late August to late October, when the migrating continental populations have built up and those bred from earlier arrivals are on the wing. Both sexes come freely to light, sugar and ivy bloom and the females lay freely if given warmth and grasses as a stimulus. The larvae are very easy to rear and when kept warm will become continuously brooded in captivity. The pupae are formed in loose cocoons at the bases of grasses or among plant debris and can last as little as ten days when kept at 25° centigrade. Most frequently seen on the south coast of England, but regularly taken further inland, especially after good summers.
Plate 36: J. Bred from a female adult to MVL. Late September. (BS)

Obscure Wainscot

Mythimna obsoleta Hübner
Larva. 37–42 mm. Body ochreous, with fine white dorsal and subdorsal lines that are edged with greyish, often with an orangish bloom subdorsally and between the segments; head light brown, speckled darker.
Foodplant. Common reed.
Habits. A single-brooded insect, being in the larval stage from about late July to the following April, overwintering when fully grown inside a slight cocoon within a hollow reed-stem in which pupation eventually takes place in the spring. The larvae can be found at night during September, but are usually not easy to rear in captivity due to the overwintering requirements. The adults fly from late May to the middle of July, coming freely to light, sugar and flowering grasses in their marshy habitats. A local species occurring mainly in southern and eastern England, although seemingly absent from many suitable localities.
Plate 36: K. Found at night, fully grown. Late September. (GAC)

Shoulder-striped Wainscot

Mythimna comma Hübner
Larva. 37–43 mm. Body various shades of light brown or ochreous, with a fine grey-edged dorsal line; thin pale subdorsal lines, above which are a series of dark brown markings; head reddish-brown with two dark vertical stripes; spiracles mainly black.
Foodplants. Various grasses, especially cock's-foot, and also reported to accept docks and sorrel.
Habits. Single-brooded, occurring in the larval stage from about late July to the following spring, after overwintering fully grown within its subterranean cocoon. The larvae may be obtained by rearing from the egg or by searching at night

during September, but can be difficult to overwinter unless kept outside in plant tubs supplied with loose soil and growing cock's-foot. The larvae must not be disturbed during this period and the pupa is formed during April or May, lasting about six to eight weeks, with the adults emerging from about mid-June to late July. These come readily to light and sugar, with most captive females laying eggs freely if given suitable grasses on which to deposit. Widespread and fairly common over much of England and Wales, local and less frequent in Scotland and Ireland.
Plate 36: L. Bred from a female adult to MVL. Early July. (SHC)

Devonshire Wainscot

Mythimna putrescens Hübner
Larva. 38–43 mm. Body various shades of light brown or ochreous, with fine white dorsal and subdorsal lines, the former edged with brownish-grey, the latter less so; head pale brown with a pair of dark vertical stripes, spiracles mostly black.
Foodplants. Various grasses, accepting annual meadow-grass and cock's-foot in captivity.
Habits. A single-brooded species, occurring as a larva from September, feeding in mild weather throughout the winter, becoming fully grown by about late February, when it forms a subterranean cocoon in which it stays unchanged until May or June. The larvae can be found by careful searching on mild nights during January and February along cliff edges and rough grassland close to the sea, and are fairly easy to rear in captivity as long as they are not disturbed after they have burrowed into the soil to pupate. The adults fly from late July to early September, coming readily to light traps, sugar and flowering plants, with the females laying in captivity if supplied with suitable grasses. A local coastal insect inhabiting Cornwall, North and South Devon and Pembrokeshire.
Plate 36: M. Found at night, nearly fully grown. Late January. (JMP)

The Cosmopolitan

Mythimna loreyi Duponchel
Larva. 40–45 mm. Body various shades of light brown, with a grey-edged fine brownish-white dorsal line and a thin subdorsal line of the same colour, this being bordered above with blackish markings; spiracular stripe broad and pale brown; head reddish-brown, with two darker stripes and other dark mottlings.
Foodplants. Various grasses, accepting cock's-foot and other broad-bladed varieties in captivity.
Habits. A formerly infrequent immigrant species that has recently been occurring in greater numbers, as in Cornwall during August 1992 when over one hundred were observed, indicating the possibility of local breeding. Most adults are recorded during August and September to light traps, and the females seem to lay quite freely if given grasses as a stimulus. The resulting larvae can be successfully reared by keeping them warm and in the dark, becoming continuously brooded in captivity if required. In Britain this insect is most likely to be encountered in Cornwall or the Isles of Scilly.
Plate 36: N. Bred from a female adult to MVL. Late August. (JC)

Flame Wainscot

Senta flammea Curtis
Larva. 32–36 mm. Body ochreous, with fine indistinct dorsal and subdorsal lines being slightly paler than the body; head light reddish-brown, delicately mottled with darker brown; spiracles small, white and ringed with black.
Foodplant. Common reed.
Habits. A single-brooded species, being in the larval state from July to October or November, hiding by day in hollow stems and feeding fully exposed on the reed-blades at night. The larvae can readily be found during the last half of September and October by searching. When taken at this point of their development, they can be bred to the adult stage by supplying them with old dry stems in which to hide and pupate for overwintering. They must be kept outside to avoid becoming too dry and constricting the cocooned pupae. The adults fly from mid-May to early July and can be taken at light and resting on reed-stems after dark, and although the females lay quite freely on supplied foodplant, the young larvae can be difficult to rear. A very local species, being found mainly in the drier parts of old large reed-beds, in Norfolk, Suffolk and Cambridgeshire; those recorded elsewhere are possibly immigrants.
Plate 36: O. Found at night, nearly fully grown. Late September. (JF)

SUBFAMILY: CUCULLIINAE

The Wormwood

Cucullia absinthii Linnaeus
Larva. 36–42 mm. Body pale grey or greyish-green, with reddish-brown and green mottlings on the dorsal and lateral areas; head pale grey with brown speckling.
Foodplants. The flowers and seeds of wormwood and mugwort.
Habits. A single-brooded species, being in the larval stage from about early August to late September or even later. These extremely well camouflaged larvae can readily be obtained by sweeping and are usually easy to rear in confinement. The pupa is formed beneath the soil in a tough cocoon from which it should not be extracted, and lasts throughout the winter, the adults emerging during the following July. These may be found feeding at flowers after dark and later are attracted to light in small numbers, with the females laying freely in captivity, if supplied with the foodplant flowers. Mainly inhabiting waste ground, commons, quarries and recently disturbed ground, such as new road embankments, locally throughout much of the southern half of England; also occurring in Wales.
Plate 36: P. Swept from wormwood, fully grown. Late September.

Scarce Wormwood

Cucullia artemisiae Hufnagel
Larva. 32–36 mm. Body green, sometimes having white mottling, with a thin pale dorsal line and distinguishing pinkish-brown conical pinacula; head green.
Foodplants. Mugwort and wormwood.
Habits. A single-brooded insect, of which a larva was discovered feeding on mugwort in Essex during September 1971 and two adults were found in Devon in 1885. Abroad, the range covers much of western and southern Europe, where the larvae occur during August and September, overwintering as pupae and with the adults flying in June and July.
Plate 49: F. Courtesy of Per Stadel Nielsen.

Chamomile Shark

Cucullia chamomillae Denis & Schiffermüller
Larva. 40–45 mm. Body usually greenish-grey, with bold

yellow or white diamond-shaped markings along the dorsal area; more blotches of the same colours and patches of reddish-brown on the subdorsal region and above the broad spiracular stripe; head pale brown or green, with darker stripes.
Foodplants. Mainly the flowers of various mayweeds, chamomiles and feverfew.
Habits. Single-brooded, being in the larval stage from about late May to the middle of July. The larvae can be found or swept, sometimes in good numbers, and are usually quite easy to rear in confinement, often accepting the leaves as well as the flowers of the foodplant when in the last instar. The pupae are formed in tough cocoons located beneath the soil, in which overwintering takes place. From late April to the end of May the adults can be found at rest on fences and posts by day, and later come in small numbers to light. Mainly to be found on waste ground and on disturbed agricultural land where the foodplants flourish, throughout much of England and Wales; local and mostly coastal in distribution in southern Scotland and Ireland.
Plate 36: Q. Swept from scentless mayweed, fully grown. Late June.

The Shark
Cucullia umbratica Linnaeus
Larva. 45–50 mm. Body various shades of brown, with darker and lighter mottlings and orange streaks from the anal plate to the last abdominal segment. Most forms have a series of dark blotches along the body below the spiracles and the underparts are ochreous; head and prothoracic plate blackish-brown.
Foodplants. Sow-thistle, wild lettuce, hawkweed and hawk's-beard.
Habits. A single-brooded insect, occurring in the larval stage from about late July to early September, feeding mainly at night and hiding beneath the lower leaves during the day. The larvae are sometimes to be found or swept at night when searching for other species, although the populations are rarely concentrated enough to make deliberate searching a worthwhile task, and rearing them from the egg is not difficult. The adults fly during June and July, coming to light and flowering plants and many females will lay freely if supplied with the foodplant flowers. The young larvae seem to prefer the flowers, but later will also readily accept the leaves. The pupa is formed in a tough cocoon underground for overwintering. Widespread and fairly common over most of the British Isles.
Plate 36: R. Bred from a female adult to MVL. Late June. (RM)

Star-wort
Cucullia asteris Denis & Schiffermüller
Larva. 45–50 mm. Body green or pinkish-purple, with a broad dark-edged yellow dorsal line, a yellowish-white subdorsal line and a pale yellow or green spiracular stripe; head green or pinkish, with minute black spots.
Foodplants. The flowers of sea aster, goldenrod and occasionally sea wormwood, accepting Michaelmas daisy flowers in captivity.
Habits. Single-brooded, occurring as a larva from late July to late August, with those of the coastal colonies feeding on sea aster and lasting well into September. The larvae can readily be obtained by searching or careful sweeping and are not difficult to rear in captivity, although some are parasitized. The pupa is formed in a strong cocoon below the soil for overwintering and should not be opened for inspection, as it will often dry out if disturbed. Most of the adults emerge between mid-June and the end of July, although they have been recorded as late as September. They come to light in small numbers and may also be taken while feeding at flowering plants. Locally common on the coast of England from Hampshire to Yorkshire, and in woodland from Dorset to Kent and in parts of Wales.
Plate 37: A. Swept from goldenrod by day, fully grown. Late August.

The Cudweed
Cucullia gnaphalii Hübner
Larva. 38–42 mm. Body various shades of green, with a broad reddish-purple dorsal stripe consisting of lozenge-shaped sections and purplish blotches surrounding each spiracle; head dull green with many small purple spots.
Foodplant. Goldenrod.
Habits. A single-brooded species, the larva of which occurs from late July to early September. When larger, during late August, the larvae hide by day and may be swept or found feeding on the leaves below the foodplant flowers, especially around dawn or dusk when they are most active, but many suffer from parasitism. The pupa is formed in a cocoon on or just under the ground for overwintering, with the adults flying from late May to early July, coming to light and flowering plants. This extremely vulnerable insect inhabited the woodlands of East Sussex and southern Kent and has not been reported since the late 1970s.
Plate 37: B. Swept at night, fully grown. Late August.

Striped Lychnis
Cucullia lychnitis Rambur
Larva. 40–45 mm. Body whitish-green, with broad yellow rings around each segment in which are black markings; head yellow, marked with black; forms without the black markings sometimes occur.
Foodplants. The flowers and seeds of black mullein and white mullein.
Habits. Single-brooded, occurring in the larval stage from about mid-July to early September, feeding fully exposed upon the flower-spikes of the foodplant. From early August the larvae can readily be located by searching and are not difficult to rear in captivity, as long as the pupae are not disturbed from within their tough subterranean cocoons, in which the insect can overwinter up to four times and they are not given peat in which to pupate, as it is too acid. The adults fly in June and early July, coming sparingly to light and more often to flowering plants. Rearing this species from the egg is not practical, unless the foodplant is readily available. A vulnerable and declining insect, mostly being found on the chalk downland of southern England.
Plate 37: C. Found on black mullein, nearly fully grown. Mid-August. (SHC)

Water Betony
Cucullia scrophulariae Denis & Schiffermüller
Larva. 42–46 mm. Body pale bluish-grey or whitish-green, with yellow rings and black markings; very similar to the following species (*C. verbasci*), although a stated distinguishing characteristic is the black coloration between the segmental divisions.
Foodplants. The flowers and seeds of figwort and mullein.
Habits. The status of this single-brooded species within the British Isles is unclear. The adults cannot be separated from *C. verbasci* without genital determination and larvae were stated to have been found in East Anglia, Kent and elsewhere

in southern England during the late nineteenth century. Since then adults have been taken in Dorset in 1949 and 1994. Abroad, in western Europe, the larval development period lasts from June to August, then overwintering as pupae, before the adults emerge in May and June.
Plate 37: D. Courtesy of B. Goater, via D. J. Carter. (NHM)

The Mullein
Cucullia verbasci Linnaeus
Larva. 44–48 mm. Body pale bluish-grey or whitish-green, usually with large black spots and yellow blotches on each ring dorsally and laterally; rarely are these blotches joined to form an unbroken band; head yellow with black spots.
Foodplants. Great mullein, dark mullein and other related species, figworts, also the leaves of garden buddleia.
Habits. A single-brooded species, being in the larval stage from late May to about the middle of July, although many become fully grown by late June. The larvae can easily be located by searching and sometimes they completely consume all of the foodplant leaves and have to move to adjacent plants to survive. The pupae are formed in tough cocoons beneath the ground and can overwinter for up to four years, before the adults emerge in late April and May. These are sometimes attracted to light and females will lay in captivity if supplied with foodplant. Widespread and fairly common, especially on calcareous soils, over the greater part of England, local in Wales and in Co. Cork in Ireland.
Plate 37: E. Found on great mullein, fully grown. Late June.

Toadflax Brocade
Calophasia lunula Hufnagel
Larva. 32–36 mm. Body bluish-grey, with bold bright yellow dorsal, subdorsal and spiracular stripes, with black blotches between; head bluish-grey with black spots.
Foodplants. Common toadflax; also recorded on pale toadflax and purple toadflax.
Habits. A mainly double-brooded insect, with the larvae occurring in July and again in late August and September. These can readily be obtained by searching or careful sweeping after dark or by close searching around the foodplant bases during the day. Usually they are easy to rear in captivity, although the larvae should be supplied with cork, balsa wood or cardboard, which they will use to construct their tough cocoons. The pupae must not be removed from the cocoons and they will last throughout the winter until the following late May or June. The adults come freely to light and those of the second generation are on the wing during August. This species is a recent colonist to the British Isles, first being recorded as breeding during 1952, since when it has established itself on the Kent and Sussex coasts and is recorded occasionally elsewhere in the south-east of England.
Plate 37: F. Found at night, fully grown. Mid-September.

Minor Shoulder-knot
Brachylomia viminalis Fabricius
Larva. 28–32 mm. Body pale bluish-green, with a broad white dorsal stripe and thinner white subdorsal and spiracular lines; head whitish-green, spiracles small and black, and small white dorsal pinacula present.
Foodplants. Sallow, willow and aspen.
Habits. Single-brooded, occurring in the larval stage from April to early June, after overwintering as an egg. The larvae spend most of the day hidden in a spinning between the foodplant leaves and can be obtained by searching or by beating after dark. They are not difficult to rear in confinement and pupate in leaf litter or just under the soil for about four to six weeks. The adults fly during July and early August, coming freely to light and sugar, with most females laying readily in confinement. A mainly woodland and marshland insect, being found over most of the British Isles; uncommon and local in Ireland.
Plate 37: G. Beaten at night, almost fully grown. Late May. (SHC)

Beautiful Gothic
Leucochlaena oditis Hübner
(*hispida* Geyer)
Larva. 30–35 mm. Body light brown, with a fine paler dorsal line and an indistinct paler subdorsal line, edged with darker markings; head brown with a pair of vertical blackish streaks.
Foodplants. Various grasses, including couch and annual meadow-grass.
Habits. A single-brooded species, of which the larva occurs from about October to the following March, feeding slowly throughout the winter months. The larvae can be found at night from late January to early March, being fairly easy to rear when taken at this stage of their development. The cocoon is formed under the soil, with the larva lying dormant within for about a month, before changing into a pupa. They should not be disturbed and kept in a shaded place to avoid desiccation during the summer. The adults emerge during September and October, responding well to light and can also be found resting on grass stems soon after dark. The females will sometimes deposit eggs in captivity when supplied with grasses and netting, and the resulting larvae can be reared quite quickly, although prone to desiccation if kept too dry. A local coastal insect, being found in the Isle of Wight, Dorset and South Devon.
Plate 37: H. Found at night, fully grown. Early March. (SHC)

The Sprawler
Brachionycha sphinx Hufnagel
Larva. 43–48 mm. Body pale green, darker below the large pinkish-white spiracles, with white dorsal and subdorsal lines and a bold yellowish spiracular line. The eleventh segment is humped dorsally and the larva adopts a characteristic posture by throwing back the anterior half of its body; head green, thoracic legs large and prolegs tipped with pinkish-brown. Young larvae are blackish-brown at first and an uncommon bluish-green form also occurs.
Foodplants. Various deciduous trees, including oak, elm, birch, beech, hawthorn, blackthorn and sallow.
Habits. Single-brooded, occurring in the larval stage from April to about early June, after overwintering as an egg. These larvae can readily be beaten from their foodplants and are relatively easy to rear as long as they are given a good depth of soil in which to pupate and kept outside during the summer. The adults hatch late in the year, during late October and November, with both sexes being attracted to light and the females laying freely if supplied with rough bark or coarse netting on which to deposit their eggs. Mainly a woodland species, being found over much of England and Wales, more commonly in the south.
Plate 37: I. Beaten from blackthorn, fully grown. Late May.

Rannoch Sprawler
Brachionycha nubeculosa Esper
Larva. 45–50 mm. Body bright green, dusted with white dots and yellow pinacula over the dorsal and lateral areas, also having an oblique yellow and white dash laterally on the

third segment and a yellow bar across the humped eleventh ring; head dark green, spiracles large and white.
Foodplants. Birch, also accepting other deciduous trees in captivity.
Habits. A single-brooded insect, occurring as a larva from May to late June or early July, occasionally being obtained by beating mature birch trees. The adults fly early in the year as soon as the weather conditions permit, usually between late March and the middle of April. Both sexes will come to light and the females can be induced to lay by supplying them with rough birch bark and coarse netting. The larvae can be difficult to rear, although sleeving them on a growing tree can prove successful. It is also necessary to give the fully grown larvae at least 25 cm of peat in which to pupate and they should not be overcrowded. Most of these pupae over-winter once, but they have been recorded as lasting four years in this stage. Distribution of this species is restricted to ancient birch woodland in the central highlands of Scotland.
Plate 37: J. Bred from a female adult to MVL. Early April. (JMP)

Brindled Ochre

Dasypolia templi Thunberg
Larva. 48–53 mm. Body dirty pinkish-white, liberally speckled with dark brown pinacula and having the dorsal vessel visible as a brownish-grey line; head orange, prothoracic plate brownish-orange, with black edging; anal plate reddish-brown.
Foodplants. The inner stems and roots of hogweed and wild angelica, accepting garden carrot in captivity.
Habits. Single-brooded, being in the larval stage from about April to early August, sometimes obtainable by splitting open hogweed stems, especially on isolated plants, from late May onwards. When taken at this point of their development the larvae can be reared on slices of carrot, and they have been bred from the egg on growing examples of this same plant. The pupa is formed just below the soil close to the hogweeds or among grass roots and lasts about six to eight weeks, with the adults emerging in early October. They can be light-trapped and only the females survive to the following spring; pairing takes place during the autumn. The females will lay eggs on foodplant roots and stems with the young larvae hatching after about three weeks and soon boring into the plants. Mainly coastal in distribution in south-western England, Wales and Ireland; inland on the Pennines and more widespread in Scotland.
Plate 37: K. Bred from a female adult to MVL. Mid-April. (JMP)

Feathered Brindle

Aporophyla australis Boisduval
Larva. 35–40 mm. Body of various shades of green or reddish-brown, with a pale dorsal line enclosed within darker triangular-shaped markings, an indistinct whitish or yellowish subdorsal line and a pale spiracular line; head dull green, minutely dotted with reddish-brown.
Foodplants. Sea campion, sorrel, bramble, wood sage and other herbaceous plants, also various grasses.
Habits. A single-brooded species, being in the larval stage from October to the following mid-May, feeding in mild weather throughout the winter months. The larvae are most easily found at night during the spring and when taken at this time are reasonably easy to rear in captivity, pupating under moss or just in the soil, until the adults emerge during late August and September. These will come to light and sugar, with the females laying in captivity if supplied with coarse netting. The eggs hatch in about three weeks and it has been stated that the larvae can be forced to develop faster by keeping them warm. Mostly a coastal insect, being found locally from Suffolk to Cornwall; again coastal in Cos. Wicklow, Wexford and Waterford in Ireland.
Plate 37: L. Found at night on grasses, fully grown. Early May. (SC)

Deep-brown Dart

Aporophyla lutulenta Denis & Schiffermüller
Larva. 36–40 mm. Body bright green, with a darker dorsal line and a whitish subdorsal line, the former of variable intensity, usually coloured black or crimson and a constant yellowish-white spiracular stripe; head large, green or brownish-green.
Foodplants. Various grasses, broom, hawthorn, blackthorn, plantains and probably other herbaceous plants.
Habits. Single-brooded, stated to occur as a larva from October to about the following early June, overwintering when still very small, although some eggs do not hatch until January. The larvae can readily be obtained by searching or careful sweeping at night during the spring and are still often difficult to rear even when taken at this point of their development. The larvae prefer to pupate in loose or sandy soil, with this stage lasting until the adults emerge during September and October, earlier in captivity. They can be obtained at light traps and are also attracted by sugar, ripe blackberries and ivy bloom. Generally distributed, inhabiting scrubland, commons and waste ground over much of southern and eastern England.
Plate 37: M. Found at night, nearly fully grown. Mid-May.

Northern Deep-brown Dart

Aporophyla lueneburgensis Freyer
Larva. 35–40 mm. Body bright green, with a dark dorsal line that is often intensified to form triangular blotches, a pale subdorsal line which can be obscured by blackish marks in the darker coloured forms and a yellowish-white spiracular stripe; head green or brownish-green.
Foodplants. Various grasses, heather, bilberry, bird's-foot trefoil and probably other herbaceous plants.
Habits. A single-brooded insect that is considered by some authors to be a subspecies of *A. lutulenta*. The larvae are very similar, but have a tendency to be more boldly marked than the previous species. They occur from September to late May, overwintering when small, and can be taken by searching or sweeping at night, most often being found where grasses and herbaceous plants are mixed with heather. Sandy soil should be given for pupation and the adults emerge from mid-August and into September, being attracted to light and flowering plants. Mainly inhabiting moorland, being found in North Wales, northern England, the Isle of Man and much of Scotland; also recorded from the coasts of northern and western Ireland.
Plate 37: N. Swept at night, nearly fully grown. Mid-May.

Black Rustic

Aporophyla nigra Haworth
Larva. 40–45 mm. Body green, with a darker green dorsal line, a whitish subdorsal line and a yellowish-white spiracular stripe, which is often edged above with a fine crimson line; head green. Brown, grey and pinkish forms also occur.
Foodplants. Various grasses and herbaceous plants, including dock, heather, clover, chickweed and dandelion, also accepting sallow, hawthorn and blackthorn in captivity.
Habits. Single-brooded, being in the larval stage from

October to the following late May, feeding slowly throughout the winter in mild weather. During the spring the larvae may be searched for or swept at night, sometimes also being found on the new growth of small sallows and blackthorns. They are not difficult to rear when taken in April and May, forming a cocooned pupa in the soil. The adults fly during September and October, with both sexes coming to light, sugar, ripe blackberries and ivy bloom, and although most females will lay freely in captivity, it is considered not an easy species to rear from the egg. Generally distributed over most of the British Isles, but much less frequent in the eastern counties of England.
Plate 37: O. Found at night on grasses, fully grown. Late May.

Golden-rod Brindle
Lithomoia solidaginis Hübner
Larva. 40–45 mm. Body reddish-brown, with a thin pale dorsal line, a broad white subspiracular line and a few whitish tubercles in the subdorsal region; head orange-brown, darker at the front; prothoracic plate mainly dark brown.
Foodplants. Heather, bilberry, bog myrtle, birch, sallow and other moorland plants.
Habits. A single-brooded species, being in the larval stage from late April to the middle of July, after overwintering as an egg. During the spring and early summer the larvae can readily be swept, by day or night, from heather and other moorland plants. Usually they are easy to rear when taken by this method, although many larvae suffer from parasitism. The pupa is formed in a cocoon under the moss or just in the ground, lasting for about four to eight weeks, with the adults being on the wing from the middle of August and throughout most of September. These come to flowering plants, light and sugar, with most females laying freely in captivity. Widely distributed on the moors and in open woodlands over much of Scotland, North Wales and parts of northern England.
Plate 37: P. Swept from heather, about half grown. Late May. (SHC)

Tawny Pinion
Lithophane semibrunnea Haworth
Larva. 37–42 mm. Body pale green, with a broad white dorsal stripe, thinner subdorsal and lateral lines and a yellowish-white spiracular line; head pale bluish-green.
Foodplants. Ash, also accepting wild privet and garden plum in captivity.
Habits. Single-brooded, occurring as a larva from May to July, possibly being obtainable by beating at night, although the populations are rarely concentrated enough. The adults fly during the autumn before overwintering and pairing takes place in the spring. They are usually obtained by sugaring or by searching ripe blackberries and ivy bloom in the autumn and sallow blossom during April, coming only infrequently to light. Females taken from April onwards are often fertile and will deposit eggs on netting, ash buds and twigs in captivity. The larvae are not difficult to rear as long as fresh food is supplied and they are not overcrowded, as they have mild cannibalistic tendencies. Pupation takes place underground in a tough cocoon; these should not be disturbed and be kept outside in a shaded place during the summer. A local species, being found in woodland, parkland and on commons throughout much of the southern half of England and in South Wales.
Plate 37: Q. Bred from a female adult to sugar. Mid-April. (DB)

Pale Pinion
Lithophane hepatica Clerck
(*socia* Hufnagel)
Larva. 38–44 mm. Body pale bluish-green, with a broad white dorsal stripe, a thinner whitish subdorsal line and a thin yellowish-white spiracular line; head pale green.
Foodplants. Birch, sallow, dock, chickweed and other trees and plants.
Habits. A single-brooded insect, being in the larval stage from early May to about late June. These larvae are occasionally beaten when attempting to obtain other species, although it would probably not be practical to deliberately try to acquire them by this method, due to their low population density. The adults are on the wing from late September to the following May, pairing in the spring, being attracted to sugar, light and sallow blossom after overwintering. Females will often deposit their eggs on netting and suitable foodplants if fed on pieces of fruit. The larvae may be successfully reared by avoiding overcrowding, as they can be cannibalistic, and by being given a variety of food throughout their development. They lie dormant for about a month in the subterranean cocoon before pupating, with some dying during this period, so they should not be disturbed. A mainly woodland species, being found throughout most of southern and south-western England, much of Wales and parts of Ireland.
Plate 37: R. Bred from a female adult to MVL. Early April. (M&JH)

Grey Shoulder-knot
Lithophane ornitopus Hufnagel
Larva. 37–42 mm. Body pale bluish-green, with a faint white subdorsal line and wholly covered with tiny white pinacula; head bluish-green, mottled with white.
Foodplant. Oak.
Habits. Single-brooded, occurring in the larval stage from about late April until the middle of June. The larvae can sometimes be beaten from mature oaks, especially in places where the moth is reasonably common, such as the New Forest and the woods on the Surrey/Sussex border. A fairly easy species to rear in captivity, although the insects should not be overcrowded and fresh food must be available. Pupation takes place in a strong cocoon under the soil, with the larva lying dormant within for about a month before changing. The adults emerge in the autumn, feed before overwintering and pair in the spring, responding well to sugar and flowering plants, also coming in small numbers to light. Mainly found in the southern half of England, much of Wales and parts of Ireland.
Plate 38: A. Bred from a female adult to MVL. Mid-April. (SHC)

The Conformist
Lithophane furcifera Hufnagel
Larva. 35–40 mm. Body olive-green, brown or grey, with yellowish-white dorsal, subdorsal and lateral lines, all interrupted with black; head dull green or brown.
Foodplants. Alder, and occasionally birch, sallow and poplar.
Habits. A single-brooded species that occurs in the larval stage from April to June, feeding at first on the membrane between the ribs of developing leaves and later consuming them wholly. This insect, the larva of which has never been reported in Britain, seems to have been established in South Wales during the latter part of the last century, with two records since from that general area (1907 and 1959). Also,

about ten individuals of the continental form have been taken this century and these are presumed to be immigrants. **Plate 49: G.** Courtesy of Per Stadel Nielsen.

The Nonconformist

Lithophane lamda Fabricius

Larva. 33–38 mm. Body bluish-green, with minute white pinacula, whitish dorsal and subdorsal lines and a yellowish-white spiracular stripe; head green (MBGBI).

Foodplants. Bog myrtle, bog bilberry and creeping willow.

Habits. Eleven adults of this species of uncertain status were taken between 1865 and 1938, with several from north-west Kent, suggesting it may have been temporarily established. The larvae occur from May to July, but are unrecorded in this country, with the hibernating adults flying from September to April.

Blair's Shoulder-knot

Lithophane leautieri Boisduval

(*lapidea* auctt.)

Larva. 34–38 mm. Body dark green, with an obvious white dorsal line, bold white markings along the subdorsal area, an indistinct whitish spiracular line and a series of dark red blotches surrounding the whitish spiracles; head green, mottled darker.

Foodplants. The flowers and leaves of cypresses, especially Monterey cypress. Also recorded on juniper.

Habits. A single-brooded insect, with the larval stage lasting from about late March to July, after overwintering as an egg. The young larvae feed on the foodplant flowers and later also on the new leaves. They can sometimes be beaten from the higher branches of mature trees and in captivity they are not difficult to rear, although the pupae, formed in the soil, should not be kept too damp. The adults emerge during late September and October, being attracted to light, and females lay in confinement if supplied with foodplant and coarse netting. This species is a recent colonist to the British Isles, being found mainly in the southern counties of England, especially in parks and gardens near the coast, but also spreading as far north as Lancashire.

Plate 38: B. Bred from an adult female to MVL. Mid-October. (MB)

Red Sword-grass

Xylena vetusta Hübner

Larva. 52–60 mm. Body usually green or occasionally brown, with a distinct yellow dorsal line, a white subdorsal line and a broadish white spiracular line that is edged above with black; small white pinacula dorsally; head and thoracic legs brownish-green, spiracles reddish.

Foodplants. Various low-growing plants, including docks, sedges, bog myrtle, heather and yellow iris, also accepting the young foliage of many deciduous trees.

Habits. Single-brooded, occurring as a larva from mid-May to about the middle of July. Although the larvae can be found by searching, sweeping and beating in areas where the populations are high, they are most often obtained by rearing from the egg stage. The adults fly from September to late May, feeding at ivy blossom and ripe blackberries during the autumn and at sallow bloom during the spring, after hibernation. They also come to sugar and light in good numbers, with most females laying their egg batches quite freely in captivity. The larvae are fairly easy to rear, seeming to prefer a varied diet, and they should not be overcrowded as some broods are susceptible to viruses. The pupa is formed underground in a slight cocoon, lasting about six to eight weeks. Mainly a moorland and damp woodland insect, being most frequently recorded in western and northern parts of the British Isles; recently declining in the south-west.

Plate 38: C. Bred from an adult female to sugar. Mid-May. (BS)

Sword-grass

Xylena exsoleta Linnaeus

Larva. 55–62 mm. Body pale green, with yellowish-white subdorsal lines above which are pairs of white pinacula enclosed in black blotches. Subspiracular line white, edged above with streaks of orange; head brownish-green, spiracles white or yellowish-white.

Foodplants. Various low-growing plants, including dock, yellow iris and bog myrtle, and occasionally garden plants such as *Chrysanthemums*.

Habits. Single-brooded, being in the larval stage from May to July. The larvae have been found in the wild on occasion, but are most readily obtained by breeding from an adult female moth. These fly from September to the following May, being attracted to sugar, flowering plants and light, often laying in captivity when fed and supplied with netting or rough cardboard on which to deposit their egg batches. The larvae are notoriously difficult to rear successfully in confinement, even when kept separately in plastic boxes with the food being changed daily. Most tend to die from virus infection after they have become about half grown, although occasionally a whole brood may develop without many casualties. The pupae are formed beneath the soil in a cocoon and again losses may occur in this stage if allowed to desiccate. Mainly a moorland species, being most often found in the highlands of Scotland, parts of northern England and North Wales; rare in Ireland and seriously declined in southern England, with most recent records being attributed to migrants.

Plate 38: D. Bred from an adult female to sugar. Late April. (JMP)

Early Grey

Xylocampa areola Esper

Larva. 40–45 mm. Body light brown, with a brown-centred yellowish dorsal line, dark brownish marks dorsally on the seventh and eighth segments and a slight hump on the eleventh ring; spiracular stripe dark brown; head greyish-brown and finely mottled.

Foodplants. Honeysuckle, of both wild and cultivated varieties.

Habits. A single-brooded species, being in the larval stage from April to early June. The larvae can readily be beaten from the foodplant from about mid-May onwards and are usually easy to rear in confinement, pupating beneath the soil in a strong cocoon, in which overwintering takes place. The adults emerge during March and April, being freely attracted to light, with the females laying their eggs readily on coarse netting or crumpled tissue-paper. Generally distributed over the southern half of England, much of Wales and parts of Ireland; local and less frequent in northern England and Scotland.

Plate 38: E. Bred from a female adult to MVL. Early April. (RM)

Green-brindled Crescent

Allophyes oxyacanthae Linnaeus

Larva. 42–48 mm. Body brownish-grey or greenish-grey, with small pale tubercles dorsally and fine brown mottling, also with a pair of small brown points on the eleventh

segment; head reddish-brown, speckled with dark brown; distinguished by the black ventral zig-zag stripe.
Foodplants. Blackthorn, hawthorn and plum.
Habits. Single-brooded, occurring in the larval state from early April to the middle of June and being readily taken by beating. The larvae are fairly easy to rear, although they do prefer deep soil in which to form their strong cocoons for pupation. The larva lies dormant for several weeks before changing and the adults emerge from late September and during October. These can be found at light, sugar and ivy bloom and will freely lay overwintering eggs in captivity. Widespread in open woodland, hedgerows and on commons throughout much of the British Isles.
Plate 38: F. Beaten from blackthorn, fully grown. Early June.

Merveille du Jour

Dichonia aprilina Linnaeus
Larva. 45–50 mm. Body greyish-brown or greyish-green, with a broken white dorsal line that is most obvious on the abdominal segments. The black chevrons along the dorsal area are infilled with dark mottling and pairs of pale spots line the subdorsal region; head brown or dull green, with a pair of bold black stripes.
Foodplant. Oak.
Habits. A single-brooded insect that occurs as a larva from April to late June, feeding at first on the developing buds and later on the leaves. When larger, the larvae spend the day hidden in bark crevices and feed only at night when they can be beaten. They tend to do well in captivity, forming their tough cocoons deep in the soil in which to pupate after lying dormant for about a month. The adults emerge during late September and October, being attracted to sugar, over-ripe blackberries and light, with the females usually laying in confinement if given rough bark or coarse netting in which to conceal the overwintering eggs. Widespread in mature oak woodland over much of England and Wales; less frequent and more local in Scotland and Ireland.
Plate 38: G. Bred from a female adult to MVL. Mid-October. (AG)

Brindled Green

Dryobotodes eremita Fabricius
(*protea* Denis & Schiffermüller)
Larva. 35–40 mm. Body bright yellowish-green, with a distinct whitish-yellow dorsal line and numerous tiny yellow mottlings over the dorsal and lateral areas; head dull green.
Foodplants. Oak; also recorded from hawthorn.
Habits. Single-brooded, occurring in the larval stage from April to June. The small larva begins feeding by boring into the buds and later forms a silken retreat by spinning together the terminal leaves, emerging to feed at night. At this point of their development and when in the last instar the larvae can readily be beaten from the lower boughs of mature trees. They are fairly easy to rear in captivity, pupating in a cocoon beneath the soil until the adults appear during late August and September. Frequent visitors to light, sugar and over-ripe berries, the females can easily be induced to lay eggs in captivity by supplying them with oak bark and twigs. Generally distributed over most of England and Wales, local in southern Scotland and considered rare in Ireland.
Plate 38: H. Beaten from oak at night, nearly fully grown. Late May.

Dark Brocade

Mniotype adusta Esper
Larva. 43–48 mm. Body usually green or brown, but occasionally yellow or even pink, with an indistinct pale dorsal line that is edged with greyish or brown. The subdorsal line is very faint, again bordered with darker colour; head brown or brownish-green.
Foodplants. Various grasses and low-growing plants, accepting sallow and hawthorn in captivity.
Habits. A single-brooded species, occurring as an active larva from June to August and then lying dormant within the underground cocoon, until pupation takes place in the following April or May. The larvae are not commonly encountered in the wild due to their nocturnal habits, but eggs may be freely obtained from adult females. These come to light and sugar during June and July, with the resulting larvae being easy to rear to the fully grown stage, when they then become difficult. Introducing them to a plant tub kept out of doors, filled with mixed vegetation and soil and leaving them undisturbed could be the answer to this problem. Widespread over much of the British Isles, being more frequent in the northern part of its range.
Plate 38: I. Bred from a female adult to sugar. Mid-June.

Flame Brocade

Trigonophora flammea Esper
Larva. 45–50 mm. Body brown or sometimes green, with an indistinct pale dorsal line often enclosed by darker diamond-shaped markings. A number of small white pinacula are to be found on the dorsal and lateral regions along with lighter and darker mottlings; head brown or green, marked with darker speckling.
Foodplants. Accepting buttercup and various grasses when small and later a mixed diet of the former and ash, privet and broom in captivity.
Habits. A single-brooded insect that currently occurs in the British Isles as an uncommon immigrant, although it was established in Sussex from 1855 to about 1919. The adults are attracted to light in September and October, and mated females may lay eggs if given netting and grasses on which to deposit them. The larvae hatch in about three weeks if kept warm and can then be either forced through by feeding them on buttercup and coarse grasses and later privet leaves or put on to potted plants and kept throughout the winter in an outhouse or garage to develop at a more natural pace. Successful rearing is a very hit and miss affair with some larvae given care and attention dying from unknown causes, while others from the same egg batch seem to thrive on neglect. Pupation takes place in a cocoon beneath the soil and even when the larvae have been forced the adults may not hatch until the following autumn. The southern coastal counties of England give the best chance of finding this attractive species.
Plate 38: J. Bred from a female adult to MVL. Mid-October. (JR)

Large Ranunculus

Polymixis flavicincta Denis & Schiffermüller
Larva. 48–53 mm. Body green, with a darker dorsal line, a subdorsal line consisting of small whitish dots and a distinct white spiracular line that is finely edged above with black; also yellowish-green between the segments. Head dull green or pale brown; spiracles light pink ringed with black.
Foodplants. Various low-growing plants, such as plantain, ragwort, dandelion, dock, red valerian and garden mint.
Habits. Single-brooded, occurring in the larval stage from

about early April to the middle of July, after overwintering as an egg. Larvae are sometimes found by searching at night, especially in rocky places where the vegetation is not too dense, and they are fairly easy to rear in captivity. Pupation takes place under the soil in a strong cocoon and lasts until the adults emerge during late September and October. These come freely to light and the females will lay eggs quite readily in captivity. Mostly to be found south of a line between the Severn and the Wash in gardens, on waste ground and coastal cliffs.

Plate 38: K. Bred from an adult female to MVL. Early October. (GAC)

Black-banded

Polymixis xanthomista Hübner

Larva. 40–45 mm. Body reddish-brown, with a dark-edged paler dorsal line and a distinct dull white spiracular line; head brown. Earlier instar larvae are green.

Foodplants. The flowers and leaves of thrift and sea plantain, accepting other plantains, sallow, birch and groundsel in captivity.

Habits. Single-brooded, probably overwintering naturally in the egg stage, although the eggs have been known to hatch two weeks after being laid in captivity. The larvae feed at night from April to early July and can sometimes be found in small numbers by searching with a lamp. They are reputed to be difficult to rear in captivity, with the most successful method being the use of potted thrift plants planted in loose soil. The subterranean pupa is formed in a tough cocoon with the adults hatching during late August and September; these are attracted to light and sugar. Essentially a coastal species occurring in Devon, Cornwall, the Scilly Isles, south-west Wales, the Isle of Man and south-west Ireland.

Plate 38: L. Located at night on thrift, about half grown. Early June.

Grey Chi

Antitype chi Linnaeus

Larva. 38–45 mm. Body dull green, with an indistinct whitish dorsal line, more obvious white subdorsal lines and a bold white spiracular stripe; head bluish-green, spiracles pinkish-white, edged with dark brown.

Foodplants. Various low-growing plants, including dock, sorrel and dandelion, also accepting sallow and hawthorn in confinement.

Habits. A single-brooded species, being in the larval stage from about April to late June after overwintering as an egg. The larvae are most easily obtained by rearing from the egg, although they can be located by searching at night. In captivity they are stated to prefer a varied diet for successful development and pupation takes place beneath the soil in a robust cocoon. The adults emerge from mid-August to the middle of September and are strongly attracted to light and sugar, with many females laying eggs freely as soon as they are boxed. Widely distributed and sometimes fairly common in the northern half of England and throughout much of Scotland and Wales; local in south-west England and Ireland.

Plate 38: M. Bred from a female adult found at rest. Mid-August. (JMP)

Feathered Ranunculus

Eumichtis lichenea Hübner

Larva. 35–40 mm. Body pale greyish-brown or light green, with an indistinct dark-edged pale dorsal line, a series of obscure dark blotches along the dorsal and subdorsal regions and a pale spiracular stripe; head pale brown mottled with darker marks.

Foodplants. A great variety of low-growing plants, such as thrift, dock, biting stonecrop, dandelion, plantains, ragwort and trefoils.

Habits. Single-brooded, occurring as a larva from about late October to the following late April, after feeding slowly during mild weather throughout the winter. During the early spring the larvae can sometimes be found at night in good numbers in sheltered situations, such as beside large rocks, fences, on banks and in ditches. Those reared from the egg stage in captivity develop faster and often the resulting specimens are undersized or the brood may fail altogether. The pupae are formed in tough subterranean cocoons and the adults emerge during September and October. Both sexes are attracted to over-ripe blackberries and ivy bloom, and the males respond well to light. Captive females sometimes lay very freely, and the eggs should be lightly sprayed with water to encourage hatching. Mainly a coastal insect, being found in most seaboard counties of England and Wales and also on the eastern side of Ireland.

Plate 38: N. Found at night on thrift, fully grown. Mid-April. (SHC)

The Satellite

Eupsilia transversa Hufnagel

(*satellitia* Linnaeus)

Larva. 45–50 mm. Body dark velvety brown or almost black, with a series of distinct white marks along the spiracular region, being especially obvious on the first and third thoracic segments and on the second and eighth abdominal rings; head is reddish-brown, heavily marked with black and the prothoracic plate is black with two bold orange stripes.

Foodplants. Oak, elm, lime, blackthorn, hawthorn, birch, sallow, aspen, poplar, apple and many other deciduous trees.

Habits. A single-brooded species, being in the larval stage from April to about early June and readily being taken by beating, especially at night when out from the daytime spun retreats and feeding. In captivity the larvae are easy to rear, but should be kept separately in individual containers as they have cannibalistic tendencies towards other larvae and have even been known to nip unwary fingers. When fully developed the larva constructs a cocoon beneath the soil and lies dormant for up to three months before pupating. The overwintering adults emerge from late September and reappear in the spring after hibernation. Then they can be taken at ivy bloom, sallow catkins, sugar and light, with most females laying eggs in captivity if required. Generally distributed over most of England and Wales; less frequent and local in Scotland and probably under recorded in Ireland.

Plate 38: O. Beaten at night from oak, fully grown. Late May.

Orange Upperwing

Jodia croceago Denis & Schiffermüller

Larva. 42–46 mm. Body light orangish-brown, with a series of darker dorsal chevron markings and an indistinct paler dorsal line; wholly covered in small vague pale spots. The eleventh segment is humped and has two more obvious pale markings dorsally; head pale brown, finely mottled darker.

Foodplant. Oak.

Habits. An increasingly uncommon single-brooded species that occurs in the larval stage from about late April to the middle of July. The larvae have been taken by beating, especially from the succulent growth on oak-stools and from the young soft leaves, which they seem to prefer in captivity.

Rearing this insect is not difficult with the larvae forming a cocoon beneath the soil, which should not be disturbed as they lie dormant for a period before changing into pupae. The adults hatch in October and are recorded as hibernating in dry curled oak leaves for overwintering. During the spring they can be taken at sallow bloom, sugar and light, with most fertilized females laying eggs in confinement if supplied with oak twigs and coarse netting; feeding them probably helps. The old mature oak woods of South Devon and Surrey are the most likely places to encounter this local and rare insect, although it seems to have been more widespread in the past.
Plate 38: P. Bred from a female adult to MVL. Early April. (AS)

The Chestnut

Conistra vaccinii Linnaeus

Larva. 30–35 mm. Body various shades of brown or greenish-grey, with indistinct dark-edged dorsal and subdorsal lines; spiracular stripe also rather indistinct and usually greyish, spiracles black and head brown. The prothoracic plate has yellowish-white subdorsal lines which are less obvious than in the following species (*C. ligula*).
Foodplants. Birch, oak, elm, dock, dandelion and various other trees and low-growing plants.
Habits. Single-brooded, being in the larval stage from late April to about the middle of June, before forming a loose subterranean cocoon in which to form the pupa after lying dormant for about two months. The larvae can be taken by beating or searching low plants at night, when they are more active, and in captivity it is an easy species to rear. The over-wintering adults emerge from the pupae during October and those females taken at sugar or light in the spring usually lay eggs freely in confinement. Widespread and fairly common over much of the British Isles.
Plate 38: Q. Bred from a female adult to sugar. Early April.

Dark Chestnut

Conistra ligula Esper

Larva. 30–34 mm. Body brown, with indistinct dark-edged dorsal and subdorsal lines, a greyish or pale brown spiracular stripe, black spiracles and a brown head. The subdorsal stripes on the prothoracic plate are whitish and tend to be brighter than those on the previous species (*C. vaccinii*).
Foodplants. Oak, birch, elm, hawthorn, blackthorn and other deciduous trees, also low-growing plants, such as docks and dandelion.
Habits. A single-brooded species that occurs in the larval stage during May and June and may be taken by beating at night. When small the larvae feed on the leaf buds or catkins of the trees, later on the foliage and when in the last instar many seem to prefer the leaves of herbaceous plants. In captivity they should be given a mixed diet and are not difficult to rear, changing into pupae some weeks after forming their subterranean cocoons. The adults emerge during October, with both sexes coming to ivy bloom, sugar and light. Females kept for eggs should be kept with males to ensure they have been mated. Most males die by December and the females may not lay until the new year begins, also usually not surviving until the spring. Widespread in much of England and Wales; local in Scotland and apparently recorded only from Co. Dublin and Co. Limerick in Ireland.
Plate 38: R. Beaten from oak, about half grown. Early May.

Dotted Chestnut

Conistra rubiginea Denis & Schiffermüller

Larva. 38–43 mm. Body dark purplish-brown or blackish-brown, with a series of cross-shaped black markings along the indistinct dorsal line and long gingery setae; head and prothoracic plate both black.
Foodplants. In captivity sallow, apple, blackthorn and plum.
Habits. Single-brooded, occurring as a larva from late April to about the middle of June. Apart from one small larva being found feeding on cultivated apple nothing is known about its natural habits. The adults fly in the late autumn and again after hibernation when they can be taken at light, sugar and sallow catkins. The adults can be difficult to sex, and when taken into captivity some females will refuse to lay even when supplied with twigs, netting and corrugated cardboard on which to deposit eggs. The larvae are very easy to rear and like others in this group lie dormant in the subterranean cocoons for a good time before changing into pupae. A local species inhabiting woodland and heathland mainly in southern England.
Plate 39: A. Bred from a female adult to sugar. Early April.

Red-headed Chestnut

Conistra erythrocephala Denis & Schiffermüller

Larva. 40–45 mm. Body pale reddish-brown or ochreous, with an indistinct greyish-edged dorsal line and black spiracles; head dark brown, marked with black; prothoracic plate black with two pale subdorsal stripes, a thin pale dorsal line and edged both anteriorly and posteriorly with bone colour.
Foodplants. Feral foodplants not known, accepting oak, elm, birch, dandelion, plantain and other plants in captivity.
Habits. A single-brooded insect that was probably resident in the British Isles between 1847 and 1932, being found in the woods of East Sussex. Since then the few records are considered to be immigrants and the early stages have never been found in Britain. The larval period lasts from April to late June, with the insect then forming a cocoon in the soil and lying dormant until pupating during August. The adults emerge from late September, visiting light and ivy bloom before they hibernate. The larva in the illustration came from an adult female taken at sugar in a north Kent copse during March 1992, laying eggs soon after capture. The larvae were very easy to rear to the adult stage by feeding them on elm and birch and avoiding overcrowding.
Plate 39: B. Bred from a female adult to sugar. Mid-March. (JMP)

The Brick

Agrochola circellaris Hufnagel

Larva. 37–42 mm. Body brown, with bold black triangular-shaped dorsal markings on the abdominal segments, fine whitish dorsal and subdorsal lines and a broad paler spiracular stripe. The ground colour on the thoracic segments is obscured by intense dark mottling; head dark brown marked with black; prothoracic plate blackish-brown with pale subdorsal stripes.
Foodplants. Wych elm, poplar, ash and sallow, especially the flowers or seeds.
Habits. Single-brooded, with the larvae occurring from late March to early June, after overwintering in the egg stage. They can readily be obtained by collecting fallen poplar catkins or by beating mature wych elms during the spring, and rearing them is easy as long as they are not overcrowded. The cocooned pupa is formed beneath the soil after the fully developed larva has lain dormant within for about six weeks, so should not be disturbed. During late August to mid-October the adults can be found at sugar, ripe berries and ivy bloom, more often than at light; most females will lay

freely in confinement. Widespread over much of the British Isles; local in Scotland.
Plate 39: C. Beaten from wych elm, half grown. Early May.

Red-line Quaker

Agrochola lota Clerck
Larva. 38–43 mm. Body greyish-brown, with an incomplete whitish dorsal line that is slightly broadened posteriorly on each segment to give the impression of spots; subdorsal line indistinct, spiracular line broad and obvious, coloured pale brown; head brown, prothoracic plate dark brown with pale subdorsal streaks.
Foodplants. Sallows and willows.
Habits. A single-brooded species, occurring in the larval stage from April to early June and readily being obtained by searching spun leaves or beating at night. The larvae are very easy to rear in captivity and should not be disturbed after forming their subterranean cocoons as they lie dormant for about six weeks before changing into pupae. The adults fly during September and October and can be taken at sugar, light and feeding on over-ripe berries. Widely distributed over most of England, Wales and Ireland; more local in Scotland.
Plate 39: D. Located in spun sallow leaves, nearly fully grown. Late May.

Yellow-line Quaker

Agrochola macilenta Hübner
Larva. 35–40 mm. Body reddish-brown, with a dull yellow dorsal line that expands posteriorly on most of the abdominal segments. Spiracles black and two small black spots also to be found close to the spiracle on the first segment; head light brown; prothoracic plate black with bold yellow subdorsal streaks.
Foodplants. Oak, beech, sallow, hawthorn, poplar catkins and low-growing plants in the later instars; also solely heather in parts of Scotland.
Habits. Single-brooded, being in the larval stage from April to early June. The larvae can be obtained by searching spun leaves of the foodplants or by beating at night during May and are not difficult to rear in captivity as long as they are given a varied diet and are not overcrowded or starved, as they have mild cannibalistic habits. The cocoon is formed under the soil, with the larva lying dormant for a few weeks before changing to a pupa. The adults fly in September and October and come freely to light, sugar, ivy bloom and ripe berries. Generally distributed over most of the British Isles, being more common in the southern counties of England.
Plate 39: E. Bred from a female adult to MVL. Late September.

Southern Chestnut

Agrochola haematidea Duponchel
Larva. 30–35 mm. Body purplish-brown, with a yellowish-white dorsal line, a broader ochreous subdorsal stripe edged above on the abdominal segments by black streaks, an indistinct pale lateral line and a pale stripe below the spiracles; prothoracic plate blackish, striped with ochreous; head reddish-brown, mottled darker. In some ways similar to the brown larva of *X. agathina* (Heath Rustic), which is less brightly coloured and has a more acute angle to the end of the body.
Foodplants. The young leaves and flowers of bell heather and cross-leaved heath, accepting other species of *Erica* in captivity.
Habits. A single-brooded species, a strong colony of which was discovered on dry heathland in West Sussex in 1990. The larval stage lasts from about late April to mid-July and the larvae may be taken by sweeping or searching at night. They are quite easy to rear in captivity, although they should be supplied with fresh heather flowers and light sandy soil in which to form their cocoons. The larvae lie dormant within these cocoons for about ten weeks before pupating and should not be disturbed at this time. The adults fly in October and early November, with both sexes coming freely to light soon after dusk, and the females lay their overwintering eggs readily in confinement.
Plate 39: F. Swept at night, over half grown. Late June. (BS)

Flounced Chestnut

Agrochola helvola Linnaeus
Larva. 40–45 mm. Body various shades of brown, with indistinct paler dorsal and subdorsal lines, a conspicuous dull white subspiracular line and wholly covered with darker speckling; head pale brown and spiracles black.
Foodplants. Oak, birch, hawthorn, elm, sallow, willow and other deciduous trees, with northern populations also feeding on bilberry and heather.
Habits. A single-brooded species, being in the larval stage from April to about the middle of June, before forming a cocoon beneath the soil in which it lies dormant until pupating during August. The larvae can be beaten or swept from the foodplants, especially at night when they are more active, and are not difficult to rear in captivity, although they are said to be cannibalistic. The adults fly during September and October, being frequently seen at sugar, ivy bloom and light. Widespread over much of England and Wales; local in Scotland and Ireland.
Plate 39: G. Beaten from oak, nearly fully grown. Late May.

Brown-spot Pinion

Agrochola litura Linnaeus
Larva. 35–42 mm. Body various shades of green, with a dark-edged pale dorsal line, a less distinct subdorsal line and a dark spiracular line, edged below with yellowish-white, also having a few small dull white pinacula on each segment; head brownish-green.
Foodplants. Various herbaceous plants and trees, including chickweed, dock, bramble, sallow and oak.
Habits. Single-brooded, occurring as a larva from about mid-April to early June, after overwintering in the egg stage. The larvae feed at first on herbaceous plants and later some also ascend trees at night to feed on the foliage, when they can be taken by beating. When fully developed they burrow into the soil and form cocoons in which they lie dormant for about six weeks before changing into pupae. The adult moths fly in September and October, being attracted to light, sugar, over-ripe berries and ivy bloom, with the females usually laying eggs freely in captivity. Widespread throughout most of England, Wales and much of Scotland.
Plate 39: H. Bred from a female adult to MVL. Late September.

Beaded Chestnut

Agrochola lychnidis Denis & Schiffermüller
Larva. 38–45 mm. Body brown or green, with dark-edged paler dorsal and subdorsal lines and a broad pale spiracular line with a small dark marking behind and slightly above each black-ringed white spiracle; head pale brown.
Foodplants. Various grasses and other plants, such as buttercup, chickweed, dandelion, dock and hawthorn.
Habits. A single-brooded insect, the larva of which occurs

from about late March to early June, feeding mainly at night on grasses and herbaceous plants, and sometimes, when larger, ascending trees and bushes to devour the foliage. The insects are not often found in the larval stage due to their retiring habits, but are easy to obtain by rearing from the overwintering eggs. Like most species in this group, they lie dormant in the subterranean cocoon for a few weeks before pupating. The adults fly in September and October, being attracted to light, sugar and ivy bloom, often in good numbers. Generally distributed over much of England and Wales; local in Scotland and Ireland.
Plate 39: I. Bred from a female adult to MVL. Early October.

Centre-barred Sallow

Atethmia centrago Haworth
(*xerampelina* sensu Hübner)
Larva. 30–35 mm. Body greyish-brown, with a white dorsal line, edged with dark brown at the segmental divisions, a less distinct white subdorsal line and an obscure pale spiracular line, bordered above with dark brown; head blackish-brown; prothoracic plate black, with pale streaks.
Foodplant. Ash.
Habits. A single-brooded insect, occurring in the larval stage from early spring to about early June, feeding at first on the buds. Later, when larger, the larvae hide in crevices and the plant debris at the base of the trunk by day, and ascend quickly at dusk to feed upon the foliage. During this part of their development they can readily be located by carefully searching behind grass tussocks and other vegetation growing at the bases of mature ash trees. They are easy to rear in captivity, forming a cocoon beneath the soil in which they pupate several weeks later. The adults fly from mid-August to early October, coming to light and sugar, with the females laying freely in confinement if supplied with ash twigs and coarse netting. Generally distributed over much of England and Wales; local in Scotland and Ireland.
Plate 39: J. Found at trunk base in crevice, fully grown. Late May.

Lunar Underwing

Omphaloscelis lunosa Haworth
Larva. 33–38 mm. Body pale brown or greyish-brown, with a dark-edged pale thin dorsal line, a whitish subdorsal line, bordered above with grey and a dark spiracular line; the body also has a few small brown pinacula and a distinguishing bone-coloured prothoracic plate; head dark brown.
Foodplants. Various grasses.
Habits. Single-brooded, occurring as a larva from October to the following May, feeding at night throughout the winter months during mild weather. The larvae can readily be taken by sweeping from February onwards, and are very easy to rear in captivity, pupating in a cocoon formed beneath the soil. The adults fly from late August to early October and both sexes come freely to light, with most females laying eggs in confinement if required to do so. Mainly inhabiting open ground, and widely distributed over most of the southern half of Britain; local elsewhere.
Plate 39: K. Swept at night, almost fully grown. Late April. (SHC)

Orange Sallow

Xanthia citrago Linnaeus
Larva. 33–38 mm. Body greyish-green or greyish-brown, with a distinct white dorsal line, a less obvious pale subdorsal line and a broad greyish-white spiracular stripe; head light brown, prothoracic plate dark brown with pale streaks.
Foodplant. Lime.
Habits. A single-brooded species, of which the larvae occur from late March to early June, feeding mainly at night, after overwintering as an egg. At first the young larvae spin leaves in which to hide by day and when larger they leave the tree to hide among plant litter and crevices at the trunk bases, ascending again at dusk to feed. During this time they are easy to find by close searching or scanning the trunks with a torch as darkness approaches, and they are easy to rear in confinement. They lie dormant in their subterranean cocoons for about six weeks before pupating, with the adults flying from the middle of August to late September. Widely distributed throughout much of England; local in Wales and Scotland.
Plate 39: L. Located in crevice at trunk base, fully grown. Late May.

Barred Sallow

Xanthia aurago Denis & Schiffermüller
Larva. 26–30 mm. Body reddish-brown, darker dorsally, with a fine pale dorsal line, an indistinct pale subdorsal line and a broad greyish line beneath the black spiracles; head dark brown, prothoracic plate dark brown with dull yellow subdorsal streaks.
Foodplants. Maple and beech.
Habits. Single-brooded, feeding in the larval stage from April to early June, mainly at night, at first on the buds and maple flowers, later on the foliage. The larvae can sometimes be taken by beating and are not difficult to rear in captivity, lying dormant for about two months within their subterranean cocoons, until pupating during August. The adults fly in September and October, coming to light and sugar, with most females laying the overwintering eggs freely in confinement. Locally common over many parts in the southern half of Britain.
Plate 39: M. Beaten at night from maple, fully grown. Late May.

Pink-barred Sallow

Xanthia togata Esper
(*lutea* Ström)
Larva. 27–32 mm. Body purplish-brown, sometimes slightly darker dorsally, with an indistinct pale dorsal line, an obscure subdorsal line and an often indistinct spiracular line; head brown, marked with darker brown; prothoracic plate with whitish subdorsal marks and anal plate with dorsal and subdorsal lines all distinct. Often indistinguishable from the following species (*X. icteritia*).
Foodplants. Sallow and poplar catkins, and later herbaceous plants.
Habits. A single-brooded insect that occurs as a larva from late March to early June, feeding at first within the catkins of sallows and poplars until they fall, and then completing its development on herbaceous plants. The larvae can easily be obtained by collecting fallen catkins and then spreading them out on white paper inside a well-ventilated container; the larvae-infested catkins can be identified by frass on the paper below. This species is easy to rear in captivity, with the larvae burrowing into the soil to form the cocoons in which they lie dormant for about six weeks before changing into pupae. The adults fly during late August and September and come freely to light, flowering plants and sugar. Widespread over much of the British Isles.
Plate 39: N. Located inside fallen sallow catkins, nearly half grown. Late April.

The Sallow

Xanthia icteritia Hufnagel
(*fulvago* sensu Linnaeus)
Larva. 29–33 mm. Body purplish-brown, sometimes slightly paler dorsally, with an indistinct pale dorsal line, an obscure subdorsal line and sometimes an indistinct spiracular line; head brown, marked darker; prothoracic plate with yellowish-white subdorsal marks; anal plate subdorsal lines usually more obvious than the dorsal line. Often indistinguishable from the previous species (*X. togata*).
Foodplants. Sallow and poplar catkins, and later herbaceous plants, such as dock and dandelion.
Habits. Single-brooded, with the larvae feeding from late March to early June, the life-cycle being very similar to that of the previous species (*X. togata*). They can be obtained by collecting fallen poplar and sallow catkins, of which the infested ones may be identified when spread out on paper by the larval frass below. This is one of the most frequent species to live in catkins, alongside several closely related insects, such as *X. togata*, *X. ocellaris* and *A. circellaris*. The insects are easy to rear in captivity, but should not be disturbed when they burrow into the soil to pupate, as the larvae lie dormant for a period before changing. The adults fly from late August to early October and are frequent visitors to light, sugar and natural food sources, with the females laying the overwintering eggs freely in confinement. Generally distributed over much of the British Isles.
Plate 39: O. Located inside fallen sallow catkins, under half grown. Late April.

Dusky-lemon Sallow

Xanthia gilvago Denis & Schiffermüller
Larva. 27–32 mm. Body greyish-brown, with a narrow whitish dorsal line, mostly obscured on the abdominal segments by dark lozenge-shaped blotches, these enclosing four small pinacula, which distinguish this species from *A. circellaris*; a dark spiracular line, below which the body is paler; head dark reddish-brown; prothoracic plate black with distinct yellow subdorsal streaks.
Foodplants. The seeds and flowers of wych elm and sometimes English elm.
Habits. Single-brooded, feeding in the larval stage from April to early June, after overwintering as an egg. When small, the larvae bore into the flower-buds and continue to feed on these until they change into seeds and fall, when the foliage will then be accepted. They can be obtained by beating and in captivity are fairly easy to rear, lying dormant inside the subterranean cocoons for about six to eight weeks before changing into pupae. The adults fly from late August to early October, coming to light and sugar. Widely distributed, but local, throughout England and Wales; less frequent in southern Scotland.
Plate 39: P. Beaten from wych elm, nearly fully grown. Late May. (PQW)

Pale-lemon Sallow

Xanthia ocellaris Borkhausen
Larva. 27–33 mm. Body purplish-brown, with an indistinct incomplete pale dorsal line, the dark edging of which forms vague dorsal blotches on the abdominal segments; a very weak pale subdorsal line and a broad pale brown spiracular line; head brown, with darker markings and prothoracic plate black with yellowish-white subdorsal streaks.
Foodplants. The catkins of mainly black poplar, later the leaves and herbaceous plants.
Habits. A single-brooded insect, the larvae of which feed mainly at night from April to early June, at first in the developing catkins until they fall to the ground and disintegrate, then upon the surrounding herbaceous vegetation. The larvae can be obtained by collecting the fresh fallen poplar catkins and keeping them in a ventilated container until they can be located by their deposits of frass. In captivity they are not difficult to rear and should be allowed to lie undisturbed within the subterranean cocoons as they do not change into pupae for about six weeks after burrowing into the soil. The adults fly in September and early October, coming to light, sugar and over-ripe berries, with the females depositing their overwintering eggs in confinement if supplied with poplar leaves and twigs. Most frequently recorded from the Breck district of East Anglia and the poplar-lined commons and avenues of north Surrey; also occurring elsewhere in south-eastern England.
Plate 39: Q. Bred from a female adult to sugar. Late September. (JMP)

SUBFAMILY: ACRONICTINAE

Scarce Merveille du Jour

Moma alpium Osbeck
(*orion* Esper)
Larva. 27–32 mm. Body black, with large yellowish-white dorsal blotches on the fourth, sixth and ninth segments, the others having reddish-orange pinacula from which emanate long grey setae and laterally another row of pinacula; head light brown, heavily marked with dark brown; prothoracic plate reddish-brown.
Foodplant. Oak.
Habits. Single-brooded, being in the larval stage from July to early September. The larvae live gregariously at first, then disperse to complete their development. Sometimes they can be beaten from the boughs of large trees growing along the edges of rides and clearings and in captivity they are fairly easy to rear, pupating in a strong cocoon among plant litter on the ground, for overwintering. The adults fly in June and July, coming to light and sugar, with the females laying their egg batches quite freely in confinement. A local species inhabiting the mature oak woodlands of Hampshire, Sussex, Kent and south-east Cornwall.
Plate 39: R. Bred from a female adult to sugar. Late June.

Poplar Grey

Acronicta megacephala Denis & Schiffermüller
Larva. 30–35 mm. Body pale grey, with dark grey dorsal markings each enclosing small orange pinacula, except the tenth segment, which has a bold white blotch; setae long and greyish-white; head dark grey; prothoracic plate pale brown.
Foodplants. Poplar, aspen and willow.
Habits. A single-brooded insect, occurring as a larva from July to September, usually pupating beneath loose bark for overwintering. The larvae can readily be obtained by searching or beating and are very easy to rear in captivity, but do prefer to use corrugated cardboard or soft wood to form their cocooned pupae. The adults fly from late May to early August, being attracted to light and sugar. Widely distributed and not uncommon over most of England and Wales; local in Scotland and Ireland.
Plate 40: A. Located on black poplar, fully grown. Early September.

The Sycamore

Acronicta aceris Linnaeus
Larva. 35–40 mm. Body pale grey, densely covered with

tufts of long yellow and brownish-orange setae and having a series of black-edged white markings along the dorsal area; head pale brown, with black streaks; prothoracic plate mainly pale brown.
Foodplants. Horse chestnut, sycamore, field maple, oak, birch and other trees.
Habits. Single-brooded, occurring as a larva from July to September, feeding fully exposed on the foliage. The larvae can be obtained by beating or searching and are not difficult to rear in captivity, requiring soft wood or cardboard with which to construct their cocoons for pupation; in which they overwinter, sometimes twice. The adults fly from about the middle of June to early August, coming to light and sugar, with most females laying eggs in confinement if required to do so. Mainly recorded from southern and south-eastern England and East Anglia; local elsewhere in the southern half of Britain.
Plate 40: B. Bred from a female adult to MVL. Late July.

The Miller

Acronicta leporina Linnaeus
Larva. 30–35 mm. Body pale green, often with brownish dorsal marks; wholly covered in long white or yellow setae of which those on one side curl forwards and on the other side rearwards; head pale green.
Foodplants. Birch and alder; also recorded on poplar and sallow.
Habits. Single-brooded, being in the larval stage from July to early October, resting on the underside of leaves with the front segments curled around to mimic the spinnings of a spider. The larvae can be obtained by beating or searching and are easy to rear in captivity. When fully developed, the larvae turn darker in colour and should then be supplied with corrugated cardboard or soft wood to burrow into and construct their cocoons for pupation, in which they may overwinter more than once. The adults fly from June to early August, with most females laying freely when supplied with foodplant. Widely distributed throughout much of England and Wales; local in Scotland and Ireland.
Plate 40: C. Bred from a female adult to MVL. Early July.

Alder Moth

Acronicta alni Linnaeus
Larva. 30–35 mm. Body black, with bold yellow transverse bands dorsally across the segments and glossy black club-tipped setae; head and prothoracic plate black. The young larvae are mainly brown and grey, with white on the last few abdominal rings.
Foodplants. Birch, oak, elm, hawthorn, sycamore and other trees.
Habits. A single-brooded insect, being in the larval stage from June to August. When about half grown the larvae live on the upper surface of the leaves resembling bird-droppings and later, when in the final instar, they continue to stay on the top of the leaves, using the warning coloration of black and yellow to deter predators. At this time they are very conspicuous but rarely found, probably because they inhabit the higher parts of the trees. The adults fly in May and June, coming to mercury-vapour light in good numbers, with most females freely laying eggs in captivity when supplied with birch leaves. Larvae are easy to rear in confinement, but do require cardboard or soft wood in which to burrow to form their overwintering cocooned pupae. Generally distributed, but somewhat local, over much of England and Wales; also recorded in Ireland.
Plate 40: D. Bred from a female adult to MVL. Early June. (RM)

Dark Dagger

Acronicta tridens Denis & Schiffermüller
Larva. 35–40 mm. Body black, with a black-centred white and orangish-red dorsal stripe on the abdominal segments; a black hump dorsally on the fourth ring and a smaller white hump on the eleventh; orange-red dorsal blotches on the second and third segments and a whitish lateral stripe; head black.
Foodplants. Hawthorn, blackthorn, sallow, apple, wild rose and other trees and shrubs.
Habits. Mainly single-brooded, with the larvae occurring from July to September, and into October from the offspring of the partial second generation that sometimes occurs in southern England. They can be obtained by beating hawthorn, especially in open woodland and fens, and are not difficult to rear in confinement. In the wild the pupa is formed under flaking bark or in a crevice within a cocoon and has been recorded as overwintering twice. The adults fly in June and July, coming to light and sugar. Widespread over much of England and Wales, although more local in the north.
Plate 40: E. Bred from a female adult to MVL. Late June. (SHC)

Grey Dagger

Acronicta psi Linnaeus
Larva. 35–40 mm. Body grey, with a distinctive yellow dorsal stripe, a dull yellowish-white spiracular line and orangish-red spots laterally; a tall fleshy hump dorsally on the fourth segment and a smaller hump on the eleventh ring; head black.
Foodplants. Birch, sallow, oak, lime, hawthorn, blackthorn, apple, wild and garden rose, rowan, elm and many other trees and shrubs.
Habits. A mostly single-brooded species, occurring in the larval stage from July to September, and later when a partial second brood occurs in southern England. The larvae are frequently found when beating or searching for other species and are very easy to rear in captivity, pupating within a cocoon for overwintering. The adults fly during June and July, and sometimes again in September, being attracted to light and sugar. Widespread and fairly common over much of England, Wales and Ireland; local in Scotland.
Plate 40: F. Bred from a female adult to MVL. Mid-June.

Marsh Dagger

Acronicta strigosa Denis & Schiffermüller
Larva. 27–33 mm. Body green, with a distinct purplish-brown dorsal stripe, small blackish pinacula from which short setae emanate; head mainly brown. A totally brown form also occurs (Buckler).
Foodplants. Hawthorn and occasionally blackthorn; also recorded on birch on the continent.
Habits. A single-brooded species that occurs in the larval stage during August and early September and used to be obtained by beating the more mature hawthorn bushes that grew on banks above marshy ground in Huntingdonshire and Cambridgeshire. It was last taken in 1939 and although several attempts have been made to rediscover this insect, none has been successful. It prefers soft wood in which to form a cocoon enclosing the overwintering pupa and the adults fly in the following late June and July. Abroad, in western Europe, it is widely distributed, but local.

Light Knot Grass

Acronicta menyanthidis Esper

Larva. 35–40 mm. Body black or blackish-brown, with an incomplete dark red subspiracular line, and large white spiracles; head black; setae long, black and gingery.

Foodplants. Heather, bog myrtle, bilberry, birch, sallow and other plants.

Habits. Single-brooded, being in the larval stage from about late June to September. The larvae can be obtained by sweeping or beating and are not difficult to rear in captivity, although overcrowded larvae bred from egg batches often suffer from viral infections and subsequently the whole brood perishes. The overwintering pupae are formed in cocoons among the plant debris and in captivity the adults will sometimes emerge after about four weeks, when kept warm. During late May and June the adults can be found at rest on fence posts, trunks and rocks in their moorland habitats, and at night they come freely to light and sugar. Widespread and locally common in suitable areas of northern England, North Wales and Scotland; less frequent and local in South Wales and parts of Ireland.

Plate 40: G. Bred from a female adult found on fence post. Late May. (BH)

Scarce Dagger

Acronicta auricoma Denis & Schiffermüller

Larva. 35–40 mm. Body greyish-black, with dull red pinacula from which reddish hairs emanate; head black and glossy (MBGBI).

Foodplants. Oak, and also bramble, birch and raspberry in captivity.

Habits. This double-brooded species was possibly a resident in Kent and East Sussex before about 1912, but became extinct. Since then about fourteen more adults have been recorded and considered to be immigrants from western Europe, where the species is widespread and locally common. The larvae occur during June and early July and again in September, before pupating in a silken cocoon for overwintering.

Sweet Gale Moth

Acronicta euphorbiae Denis & Schiffermüller

Larva. 35–40 mm. Body black, with a double row of white or yellowish-white pinacula from which long black and gingery setae emanate; a red subspiracular line and a red band dorsally behind the black prothoracic plate; spiracles white; head black.

Foodplants. Bog myrtle, heather, birch, sallow and other plants.

Habits. A mainly single-brooded insect, the larvae of which occur from June to early September. They can sometimes be obtained by sweeping or beating and female adults usually lay eggs freely in captivity. Those bred from the egg can be difficult to rear, if kept overcrowded or not cleaned out regularly, usually dying from a virus when about three-quarters grown. The overwintering cocooned pupa is formed low down among the vegetation or plant litter and often on sheltered parts of rocks and boulders. During May and early June the adults can be found resting on rocks and posts, later coming to light and sugar. Mainly inhabiting the moorlands of central and northern Scotland, and parts of western Ireland, where a second generation is known.

Plate 40: H. Bred from an adult female found at rest. Late May. (MB)

Knot Grass

Acronicta rumicis Linnaeus

Larva. 35–40 mm. Body blackish-brown, with small red dorsal spots, a series of white subdorsal markings and a red and yellow subspiracular line; setae long and reddish-brown, most dense on the fourth to seventh rings; head mainly black.

Foodplants. Various plants including heather, plantain, knotgrass, dock, bramble, sallow and hawthorn.

Habits. Mainly a single-brooded species, with the larvae occurring from about late June to September and onwards into October in southern England, where there is a second generation. They are not difficult to obtain by searching or sweeping and where mixed herbaceous plants grow against walls and fences these larvae can often be found by shaking the plants and searching on the ground below. They are very easy to rear in captivity, with the overwintering pupa being formed in a cocoon among plant litter. The adults fly from May to July, and again in August and early September in the south, being attracted to light and sugar. Widespread and generally common in England, Wales and parts of Ireland; less frequent in Scotland.

Plate 40: I. Bred from a female adult to MVL. Mid-June.

Reed Dagger

Simyra albovenosa Goeze

Larva. 37–42 mm. Body brown or black, with dull yellow or brown subdorsal lines in which are reddish-brown pinacula bearing black and pale grey setae; spiracular line yellowish-white, above which is another row of pinacula with setae; head mainly black, with yellow markings. The young larva is dull orange dorsally with a broad blackish-brown dorsal stripe; grey laterally.

Foodplants. Common reed, sallow, yellow loosestrife and sometimes tufted sedge; also accepting other broad-leaved grasses and buckthorn in captivity.

Habits. A double-brooded species, being in the larval stage during June and early July, and again in late August and September. The larvae can readily be obtained by sweeping in well-established reed-beds and are fairly easy to rear in captivity. Although they will accept alternatives to the usual foodplants, they seem to do better when given the preferred common reed. Pupation, for overwintering when necessary, takes place inside a cocoon usually located among the plant debris or low down on the foodplant under the dry blades. The adults fly in May, and during late July and August, coming to light, with the females laying egg batches freely in confinement, if supplied with fresh reed-blades. A local insect inhabiting fens, marshland and damp places, mainly in East Anglia, Essex, Kent and Hampshire.

Plate 40: J. Swept from reeds, nearly fully grown. Late June.

The Coronet

Craniophora ligustri Denis & Schiffermüller

Larva. 35–40 mm. Body pale green, darker laterally, with white dorsal and subdorsal lines and each segment having several tiny black pinacula, each with a long black seta; spiracles orange; head dull green.

Foodplants. Ash and wild privet; also recorded on hazel and alder.

Habits. Single-brooded, occurring as a larva from about mid-July to early September. The insects may be obtained by beating and are not difficult to rear, with the younger larva being whitish-green with a black head. The overwintering cocooned pupa is often formed under moss growing on ash trunks, and in captivity the larva will burrow into tissue-paper

as a substitute. During late June and July the adults visit light traps and sugar, usually in small numbers, with the females freely depositing eggs in confinement. Widespread, but local, over much of the British Isles.
Plate 40: K. Beaten from ash, over half grown. Mid-August. (BS)

Marbled Beauty

Cryphia domestica Hufnagel
(*perla* Denis & Schiffermüller)
Larva. 22–25 mm. Body greyish-black or bluish-grey, with a broad dull orange dorsal stripe containing small black spots. Black pinacula cover the subdorsal and lateral areas, each emitting a single longish grey seta; head glossy black.
Foodplants. Lichens growing on walls, roofs and rocks, including *Lecidea confluens* and *Xanthoria parietina*.
Habits. Single-brooded, being in the larval stage from September to the following late May or early June, hibernating when still very small within a silken domicile buried deep in among the foodplant. Feeding recommences in the spring, mainly at night, still hiding by day in the spinning. The larvae can sometimes be found fully exposed on or near the foodplant, after a heavy downpour when water has saturated the lichens; although generally they are rarely found, even where the moths are common at light. The pupa is formed inside a domicile, this then being sealed at both ends, and lasts about two months, with the adults flying from late July to early September. An impractical species to try to rear from the egg stage. Widespread, mainly inhabiting urban areas and coastal cliffs throughout much of the British Isles.
Plate 40: L. Found under lichen by dislodged brick, fully grown. Late May. (PJP)

Marbled Grey

Cryphia raptricula Denis & Schiffermüller
(*divisa* Esper)
Larva. 20–25 mm. Body bluish-green, with an orange-marked white dorsal line and small black pinacula; head yellowish (MBGBI).
Foodplants. Lichens, especially *Sticta pulmomacea*, growing on rocks and old stone walls.
Habits. A single-brooded insect of which several adults have been recently taken at light in south-eastern England. The larval stage, which has not been recorded in Britain, lasts from about September to the following early June and the larvae are stated to bask in sunshine. Pupation takes place in a cocoon among foodplant, with the adults flying in July and August. In western Europe it appears to be extending its range and is now not uncommon in Belgium, Holland and parts of France.

Marbled Green

Cryphia muralis Forster
Larva. 24–27 mm. Body dark greenish-grey, with a white dorsal line, a series of small white marks subdorsally and covered in longish grey setae emanating from small pinacula; head black; prothoracic plate black, with a white central streak.
Foodplants. Lichens, such as *Diploicia canescens*, growing on rocks and walls.
Habits. A single-brooded insect, occurring as a larva from about late September to the following early June, overwintering when still very small inside a silken domicile beneath the foodplant. In the spring feeding recommences, and from mid-May onwards the larvae can sometimes be located by searching for blister-like protuberances on the surface of lichens growing on rocks and can also be found exposed and wandering at night. The pupa is formed within the domicile and lasts for about two months, with the adults flying from late July to early September. Mainly a coastal species, being found in suitable localities along the south coast of England, both sides of the Bristol Channel, south-west Wales and southern and western Ireland; inland areas include the cities of Cambridge and Gloucester and Cork City in Ireland.
Plate 40: M. Found in silken domicile on side of boulder. Early June. (SHC)

SUBFAMILY: AMPHIPYRINAE

Copper Underwing

Amphipyra pyramidea Linnaeus
Larva. 37–42 mm. Body green, speckled with white, having a white dorsal line and a pronounced yellowish-tipped hump dorsally on the eleventh segment. Spiracular line whitish, finely edged with green above and being mostly absent on the third and fourth rings; thoracic legs mostly green; head bright green.
Foodplants. Oak, honeysuckle, ash, wild and garden privet, sallow, lime and various other trees and shrubs.
Habits. A single-brooded insect, occurring in the larval stage from about mid-April to early June, after overwintering as an egg. The larvae are readily obtained by beating and are usually very easy to rear in confinement. After pupating in a cocoon beneath the soil for about two months, the adults start to emerge in very late July and linger on well into October. They come freely to light and sometimes abundantly to sugar, with the females laying eggs readily in captivity on rough material. Widely distributed over much of the southern half of the British Isles; local elsewhere.
Plate 40: N. Located on sallow, about half grown. Mid-May.

Svensson's Copper Underwing

Amphipyra berbera Rungs
Larva. 33–38 mm. Body green, speckled with white, having a white dorsal line and red-tipped hump dorsally on the eleventh segment. Spiracular line whitish, boldly edged above with dark green and present on all segments; thoracic legs mostly black; head bright green.
Foodplants. Oak, birch, honeysuckle, lime, sallow and other trees and shrubs.
Habits. Single-brooded, being in the larval stage from about mid-April to the end of May. The larvae are readily taken by beating and are not difficult to rear in captivity, pupating for about two months beneath the soil in a cocoon. The adults fly from late July to about the middle of September and are greatly attracted to sugar, less so to light, with the females laying their overwintering eggs freely in confinement. Most frequently seen in the southern half of England and parts of Wales; local in northern England and also recorded from near Glasgow, in Scotland.
Plate 40: O. Beaten from birch, nearly fully grown. Mid-May.

Mouse Moth

Amphipyra tragopoginis Clerck
Larva. 33–37 mm. Body usually bright green, with bold white dorsal, subdorsal and spiracular stripes; head glossy green or yellowish-green; spiracles white, ringed with black.
Foodplants. Various herbaceous plants, also hawthorn and sallow.
Habits. A single-brooded species, being in the larval stage from April to early June, after overwintering as an egg. Although a rather common insect, the larvae are not often

met with, probably due to their nocturnal habits and to mostly living close to the ground. The pupa is formed just below the soil or among plant debris inside a cocoon, lasting about six to eight weeks, with the adults flying from late July to early September. These can be found at light, sugar or natural nectar sources and most females will lay eggs freely in captivity. Generally distributed over much of the British Isles.
Plate 40: P. Bred from an adult female to MVL. Early August. (M&JH)

Old Lady

Mormo maura Linnaeus

Larva. 60–70 mm. Body brown or greyish-brown, with a mostly inconspicuous yellowish dorsal line that is expanded on the third to fifth segments to appear as spots. The rest of the body is irrorate with dark brown or black markings, the most distinct being a band across the dorsal area of the eleventh ring; head light brown, with darker speckling; spiracles dull orange.
Foodplants. Herbaceous plants during the autumn and hawthorn, blackthorn, sallow, elm, birch, ivy and other trees and shrubs after hibernation.
Habits. Single brooded, occurring as a larva from September to May, feeding before winter low down on various herbaceous plants, such as chickweed and dock. The larvae are totally nocturnal in their habits, hiding by day in the soil or plant litter, and during the spring can easily be obtained by beating or searching the sparsely foliated twigs of hawthorn and blackthorn after dark. The pupa is formed among the soil in a cocoon and lasts about six to eight weeks before the adults begin to emerge in July. These fly until about early September and tend to shun mercury-vapour lights, but can readily be found at sugar patches or under bridges and in outbuildings during the day. Widespread over much of England, Wales, parts of Ireland and southern Scotland.
Plate 40: Q. Found at night, nearly fully grown. Early May. (SHC)

Bird's Wing

Dypterygia scabriuscula Linnaeus

Larva. 33–38 mm. Body brown, with a dark-edged pale dorsal line, greyish-brown subdorsal markings and a darker brown spiracular line that is bordered below with a thin yellowish stripe; spiracles white, ringed with black and being more obvious on the first and last segments; head brown, mottled darker.
Foodplants. Various herbaceous plants, such as dock, sorrel and knotgrass.
Habits. A mainly single-brooded species that occurs as a larva from late June to August, and during September from the occasional partial second generation. The larvae are not often found due to their nocturnal habits, although they are easily reared from the egg stage. These can be obtained from the adult females that come to sugar and light during June and July. The pupae are formed in the soil, usually overwintering, except when kept warm in captivity, when they hatch in about three weeks. Most frequently recorded from southern and eastern England and the north-west Midlands.
Plate 40: R. Bred from an adult female to MVL. Late June. (SHC)

Brown Rustic

Rusina ferruginea Esper
(*umbratica* Goeze)
(*tenebrosa* Hübner)

Larva. 32–36 mm. Body reddish-brown, with a thin yellowish-white dorsal line, which is more obvious on the first five segments, a vague paler subdorsal line, bordered by greyish dashes and an indistinct pale subspiracular line; spiracles small and black; head glossy, dark greyish-brown.
Foodplants. Various low-growing plants, including plantain, dock, grounsel and dandelion; also bramble.
Habits. Single-brooded, occurring in the larval stage from about August to the following May, entering the final instar during the autumn and overwintering when almost fully grown. The larvae are mostly nocturnal and infrequently encountered in the wild due to their retiring habits, hiding in plant litter by day. They can be obtained from eggs laid by female adults, which are more often seen at sugar than light, during June and July. The larvae seem not to respond to being forced and take a long time to mature. For successful rearing to the adult stage they should be kept outside in a pot supplied with growing foodplants and dry leaves for shelter. Pupation takes place in a cocoon beneath the soil, lasting for about a month. Generally distributed over much of the British Isles, being found in most types of habitat.
Plate 41: A. Bred from an adult female to MVL. Late June.

Straw Underwing

Thalpophila matura Hufnagel

Larva. 37–42 mm. Body pale brown or purplish-brown, with a thin yellowish dorsal line that is bordered on each side by bold black dashes on the abdominal segments; subdorsal line also pale and narrow, again edged with darker coloration; head pale brown with a pair of vertical black streaks.
Foodplants. Various grasses.
Habits. A single-brooded species, being in the larval stage from September to the following early May, feeding steadily throughout the winter. The larvae are nocturnal in their habits and from about late February onwards can be obtained, usually in small numbers, by careful sweeping in grassy places. They are not difficult to rear in captivity, pupating in the soil for about ten to twelve weeks before the adults emerge in July and August. These come freely to light, sugar and flowering plants, such as ragwort and marram. Generally distributed over most of the southern half of Britain; mainly coastal elsewhere.
Plate 41: B. Swept at night, over half grown. Late February.

Orache Moth

Trachea atriplicis Linnaeus

Larva. 43–48 mm. Body reddish- or purplish-brown, with a darker dorsal line, a yellow or dull red spiracular stripe and a yellow or red spot laterally on the eleventh ring; head pale brown.
Foodplants. Orache, goosefoot and other herbaceous plants.
Habits. A single-brooded insect that was formerly resident in the marshy places and fens of East Anglia. It probably became extinct about 1915 and since then a few adults have recently been recorded in south-eastern England, being considered immigrants from the near continent, where the species is widespread and locally common. The larvae occur from July to early September and are stated to feed at night, with the overwintering pupa being formed in a cocoon beneath the soil and the adults emerging the following June.
Plate 49: H. Bred from a female adult (Spain). (JW)

Small Angle Shades

Euplexia lucipara Linnaeus

Larva. 30–35 mm. Body green or purplish-brown, with indistinct dorsal and subdorsal lines, between which is a series of darker oblique markings on the abdominal rings and

sometimes a pair of white spots on the eleventh segment, dorsally; subspiracular line white and distinct; head dark green or brown.
Foodplants. Mostly bracken and other ferns, also birch, oak, sallow, willowherb and various herbaceous plants.
Habits. A mainly single-brooded insect, with the larvae occurring from about mid-July to early September, also later when there can be a small partial second generation in good years. They can readily be taken by sweeping bracken at night and are very easy to rear in captivity. Pupation for overwintering takes place in a cocoon beneath the soil, with the light-responsive adults flying the following June and July. Widespread over much of the British Isles.
Plate 41: C. Bred from an adult female to MVL. Late June.

Angle Shades

Phlogophora meticulosa Linnaeus
Larva. 38–45 mm. Body bright green, brown or sometimes yellow, with a pale dorsal line, a broad whitish spiracular line and vague darker oblique dorsolateral markings; head green or greenish-brown.
Foodplants. A great variety of herbaceous plants, shrubs and trees, including dock, chickweed, nettle, borage, bramble, hop, sallow, birch and oak.
Habits. Usually at least a double-brooded species, with numbers being reinforced by a steady stream of immigrants from about July onwards. The larvae overwinter and have been recorded in every month of the year. They are very easy to find and rear in confinement, with their development being more rapid under warm conditions. The pupal stage lasts for about three weeks and as with the larvae, the adults can occur at any time, with peaks being in May and June and again in the late summer and autumn. Usually a very common insect, especially in the southern counties; widely distributed throughout the British Isles.
Plate 41: D. Found at rest under borage leaves, fully grown. Late April.

Double Kidney

Ipimorpha retusa Linnaeus
Larva. 25–30 mm. Body green, with a distinct white dorsal line, a finer white subdorsal line and a wavy thin spiracular line; head pale green or black.
Foodplants. Sallow and willow.
Habits. Single-brooded, occurring in the larval stage from about early April to late May, living concealed within a silken spinning of foodplant leaves, usually those close to the ends of the branches. The larvae can be obtained by careful searching and when taken into captivity are not difficult to rear. The pupa is formed within a cocoon situated in the soil and lasts about ten weeks, with the adults flying from late July to early September. Females lay the overwintering eggs quite freely when supplied with sallow sprigs. Mainly inhabiting dampish places, local throughout most of the southern half of England and much of Wales.
Plate 41: E. Found in spun terminal shoots, over half grown. Early May.

The Olive

Ipimorpha subtusa Denis & Schiffermüller
Larva. 25–30 mm. Body pale yellowish-green and glossy, with a bold yellowish-white dorsal stripe and less distinct whitish subdorsal and spiracular lines; head greyish-green, heavily marked with black; thoracic legs black.
Foodplants. Poplars and aspen.
Habits. A single-brooded insect that overwinters in the egg stage, with the larvae occurring during April and May. These can be located by searching the higher leaves of poplars, that have been spun together, and rearing them in captivity is often easy. Pupation takes place in a cocoon beneath the soil, lasting about two months, before the adults emerge during late July and August. Widespread, but local, over much of England and Wales; also recorded from the lowlands of southern Scotland and infrequently in Ireland.
Plate 41: F. Found on poplar, fully grown. Late May. (BH)

Angle-striped Sallow

Enargia paleacea Esper
Larva. 40–45 mm. Body pale bluish-green, with a white dorsal line and less distinct subdorsal and spiracular lines of the same colour; head dull yellow.
Foodplant. Birch.
Habits. Single-brooded, being in the larval stage from about late April to the middle of June, after overwintering as an egg. During the day the larvae rest among spun leaves and sometimes can be found by careful searching or by beating after dark, usually from the more mature trees. In captivity they are not difficult to rear and pupate beneath the ground in a cocoon, until late July or August, when the adults fly. The females are attracted strongly to sugar and less so to light, laying their eggs readily in confinement. British populations are concentrated in the midland counties of England, Yorkshire and the central Highlands of Scotland, with most other records elsewhere considered to be immigrants from the east.
Plate 41: G. Bred from an adult female to sugar. Late August.

The Suspected

Parastichtis suspecta Hübner
Larva. 28–33 mm. Body reddish- or purplish-brown, with a distinct flesh-coloured dorsal line, and a slightly paler lateral area; head dark brown, mottled paler; prothoracic plate black, with paler dorsal and subdorsal streaks.
Foodplants. Birch and possibly sallow; also recorded on the continent as feeding on poplar catkins.
Habits. Single-brooded, being in the larval stage from April to early June, after overwintering as an egg. The larvae feed mainly at night, at first on the terminal shoots, and later hide by day within a spinning formed by leaves. They can be found by careful searching. In captivity they are very easy to rear and pupate within a cocoon on or just under the soil, with the adults emerging in late July and August. Females are more strongly attracted to sugar than light and most will lay eggs freely in confinement. Widely distributed over most of England, North Wales and parts of Scotland, but considered rare in Ireland.
Plate 41: H. Bred from a female adult to sugar. Early August. (PQW)

Dingy Shears

Parastichtis ypsillon Denis & Schiffermüller
(*fissipuncta* Haworth)
Larva. 35–40 mm. Body greyish-brown, with a pale yellowish-brown dorsal line, darker lateral areas and a broad pale spiracular stripe; head reddish-brown, marked finely with black.
Foodplants. Poplars, willow and sallow.
Habits. A single-brooded species, being in the larval stage from April to early June, after overwintering as an egg. Development is initiated by feeding on catkins and later at night on the leaves. During the latter half of May the larvae can readily be located by day hiding, often gregariously,

beneath loose bark or among plant debris at the base of poplar and willow trunks. The cocooned pupae are formed just in the soil or under peeling bark, lasting about a month, with the adults coming to sugar and light from late June to early August. Mostly inhabiting damp places throughout much of England and Wales; very local in Scotland and Ireland.
Plate 41: I. Found in bark crevice close to ground, fully grown. Late May.

Heart Moth

Dicycla oo Linnaeus
Larva. 34–38 mm. Body black, with bold white dorsal, subdorsal and spiracular stripes, of which the former is broken centrally on the abdominal segments; head black and glossy.
Foodplant. Oak.
Habits. Single-brooded, occurring as a larva from about mid-April to early June. This is one of the more difficult species to rear in captivity, with most females stubbornly refusing to lay eggs even when given conditions as natural as possible. The eggs overwinter and mortality among the young larvae can be high. If obtained they should be kept separately from each other to avoid viruses and to stop them being bitten by their fellows. In the wild the larvae construct strong spinnings in which to spend the day and beating, even at night in the few favoured localities, can be fruitless. The pupa is formed within a cocoon below the soil and can last as little as ten days, with the adults flying in late June and July. Both sexes come readily to sugar at dusk and later mainly males attend light traps situated beneath mature oak trees in woodland and parks. A very local insect restricted to south-east England and mostly being recorded from Surrey, Berkshire, Middlesex and Hertfordshire.
Plate 41: J. Bred from an adult female to sugar. Early July.

Lesser-spotted Pinion

Cosmia affinis Linnaeus
Larva. 24–28 mm. Body green and smooth, yellow at the segmental divisions, with white dorsal and subdorsal lines and a thinner yellowish-white subspiracular line; spiracles often with an adjacent black mark; head green. Earlier instars are darker green, with black pinacula and a black head, also having a black prothoracic plate.
Foodplants. English elm and wych elm.
Habits. A single-brooded species, occurring in the larval stage from April to early June, after overwintering as an egg. During late May the larvae can readily be beaten from hedgerow elms, but should be kept separate from other species of larvae as they have been known to devour them. They seem to do well in captivity, pupating in a silken cocoon among plant litter for about four weeks. The adults fly from mid-July to August, coming to sugar and light, the females laying eggs quite freely in confinement. Widespread, but local, mostly in the southern half of Britain.
Plate 41: K. Bred from an adult female to MVL. Late July. (SHC)

White-spotted Pinion

Cosmia diffinis Linnaeus
Larva. 25–30 mm. Body pale green, with yellowish-white dorsal and subdorsal lines, a yellowish subspiracular line and a dark brown or black head in all instars; pinacula small and black; thoracic legs and spiracles dark reddish-brown.
Foodplants. English elm and wych elm.
Habits. Single-brooded, overwintering as an egg and being in the larval stage from April to about the middle of June. It has been stated that the larvae prefer to feed on the sucker shoots that grow from the trunks of elms and can be taken by beating, although probably with a better chance at night, as they spend the day within a spinning in the earlier instars. When in captivity they are best kept separated from other larvae, as this genus is notorious for its cannibalistic tendencies. The pupa is formed in a cocoon spun among the leaves or ground litter and lasts until August when the adults are on the wing. These come to sugar and light, with females depositing their eggs, if supplied with fine netting or muslin. This always local species has greatly declined since the outbreak of Dutch elm disease, but can still be found in a few places in the southern half of Britain.
Plate 41: L. Bred from a female adult to light. Mid-August. (JW)

The Dun-bar

Cosmia trapezina Linnaeus
Larva. 27–32 mm. Body green, with a narrow white dorsal line, an indistinct pale subdorsal line and a broad pale spiracular stripe; black pinacula; head dull green.
Foodplants. Various trees and shrubs, including oak, elm, birch, sallow, hawthorn, blackthorn and hazel.
Habits. A single-brooded insect, occurring as a larva from about the middle of April to the first half of June, after overwintering in the egg stage. The larvae are readily taken by beating, especially at night when more active, often attacking other lepidopterous larvae while still on the sheet, and have also been known to nip unwary fingers when handled. They are easy to rear, but should be kept separately, pupating in a cocoon among plant litter or just in the soil for about four to eight weeks. During July and August the adults can be very common at sugar patches or lights placed in mature deciduous woodland and females usually lay their eggs freely in captivity. Widely distributed throughout most of the British Isles.
Plate 41: M. Beaten from sallow, nearly fully grown. Late May.

Lunar-spotted Pinion

Cosmia pyralina Denis & Schiffermüller
Larva. 26–30 mm. Body pale yellowish-green, with a yellowish dorsal line, a narrower subdorsal line and a distinct creamy-white subspiracular line, edged above with black on the first two rings; pinacula whitish; spiracles white, finely ringed with black; head dull green.
Foodplants. English elm, wych elm, blackthorn, hawthorn and other trees.
Habits. Single-brooded, being in the larval stage from April to early June, and can readily be taken by beating hedgerow elms near to woods and copses during the latter part of May. The larvae are fairly easy to rear, pupating inside a cocoon among plant litter for about three to four weeks. The adults come to light and sugar during July and early August, with most females depositing their overwintering eggs in captivity when supplied with foodplant and coarse netting. Generally distributed in southern Britain, ranging as far north as Lancashire.
Plate 41: N. Beaten from English elm, over half grown. Mid-May.

The Saxon

Hyppa rectilinea Esper
Larva. 37–42 mm. Body pale brown or purplish-brown, with a faint greyish bloom; thin pale dorsal and subdorsal lines, edged with darker coloration at the segmental joints

and a broad pale subspiracular stripe; body vaguely paler on the eleventh ring, subdorsally; head dark brown.
Foodplants. Sallow, bearberry and bramble, also accepting knotgrass in confinement.
Habits. A single-brooded insect that occurs as an active larva from July until October, when it then lies dormant within a hibernaculum to pass the winter, eventually pupating in the spring. The larvae can be found on occasion when searching for other species, but the best way to obtain this species is to rear it from the egg. The adults fly during very late May to early July, with both sexes coming readily to sugar and most females will lay freely in confinement. The larvae are not difficult to rear and kept warm will sometimes pupate in the autumn, with the moths emerging during the winter months. Widespread, although local, in moorland parts of central and northern Scotland, the Lake District, Northumberland and Co. Kerry in Ireland.
Plate 41: O. Bred from an adult female to sugar. Mid-June. (PQW)

Dark Arches
Apamea monoglypha Hufnagel
Larva. 40–45 mm. Body pale ochreous or pale grey, greyish-brown dorsally, with a vague whitish dorsal line and large dark brown pinacula; prothoracic and anal plates brownish-black; head glossy, usually dark reddish-brown, sometimes black.
Foodplants. The lower stems and roots of various grasses.
Habits. Mainly a single-brooded species, sometimes having a small partial second generation in the south of England, and being in the larval stage from August to the following June. The eggs are laid in grass sheaths or among the seeds and the tiny larvae feed at first on the flowers and seeds, before descending the plant and living in earthen cells at the roots to continue their development. During April and May they can be located by close searching at the bases of grass clumps, especially those growing isolated or on banks, and have also been noted when wandering over bare ground at night. Taken at this stage they are fairly easy to rear in confinement on potted grasses, pupating under the soil for about a month. The adults are strongly attracted to sugar and light, flying from about the middle of June to August, and later, in smaller numbers, in the southern parts of Britain. Widespread and common over the greater part of the British Isles.
Plate 41: P. Found wandering at night, fully grown. Late May.

Light Arches
Apamea lithoxylaea Denis & Schiffermüller
Larva. 38–43 mm. Body pale grey or ochreous, darker dorsally, with an indistinct pale dorsal line and dark brown or black pinacula; prothoracic and anal plates almost black; head dark reddish-brown.
Foodplants. The roots and lower stems of grasses.
Habits. Single-brooded, occurring in the larval stage from August to the following June, feeding initially on seeds and later on the lower parts of the plants. During the spring the larvae can occasionally be found by careful searching at the bases of grass clumps, and will survive to complete their development if kept in spacious containers in which loose soil and soft grass roots have been provided. Pupation takes place in a cell beneath the soil and lasts about four weeks, with the adults flying from late June to early August. Generally distributed over much of the British Isles.
Plate 41: Q. Bred from an adult female to MVL. Early July. (JR)

Reddish Light Arches
Apamea sublustris Esper
Larva. 36–42 mm. Body grey, darker dorsally, with an indistinct dorsal line and dark brown or black pinacula; prothoracic and anal plates almost black; head dark brown. Probably indistinguishable from the previous species (*A. lithoxylaea*).
Foodplants. The lower stems and roots of grasses.
Habits. Single-brooded, occurring in the larval state from August to the following spring and adopting the same habits as the other closely related insects (*A. monoglypha* and *A. lithoxylaea*). The females, which come freely to sugar and light during June and July, will on occasion deposit eggs within grass sheaths of plants growing in tubs. Considered a very difficult species to rear in captivity. Mostly inhabiting open grassy places on sandy or calcareous soils in the southern half of England, parts of Wales and Co. Clare in Ireland.
Plate 41: R. Bred from an adult female. Early July. (GH)

The Exile
Apamea zeta Treitschke
(*maillardi* Hübner)
(*exulis* Lefebvre)
Larva. 40–45 mm. Body glossy greyish-brown, with dark brown pinacula and visible internal vessels; prothoracic and anal plates dark brown; head orangish-brown.
Foodplants. The roots and lower stems of moorland grasses, accepting annual meadow-grass in captivity.
Habits. A single-brooded insect, the larva of which has yet to be discovered in the wild in the British Isles. Many authorities suspect that it may take more than one year to complete its development, although in captivity a few from each egg batch may attain full size within a few months. It has been stated that the larvae can be obtained by turning over moorland boulders to find them hiding from the light by day, but several attempts to confirm this habit on Cairngorm met with failure. The adults fly in July and August, coming to sugar and light, and some females will lay in confinement if supplied with stems and roots of purple moor-grass. The larvae do well at first if kept warm and constantly given fresh food and soil to burrow into and, when about two months old, seem either to die or to develop rapidly. The pupa is formed in an earthen cell, lasting from about four to eight weeks. Local, inhabiting the mountains and moorland of central and northern Scotland, and the Shetland Islands.
Plate 42: A. Bred from an adult female to MVL. Early August. (GAC)

Crescent Striped
Apamea oblonga Haworth
(*abjecta* Hübner)
Larva. 40–45 mm. Body pale ochreous or flesh-coloured, with greyish-brown pinacula; prothoracic and anal plates pale brown; head glossy, reddish-brown.
Foodplants. The roots and stem bases of saltmarsh-grass, red fescue and other allied species.
Habits. Single-brooded, being in the larval stage from about August to the following late May or June, spending most of its development in subterranean chambers among the foodplant roots. During the spring these larvae can sometimes be located by close searching among foodplant roots, especially those of isolated plants growing in fine soil. They pupate within the larval chamber, this stage lasting about four to eight weeks, with the adults flying from late June to early August. Mostly a coastal insect, occurring locally from

Hampshire northwards to Yorkshire in suitable habitats; also recorded from the fens of East Anglia.
Plate 42: B. Found among roots of foodplant, fully grown. Mid-May. (JMP)

Clouded-bordered Brindle
Apamea crenata Hufnagel
(*rurea* Fabricius)
Larva. 32–36 mm. Body of various shades of pinkish-grey, with small blackish pinacula and a pale narrow dorsal line; spiracular region paler than the dorsum; prothoracic plate blackish-brown, with distinct pale dorsal and subdorsal streaks; anal plate pale brown; head very dark brown.
Foodplants. Cock's-foot and other related grasses.
Habits. A single-brooded species that occurs in the larval stage from August to about early April, feeding initially on the seeds of grasses and later nocturnally on the blades; hiding by day close to the ground in plant litter. During the early spring the larvae can be found by searching or careful sweeping at night and with a little care can be bred through to the adult stage. The pupa is formed inside a loose chamber among the plant roots and lasts about ten weeks, with the adults flying from late May to about early July. Generally distributed over most of the British Isles.
Plate 42: C. Obtained by searching at night, fully grown. Late March. (MB)

Clouded Brindle
Apamea epomidion Haworth
(*characterea* Hübner)
(*hepatica* auctt.)
Larva. 33–38 mm. Body various shades of pinkish-grey, with a fine pale dorsal line and small black pinacula; spiracular region pale grey or brown; prothoracic plate blackish-brown, with distinct subdorsal streaks and an obscure dorsal streak; head dark brown.
Foodplants. Various grasses, including cock's-foot, tufted hair-grass and annual meadow-grass.
Habits. Single-brooded, being in the larval stage from about August to the following early March, feeding at first on grass seeds and later on the blades throughout the milder winter nights. The larvae attain full size earlier in the season than their associated species and may be taken by searching or careful sweeping after dark. The pupation period lasts for about three months, with the light- and sugar-responsive adults flying between the middle of June and late July. Inhabiting woods and gardens throughout much of England and Wales; also recorded in southern Scotland and Ireland.
Plate 42: D. Swept at night, fully grown. Late February. (BH)

Scarce Brindle
Apamea lateritia Hufnagel
Larva. 40–45 mm. Body greyish-brown, with an indistinct pale dorsal line and small black pinacula; head brown and glossy (MBGBI).
Foodplants. The roots of grasses.
Habits. A single-brooded immigrant species of which there have been twelve recorded adults. The larval stage lasts from about September to the following May, living and feeding among the roots of grasses, until pupating in the larval habitation for about four weeks. On the continent it occurs in most countries and is not uncommon.

The Confused
Apamea furva Denis & Schiffermüller
Larva. 30–35 mm. Body pale greyish-pink, with small reddish-brown tubercles and paler underparts; prothoracic plate dark reddish-brown; head dark orange-brown (Buckler).
Foodplants. The roots and lower stems of meadow-grasses (*Poa* spp.).
Habits. A single-brooded insect, occurring as a larva from September to the following June, living among the grass roots in an earthen chamber, emerging at night to feed on the lower parts of the plant. The larvae have been found by selecting plants growing on stone walls and carefully searching. The pupation takes place in the soil and lasts about four to eight weeks, with the adults flying in July and August. Widespread over much of Scotland, Wales, Ireland, northern England and the North Midlands; also recorded from the Kent coast and in south-west England.

Dusky Brocade
Apamea remissa Hübner
(*obscura* Haworth)
Larva. 32–36 mm. Body light brown or brownish-grey, with a broad distinct creamy dorsal line, a vague subdorsal line, a wide yellowish spiracular stripe and small blackish-brown pinacula; prothoracic plate brown, darker between the equally distinct dorsal and subdorsal streaks; head reddish-brown, marked with black.
Foodplants. Various grasses, including couch grass and annual meadow-grass.
Habits. Single-brooded, being in the larval stage from about August to the following April, feeding steadily at night through the winter months. The larvae can be found, usually in small numbers, by searching and careful sweeping after dusk in woodland clearings, on commons and downland slopes, and are not difficult to rear to the adult stage, requiring fine soil in which to pupate. This stage lasts for about ten weeks, with the adults flying in June and July. Widely distributed over most parts of the British Isles.
Plate 42: E. Found at night, fully grown. Early April. (MB)

Small Clouded Brindle
Apamea unanimis Hübner
Larva. 28–33 mm. Body pale brown to ochreous, with a dark-edged pale dorsal line, a vague subdorsal line and a pale spiracular stripe; prothoracic plate light brown, streaked with ochreous; head reddish-brown, marked with blackish-brown.
Foodplants. Various grasses, including reed canary-grass, couch, wavy hair-grass and annual meadow-grass.
Habits. A single-brooded species, occurring as an actively feeding larva from about mid-July to October, when it then hibernates in a sheltered place, such as under loose bark or deep in plant litter, until it wanders to find a pupation site during a mild period in late winter or early spring. The larvae can be found at night during late September and early October, before the first frosts, and can be reared to the adult stage by keeping them in a well-ventilated sheltered place out of doors. The subterranean pupa is formed in a cocoon and lasts about three months before the adults emerge during June and the early part of July, these coming to sugar patches and lights located in damp places. Widespread over the greater part of England and Wales; local in parts of southern and eastern Scotland and northern Ireland.
Plate 42: F. Bred from an adult female to MVL. Late June. (PQW)

Union Rustic
Apamea pabulatricula Brahm
Larva. 28–32 mm. Body yellowish-brown, with a dark-edged

pale dorsal line and dark brown lines laterally; head brown, marked with black streaks (MBGBI).
Foodplants. Various woodland grasses.
Habits. A single-brooded species, which occurred in Britain, mainly in South Yorkshire, Nottinghamshire and Lincolnshire, before probably becoming extinct. The larval stage lasts from September to the following May, with the adults flying from mid-July to mid-August and, even on the continent, it is considered rare and local.

Large Nutmeg

Apamea anceps Denis & Schiffermüller
(*sordida* Borkhausen)
(*infesta* Ochsenheimer)
Larva. 33–37 mm. Body brown, often darker dorsally, with a broad yellowish dorsal line, an indistinct pale subdorsal line and a series of large dark pinacula above the broad yellowish-grey spiracular stripe; prothoracic plate pale brown, with a distinct pale dorsal streak and obscure subdorsal marks; head reddish-brown, marked with black.
Foodplants. Various grasses, including cock's-foot, couch, annual meadow-grass and the leaves and grains of corn.
Habits. Single-brooded, being in the larval stage from August to April, feeding initially on the flowers and seeds and later on the blades at night, hiding by day among the dense lower parts of the foodplant in a silken cell. The larvae can sometimes be found in the early spring, by torchlight, especially in agricultural areas where the populations are often large, and in captivity they are not difficult to rear from the egg by using potted foodplants. The pupa is formed underground, lasting for about two months before the adults emerge during June and July. These come freely to flowering plants, sugar and light. Most regularly recorded from the southern and eastern counties of England; local elsewhere in England and in Wales.
Plate 42: G. Bred from an adult female to MVL. Early July. (PQW)

Rustic Shoulder-knot

Apamea sordens Hufnagel
(*basilinea* Denis & Schiffermüller)
Larva. 32–35 mm. Body drab pale brown, with a darker-edged whitish dorsal line, an indistinct subdorsal line and a broad spiracular stripe; prothoracic plate dark brown between the bold dorsal streak and less obvious subdorsal marks; head dark brown, marked with black.
Foodplants. Various grasses, such as cock's-foot, wheat, couch and other soft-bladed species.
Habits. A single-brooded insect that occurs as a larva from about mid-July to the following late March, feeding at first on the seeds and later nocturnally on the blades throughout the winter months. In some places this insect can be abundant and here the larvae may readily be found at night, when active. They are not difficult to rear in captivity, doing better if kept outside on potted grasses in a sheltered place. The pupa is formed in a cocoon situated on or just below the soil, lasting for about eight to ten weeks. Both sexes of the adults can be taken at light and sugar during late May and June, with the females laying freely in confinement when supplied with foodplant stems. Widely distributed over most of the British Isles, especially in open grassy places.
Plate 42: H. Found at night, almost fully grown. Mid-March. (SHC)

Slender Brindle

Apamea scolopacina Esper
Larva. 28–33 mm. Body dark olive-green, with a pale narrow dorsal line and contrasting greenish-white underparts; dorsal pinacula small and black, with those above the spiracles larger; prothoracic plate translucent and greyish-green; head greenish-brown, with black marks at the mandibles.
Foodplants. Woodland grasses, such as wood meadow-grass, false-brome, wood melick and others.
Habits. Single-brooded, occurring in the larval stage from August to the following May, feeding initially inside the stems and later on the blades and flowers. During late April and May the larvae can readily be swept at night from grasses growing in woodland rides, and they are fairly easy to rear in confinement when supplied with fine soil in which to form their cocooned pupae. The adults fly in July and early August, coming to light and sugar. Generally distributed over much of the southern half of Britain.
Plate 42: I. Swept at night, fully grown. Mid-May.

Double Lobed

Apamea ophiogramma Esper
Larva. 27–32 mm. Body dull pink and wrinkled, with small brown dorsal pinacula and larger pinacula mostly located close to the small black spiracles; prothoracic and anal plates blackish-brown; head dark brown or black.
Foodplants. The inner stems of reed canary-grass and occasionally reed sweet-grass.
Habits. A single-brooded insect that occurs as a larva from August to early June, spending its whole development within the stems of the plant, burrowing downwards. While searching in water-meadows, fens and damp places during May, the larvae can be located by splitting reed canary-grass stems from the top until larval frass is discovered and then carefully working down to the insect. For successful rearing, when taken at this stage, growing plants must be available or the larvae are unlikely to survive unless they are about to pupate. The cocooned pupae are formed in plant debris or just under the soil, lasting for about four to six weeks, with the adults flying during July and early August. Widespread, but local, throughout much of England and Wales; also recorded from southern Scotland and parts of Ireland, mainly in the north.
Plate 42: J. Located in lower part of stem, fully grown. Late May.

Marbled Minor

Oligia strigilis Linnaeus
Larva. 18–23 mm. Body pinkish-grey to ochreous, with a fine pale dorsal line, a broader subdorsal line and a vague darker stripe just above the small black spiracles; prothoracic and anal plates pale brown; head orangish-brown, with darker mouthparts.
Foodplants. The inner parts of cock's-foot, reed canary-grass and allied species.
Habits. Single-brooded, being in the larval stage from August to the following April or May, feeding solely within the stems of the foodplants. When larger, during the spring, the larvae may be located by carefully splitting the lower stems and are also occasionally found when changing to a fresh plant at night. They are not difficult to rear when taken at this stage of their development, if supplied regularly with replaced lower stems and not disturbed unnecessarily. The pupa is formed inside the larval habitation and lasts about a month, with the adults flying from late May to early July. Widespread and common over most of England and Wales;

local in parts of Scotland, with an uncertain distribution in Ireland.
Plate 42: K. Located in lower stem of cock's-foot, fully grown. Early May.

Rufous Minor

Oligia versicolor Borkhausen
Larva. 18–22 mm. Body dark pinkish-grey, with a fine pale dorsal line, a vague subdorsal line and a broad pale grey spiracular stripe; dorsal pinacula small, dark brown; prothoracic plate brown, darker subdorsally; head orangish-brown, with darker mouthparts.
Foodplants. The internal parts of cock's-foot and probably other grasses.
Habits. A single-brooded insect that occurs as a larva from August to the following spring. The early stages of this species were unknown until recently, when a single larva was forced to attain full growth by careful attentive rearing. The eggs were laid in a strung-out batch situated between the supplied foodplant and a plastic container, hatching in about two weeks. Most of the tiny larvae failed to survive more than a few days, being unable to establish themselves within a suitable piece of foodplant, while the remainder were kept warm and constantly supplied with fresh plants. Many more losses occurred when the larvae refused to change plant and although several were placed on a potted growing plant kept outside, none were located at a later date. Eventually a single larva remained and was fully grown during December when it pupated among the plant roots in a flimsy cocoon. The adults fly from about mid-June to mid-July, coming to light and sugar. Widespread, but local, mainly in woodland and on sea-cliffs, throughout England, Wales and parts of southern Scotland.
Plate 42: L. Bred from an adult female to MVL. Early July. (SHC)

Tawny Marbled Minor

Oligia latruncula Denis & Schiffermüller
Larva. 18–23 mm. Body pinkish-grey to ochreous, with a fine pale dorsal line, an indistinct subdorsal line and a pale area beneath the small black spiracles; prothoracic and anal plates pale brown; head orangish-brown. Probably indistinguishable from *O. strigilis*.
Foodplants. The inner parts of cock's-foot and probably other grasses.
Habits. Single-brooded, occurring as a larva from August to the following April or May, living and feeding within the inner stems of the foodplant, changing to fresh examples by entering at the leaf-axils and boring downwards, when the larvae can sometimes be found at night. The pupa is formed among the plant roots, lasting about four weeks, with the adults flying from late May to early July. Widely distributed over most of the British Isles, being more frequent in southern parts.
Plate 42: M. Located in lower stem of cock's-foot, about half grown. Early March.

Middle-barred Minor

Oligia fasciuncula Haworth
Larva. 19–23 mm. Body flesh-coloured to greyish-ochreous, with a darker dorsal line, pinkish-brown subdorsal and lateral lines and black spiracles; prothoracic and anal plates light brown; head light orangish-brown.
Foodplants. Various grasses, especially tufted hair-grass.
Habits. A single-brooded species that occurs in the larval stage from August to May, hiding by day within the sheaths and feeding on the blades at night. The larvae can be obtained by searching, or careful sweeping after dark, in grassy places, such as damp woodland clearings and marshy ground, and are not difficult to rear in captivity when taken late in their development. The cocooned pupa is formed close to the ground in plant debris, lasting about a month, with the adults being on the wing during June and July. Generally distributed over most of Britain.
Plate 42: N. Bred from an adult female to MVL. Late June. (SHC)

Cloaked Minor

Mesoligia furuncula Denis & Schiffermüller
(*bicoloria* de Villers)
Larva. 19–23 mm. Body flesh-coloured or yellowish, and plump, with the dorsal vessel obscurely visible through the skin, otherwise unmarked and without lateral chitinous plates or pinacula; prothoracic plate reddish-brown; head dark brown.
Foodplants. The inner stems of various grasses, including sheep's-fescue, tufted hair-grass, false oat-grass and tall fescue.
Habits. Single-brooded, probably occurring in the larval stage from about August to the following early June, living and feeding within the stems of the foodplants. From May onwards, the larvae can be found by carefully splitting suitable grasses in coastal localities where populations tend to be larger. They are fairly easy to rear when transferred to potted plants, or constantly given fresh lower stems when kept in small containers. Pupation takes place in a cell eaten out by the larva at the base of the foodplant, lasting about four to six weeks, and the adults fly from late July to early September. Widely distributed over much of the British Isles.
Plate 42: O. Located in lower grass stem, almost fully grown. Late May (SHC)

Rosy Minor

Mesoligia literosa Haworth
Larva. 20–24 mm. Body usually yellowish or pinkish-brown, darker dorsally, with a distinct pale dorsal line and pale brown chitinous plates laterally on the thoracic segments; spiracles black; prothoracic plate brown, edged darker; head blackish-brown.
Foodplants. The roots and stems of a great variety of grasses, including cock's-foot, marram, lyme-grass, glaucous sedge, wheat, oats and other cereals.
Habits. A single-brooded species, being in the larval stage from September to the following early June. During the spring the larvae can readily be located on coastal sandhills by carefully splitting open any sickly looking stems of lyme-grass or marram. When taken at this point of their development the larvae are fairly easy to rear in captivity. They also occur frequently inside the stems of cereal crops, often with an occupied plant showing yellowed leaves as an indicator of infestation. The cocooned pupae are formed in the soil or plant debris and last about four weeks, with the sugar- and light-responsive adults flying from mid-July to late August. Widespread and locally common throughout most of the British Isles.
Plate 42: P. Located in lower lyme-grass stem, fully grown. Late May.

Common Rustic

Mesapamea secalis Linnaeus
(*didyma* Esper)
Larva. 22–26 mm. Body green, with dull pink or purplish subdorsal markings, of variable intensity and sometimes

absent, on the abdominal segments; prothoracic and anal plates brownish-green; head light brown.
Foodplants. The inner parts of various grasses, such as cock's-foot, tufted hair-grass and tall fescue; can also be a pest of wheat and other cereal crops.
Habits. Single-brooded, occurring as a larva from September to the following May, living within the stems and sheaths of the foodplants. During the spring the larvae can easily be obtained by sweeping in grassy places at night, when they are actively moving to fresh plants, and they can be reared to the adult stage with a little care. The pupa lasts about a month and is formed in a slight cocoon just in the soil or under plant litter, with the adults flying during July and August. A widely distributed and generally common insect throughout most of Britain.
Plate 42: Q. Swept at night, nearly fully grown. Mid-May.

Lesser Common Rustic
Mesapamea didyma Esper
(*secalella* Remm)
Larva. 22–25 mm. Body green, with pink or purplish-red subdorsal markings, these often being bolder than in the previous species (*M. secalis*); prothoracic and anal plates brownish-green; head light brown.
Foodplants. The inner parts of various grasses, including cock's-foot and fescues.
Habits. A single-brooded species that was recently separated from the previous insect (*M. secalis*), occurring in the larval stage from about September to the following May, with its life-cycle and habits being very similar. The larvae may be obtained by sweeping at night, or by carefully searching within the lower stems of sickly looking plants during the spring, and they pupate inside a loose cocoon just in the soil or under the detritus. The flight period of the adults is July and August and it seems to be distributed throughout much of the British Isles.
Plate 42: R. Swept at night, nearly fully grown. Mid-May.

Least Minor
Photedes captiuncula Treitschke
Larva. 13–16 mm. Body dull ochreous, purplish-red dorsally on the abdominal segments; prothoracic and anal plates pale brown; head reddish-brown (Buckler).
Foodplants. The inner parts of glaucous sedge; also stated to accept cultivated canary-grass in captivity.
Habits. Single-brooded, being in the larval stage from August to the following late May, probably feeding within the stems throughout its development. The larvae have been found by persistent splitting and searching of the foodplant during the spring, and pupate just under the soil in a slight cocoon for about a month. The adults fly in sunshine from mid-June to early August, looking rather like a small tortrix moth when on the wing. A local insect found mainly in the limestone areas of northern England, and in the Burren district of Cos. Clare and Galway, in Ireland.

Small Dotted Buff
Photedes minima Haworth
(*arcuosa* Haworth)
Larva. 17–20 mm. Body ochreous or creamy, with an indistinct dorsal line; spiracles black; prothoracic and anal plates pale brown; head brown, darker at mouthparts.
Foodplants. The inner parts of tufted hair-grass and possibly related species.
Habits. A single-brooded insect, occurring in the larval stage from August to the following early June, living and feeding within the stems of the foodplant. During the spring the larvae can be located by carefully splitting the stems down to the crown, where their presence is often indicated by the accumulated frass. The pupation takes place in a cocoon in the soil close to the plant and lasts about a month, with the adults flying from late June to early August. Generally distributed in damp woodland clearings and marshy places over much of the British Isles.
Plate 43: A. Located in crown of foodplant, fully grown. Late May.

Morris's Wainscot
Photedes morrisii Dale
Larva. 18–22 mm. Body ochreous or cream-coloured, without any distinct markings; pinacula tiny, blackish-brown; spiracles black; prothoracic plate dark brown; anal plate pale brown, darkening to black at the tip; head dark reddish-brown.
Foodplant. The inner stems of tall fescue.
Habits. Single-brooded, being in the larval stage from August to early June, the larvae boring downwards until they reach the crown of the plant, where pupation takes place. During the late spring they can be located by carefully splitting the lower stems of the foodplant, especially those that seem unhealthy. The adults are on the wing from late June to the middle of July, and can be taken by netting them as they fly around the foodplants just after dark. A very local species, at present only found on the coasts of west Dorset and south-eastern Devon; also recorded from Kent until the 1970s.
Plate 43: B. Found in stem base of foodplant, fully grown. Late May. (SHC)

The Concolorous
Photedes extrema Hübner
(*concolor* Guenée)
Larva. 18–21 mm. Body pale ochreous, with a vague purplish tinge dorsally and an indistinct pale dorsal line; spiracles black; prothoracic and anal plates ochreous; head reddish-brown, blackish at mouthparts. Very similar to *P. fluxa*, but more slender.
Foodplants. The inner parts of wood small-reed and purple small-reed.
Habits. A single-brooded insect, occurring in the larval stage from August to late May, living and feeding head downwards inside the lowest part of the foodplant stems. The larvae can be located, usually with some difficulty, by targeting isolated plants or those looking unhealthy and carefully splitting the stem down into the root-crowns. The pupa is formed in a strong cocoon by the damaged plant and lasts about three weeks, with the adults flying from the middle of June to mid-July. A very local species mainly inhabiting the damp woods and fens of Northamptonshire and Huntingdonshire.
Plate 43: C. Found in stem base of wood small-reed, fully grown. Mid-May. (SHC)

Lyme Grass
Photedes elymi Treitschke
Larva. 24–28 mm. Body pale ochreous, with the dorsal vessel showing as a thin dark line; spiracles black; prothoracic and anal plates pale brown; head reddish-brown.
Foodplant. The inner parts of lyme-grass.
Habits. Single-brooded, becoming fully grown in early June, after probably overwintering as a small larva. The larvae can be found by splitting and searching within the lower stems

and root-crowns of the foodplant during May or early June, and may be reared to the adult stage by transferring them to potted plants. The pupae are formed in a cocoon among the roots, lasting about four to six weeks, with the adults flying from late June to early August. A local insect, being found on some of the sandhills of eastern England and eastern Scotland.

Plate 43: D. Located below soil level in lower foodplant stem, fully grown. Early June. (PQW)

Mere Wainscot

Photedes fluxa Hübner
(*hellmanni* Eversmann)

Larva. 18–21 mm. Body pale ochreous, vaguely purplish dorsally, with an indistinct paler dorsal line; prothoracic and anal plates ochreous; head reddish-brown. Similar to *P. extrema*, but less slender.

Foodplant. The inner stems of wood small-reed.

Habits. A single-brooded species that occurs as a larva from about September to the following early June, feeding within the lower stems of the foodplant and being quite difficult to find. A stated method is to clear any plant litter from around the stem bases and to give a sharp tug to any likely stems, hoping that those infested will break nearly at ground level where they have been weakened by the larva's feeding. The cocooned pupae are formed close by in the soil or detritus and last until the adults fly during July and August. Mostly recorded in the damp woods and fens of Huntingdonshire, Cambridgeshire, Northamptonshire, Lincolnshire and West Suffolk.

Plate 43: E. Located in lower stem of foodplant, nearly fully grown. Mid-May. (SHC)

Small Wainscot

Photedes pygmina Haworth
(*fulva* Hübner)

Larva. 22–24 mm. Body slender, flesh-coloured, with a vague purplish dorsal tinge and an indistinct pale dorsal line; spiracles black, slightly larger on the tenth and eleventh segments and joined by a greyish line; prothoracic and anal plates pale brown; head light reddish-brown.

Foodplants. The inner parts of various grasses, sedges and rushes.

Habits. Single-brooded, probably occurring in the larval stage from September to the following early July, being difficult to locate due to the absence of external signs and the fairly wide selection of foodplants that are accepted. The larva illustrated was found by chance inside a lower sedge stem, when randomly searching different plants in the Norfolk Broads. It pupated in a silken cocoon among the plant debris and the adult male emerged in mid-July, slightly earlier than in the wild. Widely distributed, but fairly local, over much of the British Isles.

Plate 43: F. Located in lower stem, nearly fully grown. Early June.

Fenn's Wainscot

Photedes brevilinea Fenn

Larva. 30–35 mm. Body grey, with broad pale-edged brownish dorsal and subdorsal stripes and an ochreous spiracular line; prothoracic plate grey, streaked dorsally and subdorsally paler; head brown, with two blackish stripes.

Foodplant. The inner stems and blades of common reed.

Habits. A single-brooded species that occurs in the larval stage from April to about mid-June, after overwintering as an egg. At first the larvae live and feed within the upper stems until the last instar, when they emerge at night to consume the leaf blades. During this point of their development, in late May and early June, they can be swept after dark and are fairly easy to rear in captivity when constantly supplied with fresh foodplant. The pupa is formed in a slight cocoon among plant litter and lasts about four to six weeks, with the adults flying from late July to the middle of August. Inhabiting the drier parts of well-established reed-beds in the Norfolk Broads and on the Suffolk coast.

Plate 43: G. Swept at night, almost fully grown. Early June. (GAC)

Dusky Sallow

Eremobia ochroleuca Denis & Schiffermüller

Larva. 32–38 mm. Body pale bluish-green, with distinct whitish-green dorsal, subdorsal and spiracular stripes and a good number of small black pinacula; head whitish-green, with a brown tinge to the front.

Foodplants. The flowers and seeds of cock's-foot, couch, other grasses and sometimes cultivated cereal crops.

Habits. Single-brooded, being in the larval stage from about late April to early July, after overwintering as an egg. From late May onwards the larvae can readily be swept from grasses by day or night, and have also been found within the sheaths containing the seeds of commercial crops. An easy species to rear in confinement, although many are parasitized, pupating in the soil for about three weeks in a cocoon. The adults fly in late July and August, and as well as being attracted to light, can be found resting on knapweed flowers by day. Mostly inhabiting open grassy places throughout much of southern and eastern England, ranging as far north as Yorkshire.

Plate 43: H. Found inside oat sheath, over half grown. Early June. (SHC)

Flounced Rustic

Luperina testacea Denis & Schiffermüller

Larva. 30–34 mm. Body yellowish-brown, with transverse darker banding and the dorsal vessel and other inner parts showing through the skin; prothoracic and anal plates pale brown; head orangish-brown.

Foodplants. The roots and stem bases of various grasses, also those of wheat and other cereal crops.

Habits. A single-brooded insect that occurs as a larva from September to the following June, living and feeding under the soil among the roots and lower parts of the foodplants. During the spring the larvae can readily be located by choosing isolated plants growing on mainly bare ground and searching carefully among the roots and soil. The pupa is formed in the larval habitation and lasts about six weeks, with the adults flying in August and September. Widely distributed over much of the British Isles, being more local in Scotland, and often common on the coast of southern England.

Plate 43: I. Located in soil among roots, fully grown. Mid-June.

Sandhill Rustic

Luperina nickerlii Freyer

Larva. 25–30 mm. Body glossy yellowish-brown, appearing greyish from the internal parts which are visible through the skin; prothoracic and anal plates weak, yellowish-brown; head orangish-brown.

Subspecies *knilli* Boursin. Similar, but more plump, with a strong prothoracic plate and a heavy dark chitinous band on the eleventh segment in front of the dark brown anal plate.

Foodplants. The stem bases and roots of various grasses, depending on which subspecies is being considered. Subspecies *demuthi* on saltmarsh-grass; *leechi* and *gueneei* on sand couch and *knilli* probably on red fescue. All accept annual meadow-grass in captivity.

Habits. A single-brooded insect, of which four quite separate subspecies occur within the British Isles, all being in the larval stage from September to the following July. The adults of all races fly in August and September, the females laying their eggs within the sheaths of the foodplant grasses. These hatch in about two to four weeks and the young larvae bore down the stems into the crown of the plants, until, due to their size, they eventually have to feed beneath the soil on the roots. The most widespread subspecies, *demuthi*, feeds mainly on the roots of saltmarsh-grass and can be found in June and early July by careful persistent searching at the lower parts of this plant, growing on the salterns of Kent and Essex. Both *leechi* and *gueneei* occur very locally on the sandy beaches of Cornwall, and North Wales to Lancashire, respectively. They may be located from late May to early July by raking beneath the plants with bare hands, until the insects are exposed. The final subspecies, *knilli*, occurs on the coastal cliffs of the Dingle peninsula in south-west Ireland. This larva's structure and the adult moth's habits are different from the others', and it may well prove to be a separate species, although the genitalia are indistinguishable. The larvae of *knilli* construct strong silken habitations among the soil and roots, whereas the others only form weak spinnings.

Plate 43: J. (Ssp. *leechi*) Located in gritty sand beneath foodplant, almost fully grown. Mid-June. (SHC).

Dumeril's Rustic

Luperina dumerilii Duponchel

Larva. Apparently undescribed, although probably similar to *L. testacea*.

Foodplants. Stated to feed on the roots of grasses.

Habits. About thirty adult specimens of this very rare immigrant species have been recorded in Britain during the present century. They fly in late August and September and although the earlier stages appear to be undescribed, the species probably occurs as a larva from the autumn to the following spring, adopting similar habits to allied species within this genus.

Scarce Arches

Luperina zollikoferi Freyer

Larva. Apparently undescribed, except by Spuler who states it is green.

Foodplants. Possibly low-growing plants or grasses.

Habits. Fewer than twenty adult specimens of this rare immigrant species have been recorded and it has never been proven to have bred in the British Isles. It has been stated that the larvae feed in May and June on low-growing plants and Spuler mentions meadow-rue and great fen-sedge as the natural foodplants, although confirmation of this would be desirable. The adults fly during August and September and the usual range of this insect covers eastern Europe and western Asia.

A general note on the genus *Amphipoea*. The four considered species of this genus are extremely difficult to distinguish from each other, with possibly *lucens* and *fucosa* being two geographically separated races that have been proven to hybridize where overlapping in distribution. The larvae are virtually the same in size, structure and coloration, and although the genitalia of the adults are slightly different, these could have evolved independently. The same case applies to *crinanensis* and *oculea*, with the larvae adopting basically the same habits and accepting the same foodplant, yellow iris, when successfully reared in confinement.

Large Ear

Amphipoea lucens Freyer

Larva. 26–30 mm. Body pale bluish-grey, with broad purplish-brown dorsolateral and spiracular stripes on the abdominal segments; pinacula black, largest on the thorax and final three abdominal rings; prothoracic and anal plates ochreous, darker anteriorly; head dull orange.

Foodplants. The inner stems and root-crowns of purple moor-grass, cotton-grass and probably other associated plants, accepting annual meadow-grass and cock's-foot in confinement.

Habits. Single-brooded, overwintering as an egg and occurring in the larval stage from about late April to the middle of July, mainly feeding at first within the lower parts of the stems, later among the roots. During late May and early June, the insects can sometimes be obtained by plucking stems of cotton-grass, which will break close to the base to reveal the half-grown larvae of this species, and they can then be reared in captivity on growing potted foodplants. The pupa is formed in plant litter, with the adults flying in August and September. Mostly a moorland insect, recorded from many parts of northern and western Britain and coastal localities in Ireland.

Plate 43: K. Found wandering over bare ground, nearly fully grown. Late June. (SHC)

Saltern Ear

Amphipoea fucosa Freyer

Larva. 26–30 mm. Body pale grey, with a broad purplish-brown or maroon dorsolateral stripe and a less distinct wavy line of the same colour along the spiracular region; pinacula dark brown or black; prothoracic and anal plates ochreous, both edged darker anteriorly; head orangish-brown.

Foodplants. The roots and stem bases of grasses, accepting annual meadow-grass and cock's-foot in captivity.

Habits. A single-brooded insect, overwintering as an egg and being in the larval stage from late April to July. The life-cycle in the wild is imperfectly known, although the insects have been reared from the egg on occasion. Many females seem reluctant to lay in captivity and those eggs that are deposited are often in grass sheaths or between layers of crumpled tissue-paper. The larvae hatch in the spring, bore into the foodplant by way of the leaf-axils and are best reared on growing plants of cock's-foot in containers. Pupation takes place in the soil by the root and lasts about a month, with the adults flying from late July to early September. Inhabiting saltmarshes, coastal sandhills and sometimes marshy areas inland, mainly recorded from coastal localities in the southern half of Britain and in the Outer Hebrides, where it hybridizes with *A. lucens*.

Plate 43: L. Bred from an adult female to MVL. Mid-August. (PQW)

Crinan Ear

Amphipoea crinanensis Burrows

Larva. 26–30 mm. Body pale grey, with maroon or purplish-brown dorsolateral and spiracular stripes; pinacula black; prothoracic and anal plates ochreous, both edged anteriorly with blackish-brown; head orangish-brown (Haggett).

Foodplants. Reared in captivity on the inner stems of yellow iris, possibly also accepting the stems and roots of grasses.

Habits. A single-brooded species that occurs in the larval stage from about April to July, boring and living within the inner stems of yellow iris. Newly hatched larvae should be given a choice of various grass flowers as well as the known foodplant which they seem to prefer. The pupa lasts for about four to six weeks, with the adults flying in August and September, both sexes coming to light and flowering plants. Widespread in Ireland and the mainland of Scotland; local in parts of northern England and west Wales.

Ear Moth

Amphipoea oculea Linnaeus
(*nictitans* Linnaeus)

Larva. 26–30 mm. Body pale grey, with maroon or purplish-brown dorsolateral and spiracular stripes; pinacula black; prothoracic and anal plates ochreous, both edged anteriorly with blackish-brown; head orangish-brown (Haggett).

Foodplants. The lower parts of the stems and roots of grasses and also yellow iris in captivity.

Habits. Single-brooded, being in the larval stage from April to June, after overwintering as an egg. The larvae have been reared successfully in captivity on couch, cock's-foot and yellow iris, boring into the stems and devouring the plant from within. Those bred to the adult stage on the last plant started feeding on various fine grasses while being offered yellow iris as a probable alternative. Most losses occurred during the second instar and those surviving thrived on the inner parts of iris until pupation. The adults fly, sometimes by day, from late July to early September and are attracted to light and flowering plants. Generally distributed over most parts of the British Isles, being the most likely member of this genus encountered in southern and eastern England.

Rosy Rustic

Hydraecia micacea Esper

Larva. 35–40 mm. Body flesh-coloured, with brownish transverse banding on the abdominal segments; pinacula fairly large greyish-brown; prothoracic plate bone-coloured, edged with black anteriorly; anal plate greyish-brown; head orangish-brown.

Foodplants. The inner stems and roots of dock, burdock, plantain, horse-tail and other plants.

Habits. Single-brooded, occurring in the larval stage from late April to about early August, after overwintering as an egg. At first the larvae bore into the foodplant stems and eat their way downwards into the roots to finish their development. During late May to early July they can readily be located within the lower stems of tall dock plants growing in open habitats and are not difficult to rear in captivity. The pupae are formed in the soil and last about six weeks, with the adults flying from late August to early October. Widespread throughout most of the British Isles.

Plate 43: M. Found in lower dock stem, over half grown. Late June.

The Butterbur

Hydraecia petasitis Doubleday

Larva. 37–42 mm. Body yellowish-white, with the dorsal vessel showing indistinctly through the skin; pinacula brown, quite small; prothoracic plate brownish-orange, edged darker anteriorly; anal plate brown; head dark chestnut brown.

Foodplant. The inner stem and roots of butterbur.

Habits. A single-brooded insect that occurs in the larval stage from April to mid-July, after overwintering as an egg. The tiny larvae bore into the leaf petioles of the foodplant and descend, feeding on the inner parts of the growing stem, until boring into the rootstocks to finish their development. They can be located between about late May and the middle of June by cutting through the stems about 10 cm below the leaf, and if a brown line descends further down the inner stem, it often indicates infestation by this species. By late June the larvae are usually inside the rootstocks and are much more difficult to locate. When taken into captivity they should be kept on potted foodplant, and smaller larvae have been suspected of devouring each other when short of food. The pupae are formed just under the soil, without a cocoon, and last about three to four weeks, with the adults flying in August and early September. Inhabiting river banks and damp places, locally, throughout much of England, parts of Wales and southern Scotland.

Plate 43: N. Located in lower foodplant stem, half grown. Early June.

Marsh Mallow Moth

Hydraecia osseola Staudinger

Larva. 35–40 mm. Body flesh-coloured, with the dorsal vessel showing through the skin as a greyish line; pinacula tiny on the dorsum, slightly larger laterally, pale brown; prothoracic and anal plates pale ochreous, the former with blackish edging anteriorly; head orangish-brown.

Foodplant. The inner stems and roots of marsh-mallow.

Habits. Single-brooded, occurring in the larval stage from about early May to late July, after overwintering as an egg laid on the foodplant seed-heads or nearby. The young larvae bore into the stems and gradually work their way down into the rootstocks to finish their development, reaching these about late June. They can be bred from the egg on potted foodplants, and larvae have been found among the rootstocks of heavily infested yellowing plants in July. The pupae are formed in the soil and last about a month, with the adults flying in late August and September. A very local and vulnerable species, at present restricted to the Medway valley of Kent and parts of the Romney Marsh.

Plate 43: O. Located in soil adjacent to roots of damaged foodplant, fully grown. Late July.

Frosted Orange

Gortyna flavago Denis & Schiffermüller

Larva. 33–37 mm. Body pinkish-fleshy-coloured, with large blackish pinacula; prothoracic and anal plates blackish-brown; head orangish-brown.

Foodplants. The inner stems and roots of thistles, burdock, foxglove, hemp-agrimony, common nettle and other plants.

Habits. A single-brooded species that occurs as a larva from April to early August, after overwintering in the egg stage. The larvae bore into the stems and feed in the lower parts until pupating within the damaged plant, head upwards. They may be located by finding sickly looking thistles or burdocks and carefully splitting the stems, and can be bred in captivity given fresh stems in which to live. The adults fly from late August to October, with both sexes being attracted to light. Widely distributed and fairly common in England and Wales; local and less frequent in Ireland and southern and eastern Scotland.

Plate 43: P. Located in lower stem of marsh thistle, nearly fully grown. Early July. (JMP)

Fisher's Estuarine Moth

Gortyna borelii Pierret

Larva. 44–50 mm. Body whitish, with pinkish-grey transverse banding on the anterior parts of the abdominal rings; pinacula dark brown, larger laterally; prothoracic plate

orangish-brown, with black lateral edging; anal plate black; head pale orangish-brown.
Foodplants. The inner stems and roots of hog's fennel, accepting cultivated carrot and celeriac in captivity.
Habits. A recently discovered single-brooded species that occurs in the larval stage from about late May to early August. The overwintering eggs are laid in large numbers between grass blades, or tissue-paper in captivity. After hatching the young larvae bore into the foodplant stems by way of the leaf-axils, feeding within for a period, before descending to complete the development among the roots. Infestation by larger larvae, which may burrow up to 30 cm into the soil, is sometimes indicated by piles of bleached frass accumulating at the bases of sickly looking plants. When reared from the egg in captivity, cultivated carrot plants should be established in tubs and the eggs placed at the leaf-axils of growing stems. Should these plants seem to be almost dead from the destruction of the roots, more carrots and another layer of soil may be added to the netting-covered container. In the wild pupation takes place without a cocoon in the larval borings and lasts about six to eight weeks, with the adults flying during late September and early October. A very local and vulnerable insect, inhabiting the marshy fields and banks above the saltmarshes on the Essex coast.
Plate 43: Q. Bred from an adult female found at rest on foodplant. Early October. (JMP)

Burren Green
Calamia tridens Hufnagel
(*virens* Linnaeus)
Larva. 30–34 mm. Body greyish-white, with dull purplish transverse banding and the grey dorsal vessel showing through the skin; pinacula dark brown; prothoracic and anal plates almost black; head blackish-brown.
Foodplants. Probably the stems and roots of blue moor-grass, readily accepting annual meadow-grass and cock's-foot in captivity.
Habits. A single-brooded species that occurs in the larval stage from about April to late June, after overwintering as an egg. The small larvae bore into the foodplant stems and later feed among the stem bases and roots devouring all parts of the plant available at ground level and below. They are not difficult to rear in confinement, especially when kept on potted plants or continually supplied with fresh food, and not unnecessarily disturbed when inside stems; from which they will change to fresh ones when these are laid close by. Pupation takes place among the roots and lasts about four weeks, with the adults flying in late July and August. Only recorded from the Burren district in Cos. Clare and Galway, where it can be locally common.
Plate 43: R. Bred from an adult female to MVL. Mid-August. (DJW)

Haworth's Minor
Celaena haworthii Curtis
Larva. 16–20 mm. Body purplish-brown, with indistinct paler dorsal and subdorsal lines; pinacula small, dark brown; prothoracic plate pale ochreous; head brown (Buckler).
Foodplants. The inner stems of rushes (*Juncus* spp.), club-rush (*Scirpus* spp.) and cotton-grass, also probably in other grasses.
Habits. Single-brooded, occurring in the larval stage from April to July, after overwintering as an egg. The larvae hatch in the spring and bore down into the stems, changing to fresh ones when necessary, and sometimes can be located by finding the small entrance hole low down on the plant from which frass may be ejected. The pupa lasts about a month, being formed in a cocoon among the nearby plant litter or soil, with the adults flying during August and early September. Widely distributed, inhabiting wet moorland and other damp places over much of the northern half of the British Isles; also locally recorded from fenland parts of East Anglia, Hampshire water-meadows and on boggy ground in the south-west of England.

The Crescent
Celaena leucostigma Hübner
Larva. 28–32 mm. Body flesh-coloured, heavily toned with greyish-brown dorsally; pinacula blackish-brown, large on the thoracic segments; prothoracic and anal plates blackish-brown; head glossy reddish-brown.
Foodplants. The inner stems of yellow iris, great fen-sedge and other similar plants, accepting cock's-foot and whorl-grass in captivity.
Habits. A single-brooded insect, being in the larval stage from March to early July, after overwintering as an egg. When inhabiting sedges and grasses, the larvae feed inside the stems and rootstocks; alternatively, when on yellow iris they feed predominantly inside the fleshy leaves, where they can be located by persistent searching. The pupae are formed in a flimsy cocoon among plant litter and last about three to six weeks, with the adults being on the wing from late July to early September. Generally distributed over much of the British Isles, inhabiting damp places such as fenland, boggy moorland and marshy ground near rivers.
Plate 44: A. Bred from an adult female to MVL. Early August. (PQW)

Bulrush Wainscot
Nonagria typhae Thunberg
Larva. 50–60 mm. Body slender, pinkish, with darker transverse banding; spiracles black; prothoracic plate ochreous; anal plate blackish-brown; head reddish-brown.
Foodplants. The inner stems of reedmace and less often lesser reedmace.
Habits. Single-brooded, occurring as a larva from about April to the middle of July, after overwintering in the egg stage. During June and early July the larvae can often be found by splitting the larger stems of the foodplant at the water's edge and are easily distinguished by their huge length. The pupae are formed head downwards within the plant, and below is a small eaten-out window, consisting of only the outer epidermis of the stem, from which the adult moth emerges during late July or August. These come freely to light, often wandering far from their waterside habitats. Widespread and locally common in England, Wales, parts of Ireland and southern Scotland; also recorded from eastern Scotland and Morayshire.
Plate 44: B. Located in reedmace stem, fully grown. Early July.

Twin-spotted Wainscot
Archanara geminipuncta Haworth
Larva. 27–32 mm. Body whitish, with the dorsal vessel showing through the skin as a thin grey line; pinacula small and brown; prothoracic plate ochreous; anal plate and head dark brown.
Foodplant. The inner stems of common reed.
Habits. A single-brooded species, being in the larval stage from May to July, after overwintering as an egg. The larvae bore into the stems, changing when necessary to a fresh plant and can be located by searching for plants that show

yellowing of the main leaf. Pupation takes place, head upwards, within the stem, above which is a small emergence window from which the adults escape. Sometimes a plant will be inhabited by more than one larva, each usually in a different section of the stem. The adults fly in August, with both sexes coming sparingly to light. Widespread, but local, inhabiting reedy ditches and reed-beds, south of a line between the Severn and the Wash; also recorded from coastal parts of South Wales.
Plate 44: C. Located in reed-stem, fully grown. Early July. (SHC)

Brown-veined Wainscot
Archanara dissoluta Treitschke
Larva. 25–30 mm. Body flesh-coloured, inclining to pinkish-brown; prothoracic plate pale ochreous; anal plate greyish-brown; head dark reddish-brown.
Foodplant. The inner stems of common reed.
Habits. Single-brooded, being in the larval stage from April to early July, after overwintering as an egg. The larvae usually inhabit smaller stems growing on dampish ground, entering just above the stem divisions (internodes) about half-way up the plant, and feed upwards until changing to another fresh plant to repeat the process. Pupation takes place in July, head downwards, within the lower part of a stem, lasting about two to three weeks. The adults fly from late July to late August, coming freely to light in their fen and marshland habitats. Widespread over much of southern and eastern England, ranging north to Yorkshire; also recorded more locally from Devon, North and South Wales and Lancashire.
Plate 44: D. Located in stem, fully grown. Early July. (GAC)

White-mantled Wainscot
Archanara neurica Hübner
Larva. 26–30 mm. Body flesh-coloured, inclining to pinkish, with vague paler dorsal and subdorsal lines and a narrow greyish line along the spiracles; prothoracic plate pale brown; anal plate brown, speckled darker; head blackish-brown; underparts yellowish.
Foodplant. The inner stems of common reed.
Habits. A single-brooded species, occurring as a larva from about April to late June, after overwintering in the egg stage. The larvae frequent smaller plants growing in the drier less dense parts of reed-beds, boring in about half-way up the stems, just above an internode, and change to fresh plants when necessary. Pupation takes place, head downwards, inside the lower part of an old dry stem which is entered by means of a small inconspicuous hole eaten out by the larva. The adults fly in July and early August, coming freely to light. A very local species at present restricted to the coastal reed-beds of Suffolk.
Plate 44: E. Located inside foodplant stem, fully grown. Mid-June.

Webb's Wainscot
Archanara sparganii Esper
Larva. 45–50 mm. Body green, with internal parts showing brownish through the translucent skin; prothoracic and anal plates brownish-green; head brown.
Foodplants. The inner stems of reedmace, lesser reedmace, common club-rush, branched bur-reed and yellow iris.
Habits. Single-brooded, being in the larval stage from May to early August, after overwintering as an egg. From late June onwards, the larvae can readily be located inside the stems of reedmace plants, often growing in water, in ditches, dikes and around ponds, by splitting them open carefully. Pupation takes place, head upwards, inside the stems, with the small emergence window about 3–6 cm above. The adults fly from August to early October, with both sexes being attracted to lights placed close to their damp habitats. Mostly recorded within ten kilometres of the coast in south-eastern England; also occurring locally in East Anglia, Dorset, Devon and Cornwall, and south-west Wales.
Plate 44: F. Located in reedmace stem, fully grown. Late July.

Rush Wainscot
Archanara algae Esper
(*cannae* Ochsenheimer)
Larva. 45–50 mm. Body pale green, darker at the segmental divisions, with the dorsal vessel showing darker through the skin; pinacula minute, black; prothoracic and anal plates brownish-green; head orangish-brown, freckled darker.
Foodplants. The inner stems of common club-rush, reedmace and yellow iris.
Habits. A single-brooded insect that occurs in the larval stage from about late May to early August, after overwintering as an egg. It has been stated that the young larva commences to feed in the top shoots of common club-rush, causing withering, before transferring to reedmace or yellow iris to complete the development. During July the larvae can readily be located by carefully splitting reedmace stems and the pupa is formed, head upwards, within the foodplant. The adults fly during August and early September, coming freely to a light placed among the foodplants. A local species, being found in Norfolk, Lincolnshire, Sussex, Surrey and parts of Ireland.
Plate 44: G. Found in reedmace, fully grown. Late July. (GAC)

Large Wainscot
Rhizedra lutosa Hübner
Larva. 35–42 mm. Body dull pinkish-white, with inner parts showing through the translucent skin as greyish; spiracles black and fairly large; prothoracic and anal plates dull orange; head reddish-brown.
Foodplant. The lower stems and roots of common reed.
Habits. Single-brooded, occurring as a larva from April to late July, after overwintering in the egg stage. A difficult larva to find in the wild due to its habit of living within the roots of the foodplant below ground level. The larvae can be located by finding sickly plants, with yellowing leaves, growing on the drier parts of ditches, and digging in the soil beneath. Pupation takes place in the soil and lasts from four to eight weeks, with the adults flying from late August to October, depending on the season. Generally distributed over most of the British Isles, being more frequent in the south.
Plate 44: H. Bred from an adult female to MVL. Late September. (RAB)

Blair's Wainscot
Sedina buettneri Hering
Larva. 25–28 mm. Body yellowish-white, with purplish or maroon subdorsal and spiracular stripes; head, prothoracic and anal plates pale brown (Haggett).
Foodplants. The inner stems of lesser pond-sedge, accepting reed sweet-grass in captivity.
Habits. A single-brooded insect that was formerly resident in the British Isles until the destruction of its habitat during the early 1950s. Since then isolated records of adult moths

have been noted in the southern counties of England, either immigrants or possibly indicating undiscovered colonies. The larva occurs from about April to July, after overwintering as an egg, and feeds internally within the foodplant stems changing to fresh ones whenever necessary. Pupation is stated to take place within the plant, lasting about two months, with the adults flying in late September and October.

Fen Wainscot

Arenostola phragmitidis Hübner

Larva. 28–33 mm. Body yellowish-white, with purplish-brown subdorsal blotching on the abdominal segments; pinacula black, some fairly large; prothoracic plate mainly dark brown, with a pale dorsal streak; anal plate blackish-brown; head glossy black.

Foodplant. The inner stems of common reed.

Habits. Single-brooded, occurring as a larva from April to late June, after overwintering in the egg stage. This is one of the easiest larvae of this group to find, living within the stems about half-way up the plant, entering just above a stem division causing circular scarring in the plant tissue and boring upwards leaving a trail of frass. The larvae change plants when necessary, usually at night, and may then be taken by careful sweeping. Pupation takes place in moss or among plant debris and lasts about a month, with the adults flying in July and August. Locally common in southern and eastern England, ranging northwards to Yorkshire and Cumbria.

Plate 44: I. Located in reed-stem, fully grown. Late June. (SHC)

Brighton Wainscot

Oria musculosa Hübner

Larva. 27–32 mm. Body pale green, with darker green subdorsal and lateral stripes; pinacula black, small; prothoracic and anal plates greenish-brown, both edged with blackish-brown; head pale brown (Haggett).

Foodplants. The inner stems and seeds of various grasses, wheat, barley, oats and rye.

Habits. A single-brooded species, being in the larval stage from April to early June, after overwintering as an egg. Initially, feeding begins in the stems of wayside grasses, and later the larvae move into the more succulent commercial crops to finish their development; starting again in the stem and devouring the unripe seeds within the sheaths during the final instar. Sometimes they can be located in late May and early June by targeting plants that have yellowing leaves and carefully splitting them open. Pupation takes place in a flimsy cocoon within the soil, lasting about six weeks, with the adults flying in late July and early August. This insect has suffered a noticeable contraction of range and population during the last few years with the Salisbury Plain of Wiltshire still being its stronghold.

Small Rufous

Coenobia rufa Haworth

Larva. 18–22 mm. Body flesh-pink, with whitish underparts and an indistinct pale dorsal line; prothoracic plate pale ochreous; anal plate greyish-brown; head yellowish-brown.

Foodplants. The inner stems of jointed rush and soft rush.

Habits. Single-brooded, being in the larval stage from September to the following June, overwintering when still small. During the late spring the larvae may be located by carefully splitting damaged and sickly looking plants growing in the drier parts of fenland and marshy places, their presence often indicated by an accumulation of frass at the stem bases. The larvae change plants when necessary, and eventually pupate within an old stem close to the ground, this stage lasting about a month. Both sexes of the adults can be found flying shortly before dusk from mid-July to mid-August, often ignoring light traps. Widespread, in suitable habitats, over much of southern England and East Anglia; local elsewhere, ranging as far north as Clydesdale in Scotland.

Plate 44: J. Located in stem base of foodplant, nearly fully grown. Early June. (BS)

Treble Lines

Charanyca trigrammica Hufnagel

Larva. 30–34 mm. Body of various shades of brown, with a narrow dark-edged pale dorsal line, a series of dark-edged pale oblique subdorsal markings and an indistinct dark wavy line in the spiracular region; spiracles black, fairly large; head brown.

Foodplants. Various herbaceous plants, including plantains, common knapweed, knotgrass and dandelion.

Habits. A single-brooded insect, being in the larval stage from June to April, overwintering as a fairly large larva. It feeds during mild winter weather and spends most of its development at ground level, hiding in the soil by day. The larvae are very easy to rear from the egg stage, and can sometimes be forced in captivity by keeping them warm. Pupation takes place beneath the ground, lasting about four to six weeks, with the sugar- and light-responsive adults flying from mid-May to early July. Generally distributed, inhabiting woodland, commons and downland, over much of England, Wales and Ireland.

Plate 44: K. Bred from an adult female to MVL. Early June.

The Uncertain

Hoplodrina alsines Brahm

Larva. 27–32 mm. Body of various shades of brown, with dark-edged pale dorsal and subdorsal lines; an indistinct broad pale spiracular line; spiracles black; setae yellowish, short and curved; head light brown.

Foodplants. Various herbaceous plants, such as dock, dandelion, plantain and chickweed.

Habits. Mainly single-brooded, with larvae occurring from July to the following April, probably feeding during mild conditions throughout the winter. They are nocturnal in their habits, not often being met with in the wild, although easily bred from the egg in captivity. When kept warm they may be forced, becoming fully grown in about ten weeks, and occasionally this happens naturally, producing a partial second generation of adults during the autumn. The cocooned pupa is formed in plant litter or soil, with the main brood of adults flying from mid-June to mid-August. Both sexes are attracted to light. Generally distributed over much of the British Isles; local and less frequent in Scotland and Ireland.

Plate 44: L. Bred from an adult female to MVL. Early July.

The Rustic

Hoplodrina blanda Denis & Schiffermüller

Larva. 26–30 mm. Body ochreous-brown, with dark oblique lines emanating from dark brown spots set in the thin pale dorsal line; a dark-edged paler subdorsal line; an indistinct broad greyish stripe beneath the black spiracles; setae yellowish-white, short and curved; head reddish-brown, speckled darker.

Foodplants. Various herbaceous plants, including dock, plantain, dandelion and knotgrass.

Habits. A mostly single-brooded insect, being in the larval

stage from about late July to the following May, overwintering when about half grown. The larvae are difficult to locate in the wild due to their retiring nocturnal habits, but are easily reared from the egg, often producing a second generation when kept warm; this also happens naturally in southern England. Pupation takes place inside a cocoon beneath the soil, with the adults flying from late June to the middle of August. Widely distributed over the greater part of the British Isles; local in Scotland.
Plate 44: M. Bred from an adult female to MVL. Mid-July. (BS)

Powdered Rustic
Hoplodrina superstes Ochsenheimer
Larva. 22–26 mm. Body ochreous-brown, with dark brown oblique lines surrounding the thin indistinct dorsal line and small white pinacula; head brown and mottled darker; setae short and pale grey.
Foodplants. Various herbaceous plants, including dandelion and plantain.
Habits. A single-brooded species that has been suspected of immigrating to Britain on several occasions, the latest record being two adults taken in Devon during 1945. On the continent the larvae occur from September to May with the adults flying from June to August.
Plate 44: N. Courtesy of B. Goater, via D. J. Carter. (NHM)

Vine's Rustic
Hoplodrina ambigua Denis & Schiffermüller
Larva. 27–31 mm. Body pale straw-ochreous, with greyish anterior shading on each segment, a series of distinct V-shaped markings enclosing the fine pale dorsal line on the abdominal segments; lateral area darker, often greyish, spiracular stripe pinkish-grey; head dark brown, marked paler.
Foodplants. Various herbaceous plants, such as dock, dandelion, knotgrass and chickweed.
Habits. A mainly double-brooded species, occurring as a larva from about late September to the following April, and again during the summer. The larvae are best obtained by rearing from the egg, becoming continually brooded when kept warm in captivity. Pupation takes place in an earthen cocoon, lasting about three to six weeks, and the adult insects fly between May and October, with the peaks of emergence being in June and late August to mid-September. Both sexes come freely to light, and females deposit eggs readily in confinement. Well established in southern England and East Anglia, sporadic elsewhere.
Plate 44: O. Bred from an adult female to MVL. Late June.

Small Mottled Willow
Spodoptera exigua Hübner
Larva. 28–31 mm. Body green, with a broken darker dorsal line, pairs of small white dorsal pinacula on each of the abdominal rings and a dark-edged pale spiracular line, often bordered above with lateral blotches, which can be tinged with orangish-pink; head brownish-green. A purplish form also occurs, with various intermediates between this and the more usual green larva.
Foodplants. Probably herbaceous plants in the wild, accepting dandelion, dock and groundsel in captivity.
Habits. A fairly frequent immigrant species that is continually brooded in the warmer parts of its range. The adults usually appear from late July to October, with both sexes coming readily to light and the females laying freely in confinement. It is an easy insect to rear in captivity, with the larval development being quite rapid when kept warm. Pupation takes place in a cocoon among the plant debris, or just in the soil, with this stage sometimes lasting as little as ten days. Most frequently recorded from the southern counties of England.
Plate 44: P. Bred from an adult female to MVL. Late August. (SHC)

Mediterranean Brocade
Spodoptera littoralis Boisduval
(*litura* auctt.)
Larva. 35–45 mm. Body usually purplish-grey, heavily irrorate with white speckling, with pale dorsal and subdorsal lines, a broad greyish-brown subspiracular stripe and black subdorsal blotches on the fourth and eleventh segments; prothoracic plate mainly dark grey; head dark brown. Most larvae are dull-coloured, but brighter, boldly marked forms also occur.
Foodplants. A great variety of plants, accepting *Chrysanthemum* and dandelion in captivity.
Habits. Mainly a tropical and subtropical pest species that is continuously brooded in the normal parts of its range. There have been a few records which are considered to be immigrants, but larvae were discovered during the early 1960s when *Chrysanthemum* plants were imported from the Canary Islands and kept in glass-houses all over southern Britain. The authorities quickly took steps to eradicate what could have been a potential pest to commercial tomato growers. This species has probably never bred in the wild in this country as the larvae require constant warmth to survive.
Plate 44: Q. From Canary Islands stock.

Dark Mottled Willow
Spodoptera cilium Guenée
Larva. 20–23 mm. Body grey, with bold ochreous dorsal and subdorsal stripes; head brown.
Foodplants. Various grasses.
Habits. A scarce immigrant species that has been recently taken in the adult stage on nine occasions since 1990. Abroad it occurs in North Africa, the Canaries, Spain and France with the larvae favouring short-cut grass, such as on lawns and golf-courses.
Plate 44: R. Courtesy of B. Goater, via D. J. Carter. (NHM)

Mottled Rustic
Caradrina morpheus Hufnagel
Larva. 27–32 mm. Body greyish-brown, heavily irrorate with black speckling, with the dorsal line vaguely visible on the thoracic rings where it appears as a series of small yellowish-white spots and dashes. Dorsally, the darker speckling forms indistinct chevrons and appears as dark dashes along the subdorsal ridge; head brown.
Foodplants. Various herbaceous plants, including plantain, dock, dandelion, chickweed and knotgrass.
Habits. Mainly single-brooded, occurring as an active larva from about late July to early November, when it forms an earthen cocoon in which to lie dormant until pupating in the following spring. Although a fairly common insect in southern Britain, the larva is rarely encountered in the wild due to its nocturnal ground-feeding habits, hiding by day in the soil or plant litter. The adults fly from June to early August, coming readily to light, and with the females freely depositing

their eggs in confinement. Some captive larvae feed up quite quickly producing a second generation, as sometimes happens naturally in southern England. Widely distributed over much of England and Wales; local and less frequent in Scotland and Ireland.
Plate 45: A. Bred from an adult female to MVL. Early July.

Pale Mottled Willow

Caradrina clavipalpis Scopoli
(*quadripunctata* Fabricius)
Larva. 28–32 mm. Body greyish-brown, with a fine pale interrupted dorsal line, an indistinct pale subdorsal line and greyish spiracular stripe; prothoracic plate dark greyish-brown, small; head blackish-brown.
Foodplants. The seeds of various grasses, wheat and other cereal crops, the seeds of plantains as well as the foliage; also accepting dandelion leaves in captivity.
Habits. Almost certainly double-brooded in the southern parts of Britain, with the larvae mainly occurring from September to the following spring, and again in the summer. This species may be abundant in grassy places and on agricultural ground, where the larvae have been found in large numbers in sheaves and ricks of cereals. They are very easy to rear in captivity, accepting the foliage of dandelion and plantains throughout their development. Overwintering takes place in the larval stage with most pupating during April or May, to produce the first peak of adults about a month later; although it has been noted that some of the overwintering larvae have not reached the adult stage until August. Larvae obtained from females taken in the spring will often attain full growth within six weeks to produce the second generation of adults during late August, as probably happens in the wild. Widely distributed over most of the British Isles.
Plate 45: B. Bred from an adult female to MVL. Late May.

Silky Wainscot

Chilodes maritimus Tauscher
Larva. 25–28 mm. Body dull ochreous, with a pinkish tinge; dorsal line paler, indistinct except on the thoracic rings; subdorsal line thin, brownish; spiracles small and black; head dark brown.
Foodplants. A variety of vegetable and animal matter, accepting meat fats in captivity.
Habits. A single-brooded insect, being in the larval stage from about August to the following April, living and feeding within the stems of reeds and supplementing its diet of stem-linings with any other vegetable or animal debris that may be available. The larvae can be obtained by persistent searching of old broken stems lying on banks and dryish ground by well-established reed-beds; no external signs have been noted and they cannot bore into undamaged plants. The adults fly from mid-June to mid-August, coming regularly to light. Local in southern England and East Anglia, ranging northwards, in the eastern half of Britain, to Yorkshire.
Plate 45: C. Located in old reed-stem, fully grown. Late March. (DEW)

Marsh Moth

Athetis pallustris Hübner
Larva. 24–28 mm. Body velvety, various shades of brown, with fine incomplete pale dorsal and subdorsal lines and a wavy pinkish-brown subspiracular stripe; darker brown chevrons on the dorsal area of the abdominal segments, extending to obscure the subdorsal line; spiracles black; head blackish-brown and glossy.
Foodplants. Meadow-sweet, plantain and probably other herbaceous plants, accepting dandelion in captivity.
Habits. Single-brooded, being in the larval stage from late June to the following spring, overwintering fully grown, in a flimsy spinning among plant debris, and becoming active for a period before pupating about late April. The larvae have been obtained during late August and September by earlier preparing piles of hay and other plant debris in known localities, and sifting through them carefully. Overwintering in captivity can be successful, if the larvae are kept outside in plant pots filled with growing plantains and about 10 cm of wood-shavings, straw and other dry vegetable debris. The adults fly in late May and June, with only the males coming to light. The females are rarely encountered and their habits are not fully known. A local insect, being recorded from Lincolnshire and the fens of Huntingdonshire, Cambridgeshire and Norfolk.
Plate 45: D. Found by sifting plant debris, nearly fully grown. Early September. (BS)

Porter's Rustic

Athetis hospes Freyer
Larva. 22–26 mm. Body dark grey, almost black dorsally and beneath the pale subdorsal area, a pale flesh-coloured subspiracular region and a dark brown head.
Foodplants. Various low-growing herbaceous plants, including dandelion and dock.
Habits. An irregular vagrant species that has been taken as an adult on two occasions, both in south-west England, in 1978 and 1993. Abroad, the range covers much of southern Europe, where it is at least double-brooded.
Plate 45: E. Courtesy of M. R. Honey/D. J. Carter. (NHM)

Reddish Buff

Acosmetia caliginosa Hübner
Larva. 28–32 mm. Body bright green, with fine yellowish-white dorsal and subdorsal lines and a bold yellowish-white spiracular line, below which is another thin pale line; head yellowish-green.
Foodplants. Saw-wort.
Habits. A single-brooded insect, occurring in the larval stage during July and August. The larvae feed mostly at night, hiding by day stretched out on the lower stems and under the leaves of the foodplant, where they can be found by careful searching. Pupation takes place in a cocoon just below the soil and lasts until the following late May or June, with both sexes of the adults being attracted to light. At present this species is afforded protection from collecting as it is on the verge of extinction. It was formerly found in the New Forest and other parts of Hampshire, but now seems to be restricted to the Isle of Wight.
Plate 45: F. Bred from an adult female to MVL. Mid-June. (BS)

The Anomalous

Stilbia anomala Haworth
Larva. 27–32 mm. Body yellowish-green or chestnut-brown, with fine pale dorsal and subdorsal lines and a broad spiracular stripe, which is greenish-white in the commoner form, and greyish in the brown individuals; spiracles black, especially large on the first and eleventh segments; head green or greyish-brown.
Foodplants. Wavy hair-grass and other grasses.

Habits. Single-brooded, being in the larval stage from September to the following March or April, feeding nocturnally in mild weather throughout the winter months. The larvae can be swept, or searched for, during the early spring, and are easy to rear in captivity when taken at this point of their development. The cocooned pupa is formed in the soil, with the larva lying dormant within for a few weeks before changing. Only the adult males seem to be readily attracted to light, with the females being found by searching vegetation after dark; they fly in August and September. Widespread over much of Scotland, Wales, northern and south-western England; local in the Breck district of East Anglia, the Midlands and Ireland.
Plate 45: G. Found at night on grass stem, fully grown. Mid-March. (BS)

Rosy Marbled

Elaphria venustula Hübner
Larva. 14–17 mm. Body dark reddish-brown, with swollen second to fifth segments, a fine orange dorsal line, a series of indistinct diamond-shaped markings dorsally and small red or white spots laterally on the fourth ring; head greyish-green, marked with black.
Foodplants. The flowers of cinquefoil, tormentil, bramble and broom in captivity.
Habits. A single-brooded insect, occurring in the larval stage from late June to August. The larvae are most easily obtained by rearing from the egg on potted cinquefoil plants, pupating in a subterranean cocoon for overwintering. The adults fly from late May to early July, although females do not appear to be greatly attracted to light and are more likely to be taken by netting at dusk. Widespread over parts of south-eastern England, inhabiting open woodland.
Plate 45: H. Bred from an adult female to MVL. Mid-June.

Small Yellow Underwing

Panemeria tenebrata Scopoli
(*arbuti* Fabricius)
Larva. 17–20 mm. Body whitish-green, with a darker dorsal line, a white subdorsal line and a broad yellowish-white spiracular stripe; prothoracic plate pale green; head brownish-green, with small black dots.
Foodplant. The seed capsules of common mouse-ear.
Habits. Single-brooded, occurring as a larva during June and July. The larvae can readily be obtained by picking the flowers and seed capsules of the foodplant, growing in meadows and on roadside verges, during late June and early July, then placing the plants well spread out on white paper in a spacious container. Any inhabited capsules will then be indicated by the larval frass beneath. Pupation takes place just under the soil and lasts until the following May. The adults fly in sunshine during May and early June, visiting flowers and looking very similar to several of the day-flying pyralid moths. Widely distributed, but local, over much of England and Wales; also recorded from parts of lowland Scotland.
Plate 45: I. Found in picked seed capsules, fully grown. Late June. (SHC)

SUBFAMILY: HELIOTHINAE

Pease Blossom

Periphanes delphinii Linnaeus
Larva. 30–35 mm. Body violet-grey, with a black dorsal line and streaks, yellow lateral lines and black pinacula; head yellow (MBGBI).
Foodplants. Larkspur and monk's-hood.
Habits. Twelve adult specimens of this species of uncertain status were recorded in Britain during the nineteenth century, with the last being seen in 1893. Its range covers southern and eastern Europe, being single-brooded, with the larvae occurring in July and August, overwintering as a pupa and the adults flying in May and June.

Bordered Sallow

Pyrrhia umbra Hufnagel
(*marginata* Fabricius)
Larva. 32–37 mm. Body variable in colour, usually being shades of green and also having pink, olive, brown, grey and almost black forms; dorsal line broadish, edged paler; subdorsal line pale and narrow; spiracular stripe broad, yellow or whitish; pinacula black; prothoracic and anal plates black; head reddish-brown or orange.
Foodplants. The flowers and seeds of common restharrow and spiny restharrow, also accepting the foliage of hazel, flowers of toadflax and fruits of runner beans in captivity.
Habits. A single-brooded species that occurs in the larval stage during July and August. The larvae are readily obtained by sweeping, especially at night when more active, and are very easy to rear in captivity, although they have been known to devour smaller larvae of the same species when fresh foodplant is unavailable. Pupation takes place just in the soil, and although they overwinter in this stage, those in captivity will often produce adults after about three weeks, when kept warm. The adults fly in June and July, coming to sugar and light, with most females freely laying eggs in confinement when required to do so. Widespread, on sandy and calcareous soils, over much of the southern half of England; mainly coastal in Wales, Ireland and south-eastern Scotland.
Plate 45: J. Bred from an adult female to sugar. Late June.

Scarce Bordered Straw

Heliothis armigera Hübner
Larva. 35–40 mm. Body variable in colour and markings, most being various shades of green or brown, also orange or yellow, with the heavily marked individuals having a darker dorsal line, a pale subdorsal line and sometimes a broad paler spiracular line. The pinacula can also be variable in size and either black or white; prothoracic plate weak, variable in colour; head olive-brown to brownish-green.
Foodplants. In captivity the flowers, leaves and fruits of various plants, including garden *Geranium*, marigold, carnation and tomato; also cooked chicken flesh.
Habits. A regular but uncommon immigrant species that is also accidentally imported as a larva in fruits, vegetables and flowers from southern Europe and elsewhere. The larvae are fairly easy to rear, given constant warmth, although they should not be overcrowded as cannibalistic tendencies have been noted. Growth can be rapid, the larvae taking about one month to fully develop from hatching, and the pupal stage is also quite short when kept in an incubator at a constant 25° centigrade. Most records of probable immigrant adults occur during September and October, either at light or ivy bloom, coming from the southern coastal counties of England, with the females usually being fertile and laying readily in captivity.
Plate 45: K. Bred from a female adult to MVL. Early October.

Marbled Clover
Heliothis viriplaca Hufnagel
(*dipsacea* Linnaeus)
Larva. 30–35 mm. Body green or pinkish-brown, with a darker dorsal line and yellowish-white or white subdorsal and subspiracular lines, the latter being slightly the wider; spiracles pinkish, ringed with black; head dark green or brownish-green, dotted with black.
Foodplants. The flowers and seeds of hawk's-beard, clover, white campion, bladder campion, restharrow and other plants.
Habits. A mainly single-brooded insect, usually occurring in the larval stage from late July to September, except in good seasons when the larvae of a partial second generation may still be found up to the middle of October. They can be taken by careful sweeping on waste ground and breckland, especially at dusk when they become more active, and are not difficult to rear in captivity, although many suffer from parasitism. The overwintering pupae are formed in a cocoon just below the soil and the adults often fly in sunshine during June and early July, and again in August when the second generation occurs. Locally common in the Breck district of East Anglia; also noted from parts of Wiltshire, Hampshire and elsewhere, with some records suspected to be immigrants from the continent.
Plate 45: L. Swept at dusk, nearly fully grown. Early September. (SHC)

Shoulder-striped Clover
Heliothis maritima Graslin
Larva. 30–35 mm. Body dark olive-green or rarely reddish-brown, with a darker dorsal line, a yellowish-white subdorsal line and a white subspiracular stripe; head dark green or greenish-brown, speckled with black. Very similar to the previous species (*H. viriplaca*).
Foodplants. The flowers of cross-leaved heath, bell heather and heather, also the seed-heads of bog asphodel and accepting sliced runner beans in captivity.
Habits. Single-brooded, being in the larval stage from about late July to the end of September, pupating in a silken cocoon beneath the soil for overwintering. The larvae can be obtained by sweeping from mid-August onwards, especially at night and on dull overcast days, and are fairly easy to rear in confinement, preferring sandy soil in which to pupate. In some years they suffer highly from parasites. The adults fly rapidly in bright sunshine from the middle of June to mid-July, being difficult to follow over the heather with the eye. A local species found on the open heathlands of Surrey, Hampshire, Dorset, Devon and Cornwall.
Plate 45: M. Swept at night, about half grown. Late August.

Bordered Straw
Heliothis peltigera Denis & Schiffermüller
Larva. 34–38 mm. Body usually pale green, sometimes yellowish-green, with variable amounts of pink banding around the segments, a darker incomplete dorsal line and pale yellow or white subdorsal and subspiracular lines; pinacula tiny, white or yellow; setae longish, white; head usually green, mottled darker.
Foodplants. The flowers of sticky groundsel, garden marigolds and common restharrow.
Habits. An immigrant species that occurs in variable numbers, being mainly recorded from the southern coastal counties of England. The adults usually appear from late June to late August at light traps and the larvae are most easily obtained by searching sticky groundsel plants growing on coastal shingle beaches from about mid-July to early October, preferring to be kept fairly warm, when reared in captivity. Pupation takes place in a slight cocoon in moss or the soil and paler-coloured adults will result if they have been bred throughout in an incubator.
Plate 45: N. Found on sticky groundsel, fully grown. Late August.

Eastern Bordered Straw
Heliothis nubigera Herrich-Schäffer
Larva. 32–38 mm. Body reddish-brown, with a darker dorsal line, whitish subdorsal lines, interrupted with black and a brownish lateral line (Seitz).
Foodplants. Recorded abroad on various wild and cultivated plants, including tomato and *Chrysanthemum*.
Habits. An eastern Mediterranean species that has been recorded as an adult in Britain on four occasions, three in 1958 and another in 1992. In the European parts of its range it is at least bivoltine, and continuously brooded in the subtropics.

Spotted Clover
Protoschinia scutosa Denis & Schiffermüller
Larva. 30–35 mm. Body green, with darker dorsal and lateral lines, black pinacula and a dark-marked yellow head (MBGBI).
Foodplants. Field wormwood and goosefoot.
Habits. A very scarce immigrant species that has been recorded as an adult in Britain about fifteen times this century, not including more than thirty that were observed in Devon during 1943. On the continent, in its natural range of central and southern Europe, this insect is considered to be double-brooded, with the larvae occurring in June and July and again in September and October, before overwintering as a pupa.

SUBFAMILY: ACONTIINAE

Purple Marbled
Eublemma ostrina Hübner
Larva. 14–17 mm. Body yellowish-grey, with a dull yellow dorsal line, and indistinct subdorsal and lateral lines; pinacula minute, brown; setae short, yellowish-white; prothoracic plate brown, with pale markings; head dark brown.
Foodplants. The flowers and seed-heads of thistles.
Habits. A scarce immigrant species that has several generations per year in the warmer parts of its range. Until 1992 this species had never been proven to breed in the British Isles, but in that year larvae were found in southern England and Ireland, after an unusually large migration of the species. They were found by careful searching of thistle-heads that had gone to seed and rearing them to the adult stage in captivity was not difficult. Many records of the adults in Britain have occurred during late May and June, so August would probably be the best time to search for the larvae of this insect.
Plate 45: O. Found in carline thistle seed-heads, almost fully grown. Mid-August. (BS)

Small Marbled
Eublemma parva Hübner
Larva. 10–13 mm. Body pale yellowish-green, with a purplish-red dorsal line; prothoracic plate, true legs and head black (MBGBI).

Foodplants. The flowers of common fleabane and ploughman's-spikenard.
Habits. A scarce immigrant species, of which the larvae have rarely been found in Britain, usually occurring between July and September, and most likely to be found in the coastal counties of southern England. They bore into the budding flowers and change to fresh examples when necessary, with the development taking from about three to four weeks, and pupating in a strong cocoon beneath the florets. The adults fly mainly at night and most records are from moths being found at light, during the late spring and early summer.

Marbled White Spot

Protodeltote pygarga Hufnagel
(*fasciana* auctt.)
Larva. 18–23 mm. Body reddish-brown, with a distinct dark brown dorsal stripe, a narrow dark-edged pinkish-brown subdorsal line and a pale wavy subspiracular line; first two pairs of prolegs absent; head pale reddish-brown, with darker freckling.
Foodplants. False-brome, purple moor-grass and associated species.
Habits. A single-brooded insect that occurs in the larval stage from July to September, feeding mainly at night. The larvae can readily be swept from grasses growing in woodland rides and on commons, and are not difficult to rear in captivity, pupating in a cocoon just below the soil for overwintering. The adults fly from late May to early July and are attracted to light, with females laying eggs freely in confinement, when supplied with foodplant. A fairly common species in southern England and north-west Wales; local in South Wales, parts of the Midlands and in south-western Ireland.
Plate 45: P. Bred from a female adult to MVL. Mid-June. (SHC)

Pretty Marbled

Deltote deceptoria Scopoli
Larva. 18–23 mm. Body pale green, with a dark grey dorsal line and yellowish-white subdorsal lines; head green, with white streaks (MBGBI).
Foodplants. Grasses, including timothy.
Habits. A single-brooded species that is usually considered to be a scarce immigrant. It may have bred in the woodlands around Ham Street in Kent from 1948 to 1956, as six of the fourteen records of adults come from this area. The larval period lasts from late June to August, before overwintering as a pupa, with the adults emerging in the following May and June.

Silver Hook

Deltote uncula Clerck
Larva. 23–26 mm. Body green, with yellow segmental divisions, a dark green dorsal line and an indistinct pale spiracular line; prolegs on the sixth and seventh rings absent; head green.
Foodplants. Wood-sedge, tufted hair-grass and other related sedges and grasses.
Habits. Probably single-brooded, occurring in the larval stage from about mid-July to September or later. The larvae can be swept, especially at night when more active, from sedges and grasses growing on wet heathland, in fens and other marshy places, and are not difficult to rear in captivity, overwintering as a pupa in a strong cocoon beneath moss or the soil. The adults fly mostly during June and July, with those seen later in August possibly being part of a small second generation. They come in small numbers to light and may also be disturbed from grass tussocks during the day. A local species, being widely distributed over much of west Wales, south-western and western Scotland and England, except the Midlands and north-east; also a few scattered records from Ireland.
Plate 45: Q. Swept at night on boggy heathland, fully grown. August.

Silver Barred

Deltote bankiana Fabricius
(*olivana* Denis & Schiffermüller)
(*argentula* Hübner)
Larva. 22–25 mm. Body darkish green, with a darker dorsal line, a distinct white subdorsal line and a vague yellowish spiracular line; prolegs on sixth and seventh rings almost absent; head yellowish-green.
Foodplants. Purple moor-grass, smooth meadow-grass and other grasses, accepting annual meadow-grass in captivity.
Habits. A single-brooded species, which occurs in the larval stage during July and August, and may be taken by sweeping at night. The larvae are usually very easy to rear in confinement, pupating in a silken cocoon close to the ground for overwintering. The adults fly in June and early July, being readily disturbed from herbage during warm still evenings, and later they come to light. A very local insect, being common in some of the fens of Cambridgeshire, the bogs of south-western Ireland and in a small dampish coastal site in east Kent; this locality possibly being established by immigrant moths, examples of which occasionally occur elsewhere in southern England.
Plate 45: R. Bred from an adult female netted at dusk. Early July.

Spotted Sulphur

Emmelia trabealis Scopoli
(*sulphuralis* Linnaeus)
Larva. 22–25 mm. Body dark brown, with darker dorsal and subdorsal lines and a yellow spiracular stripe; prolegs absent on the sixth segment; head brown (MBGBI).
Foodplant. The flowers and leaves of field bindweed.
Habits. A single-brooded species that was formerly found in the Breck district of East Anglia, before the last individual was seen in 1960. The larvae occurred during July and early August, before pupating in a cocoon for overwintering, with the day-flying adults emerging the following mid-June to early July. On the continent, it ranges throughout western Europe but is stated to be declining.

Pale Shoulder

Acontia lucida Hufnagel
(*solaris* Denis & Schiffermüller)
Larva. 28–35 mm. Body reddish-brown, with a small dorsal hump on the eleventh ring, oblique subdorsal marks on the fourth to sixth segments and a pale brown subspiracular line; prolegs absent on the sixth and seventh rings; head brown.
Foodplants. Field bindweed, common mallow and marsh-mallow.
Habits. A double-brooded species that was taken as an adult several times in southern England during the nineteenth century, followed by six more in recent years. The larvae occur from June to July and again in late August and September before overwintering as pupae. On the continent, its range includes central and southern France and much of Iberia.

Plate 49: I. Bred from a female adult (Portugal). Late September. (D. Warner/J. Firmin)

SUBFAMILY: CHLOEPHORINAE

Cream-bordered Green Pea

Earias clorana Linnaeus

Larva. 15–18 mm. Body plump, reddish-brown laterally, with a broad yellowish-green or yellowish-brown dorsal stripe enclosing the fine brown dorsal line; pairs of dark brown raised pinacula dorsally on the fifth and eleventh segments; head brown.

Foodplants. Sallow, willow and osier.

Habits. Mainly single-brooded, with the larval stage lasting from about late June to August, and again in September and early October from those adults of the partial second generation. In some localities, especially on coastal shingle and sand dunes, this species may be quite common and then the larvae can readily be located in the spun terminal shoots of sallow bushes; rearing them in captivity is not difficult. The overwintering pupae are formed in a tough cocoon, usually located on twigs or branches of the foodplant, with the adults flying from late May to July and again in August. A local species inhabiting damp places and fens mainly in the eastern half of England, ranging as far north as South Yorkshire.

Plate 46: A. Located in spinning, almost fully grown. Late July.

Spiny Bollworm

Earias biplaga Walker

Larva. Apparently undescribed in European literature.

Foodplants. Cotton and other plants.

Habits. A suspected immigrant or accidentally imported insect that has occurred as an adult in Britain on two occasions, in 1964 and 1982. Its natural range does not include Europe, although in tropical Africa it is considered a serious pest species.

Egyptian Bollworm

Earias insulana Boisduval

Larva. 16–20 mm. Body ochreous, with greyish subdorsal markings, small orange and black pinacula and dark brown head; setae greyish.

Foodplants. Cotton and other plants.

Habits. A suspected immigrant or accidentally imported insect that can be a serious pest of cotton crops in north-west Africa. Two adult specimens have been recorded in Britain, both during the 1960s, and larvae and pupae have been found in produce from abroad. It occurs in central Spain, Portugal, Sicily and Malta.

Plate 46: B. Courtesy of Carlos Gomez de Aizpurua.

Scarce Silver-lines

Bena bicolorana Fuessly

(*prasinana* auctt.)

Larva. 30–35 mm. Body yellowish-green, sometimes tinged with orangish-brown, with a distinct dorsal hump on the second segment, a pair of yellowish-white dorsal lines, an indistinct yellowish spiracular line and vague oblique yellowish subdorsal streaks on the abdominal rings; head green, retracted into the body when at rest.

Foodplants. Oak; has also been found and reared on birch.

Habits. A single-brooded species, being in the larval stage from August to the following late May, overwintering fully exposed among the oak buds as a small larva, being dull brown in colour during hibernation. Feeding resumes during the spring on the fresh foliage and during May the larvae can readily be beaten from mature oaks growing in woodland and parkland. When taken at this point of their development, they are easy to rear in captivity, pupating for about four to six weeks in a strong ochreous cocoon that resembles the hull of a boat, spun up on the underside of a leaf. The adults fly during late June and July, coming readily to light. Widely distributed over much of England and Wales, ranging northwards to Cumbria and Yorkshire.

Plate 46: C. Beaten from oak, fully grown. Late May.

Green Silver-lines

Pseudoips prasinana Linnaeus

(*fagana* Fabricius)

Larva. 34–38 mm. Body green, heavily mottled with small yellow markings, with yellowish-white subdorsal lines and a distinct clear yellow collar behind the bright green head.

Foodplants. Oak, beech, hazel, birch and sometimes other trees.

Habits. Mostly single-brooded, occurring as a larva from July to September and sometimes later from the very occasional second generation. The larvae can readily be obtained by beating, especially from mature oaks growing at the edges of woodland rides, and are very easy to rear in confinement. Pupation for overwintering takes place inside a strong cocoon beneath a leaf that will later fall; also sometimes in a bark crevice or among plant litter. The adults fly mainly in June and July, with both sexes coming to light. Widespread and not uncommon over much of England and Wales; local in southern Scotland and Ireland.

Plate 46: D. Beaten from oak, fully grown. Early September.

SUBFAMILY: SARROTHRIPINAE

Oak Nycteoline

Nycteola revayana Scopoli

Larva. 22–26 mm. Body green, with yellow segmental divisions and long thin white setae; spiracles tiny, surrounded by yellow; head yellowish-green.

Foodplant. Oak.

Habits. A single-brooded insect, being in the larval stage from about mid-May to late July, which can be obtained in small numbers by beating. The larvae are not difficult to rear in captivity, pupating in a cocoon for about four to six weeks before the adults emerge. These are on the wing from late August to the following May, feeding at ivy bloom and over-ripe berries before hibernating and appearing again during the spring. Widespread over much of the southern half of Britain; local and less frequent elsewhere, ranging northwards to Ross-shire.

Plate 46: E. Beaten from oak, fully grown. Late July.

SUBFAMILY: PANTHEINAE

Nut-tree Tussock

Colocasia coryli Linnaeus

Larva. 32–36 mm. Body variable in colour being greyish, pinkish or ochreous, often with a black dorsal stripe, a paler subdorsal line and usually a wavy white or yellow spiracular line. Setae mainly greyish, with the lateral setae on the second segment being longish, facing forwards and coloured orange or black, and those dorsally on the fourth, fifth and eleventh rings being orange or black; head usually reddish-brown.

Foodplants. Birch, beech, hazel, field maple and other deciduous trees.
Habits. A double-brooded insect in southern Britain, single in the north, with the larvae occurring from late May to late July and during September and early October; those in the north being found from about mid-July to early September. They can be obtained by beating at night, mainly resting between spun leaves by day, and are quite easy to rear in captivity. Pupation for overwintering takes place in a cocoon formed among plant litter or moss. The adults fly from late April to early June and again during August in the south (June and July in the north), with mostly males coming to light. Widespread in woodland, on commons and heathland over the southern half of Britain; local in northern England, North Wales, Scotland and Ireland.
Plate 46: F. Beaten from birch, fully grown. Late September.

SUBFAMILY: PLUSIINAE

Golden Twin-spot

Chrysodeixis chalcites Esper
Larva. 34–38 mm. Body pale yellowish-green, with a narrow whitish dorsal line, bordered on each side by three more wavy white lines; spiracular line darker green, edged below with a white stripe; spiracles black, fairly large; prolegs absent on sixth and seventh rings; head glassy green, with thin black lateral streaks.
Foodplants. *Chrysanthemum*, wood sage, viper's bugloss and other plants on the continent, accepting common nettle in captivity.
Habits. A very scarce immigrant species that has yet to be proven to breed in the wild in Britain. The adult moths have been taken sparingly over the years, usually in September and October, at light traps and the resulting larvae have been successfully bred by keeping them warm and supplying them with a diet of common nettle. The larval development is quite rapid, taking about a month, with the cocooned pupae lasting as little as fourteen days. In its usual range of North Africa and the Canary Islands, this species is continuously brooded.
Plate 46: G. Bred from a female adult to MVL. Early October. (AJD)

Tunbridge Wells Gem

Chrysodeixis acuta Walker
Larva. 34–38 mm. Body pale green, with a white-edged darker dorsal line, a pair of white subdorsal lines and a yellowish-white spiracular line; head green (MBGBI).
Foodplants. Recorded abroad on tomato, kidney bean and honeysuckle, accepting common nettle and pellitory-of-the-wall in captivity.
Habits. A very scarce immigrant species that has occurred in Britain only as an adult. The normal range of this insect includes the Canary Islands and North Africa, where it is continuously brooded.

Scar Bank Gem

Ctenoplusia limbirena Guenée
Larva. Apparently undescribed in European literature.
Foodplants. *Salvia*, *Verbascum*, *Althaea* and many other plants (South).
Habits. A mainly subtropical and tropical species that is continuously brooded throughout much of its range, and has occurred in Britain as an immigrant adult on ten occasions since 1947.

The Ni Moth

Trichoplusia ni Hübner
Larva. 33–38 mm. Body bluish-green, with greenish-white subdorsal lines bordered on each side by a finer line of the same colour; spiracular line white, edged above with darker green and having a black wart above each white spiracle; prolegs on sixth and seventh rings absent; head translucent brownish-green, smallish.
Foodplants. Garden marigold, sea rocket and abroad many other plants, accepting cabbage, lettuce and common nettle in captivity.
Habits. A scarce immigrant species that is most often reported from the southern coastal counties as adults during August, and has been proven to breed in the British Isles. Many times larvae have been obtained from fertile adult females, and rearing them is usually successful when kept fairly warm. The larval development can be rapid, attaining full growth in about four weeks, with the pupal duration also being short. This insect's normal distribution covers many subtropical regions, where it is sometimes considered a pest species.
Plate 46: H. Bred from a female adult to MVL. Late August. (DB)

Slender Burnished Brass

Diachrysia orichalcea Fabricius
(*aurifera* Hübner)
Larva. 30–35 mm. Body bright green, with a dark green dorsal line, a white subdorsal line, bordered on each side by finer wavy lines and a yellowish-white spiracular line, edged above with darker green; spiracles white, ringed with black and each having a prominent black wart slightly above; other pinacula white; setae whitish, quite long; true legs black; prolegs on sixth and seventh rings absent; head green, with a brownish tinge and thin black lateral streaks.
Foodplants. In captivity the leaves of potato and dandelion, also *Chrysanthemum*.
Habits. A very rare immigrant species that has never been proven to breed naturally in the British Isles. Most records of adults have been made between late August and October at light, and larvae have been bred from these on occasion. They require warmth for successful rearing, becoming fully developed in about a month and pupating inside a silken cocoon among leaves for about two weeks. Also, larvae have been noted when accidentally imported in produce from warmer regions overseas, where they are continuously brooded.
Plate 46: I. Bred from a female adult to MVL. Late August. (DB)

Burnished Brass

Diachrysia chrysitis Linnaeus
Larva. 35–40 mm. Body green, with white chevrons along the dorsal ridge, a white subdorsal line, straight on the thoracic rings, wavy on the abdominals and a bold white spiracular line, edged above with dark green; prolegs on sixth and seventh segments absent; pinacula small and white; setae white, tinged with orange; head darkish green.
Foodplants. Common nettle, white dead-nettle and probably other herbaceous plants.
Habits. A double-brooded species in the southern parts of Britain, with the larvae occurring during the summer and from September to the following May, overwintering when still quite small. Single-brooded in the north, with the larvae from about August to June. They can sometimes be found at night, during the spring and summer, when actively feeding, hiding by day low down on the plants or between spun

leaves, and are very easy to rear in captivity. The pupa is formed in a brown papery cocoon on the underside of the foodplant leaves and normally lasts about three weeks, with the adults mainly flying in June and early July, and again during August and September. Widely distributed over the greater part of the British Isles, although more local and less frequent in the north.
Plate 46: J. Bred from an adult female to MVL. Late June. (RM)

Scarce Burnished Brass
Diachrysia chryson Esper
Larva. 30–35 mm. Body yellowish-green, with a series of broken white dorsal lines, a yellowish-white subdorsal line, that is complete only on the thoracic rings and a bold white spiracular line; true legs pale green, tipped with pink; prolegs on segments six and seven absent; head plain green.
Foodplant. Hemp-agrimony.
Habits. Single-brooded, being in the larval stage from about September to the following mid-June, overwintering when still quite small. The larvae seem to prefer plants growing in the shade and during late May and early June may be located by first searching for plants showing leaf damage or having frass at the leaf-bases and then carefully examining the stems and undersides of the leaves. If disturbed, they often throw themselves from the plant and end up in the plant litter, then becoming difficult to find. When taken into captivity they are not difficult to rear and pupate in a silken cocoon beneath a foodplant leaf for about a month. The adults fly in late July and August, with both sexes being attracted to light. A local species, inhabiting river banks, water-meadows and fenland, mostly recorded from Hampshire, Berkshire, West Sussex and south-west Wales.
Plate 46: K. Located under foodplant leaf, fully grown. Early June.

Dewick's Plusia
Macdunnoughia confusa Stephens
(*gutta* Guenée)
Larva. 33–38 mm. Body green, with white dorsal lines, white or greenish-white subdorsal lines and a broad white spiracular line above which are a series of black pinacula; head green, heavily marked with black; prolegs absent on sixth and seventh rings.
Foodplants. Common nettle, yarrow, mayweed, field wormwood and other plants.
Habits. A very scarce immigrant species that has been recorded as an adult in Britain on twenty-seven occasions since 1951. In northern Europe the insect is double-brooded, with the larvae occurring during June and July, and again from October to the following early spring.
Plate 46: L. Bred from a female adult to MVL. (AJD)

Golden Plusia
Polychrysia moneta Fabricius
Larva. 33–38 mm. Body plump, bright green, with a darker green dorsal line, bordered by whitish or yellowish toning; subdorsal line white, obvious only on the thoracic rings; spiracular line white, edged above with darker green; prolegs absent on sixth and seventh rings; head green, unmarked.
Foodplants. Garden *Delphinium* and monk's-hood; also has been reared on wormwood and mugwort in captivity.
Habits. A mainly single-brooded insect, being in the larval stage from the autumn to the following June, overwintering when still very small, and in the southern counties a partial second brood may occur from the earliest adults, the larvae of these feeding up rapidly during July and August. When small the larvae live in a web, sometimes gregariously and later fully exposed, usually on the undersides of the leaves. It is almost exclusively a garden species and the larvae can readily be located by searching on plants showing leaf damage. Pupation takes place in a yellow silken cocoon on the underside of the foodplant leaves, with the adults flying from late June to early August, and sometimes again in September. Widespread, but rather local, throughout much of England and Wales; also recorded from southern Scotland.
Plate 46: M. Located on garden *Delphinium*, fully grown. Early June. (SHC)

Purple-shaded Gem
Euchalcia variabilis Pillar & Mitterpacher
(*illustris* Fabricius)
Larva. 30–35 mm. Body green, with a bold yellow spiracular stripe and small black pinacula; prolegs absent on rings six and seven; head and true legs dark brown (Spuler).
Foodplants. Monk's-hood and larkspur.
Habits. This single-brooded species was stated to have been taken as an adult during the nineteenth century. Abroad, it is mainly a montane insect occurring in the larval stage from August to the following early May, with the adults flying from June to early August.

Gold Spot
Plusia festucae Linnaeus
Larva. 36–42 mm. Body green, with a total of six thin yellowish-white lines along the dorsal and subdorsal areas and a bold pale yellowish-white spiracular line; spiracles smallish and indistinct; prolegs on segments six and seven absent; head green. Probably indistinguishable from the following species (*P. putnami*).
Foodplants. Various grasses, sedges and other low-growing plants, including yellow iris and bur-reeds, also accepting grey sallow and common nettle in captivity.
Habits. A double-brooded insect in southern Britain, univoltine in the north, occurring in the larval stage from the autumn to about late May and again during July and August in the south, overwintering when still very small. The larvae are best obtained by rearing from the egg, these being laid quite freely by adult females that may be found at light from mid-June to late July and again in late August and September. The larvae are not difficult to rear in captivity and may be forced to develop faster by keeping them warm, pupating in a strong silken cocoon spun up between leaves. Widely distributed, usually inhabiting damp places, throughout much of the British Isles.
Plate 46: N. Bred from a female adult to MVL. Late August.

Lempke's Gold Spot
Plusia putnami Grote
Larva. 36–42 mm. Body green, with six thin yellowish-white lines along the dorsal and subdorsal regions and a pale yellowish-white spiracular line; prolegs absent on sixth and seventh rings; head green. Seemingly indistinguishable from the previous species (*P. festucae*).
Foodplants. Yorkshire-fog, wood small-reed and probably other related marshland grasses.
Habits. Single-brooded, being in the larval stage from about August to the following late May, overwintering when still quite small. So far it seems that all attempts to rear this insect from the egg have been unsuccessful, with the larvae dying from an unknown cause prior to or during hiberna-

tion. They can be obtained by careful sweeping or searching at night during late April and May and when taken at this point of their development are fairly easy to rear to the adult stage. Pupation takes place in a strong silken cocoon spun up among the foodplant and lasts about six weeks, with the adults flying during July and early August. Mostly recorded from the fens and broads of East Anglia, the northern half of England and parts of southern Scotland.
Plate 46: O. Swept at night, almost fully grown. Mid-May. (JF)

Silver Y
Autographa gamma Linnaeus
Larva. 32–38 mm. Body variable in colour, usually of some shade of green, with a darker dorsal line, edged with a fine wavy white line, a broader white subdorsal line and a conspicuous yellowish spiracular line, bordered above with dark green; pinacula white, with short greyish setae; true legs pale brown; prolegs on sixth and seventh rings absent; head green or brownish-green, with a bold black lateral streak. An almost black form also occurs.
Foodplants. Various garden and wild herbaceous plants, including dandelion, dock, common nettle, common toadflax, clover and sometimes cultivated cabbage, peas and other vegetables.
Habits. A frequent immigrant species that usually occurs in good numbers in most years and can become abundant with successive migrations and home-bred individuals by the autumn. The first adults tend to appear about May and the resulting larvae can then be continuously found until they are killed by the first frosts of winter. In the wild the life-cycle from egg to adult takes about eight weeks at normal summer temperatures, with this period being dramatically shortened when they are kept warm in confinement. Pupation takes place inside a silken cocoon on the foodplant or among plant debris and can last as little as twelve days. The adults are often seen by day, and at night they can swarm to light traps in favourable seasons or during mass migrations. Recorded throughout most parts of the British Isles, being most frequent in the southern coastal counties.
Plate 46: P. Found on toadflax, fully grown. Late July.

Beautiful Golden Y
Autographa pulchrina Haworth
Larva. 33–38 mm. Body green, with a darker dorsal line, edged by a series of thin undulating white lines, an obviously separate subdorsal white line and a bold white stripe just above the spiracles; pinacula small and white, with short gingery or black setae; prolegs on sixth and seventh rings absent; true legs greenish, tipped with dark brown; head green, with a bold black lateral streak.
Foodplants. Various herbaceous plants, such as common nettle, white dead-nettle, burdock, groundsel and honeysuckle.
Habits. A single-brooded species, that occurs as a larva from about July or August to the following May, slightly later in the north, overwintering when still quite small. Feeding recommences during the spring, mainly at night, and then the larvae may be found by careful searching or by looking under burdock leaves that show signs of damage. The pupa is formed in a cocoon, usually spun up in a folded foodplant leaf, and lasts about three to four weeks, with the adults flying in June and July. Females will lay eggs freely in captivity and the resulting larvae can easily be forced by keeping them warm, to produce a second generation in confinement. Widespread and fairly common over the greater part of the British Isles.
Plate 46: Q. Bred from a female adult to MVL. Late June.

Plain Golden Y
Autographa jota Linnaeus
Larva. 35–40 mm. Body green, with a darker dorsal line, edged by a series of wavy thin white lines, a fine yellowish-white subdorsal line and a more obvious yellowish or white line just above the spiracles; pinacula whitish, with short setae; prolegs absent on rings six and seven; true legs generally tipped with green; head green, with a bold lateral black streak.
Foodplants. Various herbaceous plants, including common nettle, dead-nettle, dandelion, groundsel and honeysuckle, accepting sallow, hawthorn, chickweed and dock in captivity.
Habits. Single-brooded, occurring in the larval stage from about August to the following May or June, overwintering when still small. The larvae may be found at night after hibernation and when taken at this point of their development may be successfully reared to the adult stage. The cocooned pupae are usually formed beneath a foodplant leaf and last about four weeks, with the adults flying from late June to early August, and coming freely to light. Eggs may be obtained from female moths, but often the larvae cannot be forced and have to be overwintered outside in prepared pots containing suitable foodplants, such as nettle, and dry leaves for shelter. Fairly common and widespread over much of England, Wales and parts of Ireland; local and less frequent in Scotland.
Plate 46: R. Bred from a female adult to MVL. Early July.

Gold Spangle
Autographa bractea Denis & Schiffermüller
Larva. 32–36 mm. Body green, with six rows of thin wavy broken white lines along the dorsal area and a usually conspicuous white line just above the black-ringed white spiracles; pinacula white, with gingery setae; prolegs absent on sixth and seventh segments; true legs blackish, with brown tips; head darkish green, with black lateral streaks.
Foodplants. Various herbaceous plants, including common nettle, dead-nettle and bilberry, also accepting dandelion, plantain and dock in captivity.
Habits. A single-brooded insect, being in the larval stage from about August to the following early June, overwintering when still quite small. During the spring the larvae can sometimes be found or swept when attempting to obtain other species and are usually very easy to rear to the adult stage in captivity. The cocooned pupae are formed under the foodplant leaves or among plant litter and last about six weeks, with the light-responsive adults flying in July and early August. Stocks obtained from fertile females have been forced in captivity to produce a second generation in the autumn. Widely distributed and locally common in parts of the Midlands, the northern half of England and Scotland, and much of Wales and Ireland.
Plate 47: A. Swept at night from bilberry, fully grown. Early June. (SHC)

Stephen's Gem
Autographa biloba Stephens
Larva. 33–38 mm. Body green, with white dorsal and subdorsal stripes; head green, with black lateral streaks. Similar to *T. ni*.
Foodplants. Lettuce, clover and many other plants.
Habits. A North American insect that has been recorded

twice as an adult in the British Isles, during 1954 and 1958. It is probably continuously brooded in the warmer parts of its range and in some American states it becomes a pest of cultivated lettuce.

Scarce Silver Y

Syngrapha interrogationis Linnaeus

Larva. 32–37 mm. Body green, with a dark green dorsal line, edged on each side by three wavy white lines and a bold yellowish-white spiracular line; pinacula mainly white, except those immediately above the spiracles which are black; prolegs on sixth and seventh rings absent; head black or dark greenish-brown, speckled darker.

Foodplants. Heather and bilberry.

Habits. Single-brooded, occurring in the larval stage from about late July to the following early June, overwintering when still small. During May and early June the larvae can readily be swept from their foodplants and are easy to rear in confinement, although many tend to be parasitized. The cocooned pupa is formed among the foodplants or in plant litter and lasts about four to six weeks, with the adults flying from late June to the middle of August. Widely distributed and locally common, inhabiting moorland throughout most of Scotland, the northern half of England and parts of Wales and Ireland. Specimens recorded in southern and eastern England are usually considered to be immigrants from the continent.

Plate 47: B. Swept from bilberry, almost fully grown. Early June.

Dark Spectacle

Abrostola triplasia Linnaeus

(*trigemina* Werneburg)

Larva. 33–38 mm. Body greenish-brown or purplish-brown, sometimes green, with a fine white dorsal line on the thoracic rings, dark dorsal blotches on the humped fourth, fifth and eleventh segments, vague oblique subdorsal markings and a pale spiracular stripe; all prolegs present; head greenish-brown, with darker streaks.

Foodplants. Common nettle and hop.

Habits. A mainly single-brooded insect, being in the larval stage from about July to September, and later in south-western England where a second generation often occurs. The larvae may be obtained by searching or carefully sweeping nettles and beating hop during August and September and are not difficult to rear in captivity, overwintering in a cocooned pupa usually spun up in a folded leaf of the foodplant. The adults are on the wing during June and July, with those of the second generation in late August, coming to light in small numbers. Generally distributed, but rather local, over much of England, Wales and Ireland, being more frequent in western parts; very local in Scotland.

Plate 47: C. Found on nettle, fully grown. Early September. (BS)

The Spectacle

Abrostola tripartita Hufnagel

(*triplasia* auctt.)

Larva. 33–38 mm. Body green or olive-green, sometimes purplish-brown, with a fine white dorsal line on the thoracic rings, dark dorsal blotches on the humped fourth, fifth and eleventh segments, indistinct oblique subdorsal markings and a dark-edged pale spiracular stripe; all prolegs present; head usually dull green with darker streaks. Earlier instars bright green, without the dorsal blotching.

Foodplant. Common nettle.

Habits. A mostly single-brooded species, with the larvae occurring from July to September and later in southern Britain, where a partial second generation often takes place. They are readily obtained by sweeping in nettle-beds from early August onwards and are easy to rear in captivity. The overwintering pupae are formed inside a cocoon among plant litter, with the adults flying during late May and June and about a month later in the north. These come freely to light and females usually lay eggs in captivity when given a few foodplant leaves as a stimulus. Widely distributed over much of the British Isles.

Plate 47: D. Bred from a female adult to MVL. Mid-June. (SHC)

SUBFAMILY: CATOCALINAE

Clifden Nonpareil

Catocala fraxini Linnaeus

Larva. 65–75 mm. Body pale greyish-brown, with minute brown pinacula, a dark slightly oblique band around the humped eighth segment and a pair of small dorsal humps on the eleventh ring; spiracles brown; prolegs on sixth segment rudimentary; head light brown, heavily marked with black.

Foodplants. Aspen, also accepting poplar in captivity.

Habits. A single-brooded immigrant species that was formerly established in Norfolk and Kent during the middle part of this century. The larvae occur from about late April to mid-July and are stated to be difficult to find, feeding at night and resting well camouflaged on the bark by day. Pupation takes place in a silken cocoon spun up between the leaves or among plant litter and lasts about six weeks, with the adults flying from late August to early October. Both sexes come freely to sugar, although less attracted to light, and females kept alive to obtain livestock should be fed and supplied with rough bark and coarse netting on which to deposit their overwintering eggs. Sometimes they will wait a few days before laying, but when they start, often a good number will be produced. At present this insect is a very irregular visitor to Britain, most likely to be encountered in the south-eastern and eastern coastal counties of England.

Plate 47: E. Bred from a female adult to MVL. Early October. (AH)

Red Underwing

Catocala nupta Linnaeus

Larva. 60–70 mm. Body pale grey, with a raised hump and often a brown band on the eighth segment, another dorsal projection on the eleventh ring and a series of smallish brown subdorsal warts on the other abdominal rings; all prolegs present; head pale brown, marked with black.

Foodplants. Willows, poplars and aspen.

Habits. A single-brooded insect, being in the larval stage from about May to mid-July, after overwintering as an egg. The larvae feed at night and may sometimes be found during the day from mid-June onwards by carefully searching under loose bark or in the bark crevices of mature willows and poplars, especially those growing in parks or alongside rivers. The cocooned pupae are usually formed in a crevice or in plant litter, lasting about six weeks, with the adults flying during August and September. These are much more likely to be found at sugar than light and if livestock is obtained, the young larvae are rather delicate and should not be unnecessarily disturbed. Widely distributed over the southern half of Britain, although scarce and local in west Wales, Devon and Cornwall.

Plate 47: F. Bred from a female adult to sugar. Early September. (RL)

Rosy Underwing

Catocala electa Vieweg

Larva. 55–65 mm. Body grey, with lighter and darker mottling, small pale brown dorsal projections on the eighth and eleventh segments and pairs of subdorsal warts; all legs present; head pale brown, with darker streaks and reddish-brown at the front.

Foodplants. Willow, sallow and poplar.

Habits. A single-brooded species that has been recorded in Britain as an adult on about six occasions, having the status of a suspected immigrant. After overwintering as an egg, the larval period lasts from late April to early July, with the adults flying from late July to late September. On the continent it occurs in central and southern Europe and is stated to be uncommon and declining.

Plate 47: G. From commercial stock. (AJ)

Light Crimson Underwing

Catocala promissa Denis & Schiffermüller

Larva. 45–55 mm. Body greyish-green or sometimes dark green, with a series of black subdorsal and lateral markings, white dorsal pinacula and a small hump on the eighth segment dorsally; prolegs on the sixth and seventh rings less developed than the others; head green, with dark markings.

Foodplant. Oak.

Habits. Single-brooded, being in the larval stage from about late April to early June, feeding initially on the developing buds and later on the fresh foliage. The larvae are mainly nocturnal and although they have been located by day resting in bark crevices or among lichen, they are more likely to be obtained by beating the highest reachable branches of mature oaks after dark. Pupation takes place in a silken cocoon, usually located between leaves or on the lichen-covered branches or trunk. The adults fly from late July to late August, appearing more frequently at sugar than at light, with many females being reluctant to lay their overwintering eggs in captivity. Well established in the New Forest, occurring locally elsewhere in Hampshire, Wiltshire and West Sussex.

Plate 47: H. Beaten at night, almost fully grown. Late May. (AJP)

Dark Crimson Underwing

Catocala sponsa Linnaeus

Larva. 50–60 mm. Body brownish-grey, with a faint greyish dorsal line, a series of small reddish-brown conical subdorsal pinacula, a raised hump on the eighth segment and another, with pinacula, on the eleventh ring; all prolegs present; head reddish-brown, edged with black.

Foodplant. Oak.

Habits. A single-brooded insect, occurring in the larval stage from late April to the middle of June, feeding at night and hiding in bark crevices by day. The larvae have been beaten from the boughs of mature oaks at dusk or after dark, but never commonly. The pupae are formed in a cocoon among the foliage or in a crevice, this stage lasting for about six to eight weeks, with the adults flying during August and early September. Like others in this genus, they are greatly attracted to sugar and females can be persuaded to lay their overwintering eggs by being fed and supplied with rough bark and coarse netting. Mainly recorded from the New Forest in Hampshire, with numbers fluctuating from year to year. Formerly seen in Wiltshire, Sussex and Kent, where small colonies could still exist.

Plate 47: I. Bred from a female adult to sugar. Mid-August. (JMP)

Oak Yellow Underwing

Catocala nymphagoga Esper

Larva. 40–45 mm. Body grey, heavily speckled with lighter and darker coloration to form vague stripes; a black-edged white dorsal projection on the eighth segment and pairs of reddish-brown pinacula along the subdorsal region, with those on the eleventh ring being situated on a small hump; all legs present; head mainly pale brown, marked with black.

Foodplant. Oak.

Habits. A single-brooded species, of which two adults were recorded from widely separated localities in Britain in late July 1982. The larval stage lasts from late March to early June, after overwintering as an egg, with the adults flying in July and August. Abroad the range includes parts of central and southern Europe.

Plate 47: J. Courtesy of Carlos Gomez de Aizpurua.

Lunar Double-stripe

Minucia lunaris Denis & Schiffermüller

Larva. 60–70 mm. Body grey or greyish-brown, finely lined with darker stripes, a paler stripe subdorsally and reddish or yellowish subdorsal marks on the fourth and eleventh segments; subspiracular stripe bold and blackish, sometimes edged with red; head yellow, heavily streaked with black or dark red.

Foodplants. Oak, also accepting holm oak in captivity.

Habits. A single-brooded infrequent immigrant species that temporarily established itself in Kent from about 1942 to 1958, when both larvae and adults were found, sometimes in good numbers. The larval stage occurs during July and early August, and although nocturnal, they can be found or beaten from the fresh foliage that grows from oak-stools, even those affected by mildew. It has been stated they will not accept the foliage from the crown of the tree, and possibly died out due to the lack of suitable food when coppicing became irregular. The overwintering pupae are formed on the ground among plant litter and soil, lasting until the following mid-May to early June, when the adults fly. These come both to light and sugar. They have been recorded most recently from the southern coastal counties.

Plate 47: K. Courtesy of Carlos Gomez de Aizpurua.

The Passenger

Dysgonia algira Linnaeus

Larva. 42–48 mm. Body brown, with a reddish-brown dorsal stripe and pale brown subdorsal and spiracular lines; head brown, marked with yellow; first prolegs rudimentary and a notch, dorsally, on the eleventh segment.

Foodplants. Bramble, sallow and *Genista*.

Habits. A double-brooded suspected immigrant species that has been recorded in Britain as an adult five times between 1967 and 1996. On the continent, the range includes much of southern Europe, with the larvae occurring during June and July and again in September and October, before overwintering in the pupal stage.

Plate 47: L. Courtesy of M. R. Honey. (NHM)

Mother Shipton

Callistege mi Clerck

Larva. 33–38 mm. Body pale ochreous or whitish, wholly covered dorsally and laterally with fine pinkish-brown lines

and having a broad clear yellowish-white spiracular stripe; prolegs on sixth and seventh segments absent; head ochreous, heavily lined and speckled with brown.
Foodplants. Clovers, bird's-foot trefoil, black medick and lucerne.
Habits. A single-brooded species, occurring in the larval stage from about late June to early September, being occasionally obtained by careful sweeping. The larvae may be located at night resting on grass stems. They are quite easy to rear in captivity, pupating for overwintering inside a cocoon just below the soil or among plant debris, sometimes hatching early when kept indoors. The adults fly in sunshine from late May to early July and netted females lay eggs freely in captivity when given foodplant as a stimulus. Inhabiting downland, waste ground and other open places throughout much of the British Isles, although quite local in Scotland.
Plate 47: M. Bred from a netted female adult. Mid-June.

Burnet Companion

Euclidia glyphica Linnaeus
Larva. 32–36 mm. Body pale brown, with a pair of pale dorsal lines, darker mottling subdorsally and an indistinct paler spiracular line; prolegs absent on the sixth segment, rudimentary on the seventh; head pale brown with distinct yellow-white stripes.
Foodplants. Bird's-foot trefoil, clovers and associated plants.
Habits. Mainly single-brooded, being in the larval stage from about late June to late August, being readily obtained by careful sweeping at night on downland, where populations can be quite large. The larvae are not difficult to rear in confinement, forming their overwintering pupae in cocoons among plant litter. The adults fly in sunshine between mid-May and early July, occasionally again in August from examples of a partial second generation in southern England, with the captive females laying freely when supplied with a sprig of foodplant. Widely distributed over the southern half of England, local in northern England, Wales and southern Scotland; also commonly found in the Burren district of western Ireland.
Plate 47: N. Bred from a netted female adult. Early June.

SUBFAMILY: OPHIDERINAE

The Alchymist

Catephia alchymista Denis & Schiffermüller
Larva. 45–50 mm. Body pale brown or grey, with small black pinacula and projecting structures dorsally on the fourth and eleventh segments; prolegs on sixth and seventh rings rudimentary; head brown (MBGBI).
Foodplants. The young shoots of sapling oaks; also recorded on evergreen oak and elm.
Habits. A single-brooded, very scarce immigrant species that has been recorded twice as a larva and about fifteen times as an adult in Britain, with all but three instances being during the nineteenth century. The adults fly between May and early July, with the larvae occurring in July and August, before overwintering as pupae. Abroad, the range includes France and Belgium, as well as central and southern Europe.

The Four-spotted

Tyta luctuosa Denis & Schiffermüller
Larva. 28–33 mm. Body brown, with a pair of darker dorsal lines, a greyish line subdorsally and a thin pale spiracular line, edged above with a grey-centred dark brown stripe; underparts pale brown; subdorsal pinacula whitish; head greyish-brown, speckled darker.
Foodplant. Field bindweed.
Habits. A mainly single-brooded species, with the larvae occurring during July and August, and again in September, from the partial second generation that often occurs on the south coast of England. The populations are rarely large enough to make searching for larvae a worthwhile task, although they may readily be obtained by rearing from eggs laid by adult females. These usually fly in sunshine and later come to light during June and early July, sometimes again in August. The larvae are quite easy to rear in confinement, overwintering in a subterranean cocoon, with a few hatching in the same season when kept indoors. A very local insect, inhabiting waste ground, chalk downland, railway embankments and breckland, regularly recorded only from Dorset, the Breck district of Suffolk and from a strong colony in north-eastern Nottinghamshire; elsewhere noted from other places in southern and south-eastern England.
Plate 47: O. Bred from a netted female adult. Late June. (BS)

The Blackneck

Lygephila pastinum Treitschke
Larva. 33–38 mm. Body purplish-grey, wholly covered with small black spots, with a narrow orange dorsal line and whitish subdorsal and subspiracular lines, both edged above with orange markings; underparts very dark brown; head greyish, with a dull orange lateral streak.
Foodplants. Tufted vetch and probably closely associated plants.
Habits. Single-brooded, being in the larval stage from about August to the following late May, overwintering when still quite small. During the spring the larvae can readily be swept at night, hiding by day low down on the foodplant, and are not difficult to rear when taken at this point of their development. The pupae are formed in a cocoon usually either on or just beneath the soil, with the adults flying from mid-June to mid-July. These can readily be disturbed from the herbage by day, and are attracted to light. In captivity overwintering larvae should be kept on potted foodplants and supplied with dry leaf litter in which to hibernate. Widely distributed over the southern half of England and parts of South Wales, inhabiting commons, open woodland and downland.
Plate 47: P. Swept at night, almost fully grown. Mid-May.

Scarce Blackneck

Lygephila craccae Denis & Schiffermüller
Larva. 33–37 mm. Body pale brown, with a dull purplish-grey dorsal stripe enclosing the pale-edged grey dorsal line; another less distinct greyish stripe above the small black spiracles and underparts dark greyish-brown; head pale brown, marked darker.
Foodplants. Wood vetch, also accepting other closely related plants in confinement.
Habits. A single-brooded insect that occurs in the larval stage from about late April to early July, after overwintering as an egg. From about early June the larvae may be located by torchlight or carefully swept at night and are fairly easy to rear when brought into captivity. Pupation takes place inside a cocoon among plant litter or just in the soil and lasts about a month, with the adults flying from mid-July to the middle of August, these being most frequently encountered after being disturbed from the herbage on warm sunny days. A

very local species occurring on the rocky coasts of north Cornwall, North Devon and Somerset.
Plate 47: Q. Located on foodplant, fully grown. Early July. (AG)

Levant Blackneck

Tathorhynchus exsiccata Lederer
Larva. 28–33 mm. Body pale reddish-brown, with narrow darker dorsal and lateral lines; prolegs absent on the sixth ring, rudimentary on the seventh; head grey (MBGBI).
Foodplants. Lucerne and tree indigo.
Habits. A mainly subtropical and tropical species that has been recorded in Britain in the adult stage on about ten occasions since 1952, usually during the early spring. Even in southern Europe it is considered to be an immigrant species, with its usual range being in Africa; also resident in the Canary Islands from where those recorded in Britain may have originated.

The Herald

Scoliopteryx libatrix Linnaeus
Larva. 40–45 mm. Body bright green, with yellow segmental divisions, an obscure darker dorsal line and a narrow darker subdorsal line; spiracles reddish-orange; pinkish-tipped prolegs; head pale green.
Foodplants. Sallow, willow, aspen and poplar.
Habits. Mostly single-brooded, occurring in the larval stage from about May to September. In southern Britain those larvae that have pupated by July quickly emerge as adults and pair immediately, resulting in a second generation. The larvae may readily be obtained by beating and are very easy to rear in confinement, pupating in a cocoon between leaves for about three weeks. This insect overwinters in the adult stage, usually in old sheds, barns, caves and concrete army bunkers, and may be seen at sugar or light from about March to June and again from July to November. Generally distributed over most of the British Isles, although quite local in Scotland.
Plate 47: R. Beaten from sallow, fully grown. Late June.

Small Purple-barred

Phytometra viridaria Clerck
(*aenea* Hübner)
Larva. 22–26 mm. Body green, with a darker dorsal line, an indistinct orangish spot dorsally on the eighth segment and a whitish-green spiracular line; prolegs absent on sixth and rudimentary on the seventh rings; head pale green, mottled darker.
Foodplants. Common milkwort, also stated to feed on lousewort.
Habits. Single-brooded, possibly double-brooded in southern Britain, with the larvae occurring from about late June to early September. They can sometimes be found by careful searching or sweeping, but are easier to obtain by rearing from the eggs laid by adult females. These fly in sunshine from late May to July, sometimes later in the south, and will freely deposit eggs when supplied with foodplant and flowers from which to feed. The larval development in captivity can be quite rapid, and pupation for overwintering takes place inside a tough cocoon usually located among plant litter or on the ground. Widely distributed, inhabiting downland, sandhills, open woodland, heaths and moors, over much of the British Isles; rather local in Scotland.
Plate 48: A. Bred from a netted female adult. Mid-July. (M&JH)

Lesser Belle

Colobochyla salicalis Denis & Schiffermüller
Larva. 26–30 mm. Body green, with a darker dorsal line, yellow segmental divisions and tiny orange-ringed spiracles; true legs pale brown; prolegs on sixth segment rudimentary, those on the seventh under-developed; head pale green (Haggett).
Foodplants. The young foliage of aspen, also accepting the shoots and tender leaves of sallow in captivity.
Habits. A single-brooded insect that seems not to have been recorded in Britain since the mid-1970s. The larval period lasts throughout July and into early August, and the larvae have been located at night, when active, by searching the sapling aspens. They are stated to be easy to rear, although they will not accept the older foliage from more mature trees, and form their overwintering pupae inside a strong cocoon made from chewed bark and silk on the stems of the foodplant. The adults fly from late May to early July, being readily disturbed from herbage by day and later coming sparingly to light. A very local species, possibly now extinct, previously known to be well established at a regularly coppiced woodland site in Kent.

Beautiful Hook-tip

Laspeyria flexula Denis & Schiffermüller
Larva. 22–26 mm. Body greyish-green, with a darker dorsal line and darker mottlings, somewhat diamond-shaped, on the back; small black subdorsal pinacula, with those on the eleventh segment being modified into small humps; prolegs on sixth and seventh rings rudimentary; head greyish, marked with black.
Foodplants. Various lichens growing on the twigs and branches of hawthorn, blackthorn, larch, yew and other trees. Readily accepting in confinement the common green algae (*Desmococcus*) that grow on most tree trunks.
Habits. Single-brooded, being in the larval stage from August to the following late May, overwintering when still quite small. During the spring the larvae may be beaten, especially at night when more active, from thickets of blackthorn or hawthorn, and when taken at this point of their development are not difficult to rear. Pupation takes place in a tough cocoon on a stem or branch, lasting about four to six weeks, with the adults flying from about late June to early August. Widely distributed in woodland over most of the southern half of England and South Wales.
Plate 48: B. Beaten from lichen on hawthorn, almost fully grown. Mid-May.

Straw Dot

Rivula sericealis Scopoli
Larva. 16–20 mm. Body green, with a dark green dorsal line, bold white subdorsal lines and a distinguishing yellow dorsal patch on the eighth segment; setae long and gingery; head greenish-brown.
Foodplants. Various grasses, including false-brome, tor-grass and purple moor-grass, accepting other related species in captivity.
Habits. Probably single-brooded in the north and bivoltine in the southern half of Britain, where suspected immigration may also take place. The larvae occur from August to the following May, and again in July in the south, overwintering when small. They can be obtained by sweeping at night, especially during the spring, and are quite easy to rear in captivity, pupating in a cocoon spun between grass blades for about three to four weeks. The adults fly mainly from mid-June to late July, also in August and September where

the second generation occurs, with both sexes being readily disturbed from herbage during the day and coming freely to light after dark. A common species in the southern half of Britain and in Ireland; local in western Scotland.
Plate 48: C. Bred from a female adult to MVL. Mid-July. (SHC)

Waved Black
Parascotia fuliginaria Linnaeus
Larva. 25–30 mm. Body velvety brownish-black, with a greyish pair of dorsal lines and distinct orange pinacula; setae greyish and fairly long; prolegs absent on the sixth and seventh segments; head black.
Foodplants. Various fungi, usually varicoloured bracket (*Coriolus versicolor*), also birch polypore (*Piptoporus betulinus*), *Daldinea concentrica* and *Phaeolus schweinizii* and others growing on fallen logs, tree stumps and rotting timber.
Habits. A single-brooded species, occurring in the larval stage from August to the following mid-June, overwintering when still very small. From about mid-May onwards the larvae may be located by carefully searching under and between the fruit bodies of the common varicoloured bracket, especially those which are well established on rotting birch logs in shaded woodland. They are not difficult to rear in captivity when kept outside in a netting-covered container, placed in total shade and supplied with fresh food that should not be allowed to become desiccated. The pupae are formed in cocoons that hang from a pair of silken threads to form a hammock. This stage lasts about three to four weeks with the adults flying from late June to early August, coming sparingly to light. A local insect, most often recorded from the heaths and mature woodlands of Surrey, north Hampshire, Berkshire and parts of Middlesex and Worcestershire.
Plate 48: D. Located on varicoloured bracket fungus, almost fully grown. Early June.

SUBFAMILY: HYPENINAE

Beautiful Snout
Hypena crassalis Fabricius
(*frontis* Thunberg)
(*fontis* misspelling)
Larva. 22–26 mm. Body bright green, with yellow segmental divisions, a vague darker dorsal line, tiny black pinacula, longish black setae and brownish-pink tipped legs; prolegs on sixth ring rudimentary; head green, speckled darker.
Foodplants. Bilberry and possibly heathers.
Habits. A single-brooded insect, being in the larval stage from about mid-July to the end of September. The larger larvae are mainly nocturnal and may be taken, sometimes in good numbers, by sweeping. They are easy to rear in captivity and pupate for overwintering inside a cocoon among plant litter or just beneath the soil. The adults fly in June and July, and although they may sometimes be flushed from the foodplant by day, are more often seen at light. A widespread, but local, woodland species, occurring throughout much of southern England and Wales; also recorded from Ireland.
Plate 48: E. Swept at night, fully grown. Mid-September. (JMP)

The Snout
Hypena proboscidalis Linnaeus
Larva. 24–28 mm. Body green, with yellow segmental divisions, indistinct darker dorsal and subdorsal lines and often a white spiracular line; pinacula minute, black; setae longish and black; prolegs on sixth segment rudimentary; head dull green, with darker freckling.
Foodplant. Common nettle.
Habits. A double-brooded species, except in the northern parts of the British Isles, where it is univoltine. The larvae occur from the autumn until the following May, and again from about mid-July to mid-August, being readily obtained by sweeping nettle-beds at night. During the day they hide between spun leaves, but are not difficult to locate and when taken into captivity are very easy to rear. Pupation takes place in a cocoon spun up on the foodplant and lasts about three weeks, with the adults flying in June and July, and again in late August and September, coming freely to light and sugar. Generally distributed and fairly common over most of the British Isles.
Plate 48: F. Swept at night, nearly fully grown. Late May.

Bloxworth Snout
Hypena obsitalis Hübner
Larva. 22–26 mm. Body green, with an indistinct darker dorsal line, yellowish-white subdorsal lines and a paler green coloration in the spiracular region; pinacula greyish-black, larger on the thoracic rings; prolegs rudimentary on the sixth ring; head dull green, speckled darker.
Foodplants. Pellitory-of-the-wall and common nettle.
Habits. A double-brooded species that has established itself as a resident breeding insect on the South Devon coast from 1990, being in the larval stage from about late May to early July, and again in late August and September. Adult females usually lay freely in captivity and the larvae are very easy to rear, developing rapidly when kept warm and pupating in a loose cocoon among the foodplant leaves for about three weeks. The adults fly in late July and early August, and again in September until hibernation, then once more in the spring, and have usually been taken by netting at dusk, although they are also known to visit sugar and flowering plants.
Plate 48: G. Bred from a netted female adult. Early May. (GH)

Paignton Snout
Hypena obesalis Treitschke
Larva. 26–30 mm. Body pale green, with a whitish spiracular line; head green, marked with black (MBGBI).
Foodplant. Common nettle.
Habits. A single-brooded insect that has been recorded in Britain in the adult stage three times and holds the status of being a suspected immigrant. Abroad, in central and southern Europe, the species is mainly montane, with the larvae occurring during June and July and the overwintering adults flying in the late summer and autumn, and again in the following spring.

Buttoned Snout
Hypena rostralis Linnaeus
Larva. 22–25 mm. Body pale green, with an indistinct darker dorsal line, a white or yellowish-white subdorsal line and an incomplete white spiracular line; pinacula small, black; setae greyish; prolegs on sixth ring rudimentary; head pale yellowish-green.
Foodplant. Hop.
Habits. Single-brooded, being in the larval stage during June and July. The larvae may be obtained by locating foodplant leaves showing large holes in the central area and placing a beating tray very carefully beneath, as the larvae will throw themselves from the plant if touched or disturbed.

They are very easy to rear in confinement, pupating for about three to four weeks in a cocoon spun up under the foodplant leaves. The overwintering adults fly from about August to the following early June, with captive females, taken in the spring, freely depositing eggs when supplied with hop foliage. Local, but not uncommon, in the outer suburbs of London, Surrey, Middlesex, Essex, Kent and Berkshire; recorded casually elsewhere in southern England.
Plate 48: H. Beaten from hop, fully grown. Early July. (RGC)

White-line Snout

Schrankia taenialis Hübner
(*albistrigatis* Haworth)
(*albistrigalis* misspelling)
Larva. 11–13 mm. Body mostly pinkish-brown or purplish-brown, darker on the third and eighth segments; fourth to seventh segments greatly swollen in comparison to the others; prolegs on sixth and seventh rings obsolete; head brown, mottled darker.
Foodplants. Unknown in the wild, accepting lettuce, sliced runner beans and the flowers of heather and thyme in captivity.
Habits. A single-brooded species, of which the feral larva has still to be found. The insects have been successfully reared in captivity, usually being given a varied diet of lettuce leaves, thyme and heather flowers and seem to require a dampish environment. The larvae feed up quite quickly to produce a second generation, although it is probable that the insect overwinters as a small larva in the wild. The adults are on the wing from mid-July to mid-August, being more attracted to sugar than light and the females usually being reluctant to lay in captivity. Mainly a woodland and heathland insect, being widespread, but local, over much of southern England.
Plate 48: I. Bred from a female adult to light. Late July. (JG)

Pinion-streaked Snout

Schrankia costaestrigalis Stephens
Larva. 10–12 mm. Body purplish-brown, greatly swollen on the fourth to seventh segments and with prolegs absent on the sixth and seventh rings; head brownish-black.
Foodplants. Unknown in the wild, accepting lettuce, the flowers of thyme, marjoram and wild mint, and damp withered sallow leaves in captivity.
Habits. A mainly single-brooded insect, the wild larvae of which have yet to be discovered, probably overwintering when still small and completing their development during the spring. They have been bred in captivity and when kept indoors feed up quite rapidly to produce a second generation, as often happens naturally in southern England. The adults fly from late June to early August, again in September in the south, coming to sugar, flowering plants and in small numbers to light. Mostly inhabiting dampish places, such as fens, mosses, boggy heaths and dank woodland, over much of England, Wales and parts of western Scotland; also recorded from Ireland.
Plate 48: J. Bred from a female adult to MVL. Mid-July. (SHC)

Marsh Oblique-barred

Hypenodes humidalis Doubleday
(*turfosalis* Wocke)
Larva. 8–10 mm. Body brown, with the fourth to seventh segments swollen in comparison to the others; prolegs absent on sixth and seventh rings; head pale brown, marked darker. Similar to *S. taenialis*, but more slender (Haggett).
Foodplants. Unknown, accepting blanched lettuce in captivity.
Habits. A mainly single-brooded species, occasionally bivoltine, probably being in the larval stage from August to the following spring, yet to be found in the wild. It is suspected that the larvae may feed on some lower part of purple moor-grass, as this plant seems to occur wherever the insect is to be found, although marsh cinquefoil, cross-leaved heath, sedges and rushes have also been stated to be possible foodplants. Usually a very difficult larva to rear in captivity, dying quickly after hatching from the egg, unless the food and environment are correct. Most adults fly from late June to the middle of August, with some records during September, and both sexes may readily be netted at dusk or later attracted to light traps. A very locally common insect, inhabiting boggy heath, moorland and mosses in many lowland parts of Britain; also noted from parts of Ireland.

Common Fan-foot

Pechipogo strigilata Linnaeus
(*barbalis* Clerck)
Larva. 17–20 mm. Body pale reddish-brown, with a darker dorsal line and vague oblique darker specklings in the subdorsal region; spiracles fairly large, blackish; head pale greyish-brown.
Foodplants. Withered leaves of oak and probably those of other plants, including dandelion and bramble.
Habits. A single-brooded species, occurring in the larval stage from July to the following April, overwintering when nearly fully grown. The larvae are most easily obtained by rearing from the egg stage, these being laid quite freely by captive adult females which may be disturbed from herbage or attracted to light during late May and June. Usually it is not a difficult larva to rear in confinement and when kept warm the steady development will be completed by about September to produce more adults during the autumn. A much decreased insect, mainly inhabiting mature woodland, locally distributed over the southern half of Britain, with most recent records from north Hampshire, East Sussex, Gloucestershire and Shropshire.
Plate 48: K. Bred from a female adult to MVL. Early June. (SHC)

The Fan-foot

Herminia tarsipennalis Treitschke
Larva. 17–20 mm. Body usually brown or greyish-brown, with an indistinct darker dorsal line and pale-ringed black pinacula; head dark brown, mottled paler.
Foodplants. Withered leaves of oak, beech, bramble and other plants.
Habits. Single-brooded, possibly with a partial second generation, occurring as active larvae from about late July to October, when the cocoons are spun among plant litter, and pupation takes place in the following spring. They have been obtained in the wild by beating the dry withered foliage on broken and fallen branches, have also been found among leaves on the ground, and are quite easy to rear in confinement, often producing a second generation when kept indoors. The adults fly during June and July, coming to light and sugar in small numbers, with most females depositing their eggs quite freely when given suitable foodplant as a stimulus. Widely distributed over much of England, Wales and parts of Ireland; local and less frequent in northern England and southern Scotland.

Plate 48: L. Bred from an adult female to MVL. Early July. (JMP)

Jubilee Fan-foot

Herminia lunalis Scopoli

Larva. 17–20 mm. Body pale yellowish-brown, with a distinct reddish-pink dorsal line, less obvious lateral lines of the same colour and small black pinacula; head pale brown.
Foodplants. The withered leaves of many plants, accepting dandelion in captivity.
Habits. Single-brooded, being in the larval stage from September to the following May, overwintering when over half grown. It has been recorded in Britain on one occasion as an adult during 1976, and is stated to be widespread in western Europe.
Plate 48: M. Bred from a female adult to MVL (France). Early August. (WK)

Shaded Fan-foot

Herminia tarsicrinalis Knoch

Larva. 15–18 mm. Body warm reddish-brown, with darker dorsal chevrons and reddish oblique lateral marks on the abdominal segments; spiracles black; head dark reddish-brown.
Foodplants. Withered and fallen leaves of bramble and probably other plants, accepting both fresh and withered dandelion leaves in captivity.
Habits. Probably single-brooded, being in the larval stage from August to the following spring. This species was first confirmed as a British resident in 1982 when adults were taken in fair numbers at a site in Suffolk; also since recorded from Essex and Norfolk. The females laid readily in captivity and the larvae were not difficult to rear, some becoming fully grown in about three months to produce a second generation and others overwintering when fully grown or almost so. Pupation takes place in a cocoon among the plant debris, and the adults fly during late June and July, coming to light.
Plate 48: N. Bred from a female adult to MVL. Early July. (BS)

Small Fan-foot

Herminia grisealis Denis & Schiffermüller
(*nemoralis* Fabricius)

Larva. 14–18 mm. Body light reddish-brown, with a darker dorsal line on the abdominal segments and tiny black pinacula; head dark greyish-brown.
Foodplants. Oak, alder and bramble, consuming the living leaves as well as the withered foliage on broken branches and the ground.
Habits. A single-brooded insect, occurring in the larval stage from about late July to October, sometimes being taken when beating for other species. The larvae are fairly easy to rear in captivity, pupating in a cocoon among plant litter, in crevices or under bark for overwintering. The adults fly from late June to early August, being readily disturbed from herbage or foliage by day, later coming in small numbers to light, sugar and flowering plants. Generally distributed and not uncommon over the greater part of England, Wales and Ireland; rather local in Scotland.
Plate 48: O. Beaten from oak, almost fully grown. Early September. (SHC)

Dotted Fan-foot

Macrochilo cribrumalis Hübner

Larva. 18–22 mm. Body light reddish-brown, with a purplish-brown dorsal line and purplish lines subdorsally surrounding a greyish stripe; pinacula small, dark brown; spiracles black; head light reddish-brown, finely mottled darker.
Foodplants. Probably various marsh grasses and sedges, accepting withered dandelion leaves in captivity.
Habits. Single-brooded, being in the larval stage from about late July to the following May, overwintering when about half grown in the tufts of grasses. The larvae are best obtained by rearing from the egg stage, readily accepting withering dandelion leaves and becoming fully grown in about three months, when kept indoors, producing more adults in the autumn. Alternatively, they may be kept on potted plants of wood sedge and left outside in a sheltered place to develop naturally. The pupa is formed inside a silken cocoon among the plant debris and the adults fly from late June to early August. A very local species inhabiting fens and marshes in East Anglia, Essex, Kent, East Sussex and Hampshire.
Plate 48: P. Bred from a female adult to MVL. Early July. (GAC)

Clay Fan-foot

Paracolax tristalis Fabricius
(*derivalis* Hübner)

Larva. 15–18 mm. Body dark brown, with a velvety pubescence and indistinct darker dorsal and subdorsal lines; spiracles small, brownish-black; head brown.
Foodplants. The withered fallen leaves of oak and possibly other plants.
Habits. A single-brooded species, occurring as a larva from August to the following early June, overwintering when still quite small. Although the larvae have been beaten from oak in the autumn, they are best obtained by rearing from the egg stage, and when kept indoors will continue to feed, becoming fully grown after about four months. Pupation takes place in a cocoon among plant litter, lasting about four weeks, with the adults flying from early July to early August, both sexes coming to light and sugar, usually in small numbers. Local, mainly recorded from woodlands on heavy soils, in Sussex, Kent, Surrey and Essex.
Plate 48: Q. Bred from a female adult to MVL. Late July. (SHC)

Olive Crescent

Trisateles emortualis Denis & Schiffermüller

Larva. 16–19 mm. Body reddish-brown, occasionally pale greenish-yellow, with dull orange segmental divisions and sometimes dark dorsal blotches; pinacula small, black; prolegs rudimentary on the sixth and seventh rings; head dark brown.
Foodplants. The withered leaves of oak and less often beech.
Habits. Single-brooded, being in the larval stage from August to early October, overwintering as a cocooned pupa among plant debris. The larvae have been found by searching the skeletonized withered oak leaves on partly broken and fallen branches, also those on the ground, and are not difficult to rear in captivity. The adults fly during late June and July and on suitably warm nights will come to light. A local species recorded in fair numbers from the Chilterns and north Essex, although since 1976 it seems to have virtually disappeared from the former locality.
Plate 48: R. Courtesy of Brian R. Baker.

Colour Plates

Plate 1: *Hepialidae, Cossidae, Zygaenidae*

A. **Ghost Moth** *Hepialus humuli* Linn. Page 1.
B. **Orange Swift** *Hepialus sylvina* Linn. Page 1.
C. **Gold Swift** *Hepialus hecta* Linn. Page 1.
D. **Common Swift** *Hepialus lupulinus* Linn. Page 1.
E. **Map-winged Swift** *Hepialus fusconebulosa* DeG. Page 1.
F. **Reed Leopard** *Phragmataecia castaneae* Hb. Page 2.
G. **Leopard Moth** *Zeuzera pyrina* Linn. Page 2.
H. **Goat Moth** *Cossus cossus* Linn. Page 2.
I. **Scarce Forester** *Adscita globulariae* Hb. Page 2.
J. **Cistus Forester** *Adscita geryon* Hb. Page 2.
K. **The Forester** *Adscita statices* Linn. Page 3.
L. **Scotch Burnet** *Zygaena exulans* Hohen. Page 3.
M. **Slender Scotch Burnet** *Zygaena loti* D. & S. Page 3.
N. **New Forest Burnet** *Zygaena viciae* D. & S. Page 3.
O. **Six-spot Burnet** *Zygaena filipendulae* Linn. Page 3.
P. **Five-spot Burnet** *Zygaena trifolii* Esp. Page 3.
Q. **Narrow-bordered Five-spot Burnet** *Zygaena lonicerae* Schev. Page 4.
R. **Transparent Burnet** *Zygaena purpuralis* Brunn. Page 4.

Plate 2: *Limacodidae, Sesiidae*

A. **The Festoon** *Apoda limacodes* Hufn. Page 4.
B. **The Triangle** *Heterogenea asella* D. & S. Page 4.
C. **Hornet Moth** *Sesia apiformis* Cl. Page 5.
D. **Lunar Hornet Moth** *Sesia bembeciformis* Hb. Page 5.
E. **Currant Clearwing** *Synanthedon tipuliformis* Cl. Page 5.
F. **Yellow-legged Clearwing** *Synanthedon vespiformis* Linn. Page 5.
G. **White-barred Clearwing** *Synanthedon spheciformis* D. & S. Page 5.
H. **Welsh Clearwing** *Synanthedon scoliaeformis* Borkh. Page 6.
I. **Sallow Clearwing** *Synanthedon flaviventris* Stdgr. Page 6.
J. **Orange-tailed Clearwing** *Synanthedon andrenaeformis* Lasp. Page 6.
K. **Red-belted Clearwing** *Synanthedon myopaeformis* Borkh. Page 6.
L. **Red-tipped Clearwing** *Synanthedon formicaeformis* Esp. Page 6.
M. **Large Red-belted Clearwing** *Synanthedon culiciformis* Linn. Page 6.
N. **Six-belted Clearwing** *Bembecia scopigera* Scop. Page 6.
O. **Thrift Clearwing** *Bembecia muscaeformis* Esp. Page 7.
P. **Fiery Clearwing** *Bembecia chrysidiformis* Esp. Page 7.

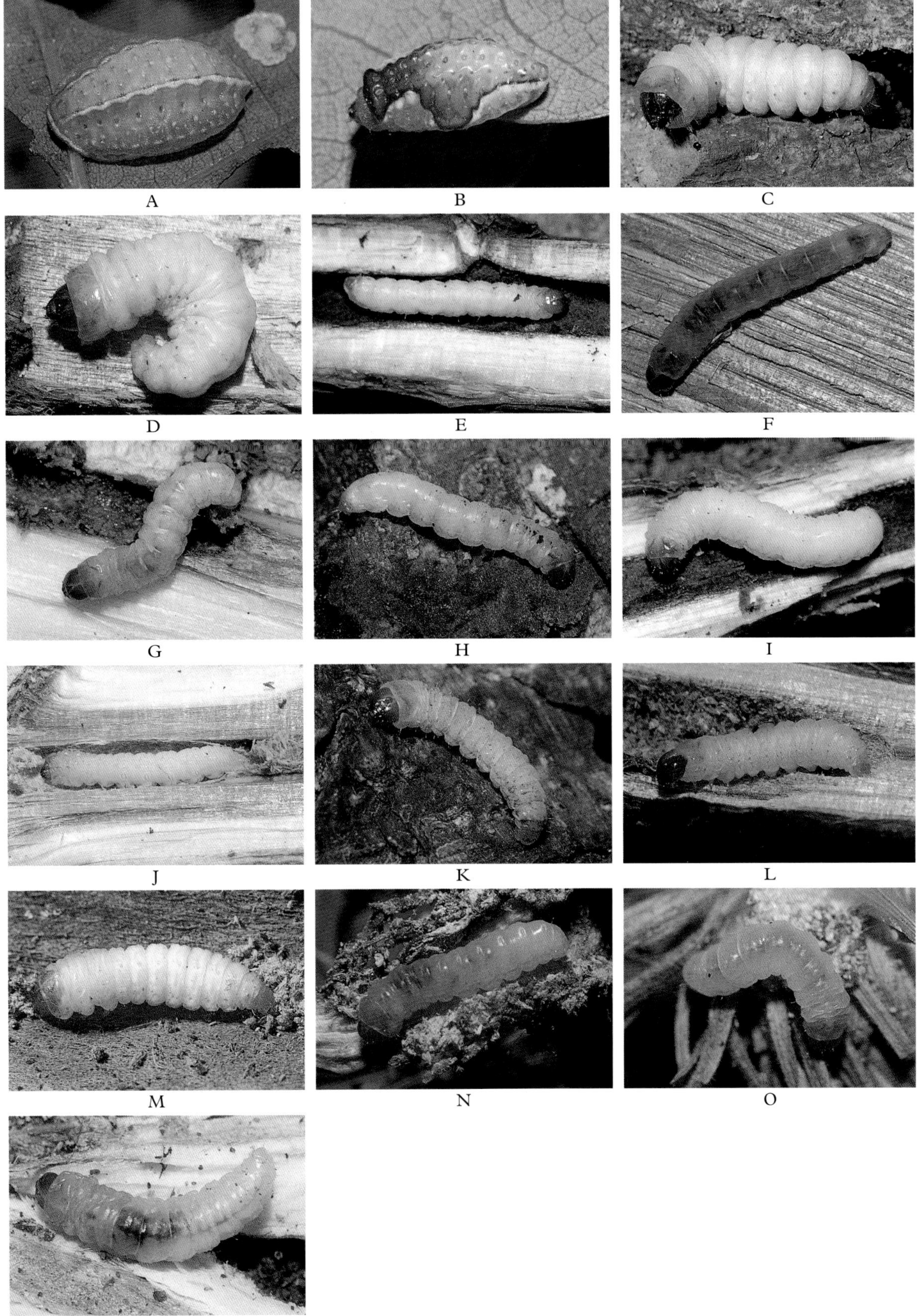
A
B
C
D
E
F
G
H
I
J
K
L
M
N
O
P

Plate 3: *Hesperiidae, Papilionidae, Pieridae*

A. **Chequered Skipper** *Carterocephalus palaemon* Pall. Page 7.
B. **Small Skipper** *Thymelicus sylvestris* Poda Page 7.
C. **Essex Skipper** *Thymelicus lineola* Ochs. Page 7.
D. **Lulworth Skipper** *Thymelicus acteon* Rott. Page 8.
E. **Silver-spotted Skipper** *Hesperia comma* Linn. Page 8.
F. **Large Skipper** *Ochlodes venata* Brem. & Grey Page 8.
G. **Dingy Skipper** *Erynnis tages* Linn. Page 8.
H. **Grizzled Skipper** *Pyrgus malvae* Linn. Page 8.
I. **The Swallowtail** *Papilio machaon* Linn. Page 9.
J. **Wood White** *Leptidea sinapis* Linn. Page 9.
K. **Pale Clouded Yellow** *Colias hyale* Linn. Page 9.
L. **Berger's Clouded Yellow** *Colias alfacariensis* Ribbe Page 9.
M. **Clouded Yellow** *Colias croceus* Geoffr. Page 9.
N. **The Brimstone** *Gonepteryx rhamni* Linn. Page 10.
O. **Black-veined White** *Aporia crataegi* Linn. Page 10.
P. **Large White** *Pieris brassicae* Linn. Page 10.
Q. **Small White** *Pieris rapae* Linn. Page 10.
R. **Green-veined White** *Pieris napi* Linn. Page 10.

A
B
C
D
E
F
G
H
I
J
K
L
M
N
O
P
Q
R

Plate 4: *Pieridae, Lycaenidae*

A. **Bath White** *Pontia daplidice* Linn. Page 10.
B. **Orange-tip** *Anthocharis cardamines* Linn. Page 10.
C. **Green Hairstreak** *Callophrys rubi* Linn. Page 11.
D. **Brown Hairstreak** *Thecla betulae* Linn. Page 11.
E. **Purple Hairstreak** *Quercusia quercus* Linn. Page 11.
F. **White-letter Hairstreak** *Satyrium w-album* Knoch Page 11.
G. **Black Hairstreak** *Satyrium pruni* Linn. Page 11.
H. **Small Copper** *Lycaena phlaeas* Linn. Page 12.
I. **Large Copper** *Lycaena dispar* Haw. Page 12.
J. **Long-tailed Blue** *Lampides boeticus* Linn. Page 12.
K. **Small Blue** *Cupido minimus* Fuess. Page 12.
L. **Silver-studded Blue** *Plebejus argus* Linn. Page 12.
M. **Brown Argus** *Aricia agestis* D. & S. Page 13.
N. **Northern Brown Argus** *Aricia artaxerxes* Fabr. Page 13.
O. **Common Blue** *Polyommatus icarus* Rott. Page 13.
P. **Chalkhill Blue** *Lysandra coridon* Poda Page 13.
Q. **Adonis Blue** *Lysandra bellargus* Rott. Page 13.
R. **Mazarine Blue** *Cyaniris semiargus* Rott. Page 13.

Plate 5: *Lycaenidae, Nemeobiidae, Nymphalidae*

A. **Holly Blue** *Celastrina argiolus* Linn. Page 14.
B. **Large Blue** *Maculinea arion* Linn. Page 14.
C. **Duke of Burgundy Fritillary** *Hamearis lucina* Linn. Page 14.
D. **White Admiral** *Ladoga camilla* Linn. Page 14.
E. **Purple Emperor** *Apatura iris* Linn. Page 15.
F. **Red Admiral** *Vanessa atalanta* Linn. Page 15.
G. **Painted Lady** *Cynthia cardui* Linn. Page 15.
H. **Small Tortoiseshell** *Aglais urticae* Linn. Page 15.
I. **Large Tortoiseshell** *Nymphalis polychloros* Linn. Page 15.
J. **Camberwell Beauty** *Nymphalis antiopa* Linn. Page 16.
K. **The Peacock** *Inachis io* Linn. Page 16.
L. **The Comma** *Polygonia c-album* Linn. Page 16.
M. **Small Pearl-bordered Fritillary** *Boloria selene* D. & S. Page 16.
N. **Pearl-bordered Fritillary** *Boloria euphrosyne* Linn. Page 16.
O. **Queen of Spain Fritillary** *Argynnis lathonia* Linn. Page 16.
P. **High Brown Fritillary** *Argynnis adippe* D. & S. Page 17.
Q. **Dark Green Fritillary** *Argynnis aglaja* Linn. Page 17.
R. **Silver-washed Fritillary** *Argynnis paphia* Linn. Page 17.

Plate 6: *Nymphalidae, Satyridae, Danaidae*

A. **Marsh Fritillary** *Eurodryas aurinia* Rott. Page 17.
B. **Glanville Fritillary** *Melitaea cinxia* Linn. Page 17.
C. **Heath Fritillary** *Mellicta athalia* Rott. Page 18.
D. **Speckled Wood** *Pararge aegeria* Linn. Page 18.
E. **The Wall** *Lasiommata megera* Linn. Page 18.
F. **Mountain Ringlet** *Erebia epiphron* Knoch Page 18.
G. **Scotch Argus** *Erebia aethiops* Esp. Page 18.
H. **Marbled White** *Melanargia galathea* Linn. Page 19.
I. **The Grayling** *Hipparchia semele* Linn. Page 19.
J. **The Gatekeeper** *Pyronia tithonus* Linn. Page 19.
K. **Meadow Brown** *Maniola jurtina* Linn. Page 19.
L. **Small Heath** *Coenonympha pamphilus* Linn. Page 19.
M. **Large Heath** *Coenonympha tullia* Müll. Page 19.
N. **The Ringlet** *Aphantopus hyperantus* Linn. Page 20.
O. **The Milkweed** or **Monarch** *Danaus plexippus* Linn. Page 20.

Plate 7: *Lasiocampidae, Saturniidae, Endromidae*

A. **December Moth** *Poecilocampa populi* Linn. Page 20.
B. **Pale Eggar** *Trichiura crataegi* Linn. Page 20.
C. **Small Eggar** *Eriogaster lanestris* Linn. Page 20.
D. **The Lackey** *Malacosoma neustria* Linn. Page 21.
E. **Ground Lackey** *Malacosoma castrensis* Linn. Page 21.
F. **Grass Eggar** *Lasiocampa trifolii* D. & S. Page 21.
G. **Oak Eggar** *Lasiocampa quercus* Linn. Page 21.
H. **Oak Eggar** *L. quercus* Linn. (early instar) Page 21.
I. **Fox Moth** *Macrothylacia rubi* Linn. Page 21.
J. **Fox Moth** *M. rubi* Linn. (early instar) Page 21.
K. **The Drinker** *Euthrix potatoria* Linn. Page 22.
L. **Small Lappet** *Phyllodesma ilicifolia* Linn. Page 22.
M. **The Lappet** *Gastropacha quercifolia* Linn. Page 22.
N. **Emperor Moth** *Pavonia pavonia* Linn. Page 22.
O. **Emperor Moth** *P. pavonia* Linn. (early instar) Page 22.
P. **Kentish Glory** *Endromis versicolora* Linn. Page 22.
Q. **Kentish Glory** *E. versicolora* Linn. (egg batch) Page 22.
R. **Small Eggar** *E. lanestris* Linn. (larval nest) Page 20.

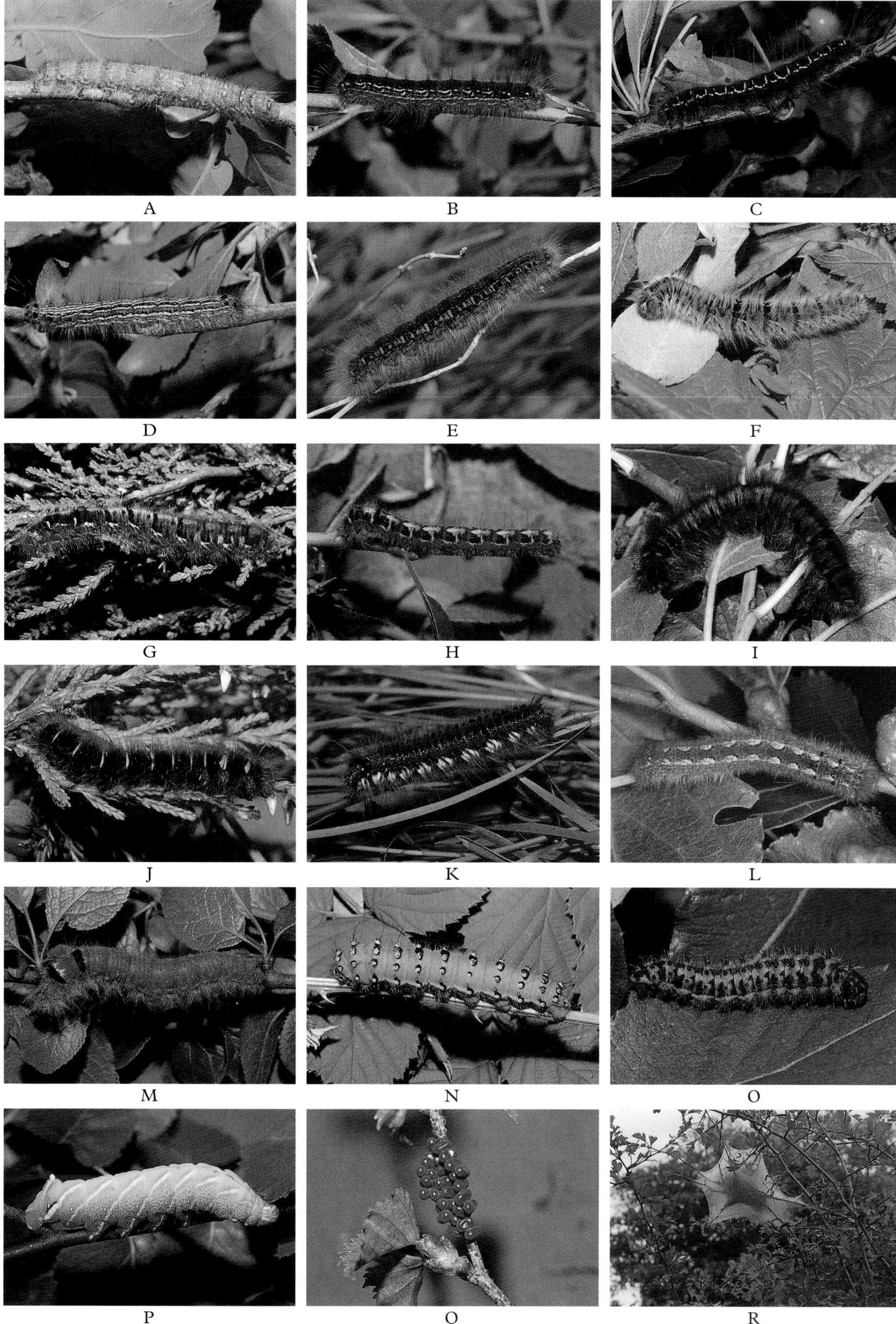

Plate 8: *Drepanidae, Thyatiridae, Geometridae*

A. **Scalloped Hook-tip** *Falcaria lacertinaria* Linn. Page 23.
B. **Oak Hook-tip** *Drepana binaria* Hufn. Page 23.
C. **Barred Hook-tip** *Drepana cultraria* Fabr. Page 23.
D. **Pebble Hook-tip** *Drepana falcataria* Linn. Page 23.
E. **Dusky Hook-tip** *Drepana curvatula* Borkh. Page 23.
F. **Scarce Hook-tip** *Sabra harpagula* Esp. Page 23.
G. **Chinese Character** *Cilix glaucata* Scop. Page 24.
H. **Peach Blossom** *Thyatira batis* Linn. Page 24.
I. **Buff Arches** *Habrosyne pyritoides* Hufn. Page 24.
J. **Figure of Eighty** *Tethea ocularis* Linn. Page 24.
K. **Poplar Lutestring** *Tethea or* D. & S. Page 24.
L. **Satin Lutestring** *Tetheella fluctuosa* Hb. Page 24.
M. **Common Lutestring** *Ochropacha duplaris* Linn. Page 25.
N. **Oak Lutestring** *Cymatophorima diluta* D. & S. Page 25.
O. **Yellow Horned** *Achlya flavicornis* Linn. Page 25.
P. **Frosted Green** *Polyploca ridens* Fabr. Page 25.
Q. **Orange Underwing** *Archiearis parthenias* Linn. Page 25.
R. **Light Orange Underwing** *Archiearis notha* Hb. Page 26.

A
B
C
D
E
F
G
H
I
J
K
L
M
N
O
P
Q
R

Plate 9: *Geometridae*

A. **March Moth** *Alsophila aescularia* D. & S. Page 26.
B. **Rest Harrow** *Aplasta ononaria* Fuess. Page 26.
C. **Grass Emerald** *Pseudoterpna pruinata* Hufn. Page 26.
D. **Large Emerald** *Geometra papilionaria* Linn. Page 26.
E. **Blotched Emerald** *Comibaena bajularia* D. & S. Page 26.
F. **Essex Emerald** *Thetidia smaragdaria* Fabr. Page 27.
G. **Common Emerald** *Hemithea aestivaria* Hb. Page 27.
H. **Small Grass Emerald** *Chlorissa viridata* Linn. Page 27.
I. **Sussex Emerald** *Thalera fimbrialis* Scop. Page 27.
J. **Small Emerald** *Hemistola chrysoprasaria* Esp. Page 27.
K. **Little Emerald** *Jodis lactearia* Linn. Page 27.
L. **Dingy Mocha** *Cyclophora pendularia* Cl. Page 28.
M. **The Mocha** *Cyclophora annulata* Schulze Page 28.
N. **Birch Mocha** *Cyclophora albipunctata* Hufn. Page 28.
O. **Blair's Mocha** *Cyclophora puppillaria* Hb. Page 28.
P. **False Mocha** *Cyclophora porata* Linn. Page 28.
Q. **Maiden's Blush** *Cyclophora punctaria* Linn. Page 28.
R. **Clay Triple-lines** *Cyclophora linearia* Hb. Page 28.

Plate 10: *Geometridae*

A. **Blood-vein** *Timandra griseata* Peters. Page 29.
B. **Lewes Wave** *Scopula immorata* Linn. Page 29.
C. **Sub-angled Wave** *Scopula nigropunctata* Hufn. Page 29.
D. **Lace Border** *Scopula ornata* Scop. Page 29.
E. **Tawny Wave** *Scopula rubiginata* Hufn. Page 29.
F. **Mullein Wave** *Scopula marginepunctata* Goeze Page 29.
G. **Small Blood-vein** *Scopula imitaria* Hb. Page 29.
H. **Rosy Wave** *Scopula emutaria* Hb. Page 30.
I. **Lesser Cream Wave** *Scopula immutata* Linn. Page 30.
J. **Cream Wave** *Scopula floslactata* Haw. Page 30.
K. **Smoky Wave** *Scopula ternata* Schr. Page 30.
L. **Bright Wave** *Idaea ochrata* Scop. Page 30.
M. **Purple-bordered Gold** *Idaea muricata* Hufn. Page 30.
N. **Least Carpet** *Idaea vulpinaria* H.-S. Page 30.
O. **Dotted Border Wave** *Idaea sylvestraria* Hb. Page 31.
P. **Small Fan-footed Wave** *Idaea biselata* Hufn. Page 31.
Q. **Rusty Wave** *Idaea inquinata* Scop. Page 31.
R. **Silky Wave** *Idaea dilutaria* Hb. Page 31.

A B C
D E F
G H I
J K L
M N O
P Q R

Plate 11: *Geometridae*

A. **Dwarf Cream Wave** *Idaea fuscovenosa* Goeze Page 31.
B. **Isle of Wight Wave** *Idaea humiliata* Hufn. Page 31.
C. **Small Dusty Wave** *Idaea seriata* Schr. Page 31.
D. **Single-dotted Wave** *Idaea dimidiata* Hufn. Page 32.
E. **Satin Wave** *Idaea subsericeata* Haw. Page 32.
F. **Weaver's Wave** *Idaea contiguaria* Hb. Page 32.
G. **Treble Brown Spot** *Idaea trigeminata* Haw. Page 32.
H. **Small Scallop** *Idaea emarginata* Linn. Page 32.
I. **Riband Wave** *Idaea aversata* Linn. Page 32.
J. **Portland Ribbon Wave** *Idaea degeneraria* Hb. Page 32.
K. **Plain Wave** *Idaea straminata* Borkh. Page 33.
L. **The Vestal** *Rhodometra sacraria* Linn. Page 33.
M. **Oblique Striped** *Phibalapteryx virgata* Hufn. Page 33.
N. **Oblique Carpet** *Orthonama vittata* Borkh. Page 33.
O. **The Gem** *Orthonama obstipata* Fabr. Page 33.
P. **Balsam Carpet** *Xanthorhoe biriviata* Borkh. Page 33.
Q. **Flame Carpet** *Xanthorhoe designata* Hufn. Page 34.
R. **Red Carpet** *Xanthorhoe munitata* Hb. Page 34.

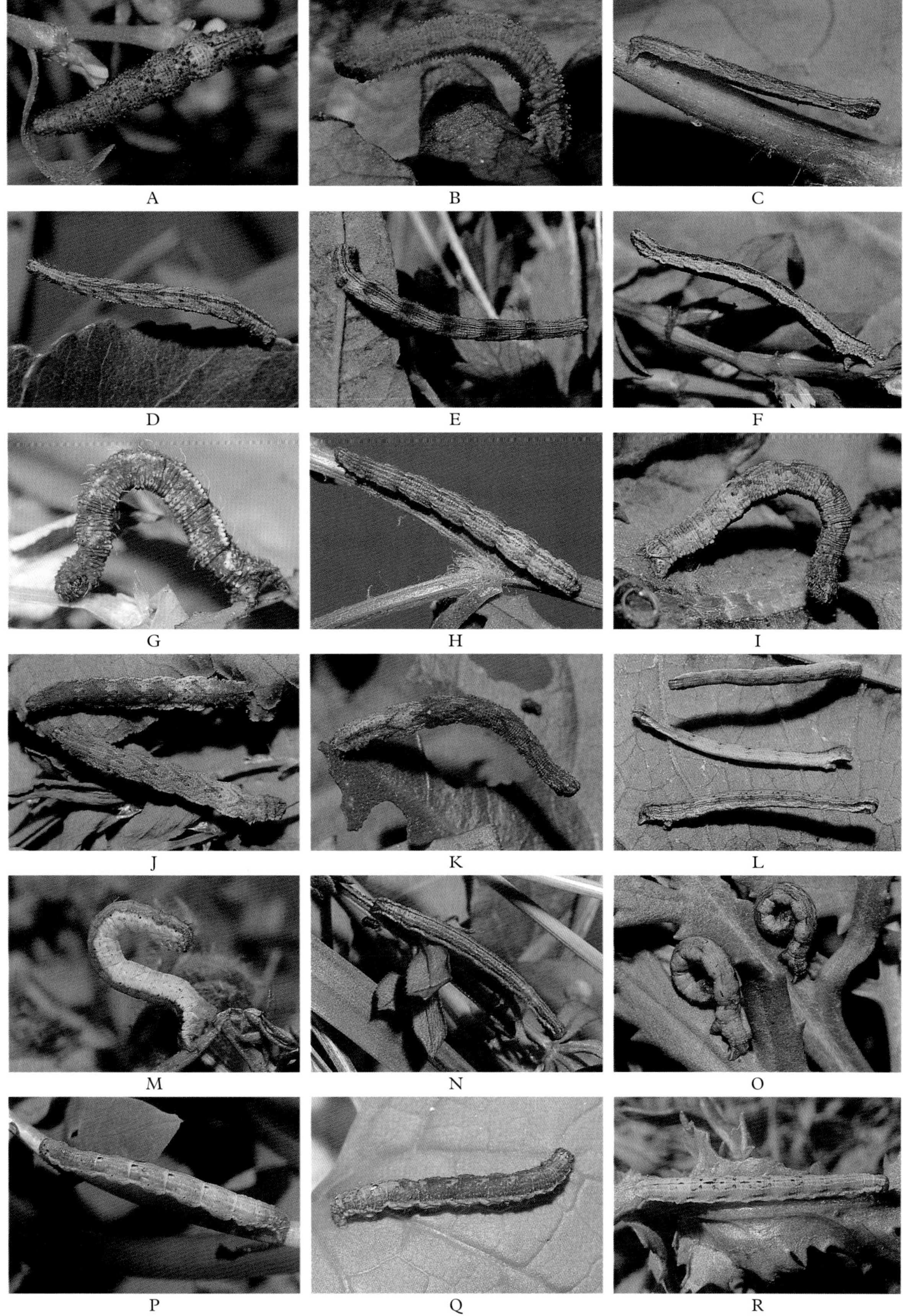

Plate 12: *Geometridae*

A. **Red Twin-spot Carpet** *Xanthorhoe spadicearia* D. & S. Page 34.
B. **Dark-barred Twin-spot Carpet** *Xanthorhoe ferrugata* Cl. Page 34.
C. **Large Twin-spot Carpet** *Xanthorhoe quadrifasiata* Cl. Page 34.
D. **Silver-ground Carpet** *Xanthorhoe montanata* D. & S. Page 34.
E. **Garden Carpet** *Xanthorhoe fluctuata* Linn. Page 35.
F. **Chalk Carpet** *Scotopteryx bipunctaria* D. & S. Page 35.
G. **Shaded Broad-bar** *Scotopteryx chenopodiata* Linn. Page 35.
H. **Lead Belle** *Scotopteryx mucronata* Scop. Page 35.
I. **July Belle** *Scotopteryx luridata* Hufn. Page 35.
J. **Ruddy Carpet** *Catarhoe rubidata* D. & S. Page 35.
K. **Royal Mantle** *Catarhoe cuculata* Hufn. Page 36.
L. **Small Argent and Sable** *Epirrhoe tristata* Linn. Page 36.
M. **Common Carpet** *Epirrhoe alternata* Müll. Page 36.
N. **Wood Carpet** *Epirrhoe rivata* Hb. Page 36.
O. **Galium Carpet** *Epirrhoe galiata* D. & S. Page 36.
P. **The Many-lined** *Costaconvexa polygrammata* Borkh. Page 36.
Q. **Yellow Shell** *Camptogramma bilineata* Linn. Page 36.
R. **The Mallow** *Larentia clavaria* Haw. Page 37.

A
B
C
D
E
F
G
H
I
J
K
L
M
N
O
P
Q
R

Plate 13: *Geometridae*

A. **Yellow-ringed Carpet** *Entephria flavicinctata* Hb. Page 37.
B. **Grey Mountain Carpet** *Entephria caesiata* D. & S. Page 37.
C. **Shoulder Stripe** *Anticlea badiata* D. & S. Page 37.
D. **The Streamer** *Anticlea derivata* D. & S. Page 37.
E. **Beautiful Carpet** *Mesoleuca albicillata* Linn. Page 37.
F. **Dark Spinach** *Pelurga comitata* Linn. Page 37.
G. **Water Carpet** *Lampropteryx suffumata* D. & S. Page 38.
H. **Devon Carpet** *Lampropteryx otregiata* Metc. Page 38.
I. **Purple Bar** *Cosmorhoe ocellata* Linn. Page 38.
J. **Striped Twin-spot Carpet** *Nebula salicata* Hb. Page 38.
K. **The Phoenix** *Eulithis prunata* Linn. Page 38.
L. **The Chevron** *Eulithis testata* Linn. Page 38.
M. **Northern Spinach** *Eulithis populata* Linn. Page 39.
N. **The Spinach** *Eulithis mellinata* Fabr. Page 39.
O. **Barred Straw** *Eulithis pyraliata* D. & S. Page 39.
P. **Small Phoenix** *Ecliptopera silaceata* D. & S. Page 39.
Q. **Red-green Carpet** *Chloroclysta siterata* Hufn. Page 39.
R. **Autumn Green Carpet** *Chloroclysta miata* Linn. Page 39.

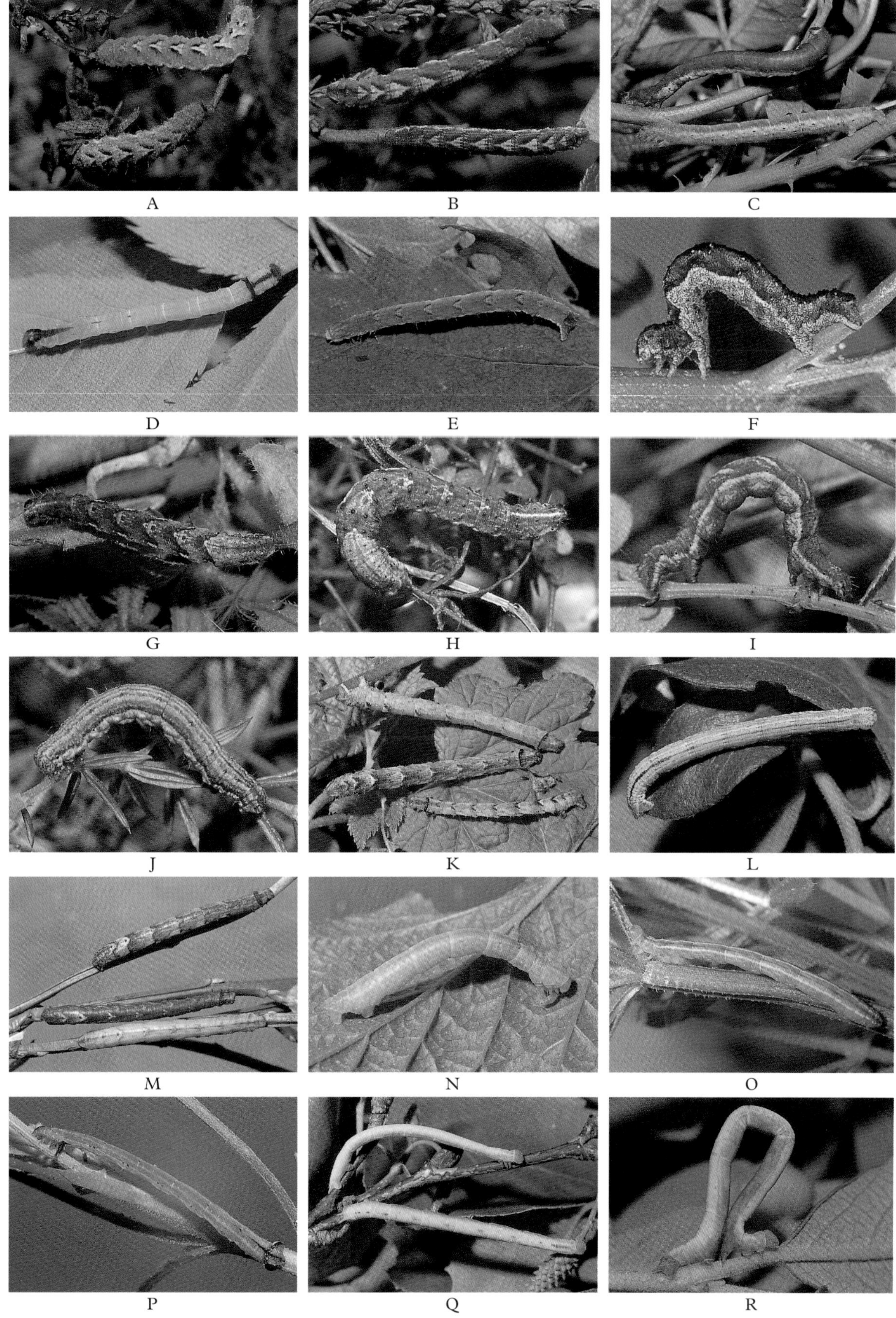

Plate 14: *Geometridae*

A. **Dark Marbled Carpet** *Chloroclysta citrata* Linn. Page 39.
B. **Arran Carpet** *Chloroclysta concinnata* Steph. Page 40.
C. **Common Marbled Carpet** *Chloroclysta truncata* Hufn. Page 40.
D. **Barred Yellow** *Cidaria fulvata* Forst. Page 40.
E. **Blue-bordered Carpet** *Plemyria rubiginata* D. & S. Page 40.
F. **Pine Carpet** *Thera firmata* Hb. Page 40.
G. **Grey Pine Carpet** *Thera obeliscata* Hb. Page 40.
H. **Spruce Carpet** *Thera britannica* Turn. Page 41.
I. **Chestnut-coloured Carpet** *Thera cognata* Thunb. Page 41.
J. **Juniper Carpet** *Thera juniperata* Linn. Page 41.
K. **Cypress Carpet** *Thera cupressata* Geyer Page 41.
L. **Netted Carpet** *Eustroma reticulatum* D. & S. Page 41.
M. **Broken-barred Carpet** *Electrophaes corylata* Thunb. Page 41.
N. **Beech-green Carpet** *Colostygia olivata* D. & S. Page 41.
O. **Mottled Grey** *Colostygia multistrigaria* Haw. Page 42.
P. **Green Carpet** *Colostygia pectinataria* Knoch Page 42.
Q. **July Highflyer** *Hydriomena furcata* Thunb. Page 42.
R. **May Highflyer** *Hydriomena impluviata* D. & S. Page 42.

A
B
C
D
E
F
G
H
I
J
K
L
M
N
O
P
Q
R

Plate 15: *Geometridae*

A. **Ruddy Highflyer** *Hydriomena ruberata* Freyer Page 42.
B. **Slender-striped Rufous** *Coenocalpe lapidata* Hb. Page 42.
C. **Small Waved Umber** *Horisme vitalbata* D. & S. Page 43.
D. **The Fern** *Horisme tersata* D. & S. Page 43.
E. **Pretty Chalk Carpet** *Melanthia procellata* D. & S. Page 43.
F. **Barberry Carpet** *Pareulype berberata* D. & S. Page 43.
G. **White-banded Carpet** *Spargania luctuata* D. & S. Page 43.
H. **Argent and Sable** *Rheumaptera hastata* Linn. Page 43.
I. **Scarce Tissue** *Rheumaptera cervinalis* Scop. Page 44.
J. **Scallop Shell** *Rheumaptera undulata* Linn. Page 44.
K. **The Tissue** *Triphosa dubitata* Linn. Page 44.
L. **Brown Scallop** *Philereme vetulata* D. & S. Page 44.
M. **Dark Umber** *Philereme transversata* Hufn. Page 44.
N. **Cloaked Carpet** *Euphyia biangulata* Haw. Page 44.
O. **Sharp-angled Carpet** *Euphyia unangulata* Haw. Page 44.
P. **November Moth** *Epirrita dilutata* D. & S. Page 45.
Q. **Pale November Moth** *Epirrita christyi* Allen Page 45.
R. **Autumnal Moth** *Epirrita autumnata* Borkh. Page 45.

Plate 16: *Geometridae*

A. **Small Autumnal Moth** *Epirrita filigrammaria* H.-S. Page 45.
B. **Winter Moth** *Operophtera brumata* Linn. Page 45.
C. **Northern Winter Moth** *Operophtera fagata* Scharf. Page 45.
D. **Barred Carpet** *Perizoma taeniata* Steph. Page 45.
E. **The Rivulet** *Perizoma affinitata* Steph. Page 46.
F. **Small Rivulet** *Perizoma alchemillata* Linn. Page 46.
G. **Barred Rivulet** *Perizoma bifaciata* Haw. Page 46.
H. **Heath Rivulet** *Perizoma minorata* Treit. Page 46.
I. **Pretty Pinion** *Perizoma blandiata* D. & S. Page 46.
J. **Grass Rivulet** *Perizoma albulata* D. & S. Page 47.
K. **Sandy Carpet** *Perizoma flavofasciata* Thunb. Page 47.
L. **Twin-spot Carpet** *Perizoma didymata* Linn. Page 47.
M. **Marsh Carpet** *Perizoma sagittata* Fabr. Page 47.
N. **Slender Pug** *Eupithecia tenuiata* Hb. Page 47.
O. **Maple Pug** *Eupithecia inturbata* Hb. Page 47.
P. **Haworth's Pug** *Eupithecia haworthiata* Doubl. Page 47.
Q. **Lead-coloured Pug** *Eupithecia plumbeolata* Haw. Page 48.
R. **Cloaked Pug** *Eupithecia abietaria* Goeze Page 48.

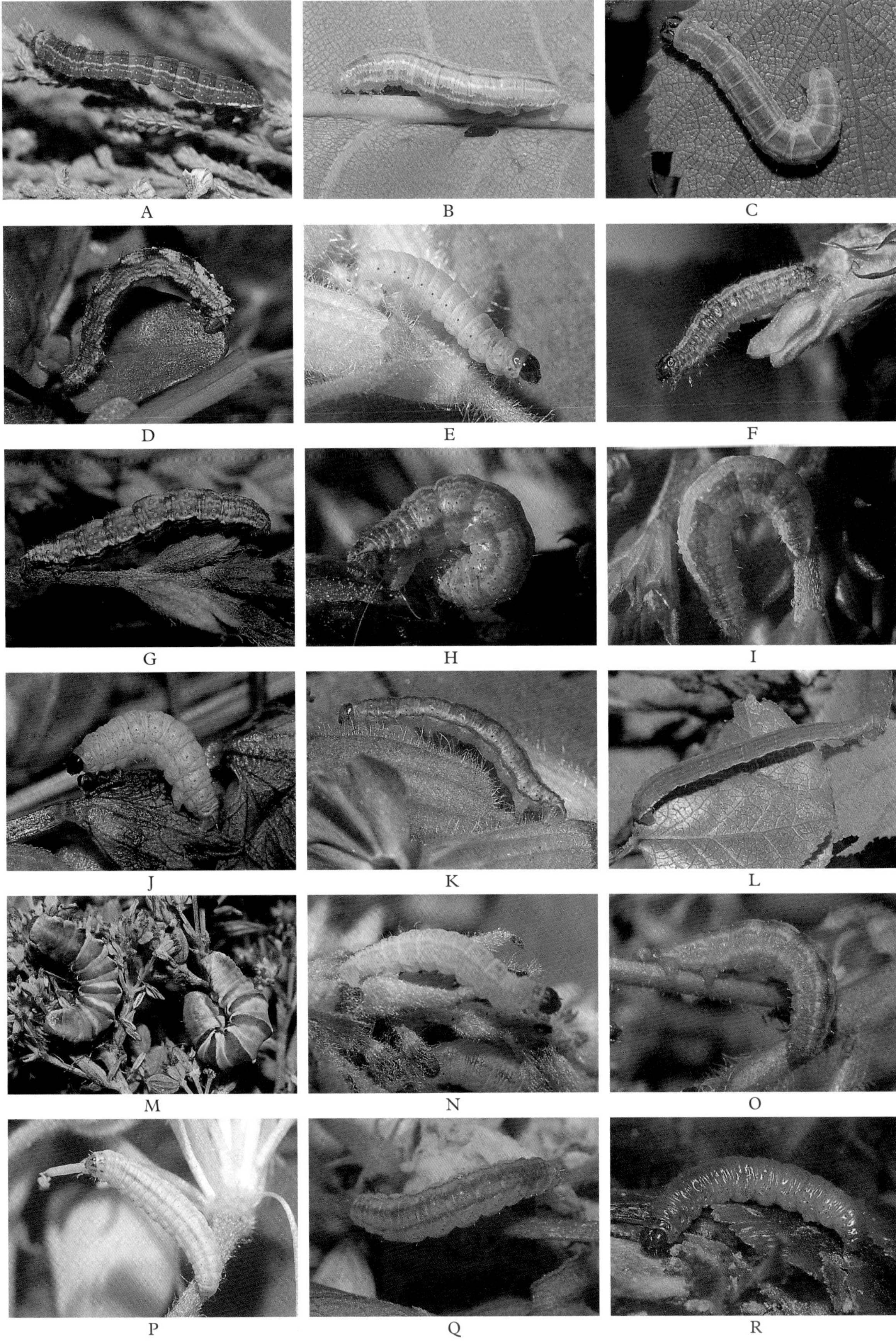
A
B
C
D
E
F
G
H
I
J
K
L
M
N
O
P
Q
R

Plate 17: *Geometridae*

A. **Toadflax Pug** *Eupithecia linariata* D. & S. Page 48.
B. **Foxglove Pug** *Eupithecia pulchellata* Steph. Page 48.
C. **Marbled Pug** *Eupithecia irriguata* Hb. Page 48.
D. **Mottled Pug** *Eupithecia exiguata* Hb. Page 48.
E. **Pinion-spotted Pug** *Eupithecia insigniata* Hb. Page 49.
F. **Valerian Pug** *Eupithecia valerianata* Hb. Page 49.
G. **Marsh Pug** *Eupithecia pygmaeata* Hb. Page 49.
H. **Netted Pug** *Eupithecia venosata* Fabr. Page 49.
I. **Pauper Pug** *Eupithecia egenaria* H.-S. Page 49.
J. **Lime-speck Pug** *Eupithecia centaureata* D. & S. Page 49.
K. **Triple-spotted Pug** *Eupithecia trisignaria* H.-S. Page 50.
L. **Freyer's Pug** *Eupithecia intricata* Zett. Page 50.
M. **Satyr Pug** *Eupithecia satyrata* Hb. Page 50.
N. **Wormwood Pug** *Eupithecia absinthiata* Cl. Page 50.
O. **Ling Pug** *Eupithecia goossensiata* Mab. Page 50.
P. **Currant Pug** *Eupithecia assimilata* Doubl. Page 50.
Q. **Bleached Pug** *Eupithecia expallidata* Doubl. Page 51.
R. **Common Pug** *Eupithecia vulgata* Haw. Page 51.

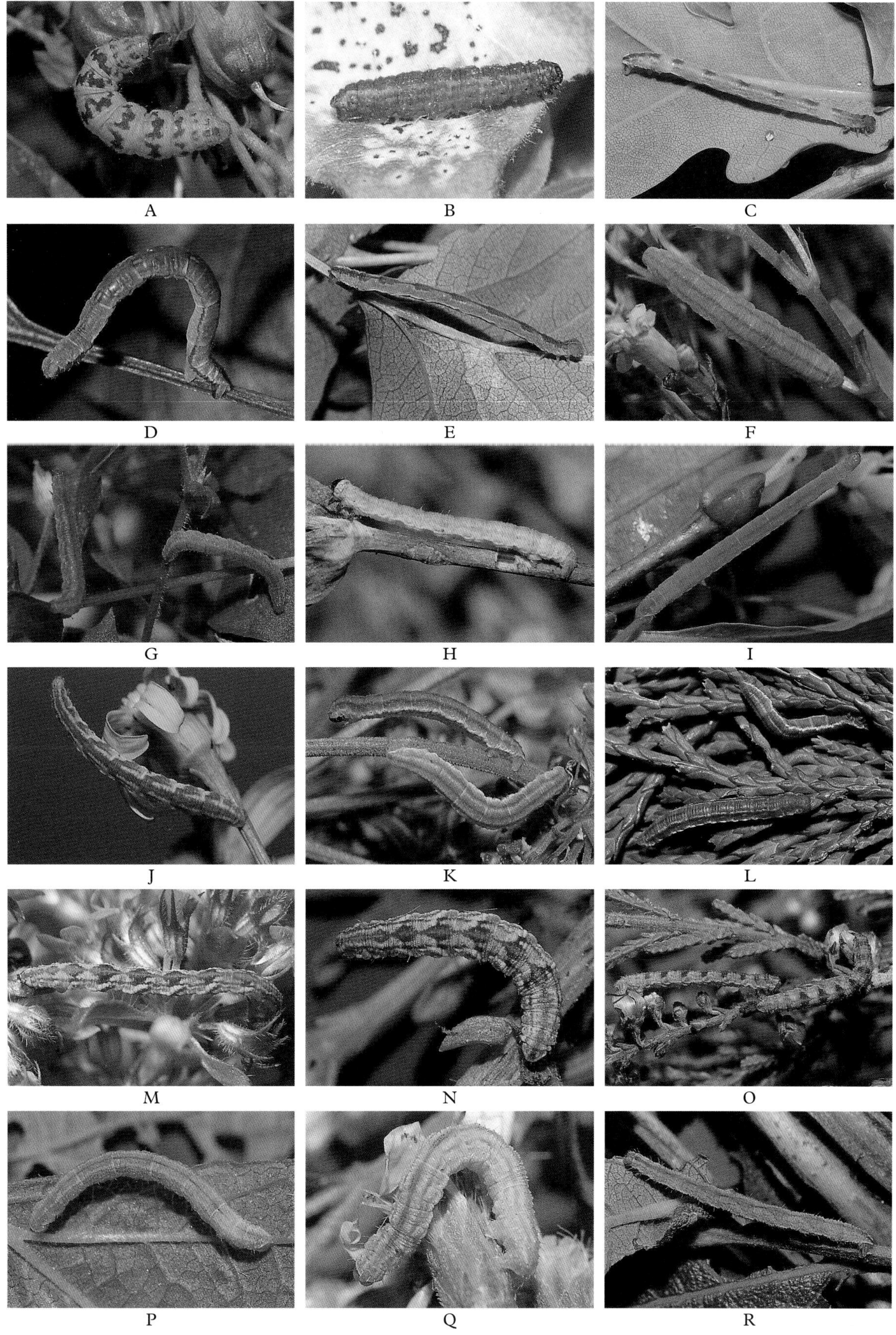

Plate 18: *Geometridae*

A. **White-spotted Pug** *Eupithecia tripunctaria* H.-S. Page 51.
B. **Campanula Pug** *Eupithecia denotata* Hb. Page 51.
C. **Jasione Pug** *Eupithecia denotata* Hb. Page 51.
D. **Grey Pug** *Eupithecia subfuscata* Haw. Page 51.
E. **Tawny Speckled Pug** *Eupithecia icterata* Vill. Page 51.
F. **Bordered Pug** *Eupithecia succenturiata* Linn. Page 51.
G. **Shaded Pug** *Eupithecia subumbrata* D. & S. Page 52.
H. **Yarrow Pug** *Eupithecia millefoliata* Rössl. Page 52.
I. **Plain Pug** *Eupithecia simpliciata* Haw. Page 52.
J. **Thyme Pug** *Eupithecia distinctaria* H.-S. Page 52.
K. **Ochreous Pug** *Eupithecia indigata* Hb. Page 52.
L. **Pimpinel Pug** *Eupithecia pimpinellata* Hb. Page 53.
M. **Narrow-winged Pug** *Eupithecia nanata* Hb. Page 53.
N. **Scarce Pug** *Eupithecia extensaria* Freyer Page 53.
O. **Ash Pug** *Eupithecia fraxinata* Crewe Page 53.
P. **Golden-rod Pug** *Eupithecia virgaureata* Doubl. Page 53.
Q. **Brindled Pug** *Eupithecia abbreviata* Steph. Page 53.
R. **Oak-tree Pug** *Eupithecia dodoneata* Guen. Page 53.

A B C D E F G H I J K L M N O P Q R

Plate 19: *Geometridae*

A. **Juniper Pug** *Eupithecia pusillata* D. & S. Page 54.
B. **Cypress Pug** *Eupithecia phoeniceata* Ramb. Page 54.
C. **Channel Islands Pug** *Eupithecia ultimaria* Boisd. Page 54.
D. **Larch Pug** *Eupithecia lariciata* Freyer Page 54.
E. **Dwarf Pug** *Eupithecia tantillaria* Boisd. Page 54.
F. **The V-Pug** *Chloroclystis v-ata* Haw. Page 54.
G. **Sloe Pug** *Chloroclystis chloerata* Mab. Page 55.
H. **Green Pug** *Chloroclystis rectangulata* Linn. Page 55.
I. **Bilberry Pug** *Chloroclystis debiliata* Hb. Page 55.
J. **Double-striped Pug** *Gymnoscelis rufifasciata* Haw. Page 55.
K. **Dentated Pug** *Anticollix sparsata* Treit. Page 55.
L. **The Streak** *Chesias legatella* D. & S. Page 55.
M. **Broom-tip** *Chesias rufata* Fabr. Page 55.
N. **Manchester Treble-bar** *Carsia sororiata* Hb. Page 56.
O. **Treble-bar** *Aplocera plagiata* Linn. Page 56.
P. **Lesser Treble-bar** *Aplocera efformata* Guen. Page 56.
Q. **Chimney Sweeper** *Odezia atrata* Linn. Page 56.
R. **Grey Carpet** *Lithostege griseata* D. & S. Page 56.

A
B
C
D
E
F
G
H
I
J
K
L
M
N
O
P
Q
R

Plate 20: *Geometridae*

A. **Blomer's Rivulet** *Discoloxia blomeri* Curt. Page 56.
B. **Welsh Wave** *Venusia cambrica* Curt. Page 56.
C. **Dingy Shell** *Euchoeca nebulata* Scop. Page 57.
D. **Small White Wave** *Asthena albulata* Hufn. Page 57.
E. **Small Yellow Wave** *Hydrelia flammeolaria* Hufn. Page 57.
F. **Waved Carpet** *Hydrelia sylvata* D. & S. Page 57.
G. **Drab Looper** *Minoa murinata* Scop. Page 57.
H. **The Seraphim** *Lobophora halterata* Hufn. Page 57.
I. **Barred Tooth-striped** *Trichopteryx polycommata* D. & S. Page 58.
J. **Early Tooth-striped** *Trichopteryx carpinata* Borkh. Page 58.
K. **Small Seraphim** *Pterapherapteryx sexalata* Retz. Page 58.
L. **Yellow-barred Brindle** *Acasis viretata* Hb. Page 58.
M. **The Magpie** *Abraxas grossulariata* Linn. Page 58.
N. **Clouded Magpie** *Abraxas sylvata* Scop. Page 58.
O. **Clouded Border** *Lomaspilis marginata* Linn. Page 58.
P. **Scorched Carpet** *Ligdia adustata* D. & S. Page 59.
Q. **Peacock Moth** *Semiothisa notata* Linn. Page 59.
R. **Sharp-angled Peacock** *Semiothisa alternaria* Hb. Page 59.

A B C D E F G H I J K L M N O P Q R

Plate 21: *Geometridae*

A. **Dusky Peacock** *Semiothisa signaria* Hb. Page 59.
B. **Tawny-barred Angle** *Semiothisa liturata* Cl. Page 59.
C. **Latticed Heath** *Semiothisa clathrata* Linn. Page 59.
D. **Netted Mountain Moth** *Semiothisa carbonaria* Cl. Page 60.
E. **Rannoch Looper** *Semiothisa brunneata* Thunb. Page 60.
F. **The V-Moth** *Semiothisa wauaria* Linn. Page 60.
G. **Frosted Yellow** *Isturgia limbaria* Fabr. Page 60.
H. **Little Thorn** *Cepphis advenaria* Hb. Page 60.
I. **Brown Silver-line** *Petrophora chlorosata* Scop. Page 60.
J. **Barred Umber** *Plagodis pulveraria* Linn. Page 61.
K. **Scorched Wing** *Plagodis dolabraria* Linn. Page 61.
L. **Horse Chestnut** *Pachycnemia hippocastanaria* Hb. Page 61.
M. **Brimstone Moth** *Opisthograptis luteolata* Linn. Page 61.
N. **Brimstone Moth** *O. luteolata* Linn. (green form) Page 61.
O. **Bordered Beauty** *Epione repandaria* Hufn. Page 61.
P. **Dark Bordered Beauty** *Epione paralellaria* D. & S. Page 61.
Q. **Speckled Yellow** *Pseudopanthera macularia* Linn. Page 62.
R. **Lilac Beauty** *Apeira syringaria* Linn. Page 62.

Plate 22: *Geometridae*

A. **Large Thorn** *Ennomos autumnaria* Werneb. Page 62.
B. **August Thorn** *Ennomos quercinaria* Hufn. Page 62.
C. **Canary-shouldered Thorn** *Ennomos alniaria* Linn. Page 62.
D. **Dusky Thorn** *Ennomos fuscantaria* Haw. Page 62.
E. **September Thorn** *Ennomos erosaria* D. & S. Page 63.
F. **Early Thorn** *Selenia dentaria* Fabr. Page 63.
G. **Lunar Thorn** *Selenia lunularia* Hb. Page 63.
H. **Purple Thorn** *Selenia tetralunaria* Hufn. Page 63.
I. **Scalloped Hazel** *Odontopera bidentata* Cl. Page 63.
J. **Scalloped Oak** *Crocallis elinguaria* Linn. Page 63.
K. **Swallow-tailed Moth** *Ourapteryx sambucaria* Linn. Page 64.
L. **Feathered Thorn** *Colotois pennaria* Linn. Page 64.
M. **Orange Moth** *Angerona prunaria* Linn. Page 64.
N. **Small Brindled Beauty** *Apocheima hispidaria* D. & S. Page 64.
O. **Pale Brindled Beauty** *Apocheima pilosaria* D. & S. Page 64.
P. **Brindled Beauty** *Lycia hirtaria* Cl. Page 64.
Q. **Belted Beauty** *Lycia zonaria* D. & S. Page 65.
R. **Rannoch Brindled Beauty** *Lycia lapponaria* Boisd. Page 65.

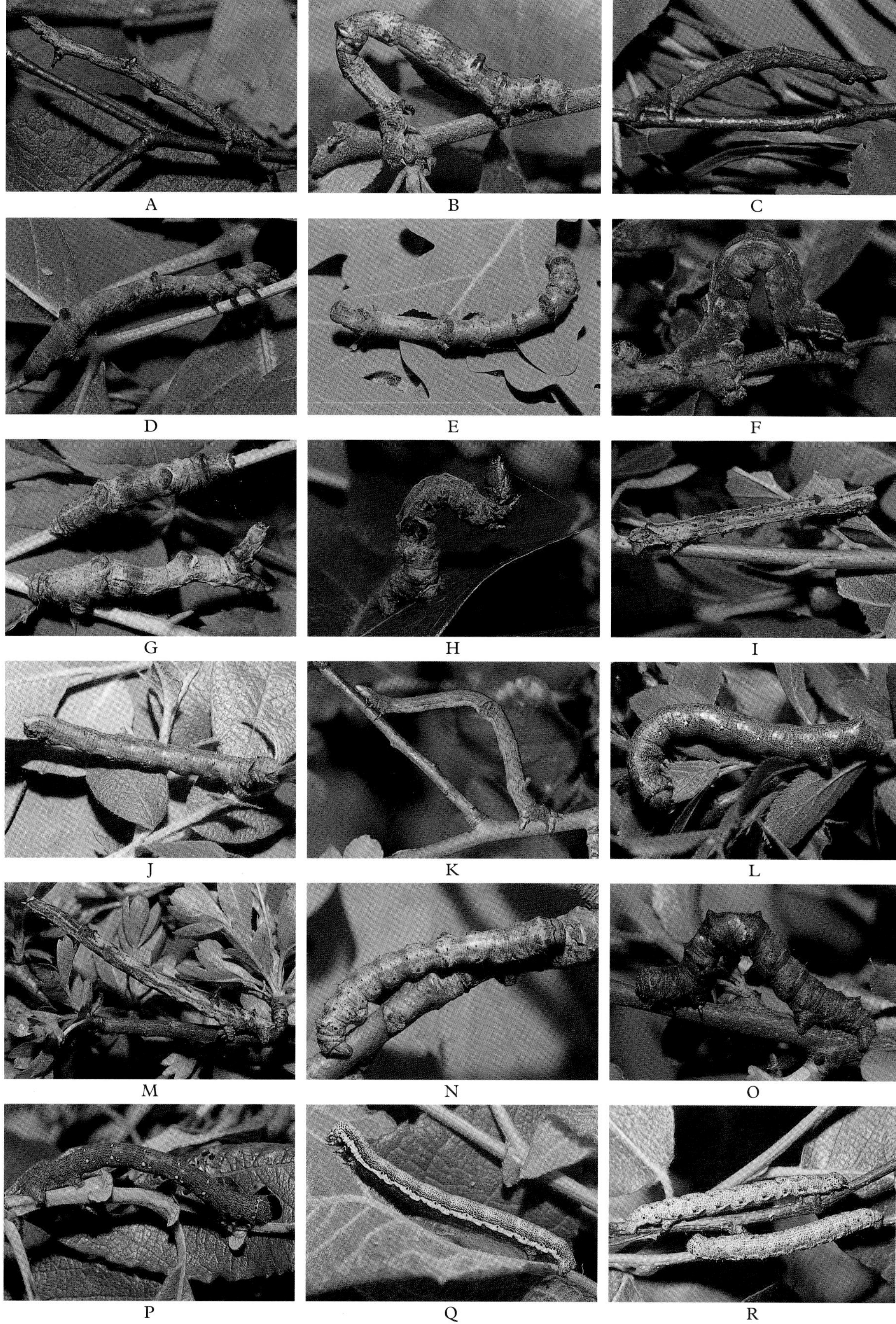

A
B
C
D
E
F
G
H
I
J
K
L
M
N
O
P
Q
R

Plate 23: *Geometridae*

A. **Oak Beauty** *Biston strataria* Hufn. Page 65.
B. **Peppered Moth** *Biston betularia* Linn. Page 65.
C. **Spring Usher** *Agriopis leucophaearia* D. & S. Page 65.
D. **Scarce Umber** *Agriopis aurantiaria* Hb. Page 66.
E. **Dotted Border** *Agriopis marginaria* Fabr. Page 66.
F. **Mottled Umber** *Erannis defoliaria* Cl. Page 66.
G. **Waved Umber** *Menophra abruptaria* Thunb. Page 66.
H. **Willow Beauty** *Peribatodes rhomboidaria* D. & S. Page 66.
I. **Feathered Beauty** *Peribatodes secundaria* Esp. Page 66.
J. **Lydd Beauty** *Peribatodes manuelaria* H.-S. Page 67.
K. **Bordered Grey** *Selidosema brunnearia* Vill. Page 67.
L. **Ringed Carpet** *Cleora cinctaria* D. & S. Page 67.
M. **Satin Beauty** *Deileptenia ribeata* Cl. Page 67.
N. **Mottled Beauty** *Alcis repandata* Linn. Page 67.
O. **Dotted Carpet** *Alcis jubata* Thunb. Page 67.
P. **Great Oak Beauty** *Hypomecis roboraria* D. & S. Page 68.
Q. **Pale Oak Beauty** *Serraca punctinalis* Scop. Page 68.
R. **Brussels Lace** *Cleorodes lichenaria* Hufn. Page 68.

A B C D E F G H I J K L M N O P Q R

Plate 24: *Geometridae*

A. **The Engrailed** *Ectropis bistortata* Goeze Page 68.
B. **Small Engrailed** *Ectropis crepuscularia* D. & S. Page 68.
C. **Square Spot** *Paradarisa consonaria* Hb. Page 69.
D. **Brindled White-spot** *Paradarisa extersaria* Hb. Page 69.
E. **Grey Birch** *Aethalura punctulata* D. & S. Page 69.
F. **Common Heath** *Ematurga atomaria* Linn. Page 69.
G. **Bordered White** *Bupalus piniaria* Linn. Page 69.
H. **Common White Wave** *Cabera pusaria* Linn. Page 69.
I. **Common Wave** *Cabera exanthemata* Scop. Page 70.
J. **White-pinion Spotted** *Lomographa bimaculata* Fabr. Page 70.
K. **Clouded Silver** *Lomographa temerata* D. & S. Page 70.
L. **Sloe Carpet** *Aleucis distinctata* H.-S. Page 70.
M. **Early Moth** *Theria primaria* Haw. Page 70.
N. **Light Emerald** *Campaea margaritata* Linn. Page 70.
O. **Barred Red** *Hylaea fasciaria* Linn. Page 70.
P. **Irish Annulet** *Odontognophos dumetata* Treit. Page 71.
Q. **Scotch Annulet** *Gnophos obfuscata* D. & S. Page 71.
R. **The Annulet** *Gnophos obscurata* D. & S. Page 71.

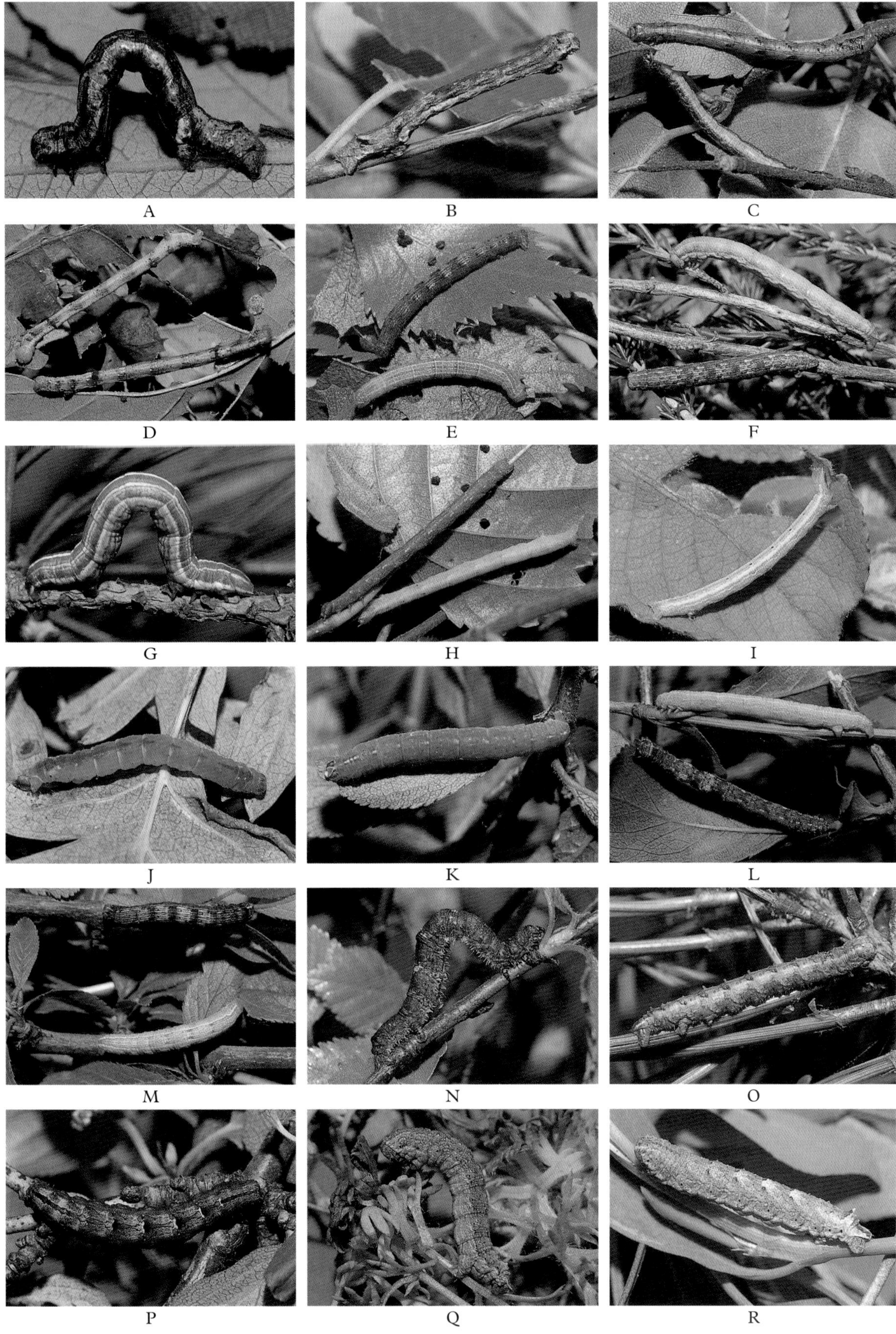
A
B
C
D
E
F
G
H
I
J
K
L
M
N
O
P
Q
R

Plate 25: *Geometridae, Sphingidae*

A. **Black Mountain Moth** *Psodos coracina* Esp. Page 71.
B. **Black-veined Moth** *Siona lineata* Scop. Page 71.
C. **Straw Belle** *Aspitates gilvaria* D. & S. Page 72.
D. **Yellow Belle** *Aspitates ochrearia* Rossi Page 72.
E. **Grey Scalloped Bar** *Dyscia fagaria* Thunb. Page 72.
F. **Grass Wave** *Perconia strigillaria* Hb. Page 72.
G. **Convolvulus Hawk-moth** *Agrius convolvuli* Linn. Page 72.
H. **Death's-head Hawk-moth** *Acherontia atropos* Linn. Page 73.
I. **Privet Hawk-moth** *Sphinx ligustri* Linn. Page 73.
J. **Pine Hawk-moth** *Hyloicus pinastri* Linn. Page 73.
K. **Lime Hawk-moth** *Mimas tiliae* Linn. Page 73.
L. **Eyed Hawk-moth** *Smerinthus ocellata* Linn. Page 73.
M. **Poplar Hawk-moth** *Laothoe populi* Linn. Page 73.
N. **Narrow-bordered Bee Hawk-moth** *Hemaris tityus* Linn. Page 73.
O. **Broad-bordered Bee Hawk-moth** *Hemaris fuciformis* Linn. Page 74.
P. **Humming-bird Hawk-moth** *Macroglossum stellatarum* Linn. Page 74.
Q. **Oleander Hawk-moth** *Daphnis nerii* Linn. Page 74.
R. **Spurge Hawk-moth** *Hyles euphorbiae* Linn. Page 74.

Plate 26: *Sphingidae, Notodontidae*

A. **Bedstraw Hawk-moth** *Hyles gallii* Rott. Page 74.
B. **Striped Hawk-moth** *Hyles livornica* Esp. Page 75.
C. **Elephant Hawk-moth** *Deilephila elpenor* Linn. Page 75.
D. **Small Elephant Hawk-moth** *Deilephila porcellus* Linn. Page 75.
E. **Silver-striped Hawk-moth** *Hippotion celerio* Linn. Page 75.
F. **Buff-tip** *Phalera bucephala* Linn. Page 75.
G. **Puss Moth** *Cerura vinula* Linn. Page 75.
H. **Alder Kitten** *Furcula bicuspis* Borkh. Page 76.
I. **Sallow Kitten** *Furcula furcula* Cl. Page 76.
J. **Poplar Kitten** *Furcula bifida* Brahm Page 76.
K. **Lobster Moth** *Stauropus fagi* Linn. Page 76.
L. **Iron Prominent** *Notodonta dromedarius* Linn. Page 76.
M. **Pebble Prominent** *Eligmodonta ziczac* Linn. Page 77.
N. **Tawny Prominent** *Harpyia milhauseri* Fabr. Page 77.
O. **Great Prominent** *Peridea anceps* Goeze Page 77.
P. **Lesser Swallow Prominent** *Pheosia gnoma* Fabr. Page 77.
Q. **Swallow Prominent** *Pheosia tremula* Cl. Page 77.
R. **Coxcomb Prominent** *Ptilodon capucina* Linn. Page 77.

A
B
C
D
E
F
G
H
I
J
K
L
M
N
O
P
Q
R

Plate 27: *Notodontidae, Thaumetopoeidae, Lymantriidae*

A. **Maple Prominent** *Ptilodontella cucullina* D. & S. Page 78.
B. **Scarce Prominent** *Odontosia carmelita* Esp. Page 78.
C. **Pale Prominent** *Pterostoma palpina* Cl. Page 78.
D. **White Prominent** *Leucodonta bicoloria* D. & S. Page 78.
E. **Plumed Prominent** *Ptilophora plumigera* D. & S. Page 78.
F. **Marbled Brown** *Drymonia dodonaea* D. & S. Page 78.
G. **Lunar Marbled Brown** *Drymonia ruficornis* Hufn. Page 79.
H. **Small Chocolate-tip** *Clostera pigra* Hufn. Page 79.
I. **Scarce Chocolate-tip** *Clostera anachoreta* D. & S. Page 79.
J. **Chocolate-tip** *Clostera curtula* Linn. Page 79.
K. **Figure of Eight** *Diloba caeruleocephala* Linn. Page 79.
L. **Oak Processionary** *Thaumetopoea processionea* Linn. Page 80.
M. **Scarce Vapourer** *Orgyia recens* Hb. Page 80.
N. **The Vapourer** *Orgyia antiqua* Linn. Page 80.
O. **Dark Tussock** *Dicallomera fascelina* Linn. Page 80.
P. **Pale Tussock** *Calliteara pudibunda* Linn. Page 80.
Q. **Brown-tail** *Euproctis chrysorrhoea* Linn. Page 81.
R. **Yellow-tail** *Euproctis similis* Fuess. Page 81.

Plate 28: *Lymantriidae, Arctiidae*

A. **White Satin Moth** *Leucoma salicis* Linn. Page 81.
B. **Black V Moth** *Arctornis l-nigrum* Müll. Page 81.
C. **Black Arches** *Lymantria monacha* Linn. Page 81.
D. **Gypsy Moth** *Lymantria dispar* Linn. Page 81.
E. **Round-winged Muslin** *Thumatha senex* Hb. Page 82.
F. **Dew Moth** *Setina irrorella* Linn. Page 82.
G. **Rosy Footman** *Miltochrista miniata* Forst. Page 82.
H. **Muslin Footman** *Nudaria mundana* Linn. Page 82.
I. **Red-necked Footman** *Atolmis rubricollis* Linn. Page 82.
J. **Four-dotted Footman** *Cybosia mesomella* Linn. Page 83.
K. **Dotted Footman** *Pelosia muscerda* Hufn. Page 83.
L. **Small Dotted Footman** *Pelosia obtusa* H.-S. Page 83.
M. **Orange Footman** *Eilema sororcula* Hufn. Page 83.
N. **Dingy Footman** *Eilema griseola* Hb. Page 83.
O. **Hoary Footman** *Eilema caniola* Hb. Page 83.
P. **Pigmy Footman** *Eilema pygmaeola* Doubl. Page 84.
Q. **Scarce Footman** *Eilema complana* Linn. Page 84.
R. **Northern Footman** *Eilema sericea* Gregs. Page 84.

A
B
C
D
E
F
G
H
I
J
K
L
M
N
O
P
Q
R

Plate 29: *Arctiidae*

A. **Buff Footman** *Eilema deplana* Esp. Page 84.
B. **Common Footman** *Eilema lurideola* Zinck. Page 84.
C. **Four-spotted Footman** *Lithosia quadra* Linn. Page 84.
D. **Feathered Footman** *Spiris striata* Linn. Page 85.
E. **Speckled Footman** *Coscinia cribraria* Linn. Page 85.
F. **Crimson Speckled** *Utetheisa pulchella* Linn. Page 85.
G. **Wood Tiger** *Parasemia plantaginis* Linn. Page 85.
H. **Garden Tiger** *Arctia caja* Linn. Page 85.
I. **Cream-spot Tiger** *Arctia villica* Linn. Page 86.
J. **Clouded Buff** *Diacrisia sannio* Linn. Page 86.
K. **White Ermine** *Spilosoma lubricipeda* Linn. Page 86.
L. **Buff Ermine** *Spilosoma luteum* Hufn. Page 86.
M. **Water Ermine** *Spilosoma urticae* Esp. Page 86.
N. **Muslin Moth** *Diaphora mendica* Cl. Page 86.
O. **Ruby Tiger** *Phragmatobia fuliginosa* Linn. Page 86.
P. **Jersey Tiger** *Euplagia quadripunctaria* Poda Page 87.
Q. **Scarlet Tiger** *Callimorpha dominula* Linn. Page 87.
R. **The Cinnabar** *Tyria jacobaeae* Linn. Page 87.

Plate 30: *Nolidae, Noctuidae*

A. **Kent Black Arches** *Meganola albula* D. & S. Page 87.
B. **Short-cloaked Moth** *Nola cucullatella* Linn. Page 88.
C. **Least Black Arches** *Nola confusalis* H.-S. Page 88.
D. **Scarce Black Arches** *Nola aerugula* Hb. Page 88.
E. **Square-spot Dart** *Euxoa obelisca* D. & S. Page 88.
F. **White-line Dart** *Euxoa tritici* Linn. Page 88.
G. **Garden Dart** *Euxoa nigricans* Linn. Page 88.
H. **Coast Dart** *Euxoa cursoria* Hufn. Page 89.
I. **Light Feathered Rustic** *Agrotis cinerea* D. & S. Page 89.
J. **Archer's Dart** *Agrotis vestigialis* Hufn. Page 89.
K. **Turnip Moth** *Agrotis segetum* D. & S. Page 89.
L. **Heart and Club** *Agrotis clavis* Hufn. Page 89.
M. **Heart and Dart** *Agrotis exclamationis* Linn. Page 90.
N. **Crescent Dart** *Agrotis trux* Hb. Page 90.
O. **Dark Sword-grass** *Agrotis ipsilon* Hufn. Page 90.
P. **Shuttle-shaped Dart** *Agrotis puta* Hb. Page 90.
Q. **Sand Dart** *Agrotis ripae* Hb. Page 90.
R. **Great Dart** *Agrotis crassa* Hb. Page 90.

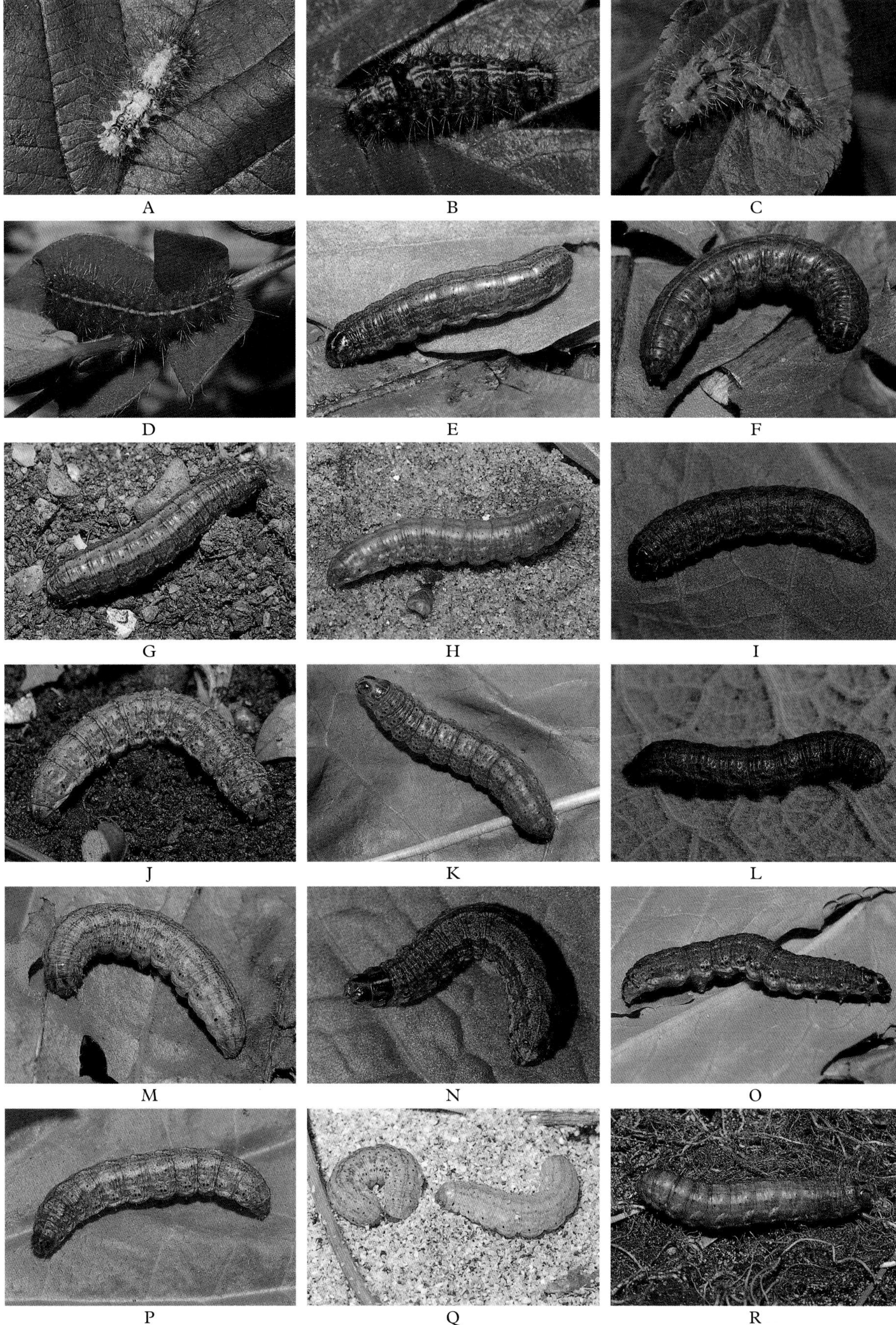
A
B
C
D
E
F
G
H
I
J
K
L
M
N
O
P
Q
R

Plate 31: *Noctuidae*

A. **Purple Cloud** *Actinotia polyodon* Cl. Page 91.
B. **The Flame** *Axylia putris* Linn. Page 91.
C. **Portland Moth** *Actebia praecox* Linn. Page 91.
D. **Flame Shoulder** *Ochropleura plecta* Linn. Page 91.
E. **Plain Clay** *Eugnorisma depuncta* Linn. Page 91.
F. **Northern Rustic** *Standfussiana lucernea* Linn. Page 92.
G. **Dotted Rustic** *Rhyacia simulans* Hufn. Page 92.
H. **Large Yellow Underwing** *Noctua pronuba* Linn. Page 92.
I. **Lunar Yellow Underwing** *Noctua orbona* Hufn. Page 92.
J. **Lesser Yellow Underwing** *Noctua comes* Hb. Page 92.
K. **Broad-bordered Yellow Underwing** *Noctua fimbriata* Schreb. Page 93.
L. **Lesser Broad-bordered Yellow Underwing** *Noctua janthe* Borkh. Page 93.
M. **Least Yellow Underwing** *Noctua interjecta* Hb. Page 93.
N. **Double Dart** *Graphiphora augur* Fabr. Page 93.
O. **Rosy Marsh Moth** *Eugraphe subrosea* Steph. Page 93.
P. **Cousin German** *Paradiarsia sobrina* Dup. Page 94.
Q. **Autumnal Rustic** *Paradiarsia glareosa* Esp. Page 94.
R. **True Lover's Knot** *Lycophotia porphyrea* D. & S. Page 94.

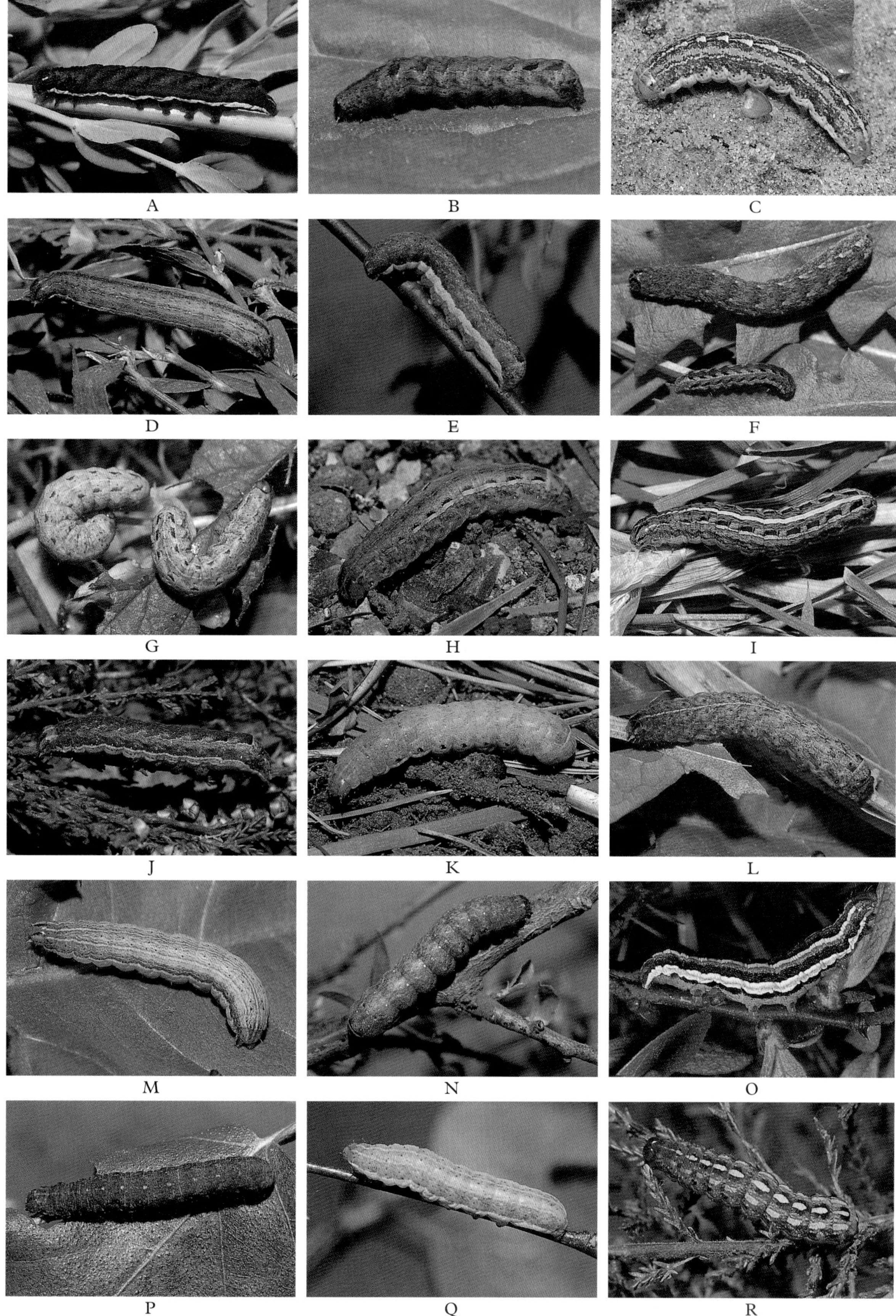

Plate 32: *Noctuidae*

A. **Pearly Underwing** *Peridroma saucia* Hb. Page 94.
B. **Ingrailed Clay** *Diarsia mendica* Fabr. Page 94.
C. **Barred Chestnut** *Diarsia dahlii* Hb. Page 94.
D. **Purple Clay** *Diarsia brunnea* D. & S. Page 95.
E. **Small Square-spot** *Diarsia rubi* View. Page 95.
F. **Fen Square-spot** *Diarsia florida* Schmidt Page 95.
G. **Northern Dart** *Xestia alpicola* Zett. Page 95.
H. **Setaceous Hebrew Character** *Xestia c-nigrum* Linn. Page 95.
I. **Triple-spotted Clay** *Xestia ditrapezium* D. & S. Page 96.
J. **Double Square-spot** *Xestia triangulum* Hufn. Page 96.
K. **Ashworth's Rustic** *Xestia ashworthii* Doubl. Page 96.
L. **Dotted Clay** *Xestia baja* D. & S. Page 96.
M. **Square-spotted Clay** *Xestia rhomboidea* Esp. Page 96.
N. **Neglected Rustic** *Xestia castanea* Esp. Page 97.
O. **Six-striped Rustic** *Xestia sexstrigata* Haw. Page 97.
P. **Square-spot Rustic** *Xestia xanthographa* D. & S. Page 97.
Q. **Heath Rustic** *Xestia agathina* Dup. Page 97.
R. **The Gothic** *Naenia typica* Linn. Page 97.

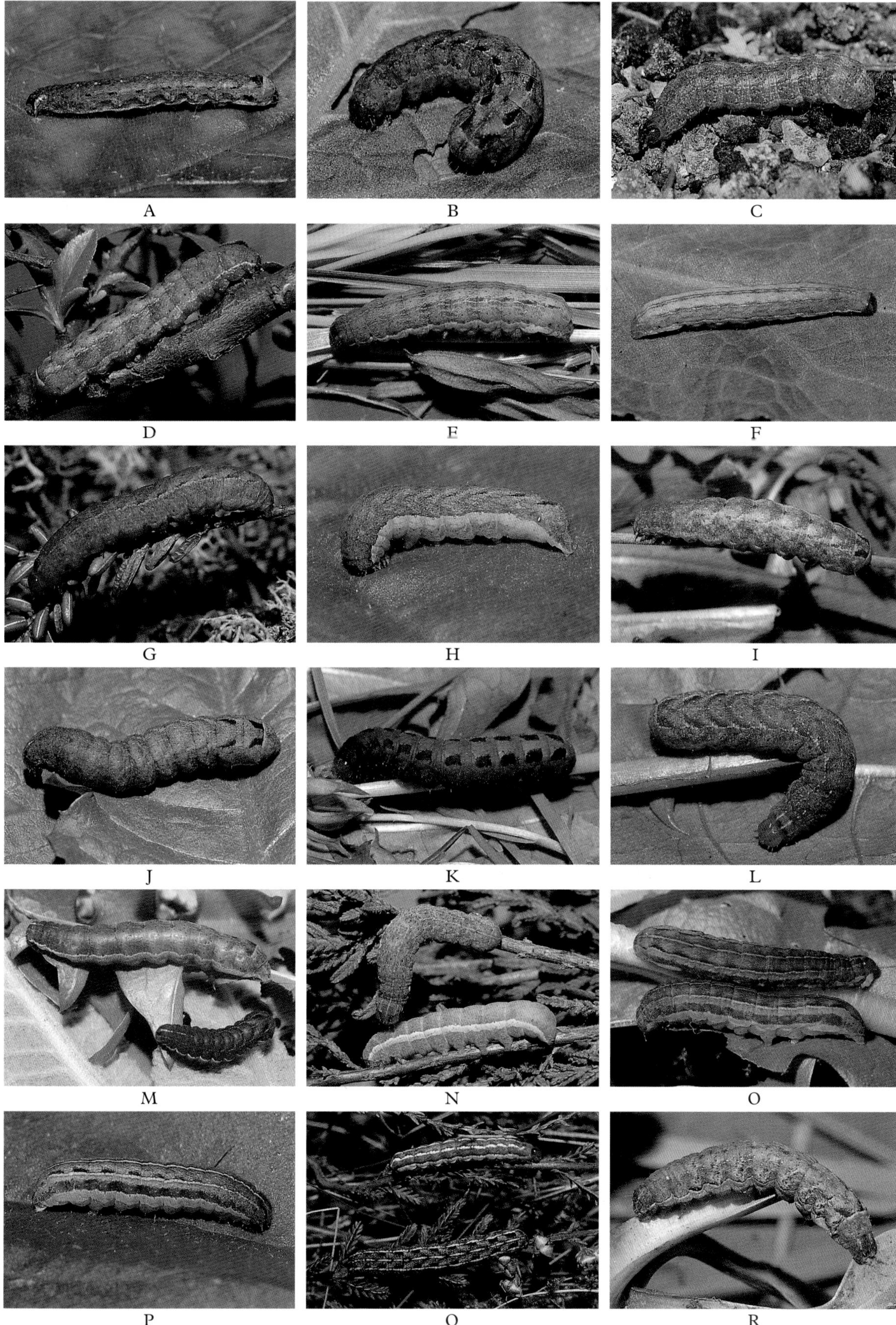
A
B
C
D
E
F
G
H
I
J
K
L
M
N
O
P
Q
R

Plate 33: *Noctuidae*

A. **Great Brocade** *Eurois occulta* Linn. Page 98.
B. **Green Arches** *Anaplectoides prasina* D. & S. Page 98.
C. **Red Chestnut** *Cerastis rubricosa* D. & S. Page 98.
D. **White-marked** *Cerastis leucographa* D. & S. Page 98.
E. **Beautiful Yellow Underwing** *Anarta myrtilli* Linn. Page 98.
F. **Small Dark Yellow Underwing** *Anarta cordigera* Thunb. Page 98.
G. **Broad-bordered White Underwing** *Anarta melanopa* Thunb. Page 99.
H. **The Nutmeg** *Discestra trifolii* Hufn. Page 99.
I. **The Shears** *Hada plebeja* Linn. Page 99.
J. **Pale Shining Brown** *Polia bombycina* Hufn. Page 99.
K. **Silvery Arches** *Polia trimaculosa* Esp. Page 99.
L. **Grey Arches** *Polia nebulosa* Hufn. Page 100.
M. **Feathered Ear** *Pachetra sagittigera* Hufn. Page 100.
N. **White Colon** *Sideridis albicolon* Hb. Page 100.
O. **Bordered Gothic** *Heliophobus reticulata* Goeze Page 100.
P. **Cabbage Moth** *Mamestra brassicae* Linn. Page 100.
Q. **Dot Moth** *Melanchra persicariae* Linn. Page 100.
R. **Beautiful Brocade** *Lacanobia contigua* D. & S. Page 101.

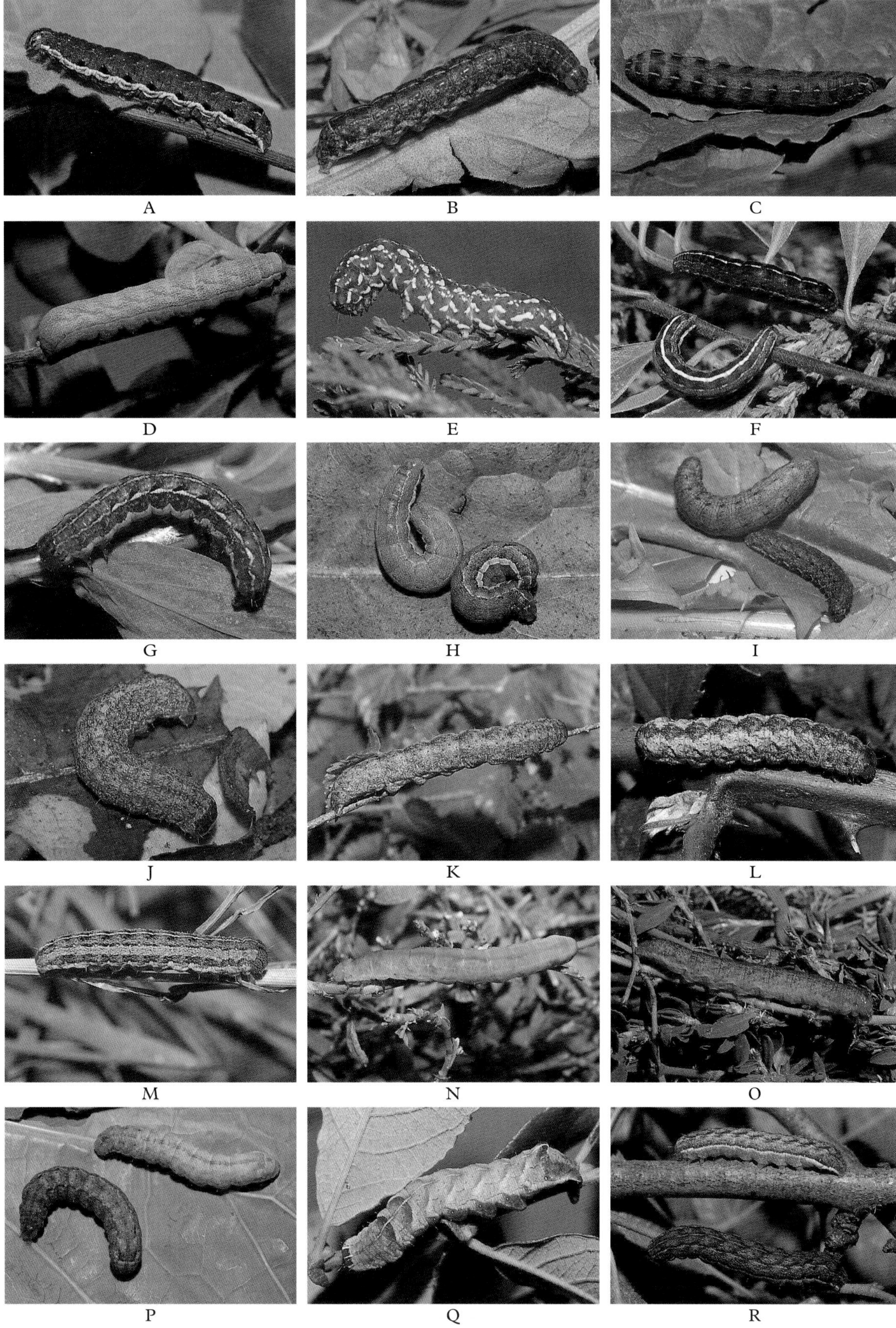
A
B
C
D
E
F
G
H
I
J
K
L
M
N
O
P
Q
R

Plate 34: *Noctuidae*

A. **Light Brocade** *Lacanobia w-latinum* Hufn. Page 101.
B. **Pale-shouldered Brocade** *Lacanobia thalassina* Hufn. Page 101.
C. **Dog's Tooth** *Lacanobia suasa* D. & S. Page 101.
D. **Bright-line Brown-eye** *Lacanobia oleracea* Linn. Page 101.
E. **The Stranger** *Lacanobia blenna* Hb. Page 102.
F. **Glaucous Shears** *Papestra biren* Goeze Page 102.
G. **Broom Moth** *Ceramica pisi* Linn. Page 102.
H. **Broad-barred White** *Hecatera bicolorata* Hufn. Page 102.
I. **Small Ranunculus** *Hecatera dysodea* D. & S. Page 102.
J. **The Campion** *Hadena rivularis* Fabr. Page 102.
K. **Tawny Shears** *Hadena perplexa* D. & S. Page 103.
L. **Viper's Bugloss** *Hadena irregularis* Hufn. Page 103.
M. **Barrett's Marbled Coronet** *Hadena luteago* D. & S. Page 103.
N. **Varied Coronet** *Hadena compta* D. & S. Page 103.
O. **Marbled Coronet** *Hadena confusa* Hufn. Page 103.
P. **White Spot** *Hadena albimacula* Borkh. Page 104.
Q. **The Lychnis** *Hadena bicruris* Hufn. Page 104.
R. **The Grey** *Hadena caesia* D. & S. Page 104.

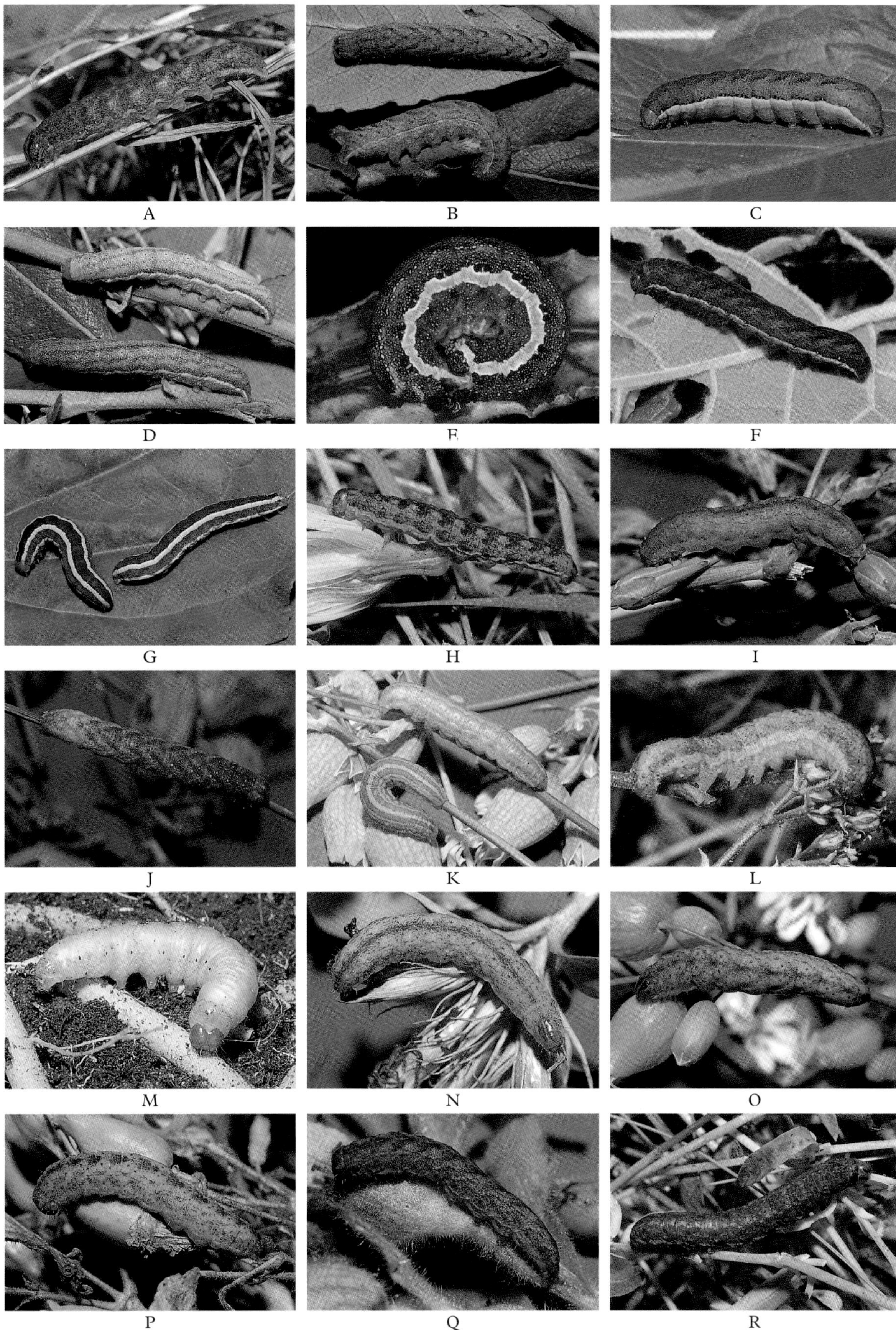
A
B
C
D
E
F
G
H
I
J
K
L
M
N
O
P
Q
R

Plate 35: *Noctuidae*

A. **The Silurian** *Eriopygodes imbecilla* Fabr. Page 104.
B. **Antler Moth** *Cerapteryx graminis* Linn. Page 104.
C. **Hedge Rustic** *Tholera cespitis* D. & S. Page 104.
D. **Feathered Gothic** *Tholera decimalis* Poda Page 105.
E. **Pine Beauty** *Panolis flammea* D. & S. Page 105.
F. **Silver Cloud** *Egira conspicillaris* Linn. Page 105.
G. **Small Quaker** *Orthosia cruda* D. & S. Page 105.
H. **Blossom Underwing** *Orthosia miniosa* D. & S. Page 105.
I. **Northern Drab** *Orthosia opima* Hb. Page 106.
J. **Lead-coloured Drab** *Orthosia populeti* Fabr. Page 106.
K. **Powdered Quaker** *Orthosia gracilis* D. & S. Page 106.
L. **Common Quaker** *Orthosia cerasi* Fabr. Page 106.
M. **Clouded Drab** *Orthosia incerta* Hufn. Page 106.
N. **Twin-spotted Quaker** *Orthosia munda* D. & S. Page 106.
O. **Hebrew Character** *Orthosia gothica* Linn. Page 107.
P. **Double Line** *Mythimna turca* Linn. Page 107.
Q. **Brown-line Bright-eye** *Mythimna conigera* D. & S. Page 107.
R. **The Clay** *Mythimna ferrago* Fabr. Page 107.

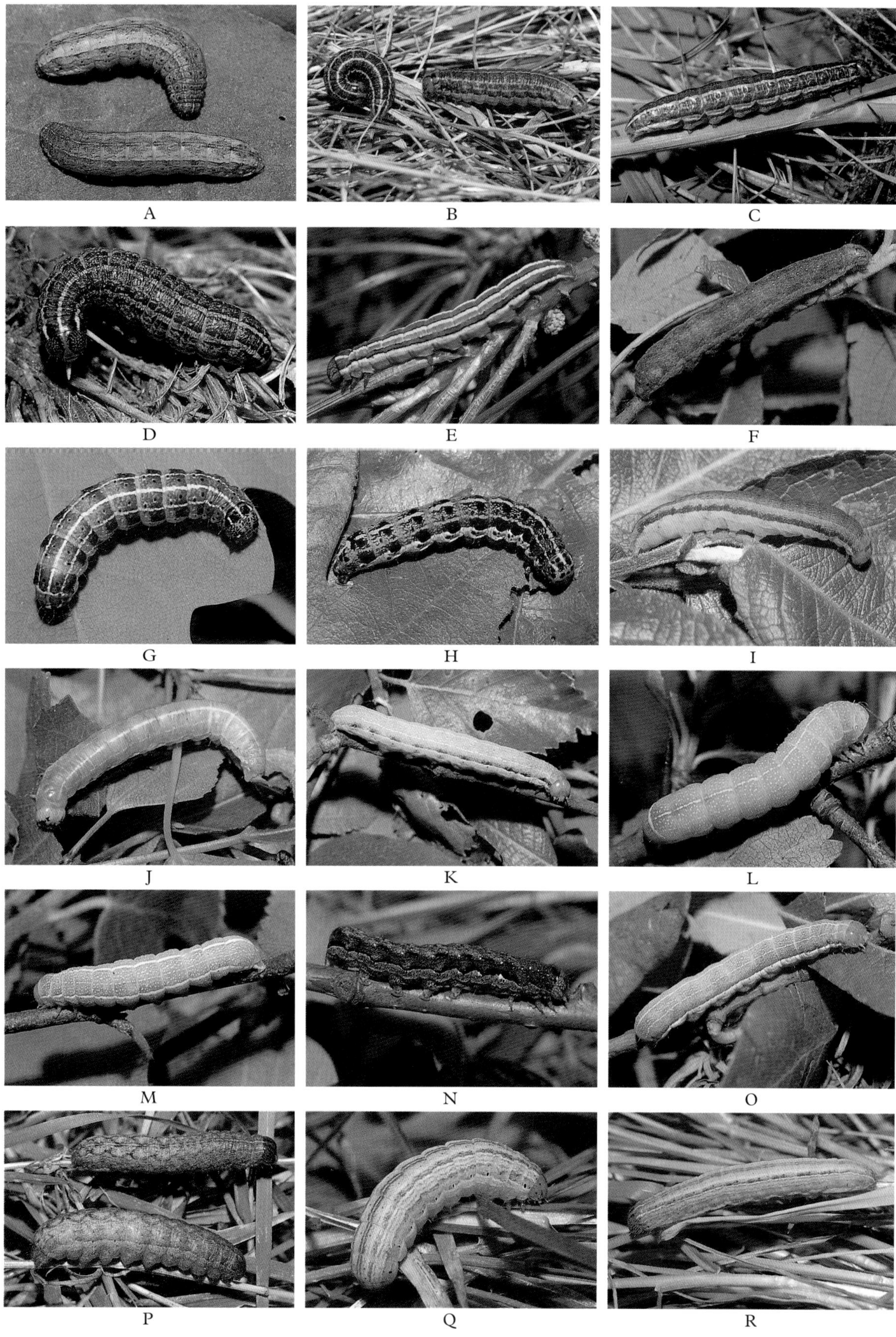
A
B
C
D
E
F
G
H
I
J
K
L
M
N
O
P
Q
R

Plate 36: *Noctuidae*

A. **White-point** *Mythimna albipuncta* D. & S. Page 107.
B. **The Delicate** *Mythimna vitellina* Hb. Page 108.
C. **Striped Wainscot** *Mythimna pudorina* D. & S. Page 108.
D. **Southern Wainscot** *Mythimna straminea* Treit. Page 108.
E. **Smoky Wainscot** *Mythimna impura* Hb. Page 108.
F. **Common Wainscot** *Mythimna pallens* Linn. Page 108.
G. **Mathew's Wainscot** *Mythimna favicolor* Barr. Page 108.
H. **Shore Wainscot** *Mythimna litoralis* Curt. Page 109.
I. **L-album Wainscot** *Mythimna l-album* Linn. Page 109.
J. **White-speck** *Mythimna unipuncta* Haw. Page 109.
K. **Obscure Wainscot** *Mythimna obsoleta* Hb. Page 109.
L. **Shoulder-striped Wainscot** *Mythimna comma* Hb. Page 109.
M. **Devonshire Wainscot** *Mythimna putrescens* Hb. Page 110.
N. **The Cosmopolitan** *Mythimna loreyi* Dup. Page 110.
O. **Flame Wainscot** *Senta flammea* Curt. Page 110.
P. **The Wormwood** *Cucullia absinthii* Linn. Page 110.
Q. **Chamomile Shark** *Cucullia chamomillae* D. & S. Page 110.
R. **The Shark** *Cucullia umbratica* Linn. Page 111.

Plate 37: *Noctuidae*

A. **Star-wort** *Cucullia asteris* D. & S. Page 111.
B. **The Cudweed** *Cucullia gnaphalii* Hb. Page 111.
C. **Striped Lychnis** *Cucullia lychnitis* Ramb. Page 111.
D. **Water Betony** *Cucullia scrophulariae* D. & S. Page 111.
E. **The Mullein** *Cucullia verbasci* Linn. Page 112.
F. **Toadflax Brocade** *Calophasia lunula* Hufn. Page 112.
G. **Minor Shoulder-knot** *Brachylomia viminalis* Fabr. Page 112.
H. **Beautiful Gothic** *Leucochlaena oditis* Hb. Page 112.
I. **The Sprawler** *Brachionycha sphinx* Hufn. Page 112.
J. **Rannoch Sprawler** *Brachionycha nubeculosa* Esp. Page 112.
K. **Brindled Ochre** *Dasypolia templi* Thunb. Page 113.
L. **Feathered Brindle** *Aporophyla australis* Boisd. Page 113.
M. **Deep-brown Dart** *Aporophyla lutulenta* D. & S. Page 113.
N. **Northern Deep-brown Dart** *Aporophyla lueneburgensis* Freyer Page 113.
O. **Black Rustic** *Aporophyla nigra* Haw. Page 113.
P. **Golden-rod Brindle** *Lithomoia solidaginis* Hb. Page 114.
Q. **Tawny Pinion** *Lithophane semibrunnea* Haw. Page 114.
R. **Pale Pinion** *Lithophane hepatica* Cl. Page 114.

Plate 38: *Noctuidae*

A. **Grey Shoulder-knot** *Lithophane ornitopus* Hufn. Page 114.
B. **Blair's Shoulder-knot** *Lithophane leautieri* Boisd. Page 115.
C. **Red Sword-grass** *Xylena vetusta* Hb. Page 115.
D. **Sword-grass** *Xylena exsoleta* Linn. Page 115.
E. **Early Grey** *Xylocampa areola* Esp. Page 115.
F. **Green-brindled Crescent** *Allophyes oxyacanthae* Linn. Page 115.
G. **Merveille du Jour** *Dichonia aprilina* Linn. Page 116.
H. **Brindled Green** *Dryobotodes eremita* Fabr. Page 116.
I. **Dark Brocade** *Mniotype adusta* Esp. Page 116.
J. **Flame Brocade** *Trigonophora flammea* Esp. Page 116.
K. **Large Ranunculus** *Polymixis flavicincta* D. & S. Page 116.
L. **Black-banded** *Polymixis xanthomista* Hb. Page 117.
M. **Grey Chi** *Antitype chi* Linn. Page 117.
N. **Feathered Ranunculus** *Eumichtis lichenea* Hb. Page 117.
O. **The Satellite** *Eupsilia transversa* Hufn. Page 117.
P. **Orange Upperwing** *Jodia croceago* D. & S. Page 117.
Q. **The Chestnut** *Conistra vaccinii* Linn. Page 118.
R. **Dark Chestnut** *Conistra ligula* Esp. Page 118.

A
B
C
D
E
F
G
H
I
J
K
L
M
N
O
P
Q
R

Plate 39: *Noctuidae*

A. **Dotted Chestnut** *Conistra rubiginea* D. & S. Page 118.
B. **Red-headed Chestnut** *Conistra erythrocephala* D. & S. Page 118.
C. **The Brick** *Agrochola circellaris* Hufn. Page 118.
D. **Red-line Quaker** *Agrochola lota* Cl. Page 119.
E. **Yellow-line Quaker** *Agrochola macilenta* Hb. Page 119.
F. **Southern Chestnut** *Agrochola haematidea* Dup. Page 119.
G. **Flounced Chestnut** *Agrochola helvola* Linn. Page 119.
H. **Brown-spot Pinion** *Agrochola litura* Linn. Page 119.
I. **Beaded Chestnut** *Agrochola lychnidis* D. & S. Page 119.
J. **Centre-barred Sallow** *Atethmia centrago* Haw. Page 120.
K. **Lunar Underwing** *Omphaloscelis lunosa* Haw. Page 120.
L. **Orange Sallow** *Xanthia citrago* Linn. Page 120.
M. **Barred Sallow** *Xanthia aurago* D. & S. Page 120.
N. **Pink-barred Sallow** *Xanthia togata* Esp. Page 120.
O. **The Sallow** *Xanthia icteritia* Hufn. Page 121.
P. **Dusky-lemon Sallow** *Xanthia gilvago* D. & S. Page 121.
Q. **Pale-lemon Sallow** *Xanthia ocellaris* Borkh. Page 121.
R. **Scarce Merveille du Jour** *Moma alpium* Osb. Page 121.

Plate 40: *Noctuidae*

A. **Poplar Grey** *Acronicta megacephala* D. & S. Page 121.
B. **The Sycamore** *Acronicta aceris* Linn. Page 121.
C. **The Miller** *Acronicta leporina* Linn. Page 122.
D. **Alder Moth** *Acronicta alni* Linn. Page 122.
E. **Dark Dagger** *Acronicta tridens* D. & S. Page 122.
F. **Grey Dagger** *Acronicta psi* Linn. Page 122.
G. **Light Knot Grass** *Acronicta menyanthidis* Esp. Page 123.
H. **Sweet Gale Moth** *Acronicta euphorbiae* D. & S. Page 123.
I. **Knot Grass** *Acronicta rumicis* Linn. Page 123.
J. **Reed Dagger** *Simyra albovenosa* Goeze Page 123.
K. **The Coronet** *Craniophora ligustri* D. & S. Page 123.
L. **Marbled Beauty** *Cryphia domestica* Hufn. Page 124.
M. **Marbled Green** *Cryphia muralis* Forst. Page 124.
N. **Copper Underwing** *Amphipyra pyramidea* Linn. Page 124.
O. **Svensson's Copper Underwing** *Amphipyra berbera* Rungs Page 124.
P. **Mouse Moth** *Amphipyra tragopoginis* Cl. Page 124.
Q. **Old Lady** *Mormo maura* Linn. Page 125.
R. **Bird's Wing** *Dypterygia scabriuscula* Linn. Page 125.

A B C D E F G H I J K L M N O P Q R

Plate 41: *Noctuidae*

A. **Brown Rustic** *Rusina ferruginea* Esp. Page 125.
B. **Straw Underwing** *Thalpophila matura* Hufn. Page 125.
C. **Small Angle Shades** *Euplexia lucipara* Linn. Page 125.
D. **Angle Shades** *Phlogophora meticulosa* Linn. Page 126.
E. **Double Kidney** *Ipimorpha retusa* Linn. Page 126.
F. **The Olive** *Ipimorpha subtusa* D. & S. Page 126.
G. **Angle-striped Sallow** *Enargia paleacea* Esp. Page 126.
H. **The Suspected** *Parastichtis suspecta* Hb. Page 126.
I. **Dingy Shears** *Parastichtis ypsillon* D. & S. Page 126.
J. **Heart Moth** *Dicycla oo* Linn. Page 127.
K. **Lesser-spotted Pinion** *Cosmia affinis* Linn. Page 127.
L. **White-spotted Pinion** *Cosmia diffinis* Linn. Page 127.
M. **The Dun-bar** *Cosmia trapezina* Linn. Page 127.
N. **Lunar-spotted Pinion** *Cosmia pyralina* D. & S. Page 127.
O. **The Saxon** *Hyppa rectilinea* Esp. Page 127.
P. **Dark Arches** *Apamea monoglypha* Hufn. Page 128.
Q. **Light Arches** *Apamea lithoxylaea* D. & S. Page 128.
R. **Reddish Light Arches** *Apamea sublustris* Esp. Page 128.

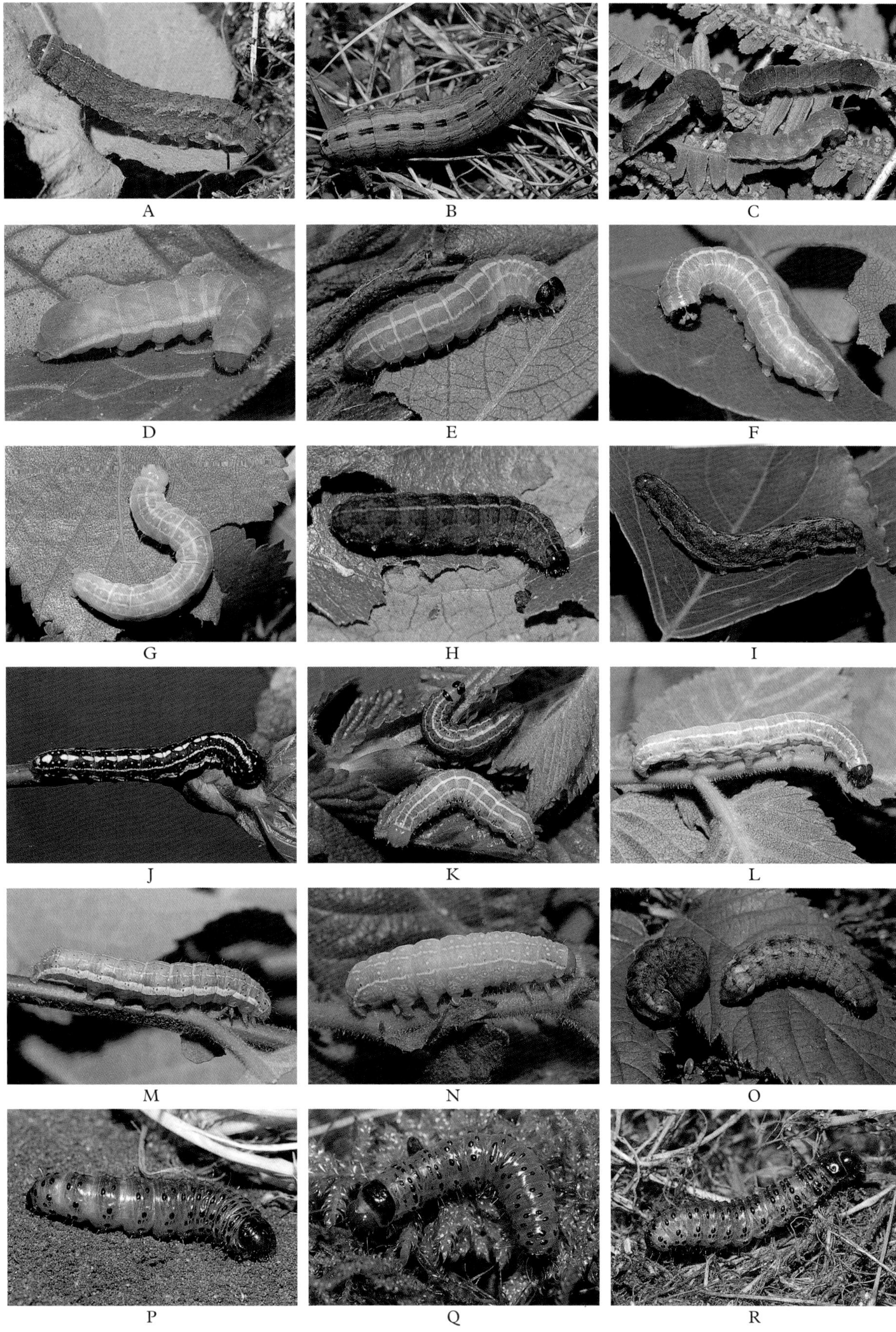

Plate 42: *Noctuidae*

A. **The Exile** *Apamea zeta* Treit. Page 128.
B. **Crescent Striped** *Apamea oblonga* Haw. Page 128.
C. **Clouded-bordered Brindle** *Apamea crenata* Hufn. Page 129.
D. **Clouded Brindle** *Apamea epomidion* Haw. Page 129.
E. **Dusky Brocade** *Apamea remissa* Hb. Page 129.
F. **Small Clouded Brindle** *Apamea unanimis* Hb. Page 129.
G. **Large Nutmeg** *Apamea anceps* D. & S. Page 130.
H. **Rustic Shoulder-knot** *Apamea sordens* Hufn. Page 130.
I. **Slender Brindle** *Apamea scolopacina* Esp. Page 130.
J. **Double Lobed** *Apamea ophiogramma* Esp. Page 130.
K. **Marbled Minor** *Oligia strigilis* Linn. Page 130.
L. **Rufous Minor** *Oligia versicolor* Borkh. Page 131.
M. **Tawny Marbled Minor** *Oligia latruncula* D. & S. Page 131.
N. **Middle-barred Minor** *Oligia fasciuncula* Haw. Page 131.
O. **Cloaked Minor** *Mesoligia furuncula* D. & S. Page 131.
P. **Rosy Minor** *Mesoligia literosa* Haw. Page 131.
Q. **Common Rustic** *Mesapamea secalis* Linn. Page 131.
R. **Lesser Common Rustic** *Mesapamea didyma* Esp. Page 132.

Plate 43: *Noctuidae*

A. **Small Dotted Buff** *Photedes minima* Haw. Page 132.
B. **Morris's Wainscot** *Photedes morrisii* Dale Page 132.
C. **The Concolorous** *Photedes extrema* Hb. Page 132.
D. **Lyme Grass** *Photedes elymi* Treit. Page 132.
E. **Mere Wainscot** *Photedes fluxa* Hb. Page 133.
F. **Small Wainscot** *Photedes pygmina* Haw. Page 133.
G. **Fenn's Wainscot** *Photedes brevilinea* Fenn Page 133.
H. **Dusky Sallow** *Eremobia ochroleuca* D. & S. Page 133.
I. **Flounced Rustic** *Luperina testacea* D. & S. Page 133.
J. **Sandhill Rustic** *Luperina nickerlii* Freyer Page 133.
K. **Large Ear** *Amphipoea lucens* Freyer Page 134.
L. **Saltern Ear** *Amphipoea fucosa* Freyer Page 134.
M. **Rosy Rustic** *Hydraecia micacea* Esp. Page 135.
N. **The Butterbur** *Hydraecia petasitis* Doubl. Page 135.
O. **Marsh Mallow Moth** *Hydraecia osseola* Stdgr. Page 135.
P. **Frosted Orange** *Gortyna flavago* D. & S. Page 135.
Q. **Fisher's Estuarine Moth** *Gortyna borelii* Pierr. Page 135.
R. **Burren Green** *Calamia tridens* Hufn. Page 136.

A
B
C
D
E
F
G
H
I
J
K
L
M
N
O
P
Q
R

Plate 44: *Noctuidae*

A. **The Crescent** *Celaena leucostigma* Hb. Page 136.
B. **Bulrush Wainscot** *Nonagria typhae* Thunb. Page 136.
C. **Twin-spotted Wainscot** *Archanara geminipuncta* Haw. Page 136.
D. **Brown-veined Wainscot** *Archanara dissoluta* Treit. Page 137.
E. **White-mantled Wainscot** *Archanara neurica* Hb. Page 137.
F. **Webb's Wainscot** *Archanara sparganii* Esp. Page 137.
G. **Rush Wainscot** *Archanara algae* Esp. Page 137.
H. **Large Wainscot** *Rhizedra lutosa* Hb. Page 137.
I. **Fen Wainscot** *Arenostola phragmitidis* Hb. Page 138.
J. **Small Rufous** *Coenobia rufa* Haw. Page 138.
K. **Treble Lines** *Charanyca trigrammica* Hufn. Page 138.
L. **The Uncertain** *Hoplodrina alsines* Brahm Page 138.
M. **The Rustic** *Hoplodrina blanda* D. & S. Page 138.
N. **Powdered Rustic** *Hoplodrina superstes* Ochs. Page 139.
O. **Vine's Rustic** *Hoplodrina ambigua* D. & S. Page 139.
P. **Small Mottled Willow** *Spodoptera exigua* Hb. Page 139.
Q. **Mediterranean Brocade** *Spodoptera littoralis* Boisd. Page 139.
R. **Dark Mottled Willow** *Spodoptera cilium* Guen. Page 139.

Plate 45: *Noctuidae*

A. **Mottled Rustic** *Caradrina morpheus* Hufn. Page 139.
B. **Pale Mottled Willow** *Caradrina clavipalpis* Scop. Page 140.
C. **Silky Wainscot** *Chilodes maritimus* Tausch. Page 140.
D. **Marsh Moth** *Athetis pallustris* Hb. Page 140.
E. **Porter's Rustic** *Athetis hospes* Freyer Page 140.
F. **Reddish Buff** *Acosmetia caliginosa* Hb. Page 140.
G. **The Anomalous** *Stilbia anomala* Haw. Page 140.
H. **Rosy Marbled** *Elaphria venustula* Hb. Page 141.
I. **Small Yellow Underwing** *Panemeria tenebrata* Scop. Page 141.
J. **Bordered Sallow** *Pyrrhia umbra* Hufn. Page 141.
K. **Scarce Bordered Straw** *Heliothis armigera* Hb. Page 141.
L. **Marbled Clover** *Heliothis viriplaca* Hufn. Page 142.
M. **Shoulder-striped Clover** *Heliothis maritima* Grasl. Page 142.
N. **Bordered Straw** *Heliothis peltigera* D. & S. Page 142.
O. **Purple Marbled** *Eublemma ostrina* Hb. Page 142.
P. **Marbled White Spot** *Protodeltote pygarga* Hufn. Page 143.
Q. **Silver Hook** *Deltote uncula* Cl. Page 143.
R. **Silver Barred** *Deltote bankiana* Fabr. Page 143.

A B C D E F G H I J K L M N O P Q R

Plate 46: *Noctuidae*

A. **Cream-bordered Green Pea** *Earias clorana* Linn. Page 144.
B. **Egyptian Bollworm** *Earias insulana* Boisd. Page 144.
C. **Scarce Silver-lines** *Bena bicolorana* Fuess. Page 144.
D. **Green Silver-lines** *Pseudoips prasinana* Linn. Page 144.
E. **Oak Nycteoline** *Nycteola revayana* Scop. Page 144.
F. **Nut-tree Tussock** *Colocasia coryli* Linn. Page 144.
G. **Golden Twin-spot** *Chrysodeixis chalcites* Esp. Page 145.
H. **The Ni Moth** *Trichoplusia ni* Hb. Page 145.
I. **Slender Burnished Brass** *Diachrysia orichalcea* Fabr. Page 145.
J. **Burnished Brass** *Diachrysia chrysitis* Linn. Page 145.
K. **Scarce Burnished Brass** *Diachrysia chryson* Esp. Page 146.
L. **Dewick's Plusia** *Macdunnoughia confusa* Steph. Page 146.
M. **Golden Plusia** *Polychrysia moneta* Fabr. Page 146.
N. **Gold Spot** *Plusia festucae* Linn. Page 146.
O. **Lempke's Gold Spot** *Plusia putnami* Grote Page 146.
P. **Silver Y** *Autographa gamma* Linn. Page 147.
Q. **Beautiful Golden Y** *Autographa pulchrina* Haw. Page 147.
R. **Plain Golden Y** *Autographa jota* Linn. Page 147.

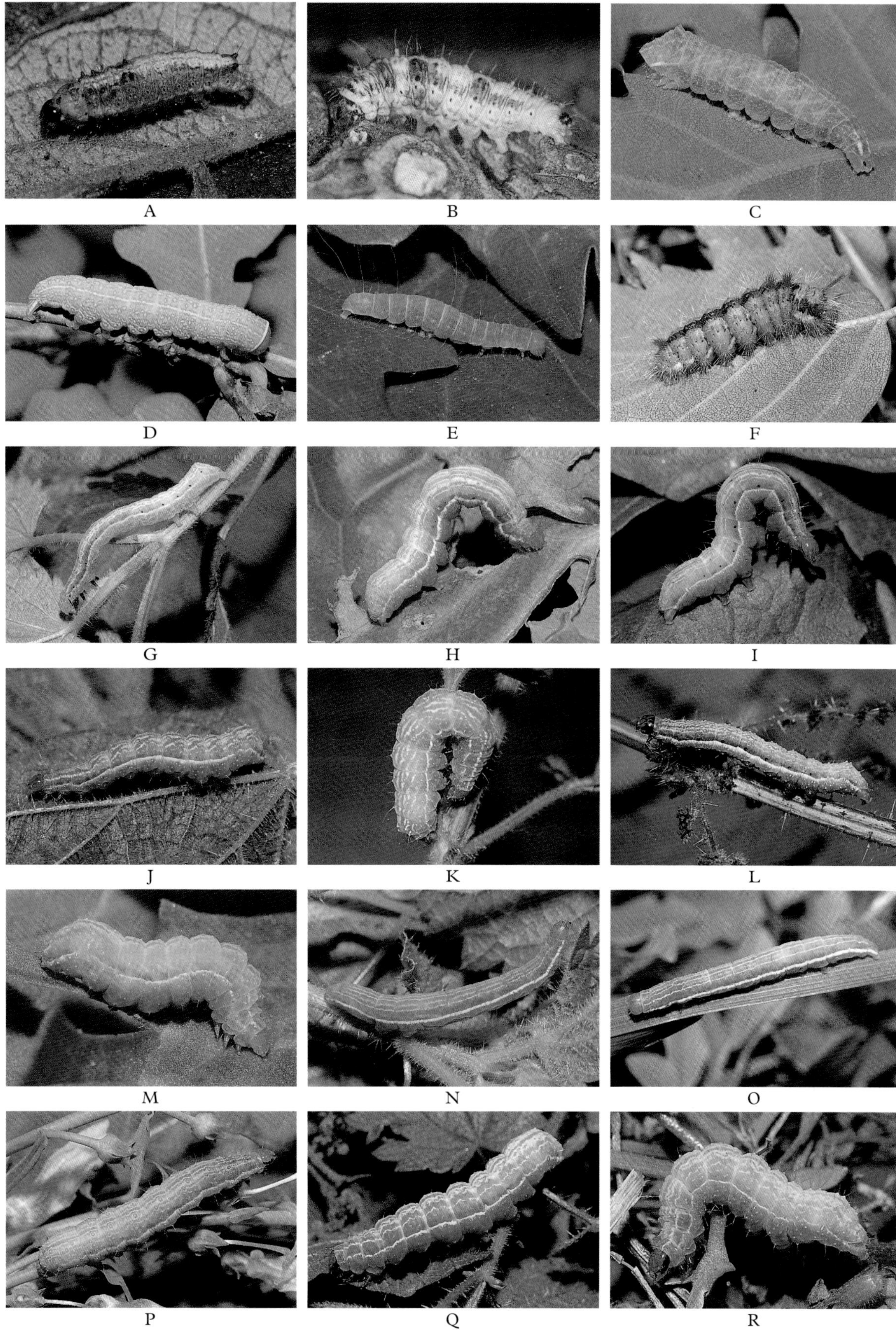

Plate 47: *Noctuidae*

A. **Gold Spangle** *Autographa bractea* D. & S. Page 147.
B. **Scarce Silver Y** *Syngrapha interrogationis* Linn. Page 148.
C. **Dark Spectacle** *Abrostola triplasia* Linn. Page 148.
D. **The Spectacle** *Abrostola tripartita* Hufn. Page 148.
E. **Clifden Nonpareil** *Catocala fraxini* Linn. Page 148.
F. **Red Underwing** *Catocala nupta* Linn. Page 148.
G. **Rosy Underwing** *Catocala electa* View. Page 149.
H. **Light Crimson Underwing** *Catocala promissa* D. & S. Page 149.
I. **Dark Crimson Underwing** *Catocala sponsa* Linn. Page 149.
J. **Oak Yellow Underwing** *Catocala nymphagoga* Esp. Page 149.
K. **Lunar Double-stripe** *Minucia lunaris* D. & S. Page 149.
L. **The Passenger** *Dysgonia algira* Linn. Page 149.
M. **Mother Shipton** *Callistege mi* Cl. Page 149.
N. **Burnet Companion** *Euclidia glyphica* Linn. Page 150.
O. **The Four-spotted** *Tyta luctuosa* D. & S. Page 150.
P. **The Blackneck** *Lygephila pastinum* Treit. Page 150.
Q. **Scarce Blackneck** *Lygephila craccae* D. & S. Page 150.
R. **The Herald** *Scoliopteryx libatrix* Linn. Page 151.

A
B
C
D
E
F
G
H
I
J
K
L
M
N
O
P
Q
R

Plate 48: *Noctuidae*

A. **Small Purple-barred** *Phytometra viridaria* Cl. Page 151.
B. **Beautiful Hook-tip** *Laspeyria flexula* D. & S. Page 151.
C. **Straw Dot** *Rivula sericealis* Scop. Page 151.
D. **Waved Black** *Parascotia fuliginaria* Linn. Page 152.
E. **Beautiful Snout** *Hypena crassalis* Fabr. Page 152.
F. **The Snout** *Hypena proboscidalis* Linn. Page 152.
G. **Bloxworth Snout** *Hypena obsitalis* Hb. Page 152.
H. **Buttoned Snout** *Hypena rostralis* Linn. Page 152.
I. **White-line Snout** *Schrankia taenialis* Hb. Page 153.
J. **Pinion-streaked Snout** *Schrankia costaestrigalis* Steph. Page 153.
K. **Common Fan-foot** *Pechipogo strigilata* Linn. Page 153.
L. **The Fan-foot** *Herminia tarsipennalis* Treit. Page 153.
M. **Jubilee Fan-foot** *Herminia lunalis* Scop. Page 154.
N. **Shaded Fan-foot** *Herminia tarsicrinalis* Knoch Page 154.
O. **Small Fan-foot** *Herminia grisealis* D. & S. Page 154.
P. **Dotted Fan-foot** *Macrochilo cribrumalis* Hb. Page 154.
Q. **Clay Fan-foot** *Paracolax tristalis* Fabr. Page 154.
R. **Olive Crescent** *Trisateles emortualis* D. & S. Page 154.

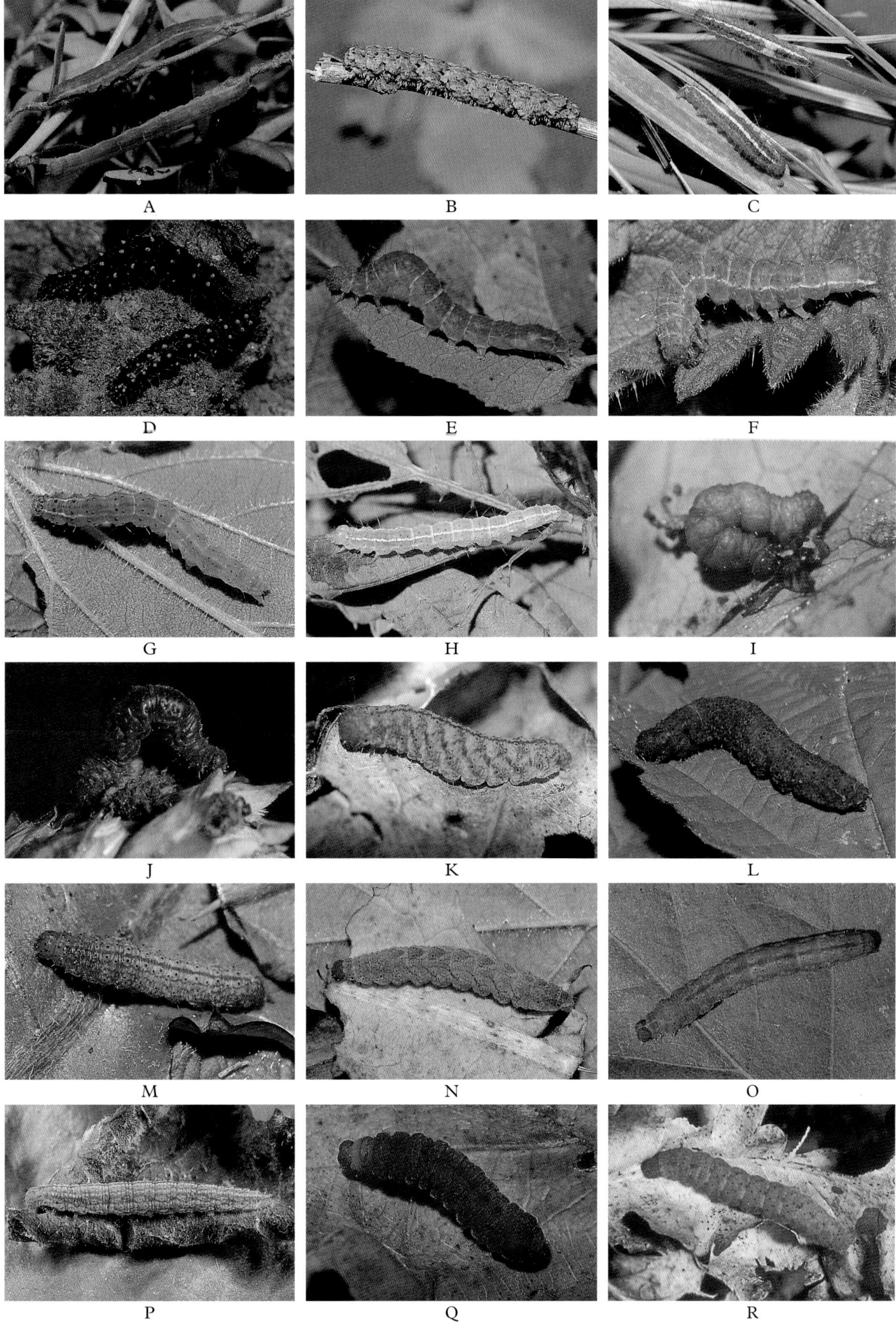

Plate 49: *Sphingidae, Notodontidae, Lymantriidae, Noctuidae*

A. **Willowherb Hawk-moth** *Proserpinus proserpina* Pall. Page 74.
B. **Large Dark Prominent** *Notodonta torva* Hb. Page 77.
C. **Three-humped Prominent** *Tritophia tritophus* D. & S. Page 77.
D. **Dusky Marbled Brown** *Gluphisia crenata* Esp. Page 79.
E. **Reed Tussock** *Laelia coenosa* Hb. Page 80.
F. **Scarce Wormwood** *Cucullia artemisiae* Hufn. Page 110.
G. **The Conformist** *Lithophane furcifera* Hufn. Page 114.
H. **Orache Moth** *Trachea atriplicis* Linn. Page 125.
I. **Pale Shoulder** *Acontia lucida* Hufn. Page 143.

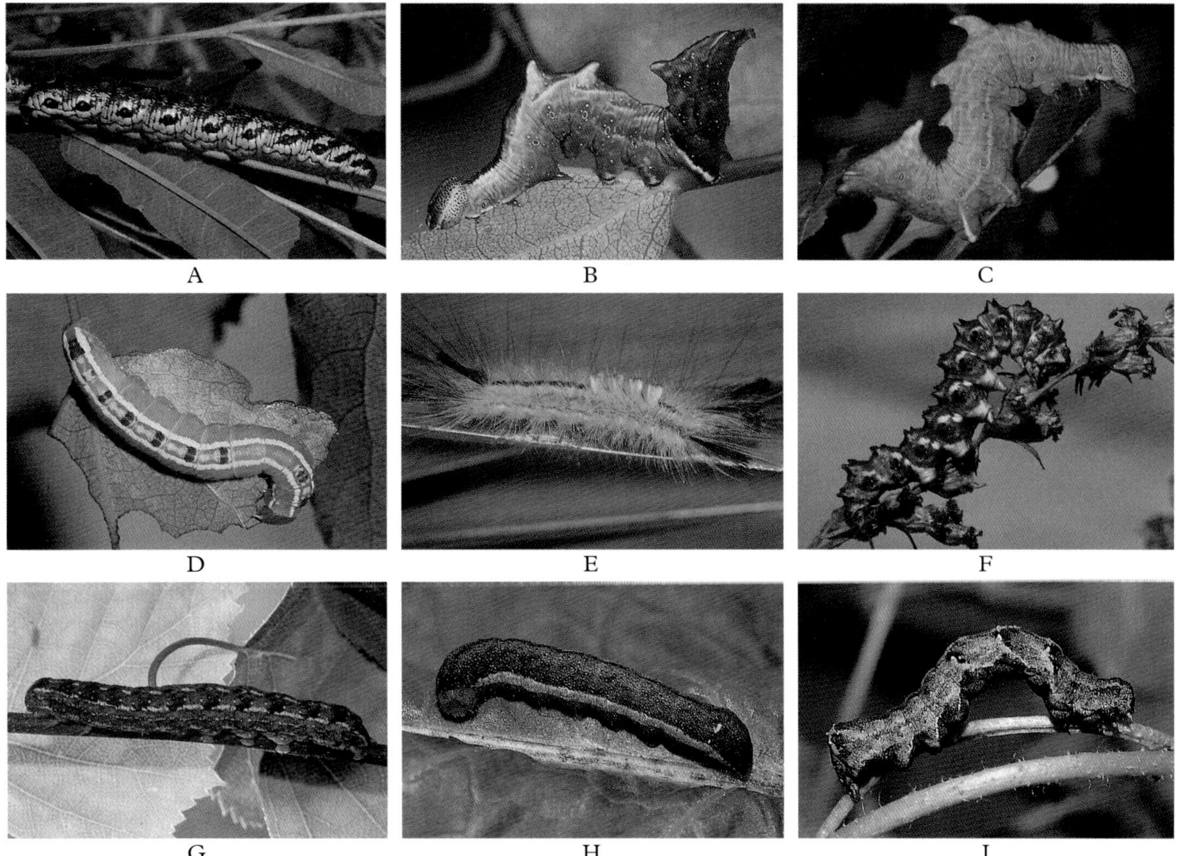

Further Information

The Wildlife and Countryside Act, 1981

The following species are at present protected by law from being collected or wilfully disturbed in any stage of their development without special licence.

New Forest Burnet, *Zygaena viciae* D. & S.
The Swallowtail, *Papilio machaon* Linn.
Large Blue, *Maculinea arion* Linn.
High Brown Fritillary, *Argynnis adippe* D. & S.
Heath Fritillary, *Mellicta athalia* Rott.
Essex Emerald, *Thetidia smaragdaria* Fabr.
Sussex Emerald, *Thalera fimbrialis* Scop.
Barberry Carpet, *Pareulype berberata* D. & S.
Black-veined Moth, *Siona lineata* Scop.
Viper's Bugloss, *Hadena irregularis* Hufn.
Reddish Buff, *Acosmetia caliginosa* Hb.

Bibliography and Further Reading

Allan, P. B. M. (1949) *Larval Foodplants*, Watkins & Doncaster, Kent.

Buckler, W. (1887–1901) *The Larvae of British Butterflies and Moths*, vols 2–9, Ray Society, London.

Carter, D. J. and Hargraves, B. (1986) *A Field Guide to Caterpillars of Butterflies and Moths of Britain and Europe*, Collins, London.

Forster, W. and Wohlfahrt, T. A. (1980–81) *Die Schmetterlinge Mittel Europus*, vols 4–5, Stuttgart.

Haggett, G. M. (1981) *Larvae of the British Lepidoptera not figured by Buckler*, British Entomological & Natural History Society, London.

Heath, J., Emmet, A. M. and others (1976–) *The Moths and Butterflies of Great Britain and Ireland*, vols 1, 2, 7, 8, 9 and 10, Harley Books, Essex.

Hoffmeyer, S. (1962/1966) *De Danske Ugler / De Danske Malere*, Aarhus.

Howarth, T. G. (1973) *South's British Butterflies*, Warne, London.

Pittaway, A. R. (1993) *The Hawkmoths of the Western Palaearctic*, Harley Books, Essex.

Scorer, A. G. (1913) *The Entomologist's Log-book*, Routledge & Son, London.

Seitz, A. (1914–38) *The Macrolepidoptera of the World*, vols 2–4 and supplements, Alfred Kernen, Stuttgart.

Skinner, B. (1984) *Colour Identification Guide to Moths of the British Isles*, Viking Books, London.

South, R. (1941) *The Butterflies of the British Isles*, Warne, London.

South, R. (1961) *The Moths of the British Isles*, 2 vols, Warne, London.

Spuler, A. (1908–1910) *Die Schmetterlinge Europas*, vols 1–4, Stuttgart.

Stokoe, W. J. (1958) *The Caterpillars of the British Moths*, 2 vols, Warne, London.

Wright, A. B. (1993) *Peterson First Guide to Caterpillars of North America*, Houghton Mifflin Co., New York.

Societies and Entomological Equipment Dealers

The Amateur Entomologists' Society, P.O. Box 8774, London SW7 5ZG.

The British Entomological & Natural History Society, Dinton Pastures Country Park, Hurst, Reading RG10 0TH.

Butterfly Conservation, P.O. Box 222, Dedham, Colchester, CO7 6EY.

Marris House Nets, 54 Richmond Park Avenue, Bournemouth BH8 9DR.

The Royal Entomological Society, 41 Queens Gate, London SW7 5HU.

Watkins & Doncaster, Four Throws, Hawkhurst, Kent TN18 5EZ.

Scientific Names of Foodplants

Common name	Scientific name
Alder	*Alnus glutinosa*
Alyssum, garden	*Alyssum* spp.
Angelica, wild	*Angelica sylvestris*
Apple	*Malus* spp.
, crab	*Malus sylvestris*
Archangel, yellow	*Lamiastrum galeobdolon*
Ash	*Fraxinus excelsior*
Aspen	*Populus tremula*
Asphodel, bog	*Narthecium ossifragum*
Aster, sea	*Aster tripolium*
Balsam, orange	*Impatiens capensis*
, small	*Impatiens parviflora*
Barberry	*Berberis vulgaris*
Barley	*Hordeum* spp.
Bartsia, red	*Odontites vernus*
Beak-sedge, white	*Rhynchospora alba*
Bearberry	*Arctostaphylos uva-ursi*
Bedstraw	*Galium* spp.
, fen	*Galium uliginosum*
, heath	*Galium saxatile*
, hedge	*Galium mollugo*
, lady's	*Galium verum*
, marsh	*Galium palustre*
Beech	*Fagus sylvatica*
Beet, sea	*Beta vulgaris*
Bellflower, giant	*Campanula latifolia*
, nettle-leaved	*Campanula trachelium*
Bilberry	*Vaccinium myrtillus*
, bog	*Vaccinium uliginosum*
Bindweed, field	*Convolvulus arvensis*
Birch	*Betula* spp.
Blackthorn	*Prunus spinosa*
Bladder-senna	*Colutea arborescens*
Borage	*Borago officinalis*
Bracken	*Pteridium aquilinum*
Bramble	*Rubus fruticosus* agg.
Broom	*Cytisus scoparius*
Buckthorn	*Rhamnus cathartica*
, alder	*Frangula alnus*
, sea	*Hippophae rhamnoides*
Buddleia, garden	*Buddleia davidii*
Bugloss, viper's	*Echium vulgare*
Burdock	*Arctium* spp.
Bur-reed, branched	*Sparganium erectum*
Burnet-saxifrage	*Pimpinella saxifraga*
Butterbur	*Petasites hybridus*
Buttercup	*Ranunculus* spp.
Cabbage	*Brassicae* spp.
, wild	*Brassica oleracea*
Campion	*Silene* spp.
, bladder	*Silene vulgaris*
, red	*Silene dioica*
, sea	*Silene uniflora*
, white	*Silene latifolia*
Canary-grass	*Phalaris* spp.
, reed	*Phalaris arundincaea*
Carnation, garden	*Dianthus caryophyllus*
Carrot	*Daucus* spp.
, wild	*Daucus carota*
Catchfly, Nottingham	*Silene nutans*
, Spanish	*Silene otites*
Cat's-tail	*Phleum pratense*
Celeriac	*Apium graveolens*
Chamomile	*Anthemis* or *chamaemelum* spp.
Charlock	*Sinapis arvensis*
Cherry	*Prunus* spp.
Chestnut, horse	*Aesculus hippocastanum*
, sweet	*Castanea sativa*
Chickweed	*Stellaria* spp.
Cinquefoil	*Potentilla* spp.
, creeping	*Potentilla reptans*
, marsh	*Potentilla palustris*
Clover	*Trifolium* spp.
, red	*Trifolium pratense*
Club-rush, common	*Schoenoplectus lacustris*
Cock's-foot	*Dactylis glomerata*
Colt's-foot	*Tussilago farfara*
Comfrey	*Symphytum* spp.
, common	*Symphytum officinale*
Cotton	*Gossypium herbaceum*
Cotton-grass	*Eriophorum* spp.
Couch	*Elytrigia* spp.
, common	*Elytrigia repens*
, sand	*Elytrigia juncea*
Cow-wheat	*Melampyrum* spp.
Cowberry	*Vaccinium vitis-idaea*
Cowslip	*Primula veris*
Cranberry	*Vaccinium oxycoccos*
Creeper, Virginia	*Parthenocissus* spp.
Cress, Water	*Rorippa nasturtium-aquaticum*
Crowberry	*Empetrum* spp.
Cudweed	*Gnaphalium* spp.
Currant	*Ribes* spp.
, black	*Ribes nigrum*
, red	*Ribes rubrum*
Cypress	*Cupressus* or *cupressocyparis* spp.
, Lawson's	*Chamaecyparis lawsoniana*
, Monterey	*Cupressus macrocarpa*
Dandelion	*Taraxacum officinale* agg.
Dead-nettle	*Lamium* spp.
, red	*Lamium purpureum*
, white	*Lamium album*
Dewberry	*Rubus caesius*
Dock	*Rumex* spp.
, broad-leaved	*Rumex obtusifolius*
, curled	*Rumex crispus*
, water or great water	*Rumex hydrolapathum*
Dogwood	*Cornus sanguinea*
Elder	*Sambucus nigra*
Elm	*Ulmus* spp.
, English	*Ulmus procera*
, small-leaved	*Ulmus minor*
, wych	*Ulmus glabra*
Eyebright	*Euphrasia officinalis* agg.
False-brome	*Brachypodium sylvaticum*
Fennel, hog's	*Peucedanum officinale*
Fen-sedge, great	*Cladium mariscus*
Fescue	*Festuca* spp.
, red	*Festuca rubra*
, tall	*Festuca arundinacea*
Feverfew	*Tanacetum parthenium*
Figwort	*Scrophularia* spp.
Fir,	*Abies* spp.
, Douglas	*Pseudotsuga menziesii*
Fleabane, common	*Pulicaria dysenterica*
Flixweed	*Descurainia sophia*
Forget-me-not	*Myosotis* spp.
Foxglove	*Digitalis purpurea*

Common name	Scientific name
Golden rod	*Solidago virguarea*
Gooseberry	*Ribes uva-crispa*
Goosefoot	*Chenopodium* spp.
Goosegrass	*Galium aparine*
Gorse	*Ulex europaeus*
Grape-vine	*Vitis vinifera*
Greenweed, dyer's	*Genista tinctoria*
Groundsel	*Senecio vulgaris*
, sticky	*Senecio viscosus*
Guelder-rose	*Viburnum opulus*
Hair-grass	*Deschampsia* spp.
, tufted	*Deschampsia cespitosa*
, wavy	*Deschampsia flexuosa*
Harebell	*Campanula rotundifolia*
Hawk's-beard	*Crepis* spp.
Hawkweed	*Hieracium* spp.
Hawthorn	*Crateagus* spp.
Hazel	*Corylus avellana*
Heath, cross-leaved	*Erica tetralix*
Heather	*Calluna vulgaris*
, bell	*Erica cinerea*
Hemlock, Western	*Tsuga heterophylla*
Hemp-agrimony	*Eupatorium cannabinum*
Hemp nettle	*Galeopsis* spp.
Herb-robert	*Geranium robertianum*
Hogweed	*Heracleum sphondylium*
Holly	*Ilex aquifolium*
Hollyhock, garden	*Althaea* spp.
Honeysuckle	*Lonicera* spp.
Hop	*Humulus lupulus*
Hornbeam	*Carpinus betulus*
Horse-tail	*Equisetum* spp.
Indigo, tree	*Indigofera tinctoria*
Iris, yellow	*Iris pseudacorus*
Ivy	*Hedera helix*
, ground	*Glechoma hederacea*
Juniper	*Juniperus communis*
Knapweed	*Centaurea* spp.
, common	*Centaurea nigra*
, greater	*Centaurea scabiosa*
Knotgrass	*Polygonum aviculare* agg.
Lady's-mantle	*Alchemilla* spp.
Larch	*Larix* spp.
Larkspur	*Consolida ajacis*
Lavender, sea	*Limonium* spp.
Lettuce	*Lactuca* spp.
, wild	*Lactuca serriola*
Lichen, beard	*Usnea* spp.
, dog	*Peltigera canina*
Lilac	*Syringa vulgaris*
Lime	*Tilia* spp.
, common	*Tilia* x *vulgaris*
, large-leaved	*Tilia platyphyllos*
, small-leaved	*Tilia cordata*
Loosestrife, purple	*Lythrum salicaria*
, yellow	*Lysimachia vulgaris*
Lousewort	*Pedicularis sylvatica*
Lucerne	*Medicago sativa*
Lupin, tree	*Lupinus arboreus*
Lyme-grass	*Elymus (Leymus) arenarius*
Madder, wild	*Rubia peregrina*
Mallow, common	*Malva sylvestris*
Maple	*Acer* spp.
, field	*Acer campestre*
Marigold, garden	*Calendula officinalis*
Marjoram	*Origanum vulgare*
Marram	*Ammophila arenaria*
Marsh-mallow	*Althaea officinalis*
Mat-grass	*Nardus stricta*
Mayweed	*Matricaria* & *Tripleurospermum* spp.
, scentless	*Tripleurospermum maritimum* agg.
Meadow-grass, annual	*Poa annua*
, smooth	*Poa pratensis*
, wood	*Poa nemoralis*
Meadow-rue, common	*Thalictrum flavum*
Meadowsweet	*Filipendula ulmaria*
Medick, black	*Medicago lupulina*
Melick, wood	*Melica uniflora*
Michaelmas-daisy	*Aster* spp.
Mignonette, wild	*Reseda lutea*
Milkweed	*Asclepias* spp.
Milkwort, common	*Polygala vulgaris*
Mint, garden	*Mentha* spp.
, water or wild	*Mentha aquatica*
Monk's-hood	*Aconitum napellus*
Moor-grass, blue	*Sesleria caerulea*
, purple	*Molinia caerulea*
Mouse-ear, common	*Cerastium fontanum*
, field	*Cerastium arvense*
Mugwort	*Artemesia vulgaris*
Mullein	*Verbascum* spp.
, dark or black	*Verbascum nigrum*
, great	*Verbascum thapsus*
, white	*Verbascum lychnitis*
Mustard, garlic	*Alliaria petiolata*
, hedge	*Sisymbrium officinale*
, treacle	*Erysimum cheiranthoides*
Myrtle, bog	*Myrica gale*
Nasturtium, garden	*Tropaeolum* spp.
Nettle	*Urtica* spp.
, common	*Urtica dioica*
, small	*Urtica urens*
Nightshade, enchanter's	*Circaea lutetiana*
Oak	*Quercus* spp.
, holm or evergreen	*Quercus ilex*
Oat	*Avena* spp.
Oat-grass, false	*Arrhenatherum elatius*
Oleander	*Nerium oleander*
Orache	*Atriplex* spp.
Osier	*Salix viminalis*
Pansy, wild	*Viola tricolor*
Parsley, cow	*Anthriscus sylvestris*
, milk	*Peucedanum palustre*
Parsnip, wild	*Pastinaca sativa*
Pea	*Pisum* spp.
, everlasting	*Lathyrus latifolius*
Pear	*Pyrus* spp.
Pellitory-of-the-wall	*Parietaria judaica*
Periwinkle	*Vinca* spp.
Persicaria	*Polygonum* spp.
, common	*Polygonum persicaria*
Pignut	*Conopodium majus*
Pine	*Pinus* spp.
, Scots	*Pinus sylvestris*
Plantain	*Plantago* spp.
, buck's-horn	*Plantago coronopus*
, greater	*Plantago major*
, ribwort	*Plantago lanceolata*
, sea	*Plantago maritima*
Ploughman's-spikenard	*Inula conyzae*
Plum	*Prunus* spp.
, wild	*Prunus domestica*
Pond-sedge, lesser	*Carex acutiformis*
Poplar	*Populus* spp.
, black	*Populus* x *canadensis*
Potato	*Solanum tuberosum*
Primrose	*Primula vulgaris*
, evening	*Oenothera biennis*
Privet	*Ligustrum* spp.
, garden	*Ligustrum ovalifolium*
,wild	*Ligustrum vulgare*
Ragged-robin	*Lychnis flos-cuculi*

Ragwort	*Senecio* spp.
Raspberry	*Rubus idaeus*
Rattle, yellow	*Rhinanthus minor*
Reed, common	*Phragmites australis*
Reedmace,	*Typha latifolia*
, lesser	*Typha angustifolia*
Restharrow	*Ononis* spp.
, common	*Ononis repens*
, spiny	*Ononis spinosa*
Rock-rose, common	*Heliathemum nummularium*
Rocket, sea	*Cakile maritima*
, sweet	*Hesperis matronalis*
Rose	*Rosa* spp.
, burnet	*Rosa pimpinellifolia*
, dog or wild	*Rosa canina*
, guelder	*Viburnum opulus*
Roseroot	*Sedum rosea*
Rowan	*Sorbus aucuparia*
Runner-bean	*Phaseolus multifloris*
Rush, jointed	*Juncus articulatus*
, soft	*Juncus effusus*
Rye	*Secale cereale*
Sage, wood	*Teucrium scorodonia*
St John's-wort	*Hypericum* spp.
Sallow	*Salix* spp.
, grey	*Salix cinerea*
Saltmarsh-grass	*Puccinellia maritima*
Saltwort, prickly	*Salsola kali*
Sandwort, sea	*Honckenya peploides*
Saw-wort	*Serratula tinctoria*
Saxifrage	*Saxifraga* spp.
Scabious	*Scabiosa columbaria*
, devil's-bit	*Succisa pratensis*
, field	*Knautia arvensis*
Sea-spurrey, rock	*Spergularia rupicola*
Sedge	*Carex* spp.
, glaucous	*Carex flacca*
, tufted	*Carex elata*
Self-heal	*Prunella vulgaris*
Sheep's-bit	*Jasione montana*
Sheep's-fescue	*Festuca ovina*
Silverweed	*Potentilla anserina*
Small-reed, purple	*Calamagrostis canescens*
, wood	*Calamagrostis epigejos*
Smock, lady's	*Cardamine pratensis*
Snapdragon	*Antirrhinum majus*
Sneezewort	*Achillea ptarmica*
Snowberry	*Symphoricarpos albus*
Soapwort	*Saponaria officinalis*
Soft-grass, creeping	*Holcus mollis*
Sorrel	*Rumex* spp.
, common	*Rumex acetosa*
, sheep's	*Rumex acetosella*
Southernwood	*Artemisia abrotanum*
Sow-thistle	*Sonchus* spp.
Speed-well, germander	*Veronica chamaedrys*
Spindle	*Euonymus europaeus*
Spruce,	*Picea* spp.
, Norway	*Picea abies*
, Sitka	*Picea sitchensis*
Spurge	*Euphorbia* spp.
, wood	*Euphorbia amygdaloides*
Stitchwort	*Stellaria* spp.
Stonecrop	*Sedum* spp.
, biting	*Sedum acre*
Stork's-bill, common	*Erodium cicutarium*
Strawberry	*Fragaria* spp.
, wild	*Fragaria vesca*
Sweet-briar	*Rosa rubiginosa*
Sweet-grass, reed	*Glyceria maxima*
Sycamore	*Acer pseudoplatanus*
Tamarisk	*Tamarix* spp.
Tansy	*Tanacetum vulgare*
Teasel	*Dipsacus* spp.
Thistle	*Carduus* & *Cirsium* spp.
, carline	*Carlina vulgaris*
, creeping	*Cirsium arvense*
, marsh	*Cirsium palustre*
, spear	*Circium vulgare*
Thrift	*Armeria maritima*
Thyme	*Thymus* spp.
, wild	*Thymus polytrichus*
Timothy	*Phleum pratense*
Toadflax	*Linaria* spp.
, common	*Linaria vulgaris*
, ivy-leaved	*Cymbalaria muralis*
, pale	*Linaria repens*
, purple	*Linaria purpurea*
Tomato	*Lycopersicon esculentum*
Tor-grass	*Brachypodium pinnatum*
Tormintel	*Potentilla erecta*
Touch-me-not	*Impatiens noli-tangere*
Traveller's-joy	*Clematis vitalba*
Trefoil	*Lotus* & *Trifolium* spp.
, bird's-foot	*Lotus corniculatus*
, greater bird's-foot	*Lotus pedunculatus*
Valerian, common	*Valeriana officinalis*
, red	*Centranthus ruber*
Vetch	*Vicia* spp.
, bitter	*Lathyrus linifolius*
, crown	*Securigera varia*
, horseshoe	*Hippocrepsis comosa*
, kidney	*Anthyllis vulneraria*
, tufted	*Vicia cracca*
, wood	*Vicia sylvatica*
Vetchling, meadow	*Lathyrus pratensis*
Violet	*Viola* spp.
, dog	*Viola riviniana*
, hairy	*Viola hirta*
, marsh	*Viola palustris*
, sweet	*Viola odorata*
Wallflower	*Erysimum cheiri*
Water-dock, great	*Rumex hydrolapathum*
Wayfaring-tree	*Viburnum lantana*
Wheat	*Triticum aestivum*
Whin, petty	*Genista anglica*
Whorl-grass	*Catabrosa aquatica*
William, sweet	*Dianthus barbatus*
Willow	*Salix* spp.
, crack	*Salix fragilis*
, creeping	*Salix repens*
, goat	*Salix caprea*
Willowherb	*Epilobium* spp.
, broad-leaved	*Epilobium montanum*
, rosebay	*Chamerion angustifolium*
Wood-rush	*Luzula* spp.
Wood-sedge	*Carex sylvatica*
Wormwood	*Artemesia* spp.
, field	*Artemesia campestris*
, sea	*Seriphidium maritima*
Woundwort	*Stachys* spp.
Yarrow	*Achillea millefolium*
Yew	*Taxus baccata*
Yorkshire-fog	*Holcus lanatus*

Index of Scientific Names

Index of English Names